Col

S

DICTIONARY

HarperCollins Publishers
Westerhill Road
Bishopbriggs
Glasgow
G64 2QT

Third Edition 2012

Reprint 10 9 8 7 6 5 4 3 2 1

ISBN 978-0-00-749276-3

www.collinslanguage.com

A catalogue record for this book is available from the British Library

Typeset by Davidson Publishing Solutions, Glasgow

Printed in Italy by Lego SpA, Lavis (Trento)

Acknowledgements

EDITORS
Gerry Breslin
Ian Brookes
Lorna Gilmour
Robert Groves
Robbie Guillory
Andrew Holmes
Persephone Lock

COMPUTING SUPPORT
Thomas Callan

FOR THE PUBLISHER
Lucy Cooper
Kerry Ferguson
Elaine Higgleton
Sharon McTeir

Introduction

The *Collins Gem Scrabble Dictionary* is the ideal reference book for people who play Scrabble for enjoyment, in a social or family setting. This dictionary doesn't include every word eligible for Scrabble, but does contain the most commonly used of the 270,000 words in *Collins Official Scrabble Words 2011*, the definitive Scrabble wordlist. The concise definitions in the *Gem Scrabble Dictionary* allow players to check the meaning of words, as well as to use the book for settling arguments during games.

The *Collins Gem Scrabble Dictionary* contains words of up to 7 letters in length. However, references to longer words playable in Scrabble are included. These longer words output in bold, and are introduced by a chevron symbol (>). Because this dictionary is designed for family play, it does not include offensive terms. Such words are, on the other hand, included in the *Collins Official Scrabble Words 2011*, the complete wordlist for tournaments and club competitions, along with words of 8–15 letters.

Words are listed in alphabetical order, although some inflected forms are grouped together or run on from the base form entry to save space. Inflected forms which are run on from the base form entry appear in bold, after the definition. Definitions are given for base forms of words where the meaning is not self-explanatory. A black triangle symbol (▶) is used to refer readers to another related entry in the dictionary. Inflections which are separate from their base form are referred back to the main entry in this way.

Two-letter words

A sound knowledge of the 124 two-letter words is crucial to success in Scrabble. Where many inexperienced Scrabble players go wrong is that they think the longer a word is, the better it is to know, as it's likely to score more. In fact, the key to a good Scrabble vocabulary is a good knowledge of short words.

The reason for that is you can use the short words to 'hook' the word you want to play on to the board, allowing you to play parallel to another word, rather than always going through it crosswise. That way you will usually make more than one word each shot, gaining you a higher score.

Notice how by using the same letters from your rack, you have scored seventeen more points. But notice also that little word **FA** which enabled you to fit the play in. And there we have the first, essential thing you have to know to improve your game: **all the allowable two letter words**. Yes, all of them.

There are 124 of these to learn, but to make the list more manageable, you can divide them into three groups:

1. The ones you already know.
2. The ones you already know, but may not have realized were words.
3. The ones you probably don't know.

There are thirty-seven two-letter words which most people would know and which would appear in most dictionaries:

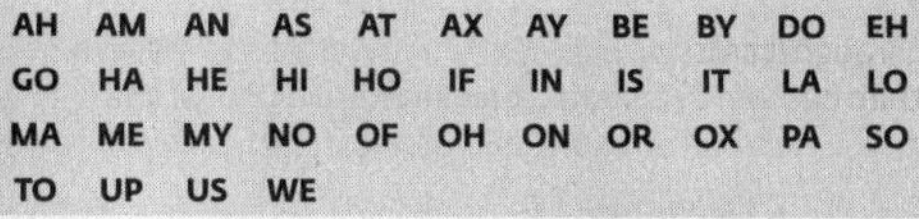

AH	AM	AN	AS	AT	AX	AY	BE	BY	DO	EH
GO	HA	HE	HI	HO	IF	IN	IS	IT	LA	LO
MA	ME	MY	NO	OF	OH	ON	OR	OX	PA	SO
TO	UP	US	WE							

So straight away you only have eighty-seven new ones to learn. But it's not even as bad as that, because now we move on to the second group: the ones you know, but don't know you know.

These include:

Contractions

AD (advertisement)	**PO** (chamberpot)
BI (bisexual)	**RE** (regarding)
MO (moment)	**TA** (thank you)
OP (operation)	

Interjections and exclamations

AW	ER	HM	MM	OI	OW	OY
SH	ST	UH	UM	UR	YA	YO

Letters of the alphabet

AR	EF	EL	EM	EN	ES	EX

Then add in **ID** (the psychiatric term), **PI** (the Greek letter and mathematical term), and **YE** (the old form of **YOU**), and that's another thirty-one taken care of with no trouble at all.

Fifty-six to go. These are the ones you probably don't know, so let's set them out where you can get the measure of them:

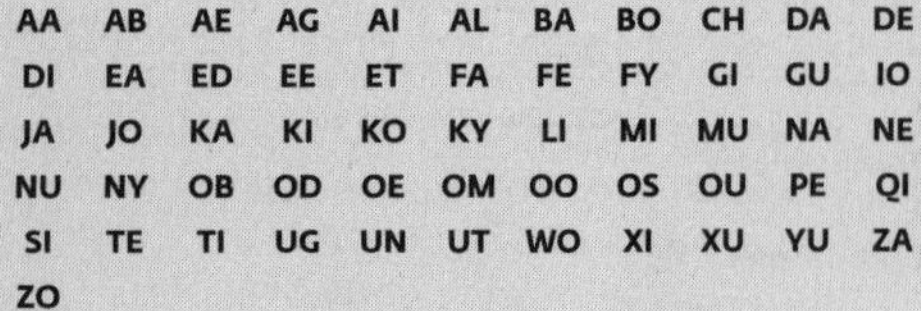

AA	AB	AE	AG	AI	AL	BA	BO	CH	DA	DE
DI	EA	ED	EE	ET	FA	FE	FY	GI	GU	IO
JA	JO	KA	KI	KO	KY	LI	MI	MU	NA	NE
NU	NY	OB	OD	OE	OM	OO	OS	OU	PE	QI
SI	TE	TI	UG	UN	UT	WO	XI	XU	YU	ZA
ZO										

Once you're happy with the common two-letter words, have a go at mastering the unusual ones. These really are the essential first step to improving your game.

Special Scrabble Words

To help family players learn and use some of the most useful words in the game, the *Collins Gem Scrabble Dictionary* includes a number of special panel entries, drawing attention to more than 200 words of particular interest or utility. For the most part these are words which are less likely to form part of a novice player's natural vocabulary, and the emphasis is on particularly useful three-letter words, on high probability seven-letter bonus words, on words that are especially useful when you have either too many vowels on your rack or too many consonants, and on selected shorter words that use the high value consonants **J**, **K**, **Q**, **X** and **Z**. But just for fun we have also featured a few of the unusual and exciting words of the kind that Scrabble players dream about. Realistically, you may well never get the chance to play words like **ZOOTAXY**, **TZADDIQ** and **QUETZAL**. But imagine the thrill (and the score!) if you did...

The *Collins Gem Scrabble Dictionary* is designed to be useful to new players and Scrabble veterans alike – we hope you enjoy using it!

Abbreviations

adj	adjective
adv	adverb
conj	conjunction
det	determiner
interj	interjection
n	noun
pl	plural
prep	preposition
pron	pronoun
vb	verb

Aa

A forms a two-letter word when followed by any one of **A, B, D, E, G, H, I, L, M, N, R, S, T, W, X** and **Y** – 16 letters out of 26 – so it's a really useful tile. There are also a number of short high-scoring words beginning with **A**. **Axe** (10 points) and **adze** (14 points) are good examples, but don't forget their US variants, **ax** (9 points) and **adz** (13 points). Also remember their plurals and the verb form **axed** (12 points). **Aye** (6) and **ay** (5) are handy for tight corners.

AA *n* volcanic rock
AAH *vb* exclaim in pleasure **aahed, aahing, aahs**
AAL *n* Asian shrub or tree

> An **aal** is an East Indian shrub, useful for getting rid of annoying multiples of A.

AALII *n* bushy shrub **aaliis**

> An **aalii** is a tropical tree, great for getting rid of surplus As and Is.

AALS ▸ **aal**
AARGH ▸ **argh**
AARRGH ▸ **argh**
AARRGHH ▸ **argh**
AARTI *n* Hindu ceremony **aartis**
AAS ▸ **aa**
AB *n* abdominal muscle
ABA *n* type of Syrian cloth
ABAC *n* mathematical diagram
ABACA *n* species of banana **abacas**
ABACI ▸ **abacus**
ABACK *adv*
ABACS ▸ **abac**
ABACTOR *n* cattle thief
ABACUS *n*
ABAFT *adv* by the rear of (a ship) ▹ *adj* closer to the stern
ABAKA *n* abaca **abakas**
ABALONE *n*
ABAMP = **abampere**
ABAMPS ▸ **abamp**
ABAND *vb* abandon **abanded**
ABANDON *vb, n*
ABANDS ▸ **aband**
ABAS ▸ **aba**
ABASE *vb* **abased, abaser, abasers, abases**
ABASH *vb* cause to feel ill at ease,
ABASHED *adj*
ABASHES ▸ **abash**
ABASIA *n* disorder affecting ability to walk **abasias**
ABASING ▸ **abase**
ABASK *adv* in pleasant warmth
ABATE *vb* **abated, abater, abaters, abates, abating**
ABATIS *n* rampart of felled trees
ABATOR *n* person who effects an abatement **abators**
ABATTIS = **abatis**
ABATTU *adj* dejected
ABATURE *n* trail left by hunted stag
ABAXIAL *adj* facing away from the axis
ABAXILE *adj* away from the axis

ABAYA *n* Arab outer garment **abayas**
ABB *n* yarn used in weaving
ABBA *n* Coptic bishop
ABBACY *n* office of abbot or abbess
ABBAS ▸ **abba**
ABBE *n* French abbot
ABBED *adj* displaying strong abdominal muscles
ABBES ▸ **abbe**
ABBESS *n* in charge of a convent
ABBEY *n* **abbeys**
ABBOT *n* **abbotcy, abbots**
ABBS ▸ **abb**
ABCEE *n* alphabet **abcees**
ABDABS *n* highly nervous state
ABDOMEN *n*
ABDUCE *vb* abduct **abduced, abduces**
ABDUCT *vb* **abducts**
ABEAM *adj* at right angles to a ship
ABEAR *vb* bear or behave **abears**
ABED *adv* in bed
ABEIGH *adv* aloof
ABELE *n* white poplar tree **abeles**
ABELIA *n* garden plant with pink or white flowers **abelian, abelias**
ABET *vb* **abets, abettal, abetted, abetter, abettor**
ABEYANT > **abeyance**
ABFARAD *n* unit of capacitance
ABHENRY *n* unit of inductance
ABHOR *vb* **abhors**
ABID ▸ **abide**
ABIDDEN ▸ **abide**
ABIDE *vb* **abided, abider, abiders, abides**
ABIDING *adj, n*
ABIES *n* fir tree
ABIETIC *adj as in* **abietic acid** yellowish powder
ABIGAIL *n* maid for a lady
ABILITY *n*
ABIOSES ▸ **abiosis**
ABIOSIS *n* absence of life **abiotic**
ABITUR *n* German examination **abiturs**
ABJECT *adj, vb* **abjects**
ABJOINT *vb* cut off
ABJURE *vb* deny or renounce on oath **abjured, abjurer, abjures**
ABLATE *vb* remove by ablation **ablated, ablates**
ABLATOR *n* heat shield of a space craft
ABLAUT *n* vowel gradation **ablauts**
ABLAZE *adj, adv*
ABLE *adj, vb*
ABLED *adj* having physical powers
ABLEISM *n* discrimination against disabled people **ableist**
ABLER ▸ **able**
ABLES ▸ **able**
ABLEST ▸ **able**
ABLET *n* freshwater fish **ablets**
ABLING ▸ **able**
ABLINGS *adv* possibly
ABLINS *adv* Scots word meaning perhaps
ABLOOM *adj* in flower
ABLOW *adj* blooming
ABLUENT *n* substance used for cleansing
ABLUSH *adj* blushing
ABLUTED *adj* washed thoroughly
ABLY *adv*
ABMHO *n* unit of electrical conductance **abmhos**
ABOARD *adv, adj*
ABODE *n, vb* **aboded, abodes, aboding**
ABOHM *n* unit of resistance **abohms**
ABOIL *adj* boiling
ABOLISH *vb*
ABOLLA *n* Roman cloak **abollae, abollas**
ABOMA *n* South American snake **abomas**
ABOMASA > **abomasum**
ABOMASI > **abomasus**
ABOON *Scots word for* ▸ **above**
ABORAL *adj* away from the mouth
ABORD *vb* accost **aborded, abords**
ABORE ▸ **abear**
ABORNE *adj* Shakespearean form of auburn
ABORT *vb, n* **aborted**
ABORTEE *n* woman having an abortion

ABORTER ▸ **abort**
ABORTS ▸ **abort**
ABORTUS *n* aborted fetus
ABOUGHT ▸ **aby**
ABOULIA = **abulia**
ABOULIC ▸ **aboulia**
ABOUND *vb* **abounds**
ABOUT *adv*
ABOUTS *prep* about
ABOVE *adv, n* **aboves**
ABRADE *vb* wear down by friction **abraded, abrader, abrades**
ABRAID *vb* awake **abraids**
ABRAM *adj* auburn
ABRASAX = **abraxas**
ABRAXAS *n* ancient charm composed of Greek letters
ABRAY *vb* awake **abrayed, abrays**
ABRAZO *n* embrace **abrazos**
ABREACT *vb* alleviate through abreaction
ABREAST *adj*
ABREGE *n* abridgment **abreges**
ABRI *n* shelter or place of refuge, esp in wartime
ABRIDGE *vb*
ABRIM *adj* full to the brim
ABRIN *n* poisonous compound **abrins**
ABRIS ▸ **abri**
ABROACH *adj* (of a cask, barrel, etc) tapped
ABROAD *adv, adj, n* **abroads**
ABROOKE *vb* bear or tolerate
ABROSIA *n* condition involving refusal to eat
ABRUPT *adj, n* **abrupts**
ABS ▸ **ab**
ABSCESS *n, vb*
ABSCIND *vb* cut off
ABSCISE *vb* separate or be separated by abscission
ABSCISS *n* cutting off
ABSCOND *vb*
ABSEIL *vb, n* **abseils**
ABSENCE *n* being away
ABSENT *adj, vb* **absents**
ABSEY *n* alphabet **abseys**
ABSINTH = **absinthe**
ABSIT *n* leave from college **absits**
ABSOLVE *vb*
ABSORB *vb* **absorbs**
ABSTAIN *vb*
ABSURD *adj, n* **absurds**
ABTHANE *n* ancient Scottish church territory
ABUBBLE *adj* bubbling
ABULIA *n* pathological inability to take decisions **abulias, abulic**
ABUNA *n* male head of Ethiopian family **abunas**
ABUNE *Scots word for* ▸ **above**
ABURST *adj* bursting
ABUSAGE *n* wrong use
ABUSE *vb, n* **abused, abuser, abusers, abuses, abusing**
ABUSION *n* wrong use or deception
ABUSIVE *adj*
ABUT *vb* **abuts**
ABUTTAL = **abutment**
ABUTTED ▸ **abut**
ABUTTER *n* owner of adjoining property
ABUZZ *adj* noisy, busy with activity etc
ABVOLT *n* unit of potential difference in the electromagnetic system **abvolts**
ABWATT *n* unit of power **abwatts**
ABY *vb* pay the penalty for

> Remember this word can be expanded to **baby** and **gaby** and also to **abye** and **abys**.

ABYE = **aby**
ABYEING ▸ **abye**
ABYES ▸ **abye**
ABYING ▸ **aby**
ABYS ▸ **aby**
ABYSM *archaic word for* ▸ **abyss**
ABYSMAL *adj*
ABYSMS ▸ **abysm**
ABYSS *n*
ABYSSAL *adj* of the ocean depths
ABYSSES ▸ **abyss**
ACACIA *n* **acacias**
ACADEME *n* place of learning
ACADEMY *n*
ACAI *n* berry **acais**
ACAJOU *n* type of mahogany **acajous**
ACALEPH *n* invertebrate

ACANTH *n* acanthus
ACANTHA *n* thorn or prickle
ACANTHI > **acanthus**
ACANTHS ▸ **acanth**
ACAPNIA *n* lack of carbon dioxide
ACARI ▸ **acarus**
ACARIAN ▸ **acarus**
ACARID *n* small arachnids ▷ *adj* of these arachnids **acarids**
ACARINE *n* acarid
ACAROID *adj* resembling a mite
ACARUS *n* type of mite
ACATER *n* buyer of provisions **acaters**
ACATES *n* provisions
ACATOUR *n* buyer of provisions
ACAUDAL *adj* having no tail
ACCA *n* academic
ACCABLE *adj* dejected or beaten
ACCAS ▸ **acca**
ACCEDE *vb* **acceded, acceder, accedes**
ACCEND *vb* set alight **accends**
ACCENT *n, vb* **accents**
ACCEPT *vb* **accepts**
ACCESS *n, vb*
ACCIDIA = **accidie**
ACCIDIE *n* spiritual sloth
ACCINGE *vb* put a belt around
ACCITE *vb* summon **accited, accites**
ACCLAIM *vb, n*
ACCLOY *vb* choke or clog **accloys**
ACCOAST *vb* accost
ACCOIED ▸ **accoy**
ACCOIL *n* welcome ▷ *vb* gather together **accoils**
ACCOMPT *vb* account
ACCORD *n, vb* **accords**
ACCOST *vb, n* **accosts**
ACCOUNT *n, vb*
ACCOURT *vb* entertain
ACCOY *vb* soothe **accoyed**
ACCOYLD ▸ **accoil**
ACCOYS ▸ **accoy**
ACCRETE *vb* grow together
ACCREW *vb* accrue **accrews**
ACCRUAL *n* act of accruing
ACCRUE *vb* **accrued, accrues**
ACCURSE *vb* curse
ACCURST = **accursed**
ACCUSAL *n* accusation
ACCUSE *vb*
ACCUSED *n* person accused of a crime
ACCUSER ▸ **accuse**
ACCUSES ▸ **accuse**
ACE *n, adj, vb* **aced**
ACEDIA = **accidie**
ACEDIAS ▸ **acedia**
ACEQUIA *n* irrigation ditch
ACER *n* type of tree
ACERATE = **acerated**
ACERB *adj* bitter **acerber**
ACERBIC *adj*
ACEROLA *n* cherry-like fruit
ACEROSE *adj* shaped like a needle **acerous**
ACERS ▸ **acer**
ACES ▸ **ace**
ACETA ▸ **acetum**
ACETAL *n* colourless liquid **acetals**
ACETATE *n* salt or ester of acetic acid
ACETIC *adj* of or involving vinegar
ACETIFY *vb* become vinegar
ACETIN *n* type of acetate **acetins**
ACETONE *n* colourless liquid used as a solvent
ACETOSE = **acetous**
ACETOUS *adj* containing acetic acid
ACETUM *n* solution that has dilute acetic acid as solvent
ACETYL *n* containing the monovalent group CH_3CO- **acetyls**
ACH *interj* Scots expression of surprise
ACHAGE *n* pain **achages**
ACHAR *n* spicy pickle made from mango
ACHARNE *adj* furiously violent
ACHARS ▸ **achar**
ACHARYA *n* religious teacher and spiritual guide
ACHATES = **acates**
ACHE *n, vb* **ached**
ACHENE *n* type of fruit **achenes**
ACHENIA > **achenium**
ACHES ▸ **ache**
ACHIER ▸ **achy**

ACHIEST ▸ **achy**
ACHIEVE *vb*
ACHING ▸ **ache**
ACHINGS ▸ **ache**
ACHIOTE *n* annatto
ACHIRAL *adj* of a tuber producing arrowroot
ACHKAN *n* man's coat in India **achkans**
ACHOLIA *n* bile condition
ACHOO *interj* sound of a sneeze
ACHY *adj* affected by a continuous dull pain
ACICULA *n* needle-shaped part
ACID *n, adj* **acider, acidest**
ACIDIC *adj* containing acid
ACIDIER ▸ **acid**
ACIDIFY *vb* convert into acid
ACIDITY *n* quality of being acid
ACIDLY ▸ **acid**
ACIDS ▸ **acid**
ACIDY ▸ **acid**
ACIFORM *adj* shaped like a needle
ACINAR *adj* of small sacs
ACING ▸ **ace**
ACINI ▸ **acinus**
ACINIC ▸ **acinus**
ACINOSE ▸ **acinus**
ACINOUS ▸ **acinus**
ACINUS *n* parts of a gland
ACKEE *n* tropical tree **ackees**
ACKER = **acca**
ACKERS ▸ **acker**
ACKNEW ▸ **acknow**
ACKNOW *vb* recognize **acknown, acknows**
ACLINIC *adj* unbending
ACMATIC *adj* highest or ultimate
ACME *n* **acmes**
ACMIC = **acmatic**
ACMITE *n* chemical with pyramid-shaped crystals **acmites**
ACNE *n*
ACNED *adj* marked by acne
ACNES ▸ **acne**
ACNODAL ▸ **acnode**
ACNODE *n* mathematical term **acnodes**
ACOCK *adv* cocked
ACOLD *adj* feeling cold
ACOLYTE *n*
ACOLYTH *n* acolyte
ACONITE *n* poisonous plant with hoodlike flowers
ACORN *n*
ACORNED *adj* covered with acorns
ACORNS ▸ **acorn**
ACOUCHI *n* South American rodent with a white-tipped tail **acouchy**
ACQUEST *n* something acquired
ACQUIRE *vb*
ACQUIS *n as in* **acquis communautaire** European Union laws
ACQUIST *n* acquisition
ACQUIT *vb*
ACQUITE *vb* acquit
ACQUITS ▸ **acquit**
ACRASIA *n* lack of willpower
ACRASIN *n* chemical
ACRATIC ▸ **acrasia**
ACRAWL *adv* crawling
ACRE *n*
ACREAGE *n, adj*
ACRED *adj* having acres of land
ACRES ▸ **acre**
ACRID *adj* **acrider**
ACRIDIN *n* acridine
ACRIDLY ▸ **acrid**
ACROBAT *n*
ACROGEN *n* flowerless plant
ACROMIA > **acromion**
ACRONIC *adj* acronical
ACRONYM *n*
ACROSS *adv*
ACROTER *n* plinth
ACROTIC *adj* of a surface
ACRYLIC *adj, n*
ACRYLYL *n* type of monovalent group
ACT *n, vb*
ACTA *n* minutes of meeting
ACTABLE ▸ **act**
ACTANT *n* grammatical term **actants**
ACTED ▸ **act**
ACTIN *n* protein
ACTINAL *adj* part of a jellyfish
ACTING *n, adj* **actings**
ACTINIA *n* type of sea anemone
ACTINIC *adj* (of radiation) producing a photochemical effect
ACTINON = **actinide**
ACTINS ▸ **actin**

ACTION *n, vb* **actions**
ACTIVE *adj, n* **actives**
ACTON *n* jacket **actons**
ACTOR *n*
ACTORLY *adj* of or relating to an actor
ACTORS ▸ **actor**
ACTRESS *n*
ACTS ▸ **act**
ACTUAL *adj*
ACTUALS *pl n* commercial commodities that can be bought and used
ACTUARY *n* statistician who calculates insurance risks
ACTUATE *vb*
ACTURE *n* action **actures**
ACUATE *adj* sharply pointed
ACUITY *n* keenness of vision or thought
ACULEI ▸ **aculeus**
ACULEUS *n* prickle or spine, such as the thorn of a rose
ACUMEN *n* **acumens**
ACUSHLA *n* Irish endearment
ACUTE *adj, n* **acutely, acuter, acutes, acutest**
ACYCLIC *adj* not cyclic
ACYL *n* member of the monovalent group of atoms RCO-
ACYLATE *vb* chemical
ACYLOIN *n* organic chemical compound
ACYLS ▸ **acyl**
AD *n*
ADAGE *n* **adages, adagial**
ADAGIO *adv, n* **adagios**
ADAMANT *adj, n*
ADAPT *vb* **adapted**
ADAPTER = **adaptor**
ADAPTOR *n*
ADAPTS ▸ **adapt**
ADAW *vb* subdue **adawed, adawing, adaws**
ADAXIAL *adj* facing the axis
ADAYS *adv* daily
ADD *vb* **addable**
ADDAX *n* antelope **addaxes**
ADDED ▸ **add**
ADDEDLY ▸ **add**
ADDEEM *vb* adjudge **addeems**
ADDEND *n* any of a set of numbers that is to be added
ADDENDA > **addendum**
ADDENDS ▸ **addend**
ADDER *n* **adders**
ADDIBLE *adj* addable
ADDICT *n, vb* **addicts**
ADDIES ▸ **addy**
ADDING *n* act or instance of addition ▹ *adj* of, for, or relating to addition **addings**
ADDIO *interj* farewell ▹ *n* cry of addio
ADDLE *vb* become muddled ▹ *adj* indicating a muddled state **addled, addles, addling**
ADDOOM *vb* adjudge **addooms**
ADDRESS *n, vb* **addrest**
ADDS ▸ **add**
ADDUCE *vb* mention something as evidence or proof **adduced, adducer, adduces**
ADDUCT *vb* movement of a muscle ▹ *n* compound **adducts**
ADDY *n* e-mail address
ADEEM *vb* cancel **adeemed, adeems**
ADENINE *n* chemical
ADENOID *adj* of or resembling a gland
ADENOMA *n* tumour occurring in glandular tissue
ADENYL *n* enzyme **adenyls**
ADEPT *n, adj* **adepter, adeptly, adepts**
ADERMIN *n* vitamin
ADHAN *n* call to prayer **adhans**
ADHARMA *n* wickedness
ADHERE *vb* **adhered, adherer, adheres**
ADHIBIT *vb* administer or apply
ADIEU *n* **adieus, adieux**

> Very useful when you want to say goodbye to a surplus of vowels. And remember its plural can be either **adieus** or **adieux**.

ADIOS *sentence substitute* Spanish for goodbye
ADIPIC *adj as in* **adipic acid** crystalline solid used in the preparation of nylon

ADIPOSE *adj* of or containing fat ▷ *n* animal fat
ADIPOUS *adj* made of fat
ADIPSIA *n* complete lack of thirst
ADIT *n* shaft into a mine, for access or drainage **adits**
ADJIGO *n* SW Australian yam plant with edible tubers **adjigos**
ADJOIN *vb* **adjoins**
ADJOINT *n* type of mathematical matrix
ADJOURN *vb*
ADJUDGE *vb*
ADJUNCT *n*
ADJURE *vb* command (to do) **adjured, adjurer, adjures, adjuror**
ADJUST *vb* **adjusts**
ADLAND *n* advertising industry and the people who work in it **adlands**
ADMAN *n* man who works in advertising
ADMASS *n* mass advertising
ADMEN ▸ **adman**
ADMIN *n* administration **admins**
ADMIRAL *n*
ADMIRE *vb* **admired, admirer, admires**
ADMIT *vb* **admits**
ADMIX *vb* mix or blend **admixed, admixes, admixt**
ADNATE *adj* growing closely attached to an adjacent part or organ
ADNEXA *pl n* organs adjoining the uterus **adnexal**
ADNOUN *n* adjective used as a noun **adnouns**
ADO *n*
ADOBE *n* sun-dried brick **adobes**
ADOBO *n* Philippine dish **adobos**
ADONIS *n* beautiful young man
ADONISE *vb* adorn
ADONIZE *vb* adorn
ADOORS *adv* at the door
ADOPT *vb*
ADOPTED *adj* having been adopted
ADOPTEE *n* one who has been adopted
ADOPTER *n* person who adopts
ADOPTS ▸ **adopt**
ADORE *vb* **adored, adorer, adorers, adores, adoring**
ADORN *vb* **adorned, adorner, adorns**
ADOS ▸ **ado**
ADOWN *adv* down
ADOZE *adv* asleep
ADPRESS *vb* press together
ADRAD *adj* afraid
ADREAD *vb* dread **adreads**
ADRED *adj* filled with dread
ADRENAL *adj* near the kidneys ▷ *n* adrenal gland
ADRIFT *adv*
ADROIT *adj*
ADRY *adj* dry
ADS ▸ **ad**
ADSORB *vb* condense to form a thin film **adsorbs**
ADSUKI = **adzuki**
ADSUKIS ▸ **adsuki**
ADSUM *sentence substitute* I am present
ADUKI = **adzuki**
ADUKIS ▸ **aduki**
ADULATE *vb* flatter or praise obsequiously
ADULT *adj, n* **adultly, adults**
ADUNC *adj* hooked
ADUST *vb* dry up or darken by heat **adusted, adusts**
ADVANCE *vb, n, adj*
ADVECT *vb* move horizontally in air **advects**
ADVENE *vb* add as extra **advened, advenes**
ADVENT *n* **advents**
ADVERB *n* **adverbs**
ADVERSE *adj*
ADVERT *n* advertisement ▷ *vb* draw attention (to) **adverts**
ADVEW *vb* look at **advewed, advews**
ADVICE *n* **advices**
ADVISE *vb*
ADVISED *adj* considered, thought-out
ADVISEE *n* person receiving advice
ADVISER *n*
ADVISES ▸ **advise**

ADVISOR = **adviser**
ADWARD *vb* award **adwards**
ADWARE *n* computer software **adwares**
ADWOMAN *n* woman working in advertising **adwomen**
ADYTA ▶ **adytum**
ADYTUM *n* sacred place in ancient temples
ADZ = **adze**

This is the American spelling of **adze**, and is one of the essential short words to know for using the Z.

ADZE *n* woodworking tool ▷ *vb* use an adze **adzed, adzes, adzing**
ADZUKI *n* type of plant **adzukis**
AE *determiner* one
AECIA ▶ **aecium**
AECIAL ▶ **aecium**
AECIDIA > **aecidium**
AECIUM *n* area of some fungi
AEDES *n* type of mosquito which transmits yellow fever and dengue
AEDILE *n* magistrate of ancient Rome **aediles**
AEDINE *adj* of a species of mosquito
AEFALD *adj* single
AEFAULD *adj* single
AEGIS *n* **aegises**
AEMULE *vb* emulate **aemuled, aemules**
AENEOUS *adj* brass-coloured or greenish-gold
AENEUS *n* aquarium fish
AEOLIAN *adj* of or relating to the wind
AEON *n* immeasurably long period of time

This little word gets played when you have too many vowels. And it has a partner **eoan**, meaning of the dawn: but beware, unlike **aeon**, it does not take a plural S.

AEONIAN *adj* everlasting
AEONIC ▶ **aeon**
AEONS ▶ **aeon**
AERATE *vb* **aerated, aerates, aerator**
AERIAL *adj*, *n* **aerials**
AERIE *a variant spelling (esp US) of* ▶ **eyrie**

This word for an eagle's nest is a great one for dealing with a surplus of vowels. And it has several variants: **aery, aiery, ayrie, eyrie** and **eyry**.

AERIED *adj* in a very high place
AERIER ▶ **aery**
AERIES ▶ **aerie**
AERIEST ▶ **aery**
AERIFY *vb* change or cause to change into a gas
AERILY ▶ **aery**
AERO *n* of or relating to aircraft or aeronautics
AEROBAT *n* person who does stunt flying
AEROBE *n* organism that requires oxygen to survive **aerobes**
AEROBIA > **aerobium**
AEROBIC *adj* designed for or relating to aerobics
AEROBOT *n* unmanned aircraft used esp in space exploration
AEROGEL *n* colloid
AEROS ▶ **aero**
AEROSAT *n* communications satellite
AEROSOL *n*
AERUGO *(esp of old bronze) another name for* > **verdigris**
AERUGOS ▶ **aerugo**
AERY *adj* lofty, insubstantial, or visionary
AESC *n* rune **aesces**
AESIR *n* chief of the Norse gods
AETHER = **ether**
AETHERS ▶ **aether**
AFALD *adj* single
AFAR *adv*, *n*
AFARA *n* African tree **afaras**
AFARS ▶ **afar**
AFAWLD *adj* single
AFEAR *vb* frighten
AFEARD *an archaic or dialect word for* ▶ **afraid**
AFEARED = **afeard**
AFEARS ▶ **afear**
AFF *adv* off
AFFABLE *adj* **affably**
AFFAIR *n*
AFFAIRE *n* love affair

AFFAIRS *pl n* personal or business interests
AFFEAR *vb* frighten **affeard**
AFFEARE *vb* frighten
AFFEARS ▸ **affear**
AFFECT *vb, n* **affects**
AFFEER *vb* assess **affeers**
AFFIANT *n* person who makes an affidavit
AFFICHE *n* poster
AFFIED ▸ **affy**
AFFIES ▸ **affy**
AFFINAL ▸ **affine**
AFFINE *adj* involving transformations which preserve collinearity ▷ *n* relation by marriage
AFFINED *adj* closely related
AFFINES ▸ **affine**
AFFIRM *vb* **affirms**
AFFIX *vb, n* **affixal, affixed, affixer, affixes**
AFFLICT *vb*
AFFLUX *n* flowing towards a point
AFFOORD *vb* consent
AFFORCE *vb* strengthen
AFFORD *vb* **affords**
AFFRAP *vb* strike **affraps**
AFFRAY *n, vb* **affrays**
AFFRET *n* furious attack **affrets**
AFFRONT *n, vb*
AFFY *vb* trust **affyde, affying**
AFGHAN *n* type of biscuit
AFGHANI *n* monetary unit of Afghanistan
AFGHANS ▸ **afghan**
AFIELD *adj*
AFIRE *adj* on fire
AFLAJ ▸ **falaj**
AFLAME *adj* burning
AFLOAT *adj, adv*
AFOOT *adj, adv*
AFORE *adv* before
AFOUL *adj* in or into a state of difficulty, confusion, or conflict (with)
AFRAID *adj*
AFREET *n* powerful evil demon or giant monster **afreets**
AFRESH *adv*
AFRIT = **afreet**
AFRITS ▸ **afrit**
AFRO *n*
AFRONT *adv* in front
AFROS ▸ **afro**
AFT *adv, adj*
AFTER *adv*
AFTERS *n* sweet course of a meal
AFTMOST *adj* furthest towards rear
AFTOSA *n* foot-and-mouth disease **aftosas**
AG *n* agriculture
AGA *n* title of respect
AGACANT *adj* irritating
AGAIN *adv*
AGAINST *prep*
AGAMA *n* small lizard **agamas**
AGAMETE *n* reproductive cell
AGAMI *n* South American bird
AGAMIC *adj* asexual
AGAMID = **agama**
AGAMIDS ▸ **agamid**
AGAMIS ▸ **agami**
AGAMOID *n* lizard of the agamid type
AGAMONT *another name for* > **schizont**
AGAMOUS *adj* without sex
AGAPAE ▸ **agape**
AGAPAI ▸ **agape**
AGAPE *adj* (of the mouth) wide open ▷ *n* love feast among the early Christians **agapeic, agapes**
AGAR *n*
AGARIC *n* type of fungus **agarics**
AGAROSE *n* gel used in chemistry
AGARS ▸ **agar**
AGAS ▸ **aga**
AGAST *adj* aghast
AGATE *n, adv* **agates**
AGATISE = **agatize**
AGATIZE *vb* turn into agate
AGATOID *adj* like agate
AGAVE *n* tropical plant **agaves**
AGAZE *adj* gazing at something
AGAZED *adj* amazed
AGE *n, vb*
AGED *adj* **agedly**
AGEE *adj* awry, crooked, or ajar ▷ *adv* awry
AGEING *n* fact or process of growing old ▷ *adj* becoming or appearing older **ageings**

AGEISM *n* discrimination against people on the grounds of age **ageisms, ageist, ageists**
AGELAST *n* someone who never laughs
AGELESS *adj* apparently never growing old
AGELONG *adj* lasting for a very long time
AGEMATE *n* person the same age as another person
AGEN *archaic form of* ▸ **again**
AGENCY *n*
AGENDA *n* **agendas, agendum**
AGENE *n* chemical used to whiten flour **agenes**
AGENISE = **agenize**
AGENIZE *vb* whiten using agene
AGENT *n, vb* **agented**
AGENTRY *n* acting as agent
AGENTS ▸ **agent**
AGER *n* something that ages **agers**
AGES ▸ **age**
AGEUSIA *n* lack of the sense of taste
AGGADA *n* explanation in Jewish literature **aggadah, aggadas**
AGGADIC *adj* of aggada
AGGADOT ▸ **aggada**
AGGER *n* rampart
AGGERS *adj* aggressive
AGGIE *n* American agricultural student **aggies**
AGGRACE *vb* add grace to
AGGRADE *vb* build up by the deposition of sediment
AGGRATE *vb* gratify
AGGRESS *vb* attack first or begin a quarrel
AGGRI *adj* of African beads
AGGRO *n* aggressive behaviour **aggros**
AGGRY *adj* of African beads
AGHA = **aga**
AGHAS ▸ **agha**
AGHAST *adj*
AGILA *n* eaglewood **agilas**
AGILE *adj* **agilely, agiler, agilest, agility**
AGIN *prep* against, opposed to
AGING = **ageing**
AGINGS ▸ **aging**
AGINNER *n* someone who is against something
AGIO *n* difference between the nominal and actual values of a currency **agios**
AGISM = **ageism**
AGISMS ▸ **agism**
AGIST *vb* care for and feed (cattle or horses) for payment **agisted**
AGISTER *n* person who grazes cattle for money
AGISTOR *n* person who grazes cattle for money
AGISTS ▸ **agist**
AGITA *n* acid indigestion
AGITANS *adj as in* **paralysis agitans** Parkinson's disease
AGITAS ▸ **agita**
AGITATE *vb*
AGITATO *adv* (to be performed) in an agitated manner
AGITPOP *n* use of pop music to promote political propaganda
AGLARE *adj* glaring
AGLEAM *adj* glowing
AGLEE = **agley**
AGLET *n* metal tag **aglets**
AGLEY *adj* awry
AGLOO = **aglu**
AGLOOS ▸ **agloo**
AGLOW *adj*
AGLU *n* breathing hole made in ice by a seal **aglus**
AGLY *Scots word for* ▸ **wrong**
AGLYCON *n* chemical compound
AGMA *n* symbol used to represent a velar nasal consonant **agmas**
AGNAIL *another name for* > **hangnail**
AGNAILS ▸ **agnail**
AGNAME *n* name additional to first name and surname
AGNAMED *adj* having an agname
AGNAMES ▸ **agname**
AGNATE *adj* related through a common male ancestor ▹ *n* descendant by male

links from a common male ancestor **agnates, agnatic**
AGNISE *vb* acknowledge **agnised, agnises**
AGNIZE *vb* acknowledge **agnized, agnizes**
AGNOMEN *n* name used by ancient Romans
AGNOSIA *n* loss of power to recognize familiar objects **agnosic**
AGO *adv*
AGOG *adj*
AGOGE *n* ancient Greek tempo **agoges**
AGOGIC *n* musical accent **agogics**
AGOING *adj* moving
AGON *n* ancient Greek festival
AGONAL *adj* of agony
AGONE *an archaic word for* ▸ **ago**
AGONES ▸ **agon**
AGONIC *adj* forming no angle
AGONIES ▸ **agony**
AGONISE = **agonize**
AGONIST *n* any muscle that is opposed in action by another muscle
AGONIZE *vb*
AGONS ▸ **agon**
AGONY *n*
AGOOD *adv* seriously or earnestly
AGORA *n* place of assembly in ancient Greece **agorae, agoras, agorot**
AGOROTH *n* agorot
AGOUTA *n* Haitian rodent **agoutas**
AGOUTI *n* rodent **agoutis**
AGOUTY *n* agouti
AGRAFE = **agraffe**
AGRAFES ▸ **agrafe**
AGRAFFE *n* loop and hook fastening
AGRAPHA > **agraphon**
AGRASTE ▸ **aggrace**
AGRAVIC *adj* of zero gravity
AGREE *vb*
AGREED *adj* determined by common consent
AGREES ▸ **agree**
AGREGE *n* winner in examination for university teaching post **agreges**
AGRIA *n* appearance of pustules **agrias**
AGRIN *adv* grinning
AGRISE *vb* fill with fear **agrised, agrises**
AGRIZE *vb* fill with fear **agrized, agrizes**
AGROUND *adv, adj*
AGRYZE *vb* fill with fear **agryzed, agryzes**
AGS ▸ **ag**
AGUE *n* periodic fever with shivering
AGUED *adj* suffering from fever
AGUES ▸ **ague**
AGUISE *vb* dress **aguised, aguises**
AGUISH ▸ **ague**
AGUIZE *vb* dress **aguized, aguizes**
AGUNA *n* (in Jewish law) woman whose husband will not grant her a divorce **agunah, agunot**
AGUTI *n* agouti **agutis**
AH *interj* exclamation expressing surprise, joy, etc ▹ *vb* say ah
AHA *interj* exclamation
AHCHOO *interj* sound made by someone sneezing
AHEAD *adv*
AHEAP *adv* in a heap
AHED ▸ **ah**
AHEIGHT *adv* at height
AHEM *interj* clearing of the throat in order to attract attention
AHENT *adv* behind
AHI *n* yellowfin tuna

> A very useful one to catch!

AHIGH *adv* at height
AHIMSA *n* the law of reverence for every form of life **ahimsas**
AHIND *adv* behind
AHING ▸ **ah**
AHINT *adv* behind
AHIS ▸ **ahi**
AHOLD *n* holding **aholds**
AHORSE *adv* on horseback
AHOY *interj*
AHS ▸ **ah**
AHULL *adv* with sails furled
AHUNGRY *adj* very hungry
AHURU *n* type of small pink cod of SW Pacific waters **ahurus**

AI *n* shaggy-coated slow-moving animal of South America
AIA *n* female servant in East **aias**
AIBLINS *Scots word for* ▸ **perhaps**
AID *n, vb*
AIDA *n* cotton fabric with a natural mesh
AIDANCE *n* help
AIDANT *adj* helping
AIDAS ▸ **aida**
AIDE *n*
AIDED ▸ **aid**
AIDER ▸ **aid**
AIDERS ▸ **aider**
AIDFUL *adj* helpful
AIDING ▸ **aid**
AIDLESS *adj* without help
AIDMAN *n* military medical assistant **aidmen**
AIDOI *adj* of the genitals
AIDOS *Greek word for* ▸ **shame**
AIDS ▸ **aid**
AIERIES ▸ **aiery**
AIERY *n* eyrie
AIGA *n* Māori word for family **aigas**
AIGHT *adv*
AIGLET = **aglet**
AIGLETS ▸ **aiglet**
AIGRET = **aigrette**
AIGRETS ▸ **aigret**
AIKIDO *n* Japanese self-defence **aikidos**
AIKONA *interj* South African expression meaning no
AIL *vb* trouble, afflict
AILANTO *n* Asian tree
AILED ▸ **ail**
AILERON *n*
AILETTE *n* shoulder armour
AILING *adj*
AILMENT *n*
AILS ▸ **ail**
AIM *vb, n* **aimed, aimer, aimers**
AIMFUL *adj* with purpose or intention
AIMING ▸ **aim**
AIMLESS *adj*
AIMS ▸ **aim**
AIN *variant of* ▸ **ayin**
AINE *adj* French word for elder (male)

> Though it doesn't score much it is useful to remember when you have too many vowels. And it can be extended to **ainee**, the feminine form.

AINEE *adj* French word for elder (female)
AINGA *n* Māori word for village **aingas**
AINS ▸ **ain**
AINSELL *n* Scots word meaning own self
AIOLI *n* garlic mayonnaise **aiolis**
AIR *n, vb*
AIRBAG *n* safety device in a car **airbags**
AIRBASE *n* centre from which military aircraft operate
AIRBOAT *n* boat
AIRBUS *n* commercial passenger aircraft
AIRCON *n* air conditioner **aircons**
AIRCREW *n*
AIRDATE *n* date of a programme broadcast
AIRDROP *n* delivery of supplies by parachute ▹ *vb* deliver (supplies, etc) by an airdrop
AIRED ▸ **air**
AIRER *n* device on which clothes are hung to dry **airers**
AIREST ▸ **air**
AIRFARE *n* money for an aircraft ticket
AIRFLOW *n* flow of air past a moving object
AIRFOIL = **aerofoil**
AIRGAP *n* gap between parts in an electrical machine **airgaps**
AIRGLOW *n* faint light in the night sky
AIRGUN *n* gun fired by compressed air **airguns**
AIRHEAD *n* stupid person
AIRHOLE *n* hole that allows the passage of air
AIRIER ▸ **airy**
AIRIEST ▸ **airy**
AIRILY *adv* in a light-hearted and casual manner
AIRING *n* exposure to air for drying or ventilation **airings**
AIRLESS *adj*
AIRLIFT *n, vb*
AIRLIKE ▸ **air**
AIRLINE *n*
AIRLOCK *n*
AIRMAIL *n, adj, vb*
AIRMAN *n* **airmen**

AIRN *Scots word for* ▸ **iron**
AIRNED ▸ **airn**
AIRNING ▸ **airn**
AIRNS ▸ **airn**
AIRPARK *n* car park at airport
AIRPLAY *n* broadcast performances of a record on radio
AIRPORT *n*
AIRPOST *n* system of delivering mail by air
AIRPROX *n* near collision involving aircraft
AIRS *pl n* manners put on to impress people
AIRSHED *n* air over a particular geographical area
AIRSHIP *n*
AIRSHOT *n* shot that misses the ball completely
AIRSHOW *n* occasion when an air base is open to the public
AIRSICK *adj* nauseated from travelling in an aircraft
AIRSIDE *n* part of an airport nearest the aircraft
AIRSTOP *n* helicopter landing-place
AIRT *n* point of the compass ▹ *vb* direct **airted, airth**
AIRTHED ▸ **airth**
AIRTHS ▸ **airth**
AIRTIME *n* time divisions on radio and TV
AIRTING ▸ **airt**
AIRTS ▸ **airt**
AIRWARD *adj* into air
AIRWAVE *n* radio wave used in radio and television broadcasting
AIRWAY *n* air route used regularly by aircraft **airways**
AIRWISE *adv* towards the air
AIRY *adj*
AIS ▸ **ai**
AISLE *n* **aisled, aisles**
AISLING *Irish word for* ▸ **dream**
AIT *n* islet, esp in a river
AITCH *n* letter *h* or the sound represented by it **aitches**
AITS ▸ **ait**
AITU *n* half-human half-divine being **aitus**

> This demigod is often played to dispose of an excess of vowels.

AIVER *n* working horse **aivers**
AIZLE *n* Scots word for hot ashes **aizles**
AJAR *adv, adj*
AJEE = **agee**

> This is a Scots word meaning ajar often useful for disposing of the J. It has an alternative spelling **agee**.

AJIVA *n* Jainist term for non-living thing **ajivas**
AJOWAN *n* plant related to caraway **ajowans**
AJUGA *n* garden plant **ajugas**
AJUTAGE *n* nozzle
AJWAN *n* plant related to caraway **ajwans**
AKA *n* type of New Zealand vine **akas**

> One of the key short words when it comes to using the K.

AKATEA *n* New Zealand vine with white flowers **akateas**
AKE *vb* old spelling of ache
AKEAKE *n* New Zealand tree **akeakes**
AKED ▸ **ake**
AKEDAH *n* binding of Isaac in Bible **akedahs**
AKEE = **ackee**
AKEES ▸ **akee**
AKELA *n* adult leader of a pack of Cub Scouts **akelas**
AKENE = **achene**
AKENES ▸ **akene**
AKENIAL ▸ **achene**
AKES ▸ **ake**
AKHARA *n* (in India) gymnasium **akharas**
AKIMBO *adj as in* **with arms akimbo**
AKIN *adj*
AKING ▸ **ake**
AKIRAHO *n* small New Zealand shrub with white flowers
AKITA *n* large dog **akitas**
AKKAS *slang word for* ▸ **money**
AKRASIA *n* weakness of will **akratic**

AKVAVIT = **aquavit**
AL = **aal**
ALA *n* winglike structure
ALAAP *n* part of raga in Indian music **alaaps**
ALACK *archaic or poetic word for* ▸ **alas**
ALAE ▸ **ala**
ALALIA *n* complete inability to speak **alalias**
ALAMEDA *n* public walk lined with trees
ALAMO *n* poplar tree
ALAMODE *n* soft light silk used for shawls and dresses, esp in the 19th century
ALAMORT *adj* exhausted and downcast
ALAMOS ▸ **alamo**
ALAN *n* member of ancient European nomadic people
ALAND *vb* come onto land **alands**
ALANE *Scots word for* ▸ **alone**
ALANG *n* type of grass in Malaysia **alangs**
ALANIN *n* alanine
ALANINE *n* chemical
ALANINS ▸ **alanin**
ALANNAH *interj* term of endearment ▹ *n* cry of alannah
ALANS ▸ **alan**
ALANT *n* flowering plant used in herbal medicine **alants**
ALANYL *n* chemical found in proteins **alanyls**
ALAP *n* Indian vocal music without words
ALAPA *n* part of raga in Indian music **alapas**
ALAPS ▸ **alap**
ALAR *adj* relating to, resembling, or having wings or alae
ALARM *n, vb* **alarmed, alarms**
ALARUM *n* alarm, esp a call to arms ▹ *vb* raise the alarm **alarums**
ALARY *adj* of, relating to, or shaped like wings
ALAS *adv*
ALASKA *n* dessert made of cake and ice cream **alaskas**
ALASTOR *n* avenging demon
ALATE *adj* having wings or winglike extensions ▹ *n* winged insect
ALATED *adj* having wings
ALATES ▸ **alate**
ALATION *n* state of having wings
ALAY *vb* allay **alayed, alaying, alays**
ALB *n* long white robe worn by a Christian priest
ALBA *n* song of lament **albas**
ALBATA *n* variety of German silver consisting of nickel, copper, and zinc **albatas**
ALBE *old word for* ▸ **albeit**
ALBEDO *n* ratio of the intensity of light **albedos**
ALBEE *archaic form of* ▸ **albeit**
ALBEIT *conj*
ALBERGO *n* Italian word for inn
ALBERT *n* watch chain **alberts**
ALBINAL ▸ **albino**
ALBINIC ▸ **albino**
ALBINO *n* **albinos**
ALBITE *n* type of mineral **albites, albitic**
ALBIZIA *n* mimosa
ALBS ▸ **alb**
ALBUGO *n* opacity of the cornea **albugos**
ALBUM *n*
ALBUMEN ▸ **albumin**
ALBUMIN *n*
ALBUMS ▸ **album**
ALCADE = **alcalde**
ALCADES ▸ **alcade**
ALCAIC *n* verse consisting of strophes with four tetrametric lines **alcaics**
ALCAIDE *n* commander of a fortress or castle
ALCALDE *n* (in Spain and Spanish America) the mayor or chief magistrate in a town
ALCAYDE *n* alcaide
ALCAZAR *n* Moorish palaces or fortresses
ALCHEMY *n*
ALCHERA *n* mythical Golden Age
ALCHYMY *old spelling of* ▸ **alchemy**

ALCID *n* bird of the auk family **alcids**
ALCO = **alko**
ALCOHOL *n*
ALCOOL *n* form of pure grain spirit distilled in Quebec **alcools**
ALCOPOP *n*
ALCORZA *n* Spanish sweet
ALCOS ▸ **alco**
ALCOVE *n*
ALCOVED *adj* with or in an alcove
ALCOVES ▸ **alcove**
ALDEA *n* Spanish village **aldeas**
ALDER *n*
ALDERN *adj* made of alder wood
ALDERS ▸ **alder**
ALDOL *n* colourless or yellowish oily liquid **aldols**
ALDOSE *n* type of sugar **aldoses**
ALDRIN *n* brown to white poisonous crystalline solid **aldrins**
ALE *n*
ALEC = **aleck**
ALECK *n* irritatingly oversmart person **alecks**
ALECOST *another name for* > **costmary**
ALECS ▸ **alec**
ALEE *adj* on or towards the lee
ALEF *n* first letter of Hebrew alphabet **alefs**
ALEFT *adv* at or to left
ALEGAR *n* malt vinegar **alegars**
ALEGGE *vb* alleviate **alegged, alegges**
ALEMBIC *n* anything that distils
ALENCON *n* elaborate lace worked on a hexagonal mesh
ALENGTH *adv* at length
ALEPH *n* first letter in the Hebrew alphabet **alephs**
ALEPINE *n* type of cloth
ALERCE *n* wood of the sandarac tree **alerces**
ALERION *n* eagle in heraldry
ALERT *adj, n, vb* **alerted, alerter, alertly, alerts**
ALES ▸ **ale**
ALETHIC *adj* of philosophical concepts
ALEURON *n* outer layer of seeds
ALEVIN *n* young fish, esp a young salmon or trout **alevins**
ALEW *n* cry to call hunting hounds
ALEWIFE *n* North American fish
ALEWS ▸ **alew**
ALEXIA *n* disorder of the central nervous system **alexias, alexic**
ALEXIN *n* complement **alexine, alexins**
ALEYE *vb* allay **aleyed, aleyes, aleying**
ALF *n* uncultivated Australian
ALFA *n* type of grass
ALFAKI *n* expert in Muslim law **alfakis**
ALFALFA *n*
ALFAQUI *n* expert in Muslim law
ALFAS ▸ **alfa**
ALFEREZ *n* Spanish standard-bearer
ALFORJA *n* saddlebag made of leather or canvas
ALFREDO *adj* cooked with a cheese and egg sauce
ALFS ▸ **alf**
ALGA *n* multicellular organism **algae, algal, algas**
ALGATE *adv* anyway
ALGATES *adv* anyway
ALGEBRA *n*
ALGESES ▸ **algesis**
ALGESIA *n* capacity to feel pain **algesic**
ALGESIS *n* feeling of pain
ALGETIC ▸ **algesia**
ALGID *adj* chilly or cold
ALGIN *n* seaweed solution
ALGINIC *adj as in* **alginic acid** powdery substance extracted from kelp
ALGINS ▸ **algin**
ALGOID *adj* resembling or relating to algae
ALGOR *n* chill **algors**
ALGUM *n* type of wood mentioned in Bible **algums**
ALIAS *adv, n* **aliases**
ALIBI *n, vb* **alibied, alibies, alibis**
ALIBLE *adj* nourishing
ALICANT *n* wine from Alicante in Spain

ALIDAD = **alidade**
ALIDADE *n* surveying instrument
ALIDADS ▸ **alidad**
ALIEN *adj, n, vb* **aliened**
ALIENEE *n* person to whom a transfer of property is made
ALIENER ▸ **alien**
ALIENLY ▸ **alien**
ALIENOR *n* person who transfers property to another
ALIENS ▸ **alien**
ALIF *n* first letter of Arabic alphabet
ALIFORM *adj* wing-shaped
ALIFS ▸ **alif**
ALIGHT *vb, adj, adv* **alights**
ALIGN *vb* **aligned, aligner, aligns**
ALIKE *adj, adv*
ALIMENT *n* something that nourishes the body ▹ *vb* support or sustain
ALIMONY *n*
ALINE *a rare spelling of* ▸ **align; alined, aliner, aliners, alines, alining**
ALIPED *n* bat-like creatures ▹ *adj* having digits connected by a membrane **alipeds**
ALIQUOT *adj* of or denoting an exact divisor of a number ▹ *n* exact divisor
ALISMA *n* marsh plant **alismas**
ALISON = **alyssum**
ALISONS ▸ **alison**
ALIST *adj* leaning over
ALIT *rare past tense and past participle of* ▸ **alight**
ALIUNDE *adj* from a source under consideration
ALIVE *adj*
ALIYA *n* immigration to Holy Land
ALIYAH *n* immigration to the Holy Land **aliyahs**
ALIYAS ▸ **aliya**
ALIYOS *n* remission of sin in Jewish faith
ALIYOT ▸ **aliyah**
ALIYOTH ▸ **aliyah**
ALIZARI *n* madder from Middle East
ALKALI *n*
ALKALIC *adj* geographical term
ALKALIN *adj* leaning over
ALKALIS ▸ **alkali**
ALKANE *n* saturated hydrocarbon **alkanes**
ALKANET *n* European plant whose roots yield a red dye
ALKENE *n* unsaturated hydrocarbon **alkenes**
ALKIE = **alky**
ALKIES ▸ **alky**
ALKINE *n* alkyne **alkines**
ALKO *n* heavy drinker or alcoholic **alkos**
ALKOXY *adj* of type of chemical compound containing oxygen
ALKY *n* heavy drinker or alcoholic
ALKYD *n* synthetic resin **alkyds**
ALKYL *n* of or containing the monovalent group C_nH_{2n+1} **alkylic, alkyls**
ALKYNE *n* any unsaturated aliphatic hydrocarbon **alkynes**
ALL *adj, adv, n*
ALLAY *vb* **allayed, allayer, allays**
ALLEDGE *vb* allege
ALLEE *n* avenue **allees**
ALLEGE *vb*
ALLEGED *adj* stated but not proved
ALLEGER ▸ **allege**
ALLEGES ▸ **allege**
ALLEGGE *vb* alleviate
ALLEGRO *adv, n*
ALLEL *n* form of gene
ALLELE *n* genes with alternative characteristics **alleles, allelic**
ALLELS ▸ **allel**
ALLERGY *n*
ALLEY *n*
ALLEYED *adj* having alleys
ALLEYS ▸ **alley**
ALLHEAL *n* plants with reputed healing powers
ALLICE *n* species of fish **allices**
ALLICIN *n* chemical found in garlic
ALLIED *adj*
ALLIES ▸ **ally**
ALLIS *n* species of fish **allises**

ALLIUM *n* type of plant **alliums**
ALLNESS *n* being all
ALLOBAR *n* form of element
ALLOD = **allodium**
ALLODIA > **allodium**
ALLODS ▸ **allod**
ALLONGE *n* paper extension to bill of exchange
ALLONS *interj* French word meaning let's go
ALLONYM *n* name assumed by a person
ALLOT *vb* **allots**
ALLOVER *n* fabric completely covered with a pattern
ALLOW *vb* **allowed, allows**
ALLOXAN *n* chemical found in uric acid
ALLOY *n, vb* **alloyed, alloys**
ALLS ▸ **all**
ALLSEED *n* type of plant
ALLUDE *vb* **alluded, alludes**
ALLURE *n, vb* **allured, allurer, allures**
ALLUVIA > **alluvium**
ALLY *vb, n* **allying**
ALLYL *n* containing the monovalent group CH_2:$CHCH_2^-$ **allylic, allyls**
ALLYOU *pron* all of you
ALMA *n* Egyptian dancing girl
ALMAH *n* Egyptian dancing girl **almahs**
ALMAIN *n* German dance **almains**
ALMANAC *n*
ALMAS ▸ **alma**
ALME *n* Egyptian dancing girl
ALMEH *n* Egyptian dancing girl **almehs**
ALMEMAR *n* area in a synagogue
ALMERY *n* cupboard for church vessels
ALMES ▸ **alme**
ALMIRAH *n* cupboard
ALMNER *n* almoner
ALMNERS ▸ **almoner**
ALMOND *n* **almonds, almondy**
ALMONER *n* formerly, a hospital social worker
ALMONRY *n* house of an almoner, usually the place where alms were given
ALMOST *adv*
ALMOUS *Scots word for* ▸ **alms**
ALMS *pl n*
ALMSMAN *n* person who gives or receives alms **almsmen**
ALMUCE *n* fur-lined hood or cape **almuces**
ALMUD *n* Spanish unit of measure
ALMUDE *n* Spanish unit of measure **almudes**
ALMUDS ▸ **almud**
ALMUG *n* type of wood mentioned in Bible **almugs**
ALNAGE *n* measurement in ells
ALNAGER *n* inspector of cloth
ALNAGES ▸ **alnage**
ALNICO *n* alloy including iron, nickel, and cobalt **alnicos**
ALOD *n* feudal estate with no superior
ALODIA ▸ **alodium**
ALODIAL ▸ **alodium**
ALODIUM = **allodium**
ALODS ▸ **alod**
ALOE *n*
ALOED *adj* containing aloes
ALOES *another name for* > **eaglewood**
ALOETIC ▸ **aloe**
ALOFT *adv, adj*
ALOGIA *n* inability to speak **alogias**
ALOHA *a Hawaiian word for* ▸ **hello**
ALOHAS ▸ **aloha**
ALOIN *n* crystalline compound **aloins**
ALONE *adv* **alonely**
ALONG *adv*
ALONGST *adv* along
ALOO *n* (in Indian cookery) potato
ALOOF *adj* **aloofly**
ALOOS ▸ **aloo**
ALOUD *adv, adj*
ALOW *adj* in or into the lower rigging of a vessel, near the deck
ALOWE *Scots word for* ▸ **ablaze**
ALP *n* high mountain
ALPACA *n* **alpacas, alpacca**
ALPEEN *n* Irish cudgel **alpeens**
ALPHA *n* first letter in the Greek alphabet **alphas**

ALPHORN *n* wind instrument
ALPHYL *n* univalent radical **alphyls**
ALPINE *adj, n* **alpines**
ALPS ▸ **alp**
ALREADY *adv*
ALRIGHT *adj*
ALS ▸ **al**
ALSIKE *n* clover native to Europe and Asia **alsikes**
ALSO *adv*
ALSOON = **alsoone**
ALSOONE *adv* as soon
ALT *n* octave directly above the treble staff
ALTAR *n* **altars**
ALTER *vb* **altered, alterer**
ALTERN *adj* alternate
ALTERNE *n* neighbouring but different plant group
ALTERS ▸ **alter**
ALTESSE *n* French word for highness
ALTEZA *n* Spanish word for highness **altezas**
ALTEZZA *n* Italian word for highness
ALTHAEA *n* type of plant **althea**
ALTHEAS ▸ **althea**
ALTHO *conj* short form of although
ALTHORN *n* valved brass musical instrument
ALTO *n, adj*
ALTOIST *n* person who plays the alto saxophone
ALTOS ▸ **alto**
ALTS ▸ **alt**
ALU ▸ **aloo**
ALUDEL *n* pear-shaped vessel **aludels**
ALULA *n* tuft of feathers **alulae, alular, alulas**
ALUM *n* double sulphate of aluminium and potassium
ALUMIN *n* aluminium oxide
ALUMINA *n* aluminium oxide
ALUMINE *n* French word for alumina
ALUMINS ▸ **alumin**
ALUMISH *adj* like alum
ALUMIUM *old name for* > **aluminium**
ALUMNA *n* female graduate of a school, college, etc **alumnae**
ALUMNI ▸ **alumnus**
ALUMNUS *n* graduate of a college
ALUMS ▸ **alum**
ALUNITE *n* white, grey, or reddish mineral
ALURE *n* area behind battlements **alures**
ALUS ▸ **alu**
ALVEARY *n* beehive
ALVEOLE *n* alveolus
ALVEOLI > **alveolus**
ALVINE *adj* of or relating to the intestines or belly
ALWAY = **always**
ALWAYS *adv*
ALYSSUM *n*
AM *see* ▸ **be**
AMA *n* vessel for water
AMABILE *adj* sweet
AMADODA *pl n* grown men
AMADOU *n* spongy substance made from fungi **amadous**
AMAH *n* (in the East, formerly) a nurse or maidservant **amahs**
AMAIN *adv* with great strength, speed, or haste
AMAKOSI ▸ **inkhosi**
AMALGAM *n*
AMANDLA *n*
AMANITA *n* type of fungus
AMARANT *n* amaranth
AMARNA *adj* pertaining to the reign of the Pharaoh Akhenaton
AMARONE *n* strong dry red Italian wine
AMAS ▸ **ama**
AMASS *vb* **amassed, amasser, amasses**
AMATE *vb* match **amated, amates**
AMATEUR *n, adj*
AMATING ▸ **amate**
AMATION *n* lovemaking
AMATIVE *a rare word for* ▸ **amorous**
AMATOL *n* explosive mixture **amatols**
AMATORY *adj* relating to romantic or sexual love
AMAUT *n* hood on an Inuit woman's parka for carrying a child **amauts**
AMAZE *vb* **amazed, amazes**
AMAZING *adj*
AMAZON *n* any tall, strong, or aggressive

woman **amazons**
AMBACH = **ambatch**
AMBAGE *n* ambiguity **ambages**
AMBAN *n* Chinese official **ambans**
AMBARI = **ambary**
AMBARIS ▸ **ambari**
AMBARY *n* tropical Asian plant that yields a fibre similar to jute
AMBASSY *n* embassy
AMBATCH *n* tree or shrub
AMBEER *n* saliva coloured by tobacco juice **ambeers**
AMBER *n, adj*
AMBERED *adj* fixed in amber
AMBERS ▸ **amber**
AMBERY *adj* like amber
AMBIENT *adj, n*
AMBIT *n* limits or boundary **ambits**
AMBITTY *adj* crystalline and brittle
AMBLE *vb, n* **ambled, ambler, amblers, ambles**
AMBLING *n* walking at a leisurely pace
AMBO *n* early Christian pulpit
AMBOINA = **amboyna ambones, ambos**
AMBOYNA *n* mottled curly-grained wood
AMBRIES ▸ **ambry**
AMBROID = **amberoid**
AMBRY *n* cupboard in the wall of a church
AMBSACE *n* double ace, the lowest throw at dice
AMBUSH *n, vb*
AME *n* soul
AMEARST *old form of* ▸ **amerce**
AMEBA = **amoeba**
AMEBAE ▸ **ameba**
AMEBAN ▸ **ameba**
AMEBAS ▸ **ameba**
AMEBEAN = **amoebean**
AMEBIC ▸ **ameba**
AMEBOID = **amoeboid**
AMEER *n* (formerly) the ruler of Afghanistan **ameers**
AMELIA *n* congenital absence of arms or legs **amelias**
AMEN *n, vb*
AMENAGE *vb* tame
AMEND *vb*
AMENDE *n* public apology
AMENDED ▸ **amend**
AMENDER ▸ **amend**
AMENDES ▸ **amende**
AMENDS *n* recompense for injury, insult, etc
AMENE *adj* pleasant
AMENED ▸ **amen**
AMENING ▸ **amen**
AMENITY *n*
AMENS ▸ **amen**
AMENT *n* mentally deficient person
AMENTA ▸ **amentum**
AMENTAL ▸ **amentum**
AMENTIA *n* severe mental deficiency, usually congenital
AMENTS ▸ **ament**
AMENTUM = **ament**
AMERCE *vb* punish by a fine **amerced, amercer, amerces**
AMES ▸ **ame**
AMESACE = **ambsace**
AMI *n* male friend
AMIA *n* species of fish
AMIABLE *adj* **amiably**
AMIAS ▸ **amia**
AMICE *n* item of clothing **amices**
AMICI ▸ **amicus**
AMICUS *n* Latin for friend
AMID *prep, n*
AMIDASE *n* enzyme
AMIDE *n* any organic compound containing the group $-CONH_2$ **amides, amidic**
AMIDIN *n* form of starch
AMIDINE *n* crystalline compound
AMIDINS ▸ **amidin**
AMIDO *adj* containing amide
AMIDOL *n* chemical used in developing photographs **amidols**
AMIDONE *n* pain-killing drug
AMIDS = **amid**
AMIDST = **amid**
AMIE *n* female friend **amies**
AMIGA *n* Spanish female friend **amigas**
AMIGO *n* friend **amigos**
AMILDAR *n* manager in India
AMIN = **amine**
AMINE *n* chemical **amines, aminic**
AMINITY *n* amenity
AMINO *n* of, consisting of, or containing the group of atoms $-NH_2$

AMINS ▸ **amin**
AMIR *n* (formerly) the ruler of Afghanistan **amirate, amirs**
AMIS ▸ **ami**
AMISES ▸ **ami**
AMISS *adv, adj, n* **amisses**
AMITIES ▸ **amity**
AMITY *n*
AMLA *n* species of Indian tree **amlas**
AMMAN = **amtman**
AMMANS ▸ **amman**
AMMETER *n*
AMMINE *n* chemical compound **ammines**
AMMINO *adj* containing ammonia molecules
AMMIRAL *old word for* ▸ **admiral**
AMMO *n* ammunition
AMMON *n* Asian wild sheep
AMMONAL *n* explosive
AMMONIA *n*
AMMONIC *adj* of ammonia
AMMONO *adj* using ammonia
AMMONS ▸ **ammon**
AMMOS ▸ **ammo**
AMNESIA *n* **amnesic**
AMNESTY *n, vb*
AMNIA ▸ **amnion**
AMNIC *adj* relating to amnion
AMNIO *n* amniocentesis
AMNION *n* innermost of two membranes enclosing an embryo **amnions**
AMNIOS ▸ **amnio**
AMNIOTE *n* group of animals
AMOEBA *n* **amoebae, amoeban, amoebas, amoebic**
AMOK *n* **amoks**
AMOKURA *n* type of sea bird
AMOLE *n* American plant **amoles**
AMOMUM *n* plant of ginger family **amomums**
AMONG *prep* **amongst**
AMOOVE *vb* stir someone's emotions **amooved, amooves**
AMORAL *adj*
AMORANT > **amorance**
AMORCE *n* small percussion cap **amorces**
AMORET *n* sweetheart **amorets**
AMORINI ▸ **amorino**
AMORINO = **amoretto**
AMORISM ▸ **amorist**
AMORIST *n* lover or a writer about love
AMOROSA *n* lover
AMOROSO *adv* (to be played) lovingly ▹ *n* sherry
AMOROUS *adj*
AMORT *adj* in low spirits
AMOSITE *n* form of asbestos
AMOTION *n* act of removing
AMOUNT *n, vb* **amounts**
AMOUR *n* (secret) love affair **amours**
AMOVE *vb* stir someone's emotions **amoved, amoves, amoving**
AMOWT = **amaut**
AMOWTS ▸ **amowt**
AMP *n* ampere ▹ *vb* excite or become excited
AMPASSY *n* ampersand
AMPED ▸ **amp**
AMPERE *n* **amperes**
AMPHORA *n* two-handled ancient Greek or Roman jar
AMPING ▸ **amp**
AMPLE *adj* **ampler, amplest**
AMPLIFY *vb*
AMPLY *adv* fully or generously
AMPOULE *n* small sealed glass vessel
AMPS ▸ **amp**
AMPUL *n* ampoule
AMPULE = **ampoule**
AMPULES ▸ **ampule**
AMPULLA *n* dilated end part of certain tubes in the body
AMPULS ▸ **ampul**
AMPUTEE *n* person who has had a limb amputated
AMREETA = **amrita**
AMRIT *n* liquid used in the Amrit Ceremony
AMRITA *n* ambrosia of the gods that bestows immortality **amritas**
AMRITS ▸ **amrit**
AMTMAN *n* magistrate in parts of Europe **amtmans**

AMTRAC *n* amphibious tracked vehicle
AMTRACK *n* amphibious tracked vehicle
AMTRACS ▸ **amtrac**
AMU *n* unit of mass
AMUCK = **amok**
AMUCKS ▸ **amuck**
AMULET *n* **amulets**
AMUS ▸ **amu**
AMUSE *vb* **amused, amuser, amusers, amuses**
AMUSIA *n* inability to recognize musical tones **amusias, amusic**
AMUSING *adj* mildly entertaining
AMUSIVE *adj* deceptive
AMYGDAL *n* almond
AMYL *n* chemical compound
AMYLASE *n* enzyme
AMYLENE *another name (no longer in technical usage) for* ▸ **pentene**
AMYLIC *adj* of or derived from amyl
AMYLOID *n* complex protein ▹ *adj* starchlike
AMYLOSE *n* type of chemical
AMYLS ▸ **amyl**
AMYLUM *another name for* ▸ **starch**
AMYLUMS ▸ **amylum**
AN *adj* form of **a** used before vowels ▹ *n* additional condition
ANA *adv* in equal quantities ▹ *n* collection of reminiscences
ANABAS *n* type of fish
ANADEM *n* garland for the head **anadems**
ANAEMIA *n*
ANAEMIC *adj* having anaemia
ANAGOGE *n* allegorical interpretation **anagogy**
ANAGRAM *n*
ANAL *adj*
ANALGIA = **analgesia**
ANALITY *n* quality of being psychologically anal
ANALLY ▸ **anal**
ANALOG = **analogue**
ANALOGA > **analogon**
ANALOGS ▸ **analog**
ANALOGY *n*
ANALYSE *vb*
ANALYST *n*
ANALYTE *n* substance that is being analyzed
ANALYZE = **analyse**
ANAN *interj* expression of failure to understand
ANANA *n* pineapple

> More than two As on your rack is bad news, but there are a number of short words that use three As, of which this word is one.

ANANAS *n* plant related to the pineapple
ANANKE *n* unalterable necessity **anankes**
ANAPEST = **anapaest**
ANAPHOR *n* word referring back to a previous word
ANARCH *n* instigator or personification of anarchy **anarchs**
ANARCHY *n*
ANAS ▸ **ana**
ANATA *n* Buddhist belief **anatas**
ANATASE *n* rare blue or black mineral
ANATMAN = **anata**
ANATOMY *n*
ANATTA *n* annatto **anattas**
ANATTO = **annatto**
ANATTOS ▸ **anatto**
ANAXIAL *adj* asymmetrical
ANBURY *n* soft spongy tumour occurring in horses and oxen
ANCE *dialect form of* ▸ **once**
ANCHO *n* chili pepper
ANCHOR *n, vb*
ANCHORS *pl n* brakes of a motor vehicle
ANCHOS ▸ **ancho**
ANCHOVY *n*
ANCHUSA *n* Eurasian plant
ANCIENT *adj, n*
ANCILE *n* mythical Roman shield **ancilia**
ANCILLA *n* Latin word for servant
ANCLE *old spelling of* ▸ **ankle**
ANCLES ▸ **ancle**
ANCOME *n* inflammation **ancomes**
ANCON *n* projecting bracket **anconal, ancone**
ANCONES ▸ **ancone**

ANCORA *adv* Italian for encore
ANCRESS *n* female anchorite
AND *n*
ANDANTE *adv, n*
ANDIRON *n* iron stand for supporting logs in a fireplace
ANDRO *n* type of sex hormone
ANDROID *n, adj*
ANDROS ▸ **andro**
ANDS ▸ **and**
ANDVILE *old form of* ▸ **anvil**
ANE *Scots word for* ▸ **one**
ANEAR *adv* nearly ▷ *vb* approach **aneared, anears**
ANEATH *Scots word for* ▸ **beneath**
ANELACE = **anlace**
ANELE *vb* anoint, esp to give extreme unction to **aneled, aneles, aneling**
ANELLI *pl n* pasta shaped like small rings
ANEMIA *n* anaemia **anemias**
ANEMIC = **anaemic**
ANEMONE *n*
ANENST *dialect word for* ▸ **against**
ANENT *prep* lying against
ANERGIA *n* anergy
ANERGIC ▸ **anergy**
ANERGY *n* lack of energy
ANERLY *Scots word for* ▸ **only**
ANEROID *adj* not containing a liquid ▷ *n* barometer that does not contain liquid
ANES ▸ **ane**
ANESTRA > **anestrus**
ANESTRI > **anestrus**
ANETHOL *n* substance derived from oil of anise
ANETIC *adj* medically soothing
ANEURIN *a less common name for* > **thiamine**
ANEW *adv*
ANGA *n* part in Indian music
ANGAKOK *n* Inuit shaman
ANGARIA *n* species of shellfish
ANGARY *n* right to use the property of a neutral state during a war
ANGAS ▸ **anga**
ANGEKOK *n* Inuit shaman
ANGEL *n, vb* **angeled**
ANGELIC *adj* very kind, pure, or beautiful
ANGELS ▸ **angel**
ANGELUS *n* series of prayers
ANGER *n, vb* **angered**
ANGERLY *adv* old form of angrily
ANGERS ▸ **anger**
ANGICO *n* South American tree **angicos**
ANGINA *n* **anginal, anginas**
ANGIOMA *n* tumour consisting of a mass of blood vessels or lymphatic vessels
ANGLE *n, vb* **angled**
ANGLER *n* **anglers**
ANGLES ▸ **angle**
ANGLICE *adv* in English
ANGLIFY = **anglicize**
ANGLING *n* art or sport of fishing with a hook and line
ANGLIST = **anglicist**
ANGLO *n* White inhabitant of the US not of Latin extraction **anglos**
ANGOLA = **angora**
ANGORA *n* **angoras**
ANGRIER ▸ **angry**
ANGRIES ▸ **angry**
ANGRILY ▸ **angry**
ANGRY *adj, n*
ANGST *n* **angsts**
ANGSTY *adj* displaying angst
ANGUINE *adj* of, relating to, or similar to a snake
ANGUISH *n, vb*
ANGULAR *adj*
ANHINGA *n* type of bird
ANI *n* tropical bird
ANICCA *n* Buddhism belief **aniccas**
ANICUT *n* dam in India **anicuts**
ANIGH *adv* near
ANIGHT *adv* at night
ANIL *n* West Indian shrub
ANILE *adj* of or like a feeble old woman
ANILIN *n* aniline
ANILINE *n* colourless oily liquid
ANILINS ▸ **anilin**
ANILITY ▸ **anile**

ANILS ▸ **anil**
ANIMA *n* feminine principle as present in the male unconscious
ANIMACY *n* state of being animate
ANIMAL *n, adj* **animals**
ANIMAS ▸ **anima**
ANIMATE *vb, adj*
ANIMATO *adv* (to be performed) in a lively manner
ANIME *n* type of Japanese animation **animes**
ANIMI ▸ **animus**
ANIMIS ▸ **animi**
ANIMISM *n* belief that natural objects possess souls **animist**
ANIMUS *n* hatred, animosity
ANION *n* ion with negative charge **anionic, anions**
ANIS ▸ **ani**
ANISE *n* plant with liquorice-flavoured seeds
ANISEED *n*
ANISES ▸ **anise**
ANISIC ▸ **anise**
ANISOLE *n* colourless pleasant-smelling liquid used as a solvent
ANKER *n* old liquid measure for wine **ankers**
ANKH *n* ancient Egyptian symbol **ankhs**
ANKLE *n, vb* **ankled, ankles**
ANKLET *n* ornamental chain worn round the ankle **anklets**
ANKLING ▸ **ankle**
ANKLONG *n* Asian musical instrument
ANKLUNG *n* Asian musical instrument
ANKUS *n* stick used, esp in India, for goading elephants **ankuses**
ANKUSH *n* Indian weapon
ANLACE *n* medieval short dagger with a broad tapering blade **anlaces**
ANLAGE *n* organ or part in the earliest stage of development **anlagen, anlages**
ANLAS = **anlace**
ANLASES ▸ **anlas**
ANN *n* old Scots word for a widow's pension
ANNA *n* former Indian coin worth one sixteenth of a rupee
ANNAL *n* recorded events of one year **annals**
ANNAS ▸ **anna**
ANNAT *n* singular of annates
ANNATES *pl n* money paid to the Pope
ANNATS ▸ **annat**
ANNATTA *n* annatto
ANNATTO *n* tropical tree
ANNEAL *vb* toughen by heating and slow cooling ▹ *n* act of annealing **anneals**
ANNELID *n* type of worm with a segmented body
ANNEX *vb* seize (territory)
ANNEXE *n* extension to a building
ANNEXED ▸ **annex**
ANNEXES ▸ **annexe**
ANNICUT *n* dam in India
ANNO *adv* Latin for in the year
ANNONA *n* American tree or shrub **annonas**
ANNOY *vb* **annoyed, annoyer, annoys**
ANNS ▸ **ann**
ANNUAL *adj, n* **annuals**
ANNUITY *n*
ANNUL *vb*
ANNULAR *adj* ring-shaped ▹ *n* ring finger
ANNULET *n* moulding in the form of a ring
ANNULI ▸ **annulus**
ANNULS ▸ **annul**
ANNULUS *n* area between two concentric circles
ANOA *n* type of small cattle **anoas**
ANOBIID *n* any type of beetle
ANODAL ▸ **anode**
ANODE *n* **anodes, anodic**
ANODISE = **anodize**
ANODIZE *vb* coat (metal) with a protective oxide film by electrolysis
ANODYNE *n, adj*
ANOESES ▸ **anoesis**
ANOESIS *n* feeling without understanding **anoetic**

ANOINT *vb* **anoints**
ANOLE *n* type of lizard **anoles**
ANOLYTE *n* part of electrolyte around anode
ANOMALY *n*
ANOMIC ▸ **anomie**
ANOMIE *n* lack of social or moral standards **anomies, anomy**
ANON *adv*
ANONYM *n* anonymous person or publication
ANONYMA *n* promiscuous woman
ANONYMS ▸ **anonym**
ANOPIA *n* inability to see **anopias**
ANOPSIA *n* squint in which the eye turns upwards
ANORAK *n* **anoraks**
ANOREXY *old name for* ▸ **anorexia**
ANOSMIA *n* loss of the sense of smell **anosmic**
ANOTHER *adj*
ANOUGH *adj* enough
ANOW *adj* old form of enough
ANOXIA *n* lack or absence of oxygen **anoxias, anoxic**
ANS *pl n as in* **ifs and ans** things that might have happened, but which did not
ANSA *n* either end of Saturn's rings **ansae**
ANSATE *adj* having a handle or handle-like part
ANSATED *adj* ansate
ANSWER *n, vb* **answers**
ANT *n*
ANTA *n* pilaster
ANTACID *n* substance that counteracts acidity ▹ *adj* having the properties of this substance
ANTAE ▸ **anta**
ANTAR *old word for* ▸ **cave**
ANTARA *n* South American panpipes **antaras**
ANTARS ▸ **antar**
ANTAS ▸ **anta**
ANTBEAR *n* aardvark
ANTBIRD *n* South American bird
ANTE *n* player's stake in poker ▹ *vb* place (one's stake) in poker **anted, anteed**
ANTEFIX *n* carved ornament
ANTEING ▸ **ante**
ANTENNA *n* insect's feeler
ANTES ▸ **ante**
ANTHEM *n, vb* **anthems**
ANTHER *n* **anthers**
ANTHILL *n* mound near an ants' nest
ANTHOID *adj* resembling a flower
ANTHRAX *n*
ANTI *adj* opposed (to) ▹ *n* opponent of a party, policy, or attitude
ANTIAIR *adj* countering attack by aircraft or missile
ANTIAR *another name for* ▸ **upas**
ANTIARS ▸ **antiar**
ANTIBUG *adj* acting against computer bugs
ANTIC *n* actor in a ludicrous or grotesque part ▹ *adj* fantastic
ANTICAL *adj* position of plant parts
ANTICAR *n* opposed to cars
ANTICK *vb* perform antics
ANTICKE *adj* old form of antique
ANTICKS ▸ **antick**
ANTICLY *adv* grotesquely
ANTICS *pl n*
ANTIENT *old spelling of* ▸ **ancient**
ANTIFAT *adj* acting to remove or prevent fat
ANTIFLU *adj* acting against influenza
ANTIFOG *adj* preventing the buildup of moisture on a surface
ANTIFUR *adj* opposed to the wearing of fur garments
ANTIGAY *adj* hostile to homosexuals
ANTIGEN *n*
ANTIGUN *adj* opposed to the possession of guns
ANTIJAM *adj* preventing jamming
ANTILOG *n* number whose logarithm to a given base is a

given number
ANTIMAN *adj* opposed to men
ANTING *n* rubbing of ants by birds on their feathers **antings**
ANTIPOT *adj* opposed to illegal use of marijuana
ANTIQUE *n, adj, vb*
ANTIRED *adj* of a particular colour of antiquark
ANTIS ▸ **anti**
ANTISAG *adj* preventing sagging
ANTISEX *adj* opposed to sexual activity
ANTITAX *adj* opposed to taxation
ANTIWAR *adj* opposed to war
ANTLER *n* **antlers**
ANTLIA *n* butterfly proboscis **antliae**
ANTLIKE *adj* of or like an ant or ants
ANTLION *n* type of insect resembling a dragonfly
ANTONYM *n*
ANTRA ▸ **antrum**
ANTRAL ▸ **antrum**
ANTRE *n* cavern or cave **antres**
ANTRUM *n* natural cavity, esp in a bone **antrums**
ANTS ▸ **ant**
ANTSIER ▸ **antsy**
ANTSY *adj* restless, nervous, and impatient
ANURAL *adj* without a tail
ANURAN *n* type of amphibian **anurans**
ANURIA *n* result of a kidney disorder **anurias, anuric**
ANUROUS *adj* lacking a tail
ANUS *n* **anuses**
ANVIL *n, vb* **anviled, anvils**
ANXIETY *n*
ANXIOUS *adj*
ANY *adj, adv*
ANYBODY *n*
ANYHOW *adv*
ANYMORE *adv* at present
ANYON *n* (in mathematics) projective representation of a Lie group
ANYONE *pron, n* **anyones**
ANYONS ▸ **anyon**
ANYROAD *a northern English dialect word for* ▸ **anyway**
ANYTIME *adv* at any time
ANYWAY *adv* **anyways**
ANYWHEN *adv* at any time
ANYWISE *adv* in any way or manner
ANZIANI *n* Italian word for councillors
AORIST *n* tense of the verb in classical Greek **aorists**
AORTA *n* **aortae, aortal, aortas, aortic**
AOUDAD *n* wild mountain sheep **aoudads**
APACE *adv* swiftly
APACHE *n* Parisian gangster or ruffian **apaches**
APADANA *n* ancient Persian palace hall
APAGE *interj* Greek word meaning go away
APAGOGE *n* reduction to absurdity
APAID ▸ **apay**
APANAGE = **appanage**
APAREJO *n* kind of packsaddle made of stuffed leather cushions
APART *adv*
APATHY *n*
APATITE *n* pale green to purple mineral, found in igneous rocks
APAY *vb* old word meaning satisfy **apayd, apaying, apays**
APE *n, vb*
APEAK *adj* in a vertical or almost vertical position
APED ▸ **ape**
APEDOM *n* state of being an ape **apedoms**
APEEK *adv* nautical word meaning vertically
APEHOOD *n* state of being ape
APELIKE ▸ **ape**
APEMAN *n* primate thought to have been the forerunner of humans **apemen**

APEPSIA *n* digestive disorder
APEPSY *n* apepsia
APER *n* person who apes
APERCU *n* outline **apercus**
APERIES ▸ **apery**
APERS ▸ **aper**
APERT *adj* open
APERY *n* imitative behaviour
APES ▸ **ape**
APETALY > **apetalous**
APEX *n* **apexes**
APGAR *n as in* **apgar score** system for determining the condition of an infant at birth
APHAGIA *n* refusal or inability to swallow
APHAKIA *n* absence of the lens of an eye
APHASIA *n* disorder of the central nervous system **aphasic**
APHELIA > **aphelion**
APHESES ▸ **aphesis**
APHESIS *n* gradual disappearance of an unstressed vowel at the beginning of a word **aphetic**
APHID *n*
APHIDES ▸ **aphis**
APHIDS ▸ **aphid**
APHIS *n* type of aphid such as the blackfly
APHONIA *n* loss of the voice caused by damage to the vocal tract
APHONIC *adj* affected with aphonia ▹ *n* person affected with aphonia
APHONY = **aphonia**
APHOTIC *adj* characterized by or growing in the absence of light
APHTHA *n* small ulceration **aphthae**
APHYLLY > **aphyllous**
APIAN *adj* of, relating to, or resembling bees
APIARY *n*
APICAL *adj* of, at, or being an apex ▹ *n* sound made with the tip of the tongue **apicals**
APICES *plural of* ▸ **apex**
APICIAN *adj* of fine or dainty food
APICULI > **apiculus**
APIECE *adv*
APIEZON *adj as in* **apiezon oil** oil left by distillation
APING ▸ **ape**
APIOL *n* substance formerly used to assist menstruation **apiols**
APISH *adj* stupid or foolish **apishly**
APISM *n* behaviour like an ape **apisms**
APLANAT *n* aplanatic lens
APLASIA *n* congenital absence of an organ
APLENTY *adv* in plenty
APLITE *n* type of igneous rock **aplites, aplitic**
APLOMB *n* **aplombs**
APNEA = **apnoea**
APNEAL ▸ **apnea**
APNEAS ▸ **apnea**
APNEIC ▸ **apnea**
APNOEA *n* temporary inability to breathe **apnoeal, apnoeas, apnoeic**
APO *n* type of protein
APOCARP *n* apocarpous gynoecium or fruit
APOCOPE *n* omission of the final sound or sounds of a word
APOD *n* animal without feet
APODAL *adj* (of snakes, eels, etc) without feet
APODE *n* animal without feet **apodes**
APODOUS = **apodal**
APODS ▸ **apod**
APOGAMY *n* type of reproduction in some ferns
APOGEAL ▸ **apogee**
APOGEAN ▸ **apogee**
APOGEE *n* point of moon's orbit **apogees, apogeic**
APOLLO *n* strikingly handsome youth **apollos**
APOLOG = **apologue**
APOLOGS ▸ **apolog**
APOLOGY *n*
APOLUNE *n* point in a lunar orbit
APOMICT *n* organism, esp a plant, produced by apomixis
APOOP *adv* on the poop deck
APOPLEX *vb* afflict with apoplexy

APORIA *n* doubt, real or professed, about what to do or say **aporias**
APORT *adj* on or towards the port side
APOS ▸ **apo**
APOSTIL *n* marginal note
APOSTLE *n*
APOTHEM *n* geometrical term
APOZEM *n* medicine dissolved in water **apozems**
APP *n* application program
APPAID ▸ **appay**
APPAIR *vb* old form of impair **appairs**
APPAL *vb* **appall**
APPALLS ▸ **appall**
APPALS ▸ **appal**
APPALTI ▸ **appalto**
APPALTO *n* Italian word for contact
APPARAT *n* Communist Party organization
APPAREL *n, vb*
APPAY *old word for* ▸ **satisfy**
APPAYD ▸ **appay**
APPAYS ▸ **appay**
APPEACH *old word for* ▸ **accuse**
APPEAL *vb, n* **appeals**
APPEAR *vb* **appears**
APPEASE *vb*
APPEL *n* stamp of the foot, used to warn of one's intent to attack **appels**
APPEND *vb* **appends**
APPERIL *old word for* ▸ **peril**
APPLAUD *vb*
APPLE *n* **apples**
APPLET *n* computing program **applets**
APPLEY *adj* resembling or tasting like an apple
APPLIED *adj*
APPLIER ▸ **apply**
APPLIES ▸ **apply**
APPLY *vb*
APPOINT *vb*
APPORT *n* production of objects at a seance **apports**
APPOSE *vb* place side by side or near to each other **apposed, apposer, apposes**
APPRESS *vb* press together
APPRISE *vb* make aware (of) **apprize**
APPRO *n* approval
APPROOF *old word for* ▸ **trial appros**
APPROVE *vb*
APPS ▸ **app**
APPUI *n* support
APPUIED ▸ **appuy**
APPUIS ▸ **appui**
APPULSE *n* close approach of two celestial bodies
APPUY *vb* support **appuyed, appuys**
APRAXIA *n* disorder of the central nervous system **apraxic**
APRES *prep* French word for after
APRICOT *n, adj*
APRON *n, vb* **aproned, aprons**
APROPOS *adv*
APROTIC *adj* (of solvents) neither accepting nor donating hydrogen ions
APSARAS *n* Hindu water sprite
APSE *n* arched or domed recess, esp in a church **apses**
APSIDAL ▸ **apsis**
APSIDES ▸ **apsis**
APSIS *n* points in the elliptical orbit of a planet or satellite
APSO *n* Tibetan terrier **apsos**
APT *adj, vb*
APTAMER *n* artificially-created DNA or RNA molecule
APTED ▸ **apt**
APTER ▸ **apt**
APTERAL *adj* (esp of a classical temple) not having columns at the sides
APTERIA > **apterium**
APTERYX *n* kiwi (the bird)
APTEST ▸ **apt**
APTING ▸ **apt**
APTLY ▸ **apt**
APTNESS ▸ **apt**
APTOTE *n* noun without inflections **aptotes, aptotic**
APTS ▸ **apt**
APYRASE *n* enzyme
AQUA *n* water **aquae**

> This Latin word for water, together with its plural **aquae** or **aquas**, comes up over and over again.

AQUAFER *n* aquifer
AQUAFIT *n* type of aerobic exercise done in water
AQUARIA > **aquarium**
AQUAS ▶ **aqua**
AQUATIC *adj, n*
AQUAVIT *n* grain- or potato-based spirit
AQUEOUS *adj* of, like, or containing water
AQUIFER *n* deposit of rock containing water used to supply wells
AQUILON *n* name for the north wind
AQUIVER *adv* quivering
AR *n* letter R
ARAARA *another name for* > **trevally**
ARAARAS ▶ **araara**
ARABA *n* Asian carriage **arabas**

> This is one of the short words that can help you deal with a surplus of As.

ARABESK = **arabesque**
ARABIC *adj as in* **gum arabic** gum exuded by certain acacia trees
ARABICA *n* high-quality coffee bean
ARABIN *n* essence of gum arabic **arabins**
ARABIS *n* type of plant
ARABISE *vb* make or become Arab
ARABIZE *vb* make or become Arab
ARABLE *adj, n* **arables**
ARACHIS *n* Brazilian plant
ARAISE *vb* old form of raise **araised, araises**
ARAK = **arrack**
ARAKS ▶ **arak**
ARALIA *n* type of plant **aralias**
ARAME *n* Japanese edible seaweed **arames**
ARAMID *n* synthetic fibre **aramids**
ARANEID *n* member of the spider family
ARAR *n* African tree
ARAROBA *n* Brazilian leguminous tree
ARARS ▶ **arar**
ARAYSE *vb* old form of raise **araysed, arayses**
ARB *short for* > **arbitrage**
ARBA *n* Asian carriage **arbas**
ARBITER *n*
ARBLAST *n* arbalest
ARBOR *n* revolving shaft or axle in a machine
ARBORED *adj* having arbors
ARBORES ▶ **arbor**
ARBORET *n* old name for an area planted with shrubs
ARBORIO *n as in* **arborio rice** variety of round-grain rice used for making risotto
ARBORS ▶ **arbor**
ARBOUR *n* **arbours**
ARBS ▶ **arb**
ARBUTE *old name for* ▶ **arbutus**
ARBUTES ▶ **arbute**
ARBUTUS *n* evergreen shrub with strawberry-like berries
ARC *n, vb*
ARCADE *n, vb* **arcaded, arcades**
ARCADIA *n* traditional idealized rural setting
ARCANA *n* either of the two divisions of a pack of tarot cards **arcanas**
ARCANE *adj*
ARCANUM *n* profound secret or mystery known only to initiates
ARCED ▶ **arc**
ARCH *n, vb, adj*
ARCHAEA *n* order of prokaryotic microorganisms
ARCHAEI > **archaeus**
ARCHAIC *adj*
ARCHEAN > **archaean**
ARCHED *adj* provided with or spanned by an arch or arches
ARCHEI ▶ **archeus**
ARCHER *n* **archers**
ARCHERY *n*
ARCHES ▶ **arch**
ARCHEST ▶ **arch**
ARCHEUS *n* spirit believed to inhabit a living thing
ARCHFOE *n* chief enemy
ARCHIL *a variant spelling of* ▶ **orchil**
ARCHILS ▶ **archil**
ARCHINE *n* Russian unit of length equal to about 71 cm
ARCHING ▶ **arch**
ARCHIVE *n, vb*
ARCHLET *n* small arch

ARCHLY ▸ **arch**
ARCHON *n* (in ancient Athens) one of the nine chief magistrates **archons**
ARCHWAY *n* passageway under an arch
ARCING ▸ **arc**
ARCINGS ▸ **arc**
ARCKED ▸ **arc**
ARCKING ▸ **arc**
ARCMIN *n* 1/60 of a degree of an angle **arcmins**
ARCO *adv* musical direction meaning with bow ▹ *n* bow of a stringed instrument **arcos**
ARCS ▸ **arc**
ARCSEC *n* 1/3600 of a degree of an angle **arcsecs**
ARCSINE *n* trigonometrical function
ARCTIC *adj*, *n* **arctics**
ARCTIID *n* type of moth
ARCTOID *adj* like a bear
ARCUATE *adj* shaped or bent like an arc or bow
ARCUS *n* circle around the cornea of the eye **arcuses**
ARD *n* primitive plough
ARDEB *n* unit of dry measure **ardebs**
ARDENCY ▸ **ardent**
ARDENT *adj*
ARDOR = **ardour**
ARDORS ▸ **ardor**
ARDOUR *n* **ardours**
ARDRI *n* Irish high king
ARDRIGH *n* Irish high king
ARDRIS ▸ **ardri**
ARDS ▸ **ard**
ARDUOUS *adj*
ARE *n*, *vb*
AREA *n*
AREACH *vb* old form of reach
AREAD *vb* old word meaning declare **areads**
AREAE ▸ **area**
AREAL ▸ **area**
AREALLY ▸ **area**
AREAR *n* old form of arrear
AREAS ▸ **area**
AREAWAY *n* passageway
ARECA *n* type of palm tree **arecas**
ARED ▸ **aread**
AREDD ▸ **aread**
AREDE *vb* old word meaning declare **aredes, areding**
AREFIED ▸ **arefy**
AREFIES ▸ **arefy**
AREFY *vb* dry up
AREG *a plural of* ▸ **erg**
AREIC *adj* relating to area
ARENA *n* **arenas**
ARENE *n* aromatic hydrocarbon **arenes**
ARENITE *n* any arenaceous rock
ARENOSE *adj* sandy
ARENOUS *adj* sandy
AREOLA *n* **areolae, areolar, areolas**
AREOLE *n* space outlined on a surface **areoles**
AREPA *n* Colombian cornmeal cake **arepas**
ARERE *adv* old word meaning backwards
ARES ▸ **are**
ARET *vb* old word meaning entrust
ARETE *n* sharp ridge separating two glacial valleys **aretes**
ARETS ▸ **aret**
ARETT *vb* old word meaning entrust **aretted, aretts**
AREW *adv* old word meaning in a row
ARF *n* barking sound **arfs**
ARGAL = **argali**
ARGALA *n* Indian stork **argalas**
ARGALI *n* wild sheep **argalis**
ARGALS ▸ **argal**
ARGAN *n* Moroccan tree
ARGAND *n* lamp with a hollow circular wick **argands**
ARGANS ▸ **argan**
ARGENT *n* silver **argents**
ARGH *interj* cry of pain
ARGHAN *n* agave plant **arghans**
ARGIL *n* clay, esp potters' clay **argils**
ARGLE *vb* quarrel **argled, argles, argling**
ARGOL *n* chemical compound **argols**
ARGON *n*
ARGONON *n* inert gas
ARGONS ▸ **argon**

ARGOSY *n* large merchant ship
ARGOT *n* **argotic, argots**
ARGUE *vb* **argued, arguer, arguers, argues**
ARGUFY *vb* argue or quarrel, esp over something trivial
ARGUING ▸ **argue**
ARGULI ▸ **argulus**
ARGULUS *n* parasite on fish
ARGUS *n* any of various brown butterflies **arguses**
ARGUTE *adj* shrill or keen
ARGYLE *adj* a diamond-shaped pattern ▹ *n* sock made of this **argyles**
ARGYLL *n* sock with diamond pattern **argylls**
ARGYRIA *n* staining of skin by exposure to silver
ARHAT *n* Buddhist who has achieved enlightenment **arhats**
ARIA *n*
ARIARY *n* currency of Madagascar
ARIAS ▸ **aria**
ARID *adj* **arider, aridest, aridity, aridly**
ARIEL *n* type of Arabian gazelle **ariels**
ARIETTA *n* short aria **ariette**
ARIGHT *adv* rightly
ARIKI *n* first-born male or female in a notable family **arikis**
ARIL *n* appendage on certain seeds
ARILED *adj* having an aril
ARILLI ▸ **arillus**
ARILLUS *n* aril
ARILS ▸ **aril**
ARIOSE *adj* songlike
ARIOSI ▸ **arioso**
ARIOSO *n* recitative with the lyrical quality of an aria **ariosos**
ARIOT *adv* riotously
ARIPPLE *adv* in ripples
ARISE *vb* **arisen, arises**
ARISH *n* field that has been mown **arishes**
ARISING ▸ **arise**
ARISTA *n* stiff bristle **aristae, aristas**
ARISTO *n* aristocrat **aristos**
ARK *n*, *vb* **arked, arking**
ARKITE *n* passenger in ark **arkites**
ARKOSE *n* type of sandstone **arkoses, arkosic**
ARKS ▸ **ark**
ARLE *vb* make downpayment **arled, arles, arling**
ARM *n* limbs from the shoulder to the wrist ▹ *vb* supply with weapons
ARMADA *n* **armadas**
ARMBAND *n* band worn on the arm
ARMED *adj*
ARMER ▸ **arm**
ARMERS ▸ **arm**
ARMET *n* close-fitting medieval visored helmet with a neck guard **armets**
ARMFUL *n* as much as can be held in the arms **armfuls**
ARMHOLE *n* opening in a garment through which the arm passes
ARMIES ▸ **army**
ARMIGER *n* person entitled to bear heraldic arms
ARMIL *n* bracelet
ARMILLA *n* bracelet
ARMILS ▸ **armil**
ARMING *n* act of taking arms or providing with arms **armings**
ARMLESS ▸ **arm**
ARMLET *n* band worn round the arm **armlets**
ARMLIKE ▸ **arm**
ARMLOAD *n* amount carried in the arms
ARMLOCK *vb* grip someone's arms
ARMOIRE *n* large cabinet
ARMOR = **armour**
ARMORED = **armoured**
ARMORER = **armourer**
ARMORS ▸ **armor**
ARMORY = **armoury**
ARMOUR *n*, *vb* **armours**
ARMOURY *n*
ARMPIT *n* **armpits**
ARMREST *n* part of a chair or sofa that supports the arm
ARMS ▸ **arm**
ARMSFUL ▸ **armful**
ARMURE *n* silk or wool

fabric with a small cobbled pattern **armures**
ARMY *n*
ARNA *n* Indian water buffalo **arnas**
ARNATTO *n* annatto
ARNICA *n* temperate or arctic plant **arnicas**
ARNOTTO *n* annatto
ARNUT *n* plant with edible tubers **arnuts**
AROBA *n* Asian carriage **arobas**
AROHA *n* love, compassion, or affection **arohas**
AROID *n* type of plant **aroids**
AROINT *vb* drive away **aroints**
AROLLA *n* European pine tree **arollas**
AROMA *n* **aromas**
AROSE *past tense of* ▸ **arise**
AROUND *adv*
AROUSAL ▸ **arouse**
AROUSE *vb* **aroused, arouser, arouses**
AROW *adv* in a row
AROYNT *vb* old word meaning to drive away **aroynts**
ARPA *n* website concerned with structure of the internet **arpas**
ARPEN *n* old French measure of land **arpens**
ARPENT *n* former French unit of length **arpents**
ARRACK *n* alcoholic drink distilled from grain or rice **arracks**
ARRAH *interj* Irish exclamation
ARRAIGN *vb*
ARRANGE *vb*
ARRANT *adj*
ARRAS *n* tapestry wall-hanging
ARRASED *adj* having an arras
ARRASES ▸ **arras**
ARRAY *n, vb* **arrayal, arrayed, arrayer, arrays**
ARREAR *n* singular of arrears
ARREARS *pl n*
ARRECT *adj* pricked up
ARREEDE *vb* old word meaning declare
ARREST *vb, n* **arrests**
ARRET *n* judicial decision **arrets**
ARRIAGE *n* Scottish feudal service
ARRIBA *interj* exclamation of pleasure or approval
ARRIDE *vb* old word meaning gratify **arrided, arrides**
ARRIERE *adj* French word meaning old-fashioned
ARRIERO *n* Spanish word for mule driver
ARRIS *n* sharp edge at the meeting of two surfaces **arrises**
ARRISH *n* corn stubble
ARRIVAL *n*
ARRIVE *vb* **arrived, arriver, arrives**
ARROBA *n* unit of weight in Spanish-speaking countries **arrobas**
ARROW *n*
ARROWED *adj* having an arrow pattern
ARROWS ▸ **arrow**
ARROWY *adj* like an arrow
ARROYO *n* usually dry stream bed **arroyos**
ARS ▸ **ar**
ARSENAL *n*
ARSENIC *n, adj*
ARSENO *adj* containing arsenic
ARSHEEN *n* old measure of length in Russia
ARSHIN *n* old measure of length in Russia
ARSHINE *n* old measure of length in Russia
ARSHINS ▸ **arshin**
ARSINE *n* colourless poisonous gas **arsines**
ARSINO *adj* containing arsine
ARSIS *n* long or stressed syllable in a metrical foot
ARSON *n* **arsons**
ART *n*
ARTAL *a plural of* ▸ **rotl**
ARTEL *n* cooperative union **artels**
ARTERY *n*
ARTFUL *adj*
ARTI *n* ritual performed in homes and temples
ARTIC *n* articulated vehicle
ARTICLE *n, vb*

ARTICS ▸ **artic**
ARTIER, arties, artiest, artily ▸ **arty**
ARTIS ▸ **arti**
ARTISAN *n*
ARTIST *n*
ARTISTE *n*
ARTISTS ▸ **artist**
ARTLESS *adj*
ARTS ▸ **art**
ARTSIER ▸ **artsy**
ARTSIES ▸ **artsy**
ARTSMAN *old word for* > **craftsman**
ARTSMEN ▸ **artsman**
ARTSY *adj* interested in the arts ▷ *n* person interested in the arts
ARTWORK *n* all the photographs and illustrations in a publication
ARTY *adj, n*
ARUGOLA *n* salad plant
ARUGULA *another name for* ▸ **rocket**
ARUHE *n* edible root of a fern **aruhes**
ARUM *n* type of plant **arums**
ARUSPEX *variant spelling of* > **haruspex**
ARVAL *adj* of ploughed land
ARVO *n* afternoon **arvos**
ARY *dialect form of* ▸ **any**
ARYL *n* of, consisting of, or containing an aromatic group **aryls**
AS *adv, n*
ASANA *n* any of various postures in yoga **asanas**
ASAR ▸ **as**
ASARUM *n* dried strong-scented root **asarums**
ASCARED *adj* afraid
ASCARID *n* type of parasitic nematode
ASCARIS *n* ascarid
ASCAUNT *adv* old word meaning slantwise
ASCEND *vb* **ascends**
ASCENT *n* **ascents**
ASCESES ▸ **ascesis**
ASCESIS *n* exercise of self-discipline
ASCETIC *adj, n*
ASCI ▸ **ascus**
ASCIAN *n* person living in the tropics **ascians**
ASCIDIA > **ascidium**
ASCITES *n* accumulation of serous fluid in the peritoneal cavity **ascitic**
ASCONCE *adv* old form of askance
ASCOT *n* type of cravat **ascots**
ASCRIBE *vb*
ASCUS *n* saclike structure in fungi
ASDIC *an early form of* ▸ **sonar**
ASDICS ▸ **asdic**
ASEA *adv* towards the sea
ASEITY *n* existence derived from itself, having no other source
ASEPSES ▸ **asepsis**
ASEPSIS *n* aseptic condition
ASEPTIC *adj, n*
ASEXUAL *adj*
ASH *n, vb*
ASHAKE *adv* shaking
ASHAME *vb* make ashamed
ASHAMED *adj*
ASHAMES ▸ **ashame**
ASHCAKE *n* cornmeal bread
ASHCAN *n* large metal dustbin **ashcans**
ASHED ▸ **ash**
ASHEN *adj*
ASHERY *n* place where ashes are made
ASHES ▸ **ash**
ASHET *n* shallow oval dish or large plate **ashets**
ASHFALL *n* dropping of ash from a volcano
ASHIER ▸ **ashy**
ASHIEST ▸ **ashy**
ASHINE *adv* old word meaning shining
ASHING ▸ **ash**
ASHIVER *adv* shivering
ASHKEY *n* winged fruit of the ash **ashkeys**
ASHLAR *n* block of hewn stone ▷ *vb* build with ashlars **ashlars, ashler**
ASHLERS ▸ **ashler**
ASHLESS ▸ **ash**
ASHMAN *n* man who shovels ashes **ashmen**
ASHORE *adv, adj*
ASHRAF ▸ **sherif**
ASHRAM *n* religious retreat where a Hindu holy man lives
ASHRAMA *n* stage in

Hindu spiritual life
ASHRAMS ▸ **ashram**
ASHTRAY *n*
ASHY *adj* pale greyish
ASIAGO *n* type of cheese **asiagos**
ASIDE *adv, n* **asides**
ASINICO *n* old Spanish word for fool
ASININE *adj*
ASK *vb* say (something) in a form that requires an answer
ASKANCE *adv, vb* **askant**
ASKANTS ▸ **askant**
ASKARI *n* (in East Africa) a soldier or policeman **askaris**
ASKED ▸ **ask**
ASKER ▸ **ask**
ASKERS ▸ **ask**
ASKESES ▸ **askesis**
ASKESIS *n* practice of self-discipline
ASKEW *adj*
ASKING ▸ **ask**
ASKINGS ▸ **ask**
ASKLENT *Scots word for* ▸ **aslant**
ASKOI ▸ **askos**
ASKOS *n* ancient Greek vase
ASKS ▸ **ask**
ASLAKE *vb* slake **aslaked, aslakes**
ASLANT *adv* at a slant (to), slanting (across)
ASLEEP *adj*
ASLOPE *adj* sloping
ASLOSH *adj* awash
ASMEAR *adj* smeared
ASOCIAL *n* person who avoids social contact
ASP *n* small poisonous snake
ASPECT *n, vb* **aspects**
ASPEN *n, adj* **aspens**
ASPER *n* former Turkish monetary unit
ASPERGE *vb* sprinkle
ASPERS ▸ **asper**
ASPERSE *vb* spread false rumours about
ASPHALT *n, vb*
ASPHYXY *n* > **asphyxia**
ASPIC *n*
ASPICK *old word for* ▸ **asp**
ASPICKS ▸ **aspick**
ASPICS ▸ **aspic**
ASPIDIA > **aspidium**
ASPINE *old word for* ▸ **aspen**
ASPINES ▸ **aspine**
ASPIRE *vb* **aspired, aspirer, aspires**
ASPIRIN *n*
ASPIS *n* horned viper **aspises**
ASPISH *adj* like an asp
ASPORT *vb* old word meaning take away **asports**
ASPOUT *adv* spouting
ASPRAWL *adv* sprawling
ASPREAD *adv* spreading
ASPRO *n* associate professor at an academic institution **aspros**
ASPROUT *adv* sprouting
ASPS ▸ **asp**
ASQUAT *adv* squatting
ASQUINT *adj* with a glance from the corner of the eye
ASRAMA *n* stage in Hindu spiritual life **asramas**
ASS *n* donkey
ASSAGAI = **assegai**
ASSAI *adv* (usually preceded by a musical direction) very ▷ *n* Brazilian palm tree
ASSAIL *vb* **assails**
ASSAIS ▸ **assai**
ASSAM *n* (in Malaysia) tamarind as used in cooking **assams**
ASSART *vb* clear ground for cultivation **assarts**
ASSAULT *n, vb*
ASSAY *n* analysis of a substance ▷ *vb* make such an analysis **assayed, assayer, assays**
ASSEGAI *n, vb*
ASSENT *n, vb* **assents**
ASSERT *vb* **asserts**
ASSES ▸ **ass**
ASSESS *vb*
ASSET *n* **assets**
ASSEVER *vb* old form of asseverate
ASSEZ *adv* (as part of a musical direction) fairly
ASSIEGE *vb* old form of besiege
ASSIGN *vb, n* **assigns**
ASSIST *vb, n* **assists**
ASSIZE *n* sitting of a legislative assembly **assized**
ASSIZER *n* weights and measures official
ASSIZES ▸ **assize**
ASSLIKE ▸ **ass**

ASSOIL *vb* absolve **assoils**
ASSORT *vb* arrange or distribute equally **assorts**
ASSOT *vb* old word meaning make infatuated **assots**
ASSOTT *vb* besot
ASSUAGE *vb*
ASSUME *vb*
ASSUMED *adj* false
ASSUMER ▸ **assume**
ASSUMES ▸ **assume**
ASSURE *vb*
ASSURED *adj, n*
ASSURER ▸ **assure**
ASSURES ▸ **assure**
ASSUROR ▸ **assure**
ASSWAGE *old spelling of* ▸ **assuage**
ASTABLE *adj* not stable
ASTARE *adv* staring
ASTART *old word for* ▸ **start**
ASTARTS ▸ **astart**
ASTASIA *n* inability to stand
ASTATIC *adj* not static
ASTATKI *n* fuel derived from petroleum
ASTEISM *n* use of irony
ASTELIC ▸ **astely**
ASTELY *n* lack of central cylinder in plants
ASTER *n* plant with daisy-like flowers
ASTERIA *n* gemstone with starlike light effect
ASTERID *n* variety of flowering plant
ASTERN *adv, adj*
ASTERS ▸ **aster**
ASTERT *vb* start **asterts**
ASTHENY = **asthenia**
ASTHMA *n* **asthmas**
ASTHORE *n* Irish endearment
ASTILBE *n* type of plant
ASTIR *adj*
ASTONE *vb old form of* > **astonish**
ASTONED ▸ **astone**
ASTONES ▸ **astone**
ASTONY *vb old form of* > **astonish**
ASTOOP *adv* stooping
ASTOUND *vb*
ASTRAL *adj* of stars ▷ *n* oil lamp **astrals**
ASTRAND *adv* on shore
ASTRAY *adv*
ASTRICT *vb* bind, confine, or constrict
ASTRIDE *adv, adj*
ASTROID *n* hypocycloid having four cusps
ASTRUT *adv* old word meaning in a protruding way
ASTUN *vb* old form of astonish **astuns**
ASTUTE *adj* **astuter**
ASTYLAR *adj* without columns or pilasters
ASUDDEN *adv* old form of suddenly
ASUNDER *adv, adj*
ASWARM *adj* filled, esp with moving things
ASWAY *adv* swaying
ASWIM *adv* floating
ASWING *adv* swinging
ASWIRL *adv* swirling
ASWOON *adv* swooning
ASYLA ▸ **asylum**
ASYLEE *n* person who is granted asylum **asylees**
ASYLUM *n* **asylums**
AT *n*
ATAATA *n* grazing marine gastropod **ataatas**
ATABAL *n* N African drum **atabals**
ATABEG *n* Turkish ruler **atabegs**
ATABEK *n* Turkish ruler **atabeks**
ATABRIN *n* drug formerly used for treating malaria
ATACTIC *adj* attribute of a polymer
ATAGHAN *a variant of* > **yataghan**
ATALAYA *n* watchtower in Spain
ATAMAN *n* elected leader of the Cossacks **atamans**
ATAP *n* palm tree of S Asia **ataps**
ATARAXY = **ataraxia**
ATAVIC ▸ **atavism**
ATAVISM *n* **atavist**
ATAXIA *n* lack of muscular coordination **ataxias, ataxic, ataxics**
ATAXIES ▸ **ataxy**
ATE *past tense of* ▸ **eat**
ATEBRIN *n* drug formerly used to treat malaria
ATELIC *adj* of action without end
ATELIER *n* workshop, artist's studio

ATEMOYA *n* tropical fruit tree
ATES *n* shop selling confectionery
ATHAME *n* witch's ceremonial knife **athames**
ATHANOR *n* alchemist's furnace
ATHEISE *vb* speak atheistically
ATHEISM *n* belief that there is no God **atheist**
ATHEIZE *vb* speak atheistically
ATHEOUS *adj* without a belief in god
ATHIRST *adj* having an eager desire
ATHLETA *n old form of* ▸ **athlete**
ATHLETE *n*
ATHODYD *another name for* ▸ **ramjet**
ATHRILL *adv* feeling thrills
ATHROB *adv* throbbing
ATHWART *adv* transversely
ATIGI *n* type of parka worn by the Inuit in Canada **atigis**
ATILT *adj* in a tilted or inclined position
ATIMIES ▸ **atimy**
ATIMY *n* loss of honour
ATINGLE *adv* tingling
ATISHOO *n* sound of a sneeze
ATLAS *n* **atlases**
ATLATL *n* Native American throwing stick **atlatls**
ATMA = **atman**
ATMAN *n* personal soul or self **atmans**
ATMAS ▸ **atma**
ATOC *n* skunk
ATOCIA *n* inability to have children **atocias**
ATOCS ▸ **atoc**
ATOK *n* skunk
ATOKAL *adj* having no children
ATOKE *n* part of a worm **atokes**
ATOKOUS *adj* having no children
ATOKS ▸ **atok**
ATOLL *n* **atolls**
ATOM *n*
ATOMIC *adj*
ATOMICS *n* science of atoms
ATOMIES ▸ **atomy**
ATOMISE = **atomize**
ATOMISM *n* ancient philosophical theory **atomist**
ATOMIZE *vb*
ATOMS ▸ **atom**
ATOMY *n* atom or minute particle
ATONAL *adj* (of music) not written in an established key
ATONE *vb* **atoned, atoner, atoners, atones**
ATONIA *n* lack of normal muscle tone **atonias**
ATONIC *adj* carrying no stress ▹ *n* unaccented or unstressed syllable **atonics**
ATONIES ▸ **atony**

> The plural of **atony**, this is another of the most frequently played 7-letter bonus words that it is essential to know.

ATONING ▸ **atone**
ATONY *n* lack of normal tone or tension, as in muscles
ATOP *adv* on top
ATOPIC *adj* of or relating to hypersensitivity to certain allergens
ATOPIES ▸ **atopy**
ATOPY *n* tendency to be hypersensitive to certain allergens
ATRESIA *n* absence of or unnatural narrowing of a body channel **atresic, atretic**
ATRIA ▸ **atrium**
ATRIAL ▸ **atrium**
ATRIP *adj* (of an anchor) no longer caught on the bottom
ATRIUM *n* upper chamber of either half of the heart **atriums**
ATROPHY *n, vb*
ATROPIA *n* atropine
ATROPIN = **atropine**
ATS ▸ **at**
ATT *n* old Siamese coin
ATTABOY *sentence substitute* expression of approval or exhortation
ATTACH *vb*
ATTACHE *n* specialist attached to a diplomatic mission

ATTACK *vb, n* **attacks**
ATTAIN *vb* **attains**
ATTAINT *vb* pass judgment of death ▷ *n* dishonour
ATTAP *n* palm tree of South Asia **attaps**
ATTAR *n* fragrant oil made from roses **attars**
ATTASK *old word for* > **criticize**
ATTASKS ▶ **attask**
ATTASKT ▶ **attask**
ATTEMPT *vb, n*
ATTEND *vb* **attends**
ATTENT *old word for* > **attention**
ATTENTS ▶ **attent**
ATTEST *vb* **attests**
ATTIC *n* **attics**
ATTIRE *n, vb* **attired, attires**
ATTONCE *adv* old word for at once
ATTONE *vb* old word meaning appease **attoned, attones**
ATTORN *vb* acknowledge a new owner of land as one's landlord **attorns**
ATTRACT *vb*
ATTRAP *vb* adorn **attraps**
ATTRIST *vb* old word meaning to sadden
ATTRIT *vb* wear down or dispose of gradually
ATTRITE *vb* wear down
ATTRITS ▶ **attrit**
ATTUENT *adj* carrying out attuition
ATTUITE *vb* perceive by attuition
ATTUNE *vb* adjust or accustom (a person or thing) **attuned, attunes**
ATUA *n* spirit or demon **atuas**
ATWAIN *adv* old word meaning into two parts
ATWEEL *Scots word for* ▶ **well**
ATWEEN *an archaic or Scots word for* ▶ **between**
ATWIXT *old word for* ▶ **between**
ATYPIC *adj* not typical
AUA *n* yellow-eye mullet **auas**

> This Maori word for a kind of mullet is very often played to balance a rack by getting rid of a surplus of vowels.

AUBADE *n* song or poem greeting the dawn **aubades**
AUBERGE *n* inn or tavern
AUBURN *adj, n* **auburns**
AUCEPS *n* old word meaning person who catches hawks
AUCTION *n, vb*
AUCUBA *n* Japanese laurel **aucubas**
AUDAD *n* wild African sheep **audads**
AUDIAL *adj* of sound
AUDIBLE *adj, n, vb* **audibly**
AUDIENT *n* person who hears
AUDILE *n* person with a faculty for auditory imagery ▷ *adj* of or relating to such a person **audiles**
AUDING *n* practice of listening to try to understand **audings**
AUDIO *adj, n* **audios**
AUDIT *n, vb* **audited**
AUDITEE *n* one who is audited
AUDITOR *n* person qualified to audit accounts
AUDITS ▶ **audit**
AUE *interj* Maori exclamation

> Another Maori exclamation, so useful for getting rid of surplus vowels. But unlike **aua** it does not take an S.

AUF *old word for* ▶ **oaf**
AUFGABE *n* word used in psychology to mean task
AUFS ▶ **auf**
AUGEND *n* number to which a number is added **augends**
AUGER *n* tool for boring holes **augers**
AUGHT *adv* in any least part ▷ *n* less common word for nought **aughts**
AUGITE *n* black or greenish-black mineral **augites, augitic**
AUGMENT *vb, n*
AUGUR *vb, n* **augural, augured, augurer,**

augurs
AUGURY *n* foretelling of the future
AUGUST *adj* dignified and imposing ▷ *n* auguste
AUGUSTE *n* type of circus clown
AUGUSTS ▶ **august**
AUK *n* sea bird with short wings
AUKLET *n* type of small auk **auklets**
AUKS ▶ **auk**
AULA *n* hall **aulas**
AULD *a Scots word for* ▶ **old**
AULDER ▶ **auld**
AULDEST ▶ **auld**
AULIC *adj* relating to a royal court
AULNAGE *n* measurement in ells
AULOI ▶ **aulos**
AULOS *n* ancient Greek pipes
AUMAIL *old word for* ▶ **enamel**
AUMAILS ▶ **aumail**
AUMBRY = **ambry**
AUMIL *n* manager in India **aumils**
AUNE *n* old French measure of length **aunes**
AUNT *n*
AUNTER *old word for* > **adventure**
AUNTERS ▶ **aunter**
AUNTIE *n* aunt
AUNTIES ▶ **aunty**
AUNTLY *adj* of or like an aunt
AUNTS ▶ **aunt**
AUNTY = **auntie**
AURA *n* **aurae**
AURAL *adj* **aurally**
AURAR *plural of* ▶ **eyrir**
AURAS ▶ **aura**
AURATE *n* salt of auric acid
AURATED *adj* combined with auric acid
AURATES ▶ **aurate**
AUREATE *adj* covered with gold, gilded
AUREI ▶ **aureus**
AUREITY *n* attributes of gold
AURELIA *n* large jellyfish
AUREOLA = **aureole**
AUREOLE *n* halo
AURES ▶ **auris**
AUREUS *n* gold coin of the Roman Empire
AURIC *adj* of or containing gold in the trivalent state
AURICLE *n* upper chamber of the heart
AURIFY *vb* turn into gold
AURIS *n* medical word for ear
AURIST *a former name for* > **audiology**
AURISTS ▶ **aurist**
AUROCHS *n* recently extinct European wild ox
AURORA *n* bands of light seen in the sky **aurorae, auroral, auroras**
AUROUS *adj* of or containing gold, esp in the monovalent state
AURUM *n* gold **aurums**
AUSFORM *vb* temper steel
AUSPEX = **augur**
AUSPICE *n* patronage or guidance
AUSTERE *adj*
AUSTRAL *adj* southern ▷ *n* former monetary unit of Argentina
AUSUBO *n* tropical tree **ausubos**
AUTARCH *n* absolute ruler
AUTARKY *n* policy of economic self-sufficiency
AUTEUR *n* director **auteurs**
AUTHOR *n*, *vb* **authors**
AUTISM *n* **autisms**
AUTIST *n* autistic person **autists**
AUTO *n* automobile ▷ *vb* travel in an automobile
AUTOBUS *n* motor bus
AUTOCAR *n* motor car
AUTOCUE *n*
AUTOED ▶ **auto**
AUTOING ▶ **auto**
AUTOMAN *n* car manufacturer
AUTOMAT *n* vending machine
AUTOMEN ▶ **automan**
AUTONYM *n* writing published under the real name of an author
AUTOPEN *n* mechanical device used to produce imitation signatures
AUTOPSY *n*
AUTOPUT *n* motorway in the former Yugoslavia

AUTOS ▸ **auto**
AUTOVAC *n* vacuum pump in a car petrol tank
AUTUMN *n* **autumns**
AUTUMNY *adj* like autumn
AUXESES ▸ **auxesis**
AUXESIS *n* increase in cell size without division
AUXETIC *n* something that promotes growth
AUXIN *n* plant hormone that promotes growth **auxinic, auxins**
AVA *adv* at all ▷ *n* Polynesian shrub
AVAIL *vb, n*
AVAILE *old word for* ▸ **lower availed**
AVAILES ▸ **availe**
AVAILS ▸ **avail**
AVAL *adj* of a grandparent
AVALE *old word for* ▸ **lower**
AVALED ▸ **avale**
AVALES ▸ **avale**
AVALING ▸ **avale**
AVANT *prep* before
AVANTI *interj* forward!
AVARICE *n*
AVAS ▸ **ava**
AVAST *sentence substitute* stop! cease!
AVATAR *n* appearance of a god in animal or human form **avatars**
AVAUNT *sentence substitute* go away! depart! ▷ *vb* go away; depart **avaunts**
AVE *n* expression of welcome or farewell
AVEL *a variant of* ▸ **ovel**
AVELLAN *adj* of hazelnuts
AVELS ▸ **avel**
AVENGE *vb* **avenged, avenger, avenges**
AVENIR *n* future **avenirs**
AVENS *n* any of several temperate or arctic rosaceous plants **avenses**
AVENTRE *old word for* ▸ **thrust**
AVENUE *n* **avenues**
AVER *vb* state to be true
AVERAGE *n, adj, vb*
AVERRED ▸ **aver**
AVERS ▸ **aver**
AVERSE *adj*
AVERT *vb* **averted, averter, averts**
AVES ▸ **ave**
AVGAS *n* aviation fuel **avgases**
AVIAN *adj* of or like a bird ▷ *n* bird **avians**
AVIARY *n*
AVIATE *vb* pilot or fly in an aircraft **aviated, aviates**
AVIATIC *adj* pertaining to aviation
AVIATOR *n*
AVID *adj* **avider, avidest**
AVIDIN *n* protein found in egg-white **avidins**
AVIDITY *n* quality or state of being avid
AVIDLY ▸ **avid**
AVIETTE *n* aeroplane driven by human strength
AVIFORM *adj* like a bird
AVINE *adj* of birds
AVION *n* aeroplane
AVIONIC > **avionics**
AVIONS ▸ **avion**
AVISE *old word for* ▸ **advise**
AVISED ▸ **avise**
AVISES ▸ **avise**
AVISING ▸ **avise**
AVISO *n* boat carrying messages **avisos**
AVITAL *adj* of a grandfather
AVIZE *old word for* ▸ **advise**
AVIZED ▸ **avize**
AVIZES ▸ **avize**
AVIZING ▸ **avize**
AVO *n* Macao currency unit
AVOCADO *n*
AVOCET *n* long-legged wading bird **avocets**
AVODIRE *n* African tree
AVOID *vb* **avoided, avoider, avoids**
AVOS ▸ **avo**
AVOSET *n* avocet **avosets**
AVOUCH *vb* vouch for
AVOURE *old word for* ▸ **avowal**
AVOURES ▸ **avoure**
AVOUTRY *old word for* > **adultery**
AVOW *vb* **avowal, avowals, avowed, avower, avowers, avowing**
AVOWRY *old word for* ▸ **avowal**
AVOWS ▸ **avow**
AVOYER *n* former Swiss magistrate **avoyers**

AVRUGA *n* herring roe **avrugas**
AVULSE *vb* take away by force **avulsed, avulses**
AVYZE *old word for* ▸ **advise**
AVYZED ▸ **avyze**
AVYZES ▸ **avyze**
AVYZING ▸ **avyze**
AW *variant of* ▸ **all**
AWA *adv* away
AWAIT *vb* **awaited, awaiter, awaits**
AWAKE *vb, adj* **awaked**
AWAKEN *vb* awake **awakens**
AWAKES ▸ **awake**
AWAKING ▸ **awake**
AWARD *vb, n* **awarded, awardee, awarder, awards**
AWARE *adj* **awarer, awarest**
AWARN *vb* old form of warn **awarned, awarns**
AWASH *adv, adj*
AWATCH *adv* watching
AWATO *n* New Zealand caterpillar **awatos**
AWAVE *adv* in waves
AWAY *adv, adj, n*
AWAYDAY *n* day trip taken for pleasure
AWAYES *old word for* ▸ **away**
AWAYS ▸ **away**
AWDL *n* traditional Welsh poem **awdls**
AWE *n, vb*
AWEARY *old form of* ▸ **weary**
AWED ▸ **awe**
AWEE *adv* for a short time
AWEEL *interj* Scots word meaning well
AWEIGH *adj* (of an anchor) no longer hooked onto the bottom
AWEING ▸ **awe**
AWELESS ▸ **awe**
AWES ▸ **awe**
AWESOME *adj*
AWETO *n* New Zealand caterpillar **awetos**
AWFUL *adj, adv*
AWFULLY *adv* in an unpleasant way
AWFY *adv*
AWHAPE *old word for* ▸ **amaze**
AWHAPED ▸ **awhape**
AWHAPES ▸ **awhape**
AWHATO *n* New Zealand caterpillar **awhatos**
AWHEEL *adv* on wheels **awheels**
AWHETO *n* New Zealand caterpillar **awhetos**
AWHILE *adv*
AWHIRL *adv* whirling
AWING ▸ **awe**
AWK *n* type of programming language **awks**

> This provides a useful high-scoring outlet for what can be the awkward letters W and K.

AWKWARD *adj*
AWL *n* pointed tool for piercing wood, leather, etc
AWLBIRD *n* woodpecker
AWLESS ▸ **awe**
AWLS ▸ **awl**
AWLWORT *n* type of aquatic plant
AWMOUS *Scots word for* ▸ **alms**
AWMRIE *n* cupboard for church vessels **awmries**
AWMRY *n* cupboard for church vessels
AWN *n* bristles on grasses **awned**
AWNER *n* machine for removing awns **awners**
AWNIER ▸ **awny**
AWNIEST ▸ **awny**
AWNING *n* **awnings**
AWNLESS ▸ **awn**
AWNS ▸ **awn**
AWNY *adj* having awns
AWOKE *past tense of* ▸ **awake**
AWOKEN ▸ **awake**
AWOL *n* person who is absent without leave **awols**
AWORK *adv* old word meaning at work
AWRACK *adv* in wrecked condition
AWRONG *adv* old word meaning wrongly
AWRY *adj*
AWSOME *adj* old form of awesome
AX = **axe**
AXAL *adj* of an axis
AXE *n, vb*
AXEBIRD *n* nightjar
AXED ▸ **axe**

AXEL *n* ice-skating movement **axels**
AXEMAN *n* man who wields an axe, esp to cut down trees **axemen**
AXENIC *adj* (of a biological culture) free from other microorganisms
AXES ▸ **axis**
AXIAL *adj* forming or of an axis **axially**
AXIL *n* angle where the stalk of a leaf joins a stem
AXILE *adj* of, relating to, or attached to the axis
AXILLA *n* area under a bird's wing **axillae**
AXILLAR = **axillary**
AXILLAS ▸ **axilla**
AXILS ▸ **axil**
AXING ▸ **axe**
AXINITE *n* crystalline substance
AXIOM *n* **axioms**
AXION *n* type of hypothetical elementary particle **axions**
AXIS *n*
AXISED *adj* having an axis
AXISES ▸ **axis**
AXITE *n* type of gunpowder **axites**
AXLE *n*
AXLED *adj* having an axle
AXLES ▸ **axle**
AXLIKE ▸ **ax**
AXMAN = **axeman**
AXMEN ▸ **axman**
AXOID *n* type of curve **axoids**
AXOLOTL *n* aquatic salamander of central America
AXON *n* threadlike extension of a nerve cell **axonal, axone**
AXONEME *n* part of cell consisting of proteins
AXONES ▸ **axone**
AXONIC ▸ **axon**
AXONS ▸ **axon**
AXSEED *n* crown vetch **axseeds**
AY *adv* ever ▷ *n* expression of agreement
AYAH *n* native maidservant or nursemaid **ayahs**
AYE *n, adv*
AYELP *adv* yelping
AYES ▸ **aye**
AYGRE *old word for* ▸ **eager**
AYIN *n* 16th letter in the Hebrew alphabet **ayins**
AYONT *adv* beyond
AYRE *old word for* ▸ **air**
AYRES ▸ **ayre**
AYRIE *old word for* ▸ **eyrie**
AYRIES ▸ **ayrie**
AYS ▸ **ay**
AYU *n* small Japanese fish **ayus**

> This comes up quite often, being an extension of both **ay** and **yu**, showing how important it is to know those little 'hook' words.

AYWORD *n* old word meaning byword **aywords**
AZALEA *n* **azaleas**
AZAN *n* call to prayer **azans**
AZERTY *n* European version of keyboard
AZIDE *n* type of chemical compound **azides**
AZIDO *adj* containing an azide
AZIMUTH *n* arc of the sky between the zenith and the horizon
AZINE *n* organic compound **azines**
AZIONE *n* musical drama **aziones**
AZLON *n* fibre made from protein **azlons**
AZO *adj* of the divalent group -N:N-

> **Azo** is a chemical term you will want to play often, but it does not take an S. It takes an N to form **azon**.

AZOIC *adj* without life
AZOLE *n* organic compound **azoles**
AZOLLA *n* tropical water fern **azollas**
AZON *n* type of drawing paper
AZONAL *adj* not divided into zones
AZONIC *adj* not confined to a zone
AZONS ▸ **azon**
AZOTE *an obsolete name for* > **nitrogen**

AZOTED ▸ **azote**
AZOTES ▸ **azote**
AZOTH *n* panacea postulated by Paracelsus **azoths**
AZOTIC *adj* of, containing, or concerned with nitrogen
AZOTISE = **azotize**
AZOTIZE *vb* combine or treat with nitrogen or a nitrogen compound
AZOTOUS *adj* containing nitrogen
AZUKI = **adzuki**
AZUKIS ▸ **azuki**
AZULEJO *n* Spanish porcelain tile

> An **azulejo** is a kind of brightly coloured tile, beautiful in its combination of the J and Z.

AZURE *n, adj*
AZUREAN *adj* azure
AZURES ▸ **azure**
AZURINE *n* blue dye
AZURITE *n* azure-blue mineral associated with copper deposits
AZURN *old word for* ▸ **azure**
AZURY *adj* bluish
AZYGIES ▸ **azygy**
AZYGOS *n* biological structure not in a pair
AZYGOUS *adj* developing or occurring singly
AZYGY *n* state of not being joined in a pair
AZYM *n* unleavened bread
AZYME *n* unleavened bread **azymes**
AZYMITE *n* member of a church using unleavened bread in the Eucharist
AZYMOUS *adj* unleavened
AZYMS ▸ **azym**

Bb

B forms a two-letter word before every vowel except **U** – and with **Y** as well. With a **B** in your rack, you can play lots of short words that will give you relatively high scores. The best of these are **box** (12 points), **bez** (14 points), and **biz** (14 points), but don't forget **bay** (8), **by** (7), **bow** (8), **boy** (8), **buy** (8), and **bye** (8).

BA *n* symbol for the soul in Ancient Egyptian religion
BAA *vb* the characteristic bleating sound of a sheep ▷ *n* cry made by a sheep **baaed, baaing, baaings**
BAAL *n* any false god or idol **baalim, baalism, baals**
BAAS *South African word for* ▸ **boss**
BAASES ▸ **baas**
BAASKAP *n* (in South Africa) control by Whites of non-Whites
BABA *n* small cake of leavened dough
BABACO *n* greenish-yellow egg-shaped fruit **babacos**
BABALAS *adj* drunk
BABAS ▸ **baba**
BABASSU *n* Brazilian palm tree with hard edible nuts
BABBITT *vb* line (a bearing) or face (a surface) with a similar soft alloy
BABBLE *vb, n* **babbled**
BABBLER *n* person who babbles
BABBLES ▸ **babble**
BABBLY ▸ **babble**
BABE *n*
BABEL *n* **babels**
BABES ▸ **babe**
BABESIA *n* parasite causing infection in cattle
BABICHE *n* thongs or lacings of rawhide
BABIED, babier, babies, babiest ▸ **baby**
BABKA *n* cake **babkas**
BABLAH *n* type of acacia **bablahs**
BABOO = **babu**
BABOOL *n* type of acacia **babools**
BABOON *n* **baboons**
BABOOS ▸ **baboo**
BABOOSH = **babouche**
BABU *n* title or form of address used in India
BABUCHE = **babouche babudom, babuism**
BABUL *n* N African and Indian tree with small yellow flowers **babuls**
BABUS ▸ **babu**
BABY *n, adj, vb* **babying, babyish**
BABYSAT ▸ **babysit**
BABYSIT *vb* look after a child in its parents' absence
BAC *n* baccalaureate
BACALAO *n* dried salt cod
BACCA *n* berry **baccae**
BACCARA = **baccarat**
BACCARE = **backare**
BACCAS ▸ **bacca**
BACCATE *adj* like a berry in form, texture, etc
BACCHIC *adj* riotously drunk

BACCHII > **bacchius**
BACCIES ▶ **baccy**
BACCO *n* tobacco **baccoes, baccos**
BACCY *n* tobacco
BACH = **batch**
BACHA *n* Indian English word for young child **bachas**
BACHCHA *n* Indian English word for young child
BACHED, baches, baching, bachs ▶ **bach**
BACILLI > **bacillus**
BACK *n, vb, adj, adv*
BACKARE *interj* instruction to keep one's distance; back off
BACKBIT > **backbite**
BACKED *adj* having a back or backing
BACKER *n* **backers**
BACKET *n* shallow box **backets**
BACKFIT *vb* overhaul nuclear power plant
BACKHOE *n* digger ▷ *vb* dig with a backhoe
BACKIE *n* ride on the back of someone's bicycle **backies**
BACKING *n*
BACKLIT *adj* illuminated from behind
BACKLOG *n*
BACKLOT *n* area outside a film or television studio used for outdoor filming
BACKOUT *n* instance of withdrawing (from an agreement, etc)
BACKRA *n* white person **backras**
BACKS ▶ **back**
BACKSAW *n* small handsaw
BACKSET *n* reversal
BACKSEY *n* sirloin
BACKUP *n* support or reinforcement **backups**
BACLAVA = **baklava**
BACON *n*
BACONER *n* pig that weighs between 83 and 101 kg, from which bacon is cut
BACONS ▶ **bacon**
BACS ▶ **bac**
BACULA ▶ **baculum**
BACULUM *n* bony support in the penis of certain mammals
BAD *adj* not good ▷ *n* unfortunate or unpleasant events collectively ▷ *adv* badly **badder, baddest**
BADDIE *n* bad character in a story, film, etc, esp an opponent of the hero
BADDIES ▶ **baddy**
BADDISH ▶ **bad**
BADDY = **baddie**
BADE ▶ **bid**
BADGE *n, vb* **badged**
BADGER *n, vb* **badgers**
BADGES ▶ **badge**
BADGING ▶ **badge**
BADIOUS *adj* chestnut; brownish-red
BADLAND > **badlands**
BADLY *adv* poorly
BADMAN *n* hired gunman, outlaw, or criminal
BADMASH *n* evil-doer ▷ *adj* naughty or bad
BADMEN ▶ **badman**
BADNESS ▶ **bad**
BADS ▶ **bad**
BADWARE *n* software designed to harm a computer system
BAEL *n* type of spiny Indian tree **baels**
BAETYL *n* magical meteoric stone **baetyls**
BAFF *vb* strike ground with golf club **baffed**
BAFFIES *pl n* slippers
BAFFING ▶ **baff**
BAFFLE *vb, n* **baffled, baffler, baffles**
BAFFS ▶ **baff**
BAFFY *n* golf club
BAFT *n* coarse fabric **bafts**
BAG *n, vb*
BAGARRE *n* brawl
BAGASS = **bagasse**
BAGASSE *n* pulp of sugar cane or similar plants
BAGEL *n* hard ring-shaped bread roll **bagels**
BAGFUL *n* amount (of something) that can be held in a bag **bagfuls**
BAGGAGE *n*
BAGGED ▶ **bag**
BAGGER *n* person who packs groceries **baggers**
BAGGIE *n* plastic bag
BAGGIER ▶ **baggy**
BAGGIES ▶ **baggy**

BAGGILY ▸ **baggy**
BAGGING ▸ **bag**
BAGGIT *n* unspawned salmon **baggits**
BAGGY = **bagie**
BAGH *n* (in India and Pakistan) a garden **baghs**
BAGIE *n* turnip **bagies**
BAGLESS *adj* (esp of a vacuum cleaner) not containing a bag
BAGLIKE ▸ **bag**
BAGMAN *n* travelling salesman **bagmen**
BAGNIO *n* brothel **bagnios**
BAGPIPE *vb* play the bagpipes
BAGS ▸ **bag**
BAGSFUL ▸ **bagful**
BAGUET = **baguette**
BAGUETS ▸ **baguet**
BAGUIO *n* hurricane **baguios**
BAGWASH *n* laundry that washes clothes without drying or pressing them
BAGWIG *n* 18th-century wig with hair pushed back into a bag **bagwigs**
BAGWORM *n* type of moth
BAH *interj* expression of contempt or disgust
BAHADA = **bajada**
BAHADAS ▸ **bahada**
BAHADUR *n* title formerly conferred by the British on distinguished Indians
BAHT *n* standard monetary unit of Thailand, divided into 100 satang **bahts**
BAHU *n* **bahus**
BAHUT *n* decorative cabinet **bahuts**
BAIL *n, vb* **bailed**
BAILEE *n* person to whom the possession of goods is transferred under a bailment **bailees**
BAILER ▸ **bail**
BAILERS ▸ **bail**
BAILEY *n* outermost wall or court of a castle **baileys**
BAILIE *n* (in Scotland) a municipal magistrate **bailies**
BAILIFF *n*
BAILING ▸ **bail**
BAILLI *n* magistrate
BAILLIE *variant of* ▸ **bailie**
BAILLIS ▸ **bailli**
BAILOR *n* person who retains ownership of goods but entrusts possession of them to another under a bailment **bailors**
BAILOUT *n* instance of helping (a person, organization, etc) out of a predicament
BAILS ▸ **bail**
BAININ *n* Irish collarless jacket made of white wool **bainins**
BAINITE *n* mixture of iron and iron carbide found in incompletely hardened steels
BAIRN *n* **bairnly, bairns**
BAIT *n, vb* **baited, baiter, baiters**
BAITH *adj* both
BAITING ▸ **bait**
BAITS ▸ **bait**
BAIZA *n* Omani unit of currency **baizas**
BAIZE *n, vb* **baized, baizes, baizing**
BAJADA *n* sloping surface formed from rock deposits **bajadas**
BAJAN *n* freshman at Aberdeen University **bajans**
BAJRA *n* Indian millet **bajras, bajree**
BAJREES ▸ **bajree**
BAJRI = **bajra**
BAJRIS ▸ **bajri**
BAJU *n* Malay jacket **bajus**
BAKE *vb, n* **baked, baken**
BAKEOFF *n* baking competition
BAKER *n* **bakers**
BAKERY *n*
BAKES ▸ **bake**
BAKGAT *adj* fine, excellent, marvellous
BAKING *n* process of cooking bread, cakes, etc ▹ *adj* (esp of weather) very hot and dry **bakings**
BAKKIE *n* **bakkies**
BAKLAVA *n* rich pastry of Middle Eastern origin **baklawa**
BAKRA *n* White person, esp one from Britain ▹ *adj* (of people) White, esp British **bakras**
BAL *n* balmoral

BALADIN *n* dancer
BALANCE *n, vb*
BALAS *n* red variety of spinel, used as a gemstone **balases**
BALATA *n* tropical American tree yielding a latex-like sap **balatas**
BALBOA *n* standard currency unit of Panama **balboas**
BALCONY *n*
BALD *adj, vb* **balded, balder, baldest**
BALDIE ▸ **baldy**
BALDIER ▸ **baldy**
BALDIES ▸ **baldy**
BALDING *adj* becoming bald
BALDISH ▸ **bald**
BALDLY ▸ **bald**
BALDRIC *n* wide silk sash or leather belt worn across the body
BALDS ▸ **bald**
BALDY *adj* bald ▹ *n* bald person
BALE = **bail**
BALED ▸ **bale**
BALEEN *n* whalebone **baleens**
BALEFUL *adj*
BALER ▸ **bail**
BALERS ▸ **bail**
BALES ▸ **bale**
BALING ▸ **bale**
BALISE *n* electronic beacon used on a railway **balises**
BALISTA = **ballista**
BALK *vb, n* **balked, balker, balkers**
BALKIER ▸ **balky**
BALKILY ▸ **balky balking, balks**
BALKY *adj* inclined to stop abruptly and unexpectedly
BALL *n, vb*
BALLAD *n, vb*
BALLADE *n* verse form
BALLADS ▸ **ballad**
BALLAN *n* species of fish **ballans**
BALLANT *vb* write a ballad
BALLAST *n, vb*
BALLAT *vb* write a ballad **ballats**
BALLED ▸ **ball**
BALLER *n* ball-game player **ballers**
BALLET *n* **ballets**
BALLIES ▸ **bally**
BALLING ▸ **ball**
BALLIUM = **bailey**
BALLON *n* light, graceful quality **ballons**
BALLOON *n, vb*
BALLOT *n, vb* **ballots**
BALLOW *n* heavy club **ballows**
BALLUTE *n* inflatable balloon parachute
BALLY *another word for* > **ballyhoo**
BALM *n, vb* **balmed**
BALMIER ▸ **balmy**
BALMILY ▸ **balmy**
BALMING ▸ **balm**
BALMS ▸ **balm**
BALMY *adj* (of weather) mild and pleasant
BALNEAL *adj* of or relating to baths or bathing
BALONEY *n* foolish talk; nonsense
BALOO *n* bear **baloos**
BALS ▸ **bal**
BALSA *n*
BALSAM *n, vb* **balsams, balsamy**
BALSAS ▸ **balsa**
BALTI *n* spicy Indian dish served in a metal dish
BALTIC *adj* very cold
BALTIS ▸ **balti**
BALU = **baloo**
BALUN *n* electrical device **baluns**
BALUS ▸ **balu**
BAM *vb* cheat
BAMBI *n* born-again middle-aged biker
BAMBINI ▸ **bambino**
BAMBINO *n* young child, esp an Italian one
BAMBIS ▸ **bambi**
BAMBOO *n* **bamboos**
BAMMED, bammer, bammers, bamming ▸ **bam**
BAMPOT *n* fool **bampots**
BAMS ▸ **bam**
BAN *vb, n*
BANAK *n* type of Central American tree **banaks**
BANAL *adj* **banaler, banally**
BANANA *n*
BANANAS *adj* crazy
BANC *n* as in **in banc** sitting as a full court
BANCO *n* call made in gambling games **bancos**
BANCS ▸ **banc**

BAND *n, vb*
BANDA *n* African thatched hut
BANDAGE *n, vb*
BANDAID *adj* (of a solution or remedy) temporary
BANDANA = **bandanna**
BANDAR *n* species of monkey
BANDARI *n* Indian English word for female monkey
BANDARS ▶ **bandar**
BANDAS ▶ **banda**
BANDBOX *n* lightweight usually cylindrical box for hats
BANDEAU *n* narrow ribbon worn round the head
BANDED ▶ **band**
BANDER ▶ **band**
BANDERS ▶ **band**
BANDH *n* (in India) a general strike **bandhs**
BANDIED ▶ **bandy**
BANDIER ▶ **bandy**
BANDIES ▶ **bandy**
BANDING *n* practice of grouping schoolchildren according to ability
BANDIT *n*
BANDITO *n* Mexican bandit
BANDITS ▶ **bandit**
BANDOG *n* ferocious dog **bandogs**
BANDOOK = **bundook**
BANDORA = **bandore**
BANDORE *n* 16th-century musical instrument
BANDROL = **banderole**
BANDS ▶ **band**
BANDSAW *n* power saw with continuous blade
BANDURA *n* type of lute
BANDY *adj, vb*
BANE *n, vb* **baned**
BANEFUL *adj* destructive, poisonous, or fatal
BANES ▶ **bane**
BANG *vb* **banged**
BANGER *n* **bangers**
BANGING ▶ **bang**
BANGKOK *n* type of straw hat
BANGLE *n* **bangled, bangles**
BANGS ▶ **bang**
BANI ▶ **ban**
BANIA = **banyan**
BANIAN = **banyan**
BANIANS ▶ **banian**
BANIAS ▶ **bania**
BANING ▶ **bane**
BANISH *vb*
BANJAX *vb* ruin; destroy

> Meaning to ruin or confound, this is a great word to remember, with its high-scoring combination of J and X.

BANJO *n* **banjoes, banjos**
BANK *n, vb* **banked**
BANKER *n* manager or owner of a bank **bankers**
BANKET *n* gold-bearing conglomerate found in South Africa **bankets**
BANKING = **bank**
BANKIT = **banquette**
BANKITS ▶ **bankit**
BANKS ▶ **bank**
BANKSIA *n*
BANNED ▶ **ban**
BANNER *n, vb, adj* **banners**
BANNET *n* bonnet **bannets**
BANNING ▶ **ban**
BANNOCK *n* round flat cake made from oatmeal or barley
BANNS *pl n*
BANOFFI = **banoffee**
BANQUET *n, vb*
BANS = **banns**
BANSELA = **bonsela**
BANSHEE *n* **banshie**
BANT *n* string ▷ *vb* tie with string
BANTAM *n* **bantams**
BANTED ▶ **bant**
BANTENG *n* wild ox
BANTER *vb, n* **banters**
BANTIES ▶ **banty**
BANTING ▶ **bant**
BANTS ▶ **bant**
BANTY *n* bantam
BANYA *n* traditional Russian steam bath
BANYAN *n* **banyans**
BANYAS ▶ **banya**
BANZAI *interj* patriotic cheer, battle cry, or salutation **banzais**
BAOBAB *n* **baobabs**
BAP *n* **baps**
BAPTISE = **baptize**
BAPTISM *n*
BAPTIST *n* one who baptizes
BAPTIZE *vb*

BAPU *n* spiritual father **bapus**
BAR *n, vb*
BARACAN = **barracan**
BARAZA *n* place where public meetings are held **barazas**
BARB *n, vb*
BARBAL *adj* of a beard
BARBATE *adj* having tufts of long hairs
BARBE *n* Waldensian missionary
BARBED ▶ **barb**
BARBEL *n* long thin growth that hangs from the jaws of certain fishes, such as the carp
BARBELL *n*
BARBELS ▶ **barbel**
BARBER *n, vb* **barbers**
BARBES ▶ **barbe**
BARBET *n* type of small tropical bird **barbets**
BARBIE *short for* > **barbecue**
BARBIES ▶ **barbie**
BARBING ▶ **barb**
BARBOLA *n* small models of flowers, etc made from plastic paste
BARBS ▶ **barb**
BARBULE *n* very small barb
BARBUT *n* open-faced helmet **barbuts**
BARBY > **barbecue**
BARCA *n* boat **barcas**
BARCHAN *n* crescent-shaped shifting sand dune
BARCODE *n*
BARD *n, vb*
BARDASH *n* kept boy in a homosexual relationship
BARDE = **bard**
BARDED ▶ **barde**
BARDES ▶ **barde**
BARDIC ▶ **bard**
BARDIE *n* type of Australian grub
BARDIER ▶ **bard**
BARDIES ▶ **bardie**
BARDING ▶ **bard**
BARDISM ▶ **bard**
BARDO *n* (in Tibetan Buddhism) the state of the soul between its death and its rebirth **bardos**
BARDS ▶ **bard**
BARDY ▶ **bard**
BARE *adj, vb* **bared**
BAREFIT > **barefoot**
BAREGE *n* light silky gauze fabric made of wool ▷ *adj* made of such a fabric **bareges**
BARELY *adv*
BARER ▶ **bare**
BARES ▶ **bare**
BAREST ▶ **bare**
BARF *vb* vomit ▷ *n* act of vomiting **barfed, barfing**
BARFLY *n* person who frequents bars
BARFS ▶ **barf**
BARFUL *adj* presenting difficulties
BARGAIN *n, vb*
BARGE *n, vb* **barged**
BARGEE *n* person in charge of a barge **bargees**
BARGES ▶ **barge**
BARGEST = **barghest**
BARGING ▶ **barge**
BARGOON *Canadian word for* ▶ **bargain**
BARHOP *vb* visit several bars in succession **barhops**
BARIC *adj* of or containing barium
BARILLA *n* impure mixture of sodium carbonate and sodium sulphate
BARING ▶ **bare**
BARISH *adj* quite thinly covered
BARISTA *n* person who makes and sells coffee in a coffee bar
BARITE *n* colourless or white mineral **barites**
BARIUM *n* **bariums**
BARK *vb*
BARKAN = **barchan**
BARKANS ▶ **barkan**
BARKED ▶ **bark**
BARKEEP *n* barkeeper
BARKEN *vb* become dry with a bark-like outer layer **barkens**
BARKER *n* person at a fairground who calls loudly to passers-by in order to attract customers **barkers**
BARKHAN = **barchan**
BARKIER ▶ **barky**
BARKING *adj* mad ▷ *adv* extremely
BARKS ▶ **bark**
BARKY *adj* having the texture or appearance of bark
BARLESS ▶ **bar**
BARLEY *n, sentence*

substitute **barleys**
BARLOW *n* type of strong knife **barlows**
BARM *n* yeasty froth on fermenting malt liquors
BARMAID *n*
BARMAN = **bartender**
BARMEN ▸ **barman**
BARMIE = **barmy**
BARMIER ▸ **barmy**
BARMKIN *n* protective wall around castle
BARMPOT *n* foolish or deranged person
BARMS ▸ **barm**
BARMY *adj*
BARN *n, vb* **barned**
BARNET *n* hair **barnets**
BARNEY *n* noisy fight or argument ▹ *vb* argue or quarrel **barneys**
BARNIER ▸ **barny**
BARNING ▸ **barn**
BARNS ▸ **barn**
BARNY *adj* reminiscent of a barn
BAROCCO = **baroque**
BAROCK = **baroque**
BAROCKS ▸ **barock**
BAROLO *n* red Italian wine **barolos**
BARON *n*
BARONET *n*
BARONG *n* broad-bladed cleaver-like knife used in the Philippines **barongs**
BARONNE *n* baroness
BARONS ▸ **baron**
BARONY *n* domain or rank of a baron
BAROQUE *n, adj*
BARP *n* hillock or bank of stones **barps**
BARQUE *n* sailing ship, esp one with three masts **barques**
BARRA *n* barramundi
BARRACE *n* record of teams entering a sports contest
BARRACK *vb*
BARRAGE *n, vb*
BARRAS ▸ **barra**
BARRAT *n* fraudulent dealings **barrats**
BARRE *n* rail at hip height used for ballet practice ▹ *vb* execute guitar chords by laying the index finger over some or all of the strings ▹ *adv* by using the barre
BARRED ▸ **bar**
BARREED ▸ **barre**
BARREL *n, vb* **barrels**
BARREN *adj*
BARRENS *pl n* (in North America) a stretch of land that is sparsely vegetated
BARRES ▸ **barre**
BARRET *n* small flat cap resembling a biretta **barrets**
BARRICO *n* small container for liquids
BARRIE *adj* very good
BARRIER *n, vb*
BARRIES ▸ **barry**
BARRING ▸ **bar**
BARRIO *n* Spanish-speaking quarter in a town or city, esp in the US **barrios**
BARRO *adj* embarrassing
BARROOM *n* room or building where alcoholic drinks are served over a counter
BARROW *n* **barrows**
BARRY *n* mistake or blunder
BARS ▸ **bar**
BARTEND *vb* serve drinks from a bar
BARTER *vb, n* **barters**
BARTON *n* farmyard **bartons**
BARTSIA *n* type of semiparasitic plant
BARWARE *n* glasses, etc used in a bar
BARWOOD *n* red wood from small African tree
BARYE *n* unit of pressure **baryes**
BARYON *n* elementary particle that has a mass greater than or equal to that of the proton **baryons**
BARYTA = **barite**
BARYTAS ▸ **baryta**
BARYTE = **baryta**
BARYTES ▸ **baryte**
BARYTIC ▸ **baryta**
BARYTON *n* bass viol with sympathetic strings as well as its six main strings
BAS ▸ **ba**
BASAL *adj* of, at, or constituting a base **basally**
BASALT *n* **basalts**
BASAN *n* sheepskin tanned in bark **basans**
BASANT *n* Pakistani spring festival **basants**

BASCULE *n* drawbridge that operates by a counterbalanced weight
BASE *n, vb, adj* **based**
BASEEJ *pl n* Iranian volunteer militia
BASELY ▶ **base**
BASEMAN *n* fielder positioned near a base **basemen**
BASEN *Spencerian spelling of* ▶ **basin**
BASENJI *n* small breed of dog
BASER ▶ **base**
BASES ▶ **basis**
BASEST ▶ **base**
BASH *vb, n*
BASHAW *n* important or pompous person **bashaws**
BASHED, basher, bashers, bashes ▶ **bash**
BASHFUL *adj*
BASHING ▶ **bash**
BASHLIK *n* Caucasian hood **bashlyk**
BASHO *n* grand tournament in sumo wrestling
BASIC *adj, n* **basics**
BASIDIA > **basidium**
BASIFY *vb* make basic
BASIJ ▶ **baseej**
BASIL *n*
BASILAR *adj* of or situated at a base
BASILIC > **basilica**
BASILS ▶ **basil**
BASIN *n* **basinal, basined**
BASINET *n* close-fitting medieval helmet of light steel usually with a visor
BASING ▶ **base**
BASINS ▶ **basin**
BASION *n* (in anatomy) midpoint on the forward border of the foramen magnum **basions**
BASIS *n*
BASK *vb* **basked**
BASKET *n* **baskets**
BASKING ▶ **bask**
BASKS ▶ **bask**
BASMATI *n* variety of long-grain rice with slender aromatic grains
BASNET = **basinet**
BASNETS ▶ **basnet**
BASOCHE *n* society of medieval French lawyers who performed comic plays
BASON = **basin**
BASONS ▶ **bason**
BASQUE *n* tight-fitting bodice for women **basqued, basques**
BASS *vb* **basse, bassed, basser, basses, bassest**
BASSET *n* breed of hound ▷ *vb* (of rock) protrude through earth's surface **bassets, bassett**
BASSI ▶ **basso**
BASSIER ▶ **bassy**
BASSING ▶ **bass**
BASSIST *n* player of a double bass, esp in a jazz band
BASSLY ▶ **bass**
BASSO *n* singer with a bass voice
BASSOON *n*
BASSOS ▶ **basso**
BASSY *adj* manifesting strong bass tones
BAST *n* fibrous material used for making rope, matting, etc
BASTA *interj* enough; stop
BASTE *vb* **basted, baster, basters, bastes**
BASTI *n* (in India) a slum inhabited by poor people
BASTIDE *n* small isolated house in France
BASTILE = **bastille**
BASTING *n* loose temporary stitches
BASTION *n*
BASTIS ▶ **basti**
BASTLE *n* fortified house **bastles**
BASTO *n* ace of clubs in certain card games **bastos**
BASTS ▶ **bast**
BASUCO *n* cocaine-based drug **basucos**
BAT *n, vb* **batable**
BATATA *n* sweet potato **batatas**
BATAVIA *n* variety of lettuce with smooth pale green leaves
BATBOY *n* boy who works at baseball games **batboys**
BATCH *n, vb* **batched,**

batcher, batches
BATE *vb* (of hawks) to jump violently from a perch or the falconer's fist
BATEAU *n* light flat-bottomed boat used on rivers in Canada and the northern US **bateaux**
BATED ▸ **bate**
BATES ▸ **bate**
BATFISH *n* type of angler fish with a flattened scaleless body
BATFOWL *vb* catch birds by temporarily blinding them with light
BATGIRL *n* girl who works at baseball games
BATH *n, vb*
BATHE *vb* **bathed, bather**
BATHERS *pl n* swimming costume
BATHES ▸ **bathe**
BATHING ▸ **bathe**
BATHMAT *n* mat to stand on after a bath
BATHMIC > **bathmism**
BATHOS *n*
BATHS ▸ **bath**
BATHTUB *n* bath, esp one not permanently fixed
BATHYAL *adj* relating to an ocean depth of between 200 and 2000 metres
BATIK *n, vb* **batiked, batiks**
BATING ▸ **bate**
BATISTE *n* fine plain-weave cotton fabric: used esp for shirts and dresses
BATLER *n* flat piece of wood for beating clothes, etc before washing **batlers, batlet**
BATLETS ▸ **batlet**
BATLIKE ▸ **bat**
BATMAN *n* **batmen**
BATON *n, vb* **batoned, batons, batoon**
BATOONS ▸ **batoon**
BATS ▸ **bat**
BATSMAN *n* **batsmen**
BATT ▸ **bat**
BATTA *n* soldier's allowance **battas**
BATTEAU = **bateau**
BATTED ▸ **bat**
BATTEL *vb* make fertile **battels**
BATTEN *n, vb* **battens**
BATTER *vb, n*
BATTERO *n* heavy club
BATTERS ▸ **batter**
BATTERY *n, adj*
BATTIER ▸ **batty**
BATTIES ▸ **batty**
BATTIK = **batik**
BATTIKS ▸ **battik**
BATTILL *old spelling of* ▸ **battle**
BATTING ▸ **bat**
BATTLE *n, vb* **battled, battler, battles**
BATTS ▸ **batt**
BATTU *adj* (in ballet) involving a beating movement
BATTUE *n* beating of woodland or cover to force game to flee in the direction of hunters **battues**
BATTUTA *n* (in music) a beat
BATTUTO *n*
BATTY *adj, n*
BATWING *adj* shaped like the wings of a bat, as a black tie, collar, etc
BAUBEE = **bawbee**
BAUBEES ▸ **baubee**
BAUBLE *n* **baubles**
BAUCHLE *vb* shuffle along
BAUD *n* unit used to measure the speed of transmission of electronic data
BAUDRIC = **baldric**
BAUDS ▸ **baud**
BAUERA *n* small evergreen Australian shrub **baueras**
BAUK = **balk**
BAUKED ▸ **bauk**
BAUKING ▸ **bauk**
BAUKS ▸ **bauk**
BAULK ▸ **balk**
BAULKED ▸ **balk**
BAULKER ▸ **balk**
BAULKS ▸ **balk**
BAULKY = **balky**
BAUR *n* humorous anecdote; joke **baurs**
BAUSOND *adj* (of animal) dappled with white spots
BAUXITE *n*
BAVIN *n* impure limestone **bavins**
BAWBEE *n* former

Scottish silver coin **bawbees**
BAWBLE = **bauble**
BAWBLES ▸ **bawble**
BAWCOCK *n* fine fellow
BAWD *n* person who runs a brothel, esp a woman
BAWDIER ▸ **bawdy**
BAWDIES ▸ **bawdy**
BAWDILY ▸ **bawdy**
BAWDKIN = **baldachin**
BAWDRIC *n* heavy belt to support sword
BAWDRY *n* obscene talk or language
BAWDS ▸ **bawd**
BAWDY *adj, n*
BAWL *vb, n* **bawled, bawler, bawlers**
BAWLEY *n* small fishing boat **bawleys**
BAWLING ▸ **bawl**
BAWLS ▸ **bawl**
BAWN *n* fortified enclosure
BAWNEEN = **bainin**
BAWNS ▸ **bawn**
BAWR = **baur**
BAWRS ▸ **bawr**
BAWSUNT *adj* black and white in colour
BAWTIE *n* name for a dog **bawties, bawty**
BAXTER *old variant of* ▸ **baker**
BAXTERS ▸ **baxter**
BAY *n, vb*
BAYAMO *n* Cuban strong wind **bayamos**
BAYARD *n* bay horse **bayards**
BAYE *vb* bathe
BAYED ▸ **bay**
BAYES ▸ **baye**
BAYING ▸ **bay**
BAYLE *n* barrier **bayles**
BAYMAN *n* fisherman **baymen**
BAYONET *n, vb*
BAYOU *n* (in the southern US) a sluggish marshy tributary of a lake or river **bayous**
BAYS ▸ **bay**
BAYT = **bate**
BAYTED ▸ **bayt**
BAYTING ▸ **bayt**
BAYTS ▸ **bayt**
BAYWOOD *n* light soft wood of a tropical American mahogany tree
BAYYAN *n* Islamic declaration **bayyans**
BAZAAR *n* **bazaars, bazar**
BAZARS ▸ **bazar**
BAZAZZ = **pizzazz**
BAZOO *a US slang word for* ▸ **mouth**
BAZOOKA *n* portable rocket launcher that fires an armour-piercing projectile
BAZOOS ▸ **bazoo**
BAZOUKI = **bouzouki**
BAZZAZZ ▸ **pizzazz**
BE *vb* exist or live
BEACH *n, vb* **beached, beaches**
BEACHY *adj* with gentle sandy slopes
BEACON *n, vb* **beacons**
BEAD *n, vb* **beaded**
BEADER *n* person making things with beads **beaders**
BEADIER ▸ **beady**
BEADILY ▸ **beady**
BEADING *n* strip of moulding used for edging furniture
BEADLE *n* (formerly) a minor parish official who acted as an usher **beadles**
BEADMAN = **beadsman**
BEADMEN ▸ **beadman**
BEADS ▸ **bead**
BEADY *adj*
BEAGLE *n, vb* **beagled**
BEAGLER *n* person who hunts with beagles
BEAGLES ▸ **beagle**
BEAK *n, vb* **beaked**
BEAKER *n* **beakers**
BEAKIER ▸ **beak**
BEAKS ▸ **beak**
BEAKY ▸ **beak**
BEAM *n, vb* **beamed**
BEAMER *n* full-pitched ball bowled at the batsman's head **beamers**
BEAMIER ▸ **beam**
BEAMILY ▸ **beam**
BEAMING ▸ **beam**
BEAMISH *adj* smiling
BEAMLET *n* small beam
BEAMS ▸ **beam**
BEAMY ▸ **beam**
BEAN *n, vb*
BEANBAG *n* small cloth bag filled with dried beans and thrown in games
BEANED ▸ **bean**
BEANERY *n* cheap restaurant
BEANIE *n* close-fitting woollen hat

BEANIES ▸ **beany**
BEANING ▸ **bean**
BEANO *n* celebration or party **beanos**
BEANS ▸ **bean**
BEANY = **beanie**
BEAR *vb, n*
BEARCAT *n* lesser panda
BEARD *n, vb* **bearded**
BEARDIE *n* another name for bearded loach
BEARDS ▸ **beard**
BEARDY *adj* having a beard
BEARE = **bear**
BEARED ▸ **bear**
BEARER *n* **bearers**
BEARES ▸ **beare**
BEARHUG *n* wrestling hold in which the arms are locked tightly round an opponent's chest and arms
BEARING ▸ **bear**
BEARISH *adj* like a bear
BEARS ▸ **bear**
BEAST *n, vb* **beasted**
BEASTIE *n* small animal
BEASTLY *adj, adv*
BEASTS ▸ **beast**
BEAT *vb, n, adj*
BEATBOX *n* drum machine simulated by a human voice
BEATEN ▸ **beat**
BEATER *n* device used for beating **beaters**
BEATH *vb* dry; heat **beathed, beaths**
BEATIER ▸ **beaty**
BEATIFY *vb* take first step towards making (a dead person) a saint
BEATING ▸ **beat**
BEATNIK *n* young person in the late 1950s who rebelled against conventional attitudes, etc
BEATS ▸ **beat**
BEATY *adj* (of music) having a strong rhythm
BEAU *n* boyfriend or admirer
BEAUFET = **buffet**
BEAUFIN = **biffin**
BEAUISH *adj* vain and showy
BEAUS ▸ **beau**
BEAUT *n, adj, interj* **beauts**
BEAUTY *n, interj, vb*
BEAUX ▸ **beau**
BEAVER *n, vb* **beavers**
BEAVERY *n* place for keeping beavers
BEBEERU *n* tropical American tree
BEBLOOD *vb* stain with blood
BEBOP = **bop**
BEBOPS ▸ **bebop**
BEBUNG *n* vibrato effect on clavichord **bebungs**
BECALL *vb* use insulting words about someone **becalls**
BECALM *vb* **becalms**
BECAME ▸ **become**
BECAP *vb* put cap on **becaps**
BECASSE *n* woodcock
BECAUSE *conj*
BECHALK *vb* mark with chalk
BECHARM *vb* delight
BECK *n, vb*
BECKE = **beak**
BECKED ▸ **beck**
BECKES ▸ **becke**
BECKET *n* clevis forming part of one end of a sheave **beckets**
BECKING ▸ **beck**
BECKON *vb, n* **beckons**
BECKS ▸ **beck**
BECLASP *vb* embrace
BECLOAK *vb* dress in cloak
BECLOG *vb* put clogs on **beclogs**
BECLOUD *vb* cover or obscure with a cloud
BECLOWN *vb* clown around
BECOME *vb* **becomes**
BECRAWL *vb* crawl all over
BECRIME *vb* make someone guilty of a crime
BECROWD *vb* crowd with something
BECRUST *vb* cover with crust
BECURL *vb* curl **becurls**
BECURSE *vb* curse **becurst**
BED *n, vb*
BEDAD *interj* by God (oath)
BEDAMN *vb* damn **bedamns**
BEDASH *vb* sprinkle with liquid
BEDAUB *vb* smear with something sticky or dirty **bedaubs**
BEDAWIN = **bedouin**
BEDAZE *vb* daze **bedazed, bedazes**

BEDBATH *n* washing of a sick person in bed
BEDBUG *n* small blood-sucking wingless insect that infests dirty houses **bedbugs**
BEDDED ▶ **bed**
BEDDER *n* (at some universities) a college servant employed to keep students' rooms in order **bedders**
BEDDING ▶ **bed**
BEDE *n* prayer
BEDECK *vb* cover with decorations **bedecks**
BEDEL *archaic spelling of* ▶ **beadle**
BEDELL ▶ **beadle**
BEDELLS ▶ **bedell**
BEDELS ▶ **bedel**
BEDEMAN = **beadsman**
BEDEMEN ▶ **bedeman**
BEDERAL = **bedral**
BEDES ▶ **bede**
BEDEVIL *vb* harass, confuse, or torment
BEDEW *vb* wet or cover with or as if with drops of dew **bedewed, bedews**
BEDFAST *an archaic word for* > **bedridden**
BEDGOWN *n* night dress
BEDHEAD *n* untidy state of hair, esp caused by sleeping
BEDIDE ▶ **bedye**
BEDIGHT *vb* array or adorn ▷ *adj* adorned or bedecked
BEDIM *vb* make dim or obscure **bedims**
BEDIRTY *vb* make dirty
BEDIZEN *vb* dress or decorate gaudily or tastelessly
BEDLAM *n*
BEDLAMP *n* bedside light
BEDLAMS ▶ **bedlam**
BEDLESS ▶ **bed**
BEDLIKE *adj* like a bed
BEDMATE *n* person who shares a bed
BEDOUIN *n* member of any of the nomadic tribes of Arabs
BEDPAN *n* **bedpans**
BEDPOST *n* vertical support on a bedstead
BEDRAIL *n* rail along the side of a bed connecting the headboard with the footboard
BEDRAL *n* minor church official **bedrals**
BEDRAPE *vb* adorn
BEDRID = **bedridden**
BEDRITE > **bedright**
BEDROCK *n*
BEDROLL *n* portable roll of bedding
BEDROOM *n, adj*
BEDROP *vb* drop on **bedrops, bedropt**
BEDRUG *vb* drug excessively **bedrugs**
BEDS ▶ **bed**
BEDSIDE *n* area beside a bed ▷ *adj* placed at or near the side of the bed
BEDSIT *n* furnished sitting room with a bed **bedsits**
BEDSORE *n*
BEDTICK *n* case containing stuffing in mattress
BEDTIME *n* time when one usually goes to bed
BEDU *adj* relating to beduins
BEDUCK *vb* duck under water **beducks**
BEDUIN *variant of* ▶ **bedouin**
BEDUINS ▶ **beduin**
BEDUMB *vb* make dumb **bedumbs**
BEDUNCE *vb* cause to look or feel foolish
BEDUNG *vb* spread with dung **bedungs**
BEDUST *vb* cover with dust **bedusts**
BEDWARD *adj* towards bed
BEDWARF *vb* hamper growth of
BEDYDE ▶ **bedye**
BEDYE *vb* dye **bedyed, bedyes**
BEE *n*
BEEBEE *n* air rifle **beebees**
BEECH *n* **beechen, beeches, beechy**
BEEDI *n* Indian cigarette **beedie, beedies**
BEEF *n, vb*
BEEFALO *n* cross between cow and buffalo
BEEFED ▶ **beef**
BEEFIER ▶ **beefy**
BEEFILY ▶ **beefy**
BEEFING ▶ **beef**
BEEFS ▶ **beef**
BEEFY *adj*
BEEGAH = **bigha**
BEEGAHS ▶ **beegah**

BEEHIVE *n*
BEELIKE ▸ **bee**
BEELINE *n, adj*
BEEN ▸ **be**
BEENAH *n* understanding; insight **beenahs**
BEENTO *n* person who has resided in Britain ▹ *adj* of, relating to, or characteristic of such a person **beentos**
BEEP *n* high-pitched sound, like that of a car horn ▹ *vb* (cause to) make this noise **beeped, beeper, beepers, beeping, beeps**
BEER *n*
BEERAGE *n* brewing industry
BEERIER ▸ **beery**
BEERILY ▸ **beery**
BEERS ▸ **beer**
BEERY *adj* smelling or tasting of beer
BEES ▸ **bee**
BEESOME = **bisson**
BEESWAX *n* wax secreted by bees, used in polishes etc ▹ *vb* polish with such wax
BEET *n, vb* **beeted**
BEETFLY *n* type of fly which is a common pest of beets and mangel-wurzels
BEETING ▸ **beet**
BEETLE *n, adj, vb* **beetled**
BEETLER *n* one who operates a beetling machine
BEETLES ▸ **beetle**
BEETS ▸ **beet**
BEEVES ▸ **beef**
BEEYARD *n* place where bees are kept
BEEZER *n* person or chap ▹ *adj* excellent **beezers**
BEFALL *vb* **befalls**
BEFANA *n* Italian gift-bearing good fairy **befanas**
BEFELD ▸ **befall**
BEFELL ▸ **befall**
BEFFANA = **befana**
BEFIT *vb* **befits**
BEFLAG *vb* decorate with flags **beflags**
BEFLEA *vb* infect with fleas **befleas**
BEFLECK *vb* fleck
BEFLUM *vb* fool; deceive **beflums**
BEFOAM *vb* cover with foam **befoams**
BEFOG *vb* surround with fog **befogs**
BEFOOL *vb* make a fool of **befools**
BEFORE *adv, prep*
BEFOUL *vb* make dirty or foul **befouls**
BEFRET *vb* fret about something **befrets**
BEG *vb*
BEGAD *interj* emphatic exclamation
BEGALL *vb* make sore by rubbing **begalls**
BEGAN ▸ **begin**
BEGAR *n* compulsory labour **begars**
BEGAT ▸ **beget**
BEGAZE *vb* gaze about or around **begazed, begazes**
BEGEM *vb* decorate with gems **begems**
BEGET *vb* **begets**
BEGGAR *n, vb* **beggars**
BEGGARY *n* extreme poverty or need
BEGGED ▸ **beg**
BEGGING ▸ **beg**
BEGHARD *n* member of a 13th century Christian brotherhood
BEGIFT *vb* give gift or gifts to **begifts**
BEGILD *vb* gild **begilds, begilt**
BEGIN *vb* start
BEGINNE = **beginning begins**
BEGIRD *vb* surround **begirds, begirt**
BEGLAD *vb* make glad **beglads**
BEGLOOM *vb* make gloomy
BEGNAW *vb* gnaw at **begnaws**
BEGO *vb* harrass; beset **begoes, begoing, begone**
BEGONIA *n*
BEGORAH = **begorra**
BEGORED *adj* smear with gore
BEGORRA *interj* emphatic exclamation, regarded as a characteristic utterance of Irishmen
BEGOT *past participle of* ▸ **beget**
BEGRIM = **begrime**
BEGRIME *vb* make dirty
BEGRIMS ▸ **begrim**
BEGROAN *vb* groan at
BEGS ▸ **beg**

BEGUILE *vb*
BEGUIN *another name for* ▸ **beghard**
BEGUINE *n* S American dance
BEGUINS ▸ **beguin**
BEGULF *vb* overwhelm **begulfs**
BEGUM *n* Muslim woman of high rank **begums**
BEGUN *past participle of* ▸ **begin**
BEGUNK *vb* delude; trick **begunks**
BEHALF *n*
BEHAVE *vb* **behaved, behaver, behaves**
BEHEAD *vb* **beheads**
BEHELD ▸ **behold**
BEHEST *n* **behests**
BEHIGHT *vb* entrust
BEHIND *adv, n, prep, adj* **behinds**
BEHOLD *vb* **beholds**
BEHOOF *n* advantage or profit **behoofs**
BEHOOVE = **behove**
BEHOTE = **behight**
BEHOTES ▸ **behote**
BEHOVE *vb* be necessary or fitting for **behoved, behoves**
BEHOWL *vb* howl at **behowls**
BEIGE *adj, n*
BEIGEL = **bagel**
BEIGELS ▸ **beigel**
BEIGES ▸ **beige**
BEIGIER ▸ **beige**
BEIGNE *variant of* ▸ **beignet**
BEIGNES ▸ **beigne**
BEIGNET *n* square deep-fried pastry served hot and sprinkled with icing sugar
BEIGY ▸ **beige**
BEIN *adj* financially comfortable
BEING ▸ **be**
BEINGS ▸ **be**
BEINKED *adj* daubed with ink
BEJADE *vb* jade; tire **bejaded, bejades**
BEJANT = **bajan**
BEJANTS ▸ **bejant**
BEJESUS *interj* exclamation of surprise ▹ *n as in* **the bejesus** mild expletive
BEJEWEL *vb* decorate with or as if with jewels
BEKAH *n* half shekel **bekahs**
BEKISS *vb* smother with kisses
BEKNAVE *vb* treat as a knave
BEKNOT *vb* tie a knot or knots in **beknots**
BEKNOWN *adj* known about
BEL *n* unit for comparing two power levels or measuring the intensity of a sound
BELABOR = **belabour**
BELACE *vb* decorate with lace **belaced, belaces**
BELADY *vb* call a lady
BELAH *n* Australian tree which yields a useful timber **belahs**
BELAMY *n* close friend
BELAR = **belah**
BELARS ▸ **belar**
BELATE *vb* cause to be late
BELATED *adj*
BELATES ▸ **belate**
BELAUD *vb* praise highly **belauds**
BELAY *vb* secure a line to a pin or cleat ▹ *n* attachment (of a climber) to a mountain **belayed, belayer, belays**
BELCH *vb, n* **belched, belcher, belches**
BELDAM *n* old woman, esp an ugly or malicious one **beldame, beldams**
BELEAP *vb* leap over **beleaps, beleapt**
BELEE *vb* put on sheltered side **beleed, belees**
BELFRY *n*
BELGA *n* former Belgian monetary unit worth five francs
BELGARD *n* kind gaze
BELGAS ▸ **belga**
BELIE *vb* **belied**
BELIEF *n* **beliefs**
BELIER ▸ **belie**
BELIERS ▸ **belie**
BELIES ▸ **belie**
BELIEVE *vb*
BELIKE *adv* perhaps
BELIVE *adv* speedily
BELL *n, vb*
BELLBOY *n* man or boy employed in a hotel, club, etc, to carry luggage and answer

calls for service
BELLE *n* beautiful woman, esp the most attractive woman at a function
BELLED ▸ **bell**
BELLEEK *n* kind of thin fragile porcelain with a lustrous glaze
BELLES ▸ **belle**
BELLHOP = **bellboy**
BELLIED ▸ **belly**
BELLIES ▸ **belly**
BELLING ▸ **bell**
BELLMAN *n* man who rings a bell, esp (formerly) a town crier **bellmen**
BELLOCK *vb* shout
BELLOW *vb, n*
BELLOWS *pl n* instrument for pumping a stream of air into something
BELLS ▸ **bell**
BELLY *n, vb*
BELON *n* type of oyster
BELONG *vb* **belongs**
BELONS ▸ **belon**
BELOVE *vb* love
BELOVED *adj, n*
BELOVES ▸ **belove**
BELOW *adv, prep*
BELOWS = **bellows**
BELS ▸ **bel**
BELT *n, vb* **belted**
BELTER *n* outstanding person or event **belters**
BELTING *n* material used to make a belt or belts ▹ *adj* excellent
BELTMAN *n* (formerly) a member of a beach life-saving team **beltmen**
BELTS ▸ **belt**
BELTWAY *n* people and institutions located in the area bounded by the Washington Beltway
BELUGA *n* large white sturgeon **belugas**
BELYING ▸ **belie**
BEMA *n* speaker's platform in the assembly in ancient Athens
BEMAD *vb* cause to become mad
BEMADAM *vb* call a person madam
BEMADS ▸ **bemad**
BEMAS ▸ **bema**
BEMATA ▸ **bema**
BEMAUL *vb* maul **bemauls**
BEMAZED *adj* amazed
BEMBEX *n* type of wasp **bembix**
BEMEAN *a less common word for* ▸ **demean**
BEMEANS ▸ **bemean**
BEMEANT ▸ **bemean**
BEMEDAL *vb* decorate with medals
BEMETE *vb* measure **bemeted, bemetes**
BEMIRE *vb* soil with or as if with mire **bemired, bemires**
BEMIST *vb* cloud with mist **bemists**
BEMIX *vb* mix thoroughly **bemixed, bemixes, bemixt**
BEMOAN *vb* **bemoans**
BEMOCK *vb* mock **bemocks**
BEMOIL *vb* soil with mud **bemoils**
BEMOUTH *vb* endow with a mouth
BEMUD *vb* cover with mud **bemuds**
BEMUSE *vb* confuse
BEMUSED *adj*
BEMUSES ▸ **bemuse**
BEN *n* mountain peak ▹ *adv* in ▹ *adj* inner
BENAME *an archaic word for* ▸ **name**
BENAMED ▸ **bename**
BENAMES ▸ **bename**
BENCH *n, vb* **benched**
BENCHER *n* member of the governing body of one of the Inns of Court
BENCHES ▸ **bench**
BENCHY *adj* (of a hillside) hollowed out in benches
BEND *vb, n*
BENDAY *vb* (printing) reproduce using Benday technique **bendays**
BENDED ▸ **bend**
BENDEE = **bendy**
BENDEES ▸ **bendee**
BENDER *n* drinking bout **benders**
BENDIER ▸ **bendy**
BENDING ▸ **bend**
BENDLET *n* narrow diagonal stripe on heraldic shield
BENDS ▸ **bend**
BENDY *adj, n* **bendys**
BENE *n* blessing
BENEATH *prep, adv*
BENEFIC *adj* a rare word for beneficent

BENEFIT *n, vb*
BENEMPT *a past participle of* ▸ **name**
BENES ▸ **bene**
BENET *vb* trap (something) in a net **benets**
BENGA *n* type of Kenyan popular music featuring guitars **bengas**
BENI *n* sesame plant
BENIGHT *vb* shroud in darkness
BENIGN *adj*
BENIS ▸ **beni**
BENISON *n* blessing, esp a spoken one
BENJ *another word for* ▸ **bhang**
BENJES ▸ **benj**
BENNE *another name for* ▸ **sesame**
BENNES ▸ **benne**
BENNET *n* Eurasian and N African plant with yellow flowers **bennets**
BENNI *n* sesame
BENNIES ▸ **benny**
BENNIS ▸ **benni**
BENNY *n* amphetamine tablet, esp benzedrine: a stimulant
BENOMYL *n* fungicide
BENS ▸ **ben**
BENT *adj, n*
BENTHAL ▸ **benthos**
BENTHIC ▸ **benthos**
BENTHON = **benthos**
BENTHOS *n* animals and plants living at the bottom of a sea or lake
BENTIER ▸ **benty**
BENTO *n* thin lightweight box used in Japanese cuisine **bentos**
BENTS ▸ **bent**
BENTY *adj* covered with bentgrass
BENUMB *vb* make numb or powerless **benumbs**
BENZAL *n* transparent crystalline substance **benzals**
BENZENE *n* flammable poisonous liquid used as a solvent, insecticide, etc
BENZIL *n* yellow compound radical **benzils**
BENZIN = **benzine**
BENZINE *n* volatile liquid used as a solvent
BENZINS ▸ **benzin**
BENZOIC *adj* of, containing, or derived from benzoic acid or benzoin
BENZOIN *n* gum resin used in ointments, perfume, etc
BENZOL *n* crude form of benzene **benzole, benzols**
BENZOYL *n* of, consisting of, or containing the monovalent group C_6H_5CO-
BENZYL *n* of, consisting of, or containing the monovalent group $C_6H_5CH_2$– **benzyls**
BEPAINT *vb* dye; paint
BEPAT *vb* pat **bepats**
BEPEARL *vb* decorate with pearls
BEPELT *vb* pelt energetically **bepelts**
BEPITY *vb* feel great pity for
BEPROSE *vb* (of poetry) reduce to prose
BEPUFF *vb* puff up **bepuffs**
BEQUEST *n*
BERAKE *vb* rake thoroughly **beraked, berakes**
BERATE *vb* **berated, berates**
BERAY *vb* soil; defile **berayed, berays**
BERBERE *n* hot-tasting Ethiopian paste
BERBICE *n as in* **berbice chair** large armchair with long arms that can be folded inwards to act as leg rests
BERCEAU *n* arched trellis for climbing plants
BERDASH = **berdache**
BERE *n* barley
BEREAVE *vb* deprive (of) something or someone valued, esp through death
BEREFT *adj*
BERES ▸ **bere**
BERET *n* **berets**
BERETTA *n* type of pistol
BERG *n* iceberg
BERGAMA *n* type of Turkish rug
BERGEN *n* large rucksack with a capacity of over 50 litres **bergens**

BERGERE *n* type of French armchair
BERGS ▸ **berg**
BERGYLT *n* large northern marine food fish
BERHYME *vb* mention in poetry **berime**
BERIMED ▸ **berime**
BERIMES ▸ **berime**
BERK *n* stupid person
BERKO *adj* berserk
BERKS ▸ **berk**
BERLEY *n* bait scattered on water to attract fish ▹ *vb* scatter (bait) on water **berleys**
BERLIN *n* fine wool yarn used for tapestry work, etc **berline, berlins**
BERM *n*, *vb* **berme, bermed**
BERMES ▸ **berme berming, berms**
BEROB *vb* rob
BEROBED *adj* wearing a robe
BEROBS ▸ **berob**
BERRET = **beret**
BERRETS ▸ **berret**
BERRIED ▸ **berry**
BERRIES ▸ **berry**
BERRY *n*, *vb*
BERSEEM *n* Mediterranean clover grown as a forage crop and to improve the soil
BERSERK *adj*, *n*
BERTH *n*, *vb*
BERTHA *n* wide deep capelike collar, often of lace, usually to cover up a low neckline **berthas**
BERTHE *n* type of lace collar
BERTHED ▸ **berth**
BERTHES ▸ **berthe**
BERTHS ▸ **berth**
BERYL *n* **beryls**
BES *variant of* ▸ **beth**
BESAINT *vb* give saint status to
BESANG ▸ **besing**
BESAT ▸ **besit**
BESAW ▸ **besee**
BESCOUR *vb* scour thoroughly
BESEE *vb* provide for; mind
BESEECH *vb* **beseeke**
BESEEM *vb* be suitable for **beseems**
BESEEN ▸ **besee**
BESEES ▸ **besee**
BESES ▸ **bes**
BESET *vb* **besets**
BESHAME *vb* cause to feel shame
BESHINE *vb* illuminate **beshone**
BESHOUT *vb* shout about
BESHREW *vb* wish evil on
BESIDE *prep*
BESIDES *prep*, *adv*
BESIEGE *vb*
BESIGH *vb* sigh for **besighs**
BESING *vb* sing about joyfully **besings**
BESIT *vb* suit; fit **besits**
BESLAVE *vb* treat as slave
BESLIME *vb* cover with slime
BESMEAR *vb* smear over
BESMILE *vb* smile on
BESMOKE *vb* blacken with smoke
BESMUT *vb* blacken with smut **besmuts**
BESNOW *vb* cover with snow **besnows**
BESOIN *n* need **besoins**
BESOM *n* broom made of twigs ▹ *vb* sweep with a besom **besomed, besoms**
BESORT *vb* fit **besorts**
BESOT *vb* make stupid or muddled **besots**
BESPAKE ▸ **bespoke**
BESPAT ▸ **bespit**
BESPATE ▸ **bespit**
BESPEAK *vb* indicate or suggest
BESPED ▸ **bespeed**
BESPEED *vb* get on with (doing something)
BESPICE *vb* flavour with spices
BESPIT *vb* cover with spittle **bespits**
BESPOKE *adj* (esp of a suit) made to the customer's specifications
BESPORT *vb* amuse oneself
BESPOT *vb* mark with spots **bespots**
BESPOUT *vb* speak pretentiously
BEST *adj* most excellent of a particular group etc ▹ *adv* in a manner surpassing all others ▹ *n* utmost effort ▹ *vb* defeat

BESTAD = **bestead**
BESTAIN *vb* stain
BESTAR *vb* decorate with stars **bestars**
BESTEAD *vb* serve; assist
BESTED ▸ **best**
BESTI *Indian English word for* ▸ **shame**
BESTIAL *adj*
BESTICK *vb* cover with sharp points
BESTILL *vb* cause to be still
BESTING ▸ **best**
BESTIR *vb* cause (oneself) to become active **bestirs**
BESTIS ▸ **besti**
BESTORM *vb* assault
BESTOW *vb* **bestows**
BESTREW *vb* scatter or lie scattered over (a surface)
BESTRID > **bestride**
BESTROW = **bestrew**
BESTS ▸ **best**
BESTUCK ▸ **bestick**
BESTUD *vb* set with, or as with studs **bestuds**
BESUNG ▸ **besing**
BESWARM *vb* swarm over
BET *n, vb*
BETA *n* second letter in the Greek alphabet, a consonant, transliterated as *b*
BETAINE *n* sweet-tasting alkaloid that occurs in the sugar beet
BETAKE *vb as in* **betake oneself** go **betaken, betakes**
BETAS ▸ **beta**
BETAXED *adj* burdened with taxes
BETCHA *interj* bet you
BETE = **beet**
BETED ▸ **bete**
BETEEM *vb* accord **beteeme, beteems**
BETEL *n* **betels**
BETES ▸ **bete**
BETH *n* second letter of the Hebrew alphabet transliterated as *b*
BETHANK *vb* thank
BETHEL *n* seaman's chapel **bethels**
BETHINK *vb* cause (oneself) to consider or meditate
BETHORN *vb* cover with thorns
BETHS ▸ **beth**
BETHUMB *vb* (of books) wear by handling
BETHUMP *vb* thump hard
BETID ▸ **betide**
BETIDE *vb* happen (to) **betided, betides, betight**
BETIME *vb* befall **betimed, betimes**
BETING ▸ **bete**
BETISE *n* folly or lack of perception **betises**
BETITLE *vb* give title to
BETOIL *vb* tire through hard work **betoils**
BETOKEN *vb* indicate or signify
BETON *n* concrete **betons**
BETONY *n* North American plant
BETOOK *the past tense of* ▸ **betake**
BETOSS *vb* toss about
BETRAY *vb* **betrays**
BETREAD *vb* tread over
BETRIM *vb* decorate **betrims**
BETROD ▸ **betread**
BETROTH *vb* promise to marry or to give in marriage
BETS ▸ **bet**
BETTA *n* fighting fish **bettas**
BETTED ▸ **bet**
BETTER *adj* more excellent than others ▹ *adv* in a more excellent manner ▹ *pl n* one's superiors ▹ *vb* improve upon **betters**
BETTIES ▸ **betty**
BETTING ▸ **bet**
BETTONG *n* short-nosed rat kangaroo
BETTOR *n* person who bets **bettors**
BETTY *n* type of short crowbar
BETWEEN *adv, prep*
BETWIXT *adv* between
BEURRE *n* butter **beurres**
BEVEL *n* slanting edge ▹ *vb* slope **beveled, beveler, bevels**
BEVER *n* snack **bevers**
BEVIES ▸ **bevy**
BEVOMIT *vb* vomit over
BEVOR *n* armour protecting lower part

of face **bevors**
BEVUE *n* careless error **bevues**
BEVVIED ▸ **bevvy**
BEVVIES ▸ **bevvy**
BEVVY *n* alcoholic drink ▷ *vb* drink alcohol
BEVY *n*
BEWAIL *vb* **bewails**
BEWARE *vb* **bewared, bewares**
BEWEARY *vb* cause to be weary
BEWEEP *vb* express grief through weeping **beweeps**
BEWENT ▸ **bego**
BEWEPT ▸ **beweep**
BEWET *vb* make wet **bewets**
BEWHORE *vb* treat as a whore
BEWIG *vb* adorn with a wig **bewigs**
BEWITCH *vb*
BEWORM *vb* fill with worms **beworms**
BEWORRY *vb* beset with worry
BEWRAP *vb* wrap up **bewraps, bewrapt**
BEWRAY *an obsolete word for* ▸ **betray**
BEWRAYS ▸ **bewray**
BEY *n* (in the Ottoman empire) a title given to senior officers, provincial governors, and certain other officials

> A **bey** was an official in the Ottoman empire. If someone plays this remember that you can of course put an O in front of it to make **obey**.

BEYLIC *n* province ruled over by a bey **beylics, beylik**
BEYLIKS ▸ **beylik**
BEYOND *prep, adv, n* **beyonds**
BEYS ▸ **bey**
BEZ *n* part of deer's horn

> This word for the tine of a deer's horn is one of the essential short words for using the Z.

BEZANT *n* medieval Byzantine gold coin **bezants**
BEZAZZ *another word for* ▸ **pizzazz**
BEZEL *n* sloping edge of a cutting tool **bezels**
BEZES ▸ **bez**
BEZIL *archaic word for* > **alcoholic**
BEZILS ▸ **bezil**
BEZIQUE *n* card game for two or more players

> This card game played with two decks of cards combines the Q and Z and would make a wonderful bonus word.

BEZOAR *n* hard mass, such as a stone or hairball, in the stomach and intestines of animals **bezoars**
BEZZANT = **bezant**
BEZZAZZ ▸ **bezazz**
BEZZLE *vb* drink to excess **bezzled, bezzles**
BHAGEE = **bhaji**
BHAGEES ▸ **bhagee**
BHAI *n* Indian form of address for a man **bhais**
BHAJAN *n* singing of devotional songs and hymns **bhajans**
BHAJEE = **bhaji**
BHAJEES ▸ **bhajee**
BHAJI *n* Indian deep-fried savoury of chopped vegetables in spiced batter **bhajia, bhajis**
BHAKTA *n* Hindu term for devotee of God **bhaktas**
BHAKTI *n* loving devotion to God leading to nirvana **bhaktis**
BHANG *n* preparation of Indian hemp used as a narcotic and intoxicant
BHANGRA *n* Punjabi folk music combined with elements of Western pop music
BHANGS ▸ **bhang**
BHARAL *n* wild Himalayan sheep **bharals**
BHAT *n* currency of Thailand
BHAVAN *n* (in India) a large house or building **bhavans, bhawan**
BHAWANS ▸ **bhawan**
BHEESTY ▸ **bhishti**

BHEL = **bael**
BHELS ▶ **bhel**
BHIKHU *n* fully ordained Buddhist monk **bhikhus**
BHINDI = **bindhi**
BHINDIS ▶ **bhindi**
BHISHTI *n* (formerly in India) a water-carrier **bhistee, bhisti, bhistie**
BHISTIS ▶ **bhisti**
BHOONA ▶ **bhuna**
BHOONAS ▶ **bhoona**
BHOOT = **bhut**
BHOOTS ▶ **bhoot**
BHUNA *n* Indian sauce **bhunas**
BHUT *n* Hindu term for type of ghost **bhuts**
BI *short for* > **bisexual**
BIALI = **bialy**
BIALIES ▶ **bialy**
BIALIS ▶ **biali**
BIALY *n* type of bagel **bialys**
BIAS *n, vb, adj, adv* **biased, biases, biasing, biassed, biasses**
BIAXAL = **biaxial**
BIAXIAL *adj* (esp of a crystal) having two axes
BIB = **bibcock**
BIBASIC *adj* with two bases
BIBB *n* wooden support on a mast for the trestletrees
BIBBED ▶ **bib**
BIBBER *n* drinker **bibbers**
BIBBERY *n* drinking to excess
BIBBING ▶ **bib**
BIBBLE *n* pebble **bibbles**
BIBBS ▶ **bibb**
BIBCOCK *n* tap with a nozzle bent downwards
BIBELOT *n* attractive or curious trinket
BIBFUL *n as in* **spill a bibful** to divulge secrets **bibfuls**
BIBLE *n* any book containing the sacred writings of a religion **bibles**
BIBLESS ▶ **bib**
BIBLIKE ▶ **bib**
BIBLIST = **biblicist**
BIBS ▶ **bib**
BICARB *n* bicarbonate of soda **bicarbs**
BICCIES ▶ **biccy**
BICCY *n* biscuit
BICE *n* medium blue colour
BICEP = **biceps**
BICEPS *n*
BICES ▶ **bice**
BICHIR *n* African freshwater fish with an elongated body **bichirs**
BICHORD *adj* having two strings for each note
BICKER *vb, n* **bickers**
BICKIE *short for* ▶ **biscuit**
BICKIES ▶ **bickie**
BICOLOR = **bicolour**
BICORN *adj* having two horns or hornlike parts **bicorne, bicorns**
BICRON *n* billionth part of a metre **bicrons**
BICYCLE *n, vb*
BID *vb, n*
BIDARKA *n* canoe covered in animal skins, esp sealskin, used by the Inuit of Alaska
BIDDEN ▶ **bid**
BIDDER ▶ **bid**
BIDDERS ▶ **bid**
BIDDIES ▶ **biddy**
BIDDING ▶ **bid**
BIDDY *n* woman, esp an old gossipy one
BIDE *vb* **bided**
BIDENT *n* instrument with two prongs **bidents**
BIDER ▶ **bide**
BIDERS ▶ **bide**
BIDES ▶ **bide**
BIDET *n* **bidets**
BIDI = **beedi**
BIDING ▶ **bide**
BIDINGS ▶ **bide**
BIDIS ▶ **bidi**
BIDON *n* oil drum **bidons**
BIDS ▶ **bid**
BIELD *n* shelter ▷ *vb* shelter or take shelter **bielded, bields**
BIELDY *adj* sheltered
BIEN *adv* well
BIENNIA > **biennium**
BIER *n* **biers**
BIFACE *n* prehistoric stone tool **bifaces**
BIFF *n* blow with the fist ▷ *vb* give (someone) such a blow **biffed**
BIFFER *n* someone, such

as a sportsperson, who has a reputation for hitting hard **biffers**
BIFFIES ▶ **biffy**
BIFFIN *n* variety of red cooking apple
BIFFING ▶ **biff**
BIFFINS ▶ **biffin**
BIFFO *n* fighting or aggressive behaviour ▷ *adj* aggressive **biffos**
BIFFS ▶ **biff**
BIFFY *n* outdoor toilet
BIFID *adj* divided into two by a cleft in the middle **bifidly**
BIFILAR *adj* having two parallel threads, as in the suspension of certain measuring instruments
BIFLEX *adj* bent or flexed in two places
BIFOCAL *adj* having two different focuses
BIFOLD *adj* that can be folded in two places
BIFORM *adj* having or combining the characteristics of two forms, as a centaur
BIFTAH *n* ▶ **bifter**
BIFTAHS ▶ **biftah**
BIFTER *n* cannabis cigarette **bifters**
BIG *adj* of considerable size, height, number, or capacity ▷ *adv* on a grand scale ▷ *vb* build
BIGA *n* chariot drawn by two horses **bigae**
BIGAMY *n*
BIGENER *n* hybrid between individuals of different genera
BIGEYE *n* type of red marine fish **bigeyes**
BIGFEET ▶ **bigfoot**
BIGFOOT *n* yeti ▷ *vb* throw one's weight around
BIGG *n* type of barley
BIGGED ▶ **big**
BIGGER ▶ **big**
BIGGEST ▶ **big**
BIGGETY = **biggity**
BIGGIE *n* something big or important **biggies**
BIGGIN *n* plain close-fitting cap
BIGGING ▶ **big**
BIGGINS ▶ **biggin**
BIGGISH ▶ **big**
BIGGITY *adj* conceited
BIGGON = **biggin**
BIGGONS ▶ **biggon**
BIGGS ▶ **bigg**
BIGGY = **biggie**
BIGHA *n* in India, unit for measuring land **bighas**
BIGHEAD *n* conceited person
BIGHORN *n* large wild mountain sheep
BIGHT *n* long curved shoreline ▷ *vb* fasten or bind with a bight **bighted, bights**
BIGLY ▶ **big**
BIGNESS ▶ **big**
BIGOS *n* Polish stew **bigoses**
BIGOT *n* **bigoted**
BIGOTRY *n* attitudes, behaviour, or way of thinking of a bigot
BIGOTS ▶ **bigot**
BIGS ▶ **big**
BIGTIME *adj* important
BIGWIG *n* important person **bigwigs**
BIJOU *adj* (of a house) small but elegant ▷ *n* something small and delicately worked **bijous, bijoux**

> A **bijou** is a French word for a jewel, and it is indeed a jewel to play, getting rid of awkward letters for a good score. And remember that the plural can be **bijous** or **bijoux**.

BIKE = **bicycle**
BIKED ▶ **bike**
BIKER *n* person who rides a motorcycle **bikers**
BIKES ▶ **bike**
BIKEWAY *n* cycle lane
BIKIE *n* member of a motorcycle gang **bikies**
BIKING ▶ **bike**
BIKINGS ▶ **bike**
BIKINI *n* **bikinis**
BIKKIE *slang word for* ▶ **biscuit**
BIKKIES ▶ **bikkie**
BILAYER *n* part of cell membrane
BILBIES ▶ **bilby**
BILBO *n* (formerly) a sword with a marked temper and elasticity **bilboa**
BILBOAS ▶ **bilboa** **bilboes, bilbos**
BILBY *n* Australian marsupial with long

pointed ears and grey fur
BILE *n, vb* **biled, biles**
BILEVEL *n* hairstyle with two different lengths
BILGE *n, vb* **bilged, bilges, bilgier, bilging, bilgy**
BILIAN *n* type of tree used for its wood **bilians**
BILIARY *adj* of bile, the ducts that convey bile, or the gall bladder ▷ *n* disease found in dogs
BILIMBI *n* type of fruit-bearing tree
BILING ▶ **bile**
BILIOUS *adj*
BILK *vb* cheat, esp by not paying ▷ *n* swindle or cheat **bilked, bilker, bilkers, bilking, bilks**
BILL *n, vb*
BILLBUG *n* type of weevil
BILLED ▶ **bill**
BILLER *n* stem of a plant **billers**
BILLET *vb, n* **billets**
BILLIE = **billy**
BILLIES ▶ **billy**
BILLING *n* prominence given in programmes, advertisements, etc, to performers or acts
BILLION *n, determiner*
BILLMAN *n* person who uses a billhook **billmen**
BILLON *n* alloy consisting of gold or silver and a base metal **billons**
BILLOW *n, vb* **billows**
BILLOWY *adj* full of or forming billows
BILLS ▶ **bill**
BILLY *n*
BILLYO *n as in* **like billyo** phrase used to emphasize or intensify something **billyoh, billyos**
BILOBAR = **bilobate**
BILOBED = **bilobate**
BILSTED *n* American gum tree
BILTONG *n* strips of dried meat
BIMA = **bema**
BIMAH = **bema**
BIMAHS ▶ **bimah**
BIMANAL = **bimanous**
BIMAS ▶ **bima**
BIMBLE *n as in* **bimble box** type of dense Australian tree
BIMETAL *n* material made from two sheets of metal
BIMODAL *adj* having two modes
BIMORPH *n* assembly of piezoelectric crystals
BIN *n, vb*
BINAL *adj* twofold
BINARY *adj, n*
BINATE *adj* occurring in two parts or in pairs
BIND *vb, n*
BINDER *n* **binders**
BINDERY *n* bookbindery
BINDHI = **bindi**
BINDHIS ▶ **bindhi**
BINDI *n* decorative dot worn in the middle of the forehead, esp by Hindu women
BINDING ▶ **bind**
BINDIS ▶ **bindi**
BINDLE *n* small packet **bindles**
BINDS ▶ **bind**
BINE *n* climbing or twining stem of various plants
BINER *n* clip used by climbers **biners**
BINES ▶ **bine**
BING *n* heap or pile, esp of spoil from a mine
BINGE *n, vb* **binged**
BINGER *n* person who is addicted to crack cocaine **bingers**
BINGES ▶ **binge**
BINGIES ▶ **bingy**
BINGING ▶ **binge**
BINGLE *n* minor crash or upset, as in a car or on a surfboard ▷ *vb* layer (hair) **bingled, bingles**
BINGO *n, sentence substitute* **bingoes, bingos**
BINGS ▶ **bing**
BINGY *Australian slang for* ▶ **stomach**
BINIOU *n* small high-pitched Breton bagpipe **binious**
BINIT *n* (computing) early form of bit **binits**
BINK *n* ledge **binks**
BINMAN *another name for* ▶ **dustman**
BINMEN ▶ **binman**
BINNED ▶ **bin**
BINNING ▶ **bin**
BINOCLE *n* binocular-style telescope
BINOCS > **binocular**
BINS ▶ **bin**

BIO *short for* > **biography**
BIOBANK *n*
BIOCHIP *n* small glass or silicon plate containing an array of biochemical molecules or structures
BIOCIDE *n* substance used to destroy living things
BIODATA *n* information regarding an individual's education and work history
BIODOT *n* temperature-sensitive device stuck to the skin in order to monitor stress **biodots**
BIOFACT *n* item of biological information
BIOFILM *n* thin layer of living organisms
BIOFUEL *n* gaseous, liquid, or solid substance of biological origin used as a fuel ▷ *vb* fuel (a vehicle, etc) using biofuel
BIOG *short form of* > **biography**
BIOGAS *n* gaseous fuel produced by the fermentation of organic waste
BIOGEN *n* hypothetical protein **biogens**
BIOGENY *n* principle that a living organism must originate from a parent form similar to itself
BIOGS ▶ **biog**
BIOHERM *n* mound of material laid down by sedentary marine organisms
BIOLOGY *n*
BIOMASS *n* total number of living organisms in a given area
BIOME *n* major ecological community **biomes**
BIONIC *adj*
BIONICS *n* study of biological functions to create electronic versions
BIONOMY *n* laws of life
BIONT *n* living thing **biontic, bionts**
BIOPHOR *n* hypothetical material particle
BIOPIC *n* film based on the life of a famous person **biopics**
BIOPSIC ▶ **biopsy**
BIOPSY *n, vb* **bioptic**
BIOS ▶ **bio**
BIOTA *n* plant and animal life of a particular region or period **biotas**
BIOTECH *n* biotechnology
BIOTIC *adj* of or relating to living organisms ▷ *n* living organism **biotics**
BIOTIN *n* vitamin of the B complex, abundant in egg yolk and liver **biotins**
BIOTITE *n* black or dark green mineral of the mica group
BIOTOPE *n* small area that supports its own distinctive community
BIOTRON *n* climate-control chamber
BIOTYPE *n* group of genetically identical plants within a species, produced by apomixis
BIPACK *n* obsolete filming process **bipacks**
BIPARTY *adj* involving two parties
BIPED *n, adj*
BIPEDAL *adj* having two feet
BIPEDS ▶ **biped**
BIPLANE *n*
BIPOD *n* two-legged support or stand **bipods**
BIPOLAR *adj* having two poles
BIPRISM *n* prism having a highly obtuse angle to facilitate beam splitting
BIRCH *n, vb* **birched, birchen, birches**
BIRCHIR ▶ **bichir**
BIRD *n, vb*
BIRDDOG *n* dog used or trained to retrieve game birds
BIRDED ▶ **bird**
BIRDER *n* birdwatcher **birders**
BIRDIE *n* score of one stroke under par for a hole ▷ *vb* play (a hole) in one stroke under par **birdied, birdies**

BIRDING ▸ **bird**
BIRDMAN *n* man concerned with birds, such as a fowler or ornithologist **birdmen**
BIRDS ▸ **bird**
BIREME *n* ancient galley having two banks of oars **biremes**
BIRETTA *n* stiff square cap worn by the Catholic clergy
BIRIANI = **biryani**
BIRK *n* birch tree ▹ *adj* consisting or made of birch
BIRKEN *adj* relating to the birch tree
BIRKIE *n* spirited or lively person ▹ *adj* lively **birkier, birkies**
BIRKS ▸ **birk**
BIRL = **burl**
BIRLE = **burl**
BIRLED ▸ **birl**
BIRLER ▸ **birl**
BIRLERS ▸ **birl**
BIRLES ▸ **birle**
BIRLING ▸ **birl**
BIRLINN *n* small Scottish book
BIRLS ▸ **birl**
BIRO *n* tradename of a kind of ballpoint pen **biros**
BIRR *vb* make or cause to make a whirring sound ▹ *n* whirring sound **birred, birring, birrs**
BIRSE *n* bristle **birses**
BIRSIER ▸ **birsy**
BIRSLE *vb* roast **birsled, birsles**
BIRSY *adj* bristly
BIRTH *n, vb* **birthed, births**
BIRYANI *n* Indian rice-based dish
BIS *adv* twice ▹ *sentence substitute* encore! again!
BISCUIT *n, adj*
BISE *n* cold dry northerly wind
BISECT *vb* **bisects**
BISES ▸ **bise**
BISH *n* mistake **bishes**
BISHOP *n, vb* **bishops**
BISK *a less common spelling of* ▸ **bisque**
BISKS ▸ **bisk**
BISMAR *n* type of weighing scale **bismars**
BISMUTH *n* pinkish-white metallic element
BISNAGA *n* type of cactus
BISOM ▸ **besom**
BISOMS ▸ **bisom**
BISON = **buffalo**
BISONS ▸ **bison**
BISQUE *n* thick rich soup made from shellfish **bisques**
BISSON *adj* blind
BIST *a form of the second person singular of* ▸ **be**
BISTATE *adj* involving two states
BISTER = **bestir**
BISTERS ▸ **bister**
BISTORT *n* Eurasian plant with a spike of small pink flowers
BISTRE *n* water-soluble pigment **bistred, bistres**
BISTRO *n* **bistros**
BIT *n* small piece, portion, or quantity
BITABLE ▸ **bite**
BITCH *n, vb* **bitched**
BITCHEN = **bitching**
BITCHES ▸ **bitch**
BITCHY *adj* spiteful or malicious
BITE *vb, n* **biter, biters, bites, biting, bitings**
BITLESS *adj* without a bit
BITMAP *n* picture created by colour or shading on a visual display unit ▹ *vb* create a bitmap of **bitmaps**
BITO *n* African and Asian tree
BITONAL *adj* consisting of black and white tones
BITOS ▸ **bito**
BITOU *n as in* **bitou bush** type of sprawling woody shrub
BITS ▸ **bit**
BITSER *n* mongrel dog **bitsers**
BITSIER ▸ **bitsy**
BITSY *adj* very small
BITT *n* strong post on the deck of a ship for securing lines ▹ *vb* secure (a line) by means of a bitt
BITTE *interj* you're welcome
BITTED ▸ **bitt**
BITTEN ▸ **bite**
BITTER *adj, n, adv, vb*
BITTERN *n*
BITTERS *pl n*

bitter-tasting spirits flavoured with plant extracts
BITTIE *n* small piece
BITTIER ▶ **bitty**
BITTIES ▶ **bittie**
BITTING ▶ **bitt**
BITTOCK *n* small amount
BITTOR *n* bittern **bittors, bittour**
BITTS ▶ **bitt**
BITTUR = **bittor**
BITTURS ▶ **bittur**
BITTY *adj* lacking unity, disjointed
BITUMED *adj* covered with bitumen
BITUMEN *n*
BIVALVE *adj* (marine mollusc) with two hinged segments to its shell ▷ *n* sea creature that has a shell consisting of two hinged valves and breathes through gills
BIVIA ▶ **bivium**
BIVINYL *another word for* > **butadiene**
BIVIOUS *adj* offering a choice of two different ways
BIVIUM *n* parting of ways
BIVOUAC *n, vb*
BIVVIED ▶ **bivvy**
BIVVIES ▶ **bivvy**
BIVVY *n* small tent or shelter ▷ *vb* camp in a bivouac
BIZ *n* business
BIZARRE *adj, n*
BIZARRO *n* bizarre person
BIZAZZ = **pizazz**
BIZE *n* dry, cold wind in France **bizes**
BIZNAGA = **bisnaga**
BIZONAL ▶ **bizone**
BIZONE *n* place comprising two zones **bizones**
BIZZES ▶ **biz**
BIZZIES ▶ **bizzy**
BIZZO *n* empty and irrelevant talk or ideas **bizzos**
BIZZY *n* policeman
BLAB *vb* **blabbed**
BLABBER *vb* talk without thinking ▷ *n* person who blabs
BLABBY *adj* talking too much; indiscreet
BLABS ▶ **blab**
BLACK *adj, n, vb* **blacked**
BLACKEN *vb*
BLACKER ▶ **black**
BLACKLY ▶ **black**
BLACKS ▶ **black**
BLAD = **blaud**
BLADDED ▶ **blad**
BLADDER *n*
BLADE *n* **bladed**
BLADER *n* person skating with in-line skates **bladers**
BLADES ▶ **blade**
BLADIER ▶ **blady**
BLADING *n* act or instance of skating with in-line skates
BLADS ▶ **blad**
BLADY *adj as in* **blady grass** coarse leafy Australasian grass
BLAE *adj* bluish-grey **blaer**
BLAES *n* hardened clay or shale
BLAEST ▶ **blae**
BLAFF *n* West Indian stew **blaffs**
BLAG *vb* obtain by wheedling or cadging ▷ *n* robbery, esp with violence **blagged, blagger, blags**
BLAGUE *n* pretentious but empty talk **blaguer, blagues**
BLAH *n* worthless or silly talk ▷ *adj* uninteresting ▷ *vb* talk nonsense or boringly **blahed, blahing, blahs**
BLAIN *n* blister, blotch, or sore on the skin **blains**
BLAISE = **blaes**
BLAIZE = **blaes**
BLAM *n* representation of the sound of a bullet being fired
BLAME *vb, n*
BLAMED *euphemistic word for* ▶ **damned** **blamer, blamers, blames, blaming**
BLAMS ▶ **blam**
BLANCH *vb*
BLANCO *n* whitening substance ▷ *vb* whiten (something) with blanco **blancos**
BLAND *adj, n, vb as in* **bland out blanded, blander, blandly, blands**
BLANK *adj, n, vb* **blanked, blanker**

BLANKET *n, adj, vb*
BLANKLY ▶ **blank**
BLANKS ▶ **blank**
BLARE *vb, n* **blared, blares, blaring**
BLARNEY *n* flattering talk ▷ *vb* cajole with flattery
BLART *vb* sound loudly and harshly **blarted, blarts**
BLASE *adj* indifferent or bored through familiarity
BLASH *n* splash **blashes**
BLASHY *adj* windy and rainy
BLAST *n, vb, interj*
BLASTED *adv* extreme or extremely ▷ *adj* blighted or withered
BLASTER ▶ **blast**
BLASTIE *n* ugly creature
BLASTS ▶ **blast**
BLASTY *adj* gusty
BLAT *vb* cry out or bleat like a sheep
BLATANT *adj*
BLATE *adj* shy; ill at ease **blater, blatest**
BLATHER *vb* speak foolishly ▷ *n* foolish talk
BLATS ▶ **blat**
BLATT *n* newspaper
BLATTED ▶ **blat**
BLATTER *n, vb* prattle
BLATTS ▶ **blatt**
BLAUBOK *n* South African antelope
BLAUD *vb* slap **blauded, blauds**
BLAW *vb* blow **blawed, blawing, blawn**
BLAWORT *n* harebell
BLAWS ▶ **blaw**
BLAY *n* small river fish **blays**
BLAZAR *n* type of active galaxy **blazars**
BLAZE *n, vb* **blazed**
BLAZER *n* **blazers**
BLAZES *pl n* hell
BLAZING ▶ **blaze**
BLAZON *vb* proclaim publicly ▷ *n* coat of arms **blazons**
BLEACH *vb, n*
BLEAK *adj, n* **bleaker, bleakly, bleaks, bleaky**
BLEAR *vb* make (eyes or sight) dim with or as if with tears ▷ *adj* bleary **bleared, blearer, blears**
BLEARY *adj*
BLEAT *vb, n* **bleated, bleater, bleats**
BLEB *n* fluid-filled blister on the skin **blebby, blebs**
BLED ▶ **bleed**
BLEE *n* complexion; hue
BLEED *vb*
BLEEDER *n* despicable person
BLEEDS ▶ **bleed**
BLEEP *n, vb* **bleeped**
BLEEPER *n* small portable radio receiver that makes a bleeping signal
BLEEPS ▶ **bleep**
BLEES ▶ **blee**
BLELLUM *n* babbler; blusterer
BLEMISH *n, vb*
BLENCH *vb*
BLEND *vb, n*
BLENDE *n* mineral consisting mainly of zinc sulphide
BLENDED ▶ **blend**
BLENDER *n*
BLENDES ▶ **blende**
BLENDS ▶ **blend**
BLENNY *n* small fish with a tapering scaleless body
BLENT *a past participle of* ▶ **blend**
BLERT *n* foolish person **blerts**
BLESBOK *n* S African antelope
BLESS *vb* **blessed, blesser, blesses, blest**
BLET *n* state of decay in certain fruits, due to overripening ▷ *vb* go soft **blets, bletted**
BLETHER = **blather**
BLEW ▶ **blow**
BLEWART = **blawort**
BLEWITS *n* type of edible fungus with a pale brown cap and a bluish stalk
BLEY = **blay**
BLEYS ▶ **bley**
BLIGHT *n, vb* **blights**
BLIGHTY *n* home country; home leave
BLIKSEM *interj* South African expression of surprise
BLIMEY *interj* exclamation of surprise or annoyance
BLIMP *n* small airship **blimps**

BLIMY = **blimey**
BLIN *Scots word for* ▸ **blind**
BLIND *adj, vb, n* **blinded, blinder, blindly, blinds**
BLING *adj, n* **blinger, blings, blingy**
BLINI *pl n* Russian pancakes made of buckwheat flour and yeast **blinis**
BLINK *vb, n* **blinked**
BLINKER *vb* provide (a horse) with blinkers ▹ *n* flashing light for sending messages
BLINKS ▸ **blink**
BLINNED ▸ **blin**
BLINS ▸ **blin**
BLINTZ *n* thin pancake folded over a filling usually of apple, cream cheese, or meat **blintze**
BLINY = **blini**
BLIP *n* a sound such as that produced by an electronic device ▹ *vb* produce such a noise **blipped, blips**
BLISS *n, vb* **blissed, blisses**
BLIST *archaic form of* ▸ **blessed**
BLISTER *n, vb*
BLIT *vb* move (a block of data) in a computer's memory
BLITE *n* type of herb **blites**
BLITHE *adj*
BLITHER = **blether**
BLITS ▸ **blit**
BLITTED ▸ **blit**
BLITTER *n* circuit that transfers large amounts of data within a computer's memory
BLITZ *n, vb* **blitzed, blitzer, blitzes**
BLIVE = **belive**
BLOAT *vb* cause to swell, as with liquid or air ▹ *n* abnormal distention of the abdomen in cattle, sheep, etc
BLOATED *adj*
BLOATER *n*
BLOATS ▸ **bloat**
BLOB *n, vb* **blobbed, blobby, blobs**
BLOC *n*
BLOCK *n, vb*
BLOCKED *adj* functionally impeded by amphetamine
BLOCKER *n* person or thing that blocks
BLOCKIE *n* owner of a small property, esp a farm
BLOCKS ▸ **block**
BLOCKY *adj* like a block, esp in shape and solidity
BLOCS ▸ **bloc**
BLOG *n, vb* **blogged, blogger, blogs**
BLOKART *n* single-seat three-wheeled vehicle propelled by the wind
BLOKE *n* **blokes**
BLOKEY = **blokeish**
BLOKIER ▸ **blokey**
BLOKISH = **blokeish**
BLOND *adj* (of men's hair) of a light colour ▹ *n* person, esp a man, having light-coloured hair and skin
BLONDE *n, adj* **blonder, blondes**
BLONDS ▸ **blond**
BLOOD *n, vb*
BLOODED *adj* (of horses, cattle, etc) of good breeding
BLOODS ▸ **blood**
BLOODY *adj, adv, vb*
BLOOEY *adj* out of order; faulty **blooie**
BLOOK *n* **blooks**
BLOOM *n, vb*
BLOOMED *adj* (of a lens) coated to reduce light lost by reflection
BLOOMER *n* stupid mistake
BLOOMS ▸ **bloom**
BLOOMY *adj* having a fine whitish coating on the surface
BLOOP *vb* (baseball) hit a ball into air beyond infield **blooped**
BLOOPER *n* stupid mistake
BLOOPS ▸ **bloop**
BLOOSME = **blossom**
BLORE *n* strong blast of wind **blores**
BLOSSOM *n, vb*
BLOT *n, vb*
BLOTCH *n, vb*
BLOTCHY *adj* covered in or marked by blotches
BLOTS ▸ **blot**
BLOTTED ▸ **blot**
BLOTTER *n* sheet of blotting paper

BLOTTO *adj* extremely drunk
BLOTTY *adj* covered in blots
BLOUBOK = **blaubok**
BLOUSE *n, vb* **bloused, blouses**
BLOUSON *n* short loose jacket with a tight waist
BLOUSY *adj* loose; blouse-like
BLOW *vb, n*
BLOWBY *n* leakage of gas past the piston of an engine at maximum pressure **blowbys**
BLOWED ▸ **blow**
BLOWER *n* mechanical device, such as a fan, that blows **blowers**
BLOWFLY *n* fly that lays its eggs in meat
BLOWGUN = **blowpipe**
BLOWIE *n* bluebottle
BLOWIER ▸ **blowy**
BLOWIES ▸ **blowie**
BLOWING *n*
BLOWN ▸ **blow**
BLOWOFF *n* discharge of a surplus fluid
BLOWOUT *n*
BLOWS ▸ **blow**
BLOWSE *n* large, red-faced woman
BLOWSED = **blowsy**
BLOWSES ▸ **blowse**
BLOWSY *adj* fat, untidy, and red-faced
BLOWUP *n* fit of temper **blowups**
BLOWY *adj* windy
BLOWZE *variant of* ▸ **blowse**
BLOWZED = **blowsy**
BLOWZES ▸ **blowze**
BLOWZY = **blowsy**
BLUB *a slang word for* ▸ **blubber**
BLUBBED ▸ **blub**
BLUBBER *n, vb, adj, n*
BLUBS ▸ **blub**
BLUCHER *n* high shoe with laces over the tongue
BLUDE *Scots form of* ▸ **blood**
BLUDES ▸ **blude**
BLUDGE *vb, n* **bludged**
BLUDGER *n* person who scrounges
BLUDGES ▸ **bludge**
BLUDIE *Scots form of* ▸ **bloody**
BLUDIER ▸ **bludie**
BLUDY = **bludie**
BLUE *n, adj, vb*
BLUECAP *another name for* ▸ **bluetit**
BLUED ▸ **blue**
BLUEFIN *another name for* ▸ **tunny**
BLUEGUM *n* widely cultivated Australian tree
BLUEING ▸ **blue**
BLUEISH = **bluish**
BLUEJAY *n* N American jay
BLUELY ▸ **blue**
BLUER ▸ **blue**
BLUES *pl n* type of music
BLUEST ▸ **blue**
BLUESY ▸ **blues**
BLUET *n* N American plant with small four-petalled blue flowers
BLUETIT *n*
BLUETS ▸ **bluet**
BLUETTE *n* short, brilliant piece of music
BLUEY *adj* bluish ▹ *n* informal Australian word meaning blanket **blueys**
BLUFF *vb, n, adj* **bluffed, bluffer, bluffly, bluffs**
BLUGGY = **bloody**
BLUID *Scots word for* ▸ **blood**
BLUIDS ▸ **bluid**
BLUIDY ▸ **bluid**
BLUIER ▸ **bluey**
BLUIEST ▸ **bluey**
BLUING ▸ **blue**
BLUINGS ▸ **blue**
BLUISH *adj* slightly blue
BLUME *Scots word for* ▸ **bloom**
BLUMED ▸ **blume**
BLUMES ▸ **blume**
BLUMING ▸ **blume**
BLUNDER *n, vb*
BLUNGE *vb* mix clay with water **blunged**
BLUNGER *n* large vat in which the contents are mixed by rotating arms
BLUNGES ▸ **blunge**
BLUNK *vb* ruin; botch **blunked, blunker, blunks**
BLUNT *adj, vb, n* **blunted, blunter, bluntly, blunts**
BLUR *vb, n*
BLURB *n, vb* **blurbed, blurbs**
BLURRED ▸ **blur**
BLURRY ▸ **blur**

BLURS ▸ **blur**
BLURT *vb* utter suddenly and involuntarily **blurted, blurter, blurts**
BLUSH *vb, n* **blushed**
BLUSHER *n* cosmetic for giving the cheeks a rosy colour
BLUSHES ▸ **blush**
BLUSHET *n* modest young woman
BLUSTER *vb, n*
BLYPE *n* piece of skin peeled off after sunburn **blypes**
BO *interj* exclamation uttered to startle or surprise someone ▹ *n* fellow, buddy
BOA *n*
BOAB *short for* ▸ **baobab**
BOABS ▸ **boab**
BOAK = **boke**
BOAKED ▸ **boak**
BOAKING ▸ **boak**
BOAKS ▸ **boak**
BOAR *n*
BOARD *n, vb* **boarded**
BOARDER *n*
BOARDS ▸ **board**
BOARISH *adj* coarse, cruel, or sensual
BOARS ▸ **boar**
BOART = **bort**
BOARTS ▸ **boart**
BOAS ▸ **boa**
BOAST *vb, n* **boasted, boaster, boasts**
BOAT *n, vb* **boated**
BOATEL *n* waterside hotel catering for boating people **boatels**
BOATER *n* **boaters**
BOATFUL ▸ **boat**
BOATIE *n* boating enthusiast **boaties**
BOATING *n* rowing, sailing, or cruising in boats as a form of recreation
BOATMAN *n* man who works on, hires out, or repairs boats **boatmen**
BOATS ▸ **boat**
BOB *vb, n*
BOBA *n* type of Chinese tea
BOBAC = **bobak**
BOBACS ▸ **bobac**
BOBAK *n* type of marmot **bobaks**
BOBAS ▸ **boba**
BOBBED ▸ **bob**
BOBBER *n* type of float for fishing **bobbers**
BOBBERY *n* mixed pack of hunting dogs ▹ *adj* noisy or excitable
BOBBIES ▸ **bobby**
BOBBIN *n*
BOBBING ▸ **bob**
BOBBINS ▸ **bobbin**
BOBBISH ▸ **cheery**
BOBBITT *vb* sever the penis of
BOBBLE *n, vb* **bobbled, bobbles**
BOBBLY *adj* (of fabric) covered in small balls; worn
BOBBY *n*
BOBCAT *n* N American feline **bobcats**
BOBECHE *n* candle drip-catcher
BOBLET *n* two-man bobsleigh **boblets**
BOBOL *n* type of fraud ▹ *vb* commit a bobol **bobols**
BOBOTIE *n* dish of curried mince
BOBS ▸ **bob**
BOBSLED = **bobsleigh**
BOBSTAY *n* stay between a bowsprit and the stem of a vessel
BOBTAIL *n* docked tail ▹ *adj* having the tail cut short ▹ *vb* dock the tail of
BOBWIG *n* type of short wig **bobwigs**
BOCAGE *n* wooded countryside characteristic of northern France **bocages**
BOCCA *n* mouth **boccas**
BOCCE = **boccie**
BOCCES ▸ **bocce**
BOCCI = **boccie**
BOCCIA = **boccie**
BOCCIAS ▸ **boccia**
BOCCIE *n* Italian version of bowls **boccies**
BOCCIS ▸ **bocci**
BOCK *a variant spelling of* ▸ **boke**
BOCKED ▸ **bock**
BOCKEDY *adj* (of a structure, piece of furniture, etc) unsteady
BOCKING ▸ **bock**
BOCKS ▸ **bock**
BOD *n* person
BODACH *n* old man **bodachs**
BODDLE = **bodle**
BODDLES ▸ **boddle**

BODE *vb* portend or presage **boded**
BODEFUL *adj* portentous
BODEGA *n* shop in a Spanish-speaking country that sells wine **bodegas**
BODES ▶ **bode**
BODGE *vb* make a mess of **bodged**
BODGER *adj* worthless or second-rate **bodgers**
BODGES ▶ **bodge**
BODGIE *n* unruly or uncouth young man, esp in the 1950s ▷ *adj* inferior **bodgier, bodgies**
BODGING ▶ **bodge**
BODHI *n as in* **bodhi tree** holy tree of Buddhists
BODHRAN *n* shallow one-sided drum popular in Irish and Scottish folk music
BODICE *n* **bodices**
BODIED ▶ **body**
BODIES ▶ **body**
BODIKIN *n* little body
BODILY *adj, adv*
BODING ▶ **bode**
BODINGS ▶ **bode**
BODKIN *n* blunt large-eyed needle **bodkins**
BODLE *n* small obsolete Scottish coin **bodles**
BODRAG *n* enemy attack **bodrags**
BODS ▶ **bod**
BODY *n* **bodying**
BOEP *n* South African word for a big belly **boeps**
BOERBUL *n* crossbred mastiff used esp as a watchdog
BOET *n* brother **boets**
BOEUF *n as in* **boeuf bourgignon** casserole of beef, vegetables, herbs, etc, cooked in red wine
BOFF *n* boffin ▷ *vb* hit **boffed**
BOFFIN *n* scientist or expert
BOFFING ▶ **boff**
BOFFINS ▶ **boffin**
BOFFO *adj* very good
BOFFOLA *n* great success
BOFFOS ▶ **boffo**
BOFFS ▶ **boff**
BOG *n, vb*
BOGAN *n* youth who dresses and behaves rebelliously **bogans**
BOGART *vb* monopolize or keep to oneself selfishly **bogarts**
BOGBEAN = **buckbean**
BOGEY *n* evil or mischievous spirit ▷ *vb* play (a hole) in one stroke over par **bogeyed, bogeys**
BOGGARD = **boggart**
BOGGART *n* ghost or poltergeist
BOGGED ▶ **bog**
BOGGER *n* lavatory **boggers**
BOGGIER ▶ **bog**
BOGGING ▶ **bog**
BOGGISH ▶ **bog**
BOGGLE *vb* **boggled, boggler, boggles**
BOGGY ▶ **bog**
BOGIE = **bogey**
BOGIED ▶ **bogie**
BOGIES ▶ **bogy**
BOGLAND *n* area of wetland
BOGLE *n* rhythmic dance performed to ragga music ▷ *vb* perform such a dance **bogled, bogles, bogling**
BOGMAN *n* body of a person found preserved in a peat bog **bogmen**
BOGOAK *n* oak or other wood found preserved in peat bogs; bogwood **bogoaks**
BOGONG *n* large nocturnal Australian moth **bogongs**
BOGS ▶ **bog**
BOGUS *adj* **bogusly**
BOGWOOD = **bogoak**
BOGY = **bogey**
BOGYISM = **bogeyism**
BOGYMAN = **bogeyman**
BOGYMEN ▶ **bogyman**
BOH = **bo**
BOHEA *n* black Chinese tea **boheas**
BOHEMIA *n* area frequented by unconventional (esp creative) people
BOHO *short for* > **bohemian**
BOHOS ▶ **boho**

BOHRIUM *n* element artificially produced in minute quantities
BOHS ▸ **boh**
BOI *n* lesbian who dresses like a boy
BOIL *vb, n* **boiled**
BOILER *n* **boilers**
BOILERY *n* place where water is boiled to extract salt
BOILING *adj, n*
BOILOFF *n* quantity of liquified gases lost in evaporation
BOILS ▸ **boil**
BOING *vb* rebound making a noise **boinged, boings, boink**
BOINKED ▸ **boink**
BOINKS ▸ **boink**
BOIS ▸ **boi**
BOITE *n* artist's portfolio **boites**
BOK *n* S African antelope

> This useful K word, meaning an antelope, that can take quite a number of front extensions, forming words like **blesbok, reitbok, rhebok**, and even, if you are lucky, **jambok** or **sjambok**.

BOKE *vb* retch or vomit ▹ *n* retch **boked, bokes, boking**
BOKO *slang word for* ▸ **nose**
BOKOS ▸ **boko**
BOKS ▸ **bok**
BOLA *n* missile used by gauchos and Indians of South America
BOLAR *adj* relating to clay
BOLAS = **bola**
BOLASES ▸ **bolas**
BOLD *adj, n*
BOLDEN *vb* make bold **boldens**
BOLDER, boldest, boldly, bolds ▸ **bold**
BOLE *n* tree trunk
BOLERO *n* **boleros**
BOLES ▸ **bole**
BOLETE *n* type of fungus **boletes**
BOLETI ▸ **boletus**
BOLETUS *n* type of fungus
BOLIDE *n* large exceptionally bright meteor that often explodes **bolides**
BOLINE *n* (in Wicca) a knife **bolines**
BOLIVAR *n* standard monetary unit of Venezuela, equal to 100 céntimos
BOLIVIA *n* type of woollen fabric
BOLL *n* rounded seed capsule of cotton, flax, etc ▹ *vb* form into a boll
BOLLARD *n*
BOLLED, bollen, bolling, bolls ▸ **boll**
BOLO *n* large single-edged knife, originating in the Philippines
BOLOGNA *n* type of sausage
BOLONEY *a variant spelling of* ▸ **baloney**
BOLOS ▸ **bolo**
BOLSHIE *adj* difficult or rebellious ▹ *n* any political radical **bolshy**
BOLSON *n* desert valley surrounded by mountains, with a shallow lake at the centre **bolsons**
BOLSTER *vb, n*
BOLT *n, vb* **bolted, bolter, bolters, bolting, bolts**
BOLUS = **bole**
BOLUSES ▸ **bolus**
BOMA *n* enclosure set up to protect a camp, herd of animals, etc **bomas**
BOMB *n, vb*
BOMBARD *vb, n*
BOMBAST *n* pompous language ▹ *vb* speak pompous language
BOMBAX *n* type of S American tree
BOMBE *n* dessert of ice cream lined or filled with custard, cake crumbs, etc ▹ *adj* (of furniture) having a projecting swollen shape
BOMBED ▸ **bomb**
BOMBER *n* **bombers**
BOMBES ▸ **bombe**
BOMBING ▸ **bomb**
BOMBLET *n* small bomb
BOMBO *n* inferior wine
BOMBORA *n* submerged reef

BOMBOS ▶ **bombo**
BOMBS ▶ **bomb**
BOMBYX *n* type of moth
BOMMIE *n* outcrop of coral reef **bommies**
BON *adj* good
BONA *n* goods
BONACI *n* type of fish **bonacis**
BONAMIA *n* parasite
BONANZA *n*
BONASUS *n* European bison
BONBON *n* sweet **bonbons**
BONCE *n* head **bonces**
BOND *n, vb*
BONDAGE *n*
BONDED *adj* consisting of, secured by, or operating under a bond or bonds
BONDER = **bondstone**
BONDERS ▶ **bonder**
BONDING *n* process by which individuals become emotionally attached to one another
BONDMAN = **bondsman**
BONDMEN ▶ **bondman**
BONDS ▶ **bond**
BONDUC *n* type of North American tree **bonducs**
BONE *n, vb* **boned**
BONER *n* blunder **boners**
BONES ▶ **bone**
BONESET *n* N American plant with flat clusters of small white flowers
BONEY = **bony**
BONEYER ▶ **boney**
BONFIRE *n*
BONG *n* deep reverberating sound, as of a large bell ▷ *vb* make a deep reverberating sound **bonged, bonging**
BONGO *n* small drum played with the fingers **bongoes, bongos**
BONGS ▶ **bong**
BONHAM *n* piglet **bonhams**
BONIATO *n* sweet potato
BONIE = **bonny**
BONIER ▶ **bony**
BONIEST ▶ **bony**
BONING ▶ **bone**
BONINGS ▶ **bone**
BONISM *n* doctrine that the world is good, although not the best of all possible worlds **bonisms, bonist, bonists**
BONITA *slang term for* ▶ **heroin**
BONITAS ▶ **bonita**
BONITO *n* small tunny-like marine food fish **bonitos**
BONJOUR *interj* hello
BONK *vb* have sex with **bonked**
BONKERS *adj* crazy
BONKING ▶ **bonk**
BONKS ▶ **bonk**
BONNE *n* housemaid or female servant **bonnes**
BONNET *n, vb* **bonnets**
BONNIE = **bonny**
BONNIER ▶ **bonny**
BONNIES ▶ **bonny**
BONNILY ▶ **bonny**
BONNOCK *n* thick oatmeal cake
BONNY *adj, adv*
BONOBO *n* type of anthropoid ape of central W Africa **bonobos**
BONSAI *n*
BONSELA *n* small gift of money
BONSOIR *interj* good evening
BONUS *n* **bonuses**
BONXIE *n* great skua **bonxies**
BONY *adj*
BONZA = **bonzer**
BONZE *n* Chinese or Japanese Buddhist priest or monk
BONZER *adj* excellent
BONZES ▶ **bonze**
BOO *interj, vb*
BOOAI ▶ **boohai**
BOOAIS ▶ **booai**
BOOAY ▶ **boohai**
BOOAYS ▶ **booay**
BOOB *n* foolish mistake ▷ *vb* make a foolish mistake ▷ *adj* of poor quality, similar to that provided in prison **boobed**
BOOBIE = **booby**
BOOBIES ▶ **booby** **boobing**
BOOBIRD *n* person who boos
BOOBISH ▶ **booby**
BOOBOO *n* blunder
BOOBOOK *n*

BOOBOOS ▸ **booboo**
BOOBS ▸ **boob**
BOOBY *n* foolish person
BOOCOO = **beaucoup**
BOOCOOS ▸ **boocoo**
BOODIE *n* type of kangaroo
BOODIED ▸ **boody**
BOODIES ▸ **boody**
BOODLE *n* money or valuables, counterfeit, or used as a bribe ▹ *vb* give or receive money corruptly or illegally **boodled, boodler, boodles**
BOODY *vb* sulk
BOOED ▸ **boo**
BOOFIER ▸ **boofy**
BOOFY *adj* muscular and strong but stupid
BOOGER *n* dried mucus from the nose **boogers**
BOOGEY = **boogie**
BOOGEYS ▸ **boogey**
BOOGIE *vb* dance to fast pop music ▹ *n* session of dancing to pop music **boogied, boogies, boogy**
BOOH = **boo**
BOOHAI *n as in* **up the boohai** thoroughly lost **boohais**
BOOHED ▸ **booh**
BOOHING ▸ **booh**
BOOHOO *vb* sob or pretend to sob noisily ▹ *n* distressed or pretended sobbing **boohoos**
BOOHS ▸ **booh**
BOOING ▸ **boo**
BOOJUM *n* American tree **boojums**
BOOK *n, vb* **booked**
BOOKEND *n* one of a pair of supports for holding books upright
BOOKER ▸ **book**
BOOKERS ▸ **book**
BOOKFUL ▸ **book**
BOOKIE *short for* > **bookmaker**
BOOKIER ▸ **booky**
BOOKIES ▸ **bookie**
BOOKING *n*
BOOKISH *adj* fond of reading
BOOKLET *n*
BOOKMAN *n* learned person **bookmen**
BOOKOO = **boocoo**
BOOKOOS ▸ **bookoo**
BOOKS ▸ **book**
BOOKSIE = **booksy**
BOOKSY *adj* inclined to be bookish or literary
BOOKY *adj* bookish
BOOL *n* bowling bowl ▹ *vb* play bowls **booled, booling, bools**
BOOM *vb, n*
BOOMBOX *n* portable stereo system
BOOMED ▸ **boom**
BOOMER *n* large male kangaroo **boomers**
BOOMIER ▸ **boomy**
BOOMING ▸ **boom**
BOOMKIN *n* short boom projecting from the deck of a ship
BOOMLET *n* small boom in business, birth rate, etc
BOOMS ▸ **boom**
BOOMY *adj* characterized by heavy bass sound
BOON *n*
BOONER *n* young working-class person from Canberra **booners**
BOONIES *short form of* > **boondocks**
BOONS ▸ **boon**
BOOR *n*
BOORD *obsolete spelling of* ▸ **board**
BOORDE *obsolete spelling of* ▸ **board**
BOORDES ▸ **boorde**
BOORDS ▸ **boord**
BOORISH *adj* ill-mannered, clumsy, or insensitive
BOORKA = **burka**
BOORKAS ▸ **boorka**
BOORS ▸ **boor**
BOOS ▸ **boo**
BOOSE = **booze**
BOOSED ▸ **boose**
BOOSES ▸ **boose**
BOOSHIT *adj* very good
BOOSING ▸ **boose**
BOOST *n, vb* **boosted**
BOOSTER *n* small additional injection of a vaccine
BOOSTS ▸ **boost**
BOOT *n, vb*
BOOTCUT *adj* (of trousers) slightly flared at the bottom of the legs
BOOTED *adj* wearing boots
BOOTEE *n* baby's soft shoe **bootees**

BOOTERY *n* shop where boots and shoes are sold
BOOTH *n* **booths**
BOOTIE *n* Royal Marine
BOOTIES ▸ **booty**
BOOTING ▸ **boot**
BOOTLEG *adj* produced, distributed, or sold illicitly ▹ *vb* make, carry, or sell (illicit goods) ▹ *n* something made or sold illicitly
BOOTS ▸ **boot**
BOOTY *n*
BOOZE *n*, *vb* **boozed**
BOOZER *n* person who is fond of drinking **boozers**
BOOZES ▸ **booze**
BOOZEY = **boozy**
BOOZIER ▸ **boozy**
BOOZILY ▸ **boozy**
BOOZING ▸ **booze**
BOOZY *adj* inclined to or involving excessive drinking of alcohol
BOP *vb* dance to pop music ▹ *n* form of jazz with complex rhythms and harmonies
BOPEEP *n* quick look; peek **bopeeps**
BOPPED, bopper, boppers, bopping, bops ▸ **bop**
BOPS ▸ **bop**
BOR *n* neighbour
BORA *n* Aboriginal ceremony
BORACES ▸ **borax**
BORACIC = **boric**
BORAGE *n* Mediterranean plant with star-shaped blue flowers **borages**
BORAK *n* rubbish **boraks**
BORAL *n* type of fine powder **borals**
BORANE *n* any compound of boron and hydrogen **boranes**
BORAS ▸ **bora**
BORATE *n* salt or ester of boric acid ▹ *vb* treat with borax, boric acid, or borate **borated, borates**
BORAX *n* soluble white mineral occurring in alkaline soils and salt deposits **boraxes**
BORAZON *n* extremely hard form of boron nitride
BORD *obsolete spelling of* ▸ **board**
BORDAR *n* smallholder who held cottage in return for menial work **bordars**
BORDE *obsolete spelling of* ▸ **board**
BORDEL = **bordello**
BORDELS ▸ **bordel**
BORDER *n*, *vb* **borders**
BORDES ▸ **borde**
BORDS ▸ **bord**
BORDURE *n* outer edge of a shield, esp when decorated distinctively
BORE *vb* make (someone) weary by being dull
BOREAL *adj* of or relating to the north or the north wind
BOREAS *n* name for the north wind
BORED ▸ **bore**
BOREDOM *n*
BOREE = **myall**
BOREEN *n* country lane or narrow road **boreens**
BOREES ▸ **boree**
BOREL *adj* unlearned
BORER *n* machine or hand tool for boring holes **borers**
BORES ▸ **bear**
BORGO *n* small attractive medieval village **borgos**
BORIC *adj* of or containing boron
BORIDE *n* compound in which boron is the most electronegative element **borides**
BORING *n*, *adj* **borings**
BORK *vb* dismiss from job unfairly **borked, borking, borks**
BORM *vb* smear with paint, oil, etc **bormed, borming, borms**
BORN *adj*
BORNA *n as in* **borna disease** viral disease found in mammals, esp horses
BORNE ▸ **bear**
BORNEOL *n* white solid terpene alcohol
BORNITE *n* type of mineral
BORNYL *n as in* **bornyl alcohol** white solid alcohol from a

Malaysian tree **bornyls**
BORON *n*
BORONIA *n* Australian aromatic flowering shrub
BORONIC ▸ **boron**
BORONS ▸ **boron**
BOROUGH *n*
BORREL *adj* ignorant **borrell**
BORROW *vb* **borrows**
BORS ▸ **bor**
BORSCH = **borscht**
BORSCHT *n* Russian soup based on beetroot **borshch, borsht**
BORSHTS ▸ **borsht**
BORSIC *n* composite material used in aviation **borsics**
BORSTAL *n*
BORT *n* inferior grade of diamond used for cutting and drilling or, in powdered form, as an industrial abrasive **bortier, borts**
BORTSCH = **borscht** **borty, bortz**
BORTZES ▸ **bortz**
BORZOI *n* **borzois**
BOS ▸ **bo**
BOSBOK = **bushbuck**
BOSBOKS ▸ **bosbok**
BOSCAGE *n* mass of trees and shrubs
BOSH *n* empty talk, nonsense
BOSHBOK = **bushbuck** **boshes**
BOSHTA = **boshter**
BOSHTER *adj* excellent
BOSIE *n* (in cricket) another term for googly **bosies**
BOSK *n* small wood of bushes and small trees
BOSKAGE = **boscage**
BOSKER *adj* excellent
BOSKET *n* clump of small trees or bushes **boskets**
BOSKIER ▸ **bosky**
BOSKS ▸ **bosk**
BOSKY *adj* containing or consisting of bushes or thickets
BOSOM *n, adj, vb* **bosomed, bosoms**
BOSOMY *adj* (of a woman) having large breasts
BOSON *n* type of elementary particle **bosonic, bosons**
BOSQUE = **bosk**
BOSQUES ▸ **bosque**
BOSQUET = **bosket**
BOSS *n, vb, adj*
BOSSBOY *n* Black African foreman of a gang of workers
BOSSDOM *n* bosses collectively
BOSSED, bosser, bosses, bossest ▸ **boss**
BOSSET *n* either of the rudimentary antlers found in young deer **bossets**
BOSSIER ▸ **bossy**
BOSSIES ▸ **bossy**
BOSSILY ▸ **bossy**
BOSSING *n* act of shaping malleable metal
BOSSISM *n* domination of political organizations by bosses
BOSSY = **boss**
BOSTON *n* card game for four, played with two packs **bostons**
BOSTRYX *n* phenomenon in which flowers develop on one side only
BOSUN = **boatswain**
BOSUNS ▸ **bosun**
BOT *n* larva of a botfly
BOTA *n* leather container
BOTANIC = **botanical**
BOTANY *n*
BOTARGO *n* relish consisting of the roe of mullet or tunny, salted and pressed into rolls
BOTAS ▸ **bota**
BOTCH *vb, n* **botched, botcher, botches**
BOTCHY *adj* clumsily done or made
BOTE *n* compensation given for injury or damage to property
BOTEL = **boatel**
BOTELS ▸ **botel**
BOTES ▸ **bote**
BOTFLY *n* type of stout-bodied hairy fly
BOTH *pron, adj, determiner*
BOTHAN *n* unlicensed drinking house **bothans**
BOTHER *vb, n, interj* **bothers**
BOTHIE = **bothy**
BOTHIES ▸ **bothy**

BOTHOLE *n* hole made by the larva of the botfly
BOTHRIA > **bothrium**
BOTHY *n* hut used for temporary shelter
BOTNET *n* network of infected computers **botnets**
BOTONE *adj* having lobes at the ends **botonee**
BOTS *n* digestive disease of horses and some other animals
BOTT = **bot**
BOTTE *n* thrust or hit
BOTTED ▸ **bot**
BOTTEGA *n* workshop; studio
BOTTES ▸ **botte**
BOTTIES ▸ **botty**
BOTTINE *n* light boot for women or children
BOTTING ▸ **bot**
BOTTLE *n, vb* **bottled**
BOTTLER *n* exceptional person or thing
BOTTLES ▸ **bottle**
BOTTOM *n, adj, vb* **bottoms**
BOTTONY = **botone**
BOTTS ▸ **bott**
BOTTY *n* diminutive for bottom
BOTULIN *n* potent toxin which causes botulism
BOUBOU *n* long flowing garment **boubous**
BOUCHE *n* notch cut in top corner of shield
BOUCHEE *n* small pastry case filled with a savoury mixture
BOUCHES ▸ **bouche**
BOUCLE *n* looped yarn giving a knobbly effect ▷ *adj* of or designating such a yarn or fabric
BOUCLEE *n* support for a cue in billiards using the hand
BOUCLES ▸ **boucle**
BOUDIN *n* French version of a black pudding **boudins**
BOUDOIR *n* woman's bedroom or private sitting room
BOUFFE *n* type of light or satirical opera common in France during the 19th century **bouffes**
BOUGE *vb* move **bouged, bouges**
BOUGET *n* budget **bougets**
BOUGH *n* **boughed, boughs**
BOUGHT ▸ **buy**
BOUGHTS ▸ **buy**
BOUGIE *n* medical instrument **bougies**
BOUGING ▸ **bouge**
BOUILLI *n* stew
BOUK *n* bulk; volume **bouks**
BOULDER *n, vb*
BOULE = **boulle**
BOULES *n* game popular in France
BOULLE *adj* relating to a type of marquetry much used on French furniture from the 17th century ▷ *n* something ornamented with such marquetry **boulles**
BOULT = **bolt**
BOULTED ▸ **boult**
BOULTER ▸ **bolt**
BOULTS ▸ **boult**
BOUN *vb* prepare to go out
BOUNCE *vb, n* **bounced**
BOUNCER *n* person employed at a disco etc to remove unwanted people
BOUNCES ▸ **bounce**
BOUNCY *adj*
BOUND ▸ **bind**
BOUNDED *adj* (of a set) having a bound
BOUNDEN *adj* morally obligatory
BOUNDER *n* morally reprehensible person
BOUNDS *pl n* limit
BOUNED ▸ **boun**
BOUNING ▸ **boun**
BOUNS ▸ **boun**
BOUNTY *n*
BOUQUET *n*
BOURBON *n* whiskey made from maize
BOURD *n* prank
BOURDER *n* prankster
BOURDON *n* 16-foot organ stop of the stopped diapason type
BOURDS ▸ **bourd**
BOURG *n* French market town, esp one beside a castle **bourgs**
BOURKHA = **burka**
BOURLAW = **byrlaw**
BOURN *n* (in S Britain) stream **bourne**
BOURNES ▸ **bourne**
BOURNS ▸ **bourn**

BOURREE *n* traditional French dance in fast duple time
BOURSE *n* stock exchange of continental Europe, esp Paris **bourses**
BOURSIN *n* tradename of a smooth white creamy cheese, often flavoured with garlic
BOUSE *vb* raise or haul with a tackle **boused, bouses**
BOUSIER ▸ **bousy**
BOUSING ▸ **bouse**
BOUSY *adj* drunken; boozy
BOUT *n*
BOUTADE *n* outburst
BOUTON *n* knob-shaped contact between nerve fibres **boutons**
BOUTS ▸ **bout**
BOUVIER *n* large powerful dog
BOVATE *n* obsolete measure of land **bovates**
BOVID *n* type of ruminant **bovids**
BOVINE *n* **bovines**
BOVVER *n* rowdiness, esp caused by gangs of teenage youths **bovvers**
BOW *vb, n*
BOWAT *n* lamp **bowats**
BOWBENT *adj* bent; bow-like
BOWED *adj* lowered, bent forward, or curved
BOWEL *n, vb* **boweled, bowels**
BOWER *n, vb* **bowered, bowers, bowery**
BOWES ▸ **bough**
BOWET = **bowat**
BOWETS ▸ **bowet**
BOWFIN *n* N American freshwater fish **bowfins**
BOWGET *obsolete variant of* ▸ **budget**
BOWGETS ▸ **bowget**
BOWHEAD *n* type of large-mouthed arctic whale
BOWIE *n as in* **bowie knife** type of hunting knife
BOWING *n* musical technique **bowings**
BOWKNOT *n* decorative knot usually having two loops and two loose ends
BOWL *n, vb*
BOWLDER = **boulder**
BOWLED ▸ **bowl**
BOWLEG *n* leg curving outwards like a bow between the ankle and the thigh **bowlegs**
BOWLER *n* player who sends (a ball) towards the batsman **bowlers**
BOWLESS ▸ **bow**
BOWLFUL = **bowl**
BOWLIKE ▸ **bow**
BOWLINE *n* line used to keep the sail taut against the wind
BOWLING *n*
BOWLS *n*
BOWMAN *n* archer **bowmen**
BOWNE = **boun**
BOWNED ▸ **bowne**
BOWNES ▸ **bowne**
BOWNING ▸ **bowne**
BOWPOT = **boughpot**
BOWPOTS ▸ **bowpot**
BOWR *n* muscle **bowrs**
BOWS ▸ **bow**
BOWSAW *n* saw with a thin blade in a bow-shaped frame **bowsaws**
BOWSE = **bouse**
BOWSED ▸ **bowse**
BOWSER *n* tanker containing fuel for aircraft, military vehicles, etc **bowsers**
BOWSES ▸ **bowse**
BOWSEY ▸ **bowsie**
BOWSEYS ▸ **bowsey**
BOWSHOT *n* distance an arrow travels from the bow
BOWSIE *n* low-class, mean or obstreperous person **bowsies**
BOWSING ▸ **bowse**
BOWWOW *n* imitation of the bark of a dog ▹ *vb* make a noise like a dog **bowwows**
BOWYANG *n* band worn round trouser leg below knee
BOWYER *n* person who makes or sells archery bows **bowyers**
BOX *n, vb*
BOXBALL *n* street ball game
BOXCAR *n* closed railway freight van **boxcars**

BOXED ▸ **box**
BOXEN ▸ **box**
BOXER *n* **boxers**
BOXES ▸ **box**
BOXFISH *another name for* > **trunkfish**
BOXFUL = **box**
BOXFULS ▸ **box**
BOXHAUL *vb* bring (a square-rigger) onto a new tack by backwinding the foresails and steering hard round
BOXIER ▸ **boxy**
BOXIEST ▸ **boxy**
BOXILY ▸ **boxy**
BOXING *n* **boxings**
BOXLIKE ▸ **box**
BOXPLOT *n* (in statistics) type of graph
BOXROOM *n* small room in which boxes, cases, etc may be stored
BOXTIES *n*
BOXTY *n* type of Irish potato pancake
BOXWOOD *n* hard yellow wood of the box tree, used to make tool handles, etc
BOXY *adj* squarish or chunky
BOY *n, vb*
BOYAR *n* member of an old order of Russian nobility **boyard**
BOYARDS ▸ **boyard**
BOYARS ▸ **boyar**
BOYAU *n* connecting trench **boyaux**
BOYCHIK *n* young boy
BOYCOTT *vb, n*
BOYED ▸ **boy**
BOYF *n* boyfriend **boyfs**
BOYG *n* troll-like mythical creature **boygs**
BOYHOOD *n* state or time of being a boy
BOYING ▸ **boy**
BOYISH *adj* of or like a boy in looks, behaviour, or character
BOYKIE *n* **boykies**
BOYLA *n* Australian Aboriginal word for magician **boylas**
BOYO *n* boy or young man: often used in direct address **boyos**
BOYS ▸ **boy**
BOYSIER ▸ **boysy**
BOYSY *adj* suited to or typical of boys or young men
BOZO *n* man, esp a stupid one **bozos**
BRA = **brassiere**
BRAAI *vb* grill or roast (meat) over open coals **braaied, braais**
BRAATA *n* small portion added to a purchase to encourage the customer to return **braatas**
BRABBLE *rare word for* > **squabble**
BRACCIA ▸ **braccio**
BRACCIO *n* former unit of measurement; length of man's arm
BRACE *n, vb* **braced**
BRACER *n* person or thing that braces
BRACERO *n* Mexican World War II labourer
BRACERS ▸ **bracer**
BRACES *pl n* pair of straps worn over the shoulders for holding up the trousers
BRACH *n* bitch hound
BRACHAH *n* blessing
BRACHES ▸ **brach**
BRACHET = **brach**
BRACHIA > **brachium**
BRACHOT ▸ **brachah**
BRACHS ▸ **brach**
BRACING *adj, n*
BRACK = **barmbrack**
BRACKEN *n*
BRACKET *n, vb*
BRACKS ▸ **brack**
BRACT *n* **bracted, bracts**
BRAD *n* small tapered nail with a small head
BRADAWL *n* small boring tool
BRADDED ▸ **brad**
BRADOON = **bridoon**
BRADS ▸ **brad**
BRAE *n* hill or slope **braes**
BRAG *vb, n* **bragged, bragger**
BRAGGY *adj* boastful
BRAGLY ▸ **brag**
BRAGS ▸ **brag**
BRAHMA *n* breed of domestic fowl
BRAHMAN *n* member of highest Hindu caste
BRAHMAS ▸ **brahma**
BRAHMIN = **brahman**
BRAID *vb, n, adj, adv*
BRAIDE *adj* given to deceit

BRAIDED *adj* (of a river or stream) flowing in several shallow interconnected channels
BRAIDER ▶ **braid**
BRAIDS ▶ **braid**
BRAIL *n* one of several lines fastened to a fore-and-aft sail to aid in furling it ▷ *vb* furl (a fore-and-aft sail) using brails **brailed**
BRAILLE *n* system of writing for the blind ▷ *vb* print or write using this method
BRAILS ▶ **brail**
BRAIN *n, vb* **brained, brains**
BRAINY *adj*
BRAIRD *vb* appear as shoots **brairds**
BRAISE *vb* **braised, braises, braize**
BRAIZES ▶ **braize**
BRAK *n* crossbred dog ▷ *adj* (of water) slightly salty
BRAKE = **bracken**
BRAKED ▶ **brake**
BRAKES ▶ **brake**
BRAKIER ▶ **braky**
BRAKING ▶ **brake**
BRAKS ▶ **brak**
BRAKY *adj* brambly
BRALESS ▶ **bra**
BRAMBLE *n* Scots word for blackberry **brambly**
BRAME *n* powerful feeling of emotion **brames**
BRAN *n*
BRANCH *n, vb* **branchy**
BRAND *n, vb*
BRANDED *adj* identifiable as being the product of a particular company
BRANDER ▶ **brand**
BRANDS ▶ **brand**
BRANDY *n, vb*
BRANE *n* hypothetical component of string theory **branes**
BRANGLE *vb* quarrel noisily
BRANK *vb* walk with swaggering gait **branked**
BRANKS *pl n* (formerly) iron bridle used to restrain scolding women
BRANKY *adj* ostentatious
BRANLE *n* old French country dance performed in a linked circle **branles**
BRANNED ▶ **bran**
BRANNER *n* person or machine that treats metal with bran
BRANNY *adj* having the appearance or texture of bran
BRANS ▶ **bran**
BRANSLE *another word for* ▶ **brantle**
BRANT *n* type of small goose
BRANTLE *n* French country dance
BRANTS ▶ **brant**
BRAS ▶ **bra**
BRASCO *n* lavatory **brascos**
BRASERO *n* metal grid for burning coals
BRASES ▶ **bra**
BRASH *adj, n, vb* **brashed, brasher, brashes, brashly**
BRASHY *adj* loosely fragmented
BRASIER = **brazier**
BRASIL = **brazil**
BRASILS ▶ **brasil**
BRASS *n, vb* **brassed, brasses**
BRASSET = **brassart**
BRASSIE *n* former name for a golf club **brassy**
BRAST = **burst**
BRASTS ▶ **brast**
BRAT *n* **brats**
BRATTLE *vb* make a rattling sound
BRATTY ▶ **brat**
BRAUNCH *old variant of* ▶ **branch**
BRAVA *n* professional assassin
BRAVADO *n, vb*
BRAVAS ▶ **brava**
BRAVE *adj, n, vb* **braved, bravely, braver, bravers, bravery, braves, bravest**
BRAVI ▶ **bravo**
BRAVING ▶ **brave**
BRAVO *interj, n, vb* **bravoed, bravoes, bravos**
BRAVURA *n* display of boldness or daring **bravure**
BRAW *adj* fine or excellent, esp in appearance or dress

▷ *pl n* best clothes **brawer, brawest**
BRAWL *n, vb* **brawled, brawler**
BRAWLIE *adj* in good health
BRAWLS ▶ **brawl**
BRAWLY ▶ **braw**
BRAWN *n* **brawned, brawns**
BRAWNY *adj* muscular and strong
BRAWS *n* fine apparel
BRAXIES ▶ **braxy**
BRAXY *n* acute and usually fatal bacterial disease of sheep
BRAY *vb, n* **brayed, brayer, brayers, braying, brays**
BRAZA *n* Spanish unit of measurement **brazas**
BRAZE *vb* join (two metal surfaces) with brass ▷ *n* high-melting solder or alloy used in brazing **brazed**
BRAZEN *adj, vb* **brazens**
BRAZER ▶ **braze**
BRAZERS ▶ **braze**
BRAZES ▶ **braze**
BRAZIER *n*
BRAZIL *n* red wood used for cabinetwork **brazils**
BRAZING ▶ **braze**
BREACH *n, vb*
BREAD *n, vb* **breaded, breads**
BREADTH *n*
BREADY *adj* having the appearance or texture of bread
BREAK ▶ **bracken**
BREAKER *n*
BREAKS ▶ **bracken**
BREAKUP *n* separation or disintegration
BREAM *n, vb* **breamed, breams**
BREARE = **brier**
BREARES ▶ **breare**
BREAST *n, vb* **breasts**
BREATH *n*
BREATHE *vb*
BREATHS ▶ **breath**
BREATHY *adj* (of the speaking voice) accompanied by an audible emission of breath
BRECCIA *n* type of rock
BRECHAM *n* straw horse-collar **brechan**
BRED *n*
BREDE *archaic spelling of* ▶ **braid**
BREDED ▶ **brede**
BREDES ▶ **brede**
BREDIE *n* meat and vegetable stew **bredies**
BREDING ▶ **brede**
BREDREN > **brethren**
BREDRIN > **brethren**
BREDS ▶ **bred**
BREE *n* broth, stock, or juice
BREECH *n* buttocks ▷ *vb* fit (a gun) with a breech
BREED *vb, n*
BREEDER *n* person who breeds plants or animals
BREEDS ▶ **breed**
BREEKS *pl n* trousers
BREEM = **breme**
BREENGE *vb* lunge forward ▷ *n* violent movement
BREER *another word for* ▶ **braird**
BREERED ▶ **breer**
BREERS ▶ **breer**
BREES ▶ **bree**
BREESE = **breeze**
BREESES ▶ **breese**
BREEST ▶ **breast**
BREESTS ▶ **breast**
BREEZE *n, vb* **breezed, breezes**
BREEZY *adj* windy
BREGMA *n* point on the top of the skull
BREHON *n* (formerly) judge in Ireland **brehons**
BREI *vb* speak with a uvular r, esp in Afrikaans
BREID *n* bread **breids**
BREIING ▶ **brei**
BREINGE = **breenge**
BREIS ▶ **brei**
BREIST *Scot word for* ▶ **breast**
BREISTS ▶ **breist**
BREKKY *slang word for* > **breakfast**
BREME *adj* well-known
BREN *n* type of machine gun
BRENNE *vb* burn **brennes**
BRENS ▶ **bren**
BRENT *n* type of goose ▷ *adj* steep **brenter, brents**
BRER *n* brother: usually prefixed to a name
BRERE = **brier**

BRERES ▶ **brere**
BRERS ▶ **brer**
BRETON *n* hat with an upturned brim and a rounded crown **bretons**
BREVE *n* accent placed over a vowel to indicate shortness **breves**
BREVET *n* document entitling a commissioned officer to hold temporarily a higher military rank ▷ *vb* promote by brevet
BREVETE *adj* patented
BREVETS ▶ **brevet**
BREVIER *n* (formerly) size of printer's type approximately equal to 8 point
BREVIS = **brewis**
BREVITY *n*
BREW *vb*, *n*
BREWAGE *n* product of brewing
BREWED ▶ **brew**
BREWER ▶ **brew**
BREWERS ▶ **brew**
BREWERY *n*
BREWING *n* quantity of a beverage brewed at one time
BREWIS *n* bread soaked in broth, gravy, etc
BREWPUB *n* pub that incorporates a brewery on its premises
BREWS ▶ **brew**
BREWSKI *n* beer
BREY = **brei**
BREYED ▶ **brey**
BREYING ▶ **brey**
BREYS ▶ **brey**
BRIAR *n*
BRIARD *n* medium-sized dog **briards**
BRIARED ▶ **briar**
BRIARS ▶ **briar**
BRIARY ▶ **briar**
BRIBE *vb*, *n* **bribed**
BRIBEE *n* one who is bribed **bribees**
BRIBER ▶ **bribe**
BRIBERS ▶ **bribe**
BRIBERY *n* process of giving or taking bribes
BRIBES ▶ **bribe**
BRIBING ▶ **bribe**
BRICHT *Scot word for* ▶ **bright**
BRICK *n*, *vb* **bricked**
BRICKEN *adj* made of brick
BRICKIE *n* bricklayer
BRICKLE *variant of* ▶ **brittle**
BRICKS ▶ **brick**
BRICKY = **brickie**
BRICOLE *n* billiards shot
BRIDAL *adj* of a bride or a wedding ▷ *n* wedding or wedding feast **bridals**
BRIDE *n* **brided, brides**
BRIDGE *n*, *vb* **bridged, bridges**
BRIDIE *n* semicircular pie containing meat and onions **bridies**
BRIDING ▶ **bride**
BRIDLE *n*, *vb* **bridled, bridler, bridles**
BRIDOON *n* horse's bit: small snaffle used in double bridles
BRIE = **bree**
BRIEF *adj*, *n*, *vb* **briefed, briefer, briefly**
BRIEFS *pl n* men's or women's underpants without legs
BRIER = **briar**
BRIERED ▶ **brier**
BRIERS ▶ **brier**
BRIERY ▶ **brier**
BRIES ▶ **brie**
BRIG *n* two-masted square-rigged ship
BRIGADE *n*, *vb*
BRIGAND *n*
BRIGHT *adj*, *adv*
BRIGHTS *pl n* high beam of the headlights of a motor vehicle
BRIGS ▶ **brig**
BRIGUE *vb* solicit **brigued, brigues**
BRIK *n* Tunisian pastry
BRIKI = **cezve**
BRIKIS ▶ **briki**
BRIKS ▶ **brik**
BRILL *n* type of European flatfish popular as a food fish **briller**
BRILLO *n* tradename for a type of scouring pad impregnated with a detergent **brillos**
BRILLS ▶ **brill**
BRIM *n*, *vb*
BRIMFUL *adj* completely filled with
BRIMING *n* phosphorescence of sea
BRIMMED ▶ **brim**
BRIMMER *n* vessel, such as a glass or bowl, filled to the brim
BRIMS ▶ **brim**
BRIN *n* thread of silk

from silkworm
BRINDED *adj* streaky or patchy
BRINDLE *n* brindled animal
BRINE *n, vb* **brined, briner, briners, brines**
BRING *vb* **bringer, brings**
BRINIER ▶ **briny**
BRINIES ▶ **briny**
BRINING ▶ **brine**
BRINISH ▶ **brine**
BRINJAL *n*
BRINK *n* **brinks**
BRINNY *n* stone, esp when thrown
BRINS ▶ **brin**
BRINY *adj* very salty
BRIO *n* liveliness
BRIOCHE *n* soft roll or loaf made from a very light yeast dough, sometimes mixed with currants
BRIONY = **bryony**
BRIOS ▶ **brio**
BRIQUET = **briquette**
BRIS *n* ritual circumcision of male babies
BRISANT > **brisance**
BRISE *n* type of jump
BRISES ▶ **bris**
BRISK *adj, vb* **brisked**
BRISKEN *vb* make or become more lively or brisk
BRISKER ▶ **brisk**
BRISKET *n* beef from the breast of a cow
BRISKLY ▶ **brisk**
BRISKS ▶ **brisk**
BRISKY *another word for* ▶ **brisk**
BRISS = **bris**
BRISSES ▶ **bris**
BRISTLE *n, vb* **bristly**
BRISTOL *n as in* **bristol board** type of heavy cardboard
BRISURE *n* mark of cadency in heraldry
BRIT *n* young of a herring, sprat, or similar fish
BRITH = **bris**
BRITHS ▶ **brith**
BRITS ▶ **brit**
BRITSKA = **britzka**
BRITT *n* young herring or sprat
BRITTLE *adj, n* **brittly**
BRITTS ▶ **britt**
BRITZKA *n* long horse-drawn carriage
BRIZE = **breeze**
BRIZES ▶ **brize**
BRO *n* family member
BROACH *vb, n*
BROAD *adj, n*
BROADAX = **broadaxe**
BROADEN *vb*
BROADER ▶ **broad**
BROADLY ▶ **broad**
BROADS ▶ **broad**
BROCADE *n, vb*
BROCAGE *another word for* > **brokerage**
BROCARD *n* basic principle of civil law
BROCH *n* (in Scotland) a circular dry-stone tower large enough to serve as a fortified home
BROCHAN *n* type of thin porridge
BROCHE *adj* woven with a raised design, as brocade **broched, broches**
BROCHO = **brachah**
BROCHOS ▶ **brocho**
BROCHS ▶ **broch**
BROCK *n* badger
BROCKED *adj* having different colours
BROCKET *n* small tropical American deer with small unbranched antlers
BROCKIT = **brocked**
BROCKS ▶ **brock**
BROCOLI = **broccoli**
BROD *vb* prod **brodded**
BRODDLE *vb* poke or pierce (something)
BRODKIN = **brodekin**
BRODS ▶ **brod**
BROG *n* bradawl
BROGAN *n* heavy laced, usually ankle-high, work boot **brogans**
BROGGED ▶ **brog**
BROGH = **broch**
BROGHS ▶ **brogh**
BROGS ▶ **brog**
BROGUE *n* **brogues**
BROIDER *archaic word for* > **embroider**
BROIL *vb* cook by direct heat under a grill ▷ *n* process of broiling **broiled**
BROILER *n* young tender chicken for roasting
BROILS ▶ **broil**
BROKAGE *another word for* > **brokerage**
BROKE *vb* **broked**
BROKEN ▶ **bracken**

BROKER *n, vb* **brokers**
BROKERY *n* work done by a broker
BROKES ▸ **broke**
BROKING ▸ **broke**
BROLGA *n* **brolgas**
BROLLY *n*
BROMAL *n* synthetic liquid formerly used medicinally **bromals**
BROMATE = **brominate**
BROME *n* type of grass **bromes**
BROMIC *adj* of or containing bromine in the trivalent or pentavalent state
BROMID = **bromide**
BROMIDE *n* chemical compound used in medicine and photography
BROMIDS ▸ **bromid**
BROMIN = **bromine**
BROMINE *n*
BROMINS ▸ **bromin**
BROMISE = **bromize**
BROMISM *n* bromine poisoning
BROMIZE *vb* treat with bromine
BROMMER *n* S African word for bluebottle
BROMO *n* something that contains bromide **bromos**
BRONC = **bronco**
BRONCHI > **bronchus**
BRONCHO = **bronco**
BRONCO *n* (in the US) wild or partially tamed pony **broncos**
BRONCS ▸ **bronc**
BROND *n* old form of brand **bronds**
BRONZE *n, adj, vb* **bronzed**
BRONZEN *adj* made of or the colour of bronze
BRONZER *n* cosmetic applied to the skin to simulate a sun tan
BRONZES ▸ **bronze**
BRONZY ▸ **bronze**
BROO *n* brow of hill
BROOCH *n, vb*
BROOD *n, vb* **brooded**
BROODER *n* structure used for rearing young chickens or other fowl
BROODS ▸ **brood**
BROODY *adj* moody and sullen
BROOK *n, vb* **brooked**
BROOKIE *n* brook trout
BROOKS ▸ **brook**
BROOL *n* low roar **brools**
BROOM *n, vb* **broomed, brooms**
BROOMY *adj* covered with growth of broom
BROOS ▸ **broo**
BROOSE *n* race at country wedding **brooses**
BROS ▸ **bro**
BROSE *n* oatmeal or pease porridge, sometimes with butter or fat added **broses**
BROSIER ▸ **brosy**
BROSY *adj* smeared with porridge
BROTH *n*
BROTHEL *n*
BROTHER *n, interj, vb*
BROTHS ▸ **broth**
BROTHY *adj* having appearance or texture of broth
BROUGH = **broch**
BROUGHS ▸ **brough**
BROUGHT ▸ **bring**
BROUZE = **broose**
BROUZES ▸ **brouze**
BROW *n*
BROWED *adj* having a brow
BROWN *n, adj, vb* **browned, browner**
BROWNIE *n*
BROWNS ▸ **brown**
BROWNY ▸ **brown**
BROWS ▸ **brow**
BROWSE *vb, n* **browsed**
BROWSER *n*
BROWSES ▸ **browse**
BROWST *n* brewing (of ale, tea) **browsts**
BROWSY ▸ **browse**
BRR = **brrr**

> This is useful if your consonant-heavy rack is giving you the shivers. And if you are even colder, **brrr** is available.

BRRR *interj* used to suggest shivering
BRU *South African word for* ▸ **friend**
BRUCHID *n* type of beetle
BRUCIN = **brucine**
BRUCINE *n* bitter poisonous alkaloid resembling strychnine
BRUCINS ▸ **brucin**
BRUCITE *n* white

translucent mineral
BRUCKLE *adj* brittle
BRUGH *n* large house **brughs**
BRUHAHA = **brouhaha**
BRUIN *n* name for a bear, used in children's tales, fables, etc **bruins**
BRUISE *n*, *vb* **bruised**
BRUISER *n* strong tough person
BRUISES ▸ **bruise**
BRUIT *vb* report ▹ *n* abnormal sound heard within the body **bruited, bruiter, bruits**
BRULE *n* a mixed-race person of Canadian Indian and White (usually French-Canadian) ancestry **brules**
BRULOT *n* coffee-based alcoholic drink, served flaming **brulots**
BRULYIE = **brulyie**
BRULZIE *n* noisy dispute
BRUMAL *adj* of, characteristic of, or relating to winter
BRUMBY *n*
BRUME *n* heavy mist or fog **brumes**
BRUMMER = **brommer** **brumous**
BRUNCH *n* breakfast and lunch combined ▹ *vb* eat brunch
BRUNET *adj* dark brown **brunets**
BRUNG ▸ **bring**
BRUNT *n*, *vb* **brunted, brunts**
BRUS ▸ **bru**
BRUSH *n*, *vb*
BRUSHED *adj* treated with a brushing process
BRUSHER ▸ **brush**
BRUSHES ▸ **brush**
BRUSHUP *n* the act or an instance of tidying one's appearance
BRUSHY *adj* like a brush
BRUSK = **brusque**
BRUSKER ▸ **brusk**
BRUSQUE *adj*
BRUSSEN *adj* bold
BRUST = **burst**
BRUSTS ▸ **brust**
BRUT *adj* (of champagne or sparkling wine) very dry ▹ *n* very dry champagne
BRUTAL *adj*
BRUTE *n*, *adj* **bruted, brutely**
BRUTER *n* diamond cutter **bruters**
BRUTES ▸ **brute**
BRUTIFY *less common word for* > **brutalize**
BRUTING *n* diamond cutting
BRUTISH *adj* of or like an animal
BRUTISM *n* stupidity; vulgarity
BRUTS ▸ **brut**
BRUX *vb* grind one's teeth **bruxed, bruxes, bruxing**
BRUXISM *n* habit of grinding the teeth, esp unconsciously
BRYONY *n* wild climbing hedge plant
BUAT = **bowat**
BUATS ▸ **buat**
BUAZE *n* fibrous African plant **buazes**
BUB *n* youngster
BUBA *another name for* ▸ **yaws**
BUBAL *n* any of various antelopes
BUBALE *n* large antelope **bubales**
BUBALIS = **bubal**
BUBALS ▸ **bubal**
BUBAS ▸ **buba**
BUBBA *n* ordinary American person **bubbas**
BUBBLE *n*, *vb* **bubbled**
BUBBLER *n* drinking fountain
BUBBLES ▸ **bubble**
BUBBLY *adj* excited and lively ▹ *n* champagne
BUBINGA *n* reddish-brown wood from African tree
BUBKES *n* very small amount
BUBKIS *n*
BUBO *n* inflammation and swelling of a lymph node, esp in the armpit or groin **buboed, buboes, bubonic**
BUBS ▸ **bub**
BUBU = **boubou**
BUBUKLE *n* red spot on skin
BUBUS ▸ **bubu**
BUCARDO *n* type of

Spanish mountain goat, recently extinct

BUCCAL *adj* of or relating to the cheek

BUCCINA *n* curved Roman horn

BUCHU *n* S African shrub whose leaves are used as an antiseptic and diuretic **buchus**

BUCK *n, vb* **bucked**

BUCKEEN *n* (in Ireland) poor young man who aspires to the habits and dress of the wealthy

BUCKER ▶ **buck**

BUCKERS ▶ **buck**

BUCKET *vb* **buckets**

BUCKEYE *n* N American tree with erect clusters of white or red flowers and prickly fruits

BUCKIE *n* whelk or its shell **buckies**

BUCKING ▶ **buck**

BUCKISH ▶ **buck**

BUCKLE *n, vb* **buckled**

BUCKLER *n* small round shield worn on the forearm ▷ *vb* defend

BUCKLES ▶ **buckle**

BUCKO *n* lively young fellow: often a term of address **buckoes, buckos**

BUCKRAM *n* cotton or linen cloth stiffened with size, etc ▷ *vb* stiffen with buckram

BUCKS ▶ **buck**

BUCKSAW *n* woodcutting saw

BUCKSOM = **buxom**

BUCKU = **buchu**

BUCKUS ▶ **bucku**

BUCOLIC *adj, n*

BUD *n* swelling on a plant that develops into a leaf or flower ▷ *vb* produce buds **budded, budder, budders**

BUDDHA *n* person who has achieved a state of perfect enlightenment **buddhas**

BUDDIED, buddier, buddies, buddiest ▶ **buddy**

BUDDLE *n* sloping trough in which ore is washed ▷ *vb* wash (ore) in a buddle **buddled, buddles**

BUDDY *n* friend ▷ *vb* act as a friend to ▷ *adj* friendly

BUDGE *vb, n* **budged, budger**

BUDGERO = **budgerow**

BUDGERS ▶ **budge**

BUDGES ▶ **budge**

BUDGET *n, vb, adj* **budgets**

BUDGIE *n* short form of budgerigar **budgies**

BUDGING ▶ **budge**

BUDLESS ▶ **bud**

BUDLIKE ▶ **bud**

BUDMASH ▶ **badmash**

BUDO *n* combat and spirit in martial arts **budos**

BUDS ▶ **bud**

BUDWORM *n* pest that eats tree leaves and buds

BUFF *n, adj, vb*

BUFFA ▶ **buffo**

BUFFALO *n, vb*

BUFFE ▶ **buffo**

BUFFED ▶ **buff**

BUFFEL *adj as in* **buffel grass** grass used for pasture in Africa, India, and Australia

BUFFER = **buff**

BUFFERS ▶ **buffer**

BUFFEST ▶ **buff**

BUFFET *n, vb* **buffets**

BUFFI ▶ **buffo**

BUFFIER ▶ **buffy**

BUFFING ▶ **buff**

BUFFO *n* (in Italian opera of the 18th century) comic part, esp one for a bass

BUFFOON *n*

BUFFOS ▶ **buffo**

BUFFS ▶ **buff**

BUFFY *adj* having appearance or texture of buff

BUFO *n* type of toad **bufos**

BUG *n, vb*

BUGABOO *n* imaginary source of fear

BUGBANE *n* European plant whose flowers are reputed to repel insects

BUGBEAR *n* thing that causes obsessive anxiety

BUGEYE *n* oyster-dredging boat **bugeyes**

BUGGAN *n* evil spirit

buggane, buggans
BUGGED ▸ **bug**
BUGGERY *n* anal intercourse
BUGGIER ▸ **buggy**
BUGGIES ▸ **buggy**
BUGGIN = **buggan**
BUGGING ▸ **bug**
BUGGINS ▸ **buggin**
BUGGY *n* light horse-drawn carriage ▹ *adj* infested with bugs
BUGLE *n, vb* **bugled, bugler, buglers, bugles**
BUGLET *n* small bugle **buglets**
BUGLING ▸ **bugle**
BUGLOSS *n* hairy Eurasian plant with clusters of blue flowers
BUGONG = **bogong**
BUGONGS ▸ **bugong**
BUGOUT *n* act of running away **bugouts**
BUGS ▸ **bug**
BUGSEED *n* form of tumbleweed
BUGSHA = **buqsha**
BUGSHAS ▸ **bugsha**
BUGWORT *another name for* ▸ **bugbane**
BUHL = **boulle**
BUHLS ▸ **buhl**
BUHR ▸ **burr**
BUHRS ▸ **burr**
BUHUND *n* type of Norwegian dog **buhunds**
BUIBUI *n* black cloth worn as a shawl by Muslim women **buibuis**
BUIK = **book**
BUIKS ▸ **buik**
BUILD *vb, n* **builded**
BUILDER *n* person who constructs houses and other buildings
BUILDS ▸ **build**
BUILDUP *n* gradual approach to a climax or critical point
BUILT ▸ **build**
BUIRDLY *adj* well-built
BUIST *vb* brand sheep with identification mark **buisted, buists**
BUKE = **book**
BUKES ▸ **buke**
BUKSHEE *n* person in charge of paying wages **bukshi**
BUKSHIS ▸ **bukshi**
BULB *n, vb*
BULBAR *adj* of or relating to a bulb, esp the medulla oblongata
BULBED ▸ **bulb**
BULBEL = **bulbil**
BULBELS ▸ **bulbel**
BULBIL *n* small bulblike organ growing on plants such as the onion and tiger lily **bulbils**
BULBING ▸ **bulb**
BULBLET *n* small bulb at base of main bulb
BULBOUS *adj*
BULBS ▸ **bulb**
BULBUL *n* songbird of tropical Africa and Asia **bulbuls**
BULGE *n, vb* **bulged, bulger, bulgers, bulges**
BULGHUR = **bulgur**
BULGIER ▸ **bulge**
BULGINE = **bullgine**
BULGING ▸ **bulge**
BULGUR *n* kind of dried cracked wheat **bulgurs**
BULGY ▸ **bulge**
BULIMIA *n* eating disorder **bulimic, bulimus, bulimy**
BULK *n, vb* **bulkage, bulked**
BULKER *n* ship that carries unpackaged cargo **bulkers**
BULKIER ▸ **bulky**
BULKILY ▸ **bulky**
BULKING *n* expansion of excavated material to a volume greater than that of the excavation from which it came
BULKS ▸ **bulk**
BULKY *adj*
BULL *adj*
BULLA *n* leaden seal affixed to a papal bull
BULLACE *n* small Eurasian tree of which the damson is the cultivated form
BULLAE ▸ **bulla**
BULLARY *n* boilery for preparing salt
BULLATE *adj* puckered or blistered in appearance
BULLBAT *another name for* > **nighthawk**
BULLDOG *n*
BULLED ▸ **bull**
BULLER *vb* make

bubbling sound **bullers**
BULLET *n, vb* **bullets**
BULLIED ▸ **bully**
BULLIER ▸ **bully**
BULLIES ▸ **bully**
BULLING ▸ **bull**
BULLION *n*
BULLISH *adj* like a bull
BULLOCK *n, vb*
BULLOSA *adj as in* **epidermolysis bullosa** type of genetic skin disorder
BULLOUS *adj* blistered
BULLPEN *n* large cell where prisoners are confined together temporarily
BULLS ▸ **bull**
BULLY *n, vb, adj*
BULRUSH *n*
BULSE *n* purse or bag for diamonds **bulses**
BULWARK *n, vb*
BUM *n* buttocks or anus ▹ *vb* get by begging ▹ *adj* of poor quality
BUMALO = **bummalo**
BUMBAG *n* small bag attached to a belt and worn round the waist **bumbags**
BUMBAZE *vb* confuse; bewilder
BUMBLE *vb* speak, do, or move in a clumsy way ▹ *n* blunder or botch **bumbled, bumbler, bumbles**
BUMBO *n* drink with gin or rum, nutmeg, lemon juice, etc
BUMBOAT *n* any small boat used for ferrying goods to a ship at anchor or at a mooring
BUMBOS ▸ **bumbo**
BUMELIA *n* thorny shrub
BUMF *n* official documents or forms **bumfs**
BUMKIN = **bumpkin**
BUMKINS ▸ **bumkin**
BUMMALO *n* Bombay duck
BUMMED ▸ **bum**
BUMMEL *n* stroll
BUMMELS ▸ **stroll**
BUMMER *n* unpleasant or disappointing experience **bummers**
BUMMEST ▸ **bum**
BUMMING ▸ **bum**
BUMMLE *Scots variant of* ▸ **bumble**
BUMMLED ▸ **bummle**
BUMMLES ▸ **bummle**
BUMMOCK *n* submerged mass of ice projecting downwards
BUMP *vb, n* **bumped**
BUMPER *n, adj, vb* **bumpers**
BUMPH = **bumf**
BUMPHS ▸ **bumph**
BUMPIER ▸ **bumpy**
BUMPILY ▸ **bumpy**
BUMPING ▸ **bump**
BUMPKIN *n*
BUMPS ▸ **bump**
BUMPY *adj* having an uneven surface
BUMS ▸ **bum**
BUMSTER *adj* (of trousers) cut low so as to reveal the top part of the buttocks
BUN *n*
BUNA *n* synthetic rubber **bunas**
BUNCE *n* windfall; boom ▹ *vb* charge someone too much money **bunced, bunces**
BUNCH *n, vb* **bunched**
BUNCHES *pl n* hair tied into two sections
BUNCHY *adj* composed of or resembling bunches
BUNCING ▸ **bunce**
BUNCO *n* swindle, esp one by confidence tricksters ▹ *vb* swindle **buncoed, buncos**
BUND *n* embankment or German federation ▹ *vb* form into an embankment **bunde, bunded**
BUNDH = **bandh**
BUNDHS ▸ **bundh**
BUNDIED ▸ **bundy**
BUNDIES ▸ **bundy**
bunding, bundist
BUNDLE *n, vb* **bundled, bundler, bundles**
BUNDOOK *n* rifle
BUNDS ▸ **bund**
BUNDT *n* type of sweet cake **bundts**
BUNDU *n* largely uninhabited wild region far from towns **bundus**
BUNDY *n* time clock at work ▹ *vb* register arrival or departure from work on a time clock
BUNG *n, vb* **bunged**
BUNGEE *n* strong elastic

cable **bungees**
BUNGER *n* firework **bungers**
BUNGEY = **bungee**
BUNGEYS ▸ **bungey**
BUNGIE = **bungee**
BUNGIES ▸ **bungy**
BUNGING ▸ **bung**
BUNGLE *vb*, *n* **bungled, bungler, bungles**
BUNGS ▸ **bung**
BUNGY ▸ **bungee**
BUNIA = **bunnia**
BUNIAS ▸ **bunia**
BUNION *n* **bunions**
BUNJE = **bungee**
BUNJEE = **bungee**
BUNJEES ▸ **bunjee**
BUNJES ▸ **bunje**
BUNJIE = **bungee**
BUNJIES ▸ **bunjie**
BUNJY = **bungee**
BUNK *n*, *vb* **bunked**
BUNKER *n*, *vb* **bunkers**
BUNKING ▸ **bunk**
BUNKO = **bunco**
BUNKOED ▸ **bunko**
BUNKOS ▸ **bunko**
BUNKS ▸ **bunk**
BUNKUM *n* nonsense **bunkums**
BUNN = **bun**
BUNNET = **bonnet**
BUNNETS ▸ **bunnet**
BUNNIA *n* Hindu shopkeeper **bunnias**
BUNNIES ▸ **bunny**
BUNNS ▸ **bunn**
BUNNY *n* child's word for a rabbit
BUNRAKU *n* Japanese puppet theatre
BUNS *pl n* buttocks
BUNSEN *n as in* **bunsen burner** gas burner used in scientific labs **bunsens**
BUNT *vb* (of an animal) butt (something) with the head or horns ▷ *n* act or an instance of bunting
BUNTAL *n* straw obtained from leaves of the talipot palm **buntals**
BUNTED ▸ **bunt**
BUNTER *n* batter who deliberately taps ball lightly **bunters**
BUNTIER ▸ **bunt**
BUNTING *n*
BUNTS ▸ **bunt**
BUNTY ▸ **bunt**
BUNYA *n* tall dome-shaped Australian coniferous tree **bunyas**
BUNYIP *n* **bunyips**
BUOY *n*, *vb*
BUOYAGE *n* system of buoys
BUOYANT *adj*
BUOYED ▸ **buoy**
BUOYING ▸ **buoy**
BUOYS ▸ **buoy**
BUPKES = **bubkes**
BUPKIS ▸ **bubkis**
BUPKUS = **bubkes**
BUPPIE *n* affluent young Black person
BUPPIES ▸ **buppy**
BUPPY ▸ **buppie**
BUQSHA *n* former Yemeni coin **buqshas**
BUR ▸ **burr**
BURA = **buran**
BURAN *n* blizzard, with the wind blowing from the north and reaching gale force **burans**
BURAS ▸ **bura**
BURB *n* suburb
BURBLE *vb*, *n* **burbled, burbler, burbles**
BURBLY *adj* burbling
BURBOT *n* freshwater fish of the cod family that has barbels around its mouth **burbots**
BURBS ▸ **burb**
BURD *Scots form of* ▸ **bird**
BURDASH *n* fringed sash worn over coat
BURDEN *n*, *vb* **burdens**
BURDIE *Scots form of* ▸ **birdie**
BURDIES ▸ **burdie**
BURDOCK *n* weed with prickly burrs
BURDS ▸ **burd**
BUREAU *n* **bureaus, bureaux**
BURET = **burette**
BURETS ▸ **buret**
BURETTE *n* glass tube for dispensing known volumes of fluids
BURG *n* fortified town
BURGAGE *n* (in England) tenure of land or tenement in a town or city, which originally involved a fixed money rent
BURGEE *n* triangular or swallow-tailed flag flown from the mast of a merchant ship **burgees**

BURGEON *vb, n*
BURGER *n* hamburger **burgers**
BURGESS *n* (in England) citizen or freeman of a borough
BURGH *n* Scottish borough **burghal**
BURGHER *n* citizen
BURGHS ▸ **burgh**
BURGHUL = **bulgur**
BURGLAR *n, vb*
BURGLE *vb* **burgled, burgles**
BURGOO *n* porridge **burgoos, burgout**
BURGS ▸ **burg**
BURHEL = **bharal**
BURHELS ▸ **burhel**
BURIAL *n* **burials**
BURIED ▸ **bury**
BURIER *n* person or thing that buries **buriers**
BURIES ▸ **bury**
BURIN *n* steel chisel used for engraving metal, wood, or marble **burins**
BURITI *n* type of palm tree **buritis**
BURK = **berk**
BURKA = **burqa**
BURKAS ▸ **burka**
BURKE *vb* murder in such a way as to leave no marks on the body, usually by suffocation **burked, burker, burkers, burkes**
BURKHA *n* all-enveloping garment worn by Muslim women **burkhas**
BURKING ▸ **burke**
BURKITE ▸ **burke**
BURKS ▸ **burk**
BURL *n* small knot or lump in wool ▹ *vb* remove the burls from (cloth)
BURLAP *n* coarse fabric woven from jute, hemp, or the like **burlaps**
BURLED ▸ **burl**
BURLER ▸ **burl**
BURLERS ▸ **burl**
BURLESK = **burlesque**
BURLEY = **berley**
BURLEYS ▸ **burley**
BURLIER ▸ **burly**
BURLILY ▸ **burly**
BURLING ▸ **burl**
BURLS ▸ **burl**
BURLY *adj*
BURN *vb, n* **burned**
BURNER *n* part of a stove or lamp that produces the flame **burners**
BURNET *n* type of rose **burnets**
BURNIE *n* sideburn **burnies**
BURNING ▸ **burn**
BURNISH *vb, n*
BURNOUS *n* long circular cloak with a hood, worn esp by Arabs
BURNOUT *n* failure of a mechanical device from excessive heating
BURNS ▸ **burn**
BURNT ▸ **burn**
BUROO *n* government office from which unemployment benefit is distributed **buroos**
BURP *n, vb* **burped**
BURPEE *n* type of physical exercise movement **burpees**
BURPING ▸ **burp**
BURPS ▸ **burp**
BURQA *n* garment worn by Muslim women in public **burqas**

> This Arab garment illustrates the fact that Q doesn't always have to be followed by U. It has several variants including **burka** and **burkha**.

BURR *n* small rotary file ▹ *vb* form a rough edge on (a workpiece) **burred**
BURREL = **bharal**
BURRELL *variant of* ▸ **bharal**
BURRELS ▸ **burrel**
BURRER *n* person who removes burrs **burrers**
BURRHEL = **burrel**
BURRIER ▸ **burry**
BURRING ▸ **burr**
BURRITO *n* tortilla folded over a filling of minced beef, chicken, cheese, or beans
BURRO *n* donkey, esp one used as a pack animal **burros**
BURROW *n, vb* **burrows**
BURRS ▸ **burr**
BURRY *adj* full of or covered in burs

BURS ▶ **burr**
BURSA *n* small fluid-filled sac that reduces friction between movable parts of the body **bursae, bursal**
BURSAR *n* **bursars**
BURSARY *n*
BURSAS ▶ **bursa**
BURSATE ▶ **bursa**
BURSE *n* flat case used at Mass as a container for the corporal
BURSEED *n* type of plant
BURSERA *adj* of a type of gum tree
BURSES ▶ **burse**
BURST *vb, n, adj* **bursted, bursten, burster, bursts**
BURTHEN *archaic word for* ▶ **burden**
BURTON *n* type of hoisting tackle **burtons**
BURWEED *n* any of various plants that bear burs, such as the burdock
BURY *vb* **burying**
BUS *n, vb*
BUSBAR *n* electrical conductor **busbars**
BUSBIES ▶ **busby**
BUSBOY *n* waiter's assistant **busboys**
BUSBY *n* tall fur hat worn by some soldiers
BUSED ▶ **bus**
BUSERA *n* Ugandan alcoholic drink made from millet: sometimes mixed with honey **buseras**
BUSES ▶ **bus**
BUSGIRL *n* waiter's assistant
BUSH *n, vb*
BUSHED *adj* extremely tired
BUSHEL *n* obsolete unit of measure equal to 8 gallons ▷ *vb* alter or mend (a garment) **bushels**
BUSHER ▶ **bush**
BUSHERS ▶ **bush**
BUSHES ▶ **bush**
BUSHFLY *n* small black Australian fly that breeds in faeces and dung
BUSHIDO *n* feudal code of the Japanese samurai
BUSHIE = **bushy**
BUSHIER ▶ **bushy**
BUSHIES ▶ **bushy**
BUSHILY ▶ **bushy**
BUSHING = **bush**
BUSHMAN *n* **bushmen**
BUSHPIG *n* wild brown or black forest pig of tropical Africa and Madagascar
BUSHTIT *n* small grey active North American songbird
BUSHWA *n* nonsense **bushwah, bushwas**
BUSHY *adj, n*
BUSIED, busier, busies, busiest ▶ **busy**
BUSILY *adv* in a busy manner
BUSING ▶ **bus**
BUSINGS ▶ **bus**
BUSK *vb* act as a busker ▷ *n* strip of whalebone, wood, steel, etc, inserted into the front of a corset **busked, busker, buskers**
BUSKET *n* bouquet **buskets**
BUSKIN *n* (formerly) sandal-like covering
BUSKING ▶ **busk**
BUSKINS ▶ **buskin**
BUSKS ▶ **busk**
BUSKY = **bosky**
BUSLOAD *n* number of people bus carries
BUSMAN *n* person who drives a bus **busmen**
BUSS *archaic or dialect word for* ▶ **kiss**
BUSSED ▶ **bus**
BUSSES ▶ **bus**
BUSSING ▶ **bus**
BUSSU *n* type of palm tree **bussus**
BUST *n, adj, vb*
BUSTARD *n* type of bird
BUSTED ▶ **bust**
BUSTEE = **basti**
BUSTEES ▶ **bustee**
BUSTER *n* person or thing destroying something as specified **busters**
BUSTI = **basti**
BUSTIC *n* type of small American tree **bustics**
BUSTIER *n* close-fitting strapless women's top
BUSTING ▶ **bust**
BUSTIS ▶ **busti**
BUSTLE *vb, n* **bustled, bustler, bustles**

BUSTS ▸ **bust**
BUSTY *adj* (of a woman) having a prominent bust
BUSUUTI *n* garment worn by Ugandan women
BUSY *adj, vb* **busying**
BUT *prep, adv, n*
BUTANE *n* gas used for fuel **butanes**
BUTANOL *n* colourless substance
BUTCH *adj* markedly or aggressively masculine ▹ *n* lesbian who is noticeably masculine
BUTCHER *n, vb*
BUTCHES ▸ **butch**
BUTE *n* drug used illegally to dope horses
BUTENE *n* pungent colourless gas **butenes**
BUTEO *n* type of American hawk **buteos**
BUTES ▸ **bute**
BUTLE *vb* act as butler **butled**
BUTLER *n, vb* **butlers**
BUTLERY *n* butler's room
BUTLES ▸ **butle**
BUTLING ▸ **butle**
BUTMENT = **abutment**
BUTS ▸ **but**
BUTT *n, vb*
BUTTALS *n* abuttal
BUTTE *n* isolated steep flat-topped hill
BUTTED ▸ **butt**
BUTTER *n, vb* **butters**
BUTTERY *n* (in some universities) room in which food and drink are sold to students ▹ *adj* containing, like, or coated with butter
BUTTES ▸ **butte**
BUTTIES ▸ **butty**
BUTTING ▸ **butt**
BUTTLE *vb* act as butler **buttled, buttles**
BUTTOCK *n* either of the two fleshy masses that form the human rump ▹ *vb* perform a kind of wrestling manoeuvre on a person
BUTTON *n, vb*
BUTTONS *n* page boy
BUTTONY ▸ **button**
BUTTS ▸ **butt**
BUTTY *n* sandwich
BUTUT *n* Gambian monetary unit worth one hundredth of a dalasi **bututs**
BUTYL *adj* of or containing any of four isomeric forms of the group C_4H_9- ▹ *n* of, consisting of, or containing any of four isomeric forms of the group C_4H_9- **butyls**
BUTYRAL *n* type of resin
BUTYRIC *adj as in* **butyric acid** type of acid
BUTYRIN *n* colourless liquid found in butter
BUTYRYL *n* radical of butyric acid
BUVETTE *n* roadside café
BUXOM *adj* **buxomer, buxomly**
BUY *vb, n* **buyable**
BUYBACK *n* repurchase by a company of some or all of its shares from an early investor
BUYER *n* customer **buyers**
BUYING *n as in* **panic buying**
BUYINGS ▸ **buying**
BUYOFF *n* purchase **buyoffs**
BUYOUT *n* purchase of a company **buyouts**
BUYS ▸ **buy**
BUZUKI = **bouzouki**
BUZUKIA ▸ **buzuki**
BUZUKIS ▸ **buzuki**
BUZZ *n, vb*
BUZZARD *n*
BUZZCUT *n* very short haircut
BUZZED ▸ **buzz**
BUZZER *n* **buzzers**
BUZZES ▸ **buzz**
BUZZIER ▸ **buzzy**
BUZZING ▸ **buzz**
BUZZWIG *n* bushy wig
BUZZY *adj* making a buzzing sound
BWANA *n* (in E Africa) master, often used as a respectful form of address **bwanas**
BWAZI = **buaze**
BWAZIS ▸ **bwazi**
BY *prep, adv, n*
BYCATCH *n* unwanted fish and sea animals caught along with the desired kind

BYCOKET *n* former Italian high-crowned hat
BYDE = **bide**
BYDED ▸ **byde**
BYDES ▸ **byde**
BYDING ▸ **byde**
BYE *n* situation where a player or team wins a round by having no opponent ▹ *interj* goodbye ▹ *sentence substitute* goodbye
BYELAW *n* rule made by a local authority **byelaws**
BYES ▸ **bye**
BYGONE *adj* **bygones**
BYKE ▸ **bicycle; byked, bykes, byking**
BYLANE *n* side lane or alley off a road **bylanes**
BYLAW *n* rule made by a local authority **bylaws**
BYLINE *n* line under the title of a newspaper or magazine article giving the author's name ▹ *vb* give a byline to **bylined, byliner, bylines**
BYLIVE = **belive**
BYNAME *n* nickname **bynames**
BYNEMPT ▸ **bename**
BYPASS *n*, *vb* **bypast**
BYPATH *n* little-used path or track, esp in the country **bypaths**
BYPLACE *n* private place
BYPLAY *n* secondary action or talking carried on apart while the main action proceeds **byplays**
BYRE *n* shelter for cows
BYREMAN *n* man who works in byre **byremen**
BYRES ▸ **byre**
BYRL = **birl**
BYRLADY *interj* short for By Our Lady
BYRLAW = **bylaw**
BYRLAWS ▸ **byrlaw**
BYRLED ▸ **byrl**
BYRLING ▸ **byrl**
BYRLS ▸ **byrl**
BYRNIE *n* archaic word for coat of mail **byrnies**
BYROAD *n* secondary or side road **byroads**
BYROOM *n* private room **byrooms**
BYS ▸ **by**
BYSSAL *adj* of mollusc's byssus
BYSSI ▸ **byssus**
BYSSINE *adj* made from flax
BYSSOID *adj* consisting of fine fibres
BYSSUS *n* mass of threads that attaches an animal to a hard surface
BYTALK *n* trivial conversation **bytalks**
BYTE *n* **bytes**
BYWAY *n* minor road **byways**
BYWONER *n* poor tenant-farmer
BYWORD *n* **bywords**
BYWORK *n* work done outside usual working hours **byworks**
BYZANT = **bezant**
BYZANTS ▸ **byzant**

Cc

C can be a tricky letter to use, especially as it only forms a single two-letter word **ch**. But if you remember this, you won't waste time racking your brains for two-letter words. There are, however, plenty of good three-letter words beginning with **C**. **Cox** scores 12 points, while **caw**, **cow**, and **coy** are each worth 8 and **caz**, **coz**, and **cuz** are worth 14. It's also a good idea to remember the short words starting with **C** that don't contain any vowels: **cly** and **cwm** as well as **ch**.

CAA *a Scot word for* ▶ **call**
CAAED ▶ **caa**
CAAING ▶ **caa**
CAAS ▶ **caa**
CAB *n, vb*
CABA = **cabas**
CABAL *n, vb*
CABALA *a variant spelling of* > **kabbalah**
CABALAS ▶ **cabala**
CABALS ▶ **cabal**
CABANA *n* tent used as a dressing room by the sea **cabanas**
CABARET *n*
CABAS *n* reticule
CABBAGE *n, vb* **cabbagy**
CABBALA *a variant spelling of* > **kabbalah**
CABBED ▶ **cab**
CABBIE *n* taxi driver **cabbies**
CABBING ▶ **cab cabby**
CABER *n* tree trunk tossed in competition at Highland games **cabers**
CABEZON *n* large fish
CABILDO *n* Spanish municipal council
CABIN *n, vb* **cabined**
CABINET *n*
CABINS ▶ **cabin**
CABLE *n, vb* **cabled**
CABLER *n* cable broadcasting company **cablers**
CABLES ▶ **cable**
CABLET *n* small cable **cablets**
CABLING ▶ **cable**
CABMAN *n* driver of a cab **cabmen**
CABOB *vb* roast on a skewer **cabobs**
CABOC *n* type of Scottish cheese **cabocs**
CABOMBA *n* type of aquatic plant
CABOOSE *n* guard's van on a train
CABOVER *adj* of a truck or lorry in which the cab is over the engine
CABRE *adj* heraldic term designating an animal rearing
CABRIE *n* pronghorn antelope **cabries**
CABRIO *short for* > **cabriolet**
CABRIOS ▶ **cabrio**
CABRIT *n* pronghorn antelope **cabrits**
CABS ▶ **cab**
CACA *n* heroin
CACAO = **cocoa**
CACAOS ▶ **cocoa**
CACAS ▶ **caca**
CACHACA *n* white Brazilian rum made from sugar cane
CACHE *n, vb* **cached, caches**

CACHET *n, vb* **cachets**
CACHEXY = **cachexia**
CACHING ▸ **cache**
CACHOU = **catechu**
CACHOUS ▸ **catechu**
CACIQUE *n* American Indian chief in a Spanish-speaking region
CACKIER ▸ **cacky**
CACKLE *vb, n* **cackled, cackler, cackles**
CACKY *adj* of or like excrement
CACODYL *n* oily poisonous liquid with a strong garlic smell
CACOEPY *n* bad or mistaken pronunciation
CACOLET *n* seat fitted to the back of a mule
CACONYM *n* erroneous name
CACOON *n* large seed of the sword-bean **cacoons**
CACTI ▸ **cactus**
CACTOID *adj* resembling a cactus
CACTUS *n*
CACUMEN *n* apex
CAD *n*
CADAGA *n* eucalyptus tree **cadagas, cadagi**
CADAGIS ▸ **cadagi**
CADAVER *n* corpse
CADDICE = **caddis**
CADDIE *n, vb* **caddied, caddies**
CADDIS *n* type of coarse woollen yarn, braid, or fabric
CADDISH ▸ **cad**
CADDY = **caddie**
CADDYSS = **caddis**
CADE *n* juniper tree ▹ *adj* (of a young animal) left by its mother and reared by humans
CADEAU *n* present **cadeaux**
CADEE *old form of* ▸ **cadet**
CADEES ▸ **cadee**
CADELLE *n* type of beetle that feeds on flour, grain, and other stored foods
CADENCE *n, vb* **cadency**
CADENT *adj* having cadence
CADENZA *n*
CADES ▸ **cade**
CADET *n* **cadets**
CADGE *vb* **cadged**
CADGER *n* person who cadges **cadgers**
CADGES ▸ **cadge**
CADGIER ▸ **cadgy**
CADGING ▸ **cadge**
CADGY *adj* cheerful
CADI *n* judge in a Muslim community
CADIE *n* messenger **cadies**
CADIS ▸ **cadi**
CADMIC ▸ **cadmium**
CADMIUM *n*
CADRANS *n* instrument used in gemcutting
CADRE *n* group of people trained to form the core of a political or military unit **cadres**
CADS ▸ **cad**
CADUAC *n* windfall **caduacs**
CADUCEI > **caduceus**
CAECA ▸ **caecum**
CAECAL ▸ **caecum**
CAECUM *n* pouch at the beginning of the large intestine
CAEOMA *n* aecium in some rust fungi that has no surrounding membrane **caeomas**
CAERULE = **cerule**
CAESAR *n* any emperor, autocrat, dictator, or other powerful ruler **caesars**
CAESE *interj* Shakespearean interjection
CAESIUM *n*
CAESTUS = **cestus**
CAESURA *n*
CAFARD *n* feeling of severe depression **cafards**
CAFE *n* small or inexpensive restaurant serving light refreshments **cafes**
CAFF *n* café
CAFFEIN = **caffeine**
CAFFILA *n* caravan train
CAFFS ▸ **caff**
CAFILA = **caffila**
CAFILAS ▸ **cafila**
CAFTAN = **kaftan**
CAFTANS ▸ **caftan**
CAG = **cagoule**
CAGANER *n* figure of a squatting defecating person
CAGE *n, vb* **caged**
CAGEFUL *n* amount which fills a cage to capacity

CAGER *n* basketball player **cagers**
CAGES ▶ **cage**
CAGEY *adj* **cagier, cagiest, cagily**
CAGING ▶ **cage**
CAGMAG *adj* done shoddily ▷ *vb* chat idly **cagmags**
CAGOT *n* member of a class of French outcasts **cagots**
CAGOUL = **cagoule**
CAGOULE *n*
CAGOULS ▶ **cagoul**
CAGS ▶ **cag**
CAGY = **cagey**
CAHIER *n* notebook **cahiers**
CAHOOT *n* partnership **cahoots**
CAHOW *n* Bermuda petrel **cahows**
CAID *n* Moroccan district administrator **caids**
CAILLE *n* quail **cailles**
CAIMAC = **caimacam**
CAIMACS ▶ **caimac**
CAIMAN = **cayman**
CAIMANS ▶ **caiman**
CAIN *n* (in Scotland and Ireland) payment in kind **cains**
CAIQUE *n* long narrow light rowing skiff used on the Bosporus **caiques**
CAIRD *n* travelling tinker **cairds**
CAIRN *n*
CAIRNED *adj* marked by a cairn
CAIRNS ▶ **cairn**
CAIRNY *adj* covered with cairns
CAISSON > **cofferdam**
CAITIFF *n* cowardly or base person ▷ *adj* cowardly
CAITIVE *n* captive
CAJAPUT = **cajuput**
CAJEPUT = **cajuput**
CAJOLE *vb* **cajoled, cajoler, cajoles**
CAJON *n* Peruvian wooden box used as a drum **cajones**
CAJUN *n* music of the Cajun people
CAJUPUT *n* small tree or shrub
CAKE *n*, *vb* **caked, cakes, cakey, cakier, cakiest, caking, cakings, caky**
CALALOO = **calalu**
CALALU *n* edible leaves of various plants **calalus**
CALAMAR *n* any member of the squid family
CALAMI ▶ **calamus**
CALAMUS *n* tropical Asian palm
CALANDO *adv* (to be performed) with gradually decreasing tone and speed
CALASH *n* horse-drawn carriage with low wheels and a folding top
CALATHI > **calathus**
CALCAR *n* spur or spurlike process **calcars**
CALCED *adj* wearing shoes
CALCES ▶ **calx**
CALCIC *adj* of, containing, or concerned with lime or calcium
CALCIFY *vb* harden by the depositing of calcium salts
CALCINE *vb* oxidize (a substance) by heating
CALCITE *n* colourless or white form of calcium carbonate
CALCIUM *n*
CALCULI > **calculus**
CALDERA *n* large basin-shaped crater at the top of a volcano
CALDRON = **cauldron**
CALECHE *a variant of* ▶ **calash**
CALEFY *vb* make warm
CALENDS *pl n* first day of each month in the ancient Roman calendar
CALESA *n* horse-drawn buggy **calesas**
CALF *n* **calfs**
CALIBER = **calibre**
CALIBRE *n*
CALICES ▶ **calix**
CALICHE *n* bed of sand or clay in arid regions
CALICLE = **calycle**
CALICO *n* **calicos**
CALID *adj* warm
CALIF = **caliph**
CALIFS ▶ **calif**
CALIGO *n* speck on the cornea causing poor vision **caligos**

CALIMA *n* Saharan dust-storm **calimas**
CALIPEE *n* edible part of the turtle found next to the lower shell
CALIPER = **calliper**
CALIPH *n* Muslim ruler **caliphs**
CALIVER *n* type of musket
CALIX *n* cup
CALK = **caulk**
CALKED, calker, calkers, calkin, calking, calkins, calks ▸ **calk**
CALL *vb* name ▹ *n* cry, shout
CALLA *n* S African plant with a white funnel-shaped spathe enclosing a yellow spadix
CALLAIS *n* type of green stone
CALLAN = **callant**
CALLANS ▸ **callan**
CALLANT *n* youth
CALLAS ▸ **calla**
CALLBOY *n* person who notifies actors when it is time to go on stage
CALLED ▸ **call**
CALLEE *n* computer function being used **callees**
CALLER *n* person or thing that calls, esp a person who makes a brief visit ▹ *adj* (of food, esp fish) fresh **callers**
CALLET *n* scold **callets**
CALLID *adj* cunning
CALLING *n*
CALLOP *n* edible Australian freshwater fish **callops**
CALLOSE *n* carbohydrate found in plants
CALLOUS *adj, vb*
CALLOW *adj, n* **callows**
CALLS ▸ **call**
CALLUNA *n* type of heather
CALLUS *n, vb*
CALM *adj, n, vb*
CALMANT *n* sedative
CALMED ▸ **calm**
CALMER ▸ **calm**
CALMEST ▸ **calm**
CALMIER ▸ **calmy**
CALMING ▸ **calm**
CALMLY ▸ **calm**
CALMS ▸ **calm**
CALMY *adj* tranquil
CALO *n* military servant
CALOMEL *n* colourless tasteless powder
CALORIC *adj* of heat or calories ▹ *n* hypothetical fluid formerly postulated as the embodiment of heat
CALORIE *n* **calory**
CALOS ▸ **calo**
CALOTTE *n* skullcap worn by Roman Catholic clergy
CALOYER *n* monk of the Greek Orthodox Church, esp of the Basilian Order
CALP *n* type of limestone
CALPA *n* Hindu unit of time
CALPAC *n* large black brimless hat **calpack, calpacs**
CALPAIN *n* type of enzyme
CALPAS ▸ **calpa**
CALPS ▸ **calp**
CALQUE ▸ **caulk**
CALQUED ▸ **calque**
CALQUES ▸ **calque**
CALTHA *n* marsh marigold **calthas**
CALTRAP = **caltrop**
CALTROP *n* floating Asian plant
CALUMBA *n* Mozambiquan root used for medicinal purposes
CALUMET *n* peace pipe
CALUMNY *n*
CALVARY *n* representation of Christ's crucifixion
CALVE *vb* **calved**
CALVER *vb* prepare fish for cooking **calvers**
CALVES ▸ **calf**
CALVING ▸ **calve**
CALX *n* powdery metallic oxide formed when an ore or mineral is roasted **calxes**
CALYCES ▸ **calyx**
CALYCLE *n* cup-shaped structure, as in the coral skeleton
CALYPSO *n*
CALYX *n* **calyxes**
CALZONE *n* folded pizza filled with cheese, tomatoes, etc **calzoni**
CAM *n, vb*
CAMA *n* hybrid offspring

of a camel and a llama
CAMAIEU *n* cameo
CAMAIL *n* covering of chain mail **camails**
CAMAN *n* wooden stick used to hit the ball in shinty **camans**
CAMARON *n* shrimp
CAMAS = **camass**
CAMASES ▸ **camas**
CAMASH = **camass**
CAMASS *n* type of North American plant
CAMBER *n*, *vb* **cambers**
CAMBIA ▸ **cambium**
CAMBIAL ▸ **cambium**
CAMBISM ▸ **cambist**
CAMBIST *n* dealer or expert in foreign exchange
CAMBIUM *n* meristem that increases the girth of stems and roots
CAMBOGE *n* type of gum resin
CAMBREL *a variant of* ▸ **gambrel**
CAMBRIC *n* fine white linen fabric
CAME ▸ **come**
CAMEL *n*
CAMELIA = **camellia**
CAMELID *adj* of or relating to camels ▹ *n* any animal of the camel family
CAMELOT *n* supposedly idyllic period or age
CAMELRY *n* troops mounted on camels
CAMELS ▸ **camel**
CAMEO *n*, *vb* **cameoed, cameos**
CAMERA *n* **camerae**
CAMERAL *adj* of or relating to a judicial or legislative chamber
CAMERAS ▸ **camera**
CAMES ▸ **canvas**
CAMESE = **camise**
CAMESES ▸ **camese**
CAMION *n* lorry, or, esp formerly, a large dray **camions**
CAMIS *n* light robe
CAMISA *n* smock **camisas**
CAMISE *n* loose light shirt, smock, or tunic originally worn in the Middle Ages **camises**
CAMISIA *n* surplice
CAMLET *n* tough waterproof cloth **camlets**
CAMMED ▸ **cam**
CAMMIE *n* webcam award **cammies**
CAMMING ▸ **cam**
CAMO *n* short for camouflage
CAMOGIE *n* form of hurling played by women
CAMOODI *a Caribbean name for* > **anaconda**
CAMORRA *n* secret criminal group
CAMOS ▸ **camo**
CAMOTE *n* type of sweet potato **camotes**
CAMP *vb*, *adj*
CAMPANA *n* bell or bell shape
CAMPED ▸ **camp**
CAMPER *n* person who lives or temporarily stays in a tent, cabin, etc **campers**
CAMPERY *n* campness
CAMPEST ▸ **camp**
CAMPHOL *another word for* ▸ **borneol**
CAMPHOR *n*
CAMPI ▸ **campo**
CAMPIER ▸ **campy**
CAMPILY ▸ **campy**
CAMPING ▸ **camp**
CAMPION *n* red, pink, or white wild flower
CAMPLE *vb* argue **campled, camples**
CAMPLY ▸ **camp**
CAMPO *n* level or undulating savanna country
CAMPONG *n* in Malaysia, a village
CAMPOS ▸ **campo**
CAMPOUT *n* camping trip
CAMPS ▸ **camp**
CAMPUS *n*, *vb*
CAMPY *adj* effeminate
CAMS ▸ **cam**
CAMSHO *adj* crooked
CAMUS *n* type of loose robe **camuses**
CAMWOOD *n* W African leguminous tree
CAN *vb*, *n*
CANADA *n* canada goose **canadas**
CANAKIN = **cannikin**
CANAL *n*, *vb* **canaled, canals**
CANAPE *n* small piece of bread or toast with a savoury topping **canapes**
CANARD *n* false report

canards
CANARY *n, vb*
CANASTA *n* card game like rummy, played with two packs
CANBANK *n* container for receiving cans for recycling
CANCAN *n* lively high-kicking dance performed by a female group **cancans**
CANCEL *vb, n* **cancels**
CANCER *n* **cancers**
CANCHA *n* toasted maize **canchas**
CANDELA *n*
CANDENT *adj* emitting light as a result of being heated to a high temperature
CANDID *adj, n*
CANDIDA *n* yeastlike parasitic fungus which causes thrush
CANDIDS ▸ **candid**
CANDIE *n* South Indian unit of weight
CANDIED *adj*
CANDIES ▸ **candy**
CANDIRU *n* parasitic freshwater catfish of the Amazon region
CANDLE *n, vb* **candled, candler, candles**
CANDOCK *n* type of water lily, or horsetail
CANDOR = **candour**
CANDORS ▸ **candor**
CANDOUR *n* honesty and straightforwardness
CANDY *n, vb*
CANE *n, vb* **caned**
CANEH *n* Hebrew unit of length **canehs**
CANELLA *n* fragrant cinnamon-like inner bark of a W Indian tree, used as a spice and in medicine
CANER ▸ **cane**
CANERS ▸ **cane**
CANES ▸ **cane**
CANFUL *n* amount a can will hold **canfuls**
CANG = **cangue**
CANGLE *vb* wrangle **cangled, cangles**
CANGS ▸ **cang**
CANGUE *n* (formerly in China) a wooden collar worn as a punishment **cangues**
CANID *n* animal of the dog family **canids**
CANIER ▸ **cany**
CANIEST ▸ **cany**
CANIKIN = **cannikin**
CANINE *adj, n* **canines**
CANING *n* beating with a cane as a punishment **canings**
CANKER *n, vb* **cankers**
CANKERY *adj* like a canker
CANKLE *n* thickened calfs on an overweight person **cankles**
CANN *vb* direct a ship's steering
CANNA *n* type of tropical plant
CANNACH *n* cotton grass
CANNAE *vb* can not
CANNAS ▸ **canna**
CANNED ▸ **can**
CANNEL *n* type of dull coal **cannels**
CANNER *n* person or organization whose job is to can foods **canners**
CANNERY *n* factory where food is canned
CANNIE = **canny**
CANNIER ▸ **canny**
CANNILY ▸ **canny**
CANNING ▸ **can**
CANNOLI *n* Sicilian pudding of pasta shells filled with sweetened ricotta
CANNON *n, vb* **cannons**
CANNOT *vb*
CANNS ▸ **cann**
CANNULA *n* narrow tube for insertion into a bodily cavity
CANNY *adj, adv*
CANOE *n, vb* **canoed, canoer, canoers, canoes**
CANOLA *n* cooking oil extracted from a variety of rapeseed **canolas**
CANON *n*
CANONIC = **canonical**
CANONRY *n* office, benefice, or status of a canon
CANONS ▸ **canon**
CANOPIC *adj* of ancient Egyptian vase
CANOPY *n, vb*
CANS ▸ **can**
CANSFUL ▸ **canful**
CANSO *n* love song **cansos**

CANST *vb* form of 'can' used with the pronoun *thou* or its relative form
CANT *n, vb, adj*
CANTAL *n* French cheese
CANTALA *n* tropical American plant, the agave
CANTALS ▸ **cantal**
CANTAR *variant form of* ▸ **kantar**
CANTARS ▸ **cantar**
CANTATA *n* musical work consisting of arias, duets, and choruses
CANTATE *n* 98th psalm sung as a nonmetrical hymn
CANTDOG = **canthook**
CANTED ▸ **cant**
CANTEEN *n*
CANTER *vb* move at gait between trot and gallop **canters**
CANTEST ▸ **cant**
CANTHAL ▸ **canthus**
CANTHI ▸ **canthus**
CANTHUS *n* inner or outer corner or angle of the eye
CANTIC ▸ **cant**
CANTICO *vb* dance as part of an act of worship
CANTIER ▸ **canty**
CANTILY ▸ **canty**
CANTINA *n* bar or wine shop, esp in a Spanish-speaking country
CANTING ▸ **cant**
CANTION *n* song
CANTLE *n* back part of a saddle that slopes upwards ▷ *vb* set up, or stand, on high **cantled, cantles**
CANTLET *n* piece
CANTO = **cantus**
CANTON *n, vb* **cantons**
CANTOR *n* man employed to lead services in a synagogue **cantors**
CANTOS ▸ **canto**
CANTRAP = **cantraip**
CANTRED *n* district comprising a hundred villages **cantref**
CANTRIP *n* magic spell ▷ *adj* (of an effect) produced by black magic
CANTS ▸ **cant**
CANTUS *n* medieval form of church singing
CANTY *adj* lively
CANULA = **cannula**
CANULAE ▸ **canula**
CANULAR *adj* shaped like a cannula
CANULAS ▸ **canula**
CANVAS *n, vb*
CANVASS *vb, n*
CANY *adj* cane-like
CANYON *n* **canyons**
CANZONA *n* type of 16th- or 17th-century contrapuntal music
CANZONE *n* Provençal or Italian lyric, often in praise of love or beauty **canzoni**
CAP *n, vb*
CAPA *n* type of Spanish cloak
CAPABLE *adj* **capably**
CAPAS ▸ **capa**
CAPE *n, vb* **caped**
CAPELAN *another word for* ▸ **capelin**
CAPELET *n* small cape
CAPELIN *n* type of small marine food fish
CAPER *n, vb* **capered, caperer**
CAPERS *pl n* pickled flower buds of a Mediterranean shrub used in sauces
CAPES ▸ **cape**
CAPEX *n* capital expenditure **capexes**
CAPFUL *n* quantity held by a (usually bottle) cap **capfuls**
CAPH *n* letter of the Hebrew alphabet **caphs**
CAPI ▸ **capo**
CAPIAS *n* (formerly) a writ directing the arrest of a named person
CAPING ▸ **cape**
CAPITA ▸ **caput**
CAPITAL *n, adj*
CAPITAN *another name for* ▸ **hogfish**
CAPITOL *n* (in America) building housing the state legislature
CAPIZ *n* bivalve shell of a mollusc **capizes**
CAPLE *n* horse **caples**
CAPLESS ▸ **cap**
CAPLET *n* medicinal tablet, usually oval in shape, coated in a soluble substance

caplets
CAPLIN = **capelin**
CAPLINS ▸ **caplin**
CAPO *n* device used to raise the pitch of a stringed instrument
CAPON *n* castrated cock fowl fattened for eating **capons**
CAPORAL *n* strong coarse dark tobacco
CAPOS ▸ **capo**
CAPOT *n* winning of all the tricks by one player ▹ *vb* score a capot (against)
CAPOTE *n* long cloak or soldier's coat, usually with a hood **capotes**
CAPOTS ▸ **capot**
CAPOUCH = **capuche**
CAPPED, capper, cappers, capping ▸ **cap**
CAPRATE *n* any salt of capric acid
CAPRIC *adj* (of a type of acid) smelling of goats
CAPRICE = **capriccio**
CAPRID *n* any member of the goat family **caprids**
CAPRIFY *vb* induce figs to ripen
CAPRINE *adj* of or resembling a goat
CAPRIS *pl n* women's tight-fitting trousers
CAPROCK *n* layer of rock that overlies a salt dome
CAPROIC *adj as in* **caproic acid** oily acid found in milk
CAPS ▸ **cap**
CAPSID *n* outer protein coat of a mature virus **capsids**
CAPSIZE *vb*
CAPSTAN *n* rotating cylinder round which a ship's rope is wound
CAPSULE *n, adj, vb*
CAPTAIN *n, vb*
CAPTAN *n* type of fungicide **captans**
CAPTION *n, vb*
CAPTIVE *n, adj, vb*
CAPTOR *n* **captors**
CAPTURE *vb, n*
CAPUCHE *n* large hood or cowl, esp that worn by Capuchin friars
CAPUERA *variant of* > **capoeira**
CAPUL = **caple**
CAPULS ▸ **capul**
CAPUT *n* main or most prominent part of an organ or structure
CAR *n*
CARABAO *n* water buffalo
CARABID *n* type of beetle
CARABIN = **carbine**
CARACAL *n* lynx with reddish fur, which inhabits deserts of N Africa and S Asia
CARACK = **carrack**
CARACKS ▸ **carack**
CARACOL = **caracole**
CARACT *n* sign or symbol **caracts**
CARACUL *n* fur from the skins of newly born lambs of the karakul sheep
CARAFE *n* **carafes**
CARAMBA *n* Spanish interjection similar to 'wow!'
CARAMEL *n, vb*
CARANNA *n* gumlike substance
CARAP *n* crabwood
CARAPAX *n* carapace
CARAPS ▸ **carap**
CARAT *n*
CARATE *n* tropical disease **carates**
CARATS ▸ **carat**
CARAUNA = **caranna**
CARAVAN *n, vb*
CARAVEL *n* two- or three-masted sailing ship
CARAWAY *n*
CARB *n* carbohydrate
CARBARN *n* streetcar depot
CARBEEN *n* Australian eucalyptus tree
CARBENE *n* neutral divalent free radical, such as methylene: CH_2
CARBIDE *n*
CARBIES ▸ **carby**
CARBINE *n*
CARBO *n* carbohydrate
CARBON *n* **carbons**
CARBORA *n* former name for the koala
CARBOS ▸ **carbo**
CARBOY *n* large bottle with a protective casing **carboys**

CARBS ▶ **carb**
CARBY *n* short for carburettor
CARCAKE *n* (formerly, in Scotland) a cake traditionally made for Shrove Tuesday
CARCASE ▶ **carcass**
CARCASS *n*, *vb*
CARCEL *n* French unit of light **carcels**
CARD *n*, *vb*
CARDAN *n as in* **cardan joint** type of universal joint
CARDECU *n* old French coin (a quarter of a crown)
CARDED ▶ **card**
CARDER ▶ **card**
CARDERS ▶ **card**
CARDI *n* cardigan
CARDIA *n* lower oesophageal sphincter
CARDIAC *adj*, *n*
CARDIAE ▶ **cardia**
CARDIAS ▶ **cardia**
CARDIE *short for* > **cardigan**
CARDIES ▶ **cardie**
CARDING ▶ **card**
CARDIO *adj* exercising heart ▷ *n* cardiovascular exercise **cardios**
CARDIS ▶ **cardi**
CARDON *n* variety of cactus **cardons**
CARDOON *n* thistle-like S European plant
CARDS ▶ **card**
CARDUUS *n* thistle
CARDY = **cardie**
CARE *vb*, *n* **cared**
CAREEN *vb* tilt over to one side **careens**
CAREER *n*, *vb*, *adj* **careers**
CAREFUL *adj*
CAREME *n* period of Lent **caremes**
CARER *n* person who looks after someone who is ill or old, often a relative **carers**
CARES ▶ **care**
CARESS *n*, *vb*
CARET *n* proofreading symbol **carets**
CAREX *n* any member of the sedge family
CARFARE *n* fare that a passenger is charged for a ride on a bus, etc
CARFAX *n* place where principal roads or streets intersect **carfox**
CARFUL *n* maximum number of people a car will hold **carfuls**
CARGO *n*, *vb* **cargoed, cargoes, cargos**
CARHOP *n* waiter or waitress at a drive-in restaurant ▷ *vb* work as a carhop **carhops**
CARIAMA *another word for* ▶ **seriema**
CARIBE *n* piranha **caribes**
CARIBOU *n*
CARICES ▶ **carex**
CARIED *adj* (of teeth) decayed
CARIERE *obsolete word for* ▶ **career**
CARIES *n*
CARINA *n* keel-like part or ridge **carinae**
CARINAL *adj* keel-like
CARINAS ▶ **carina**
CARING *adj* feeling or showing care and compassion for other people ▷ *n* practice or profession of providing social or medical care **carings**
CARIOCA *n* Brazilian dance similar to the samba
CARIOLE *n* small open two-wheeled horse-drawn vehicle
CARIOSE = **carious**
CARIOUS *adj* (of teeth or bone) affected with caries
CARITAS *n* divine love; charity
CARJACK *vb*
CARK *vb* break down **carked, carking, carks**
CARL *another word for* ▶ **churl**
CARLE = **carl**
CARLES ▶ **carle**
CARLESS ▶ **car**
CARLIN ▶ **carling**
CARLINE = **carling**
CARLING *n* fore-and-aft beam in a vessel **carlins**
CARLISH *adj* churlish
CARLOAD *n* amount that can be carried by a car
CARLOCK *n* type of Russian isinglass
CARLOT *n* boor **carlots**

CARLS ▸ **carl**
CARMAN *n* man who drives a car or cart **carmen**
CARMINE *adj, n*
CARN *n* cairn
CARNAGE *n*
CARNAL *adj, vb* **carnals**
CARNET *n* type of customs licence **carnets**
CARNEY = **carny**
CARNEYS ▸ **carney**
CARNIE = **carny**
CARNIED ▸ **carny**
CARNIER ▸ **carny**
CARNIES ▸ **carny**
CARNIFY *vb* be altered so as to resemble skeletal muscle
CARNOSE *adj* fleshy
CARNS ▸ **carn**
CARNY *vb* coax or cajole or act in a wheedling manner ▹ *n* person who works in a carnival ▹ *adj* sly
CARNYX *n* bronze Celtic war trumpet
CAROACH = **caroche**
CAROB *n* pod of a Mediterranean tree, used as a chocolate substitute **carobs**
CAROCH = **caroche**
CAROCHE *n* stately ceremonial carriage used in the 16th and 17th centuries
CAROL *n, vb* **caroled, caroler**
CAROLI ▸ **carolus**
CAROLS ▸ **carol**
CAROLUS *n* any of several coins struck in the reign of a king called Charles
CAROM *n* shot in which the cue ball is caused to contact one object ball after another ▹ *vb* carambole **caromed**
CAROMEL *vb* turn into caramel
CAROMS ▸ **carom**
CARON *n* inverted circumflex **carons**
CAROTID *n* either of the two arteries supplying blood to the head ▹ *adj* of either of these arteries
CAROTIN = **carotene**
CAROUSE *vb*
CARP *n, vb*
CARPAL *n* wrist bone **carpale, carpals**
CARPED ▸ **carp**
CARPEL *n* **carpels**
CARPER ▸ **carp**
CARPERS ▸ **carp**
CARPET *n, vb* **carpets**
CARPI ▸ **carpus**
CARPING *adj* tending to make petty complaints ▹ *n* petty complaint
CARPOOL *vb* share the use of a single car to travel to work or school
CARPORT *n* shelter for a car, consisting of a roof supported by posts
CARPS ▸ **carp**
CARPUS *n* set of eight bones of the wrist
CARR *n* area of bog or fen in which scrub has become established
CARRACK *n* galleon used as a merchantman **carract**
CARRAT = **carat**
CARRATS ▸ **carrat**
CARRECT = **carrack**
CARREL *n* small individual study room or private desk **carrell, carrels**
CARRICK *n as in* **carrick bend** type of knot
CARRIED ▸ **carry**
CARRIER *n*
CARRIES ▸ **carry**
CARRION *n*
CARROCH *variant of* ▸ **caroche**
CARROM ▸ **carom**
CARROMS ▸ **carrom**
CARRON *n as in* **carron oil** ointment of limewater and linseed oil
CARROT *n* **carrots**
CARROTY *adj* (of hair) reddish-orange
CARRS ▸ **carr**
CARRY *vb*
CARRYON *n* fuss or commotion
CARS ▸ **car**
CARSE *n* riverside area of flat fertile alluvium **carses**
CARSEY *slang word for* ▸ **toilet**
CARSEYS ▸ **carsey**
CARSICK *adj* nauseated from riding in a car
CART *n, vb*

CARTA *n* charter
CARTAGE *n* process or cost of carting
CARTAS ▸ **carta**
CARTE *n* fencing position
CARTED ▸ **cart**
CARTEL *n* association of competing firms formed to fix prices **cartels**
CARTER ▸ **cart**
CARTERS ▸ **cart**
CARTES ▸ **carte**
CARTFUL *n* amount a cart can hold
CARTING ▸ **cart**
CARTON *n, vb* **cartons**
CARTOON *n, vb*
CARTOP *adj* designed to be transported on top of a vehicle
CARTS ▸ **cart**
CARTWAY *n* way by which carts travel
CARVE *vb* **carved**
CARVEL = **caravel**
CARVELS ▸ **carvel**
CARVEN ▸ **carve**
CARVER *n* carving knife **carvers**
CARVERY *n* restaurant where customers pay a set price for unrestricted helpings
CARVES ▸ **carve**
CARVIES ▸ **carvy**
CARVING *n*
CARVY *n* caraway seed
CARWASH *n* drive-through structure containing automated equipment for washing cars
CASA *n* house
CASABA *n* kind of winter muskmelon **casabas**
CASAS ▸ **casa**
CASAVA = **cassava**
CASAVAS ▸ **casava**
CASBAH *n* citadel of a N African city **casbahs**
CASCADE *n, vb*
CASCARA *n* bark of a N American shrub, used as a laxative
CASCO *n* Argentinian homestead **cascos**
CASE *n, vb*
CASEASE *n* proteolytic enzyme
CASEATE *vb* undergo caseation
CASED ▸ **case**
CASEFY *vb* make or become similar to cheese
CASEIC *adj* relating to cheese
CASEIN *n* phosphoprotein forming the basis of cheese **caseins**
CASEMAN *n* in printing, a person who sets and corrects type **casemen**
CASEMIX *n* mix or type of patients treated by a hospital or medical unit
CASEOSE *n* peptide produced by the peptic digestion of casein
CASEOUS *adj* of or like cheese
CASERN *n* (formerly) a billet or accommodation for soldiers in a town **caserne, caserns**
CASES ▸ **case**
CASETTE *variant of* > **cassette**
CASEVAC *vb* evacuate (a casualty) from a combat zone, usu by air
CASH *n, adj, vb*
CASHAW *n* winter squash **cashaws**
CASHBOX *n* box for holding cash
CASHED ▸ **cash**
CASHES ▸ **cash**
CASHEW *n* **cashews**
CASHIER *n, vb*
CASHING ▸ **cash**
CASHOO *n* catechu **cashoos**
CASING *n* **casings**
CASINI ▸ **casino**
CASINO *n* **casinos**
CASITA *n* small house **casitas**
CASK *n, vb* **casked**
CASKET *n, vb* **caskets**
CASKIER ▸ **casky**
CASKING ▸ **cask**
CASKS ▸ **cask**
CASKY *adj* (of wine) having a musty smell due to resting too long in the cask
CASPASE *n* type of enzyme
CASQUE *n* helmet or a helmet-like process or structure **casqued, casques**
CASSABA = **casaba**
CASSATA *n* ice cream usually containing nuts and candied fruit

CASSAVA *n*
CASSENA = **cassina**
CASSENE = **cassina**
CASSIA *n* tropical plant whose pods yield a mild laxative **cassias**
CASSINA *n* American tree **cassine**
CASSINO *n* card game for two to four players
CASSIS *n* blackcurrant cordial
CASSOCK *n*
CASSONE *n* highly-decorated Italian dowry chest
CASSPIR *n* armoured military vehicle
CAST *n, vb*
CASTE *n*
CASTED *adj* having a caste
CASTER *n* person or thing that casts **casters**
CASTES ▸ **caste**
CASTING ▸ **cast**
CASTLE *n, vb*
CASTLED *adj* like a castle in construction
CASTLES ▸ **castle**
CASTOCK *n* kale stalk
CASTOFF *n* person or thing that has been discarded or abandoned
CASTOR = **caster**
CASTORS ▸ **castor**
CASTORY *n* dye derived from beaver pelts
CASTRAL *adj* relating to camps
CASTS ▸ **cast**
CASUAL *adj, n* **casuals**
CASUIST *n* person who attempts to resolve moral dilemmas
CASUS *n* event
CAT *n, vb*
CATALO = **cattalo**
CATALOG = **catalogue**
CATALOS ▸ **catalo**
CATALPA *n* tree of N America and Asia with bell-shaped whitish flowers
CATAPAN *n* governor in the Byzantine Empire
CATARRH *n*
CATASTA *n* platform on which slaves were presented for sale
CATAWBA *n* type of red North American grape
CATBIRD *n* North American songbird
CATBOAT *n* sailing vessel
CATCALL *n, vb*
CATCH *vb* seize, capture ▹ *n* device for fastening a door, window, etc **catched, catchen**
CATCHER *n* person or thing that catches, esp in a game or sport
CATCHES ▸ **catch**
CATCHT = **catched**
CATCHUP *a variant spelling (esp US) of* ▸ **ketchup**
CATCHY *adj*
CATCLAW *n* type of shrub; black bead
CATCON *n* **catcons**
CATE *n* delicacy
CATECHU *n* astringent resinous substance
CATELOG *obsolete word for* > **catalogue**
CATENA *n* connected series, esp of patristic comments on the Bible **catenae, catenas**
CATER *vb*
CATERAN *n* (formerly) a member of a band of brigands in the Scottish highlands
CATERED ▸ **cater**
CATERER *n*
CATERS ▸ **cater**
CATES *pl n* choice dainty food
CATFACE *n* deformity of the surface of a tree trunk, caused by fire or disease
CATFALL *n* line used as a tackle for hoisting an anchor to the cathead
CATFISH *n* fish with whisker-like barbels round the mouth
CATFLAP *n* small flap in a door to let a cat go through
CATGUT *n* strong cord used to string musical instruments and sports rackets **catguts**
CATHEAD *n* fitting at the bow of a vessel for securing the anchor when raised
CATHECT *vb* invest mental or emotional energy in
CATHODE *n*
CATHOLE *n* hole in a ship through which ropes are passed

CATHOOD *n* state of being a cat
CATION *n* positively charged ion **cations**
CATJANG *n* tropical shrub
CATKIN *n* **catkins**
CATLIKE ▸ **cat**
CATLIN = **catling**
CATLING *n* long double-edged surgical knife for amputations
CATLINS ▸ **catlin**
CATMINT *n* Eurasian plant with scented leaves that attract cats
CATNAP *vb* doze ▹ *n* short sleep or doze **catnaps**
CATNEP = **catmint**
CATNEPS ▸ **catnep**
CATNIP = **catmint**
CATNIPS ▸ **catmint**
CATS ▸ **cat**
CATSKIN *n* skin and/or fur of a cat
CATSPAW *n* person used by another as a tool
CATSUIT *n* one-piece usually close-fitting trouser suit
CATSUP *a variant (esp US) of* ▸ **ketchup**
CATSUPS ▸ **catsup**
CATTABU *n* cross between common cattle and zebu
CATTAIL *n* reed mace
CATTALO *n* hardy breed of cattle
CATTED ▸ **cat**
CATTERY *n* place where cats are bred or looked after
CATTIE = **catty**
CATTIER ▸ **catty**
CATTIES ▸ **catty**
CATTILY ▸ **catty**
CATTING ▸ **cat**
CATTISH ▸ **cat**
CATTLE *pl n*
CATTY *adj, n*
CATWALK *n*
CATWORM *n* type of carnivorous worm
CAUCUS *n, vb*
CAUDA *n* area behind the anus of an animal
CAUDAD *adv* towards the tail or posterior part
CAUDAE ▸ **cauda**
CAUDAL *adj* at or near an animal's tail
CAUDATE *adj* having a tail or a tail-like appendage ▹ *n* lizard-like amphibian
CAUDEX *n* thickened persistent stem base of some herbaceous perennial plants
CAUDLE *n* hot spiced wine drink made with gruel, formerly used medicinally ▹ *vb* make such a drink **caudled, caudles**
CAUDRON *Spenserian spelling of* > **cauldron**
CAUF *n* cage for holding live fish in the water
CAUGHT ▸ **catch**
CAUK *n* type of barite
CAUKER *n* one who caulks **caukers**
CAUKS ▸ **cauk**
CAUL *n* membrane sometimes covering a child's head at birth
CAULD *a Scot word for* ▸ **cold**
CAULDER ▸ **cauld**
CAULDS ▸ **cauld**
CAULES ▸ **caulis**
CAULINE *adj* relating to or growing from a plant stem
CAULIS *n* main stem of a plant
CAULK *vb* fill in (cracks) with paste etc **caulked, caulker, caulks**
CAULOME *n* plant's stem structure, considered as a whole
CAULS ▸ **caul**
CAUM = **cam**
CAUMED ▸ **caum**
CAUMING ▸ **caum**
CAUMS ▸ **caum**
CAUP *n* type of quaich **caups**
CAUSA *n* reason or cause **causae**
CAUSAL *adj* of or being a cause ▹ *n* something that suggests a cause **causals**
CAUSE *n* something that produces a particular effect ▹ *vb* be the cause of **caused, causen, causer, causers, causes**
CAUSEY *n* cobbled street ▹ *vb* cobble **causeys**
CAUSING ▸ **cause**

CAUSTIC *adj, n*
CAUTEL *n* craftiness **cautels**
CAUTER *n* cauterising instrument **cauters**
CAUTERY *n* coagulation of blood or destruction of body tissue by cauterizing
CAUTION *n, vb*
CAUVES ▶ **cauf**
CAVA *n* Spanish sparkling wine
CAVALLA *n* type of tropical fish **cavally**
CAVALRY *n*
CAVAS ▶ **cava**
CAVASS *n* Turkish armed police officer
CAVE *n, vb*
CAVEAT *n* warning ▷ *vb* introduce a caveat **caveats**
CAVED ▶ **cave**
CAVEL *n* drawing of lots among miners for an easy and profitable place at the coalface **cavels**
CAVEMAN *n* **cavemen**
CAVER ▶ **caving**
CAVERN *n, vb* **caverns**
CAVERS ▶ **caving**
CAVES ▶ **cave**
CAVETTI ▶ **cavetto**
CAVETTO *n* concave moulding, shaped to a quarter circle in cross section
CAVIAR *n* **caviare, caviars**
CAVIE *n* hen coop
CAVIER = **caviar**
CAVIERS ▶ **cavier**
CAVIES ▶ **cavy**
CAVIL *vb, n* **caviled, caviler, cavils**
CAVING *n* sport of exploring caves **cavings**
CAVITY *n*
CAVORT *vb* **cavorts**
CAVY *n* type of small rodent
CAW *n, vb* **cawed, cawing, cawings**
CAWK = **cauk**
CAWKER *n* metal projection on a horse's shoe to prevent slipping **cawkers**
CAWKS ▶ **cawk**
CAWS ▶ **caw**
CAXON *n* type of wig **caxons**
CAY *n* low island or bank composed of sand and coral fragments
CAYENNE *n* very hot condiment
CAYMAN *n* S American reptile similar to an alligator **caymans**
CAYS ▶ **cay**
CAYUSE *n* small American Indian pony used by cowboys **cayuses**
CAZ *short for* ▶ **casual**

> **Caz** is slang for casual, and is one of the essential short words for using the Z.

CAZIQUE = **cacique**

> This word means an American Indian chief, and its plural **caziques** was once played as a 9-timer (that is, a word spanning two triple-word squares) earning the highest score for a single word ever officially recorded in a game of Scrabble, 392 points.

CEAS = **caese**
CEASE *vb* **ceased, ceases, ceasing**
CEAZE *obsolete spelling of* ▶ **seize**
CEAZED ▶ **ceaze**
CEAZES ▶ **ceaze**
CEAZING ▶ **ceaze**
CEBID *n* any member of the Cebidae family of New World monkeys **cebids, ceboid**
CEBOIDS ▶ **ceboid**
CECA ▶ **cecum**
CECAL ▶ **cecum**
CECALLY ▶ **cecum**
CECILS *pl n* fried meatballs
CECITIS *n* inflammation of the c(a)ecum
CECITY *n* rare word for blindness
CECUM = **caecum**
CEDAR *n, adj*
CEDARED *adj* covered with cedars
CEDARN *adj* relating to cedar
CEDARS ▶ **cedar**
CEDARY *adj* like cedar
CEDE *vb* **ceded, ceder, ceders, cedes**
CEDI *n* standard monetary unit of

Ghana, divided into 100 pesewas
CEDILLA *n*
CEDING ▸ **cede**
CEDIS ▸ **cedi**
CEDRATE *n* citron
CEDRINE *adj* relating to cedar
CEDULA *n* form of identification in Spanish-speaking countries **cedulas**
CEE *n* third letter of the alphabet **cees**
CEIBA *n* type of tropical tree **ceibas**
CEIL *vb* line (a ceiling) with plaster, boarding, etc **ceiled, ceiler, ceilers**
CEILI *variant spelling of* ▸ **ceilidh**
CEILIDH *n*
CEILING *n, vb*
CEILIS ▸ **ceili**
CEILS ▸ **ceil**
CEL *short for* > **celluloid**
CELADON *n* type of porcelain having a greyish-green glaze: mainly Chinese
CELEB *n* celebrity **celebs**
CELERY *n*
CELESTA *n* instrument like a small piano **celeste**
CELIAC = **coeliac**
CELIACS ▸ **celiac**
CELL *n*
CELLA *n* inner room of a classical temple **cellae**
CELLAR *n, vb* **cellars**
CELLED *adj* cellular
CELLI ▸ **cello**
CELLING *n* formation of cells
CELLIST ▸ **cello**
CELLO *n* **cellos**
CELLOSE *n* disaccharide obtained by the hydrolysis of cellulose by cellulase
CELLS ▸ **cell**
CELLULE *n* very small cell
CELOM = **coelom**
CELOMIC ▸ **celom**
CELOMS ▸ **celom**
CELOSIA = **cockscomb**
CELOTEX *n* tradename for a type of insulation board
CELS ▸ **cel**
CELT *n* stone or metal axelike instrument with a bevelled edge **celts**
CEMBALI ▸ **cembalo**
CEMBALO *n* harpsichord
CEMBRA *n* Swiss pine **cembras**
CEMENT *n, vb*
CEMENTA > **cementum**
CEMENTS ▸ **cement**
CENACLE *n* supper room, esp one on an upper floor
CENDRE *adj* ash-blond
CENOTE *n* natural well formed by the collapse of an overlying limestone crust **cenotes**
CENS *n* type of annual property rent
CENSE *vb* burn incense near or before (an altar, shrine, etc) **censed**
CENSER *n* container for burning incense **censers**
CENSES ▸ **cense**
CENSING ▸ **cense**
CENSOR *n, vb* **censors**
CENSUAL ▸ **census**
CENSURE *n, vb*
CENSUS *n, vb*
CENT *n*
CENTAGE *n* rate per hundred
CENTAI ▸ **centas**
CENTAL *n* unit of weight equal to 100 pounds (45.3 kilograms) **centals**
CENTARE = **centiare**
CENTAS *n* monetary unit of Lithuania
CENTAUR *n*
CENTAVO *n* monetary unit in Portugal and many Latin American countries
CENTER = **centre**
CENTERS ▸ **center**
CENTILE *n* (in statistics) another word for percentile
CENTIME *n*
CENTIMO *n* monetary unit of Costa Rica, Paraguay, Peru, and Venezuela
CENTNER *n* unit of weight equivalent to 100 pounds (45.3 kilograms)
CENTO *n* piece of writing composed of quotations from other authors **centos**
CENTRA ▸ **centrum**

CENTRAL *adj, n*
CENTRE *n, vb*
CENTRED *adj* mentally and emotionally confident, focused, and well-balanced
CENTRES ▸ **centre**
CENTRIC *adj* being central or having a centre
CENTRUM *n* main part or body of a vertebra
CENTRY *obsolete variant of* ▸ **sentry**
CENTS ▸ **cent**
CENTU *n* Lithuanian money unit
CENTUM *adj* denoting or belonging to the Indo-European languages in which original velar stops (*k*) were not palatalized ▹ *n* hundred **centums**
CENTURY *n*
CEORL *n* freeman of the lowest class in Anglo-Saxon England **ceorls**
CEP *another name for* ▸ **porcino**
CEPAGE *n* grape variety or type of wine **cepages**
CEPE *another spelling of* ▸ **cep**
CEPES ▸ **cepe**
CEPHEID *n* type of variable star with a regular cycle of variations in luminosity
CEPS ▸ **cep**
CERAMAL = **cermet**
CERAMIC *n, adj*
CERASIN *n* meta-arabinic acid
CERATE *n* hard ointment or medicated paste
CERATED *adj* (of certain birds, such as the falcon) having a cere
CERATES ▸ **cerate**
CERATIN = **keratin**
CERCAL *adj* of or relating to a tail
CERCI ▸ **cercus**
CERCIS *n* type of tree or shrub
CERCUS *n* one of a pair of sensory appendages on some insects and other arthropods
CERE *n* soft waxy swelling at the base of the upper beak of a parrot ▹ *vb* wrap (a corpse) in a cerecloth
CEREAL *n* **cereals**
CEREBRA > **cerebrum**
CERED ▸ **cere**
CEREOUS *adj* waxlike
CERES ▸ **cere**
CERESIN *n* white wax extracted from ozocerite
CEREUS *n* type of tropical American cactus
CERGE *n* large altar candle **cerges**
CERIA *n* ceric oxide **cerias**
CERIC *adj* of or containing cerium in the tetravalent state
CERING ▸ **cere**
CERIPH = **serif**
CERIPHS ▸ **ceriph**
CERISE *adj* cherry-red ▹ *n* moderate to dark red colour **cerises**
CERITE *n* hydrous silicate of cerium **cerites**
CERIUM *n* steel-grey metallic element **ceriums**
CERMET *n* materials consisting of a metal matrix with ceramic particles disseminated through it **cermets**
CERNE *obsolete variant of* > **encircle**
CERNED ▸ **cerne**
CERNES ▸ **cerne**
CERNING ▸ **cerne**
CERO *n* type of large food fish
CEROON *n* hide-covered bale **ceroons**
CEROS ▸ **cero**
CEROTIC *adj as in* **cerotic acid** white insoluble odourless wax
CEROUS *adj* of or containing cerium in the trivalent state
CERRADO *n* vast area of tropical savanna in Brazil
CERRIAL *adj* relating to the cerris
CERRIS *n* Turkey oak
CERT *n* certainty
CERTAIN *adj*
CERTES *adv* with certainty
CERTIE *n as in* **by my certie** assuredly

CERTIFY *vb*
CERTS ▸ **cert**
CERTY *n as in* **by my certy** assuredly
CERULE *adj* sky-blue
CERUMEN *n* wax secreted by glands in the external ear
CERUSE *n* white lead **ceruses**
CERVEZA *n* Spanish word for beer
CERVID *n* type of ruminant mammal characterized by the presence of antlers **cervids**
CERVINE *adj* resembling or relating to a deer
CERVIX *n*
CESIOUS = **caesious**
CESIUM = **caesium**
CESIUMS ▸ **cesium**
CESS *n* any of several special taxes, such as a land tax in Scotland ▹ *vb* tax or assess for taxation
CESSE *obsolete variant of* ▸ **cease**
CESSED ▸ **cess**
CESSER *n* coming to an end of a term interest or annuity **cessers**
CESSES ▸ **cess**
CESSING ▸ **cess**
CESSION *n* ceding
CESSPIT = **cesspool**
CESTA *n* in jai alai, the basket used to throw and catch the pelota **cestas**
CESTI ▸ **cestus**
CESTODE *n* type of parasitic flatworm such as the tapeworms
CESTOI ▸ **cestos**
CESTOID *adj* (esp of tapeworms and similar animals) ribbon-like in form ▹ *n* ribbon-like worm
CESTOS = **cestus**
CESTUI *n* legal term to designate a person **cestuis**
CESTUS *n* girdle of Aphrodite (Venus) decorated to cause amorousness
CESURA *a variant spelling of* ▸ **caesura**
CESURAE ▸ **cesura**
CESURAL ▸ **cesura**
CESURAS ▸ **cesura**
CESURE = **caesura**
CESURES ▸ **cesure**
CETANE *n* colourless liquid hydrocarbon, used as a solvent **cetanes**
CETE *n* group of badgers **cetes**
CETYL *n* univalent alcohol radical **cetyls**
CEVICHE *n* Peruvian seafood dish
CEZVE *n* **cezves**
CH *pron* obsolete from of I
CHA *n* tea
CHABLIS *n* dry white French wine
CHABOUK *n* type of whip **chabuk**
CHABUKS ▸ **chabuk**
CHACE *obsolete variant of* ▸ **chase**
CHACED ▸ **chace**
CHACES ▸ **chace**
CHACHKA *n* cheap trinket
CHACING ▸ **chace**
CHACK *vb* bite **chacked, chacks**
CHACMA *n* type of baboon with coarse greyish hair, occurring in S and E Africa **chacmas**
CHACO = **shako**
CHACOES ▸ **chaco**
CHACOS ▸ **chaco**
CHAD *n* small pieces removed during the punching of holes in punch cards, printer paper, etc
CHADAR = **chuddar**
CHADARS ▸ **chadar**
CHADDAR = **chuddar**
CHADDOR = **chuddar**
CHADO *n* Japanese tea ceremony
CHADOR = **chuddar**
CHADORS ▸ **chador**
CHADOS ▸ **chado**
CHADRI *n* shroud which covers the body from head to foot
CHADS ▸ **chad**
CHAEBOL *n* large, usually family-owned, business group in South Korea
CHAETA *n* the chitinous bristles on the body of annelids **chaetae, chaetal**
CHAFE *vb* **chafed**
CHAFER *n* large beetle **chafers**

CHAFES ▸ **chafe**
CHAFF *n, vb* **chaffed**
CHAFFER *vb* haggle
CHAFFS ▸ **chaff**
CHAFFY ▸ **chaff**
CHAFING ▸ **chafe**
CHAFT *n* jaw **chafts**
CHAGAN *n* Mongolian royal or imperial title **chagans**
CHAGRIN *n, vb*
CHAI *n* tea, esp as made in India with added spices
CHAIN *n, vb*
CHAINE *adj* (of a dance turn) producing a full rotation for every two steps taken ▹ *vb* produce a full rotation for every two steps taken
CHAINED ▸ **chain**
CHAINES ▸ **chaine**
CHAINS ▸ **chain**
CHAIR *n, vb* **chaired, chairs**
CHAIS ▸ **chai**
CHAISE *n* light horse-drawn carriage **chaises**
CHAKRA *n* (in yoga) any of the seven major energy centres in the body **chakras**
CHAL *n* in Romany, person or fellow
CHALAH = **challah**
CHALAHS ▸ **chalah**
CHALAN *vb* (in India) to cause an accused person to appear before a magistrate **chalans**
CHALAZA *n* one of a pair of spiral threads holding the yolk of a bird's egg in position
CHALCID *n* type of tiny insect
CHALDER *n* former Scottish dry measure
CHALEH = **challah**
CHALEHS ▸ **chaleh**
CHALET *n* **chalets**
CHALICE *n*
CHALK *n, vb* **chalked, chalks, chalky**
CHALLA = **challah**
CHALLAH *n* type of bread
CHALLAN = **chalan**
CHALLAS ▸ **challa**
CHALLIE = **challis**
CHALLIS *n* lightweight plain-weave fabric
CHALLOT ▸ **challah**
CHALLY = **challis**
CHALONE *n* any internal secretion that inhibits a physiological process or function
CHALOT ▸ **chalah**
CHALOTH ▸ **chalah**
CHALS ▸ **chal**
CHALUPA *n* Mexican dish
CHALUTZ *n* member of an organization of immigrants to Israeli agricultural settlements
CHAM *an archaic word for* ▸ **khan**
CHAMADE *n* (formerly) a signal by drum or trumpet inviting an enemy to a parley
CHAMBER *n, vb*
CHAMBRE *adj* (of wine) at room temperature
CHAMETZ *n* leavened food which may not be eaten during Passover
CHAMFER = **chase**
CHAMISA *n* American shrub
CHAMISE = **chamiso**
CHAMISO *n* fourwing saltbush
CHAMLET = **camlet**
CHAMMY = **chamois**
CHAMOIS *n* small mountain antelope or a pice of leather from its skin, used for polishing ▹ *vb* polish with a chamois **chamoix**
CHAMP *vb*
CHAMPAC *n* type of tree **champak**
CHAMPED ▸ **champ**
CHAMPER ▸ **champ**
CHAMPS ▸ **champ**
CHAMPY *adj* (of earth) churned up (by cattle, for example)
CHAMS ▸ **cham**
CHANA *n* (in Indian cookery) chickpeas **chanas**
CHANCE *n, vb* **chanced**
CHANCEL *n*
CHANCER *n* unscrupulous or dishonest opportunist
CHANCES ▸ **chance**
CHANCEY = **chancy**
CHANCRE *n* small hard growth which is the first sign of syphilis

CHANCY *adj*
CHANG *n* loud discordant noise
CHANGA *interj* in Indian English, an expression of approval or agreement
CHANGE *n, vb* **changed, changer, changes**
CHANGS ▸ **chang**
CHANK *n* shell of several types of sea conch, used to make bracelets **chanks**
CHANNEL *n, vb*
CHANNER *n* gravel
CHANOYO *a variant of* ▸ **chado**
CHANOYU = **chado**
CHANSON *n* song
CHANT *vb, n* **chanted**
CHANTER *n* (on bagpipes) pipe on which the melody is played
CHANTEY *the usual US spelling of* ▸ **shanty**
CHANTIE *n* chamber pot
CHANTOR = **chanter**
CHANTRY *n* endowment for the singing of Masses for the soul of the founder or others designated by him
CHANTS ▸ **chant**
CHANTY = **shanty**
CHAO *n* Vietnamese rice porridge
CHAOS *n* **chaoses, chaotic**
CHAP *n, vb*
CHAPATI *n* (in Indian cookery) flat thin unleavened bread
CHAPE *n* metal tip or trimming for a scabbard
CHAPEAU *n* hat
CHAPEL *n* **chapels**
CHAPES ▸ **chape**
CHAPESS *n* woman
CHAPKA = **czapka**
CHAPKAS ▸ **chapka**
CHAPLET *n* garland for the head ▹ *vb* create a garland
CHAPMAN *n* travelling pedlar **chapmen**
CHAPPAL *n* one of a pair of sandals, usually of leather, worn in India
CHAPPED ▸ **chap**
CHAPPIE *n* man or boy
CHAPPY *adj* (of skin) chapped
CHAPS ▸ **chap**
CHAPT *adj* chapped
CHAPTER *n, vb*
CHAR *vb, n*
CHARA *n* type of green freshwater algae
CHARACT *n* distinctive mark
CHARADE *n*
CHARAS *another name for* ▸ **hashish**
CHARD *n* variety of beet **chards**
CHARE = **char**
CHARED ▸ **char**
CHARES ▸ **char**
CHARET *obsolete variant of* ▸ **chariot**
CHARETS ▸ **charet**
CHARGE *vb, n* **charged**
CHARGER *n*
CHARGES ▸ **charge**
CHARIER ▸ **chary**
CHARILY *adv* cautiously
CHARING ▸ **char**
CHARIOT *n, vb*
CHARISM = **charisma**
CHARITY *n*
CHARK *vb* char
CHARKA = **charkha**
CHARKAS ▸ **charka**
CHARKED ▸ **chark**
CHARKHA *n* (in India) a spinning wheel, esp for cotton
CHARKS ▸ **chark**
CHARLEY *n as in* **charley horse** muscle stiffness after strenuous exercise
CHARLIE *n* fool
CHARM *n, vb*
CHARMED *adj* delighted or fascinated
CHARMER *n*
CHARMS ▸ **charm**
CHARNEL *adj* ghastly ▹ *n* ghastly thing
CHARPAI = **charpoy**
CHARPIE *n* lint pieces used to make surgical dressings
CHARPOY *n* type of bedstead
CHARQUI *n* meat, esp beef, cut into strips and dried
CHARR = **char**
CHARRED ▸ **char**
CHARRO *n* Mexican cowboy **charros**
CHARRS ▸ **charr**
CHARRY *adj* of or relating to charcoal
CHARS ▸ **char**
CHART *n, vb*

CHARTA *n* charter **chartas**
CHARTED ▸ **chart**
CHARTER *n, vb*
CHARTS ▸ **chart**
CHARY *adj*
CHAS ▸ **cha**
CHASE *vb, n* **chased**
CHASER *n* milder drink drunk after another stronger one **chasers**
CHASES ▸ **chase**
CHASING ▸ **chase**
CHASM *n, vb* **chasmal, chasmed, chasmic, chasms**
CHASMY *adj* full of chasms
CHASSE *n* one of a series of gliding steps in ballet ▹ *vb* perform either of these steps **chassed, chasses**
CHASSIS *n*
CHASTE *adj*
CHASTEN *vb*
CHASTER ▸ **chaste**
CHAT *n, vb*
CHATBOT *n* computer program
CHATEAU *n*
CHATON *n* in jewellery, a stone with a reflective metal foil backing **chatons**
CHATS ▸ **chat**
CHATTA *n* umbrella **chattas**
CHATTED ▸ **chat**
CHATTEL *n*
CHATTER *vb, n*
CHATTI *n* (in India) an earthenware pot **chattis**
CHATTY *adj*
CHAUFE *obsolete variant of* ▸ **chafe**
CHAUFED ▸ **chaufe**
CHAUFER = **chauffer**
CHAUFES ▸ **chaufe**
CHAUFF *obsolete variant of* ▸ **chafe**
CHAUFFS ▸ **chauff**
CHAUMER *n* chamber
CHAUNCE *archaic variant of* ▸ **chance**
CHAUNGE *archaic variant of* ▸ **change**
CHAUNT *a less common variant of* ▸ **chant**
CHAUNTS ▸ **chaunt**
CHAUVIN *n* chauvinist
CHAVE *vb* old dialect term for "I have"
CHAVVY *adj* relating to or like a chav
CHAW *vb* chew (tobacco), esp without swallowing it ▹ *n* something chewed, esp a plug of tobacco **chawed, chawer, chawers, chawing**
CHAWK *n* jackdaw **chawks**
CHAWS ▸ **chaw**
CHAY *n* plant of the madder family **chaya**
CHAYAS ▸ **chaya**
CHAYOTE *n* tropical climbing plant
CHAYS ▸ **chay**
CHAZAN = **cantor**
CHAZANS ▸ **chazan**
CHAZZAN *variant of* ▸ **chazan**
CHAZZEN = **chazzan**
CHE *pron* dialectal form meaning "I"
CHEAP *adj, adv, n, vb* **cheaped**
CHEAPEN *vb* lower the reputation of
CHEAPER ▸ **cheap**
CHEAPIE *n* something inexpensive
CHEAPLY ▸ **cheap**
CHEAPO *n* very cheap and possibly shoddy thing **cheapos**
CHEAPS ▸ **cheap**
CHEAPY = **cheapie**
CHEAT *vb, n* **cheated, cheater, cheats**
CHEBEC *n* type of boat **chebecs**
CHECHIA *n* Berber skullcap
CHECK *vb, n* **checked**
CHECKER = **chequer**
CHECKS ▸ **check**
CHECKUP *n*
CHECKY *adj* having squares of alternating tinctures or furs
CHEDDAR *n* type of smooth hard yellow or whitish cheese
CHEDER *n* Jewish religious education **cheders**
CHEDITE = **cheddite**
CHEEK *n, vb* **cheeked, cheeks**
CHEEKY *adj*
CHEEP *n* young bird's high-pitched cry ▹ *vb* utter a cheep **cheeped, cheeper, cheeps**
CHEER *vb, n* **cheered, cheerer**

CHEERIO *interj, n, sentence substitute*
CHEERLY *adv* cheerful or cheerfully
CHEERO = **cheerio**
CHEEROS ▸ **cheero**
CHEERS *interj* drinking toast ▹ *sentence substitute* drinking toast
CHEERY *adj*
CHEESE *n, vb* **cheesed, cheeses**
CHEESY *adj* like cheese
CHEETAH *n*
CHEF *n, vb*
CHEFDOM *n* state or condition of being a chef
CHEFED, cheffed, chefing, chefs ▸ **chef**
CHEGOE = **chigger**
CHEGOES ▸ **chigger**
CHEKA *n* secret police set up in Russia in 1917 **chekas**
CHEKIST *n* member of the cheka
CHELA *n* disciple of a religious teacher **chelae, chelas**
CHELATE *n* coordination compound ▹ *adj* of or possessing chelae ▹ *vb* form a chelate
CHELLUP *n* noise
CHELOID *a variant spelling of* ▸ **keloid**
CHELONE *n* hardy N American plant
CHELP *vb* (esp of women or children) to chatter or speak out of turn **chelped, chelps**
CHEMIC *vb* bleach ▹ *n* chemist **chemics**
CHEMISE *n* woman's loose-fitting slip
CHEMISM *n* chemical action
CHEMIST *n*
CHEMMY *n* gambling card game
CHEMO *n* short form of chemotherapy **chemos**
CHENAR *n* oriental plane tree **chenars**
CHENET *another word for* ▸ **genip**
CHENETS ▸ **chenet**
CHENIX *n* ancient measure, slightly more than a quart
CHEQUE *n*
CHEQUER *n* piece used in Chinese chequers ▹ *vb* make irregular in colour or character
CHEQUES ▸ **cheque**
CHEQUY = **checky**
CHER *adj* dear or expensive **chere**
CHERISH *vb*
CHEROOT *n* cigar with both ends cut flat
CHERRY *n, adj, vb*
CHERT *n* microcrystalline form of silica **cherts, cherty**
CHERUB *n* **cherubs**
CHERUP = **chirrup**
CHERUPS ▸ **cherup**
CHERVIL *n* aniseed-flavoured herb
CHESIL *n* gravel or shingle **chesils**
CHESNUT *rare variant of* > **chestnut**
CHESS *n*
CHESSEL *n* mould used in cheese-making
CHESSES ▸ **chess**
CHEST *n, vb* **chested, chests**
CHESTY *adj* symptomatic of chest disease
CHETAH = **cheetah**
CHETAHS ▸ **chetah**
CHETH = **heth**
CHETHS ▸ **cheth**
CHETNIK *n* member of a Serbian nationalist paramilitary group
CHETRUM *n* monetary unit in Bhutan
CHEVAL *n as in* **cheval glass** full-length mirror that can swivel
CHEVEN *n* chub **chevens**
CHEVET *n* semicircular or polygonal east end of a church **chevets**
CHEVIED ▸ **chevy**
CHEVIES ▸ **chevy**
CHEVIN = **cheven**
CHEVINS ▸ **chevin**
CHEVIOT *n* type of British sheep reared for its wool
CHEVRE *n* any cheese made from goats' milk **chevres**
CHEVRET *n* type of goats' cheese
CHEVRON *n, vb*
CHEVY = **chivy**
CHEW *vb, n* **chewed, chewer, chewers**

CHEWET *n* type of meat pie **chewets**
CHEWIE *n* chewing gum
CHEWIER ▶ **chewy**
CHEWIES ▶ **chewy**
CHEWING ▶ **chew**
CHEWINK *n* towhee
CHEWS ▶ **chew**
CHEWY *adj* requiring a lot of chewing ▷ *n* dog's rubber toy
CHEZ *prep* at the home of
CHI *n* 22nd letter of the Greek alphabet

> **Chi** is a letter of the Greek alphabet, and can also be spelt **khi**.

CHIA *n* plant of the mint family
CHIACK *vb* tease or banter ▷ *n* good-humoured banter **chiacks**
CHIANTI *n* dry red Italian wine
CHIAO *n* Chinese coin equal to one tenth of one yuan
CHIAS ▶ **chia**
CHIASM = **chiasma**
CHIASMA *n* biological term
CHIASMI > **chiasmus**
CHIASMS ▶ **chiasma**
CHIAUS = **chouse**
CHIB *vb* in Scots English, stab or slash with a sharp weapon ▷ *n* sharp weapon **chibbed**
CHIBOL *n* spring onion **chibols**
CHIBOUK *n* Turkish tobacco pipe with an extremely long stem
CHIBS ▶ **chib**
CHIC *adj, n*
CHICA *n* Spanish young girl
CHICANA *n* female chicano
CHICANE *n* obstacle in a motor-racing circuit ▷ *vb* deceive or trick by chicanery
CHICANO *n* American citizen of Mexican origin
CHICAS ▶ **chica**
CHICER ▶ **chic**
CHICEST ▶ **chic**
CHICH *another word for* > **chickpea**
CHICHA *n* Andean drink made from fermented maize **chichas**
CHICHES > **chickpea**
CHICHI *adj* affectedly pretty or stylish ▷ *n* quality of being affectedly pretty or stylish **chichis**
CHICK *n*
CHICKEE *n* opensided, thatched building on stilts
CHICKEN *n, adj, vb*
CHICKS ▶ **chick**
CHICLE *n* gumlike substance obtained from the sapodilla **chicles**
CHICLY ▶ **chic**
CHICO *n* spiny chenopodiaceous shrub
CHICON = **chicory**
CHICONS ▶ **chicon**
CHICORY *n*
CHICOS ▶ **chico**
CHICS ▶ **chic**
CHID ▶ **chide**
CHIDDEN ▶ **chide**
CHIDE *vb* **chided, chider, chiders, chides, chiding**
CHIEF *n, adj* **chiefer**
CHIEFLY *adv* especially ▷ *adj* of or relating to a chief or chieftain
CHIEFRY = **chiefery**
CHIEFS ▶ **chief**
CHIEL *n* young man **chield, chields, chiels**
CHIFFON *n, adj*
CHIGGER *n* parasitic larva of various mites
CHIGNON *n* knot of hair pinned up at the back of the head ▷ *vb* make a chignon
CHIGOE = **chigger**
CHIGOES ▶ **chigoe**
CHIGRE = **chigger**
CHIGRES ▶ **chigre**
CHIK *n* slatted blind
CHIKARA *n* Indian seven-stringed musical instrument
CHIKHOR = **chukar**
CHIKOR = **chukar**
CHIKORS ▶ **chikor**
CHIKS ▶ **chik**
CHILD *n, vb*
CHILDE *n* young man of noble birth
CHILDED ▶ **child**
CHILDER *dialect variant of* > **children**
CHILDES ▶ **childe**

CHILDLY ▸ **child**
CHILDS ▸ **child**
CHILE *a variant spelling of* ▸ **chilli**
CHILES ▸ **chile**
CHILI = **chilli**
CHILIAD *n* group of one thousand
CHILIES ▸ **chili**
CHILIS ▸ **chili**
CHILL *n, vb, adj* **chilled**
CHILLER *n* cooling or refrigerating device
CHILLI *n* **chillis**
CHILLS ▸ **chill**
CHILLUM *n* short pipe, usually of clay, used esp for smoking cannabis
CHILLY *adj*
CHIMAR = **chimere**
CHIMARS ▸ **chimar**
CHIMB = **chime**
CHIMBLY = **chimney**
CHIMBS ▸ **chime**
CHIME *n, vb* **chimed, chimer**
CHIMERA *n* unrealistic hope or idea
CHIMERE *n* gown worn by bishops
CHIMERS ▸ **chime**
CHIMES ▸ **chime**
CHIMING ▸ **chime**
CHIMLA = **chimney**
CHIMLAS ▸ **chimla**
CHIMLEY = **chimney**
CHIMNEY *n, vb*
CHIMO *interj* Inuit greeting and toast
CHIMP *n* chimpanzee **chimps**
CHIN *n, vb*
CHINA *n*
CHINAR = **chenar**
CHINARS ▸ **chinar**
CHINAS ▸ **china**
CHINCH *another name for a* ▸ **bedbug**
CHINCHY *adj* tightfisted
CHINDIT *n* Allied soldier fighting behind the Japanese lines in Burma during World War II
CHINE = **chime**
CHINED ▸ **chine**
CHINES ▸ **chine**
CHINESE *adj* of or relating to China
CHINING ▸ **chine**
CHINK *n, vb* **chinked, chinks, chinky**
CHINNED ▸ **chin**
CHINO *n* durable cotton twill cloth
CHINONE *n* benzoquinone
CHINOOK *n* wind found in the Rocky Mountains
CHINOS *pl n* trousers made of a kind of hard-wearing cotton
CHINS ▸ **chin**
CHINTS *obsolete variant of* ▸ **chintz**
CHINTZ *n*
CHINTZY *adj* of or covered with chintz
CHINWAG *n* chat
CHIP *n, vb* **chipped**
CHIPPER *vb* chirp or chatter
CHIPPIE = **chippy**
CHIPPY *n* fish-and-chip shop ▹ *adj* resentful or oversensitive about being perceived as inferior
CHIPS ▸ **chip**
CHIPSET *n* highly integrated circuit on the motherboard of a computer
CHIRAL > **chirality**
CHIRK *vb* creak, like a door ▹ *adj* spritely; high-spirited **chirked, chirker, chirks**
CHIRL *vb* warble **chirled, chirls**
CHIRM *n* chirping of birds ▹ *vb* (esp of a bird) to chirp **chirmed, chirms**
CHIRO *n* informal name for chiropractor **chiros**
CHIRP *vb, n* **chirped, chirper, chirps**
CHIRPY *adj*
CHIRR *vb* (esp of certain insects, such as crickets) to make a shrill trilled sound ▹ *n* sound of chirring **chirre, chirred**
CHIRREN *n* dialect form of children
CHIRRES ▸ **chirre**
CHIRRS ▸ **chirr**
CHIRRUP *vb, n*
CHIRT *vb* squirt **chirted, chirts**
CHIRU *n* Tibetan antelope **chirus**
CHIS ▸ **chi**
CHISEL *n, vb* **chisels**
CHIT *n, vb*
CHITAL *n* type of deer **chitals**

CHITIN *n* outer layer of the bodies of arthropods **chitins**
CHITLIN *n* pig intestine cooked and served as a dish
CHITON *n* (in ancient Greece and Rome) a loose woollen tunic **chitons**
CHITS ▸ **chit**
CHITTED ▸ **chit**
CHITTER *vb* twitter or chirp
CHITTY *adj, vb*
CHIV *n* knife ▹ *vb* stab (someone)
CHIVARI = **charivari**
CHIVE *n, vb* **chived, chives**
CHIVIED ▸ **chivy**
CHIVIES ▸ **chivy**
CHIVING ▸ **chive**
CHIVS ▸ **chiv**
CHIVVED ▸ **chiv**
CHIVVY = **chivy**
CHIVY *vb* harass or nag ▹ *n* hunt
CHIZ *n* cheat ▹ *vb* cheat **chizz, chizzed, chizzes**
CHLAMYS *n* woollen cloak worn by ancient Greek soldiers
CHLORAL *n* colourless oily liquid with a pungent odour
CHLORIC *adj* of or containing chlorine in the pentavalent state
CHLORID *n* type of chlorine compound
CHLORIN = **chlorine**
CHOANA *n* posterior nasal aperture **choanae**
CHOBDAR *n* in India and Nepal, king's macebearer or attendant
CHOC *short form of* > **chocolate**
CHOCCY *n* chocolate ▹ *adj* made of, tasting of, smelling of, or resembling chocolate
CHOCHO = **chayote**
CHOCHOS ▸ **chocho**
CHOCK *n, vb, adv* **chocked**
CHOCKER *adj* full up
CHOCKO = **choco**
CHOCKOS ▸ **chocko**
CHOCKS ▸ **chock**
CHOCO *n* member of the Australian army **chocos**
CHOCS ▸ **choc**
CHOCTAW *n* movement in ice-skating
CHODE ▸ **chide**
CHOENIX = **chenix**
CHOG *n* core of a piece of fruit **chogs**
CHOICE *n, adj* **choicer, choices**
CHOIR *n, vb* **choired, choirs**
CHOKE *vb, n*
CHOKED *adj* disappointed or angry
CHOKER *n* tight-fitting necklace **chokers**
CHOKES ▸ **choke**
CHOKEY *n* slang word for prison ▹ *adj* involving, caused by, or causing choking **chokeys, chokier, chokies**
CHOKING ▸ **choke**
CHOKO *n* **chokos**
CHOKRA *n* in India, a boy or young man **chokras**
CHOKRI *n* in India, a girl or young woman **chokris**
CHOKY = **chokey**
CHOLA *n* Hispanic girl **cholas**
CHOLATE *n* salt of cholic acid
CHOLENT *n* meal prepared on Friday and left to cook until eaten for Sabbath lunch
CHOLER *n* bad temper
CHOLERA *n*
CHOLERS ▸ **choler**
CHOLI *n* short-sleeved bodice, as worn by Indian women
CHOLIC *adj as in* **cholic acid** crystalline acid found in bile
CHOLINE *n* colourless viscous soluble alkaline substance present in animal tissues
CHOLIS ▸ **choli**
CHOLLA *n* type of spiny cactus **chollas**
CHOLO *n* chicano gangster **cholos**
CHOLTRY *n* caravanserai
CHOMETZ = **chametz**
CHOMMIE *n* (in informal South African English) friend

CHOMP *vb* chew noisily ▷ *n* act or sound of chewing in this manner **chomped, chomper, chomps**
CHON *n* North and South Korean monetary unit
CHONDRE *another word for* > **chondrule**
CHONDRI > **chondrus**
CHOOF *vb* go away **choofed, choofs**
CHOOK *n, vb* **chooked, chookie, chooks**
CHOOM *n* Englishman **chooms**
CHOON *n* **choons**
CHOOSE *vb* **chooser, chooses**
CHOOSEY = **choosy**
CHOOSY *adj*
CHOP *vb, n*
CHOPIN = **chopine**
CHOPINE *n* sandal-like shoe popular in the 18th century
CHOPINS ▶ **chopin**
CHOPPED ▶ **chop**
CHOPPER *n, vb*
CHOPPY *adj*
CHOPS ▶ **chop**
CHORAGI > **choragus**
CHORAL *adj*
CHORALE *n* slow stately hymn tune
CHORALS ▶ **choral**
CHORD *n* straight line joining two points on a curve ▷ *vb* provide (a melodic line) with chords
CHORDA *n* in anatomy, a cord **chordae**
CHORDAL ▶ **chord**
CHORDED ▶ **chord**
CHORDEE *n* painful penile erection, a symptom of gonorrhoea
CHORDS ▶ **chord**
CHORE *n, vb*
CHOREA *n* disorder of the nervous system **choreal, choreas**
CHORED ▶ **chore**
CHOREE *n* trochee **chorees**
CHOREGI > **choregus**
CHOREIC ▶ **chorea**
CHORES ▶ **chore**
CHOREUS = **choree**
CHORIA ▶ **chorion**
CHORIAL ▶ **chorion**
CHORIC *adj* in the manner of a chorus
CHORINE *n* chorus girl
CHORING ▶ **chore**
CHORION *n* outer membrane forming a sac around an embryo
CHORISM > **chorisis**
CHORIST *n* choir member
CHORIZO *n* kind of highly seasoned pork sausage of Spain or Mexico
CHOROID *adj* resembling the chorion, esp in being vascular ▷ *n* vascular membrane of the eyeball
CHORRIE *n* dilapidated old car
CHORTEN *n* Buddhist shrine
CHORTLE *vb, n*
CHORUS *n* large choir ▷ *vb* sing or say together
CHOSE ▶ **choose**
CHOSEN ▶ **choose**
CHOSES ▶ **choose**
CHOTA *adj* (in British Empire Indian usage) small
CHOTT *a variant spelling of* ▶ **shott**
CHOTTS ▶ **chott**
CHOU *n* type of cabbage
CHOUGH *n* large black Eurasian and N African bird of the crow family **choughs**
CHOUSE *vb* to cheat **choused, chouser, chouses**
CHOUSH *n* Turkish messenger
CHOUT *n* blackmail **chouts**
CHOUX ▶ **chou**
CHOW *n, vb*
CHOWDER *n* thick soup containing clams or fish ▷ *vb* to make a chowder of
CHOWED ▶ **chow**
CHOWING ▶ **chow**
CHOWK *n* marketplace or market area **chowks**
CHOWRI *n* fly-whisk **chowris, chowry**
CHOWS ▶ **chow**
CHOWSE = **chouse**
CHOWSED ▶ **chowse**
CHOWSES ▶ **chowse**
CHRISM *n* consecrated oil used for anointing in some churches

CHRISMA > **chrismon**
CHRISMS ▶ **chrism**
CHRISOM = **chrism**
CHRISTY *n* skiing turn for stopping or changing direction quickly
CHROMA *n* attribute of a colour **chromas**
CHROME *n*, *vb*, *adj* **chromed**
CHROMEL *n* nickel-based alloy
CHROMES ▶ **chrome**
CHROMIC *adj* of or containing chromium in the trivalent state
CHROMO *n* picture produced by lithography **chromos**
CHROMY ▶ **chrome**
CHROMYL *n* of, consisting of, or containing the divalent radical CrO_2
CHRONIC *adj*, *n*
CHRONON *n* unit of time
CHUB *n* European freshwater fish of the carp family
CHUBBY *adj*
CHUBS ▶ **chub**
CHUCK *vb*, *n* **chucked**
CHUCKER *n* person who throws something
CHUCKIE *n* small stone
CHUCKLE *vb*, *n*
CHUCKS ▶ **chuck**
CHUCKY = **chuckie**
CHUDDAH = **chuddar**
CHUDDAR *n* large shawl or veil **chudder**
CHUDDY *n* chewing gum
CHUFA *n* type of sedge **chufas**
CHUFF *vb* (of a steam engine) move while making a puffing sound ▷ *n* puffing sound of or as if of a steam engine ▷ *adj* boorish
CHUFFED *adj* very pleased
CHUFFER ▶ **chuff**
CHUFFS ▶ **chuff**
CHUFFY *adj* boorish and surly
CHUG *n*, *vb* **chugged, chugger, chugs**
CHUKAR *n* common Indian partridge **chukars**
CHUKKA *n* period of play in polo **chukkar, chukkas, chukker**
CHUKOR = **chukar**
CHUKORS ▶ **chukor**
CHUM *n*, *vb*
CHUMASH *n* printed book containing one of the Five Books of Moses
CHUMLEY = **chimney**
CHUMMED ▶ **chum**
CHUMMY *adj* friendly ▷ *n* chum
CHUMP *n*, *vb* **chumped, chumps**
CHUMS ▶ **chum**
CHUNDER *vb* vomit ▷ *n* vomit
CHUNK *n*, *vb* **chunked, chunks**
CHUNKY *adj*
CHUNNEL *n* rail tunnel linking England and France
CHUNNER = **chunter**
CHUNTER *vb* mutter or grumble incessantly in a meaningless fashion
CHUPATI = **chupatti**
CHUPPA *variant of* ▶ **chuppah**
CHUPPAH *n* canopy under which a marriage is performed
CHUPPAS ▶ **chuppa**
CHUPPOT ▶ **chuppah**
CHUR *interj* expression of agreement
CHURCH *n*, *vb*
CHURCHY *adj* like a church, church service, etc
CHURL *n* surly ill-bred person **churls**
CHURN *n*, *vb* **churned, churner, churns**
CHURR = **chirr**
CHURRED ▶ **churr**
CHURRO *n* Spanish dough stick snack **churros**
CHURRS ▶ **churr**
CHURRUS *n* hemp resin
CHUSE *obsolete variant of* ▶ **choose**
CHUSES ▶ **chuse**
CHUSING ▶ **chuse**
CHUT *interj* expression of surprise or annoyance ▷ *vb* make such an expression
CHUTE *n*, *vb* **chuted, chutes, chuting, chutist**
CHUTNEE = **chutney**
CHUTNEY *n*
CHUTZPA = **chutzpah**
CHYACK = **chiack**

CHYACKS ▸ **chyack**
CHYLDE *archaic word for* ▸ **child**
CHYLE *n* milky fluid formed in the small intestine during digestion **chyles**
CHYLIFY *vb* to be turned into chyle
CHYLOUS ▸ **chyle**
CHYME *n* partially digested food that leaves the stomach **chymes**
CHYMIC = **chemic**
CHYMICS ▸ **chymic**
CHYMIFY *vb* to form into chyme
CHYMIST = **chemist**
CHYMOUS ▸ **chyme**
CHYND *adj* chined
CHYPRE *n* perfume made from sandalwood **chypres**
CHYTRID *n* variety of fungus
CIAO *an informal word for* ▸ **hello**
CIBOL = **chibol**
CIBOLS ▸ **cibol**
CIBORIA > **ciborium**
CIBOULE = **chibol**
CICADA *n* **cicadae, cicadas, cicala**
CICALAS ▸ **cicala**
CICALE ▸ **cicala**
CICELY *n* type of plant
CICERO *n* measure for type that is somewhat larger than the pica **ciceros**
CICHLID *n* type of tropical freshwater fish popular in aquariums
CICOREE = **chicory**
CICUTA *n* spotted hemlock **cicutas**
CID *n* leader
CIDARIS *n* sea urchin
CIDE *Shakespearean variant of* ▸ **decide**
CIDED ▸ **cide**
CIDER *n* **ciders, cidery**
CIDES ▸ **cide**
CIDING ▸ **cide**
CIDS ▸ **cid**
CIEL = **ceil**
CIELED ▸ **ciel**
CIELING ▸ **ciel**
CIELS ▸ **ciel**
CIERGE = **cerge**
CIERGES ▸ **cierge**
CIG = **cigarette**
CIGAR *n*
CIGARET = **cigarette**
CIGARS ▸ **cigar**
CIGGIE = **cigarette**
CIGGIES ▸ **ciggie**
CIGGY > **cigarette**
CIGS ▸ **cig**
CILIA ▸ **cilium**
CILIARY *adj* of or relating to cilia
CILIATE *n* type of protozoan
CILICE *n* haircloth fabric or garment **cilices**
CILIUM *n* short thread projecting from a cell that causes movement
CILL *a variant spelling (used in the building industry) for* ▸ **sill**
CILLS ▸ **cill**
CIMAR = **cymar**
CIMARS ▸ **cimar**
CIMELIA *n* (especially, ecclesiastical) treasures
CIMEX *n* type of heteropterous insect, esp the bedbug **cimices**
CIMIER *n* crest of a helmet **cimiers**
CINCH *n* easy task ▹ *vb* fasten a girth around (a horse) **cinched, cinches**
CINCT *adj* encircled
CINDER *n*, *vb* **cinders, cindery**
CINE *n as in* **cine camera** camera able to film moving pictures
CINEAST = **cineaste**
CINEMA *n* **cinemas**
CINEOL *n* colourless oily liquid with a camphor-like odour and a spicy taste **cineole, cineols**
CINEREA *n* grey matter of the brain and nervous system
CINERIN *n* either of two organic compounds used as insecticides
CINES ▸ **cine**
CINGULA > **cingulum**
CINQUE *n* number five in cards, dice, etc **cinques**
CION = **scion**
CIONS ▸ **cion**
CIPHER *n*, *vb* **ciphers**
CIPHONY *n* ciphered telephony
CIPOLIN *n* Italian marble with alternating white and

green streaks
CIPPI ▸ **cippus**
CIPPUS *n* pillar bearing an inscription
CIRCA *prep*
CIRCAR *n* in India, part of a province **circars**
CIRCLE *n*, *vb* **circled, circler, circles**
CIRCLET *n* circular ornament worn on the head
CIRCLIP *n* type of fastener
CIRCS *pl n* circumstances
CIRCUIT *n*, *vb*
CIRCUS *n* **circusy**
CIRE *adj* (of fabric) treated with a heat or wax process to make it smooth ▹ *n* such a surface on a fabric **cires**
CIRL *n* bird belonging to the bunting family **cirls**
CIRQUE *n* steep-sided semicircular hollow found in mountainous areas **cirques**
CIRRATE *adj* bearing or resembling cirri
CIRRI ▸ **cirrus**
CIRROSE = **cirrate**
CIRROUS = **cirrate**
CIRRUS *n*
CIRSOID *adj* resembling a varix
CIS *adj* having two groups of atoms on the same side of a double bond
CISCO *n* whitefish, esp the lake herring of cold deep lakes of North America **ciscoes, ciscos**
CISSIER ▸ **cissy**
CISSIES ▸ **cissy**
CISSING *n* appearance of pinholes, craters, etc, in paintwork
CISSOID *n* geometric curve whose two branches meet in a cusp at the origin and are asymptotic to a line parallel to the *y*-axis
CISSUS *n* type of climbing plant
CISSY = **sissy**
CIST *n* wooden box for holding ritual objects used in ancient Rome and Greece ▹ *vb* make a cist **cisted**
CISTERN *n*
CISTIC *adj* cist-like
CISTRON *n* section of a chromosome that encodes a single polypeptide chain
CISTS ▸ **cist**
CISTUS *n* type of plant
CIT *n* pejorative term for a town dweller
CITABLE ▸ **cite**
CITADEL *n*
CITAL *n* court summons **citals**
CITATOR *n* legal publication
CITE *vb* **cited, citer, citers, cites**
CITESS *n* female cit
CITHARA *n* ancient stringed musical instrument
CITHER = **cittern**
CITHERN ▸ **cittern**
CITHERS ▸ **cither**
CITHREN = **cithara**
CITIED *adj* having cities
CITIES ▸ **city**
CITIFY *vb* cause to conform to or adopt the customs, habits, or dress of city people
CITING ▸ **cite**
CITIZEN *n*
CITO *adv* swiftly
CITOLA *n* type of medieval stringed instrument **citolas**
CITOLE *a rare word for* ▸ **cittern**
CITOLES ▸ **citole**
CITRAL *n* volatile liquid with a lemon-like odour **citrals**
CITRATE *n* any salt or ester of citric acid
CITRIC *adj* of or derived from citrus fruits or citric acid
CITRIN *n* vitamin P
CITRINE *n* brownish-yellow variety of quartz: a gemstone
CITRINS ▸ **citrin**
CITRON *n* lemon-like fruit of a small Asian tree **citrons**
CITROUS = **citrus**
CITRUS *n* type of tropical or subtropical tree or shrub
CITRUSY = **citrussy**
CITS ▸ **cit**
CITTERN *n* medieval

stringed instrument
CITY *n*
CITYFY = **citify**
CIVE = **chive**
CIVES ▸ **cive**
CIVET *n* spotted catlike African mammal **civets**
CIVIC *adj*
CIVICS *n* study of the rights and responsibilities of citizenship
CIVIE = **civvy**
CIVIES ▸ **civie**
CIVIL *adj* **civilly, civils**
CIVISM *n* good citizenship **civisms**
CIVVIES ▸ **civvy**
CIVVY *n* civilian
CIZERS *archaic spelling of* ▸ **scissors**
CLABBER *vb* to cover with mud
CLACH *n* stone
CLACHAN *n* small village
CLACHS ▸ **clach**
CLACK *n* sound made by two hard objects striking each other ▹ *vb* make this sound **clacked**
CLACKER *n* object that makes a clacking sound
CLACKS ▸ **clack**
CLAD *vb*
CLADDED *adj* covered with cladding
CLADDER ▸ **clad**
CLADDIE *another name for* ▸ **korari**
CLADE *n* group of organisms sharing a common ancestor **clades**
CLADISM ▸ **cladist**
CLADIST *n* proponent of cladistics
CLADODE *n* stem resembling and functioning as a leaf
CLADS ▸ **clad**
CLAES *Scots word for* ▸ **clothes**
CLAG *n* sticky mud ▹ *vb* stick, as mud **clagged**
CLAGGY *adj* stickily clinging, as mud
CLAGS ▸ **clag**
CLAIM *vb, n* **claimed, claimer, claims**
CLAM *n, vb*
CLAMANT *adj* noisy
CLAMBE *old variant of* ▸ **climb**
CLAMBER *vb, n*
CLAME *archaic variant of* ▸ **claim**
CLAMES ▸ **claim**
CLAMMED ▸ **clam**
CLAMMER *n* person who gathers clams
CLAMMY *adj*
CLAMOR = **clamour**
CLAMORS ▸ **clamor**
CLAMOUR *n, vb*
CLAMP *n, vb* **clamped**
CLAMPER *n* spiked metal frame fastened to the sole of a shoe ▹ *vb* to tread heavily
CLAMPS ▸ **clamp**
CLAMS ▸ **clam**
CLAN *n*
CLANG *vb, n* **clanged**
CLANGER *n*
CLANGOR = **clangour**
CLANGS ▸ **clang**
CLANK *n, vb* **clanked, clanks**
CLANKY *adj* making clanking sounds
CLANS ▸ **clan**
CLAP *vb, n*
CLAPNET *n* net that can be closed instantly by pulling a string
CLAPPED ▸ **clap**
CLAPPER *n, vb*
CLAPS ▸ **clap**
CLAPT ▸ **clap**
CLAQUE *n* group of people hired to applaud
CLAQUER = **claqueur**
CLAQUES ▸ **claque**
CLARAIN *n* one of the four major lithotypes of banded coal
CLARET *n, adj, vb* **clarets**
CLARIES ▸ **clary**
CLARIFY *vb*
CLARINI ▸ **clarino**
CLARINO *adj* relating to a high passage for the trumpet in 18th-century music ▹ *n* high register of the trumpet
CLARION *n* obsolete high-pitched trumpet ▹ *adj* clear and ringing ▹ *vb* proclaim loudly
CLARITY *n*
CLARKIA *n* N American plant cultivated for its red, purple, or pink flowers
CLARO *n* mild light-coloured cigar

claroes, claros
CLART *vb* to dirty **clarted**
CLARTS *pl n* lumps of mud, esp on shoes
CLARTY *adj* dirty, esp covered in mud
CLARY *n* European plant with aromatic leaves and blue flowers
CLASH *vb, n* **clashed, clasher, clashes**
CLASP *n, vb* **clasped, clasper, clasps, claspt**
CLASS *n, vb* **classed, classer**
CLASSES ▸ **classis**
CLASSIC *adj, n*
CLASSIS *n* governing body of elders or pastors
CLASSON *n* elementary atomic particle
CLASSY *adj*
CLAST *n* fragment of a clastic rock
CLASTIC *adj* composed of fragments ▹ *n* clast
CLASTS ▸ **clast**
CLAT *n* irksome or troublesome task ▹ *vb* to scrape
CLATCH *vb* to move making a squelching sound
CLATS ▸ **clat**
CLATTED ▸ **clat**
CLATTER *n, vb*
CLAUCHT *vb* to seize by force **claught**
CLAUSAL ▸ **clause**
CLAUSE *n* **clauses**
CLAUT = **clat**
CLAUTED ▸ **claut**
CLAUTS ▸ **claut**
CLAVATE *adj* shaped like a club with the thicker end uppermost
CLAVE *n* one of a pair of hardwood sticks struck together to make a hollow sound
CLAVER *vb* talk idly ▹ *n* idle talk **clavers**
CLAVES ▸ **clave**
CLAVI ▸ **clavus**
CLAVIE *n* tar-barrel traditionally set alight in Moray in Scotland on Hogmanay
CLAVIER *n* any keyboard instrument
CLAVIES ▸ **clavie**
CLAVIS *n* key
CLAVUS *n* corn on the toe
CLAW *n, vb* **clawed, clawer, clawers, clawing, claws**
CLAXON = **klaxon**
CLAXONS ▸ **claxon**
CLAY *n, vb* **clayed, clayey, clayier, claying, clayish**
CLAYPAN *n* layer of stiff impervious clay situated just below the surface of the ground
CLAYS ▸ **clay**
CLEAN *adj, vb, adv* **cleaned**
CLEANER *n* person or thing that removes dirt
CLEANLY *adv* easily or smoothly ▹ *adj* habitually clean or neat
CLEANS ▸ **clean**
CLEANSE *vb*
CLEANUP *n* process of cleaning up or eliminating something
CLEAR *adj, adv, vb* **cleared, clearer**
CLEARLY *adv* in a clear, distinct, or obvious manner
CLEARS ▸ **clear**
CLEAT *n* wedge ▹ *vb* supply or support with a cleat or cleats **cleated, cleats**
CLEAVE *vb* split apart ▹ *n* split **cleaved**
CLEAVER *n*
CLEAVES ▸ **cleave**
CLECHE *adj* (in heraldry) voided so that only a narrow border is visible
CLECK *vb* (of birds) to hatch ▹ *n* piece of gossip **clecked, clecks, clecky**
CLEEK *n* large hook, such as one used to land fish ▹ *vb* to seize **cleeked, cleekit, cleeks**
CLEEP = **clepe**
CLEEPED ▸ **cleep**
CLEEPS ▸ **cleep**
CLEEVE *n* cliff **cleeves**
CLEF *n* **clefs**
CLEFT ▸ **cleave**
CLEFTED ▸ **cleave**
CLEFTS ▸ **cleave**
CLEG *another name for a* > **horsefly**
CLEGS ▸ **cleg**
CLEIK = **cleek**

CLEIKS ▶ **cleek**
CLEM *vb* be hungry or cause to be hungry
CLEMENT *adj* (of weather) mild
CLEMMED ▶ **clem**
CLEMS ▶ **clem**
CLENCH *vb, n*
CLEOME *n* type of herbaceous or shrubby plant **cleomes**
CLEPE *vb* call by the name of **cleped, clepes, cleping, clept**
CLERGY *n*
CLERIC *n* **clerics**
CLERID *n* beetle that preys on other insects **clerids**
CLERISY *n* learned or educated people
CLERK *n, vb* **clerked**
CLERKLY *adj* of or like a clerk ▷ *adv* in the manner of a clerk
CLERKS ▶ **clerk**
CLERUCH *n* settler in a cleruchy
CLEUCH = **clough**
CLEUCHS ▶ **cleuch**
CLEUGH = **clough**
CLEUGHS ▶ **cleugh**
CLEVE = **cleeve**
CLEVER *adj*
CLEVES ▶ **cleeve**
CLEVIS *n* type of fastening used in agriculture
CLEW *n* ball of thread, yarn, or twine ▷ *vb* coil or roll into a ball **clewed, clewing, clews**
CLICHE *n* expression or idea that is no longer effective because of overuse ▷ *vb* use a cliché (in speech or writing) **cliched, cliches**
CLICK *n, vb* **clicked, clicker**
CLICKET *vb* make a click
CLICKS ▶ **click**
CLIED ▶ **cly**
CLIENT *n* **clients**
CLIES ▶ **cly**
CLIFF *n, vb* **cliffed, cliffs, cliffy, clift, clifted, clifts, clifty**
CLIMATE *n, vb*
CLIMAX *n, vb*
CLIMB *vb, n* **climbed**
CLIMBER *n* person or thing that climbs
CLIMBS ▶ **climb**
CLIME *n* place or its climate **climes**
CLINAL ▶ **cline**
CLINCH *vb, n*
CLINE *n* variation within a species **clines**
CLING *vb, n* **clinged, clinger, clings, clingy**
CLINIC *n* **clinics**
CLINK *n, vb* **clinked**
CLINKER *n* fused coal left over in a fire or furnace ▷ *vb* form clinker during burning
CLINKS ▶ **clink**
CLINT *n* section of a limestone pavement separated from others by fissures **clints**
CLIP *vb, n*
CLIPART *n* large collection of simple drawings stored in a computer
CLIPE = **clype**
CLIPED ▶ **clipe**
CLIPES ▶ **clipe**
CLIPING ▶ **clipe**
CLIPPED ▶ **clip**
CLIPPER *n*
CLIPPIE *n* bus conductress
CLIPS ▶ **clip**
CLIPT *old inflection of* ▶ **clip**
CLIQUE *n, vb* **cliqued, cliques**
CLIQUEY *adj* exclusive, confined to a small group **cliquy**
CLIT > **clitoris**
CLITIC *adj* (of a word) incapable of being stressed ▷ *n* clitic word **clitics**
CLITS ▶ **clit**
CLITTER *vb* to stridulate
CLIVERS = **cleavers**
CLIVIA *n* plant belonging to the Amaryllid family **clivias**
CLOACA *n* cavity in most animals into which the alimentary canal and the genital and urinary ducts open **cloacae, cloacal, cloacas**
CLOAK *n, vb* **cloaked, cloaks**
CLOAM *adj* made of clay or earthenware ▷ *n* clay or earthenware pots, dishes, etc,

collectively **cloams**
CLOBBER *vb, n*
CLOCHE *n* **cloches**
CLOCK *n, vb* **clocked, clocker, clocks**
CLOD *n, vb* **clodded, cloddy, clodly, clods**
CLOFF *n* cleft of a tree **cloffs**
CLOG *vb, n* **clogged**
CLOGGER *n* clogmaker
CLOGGY ▸ **clog**
CLOGS ▸ **clog**
CLOISON *n* partition
CLOKE = **cloak**
CLOKED ▸ **cloke**
CLOKES ▸ **cloke**
CLOKING ▸ **cloke**
CLOMB *a past tense and past participle of* ▸ **climb**
CLOMP = **clump**
CLOMPED ▸ **clomp**
CLOMPS ▸ **clomp**
CLON = **clone**
CLONAL ▸ **clone**
CLONE *n, vb* **cloned, cloner, cloners, clones**
CLONIC ▸ **clonus**
CLONING ▸ **clone**
CLONISM *n* series of clonic spasms
CLONK *vb* make a loud dull thud ▹ *n* loud thud **clonked, clonks**
CLONS ▸ **clon**
CLONUS *n* type of convulsion
CLOOP *n* sound made when a cork is drawn from a bottle **cloops**
CLOOT *n* hoof
CLOOTIE *adj as in* **clootie dumpling** kind of dumpling
CLOOTS ▸ **cloot**
CLOP *vb, n* **clopped, clops**
CLOQUE *n* fabric with an embossed surface **cloques**
CLOSE *vb* shut ▹ *n* end, conclusion ▹ *adj* near ▹ *adv* closely, tightly **closed, closely, closer, closers, closes, closest**
CLOSET *n, adj, vb* **closets**
CLOSEUP *n* photo taken close to subject
CLOSING ▸ **close**
CLOSURE *n, vb*
CLOT *n, vb*
CLOTBUR *n* burdock
CLOTE *n* burdock **clotes**
CLOTH *n*
CLOTHE *vb* **clothed**
CLOTHES *n* garments
CLOTHS ▸ **cloth**
CLOTS ▸ **clot**
CLOTTED ▸ **clot**
CLOTTER *vb* to clot
CLOTTY *adj* full of clots
CLOTURE *n* closure in the US Senate ▹ *vb* end (debate) in the US Senate by cloture
CLOU *n* crux; focus
CLOUD *n, vb* **clouded, clouds**
CLOUDY *adj*
CLOUGH *n* gorge or narrow ravine **cloughs**
CLOUR *vb* to thump or dent **cloured, clours**
CLOUS ▸ **clou**
CLOUT *n, vb* **clouted, clouter, clouts**
CLOVE *n* tropical evergreen myrtaceous tree
CLOVEN ▸ **cleave**
CLOVER *n* **clovers, clovery**
CLOVES ▸ **clove**
CLOVIS *n as in* **clovis point** flint projectile dating from the 10th millennium bc
CLOW *n* clove
CLOWDER *n* collective term for a group of cats
CLOWN *n, vb* **clowned, clowns**
CLOWS ▸ **clow**
CLOY *vb* cause weariness through an excess of something initially pleasurable
CLOYE *vb* to claw
CLOYED ▸ **cloy**
CLOYES ▸ **cloye**
CLOYING *adj*
CLOYS ▸ **cloy**
CLOZE *adj as in* **cloze test** test of the ability to understand text **clozes**
CLUB *n, vb* **clubbed**
CLUBBER *n* person who regularly frequents nightclubs
CLUBBY *adj* sociable, esp effusively so
CLUBMAN *n* man who is an enthusiastic member of a club or clubs **clubmen**

CLUBS ▸ **club**
CLUCK *n, vb* **clucked, clucks**
CLUCKY *adj* wishing to have a baby
CLUDGIE *n* toilet
CLUE *n, vb* **clued, clueing, clues, cluing**
CLUMBER *n* type of thickset spaniel
CLUMP *n, vb* **clumped, clumper, clumps, clumpy**
CLUMSY *adj*
CLUNCH *n* hardened clay
CLUNG ▸ **cling**
CLUNK *n* dull metallic sound ▷ *vb* make such a sound **clunked**
CLUNKER *n* dilapidated old car or other machine
CLUNKS ▸ **clunk**
CLUNKY *adj* making a clunking noise
CLUPEID *n* type of fish
CLUSIA *n* tree of the tropical American genus Clusia **clusias**
CLUSTER *n, vb*
CLUTCH *vb, n*
CLUTCHY *adj* (of a person) tending to cling
CLUTTER *vb, n*
CLY *vb* to steal or seize **clying**

> A little word meaning to seize or steal, this can be useful when you are short of vowels.

CLYPE *vb* tell tales ▷ *n* person who tells tales
CLYPEAL ▸ **clypeus**
CLYPED ▸ **clype**
CLYPEI ▸ **clypeus**
CLYPES ▸ **clype**
CLYPEUS *n* cuticular plate on the head of some insects
CLYPING ▸ **clype**
CLYSTER *a former name for an* ▸ **enema**
CNEMIAL ▸ **cnemis**
CNEMIS *n* shin or tibia
CNIDA *n* nematocyst **cnidae**
COACH *n, vb* **coached**
COACHEE *n* person who receives training from a coach
COACHER ▸ **coach**
COACHES ▸ **coach**
COACHY *n* coachman ▷ *adj* resembling or pertaining to a coach
COACT *vb* to act together **coacted, coactor, coacts**
COADMIT *vb* to admit together
COAEVAL *n* contemporary
COAGENT > **coagency**
COAGULA > **coagulum**
COAITA *n* spider monkey **coaitas**
COAL *n, vb*
COALA = **koala**
COALAS ▸ **coala**
COALBIN *n* bin for holding coal
COALBOX *n* box for holding coal
COALED ▸ **coal**
COALER *n* ship, train, etc, used to carry or supply coal **coalers**
COALIER ▸ **coal**
COALIFY *vb* to turn into coal
COALING ▸ **coal**
COALISE *vb* to form a coalition **coalize**
COALMAN *n* man who delivers coal **coalmen**
COALPIT *n* pit from which coal is extracted
COALS ▸ **coal**
COALY ▸ **coal**
COAMING *n* raised frame round a ship's hatchway for keeping out water
COANNEX *vb* to annex with something else
COAPT *vb* to secure **coapted, coapts**
COARB *n* spiritual successor **coarbs**
COARSE *adj*
COARSEN *vb*
COARSER ▸ **coarse**
COAST *n, vb* **coastal, coasted**
COASTER *n* small mat placed under a glass
COASTS ▸ **coast**
COAT *n, vb*
COATE = **quote**
COATED *adj* covered with an outer layer, film, etc
COATEE *n* short coat, esp for a baby **coatees**
COATER *n* machine that applies a coating to something **coaters**
COATES ▸ **coate**

COATI *n* type of omnivorous mammal
COATING *n*
COATIS ▸ **coati**
COATS ▸ **coat**
COAX *vb*
COAXAL = **coaxial**
COAXED, coaxer, coaxers, coaxes ▸ **coax**
COAXIAL *adj* (of a cable) transmitting by means of two concentric conductors separated by an insulator
COAXING ▸ **coax**
COB *n* stalk of an ear of maize ▹ *vb* beat, esp on the buttocks
COBAEA *n* tropical climbing shrub **cobaeas**
COBALT *n* **cobalts**
COBB = **cob**
COBBED ▸ **cob**
COBBER *n* friend **cobbers**
COBBIER ▸ **cobby**
COBBING ▸ **cob**
COBBLE *n, vb* **cobbled**
COBBLER *n*
COBBLES *pl n* coal in small rounded lumps
COBBS ▸ **cobb**
COBBY *adj* short and stocky
COBIA *n* large dark-striped game fish **cobias**
COBLE *n* small single-masted flat-bottomed fishing boat **cobles**
COBLOAF *n* round loaf of bread
COBNUT *another name for* > **hazelnut**
COBNUTS ▸ **cobnut**
COBRA *n* **cobras, cobric**
COBS ▸ **cob**
COBURG *n* rounded loaf with a cross cut on the top **coburgs**
COBWEB *n* **cobwebs**
COBZA *n* Romanian lute **cobzas**
COCA *n* dried leaves of a S American shrub which contain cocaine
COCAIN = **cocaine**
COCAINE *n*
COCAINS ▸ **cocain**
COCAS ▸ **coca**
COCCAL ▸ **coccus**
COCCI ▸ **coccus**
COCCIC ▸ **coccus**
COCCID *n* type of homopterous insect **coccids**
COCCO *n* taro
COCCOID ▸ **coccus**
COCCOS ▸ **cocco**
COCCOUS ▸ **coccus**
COCCUS *n* any spherical or nearly spherical bacterium
COCCYX *n*
COCH *obsolete variant of* ▸ **coach**
COCHAIR *vb* to chair jointly
COCHES ▸ **coch**
COCHIN *n* large breed of domestic fowl **cochins**
COCHLEA *n* spiral tube in the internal ear
COCK *n, vb*
COCKADE *n* feather or rosette worn on a hat as a badge
COCKED ▸ **cock**
COCKER *n* devotee of cockfighting ▹ *vb* pamper or spoil by indulgence **cockers**
COCKET *n* document issued by a customs officer **cockets**
COCKEYE *n* eye affected with strabismus or one that squints
COCKIER ▸ **cocky**
COCKIES ▸ **cocky**
COCKILY ▸ **cocky**
COCKING ▸ **cock**
COCKISH *adj* wanton
COCKLE *n, vb* **cockled**
COCKLER *n* person employed to gather cockles
COCKLES ▸ **cockle**
COCKNEY *n* native of London, esp of its East End ▹ *adj* characteristic of cockneys or their dialect
COCKPIT *n*
COCKS ▸ **cock**
COCKSHY *n* target aimed at in throwing games
COCKSY *adj* cocky
COCKUP *n* something done badly ▹ *vb* ruin or spoil **cockups**
COCKY *adj, n*
COCO *n* coconut palm
COCOA *n* **cocoas**
COCOMAT *n* mat made from coconut fibre
COCONUT *n*

COCOON *n, vb* **cocoons**
COCOPAN *n* (in South Africa) a small wagon running on narrow-gauge railway lines used in mines
COCOS ▸ coco
COCOTTE *n* small fireproof dish in which individual portions of food are cooked
COCOYAM *n* food plant of West Africa with edible underground stem
COCTILE *adj* made by exposing to heat
COCTION *n* boiling
COD *n, adj, vb*
CODA *n* final part of a musical composition
CODABLE *adj* capable of being coded
CODAS ▸ coda
CODDED ▸ cod
CODDER *n* cod fisherman or his boat **codders**
CODDING ▸ cod
CODDLE *vb, n* **coddled, coddler, coddles**
CODE *n, vb*
CODEC *n* set of electrical equipment **codecs**
CODED ▸ code
CODEIA *n* codeine **codeias**
CODEIN = codeine
CODEINA *obsolete variant of* **▸ codeine**
CODEINE *n* drug used as a painkiller
CODEINS ▸ codein
CODEN *n* identification code assigned to a publication **codens**
CODER *n* person or thing that codes **coders**
CODES ▸ code
CODETTA *n* short coda
CODEX *n* volume of manuscripts of an ancient text
CODFISH *n* cod
CODGER *n* old man **codgers**
CODICES ▸ codex
CODICIL *n* addition to a will
CODIFY *vb*
CODILLA *n* coarse tow of hemp and flax
CODILLE *n* in the cardgame ombre, term indicating that the game is won
CODING ▸ code
CODINGS ▸ code
CODIST *n* codifier **codists**
CODLIN = codling
CODLING *n* young cod
CODLINS ▸ codlin
CODON *n* part of a DNA molecule **codons**
CODRIVE *vb* take alternate turns driving a car with another person **codrove**
CODS ▸ cod
COED *adj* educating both sexes together ▹ *n* school or college that educates both sexes together
COEDIT *vb* edit (a book, newspaper, etc) jointly **coedits**
COEDS ▸ coed
COEHORN *n* type of small artillery mortar
COELIAC *adj* of or relating to the abdomen ▹ *n* person who has coeliac disease
COELOM *n* body cavity of many multicellular animals **coelome, coeloms**
COEMPT *vb* buy up something in its entirety **coempts**
COENACT *vb* to enact jointly
COENURE *variant form of* > **coenurus**
COENURI > coenurus
COEQUAL *n* equal ▹ *adj* of the same size, rank, etc
COERCE *vb* **coerced, coercer, coerces**
COERECT *vb* to erect together
COESITE *n* polymorph of silicon dioxide
COEVAL *n* contemporary ▹ *adj* contemporary **coevals**
COEXERT *vb* to exert together
COEXIST *vb*
COFF *vb* buy **coffed**
COFFEE *n, adj* **coffees**
COFFER *n* chest, esp for storing valuables ▹ *vb* store
COFFERS > cofferdam
COFFIN *n, vb*
COFFING ▸ coff

COFFINS ▸ **coffin**
COFFLE *n* (esp formerly) a line of slaves, beasts, etc, fastened together ▹ *vb* to fasten together in a coffle **coffled, coffles**
COFFRET *n* small coffer
COFFS ▸ **coff**
COFOUND *vb* to found jointly
COFT ▸ **coff**
COG *n, vb*
COGENCE ▸ **cogent**
COGENCY ▸ **cogent**
COGENER *n* congener
COGENT *adj*
COGGED ▸ **cog**
COGGER *n* deceiver **coggers**
COGGIE *n* quaich or drinking cup **coggies**
COGGING ▸ **cog**
COGGLE *vb* wobble or rock **coggled, coggles, coggly**
COGIE = **coggie**
COGIES ▸ **cogie**
COGITO *n* philosophical theory **cogitos**
COGNAC *n* **cognacs**
COGNATE *adj* derived from a common original form ▹ *n* cognate word or language
COGNISE = **cognize**
COGNIZE *vb* perceive, become aware of, or know
COGON *n* type of coarse tropical grass used for thatching **cogons**
COGS ▸ **cog**
COGUE *n* wooden pail or drinking vessel **cogues**
COGWAY *n* rack railway **cogways**
COHAB *n* cohabitor
COHABIT *vb*
COHABS ▸ **cohab**
COHEAD *vb* to head jointly **coheads**
COHEIR *n* person who inherits jointly with others **coheirs**
COHEN ▸ **kohen**
COHENS ▸ **cohen**
COHERE *vb* hold or stick together **cohered**
COHERER *n* electrical component
COHERES ▸ **cohere**
COHIBIT *vb* to restrain
COHO *n* type of Pacific salmon **cohoe, cohoes**
COHOG *n* quahog, an edible clam **cohogs**
COHORN = **coehorn**
COHORNS ▸ **coehorn**
COHORT *n* band of associates **cohorts**
COHOS ▸ **coho**
COHOSH *n* type of North American plant
COHOST *vb* to host jointly **cohosts**
COHUNE *n* tropical feather palm **cohunes**
COIF *vb* arrange the hair of ▹ *n* close-fitting cap worn in the Middle Ages
COIFED *adj* wearing a coif
COIFFE *vb* to coiffure
COIFFED ▸ **coif**
COIFFES ▸ **coiffe**
COIFING ▸ **coif**
COIFS ▸ **coif**
COIGN *vb* wedge ▹ *n* quoin **coigne, coigned**
COIGNES ▸ **coigne**
COIGNS ▸ **coign**
COIL *vb, n* **coiled, coiler, coilers, coiling, coils**
COIN *n, vb*
COINAGE *n*
COINED ▸ **coin**
COINER ▸ **coin**
COINERS ▸ **coin**
COINFER *vb* infer jointly
COINING ▸ **coin**
COINOP *adj* (of a machine) operated by putting a coin in a slot
COINS ▸ **coin**
COINTER *vb* to inter together
COIR *n* coconut fibre, used for matting **coirs**
COIT *n* buttocks
COITAL ▸ **coitus**
COITION = **coitus**
COITS ▸ **coit**
COITUS *n*
COJOIN *vb* to conjoin **cojoins**
COJONES *pl n* testicles
COKE *n, vb* **coked**
COKES *n* fool **cokeses**
COKIER ▸ **coky**
COKIEST ▸ **coky**
COKING ▸ **coke**
COKY *adj* like coke
COL *n* high mountain pass
COLA *n* dark brown fizzy soft drink **colas**
COLBIES ▸ **colby**

COLBY *n* type of mild-tasting hard cheese **colbys**
COLD *adj*, *n* **colder, coldest**
COLDIE *n* cold can or bottle of beer **coldies**
COLDISH ▸ **cold**
COLDLY ▸ **cold**
COLDS ▸ **cold**
COLE = **cabbage**
COLEAD *vb* to lead together **coleads, coled**
COLES ▸ **cole**
COLETIT *n* coal tit
COLEUS *n* Old World plant
COLEY = **coalfish**
COLEYS ▸ **coley**
COLIBRI *n* hummingbird
COLIC *n*
COLICIN *n* bacteriocidal protein
COLICKY *adj* relating to or suffering from colic
COLICS ▸ **colic**
COLIES ▸ **coly**
COLIN *n* quail **colins**
COLITIC ▸ **colitis**
COLITIS *n* inflammation of the colon
COLL *vb* to embrace
COLLAGE *n*, *vb*
COLLAR *n*, *vb*
COLLARD *n* variety of the cabbage with a crown of edible leaves
COLLARS ▸ **collar**
COLLATE *vb*
COLLECT *vb*, *n*
COLLED ▸ **coll**
COLLEEN *n* girl
COLLEGE *n*
COLLET *n* (in a jewellery setting) a band or coronet-shaped claw that holds an individual stone ▹ *vb* mount in a collet **collets**
COLLIDE *vb*
COLLIE *n*
COLLIED ▸ **colly**
COLLIER *n* coal miner
COLLIES ▸ **colly**
COLLING *n* embrace
COLLINS *n* type of cocktail
COLLOID *n* suspension of particles in a solution ▹ *adj* of or relating to the gluelike translucent material found in certain degenerating tissues
COLLOP *n* small slice of meat **collops**
COLLS ▸ **coll**
COLLUDE *vb*
COLLY *n* soot or grime, such as coal dust ▹ *vb* begrime
COLOBI ▸ **colobus**
COLOBID ▸ **colobus**
COLOBUS *n* type of Old World monkey
COLOG *n* logarithm of the reciprocal of a number
COLOGNE *n*
COLOGS ▸ **colog**
COLON *n* **colone**
COLONEL *n*
COLONES ▸ **colone**
COLONI ▸ **colonus**
COLONIC *adj* of or relating to the colon ▹ *n* irrigation of the colon
COLONS ▸ **colon**
COLONUS *n* ancient Roman farmer
COLONY *n*
COLOR = **colour**
COLORED *US spelling of* > **coloured**
COLORER ▸ **color**
COLORS ▸ **color**
COLORY = **coloury**
COLOSSI > **colossus**
COLOUR *n* appearance of things as a result of reflecting light ▹ *vb* apply colour to **colours**
COLOURY *adj* possessing colour
COLS ▸ **col**
COLT *n*, *vb*
COLTAN *n* metallic ore **coltans**
COLTED ▸ **colt**
COLTER = **coulter**
COLTERS ▸ **coulter**
COLTING ▸ **colt**
COLTISH *adj* inexperienced
COLTS ▸ **colt**
COLUGO *n* flying lemur **colugos**
COLUMEL *n* in botany, the central column in a capsule
COLUMN *n*, *vb* **columns**
COLURE *n* either of two great circles on the celestial sphere **colures**
COLY *n* S African arboreal bird

COLZA *n* oilseed rape, a Eurasian plant with bright yellow flowers **colzas**
COMA *n*
COMADE ▸ **comake**
COMAE ▸ **coma**
COMAKE *vb* to make together **comaker, comakes**
COMAL ▸ **coma**
COMARB = **coarb**
COMARBS ▸ **comarb**
COMART *n* covenant **comarts**
COMAS ▸ **coma**
COMATE *adj* having tufts of hair ▹ *n* companion **comates**
COMATIC ▸ **coma**
COMATIK *variant of* ▸ **komatik**
COMB *n, vb*
COMBAT *vb, n* **combats**
COMBE = **comb**
COMBED ▸ **comb**
COMBER *n* long curling wave **combers**
COMBES ▸ **combe**
COMBI *n* combination boiler
COMBIER ▸ **comby**
COMBIES ▸ **comby**
COMBINE *vb, n*
COMBING ▸ **comb**
COMBIS ▸ **combi**
COMBLE *n* apex; zenith **combles**
COMBO *n* small group of jazz musicians **combos**
COMBS ▸ **comb**
COMBUST *adj* invisible due to proximity to the sun ▹ *vb* burn
COMBY *adj* comb-like ▹ *n* combination boiler
COME *vb*
COMEDIC *adj* of or relating to comedy
COMEDO *the technical name for* > **blackhead**
COMEDOS ▸ **comedo**
COMEDY *n*
COMELY *adj*
COMER *n* person who comes **comers**
COMES ▸ **come**
COMET *n*
COMETH ▸ **come**
COMETIC ▸ **comet**
COMETS ▸ **comet**
COMFIER ▸ **comfy**
COMFIT *n* sugar-coated sweet **comfits**
COMFORT *n, vb*
COMFREY *n* tall plant with bell-shaped flowers
COMFY *adj* comfortable
COMIC *adj, n*
COMICAL *adj*
COMICE *n* kind of pear **comices**
COMICS ▸ **comic**
COMING ▸ **come**
COMINGS ▸ **come**
COMIQUE *n* comic actor
COMITAL *adj* relating to a count or earl
COMITIA *n* ancient Roman assembly
COMITY *n* friendly politeness, esp between different countries
COMIX *n* comic books in general
COMM *n as in* **comm badge** small wearable badge-shaped radio transmitter and receiver
COMMA *n*
COMMAND *vb, n*
COMMAS ▸ **comma**
COMMATA ▸ **comma**
COMMEND *vb*
COMMENT *n, vb*
COMMER = **comer**
COMMERE *n* female compere
COMMERS ▸ **commer**
COMMIE *adj* communist **commies**
COMMIS *n* apprentice waiter or chef ▹ *adj* (of a waiter or chef) apprentice
COMMIT *vb* **commits**
COMMIX *a rare word for* ▸ **mix**
COMMIXT ▸ **commix**
COMMO *short for* > **communist**
COMMODE *n* seat with a hinged flap concealing a chamber pot
COMMODO = **comodo**
COMMON *adj, n, vb*
COMMONS *n* people not of noble birth viewed as forming a political order
COMMOS ▸ **commo**
COMMOT *n* in medieval Wales, a division of land **commote, commots**
COMMOVE *vb* disturb
COMMS *pl n* communications

COMMUNE *n, vb*
COMMUTE *vb, n*
COMMY = **commie**
COMODO *adv* (to be performed) at a convenient relaxed speed
COMOSE *another word for* ▸ **comate**
COMOUS *adj* hairy
COMP *n* person who sets and corrects type ▹ *vb* set or correct type
COMPACT *adj, n, vb*
COMPAGE *obsolete form of* > **compages**
COMPAND *vb* (of a transmitter signal) to compress before, and expand after, transmission
COMPANY *n, vb*
COMPARE *vb*
COMPART *vb* to divide into parts
COMPAS *n* rhythm in flamenco
COMPASS *n, vb*
COMPAST *adj* rounded
COMPEAR *vb* in Scots law, to appear in court
COMPED > **compositor**
COMPEER *n* person of equal rank, status, or ability ▹ *vb* to equal
COMPEL *vb* **compels**
COMPEND *n* compendium
COMPER *n* person who regularly enters competitions
COMPERE *n, vb*
COMPERS ▸ **comper**
COMPETE *vb*
COMPILE *vb*
COMPING ▸ **comp**
COMPLEX *adj, n, vb*
COMPLIN = **compline**
COMPLOT *n* plot or conspiracy ▹ *vb* plot together
COMPLY *vb*
COMPO *n* mixture of materials, such as mortar, plaster, etc ▹ *adj* intended to last for several days
COMPONE = **compony**
COMPONY *adj* made up of alternating metal and colour, colour and fur, or fur and metal
COMPORT *vb* behave (oneself) in a specified way
COMPOS ▸ **compo**
COMPOSE *vb*
COMPOST *n, vb*
COMPOT = **compote**
COMPOTE *n* fruit stewed with sugar
COMPOTS ▸ **compot**
COMPS ▸ **comp**
COMPT *obsolete variant of* ▸ **count**
COMPTED ▸ **compt**
COMPTER *n* formerly, a prison
COMPTS ▸ **count**
COMPUTE *vb, n*
COMRADE *n*
COMS *pl n* one-piece woollen undergarment with long sleeves and legs
COMTE *n* European nobleman **comtes**
COMUS *n* wild party **comuses**
CON *vb, n, prep*
CONACRE *n* farming land let for a season or for eleven months ▹ *vb* to let conacre
CONARIA > **conarium**
CONATUS *n* effort or striving of natural impulse
CONCAVE *adj, vb*
CONCEAL *vb*
CONCEDE *vb*
CONCEDO *interj* I allow; I concede (a point)
CONCEIT *n, vb*
CONCENT *n* concord, as of sounds, voices, etc
CONCEPT *n*
CONCERN *n, vb*
CONCERT *n*
CONCH = **concha**
CONCHA *n* any bodily organ or part resembling a shell in shape **conchae, conchal, conchas**
CONCHE *vb* (in chocolate-making) to use a conche **conched, conches**
CONCHIE *n* conscientious objector
CONCHO *n* American metal ornament **conchos**
CONCHS ▸ **conch**
CONCHY = **conchie**
CONCISE *adj, vb*
CONCOCT *vb*
CONCORD *n* state of peaceful agreement, harmony ▹ *vb* to agree

CONCREW *vb* to grow together
CONCUPY *n* concupiscence
CONCUR *vb* **concurs**
CONCUSS *vb* injure (the brain) by a fall or blow
COND *old inflection of* ▸ **con**
CONDEMN *vb*
CONDER *n* person who directs the steering of a vessel **conders**
CONDIE *n* culvert; tunnel **condies**
CONDIGN *adj* (esp of a punishment) fitting
CONDO *n* condominium **condoes**
CONDOLE *vb* express sympathy with someone in grief, pain, etc
CONDOM *n* **condoms**
CONDONE *vb*
CONDOR *n* large vulture of S America **condors**
CONDOS ▸ **condo**
CONDUCE *vb* lead or contribute (to a result)
CONDUCT *n*, *vb*
CONDUIT *n*
CONDYLE *n* rounded projection on the articulating end of a bone
CONE *n*, *vb* **coned, cones**
CONEY = **cony**
CONEYS ▸ **coney**
CONF *n* online forum
CONFAB *n* conversation ▹ *vb* converse **confabs**
CONFECT *vb* prepare by combining ingredients
CONFER *vb* **confers**
CONFESS *vb*
CONFEST *adj* admitted
CONFIDE *vb*
CONFINE *vb*, *n*
CONFIRM *vb*
CONFIT *n* preserve **confits**
CONFIX *vb* to fasten
CONFLUX *n* merging or folowing togther, especially of rivers
CONFORM *vb*
CONFS ▸ **conf**
CONFUSE *vb*
CONFUTE *vb* prove wrong
CONGA *n* dance performed by a number of people in single file ▹ *vb* dance the conga **congaed, congas**
CONGE *n* permission to depart or dismissal, esp when formal ▹ *vb* to take one's leave
CONGEAL *vb*
CONGED ▸ **conge**
CONGEE = **conge**
CONGEED ▸ **congee**
CONGEES ▸ **congee**
CONGER *n* **congers**
CONGES ▸ **conge**
CONGEST *vb* crowd or become crowded to excess
CONGII ▸ **congius**
CONGIUS *n* unit of liquid measure equal to 1 Imperial gallon
CONGO = **congou**
CONGOES ▸ **congou**
CONGOS ▸ **congo**
CONGOU *n* kind of black tea from China **congous**
CONGREE *vb* to agree
CONGRUE *vb* to agree
CONI ▸ **conus**
CONIA = **coniine**
CONIAS ▸ **coniine**
CONIC *adj* having the shape of a cone
CONICAL *adj*
CONICS *n* branch of geometry
CONIDIA > **conidium**
CONIES ▸ **cony**
CONIFER *n*
CONIINE *n* colourless poisonous soluble liquid alkaloid found in hemlock
CONIMA *n* gum resin from the conium hemlock tree **conimas**
CONIN = **coniine**
CONINE = **coniine**
CONINES ▸ **conine**
CONING ▸ **cone**
CONINS ▸ **conin**
CONIUM *n* N temperate umbelliferous plant, esp hemlock **coniums**
CONJECT *vb* to conjecture
CONJEE *vb* prepare as, or in, a conjee (a gruel of boiled rice and water) **conjeed, conjees**
CONJOIN *vb* join or become joined
CONJURE *vb* perform tricks that appear to

be magic
CONJURY *n* magic
CONK *n* nose ▷ *vb* strike (someone) on the head or nose **conked**
CONKER *n*
CONKERS *n* game played with conkers tied on strings
CONKIER ▶ **conky**
CONKING ▶ **conk**
CONKS ▶ **conk**
CONKY *adj* affected by the timber disease, conk
CONN = **con**
CONNATE *adj* existing in a person or thing from birth
CONNE = **con**
CONNECT *vb*
CONNED ▶ **con**
CONNER = **conder**
CONNERS ▶ **conner**
CONNES ▶ **conne**
CONNIE *n* **connies**
CONNING ▶ **con**
CONNIVE *vb*
CONNOTE *vb* imply or suggest
CONNS ▶ **conn**
CONOID *n* geometric surface ▷ *adj* conical, cone-shaped **conoids**
CONQUER *vb*
CONS ▶ **con**
CONSEIL *n* advice
CONSENT *n*, *vb*
CONSIGN *vb*
CONSIST *vb*
CONSOL *n* consolidated annuity, a British government bond
CONSOLE *vb*, *n*
CONSOLS *pl n* irredeemable British government securities
CONSORT *vb*, *n*
CONSPUE *vb* spit on with contempt
CONSTER *obsolete variant of* > **construe**
CONSUL *n* **consuls**
CONSULT *vb*
CONSUME *vb*
CONTACT *n*, *vb*, *interj*
CONTAIN *vb*
CONTE *n* tale or short story, esp of adventure
CONTECK *n* contention
CONTEMN *vb* regard with contempt
CONTEND *vb*
CONTENT *n* meaning or substance of a piece of writing ▷ *adj* satisfied with things as they are ▷ *vb* make (someone) content
CONTES ▶ **conte**
CONTEST *n*, *vb*
CONTEXT *n*
CONTO *n* former Portuguese monetary unit worth 1000 escudos
CONTORT *vb* twist out of shape
CONTOS ▶ **conto**
CONTOUR *n*, *vb*
CONTRA *n* counter-argument **contras**
CONTRAT *old form of* > **contract**
CONTROL *n*, *vb*
CONTUND *vb* to pummel
CONTUSE *vb* injure (the body) without breaking the skin
CONURE *n* small American parrot **conures**
CONUS *n* any of several cone-shaped structures
CONVECT *vb* to circulate hot air by convection
CONVENE *vb*
CONVENT *n*, *vb*
CONVERT *vb*, *n*
CONVEX *adj*, *vb*
CONVEY *vb* **conveys**
CONVICT *vb*, *n*, *adj*
CONVIVE *vb* to feast together
CONVO *n* conversation
CONVOKE *vb* call together
CONVOS ▶ **convo**
CONVOY *n*, *vb* **convoys**
CONY *n* rabbit
COO *vb*, *n*, *interj*
COOCOO *old spelling of* ▶ **cuckoo**
COOED ▶ **coo**
COOEE *interj* call to attract attention ▷ *vb* utter this call ▷ *n* calling distance **cooeed, cooees**
COOER ▶ **coo**
COOERS ▶ **coo**
COOEY = **cooee**
COOEYED ▶ **cooey**
COOEYS ▶ **cooey**
COOF *n* simpleton **coofs**
COOING ▶ **coo**
COOINGS ▶ **coo**

COOK *vb, n* **cooked**
COOKER *n* **cookers**
COOKERY *n*
COOKEY = **cookie**
COOKEYS ▸ **cookey**
COOKIE *n* **cookies**
COOKING ▸ **cook**
COOKOFF *n* cookery competition
COOKOUT *n* party where a meal is cooked and eaten out of doors
COOKS ▸ **cook**
COOKTOP *n* flat unit for cooking in saucepans or the top part of a stove
COOKY = **cookie**
COOL *adj, vb, n*
COOLANT *n*
COOLED ▸ **cool**
COOLER *n* container for making or keeping things cool **coolers**
COOLEST ▸ **cool**
COOLIE *n* unskilled Oriental labourer **coolies**
COOLING *n as in* **regenerative cooling**
COOLISH ▸ **cool**
COOLLY ▸ **cool**
COOLS ▸ **cool**
COOLTH *n* coolness **coolths**
COOLY = **coolie**
COOM *n* waste material ▹ *vb* to blacken
COOMB = **comb**
COOMBE ▸ **comb**
COOMBES ▸ **coombe**
COOMBS ▸ **coomb**
COOMED ▸ **coom**
COOMIER ▸ **coomy**
COOMING ▸ **coom**
COOMS ▸ **coom**
COOMY *adj* grimy
COON *n* raccoon
COONCAN *n* card game for two players, similar to rummy
COONDOG *n* dog trained to hunt raccoons
COONS ▸ **coon**
COONTIE *n* evergreen plant of S Florida **coonty**
COOP *n, vb* **cooped**
COOPER *n* person who makes or repairs barrels ▹ *vb* make or mend (barrels, casks, etc) **coopers**
COOPERY = **cooperage**
COOPING ▸ **coop**
COOPS ▸ **coop**
COOPT *vb* **coopted, coopts**
COORIE = **courie**
COORIED ▸ **coorie**
COORIES ▸ **coorie**
COOS ▸ **coo**
COOSEN = **cozen**
COOSENS ▸ **coosen**
COOSER *n* stallion **coosers**
COOSIN = **cozen**
COOSINS ▸ **coosin**
COOST *Scots form of* ▸ **cast**
COOT *n*
COOTCH *n* hiding place ▹ *vb* hide
COOTER *n* type of freshwater turtle **cooters**
COOTIE ▸ **louse**
COOTIES ▸ **cootie**
COOTS ▸ **coot**
COP = **copper**
COPAIBA *n* resin obtained from certain tropical trees **copaiva**
COPAL *n* resin used in varnishes
COPALM *n* aromatic resin **copalms**
COPALS ▸ **copal**
COPAY *n* amount payable for treatment by person with medical insurance **copays**
COPE *vb, n*
COPECK = **kopeck**
COPECKS ▸ **copeck**
COPED ▸ **cope**
COPEN *n* shade of blue **copens**
COPEPOD *n* type of minute crustacean
COPER *n* horse-dealer ▹ *vb* smuggle liquor to deep-sea fishermen **copered, copers**
COPES ▸ **cope**
COPIED ▸ **copy**
COPIER *n* machine that copies **copiers**
COPIES ▸ **copy**
COPIHUE *n* Chilean bellflower
COPILOT *n* second pilot of an aircraft
COPING *n* sloping top row of a wall **copings**
COPIOUS *adj*
COPITA *n* tulip-shaped sherry glass **copitas**

COPLOT *vb* plot together **coplots**
COPOUT *n* act of avoiding responsibility **copouts**
COPPED ▸ **copper**
COPPER *n, adj, vb* **coppers, coppery**
COPPICE *n, vb*
COPPIES ▸ **coppy**
COPPIN *n* ball of thread
COPPING ▸ **copper**
COPPINS ▸ **coppin**
COPPLE *n* hill rising to a point **copples**
COPPRA = **copra**
COPPRAS ▸ **coppra**
COPPY *n* small wooden stool
COPRA *n* dried oil-yielding kernel of the coconut **coprah**
COPRAHS ▸ **coprah**
COPRAS ▸ **copra**
COPS ▸ **copper**
COPSE = **coppice**
COPSED ▸ **copse**
COPSES ▸ **copse**
COPSHOP *n* police station
COPSIER ▸ **copsy**
COPSING ▸ **copse**
COPSY *adj* having copses
COPTER *n* helicopter **copters**
COPULA *n* verb used to link the subject and complement of a sentence **copulae, copular, copulas**
COPY *n, vb*
COPYBOY *n* formerly, in journalism, boy who carried copy and ran errands
COPYCAT *n* person who imitates or copies someone ▹ *vb* to imitate with great attention to detail
COPYING ▸ **copy**
COPYISM *n* slavish copying
COPYIST *n* person who makes written copies
COQUET *vb* behave flirtatiously **coquets**
COQUINA *n* soft limestone
COQUITO *n* Chilean palm tree yielding edible nuts and a syrup
COR *interj* exclamation of surprise, amazement, or admiration
CORACLE *n*
CORAL *n, adj*
CORALLA > **corallum**
CORALS ▸ **coral**
CORAM *prep* before, in the presence of
CORANTO = **courante**
CORBAN *n* gift to God **corbans**
CORBE *obsolete variant of* ▸ **corbel**
CORBEAU *n* blackish green colour
CORBEIL *n* carved ornament in the form of a basket of fruit, flowers, etc
CORBEL *n* stone or timber support sticking out of a wall ▹ *vb* lay (a stone or brick) so that it forms a corbel **corbels**
CORBES ▸ **corbe**
CORBIE *n* raven or crow **corbies**
CORBINA *n* type of North American whiting
CORBY = **corbie**
CORCASS *n* in Ireland, marshland
CORD *n, adj, vb*
CORDAGE *n* lines and rigging of a vessel
CORDATE *adj* heart-shaped
CORDED *adj* tied or fastened with cord
CORDER ▸ **cord**
CORDERS ▸ **cord**
CORDIAL *adj, n*
CORDING ▸ **cord**
CORDITE *n*
CORDOBA *n* standard monetary unit of Nicaragua
CORDON *n, vb* **cordons**
CORDS *pl n* trousers made of corduroy
CORE *n, vb* **cored**
COREIGN *vb* to reign jointly
CORELLA *n* white Australian cockatoo
COREMIA > **coremium**
CORER ▸ **core**
CORERS ▸ **core**
CORES ▸ **core**
CORF *n* wagon or basket used formerly in mines
CORGI *n* short-legged sturdy dog **corgis**
CORIA ▸ **corium**

CORIES ▸ **cory**
CORING ▸ **core**
CORIOUS *adj* leathery
CORIUM *n* deep inner layer of the skin **coriums**
CORIVAL = **corrival**
CORIXID *n* type of water bug
CORK *n, vb, adj*
CORKAGE *n* restaurant's charge for serving wine bought elsewhere
CORKED *adj* (of wine) spoiled through having a decayed cork
CORKER *n* splendid or outstanding person or thing **corkers**
CORKIER ▸ **corky**
CORKING *adj* excellent
CORKIR *n* lichen from which red or purple dye is made **corkirs**
CORKS ▸ **cork**
CORKY = **corked**
CORM *n*
CORMEL *n* new small corm arising from the base of a fully developed one **cormels**
CORMOID *adj* like a corm
CORMOUS ▸ **corm**
CORMS ▸ **corm**
CORMUS *n* corm
CORN *n, vb*
CORNAGE *n* rent fixed according to the number of horned cattle pastured
CORNCOB *n* core of an ear of maize, to which the kernels are attached
CORNEA *n* **corneae, corneal, corneas**
CORNED *adj* preserved in salt or brine
CORNEL *n* type of plant such as the dogwood and dwarf cornel **cornels**
CORNER *n, vb* **corners**
CORNET = **cornett**
CORNETS ▸ **cornet**
CORNETT *n* musical instrument
CORNFED *adj* fed on corn
CORNFLY *n* small fly
CORNI ▸ **corno**
CORNICE *n, vb*
CORNIER ▸ **corny**
CORNIFY *vb* turn soft tissue hard
CORNILY ▸ **corny**
CORNING ▸ **corn**
CORNIST *n* horn-player
CORNO *n* French horn
CORNROW *n* hairstyle in which the hair is plaited in close parallel rows ▹ *vb* style the hair in a cornrow
CORNS ▸ **corn**
CORNU *n* part or structure resembling a horn or having a hornlike pattern **cornua, cornual**
CORNUS *n* any member of the genus Cornus, such as dogwood
CORNUTE *adj* having or resembling cornua ▹ *vb* to make a cuckold of
CORNUTO *n* cuckold
CORNY *adj*
CORODY *n* feudal law
COROLLA *n* petals of a flower collectively
CORONA *n* ring of light round the moon or sun **coronae**
CORONAL *n* circlet for the head ▹ *adj* of or relating to a corona or coronal
CORONAS ▸ **corona**
CORONEL *n* iron head of a tilting spear
CORONER *n*
CORONET *n*
CORONIS *n* symbol used in Greek writing
COROZO *n* tropical American palm whose seeds yield a useful oil **corozos**
CORPORA ▸ **corpus**
CORPS *n*
CORPSE *n, vb* **corpsed, corpses**
CORPUS *n* collection of writings, esp by a single author
CORRADE *vb* to erode by the abrasive action of rock particles
CORRAL *n* enclosure for cattle or horses ▹ *vb* put in a corral **corrals**
CORREA *n* **correas**
CORRECT *adj, vb*
CORRIDA *the Spanish word for* > **bullfight**
CORRIE = **cirque**

CORRIES ▸ **corrie**
CORRODE *vb*
CORRODY = **corody**
CORRUPT *adj*, *vb*
CORS ▸ **cor**
CORSAC *n* type of fox of central Asia **corsacs**
CORSAGE *n* small bouquet worn on the bodice of a dress
CORSAIR *n* pirate
CORSE *n* corpse **corses**
CORSET *n*, *vb* **corsets**
CORSEY *n* pavement or pathway **corseys**
CORSIVE *n* corrodent
CORSLET = **corselet**
CORSNED *n* ordeal to discover innocence or guilt
CORSO *n* promenade **corsos**
CORTEGE *n*
CORTEX *n*
CORTILE *n* open, internal courtyard **cortili**
CORTIN *n* adrenal cortex extract
CORTINA *n* weblike part of certain mushrooms
CORTINS ▸ **cortin**
CORULER *n* joint ruler
CORVEE *n* day's unpaid labour owed by a feudal vassal to his lord **corvees**
CORVES ▸ **corf**
CORVET = **curvet**
CORVETS ▸ **corvet**
CORVID *n* any member of the crow family **corvids**
CORVINA = **corbina**
CORVINE *adj* of, relating to, or resembling a crow
CORVUS *n* type of ancient hook
CORY *n* catfish belonging to the South American Corydoras genus
CORYLUS *n* hazel genus
CORYMB *n* flat-topped flower cluster ▷ *vb* be corymb-like **corymbs**
CORYPHE *n* coryphaeus
CORYZA *n* acute inflammation in the nose **coryzal, coryzas**
COS = **cosine**
COSE *vb* get cosy
COSEC = **cosecant**
COSECH *n* hyperbolic cosecant **cosechs**
COSECS ▸ **cosec**
COSED ▸ **cose**
COSES ▸ **cose**
COSET *n* mathematical set **cosets**
COSEY *n* tea cosy **coseys**
COSH *n* heavy blunt weapon ▷ *vb* hit with a cosh **coshed**
COSHER *vb* pamper or coddle **coshers**
COSHERY *n* Irish chief's right to lodge at his tenants' houses
COSHES ▸ **cosh**
COSHING ▸ **cosh**
COSIE = **cosy**
COSIED ▸ **cosy**
COSIER *n* cobbler **cosiers**
COSIES ▸ **cosy**
COSIEST ▸ **cosy**
COSIGN *vb* to sign jointly **cosigns**
COSILY ▸ **cosy**
COSINE *n* **cosines**
COSING ▸ **cose**
COSMEA *n* plant of the genus Cosmos **cosmeas**
COSMIC *adj*
COSMID *n* segment of DNA **cosmids**
COSMIN = **cosmine**
COSMINE *n* substance resembling dentine
COSMINS ▸ **cosmin**
COSMISM *n* Russian cultural and philosophical movement **cosmist**
COSMOID *adj* (of the scales of coelacanths and lungfish) consisting of two inner bony layers and an outer layer of cosmine
COSMOS *n*
COSS *another name for* ▸ **kos**
COSSACK *n* Slavonic warrior-peasant
COSSES ▸ **coss**
COSSET *vb*, *n* **cossets**
COSSIE *n* informal name for a swimming costume **cossies**
COST *n*, *vb*
COSTA *n* riblike part, such as the midrib of a plant leaf **costae**
COSTAL *n* strengthening rib of an insect's wing **costals**

COSTAR *n* actor who shares the billing with another ▷ *vb* share the billing with another actor
COSTARD *n* English variety of apple tree
COSTARS ▶ **costar**
COSTATE *adj* having ribs
COSTE *vb* to draw near
COSTEAN *vb* to mine for lodes
COSTED ▶ **cost**
COSTER *n* person who sells fruit, vegetables etc from a barrow **costers**
COSTES ▶ **coste**
COSTING *n as in* **marginal costing**
COSTIVE *adj* having or causing constipation
COSTLY *adj*
COSTREL *n* flask, usually of earthenware or leather
COSTS ▶ **cost**
COSTUME *n*, *vb*
COSTUS *n* Himalayan herb with an aromatic root
COSY *adj*, *n*, *vb* **cosying**
COT *n*, *vb*
COTAN = **cotangent**
COTANS > **cotangent**
COTE ▶ **cot**
COTEAU *n* hillside **coteaux**
COTED ▶ **cot**
COTERIE *n* exclusive group, clique
COTES ▶ **cote**
COTH *n* hyperbolic cotangent **coths**
COTHURN = **cothurnus**
COTIDAL *adj* (of a line on a tidal chart) joining points at which high tide occurs simultaneously
COTING ▶ **cot**
COTINGA *n* tropical bird
COTISE = **cottise**
COTISED ▶ **cotise**
COTISES ▶ **cotise**
COTLAND *n* grounds that belong to a cotter
COTS ▶ **cot**
COTT = **cot**
COTTA *n* short form of surplice **cottae**
COTTAGE *n*, *vb*
COTTAR = **cotter**
COTTARS ▶ **cottar**
COTTAS ▶ **cotta**
COTTED ▶ **cot**
COTTER *n* pin or wedge used to secure machine parts ▷ *vb* secure (two parts) with a cotter
COTTERS ▶ **cottier**
COTTID *n* type of fish typically with a large head, tapering body, and spiny fins **cottids**
COTTIER = **cotter**
COTTING ▶ **cot**
COTTISE *n* type of heraldic decoration ▷ *vb* (in heraldry) decorate with a cottise
COTTOID *adj* resembing a fish of the genus Cottus
COTTON *n*, *vb* **cottons, cottony, cottown**
COTTS ▶ **cott**
COTTUS *n* type of fish with four yellowish knobs on its head
COTWAL *n* Indian police officer **cotwals**
COTYLAE ▶ **cotyle**
COTYLE *n* cuplike cavity **cotyles**
COTYPE *n* type specimen in biological study **cotypes**
COUCAL *n* type of ground-living bird of Africa, S Asia, and Australia, with long strong legs **coucals**
COUCH *n*, *vb*
COUCHE *adj* in heraldry (of a shield), tilted
COUCHED ▶ **couch**
COUCHEE *n* reception held late at night
COUCHER ▶ **couch**
COUCHES ▶ **couch**
COUDE *adj* relating to the construction of a reflecting telescope
COUGAN *n* drunk and rowdy person **cougans**
COUGAR *n* **cougars**
COUGH *vb*, *n* **coughed, cougher, coughs**
COUGUAR = **cougar**
COULD ▶ **can**
COULDST *vb* form of 'could' used with the pronoun *thou* or its relative form
COULEE *n* flow of molten lava **coulees**
COULIS *n* thin purée of vegetables or fruit

COULOIR *n* deep gully on a mountain side, esp in the French Alps
COULOMB *n*
COULTER *n* blade at the front of a ploughshare
COUNCIL *n, adj*
COUNSEL *n, vb*
COUNT *vb, n* **counted**
COUNTER *n, vb, adv*
COUNTRY *n*
COUNTS ▸ **count**
COUNTY *n, adj*
COUP *n, vb*
COUPE *n* sports car with two doors and a sloping fixed roof
COUPED ▸ **coup**
COUPEE *n* dance movement **coupees**
COUPER *n* dealer **coupers**
COUPES ▸ **coupe**
COUPING ▸ **coup**
COUPLE *n, vb* **coupled**
COUPLER *n* mechanical device
COUPLES ▸ **couple**
COUPLET *n*
COUPON *n* **coupons**
COUPS ▸ **coup**
COUPURE *n* entrenchment made by beseiged forces behind a breach
COUR *obsolete variant of* ▸ **cover**
COURAGE *n*
COURANT *n* courante ▹ *adj* (of an animal) running
COURB *vb* to bend **courbed, courbs**
COURD *obsolete variant of* ▸ **covered**
COURE *obsolete variant of* ▸ **cover**
COURED ▸ **coure**
COURES ▸ **coure**
COURIE *vb* nestle or snuggle **couried**
COURIER *n, vb*
COURIES ▸ **courie**
COURING ▸ **cour**
COURLAN *another name for* ▸ **limpkin**
COURS ▸ **cour**
COURSE *n, vb* **coursed**
COURSER *n* swift horse
COURSES *another word for* ▸ **menses**
COURT *n, vb* **courted**
COURTER *n* suitor
COURTLY *adj* ceremoniously polite
COURTS ▸ **court**
COUSIN *n* **cousins**
COUTA *n* **coutas**
COUTEAU *n* large two-edged knife used formerly as a weapon
COUTER *n* armour designed to protect the elbow **couters**
COUTH *adj* refined ▹ *n* refinement **couther**
COUTHIE *adj* sociable
COUTHS ▸ **couth**
COUTHY = **couthie**
COUTIL *n* type of tightly-woven twill cloth **coutils**
COUTURE *n, adj*
COUVADE *n* custom in certain cultures relating to childbirth
COUVERT *another word for* ▸ **cover**
COUZIN *n* South African word for a friend **couzins**
COVARY *vb* vary together maintaining a certain mathematical relationship
COVE *n, vb* **coved**
COVELET *n* small cove
COVEN *n* meeting of witches **covens**
COVENT = **convent**
COVENTS ▸ **covent**
COVER *vb, n* **covered, coverer, covers**
COVERT *adj, n* **coverts**
COVERUP *n* concealment of a mistake, crime, etc
COVES ▸ **cove**
COVET *vb* **coveted, coveter, covets**
COVEY *n* small flock of grouse or partridge **coveys**
COVIN *n* conspiracy between two or more persons
COVING = **cove**
COVINGS ▸ **coving**
COVINS ▸ **covin**
COVYNE = **covin**
COVYNES ▸ **covyne**
COW *n, vb*
COWAGE *n* tropical climbing plant **cowages**
COWAL *n* shallow lake or swampy depression supporting vegetation **cowals**
COWAN *n* drystone waller **cowans**
COWARD *n, vb* **cowards**

COWBANE *n* poisonous marsh plant
COWBELL *n* bell hung around a cow's neck
COWBIND *n* any of various bryony plants, esp the white bryony
COWBIRD *n* American oriole with a dark plumage and short bill
COWBOY *n, vb* **cowboys**
COWED ▶ **cow**
COWEDLY ▶ **cow**
COWER *vb* **cowered, cowers**
COWFISH *n* type of trunkfish with hornlike spines over the eyes
COWFLAP *n* cow dung
COWFLOP *n* foxglove
COWGIRL *n* female cowboy
COWHAGE = **cowage**
COWHAND = **cowboy**
COWHEEL *n* heel of a cow, used as cooking ingredient
COWHERB *n* European plant with clusters of pink flowers
COWHERD *n* person employed to tend cattle
COWHIDE *n* hide of a cow ▷ *vb* to lash with a cowhide whip
COWIER ▶ **cowy**
COWIEST ▶ **cowy**
COWING ▶ **cow**
COWISH *adj* cowardly
COWITCH *another name for* ▶ **cowage**
COWK *vb* retch or feel nauseated **cowked, cowking, cowks**
COWL = **cowling**
COWLED *adj* wearing a cowl
COWLICK *n* tuft of hair over the forehead
COWLING *n* cover on an engine
COWLS ▶ **cowl**
COWMAN *n* man who owns cattle **cowmen**
COWP = **coup**
COWPAT *n* pool of cow dung **cowpats**
COWPEA *n* type of tropical climbing plant **cowpeas**
COWPED ▶ **cowp**
COWPIE *n* cowpat **cowpies**
COWPING ▶ **cowp**
COWPLOP *n* cow dung
COWPOKE *n* cowboy
COWPOX *n* disease of cows
COWPS ▶ **cowp**
COWRIE *n* brightly-marked sea shell **cowries**
COWRITE *vb* to write jointly **cowrote**
COWRY = **cowrie**
COWS ▶ **cow**
COWSHED *n* byre
COWSKIN = **cowhide**
COWSLIP *n*
COWTREE *n* South American tree that produces latex
COWY *adj* cowlike
COX *n, vb*
COXA *n* technical name for the hipbone or hip joint **coxae, coxal**
COXALGY = **coxalgia**
COXCOMB = **cockscomb**
COXED ▶ **cox**
COXES ▶ **cox**
COXIB *n* anti-inflammatory drug **coxibs**
COXIER ▶ **coxy**
COXIEST ▶ **coxy**
COXING ▶ **cox**
COXITIS *n* inflammation of the hip joint
COXLESS ▶ **cox**
COXY *adj* cocky
COY *adj, vb*
COYDOG *n* cross between a coyote and a dog **coydogs**
COYED, coyer, coyest, coying, coyish, coyly, coyness ▶ **coy**
COYOTE *n* **coyotes**
COYPOU = **coypu**
COYPOUS ▶ **coypou**
COYPU *n* **coypus**
COYS ▶ **coy**
COZ *archaic word for* ▶ **cousin**

> **Coz** is an old word for **cousin**, and a good one to know for using the Z.

COZE *vb* to chat **cozed**
COZEN *vb* cheat, trick **cozened, cozener, cozens**
COZES ▶ **coze**
COZEY *n* tea cosy **cozeys, cozie**
COZIED ▶ **cosy**
COZIER *n* cobbler **coziers**

COZIES ▸ **cozey**
COZIEST ▸ **cozy**
COZILY ▸ **cozy**
COZING ▸ **coze**
COZY ▸ **cosy**
COZYING ▸ **cozy**
COZZES ▸ **coz**
CRAAL *vb* to enclose in a craal (or kraal) **craaled, craals**
CRAB *n* **crabbed**
CRABBER *n* crab fisherman
CRABBIT *adj* bad-tempered
CRABBY *adj* bad-tempered
CRABS ▸ **crab**
CRACK *vb, n, adj*
CRACKED *adj* damaged by cracking ▹ *n* sharp noise
CRACKER *n*
CRACKET *n* low stool, often with three legs
CRACKLE *vb, n*
CRACKLY *adj* making a cracking sound
CRACKS ▸ **crack**
CRACKUP *n* physical or mental breakdown
CRACKY *adj* full of cracks
CRACOWE *n* medieval shoe with a sharply pointed toe
CRADLE *n, vb* **cradled, cradler, cradles**
CRAFT *n, vb* **crafted**
CRAFTER *n* person doing craftwork
CRAFTS ▸ **craft**
CRAFTY *adj*
CRAG *n*
CRAGGED = **craggy**
CRAGGY *adj*
CRAGS ▸ **crag**
CRAIC *n* Irish word meaning fun **craics**
CRAIG *a Scot word for* ▸ **crag**
CRAIGS ▸ **craig**
CRAKE *n* bird of the rail family, such as the corncrake ▹ *vb* to boast **craked, crakes, craking**
CRAM *vb, n*
CRAMBE *n* any plant of the genus Crambe **crambes**
CRAMBO *n* word game **crambos**
CRAME *n* merchant's booth or stall **crames**
CRAMESY = **cramoisy**
CRAMMED ▸ **cram**
CRAMMER *n* person or school that prepares pupils for an examination
CRAMP *n, vb*
CRAMPED *adj*
CRAMPER *n* spiked metal plate used as a brace for the feet in throwing the stone
CRAMPET *n* cramp iron **crampit**
CRAMPON *n* spiked plate strapped to a boot for climbing on ice ▹ *vb* climb using crampons
CRAMPS ▸ **cramp**
CRAMPY *adj* affected with cramp
CRAMS ▸ **cram**
CRAN *n* unit of capacity used for measuring fresh herring, equal to 37.5 gallons
CRANAGE *n* use of a crane
CRANCH *vb* to crunch
CRANE *n, vb* **craned, cranes**
CRANIA ▸ **cranium**
CRANIAL *adj* of or relating to the skull
CRANING ▸ **crane**
CRANIUM *n*
CRANK *n, vb, adj* **cranked, cranker**
CRANKLE *vb* to bend or wind
CRANKLY *adj* vigorously
CRANKS ▸ **crank**
CRANKY = **crank**
CRANNOG *n* ancient Celtic lake or bog dwelling
CRANNY *n, vb*
CRANS ▸ **cran**
CRANTS *n* garland carried in front of a maiden's bier
CRAP *n* rubbish, nonsense ▹ *vb* defecate
CRAPAUD *n* frog or toad
CRAPE = **crepe; craped, crapes, crapier, craping**
CRAPLE = **grapple**
CRAPLES ▸ **craple**
CRAPOLA *n* rubbish
CRAPPED ▸ **crap**
CRAPPIE *n* N American freshwater fish)

CRAPPY *adj* worthless, lousy
CRAPS ▸ **crap**
CRAPY ▸ **crape**
CRARE *n* type of trading vessel **crares**
CRASES ▸ **crasis**
CRASH *n, vb, adj* **crashed, crasher, crashes**
CRASIS *n* fusion or contraction of two adjacent vowels into one
CRASS *adj* **crasser, crassly**
CRATCH *n* rack for holding fodder for cattle, etc
CRATE *n, vb* **crated**
CRATER *n* bowl-shaped opening at the top of a volcano ▹ *vb* make or form craters **craters**
CRATES ▸ **crate**
CRATHUR *n* ▸ **cratur**
CRATING ▸ **crate**
CRATON *n* stable part of the earth's continental crust **cratons**
CRATUR *n* whisky or whiskey **craturs**
CRAUNCH = **crunch**
CRAVAT *n, vb* **cravats**
CRAVE *vb* **craved**
CRAVEN *adj, n, vb* **cravens**
CRAVER ▸ **crave**
CRAVERS ▸ **crave**
CRAVES ▸ **crave**
CRAVING *n* intense desire or longing
CRAW *n* pouchlike part of a bird's oesophagus
CRAWDAD *n* crayfish
CRAWL *vb, n* **crawled**
CRAWLER *n* servile flatterer
CRAWLS ▸ **crawl**
CRAWLY *adj* feeling like creatures are crawling on one's skin
CRAWS ▸ **craw**
CRAY *n* crayfish
CRAYER = **crare**
CRAYERS ▸ **crayer**
CRAYON *n, vb* **crayons**
CRAYS ▸ **cray**
CRAZE *n, vb*
CRAZED *adj* wild and uncontrolled
CRAZES ▸ **craze**
CRAZIER ▸ **crazy**
CRAZIES ▸ **crazy**
CRAZILY ▸ **crazy**
CRAZING ▸ **craze**
CRAZY *adj, n*
CREACH = **creagh**
CREACHS ▸ **creach**
CREAGH *n* foray **creaghs**
CREAK *n, vb* **creaked, creaks, creaky**
CREAM *n, adj, vb* **creamed**
CREAMER *n* powdered milk substitute for use in coffee
CREAMS ▸ **cream**
CREAMY *adj* resembling cream in colour, taste, or consistency
CREANCE *n* long light cord used in falconry
CREANT *adj* formative
CREASE *n, vb* **creased, creaser, creases, creasy**
CREATE *vb* **created, creates**
CREATIC *adj* relating to flesh or meat
CREATIN = **creatine**
CREATOR *n* person who creates
CRECHE *n* place where small children are looked after **creches**
CRED *n* short for credibility
CREDAL ▸ **creed**
CREDENT *adj* believing or believable
CREDIT *n, vb*
CREDITS *pl n* list of people responsible for the production of a film, programme, or record
CREDO *n* creed **credos**
CREDS ▸ **cred**
CREE *vb* to soften grain by boiling or soaking
CREED *n* **creedal, creeds**
CREEING ▸ **cree**
CREEK *n* **creeks**
CREEKY *adj* abounding in creeks
CREEL *n* wicker basket used by anglers ▹ *vb* to fish using creels **creeled, creels**
CREEP *vb, n* **creeped**
CREEPER *n, vb*
CREEPIE *n* low stool
CREEPS ▸ **creep**
CREEPY *adj*
CREES ▸ **cree**
CREESE ▸ **kris**
CREESED ▸ **creese**
CREESES ▸ **creese**

CREESH *vb* to lubricate
CREESHY *adj* greasy
CREM *n* crematorium
CREMANT *adj* (of wine) moderately sparkling
CREMATE *vb*
CREME *n* cream ▷ *adj* (of a liqueur) rich and sweet **cremes**
CREMINI *n* variety of mushroom
CREMONA = **cromorna**
CREMOR *n* cream **cremors**
CREMS ▸ **crem**
CREMSIN = **cremosin**
CRENA *n* cleft or notch **crenas**
CRENATE *adj* having a scalloped margin, as certain leaves
CRENEL *n* opening formed in the top of a wall having slanting sides ▷ *vb* crenellate **crenels**
CREOLE *n*, *adj* **creoles**
CREOSOL *n* insoluble oily liquid
CREPE *n*, *vb* **creped, crepes**
CREPEY = **crepy**
CREPIER ▸ **crepy**
CREPING ▸ **crepe**
CREPON *n* thin material made of fine wool and/or silk **crepons**
CREPS *pl n*
CREPT ▸ **creep**
CREPY *adj* (esp of the skin) having a dry wrinkled appearance like crepe
CRESOL *n* aromatic compound **cresols**
CRESS *n* **cresses**
CRESSET *n* metal basket mounted on a pole
CRESSY ▸ **cress**
CREST *n*, *vb*
CRESTA *adj* *as in* **cresta run** high-speed tobogganing down a steep narrow passage
CRESTAL ▸ **crest**
CRESTED ▸ **crest**
CRESTON *n* hogback
CRESTS ▸ **crest**
CRESYL *n* tolyl **cresyls**
CRETIC *n* metrical foot **cretics**
CRETIN *n* stupid person **cretins**
CRETISM *n* lying
CRETONS *pl n*
CREVICE *n*
CREW *n*, *vb*
CREWCUT *n* very short haircut
CREWE *n* type of pot
CREWED ▸ **crew**
CREWEL *n* fine worsted yarn used in embroidery ▷ *vb* to embroider in crewel **crewels**
CREWES ▸ **crewe**
CREWING ▸ **crew**
CREWMAN *n* member of a ship's crew **crewmen**
CREWS ▸ **crew**
CRIA *n* baby llama, alpaca, or vicu
CRIANT *adj* garish
CRIAS ▸ **cria**
CRIB *n*, *vb* **cribbed, cribber**
CRIBBLE *vb* to sift
CRIBLE *adj* dotted
CRIBS ▸ **crib**
CRICK *n*, *vb* **cricked**
CRICKET *n*, *vb*
CRICKEY = **crikey**
CRICKS ▸ **crick**
CRICKY = **crikey**
CRICOID *adj* of or relating to part of the larynx ▷ *n* this cartilage
CRIED ▸ **cry**
CRIER *n* (formerly) official who made public announcements **criers**
CRIES ▸ **cry**
CRIKEY *interj* expression of surprise
CRIM *short for* > **criminal**
CRIME *n*, *vb* **crimed**
CRIMEN *n* crime
CRIMES ▸ **crime**
CRIMINA ▸ **crimen**
CRIMINE *interj* expression of surprise
CRIMING ▸ **crime**
CRIMINI ▸ **crimine**
CRIMINY *interj* cry of surprise
CRIMMER *a variant spelling of* ▸ **krimmer**
CRIMP *vb* fold or press into ridges ▷ *n* act or result of crimping **crimped, crimper**
CRIMPLE *vb* crumple, wrinkle, or curl
CRIMPS ▸ **crimp**
CRIMPY ▸ **crimp**
CRIMS ▸ **crim**

CRIMSON *adj, n, vb*
CRINAL *adj* relating to the hair
CRINATE *adj* having hair
CRINE *vb* to shrivel **crined, crines**
CRINGE *vb, n* **cringed, cringer, cringes**
CRINGLE *n* eye at the edge of a sail
CRINING ▸ **crine**
CRINITE *adj* covered with soft hairs or tufts ▹ *n* sedimentary rock
CRINKLE *n, vb*
CRINKLY *adj* wrinkled ▹ *n* old person
CRINOID *n* type of primitive echinoderm
CRINOSE *adj* hairy
CRINUM *n* type of mostly tropical plant **crinums**
CRIOLLO *n* native or inhabitant of Latin America of European descent ▹ *adj* of, relating to, or characteristic of a criollo or criollos
CRIOS *n* multicoloured woven woollen belt **crioses**
CRIPE *variant of* ▸ **cripes**
CRIPES *interj* expression of surprise
CRIPPLE *n, vb*
CRIS *variant of* ▸ **kris**
CRISE *n* crisis
CRISES ▸ **crisis**
CRISIC *adj* relating to a crisis
CRISIS *n*
CRISP *adj, n, vb*
CRISPED = **crispate**
CRISPEN *vb* to make crisp
CRISPER *n* compartment in a refrigerator
CRISPIN *n* cobbler
CRISPLY ▸ **crisp**
CRISPS ▸ **crisp**
CRISPY *adj*
CRISSA ▸ **crissum**
CRISSAL ▸ **crissum**
CRISSUM *n* area or feathers surrounding the cloaca of a bird
CRISTA *n* structure resembling a ridge or crest **cristae**
CRIT *abbreviation of* > **criticism**
CRITH *n* unit of weight for gases **criths**
CRITIC *n* **critics**
CRITS ▸ **crit**
CRITTER *a dialect word for* > **creature**
CRITTUR = **critter**
CRIVENS *interj* expression of surprise
CROAK *vb, n* **croaked**
CROAKER *n* animal, bird, etc, that croaks
CROAKS ▸ **croak**
CROAKY ▸ **croak**
CROC *short for* > **crocodile**
CROCEIN *n* any one of a group of red or orange acid azo dyes
CROCHE *n* knob at the top of a deer's horn **croches**
CROCHET *vb, n*
CROCI ▸ **crocus**
CROCINE *adj* relating to the crocus
CROCK *n* earthenware pot or jar ▹ *vb* become or cause to become weak or disabled
CROCKED *adj* injured
CROCKET *n* carved ornament in the form of a curled leaf or cusp
CROCKS ▸ **crock**
CROCS ▸ **croc**
CROCUS *n* flowering plant
CROFT *n, vb* **crofted**
CROFTER *n* owner or tenant of a small farm, esp in Scotland or northern England
CROFTS ▸ **croft**
CROG *vb* ride on a bicycle as a passenger **crogged**
CROGGY *n* ride on a bicycle as a passenger
CROGS ▸ **crog**
CROJIK *n* triangular sail **crojiks**
CROMACK = **crummock**
CROMB = **crome**
CROMBEC *n* African Old World warbler with colourful plumage
CROMBED ▸ **cromb**
CROMBS ▸ **cromb**
CROME *n* hook ▹ *vb* use a crome **cromed, cromes, croming**
CRONE *n* **crones**
CRONET *n* hair which grows over the top of a horse's hoof **cronets**
CRONIES ▸ **crony**

CRONISH ▸ **crone**
CRONK *adj* unfit **cronker**
CRONY *n*
CROODLE *vb* to nestle close
CROOK *n, vb*
CROOKED *adj*
CROOKER ▸ **crook**
CROOKS ▸ **crook**
CROOL *vb* spoil **crooled, crools**
CROON *vb, n* **crooned, crooner, croons**
CROOVE *n* animal enclosure **crooves**
CROP *n, vb*
CROPFUL *n* quantity that can be held in the craw
CROPPED ▸ **crop**
CROPPER *n* person who cultivates or harvests a crop
CROPPIE = **croppy**
CROPPY *n* rebel in the Irish rising of 1798
CROPS ▸ **crop**
CROQUET *n, vb*
CROQUIS *n* rough sketch
CRORE *n* (in Indian English) ten million **crores**
CROSIER *n* staff carried by bishops as a symbol of pastoral office ▹ *vb* bear or carry such a cross
CROSS *vb, n, adj*
CROSSE *n* light staff used in playing lacrosse
CROSSED, crosser, crosses, crossly, crost ▸ **cross**
CROTAL *n* any of various lichens used in dyeing wool
CROTALA > **crotalum**
crotals
CROTCH *n, vb*
CROTON *n* type of shrub or tree, the seeds of which yield croton oil **crotons**
CROTTLE = **crotal**
CROUCH *vb, n*
CROUP *n, vb* **croupe, crouped**
CROUPER *obsolete variant of* ▸ **crupper**
CROUPES ▸ **croupe**
CROUPON *n* type of highly-polished flexible leather
CROUPS ▸ **croup**
CROUPY ▸ **croup**
CROUSE *adj* lively, confident, or saucy
CROUT *n* sauerkraut
CROUTE *n* small round of toasted bread on which a savoury mixture is served **croutes**
CROUTON *n*
CROUTS ▸ **crout**
CROW *n, vb*
CROWBAR *n, vb*
CROWD *n, vb* **crowded, crowder**
CROWDIE *n* porridge of meal and water
CROWDS ▸ **crowd**
crowdy
CROWEA *n* Australian shrub with pink flowers **croweas**
CROWED, crower, crowers, crowing ▸ **crow**
CROWN *n, vb* **crowned**
CROWNER *n* promotional label
CROWNET *n* coronet
CROWNS ▸ **crown**
CROWS ▸ **crow**
CROZE *n* recess cut at the end of a barrel or cask to receive the head
CROZER *n* machine which cuts grooves in cask staves **crozers**
CROZES ▸ **croze**
CROZIER = **crosier**
CRU *n* (in France) a vineyard, group of vineyards, or wine-producing region
CRUBEEN *n* pig's trotter
CRUCES ▸ **crux**
CRUCIAL *adj*
CRUCIAN *n* European fish
CRUCIFY *vb*
CRUCK *n* wooden timber supporting the end of certain roofs **crucks**
CRUD *n* sticky or encrusted substance ▹ *interj* expression of disgust, disappointment, etc ▹ *vb* cover with a sticky or encrusted substance **crudded**
CRUDDLE *vb* to curdle
CRUDDY *adj* dirty or unpleasant

CRUDE *adj, n* **crudely, cruder, crudes, crudest, crudity**
CRUDS ▸ **crud**
CRUDY *adj* raw
CRUE *obsolete variant of* ▸ **crew**
CRUEL *adj* **crueler**
CRUELLS = **cruels**
CRUELLY ▸ **cruel**
CRUELS *n* disease of cattle and sheep
CRUELTY *n*
CRUES ▸ **crew**
CRUET *n* **cruets**
CRUISE *n, vb* **cruised**
CRUISER *n*
CRUISES ▸ **cruise**
CRUISIE = **cruizie**
CRUIVE *n* animal enclosure **cruives**
CRUIZIE *n* oil lamp
CRULLER *n* light sweet ring-shaped cake, fried in deep fat
CRUMB *n, vb, adj* **crumbed, crumber**
CRUMBLE *vb, n*
CRUMBLY *adj*
CRUMBS *interj* expression of dismay or surprise
CRUMBUM *n* rogue
CRUMBY *adj* full of crumbs
CRUMEN *n* deer's larmier or tear-pit **crumens**
CRUMMIE *n* cow with a crumpled horn
CRUMMY *adj* of poor quality ▷ *n* lorry that carries loggers to work from their camp
CRUMP *vb* thud or explode with a loud dull sound ▷ *n* crunching, thudding, or exploding noise ▷ *adj* crooked **crumped, crumper**
CRUMPET *n*
CRUMPLE *vb, n* **crumply**
CRUMPS ▸ **crump**
CRUMPY *adj* crisp
CRUNCH *vb, n* **crunchy**
CRUNK *n* form of hip-hop music originating in the Southern US
CRUNKED *adj* excited or intoxicated
CRUNKLE *Scots variant of* ▸ **crinkle**
CRUNKS ▸ **crunk**
CRUNODE *n* mathematical term
CRUOR *n* blood clot **cruores, cruors**
CRUPPER *n* strap that passes from the back of a saddle under a horse's tail
CRURA ▸ **crus**
CRURAL *adj* of or relating to the leg or thigh
CRUS *n* leg, esp from the knee to the foot
CRUSADE *n, vb*
CRUSADO *n* former gold or silver coin of Portugal
CRUSE *n* small earthenware jug or pot **cruses**
CRUSET *n* goldsmith's crucible **crusets**
CRUSH *vb, n* **crushed, crusher, crushes**
CRUSIAN *variant of* ▸ **crucian**
CRUSIE = **cruizie**
CRUSIES ▸ **crusie**
CRUSILY *adj* (in heraldry) strewn with crosses
CRUST *n, vb*
CRUSTA *n* hard outer layer **crustae**
CRUSTAL *adj* of or relating to the earth's crust
CRUSTED ▸ **crust**
CRUSTS ▸ **crust**
CRUSTY *adj, n*
CRUSY = **cruizie**
CRUTCH *n, vb*
CRUVE = **cruive**
CRUVES ▸ **cruve**
CRUX *n* **cruxes**
CRUZADO = **crusado**
CRUZIE = **cruizie**
CRUZIES ▸ **cruzie**
CRWTH *n* ancient stringed instrument of Celtic origin **crwths**

> This old Celtic musical instrument makes a fine tune when your rack is all consonants.

CRY *vb* shed tears ▷ *n* fit of weeping
CRYBABY *n* person, esp a child, who cries too readily
CRYING ▸ **cry**
CRYINGS ▸ **cry**
CRYOGEN *n* substance used to produce low temperatures

CRYONIC > **cryonics**
CRYPT *n* **cryptal**
CRYPTIC *adj*
CRYPTO *n* person who is a secret member of an organization or sect
CRYPTON *n* krypton
CRYPTOS ▶ **crypto**
CRYPTS ▶ **crypt**
CRYSTAL *n, adj*
CSARDAS *n* type of Hungarian folk dance
CTENE *n* locomotor organ found in ctenophores (or comb jellies) **ctenes**
CTENOID *adj* toothed like a comb, as the scales of perches
CUATRO *n* four-stringed guitar **cuatros**
CUB *n, adj, vb*
CUBAGE = **cubature**
CUBAGES > **cubature**
CUBANE *n* rare octahedral hydrocarbon **cubanes**
CUBBED ▶ **cub**
CUBBIER ▶ **cubby**
CUBBIES ▶ **cubby**
CUBBING ▶ **cub**
CUBBISH ▶ **cub**
CUBBY *n, adj*
CUBE *n, vb*
CUBEB *n* SE Asian woody climbing plant with brownish berries **cubebs**
CUBED ▶ **cube**
CUBER ▶ **cube**
CUBERS ▶ **cube**
CUBES ▶ **cube**
CUBHOOD *n* state of being a cub
CUBIC *adj, n*
CUBICA *n* fine shalloon-like fabric
CUBICAL *adj* of or related to volume
CUBICAS ▶ **cubica**
CUBICLE *n*
CUBICLY ▶ **cubic**
CUBICS ▶ **cubic**
CUBING ▶ **cube**
CUBISM *n* style of art in which objects are represented by geometrical shapes **cubisms, cubist, cubists**
CUBIT *n* old measure of length based on the length of the forearm
CUBITAL *adj* of or relating to the forearm
CUBITI ▶ **cubitus**
CUBITS ▶ **cubit**
CUBITUS *n* elbow
CUBLESS *adj* having no cubs
CUBOID *adj* shaped like a cube ▷ *n* geometric solid whose six faces are rectangles **cuboids**
CUBS ▶ **cub**
CUCKING *adj as in* **cucking stool** stool in which suspected witches were tested
CUCKOLD *n* man whose wife has been unfaithful ▷ *vb* be unfaithful to (one's husband)
CUCKOO *n, adj, interj, vb* **cuckoos**
CUD *n*
CUDBEAR *another name for* ▶ **orchil**
CUDDEN *n* young coalfish **cuddens**
CUDDIE = **cuddy**
CUDDIES ▶ **cuddy**
CUDDIN = **cudden**
CUDDINS ▶ **cuddin**
CUDDLE *n, vb* **cuddled, cuddler, cuddles, cuddly**
CUDDY *n* small cabin in a boat
CUDGEL *n, vb* **cudgels**
CUDS ▶ **cud**
CUDWEED *n* type of temperate plant
CUE *n, vb* **cued, cueing**
CUEINGS ▶ **cueing**
CUEIST *n* snooker or billiards player **cueists**
CUES ▶ **cue**
CUESTA *n* long low ridge with a steep scarp slope and a gentle back slope **cuestas**
CUFF *n, vb* **cuffed**
CUFFIN *n* man
CUFFING ▶ **cuff**
CUFFINS ▶ **cuffin**
CUFFLE *vb* scuffle **cuffled, cuffles**
CUFFO *adv* free of charge
CUFFS ▶ **cuff**
CUIF = **coof**
CUIFS ▶ **cuif**
CUING ▶ **cue**
CUIRASS *n* piece of armour, of leather or metal covering the chest and back ▷ *vb* equip with a cuirass

CUISH = **cuisse**
CUISHES ▸ **cuish**
CUISINE *n*
CUISSE *n* piece of armour for the thigh
CUISSER = **cooser** **cuisses**
CUIT *n* ankle
CUITER *vb* to pamper **cuiters**
CUITS ▸ **cuit**
CUITTLE *vb* to wheedle
CUKE *n* cucumber **cukes**
CULCH *n* the basis of an oyster bed **culches**
CULCHIE *n* rough or unsophisticated country-dweller from outside Dublin
CULET *n* flat face at the bottom of a gem **culets**
CULEX *n* type of mosquito **culexes, culices**
CULICID *n* type of dipterous insect
CULL *vb, n*
CULLAY *n* soapbark tree **cullays**
CULLED ▸ **cull**
CULLER *n* person employed to cull animals **cullers**
CULLET *n* waste glass for melting down to be reused **cullets**
CULLIED ▸ **cully**
CULLIES ▸ **cully**
CULLING ▸ **cull**
CULLION *n* rascal
CULLIS = **coulisse**
CULLS ▸ **cull**
CULLY *n* pal ▹ *vb* to trick
CULM *n* coal-mine waste ▹ *vb* to form a culm or grass stem **culmed**
CULMEN *n* summit **culmina**
CULMING ▸ **culm**
CULMS ▸ **culm**
CULOTTE > **culottes**
CULPA *n* act of neglect **culpae**
CULPRIT *n*
CULT *n, adj*
CULTCH = **culch**
CULTER = **coulter**
CULTERS ▸ **culter**
CULTI ▸ **cultus**
CULTIC *adj* of or relating to a religious cult
CULTIER ▸ **culty**
CULTISH *adj* intended to appeal to a small group of fashionable people
CULTISM ▸ **cult**
CULTIST ▸ **cult**
CULTS ▸ **cult**
CULTURE *n, vb*
CULTUS *another word for* ▸ **cult**
CULTY = **cultish**
CULVER *an archaic or poetic name for* ▸ **pigeon**
CULVERS ▸ **culver**
CULVERT *n*
CUMARIC ▸ **cumarin**
CUMARIN = **coumarin**
CUMBENT *adj* lying down
CUMBER *vb* obstruct or hinder ▹ *n* hindrance or burden **cumbers**
CUMBIA *n* Colombian style of music **cumbias**
CUMEC *n* unit of volumetric rate of flow **cumecs**
CUMIN *n* **cumins**
CUMMER *n* gossip **cummers**
CUMMIN = **cumin**
CUMMINS ▸ **cummin**
CUMQUAT = **kumquat**
CUMSHAW *n* (used, esp formerly, by beggars in Chinese ports) a present or tip
CUMULET *n* variety of domestic fancy pigeon
CUMULI ▸ **cumulus**
CUMULUS *n*
CUNDIES ▸ **cundy**
CUNDUM *n* early form of condom **cundums**
CUNDY *n* sewer
CUNEAL = **cuneiform**
CUNEATE *adj* wedge-shaped: cuneate leaves are attached at the narrow end
CUNEI ▸ **cuneus**
CUNETTE *n* small trench dug in the main ditch of a fortification
CUNEUS *n* small wedge-shaped area of the cerebral cortex
CUNNER *n* fish of the wrasse family **cunners**
CUNNING *adj, n*
CUP *n, vb*
CUPCAKE *n* small cake baked in a cup-shaped

foil or paper case
CUPEL *n* refractory pot in which gold or silver is refined ▷ *vb* refine (gold or silver) by means of cupellation **cupeled, cupeler, cupels**
CUPFUL *n* amount a cup will hold **cupfuls**
CUPGALL *n* gall found on oakleaves
CUPHEAD *n* type of bolt or rivet with a cup-shaped head
CUPID *n* figure representing the Roman god of love **cupids**
CUPLIKE ▸ **cup**
CUPMAN *n* drinking companion **cupmen**
CUPOLA *n, vb* **cupolar, cupolas**
CUPPA *n* cup of tea **cuppas**
CUPPED ▸ **cup**
CUPPER = **cuppa**
CUPPERS ▸ **cupper**
CUPPIER ▸ **cuppy**
CUPPING ▸ **cup**
CUPPY *adj* cup-shaped
CUPRIC *adj* of or containing copper in the divalent state
CUPRITE *n* red secondary mineral
CUPROUS *adj* of or containing copper in the monovalent state
CUPRUM *an obsolete name for* ▸ **copper**
CUPRUMS ▸ **cuprum**
CUPS ▸ **cup**
CUPSFUL ▸ **cupful**
CUPULA *n* dome-shaped structure **cupulae**
CUPULAR = **cupulate**
CUPULE *n* cup-shaped part or structure **cupules**
CUR *n* mongrel dog
CURABLE *adj* **curably**
CURACAO *n* orange-flavoured liqueur **curacoa**
CURACY *n* work or position of a curate
CURAGH = **currach**
CURAGHS ▸ **curagh**
CURARA = **curare**
CURARAS ▸ **curara**
CURARE *n* poisonous resin of a S American tree **curares, curari**
CURARIS ▸ **curari**
CURAT *n* cuirass
CURATE *n, vb* **curated, curates**
CURATOR *n*
CURATS ▸ **curat**
CURB *n, vb* **curbed, curber, curbers**
CURBING *the US spelling of* ▸ **kerbing**
CURBS ▸ **curb**
CURCH *n* woman's plain cap or kerchief **curchef, curches**
CURCUMA *n* type of tropical Asian tuberous plant
CURD *n* coagulated milk, used to make cheese ▷ *vb* turn into or become curd **curded, curdier, curding**
CURDLE *vb* **curdled, curdler, curdles**
CURDS ▸ **curd**
CURDY ▸ **curd**
CURE *vb, n* **cured, curer, curers, cures**
CURET = **curette**
CURETS ▸ **curet**
CURETTE *n* surgical instrument for scraping tissue from body cavities ▷ *vb* scrape with a curette
CURF *n* type of limestone
CURFEW *n* **curfews**
CURFS ▸ **curf**
CURIA *n* papal court and government of the Roman Catholic Church **curiae, curial, curias**
CURIE *n* standard unit of radioactivity **curies**
CURIET *n* cuirass **curiets**
CURING ▸ **cure**
CURIO *n* **curios**
CURIOSA *n* curiosities
CURIOUS *adj*
CURITE *n* oxide of uranium and lead **curites**
CURIUM *n* radioactive element artificially produced from plutonium **curiums**
CURL *n, vb* **curled**
CURLER *n* **curlers**
CURLEW *n* **curlews**
CURLI *pl n* curled hairlike processes on the surface of the E. coli bacterium

CURLIER ▸ **curly**
CURLIES *pl n as in* **have by the short and curlies** have completely in one's power
CURLILY ▸ **curly**
CURLING *n* game like bowls, played with heavy stones on ice
CURLS ▸ **curl**
CURLY *adj* tending to curl
CURN *n* grain (of corn etc)
CURNEY = **curny**
CURNIER ▸ **curny**
CURNS ▸ **curn**
CURNY *adj* granular
CURPEL = **crupper**
CURPELS ▸ **curpel**
CURR *vb* to purr
CURRACH *a Scot or Irish name for* ▸ **coracle**
CURRAGH = **currach**
CURRAN *n* black bun **currans**
CURRANT *n*
CURRED ▸ **curr**
CURRENT *adj, n*
CURRIE = **curry**
CURRIED ▸ **curry**
CURRIER *n* person who curries leather
CURRIES ▸ **curry**
CURRING ▸ **curr**
CURRISH *adj* of or like a cur
CURRS ▸ **curr**
CURRY *n, vb*
CURS ▸ **cur**
CURSAL ▸ **cursus**
CURSE *vb, n* **cursed, curser, cursers, curses**
CURSI ▸ **cursus**
CURSING ▸ **curse**
CURSIVE *n, adj*
CURSOR *n* **cursors**
CURSORY *adj*
CURST ▸ **curse**
CURSUS *n* Neolithic parallel earthworks
CURT *adj*
CURTAIL *vb*
CURTAIN *n, vb*
CURTAL *adj* cut short ▷ *n* animal whose tail has been docked **curtals**
CURTANA *n* unpointed sword displayed at a coronation as an emblem of mercy
CURTATE *adj* shortened
CURTAXE = **curtalaxe**
CURTER ▸ **curt**
CURTEST ▸ **curt**
CURTESY *n* widower's life interest in his wife's estate
CURTLY ▸ **curt**
CURTSEY = **curtsy**
CURTSY *n, vb*
CURULE *adj* (in ancient Rome) of the highest rank, esp one entitled to use a curule chair
CURVATE *adj* curved
CURVE *n, vb* **curved, curves**
CURVET *n* horse's low leap with all four feet off the ground ▷ *vb* make such a leap **curvets**
CURVEY = **curvy**
CURVIER ▸ **curve**
CURVING ▸ **curve**
CURVITY *n* curvedness
CURVY ▸ **curve**
CUSCUS *n* large Australian nocturnal possum
CUSEC *n* unit of flow equal to 1 cubic foot per second **cusecs**
CUSH *n* cushion
CUSHAT *n* wood pigeon **cushats**
CUSHAW = **cashaw**
CUSHAWS ▸ **cushaw**
CUSHES ▸ **cush**
CUSHIE = **cushat**
CUSHIER ▸ **cushy**
CUSHIES ▸ **cushie**
CUSHILY ▸ **cushy**
CUSHION *n, vb*
CUSHTY *interj* exclamation of pleasure, agreement, approval, etc
CUSHY *adj*
CUSK *n* type of food fish of northern coastal waters, with a single long dorsal fin **cusks**
CUSP *n* pointed end, esp on a tooth **cuspal**
CUSPATE *adj* having a cusp or cusps **cusped**
CUSPID *n* tooth having one point **cuspids**
CUSPIER ▸ **cuspy**
CUSPIS *n* (in anatomy), tapering structure
CUSPS ▸ **cusp**
CUSPY *adj* (of a computer program) well-designed and user-friendly
CUSS *n* curse, oath ▷ *vb* swear (at)

CUSSED *adj* obstinate
CUSSER = **cooser**
CUSSERS ▸ **cusser**
CUSSES ▸ **cuss**
CUSSING ▸ **cuss**
CUSSO *n* tree of the rose family **cussos**
CUSTARD *n*
CUSTOCK = **castock**
CUSTODE *n* custodian
CUSTODY *n*
CUSTOM *n, adj*
CUSTOMS *n* duty charged on imports or exports
CUSTOS *n* superior in the Franciscan religious order
CUSTREL *n* knave
CUSUM *n* analysis technique used in statistics **cusums**
CUT *vb*
CUTAWAY *adj* (of a drawing or model) having part of the outside omitted to reveal the inside ▷ *n* man's coat cut diagonally from the front waist to the back of the knees
CUTBACK *n* decrease or reduction ▷ *vb* shorten by cutting
CUTBANK *n* steep banking at a bend in a river
CUTCH = **catechu**
CUTCHA *adj* crude
CUTCHES ▸ **cutch**
CUTDOWN *n* decrease
CUTE *adj* **cutely, cuter**
CUTES ▸ **cutis**
CUTESIE = **cutesy**
CUTEST ▸ **cute**
CUTESY *adj* affectedly cute or coy
CUTEY = **cutie**
CUTEYS ▸ **cutey**
CUTICLE *n*
CUTIE *n* person regarded as appealing or attractive, esp a girl or woman **cuties**
CUTIKIN = **cutikin**
CUTIN *n* waxy waterproof substance **cutins**
CUTIS *a technical name for the* ▸ **skin**
CUTISES ▸ **cutis**
CUTLAS = **cutlass**
CUTLASS *n*
CUTLER *n* maker of cutlery **cutlers**
CUTLERY *n*
CUTLET *n* **cutlets**
CUTLINE *n* caption
CUTOFF *n* limit or termination **cutoffs**
CUTOUT *n* **cutouts**
CUTOVER *n* transitional period in IT system changeover
CUTS ▸ **cut**
CUTTAGE *n* propagation by using parts taken from growing plants
CUTTER *n* person or tool that cuts **cutters**
CUTTIER ▸ **cutty**
CUTTIES ▸ **cutty**
CUTTING ▸ **cut**
CUTTLE *vb* to whisper **cuttled, cuttles**
CUTTO *n* large knife **cuttoe, cuttoes**
CUTTY *adj* short or cut short ▷ *n* something cut short
CUTUP *n* joker or prankster **cutups**
CUTWORK *n* type of openwork embroidery
CUTWORM *n* caterpillar of various types of moth
CUVEE *n* individual batch or blend of wine **cuvees**
CUVETTE *n* shallow dish or vessel for holding liquid
CUZ *n* cousin **cuzzes**

> **Cuz** is another word for **cousin**, great for using the Z.

CUZZIE *n* close friend or family member **cuzzies**
CWM = **cirque**

> **Cwm** is a Welsh word meaning a valley, a useful one to remember because it doesn't contain any vowels.

CWMS ▸ **cwm**
CWTCH *vb* be snuggled up **cwtched, cwtches**

> This delightful Welsh word meaning to cuddle is not likely to come up, but might just help you out of a tight spot one day when your rack is all consonants.

CYAN *n* highly saturated green-blue ▷ *adj* of this colour

CYANATE *n* any salt or ester of cyanic acid
CYANIC *adj as in* **cyanic acid** colourless poisonous volatile liquid acid
CYANID = **cyanide**
CYANIDE *n, vb*
CYANIDS ▸ **cyanid**
CYANIN = **cyanine**
CYANINE *n* blue dye used in photography
CYANINS ▸ **cyanin**
CYANISE *vb* turn into cyanide
CYANITE *a variant spelling of* ▸ **kyanite**
CYANIZE = **cyanise**
CYANO *adj* containing cyanogen
CYANS ▸ **cyan**
CYATHI ▸ **cyathus**
CYATHIA > **cyathium**
CYATHUS *n* ancient measure of wine
CYBER *adj* involving computers
CYBORG *n* (in science fiction) a living being enhanced by computer implants **cyborgs**
CYBRID *n* cytoplasmic hybrid **cybrids**
CYCAD *n* type of tropical or subtropical plant **cycads**
CYCAS *n* palm tree of the genus Cycas **cycases**
CYCASIN *n* glucoside, toxic to mammals, occurring in cycads
CYCLASE *n* enzyme which acts as a catalyst in the formation of a cyclic compound
CYCLE *vb, n* **cycled**
CYCLER = **cyclist**
CYCLERS ▸ **cyclist**
CYCLERY *n* business dealing in bicycles and bicycle accessories
CYCLES ▸ **cycle**
CYCLIC *adj* recurring or revolving in cycles
CYCLIN *n* type of protein
CYCLING ▸ **cycle**
CYCLINS ▸ **cyclin**
CYCLISE = **cyclize**
CYCLIST *n*
CYCLIZE *vb* be cyclical
CYCLO *n* type of rickshaw
CYCLOID *adj* resembling a circle ▷ *n* mathematical curve
CYCLONE *n*
CYCLOPS *n* type of copepod characterized by having one eye
CYCLOS ▸ **cyclo**
CYCLUS *n* cycle
CYDER = **cider**
CYDERS ▸ **cyder**
CYESES ▸ **cyesis**
CYESIS *the technical name for* > **pregnancy**
CYGNET *n* **cygnets**
CYLICES ▸ **cylix**
CYLIX *a variant of* ▸ **kylix**
CYMA *n* moulding with a double curve, part concave and part convex **cymae**
CYMAR *n* woman's short fur-trimmed jacket, popular in the 17th and 18th centuries **cymars**
CYMAS ▸ **cyma**
CYMATIA > **cymatium**
CYMBAL *n*
CYMBALO *another name for* > **dulcimer** **cymbals**
CYME *n* type of flower cluster
CYMENE *n* colourless insoluble liquid **cymenes**
CYMES ▸ **cyme**
CYMLIN = **cymling**
CYMLING *n* pattypan squash
CYMLINS ▸ **cymlin**
CYMOID *adj* resembling a cyme or cyma
CYMOL = **cymene**
CYMOLS ▸ **cymol**
CYMOSE *adj* having the characteristics of a cyme
CYMOUS *adj* relating to a cyme
CYNIC *n, adj*
CYNICAL *adj*
CYNICS ▸ **cynic**
CYPHER = **cipher**
CYPHERS ▸ **cypher**
CYPRES *n* legal doctrine
CYPRESS *n*
CYPRIAN *n* prostitute or dancer
CYPRID *n* cypris **cyprids**
CYPRINE *adj* relating to carp
CYPRIS *n* member of the genus Cypris (small bivalve freshwater crustaceans)
CYPRUS = **cypress**
CYPSELA *n* dry

one-seeded fruit of the daisy and related plants
CYST *n*
CYSTEIN = **cysteine**
CYSTIC *adj* of, relating to, or resembling a cyst
CYSTID *n* cystidean **cystids**
CYSTINE *n* sulphur-containing amino acid
CYSTOID *adj* resembling a cyst or bladder ▷ *n* tissue mass that resembles a cyst but lacks an outer membrane
CYSTS ▸ **cyst**
CYTASE *n* cellulose-dissolving enzyme **cytases**
CYTE *n* biological cell **cytes**
CYTISI ▸ **cytisus**
CYTISUS *n* any plant of the broom genus, Cytisus
CYTODE *n* mass of protoplasm without a nucleus **cytodes**
CYTOID *adj* resembling a cell
CYTON *n* main part of a neuron **cytons**
CYTOSOL *n* solution in a biological cell
CZAPKA *n* leather and felt peaked military helmet of Polish origin **czapkas**
CZAR = **tsar**
CZARDAS *n* Hungarian national dance of alternating slow and fast sections
CZARDOM ▸ **czar**
CZARINA *variant spellings (esp US) of* ▸ **tsarina**
CZARISM *a variant spelling (esp US) of* ▸ **tsarism**
CZARIST ▸ **czarism**
CZARS ▸ **czar**

Dd

D forms a two-letter word before every vowel except **U**. There are plenty of good three-letter words beginning with **D**, particularly those with a **Y** or **W**: **day, dye** and **dew** are worth 7 points each, for example. And don't forget **dex** and **dux** for 11 points each and the invaluable **dzo** for 13 points.

DA *n* Burmese knife
DAAL *n* (in Indian cookery) split pulses **daals**
DAB *vb, n*
DABBA *n* in Indian cookery, round metal box used to transport hot food **dabbas**
DABBED ▸ **dab**
DABBER *n* pad used by printers for applying ink by hand **dabbers**
DABBING ▸ **dab**
DABBITY *n* temporary tattoo
DABBLE *vb* **dabbled, dabbler, dabbles**
DABS ▸ **dab**
DABSTER *n* incompetent or amateurish worker
DACE *n* **daces**
DACHA *n* country cottage in Russia **dachas**
DACITE *n* volcanic rock **dacites**
DACK *vb* remove the trousers from (someone) by force **dacked**
DACKER *vb* walk slowly **dackers**
DACKING ▸ **dack**
DACKS ▸ **dack**
DACOIT *n* (in India and Myanmar) a member of a gang of armed robbers **dacoits**
DACOITY *n* (in India and Myanmar) robbery by an armed gang
DACRON *n* US tradename for a synthetic polyester fibre or fabric **dacrons**
DACTYL *n* metrical foot of three syllables, one long followed by two short
DACTYLI > **dactylus**
DACTYLS ▸ **dactyl**
DAD *n, vb*
DADA *n* nihilistic artistic movement of the early 20th century
DADAH *n* illegal drugs **dadahs**
DADAISM = **dada**
DADAIST ▸ **dada**
DADAS ▸ **dada**
DADDED ▸ **dad**
DADDIES ▸ **daddy**
DADDING ▸ **dad**
DADDLE *vb* walk unsteadily **daddled, daddles**
DADDOCK *n* core of a dead tree
DADDY *n* father
DADGUM *mild form of* ▸ **damned**
DADO *n, vb* **dadoed, dadoes, dadoing, dados**
DADS ▸ **dad**
DAE *a Scot word for* ▸ **do**
DAEDAL *adj* skilful or intricate

DAEING ▶ **dae**
DAEMON = **demon**
DAEMONS ▶ **daemon**
DAES ▶ **dae**
DAFF *vb* frolic **daffed**
DAFFIER ▶ **daffy**
DAFFIES ▶ **daffy**
DAFFILY ▶ **daffy**
DAFFING ▶ **daff**
DAFFS ▶ **daff**
DAFFY *another word for* ▶ **daft**
DAFT *adj*
DAFTAR *Indian word for* ▶ **office**
DAFTARS ▶ **daftar**
DAFTER ▶ **daft**
DAFTEST ▶ **daft**
DAFTIE *n* foolish person **dafties**
DAFTLY ▶ **daft**
DAG *n* character ▷ *vb* cut daglocks from sheep
DAGABA *n* shrine for Buddhist relics **dagabas**
DAGGA *n* **daggas**
DAGGED ▶ **dag**
DAGGER ▶ **dag**
DAGGERS ▶ **dag**
DAGGIER ▶ **daggy**
DAGGING ▶ **dag**
DAGGLE *vb* trail through water **daggled, daggles**
DAGGY *adj* amusing
DAGLOCK *n* dung-caked lock of wool around the hindquarters of a sheep
DAGOBA *n* dome-shaped Buddhist shrine **dagobas**
DAGS ▶ **dag**
DAGWOOD *n* European shrub
DAH *n* long sound used in combination with the short sound in the spoken representation of Morse and other telegraphic codes
DAHL = **dhal**
DAHLIA *n* **dahlias**
DAHLS ▶ **dahl**
DAHOON *n* evergreen shrub **dahoons**
DAHS ▶ **dah**
DAIDLE *vb* waddle about **daidled, daidles**
DAIKER *vb* walk slowly **daikers**
DAIKO *n* Japanese drum
DAIKON *another name for* ▶ **mooli**
DAIKONS ▶ **daikon**
DAIKOS ▶ **daiko**
DAILIES ▶ **daily**
DAILY *adj, adv, n*
DAIMEN *adj* occasional
DAIMIO = **daimyo**
DAIMIOS ▶ **daimio**
DAIMOKU *n* Nichiren Buddhist chant
DAIMON = **demon**
DAIMONS ▶ **daimon**
DAIMYO *n* magnate in Japan from the 11th to the 19th century **daimyos**
DAINE *vb* condescend **dained, daines, daining**
DAINT *adj* dainty
DAINTY *adj, n*
DAIRIES ▶ **dairy**
DAIRY *n, adj*
DAIS *n* **daises**
DAISIED ▶ **daisy**
DAISIES ▶ **daisy**
DAISY *n*
DAK *n* system of mail delivery or passenger transport

> A **dak** is an old mail or transport system, often useful for disposing of the K.

DAKER *vb* walk slowly **dakered, dakers**
DAKOIT = **dacoit**
DAKOITI = **dakoit**
DAKOITS ▶ **dakoit**
DAKOITY *n* armed robbery
DAKS *an informal name for* > **trousers**
DAL = **decalitre**
DALAPON *n* herbicide
DALASI *n* standard monetary unit of The Gambia, divided into 100 bututs **dalasis**
DALE *n*
DALED = **daleth**
DALEDH *n* letter of Hebrew alphabet **daledhs**
DALEDS ▶ **daled**
DALES ▶ **dale**
DALETH *n* fourth letter of the Hebrew alphabet, transliterated as *d* or, when final, *dh* **daleths**
DALGYTE *another name for* ▶ **bilby**
DALI *n* type of tree **dalis**
DALLE ▶ **dalles**

DALLES *pl n* stretch of a river between high rock walls, with rapids and dangerous currents
DALLIED ▶ **dally**
DALLIER ▶ **dally**
DALLIES ▶ **dally**
DALLOP *n* semisolid lump **dallops**
DALLY *vb*
DALS ▶ **dal**
DALT *n* foster child
DALTON *n* atomic mass unit **daltons**
DALTS ▶ **dalt**
DAM *n, vb*
DAMAGE *vb, n* **damaged, damager**
DAMAGES *pl n* money awarded as compensation for injury or loss
DAMAN *n* the Syrian rock hyrax **damans**
DAMAR = **dammar**
DAMARS ▶ **dammar**
DAMASK *n, vb* **damasks**
DAMBROD *n* draughtboard
DAME *n* **dames**
DAMFOOL *adj* foolish
DAMIANA *n* herbal medicine
DAMMAR *n* any of various resins obtained from SE Asian trees **dammars**
DAMME *interj* exclamation of surprise
DAMMED ▶ **dam**
DAMMER = **dammar**
DAMMERS ▶ **dammer**
DAMMING ▶ **dam**
DAMMIT *interj* exclamation of surprise
DAMN *interj, adj, vb*
DAMNED *adj* condemned to hell ▷ *adv* extreme or extremely
DAMNER *n* person who damns **damners**
DAMNIFY *vb* cause loss or damage to (a person)
DAMNING ▶ **damn**
DAMNS ▶ **damn**
DAMOSEL = **damsel**
DAMOZEL = **damoiselle**
DAMP *adj, n, vb* **damped**
DAMPEN *vb* **dampens**
DAMPER *n* **dampers**
DAMPEST ▶ **damp**
DAMPIER ▶ **dampy**
DAMPING *n* moistening or wetting
DAMPISH ▶ **damp**
DAMPLY ▶ **damp**
DAMPS ▶ **damp**
DAMPY *adj* damp
DAMS ▶ **dam**
DAMSEL *n* **damsels**
DAMSON *n* **damsons**
DAN *n*
DANAZOL *n* type of drug
DANCE *vb, n* **danced, dancer, dancers, dances**
DANCEY *adj* of, relating to, or resembling dance music **dancier**
DANCING ▶ **dance**
DANCY *adj* (of music) appropriate for dancing
DANDER *n* stroll ▷ *vb* stroll **danders**
DANDIER ▶ **dandy**
DANDIES ▶ **dandy**
DANDIFY *vb* dress like or cause to resemble a dandy
DANDILY ▶ **dandy**
DANDLE *vb* move (a child) up and down on one's knee **dandled, dandler, dandles**
DANDY *n, adj*
DANELAW *n* Danish law in parts of Anglo-Saxon England
DANG *a euphemistic word for* ▶ **damn**
DANGED ▶ **dang**
DANGER *n, vb* **dangers**
DANGING ▶ **dang**
DANGLE *vb, n* **dangled, dangler, dangles, dangly**
DANGS ▶ **dang**
DANIO *n* type of tropical freshwater fish **danios**
DANISH *n* sweet pastry
DANK *adj, n* **danker, dankest, dankish, dankly, danks**
DANNIES ▶ **danny**
DANNY *n* hand (used esp when addressing children)
DANS ▶ **dan**
DANSEUR *n* male ballet dancer
DANT *vb* intimidate **danted, danting**
DANTON = **daunton**

DANTONS ▸ **danton**
DANTS ▸ **dant**
DAP *vb* engage in type of fly fishing
DAPHNE *n* ornamental Eurasian shrub **daphnes**
DAPHNIA *n*
DAPHNID *n* water flea
DAPPED ▸ **dap**
DAPPER *adj, n* **dappers**
DAPPING ▸ **dap**
DAPPLE *vb* mark or become marked with spots or patches of a different colour ▷ *n* mottled or spotted markings ▷ *adj* marked with dapples or spots **dappled, dapples**
DAPS ▸ **dap**
DAPSONE *n* antimicrobial drug
DAQUIRI *n* rum cocktail
DARAF *n* unit of elastance equal to a reciprocal farad **darafs**
DARB *n* something excellent
DARBAR *n* hall in Sikh temple **darbars**
DARBIES > **handcuffs**
DARBS ▸ **darb**
DARCIES ▸ **darcy**
DARCY *n* unit expressing the permeability coefficient of rock **darcys**
DARE *vb, n* **dared**
DAREFUL *adj* daring
DARER ▸ **dare**
DARERS ▸ **dare**
DARES ▸ **dare**
DARESAY *vb* venture to say
DARG *n* day's work
DARGA *n* Muslim shrine
DARGAH *n* tomb of a Muslim saint **dargahs**
DARGAS ▸ **darga**
DARGLE *n* wooded hollow **dargles**
DARGS ▸ **darg**
DARI *n* variety of sorghum
DARIC *n* gold coin of ancient Persia **darics**
DARING *adj, n* **darings**
DARIOLE *n* small cup-shaped mould
DARIS ▸ **dari**
DARK *adj, n, vb* **darked**
DARKEN *vb* **darkens**
DARKER, darkest, darking, darkish ▸ **dark**
DARKLE *vb* grow dark **darkled, darkles**
DARKLY ▸ **dark**
DARKNET *n* covert communication network on the Internet
DARKS ▸ **dark**
DARLING *n, adj*
DARN *vb, n*
DARNED *adj* damned
DARNEL *n* weed that grows in grain fields **darnels**
DARNER, darners, darning, darns ▸ **darn**
DAROGHA *n* in India, manager
DARRAIN *vb* clear of guilt
DARRAYN *vb* clear of guilt
DARRE *vb* dare **darred, darres, darring**
DARSHAN *n* Hindu blessing
DART *n, vb* **darted**
DARTER *n* type of aquatic bird **darters**
DARTING ▸ **dart**
DARTLE *vb* move swiftly **dartled, dartles**
DARTRE *n* skin disease **dartres**
DARTS *n* game in which darts are thrown at a dartboard
DARZI *n* tailor in India **darzis**
DAS ▸ **da**
DASH *vb, n* **dashed**
DASHEEN *another name for* ▸ **taro**
DASHEKI *n* upper garment
DASHER *n* one of the boards surrounding an ice-hockey rink **dashers**
DASHES ▸ **dash**
DASHI *n* clear stock made from dried fish and kelp
DASHIER ▸ **dashy**
DASHIKI *n* large loose-fitting buttonless upper garment
DASHING *adj*
DASHIS ▸ **dashi**
DASHPOT *n* device for damping vibrations
DASHY *adj* showy

DASSIE *n* type of hoofed rodent-like animal **dassies**
DASTARD *n* contemptible sneaking coward
DASYPOD *n* armadillo
DASYURE *n*
DATA *n*
DATABLE ▸ **date**
DATABUS *n* computing term
DATAL *adj* slow-witted ▹ *n* day labour **datals**
DATARIA *n* Roman Catholic office
DATARY *n* head of the dataria
DATCHA = **dacha**
DATCHAS ▸ **datcha**
DATE *n*, *vb*
DATED *adj* **datedly**
DATER *n* person who dates **daters**
DATES ▸ **date**
DATING *n* any of several techniques for establishing the age of objects **datings**
DATIVAL ▸ **dative**
DATIVE *adj*, *n* **datives**
DATO *n* chief of any of certain Muslim tribes in the Philippine Islands **datos**
DATTO *n* Datsun car **dattos**
DATUM *n* **datums**
DATURA *n* type of plant **daturas, daturic**
DAUB *vb*, *n*
DAUBE *n* braised meat stew
DAUBED ▸ **daub**
DAUBER ▸ **daub**
DAUBERS ▸ **daub**
DAUBERY *n* act or an instance of daubing
DAUBES ▸ **daube**
DAUBIER ▸ **daub**
DAUBING ▸ **daub**
DAUBRY *n* unskilful painting
DAUBS ▸ **daub**
DAUBY ▸ **daub**
DAUD *n* lump or chunk of something ▹ *vb* (in dialect) whack **dauded, dauding, dauds**
DAULT *n* foster child **daults**
DAUNDER *vb* stroll
DAUNER *vb* stroll **dauners**
DAUNT *vb* **daunted, daunter**
DAUNTON *vb* dishearten
DAUNTS ▸ **daunt**
DAUPHIN *n*
DAUR *a Scot word for* ▸ **dare**
DAURED ▸ **daur**
DAURING ▸ **daur**
DAURS ▸ **daur**
DAUT *vb* fondle **dauted**
DAUTIE *n* darling **dauties**
DAUTING ▸ **daut**
DAUTS ▸ **daut**
DAVEN *vb* pray **davened, davens**
DAVIDIA *n* Chinese shrub
DAVIES ▸ **davy**
DAVIT *n* crane, usu one of a pair, at a ship's side, for lowering and hoisting a lifeboat **davits**
DAVY *n* miner's safety lamp
DAW *n* archaic, dialect, or poetic name for a jackdaw ▹ *vb* old word for dawn

> This is another name for a **jackdaw**. It is worth remembering that not only does this little word take D, K, N, S and T at the back, to make **dawd, dawk, dawn, daws** and **dawt**, but you can put an A on the front of it to make **adaw**.

DAWAH *n* practice of educating non-Muslims about the message of Islam **dawahs**
DAWBAKE *n* foolish or slow-witted person
DAWBRY *n* unskilful painting
DAWCOCK *n* male jackdaw
DAWD *vb* thump **dawded, dawding**
DAWDLE *vb* **dawdled, dawdler, dawdles**
DAWDS ▸ **dawd**
DAWED, dawen, dawing, dawish ▸ **daw**
DAWK = **dak**
DAWKS ▸ **dawk**
DAWN *n*, *vb* **dawned**

DAWNER *vb* stroll **dawners**
DAWNEY *adj* (of a person) dull or slow
DAWNING ▸ **dawn**
DAWNS ▸ **dawn**
DAWS ▸ **daw**
DAWT *vb* fondle **dawted**
DAWTIE *n* darling **dawties**
DAWTING ▸ **dawt**
DAWTS ▸ **dawt**
DAY *n*
DAYAN *n* senior rabbi, esp one who sits in a religious court **dayanim, dayans**
DAYBED *n* narrow bed for day use **daybeds**
DAYBOAT *n* small sailing boat with no sleeping accommodation
DAYBOOK *n* book in which transactions are recorded as they occur
DAYBOY *n* boy who attends a boarding school but returns home each evening **dayboys**
DAYCARE *n*
DAYCH *vb* thatch **dayched, dayches**
DAYFLY *another name for* ▸ **mayfly**
DAYGIRL *n* girl who attends a boarding school but returns home each evening
DAYGLO *n* fluorescent colours
DAYGLOW *n* fluorescent colours
DAYLILY *n* any of various plants having lily-like flowers
DAYLIT > **daylight**
DAYLONG *adv* lasting the entire day
DAYMARE *n* bad dream during the day
DAYMARK *n* navigation aid
DAYNT *adj* dainty
DAYPACK *n* small rucksack
DAYROOM *n* communal living room in a residential institution
DAYS *adv* during the day, esp regularly
DAYSACK *n* rucksack
DAYSIDE *n* side of a planet nearest the sun
DAYSMAN *n* umpire **daysmen**
DAYSTAR *a poetic word for* ▸ **sun**
DAYTALE *n* day labour
DAYTIME *n* time from sunrise to sunset
DAYWEAR *n* clothes for everyday or informal wear
DAYWORK *n* daytime work
DAZE *vb, n* **dazed, dazedly, dazer, dazers, dazes, dazing**
DAZZLE *vb, n* **dazzled, dazzler, dazzles**
DE *prep* of or from
DEACON *n, vb* **deacons**
DEAD *adj, n, adv, vb*
DEADBOY ▸ **deadman**
DEADED ▸ **dead**
DEADEN *vb* **deadens**
DEADER ▸ **dead**
DEADERS ▸ **dead**
DEADEST ▸ **dead**
DEADEYE *n* either of two disclike blocks used to tighten a shroud on a boat
DEADING ▸ **dead**
DEADLY *adj, adv*
DEADMAN *n* item used in construction **deadmen**
DEADPAN *adv, adj, n*
DEADS ▸ **dead**
DEAF *adj*
DEAFEN *vb* **deafens**
DEAFER, deafest, deafish, deafly ▸ **deaf**
DEAIR *vb* remove air from **deaired, deairs**
DEAL *n, vb, adj*
DEALATE *adj* (of insects) having lost their wings after mating ▹ *n* insect that has shed its wings
DEALER *n* **dealers**
DEALING ▸ **deal**
DEALS ▸ **deal**
DEALT ▸ **deal**
DEAN *n, vb* **deaned**
DEANER *n* shilling **deaners**
DEANERY *n* office or residence of a dean
DEANING ▸ **dean**
DEANS ▸ **dean**
DEAR *n, adj*
DEARE *vb* harm **deared**
DEARER ▸ **dear**
DEARES ▸ **deare**
DEAREST ▸ **dear**

DEARIE = **deary**
DEARIES ▸ **deary**
DEARING ▸ **deare**
DEARLY *adv* very much
DEARN *vb* hide **dearnly, dearns**
DEARS ▸ **dear**
DEARTH *n* **dearths**
DEARY *n* term of affection: now often sarcastic or facetious
DEASH *vb* remove ash from **deashed, deashes**
DEASIL *adv* in the direction of the apparent course of the sun ▹ *n* motion in this direction **deasils**
DEASIUL *n* motion towards the sun
DEASOIL *n* motion towards the sun
DEATH *n*
DEATHLY *adv, adj*
DEATHS ▸ **death**
DEATHY ▸ **death**
DEAVE *vb* deafen **deaved, deaves, deaving**
DEAW *n* dew **deawie, deaws, deawy**
DEB *n* debutante
DEBACLE *n*
DEBAG *vb* remove the trousers from (someone) by force **debags**
DEBAR *vb*
DEBARK *vb* remove the bark from (a tree) **debarks**
DEBARS ▸ **debar**
DEBASE *vb* **debased, debaser, debases**
DEBATE *n, vb* **debated, debater, debates**
DEBAUCH *vb* make (someone) bad or corrupt, esp sexually ▹ *n* instance or period of extreme dissipation
DEBBIER ▸ **debby**
DEBBIES ▸ **debby**
DEBBY *n* debutante ▹ *adj* of, or resembling a debutante
DEBE *n* tin
DEBEAK *vb* remove part of the beak of poultry to reduce the risk of such habits as feather-picking or cannibalism **debeaks**
DEBEARD *vb* remove beard from mussel
DEBEL *vb* beat in war **debels**
DEBES ▸ **debe**
DEBILE *adj* lacking strength
DEBIT *n, vb* **debited**
DEBITOR *n* person in debt
DEBITS ▸ **debit**
DEBONE *vb* remove bones from **deboned, deboner, debones**
DEBOSH *vb* debauch
DEBOSS *vb* carve a design into
DEBOUCH *vb* move out from a narrow place to a wider one ▹ *n* outlet or passage, as for the exit of troops
DEBRIDE *vb* remove dead tissue from
DEBRIEF *vb*
DEBRIS *n*
DEBS ▸ **deb**
DEBT *n*
DEBTED *adj* in debt
DEBTEE *n* person owed a debt **debtees**
DEBTOR *n* **debtors**
DEBTS ▸ **debt**
DEBUD = **disbud**
DEBUDS ▸ **debud**
DEBUG *vb, n* **debugs**
DEBUNK *vb* expose the falseness of **debunks**
DEBUR *vb* remove burs from (a piece of machined metal)
DEBURR *vb* remove burrs from (a workpiece) **deburrs**
DEBURS ▸ **debur**
DEBUS *vb* unload (goods) or (esp of troops) to alight from a motor vehicle **debused, debuses**
DEBUT *n, vb* **debuted, debuts**
DEBYE *n* unit of electric dipole moment **debyes**
DECAD *n* ten years
DECADAL ▸ **decade**
DECADE *n* **decades**
DECADS ▸ **decad**
DECAF *n* decaffeinated coffee ▹ *adj* decaffeinated
DECAFF *n* decaffeinated coffee **decaffs**
DECAFS ▸ **decaf**
DECAGON *n* geometric figure with ten faces
DECAL *vb* transfer

(a design) by decalcomania **decaled**
DECALOG = **decalogue decals**
DECAMP *vb* **decamps**
DECANAL *adj* of or relating to a dean or deanery
DECANE *n* liquid alkane hydrocarbon **decanes**
DECANI *adv* be sung by the decanal side of a choir
DECANT *vb* **decants**
DECAPOD *n* creature, such as a crab, with five pairs of walking limbs ▷ *adj* of, relating to, or belonging to these creatures
DECARB *vb* decoke **decarbs**
DECARE *n* ten ares or 1000 square metres **decares**
DECAY *vb, n* **decayed, decayer, decays**
DECCIE *n* decoration **deccies**
DECEASE *n*
DECEIT *n* **deceits**
DECEIVE *vb*
DECENCY *n*
DECENT *adj*
DECERN *vb* decree or adjudge **decerns**
DECIARE *n* one tenth of an are or 10 square metres
DECIBEL *n*
DECIDE *vb*
DECIDED *adj*
DECIDER *n* thing that determines who wins a match or championship
DECIDES ▸ **decide**
DECIDUA *n* membrane lining the uterus of some mammals during pregnancy
DECILE *n* one of nine actual or notional values of a variable dividing its distribution into ten groups with equal frequencies **deciles**
DECIMAL *n, adj*
DECIME *n* former French coin **decimes**
DECK *n, vb*
DECKED *adj* having a wooden deck or platform
DECKEL = **deckle**
DECKELS ▸ **deckel**
DECKER ▸ **deck**
DECKERS ▸ **deck**
DECKING *n* wooden platform in a garden
DECKLE *n* frame used to contain pulp on the mould in the making of handmade paper **deckled, deckles**
DECKO *n* look ▷ *vb* have a look **deckoed, deckos**
DECKS ▸ **deck**
DECLAIM *vb*
DECLARE *vb*
DECLASS *vb* lower in social status or position
DECLAW *vb* remove claws from **declaws**
DECLINE *vb, n*
DECO *adj as in* **art deco** style of art, jewellery, design, etc
DECOCT *vb* extract the essence from (a substance) by boiling **decocts**
DECODE *vb* **decoded, decoder, decodes**
DECOKE *n* decarbonize **decoked, decokes**
DECOLOR *vb* bleach
DECOR *n* **decors**
DECORUM *n*
DECOS ▸ **deco**
DECOY *n, vb* **decoyed, decoyer, decoys**
DECREE *n, vb* **decreed, decreer, decrees**
DECREET *n* final judgment or sentence of a court
DECREW *vb* decrease **decrews**
DECRIAL, decried, decrier, decries ▸ **decry**
DECROWN *vb* depose
DECRY *vb*
DECRYPT *vb* decode (a message)
DECTET *n* ten musicians **dectets**
DECUMAN *n* large wave
DECUPLE *vb* increase by ten times ▷ *n* amount ten times as large as a given reference ▷ *adj* increasing tenfold
DECURIA *n* group of ten
DECURVE *vb* curve downwards
DECURY *n* (in ancient

Rome) a body of ten men
DEDAL = **daedal**
DEDANS *n* open gallery at the server's end of the court
DEDIMUS *n* legal term
DEDUCE *vb* **deduced, deduces**
DEDUCT *vb* **deducts**
DEE *a Scot word for* ▸ **die**
DEED *n, vb, adj* **deeded, deeder, deedest**
DEEDFUL *adj* full of exploits
DEEDIER ▸ **deedy**
DEEDILY ▸ **deedy**
DEEDING ▸ **deed**
DEEDS ▸ **deed**
DEEDY *adj* hard-working
DEEING ▸ **dee**
DEEJAY *n* disc jockey ▹ *vb* work or act as a disc jockey **deejays**
DEEK *vb* look at
DEELY *adj as in* **deely boppers** hairband with two bobbing antennae-like attachments
DEEM *vb* **deemed, deeming, deems**
DEEN *n* din **deens**
DEEP *adj, n*
DEEPEN *vb* **deepens**
DEEPER ▸ **deep**
DEEPEST ▸ **deep**
DEEPIE *n* 3D film **deepies**
DEEPLY ▸ **deep**
DEEPS ▸ **deep**
DEER *n*
DEERE *adj* serious
DEERFLY *n* insect related to the horsefly
DEERLET *n* ruminant mammal
DEERS ▸ **deer**
DEES ▸ **dee**
DEET *n* insect-repellent **deets**
DEEV *n* mythical monster
DEEVE *vb* deafen **deeved, deeves, deeving**
DEEVS ▸ **deev**
DEEWAN *n* chief of a village in India **deewans**
DEF *adj* very good
DEFACE *vb* **defaced, defacer, defaces**
DEFAME *vb* attack the good reputation of **defamed, defamer, defames**
DEFANG *vb* remove the fangs of **defangs**
DEFAST *adj* defaced
DEFASTE *adj* defaced
DEFAT *vb* remove fat from **defats**
DEFAULT *n, vb*
DEFEAT *vb, n* **defeats**
DEFECT *n, vb* **defects**
DEFENCE *n*
DEFEND *vb* **defends**
DEFENSE = **defence**
DEFER *vb* **defers**
DEFFER ▸ **def**
DEFFEST ▸ **def**
DEFFLY *archaic word* = **deftly**
DEFFO *interj* definitely: an expression of agreement or consent
DEFI *n* challenge
DEFIANT *adj* marked by resistance or bold opposition, as to authority
DEFICIT *n*
DEFIED, defier, defiers, defies ▸ **defy**
DEFILE *vb, n* **defiled, defiler, defiles**
DEFINE *vb* **defined, definer, defines**
DEFIS ▸ **defi**
DEFLATE *vb*
DEFLEA *vb* remove fleas from **defleas**
DEFLECT *vb*
DEFLEX *vb* turn downwards
DEFO *interj*
DEFOAM *vb* remove foam from **defoams**
DEFOCUS *vb* put out of focus
DEFOG *vb* clear of vapour **defogs**
DEFORCE *vb* withhold (property, esp land) wrongfully or by force from the rightful owner
DEFORM *vb* **deforms**
DEFOUL *vb* defile **defouls**
DEFRAG *vb* defragment **defrags**
DEFRAUD *vb*
DEFRAY *vb* **defrays**
DEFROCK *vb* deprive (a priest) of priestly status
DEFROST *vb*
DEFROZE > **defreeze**
DEFT *adj* **defter,**

deftest, deftly
DEFUEL *vb* remove fuel from **defuels**
DEFUNCT *adj, n*
DEFUND *vb* stop funds to **defunds**
DEFUSE *vb* **defused, defuser, defuses, defuze**
DEFUZED ▸ **defuze**
DEFUZES ▸ **defuze**
DEFY *vb* **defying**
DEG *vb* water (a plant, etc)
DEGAGE *adj* unconstrained in manner
DEGAME *n* tree of South and Central America **degames, degami**
DEGAMIS ▸ **degami**
DEGAS *vb* remove gas from (a container, vacuum tube, liquid, adsorbent, etc) **degases**
DEGAUSS *n* demagnetize
DEGERM *vb* remove germs from **degerms**
DEGGED ▸ **deg**
DEGGING ▸ **deg**
DEGLAZE *vb* dilute meat sediments in (a pan) in order to make a sauce or gravy
DEGOUT *n* disgust **degouts**
DEGRADE *vb*
DEGRAS *n* emulsion used for dressing hides
DEGREE *n*
DEGREED *adj* having a degree
DEGREES ▸ **degree**
DEGS ▸ **deg**
DEGU *n* small S American rodent
DEGUM *vb* remove gum from **degums**
DEGUS ▸ **degu**
DEGUST *vb* taste, esp with care or relish **degusts**
DEHISCE *vb* (of the seed capsules of some plants) to burst open spontaneously
DEHORN *vb* remove or prevent the growth of the horns of (cattle, sheep, or goats) **dehorns**
DEHORT *vb* dissuade **dehorts**
DEI ▸ **deus**
DEICE *vb* free or be freed of ice **deiced, deicer, deicers, deices**
DEICIDE *n* act of killing a god
DEICING ▸ **deice**
DEICTIC *adj* proving by direct argument
DEID *a Scot word for* ▸ **dead**
DEIDER ▸ **deid**
DEIDEST ▸ **deid**
DEIDS ▸ **deid**
DEIF *a Scot word for* ▸ **deaf**
DEIFER ▸ **deif**
DEIFEST ▸ **deif**
DEIFIC *adj* making divine or exalting to the position of a god
DEIFIED ▸ **deify**
DEIFIER ▸ **deify**
DEIFIES ▸ **deify**
DEIFORM *adj* having the form or appearance of a god
DEIFY *vb*
DEIGN *vb* **deigned, deigns**
DEIL *a Scot word for* ▸ **devil**
DEILS ▸ **deil**
DEINDEX *vb* cause to become no longer index-linked
DEISEAL *n* clockwise motion
DEISM *n* belief in God but not in divine revelation **deisms, deist, deistic, deists**
DEITIES ▸ **deity**
DEITY *n*
DEIXES ▸ **deixis**
DEIXIS *n* use or reference of a deictic word
DEJECT *vb* have a depressing effect on ▷ *adj* downcast
DEJECTA *pl n* waste products excreted through the anus
DEJECTS ▸ **deject**
DEJEUNE *n* lunch
DEKARE *n* unit of measurement equal to ten ares **dekares**
DEKE *vb* movement used in ice hockey or box lacrosse ▷ *n* such a shot or movement **deked, dekeing, dekes, deking**
DEKKO *n* look ▷ *vb* have a look **dekkoed, dekkos**

DEL *n* differential operator
DELAINE *n* sheer wool or wool and cotton fabric
DELAPSE *vb* be inherited
DELATE *vb* (formerly) to bring a charge against **delated, delates, delator**
DELAY *vb, n* **delayed, delayer, delays**
DELE *n* sign indicating that typeset matter is to be deleted ▷ *vb* mark (matter to be deleted) with a dele
DELEAD *vb* remove lead from **deleads**
DELEAVE *vb* separate copies
DELEBLE *adj* able to be deleted
DELED ▸ **dele**
DELEING ▸ **dele**
DELENDA *pl n* items for deleting
DELES ▸ **dele**
DELETE *vb* **deleted, deletes**
DELF *n* kind of earthenware **delfs**
DELFT *n* tin-glazed earthenware, typically having blue designs on white **delfts**
DELI *n* delicatessen
DELIBLE *adj* able to be deleted
DELICE *n* delicacy **delices**
DELICT *n* wrongful act for which the person injured has the right to a civil remedy **delicts**
DELIGHT *n, vb*
DELIME *vb* remove lime from **delimed, delimes**
DELIMIT *vb*
DELIRIA > **delirium**
DELIS ▸ **deli**
DELISH *adj* delicious
DELIST *vb* remove from a list **delists**
DELIVER *vb*
DELL *n*
DELLIES ▸ **delly**
DELLS ▸ **dell**
DELLY *n* delicatessen
DELO *an informal word for* > **delegate**
DELOPE *vb* shoot into the air **deloped, delopes**
DELOS ▸ **delo**
DELOUSE *vb* rid (a person or animal) of lice
DELPH *n* kind of earthenware
DELPHIC *adj* obscure or ambiguous
DELPHIN *n* fatty substance from dolphin oil
DELPHS ▸ **delph**
DELS ▸ **del**
DELT *n* deltoid muscle
DELTA *n* **deltaic, deltas, deltic**
DELTOID *n* muscle acting to raise the arm ▷ *adj* shaped like a Greek capital delta
DELTS ▸ **delt**
DELUDE *vb* **deluded, deluder, deludes**
DELUGE *n, vb* **deluged, deluges**
DELUXE *adj* rich, elegant, superior, or sumptuous
DELVE *vb* **delved, delver, delvers, delves, delving**
DEMAGOG = **demagogue**
DEMAIN *n* demesne
DEMAINE *n* demesne
DEMAINS ▸ **demain**
DEMAN *vb* reduce the workforce of (a plant, industry, etc)
DEMAND *vb, n* **demands**
DEMANS ▸ **deman**
DEMARK *vb* demarcate **demarks**
DEMAST *vb* remove the mast from **demasts**
DEMAYNE *n* demesne
DEME *n* (in preclassical Greece) the territory inhabited by a tribe
DEMEAN *vb*
DEMEANE *n* demesne
DEMEANS ▸ **demean**
DEMENT *vb* deteriorate mentally, esp because of old age
DEMENTI *n* denial
DEMENTS ▸ **dement**
DEMERGE *vb* separate a company from another
DEMERIT *n* fault, disadvantage ▷ *vb* deserve
DEMERSE *vb* immerse
DEMES ▸ **deme**

DEMESNE *n* land surrounding a house
DEMETON *n* insecticide
DEMIC *adj* of population
DEMIES ▸ **demy**
DEMIGOD *n* being who is part mortal, part god
DEMIREP *n* woman of bad repute, esp a prostitute
DEMISE *n*, *vb* **demised, demises**
DEMISS *adj* humble
DEMIST *vb* remove condensation from (a windscreen) **demists**
DEMIT *vb* resign (an office, position, etc) **demits**
DEMIVEG *n* person who eats poultry and fish, but no red meat ▹ *adj* denoting a person who eats poultry and fish, but no red meat
DEMO *n*, *vb*
DEMOB *vb* demobilize **demobs**
DEMODE *adj* out of fashion
DEMODED *adj* out of fashion
DEMOED ▸ **demo**
DEMOING ▸ **demo**
DEMON *n*
DEMONIC *adj* evil
DEMONRY ▸ **demon**
DEMONS ▸ **demon**
DEMOS *n* people of a nation regarded as a political unit **demoses**
DEMOTE *vb* **demoted, demotes**
DEMOTIC *adj* of the common people ▹ *n* demotic script of ancient Egypt
DEMOUNT *vb* remove (a motor, gun, etc) from its mounting or setting
DEMPT ▸ **deem**
DEMUR *vb*, *n*
DEMURE *adj*, *vb*, *n* **demured, demurer, demures**
DEMURS ▸ **demur**
DEMY *n* size of printing paper, 17½ by 22½ inches (444.5 x 571.5 mm)
DEN *n*, *vb*
DENAR *n* standard monetary unit of Macedonia, divided into 100 deni **denari**
DENARII > **denarius**
DENARS ▸ **denar**
DENARY *adj* calculated by tens
DENAY *vb* deny **denayed, denays**
DENDRON = **dendrite**
DENE *n* narrow wooded valley **denes**
DENET *vb* remove from the Net Book Agreement **denets**
DENGUE *n* viral disease transmitted by mosquitoes **dengues**
DENI *n* monetary unit of the Former Yugoslav Republic of Macedonia, worth one hundredth of a denar
DENIAL *n* **denials**
DENIED ▸ **deny**
DENIER *n* **deniers**
DENIES ▸ **deny**
DENIM *n*
DENIMED *adj* wearing denim
DENIMS *pl n* jeans or overalls made of denim
DENIS ▸ **deni**
DENIZEN *n* inhabitant ▹ *vb* make a denizen
DENNED ▸ **den**
DENNET *n* carriage for one horse **dennets**
DENNING ▸ **den**
DENOTE *vb* **denoted, denotes**
DENS ▸ **den**
DENSE *adj* **densely, denser, densest**
DENSIFY *vb* make or become dense
DENSITY *n*
DENT *n*, *vb*
DENTAL *adj*, *n* **dentals**
DENTARY *n* lower jawbone with teeth
DENTATE *adj* having teeth or teethlike notches
DENTED ▸ **dent**
DENTEL *n* architectural term **dentels**
DENTEX *n* large predatory fish
DENTIL *n* architectural ornament **dentils**
DENTIN = **dentine**
DENTINE *n*
DENTING ▸ **dent**

DENTINS ▸ **dentin**
DENTIST *n*
DENTOID *adj* resembling a tooth
DENTS ▸ **dent**
DENTURE *n* false tooth
DENUDE *vb* **denuded, denuder, denudes**
DENY *vb* **denying**
DEODAND *n* (formerly) a thing that had caused a death and was forfeited to the crown for a charitable purpose
DEODAR *n* Himalayan cedar with drooping branches **deodara, deodars**
DEODATE *n* offering to God
DEONTIC *adj* of or relating to such ethical concepts as obligation and permissibility
DEORBIT *vb* go out of orbit
DEOXY *adj* having less oxygen than a specified related compound
DEPAINT *vb* depict
DEPART *vb* **departs**
DEPECHE *n* message
DEPEND *vb* **depends**
DEPERM *vb* demagnetize **deperms**
DEPICT *vb* **depicts**
DEPLANE *vb* disembark from an aeroplane
DEPLETE *vb*
DEPLORE *vb*
DEPLOY *vb* **deploys**
DEPLUME *vb* deprive of feathers
DEPONE *vb* declare (something) under oath **deponed, depones**
DEPORT *vb* **deports**
DEPOSAL *n* deposition; giving of testimony under oath
DEPOSE *vb* **deposed, deposer, deposes**
DEPOSIT *vb, n*
DEPOT *n, adj* **depots**
DEPRAVE *vb*
DEPRESS *vb*
DEPRIVE *vb*
DEPSIDE *n* organic chemical compound
DEPTH *n* **depths**
DEPUTE *vb, n* **deputed, deputes**
DEPUTY *n*
DEQUEUE *vb* remove (an item) from a queue of computing tasks
DERAIGN *vb* contest (a claim, suit, etc)
DERAIL *vb, n* **derails**
DERANGE *vb* disturb the order or arrangement of
DERAT *vb* remove rats from
DERATE *vb* assess the value of some types of property at a lower rate than others for local taxation **derated, derates**
DERATS ▸ **derat**
DERAY *vb* go mad **derayed, derays**
DERBIES ▸ **derby**
DERBY *n*
DERE *vb* injure **dered, deres**
DERHAM = **dirham**
DERHAMS ▸ **derham**
DERIDE *vb* **derided, derider, derides**
DERIG *vb* remove equipment, e.g. from stage set **derigs**
DERING ▸ **dere**
DERIVE *vb* **derived, deriver, derives**
DERM = **derma**
DERMA *n* beef or fowl intestine used as a casing for certain dishes, esp kishke
DERMAL *adj* of or relating to the skin
DERMAS ▸ **derma**
DERMIC ▸ **dermis**
DERMIS *another name for* ▸ **corium**
DERMOID *adj* of or resembling skin ▹ *n* congenital cystic tumour whose walls are lined with epithelium
DERMS ▸ **derm**
DERN *n* concealment
DERNFUL *adj* sorrowful
DERNIER *adj* last
DERNLY *adv* sorrowfully
DERNS ▸ **dern**
DERO *n* tramp or derelict **deros**
DERRICK *n, vb*
DERRIES ▸ **derry**
DERRIS *n* E Indian woody climbing plant
DERRO *n* vagrant **derros**
DERRY *n* derelict house, esp one used by tramps, drug addicts, etc

DERTH = **dearth**
DERTHS ▶ **derth**
DERV *n*
DERVISH *n* member of a Muslim religious order noted for a frenzied whirling dance
DERVS ▶ **derv**
DESALT *vb* **desalts**
DESAND *vb* remove sand from **desands**
DESCALE *vb* remove a hard coating from inside (a kettle or pipe)
DESCANT *n, adj, vb*
DESCEND *vb*
DESCENT *n*
DESCRY *vb* catch sight of
DESEED *vb* remove the seeds from (eg a fruit) **deseeds**
DESERT *n, vb* **deserts**
DESERVE *vb*
DESEX *n* desexualize **desexed, desexes**
DESHI = **desi**
DESI *adj* in Indian English, indigenous or local
DESIGN *vb, n* **designs, desine**
DESINED ▶ **desine**
DESINES ▶ **desine**
DESIRE *vb, n* **desired, desirer, desires**
DESIST *vb* **desists**
DESK *n*
DESKILL *vb* mechanize or computerize (a job) thereby reducing the skill required to do it
DESKING *n* desks and related furnishings in a given space, eg an office
DESKMAN *n* police officer in charge in police station **deskmen**
DESKS ▶ **desk**
DESKTOP *adj, n*
DESMAN *n* either of two molelike amphibious mammals **desmans**
DESMID *n* type of mainly unicellular freshwater green alga **desmids**
DESMINE *n* type of mineral
DESMOID *adj* resembling a tendon or ligament ▷ *n* very firm tumour of connective tissue
DESNOOD *vb* remove the snood of a turkey poult to reduce the risk of cannibalism
DESORB *vb* change from an adsorbed state to a gaseous or liquid state **desorbs**
DESOXY = **deoxy**
DESPAIR *n, vb*
DESPISE *vb*
DESPITE *prep, n, vb*
DESPOIL *vb*
DESPOND *vb* lose heart or hope
DESPOT *n* **despots**
DESSE *n* desk
DESSERT *n*
DESSES ▶ **desse**
DESTAIN *vb* remove stain from
DESTINE *vb* set apart or appoint
DESTINY *n*
DESTOCK *vb* reduce the amount of stock
DESTROY *vb*
DESUGAR *vb* remove sugar from
DESYNE = **design**
DESYNED ▶ **desyne**
DESYNES ▶ **desyne**
DETACH *vb*
DETAIL *n, vb* **details**
DETAIN *vb* **detains**
DETECT *vb* **detects**
DETENT *n* locking piece of a mechanism, often spring-loaded to check the movement of a wheel in one direction only
DETENTE *n*
DETENTS ▶ **detent**
DETENU *n* prisoner
DETENUE *n* female prisoner
DETENUS ▶ **detenu**
DETER *vb*
DETERGE *vb* wash or wipe away
DETERS ▶ **deter**
DETEST *vb* **detests**
DETICK *vb* remove ticks from **deticks**
DETINUE *n* action brought by a plaintiff to recover goods wrongfully detained
DETORT *vb* pervert **detorts**
DETOUR *n, vb* **detours**
DETOX *n* treatment to rid the body of poisonous substances

▷ *vb* undergo treatment to rid the body of poisonous substances **detoxed, detoxes**
DETRACT *vb*
DETRAIN *vb* leave or cause to leave a railway train, as passengers, etc
DETRUDE *vb* force down or thrust away or out
DETUNE *vb* change pitch of (stringed instrument) **detuned, detunes**
DEUCE *vb, n*
DEUCED *adj* damned
DEUCES ▶ **deuce**
DEUCING ▶ **deuce**
DEUS *n* god
DEUTON *old form of* > **deuteron**
DEUTONS ▶ **deuton**
DEUTZIA *n* shrub with clusters of pink or white flowers
DEV = **deva**

> **Dev** is a Sanskrit word for a good spirit; related words are **deev** and **deva**

DEVA *n* (in Hinduism and Buddhism) divine being or god
DEVALL *vb* stop **devalls**
DEVALUE *vb*
DEVAS ▶ **deva**
DEVEIN *vb* remove vein from **deveins**
DEVEL = **devvel**
DEVELED ▶ **devel**
DEVELOP *vb*
DEVELS ▶ **devel**
DEVEST *variant spelling of* ▶ **divest**
DEVESTS ▶ **devest**
DEVIANT *adj, n*
DEVIATE *vb*
DEVICE *n* **devices**
DEVIL *n, vb* **deviled**
DEVILET *n* young devil
DEVILRY *n*
DEVILS ▶ **devil**
DEVIOUS *adj*
DEVISAL *n* act of inventing, contriving, or devising
DEVISE *vb, n* **devised**
DEVISEE *n* person to whom property, esp realty, is devised by will
DEVISER ▶ **devise**
DEVISES ▶ **devise**
DEVISOR *n* person who devises property, esp realty, by will
DEVLING *n* young devil
DEVOICE *vb* make (a voiced speech sound) voiceless
DEVOID *adj*
DEVOIR *n* duty **devoirs**
DEVOLVE *vb*
DEVON *n* bland processed meat in sausage form, eaten cold in slices **devons**
DEVORE *n* velvet fabric with a raised pattern **devores**
DEVOT *n* devotee
DEVOTE *vb*
DEVOTED *adj*
DEVOTEE *n*
DEVOTES ▶ **devote**
DEVOTS ▶ **devot**
DEVOUR *vb* **devours**
DEVOUT *adj*
DEVS ▶ **dev**
DEVVEL *vb* strike with blow **devvels**
DEW *n, vb*
DEWAN *n* (formerly in India) the chief or finance minister of a state ruled by an Indian prince
DEWANI *n* post of dewan **dewanis, dewanny**
DEWANS ▶ **dewan**
DEWAR *n as in* **dewar flask** type of vacuum flask **dewars**
DEWATER *vb* remove water from
DEWAX *vb* remove wax from **dewaxed, dewaxes**
DEWCLAW *n* nonfunctional claw on a dog's leg
DEWDROP *n* drop of dew
DEWED ▶ **dew**
DEWFALL *n* formation of dew
DEWFULL *obsolete form of* ▶ **due**
DEWIER ▶ **dewy**
DEWIEST ▶ **dewy**
DEWILY ▶ **dewy**
DEWING ▶ **dew**
DEWITT *vb* kill, esp hang unlawfully **dewitts**
DEWLAP *n* **dewlaps, dewlapt**
DEWLESS ▶ **dew**
DEWOOL *vb* remove wool from **dewools**

DEWORM *vb* rid of worms **deworms**
DEWS ▸ **dew**
DEWY *adj*
DEX *n* dextroamphetamine **dexes**

> Short for Dexedrine®, a stimulant drug, this is another of the key words to know for using the X. It can be extended to **dexy** or **dexie**.

DEXIE *n* pill containing dextroamphetamine **dexies**
DEXTER *adj* of or on the right side of a shield, etc, from the bearer's point of view ▹ *n* small breed of beef cattle **dexters**
DEXTRAL *adj* of, relating to, or located on the right side, esp of the body
DEXTRAN *n* polysaccharide compound
DEXTRIN *n* sticky substance obtained from starch
DEXTRO *adj* dextrorotatory or rotating to the right
DEXY = **dexie**
DEY *n* title given to commanders or governors of the Janissaries of Algiers **deys**
DEZINC *vb* remove zinc from **dezincs**
DHAK *n* tropical Asian tree **dhaks**
DHAL *n* **dhals**
DHAMMA *variant of* ▸ **dharma**
DHAMMAS ▸ **dhamma**
DHANSAK *n* any of a variety of Indian dishes
DHARMA *n* **dharmas, dharmic**
DHARNA *n* (in India) a method of obtaining justice **dharnas**
DHIMMI *n* non-Muslim living in a state governed by sharia law **dhimmis**
DHOBI *n* (in India, Malaya, East Africa, etc, esp formerly) a washerman **dhobis**
DHOL *n* type of Indian drum
DHOLE *n* fierce canine mammal **dholes**
DHOLL = **dhal**
DHOLLS ▸ **dholl**
DHOLS ▸ **dhol**
DHOOLY = **doolie**
DHOORA = **durra**
DHOORAS ▸ **dhoora**
DHOOTI = **dhoti**
DHOOTIE = **dhoti**
DHOOTIS ▸ **dhooti**
DHOTI *n* **dhotis**
DHOURRA = **durra**
DHOW *n* Arab sailing ship **dhows**
DHURNA = **dharna**
DHURNAS ▸ **dhurna**
DHURRA = **durra**
DHURRAS ▸ **dhurra**
DHURRIE = **durrie**
DHUTI = **dhoti**
DHUTIS ▸ **dhuti**
DI ▸ **deus**
DIABASE *n* altered dolerite
DIABLE *n* type of sauce **diables**
DIABOLO *n* game using a spinning top and a cord fastened to two sticks
DIACID *n* lead plaster **diacids**
DIACT *n* two-rayed
DIADEM *n, vb* **diadems**
DIADROM *n* complete course of pendulum
DIAGRAM *n, vb*
DIAGRID *n* diagonal structure network
DIAL *n, vb*
DIALECT *n*
DIALED, dialer, dialers, dialing ▸ **dial**
DIALIST *n* dial-maker
DIALLED ▸ **dial**
DIALLEL *n* interbreeding among a group of parents
DIALLER ▸ **dial**
DIALOG = **dialogue**
DIALOGS ▸ **dialog**
DIALS ▸ **dial**
DIALYSE *vb* separate by dialysis **dialyze**
DIAMIDE *n* compound containing two amido groups
DIAMIN = **diamine**
DIAMINE *n* any chemical compound containing two amino groups in its molecules
DIAMINS ▸ **diamin**
DIAMOND *n, adj, vb*

DIAMYL *adj* with two amyl groups
DIANDRY *n* practice of having two husbands
DIANE *adj as in* **steak diane** kind of steak
DIANOIA *n* perception and experience regarded as lower modes of knowledge
DIAPASE = **diapason**
DIAPER *n* nappy ▷ *vb* decorate with a geometric pattern **diapers**
DIAPIR *n* anticlinal fold in which the brittle overlying rock has been pierced by material, such as salt, from beneath **diapirs**
DIAPSID *n* reptile with two holes in rear of skull
DIARCH *adj* (of a vascular bundle) having two strands of xylem
DIARCHY *n* government by two states, individuals, etc
DIARIAL ▸ **diary**
DIARIAN ▸ **diary**
DIARIES ▸ **diary**
DIARISE = **diarize**
DIARIST *n* person who writes a diary
DIARIZE *vb* record in diary
DIARY *n*
DIASCIA *n* S African plant, usu with pink flowers
DIASTEM = **diastema**
DIASTER *n* stage in cell division
DIATOM *n* microscopic unicellular alga **diatoms**
DIATRON *n* circuit that uses diodes
DIAXON *n* bipolar cell **diaxons**
DIAZIN = **diazine**
DIAZINE *n* organic compound
DIAZINS ▸ **diazin**
DIAZO *adj* relating to a method for reproducing documents ▷ *n* document produced by this method **diazoes**
DIAZOLE *n* type of organic compound
DIAZOS ▸ **diazo**
DIB *vb* fish by allowing the bait to bob and dip on the surface
DIBASIC *adj* (of an acid) containing two acidic hydrogen atoms
DIBBED ▸ **dib**
DIBBER = **dibble**
DIBBERS ▸ **dibber**
DIBBING ▸ **dib**
DIBBLE *n* small gardening tool ▷ *vb* make a hole in (the ground) with a dibble **dibbled, dibbler, dibbles**
DIBBS *n* money
DIBBUK *variant spelling of* ▸ **dybbuk**
DIBBUKS ▸ **dibbuk**
DIBS ▸ **dib**
DIBUTYL *adj* with two butyl groups
DICAMBA *n* type of weedkiller
DICAST *n* juror in ancient Athens **dicasts**
DICE *n, vb* **diced, dicer, dicers, dices**
DICEY *adj*
DICH *interj* archaic expression meaning "may it do"
DICHORD *n* two-stringed musical instrument
DICHT *vb* wipe **dichted, dichts**
DICIER ▸ **dicey**
DICIEST ▸ **dicey**
DICING ▸ **dice**
DICINGS ▸ **dice**
DICKENS *n* euphemism for devil
DICKER *vb* trade (goods) by bargaining ▷ *n* petty bargain or barter **dickers**
DICKEY = **dicky**
DICKEYS ▸ **dickey**
DICKIE = **dicky**
DICKIER ▸ **dicky**
DICKIES ▸ **dicky**
DICKTY = **dicty**
DICKY *n, adj*
DICLINY > **diclinous**
DICOT *n* type of flowering plant **dicots**
DICOTYL *n* type of flowering plant
DICT *vb* dictate
DICTA ▸ **dictum**
DICTATE *vb, n*
DICTED ▸ **dict**
DICTIER ▸ **dicty**

DICTING ▸ **dict**
DICTION *n*
DICTS ▸ **dict**
DICTUM *n* **dictums**
DICTY *adj* conceited; snobbish
DICYCLY > **dicyclic**
DID ▸ **do**
DIDACT *n* instructive person **didacts**
DIDAKAI = **didicoy**
DIDAKEI = **didicoy**
DIDDER *vb* shake with fear **didders**
DIDDIER ▸ **diddy**
DIDDIES ▸ **diddy**
DIDDLE *vb* **diddled, diddler, diddles**
DIDDLEY *n* worthless amount
DIDDLY *n* worthless amount
DIDDY *n* female breast or nipple ▹ *adj* of or relating to a diddy
DIDICOI = **didicoy**
DIDICOY *n* (in Britain) a person who lives like a Gypsy but is not a true Romany
DIDIE = **didy**
DIDIES ▸ **didy**
DIDO *n* antic **didoes, didos**
DIDST *form of the past tense of* ▸ **do**
DIDY *n* woman's breast
DIE *vb, n*
DIEB *n* N African jackal
DIEBACK *n* disease of trees and shrubs ▹ *vb* (of plants) to suffer from dieback
DIEBS ▸ **dieb**
DIED ▸ **die**
DIEDRAL = **dihedral**
DIEDRE *n* large shallow groove or corner in a rock face **diedres**
DIEHARD *n*
DIEING ▸ **die**
DIEL *n* 24-hour period
DIENE *n* type of hydrocarbon **dienes**
DIEOFF *n* process of dying in large numbers **dieoffs**
DIES ▸ **die**
DIESEL *vb, n* **diesels**
DIESES ▸ **diesis**
DIESIS *n* (in ancient Greek theory) any interval smaller than a whole tone
DIESTER *n* synthetic lubricant
DIET *n, vb, adj*
DIETARY *adj* of or relating to a diet ▹ *n* regulated diet
DIETED ▸ **diet**
DIETER ▸ **diet**
DIETERS ▸ **diet**
DIETHER *n* chemical compound
DIETHYL *adj as in* **diethyl ether**
DIETINE *n* low-ranking diet
DIETING ▸ **diet**
DIETIST *another word for* > **dietitian**
DIETS ▸ **diet**
DIF = **diff**
DIFF *n* (slang) difference
DIFFER *vb* **differs**
DIFFORM *adj* irregular in form
DIFFS ▸ **diff**
DIFFUSE *vb, adj*
DIFS ▸ **dif**
DIG *vb, n*
DIGAMMA *n* letter of the Greek alphabet
DIGAMY *n* second marriage
DIGEST *vb, n* **digests**
DIGGED *a past tense of* ▸ **dig**
DIGGER *n* **diggers**
DIGGING ▸ **dig**
DIGHT *vb* adorn or equip, as for battle **dighted, dights**
DIGICAM *n* digital camera
DIGIT *n*
DIGITAL *adj, n*
DIGITS ▸ **digit**
DIGLOT *n* bilingual book **diglots**
DIGLYPH *n* ornament in Doric frieze with two grooves
DIGNIFY *vb*
DIGNITY *n*
DIGONAL *adj* of or relating to a symmetry operation
DIGOXIN *n* glycoside extracted from the leaves of the woolly foxglove
DIGRAPH *n* two letters used to represent a single sound
DIGRESS *vb*
DIGS ▸ **dig**
DIHEDRA > **dihedron**
DIKA *n* wild mango **dikas**
DIKAST = **dicast**

DIKASTS ▸ **dikast**
DIKDIK *n* small African antelope **dikdiks**
DIKE = **dyke**
DIKED ▸ **dike**
DIKER *n* builder of dikes **dikers**
DIKES ▸ **dike**
DIKING ▸ **dike**
DIKKOP *n* type of brownish shore bird with a large head and eyes **dikkops**
DIKTAT *n* dictatorial decree **diktats**
DILATE *vb* **dilated**
DILATER = **dilator**
DILATES ▸ **dilate**
DILATOR *n* something that dilates an object
DILDO *n* object used as a substitute for an erect penis **dildoe**
DILDOES ▸ **dildo**
DILDOS ▸ **dildo**
DILEMMA *n*
DILL *vb, n* **dilled**
DILLI *n* dilly bag; small bag, esp one made of plaited grass and used for carrying food
DILLIER ▸ **dilly**
DILLIES ▸ **dilly**
DILLING ▸ **dill**
DILLIS ▸ **dilli**
DILLS ▸ **dill**
DILLY *adj* foolish ▹ *n* person or thing that is remarkable
DILUENT *adj* causing dilution or serving to dilute ▹ *n* substance used for or causing dilution
DILUTE *vb, adj* **diluted, dilutee, diluter, dilutes**
DILUTOR *n* thing intended to have a diluting effect
DILUVIA > **diluvium**
DIM *adj, vb*
DIMBLE *n* wooded hollow; dingle **dimbles**
DIME *n*
DIMER *n* type of molecule
DIMERIC *adj* of a dimer
DIMERS ▸ **dimer**
DIMES ▸ **dime**
DIMETER *n* type of verse
DIMITY *n* light strong cotton fabric with woven stripes or squares
DIMLY, dimmed, dimmer, dimmers, dimmest ▸ **dim**
DIMMING *n as in* **global dimming** decrease in the amount of sunlight reaching the earth
DIMMISH ▸ **dim**
DIMNESS ▸ **dim**
DIMORPH *n* either of two forms of a substance that exhibits dimorphism
DIMOUT *n* reduction of lighting **dimouts**
DIMP *n* in Northern English dialect, a cigarette butt
DIMPLE *n, vb* **dimpled, dimples, dimply**
DIMPS ▸ **dimp**
DIMPSY *n* twilight
DIMS ▸ **dim**
DIMWIT *n* stupid person **dimwits**
DIN *n, vb*
DINAR *n* **dinars**
DINDLE *another word for* ▸ **dinnle**
DINDLED ▸ **dindle**
DINDLES ▸ **dindle**
DINE *vb* **dined**
DINER *n*
DINERIC *adj* of or concerned with the interface between immiscible liquids
DINERO *n* money **dineros**
DINERS ▸ **diner**
DINES ▸ **dine**
DINETTE *n* alcove or small area for use as a dining room
DINFUL *adj* noisy
DING *n* small dent in a vehicle ▹ *vb* ring or cause to ring, esp with tedious repetition
DINGBAT *n* any unnamed object
DINGE *n* dent ▹ *vb* make a dent in (something) **dinged**
DINGER *n* (in baseball) home run **dingers**
DINGES *n* jocular word for something whose name is unknown or forgotten
DINGEY = **dinghy**
DINGEYS ▸ **dingey**
DINGHY *n, vb*
DINGIED ▸ **dingey**

DINGIER ▸ **dingy**
DINGIES ▸ **dingy**
DINGILY ▸ **dingy**
DINGING ▸ **dinge**
DINGLE *n* small wooded hollow or valley **dingles**
DINGO *n*, *vb* **dingoed, dingoes**
DINGS ▸ **ding**
DINGUS = **dinges**
DINGY *adj*, *vb*
DINIC *n* remedy for vertigo **dinics**
DINING ▸ **dine**
DINITRO *adj* containing two nitro groups
DINK *adj* neat or neatly dressed ▹ *vb* carry (a second person) on a horse, bicycle, etc ▹ *n* ball struck delicately **dinked, dinker, dinkest**
DINKEY *n* small locomotive **dinkeys**
DINKIE *n* affluent married childless person ▹ *adj* designed for or appealing to dinkies
DINKIER ▸ **dinky**
DINKIES ▸ **dinkie**
DINKING ▸ **dink**
DINKLY *adj* neat
DINKS ▸ **dink**
DINKUM *n* **dinkums**
DINKY *adj* small and neat
DINMONT *n* neutered sheep
DINNA *vb* a Scots word for do not
DINNAE *vb* (Scots) do not
DINNED ▸ **din**
DINNER *vb*, *n* **dinners**
DINNING ▸ **din**
DINNLE *vb* shake **dinnled, dinnles**
DINO *n* dinosaur **dinos**
DINS ▸ **din**
DINT *variant of* ▸ **dent**
DINTED ▸ **dint**
DINTING ▸ **dint**
DINTS ▸ **dint**
DIOBOL *n* ancient Greek coin **diobols**
DIOCESE *n*
DIODE *n* **diodes**
DIOECY *n* state of being dioecious
DIOL *n* any of a class of alcohols that have two hydroxyl groups in each molecule **diols**
DIOPTER = **dioptre**
DIOPTRE *n* unit for measuring the refractive power of a lens
DIORAMA *n* miniature three-dimensional scene
DIORISM *n* definition; clarity
DIORITE *n* dark coarse-grained igneous plutonic rock
DIOTA *n* type of ancient vase **diotas**
DIOXAN *n* colourless insoluble toxic liquid **dioxane, dioxans**
DIOXID = **dioxide**
DIOXIDE *n*
DIOXIDS ▸ **dioxid**
DIOXIN *n* poisonous chemical by-products of certain weedkillers **dioxins**
DIP *vb*, *n*
DIPHASE *adj* of, having, or concerned with two phases
DIPHONE *n* combination of two speech sounds
DIPLEX *adj* (in telecommunications) permitting the transmission of simultaneous signals in both directions
DIPLOE *n* spongy bone separating the two layers of compact bone of the skull **diploes**
DIPLOIC *adj* relating to diploe
DIPLOID *adj* denoting a cell or organism with pairs of homologous chromosomes ▹ *n* diploid cell or organism
DIPLOMA *vb*, *n*
DIPLON *another name for* ▹ **deuteron**
DIPLONS ▸ **diplon**
DIPLONT *n* animal or plant that has the diploid number of chromosomes in its somatic cells
DIPNET *vb* fish using fishing net on pole **dipnets**
DIPNOAN *n* lungfish
DIPODIC ▸ **dipody**
DIPODY *n* metrical unit consisting of two feet
DIPOLAR ▸ **dipole**

DIPOLE *n* two equal but opposite electric charges or magnetic poles separated by a small distance **dipoles**
DIPPED ▶ **dip**
DIPPER *n* ladle used for dipping **dippers**
DIPPIER ▶ **dippy**
DIPPING ▶ **dip**
DIPPY *adj* odd, eccentric, or crazy
DIPS ▶ **dip**
DIPSAS *n* type of snake
DIPSHIT *n* stupid person
DIPSO *n* (slang) dipsomaniac or alcoholic **dipsos**
DIPT ▶ **dip**
DIPTERA *n* order of insects with two wings
DIPTYCA = **diptych**
DIPTYCH *n* painting on two hinged panels
DIQUARK *n* particle in physics
DIQUAT *n* type of herbicide **diquats**
DIRAM *n* money unit of Tajikistan **dirams**
DIRDAM = **dirdum**
DIRDAMS ▶ **dirdam**
DIRDUM *n* tumult **dirdums**
DIRE *adj*
DIRECT *adj, adv, vb* **directs**
DIREFUL = **dire**
DIRELY ▶ **dire**
DIREMPT *vb* separate with force
DIRER ▶ **dire**
DIREST ▶ **dire**
DIRGE *n* **dirges**
DIRHAM *n* standard monetary unit of Morocco **dirhams, dirhem**
DIRHEMS ▶ **dirhem**
DIRIGE *n* dirge **diriges**
DIRK *n* dagger, formerly worn by Scottish Highlanders ▷ *vb* stab with a dirk **dirke, dirked**
DIRKES ▶ **dirke**
DIRKING ▶ **dirk**
DIRKS ▶ **dirk**
DIRL *vb* tingle; vibrate **dirled, dirling, dirls**
DIRNDL *n* full gathered skirt **dirndls**
DIRT *vb, n*
DIRTBAG *n* filthy person
DIRTED ▶ **dirt**
DIRTIED, dirtier, dirties, dirtily ▶ **dirty**
DIRTING ▶ **dirt**
DIRTS ▶ **dirt**
DIRTY *adj, vb*
DIS = **diss**
DISA *n* type of orchid
DISABLE *vb*
DISALLY *vb* separate
DISARM *vb* **disarms**
DISAS ▶ **disa**
DISAVOW *vb*
DISBAND *vb*
DISBAR *vb* deprive (a barrister) of the right to practise
DISBARK = **disembark**
DISBARS ▶ **disbar**
DISBUD *vb* remove superfluous buds from (a plant, esp a fruit tree) **disbuds**
DISC *n, vb*
DISCAGE *vb* release from cage
DISCAL *adj* relating to or resembling a disc
DISCANT = **descant**
DISCARD *vb, n*
DISCASE *vb* remove case from
DISCED ▶ **disc**
DISCEPT *vb* discuss
DISCERN *vb*
DISCERP *vb* divide
DISCI ▶ **discus**
DISCIDE *vb* split
DISCING ▶ **disc**
DISCO *vb, n* **discoed, discoer**
DISCOID *adj* like a disc ▷ *n* disclike object
DISCORD *n, vb*
DISCOS ▶ **disco**
DISCS ▶ **disc**
DISCURE *old form of* > **discover**
DISCUS *n*
DISCUSS *vb*
DISDAIN *n, vb*
DISEASE *vb, n*
DISEDGE *vb* render blunt
DISEUR = **diseuse**
DISEURS ▶ **diseur**
DISEUSE *n* (esp formerly) an actress who presents dramatic recitals
DISFAME *n* discredit
DISFORM *vb* change form of
DISGEST *vb* digest
DISGOWN *vb* remove gown from
DISGUST *n, vb*

DISH *n, vb*
DISHED *adj* shaped like a dish
DISHELM *vb* remove helmet from
DISHES ▸ **dish**
DISHFUL *n* the amount that a dish is able to hold
DISHIER ▸ **dishy**
DISHING ▸ **dish**
DISHOME *vb* deprive of home
DISHORN *vb* remove horns from
DISHPAN *n* large pan for washing dishes, pots, etc
DISHRAG *n* dishcloth
DISHY *adj* good-looking
DISJECT *vb* break apart
DISJOIN *vb* disconnect or become disconnected
DISJUNE *n* breakfast
DISK = **disc**
DISKED ▸ **disk**
DISKING ▸ **disk**
DISKS ▸ **disk**
DISLEAF *vb* remove leaf or leaves from
DISLEAL *archaic form of* > **disloyal**
DISLIKE *vb, n*
DISLIMB *vb* remove limbs from
DISLIMN *vb* efface
DISLINK *vb* disunite
DISLOAD *vb* unload
DISMAL *adj*
DISMALS *pl n* gloomy state of mind
DISMAN *vb* remove men from **dismans**
DISMASK *vb* remove mask from
DISMAST *vb* break off the mast or masts of (a sailing vessel)
DISMAY *vb, n* **dismayed**
DISMAYL *vb* remove a coat of mail from
DISMAYS ▸ **dismay**
DISME *old form of* ▸ **dime**
DISMES ▸ **disme**
DISMISS *vb, sentence substitute*
DISNEST *vb* remove from nest
DISOBEY *vb*
DISOMIC *adj* having an extra chromosome in the haploid state **disomy**
DISOWN *vb* **disowns**
DISPACE *vb* move or travel about
DISPARK *vb* release
DISPART *vb* separate
DISPEL *vb* **dispels**
DISPEND *vb* spend
DISPLAY *vb, n*
DISPLE *vb* punish **displed, disples**
DISPONE *vb* transfer ownership
DISPORT *vb* indulge (oneself) in pleasure ▷ *n* amusement
DISPOSE *vb*
DISPOST *vb* remove from post
DISPRAD *old form of* > **dispread**
DISPRED *old spelling of* > **dispread**
DISPUTE *n, vb*
DISRANK *vb* demote
DISRATE *vb* punish (an officer) by lowering in rank
DISROBE *vb* undress
DISROOT *vb* uproot
DISRUPT *vb*
DISS *vb* treat (a person) with contempt
DISSAVE *vb* spend savings
DISSEAT *vb* unseat
DISSECT *vb*
DISSED ▸ **diss**
DISSENT *vb, n*
DISSERT *n* give or make a dissertation; dissertate
DISSES ▸ **diss**
DISSING ▸ **diss**
DISTAFF *n* rod on which wool etc is wound for spinning
DISTAIN *vb* stain; tarnish
DISTAL *adj* (of a bone, limb, etc) situated farthest from the point of attachment
DISTANT *adj*
DISTEND *vb*
DISTENT *adj* bloated; swollen
DISTICH *n* unit of two verse lines
DISTIL *vb* **distill, distils**
DISTOME *n* parasitic flatworm
DISTORT *vb*
DISTRIX *n* splitting of the ends of hairs
DISTUNE *vb* cause to be out of tune

DISTURB *vb*
DISTYLE *n* temple with two columns
DISUSE *vb, n*
DISUSED *adj* no longer used
DISUSES ▶ **disuse**
DISYOKE *vb* unyoke
DIT *vb* stop something happening ▷ *n* short sound used in the spoken representation of telegraphic codes
DITA *n* tropical shrub
DITAL *n* key for raising pitch of lute string **ditals**
DITAS ▶ **dita**
DITCH *n, vb* **ditched, ditcher, ditches**
DITE *vb* set down in writing **dited, dites**
DITHER *vb, n* **dithers, dithery**
DITHIOL *n* chemical compound
DITING ▶ **dite**
DITONE *n* interval of two tones **ditones**
DITS ▶ **dit**
DITSIER ▶ **ditsy**
DITSY = **ditzy**
DITT = **dit**
DITTANY *n* aromatic plant
DITTAY *n* accusation; charge **dittays**
DITTED ▶ **dit**
DITTIED ▶ **ditty**
DITTIES ▶ **ditty**
DITTING ▶ **dit**
DITTIT ▶ **dit**
DITTO *n, adv, sentence substitute, vb* **dittoed, dittos**
DITTS ▶ **ditt**
DITTY *vb, n*
DITZ *n* silly scatterbrained person **ditzes**
DITZIER ▶ **ditzy**
DITZY *adj* silly and scatterbrained
DIURNAL *adj* happening during the day or daily ▷ *n* service book containing all the canonical hours except matins
DIURON *n* type of herbicide **diurons**
DIV *n* stupid or foolish person
DIVA *n*
DIVAN *n* **divans**
DIVAS ▶ **diva**
DIVE *vb, n* **dived**
DIVER *n* person who works or explores underwater
DIVERGE *vb*
DIVERS *adj* various ▷ *determiner* various
DIVERSE *vb, adj*
DIVERT *vb* **diverts**
DIVES ▶ **dive**
DIVEST *vb* **divests**
DIVI *alternative spelling of* ▶ **divvy**
DIVIDE *vb, n*
DIVIDED *adj* split
DIVIDER *n*
DIVIDES ▶ **divide**
DIVIED ▶ **divvied**
DIVINE *adj, vb, n* **divined, diviner, divines**
DIVING ▶ **dive**
DIVINGS ▶ **dive**
DIVIS ▶ **divi**
DIVISIM *adv* separately
DIVISOR *n*
DIVNA *vb* do not
DIVO *n* male diva
DIVORCE *n, vb*
DIVOS ▶ **divo**
DIVOT *n* small piece of turf **divots**
DIVS ▶ **div**
DIVULGE *vb*
DIVULSE *vb* tear apart
DIVVIED ▶ **divvy**
DIVVIER ▶ **divvy**
DIVVIES ▶ **divvy**
DIVVY *vb* divide and share ▷ *adj* stupid ▷ *n* stupid person
DIVYING > **divvying**
DIWAN = **dewan**
DIWANS ▶ **diwan**
DIXI *interj* I have spoken
DIXIE *n* large metal pot for cooking, brewing tea, etc **dixies**
DIXIT *n* statement **dixits**
DIXY = **dixie**
DIYA *n* small oil lamp, usu made from clay **diyas**
DIZAIN *n* ten-line poem **dizains**
DIZEN *archaic word for* ▶ **bedizen**
DIZENED ▶ **dizen**
DIZENS ▶ **dizen**
DIZZARD *n* dunce
DIZZIED, dizzier, dizzies, dizzily ▶ **dizzy**
DIZZY *adj, vb*
DJEBEL *a variant spelling of* ▶ **jebel**

DJEBELS ▸ **djebel**
DJEMBE *n* W African drum **djembes**
DJIBBAH = **jubbah**
DJIN = **jinn**
DJINN ▸ **djinni**
DJINNI = **jinni**
DJINNS ▸ **djinn**
DJINNY = **jinni**
DJINS ▸ **djin**
DO *vb* perform or complete (a deed or action) ▹ *n* party, celebration
DOAB *n* alluvial land between two converging rivers
DOABLE *adj* capable of being done
DOABS ▸ **doab**
DOAT = **dote; doated, doater, doaters, doating, doats**
DOB *vb as in* **dob in** inform against or report **dobbed**
DOBBER *n* informant or traitor **dobbers**
DOBBIE = **dobby**
DOBBIES ▸ **dobby**
DOBBIN *n* name for a horse
DOBBING ▸ **dob**
DOBBINS ▸ **dobbin**
DOBBY *n* attachment to a loom, used in weaving small figures
DOBHASH *n* interpreter
DOBIE *n* cannabis **dobies**
DOBLA *n* medieval Spanish gold coin, probably worth 20 maravedis **doblas**
DOBLON *a variant spelling of* > **doubloon**
DOBLONS ▸ **doblon**
DOBRA *n* standard monetary unit of São Tomé e Principe **dobras**
DOBRO *n* type of acoustic guitar **dobros**
DOBS ▸ **dob**
DOBSON *n* larva of dobsonfly **dobsons**
DOBY = **dobie**
DOC = **doctor**
DOCENT *n* voluntary worker who acts as a guide **docents**
DOCETIC *adj* believing in docetism
DOCHMII > **dochmius**
DOCHT ▸ **dow**
DOCIBLE *adj* easily tamed
DOCILE *adj* **dociler**
DOCK *n, vb*
DOCKAGE *n* charge levied upon a vessel for using a dock
DOCKED ▸ **dock**
DOCKEN *n* something of no value or importance **dockens**
DOCKER *n* person employed to load and unload ships **dockers**
DOCKET *n, vb* **dockets**
DOCKING ▸ **dock**
DOCKISE = **dockize**
DOCKIZE *vb* convert into docks
DOCKS ▸ **dock**
DOCO *n* (slang) documentary **docos**
DOCQUET = **docket**
DOCS ▸ **doc**
DOCTOR *n, vb* **doctors**
DOD *vb* clip
DODDARD *adj* archaic word for missing branches; rotten
DODDED ▸ **dod**
DODDER *vb, n* **dodders, doddery**
DODDIER ▸ **doddy**
DODDIES ▸ **doddy**
DODDING ▸ **dod**
DODDLE *n* something easily accomplished **doddles**
DODDY *n* bad mood ▹ *adj* sulky
DODGE *vb, n* **dodged**
DODGEM *n* bumper car **dodgems**
DODGER *n* person who evades a responsibility or duty **dodgers**
DODGERY *n* deception
DODGES ▸ **dodge**
DODGIER ▸ **dodgy**
DODGING ▸ **dodge**
DODGY *adj*
DODKIN *n* coin of little value **dodkins**
DODMAN *n* snail **dodmans**
DODO *n* **dodoes, dodoism, dodos**
DODS ▸ **dod**
DOE *n*
DOEK *n* square of cloth worn on the head by women **doeks**
DOEN ▸ **do**
DOER *n* active or energetic person **doers**
DOES ▸ **do**
DOESKIN *n* skin of a

deer, lamb, or sheep
DOEST ▸ **do**
DOETH ▸ **do**
DOF *informal South African word for* ▸ **stupid**
DOFF *vb* **doffed, doffer, doffers, doffing, doffs**
DOG *n, vb*
DOGATE *n* office of doge **dogates**
DOGBANE *n* N American plant
DOGBOLT *n* bolt on cannon
DOGCART *n* light horse-drawn two-wheeled cart
DOGDOM *n* world of dogs **dogdoms**
DOGE *n* (formerly) chief magistrate of Venice or Genoa
DOGEAR *vb* fold down the corner of (a page) ▹ *n* folded-down corner of a page **dogears**
DOGEATE *n* office of doge
DOGEDOM *n* domain of doge
DOGES ▸ **doge**
DOGEY = **dogie**
DOGEYS ▸ **dogey**
DOGFACE *n* WW2 US soldier
DOGFISH *n* small shark
DOGFOX *n* male fox
DOGGED ▸ **dog**
DOGGER *n* Dutch fishing vessel with two masts **doggers**
DOGGERY *n* surly behaviour
DOGGESS *n* female dog
DOGGIE = **doggy**
DOGGIER ▸ **doggy**
DOGGIES ▸ **doggy**
DOGGING ▸ **dog**
DOGGISH *adj* of or like a dog
DOGGO *adv*
DOGGONE *interj* exclamation of annoyance, disappointment, etc ▹ *vb* damn ▹ *adj* damnedest
DOGGREL = **doggerel**
DOGGY *n* child's word for a dog ▹ *adj* of or like a dog
DOGHOLE *n* squalid dwelling place
DOGIE *n* motherless calf
DOGIES ▸ **dogy**
DOGLEG *n* sharp bend ▹ *vb* go off at an angle ▹ *adj* of or with the shape of a dogleg **doglegs**
DOGLIKE ▸ **dog**
DOGMA *n*
DOGMAN *n* person who directs a crane whilst riding on an object being lifted by it
DOGMAS ▸ **dogma**
DOGMATA ▸ **dogma**
DOGMEN ▸ **dogman**
DOGNAP *vb* carry off and hold (a dog), usually for ransom **dognaps**
DOGS ▸ **dog**
DOGSHIP *n* condition of being a dog
DOGSKIN *n* leather from dog's skin
DOGSLED *n* sleigh drawn by dogs
DOGTOWN *n* community of prairie dogs
DOGTROT *n* gently paced trot
DOGVANE *n* light windvane mounted on the side of a vessel
DOGWOOD *n* type of tree or shrub
DOGY = **dogie**
DOH *n* in tonic sol-fa, first degree of any major scale ▹ *interj* exclamation of annoyance when something goes wrong **dohs**

> This is one of the very useful short words denoting a note of the musical scale.

DOHYO *n* sumo wrestling ring **dohyos**
DOILED = **doilt**
DOILIES ▸ **doily**
DOILT *adj* foolish **doilter**
DOILY *n*
DOING ▸ **do**
DOINGS *pl n* deeds or actions
DOIT *n* former small copper coin of the Netherlands
DOITED *adj* foolish or childish, as from senility **doitit**
DOITKIN = **doit**
DOITS ▸ **doit**

DOJO *n* room or hall for the practice of martial arts **dojos**
DOL *n* unit of pain intensity, as measured by dolorimetry
DOLCE *n* dessert ▷ *adv* (to be performed) gently and sweetly **dolces, dolci**
DOLE *n, vb* **doled**
DOLEFUL *adj*
DOLENT *adj* sad
DOLENTE *adv* (to be performed) in a sorrowful manner
DOLES ▶ **dole**
DOLIA ▶ **dolium**
DOLINA = **doline**
DOLINAS ▶ **dolina**
DOLINE *n* depression of the ground surface formed in limestone regions **dolines**
DOLING ▶ **dole**
DOLIUM *n* genus of molluscs
DOLL *n, vb as in* **doll up**
DOLLAR *n* **dollars**
DOLLDOM ▶ **doll**
DOLLED ▶ **doll**
DOLLIED ▶ **dolly**
DOLLIER *n* person who operates a dolly
DOLLIES ▶ **dolly**
DOLLING ▶ **doll**
DOLLISH ▶ **doll**
DOLLOP *n, vb* **dollops**
DOLLS ▶ **doll**
DOLLY *adj, n, vb*
DOLMA *n* vine leaf stuffed with a filling of meat and rice
DOLMAN *n* long Turkish outer robe **dolmans**
DOLMAS ▶ **dolma**
DOLMEN *n* prehistoric monument **dolmens**
DOLOR = **dolour**
DOLORS ▶ **dolor**
DOLOS *n* knucklebone of a sheep, buck, etc, used esp by diviners **dolosse**
DOLOUR *n* grief or sorrow **dolours**
DOLPHIN *n*
DOLS ▶ **dol**
DOLT *n* **doltish, dolts**
DOM *n* title given to various monks and to certain of the canons regular
DOMAIN *n*
DOMAINE *n* French estate where wine is made
DOMAINS ▶ **domain**
DOMAL *adj* of a house
DOMATIA > **domatium**
DOME *n, vb* **domed, domes**
DOMETT *n* wool and cotton cloth **dometts**
DOMIC *adj* dome-shaped
DOMICAL ▶ **dome**
DOMICIL = **domicile**
DOMIER ▶ **domy**
DOMIEST ▶ **domy**
DOMINE *n* clergyman
DOMINEE *n* minister of the Dutch Reformed Church
DOMINES ▶ **domine**
DOMING ▶ **dome**
DOMINIE *n* minister or clergyman: also used as a term of address
DOMINO *n* **dominos**
DOMOIC *adj as in* **domoic acid** kind of amino acid
DOMS ▶ **dom**
DOMY *adj* having a dome or domes
DON *vb, n*
DONA *n* Spanish lady
DONAH *n* woman **donahs**
DONARY *n* thing given for holy use
DONAS ▶ **dona**
DONATE *vb* **donated, donates, donator**
DONDER *vb* beat (someone) up ▷ *n* wretch **donders**
DONE ▶ **do**
DONEE *n* person who receives a gift **donees**
DONER *n as in* **doner kebab** grilled meat and salad served in pitta bread with chilli sauce
DONG *n* deep reverberating sound of a large bell ▷ *vb* (of a bell) to make a deep reverberating sound
DONGA *n* steep-sided gully created by soil erosion **dongas**
DONGED ▶ **dong**
DONGING ▶ **dong**
DONGLE *n* electronic device **dongles**
DONGOLA *n* leather tanned using a particular method

DONGS ▸ **dong**
DONING *n* act of giving blood **donings**
DONJON *n* heavily fortified central tower of a castle **donjons**
DONKEY *n* **donkeys**
DONKO *n* tearoom or cafeteria in a factory, wharf area, etc **donkos**
DONNA *n* Italian lady
DONNARD = **donnert**
DONNART = **donnert**
DONNAS ▸ **donna**
DONNAT *n* lazy person **donnats**
DONNE = **donnee**
DONNED ▸ **don**
DONNEE *n* subject or theme **donnees**
DONNERD *adj* stupid
DONNERT *adj* stunned
DONNES ▸ **donne**
DONNIES ▸ **donny**
DONNING ▸ **don**
DONNISH *adj* serious and academic
DONNISM *n* loftiness
DONNOT *n* lazy person **donnots**
DONNY = **danny**
DONOR *n* **donors**
DONS ▸ **don**
DONSHIP *n* state or condition of being a don
DONSIE *adj* rather unwell **donsier, donsy**
DONUT = **doughnut**
DONUTS ▸ **donut**
DONZEL *n* man of high birth **donzels**
DOO *a Scot word for* ▸ **dove**
DOOB *n* cannabis cigarette **doobie**
DOOBIES ▸ **doobie**
DOOBREY *n* thingumabob **doobrie**
DOOBS ▸ **doob**
DOOCE *vb* dismiss (an employee) because of comments they have posted on the Internet **dooced, dooces, doocing**
DOOCOT *n* dovecote **doocots**
DOODAD = **doodah**
DOODADS ▸ **doodad**
DOODAH *n* unnamed thing **doodahs**
DOODIES ▸ **doody**
DOODLE *vb, n* **doodled, doodler, doodles**
DOODOO *n* excrement **doodoos, doody**
DOOFER *n* thingamajig **doofers**
DOOFUS *n* slow-witted or stupid person
DOOK *n* wooden plug driven into a wall to hold a nail, screw, etc ▹ *vb* dip or plunge **dooked**
DOOKET *n* dovecote **dookets**
DOOKING ▸ **dook**
DOOKS ▸ **dook**
DOOL *n* boundary marker
DOOLAN *n* Roman Catholic **doolans**
DOOLE = **dool**
DOOLEE = **doolie**
DOOLEES ▸ **doolee**
DOOLES ▸ **doole**
DOOLIE *n* enclosed couch on poles for carrying passengers **doolies**
DOOLS ▸ **dool**
DOOLY = **doolie**
DOOM *n, vb* **doomed, doomful**
DOOMIER ▸ **doomy**
DOOMILY ▸ **doomy**
DOOMING ▸ **doom**
DOOMS ▸ **doom**
DOOMY *adj* despondent or pessimistic
DOON = **down**
DOONA *n* large quilt used as a bed cover **doonas**
DOOR *n*
DOORMAN *n* man employed to be on duty at the entrance to a large public building
DOORMAT *n* mat for wiping dirt from shoes before going indoors
DOORMEN ▸ **doorman**
DOORN *n* thorn **doorns**
DOORS ▸ **door**
DOORWAY *n*
DOOS ▸ **doo**
DOOSRA *n* delivery in cricket **doosras**
DOOWOP *n* style of singing in harmony **doowops**
DOOZER = **doozy**
DOOZERS ▸ **doozer**
DOOZIE = **doozy**
DOOZIES ▸ **doozie**
DOOZY *n* something excellent

DOP *vb* curtsy ▷ *n* tot or small drink, usually alcoholic ▷ *vb* fail to reach the required standard in (an examination, course, etc)
DOPA *n* precursor to dopamine
DOPANT *n* element or compound used to dope a semiconductor **dopants**
DOPAS ▸ **dopa**
DOPATTA *n* headscarf
DOPE *n, vb, adj* **doped**
DOPER *n* person who administers dope **dopers**
DOPES ▸ **dope**
DOPEY *adj*
DOPIAZA *n* Indian meat or fish dish cooked in onion sauce
DOPIER ▸ **dopy**
DOPIEST ▸ **dopy**
DOPILY ▸ **dopey**
DOPING ▸ **dope**
DOPINGS ▸ **dope**
DOPPED ▸ **dop**
DOPPER *n* member of an Afrikaner church that practises a stict Calvinism **doppers**
DOPPIE *n* cartridge case **doppies**
DOPPING ▸ **dop**
DOPPIO *n* double measure, esp of espresso coffee **doppios**
DOPS ▸ **dop**
DOPY = **dopey**
DOR *n* European dung beetle
DORAD *n* South American river fish
DORADO *n* large marine percoid fish **dorados**
DORADS ▸ **dorad**
DORB = **dorba**
DORBA *n* stupid, inept, or clumsy person **dorbas**
DORBS ▸ **dorb**
DORBUG *n* type of beetle **dorbugs**
DORE *n* walleye fish
DOREE *n* type of fish **dorees**
DORES ▸ **dore**
DORHAWK *n* nightjar
DORIC *adj* rustic
DORIES ▸ **dory**
DORIS *n* woman
DORISE = **dorize**
DORISED ▸ **dorise**
DORISES ▸ **dorise**
DORIZE *vb* become Doric **dorized, dorizes**
DORK *n* stupid person **dorkier**
DORKISH *adj* stupid or contemptible
DORKS ▸ **dork**
DORKY ▸ **dork**
DORLACH *n* quiver of arrows
DORM = **dormitory**
DORMANT *n, adj*
DORMER *n* **dormers**
DORMICE > **dormouse**
DORMIE *adj* (in golf) leading by as many holes as there are left
DORMIN *n* hormone found in plants **dormins**
DORMS ▸ **dorm**
DORMY = **dormie**
DORNECK = **dornick**
DORNICK *n* heavy damask cloth
DORNOCK *n* type of coarse fabric
DORP *n* small town
DORPER *n* breed of sheep **dorpers**
DORPS ▸ **dorp**
DORR = **dor**
DORRED ▸ **dor**
DORRING ▸ **dor**
DORRS ▸ **dorr**
DORS ▸ **dor**
DORSA ▸ **dorsum**
DORSAD *adj* towards the back or dorsal aspect
DORSAL *adj, n* **dorsals**
DORSE *n* type of small fish
DORSEL *another word for* ▸ **dossal**
DORSELS ▸ **dorsel**
DORSER *n* hanging tapestry **dorsers**
DORSES ▸ **dorse**
DORSUM *n* the back
DORT *vb* sulk **dorted**
DORTER *n* dormitory **dorters**
DORTIER ▸ **dorty**
DORTING ▸ **dort**
DORTOUR = **dorter**
DORTS ▸ **dort**
DORTY *adj* haughty, or sullen
DORY *n* spiny-finned edible sea fish

DOS ▸ **do**
DOSAGE = **dose**
DOSAGES ▸ **dosage**
DOSE *n, vb* **dosed**
DOSEH *n* former Egyptian religious ceremony **dosehs**
DOSER ▸ **dose**
DOSERS ▸ **dose**
DOSES ▸ **dose**
DOSH *n* money **doshes**
DOSING ▸ **dose**
DOSS *vb, n*
DOSSAL *n* ornamental hanging used in churches **dossals**
DOSSED ▸ **doss**
DOSSEL = **dossal**
DOSSELS ▸ **dossel**
DOSSER *n* bag or basket for carrying objects on the back **dossers**
DOSSES ▸ **doss**
DOSSIER *n*
DOSSIL *n* lint for dressing wound **dossils**
DOSSING ▸ **doss**
DOST *a singular form of the present tense (indicative mood) of* ▸ **do**
DOT *n, vb*
DOTAGE *n* **dotages**
DOTAL ▸ **dot**
DOTANT *another word for* ▸ **dotard**
DOTANTS ▸ **dotant**
DOTARD *n* person who is feeble-minded through old age **dotards**
DOTCOM *n* **dotcoms**
DOTE *vb* **doted, doter, doters, dotes**
DOTH *a singular form of the present tense of* ▸ **do**
DOTIER ▸ **doty**
DOTIEST ▸ **doty**
DOTING ▸ **dote**
DOTINGS ▸ **dote**
DOTISH *adj* foolish
DOTS ▸ **dot**
DOTTED ▸ **dot**
DOTTEL = **dottle**
DOTTELS ▸ **dottel**
DOTTER ▸ **dot**
DOTTERS ▸ **dot**
DOTTIER ▸ **dotty**
DOTTILY ▸ **dotty**
DOTTING ▸ **dot**
DOTTLE *n* tobacco left in a pipe after smoking ▹ *adj* relating to dottle
DOTTLED *adj* foolish
DOTTLER ▸ **dottle**
DOTTLES ▸ **dottle**
DOTTREL = **dotterel**
DOTTY *adj*
DOTY *adj* (of wood) rotten
DOUANE *n* customs house **douanes**
DOUAR = **duar**
DOUARS ▸ **douar**
DOUBLE *adj, adv, n, vb* **doubled, doubler**
DOUBLES *n* game between two pairs of players
DOUBLET *n* man's close-fitting jacket, with or without sleeves
DOUBLY *adv* in a greater degree, quantity, or measure
DOUBT *n, vb* **doubted, doubter, doubts**
DOUC *n* Old World monkey
DOUCE *adj* quiet **doucely, doucer, doucest**
DOUCET *n* former flute-like instrument **doucets**
DOUCEUR *n* gratuity, tip, or bribe
DOUCHE *n* stream of water onto or into the body ▹ *vb* cleanse or treat by means of a douche **douched, douches**
DOUCINE *n* type of moulding for cornice
DOUCS ▸ **douc**
DOUGH *n* **doughs**
DOUGHT ▸ **dow**
DOUGHTY *adj* brave and determined
DOUGHY *adj* resembling dough in consistency, colour, etc
DOUK = **dook**
DOUKED ▸ **douk**
DOUKING ▸ **douk**
DOUKS ▸ **douk**
DOULA *n* woman trained to provide support to families during pregnancy, childbirth, and time following the birth **doulas**
DOULEIA = **dulia**

> This word refers to the inferior veneration accorded to saints and angels,

as distinct from **latria**, the veneration accorded to God alone, and is another of the few seven-letter words that use all five vowels. It's surprising how often you want to do this!

DOUM *n as in* **doum palm** variety of palm tree
DOUMA = **duma**
DOUMAS ▸ **douma**
DOUMS ▸ **doum**
DOUN = **down**
DOUP *n* bottom **doups**
DOUR *adj*
DOURA = **durra**
DOURAH = **durra**
DOURAHS ▸ **dourah**
DOURAS ▸ **doura**
DOURER ▸ **dour**
DOUREST ▸ **dour**
DOURINE *n* infectious venereal disease of horses
DOURLY ▸ **dour**
DOUSE *vb, n* **doused, douser, dousers, douses, dousing**
DOUT *vb* extinguish **douted, douter, douters, douting, douts**
DOUX *adj* sweet
DOVE *vb, n*
DOVECOT = **dovecote doved**
DOVEISH *adj* dovelike
DOVEKEY = **dovekie**
DOVEKIE *n* small short-billed auk
DOVELET *n* small dove
DOVEN *vb* pray **dovened, dovens**
DOVER *vb* doze ▹ *n* doze **dovered, dovers**
DOVES ▸ **dove**
DOVIE *Scots word for* ▸ **stupid**
DOVIER ▸ **dovie**
DOVIEST ▸ **dovie**
DOVING ▸ **dove**
DOVISH ▸ **dove**
DOW *vb* archaic word meaning be of worth
DOWABLE *adj* capable of being endowed
DOWAGER *n*
DOWAR = **duar**
DOWARS ▸ **dowar**
DOWD *n* woman who wears unfashionable clothes
DOWDIER ▸ **dowdy**
DOWDIES ▸ **dowdy**
DOWDILY ▸ **dowdy**
DOWDS ▸ **dowd**
DOWDY *adj, n*
DOWED ▸ **dow**
DOWEL *n, vb* **doweled, dowels**
DOWER *n* life interest in a part of her husband's estate allotted to a widow by law ▹ *vb* endow **dowered, dowers**
DOWERY = **dowry**
DOWF *adj* dull; listless
DOWIE *adj* dull and dreary **dowier, dowiest**
DOWING ▸ **dow**
DOWL *n* fluff
DOWLAS *n* coarse fabric
DOWLE = **dowl**
DOWLES ▸ **dowle**
DOWLIER ▸ **dowly**
DOWLNE *obsolete form of* ▸ **down**
DOWLNES ▸ **dowlne**
DOWLNEY ▸ **dowlne**
DOWLS ▸ **dowl**
DOWLY *adj* dull
DOWN *adv, adj, vb, n*
DOWNA *obsolete Scots form of* ▸ **cannot**
DOWNBOW *n* (in music) a downward stroke of the bow across the strings
DOWNED ▸ **down**
DOWNER *n* barbiturate, tranquillizer, or narcotic **downers**
DOWNIER ▸ **downy**
DOWNING ▸ **down**
DOWNS *pl n*
DOWNY *adj*
DOWP = **doup**
DOWPS ▸ **dowp**
DOWRIES ▸ **dowry**
DOWRY *n*
DOWS ▸ **dow**
DOWSE = **douse; dowsed, dowser, dowsers, dowses**
DOWSET = **doucet**
DOWSETS ▸ **dowset**
DOWSING ▸ **dowse**
DOWT *n* cigarette butt **dowts**
DOXIE = **doxy**
DOXIES ▸ **doxy**
DOXY *n* opinion or doctrine, esp concerning religious matters
DOY *n* beloved person:

used esp as an endearment
DOYEN *n* **doyenne, doyens**
DOYLEY = **doily**
DOYLEYS ▸ **doyley**
DOYLIES ▸ **doyly**
DOYLY = **doily**
DOYS ▸ **doy**
DOZE *vb, n*
DOZED *adj* (of timber or rubber) rotten or decayed
DOZEN *vb* **dozened, dozens, dozenth**
DOZER ▸ **doze**
DOZERS ▸ **doze**
DOZES ▸ **doze**
DOZIER ▸ **dozy**
DOZIEST ▸ **dozy**
DOZILY ▸ **dozy**
DOZING ▸ **doze**
DOZINGS ▸ **doze**
DOZY *adj*
DRAB *adj, n, vb* **drabbed**
DRABBER *n* one who frequents low women
DRABBET *n* yellowish-brown fabric of coarse linen
DRABBLE *vb* make or become wet or dirty
DRABBY *adj* promiscuous
DRABLER = **drabble**
DRABLY ▸ **drab**
DRABS ▸ **drab**
DRAC = **drack**
DRACENA = **dracaena**
DRACHM = **dram**
DRACHMA *n* former monetary unit of Greece
DRACHMS ▸ **drachm**
DRACK *adj* (esp of a woman) unattractive
DRACO *n as in* **draco lizard** flying lizard
DRACONE *n* large container towed by a ship
DRAD ▸ **dread**
DRAFF *n* residue of husks used as a food for cattle **draffs, draffy**
DRAFT = **draught**
DRAFTED ▸ **draft**
DRAFTEE *n* conscript
DRAFTER ▸ **draft**
DRAFTS ▸ **draft**
DRAFTY = **draughty**
DRAG *vb, n*
DRAGEE *n* sweet made of a nut, fruit, etc, coated with a hard sugar icing **dragees**
DRAGGED ▸ **drag**
DRAGGER ▸ **drag**
DRAGGLE *vb* make or become wet or dirty by trailing on the ground
DRAGGY *adj* slow or boring
DRAGNET *n* net used to scour the bottom of a pond or river
DRAGON *n* **dragons**
DRAGOON *n, vb*
DRAGS ▸ **drag**
DRAIL *n* weighted hook used in trolling ▹ *vb* fish with a drail **drailed, drails**
DRAIN *n, vb* **drained**
DRAINER *n* person or thing that drains
DRAINS ▸ **drain**
DRAKE *n* **drakes**
DRAM *n* small amount of a strong alcoholic drink, esp whisky ▹ *vb* drink a dram
DRAMA *n*
DRAMADY = **dramedy**
DRAMAS ▸ **drama**
DRAMEDY *n* television or film drama in which there are important elements of comedy
DRAMMED ▸ **dram**
DRAMS ▸ **dram**
DRANK ▸ **drink**
DRANT *vb* drone **dranted, drants**
DRAP *a Scot word for* ▸ **drop**
DRAPE *vb, n* **draped**
DRAPER *n* **drapers**
DRAPERY *n*
DRAPES *pl n* material hung at an opening or window to shut out light or to provide privacy
DRAPET *n* cloth **drapets**
DRAPEY *adj* hanging in loose folds
DRAPIER *n* draper
DRAPING ▸ **drape**
DRAPPED ▸ **drap**
DRAPPIE *n* little drop, esp a small amount of spirits
DRAPPY *n* drop (of liquid)
DRAPS ▸ **drap**
DRASTIC *n, adj*
DRAT *interj* exclamation of annoyance ▹ *vb* curse **drats**

DRATTED *adj* wretched
DRAUGHT *vb, n, adj*
DRAUNT = **drant**
DRAUNTS ▸ **draunt**
DRAVE *archaic past of* ▸ **drive**
DRAW *vb, n*
DRAWBAR *n* strong metal bar on a tractor, locomotive, etc
DRAWEE *n* person or organization on which payment is drawn **drawees**
DRAWER *n*
DRAWERS *pl n* undergarment worn on the lower part of the body
DRAWING ▸ **draw**
DRAWL *vb, n* **drawled, drawler, drawls, drawly**
DRAWN ▸ **draw**
DRAWS ▸ **draw**
DRAY *vb* pull using cart ▹ *n* low cart used for carrying heavy loads
DRAYAGE *n* act of transporting something a short distance
DRAYED ▸ **dray**
DRAYING ▸ **dray**
DRAYMAN *n* driver of a dray **draymen**
DRAYS ▸ **dray**
DRAZEL *n* low woman **drazels**
DREAD *vb, n, adj* **dreaded, dreader, dreadly, dreads**
DREAM *n, vb, adj* **dreamed**
DREAMER *n* person who dreams habitually
DREAMS ▸ **dream**
DREAMT ▸ **dream**
DREAMY *adj*
DREAR = **dreary**
DREARE *obsolete form of* ▸ **drear**
DREARER ▸ **drear**
DREARES ▸ **dreare**
DREARS ▸ **drear**
DREARY *adj, n*
DRECK *n* rubbish **drecks, drecky**
DREDGE *vb, n* **dredged, dredger, dredges**
DREE *vb* endure **dreed, dreeing, drees**
DREG *n* small quantity
DREGGY *adj* like or full of dregs
DREGS *pl n*
DREICH *adj* dreary
DREIDEL *n* spinning top **dreidl**
DREIDLS ▸ **dreidl**
DREIGH = **dreich**
DREK = **dreck**
DREKS ▸ **drek**
DRENCH *vb, n* **drent**
DRERE *obsolete form of* ▸ **drear**
DRERES ▸ **drere**
DRESS *n, vb, adj* **dressed**
DRESSER *n*
DRESSES ▸ **dress**
DRESSY *adj* (of clothes) elegant
DREST ▸ **dress**
DREVILL *n* offensive person
DREW ▸ **draw**
DREY *n* squirrel's nest **dreys**
DRIB *vb* flow in drops **dribbed, dribber**
DRIBBLE *vb, n* **dribbly**
DRIBLET *n* small amount
DRIBS ▸ **drib**
DRICE *n* pellets of frozen carbon dioxide **drices**
DRIED ▸ **dry**
DRIEGH *adj* tedious
DRIER, driers, dries, driest ▸ **dry**
DRIFT *vb, n* **drifted**
DRIFTER *n* person who moves aimlessly from place to place or job to job
DRIFTS ▸ **drift**
DRIFTY ▸ **drift**
DRILL *n, vb* **drilled, driller, drills**
DRILY *adv* in a dry manner
DRINK *vb, n*
DRINKER *n* person who drinks
DRINKS ▸ **drink**
DRIP *vb, n* **dripped, dripper**
DRIPPY *adj* mawkish, insipid, or inane
DRIPS ▸ **drip**
DRIPT ▸ **drip**
DRIVE *vb* guide the movement of (a vehicle) ▹ *n* journey by car, van, etc
DRIVEL *n, vb* **drivels**
DRIVEN ▸ **drive**
DRIVER *n* person who drives a vehicle **drivers**
DRIVES ▸ **drive**

DRIVING ▸ **drive**
DRIZZLE *n, vb* **drizzly**
DROGER *n* W Indian boat **drogers, drogher**
DROGUE *n* any funnel-like device used as a sea anchor **drogues**
DROGUET *n* woollen fabric
DROICH *n* dwarf **droichs**
DROICHY *adj* dwarfish
DROID = **android**
DROIDS ▸ **droid**
DROIL *vb* carry out boring menial work **droiled, droils**
DROIT *n* legal or moral right or claim **droits**
DROLE *adj* amusing ▹ *n* scoundrel **droler, droles, drolest**
DROLL *vb, adj* **drolled, droller, drolls, drolly**
DROME > **aerodrome**
DROMES ▸ **drome**
DROMIC *adj* relating to running track
DROMOI ▸ **dromos**
DROMON = **dromond**
DROMOND *n* sailing vessel of the 12th to 15th centuries
DROMONS ▸ **dromon**
DROMOS *n* Greek passageway
DRONE *n, vb* **droned, droner, droners, drones**
DRONGO *n* tropical songbird **drongos**
DRONIER ▸ **drony**
DRONING ▸ **drone**
DRONISH ▸ **drone**
DRONY *adj* monotonous
DROOB *n* pathetic person **droobs**
DROOG *n* ruffian **droogs**
DROOK = **drouk**
DROOKED ▸ **drook**
DROOKIT = **droukit**
DROOKS ▸ **drook**
DROOL *vb* **drooled, drools**
DROOLY *adj* tending to drool
DROOME *obsolete form of* ▸ **drum**
DROOMES ▸ **drum**
DROOP *vb, n* **drooped, droops**
DROOPY *adj* hanging or sagging downwards
DROP *vb, n*
DROPFLY *n* (angling) artificial fly
DROPLET *n*
DROPOUT *n* person who rejects conventional society ▹ *vb* abandon or withdraw (from an institution or group)
DROPPED ▸ **drop**
DROPPER *n* small tube with a rubber part at one end
DROPPLE *n* trickle
DROPS ▸ **drop**
DROPSY *n* illness in which watery fluid collects in the body
DROPT ▸ **drop**
DROSERA *n* insectivorous plant
DROSHKY *n* four-wheeled carriage, formerly used in Russia **drosky**
DROSS *n* **drosses, drossy**
DROSTDY *n* office of landdrost
DROUGHT *n*
DROUK *vb* drench **drouked**
DROUKIT *adj* drenched
DROUKS ▸ **drouk**
DROUTH = **drought**
DROUTHS ▸ **drouth**
DROUTHY *adj* thirsty or dry
DROVE ▸ **drive**
DROVED ▸ **drive**
DROVER *n* person who drives sheep or cattle **drovers**
DROVES ▸ **drive**
DROVING ▸ **drive**
DROW *n* sea fog
DROWN *vb* **drownd**
DROWNDS ▸ **drownd**
DROWNED ▸ **drown**
DROWNER ▸ **drown**
DROWNS ▸ **drown**
DROWS ▸ **drow**
DROWSE *vb, n* **drowsed, drowses**
DROWSY *adj*
DRUB *vb* beat as with a stick ▹ *n* blow, as from a stick **drubbed, drubber, drubs**
DRUCKEN *adj* drunken
DRUDGE *n, vb* **drudged, drudger, drudges**
DRUG *n, vb* **drugged**
DRUGGER *n* druggist
DRUGGET *n* coarse

fabric used as a protective floor-covering, etc
DRUGGIE *n* drug addict
DRUGGY ▸ **drug**
DRUGS ▸ **drug**
DRUID *n* **druidic, druidry, druids**
DRUM *n, vb*
DRUMBLE *vb* be inactive
DRUMLIN *n* streamlined mound of glacial drift
DRUMLY *adj* dismal; dreary
DRUMMED ▸ **drum**
DRUMMER *n* person who plays a drum or drums
DRUMMY *n* (in South Africa) drum majorette
DRUMS ▸ **drum**
DRUNK ▸ **drink**
DRUNKEN *adj* drunk or frequently drunk
DRUNKER ▸ **drink**
DRUNKS ▸ **drink**
DRUPE *n* fleshy fruit with a stone, such as the peach or cherry
DRUPEL = **drupelet**
DRUPELS ▸ **drupel**
DRUPES ▸ **drupe**
DRUSE *n* aggregate of small crystals within a cavity
DRUSEN *pl n* small deposits of material on the retina
DRUSES ▸ **druse**
DRUSIER ▸ **drusy**
DRUSY *adj* made of tiny crystals
DRUXIER ▸ **druxy**
DRUXY *adj* (of wood) having decayed white spots
DRY *adj, vb* **dryable**
DRYAD *n* wood nymph **dryades, dryadic, dryads**
DRYBEAT *vb* beat severely
DRYER, dryers, dryest, drying, dryings ▸ **dry**
DRYISH *adj* fairly dry
DRYLAND *adj* of an arid area
DRYLOT *n* livestock enclosure **drylots**
DRYLY = **drily**
DRYNESS ▸ **dry**
DRYS ▸ **dry**
DRYSUIT *n* waterproof rubber suit for wearing in esp cold water
DRYWALL *n* wall built without mortar ▹ *vb* build a wall without mortar
DRYWELL *n* type of sewage disposal system
DSO = **zho**

> A **dso** is a kind of Himalayan ox; the other forms are **dzo, zho, dzho** and **zo** and it's worth remembering all of them.

DSOBO = **zobo**
DSOBOS ▸ **dsobo**
DSOMO = **zhomo**
DSOMOS ▸ **dsomo**
DSOS ▸ **dso**
DUAD *a rare word for* ▸ **pair**
DUADS ▸ **duad**
DUAL *adj, n, vb*
DUALIN *n* explosive substance **dualins**
DUALISE = **dualize**
DUALISM *n* state of having two distinct parts **dualist**
DUALITY *n* state or quality of being two or in two parts
DUALIZE *vb* cause to have two parts
DUALLED ▸ **dual**
DUALLY ▸ **dual**
DUALS ▸ **dual**
DUAN *n* poem **duans**
DUAR *n* Arab camp
DUARCHY = **diarchy**
DUARS ▸ **duar**
DUB *vb, n* **dubbed, dubber, dubbers**
DUBBIN *n* thick grease applied to leather to soften and waterproof it
DUBBING ▸ **dub**
DUBBINS ▸ **dubbin**
DUBBO *adj* stupid ▹ *n* stupid person **dubbos**
DUBIETY *n*
DUBIOUS *adj*
DUBNIUM *n* chemical element
DUBS ▸ **dub**
DUBSTEP *n*
DUCAL *adj* of a duke **ducally**
DUCAT *n* former European gold or silver coin **ducats**
DUCDAME *interj*

Shakespearean nonsense word
DUCE *n* leader **duces**
DUCHESS *n, vb*
DUCHIES ▸ **duchy**
DUCHY *n*
DUCI ▸ **duce**
DUCK *n, vb* **ducked, ducker, duckers**
DUCKIE = **ducky**
DUCKIER ▸ **ducky**
DUCKIES ▸ **ducky**
DUCKING ▸ **duck**
DUCKPIN *n* short bowling pin
DUCKS ▸ **duck**
DUCKY *n* darling or dear ▹ *adj* delightful
DUCT *vb, n* **ductal, ducted**
DUCTILE *adj*
DUCTING ▸ **duct**
DUCTS ▸ **duct**
DUCTULE *n* small duct
DUD *n, adj*
DUDDER *n* door-to-door salesman **dudders**
DUDDERY *n* place where old clothes are sold
DUDDIE *adj* ragged **duddier, duddy**
DUDE *vb* dress fashionably ▹ *n* man **duded**
DUDEEN *n* clay pipe with a short stem **dudeens**
DUDES ▸ **dude**
DUDGEON *n* anger or resentment
DUDHEEN *n* type of pipe
DUDING ▸ **dude**
DUDISH ▸ **dude**
DUDISM *n* being a dude **dudisms**
DUDS ▸ **dud**
DUE *vb, adj, n, adv* **dued**
DUEFUL *adj* proper
DUEL *n, vb* **dueled, dueler, duelers, dueling, duelist, duelled, dueller**
DUELLI ▸ **duello**
DUELLO *n* art of duelling **duellos**
DUELS ▸ **duel**
DUENDE *n* Spanish goblin **duendes**
DUENESS ▸ **due**
DUENNA *n* (esp in Spain) elderly woman acting as chaperone to a young woman **duennas**
DUES *pl n* membership fees
DUET *n, vb* **dueted, dueting, duets, duett, duetted**
DUETTI ▸ **duetto**
DUETTO = **duet**
DUETTOS ▸ **duetto**
DUETTS ▸ **duett**
DUFF *adj* broken or useless ▹ *vb* change the appearance of or give a false appearance to (old or stolen goods) ▹ *n* rump or buttocks **duffed**
DUFFEL *n* **duffels**
DUFFER *n* **duffers**
DUFFEST ▸ **duff**
DUFFING ▸ **duff**
DUFFLE = **duffel**
DUFFLES ▸ **duffle**
DUFFS ▸ **duff**
DUFUS = **doofus**
DUFUSES ▸ **dufus**
DUG ▸ **dig**
DUGITE *n* medium-sized Australian venomous snake **dugites**
DUGONG *n* **dugongs**
DUGOUT *n* **dugouts**
DUGS ▸ **dig**
DUH *interj* ironic response to a question or statement

> This word provides a useful front hook to **uh**.

DUHKHA = **dukkha**
DUHKHAS ▸ **duhkha**
DUI ▸ **duo**
DUIKER *n* small African antelope **duikers**
DUING ▸ **due**
DUIT *n* former Dutch coin **duits**
DUKA *n* shop **dukas**
DUKE *vb, n* **duked**
DUKEDOM *n*
DUKERY *n* duke's domain
DUKES *pl n* fists
DUKING ▸ **duke**
DUKKA *n* mix of ground roast nuts and spices **dukkah**
DUKKAHS ▸ **dukkah**
DUKKAS ▸ **dukka**
DUKKHA *n* Buddhist belief that all things are suffering **dukkhas**
DULCET *adj, n* **dulcets**
DULCIAN *n* precursor to the bassoon
DULCIFY *vb* make

pleasant or agreeable
DULCITE *n* sweet substance **dulcose**
DULE *n* suffering; misery **dules**
DULIA *n* veneration accorded to saints **dulias**
DULL *adj, vb*
DULLARD *n* dull or stupid person
DULLED, duller, dullest, dullier, dulling, dullish, dulls, dully, dulness ▶ **dull**
DULOSES ▶ **dulosis**
DULOSIS *n* behaviour where one species of ant forces members of another to work for them **dulotic**
DULSE *n* seaweed with large red edible fronds **dulses**
DULY *adv*
DUMA *n* elective legislative assembly established by Tsar Nicholas II
DUMAIST *n* member of duma
DUMAS ▶ **duma**
DUMB *vb, adj* **dumbed, dumber, dumbest, dumbing, dumbly**
DUMBO *n* slow-witted unintelligent person **dumbos**
DUMBS ▶ **dumb**
DUMDUM *n* soft-nosed bullet **dumdums**
DUMELA *sentence substitute* hello
DUMKA *n* Slavonic lyrical song **dumky**
DUMMIED ▶ **dummy**
DUMMIER ▶ **dummy**
DUMMIES ▶ **dummy**
DUMMY *adj, n, vb*
DUMOSE *adj* bushlike **dumous**
DUMP *vb, n*
DUMPBIN *n* unit in a bookshop displaying a particular publisher's books
DUMPED ▶ **dump**
DUMPEE *n* person dumped from a relationship **dumpees**
DUMPER ▶ **dump**
DUMPERS ▶ **dump**
DUMPIER ▶ **dumpy**
DUMPIES ▶ **dumpy**
DUMPILY ▶ **dumpy**
DUMPING ▶ **dump**
DUMPISH = **dumpy**
DUMPLE *vb* form into dumpling shape **dumpled, dumples**
DUMPS *pl n* state of melancholy or depression
DUMPY *n, adj*
DUN *adj, vb, n*
DUNAM *n* unit of area measurement **dunams**
DUNCE *n*
DUNCERY *n* duncelike behaviour
DUNCES ▶ **dunce**
DUNCH *vb* push against gently **dunched, dunches**
DUNCISH *adj* duncelike
DUNDER *n* cane juice lees **dunders**
DUNE *n* **dunes**
DUNG *n, vb* **dunged**
DUNGEON *vb, n*
DUNGER *n* old decrepit car **dungers**
DUNGIER, dunging, dungs, dungy ▶ **dung**
DUNITE *n* ultrabasic igneous rock **dunites, dunitic**
DUNK *vb* **dunked, dunker, dunkers, dunking, dunks**
DUNLIN *n* small sandpiper **dunlins**
DUNNAGE *n* loose material used for packing cargo
DUNNART *n* type of insectivorous marsupial
DUNNED, dunner, dunness, dunnest ▶ **dun**
DUNNIER ▶ **dunny**
DUNNIES ▶ **dunny**
DUNNING ▶ **dun**
DUNNISH ▶ **dun**
DUNNITE *n* explosive containing ammonium picrate
DUNNO *vb* slang for don't know
DUNNOCK *n* hedge sparrow
DUNNY *n* in Australia, toilet ▷ *adj* relating to dunny
DUNS ▶ **dun**
DUNSH = **dunch**
DUNSHED ▶ **dunsh**
DUNSHES ▶ **dunsh**
DUNT *n* blow ▷ *vb* strike

or hit **dunted, dunting, dunts**
DUO = **duet**
DUODENA > **duodenum**
DUOLOG = **duologue**
DUOLOGS ▸ **duolog**
DUOMI ▸ **duomo**
DUOMO *n* cathedral in Italy **duomos**
DUOPOLY *n* siuation when control of a commodity is vested in two producers or suppliers
DUOS ▸ **duo**
DUOTONE *n* process for producing halftone illustrations
DUP *vb* open
DUPABLE ▸ **dupe**
DUPATTA *n* scarf worn in India
DUPE *vb*, *n* **duped, duper, dupers, dupery, dupes, duping**
DUPION *n* silk fabric made from the threads of double cocoons **dupions**
DUPLE *adj* having two beats in a bar
DUPLET *n* pair of electrons shared between two atoms in a covalent bond **duplets**
DUPLEX *vb* duplicate ▷ *n* apartment on two floors ▷ *adj* having two parts
DUPLIED ▸ **duply**
DUPLIES ▸ **duply**
DUPLY *vb* give a second reply
DUPPED ▸ **dup**
DUPPIES ▸ **duppy**
DUPPING ▸ **dup**
DUPPY *n* spirit or ghost
DUPS ▸ **dup**
DURA = **durra**
DURABLE *adj* **durably**
DURAL *n* alloy of aluminium and copper **durals**
DURAMEN *another name for* > **heartwood**
DURANCE *n* imprisonment
DURANT *n* tough, leathery cloth **durants**
DURAS ▸ **dura**
DURBAR *n* (formerly) the court of a native ruler or a governor in India **durbars**
DURDUM = **dirdum**
DURDUMS ▸ **durdum**
DURE *vb* endure **dured**
DUREFUL *adj* lasting
DURES ▸ **dure**
DURESS *n* **duresse**
DURGAH = **dargah**
DURGAHS ▸ **durgah**
DURGAN *n* dwarf **durgans**
DURGIER ▸ **durgy**
DURGY *adj* dwarflike
DURIAN *n* SE Asian tree whose very large oval fruits have a hard spiny rind and an evil smell **durians**
DURING *prep*
DURION = **durian**
DURIONS ▸ **durion**
DURMAST *n* large Eurasian oak tree with lobed leaves
DURN ▸ **darn**
DURNED ▸ **durn**
DURNING ▸ **durn**
DURNS ▸ **durn**
DURO *n* silver peso of Spain or Spanish America
DUROC *n* breed of pig **durocs**
DUROS ▸ **duro**
DUROY *n* coarse woollen fabric **duroys**
DURR = **durra**
DURRA *n* Old World variety of sorghum with hairy flower spikes and round seeds, cultivated for grain and fodder **durras**
DURRIE *n* cotton carpet made in India, often in rectangular pieces fringed at the ends
DURRIES ▸ **durry**
DURRS ▸ **durr**
DURRY *n* cigarette
DURST *a past tense of* ▸ **dare**
DURUM *n* variety of wheat cultivated mainly in the Mediterranean region, used chiefly to make pastas **durums**
DURZI *n* Indian tailor **durzis**
DUSH *vb* strike hard **dushed, dushes, dushing**

DUSK *n, adj, vb* **dusked**
DUSKEN *vb* grow dark **duskens**
DUSKER ▸ **dusk**
DUSKEST ▸ **dusk**
DUSKIER ▸ **dusky**
DUSKILY ▸ **dusky**
DUSKING, duskish, duskly, dusks ▸ **dusk**
DUSKY *adj*
DUST *n, vb*
DUSTBIN *n*
DUSTED ▸ **dust**
DUSTER *n* **dusters**
DUSTIER ▸ **dusty**
DUSTILY ▸ **dusty**
DUSTING ▸ **dust**
DUSTMAN *n* **dustmen**
DUSTOFF *n* casualty evacuation helicopter
DUSTPAN *n* short-handled shovel
DUSTRAG *n* cloth for dusting
DUSTS ▸ **dust**
DUSTUP *n* quarrel, fight, or argument **dustups**
DUSTY *adj*
DUTCH *n* wife **dutches**
DUTEOUS *adj* dutiful or obedient
DUTIED *adj* liable for duty
DUTIES ▸ **duty**
DUTIFUL *adj*
DUTY *n*
DUUMVIR *n* one of two coequal magistrates or officers
DUVET = **doona**
DUVETS ▸ **duvet**
DUVETYN *n* soft napped velvety fabric of cotton, silk, wool, or rayon
DUX *n* (in Scottish and certain other schools) the top pupil in a class or school **duxes**

> A **dux** is a leader, and is often useful for disposing of the X.

DUYKER = **duiker**
DUYKERS ▸ **duyker**
DVANDVA *n* class of compound words
DVORNIK *n* Russian doorkeeper
DWAAL *n* state of absent-mindedness **dwaals**
DWALE *n* deadly nightshade **dwales**
DWALM *vb* faint **dwalmed, dwalms**
DWAM *n* stupor or daydream ▹ *vb* faint or fall ill **dwammed, dwams**
DWANG *n* short piece of wood inserted in a timber-framed wall **dwangs**
DWARF *adj, n, vb* **dwarfed, dwarfer, dwarfs, dwarves**
DWAUM = **dwam**
DWAUMED ▸ **dwaum**
DWAUMS ▸ **dwaum**
DWEEB *n* stupid or uninteresting person **dweebs**
DWEEBY *adj* like or typical of a dweeb
DWELL *vb, n* **dwelled, dweller, dwells, dwelt**
DWILE *n* floor cloth **dwiles**
DWINDLE *vb*
DWINE *vb* languish **dwined, dwines, dwining**
DYABLE ▸ **dye**
DYAD *n* operator that is the unspecified product of two vectors
DYADIC *adj* of or relating to a dyad ▹ *n* sum of a particular number of dyads **dyadics**
DYADS ▸ **dyad**
DYARCHY = **diarchy**
DYBBUK *n* (in Jewish folklore) the body of a person possessed by the soul of a dead sinner **dybbuks**
DYE *n, vb* **dyeable, dyed, dyeing, dyeings**
DYELINE = **diazo**
DYER ▸ **dye**
DYERS ▸ **dye**
DYES ▸ **dye**
DYESTER *n* dyer
DYEWEED *n* plant that produces dye
DYEWOOD *n* any wood from which dyes and pigments can be obtained
DYING ▸ **die**
DYINGLY ▸ **die**
DYINGS ▸ **die**
DYKE *n, vb* **dyked, dykes, dyking**
DYKON *n* **dykons**
DYNAMIC *adj, n*
DYNAMO *n* **dynamos**
DYNAST *n* hereditary ruler **dynasts**

DYNASTY *n*
DYNE *n* cgs unit of force
DYNEIN *n* class of proteins **dyneins**
DYNEL *n* trade name for synthetic fibre **dynels**
DYNES ▸ **dyne**
DYNODE *n* electrical component **dynodes**
DYSLOGY *n* uncomplimentary remarks
DYSODIL *n* yellow or green mineral
DYSPNEA = **dyspnoea**
DYSURIA *n* difficult or painful urination **dysuric, dysury**
DYVOUR *n* debtor **dyvours**
DYVOURY *n* bankruptcy
DZEREN *n* Chinese yellow antelope **dzerens**
DZHO = **zho**
DZHOS ▸ **dzho**
DZO *a variant spelling of* ▸ **zo**
DZOS ▸ **zo**

Ee

E is the most common tile in the game and, while it is only worth one point, as the most frequent letter in English it is extremely useful, especially when it comes to forming bonus words scoring an extra 50 points. Many words contain two or more **E**s, so, unlike many tiles, it does no harm to have two **E**s on your rack and even three can be manageable. Keep in mind three-letter words formed by an **E** on either side of a consonant, like **eye, ewe** and **eve** (6 points each), and **eke** (7). **E** can also be handy for getting rid of double consonants: think of words like **egg** or **ebb** (each 5 points). **E** also combines well with **K**: as well as **eke**, we have **elk** and **eek** (both 7), and **ewk** (10). If you have an **X** on your rack, **E** offers you all kinds of options: just think of all the words that begin with **ex-**, like **exhaust** (17), which will give you a 50-point bonus if you use all of your tiles to form it. And don't forget **ex** itself, a nice little word that earns you 9 points, and also the very useful **exo** for 10 points. Just as important are **jee** for 10 points, **zee** for 12 points and **zed** for 13 points.

EA *n* river
EACH *pron, determiner, adv*
EADISH *n* aftermath
EAGER *adj, n* **eagerer, eagerly, eagers**
EAGLE *n, vb* **eagled, eagles**
EAGLET *n* young eagle **eaglets**
EAGLING ▸ **eagle**
EAGRE *n* tidal bore, esp of the Humber or Severn estuaries **eagres**
EALE *n* beast in Roman legend **eales**
EAN *vb* give birth **eaned, eaning**
EANLING *n* newborn lamb
EANS ▸ **ean**
EAR *n, vb*
EARACHE *n* pain in the ear
EARBALL *n* device used in acupressure
EARBASH *vb* talk incessantly
EARBOB *n* earring **earbobs**
EARBUD *n* small earphone **earbuds**
EARCON *n* sound representing object or event **earcons**
EARD *vb* bury **earded, earding**
EARDROP *n* pendant earring
EARDRUM *n*
EARDS ▸ **eard**

EARED *adj* having an ear or ears
EARFLAP *n* either of two pieces of fabric or fur attached to a cap
EARFUL *n* scolding or telling-off **earfuls**
EARING *n* line fastened to a corner of a sail for reefing **earings**
EARL *n*
EARLAP = **earflap**
EARLAPS ▸ **earlap**
EARLDOM *n* rank, title, or dignity of an earl or countess
EARLESS ▸ **ear**
EARLIER ▸ **early**
EARLIES ▸ **early**
EARLIKE ▸ **ear**
EARLOBE *n* fleshy lower part of the outer ear
EARLOCK *n* curl of hair close to ear
EARLS ▸ **earl**
EARLY *adv* before the expected or usual time ▹ *adj* occurring or arriving before the correct or expected time ▹ *n* something which is early
EARMARK *vb, n*
EARMUFF *n* item of clothing for keeping the ears warm
EARN *vb* **earned, earner, earners**
EARNEST *adj, n*
EARNING ▸ **earn**
EARNS ▸ **earn**
EARPICK *n* instrument for removing ear wax
EARPLUG *n* piece of soft material placed in the ear to keep out water or noise
EARRING *n*
EARS ▸ **ear**
EARSHOT *n*
EARST *adv* first; previously
EARTH *n, vb* **earthed**
EARTHEN *adj* made of baked clay or earth
EARTHLY *adj, n*
EARTHS ▸ **earth**
EARTHY *adj*
EARWAX *nontechnical name for* ▸ **cerumen**
EARWIG *n, vb* **earwigs**
EARWORM *n* irritatingly catchy tune
EAS ▸ **ea**
EASE *n, vb* **eased**
EASEFUL *adj* characterized by or bringing ease
EASEL *n*
EASELED *adj* mounted on easel
EASELS ▸ **easel**
EASER ▸ **ease**
EASERS ▸ **ease**
EASES ▸ **ease**
EASIED, easier, easies, easiest ▸ **easy**
EASILY *adv*
EASING *n as in* **quantitative easing easings**
EASLE *n* hot ash **easles**
EASSEL *adv* easterly
EASSIL *adv* easterly
EAST *n, adj, adv, vb* **easted**
EASTER *n* most important festival of the Christian Church
EASTERN *adj*
EASTERS ▸ **easter**
EASTING *n* net distance eastwards made by a vessel moving towards the east
EASTLIN *adj* easterly
EASTS ▸ **east**
EASY *adj, vb* **easying**
EAT *vb*
EATABLE *adj* fit or suitable for eating
EATAGE *n* grazing rights **eatages**
EATCHE *n* adze **eatches**
EATEN ▸ **eat**
EATER ▸ **eat**
EATERIE = **eatery**
EATERS ▸ **eat**
EATERY *n* restaurant or eating house
EATH *adj* easy **eathe, eathly**
EATING ▸ **eat**
EATINGS ▸ **eat**
EATS ▸ **eat**
EAU = **ea**
EAUS ▸ **eau**
EAUX ▸ **eau**
EAVE *n* overhanging edge of a roof
EAVED *adj* having eaves
EAVES ▸ **eave**
EBAUCHE *n* rough sketch
EBAYER *n* any person who uses eBay **ebayers**
EBAYING *n* buying or selling using eBay
EBB *vb, n* **ebbed**
EBBET *n* type of newt **ebbets**
EBBING ▸ **ebb**

EBBLESS ▶ **ebb**
EBBS ▶ **ebb**
EBON *poetic word for* ▶ **ebony**
EBONICS *n* dialect used by African-Americans
EBONIES ▶ **ebony**
EBONISE = **ebonize**
EBONIST *n* carver of ebony
EBONITE *another name for* > **vulcanite**
EBONIZE *vb* stain or otherwise finish in imitation of ebony
EBONS ▶ **ebon**
EBONY *n, adj*
EBOOK *n* book in electronic form **ebooks**
EBRIATE *adj* drunk
EBRIETY *n* drunkenness
EBRIOSE *adj* drunk
ECAD *n* organism whose form has been affected by its environment **ecads**
ECARTE *n* card game for two, played with 32 cards and king high **ecartes**
ECBOLE *n* digression **ecboles**
ECBOLIC *adj* hastening labour or abortion ▷ *n* drug or agent that hastens labour or abortion
ECCE *interj* behold
ECCO *interj* look there
ECCRINE *adj* of or denoting glands that secrete externally
ECDEMIC *adj* not indigenous or endemic
ECDYSES ▶ **ecdysis**
ECDYSIS *n* shedding of the cuticle in arthropods or the outer epidermal layer in reptiles
ECDYSON > **ecdysone**
ECESIC ▶ **ecesis**
ECESIS *n* establishment of a plant in a new environment
ECH = **eche**
ECHAPPE *n* leap in ballet
ECHARD *n* water that is present in the soil but cannot be utilized by plants **echards**
ECHE *vb* eke out **eched**
ECHELLE *n* ladder; scale
ECHELON *n, vb*
ECHES ▶ **eche**
ECHIDNA *n*
ECHING ▶ **eche**
ECHINI ▶ **echinus**
ECHINUS *n* ovolo moulding between the shaft and the abacus of a Doric column
ECHIUM *n* type of Eurasian and African plant **echiums**
ECHO *n, vb* **echoed, echoer, echoers, echoes**
ECHOEY *adj*
ECHOIC *adj* characteristic of or resembling an echo
ECHOIER ▶ **echoey**
ECHOING ▶ **echo**
ECHOISE = **echoize**
ECHOISM *n* onomatopoeia as a source of word formation **echoist**
ECHOIZE *vb* repeat like echo
ECHOS ▶ **echo**
ECHT *adj* real
ECLAIR *n* finger-shaped pastry filled with cream and covered with chocolate **eclairs**
ECLAT *n* brilliant success **eclats**
ECLIPSE *n, vb*
ECLOGUE *n* pastoral or idyllic poem, usually in the form of a conversation or soliloquy
ECLOSE *vb* emerge **eclosed, ecloses**
ECO *n* ecology activist
ECOCIDE *n* total destruction of an area of the natural environment
ECOD = **egad**
ECOLOGY *n*
ECOMAP *n* diagram showing the links between an individual and their community **ecomaps**
ECONOMY *n, adj*
ECONUT *n* environmentalist **econuts**
ECORCHE *n* anatomical figure without the skin
ECOS ▶ **eco**
ECOTAGE *n* sabotage for ecological motives
ECOTONE *n* zone between two major

ecological communities
ECOTOUR *n* holiday taking care not to damage environment
ECOTYPE *n* organisms within a species that have adapted to a particular environment
ECRU *adj* pale creamy-brown ▷ *n* greyish-yellow to a light greyish colour **ecrus**
ECSTASY *n*
ECTASES ▸ **ectasis**
ECTASIA *n* distension or dilation of a duct, vessel, or hollow viscus **ectasis, ectatic**
ECTHYMA *n* local inflammation of the skin
ECTOPIA *n* congenital displacement of an organ or part **ectopic, ectopy**
ECTOZOA > **ectozoon**
ECTYPAL ▸ **ectype**
ECTYPE *n* copy as distinguished from a prototype **ectypes**
ECU *n* any of various former French gold or silver coins
ECUELLE *n* covered soup bowl with handles
ECURIE *n* team of motor-racing cars **ecuries**
ECUS ▸ **ecu**
ECZEMA *n* **eczemas**
ED *n* education
EDACITY > **edacious**
EDAMAME *n* immature soybeans boiled in the pod
EDAPHIC *adj* of or relating to the physical and chemical conditions of the soil
EDDIED ▸ **eddy**
EDDIES ▸ **eddy**
EDDISH *n* pasture grass
EDDO = **taro**
EDDOES ▸ **eddo**
EDDY *n, vb* **eddying**
EDEMA = **oedema**
EDEMAS ▸ **edema**
EDEMATA ▸ **edema**
EDENIC *adj* delightful, like the Garden of Eden
EDENTAL *adj* having few or no teeth
EDGE *n, vb* **edged, edger, edgers, edges**
EDGIER ▸ **edgy**
EDGIEST ▸ **edgy**
EDGILY ▸ **edgy**
EDGING *n* anything placed along an edge to finish it ▷ *adj* relating to or used for making an edge **edgings**
EDGY *adj*
EDH *n* character of the runic alphabet **edhs**
EDIBLE *adj*
EDIBLES *pl n* articles fit to eat
EDICT *n* **edictal, edicts**
EDIFICE *n*
EDIFIED ▸ **edify**
EDIFIER ▸ **edify**
EDIFIES ▸ **edify**
EDIFY *vb*
EDILE *variant spelling of* ▸ **aedile**
EDILES ▸ **edile**
EDIT *vb, n* **edited, editing**
EDITION *n, vb*
EDITOR *n* **editors**
EDITRIX *n* female editor
EDITS ▸ **edit**
EDS ▸ **ed**
EDUCATE *vb*
EDUCE *vb* evolve or develop **educed, educes, educing**
EDUCT *n* substance separated from a mixture without chemical change
EDUCTOR ▸ **educe**
EDUCTS ▸ **educt**
EE *Scots word for* ▸ **eye**
EECH = **eche**
EECHED ▸ **eech**
EECHES ▸ **eech**
EECHING ▸ **eech**
EEJIT *Scots and Irish word for* ▸ **idiot**
EEJITS ▸ **eejit**
EEK *interj* indicating shock or fright
EEL *n*
EELFARE *n* young eel
EELIER ▸ **eel**
EELIEST ▸ **eel**
EELLIKE *adj* resembling an eel
EELPOUT *n* marine eel-like blennioid fish
EELS ▸ **eel**
EELWORM *n* any of various nematode worms
EELY ▸ **eel**
EEN ▸ **ee**
EERIE *adj* **eerier, eeriest, eerily, eery**

EEVEN *n* evening **eevens**
EEVN *n* evening
EEVNING *n* evening
EEVNS ▸ **eevn**
EF *n* the letter F
EFF *vb* say the word 'fuck'
EFFABLE *adj* capable of being expressed in words
EFFACE *vb* **effaced, effacer, effaces**
EFFECT *n, vb*
EFFECTS *pl n* personal belongings
EFFED ▸ **eff**
EFFEIR *vb* suit **effeirs**
EFFENDI *n* (in the Ottoman Empire) a title of respect
EFFERE = **effeir**
EFFERED ▸ **effere**
EFFERES ▸ **effere**
EFFETE *adj*
EFFIGY *n*
EFFING ▸ **eff**
EFFINGS ▸ **eff**
EFFLUX = **effluence**
EFFORCE *vb* force
EFFORT *n* **efforts**
EFFRAY = **affray**
EFFRAYS ▸ **effray**
EFFS ▸ **eff**
EFFULGE *vb* radiate
EFFUSE *vb* pour or flow out ▹ *adj* (esp of an inflorescence) spreading out loosely **effused, effuses**
EFS ▸ **ef**
EFT *n* dialect or archaic name for a newt ▹ *adv* again
EFTEST *adj* nearest at hand
EFTS ▸ **eft**
EFTSOON > **eftsoons**
EGAD *n* mild oath or expression of surprise **egads**
EGAL *adj* equal
EGALITE *n* equality
EGALITY *n* equality
EGALLY ▸ **egal**
EGENCE *n* need **egences, egency**
EGER = **eagre**
EGERS ▸ **eger**
EGEST *vb* excrete (waste material)
EGESTA *pl n* anything egested, as waste material from the body
EGESTED ▸ **egest**
EGESTS ▸ **egest**
EGG *n, vb*
EGGAR = **egger**
EGGARS ▸ **eggar**
EGGCUP *n* cup for holding a boiled egg **eggcups**
EGGED ▸ **egg**
EGGER *n* moth with brown body and wings **eggers**
EGGERY *n* place where eggs are laid
EGGHEAD *n* intellectual person
EGGIER ▸ **eggy**
EGGIEST ▸ **eggy**
EGGING ▸ **egg**
EGGLER *n* egg dealer: sometimes itinerant **egglers**
EGGLESS ▸ **egg**
EGGMASS *n* intelligentsia
EGGNOG *n* drink made of raw eggs, milk, sugar, spice, and brandy or rum **eggnogs**
EGGS ▸ **egg**
EGGWASH *n* beaten egg for brushing on pastry
EGGY *adj* soaked in or tasting of egg
EGIS *rare spelling of* ▸ **aegis**
EGISES ▸ **egis**
EGMA *mispronunciation of* ▸ **enigma**
EGMAS ▸ **egma**
EGO *n*
EGOISM *n* **egoisms**
EGOIST *n* person who is preoccupied with his own interests **egoists**
EGOITY *n* essence of the ego
EGOLESS *adj* without an ego
EGOS ▸ **ego**
EGOTISE = **egotize**
EGOTISM *n* concern only for one's own interests and feelings
EGOTIST *n* conceited boastful person
EGOTIZE *vb* talk or write in self-important way
EGRESS = **emersion**
EGRET *n* lesser white heron **egrets**
EH *interj* exclamation of surprise or inquiry ▹ *vb* say 'eh' **ehed, ehing, ehs**
EIDE ▸ **eidos**
EIDENT *adj* diligent

EIDER *n* Arctic duck **eiders**
EIDETIC *adj* (of images) exceptionally vivid, allowing detailed recall of something ▷ *n* person with eidetic ability
EIDOLA ▸ **eidolon**
EIDOLIC ▸ **eidolon**
EIDOLON *n* unsubstantial image
EIDOS *n* intellectual character of a culture or a social group
EIGHT *n, adj*
EIGHTH *n* number eight in a series ▷ *adj* coming after the seventh and before the ninth ▷ *adv* after the seventh person, position, event, etc **eighths**
EIGHTS ▸ **eight**
EIGHTVO *another word for* ▸ **octavo**
EIGHTY *n, adj, determiner*
EIGNE *adj* firstborn
EIK *variant form of* ▸ **eke**
EIKED ▸ **eik**
EIKING ▸ **eik**
EIKON *variant spelling of* ▸ **icon**
EIKONES ▸ **eikon**
EIKONS ▸ **eikon**
EIKS ▸ **eik**
EILD *n* old age
EILDING *n* fuel
EILDS ▸ **eild**
EINA *interj* exclamation of pain
EINE *pl n* eyes
EINKORN *n* variety of wheat of Greece and SW Asia
EIRACK *n* young hen **eiracks**
EIRENIC *variant spelling of* ▸ **irenic**
EISEL *n* vinegar **eisell**
EISELLS ▸ **eisell**
EISELS ▸ **eisel**
EISH *interj* South African exclamation
EISWEIN *n* wine made from grapes frozen on the vine
EITHER *pron, adv, determiner*
EJECT *vb*
EJECTA *pl n* matter thrown out by a volcano or during a meteorite impact
EJECTED ▸ **eject**
EJECTOR *n* person or thing that ejects
EJECTS ▸ **eject**
EKE *vb* increase, enlarge, or lengthen **eked, ekes, eking**
EKISTIC > **ekistics**
EKKA *n* type of one-horse carriage **ekkas**
EKPWELE *n* former monetary unit of Equatorial Guinea **ekuele**
EL *n* American elevated railway
ELAIN = **triolein**
ELAINS ▸ **elain**
ELAN *n* style and vigour
ELANCE *vb* throw a lance **elanced, elances**
ELAND *n* **elands**
ELANET *n* bird of prey **elanets**
ELANS ▸ **elan**
ELAPID *n* mostly tropical type of venomous snake **elapids**
ELAPINE *adj* of or like an elapid
ELAPSE *vb* **elapsed, elapses**
ELASTIC *adj, n*
ELASTIN *n* fibrous scleroprotein
ELATE *vb* fill with high spirits, exhilaration, pride or optimism
ELATED *adj* extremely happy and excited
ELATER *n* elaterid beetle **elaters**
ELATES ▸ **elate**
ELATING ▸ **elate**
ELATION *n*
ELATIVE *adj* denoting a grammatical case in Finnish and other languages ▷ *n* elative case
ELBOW *n, vb* **elbowed, elbows**
ELCHEE *n* ambassador **elchees, elchi**
ELCHIS ▸ **elchi**
ELD *n* old age
ELDER *adj, n*
ELDERLY *adj*
ELDERS ▸ **elder**
ELDEST *adj* oldest
ELDIN *n* fuel **elding**
ELDINGS ▸ **elding**
ELDINS ▸ **eldin**
ELDRESS *n* woman elder

ELDRICH = **eldritch**
ELDS ▸ **eld**
ELECT *vb, adj* **elected**
ELECTEE *n* someone who is elected
ELECTOR *n* someone who has the right to vote in an election
ELECTRO *vb* (in printing) make a metallic copy of a page
ELECTS ▸ **elect**
ELEGANT *adj*
ELEGIAC *adj, n*
ELEGIES ▸ **elegy**
ELEGISE = **elegize**
ELEGIST ▸ **elegize**
ELEGIT *n* writ delivering debtor's property to plaintiff **elegits**
ELEGIZE *vb* compose an elegy or elegies (in memory of)
ELEGY *n*
ELEMENT *n*
ELEMI *n* fragrant resin obtained from various tropical trees **elemis**
ELENCH *n* refutation in logic
ELENCHI > **elenchus**
ELENCHS ▸ **elench**
ELEVATE *vb*
ELEVEN *n, adj, determiner* **elevens**
ELEVON *n* aircraft control surface usually fitted to tailless or delta-wing aircraft **elevons**
ELF *n, vb* **elfed, elfhood**
ELFIN *adj, n*
ELFING ▸ **elf**
ELFINS ▸ **elfin**
ELFISH *adj* of, relating to, or like an elf or elves ▹ *n* supposed language of elves
ELFLAND *another name for* > **fairyland**
ELFLIKE ▸ **elf**
ELFLOCK *n* lock of hair
ELFS ▸ **elf**
ELHI *adj* informal word for or relating to elementary high school
ELIAD *n* glance **eliads**
ELICHE *n* pasta in the form of spirals **eliches**
ELICIT *vb* **elicits**
ELIDE *vb* **elided, elides, eliding**
ELINT *n* electronic intelligence **elints**
ELISION *n*
ELITE *n, adj* **elites**
ELITISM *n* **elitist**
ELIXIR *n* **elixirs**
ELK *n*
ELKHORN *n as in* **elkhorn fern** fern with a large leaf like an elk's horn
ELKS ▸ **elk**
ELL *n* obsolete unit of length
ELLAGIC *adj* of an acid derived from gallnuts
ELLIPSE *n*
ELLOPS = **elops**
ELLS ▸ **ell**
ELLWAND *n* stick for measuring lengths
ELM *n*
ELMEN *adj* of or relating to elm trees
ELMIER ▸ **elmy**
ELMIEST ▸ **elmy**
ELMS ▸ **elm**
ELMWOOD *n* wood from an elm tree
ELMY *adj* of or relating to elm trees
ELOCUTE *vb* speak as if practising elocution
ELODEA *n* type of American plant **elodeas**
ELOGE = **eulogy**
ELOGES ▸ **eloge**
ELOGIES ▸ **elogy**
ELOGIST ▸ **elogy**
ELOGIUM = **eulogy**
ELOGY = **eulogy**
ELOIGN *vb* remove (oneself, one's property, etc) to a distant place **eloigns, eloin**
ELOINED ▸ **eloin**
ELOINER ▸ **eloign**
ELOINS ▸ **eloin**
ELOPE *vb* **eloped, eloper, elopers, elopes, eloping**
ELOPS *n* type of fish **elopses**
ELPEE *n* LP, long-playing record **elpees**
ELS ▸ **el**
ELSE *adv*
ELSHIN *n* cobbler's awl **elshins, elsin**
ELSINS ▸ **elsin**
ELT *n* young female pig
ELTCHI *variant of* ▸ **elchee**
ELTCHIS ▸ **eltchi**
ELTS ▸ **elt**
ELUANT = **eluent**
ELUANTS ▸ **eluant**

ELUATE *n* solution of adsorbed material obtained during the process of elution **eluates**
ELUDE *vb* **eluded, eluder, eluders, eludes, eluding**
ELUENT *n* solvent used for eluting **eluents**
ELUSION ▸ **elude**
ELUSIVE *adj*
ELUSORY *adj* avoiding the issue
ELUTE *vb* wash out (a substance) by the action of a solvent **eluted, elutes, eluting, elution, elutor, elutors**
ELUVIA ▸ **eluvium**
ELUVIAL ▸ **eluvium**
ELUVIUM *n* mass of sand, silt, etc
ELVAN *n* type of rock **elvans**
ELVER *n* young eel **elvers**
ELVES ▸ **elf**
ELVISH = **elfish**
ELYSIAN *adj* delightful, blissful
ELYTRA ▸ **elytrum**
ELYTRAL ▸ **elytron**
ELYTRON *n* either of the horny front wings of beetles and some other insects **elytrum**
EM *n* square of a body of any size of type, used as a unit of measurement
EMACS *n* powerful computer program **emacsen**
EMAIL *n* electronic mail ▹ *vb* send a message by electronic mail **emailed, emailer, emails**
EMANANT ▸ **emanate**
EMANATE *vb*
EMBACE *variant of* ▸ **embase**
EMBACES ▸ **embace**
EMBAIL *vb* enclose in a circle **embails**
EMBALE *vb* bind **embaled, embales**
EMBALL *vb* enclose in a circle **emballs**
EMBALM *vb* **embalms**
EMBANK *vb* protect, enclose, or confine with an embankment **embanks**
EMBAR *vb* close in with bars
EMBARGO *n, vb*
EMBARK *vb* **embarks**
EMBARS ▸ **embar**
EMBASE *vb* degrade or debase **embased, embases**
EMBASSY *n*
EMBASTE ▸ **embase**
EMBATHE *vb* bathe with water
EMBAY *vb* form into a bay **embayed**
EMBAYLD ▸ **embail**
EMBAYS ▸ **embay**
EMBED *vb, n* **embeds**
EMBER *n* **embers**
EMBLAZE *vb* cause to light up
EMBLEM *n, vb*
EMBLEMA *n* mosaic decoration
EMBLEMS ▸ **emblem**
EMBLIC *n* type of Indian tree **emblics**
EMBLOOM *vb* adorn with blooms
EMBODY *vb*
EMBOG *vb* sink down into a bog **embogs**
EMBOGUE *vb* go out through a narrow channel or passage
EMBOIL *vb* enrage or be enraged **emboils**
EMBOLI ▸ **embolus**
EMBOLIC *adj* of or relating to an embolus or embolism
EMBOLUS *n* material that blocks a blood vessel
EMBOLY *n* infolding of an outer layer of cells so as to form a pocket in the surface
EMBOSK *vb* hide or cover **embosks**
EMBOSOM *vb* enclose or envelop, esp protectively
EMBOSS *vb* create a decoration that stands out on (a surface) **embost**
EMBOUND *vb* surround or encircle
EMBOW *vb* design or create (a structure) in the form of an arch or vault **embowed**
EMBOWEL *vb* bury or embed deeply
EMBOWER *vb* enclose in or as in a bower

EMBOWS ▸ **embow**
EMBOX *vb* put in a box **emboxed, emboxes**
EMBRACE *vb, n*
EMBRAID *vb* braid or interweave
EMBRAVE *vb* adorn or decorate
EMBREAD *vb* braid
EMBROIL *vb*
EMBROWN *vb* make or become brown
EMBRUE *variant spelling of* ▸ **imbrue**
EMBRUED ▸ **embrue**
EMBRUES ▸ **embrue**
EMBRUTE *variant of* ▸ **imbrute**
EMBRYO *n* **embryon, embryos**
EMBUS *vb* cause (troops) to board a transport vehicle **embused, embuses**
EMBUSY *vb* keep occupied
EMCEE *n* master of ceremonies ▹ *vb* act as master of ceremonies (for or at) **emceed, emcees**
EMDASH *n* long dash in punctuation
EME *n* uncle
EMEER *variant of* ▸ **emir**
EMEERS ▸ **emeer**
EMEND *vb* **emended, emender, emends**
EMERALD *n, adj*
EMERGE *vb* **emerged, emerges**
EMERIED ▸ **emery**
EMERIES ▸ **emery**
EMERITA *adj* retired, but retaining an honorary title ▹ *n* woman who is retired, but retains an honorary title
EMERITI > **emeritus**
EMEROD *n* haemorrhoid **emerods, emeroid**
EMERSE ▸ **emersed**
EMERSED *adj* protruding above the surface of the water
EMERY *n* hard mineral used for smoothing and polishing ▹ *vb* apply emery to
EMES ▸ **eme**
EMESES ▸ **emesis**
EMESIS *technical name for* > **vomiting**
EMETIC *n, adj* **emetics**
EMETIN = **emetine**
EMETINE *n* white bitter poisonous alkaloid
EMETINS ▸ **emetin**
EMEU *variant of* ▸ **emu**
EMEUS ▸ **emeu**
EMEUTE *n* uprising or rebellion **emeutes**
EMIC *adj* of or relating to a significant linguistic unit
EMICANT ▸ **emicate**
EMICATE *vb* twinkle
EMIGRE *n* someone who has left his native country for political reasons **emigres**
EMINENT *adj*
EMIR *n*
EMIRATE *n* emir's country
EMIRS ▸ **emir**
EMIT *vb* **emits, emitted**
EMITTER *n* person or thing that emits
EMLETS *pl n as in* **blood-drop emlets** Chilean plant
EMMA *n* former communications code for the letter A **emmas**
EMMER *n* variety of wheat **emmers**
EMMESH *variant of* ▸ **enmesh**
EMMET *n* tourist or holiday-maker **emmets**
EMMEW *vb* restrict **emmewed, emmews**
EMMOVE *vb* cause emotion in **emmoved, emmoves**
EMMY *n* award for outstanding television performances and productions **emmys**
EMO *n* type of music
EMODIN *n* type of chemical compound **emodins**
EMONG *variant of* ▸ **among**
EMONGES *variant of* ▸ **among**
EMONGST *variant of* ▸ **amongst**
EMOS ▸ **emo**
EMOTE *vb* display exaggerated emotion, as if acting **emoted, emoter, emoters, emotes, emoting**
EMOTION *n*
EMOTIVE *adj*
EMOVE *vb* cause to feel emotion **emoved,**

emoves, emoving
EMPAIRE *variant of* ▸ **impair**
EMPALE *less common spelling of* ▸ **impale**
EMPALED ▸ **empale**
EMPALER ▸ **empale**
EMPALES ▸ **empale**
EMPANEL *vb* enter on a list (names of persons to be summoned for jury service)
EMPARE *variant of* ▸ **impair**
EMPARED ▸ **empare**
EMPARES ▸ **empare**
EMPARL *variant of* ▸ **imparl**
EMPARLS ▸ **emparl**
EMPART *variant of* ▸ **impart**
EMPARTS ▸ **empart**
EMPATHY *n* ability to understand someone else's feelings
EMPAYRE *variant of* ▸ **impair**
EMPEACH *variant of* ▸ **impeach**
EMPERCE *variant of* > **empierce**
EMPEROR *n*
EMPERY *n* dominion or power
EMPIGHT *adj* attached or positioned
EMPIRE *n* **empires**
EMPIRIC *n* person who relies on empirical methods
EMPLACE *vb* put in place or position
EMPLANE *vb* board or put on board an aeroplane
EMPLOY *vb, n*
EMPLOYE = **employee**
EMPLOYS ▸ **employ**
EMPLUME *vb* put a plume on
EMPORIA > **emporium**
EMPOWER *vb*
EMPRESS *n*
EMPRISE *n* chivalrous or daring enterprise **emprize**
EMPT *vb* empty **empted**
EMPTIED, emptier, empties, emptily ▸ **empty**
EMPTING ▸ **empt**
EMPTINS *pl n* liquid leavening agent made from potatoes
EMPTION *n* process of buying something
EMPTS ▸ **empt**
EMPTY *adj, vb, n*
EMPUSA *n* goblin in Greek mythology **empusas, empuse**
EMPUSES ▸ **empuse**
EMPYEMA *n* collection of pus in a body cavity
EMS ▸ **em**
EMU *n*
EMULATE *vb* **emule**
EMULED ▸ **emule**
EMULES ▸ **emule**
EMULGE *vb* remove liquid from **emulged, emulges**
EMULING ▸ **emule**
EMULOUS *adj* desiring or aiming to equal or surpass another
EMULSIN *n* enzyme that is found in almonds
EMULSOR *n* device that emulsifies
EMUNGE *vb* clean or clear out **emunged, emunges**
EMURE *variant of* ▸ **immure**
EMURED ▸ **emure**
EMURES ▸ **emure**
EMURING ▸ **emure**
EMUS ▸ **emu**
EMYD *n* freshwater tortoise or terrapin **emyde**
EMYDES ▸ **emyde**
EMYDS ▸ **emyd**
EMYS *n* freshwater tortoise or terrapin
EN *n* unit of measurement, half the width of an em
ENABLE *vb* **enabled, enabler, enables**
ENACT *vb* **enacted, enactor, enacts**
ENAMEL *n, vb* **enamels**
ENAMINE *n* type of unsaturated compound
ENAMOR = **enamour**
ENAMORS ▸ **enamor**
ENAMOUR *vb* inspire with love
ENARCH *variant of* ▸ **inarch**
ENARM *vb* provide with arms **enarmed, enarms**
ENATE *adj* growing out or outwards ▹ *n* relative on the mother's side **enates**
ENATIC *adj* related on one's mother's side
ENATION ▸ **enate**

ENCAGE *vb* confine in or as in a cage **encaged, encages**
ENCALM *vb* becalm, settle **encalms**
ENCAMP *vb* **encamps**
ENCASE *vb* **encased, encases**
ENCASH *vb* exchange (a cheque) for cash
ENCAVE *variant of* ▸ **incave**
ENCAVED ▸ **encave**
ENCAVES ▸ **encave**
ENCHAFE *vb* heat up
ENCHAIN *vb* bind with chains
ENCHANT *vb*
ENCHARM *vb* enchant
ENCHASE *less common word for* ▸ **chase**
ENCHEER *vb* cheer up
ENCINA *n* type of oak **encinal, encinas**
ENCLASP *vb* clasp
ENCLAVE *n, vb*
ENCLOSE *vb*
ENCLOUD *vb* hide with clouds
ENCODE *vb* convert (a message) into code **encoded, encoder, encodes**
ENCOMIA > **encomium**
ENCORE *interj, n, vb* **encored, encores**
ENCRATY *n* control of one's desires, actions, etc
ENCRUST *vb* cover with a layer of something
ENCRYPT *vb* put (a message) into code
ENCYST *vb* enclose or become enclosed by a cyst, thick membrane, or shell **encysts**
END *n* furthest point or part ▹ *vb* bring or come to a finish
ENDARCH *adj* having the first-formed xylem internal to that formed later
ENDART *variant of* ▸ **indart**
ENDARTS ▸ **endart**
ENDASH *n* short dash in punctuation
ENDEAR *vb* **endears**
ENDED ▸ **end**
ENDEMIC *adj, n*
ENDER ▸ **end**
ENDERON *variant of* ▸ **andiron**
ENDERS ▸ **end**
ENDEW *variant of* ▸ **endue**
ENDEWED ▸ **endew**
ENDEWS ▸ **endew**
ENDGAME *n* closing stage of a game of chess
ENDGATE *n* tailboard of a vehicle
ENDING *n* **endings**
ENDIRON *variant of* ▸ **andiron**
ENDITE *variant of* ▸ **indict**
ENDITED ▸ **endite**
ENDITES ▸ **endite**
ENDIVE *n* curly-leaved plant used in salads **endives**
ENDLANG *variant of* ▸ **endlong**
ENDLEAF *n* endpaper in a book
ENDLESS *adj*
ENDLONG *adv* lengthways or on end
ENDMOST *adj* nearest the end
ENDNOTE *n* note at the end of a section of writing
ENDOGEN *n* plant that increases in size by internal growth
ENDOPOD *n* inner branch of a two-branched crustacean
ENDORSE *vb*
ENDOSS *vb* endorse
ENDOW *vb* **endowed, endower, endows**
ENDOZOA > **endozoon**
ENDPLAY *n* technique in card games ▹ *vb* force (an opponent) to make a particular lead near the end of a hand
ENDRIN *n* type of insecticide **endrins**
ENDS ▸ **end**
ENDSHIP *n* small village
ENDUE *vb* invest or provide, as with some quality or trait **endued, endues, enduing**
ENDURE *vb* **endured, endurer, endures**
ENDURO *n* long-distance race for vehicles **enduros**
ENDWAYS *adv* having the end forwards or upwards ▹ *adj* vertical or upright **endwise**
ENDYSES ▸ **endysis**

ENDYSIS *n* formation of new layers of integument after ecdysis
ENDZONE *n* (in American football) area at either end of the playing field
ENE *variant of* ▸ **even**
ENEMA *n* **enemas, enemata**
ENEMIES ▸ **enemy**
ENEMY *n, adj*
ENERGIC ▸ **energy**
ENERGID *n* nucleus and cytoplasm in a syncytium
ENERGY *n*
ENERVE *vb* enervate **enerved, enerves**
ENES ▸ **ene**
ENEW *vb* force a bird into water **enewed, enewing, enews**
ENFACE *vb* write, print, or stamp (something) on the face of (a document) **enfaced, enfaces**
ENFANT *n* French child **enfants**
ENFELON *vb* infuriate
ENFEOFF *vb* invest (a person) with possession of a freehold estate in land
ENFEVER *vb* make feverish
ENFILED *adj* passed through
ENFIRE *vb* set alight **enfired, enfires**
ENFIX *variant of* ▸ **infix**
ENFIXED ▸ **enfix**
ENFIXES ▸ **enfix**
ENFLAME *variant of* ▸ **inflame**
ENFLESH *vb* make flesh
ENFOLD *vb* **enfolds**
ENFORCE *vb*
ENFORM *variant of* ▸ **inform**
ENFORMS ▸ **enform**
ENFRAME *vb* put inside a frame
ENFREE *vb* release, make free **enfreed, enfrees**
ENFROZE > **enfreeze**
ENG *another name for* ▸ **agma**
ENGAGE *vb, adj*
ENGAGED *adj*
ENGAGEE *adj* (of a female artist) morally or politically committed to some ideology
ENGAGER ▸ **engage**
ENGAGES ▸ **engage**
ENGAOL *vb* put into gaol **engaols**
ENGILD *vb* cover with or as if with gold **engilds, engilt**
ENGINE *n, vb* **engined, enginer, engines**
ENGIRD *vb* surround **engirds, engirt**
ENGLISH *vb* put spin on a billiard ball
ENGLOBE *vb* surround as if in a globe
ENGLOOM *vb* make dull or dismal
ENGLUT *vb* devour ravenously **engluts**
ENGOBE *n* liquid put on pottery before glazing **engobes**
ENGORE *vb* pierce or wound **engored, engores**
ENGORGE *vb* clog with blood
ENGRACE *vb* give grace to
ENGRAFF *variant of* ▸ **engraft**
ENGRAFT *vb* graft (a shoot, bud, etc) onto a stock
ENGRAIL *vb* decorate or mark with small carved notches
ENGRAIN *variant spelling of* ▸ **ingrain**
ENGRAM *n* physical basis of an individual memory in the brain **engrams**
ENGRASP *vb* grasp or seize
ENGRAVE *vb*
ENGROSS *vb*
ENGS ▸ **eng**
ENGUARD *vb* protect or defend
ENGULF *vb* **engulfs, engulph**
ENHALO *vb* surround with or as if with a halo **enhalos**
ENHANCE *vb*
ENIAC *n* early type of computer built in the 1940s **eniacs**
ENIGMA *n* **enigmas**
ENISLE *vb* put on or make into an island **enisled, enisles**
ENJAMB *vb* (of a line of verse) run over into the next line **enjambs**

ENJOIN *vb* **enjoins**
ENJOY *vb* **enjoyed, enjoyer, enjoys**
ENLACE *vb* bind or encircle with or as with laces **enlaced, enlaces**
ENLARD *vb* put lard on **enlards**
ENLARGE *vb*
ENLEVE *adj* having been abducted
ENLIGHT *vb* light up
ENLINK *vb* link together **enlinks**
ENLIST *vb* **enlists**
ENLIT ▸ **enlight**
ENLIVEN *vb*
ENLOCK *vb* lock or secure **enlocks**
ENMESH *vb*
ENMEW *variant of* ▸ **emmew**
ENMEWED ▸ **enmew**
ENMEWS ▸ **enmew**
ENMITY *n*
ENMOVE *variant of* ▸ **emmove**
ENMOVED ▸ **enmove**
ENMOVES ▸ **enmove**
ENNAGE *n* number of ens in printed matter **ennages**
ENNEAD *n* group or series of nine **enneads**
ENNOBLE *vb*
ENNOG *n* back alley **ennogs**
ENNUI *n*, *vb* **ennuied, ennuis**
ENNUYE *adj* bored
ENNUYED ▸ **ennui**
ENNUYEE = **ennuye**
ENODAL *adj* having no nodes
ENOKI *variant of* > **enokitake**
ENOKIS ▸ **enoki**
ENOL *n* type of organic compound
ENOLASE *n* type of enzyme
ENOLIC ▸ **enol**
ENOLOGY *usual US spelling of* > **oenology**
ENOLS ▸ **enol**
ENOMOTY *n* division of the Spartan army in ancient Greece
ENORM *variant of* > **enormous**
ENOSES ▸ **enosis**
ENOSIS *n* union of Greece and Cyprus
ENOUGH *adj*, *n*, *adv* **enoughs**
ENOUNCE *vb* enunciate
ENOW *archaic word for* ▸ **enough**
ENOWS ▸ **enow**
ENPLANE *vb* board an aircraft
ENPRINT *n* standard photographic print
ENQUEUE *vb* add (an item) to a queue of computing tasks
ENQUIRE = **inquire**
ENQUIRY ▸ **enquire**
ENRACE *vb* bring in a race of people **enraced, enraces**
ENRAGE *vb* **enraged, enrages**
ENRANGE *vb* arrange, organize
ENRANK *vb* put in a row **enranks**
ENRAPT > **enrapture**
ENRHEUM *vb* pass a cold on to
ENRICH *vb*
ENRING *vb* put a ring round **enrings**
ENRIVEN *adj* ripped
ENROBE *vb* dress in or as if in a robe **enrobed, enrober, enrobes**
ENROL *vb* **enroll**
ENROLLS ▸ **enroll**
ENROLS ▸ **enrol**
ENROOT *vb* establish (plants) by fixing their roots in the earth **enroots**
ENROUGH *vb* roughen
ENROUND *vb* encircle
ENS *n* being or existence in the most general abstract sense
ENSATE *adj* shaped like a sword
ENSEAL *vb* seal up **enseals**
ENSEAM *vb* put a seam on **enseams**
ENSEAR *vb* dry **ensears**
ENSERF *vb* enslave **enserfs**
ENSEW *variant of* ▸ **ensue**
ENSEWED ▸ **ensew**
ENSEWS ▸ **ensew**
ENSHELL *variant of* ▸ **inshell**
ENSIGN *n*, *vb* **ensigns**
ENSILE *vb* store and preserve (green fodder) in an enclosed pit or silo **ensiled, ensiles**

ENSKIED ▸ **ensky**
ENSKIES ▸ **ensky**
ENSKY *vb* put in the sky **enskyed**
ENSLAVE *vb*
ENSNARE *vb*
ENSNARL *vb* become tangled in
ENSOUL *vb* endow with a soul **ensouls**
ENSTAMP *vb* imprint with a stamp
ENSTEEP *vb* soak in water
ENSTYLE *vb* give a name to
ENSUE *vb* **ensued, ensues**
ENSUING *adj* following subsequently or in order
ENSURE *vb* **ensured, ensurer, ensures**
ENSWEEP *vb* sweep across **enswept**
ENTAIL *vb, n* **entails**
ENTAME *vb* make tame **entamed, entames**
ENTASES ▸ **entasis**
ENTASIA = **entasis**
ENTASIS *n* slightly convex curve given to the shaft of a structure
ENTAYLE *variant of* ▸ **entail**
ENTENTE *n*
ENTER *vb*
ENTERA ▸ **enteron**
ENTERAL = **enteric**
ENTERED ▸ **enter**
ENTERER ▸ **enter**
ENTERIC *adj* intestinal ▹ *n* infectious disease of the intestines
ENTERON *n* alimentary canal
ENTERS ▸ **enter**
ENTETE *adj* obsessed **entetee**
ENTHRAL *vb*
ENTHUSE *vb*
ENTIA ▸ **ens**

> This means entities, and because of the common letters it uses is one of the most frequently played five-letter words, at least towards the end of the game.

ENTICE *vb* **enticed, enticer, entices**
ENTIRE *adj, n* **entires**
ENTITLE *vb*
ENTITY *n*
ENTOIL *archaic word for* ▸ **ensnare**
ENTOILS ▸ **entoil**
ENTOMB *vb* place (a corpse) in a tomb **entombs**
ENTOMIC *adj* denoting or relating to insects
ENTOPIC *adj* situated in its normal place or position
ENTOTIC *adj* of or relating to the inner ear
ENTOZOA > **entozoon**
ENTRAIL *vb* twist or entangle
ENTRAIN *vb* board or put aboard a train
ENTRALL *variant of* > **entrails**
ENTRANT *n*
ENTRAP *vb* trick into difficulty etc **entraps**
ENTREAT *vb*
ENTREE *n* dish served before a main course **entrees**
ENTREZ *interj* enter
ENTRIES ▸ **entry**
ENTRISM *variant of* > **entryism**
ENTRIST > **entryism**
ENTROLD *adj* surrounded
ENTROPY *n* lack of organization
ENTRUST *vb*
ENTRY *n, adj*
ENTWINE *vb*
ENTWIST *vb* twist together or around
ENUF *common intentional literary misspelling of* ▸ **enough**
ENURE *variant spelling of* ▸ **inure**
ENURED ▸ **enure**
ENURES ▸ **enure**
ENURING ▸ **enure**
ENURN ▸ **inurn**
ENURNED ▸ **inurned**
ENURNS ▸ **inurns**
ENVAULT *vb* enclose in a vault; entomb
ENVELOP *vb*
ENVENOM *vb* fill or impregnate with venom
ENVIED, envier, enviers, envies ▸ **envy**
ENVIOUS *adj*
ENVIRO *n* environmentalist

ENVIRON *vb* encircle or surround
ENVIROS ▸ **enviro**
ENVOI = **envoy**
ENVOIS ▸ **envoi**
ENVOY *n* **envoys**
ENVY *n*, *vb* **envying**
ENWALL *vb* wall in **enwalls**
ENWHEEL *archaic word for* > **encircle**
ENWIND *vb* wind or coil around **enwinds**
ENWOMB *vb* enclose in or as if in a womb **enwombs**
ENWOUND ▸ **enwind**
ENWRAP *vb* wrap or cover up **enwraps**
ENZIAN *n* gentian violet **enzians**
ENZONE *vb* enclose in a zone **enzoned, enzones**
ENZYM = **enzyme**
ENZYME *n* **enzymes, enzymic**
ENZYMS ▸ **enzym**
EOAN *adj* of or relating to the dawn
EOBIONT *n* hypothetical chemical precursor of a living cell
EOCENE *adj* of, denoting, or formed in the second epoch of the Tertiary period
EOLIAN *adj* of or relating to the wind

> 6-letter words tend to be among the least known and least used, because they leave you at the mercy of the tile bag without scoring that extra 50 points you would get for using all 7 letters. This word, meaning related to the wind, often comes in useful for dumping a surplus of vowels. And its alternative spelling **aeolian** is even better for this and what's more will get you a bonus!

EOLITH *n* stone used as a primitive tool in Eolithic times **eoliths**
EON *n* two or more eras
EONIAN *adj* of or relating to an eon
EONISM *n* adoption of female dress and behaviour by a male **eonisms**
EONS ▸ **eon**
EORL *n* Anglo-Saxon nobleman **eorls**
EOSIN *n* red crystalline water-insoluble derivative of fluorescein **eosine**
EOSINES ▸ **eosine**
EOSINIC ▸ **eosin**
EOSINS ▸ **eosin**
EOTHEN *adv* from the East
EPACRID *n* type of heath-like plant
EPACRIS *n* genus of the epacrids
EPACT *n* difference in time between the solar year and the lunar year **epacts**
EPAGOGE *n* inductive reasoning
EPARCH *n* bishop or metropolitan in charge of an eparchy **eparchs**
EPARCHY *n* diocese of the Eastern Christian Church
EPATANT *adj* startling or shocking
EPAULE *n* shoulder of a fortification **epaules**
EPAULET = **epaulette**
EPAXIAL *adj* above the axis
EPAZOTE *n* type of herb
EPEE *n* straight-bladed sword used in fencing
EPEEIST *n* one who uses or specializes in using an epee
EPEES ▸ **epee**
EPEIRA = **epeirid**
EPEIRAS ▸ **epeira**
EPEIRIC *adj* in, of, or relating to a continent
EPEIRID *n* type of spider
EPERDU *adj* distracted
EPERDUE *adj* distracted
EPERGNE *n* ornamental centrepiece for a table
EPHA = **ephah**
EPHAH *n* Hebrew unit of dry measure **ephahs**
EPHAS ▸ **epha**
EPHEBE *n* (in ancient Greece) youth about to enter full citizenship **ephebes, ephebi, ephebic**
EPHEBOI ▸ **ephebos**
EPHEBOS = **ephebe**
EPHEBUS = **ephebe**

EPHEDRA *n* gymnosperm shrub
EPHELIS *n* freckle
EPHOD *n* embroidered vestment worn by priests **ephods**
EPHOR *n* (in ancient Greece) one of a board of senior magistrates in any of several Dorian states **ephoral, ephori, ephors**
EPIBLEM *n* outermost cell layer of a root
EPIBOLY *n* process that occurs during gastrulation in vertebrates
EPIC *n, adj* **epical**
EPICARP *n* outermost layer of the pericarp of fruits
EPICEDE = **epicedium**
EPICENE *adj* having the characteristics of both sexes; hermaphroditic ▷ *n* epicene person or creature
EPICIER *n* grocer
EPICISM *n* style or trope characteristic of epics
EPICIST *n* writer of epics
EPICS ▶ **epic**
EPICURE *n*
EPIDERM = **epidermis**
EPIDOTE *n* green mineral
EPIGEAL *adj* of or relating to a form of seed germination **epigean, epigeic**
EPIGENE *adj* formed or taking place at or near the surface of the earth
EPIGON = **epigone**
EPIGONE *n* inferior follower or imitator **epigoni**
EPIGONS ▶ **epigon**
EPIGRAM *n*
EPIGYNY > **epigynous**
EPILATE *vb* remove hair from
EPILOG = **epilogue**
EPILOGS ▶ **epilog**
EPIMER *n* isomer
EPIMERE *n* dorsal part of the mesoderm of a vertebrate embryo
EPIMERS ▶ **epimer**
EPINAOI ▶ **epinaos**
EPINAOS *n* rear vestibule
EPISCIA *n* creeping plant
EPISODE *n*
EPISOME *n* unit of genetic material (DNA) in bacteria that can be replicated
EPISTLE *n, vb*
EPITAPH *n, vb*
EPITAXY *n* growth of a thin layer on the surface of a crystal
EPITHEM *n* external topical application
EPITHET *n, vb*
EPITOME *n*
EPITOPE *n* site on an antigen at which a specific antibody becomes attached
EPIZOA ▶ **epizoon**
EPIZOAN = **epizoon**
EPIZOIC *adj* (of an animal or plant) growing or living on the exterior of a living animal
EPIZOON *n* animal that lives on the body of another animal
EPOCH *n* **epocha, epochal**
EPOCHAS ▶ **epocha**
EPOCHS ▶ **epoch**
EPODE *n* part of a lyric ode that follows the strophe and the antistrophe **epodes, epodic**
EPONYM *n* name derived from the name of a real or mythical person **eponyms**
EPONYMY *n* derivation of names of places, etc, from those of persons
EPOPEE *n* epic poem **epopees**
EPOPT *n* one initiated into mysteries **epopts**
EPOS *n* body of poetry in which the tradition of a people is conveyed **eposes**
EPOXIDE *n* chemical compound
EPOXIED ▶ **epoxy**
EPOXIES ▶ **epoxy**
EPOXY *adj* of or containing a specific type of chemical compound ▷ *n* epoxy resin ▷ *vb* glue with epoxy resin **epoxyed**
EPRIS *adj* enamoured **eprise**
EPSILON *n* fifth letter of the Greek alphabet

EPUISE *adj* exhausted **epuisee**
EPULARY *adj* of or relating to feasting
EPULIS *n* swelling of the gum
EPURATE *vb* purify
EPYLLIA > **epyllion**
EQUABLE *adj* **equably**
EQUAL *adj, n, vb* **equaled**
EQUALI *pl n* pieces for a group of instruments of the same kind
EQUALLY ▸ **equal**
EQUALS ▸ **equal**
EQUANT *n* circle in which a planet was formerly believed to move **equants**
EQUATE *vb* **equated, equates**
EQUATOR *n*
EQUERRY *n* attendant to a member of a royal family
EQUID *n* any animal of the horse family **equids**
EQUINAL = **equine**
EQUINE *adj, n* **equines**
EQUINIA *n* glanders
EQUINOX *n*
EQUIP *vb*
EQUIPE *n* (esp in motor racing) team **equipes**
EQUIPS ▸ **equip**
EQUITES *pl n* cavalry
EQUITY *n*
ER *interj* sound made when hesitating in speech
ERA *n* **eras**
ERASE *vb* **erased**
ERASER *n* **erasers**
ERASES ▸ **erase**
ERASING ▸ **erase**
ERASION *n* act of erasing

> This means the state of being erased: not an exciting word, but its combination of common letters makes it one of the most frequently played of 7-letter bonus words.

ERASURE *n* erasing
ERATHEM *n* stratum of rocks representing a specific geological era
ERBIA *n* oxide of erbium **erbias**
ERBIUM *n* metallic element of the lanthanide series **erbiums**
ERE *prep* before ▹ *vb* plough
ERECT *vb, adj* **erected**
ERECTER = **erector**
ERECTLY ▸ **erect**
ERECTOR *n* any muscle that raises a part or makes it erect
ERECTS ▸ **erect**
ERED ▸ **ere**
ERELONG *adv* before long
EREMIC *adj* of or relating to deserts
EREMITE *n* Christian hermit
EREMURI > **eremurus**
ERENOW *adv* long before the present
EREPSIN *n* mixture of proteolytic enzymes secreted by the small intestine
ERES ▸ **ere**
ERETHIC > **erethism**
EREV *n* day before **erevs**
ERF *n* plot of land marked off for building purposes
ERG = **ergometer**
ERGATE *n* worker ant **ergates**
ERGO = **ergometer**
ERGODIC *adj* of or relating to the probability that any state will recur
ERGON *n* work **ergons**
ERGOS ▸ **ergo**
ERGOT *n* fungal disease of cereal **ergotic, ergots**
ERGS ▸ **erg**
ERHU *n* Chinese two-stringed violin **erhus**
ERIACH = **eric**
ERIACHS ▸ **eriach**
ERIC *n* (in old Irish law) fine paid by a murderer to the family of his victim
ERICA *n* genus of plants including heathers **ericas**
ERICK = **eric**
ERICKS ▸ **erick**
ERICOID *adj* (of leaves) small and tough, resembling those of heather

ERICS ▸ **eric**
ERING ▸ **ere**
ERINGO = **eryngo**
ERINGOS ▸ **eringo**
ERINITE *n* arsenate of copper
ERINUS *n* type of plant
ERISTIC *adj* of, relating, or given to controversy or logical disputation ▹ *n* person who engages in logical disputes
ERK *n* aircraftman or naval rating **erks**
ERLANG *n* unit of traffic intensity in a telephone system **erlangs**
ERLKING *n* malevolent spirit who carries off children
ERM *interj*
ERMELIN *n* ermine
ERMINE *n*
ERMINED *adj* clad in the fur of the ermine
ERMINES ▸ **ermine**
ERN *archaic variant of* ▸ **earn**
ERNE *n* fish-eating (European) sea eagle
ERNED ▸ **ern**
ERNES ▸ **erne**
ERNING ▸ **ern**
ERNS ▸ **ern**
ERODE *vb* **eroded, erodent, erodes, eroding**
ERODIUM *n* type of geranium
EROS *n* lust
EROSE *adj* jagged or uneven, as though gnawed or bitten **erosely**
EROSES ▸ **eros**
EROSION *n* **erosive**
EROTEMA *n* rhetorical question **eroteme**
EROTIC *adj, n*
EROTICA *n*
EROTICS ▸ **erotic**
EROTISE = **erotize**
EROTISM = **eroticism**
EROTIZE *vb* make erotic
ERR *vb*
ERRABLE *adj* capable of making a mistake
ERRANCY *n* state or an instance of erring or a tendency to err
ERRAND *n* **errands**
ERRANT *adj* behaving in a manner considered to be unacceptable ▹ *n* knight-errant **errants**
ERRATA ▸ **erratum**
ERRATAS *informal variant of* ▸ **errata**
ERRATIC *adj, n*
ERRATUM *n* error in writing or printing
ERRED ▸ **err**
ERRHINE *adj* causing nasal secretion ▹ *n* errhine drug or agent
ERRING ▸ **err**
ERRINGS ▸ **err**
ERROR *n* **errors**
ERRS ▸ **err**
ERS = **ervil**
ERSATZ *adj* made in imitation ▹ *n* ersatz substance or article
ERSES ▸ **ers**
ERST *adv* long ago
ERUCIC *adj as in* **erucic acid** crystalline fatty acid
ERUCT *vb* belch **eructed, eructs**
ERUDITE *adj, n*
ERUGO *n* verdigris **erugos**
ERUPT *vb* **erupted, erupts**
ERUV *n* area within which certain activities forbidden to be done on the Sabbath are permitted **eruvim, eruvin, eruvs**
ERVEN ▸ **erf**
ERVIL *n* type of vetch **ervils**
ERYNGO *n* type of plant with toothed or lobed leaves **eryngos**
ES *n* letter S
ESCALOP *another word for* ▸ **scallop**
ESCAPE *vb, n* **escaped**
ESCAPEE *n*
ESCAPER ▸ **escape**
ESCAPES ▸ **escape**
ESCAR = **esker**
ESCARP *n* inner side of the ditch separating besiegers and besieged ▹ *vb* make into a slope **escarps**
ESCARS ▸ **escar**
ESCHAR *n* dry scab or slough **eschars**
ESCHEAT *n* possessions that become state property in the absence of an heir ▹ *vb* attain such property
ESCHEW *vb* **eschews**

ESCOLAR *n* slender spiny-finned fish
ESCORT *n, vb* **escorts**
ESCOT *vb* maintain **escoted, escots**
ESCRIBE *vb* make a mathematical drawing
ESCROC *n* conman **escrocs**
ESCROL = **escroll**
ESCROLL *n* scroll
ESCROLS ▸ **escrol**
ESCROW *n* item delivered to a third party pending fulfilment of a condition ▹ *vb* place (money, a document, etc) in escrow **escrows**
ESCUAGE *(in medieval Europe) another word for* ▸ **scutage**
ESCUDO *n* former monetary unit of Portugal **escudos**
ESERINE *n* crystalline alkaloid
ESES ▸ **es**
ESILE *n* vinegar **esiles**
ESKAR = **esker**
ESKARS ▸ **eskar**
ESKER *n* long ridge of gravel, sand, etc **eskers**
ESKIES ▸ **esky**
ESKY *n* portable insulated container
ESLOIN = **eloign**
ESLOINS ▸ **esloin**
ESLOYNE = **eloign**
ESNE *n* household slave
ESNECY *n* inheritance law
ESNES ▸ **esne**
ESOTERY > **esoteric**
ESPADA *n* sword **espadas**
ESPANOL *n* Spanish person
ESPARTO *n* grass of S Europe and N Africa
ESPIAL *n* act or fact of being seen or discovered **espials**
ESPIED, espier, espiers, espies ▸ **espy**
ESPOUSE *vb*
ESPRIT *n* spirit, liveliness, or wit **esprits**
ESPY *vb* **espying**
ESQUIRE *n* courtesy title placed after a man's name ▹ *vb* escort
ESS *n* letter S
ESSAY *n, vb* **essayed, essayer, essays**
ESSE *n* existence
ESSENCE *n*
ESSES ▸ **ess**
ESSIVE *n* grammatical case **essives**
ESSOIN *n* excuse **essoins, essoyne**
EST *n* treatment intended to help people towards psychological growth
ESTATE *n, vb* **estated, estates**
ESTEEM *n, vb* **esteems**
ESTER *n* chemical compound **esters**
ESTHETE *US spelling of* > **aesthete**
ESTIVAL *usual US spelling of* > **aestival**
ESTOC *n* short stabbing sword **estocs**
ESTOILE *n* heraldic star with wavy points
ESTOP *vb* preclude by estoppel **estops**
ESTOVER = **estovers**
ESTRADE *n* dais or raised platform
ESTRAL *US spelling of* ▸ **oestral**
ESTRAY *n* stray domestic animal of unknown ownership ▹ *vb* stray **estrays**
ESTREAT *n* true copy of or extract from a court record ▹ *vb* send an extract of the court record
ESTREPE *vb* lay waste
ESTRICH *n* ostrich
ESTRIN *US spelling of* ▸ **oestrin**
ESTRINS ▸ **estrin**
ESTRIOL *usual US spelling of* > **oestriol**
ESTRO *n* poetic inspiration
ESTRONE *usual US spelling of* > **oestrone**
ESTROS ▸ **estro**
ESTROUS ▸ **estrus**
ESTRUAL ▸ **estrus**
ESTRUM *usual US spelling of* ▸ **oestrum**
ESTRUMS ▸ **estrum**
ESTRUS *usual US spelling of* ▸ **oestrus**
ESTS ▸ **est**
ESTUARY *n*
ET *dialect past tense of* ▸ **eat**
ETA *n* seventh letter in the Greek alphabet

ETACISM *n* pronunciation of eta as a long vowel sound
ETAERIO *n* aggregate fruit

> This strange-looking word is a type of fruit, and because it uses the commonest letters is, along with **otarine**, the most frequently played of all bonus words.

ETAGE *n* floor in a multi-storey building
ETAGERE *n* stand with open shelves for displaying ornaments, etc
ETAGES ▸ **etage**
ETALAGE *n* display
ETALON *n* device used in spectroscopy **etalons**
ETAMIN = **etamine**
ETAMINE *n* cotton or worsted fabric of loose weave
ETAMINS ▸ **etamin**
ETAPE *n* public storehouse **etapes**
ETAS ▸ **eta**
ETAT *n* state
ETATISM = **etatisme**
ETATIST > **etatisme**
ETATS ▸ **etat**
ETCH *vb*
ETCHANT *n* any acid or corrosive used for etching
ETCHED, etcher, etchers, etches ▸ **etch**
ETCHING *n*
ETEN *n* giant **etens**
ETERNAL *adj, n* **eterne**
ETESIAN *adj* (of NW winds) recurring annually in the summer in the E Mediterranean ▹ *n* etesian wind
ETH = **edh**
ETHAL *n* cetyl alcohol **ethals**
ETHANAL *n* colourless volatile pungent liquid
ETHANE *n* odourless flammable gas **ethanes**
ETHANOL = **alcohol**
ETHE *adj* easy
ETHENE = **ethylene**
ETHENES ▸ **ethene**
ETHER *n* **etheric, ethers**
ETHIC *n* moral principle
ETHICAL *adj, n*
ETHICS *n*
ETHINYL = **ethynyl**
ETHION *n* type of pesticide **ethions**
ETHIOPS *n* dark-coloured chemical compound
ETHMOID *adj* denoting or relating to a specific bone of the skull ▹ *n* ethmoid bone
ETHNIC *adj, n* **ethnics**
ETHNOS *n* ethnic group
ETHOS *n* **ethoses**
ETHOXY ▸ **ethoxyl**
ETHOXYL *n* univalent radical
ETHS ▸ **eth**
ETHYL *adj* type of chemical hydrocarbon group **ethylic, ethyls**
ETHYNE *another name for* > **acetylene**
ETHYNES ▸ **ethyne**
ETHYNYL *n* univalent radical
ETIC *adj* relating to linguistic terms analysed without regard to structural function
ETIOLIN *n* yellow pigment
ETNA *n* container used to heat liquids **etnas**
ETOILE *n* star **etoiles**
ETOURDI *adj* foolish
ETRENNE *n* New Year's gift
ETRIER *n* short portable ladder or set of webbing loops **etriers**
ETTIN *n* giant **ettins**
ETTLE *vb* intend **ettled, ettles, ettling**
ETUDE *n* short musical composition for a solo instrument **etudes**
ETUI *n* small usually ornamented case **etuis, etwee, etwees**
ETYMA ▸ **etymon**
ETYMIC ▸ **etymon**
ETYMON *n* earliest form of a word or morpheme from which another is derived **etymons**
ETYPIC *n* unable to conform to type
EUCAIN = **eucaine**
EUCAINE *n* crystalline optically active substance

EUCAINS ▸ **eucain**
EUCHRE *n* US and Canadian card game ▹ *vb* prevent (a player) from making his contracted tricks **euchred, euchres**
EUCLASE *n* brittle green gem
EUCRITE *n* type of stony meteorite
EUDEMON *n* benevolent spirit or demon
EUGARIE *another name for* ▸ **pipi**
EUGE *interj* well done!
EUGENIA *n* plant of the clove family
EUGENIC > **eugenics**
EUGENOL *n* oily liquid used in perfumery
EUGH *archaic form of* ▸ **yew**
EUGHEN *archaic form of* ▸ **yew**
EUGHS ▸ **eugh**
EUGLENA *n* type of freshwater unicellular organism
EUK *vb* itch **euked, euking, euks**
EULOGIA *n* blessed bread

> This is one of the few 7-letter words that use all the vowels. What's more, it can take a plural in E as well as S, giving **eulogiae**, which can be great for getting you out of vowel trouble.

EULOGY *n*
EUMONG = **eumung**
EUMONGS ▸ **eumong**
EUMUNG *n* any of various Australian acacias **eumungs**
EUNUCH *n* **eunuchs**
EUOI *n* cry of Bacchic frenzy

> This is a cry expressing Bacchic frenzy, and is forever coming in useful to dispose of a surplus of vowels. It has the less commonly played but still useful variants **evoe, evhoe** and **evohe**.

EUOUAE *n* musical term **euouaes**

> This word is remarkable in containing no consonants. You will be surprised at how often you will be glad to play it!

EUPAD *n* antiseptic powder **eupads**
EUPEPSY = **eupepsia**
EUPHON *n* glass harmonica **euphons**
EUPHONY *n* pleasing sound
EUPHORY = **euphoria**
EUPHROE *n* wooden block through which the lines of a crowfoot are rove
EUPLOID *adj* having chromosomes in an exact multiple of the haploid number ▹ *n* euploid cell or individual
EUPNEA = **eupnoea**
EUPNEAS ▸ **eupnea**
EUPNEIC ▸ **eupnoea**
EUPNOEA *n* normal relaxed breathing
EUREKA *n* **eurekas**
EURIPI ▸ **euripus**
EURIPUS *n* strait or channel with a strong current or tide
EURO *n*
EUROKY *n* ability of an organism to live under different conditions
EUROPOP *n* type of pop music by European artists
EUROS ▸ **euro**
EURYOKY = **euroky**
EUSOL *n* solution of eupad in water **eusols**
EUSTACY > **eustatic**
EUSTASY > **eustatic**
EUSTELE *n* central cylinder of a seed plant
EUSTYLE *n* building with columns optimally spaced
EUTAXIA *n* condition of being easily melted
EUTAXY *n* good order
EUTEXIA = **eutaxia**
EUTROPY *n* chemical structure
EVACUEE *n* person evacuated from a place of danger
EVADE *vb* **evaded, evader, evaders, evades, evading**
EVANGEL *n* gospel of Christianity

EVANISH *poetic word for* ▸ **vanish**
EVASION *n*
EVASIVE *adj*
EVE *n*
EVEJAR *n* nightjar **evejars**
EVEN *adj, adv, vb, n* **evened, evener, eveners, evenest**
EVENING *n, adj*
EVENLY ▸ **even**
EVENS *adv* (of a bet) winning the same as the amount staked if successful
EVENT *n, vb* **evented**
EVENTER > **eventing**
EVENTS ▸ **event**
EVER *adv*
EVERNET *n* hypothetical form of internet
EVERT *vb* turn (some bodily part) outwards or inside out **everted**
EVERTOR *n* any muscle that turns a part outwards
EVERTS ▸ **evert**
EVERY *adj*
EVES ▸ **eve**
EVET *n* eft **evets**
EVHOE *interj* cry of Bacchic frenzy
EVICT *vb* **evicted, evictee, evictor, evicts**
EVIDENT *adj, n*
EVIL *n, adj, adv* **eviler, evilest, eviller, evilly, evils**
EVINCE *vb* **evinced, evinces**
EVIRATE *vb* castrate
EVITATE *archaic word for* ▸ **avoid**
EVITE *archaic word for* ▸ **avoid**
EVITED ▸ **evite**
EVITES ▸ **evite**
EVITING ▸ **evite**
EVO *informal word for* ▸ **evening**
EVOCATE *vb* evoke
EVOE *interj* cry of Bacchic frenzy
EVOHE *interj* cry of Bacchic frenzy
EVOKE *vb* **evoked, evoker, evokers, evokes, evoking**
EVOLUE *n* colonial term for an African educated according to European principles **evolues**
EVOLUTE *n* geometric curve ▹ *adj* having the margins rolled outwards ▹ *vb* evolve
EVOLVE *vb* **evolved, evolver, evolves**
EVOS ▸ **evo**
EVOVAE *n* mnemonic used in sacred music **evovaes**
EVULSE *vb* extract by force **evulsed, evulses**
EVZONE *n* soldier in an elite Greek infantry regiment **evzones**
EWE *n*
EWER *n* **ewers**
EWES ▸ **ewe**
EWEST *Scots word for* ▸ **near**
EWFTES *Spenserian plural of* ▸ **eft**
EWGHEN *archaic form of* ▸ **yew**
EWHOW *interj* expression of pity or regret
EWK *vb* itch **ewked, ewking, ewks**

> **Ewk** is a dialect word for **itch**. It's a handy little word and a good one to remember in case you end up with both K and W, and remember that it's a verb so you can have **ewks, ewked** and **ewking**. It's also worth knowing its variants **euk, yeuk, youk, yuck** and **yuke**.

EWT *archaic form of* ▸ **newt**
EWTS ▸ **ewt**
EX *prep* not including ▹ *n* former husband, wife etc ▹ *vb* cross out or delete
EXABYTE *n* very large unit of computer memory
EXACT *adj, vb*
EXACTA *n* horse-racing bet **exactas**
EXACTED ▸ **exact**
EXACTER ▸ **exact**
EXACTLY *adv, interj*
EXACTOR ▸ **exact**
EXACTS ▸ **exact**
EXACUM *n* type of tropical plant **exacums**
EXALT *vb*
EXALTED *adj*

EXALTER ▸ **exalt**
EXALTS ▸ **exalt**
EXAM *n*
EXAMEN *n* examination of conscience **examens**
EXAMINE *vb*
EXAMPLE *n*
EXAMS ▸ **exam**
EXAPTED *adj* biologically adapted
EXARATE *adj* (of the pupa of some insects) having legs, wings, antennae, etc, free and movable
EXARCH *n* head of certain autonomous Orthodox Christian Churches ▷ *adj* (of a xylem strand) having the first-formed xylem external to that formed later **exarchs**
EXARCHY = **exarchate**
EXCAMB *vb* exchange **excambs**
EXCEED *vb* **exceeds**
EXCEL *vb* **excels**
EXCEPT *prep, vb* **excepts**
EXCERPT *n, vb*
EXCESS *n, vb*
EXCHEAT = **escheat**
EXCIDE *vb* cut out **excided, excides**
EXCIMER *n* excited dimer which would remain dissociated in the ground state
EXCIPLE *n* part of a lichen
EXCISE *n, vb* **excised, excises**
EXCITE *vb*
EXCITED *adj*
EXCITER *n* person or thing that excites
EXCITES ▸ **excite**
EXCITON *n* excited electron bound to the hole produced by its excitation
EXCITOR *n* type of nerve
EXCLAIM *vb*
EXCLAVE *n* territory owned by a country, but surrounded by another
EXCLUDE *vb*
EXCRETA *n* excrement
EXCRETE *vb*
EXCUDIT *sentence substitute* (named person) made this
EXCURSE *vb* wander
EXCUSAL ▸ **excuse**
EXCUSE *n, vb* **excused, excuser, excuses**
EXEAT *n* leave of absence from school or some other institution **exeats**
EXEC *n* executive **execs**
EXECUTE *vb*
EXED ▸ **ex**
EXEDRA *n* building, room, portico, or apse containing a continuous bench **exedrae**
EXEEM = **exeme**
EXEEMED ▸ **exeem**
EXEEMS ▸ **exeem**
EXEGETE *n* person who practises exegesis
EXEME *vb* set free **exemed, exemes, exeming**
EXEMPLA > **exemplum**
EXEMPLE = **example**
EXEMPT *adj, vb, n* **exempts**
EXEQUY *n* funeral rite

> Meaning a funeral rite, this word combines X and Q. Even better is its plural **exequies**, which would earn an extra 50 points for using all your tiles.

EXERGUE *n* space on the reverse of a coin or medal
EXERGY *n* maximum amount of useful work obtainable from a system
EXERT *vb* **exerted, exerts**
EXES ▸ **ex**
EXEUNT *vb* (they) go out
EXHALE *vb* **exhaled, exhales**
EXHAUST *vb, n*
EXHEDRA = **exedra**
EXHIBIT *vb, n*
EXHORT *vb* **exhorts**
EXHUME *vb* **exhumed, exhumer, exhumes**
EXIES *n* hysterics
EXIGENT *adj* urgent ▷ *n* emergency
EXILE *n, vb* **exiled, exiler, exilers, exiles, exilian, exilic, exiling**
EXILITY *n* poverty or meagreness
EXINE *n* outermost coat of a pollen grain or a spore **exines**

EXING ▸ **ex**
EXIST *vb* **existed, exists**
EXIT *n, vb* **exited, exiting, exits**
EXO *informal word for* > **excellent**

> **Exo** is an informal Australian way of saying excellent. This is a great little word as it allows you to combine X with two of the most common tiles in the game, E and O.

EXOCARP = **epicarp**
EXODE *n* exodus
EXODERM = **ectoderm**
EXODES ▸ **exode**
EXODIC ▸ **exode**
EXODIST ▸ **exodus**
EXODOI ▸ **exodos**
EXODOS *n* processional song performed at the end of a play
EXODUS *n*
EXOGAMY *n* act of marrying a person from another tribe, clan, etc
EXOGEN *n* type of plant **exogens**
EXOMION = **exomis**
EXOMIS *n* sleeveless jacket
EXON *n* one of the officers who command the Yeomen of the Guard **exonic, exons**
EXONYM *n* name given to a place by foreigners **exonyms**
EXOPOD = **exopodite**
EXOPODS ▸ **exopod**
EXORDIA > **exordium**
EXOSMIC > **exosmosis**
EXOTIC *adj, n*
EXOTICA *pl n* (collection of) exotic objects
EXOTICS ▸ **exotic**
EXOTISM ▸ **exotic**
EXPAND *vb* **expands**
EXPANSE *n*
EXPAT *n* short for **expats**
EXPECT *vb* **expects**
EXPEL *vb* **expels**
EXPEND *vb* **expends**
EXPENSE *n*
EXPERT *n, adj, vb* **experts**
EXPIATE *vb*
EXPIRE *vb* **expired, expirer, expires**
EXPIRY *n* end, esp of a contract period
EXPLAIN *vb*
EXPLANT *vb* transfer (living tissue) from its natural site to a new site or to a culture medium ▹ *n* piece of tissue treated in this way
EXPLODE *vb*
EXPLOIT *vb, n*
EXPLORE *vb*
EXPO *n* exposition, large public exhibition
EXPORT *n, vb* **exports**
EXPOS ▸ **expo**
EXPOSAL ▸ **expose**
EXPOSE *vb, n*
EXPOSED *adj* not concealed
EXPOSER ▸ **expose**
EXPOSES ▸ **expose**
EXPOSIT *vb* state
EXPOUND *vb*
EXPRESS *vb, adj, n, adv*
EXPUGN *vb* storm **expugns**
EXPULSE *vb* expel
EXPUNCT *vb* expunge
EXPUNGE *vb*
EXPURGE *vb* purge
EXSCIND *vb* cut off or out
EXSECT *vb* cut out **exsects**
EXSERT *vb* thrust out ▹ *adj* protruded or stretched out from (something) **exserts**
EXTANT *adj*
EXTASY = **ecstasy**
EXTATIC = **ecstatic**
EXTEND *vb* **extends**
EXTENSE *adj* extensive
EXTENT *n* **extents**
EXTERN *n* person with an official connection to an institution but does not reside in it **externe, externs**
EXTINCT *adj, vb*
EXTINE = **exine**
EXTINES ▸ **extine**
EXTIRP *vb* extirpate **extirps**
EXTOL *vb* **extold, extoll**
EXTOLLS ▸ **extoll**
EXTOLS ▸ **extol**
EXTORT *vb* **extorts**
EXTRA *adj, n, adv*
EXTRACT *vb, n*
EXTRAIT *n* extracts
EXTRAS ▸ **extra**
EXTREAT *n* extraction
EXTREMA > **extremum**
EXTREME *adj, n*

EXTRUDE *vb*
EXUDATE = **exudation**
EXUDE *vb* **exuded, exudes, exuding**
EXUL *n* exile **exuls**
EXULT *vb* **exulted, exults**
EXURB *n* residential area beyond suburbs
EXURBAN ▸ **exurbia**
EXURBIA *n* region outside the suburbs of a city
EXURBS ▸ **exurb**
EXUVIA *n* cast-off exoskeleton of animal **exuviae, exuvial**
EXUVIUM *n* cast-off exoskeleton of animal
EYALET *n* province of Ottoman Empire **eyalets**
EYAS *n* nestling hawk or falcon **eyases, eyass**
EYASSES ▸ **eyass**
EYE *n*, *vb*
EYEABLE *adj* pleasant to look at
EYEBALL *n*, *vb*
EYEBANK *n* place in which corneas are stored
EYEBAR *n* bar with flattened ends with holes for connecting pins **eyebars**
EYEBATH = **eyecup**
EYEBEAM *n* glance
EYEBOLT *n* type of threaded bolt
EYEBROW *n*, *vb*
EYECUP = **eyebath**
EYECUPS ▸ **eyecup**
EYED ▸ **eye**
EYEFOLD *n* fold of skin above eye
EYEFUL *n* view **eyefuls**
EYEHOLE *n* hole through which something is passed
EYEHOOK *n* hook attached to a ring at the extremity of a rope or chain
EYEING ▸ **eye**
EYELASH *n*
EYELESS ▸ **eye**
EYELET *n*, *vb* **eyelets**
EYELIAD = **oeillade**
EYELID *n* **eyelids**
EYELIFT *n* cosmetic surgery for eyes
EYELIKE ▸ **eye**
EYEN *pl n* eyes
EYER *n* someone who eyes **eyers**
EYES ▸ **eye**
EYESHOT *n* range of vision
EYESOME *adj* attractive
EYESORE *n*
EYESPOT *n* small area of pigment
EYEWASH *n* nonsense
EYEWEAR *n* spectacles; glasses
EYEWINK *n* wink of the eye; instant
EYING ▸ **eye**
EYLIAD = **oeillade**
EYLIADS ▸ **eyliad**
EYNE *poetic plural of* ▸ **eye**
EYOT *n* island **eyots**
EYRA *n* reddish-brown variety of the jaguarondi **eyras**
EYRE *n* obsolete circuit court **eyres**
EYRIE *n* **eyries**
EYRIR *n* Icelandic monetary unit
EYRY = **eyrie**

Ff

F is a useful letter in Scrabble: it begins three two-letter words (**fa, fe** and **fy**). There are also quite a few words that combine **F** with **X** or **Z**, allowing high scores, particularly if you can hit a bonus square with them. **Fax, fix** and **fox** are good examples (13 points each), and don't forget **fez** and **fiz** (15 points each). **Fay, fey, fly, foy** and **fry** can also be useful (9 each).

FA = **fah**
FAA *Scot word for* ▶ **fall**
FAAING ▶ **faa**
FAAN ▶ **faa**
FAAS ▶ **faa**
FAB *adj* excellent ▷ *n* fabrication **fabber, fabbest**
FABBIER ▶ **fabby**
FABBY = **fab**
FABLE *n, vb*
FABLED *adj*
FABLER ▶ **fable**
FABLERS ▶ **fable**
FABLES ▶ **fable**
FABLIAU *n* comic usually ribald verse tale
FABLING ▶ **fable**
FABRIC *n, vb* **fabrics**
FABS ▶ **fab**
FABULAR *adj* relating to fables
FACADE *n* **facades**
FACE *n, vb*
FACEBAR *n* wrestling hold
FACED ▶ **face**
FACEMAN *n* miner who works at the coalface **facemen**
FACER *n* difficulty or problem **facers**
FACES ▶ **face**
FACET *n, vb*
FACETE *adj* witty and humorous
FACETED ▶ **facet**
FACETS ▶ **facet**
FACEUP *adj* with the face or surface exposed
FACIA = **fascia**
FACIAE ▶ **facia**
FACIAL *adj, n* **facials**
FACIAS ▶ **facia**
FACIEND *n* multiplicand
FACIES *n* general form and appearance
FACILE *adj*
FACING *n* lining or covering for decoration or reinforcement **facings**
FACONNE *adj* denoting a fabric with the design woven in ▷ *n* such a fabric
FACT *n* **factful**
FACTICE *n* soft rubbery material
FACTION *n*
FACTIS *variant of* ▶ **factice**
FACTIVE *adj* giving rise to the presupposition that a sentence is true
FACTOID *n* piece of unreliable information believed to be true
FACTOR *n, vb* **factors**
FACTORY *n*
FACTS ▶ **fact**
FACTUAL *adj* concerning facts rather than opinions or theories
FACTUM *n* something done, deed **factums**
FACTURE *n* construction

FACULA *n* any of the bright areas on the sun's surface **faculae, facular**
FACULTY *n*
FAD *n*
FADABLE ▸ **fade**
FADAISE *n* silly remark
FADDIER ▸ **faddy**
FADDISH ▸ **fad**
FADDISM ▸ **fad**
FADDIST ▸ **fad**
FADDLE *vb* mess around, toy with **faddled, faddles**
FADDY *adj*
FADE *vb, n* **faded, fadedly**
FADEIN *n* gradual appearance of image on film **fadeins**
FADEOUT *n* gradual disappearance of image on film
FADER ▸ **fade**
FADERS ▸ **fade**
FADES ▸ **fade**
FADEUR *n* blandness, insipidness **fadeurs**
FADGE *vb* agree ▹ *n* package of wool in a wool-bale **fadged, fadges, fadging**
FADIER ▸ **fady**
FADIEST ▸ **fady**
FADING *n* variation in strength of received radio signals **fadings**
FADLIKE ▸ **fad**
FADO *n* type of melancholy Portuguese folk song **fados**
FADS ▸ **fad**
FADY *adj* faded
FAE *Scot word for* ▸ **from**
FAECAL *adj* of, relating to, or consisting of faeces
FAECES *pl n*
FAENA *n* matador's final actions before the kill **faenas**
FAERIE *n* land of fairies
FAERIES ▸ **faery**
FAERY = **faerie**
FAFF *vb* dither or fuss **faffed, faffing, faffs**
FAG = **faggot**
FAGGED ▸ **fag**
FAGGING ▸ **fag**
FAGGOT *n, vb* **faggots**
FAGIN *n* criminal **fagins**
FAGOT = **faggot**
FAGOTED ▸ **fagot**
FAGOTER ▸ **fagot**
FAGOTS ▸ **fagot**
FAGOTTI ▸ **fagotto**
FAGOTTO *n* bassoon
FAGS ▸ **fag**
FAH *n* (in tonic sol-fa) fourth degree of any major scale
FAHLERZ *n* copper ore
FAHLORE *n* copper ore
FAHS ▸ **fah**
FAIBLE *variant of* ▸ **foible**
FAIBLES ▸ **faible**
FAIENCE *n* tin-glazed earthenware
FAIK *vb* grasp **faiked, faikes, faiking, faiks**
FAIL *vb, n* **failed**
FAILING *n, prep*
FAILLE *n* soft light ribbed fabric of silk, rayon, or taffeta **failles**
FAILS ▸ **fail**
FAILURE *n*
FAIN *adv, adj* **faine, fained, fainer**
FAINES ▸ **faine**
FAINEST ▸ **fain**
FAINING ▸ **fain**
FAINLY ▸ **fain**
FAINNE *n* badge worn by advocates of the Irish language **fainnes**
FAINS = **fainites**
FAINT *adj, vb, n* **fainted, fainter, faintly, faints, fainty**
FAIR *adj, adv, n, vb* **faired, fairer, fairest**
FAIRIES ▸ **fairy**
FAIRILY ▸ **fairy**
FAIRING *n* structure fitted round part of a vehicle to reduce drag
FAIRISH *adj* moderately good, well, etc
FAIRLY *adv* moderately
FAIRS ▸ **fair**
FAIRWAY *n*
FAIRY *n*
FAITH *n*
FAITHED *adj* having faith or a faith
FAITHER *Scot word for* ▸ **father**
FAITHS ▸ **faith**
FAITOR *n* traitor, impostor **faitors**
FAITOUR *n* impostor
FAIX *interj* have faith
FAJITA ▸ **fajitas**
FAJITAS *pl n* Mexican dish
FAKE *vb, n, adj* **faked**
FAKEER = **fakir**

FAKEERS ▸ **fakeer**
FAKER, fakers, fakery, fakes ▸ **fake**
FAKEY *adj, adv* (of a skateboarding or snowboarding manoeuvre) travelling backwards **fakie, fakier**
FAKIES ▸ **fakie**
FAKIEST ▸ **fakey**
FAKING ▸ **fake**
FAKIR *n* Muslim who spurns worldly possessions **fakirs**
FALAFEL *n* ball or cake made from chickpeas
FALAJ *n* kind of irrigation channel in ancient Oman
FALBALA *n* gathered flounce, frill, or ruffle
FALCADE *n* movement of a horse
FALCATE *adj* shaped like a sickle
FALCES ▸ **falx**
FALCON *n* **falcons**
FALCULA *n* sharp curved claw, esp of a bird
FALDAGE *n* feudal right
FALL *vb, n*
FALLACY *n*
FALLAL *n* showy ornament, trinket, or article of dress **fallals**
FALLEN ▸ **fall**
FALLER *n* any device that falls or operates machinery by falling **fallers**
FALLING ▸ **fall**
FALLOFF *n* decline or drop
FALLOUT *n, vb, sentence substitute*
FALLOW *adj, n, vb* **fallows**
FALLS ▸ **fall**
FALSE *adj, adv, vb* **falsed, falsely, falser**
FALSERS *n* colloquial term for false teeth
FALSES ▸ **false**
FALSEST ▸ **false**
FALSIE *n* pad used to enlarge breast shape **falsies**
FALSIFY *vb*
FALSING ▸ **false**
FALSISH ▸ **false**
FALSISM ▸ **false**
FALSITY *n* state of being false
FALTER *vb, n* **falters**
FALX *n* sickle-shaped anatomical structure
FAME *n, vb* **famed, fames**
FAMILLE *n* type of Chinese porcelain
FAMILY *n, adj*
FAMINE *n* **famines**
FAMING ▸ **fame**
FAMISH *vb* be or make very hungry or weak
FAMOUS *adj, vb*
FAMULI ▸ **famulus**
FAMULUS *n* (formerly) the attendant of a sorcerer or scholar
FAN *n, vb*
FANAL *n* lighthouse **fanals**
FANATIC *n, adj*
FANBASE *n* body of admirers
FANBOY *n* obsessive fan of a subject or hobby **fanboys**
FANCIED *adj* imaginary
FANCIER *n* person interested in plants or animals
FANCIES ▸ **fancy**
FANCIFY *vb* make more beautiful
FANCILY ▸ **fancy**
FANCY *adj, n, vb*
FAND *vb* try **fanded, fanding**
FANDOM *n* collectively, the fans of a sport, pastime or person **fandoms**
FANDS ▸ **fand**
FANE *n* temple or shrine
FANEGA *n* Spanish unit of measurement **fanegas**
FANES ▸ **fane**
FANFARE *n, vb*
FANFIC *n* fiction based on work by other authors **fanfics**
FANFOLD *vb* fold (paper) like a fan
FANG *n, vb*
FANGA = **fanega**
FANGAS ▸ **fanga**
FANGED ▸ **fang**
FANGING ▸ **fang**
FANGLE *vb* fashion **fangled, fangles**
FANGO *n* mud from thermal springs in Italy **fangos**
FANGS ▸ **fang**
FANION *n* small flag used by surveyors **fanions**
FANJET = **turbofan**

FANJETS ▸ **fanjet**
FANK *n* sheep pen
FANKLE *vb* entangle ▹ *n* tangle **fankled, fankles**
FANKS ▸ **fank**
FANLIKE ▸ **fan**
FANNED ▸ **fan**
FANNEL *n* ecclesiastical vestment **fannell, fannels**
FANNER ▸ **fan**
FANNERS ▸ **fan**
FANNING ▸ **fan**
FANO = **fanon**
FANON *n* collar-shaped vestment **fanons**
FANOS ▸ **fano**
FANS ▸ **fan**
FANSITE *n* website aimed at fans of a celebrity, film, etc
FANSUB *n* **fansubs**
FANTAD *n* nervous, agitated state **fantads**
FANTAIL *n*
FANTASM *archaic spelling of* > **phantasm**
FANTAST *n* dreamer or visionary
FANTASY *n, adj, vb*
FANTEEG *n* nervous, agitated state
FANTOD *n* crotchety or faddish behaviour **fantods**
FANTOM *archaic spelling of* ▸ **phantom**
FANTOMS ▸ **fantom**
FANUM *n* temple **fanums**
FANWISE *adj* like a fan
FANWORT *n* aquatic plant
FANZINE *n* magazine produced by fans
FAP *adj* drunk
FAQIR = **fakir**

Meaning a Hindu ascetic, this is one of those invaluable words allowing you to play the Q without a U. It can also be spelt **fakeer, fakir** and **faquir**.

FAQIRS ▸ **faqir**
FAQUIR *variant of* ▸ **faqir**
FAQUIRS ▸ **faquir**
FAR *adv, adj, vb*
FARAD *n* unit of electrical capacitance
FARADAY *n* quantity of electricity
FARADIC *adj* of an intermittent asymmetric alternating current
FARADS ▸ **farad**
FARAND *adj* pleasant or attractive in manner or appearance
FARAWAY *adj* very distant
FARCE *n, vb* **farced**
FARCER = **farceur**
FARCERS ▸ **farcer**
FARCES ▸ **farce**
FARCEUR *n* writer of or performer in farces
FARCI *adj* (of food) stuffed **farcie**
FARCIED *adj* afflicted with farcy
FARCIES ▸ **farcy**
FARCIFY *vb* turn into a farce
FARCIN *n* equine disease
FARCING ▸ **farce**
FARCINS ▸ **farcin**
FARCY *n* form of glanders, a bacterial disease of horses
FARD *n* paint for the face, esp white paint ▹ *vb* paint (the face) with fard
FARDAGE *n* material laid beneath or between cargo
FARDED ▸ **fard**
FARDEL *n* bundle or burden **fardels**
FARDEN *n* farthing **fardens**
FARDING ▸ **fard**
FARDS ▸ **fard**
FARE *n, vb*
FAREBOX *n* box where money for bus fares is placed
FARED, farer, farers, fares ▸ **fare**
FARFAL = **felafel**
FARFALS ▸ **farfal**
FARFEL = **felafel**
FARFELS = **farfel**
FARFET *adj* far-fetched
FARINA *n* flour or meal made from any kind of cereal grain **farinas**
FARING ▸ **fare**
FARINHA *n* cassava meal
FARL *n* thin cake of oatmeal, often triangular in shape **farle**
FARLES ▸ **farle**
FARLS ▸ **farl**

FARM *n, vb*
FARMED *adj* (of fish or game) reared on a farm
FARMER *n* person who owns or runs a farm **farmers**
FARMERY *n* farm buildings
FARMING *n* business or skill of agriculture
FARMOST ▸ **far**
FARMS ▸ **farm**
FARNESS ▸ **far**
FARO *n* gambling game **faros**
FARRAGO *n* jumbled mixture of things
FARRAND *variant of* ▸ **farand**
FARRANT *variant of* ▸ **farand**
FARRED ▸ **far**
FARREN *n* allotted ground **farrens**
FARRIER *n*
FARRING ▸ **far**
FARROW *n, vb, adj* **farrows**
FARRUCA *n* flamenco dance performed by men
FARS ▸ **far**
FARSE *vb* insert into **farsed, farses**
FARSIDE *n* part of the Moon facing away from the Earth
FARSING ▸ **farse**
FARTHEL = **farl**
FARTHER ▸ **far**
FARTLEK *n* in sport, another name for interval training
FAS ▸ **fa**
FASCES *pl n* (in ancient Rome) a bundle of rods containing an axe
FASCI ▸ **fascio**
FASCIA *n* outer surface of a dashboard **fasciae, fascial, fascias**
FASCINE *n* bundle of long sticks used in construction
FASCIO *n* political group
FASCIS ▸ **fasci**
FASCISM *n*
FASCIST *n* adherent or practitioner of fascism ▹ *adj* characteristic of or relating to fascism
FASH *n* worry ▹ *vb* trouble **fashed**
FASHERY *n* difficulty, trouble
FASHES ▸ **fash**
FASHING ▸ **fash**
FASHION *n, vb*
FAST *adj, adv, vb, n* **fasted**
FASTEN *vb* **fastens**
FASTER, fasters, fastest ▸ **fast**
FASTI *pl n* in ancient Rome, business days
FASTIE *n* deceitful act **fasties**
FASTING, fastish, fastly, fasts ▸ **fast**
FAT *adj* having excess flesh on the body ▹ *n* extra flesh on the body
FATAL *adj*
FATALLY *adv* resulting in death or disaster
FATBACK *n* fat from the upper part of a side of pork
FATBIRD *n* nocturnal bird
FATE *n, vb*
FATED *adj*
FATEFUL *adj*
FATES ▸ **fate**
FATHEAD *n* stupid person
FATHER *n, vb* **fathers**
FATHOM *n, vb* **fathoms**
FATIDIC *adj* prophetic
FATIGUE *n, vb*
FATING ▸ **fate**
FATLESS ▸ **fat**
FATLIKE ▸ **fat**
FATLING *n* young farm animal fattened for killing
FATLY ▸ **fat**
FATNESS ▸ **fat**
FATS ▸ **fat**
FATSIA *n* type of shrub **fatsias**
FATTED ▸ **fat**
FATTEN *vb* **fattens**
FATTER ▸ **fat**
FATTEST ▸ **fat**
FATTIER ▸ **fatty**
FATTIES ▸ **fatty**
FATTILY ▸ **fatty**
FATTING ▸ **fat**
FATTISH ▸ **fat**
FATTISM *n* discrimination on the basis of weight **fattist**
FATTY *adj* containing fat ▹ *n* fat person
FATUITY *n* foolish thoughtlessness
FATUOUS *adj*
FATWA *n* religious decree issued by a

Muslim leader ▷ *vb* issue a fatwa **fatwah**
FATWAHS ▶ **fatwah**
FATWAS ▶ **fatwa**
FATWOOD *n* wood used for kindling
FAUCAL *adj* of or relating to the fauces **faucals**
FAUCES *n* area of the mouth
FAUCET *n* **faucets**
FAUCHON *variant of* > **fauchion**
FAUCIAL = **faucal**
FAUGH *interj* exclamation of disgust, scorn, etc
FAULD *n* piece of armour **faulds**
FAULT *n, vb* **faulted, faults**
FAULTY *adj*
FAUN *n* (in Roman legend) mythological creature
FAUNA *n* **faunae, faunal, faunas, faunist**
FAUNS ▶ **faun**
FAUNULA *n* fauna of a small single environment **faunule**
FAUR *Scot word for* ▶ **far**
FAURD *adj* favoured
FAURER ▶ **faur**
FAUREST ▶ **faur**
FAUT *Scot word for* ▶ **fault**
FAUTED ▶ **faut**
FAUTING ▶ **faut**
FAUTOR *n* patron **fautors**
FAUTS ▶ **faut**
FAUVE *adj* of the style of the Fauve art movement ▷ *n* member of the Fauve art movement **fauves, fauvism**
FAUVIST *n* artist following the Fauve style of painting
FAUX *adj* false
FAVA *n* type of bean **favas**
FAVE *short for* > **favourite**
FAVEL *adj* (of a horse) dun-coloured
FAVELA *n* (in Brazil) a shanty or shantytown **favelas**
FAVELL *variant of* ▶ **favel**
FAVELLA *n* group of spores
FAVER ▶ **fave**
FAVES ▶ **fave**
FAVEST ▶ **fave**
FAVICON *n* icon displayed before a website's URL
FAVISM *n* type of anaemia **favisms**
FAVOR = **favour**
FAVORED ▶ **favor**
FAVORER ▶ **favour**
FAVORS = **favours**
FAVOSE = **faveolate**
FAVOUR *n, vb*
FAVOURS *pl n* sexual intimacy
FAVOUS *adj* resembling honeycomb
FAVRILE *n* type of iridescent glass
FAVUS *n* infectious fungal skin disease **favuses**
FAW *n* gypsy

> A **faw** is a gypsy, a good word for taking advantage of a nearby bonus square.

FAWN *n, adj, vb* **fawned, fawner, fawners**
FAWNIER ▶ **fawny**
FAWNING ▶ **fawn**
FAWNS ▶ **fawn**
FAWNY *adj* of a fawn colour
FAWS ▶ **faw**
FAX *n, vb* **faxed, faxes, faxing**
FAY *n* fairy or sprite ▷ *adj* of or resembling a fay ▷ *vb* fit or be fitted closely or tightly **fayed**

> A **fay** is a fairy but it can also be a verb, meaning to fit directly. It has a variant **fey**. Both are useful high-scoring short words.

FAYENCE *variant of* ▶ **faience**
FAYER ▶ **fay**
FAYEST ▶ **fay**
FAYING ▶ **fay**
FAYNE *vb* pretend **fayned, faynes, fayning**
FAYRE *pseudo-archaic spelling of* ▶ **fair**
FAYRES ▶ **fayre**
FAYS ▶ **fay**
FAZE *vb*
FAZED *adj* worried or disconcerted
FAZENDA *n* large estate or ranch

FAZES ▸ **faze**
FAZING ▸ **faze**
FE *n*
FEAGUE *vb* whip or beat **feagued, feagues**
FEAL *vb* conceal **fealed, fealing, feals**
FEALTY *n* (in feudal society) subordinate's loyalty
FEAR *n*, *vb*
FEARE *n* companion, spouse
FEARED ▸ **fear**
FEARER ▸ **fear**
FEARERS ▸ **fear**
FEARES ▸ **feare**
FEARFUL *adj*
FEARING ▸ **fear**
FEARS ▸ **fear**
FEART *adj*
FEASE *vb* perform an act **feased, feases, feasing**
FEAST *n*, *vb* **feasted, feaster, feasts**
FEAT *n* **feated, feater, featest**
FEATHER *n*, *vb*
FEATING ▸ **feat**
FEATLY ▸ **feat**
FEATOUS *variant of* > **featеous**
FEATS ▸ **feat**
FEATURE *n*, *vb*
FEAZE = **feeze**
FEAZED ▸ **feaze**
FEAZES ▸ **feaze**
FEAZING ▸ **feaze**
FEBRILE *adj* very active and nervous
FECAL = **faecal**
FECES = **faeces**
FECHT *Scot word for* ▸ **fight**
FECHTER ▸ **fecht**
FECHTS ▸ **fecht**
FECIAL *adj* heraldic **fecials**
FECIT *vb* (he or she) made it
FECULA *n* type of starch **feculae, feculas**
FECUND *adj* fertile
FED *n*
FEDARIE *n* accomplice
FEDAYEE *n* (in Arab states) a commando
FEDERAL *adj*, *n*
FEDEX *vb* send by FedEx **fedexed, fedexes**
FEDORA *n* man's soft hat with a brim **fedoras**
FEDS ▸ **fee**
FEE *n*, *vb*
FEEB *n* contemptible person
FEEBLE *adj*, *vb* **feebled, feebler, feebles, feebly**
FEEBS ▸ **feeb**
FEED *vb*, *n*
FEEDBAG *n* any bag in which feed for livestock is sacked
FEEDBOX *n* trough, manger
FEEDER *n* baby's bib **feeders**
FEEDING ▸ **feed**
FEEDLOT *n* area where livestock are fattened rapidly
FEEDS ▸ **feed**
FEEING ▸ **fee**
FEEL *vb*, *n*
FEELBAD *n* something inducing depression
FEELER *n* **feelers**
FEELESS ▸ **fee**
FEELING ▸ **feel**
FEELS ▸ **feel**
FEEN *n* in Irish dialect, an informal word for 'man' **feens**
FEER *vb* make a furrow **feered**
FEERIE *n* fairyland **feeries**
FEERIN *n* furrow
FEERING ▸ **feer**
FEERINS ▸ **feerin**
FEERS ▸ **feer**
FEES ▸ **fee**
FEESE *vb* perturb **feesed, feeses, feesing**
FEET ▸ **foot**
FEEZE *vb* beat ▷ *n* rush **feezed, feezes, feezing**
FEG = **fig**
FEGARY *variant of* ▸ **vagary**
FEGS ▸ **feg**
FEH ▸ **fe**
FEHM *n* medieval German court **fehme, fehmic**
FEHS ▸ **feh**
FEIGN *vb* **feigned, feigner, feigns**
FEIJOA *n* evergreen myrtaceous shrub of S America **feijoas**
FEINT *n*, *vb*, *adj* **feinted, feinter**
FEINTS *pl n* leavings of the second distillation of Scotch malt whisky

FEIRIE *adj* nimble **feirier**
FEIS *n* Irish music and dance festival
FEIST *n* small aggressive dog **feists**
FEISTY *adj* showing courage or spirit
FELAFEL = **falafel**
FELICIA *n* type of African herb
FELID *n* any animal belonging to the cat family **felids**
FELINE *adj, n* **felines**
FELL *vb, adj*
FELLA *nonstandard variant of* ▸ **fellow**
FELLAH *n* peasant in Arab countries **fellahs**
FELLAS ▸ **fella**
FELLATE *vb* perform fellatio on (a person)
FELLED ▸ **fell**
FELLER *n* person or thing that fells **fellers**
FELLEST ▸ **fell**
FELLIES ▸ **felly**
FELLING ▸ **fell**
FELLOE *n* (segment of) the rim of a wheel **felloes**
FELLOW *n, adj* **fellows**
FELLS ▸ **fell**
FELLY = **felloe**
FELON *n, adj*
FELONRY *n* felons collectively
FELONS ▸ **felon**
FELONY *n* serious crime
FELSIC *adj* relating to igneous rock
FELSITE *n* any fine-grained igneous rock
FELSPAR = **feldspar**
FELT *n, vb* **felted**
FELTER *vb* mat together **felters**
FELTIER ▸ **felt**
FELTING *n* felted material
FELTS ▸ **felt**
FELTY ▸ **felt**
FELUCCA *n* narrow lateen-rigged vessel
FELWORT *n* type of plant
FEM *n* passive homosexual
FEMAL *adj* effeminate ▹ *n* effeminate person
FEMALE *adj, n* **females**
FEMALS ▸ **femal**
FEME *n* woman or wife **femes**
FEMINAL *adj* feminine, female
FEMINIE *n* women collectively
FEMITER *variant of* > **fumitory**
FEMME *n* woman or wife **femmes**
FEMMIER ▸ **femmy**
FEMMY *adj* markedly or exaggeratedly feminine
FEMORA ▸ **femur**
FEMORAL *adj* of the thigh
FEMS ▸ **fem**
FEMUR *n* **femurs**
FEN *n*
FENAGLE *variant of* ▸ **finagle**
FENCE *n, vb* **fenced**
FENCER *n* person who fights with a sword **fencers**
FENCES ▸ **fence**
FENCING *n*
FEND *vb, n* **fended**
FENDER *n* **fenders**
FENDIER ▸ **fendy**
FENDING ▸ **fend**
FENDS ▸ **fend**
FENDY *adj* thrifty
FENI *n* Goan alcoholic drink **fenis**
FENITAR *variant of* > **fumitory**
FENKS *n* whale blubber
FENLAND ▸ **fen**
FENMAN ▸ **fen**
FENMEN ▸ **fen**
FENNEC *n* type of nocturnal desert fox **fennecs**
FENNEL *n* **fennels**
FENNIER ▸ **fenny**
FENNIES ▸ **fenny**
FENNISH ▸ **fen**
FENNY *adj* boggy or marshy ▹ *n* feni
FENS ▸ **fen**
FENT *n* piece of waste fabric **fents**
FENURON *n* type of herbicide
FEOD = **feud**
FEODAL ▸ **feod**
FEODARY ▸ **feod**
FEODS ▸ **feod**
FEOFF = **fief**
FEOFFED ▸ **feoff**
FEOFFEE *n* (in feudal society) a vassal granted a fief by his lord
FEOFFER ▸ **feoff**
FEOFFOR ▸ **feoff**
FEOFFS ▸ **feoff**
FER = **far**
FERAL *adj, n* **ferals**

FERBAM *n* powder used as a fungicide **ferbams**
FERE *n* companion ▷ *adj* fierce **ferer, feres, ferest**
FERIA *n* weekday on which no feast occurs **feriae**
FERIAL *adj* of or relating to a feria
FERIAS ▸ **feria**
FERINE = **feral**
FERITY ▸ **feral**
FERLIE = **ferly**
FERLIED ▸ **ferly**
FERLIER ▸ **ferly**
FERLIES ▸ **ferly**
FERLY *adj* wonderful ▷ *n* wonder ▷ *vb* wonder
FERM *variant of* ▸ **farm**
FERMATA *another word for* ▸ **pause**
FERMATE ▸ **fermata**
FERMENT *n, vb*
FERMI *n* unit of length
FERMION *n* type of particle
FERMIS ▸ **fermi**
FERMIUM *n* chemical element
FERMS ▸ **ferm**
FERN *n*
FERNERY *n* place where ferns are grown
FERNIER ▸ **fern**
FERNING *n* production of a fern-like pattern
FERNS ▸ **fern**
FERNY ▸ **fern**
FERRATE *n* type of salt
FERREL *variant of* ▸ **ferrule**
FERRELS ▸ **ferrel**
FERRET *n, vb* **ferrets, ferrety**
FERRIC *adj* of or containing iron
FERRIED ▸ **ferry**
FERRIES ▸ **ferry**
FERRITE *n* type of ceramic compound
FERROUS *adj*
FERRUGO *n* disease affecting plants
FERRULE *n* metal cap to strengthen the end of a stick ▷ *vb* equip (a stick, etc) with a ferrule
FERRUM *Latin word for* ▸ **iron**
FERRUMS ▸ **ferrum**
FERRY *n, vb*
FERTILE *adj*
FERULA *n* large Mediterranean plant **ferulae, ferulas**
FERULE = **ferrule**
FERULED ▸ **ferule**
FERULES ▸ **ferule**
FERVENT *adj* **fervid**
FERVOR = **fervour**
FERVORS ▸ **fervor**
FERVOUR *n*
FES ▸ **fe**
FESCUE *n* pasture and lawn grass with stiff narrow leaves **fescues**
FESS = **fesse**
FESSE *n* horizontal band across a shield
FESSED ▸ **fess**
FESSES ▸ **fesse**
FESSING ▸ **fess**
FEST *n* event at which the emphasis is on a particular activity
FESTA *n* festival
FESTAL *adj* festive ▷ *n* festivity **festals**
FESTAS ▸ **festa**
FESTER *vb, n* **festers**
FESTIER ▸ **festy**
FESTIVE *adj*
FESTOON *vb, n*
FESTS ▸ **fest**
FESTY *adj* dirty
FET *vb* fetch
FETA *n* white salty Greek cheese
FETAL *adj* of, relating to, or resembling a fetus
FETAS ▸ **feta**
FETCH *vb, n* **fetched**
FETCHER *n* person or animal that fetches
FETCHES ▸ **fetch**
FETE *n, vb* **feted, fetes**
FETIAL *n* ancient Roman herald ▷ *adj* of or relating to the fetiales **fetials**
FETICH = **fetish**
FETICHE *variant of* ▸ **fetich**
FETID *adj* **fetider, fetidly**
FETING ▸ **fete**
FETISH *n*
FETLOCK *n*
FETOR *n* offensive stale or putrid odour **fetors**
FETS ▸ **fet**
FETT *variant of* ▸ **fet**
FETTA *variant of* ▸ **feta**
FETTAS ▸ **fetta**
FETTED ▸ **fet**
FETTER *n, vb* **fetters**
FETTING ▸ **fet**
FETTLE = **fettling**
FETTLED ▸ **fettle**
FETTLER *n* person employed to maintain railway tracks

FETTLES ▸ **fettle**
FETTS ▸ **fett**
FETUS *n* **fetuses**
FETWA *variant of* ▸ **fatwa**
FETWAS ▸ **fetwa**
FEU *n* (in Scotland) type of rent
FEUAR *n* tenant of a feu **feuars**
FEUD *n, vb*
FEUDAL *adj* of or like feudalism
FEUDARY *n* holder of land through feudal right
FEUDED ▸ **feud**
FEUDING ▸ **feud**
FEUDIST *n* person who takes part in a feud or quarrel
FEUDS ▸ **feud**
FEUED ▸ **feu**
FEUING ▸ **feu**
FEUS ▸ **feu**
FEUTRE *vb* place in a resting position **feutred, feutres**
FEVER *n, vb* **fevered, fevers**
FEW *adj as in* **the few**
FEWER ▸ **few**
FEWEST ▸ **few**
FEWMET *variant of* ▸ **fumet**
FEWMETS ▸ **fewmet**
FEWNESS ▸ **few**
FEWS ▸ **few**
FEWTER *variant of* ▸ **feutre**
FEWTERS ▸ **feutre**
FEY *adj, vb* **feyed, feyer, feyest, feying, feyly, feyness, feys**
FEZ *n* **fezes**
FEZZED *adj* wearing a fez
FEZZES ▸ **fez**
FEZZY ▸ **fez**
FIACRE *n* small four-wheeled horse-drawn carriage **fiacres**
FIANCE *n* man engaged to be married
FIANCEE *n* woman who is engaged to be married
FIANCES ▸ **fiance**
FIAR *n* property owner
FIARS *n* legally fixed price of corn
FIASCHI ▸ **fiasco**
FIASCO *n* **fiascos**
FIAT *n, vb* **fiated, fiating, fiats**
FIAUNT *n* fiat **fiaunts**
FIB *n, vb* **fibbed, fibber, fibbers, fibbery, fibbing**
FIBER = **fibre**
FIBERED ▸ **fibre**
FIBERS ▸ **fiber**
FIBRATE *n* drug used to lower fat levels in the body
FIBRE *n* **fibred, fibres**
FIBRIL *n* small fibre **fibrils**
FIBRIN *n* **fibrins**
FIBRO *n* mixture of cement and asbestos fibre
FIBROID *adj, n*
FIBROIN *n* tough elastic protein
FIBROMA *n* type of benign tumour
FIBROS ▸ **fibro**
FIBROSE *vb* become fibrous
FIBROUS *adj* consisting of, containing, or resembling fibres
FIBS ▸ **fib**
FIBSTER *n* fibber
FIBULA *n* **fibulae, fibular, fibulas**
FICE *n* small aggressive dog **fices**
FICHE *n* film for storing publications in miniature **fiches**
FICHU *n* woman's shawl or scarf **fichus**
FICIN *n* enzyme **ficins**
FICKLE *adj, vb* **fickled, fickler, fickles, fickly**
FICO *n* worthless trifle **ficoes, ficos**
FICTILE *adj* moulded or capable of being moulded from clay
FICTION *n*
FICTIVE *adj* of, relating to, or able to create fiction
FICTOR *n* sculptor **fictors**
FICUS *n* type of plant **ficuses**
FID *n* spike for separating strands of rope in splicing
FIDDLE *n, vb* **fiddled**
FIDDLER *n* person who plays the fiddle
FIDDLES ▸ **fiddle**
FIDDLEY *n* area of a vessel
FIDDLY *adj*
FIDEISM *n* theological doctrine **fideist**

FIDES *n* faith or trust
FIDGE *obsolete word for* ▸ **fidget**
FIDGED ▸ **fidge**
FIDGES ▸ **fidge**
FIDGET *vb, n* **fidgets, fidgety**
FIDGING ▸ **fidge**
FIDIBUS *n* spill for lighting a candle or pipe
FIDO *n* generic term for a dog **fidos**
FIDS ▸ **fid**
FIE *adj* ▸ **fey**
FIEF *n* land granted by a lord in return for war service
FIEFDOM *n* (in Feudal Europe) the property owned by a lord
FIEFS ▸ **fief**
FIELD *n, vb* **fielded**
FIELDER *n*
FIELDS ▸ **field**
FIEND *n* **fiends**
FIENT *n* fiend **fients**
FIER = **fere**
FIERCE *adj* **fiercer**
FIERE ▸ **fere**
FIERES ▸ **fere**
FIERIER ▸ **fiery**
FIERILY ▸ **fiery**
FIERS ▸ **fier**
FIERY *adj*
FIEST ▸ **fie**
FIESTA *n* **fiestas**
FIFE *n, vb* **fifed, fifer, fifers, fifes, fifing**
FIFTEEN *n, adj, determiner*
FIFTH *n, adj, adv* **fifthly, fifths**
FIFTIES ▸ **fifty**
FIFTY *n, adj, determiner*
FIG *n, vb* **figged**
FIGGERY *n* adornment, ornament
FIGGING ▸ **fig**
FIGHT *vb, n*
FIGHTER *n*
FIGHTS ▸ **fight**
FIGMENT *n*
FIGO *variant of* ▸ **fico**
FIGOS ▸ **figo**
FIGS ▸ **fig**
FIGURAL *adj* composed of or relating to human or animal figures
FIGURE *n, vb*
FIGURED *adj* decorated with a design
FIGURER ▸ **figure**
FIGURES ▸ **figure**
FIGWORT *n* N temperate plant
FIKE *vb* fidget **fiked**
FIKERY *n* fuss
FIKES ▸ **fike**
FIKIER ▸ **fiky**
FIKIEST ▸ **fiky**
FIKING ▸ **fike**
FIKISH *adj* fussy
FIKY *adj* fussy
FIL = **fils**
FILA ▸ **filum**
FILABEG *variant of* ▸ **filibeg**
FILACER *n* formerly, English legal officer
FILAR *adj* of thread
FILAREE *n* type of storksbill, a weed
FILARIA *n* type of parasitic nematode worm
FILASSE *n* vegetable fibre such as jute
FILAZER *variant of* ▸ **filacer**
FILBERD *variant of* ▸ **filbert**
FILBERT *n* hazelnut
FILCH *vb* **filched, filcher, filches**
FILE *n, vb* **filed**
FILEMOT *n* type of brown colour
FILER ▸ **file**
FILERS ▸ **file**
FILES ▸ **file**
FILET *variant of* ▸ **fillet**
FILETED ▸ **filet**
FILETS ▸ **filet**
FILFOT *variant of* ▸ **fylfot**
FILFOTS ▸ **filfot**
FILIAL *adj*
FILIATE *vb* fix judicially the paternity of (a child)
FILIBEG *n* kilt worn by Scottish Highlanders
FILII ▸ **filius**

> This plural of **filius**, a Latin word for son, is the only 5-letter word that lets you get rid of three Is!

FILING ▸ **file**
FILINGS *pl n*
FILIUS *n* son
FILL *vb*
FILLE *n* girl
FILLED ▸ **fill**
FILLER *n* **fillers**
FILLES ▸ **fille**
FILLET *n, vb* **fillets**
FILLIES ▸ **filly**
FILLING *n, adj*
FILLIP *n, vb* **fillips**
FILLO *variant of* ▸ **filo**

FILLOS ▸ **fillo**
FILLS ▸ **fill**
FILLY *n*
FILM *n, vb, adj*
FILMDOM *n* cinema industry
FILMED ▸ **film**
FILMER *n* film-maker **filmers**
FILMI *adj* of or relating to Indian films
FILMIC *adj* of or suggestive of films or the cinema
FILMIER ▸ **filmy**
FILMILY ▸ **filmy**
FILMING ▸ **film**
FILMIS ▸ **filmi**
FILMISH ▸ **film**
FILMS ▸ **film**
FILMSET *vb* set (type matter) by filmsetting
FILMY *adj*
FILO *n* type of flaky Greek pastry in very thin sheets **filos**
FILOSE *adj* resembling a thread or threadlike process
FILS *n* monetary unit of Bahrain, Iraq, Jordan, and Kuwait
FILTER *n, vb* **filters**
FILTH *n* **filths**
FILTHY *adj* characterized by or full of filth ▹ *adv* extremely
FILTRE *adj as in* **cafe filtre** a strong black filtered coffee
FILUM *n* any threadlike structure or part
FIMBLE *n* male plant of the hemp **fimbles**
FIMBRIA *n* fringe or fringelike margin or border
FIN *n, vb*
FINABLE *adj* liable to a fine
FINAGLE *vb* get or achieve by craftiness or trickery
FINAL *adj, n*
FINALE *n* **finales**
FINALIS *n* musical finishing note
FINALLY *adv*
FINALS *pl n* deciding part of a competition
FINANCE *vb, n*
FINBACK *another name for* ▸ **rorqual**
FINCA *n* Spanish villa **fincas**
FINCH *n*
FINCHED *adj* with streaks or spots on the back
FINCHES ▸ **finch**
FIND *vb* discover by chance ▹ *n* person or thing found, esp when valuable
FINDER *n* small telescope fitted to a larger one **finders**
FINDING ▸ **find**
FINDRAM *variant of* ▸ **finnan**
FINDS ▸ **find**
FINE *adj, n, vb* **fined**
FINEER *variant of* ▸ **veneer**
FINEERS ▸ **fineer**
FINEISH ▸ **fine**
FINELY *adv* into small pieces
FINER ▸ **fine**
FINERS ▸ **fine**
FINERY *n*
FINES ▸ **fine**
FINESSE *n, vb*
FINEST ▸ **fine**
FINFISH *n* fish with fins, as opposed to shellfish
FINFOOT *n* type of aquatic bird
FINGAN *variant of* ▸ **finjan**
FINGANS ▸ **fingan**
FINGER *n, vb* **fingers**
FINI *n* end; finish
FINIAL *n* ornament at the apex of a gable or spire **finials**
FINICAL *another word for* ▸ **finicky**
FINICKY *adj* **finikin**
FINING *n* process of removing bubbles from molten glass **finings**
FINIS ▸ **fini**
FINISES ▸ **finis**
FINISH *vb, n*
FINITE *adj, n* **finites**
FINITO *adj* finished
FINJAN *n* small, handleless coffee cup **finjans**
FINK *n* strikebreaker ▹ *vb* inform (on someone), as to the police **finked, finking, finks**
FINLESS ▸ **fin**
FINLIKE ▸ **fin**
FINMARK *n* monetary unit of Finland
FINNAC *variant of* ▸ **finnock**

FINNACK *variant of* ▸ **finnock**
FINNACS ▸ **finnac**
FINNAN *n* smoked haddock **finnans**
FINNED ▸ **fin**
FINNER *another name for* ▸ **rorqual**
FINNERS ▸ **finner**
FINNIER ▸ **finny**
FINNING ▸ **fin**
FINNOCK *n* young sea trout on its first return to fresh water
FINNSKO *variant of* > **finnesko**
FINNY *adj* relating to or containing many fishes
FINO *n* very dry sherry **finos**
FINS ▸ **fin**
FINSKO *variant of* > **finnesko**
FIORD = **fjord**
FIORDS ▸ **fiord**
FIORIN *n* type of temperate perennial grass **fiorins**
FIPPLE *n* wooden plug forming a flue in the end of a pipe **fipples**
FIQH *n* Islamic jurisprudence **fiqhs**
FIQUE *n* hemp **fiques**
FIR *n*
FIRE *n, vb*
FIREARM *n*
FIREBOX *n* furnace chamber of a boiler in a steam locomotive
FIREBUG *n* person who deliberately sets fire to property
FIRED ▸ **fire**
FIREDOG *n* either of two metal stands supporing logs in a fire
FIREFLY *n*
FIRELIT *adj* lit by firelight
FIREMAN *n* **firemen**
FIREPAN *n* metal container for a fire in a room
FIREPOT *n* Chinese fondue-like cooking pot
FIRER ▸ **fire**
FIRERS ▸ **fire**
FIRES ▸ **fire**
FIRIE *n* in Australian English, informal word for a firefighter **firies**
FIRING *n* discharge of a firearm **firings**
FIRK *vb* beat **firked**
FIRKIN *n* small wooden barrel or similar container
FIRKING ▸ **firk**
FIRKINS ▸ **firkin**
FIRKS ▸ **firk**
FIRLOT *n* unit of measurement for grain **firlots**
FIRM *adj, adv, vb, n*
FIRMAN *n* edict of an Oriental sovereign **firmans**
FIRMED, firmer, firmers, firmest, firming, firmly, firms ▸ **firm**
FIRN *another name for* ▸ **neve**
FIRNS ▸ **firn**
FIRRIER ▸ **firry**
FIRRING *n* wooden battens used in building construction
FIRRY *adj* of, relating to, or made from fir trees
FIRS ▸ **fir**
FIRST *adj* earliest in time or order ▹ *n* person or thing coming before all others ▹ *adv* before anything else
FIRSTLY *adv* coming before other points, questions, etc
FIRSTS *pl n* saleable goods of the highest quality
FIRTH *n* narrow inlet of the sea, esp in Scotland **firths**
FIRWOOD *n* wood of the fir tree
FISC *n* state or royal treasury
FISCAL *adj, n* **fiscals**
FISCS ▸ **fisc**
FISGIG *variant of* ▸ **fishgig**
FISGIGS ▸ **fisgig**
FISH *n, vb* **fished**
FISHER *n* fisherman **fishers**
FISHERY *n*
FISHES ▸ **fish**
FISHEYE *n* type of lens
FISHFUL *adj* teeming with fish
FISHGIG *n* pole with barbed prongs for impaling fish
FISHIER ▸ **fishy**
FISHIFY *vb* change into fish

FISHILY ▸ **fishy**
FISHING *n* job or pastime of catching fish
FISHNET *n* open mesh fabric resembling netting
FISHWAY *n* fish ladder
FISHY *adj*
FISK *vb* frisk **fisked, fisking, fisks**
FISSATE ▸ **fissile**
FISSILE *adj*
FISSION *n*
FISSIVE ▸ **fissile**
FISSLE *vb* rustle **fissled, fissles**
FISSURE *n, vb*
FIST *n, vb* **fisted**
FISTFUL *n* quantity that can be held in a fist or hand
FISTIC *adj* of or relating to fisticuffs or boxing
FISTIER ▸ **fist**
FISTING ▸ **fist**
FISTS ▸ **fist**
FISTULA *n* long narrow ulcer
FISTY ▸ **fist**
FIT *vb* be appropriate or suitable for ▹ *adj* appropriate ▹ *n* way in which something fits
FITCH *n* fur of the polecat or ferret
FITCHE *adj* pointed **fitchee**
FITCHES ▸ **fitch**
FITCHET = **fitch**
FITCHEW *archaic name for* ▸ **polecat**
FITCHY = **fitche**
FITFUL *adj*
FITLIER ▸ **fitly**
FITLY *adv* in a proper manner or place or at a proper time
FITMENT *n* accessory attached to a machine
FITNA *n* state of trouble or chaos **fitnas**
FITNESS *n* state of being fit
FITS ▸ **fit**
FITT *n* song **fitte**
FITTED ▸ **fit**
FITTER ▸ **fit**
FITTERS ▸ **fit**
FITTES ▸ **fitte**
FITTEST ▸ **fit**
FITTING ▸ **fit**
FITTS ▸ **fitt**
FIVE *n, adj, determiner*
FIVEPIN > **fivepins**
FIVER *n* five-pound note **fivers**
FIVES *n* ball game resembling squash
FIX *vb, n* **fixable**
FIXATE *vb* become or cause to become fixed **fixated, fixates**
FIXATIF *variant of* > **fixative**
FIXED *adj* attached or placed so as to be immovable **fixedly**
FIXER *n* solution used to make a photographic image permanent **fixers**
FIXES ▸ **fix**
FIXING *n* means of attaching one thing to another
FIXINGS *pl n* apparatus or equipment
FIXIT *n* solution to a complex problem
FIXITY *n*
FIXIVE ▸ **fix**
FIXT *adj* fixed
FIXTURE *n*
FIXURE *n* firmness **fixures**
FIZ *variant of* ▸ **fizz**
FIZGIG *vb* inform on someone to the police **fizgigs**
FIZZ *vb, n* **fizzed**
FIZZEN *variant of* ▸ **foison**
FIZZENS ▸ **fizzen**
FIZZER *n* anything that fizzes **fizzers**
FIZZES ▸ **fizz**
FIZZGIG *variant of* ▸ **fishgig**
FIZZIER ▸ **fizz**
FIZZING ▸ **fizz**
FIZZLE *vb, n* **fizzled, fizzles**
FIZZY ▸ **fizz**
FJELD *n* high rocky plateau **fjelds**
FJORD *n* **fjordic, fjords**
FLAB *n*
FLABBY *adj*
FLABS ▸ **flab**
FLACCID *adj*
FLACK *vb* flutter **flacked**
FLACKER *vb* flutter like a bird
FLACKET *n* flagon
FLACKS ▸ **flack**
FLACON *n* small stoppered bottle or flask **flacons**
FLAFF *vb* flap **flaffed**

FLAFFER *vb* flutter
FLAFFS ▸ **flaff**
FLAG *n, vb* **flagged, flagger**
FLAGGY *adj* drooping
FLAGMAN *n* person who has charge of a flag **flagmen**
FLAGON *n* **flagons**
FLAGS ▸ **flag**
FLAIL *vb, n* **flailed, flails**
FLAIR *n* **flairs**
FLAK *n*
FLAKE *n, vb* **flaked, flaker, flakers, flakes**
FLAKEY = **flaky**
FLAKIER ▸ **flaky**
FLAKIES *n* dandruff
FLAKILY ▸ **flaky**
FLAKING ▸ **flake**
FLAKS ▸ **flak**
FLAKY *adj* like or made of flakes
FLAM *n* falsehood, deception, or sham ▹ *vb* cheat or deceive
FLAMBE *vb* cook or serve (food) in flaming brandy ▹ *adj* (of food) served in flaming brandy **flambee, flambes**
FLAME *n, vb* **flamed**
FLAMEN *n* (in ancient Rome) type of priest **flamens**
FLAMER ▸ **flame**
FLAMERS ▸ **flame**
FLAMES ▸ **flame**
FLAMFEW *n* fantastic trifle
FLAMIER ▸ **flame**
FLAMING *adj* burning with flames ▹ *adv* extremely
FLAMM *variant of* ▸ **flam**
FLAMMED ▸ **flam**
FLAMMS ▸ **flamm**
FLAMS ▸ **flam**
FLAMY ▸ **flame**
FLAN *n*
FLANCH *variant of* ▸ **flaunch**
FLANES *n* arrows
FLANEUR *n* idler or loafer
FLANGE *n, vb* **flanged, flanger, flanges**
FLANK *n, vb* **flanked**
FLANKEN *n* cut of beef
FLANKER *n* one of a detachment of soldiers guarding the flanks
FLANKS ▸ **flank**
FLANNEL *n, vb*
FLANNEN *adj* made of flannel
FLANNIE ▸ **flanny**
FLANNY *n* shirt made of flannel
FLANS ▸ **flan**
FLAP *vb, n* **flapped**
FLAPPER *n*
FLAPPY *adj* loose
FLAPS ▸ **flap**
FLARE *vb, n* **flared**
FLARES *pl n* trousers with legs that widen below the knee
FLAREUP *n* outbreak of something
FLARIER ▸ **flare**
FLARING ▸ **flare**
FLARY ▸ **flare**
FLASER *n* type of sedimentary structure in rock **flasers**
FLASH *n, adj, vb* **flashed**
FLASHER *n* man who exposes himself indecently
FLASHES ▸ **flash**
FLASHY *adj*
FLASK *n*
FLASKET *n* long shallow basket
FLASKS ▸ **flask**
FLAT *adj, adv, n, vb*
FLATBED *n* type of printing machine
FLATCAP *n* Elizabethan man's hat
FLATCAR *n* flatbed
FLATLET *n* small flat
FLATLY ▸ **flat**
FLATS ▸ **flat**
FLATTED ▸ **flat**
FLATTEN *vb*
FLATTER *vb*
FLATTIE *n* flat tyre
FLATTOP *n* informal name for an aircraft carrier
FLATTY *n* flat shoe
FLATUS *n* gas generated in the alimentary canal
FLAUGHT *vb* flutter
FLAUNCH *n* cement or mortar slope to throw off water ▹ *vb* cause to slope in this manner
FLAUNE *variant of* ▸ **flam**
FLAUNES ▸ **flaune**
FLAUNT *vb, n* **flaunts**
FLAUNTY *adj* characterized by or inclined to ostentatious display

FLAUTA *n* tortilla rolled around a filling **flautas**
FLAVA *n* individual style **flavas**
FLAVIN *n* heterocyclic ketone **flavine, flavins**
FLAVONE *n* crystalline compound occurring in plants
FLAVOR = **flavour**
FLAVORS ▸ **flavor**
FLAVORY *adj* flavoursome
FLAVOUR *n, vb*
FLAW *n, vb* **flawed, flawier, flawing**
FLAWN *variant of* ▸ **flam**
FLAWNS ▸ **flawn**
FLAWS ▸ **flaw**
FLAWY ▸ **flaw**
FLAX *n*
FLAXEN *adj*
FLAXES ▸ **flax**
FLAXIER ▸ **flaxy**
FLAXY = **flaxen**
FLAY = **fley; flayed, flayer, flayers, flaying, flay**
FLEA *n*
FLEABAG *n* dirty or unkempt person, esp a woman
FLEADH *n* festival of Irish music, dancing, and culture **fleadhs**
FLEAM *n* lancet used for letting blood **fleams**
FLEAPIT *n* shabby cinema or theatre
FLEAS ▸ **flea**
FLECHE *n* slender spire **fleches**
FLECK *n, vb* **flecked, flecker, flecks, flecky**
FLED ▸ **flee**
FLEDGE *vb* feed and care for (a young bird) until it is able to fly **fledged, fledges**
FLEDGY *adj* feathery or feathered
FLEE *vb*
FLEECE *n, vb* **fleeced, fleecer, fleeces**
FLEECH *vb* flatter
FLEECIE *n* person who collects fleeces for baling
FLEECY *adj* made of or like fleece ▹ *n* person who collects fleeces after shearing and prepares them for baling
FLEEING ▸ **flee**
FLEER *vb* grin or laugh at ▹ *n* derisory glance or grin **fleered, fleerer, fleers**
FLEES ▸ **flee**
FLEET *n, adj, vb* **fleeted, fleeter, fleetly, fleets**
FLEG *vb* scare **flegged, flegs**
FLEHMEN *vb* (of mammal) grimace
FLEME *vb* drive out **flemes**
FLEMING *n* inhabitant of Flanders or a Flemish-speaking Belgian
FLEMISH *vb* stow (a rope) in a Flemish coil
FLEMIT ▸ **fleme**
FLENCH = **flense**
FLENSE *vb* strip (a whale, seal, etc) of (its blubber or skin) **flensed, flenser, flenses**
FLESH *n* **fleshed**
FLESHER *n* person or machine that fleshes hides or skins
FLESHES ▸ **flesh**
FLESHLY *adj* carnal
FLESHY *adj* plump
FLETCH = **fledge**
FLETTON *n* type of brick
FLEURET = **fleurette**
FLEURON *n* decorative piece of pastry
FLEURY = **flory**
FLEW ▸ **fly**
FLEWED *adj* having large flews
FLEWS *pl n* upper lip of a bloodhound or similar dog
FLEX *n, vb* **flexed, flexes**
FLEXILE = **flexible**
FLEXING ▸ **flex**
FLEXION *n* act of bending a joint or limb
FLEXO *n, adj, adv* flexography
FLEXOR *n* type of muscle **flexors**
FLEXOS ▸ **flexo**
FLEXURE *n* act of flexing or the state of being flexed
FLEY *vb* be afraid or cause to be afraid **fleyed, fleying, fleys**
FLIC *n* French police officer
FLICK *vb, n* **flicked**
FLICKER *vb, n*
FLICKS ▸ **flick**

FLICS ▸ **flic**
FLIED, flier, fliers, flies, fliest ▸ **fly**
FLIGHT *n, vb* **flights**
FLIGHTY *adj*
FLIM *n* five-pound note
FLIMP *vb* steal **flimped, flimps**
FLIMS ▸ **flim**
FLIMSY *adj, n*
FLINCH = **flense**
FLINDER *n* fragment
FLING *vb, n* **flinger, flings**
FLINT *n, vb* **flinted, flints**
FLINTY *adj*
FLIP *vb, n, adj* **flipped**
FLIPPER *n*
FLIPPY *adj* (of clothes) moving to and fro as the wearer walks
FLIPS ▸ **flip**
FLIR *n* forward looking infrared radar **flirs**
FLIRT *vb, n* **flirted, flirter, flirts, flirty**
FLISK *vb* skip **flisked, flisks, flisky**
FLIT *vb, n*
FLITCH *n* side of pork salted and cured ▹ *vb* cut (a tree trunk) into flitches
FLITE *vb* scold or rail at ▹ *n* dispute or scolding **flited, flites, fliting**
FLITS ▸ **flit**
FLITT *adj* fleet
FLITTED ▸ **flit**
FLITTER ▸ **flit**
FLIVVER *n* old, cheap, or battered car
FLIX *n* fur ▹ *vb* have fur **flixed, flixes, flixing**
FLOAT *vb, n* **floated**
FLOATEL = **flotel**
FLOATER *n* person or thing that floats
FLOATS *pl n* footlights
FLOATY *adj* filmy and light
FLOB *vb* **flobbed, flobs**
FLOC = **flock**
FLOCCED ▸ **floc**
FLOCCI ▸ **floccus**
FLOCCUS *n* downy or woolly covering ▹ *adj* (of a cloud) having the appearance of woolly tufts
FLOCK *n, vb, adj* **flocked, flocks, flocky**
FLOCS ▸ **floc**
FLOE *n* **floes**
FLOG *vb* **flogged, flogger, flogs**
FLOKATI *n* Greek hand-woven shaggy woollen rug
FLONG *n* material used for making moulds in stereotyping **flongs**
FLOOD *n, vb* **flooded, flooder, floods**
FLOOEY *adj* awry **flooie**
FLOOR *n, vb* **floored**
FLOORER *n* coup de grâce
FLOORS ▸ **floor**
FLOOSIE = **floozy**
FLOOSY *variant of* ▸ **floosie**
FLOOZIE = **floozy**
FLOOZY *n* disreputable woman
FLOP *vb, n* **flopped, flopper**
FLOPPY *adj, n*
FLOPS ▸ **flop**
FLOR *n* type of yeast
FLORA *n* **florae**
FLORAL *adj, n* **florals**
FLORAS ▸ **flora**
FLOREAT *vb* may (a person, institution, etc) flourish
FLORET *n* **florets**
FLORID *adj*
FLORIER ▸ **flory**
FLORIN *n* former British and Australian coin **florins**
FLORIST *n*
FLORS ▸ **flor**
FLORUIT *prep* (he or she) flourished in ▹ *n* such a period in a person's life
FLORULA *n* flora of a small single environment **florule**
FLORY *adj* containing a fleur-de-lys
FLOSH *n* hopper-shaped box **floshes**
FLOSS *n, vb* **flossed, flosser, flosses**
FLOSSIE *variant of* ▸ **flossy**
FLOSSY *adj* consisting of or resembling floss ▹ *n* floozy
FLOTA *n* formerly, Spanish commercial fleet
FLOTAGE *n* act or state of floating
FLOTANT *adj* in heraldry, flying in the air
FLOTAS ▸ **flota**
FLOTE *n* aquatic

perennial grass
FLOTEL *n* (in the oil industry) a rig or boat used as accommodation **flotels**
FLOTES ▸ **flote**
FLOTSAM *n*
FLOUNCE *vb, n* **flouncy**
FLOUR *n, vb* **floured, flours, floury**
FLOUSE *vb* splash **floused, flouses, floush**
FLOUT *vb* **flouted, flouter, flouts**
FLOW *vb, n*
FLOWAGE *n* act of overflowing or the state of having overflowed
FLOWED ▸ **flow**
FLOWER *n, vb* **flowers**
FLOWERY *adj*
FLOWING ▸ **flow**
FLOWN ▸ **fly**
FLOWS ▸ **flow**
FLOX *adj as in* **flox silk** type of silk
FLU *n*
FLUATE *n* fluoride **fluates**
FLUB *vb* bungle **flubbed, flubber**
FLUBDUB *n* bunkum
FLUBS ▸ **flub**
FLUE *n*
FLUED *adj* having a flue
FLUENCE ▸ **fluency**
FLUENCY *n* quality of being fluent
FLUENT *adj, n* **fluents**
FLUERIC *adj* of or relating to fluidics
FLUES ▸ **flue**
FLUEY *adj* involved in, caused by, or like influenza
FLUFF *n, vb* **fluffed**
FLUFFER *n* person employed on a pornographic film set
FLUFFS ▸ **fluff**
FLUFFY *adj* of, resembling, or covered with fluff
FLUGEL *n* grand piano or harpsichord **flugels**
FLUID *n, adj* **fluidal**
FLUIDIC > **fluidics**
FLUIDLY ▸ **fluid**
FLUIDS ▸ **fluid**
FLUIER ▸ **fluey**
FLUIEST ▸ **fluey**
FLUISH ▸ **flu**
FLUKE *n, vb* **fluked, flukes**
FLUKEY = **fluky**
FLUKIER ▸ **fluky**
FLUKILY ▸ **fluky**
FLUKING ▸ **fluke**
FLUKY *adj* done or gained by an accident
FLUME *n* narrow sloping channel for water ▹ *vb* transport (logs) in a flume **flumed, flumes, fluming**
FLUMMOX *vb*
FLUMP *vb* move or fall heavily **flumped, flumps**
FLUNG ▸ **fling**
FLUNK *vb, n* **flunked, flunker**
FLUNKEY = **flunky**
FLUNKIE = **flunky**
FLUNKS ▸ **flunk**
FLUNKY *n* servile person
FLUOR > **fluorspar**
FLUORIC *adj* of, concerned with, or produced from fluorine or fluorspar
FLUORID = **fluoride**
FLUORIN = **fluorine**
FLUORS ▸ **fluor**
FLURR *vb* scatter **flurred, flurrs**
FLURRY *n, vb*
FLUS ▸ **flu**
FLUSH *vb, n, adj, adv* **flushed, flusher, flushes**
FLUSHY *adj* ruddy
FLUSTER *vb, n*
FLUTE *n, vb*
FLUTED *adj*
FLUTER *n* craftsman who makes flutes or fluting **fluters**
FLUTES ▸ **flute**
FLUTEY ▸ **flute**
FLUTIER ▸ **flute**
FLUTINA *n* type of accordion
FLUTING *n* design of decorative grooves
FLUTIST = **flautist**
FLUTTER *vb, n*
FLUTY ▸ **flute**
FLUVIAL *adj*
FLUX *n, vb* **fluxed, fluxes, fluxing**
FLUXION *n* rate of change of a function
FLUXIVE ▸ **flux**
FLUYT *n* Dutch sailing ship **fluyts**
FLY *vb, n, adj* **flyable**
FLYAWAY *adj* (of hair) very fine and soft ▹ *n* person who is frivolous

or flighty
FLYBACK *n* item of electrical equipment
FLYBANE *n* type of campion
FLYBELT *n* strip of tsetse-infested land
FLYBLEW ▸ **flyblow**
FLYBLOW *vb* contaminate ▹ *n* egg or young larva of a blowfly
FLYBOAT *n* any small swift boat
FLYBOOK *n* small case or wallet for storing artificial flies
FLYBOY *n* air force pilot **flyboys**
FLYBY *n* flight past a particular position or target **flybys**
FLYER ▸ **fly**
FLYERS ▸ **fly**
FLYEST ▸ **fly**
FLYHAND *n* device on a printing press
FLYING ▸ **fly**
FLYINGS ▸ **fly**
FLYLEAF *n*
FLYLESS ▸ **fly**
FLYMAN *n* stagehand **flymen**
FLYOFF *n* all water transferred from the earth to the atmosphere **flyoffs**
FLYOVER *n*
FLYPAST *n* ceremonial flight of aircraft over a given area
FLYPE *vb* fold back **flyped, flypes, flyping**
FLYSCH *n* type of marine sedimentary facies
FLYTE = **flite**
FLYTED ▸ **flyte**
FLYTES ▸ **flyte**
FLYTIER *n* person who makes his own fishing flies
FLYTING ▸ **flyte**
FLYTRAP *n* any of various insectivorous plants
FLYWAY *n* usual route used by birds when migrating **flyways**
FOAL *n, vb* **foaled, foaling, foals**
FOAM *n, vb* **foamed**
FOAMER *n* (possibly obsessive) enthusiast **foamers**
FOAMIER ▸ **foamy**
FOAMILY ▸ **foamy**
FOAMING ▸ **foam**
FOAMS ▸ **foam**
FOAMY *adj* of, resembling, consisting of, or covered with foam
FOB *n* short watch chain ▹ *vb* cheat **fobbed, fobbing, fobs**
FOCAL *adj* of or at a focus **focally**
FOCI ▸ **focus**
FOCUS *n, vb* **focused, focuser, focuses**
FODDER *n, vb* **fodders**
FODGEL *adj* buxom
FOE *n*
FOEHN = **fohn**
FOEHNS ▸ **foehn**
FOEMAN *n* enemy in war **foemen**
FOEN ▸ **foe**
FOES ▸ **foe**
FOETAL = **fetal**
FOETID = **fetid**
FOETOR = **fetor**
FOETORS ▸ **foetor**
FOETUS = **fetus**
FOG *n, vb*
FOGASH *n* type of Hungarian pike perch
FOGBOW *n* faint arc of light sometimes seen in a fog bank **fogbows**
FOGDOG *n* spot sometimes seen in fog near the horizon **fogdogs**
FOGEY *n* **fogeys**
FOGGAGE *n* grass grown for winter grazing
FOGGED ▸ **fog**
FOGGER *n* device that generates a fog **foggers**
FOGGIER, foggily, fogging, foggy ▸ **fog**
FOGHORN *n*
FOGIE *variant of* ▸ **fogey**
FOGIES ▸ **fogie**
FOGLE *n* silk handkerchief **fogles**
FOGLESS ▸ **fog**
FOGMAN *n* person in charge of railway fog-signals **fogmen**
FOGOU *n* subterranean building found in Cornwall **fogous**
FOGRAM *n* fogey **fograms**
FOGS ▸ **fog**
FOGY = **fogey**
FOGYDOM ▸ **fogy**

FOGYISH ▸ **fogy**
FOGYISM ▸ **fogy**
FOH *interj* expression of disgust
FOHN *n* type of warm dry wind **fohns**
FOIBLE *n* **foibles**
FOID *n* rock-forming mineral similar to feldspar **foids**
FOIL *vb, n* **foiled, foiling, foils**
FOIN *n* thrust or lunge with a weapon ▹ *vb* thrust with a weapon **foined, foining, foins**
FOISON *n* plentiful supply or yield **foisons**
FOIST *vb* **foisted, foister, foists**
FOLACIN *n* folic acid
FOLATE *n* folic acid
FOLATES ▸ **folic**
FOLD *vb, n* **folded**
FOLDER *n* **folders**
FOLDING ▸ **fold**
FOLDOUT *another name for* > **gatefold**
FOLDS ▸ **fold**
FOLDUP *n* something that folds up **foldups**
FOLEY *n* footsteps editor **foleys**
FOLIA ▸ **folium**
FOLIAGE *n*
FOLIAR *adj* of or relating to a leaf or leaves
FOLIATE *adj* relating to, possessing, or resembling leaves ▹ *vb* ornament with foliage or with leaf forms such as foils
FOLIC *adj as in* **folic acid** any of a group of vitamins of the B complex
FOLIE *n* madness **folies**
FOLIO *n* sheet of paper folded in half to make two leaves of a book ▹ *adj* of or made in the largest book size, common esp in early centuries of European printing ▹ *vb* number the leaves of (a book) consecutively **folioed**
FOLIOLE *n* part of a compound leaf
FOLIOS ▸ **folio**
FOLIOSE *adj* (of a tree) leaf-bearing
FOLIOUS *adj* foliose
FOLIUM *n* plane geometrical curve **foliums**
FOLK *n, adj*
FOLKIE *n* devotee of folk music ▹ *adj* of or relating to folk music **folkier, folkies**
FOLKISH ▸ **folk**
FOLKMOT = **folkmoot**
FOLKS ▸ **folk**
FOLKSY *adj* simple and unpretentious
FOLKWAY *singular form of* > **folkways**
FOLKY = **folkie**
FOLLES ▸ **follis**
FOLLIED ▸ **folly**
FOLLIES ▸ **folly**
FOLLIS *n* Roman coin
FOLLOW *vb* **follows**
FOLLY *n, vb*
FOMENT *vb* **foments**
FOMES *n* any material that may harbour pathogens **fomite, fomites**
FON *vb* compel
FOND *adj, n, vb*
FONDA *n* Spanish hotel
FONDANT *n* (sweet made from) flavoured paste of sugar and water ▹ *adj* (of a colour) soft
FONDAS ▸ **fonda**
FONDED, fonder, fondest, fonding ▸ **fond**
FONDLE *vb* **fondled, fondler, fondles**
FONDLY ▸ **fond**
FONDS ▸ **fond**
FONDU *n* ballet movement
FONDUE *n, vb* **fondued, fondues**
FONDUS ▸ **fondu**
FONE *variant of* ▸ **foe**
FONLY *adv* foolishly
FONNED ▸ **fon**
FONNING ▸ **fon**
FONS ▸ **fon**
FONT *n* **fontal**
FONTINA *n* mild Italian cheese
FONTLET ▸ **font**
FONTS ▸ **font**
FOOBAR = **fubar**
FOOD *n*
FOODFUL *adj* supplying abundant food
FOODIE *n* gourmet **foodies**
FOODISM *n* enthusiasm for and interest in good food
FOODS ▸ **food**

FOODY = **foodie**
FOOL *n, vb* **fooled**
FOOLERY *n* foolish behaviour
FOOLING ▸ **fool**
FOOLISH *adj*
FOOLS ▸ **fool**
FOOT *n, vb*
FOOTAGE *n*
FOOTBAG *n* type of sport
FOOTBAR *n* any bar used by the foot
FOOTBOY *n* boy servant
FOOTED ▸ **foot**
FOOTER *n* person who goes on foot ▹ *vb* potter **footers**
FOOTIE = **footy**
FOOTIER ▸ **footy**
FOOTIES ▸ **footie**
FOOTING *n*
FOOTLE *vb* loiter aimlessly ▹ *n* foolishness **footled, footler, footles**
FOOTMAN *n* **footmen**
FOOTPAD *n* highwayman, on foot rather than horseback
FOOTRA *variant of* ▸ **foutra**
FOOTRAS ▸ **footra**
FOOTS *pl n* sediment that accumulates at the bottom of a vessel
FOOTSIE *n* flirtation involving the touching together of feet **footsy**
FOOTWAY *n* way or path for pedestrians
FOOTY *n* football ▹ *adj* mean
FOOZLE *vb* bungle (a shot) ▹ *n* bungled shot **foozled, foozler, foozles**
FOP *n, vb*
FOPLING *n* vain affected dandy
FOPPED ▸ **fop**
FOPPERY *n* clothes, affectations, etc, of or befitting a fop
FOPPING ▸ **fop**
FOPPISH ▸ **fop**
FOPS ▸ **fop**
FOR *prep*
FORA ▸ **forum**
FORAGE *vb, n* **foraged, forager, forages**
FORAM *n* marine protozoan
FORAMEN *n* natural hole
FORAMS ▸ **foram**
FORANE *adj as in* **vicar forane** type of Roman Catholic priest
FORAY *n, vb* **forayed, forayer, forays**
FORB *n* any herbaceous plant that is not a grass
FORBAD ▸ **forbid**
FORBADE ▸ **forbid**
FORBARE ▸ **forbear**
FORBEAR *vb*
FORBID *vb* **forbids**
FORBODE *vb* obsolete word meaning forbid ▹ *n* obsolete word meaning forbidding
FORBORE *past tense of* ▸ **forbear**
FORBS ▸ **forb**
FORBY *adv* besides **forbye**
FORCAT *n* convict or galley slave **forcats**
FORCE *n, vb*
FORCED *adj*
FORCEPS *pl n*
FORCER, forcers, forces, forcing ▸ **force**
FORD *n, vb* **forded**
FORDID ▸ **fordo**
FORDING ▸ **ford**
FORDO *vb* destroy **fordoes, fordone**
FORDS ▸ **ford**
FORE *adj, n, interj*
FOREARM *n, vb*
FOREBAY *n* reservoir or canal
FOREBY *variant of* ▸ **forby**
FOREBYE *variant of* ▸ **forby**
FORECAR *n* vehicle attached to a motorcycle
FOREDID ▸ **foredo**
FOREDO = **fordo**
FOREGO = **forgo**
FOREGUT *n* anterior part of the digestive tract of vertebrates
FOREIGN *adj*
FOREL *n* type of parchment
FORELAY *archaic word for* ▸ **ambush**
FORELEG *n* either of the front legs of an animal
FORELIE *vb* lie in front of
FORELS ▸ **forel**
FOREMAN *n* **foremen**
FOREPAW *n* either of the front feet of a land mammal
FORERAN ▸ **forerun**

FORERUN *vb* serve as a herald for
FORES ▸ **fore**
FORESAW ▸ **foresee**
FORESAY *vb* foretell
FORESEE *vb*
FOREST *n*, *vb* **forests**
FORETOP *n* platform at the top of the foremast
FOREVER *adv*
FOREX *n* foreign exchange **forexes**
FORFAIR *vb* perish
FORFEIT *n*, *vb*, *adj*
FORFEND *vb* protect or secure
FORFEX *n* pair of pincers, esp the paired terminal appendages of an earwig
FORGAT *past tense of* ▸ **forget**
FORGAVE ▸ **forgive**
FORGE *n*, *vb* **forged, forger, forgers**
FORGERY *n*
FORGES ▸ **forge**
FORGET *vb* **forgets**
FORGING *n* process of producing a metal component by hammering
FORGIVE *vb*
FORGO *vb* **forgoer, forgoes, forgone**
FORGOT *past tense of* ▸ **forget**
FORHENT *variant of* > **forehent**
FORHOO *vb* forsake **forhoos, forhow**
FORHOWS ▸ **forhow**
FORINT *n* standard monetary unit of Hungary **forints**
FORK *n*, *vb*
FORKED *adj* having a fork or forklike parts
FORKER ▸ **fork**
FORKERS ▸ **fork**
FORKFUL ▸ **fork**
FORKIER ▸ **forky**
FORKING ▸ **fork**
FORKS ▸ **fork**
FORKY *adj* forked
FORLANA *n* Venetian dance
FORLEND *variant of* > **forelend**
FORLENT ▸ **forlend**
FORLORN *adj*, *n*
FORM *n*, *vb*
FORMAL *adj* **formals**
FORMANT *n* any of several frequency ranges
FORMAT *n*, *vb*
FORMATE *n* type of salt or ester of formic acid ▹ *vb* fly aircraft in formation
FORMATS ▸ **format**
FORME *n* type matter assembled and ready for printing
FORMED ▸ **form**
FORMEE *n* type of heraldic cross
FORMER *adj*, *n* **formers**
FORMES ▸ **forme**
FORMFUL *adj* imaginative
FORMIC *adj* of, relating to, or derived from ants
FORMICA *n* tradename for any of various laminated plastic sheets
FORMING ▸ **form**
FORMOL = **formalin**
FORMOLS ▸ **formol**
FORMS ▸ **form**
FORMULA *n*
FORMYL *n* of, consisting of, or containing the monovalent group HCO- **formyls**
FORNENT *variant of* > **fornenst**
FORNIX *n* any archlike structure
FORPET *n* quarter of a peck (measure) **forpets**
FORPINE *vb* waste away
FORPIT *variant of* ▸ **forpet**
FORPITS ▸ **forpit**
FORRAD *adv* forward
FORRAY *archaic variant of* ▸ **foray**
FORRAYS ▸ **forray**
FORREN *adj* foreign
FORRIT *adv* forward(s)
FORSAID ▸ **forsay**
FORSAKE *vb*
FORSAY *vb* renounce **forsays**
FORSLOE *variant of* ▸ **forslow**
FORSLOW *vb* hinder
FORSOOK *past tense of* ▸ **forsake**
FORT *n*, *vb*
FORTE *n*, *adv*
FORTED ▸ **fort**
FORTES ▸ **fortis**
FORTH *adv*, *prep*
FORTHY *adv* therefore

FORTIES ▸ **forty**
FORTIFY *vb*
FORTING ▸ **fort**
FORTIS *adj* (of a consonant) articulated with considerable muscular tension ▹ *n* type of consonantal pronunciation
FORTLET ▸ **fort**
FORTS ▸ **fort**
FORTUNE *n, vb*
FORTY *n, adj, determiner*
FORUM *n* **forums**
FORWARD = **forwards**
FORWARN *archaic word for* ▸ **forbid**
FORWENT *past tense of* ▸ **forgo**
FORWHY *adv* for what reason
FORWORN *adj* weary
FORZA *n* force
FORZATI ▸ **forzato**
FORZATO *variant of* > **forzando**
FORZE ▸ **forza**
FOSS = **fosse**
FOSSA *n* anatomical depression, trench, or hollow area **fossae, fossas**
FOSSATE *adj* having cavities or depressions
FOSSE *n* ditch or moat, esp one dug as a fortification
FOSSED *adj* having a ditch or moat
FOSSES ▸ **fosse**
FOSSICK *vb*
FOSSIL *n, adj* **fossils**
FOSSOR *n* grave digger **fossors**
FOSSULA *n* small fossa
FOSTER *vb, adj* **fosters**
FOTHER *vb* stop a leak in a ship's hull **fothers**
FOU *adj* full ▹ *n* bushel
FOUAT *n* succulent pink-flowered plant **fouats**
FOUD *n* sheriff in Orkney and Shetland
FOUDRIE *n* foud's district or office
FOUDS ▸ **foud**
FOUER ▸ **fou**
FOUEST ▸ **fou**
FOUET *n* archaic word for a whip **fouets**
FOUETTE *n* step in ballet
FOUGADE *n* booby-trapped pit or type of mine
FOUGHT ▸ **fight**
FOUGHTY *adj* musty
FOUL *adj, n, vb*
FOULARD *n* soft light fabric
FOULDER *vb* flash like lightning
FOULE *n* type of woollen cloth
FOULED ▸ **foul**
FOULER ▸ **foul**
FOULES ▸ **foule**
FOULEST ▸ **foul**
FOULIE *n* bad mood **foulies**
FOULING ▸ **foul**
FOULLY ▸ **foul**
FOULS ▸ **foul**
FOUMART *former name for the* ▸ **polecat**
FOUND *vb* **founded**
FOUNDER *vb, n*
FOUNDRY *n*
FOUNDS ▸ **found**
FOUNT = **font**
FOUNTS ▸ **fount**
FOUR *n, adj, determiner*
FOURGON *n* long covered wagon
FOURS ▸ **four**
FOURSES *n* snack eaten at four o'clock
FOURTH *n, adj, adv* **fourths**
FOUS ▸ **fou**
FOUSSA *n* Madagascan civet-like animal **foussas**
FOUSTY *archaic variant of* ▸ **fusty**
FOUTER = **footer**
FOUTERS ▸ **fouter**
FOUTH *n* abundance **fouths**
FOUTRA *n* fig; expression of contempt **foutras**
FOUTRE *vb* footer **foutred, foutres**
FOVEA *n* any small pit in the surface of a bodily organ or part **foveae, foveal, foveas, foveate**
FOVEOLA *n* small fovea **foveole**
FOWL *n, vb* **fowled**
FOWLER ▸ **fowling**
FOWLERS ▸ **fowling**
FOWLING *n* shooting or trapping of birds for sport or as a livelihood
FOWLPOX *n* viral infection of poultry and other birds
FOWLS ▸ **fowl**
FOWTH *variant of*

▸ fouth
FOWTHS ▸ **fowth**
FOX *n, vb* **foxed, foxes**
FOXFIRE *n* glow emitted by certain fungi
FOXFISH *n* type of shark
FOXHOLE *n* small pit dug for protection
FOXHUNT *n* hunting of foxes with hounds ▹ *vb* hunt foxes with hounds
FOXIE *n* fox terrier
FOXIER ▸ **foxy**
FOXIES ▸ **foxie**
FOXIEST ▸ **foxy**
FOXILY ▸ **foxy**
FOXING *n* piece of leather used on part of the upper of a shoe **foxings**
FOXLIKE ▸ **fox**
FOXSHIP *n* cunning
FOXSKIN *adj* made from the skin of a fox ▹ *n* skin of a fox
FOXTAIL *n* type of grass
FOXTROT *n* ballroom dance with slow and quick steps ▹ *vb* perform this dance
FOXY *adj* of or like a fox, esp in craftiness
FOY *n* loyalty

> This unusual word for loyalty can be a good scorer.

FOYBOAT *n* small rowing boat
FOYER *n* **foyers**
FOYLE *variant of* ▸ **foil**
FOYLED ▸ **foyle**
FOYLES ▸ **foyle**
FOYLING ▸ **foyle**
FOYNE *variant of* ▸ **foin**
FOYNED ▸ **foyne**
FOYNES ▸ **foyne**
FOYNING ▸ **foyne**
FOYS ▸ **foy**
FOZIER ▸ **fozy**
FOZIEST ▸ **fozy**
FOZY *adj* spongy
FRA *n* brother: a title given to an Italian monk or friar
FRAB *vb* nag **frabbed**
FRABBIT *adj* peevish
FRABS ▸ **frab**
FRACAS *n*
FRACK *adj* bold
FRACT *vb* break
FRACTAL *n* mathematically repeating structure ▹ *adj* of, relating to, or involving such a process
FRACTED ▸ **fract**
FRACTI ▸ **fractus**
FRACTS ▸ **fract**
FRACTUR *variant of* ▸ **fraktur**
FRACTUS *n* ragged-shaped cloud formation
FRAE *Scot word for* ▸ **from**
FRAENA ▸ **fraenum**
FRAENUM *n* fold of membrane or skin that supports an organ
FRAG *vb* kill or wound (a fellow soldier or superior officer) deliberately **fragged**
FRAGILE *adj*
FRAGOR *n* sudden sound **fragors**
FRAGS ▸ **frag**
FRAIL *adj, n* **frailer, frailly, frails**
FRAILTY *n* physical or moral weakness
FRAIM *n* stranger **fraims**
FRAISE *n* neck ruff worn during the 16th century ▹ *vb* provide a rampart with a palisade **fraised, fraises**
FRAKTUR *n* style of typeface
FRAME *n, vb* **framed, framer, framers, frames**
FRAMING *n* frame, framework, or system of frames
FRAMPAL = **frampold**
FRANC *n*
FRANCO *adj* post-free
FRANCS ▸ **franc**
FRANGER *n* condom
FRANION *n* lover, paramour
FRANK *adj, n, vb* **franked, franker**
FRANKLY *adv* in truth
FRANKS ▸ **frank**
FRANTIC *adj*
FRANZY *adj* irritable
FRAP *vb* lash down or together
FRAPE *adj* tightly bound
FRAPPE *adj* (of drinks) chilled ▹ *n* type of drink
FRAPPED ▸ **frap**
FRAPPEE ▸ **frappe**
FRAPPES ▸ **frappe**
FRAPS ▸ **frap**
FRAS ▸ **fra**

FRASS *n* refuse left by insects and insect larvae **frasses**
FRAT *n* member of a fraternity
FRATCH *n* quarrel
FRATCHY *adj* quarrelsome
FRATE *n* friar
FRATER *n* mendicant friar or a lay brother in a monastery or priory **fraters, fratery**
FRATI ▶ **frate**
FRATRY ▶ **frater**
FRATS ▶ **frat**
FRAU *n* married German woman
FRAUD *n* **frauds**
FRAUGHT *adj, vb, n*
FRAUS ▶ **frau**
FRAWZEY *n* celebration
FRAY *n, vb* **frayed, fraying, frays**
FRAZIL *n* small pieces of ice that form in turbulently moving water **frazils**
FRAZZLE *n* exhausted state ▷ *vb* tire out
FREAK *n, adj, vb* **freaked, freaks**
FREAKY *adj* weird, peculiar
FRECKLE *n, vb* **freckly**
FREE *adj, vb*
FREEBEE *variant of* ▶ **freebie**
FREEBIE *n* something provided without charge ▷ *adj* without charge
FREED ▶ **free**
FREEDOM *n*
FREEGAN *n* person who avoids buying consumer goods
FREEING ▶ **free**
FREELY ▶ **free**
FREEMAN *n* person who has been given the freedom of a city **freemen**
FREER *n* liberator **freers**
FREES ▶ **free**
FREESIA *n*
FREEST ▶ **free**
FREET *n* omen or superstition **freets**
FREETY *adj* superstitious
FREEWAY *n*
FREEZE *vb, n*
FREEZER *n*
FREEZES ▶ **freeze**
FREIGHT *n, vb*
FREIT *variant of* ▶ **freet**
FREITS ▶ **freit**
FREITY *adj* superstitious
FREMD *adj, n* alien or strange (person or thing) **fremds, fremit**
FREMITS ▶ **fremit**
FRENA ▶ **frenum**
FRENCH *vb* (of food) cut into thin strips
FRENNE *variant of* ▶ **fremd**
FRENNES ▶ **frenne**
FRENULA > **frenulum**
FRENUM = **fraenum**
FRENUMS ▶ **frenum**
FRENZY *n, vb*
FRERE *n* friar **freres**
FRESCO *n, vb* **frescos**
FRESH *adj, adv, vb* **freshed**
FRESHEN *vb*
FRESHER *n*
FRESHES ▶ **fresh**
FRESHET *n* sudden overflowing of a river
FRESHIE *n* new Indian immigrant to the UK
FRESHLY ▶ **fresh**
FRESNEL *n* unit of frequency equivalent to 10^{12} hertz
FRET *vb, n*
FRETFUL *adj* irritable
FRETS ▶ **fret**
FRETSAW *n* fine saw with a narrow blade, used for fretwork
FRETTED ▶ **fret**
FRETTER ▶ **fret**
FRETTY *adj* decorated with frets
FRIABLE *adj* easily crumbled
FRIAND *n* small almond cake **friande, friands**
FRIAR *n* **friarly, friars**
FRIARY *n* house of friars
FRIB *n* piece of wool removed from a fleece during classing
FRIBBLE *vb* fritter away ▷ *n* wasteful or frivolous person or action ▷ *adj* frivolous
FRIBS ▶ **frib**
FRICHT *vb* frighten **frichts**
FRIDGE *n, vb* **fridged, fridges**
FRIED ▶ **fry**
FRIEND *n, vb* **friends**
FRIER = **fryer**
FRIERS ▶ **frier**
FRIES ▶ **fry**
FRIEZE *n, vb* **friezed, friezes**

FRIGATE *n*
FRIGHT *n* **frights**
FRIGID *adj*
FRIGOT *variant of* ▸ **frigate**
FRIGOTS ▸ **frigot**
FRIJOL *n* variety of bean **frijole**
FRILL *n, vb* **frilled, friller, frills**
FRILLY *adj* with a frill or frills
FRINGE *n, vb, adj* **fringed, fringes**
FRINGY *adj* having a fringe
FRIPON *n* rogue **fripons**
FRIPPER *n* dealer in old clothes
FRIPPET *n* frivolous or flamboyant young woman
FRIS ▸ **friska**
FRISBEE *n* tradename of a light plastic disc
FRISE *n* fabric with a long normally uncut nap used for upholstery and rugs
FRISEE *n* endive **frisees**
FRISES ▸ **fris**
FRISEUR *n* hairdresser
FRISK *vb, n*
FRISKA *n* (in Hungarian music) the fast movement of a piece **friskas**
FRISKED ▸ **frisk**
FRISKER ▸ **frisk**
FRISKET *n* part of a hand printing press
FRISKS ▸ **frisk**
FRISKY *adj*
FRISSON *n* shiver of fear or excitement
FRIST *archaic word for* > **postpone**
FRISTED ▸ **frist**
FRISTS ▸ **frist**
FRISURE *n* styling the hair into curls
FRIT *n* basic materials for making glass, glazes for pottery, etc ▷ *vb* fuse (materials) in making frit
FRITES *pl n* chipped potatoes
FRITFLY *n* type of small black fly
FRITH = **firth**
FRITHS ▸ **frith**
FRITS ▸ **frit**
FRITT = **frit**
FRITTED ▸ **frit**
FRITTER *n, vb*
FRITTS ▸ **fritt**
FRITURE *archaic word for* ▸ **fritter**
FRITZ *n as in* **on the fritz** state of disrepair
FRIVOL *vb* behave frivolously **frivols**
FRIZ *variant of* ▸ **frizz**
FRIZE *n* coarse woollen fabric ▷ *vb* freeze **frized**
FRIZER *n* person who gives nap to cloth **frizers**
FRIZES ▸ **frize**
FRIZING ▸ **frize**
FRIZZ *vb* form (hair) into stiff wiry curls ▷ *n* hair that has been frizzed **frizzed, frizzer, frizzes**
FRIZZLE *vb* cook or heat until crisp and shrivelled ▷ *n* tight curl **frizzly**
FRIZZY *adj*
FRO *adv* away ▷ *n* afro
FROCK *n, vb* **frocked, frocks**
FROE *n* cutting tool **froes**
FROG *n*
FROGBIT *n* floating aquatic Eurasian plant
FROGEYE *n* plant disease
FROGGED *adj* decorated with frogging
FROGGY *adj* like a frog
FROGLET *n* young frog
FROGMAN *n* **frogmen**
FROGS ▸ **frog**
FROING *n as in* **toing and froing** going back and forth **froings**
FROISE *n* kind of pancake **froises**
FROLIC *vb, n, adj* **frolics**
FROM *prep*
FROMAGE *n as in* **fromage frais** low-fat soft cheese
FROND *n*
FRONDED *adj* having fronds
FRONDS ▸ **frond**
FRONS *n* plate on the head of some insects
FRONT *n, adj, vb*
FRONTAL *adj* of, at, or in the front ▷ *n* decorative hanging for the front of an altar
FRONTED ▸ **front**
FRONTER ▸ **front**
FRONTES ▸ **frons**
FRONTON *n* wall

against which pelota or jai alai is played
FRONTS ▸ **front**
FRORE *adj* very cold or frosty **froren, frorn, frorne**
FRORY *adj* frozen
FROS ▸ **fro**
FROSH *n* freshman **froshes**
FROST *n, vb*
FROSTED *adj, n*
FROSTS ▸ **frost**
FROSTY *adj*
FROTH *n, vb* **frothed, frother, froths, frothy**
FROUGHY *adj* rancid
FROUNCE *vb* wrinkle
FROUZY = **frowzy**
FROW = **froe**
FROWARD *adj* obstinate
FROWIE *variant of* ▸ **froughy**
FROWIER ▸ **frowie**
FROWN *vb, n* **frowned, frowner, frowns**
FROWS ▸ **frow**
FROWST *n* hot and stale atmosphere ▹ *vb* abandon oneself to such an atmosphere **frowsts**
FROWSTY *adj* stale or musty
FROWSY = **frowzy**
FROWY *variant of* ▸ **froughy**
FROWZY *adj* dirty or unkempt
FROZE ▸ **freeze**
FROZEN ▸ **freeze**
FRUCTAN *n* type of polymer of fructose
FRUCTED *adj* fruit-bearing
FRUG *vb* perform the frug, a 1960s dance
FRUGAL *adj*
FRUGGED ▸ **frug**
FRUGS ▸ **frug**
FRUICT *obsolete variant of* ▸ **fruit**
FRUICTS ▸ **fruict**
FRUIT *n, vb* **fruited**
FRUITER *n* fruit grower
FRUITS ▸ **fruit**
FRUITY *adj*
FRUMP *n, vb* **frumped**
FRUMPLE *vb* wrinkle or crumple
FRUMPS ▸ **frump**
FRUMPY *adj* (of a woman, clothes, etc) dowdy or unattractive
FRUSH *vb* break into pieces **frushed, frushes**
FRUST *n* fragment
FRUSTA ▸ **frustum**
FRUSTS ▸ **frust**
FRUSTUM *n* part of a solid
FRUTEX *n* shrub
FRUTIFY *vb* malapropism for notify
FRY *vb, n* **fryable**
FRYER *n* person or thing that fries **fryers**
FRYING ▸ **fry**
FRYINGS ▸ **fry**
FRYPAN *n* long-handled shallow pan used for frying **frypans**
FUB *vb* cheat
FUBAR *adj* irreparably damaged or bungled
FUBBED ▸ **fub**
FUBBERY *n* cheating
FUBBIER ▸ **fubby**
FUBBING ▸ **fub**
FUBBY *adj* chubby
FUBS ▸ **fub**
FUBSIER ▸ **fubsy**
FUBSY *adj* short and stout
FUCHSIA *n*
FUCHSIN *n* greenish crystalline substance
FUCI ▸ **fucus**
FUCOID *n* type of seaweed **fucoids**
FUCOSE *n* aldose **fucoses**
FUCOUS = **fucoidal**
FUCUS *n* type of seaweed
FUCUSED *adj* archaic word meaning made up with cosmetics
FUCUSES ▸ **fucus**
FUD *n* rabbit's tail
FUDDIES ▸ **fuddy**
FUDDLE *vb* cause to be intoxicated or confused ▹ *n* confused state **fuddled, fuddler, fuddles**
FUDDY *n* old-fashioned person
FUDGE *n, vb, interj* **fudged, fudges, fudging**
FUDS ▸ **fud**
FUEHRER *n* leader: applied esp to Adolf Hitler
FUEL *n, vb* **fueled, fueler, fuelers, fueling, fuelled, fueller, fuels**
FUERO *n* Spanish code

of laws **fueros**
FUFF *vb* puff **fuffed**
FUFFIER ▸ **fuffy**
FUFFING ▸ **fuff**
FUFFS ▸ **fuff**
FUFFY *adj* puffy
FUG *n, vb*
FUGAL *adj* of, relating to, or in the style of a fugue **fugally**
FUGATO *adj* in the manner or style of a fugue ▹ *n* movement, section, or piece in this style **fugatos**
FUGGED, fuggier, fuggily, fugging, fuggy ▸ **fug**
FUGIE *n* runaway **fugies**
FUGIO *n* former US copper coin **fugios**
FUGLE *vb* act as a fugleman **fugled, fugles, fugling**
FUGS ▸ **fug**
FUGU *n* puffer fish

> U is not normally a desirable letter to have on your rack unless you happen to have the Q, and two Us can be trouble. This Japanese fish can help you out.

FUGUE *n, vb* **fugued, fugues, fuguing**
FUGUIST *n* composer of fugues
FUGUS ▸ **fugu**
FUHRER = **fuehrer**
FUHRERS ▸ **fuhrer**
FUJI *n* type of African music **fujis**
FULCRA ▸ **fulcrum**
FULCRUM *n*
FULFIL *vb* **fulfill, fulfils**
FULGENT *adj* shining brilliantly **fulgid**
FULGOR *n* brilliance **fulgors, fulgour**
FULHAM *n* loaded die **fulhams**
FULL *adj, adv, vb*
FULLAGE *n* price charged for fulling cloth
FULLAM *variant of* ▸ **fulham**
FULLAMS ▸ **fullam**
FULLAN *variant of* ▸ **fulham**
FULLANS ▸ **fullan**
FULLED ▸ **full**
FULLER *n* person who fulls cloth for his living ▹ *vb* forge (a groove) or caulk (a riveted joint) with a fuller **fullers**
FULLERY *n* place where fulling is carried out
FULLEST, fulling, fullish, fulls ▸ **full**
FULLY *adv* greatest degree or extent
FULMAR *n* Arctic sea bird **fulmars**
FULMINE *vb* fulminate
FULNESS ▸ **full**
FULSOME *adj*
FULVID *variant of* ▸ **fulvous**
FULVOUS *adj* of a dull brownish-yellow colour
FUM *n* phoenix, in Chinese mythology
FUMADO *n* salted, smoked fish **fumados**
FUMAGE *n* hearth money **fumages**
FUMARIC *adj as in* **fumaric acid** colourless crystalline acid
FUMBLE *vb, n* **fumbled, fumbler, fumbles**
FUME *vb*
FUMED *adj* (of wood) having been exposed to ammonia fumes
FUMER ▸ **fume**
FUMERS ▸ **fume**
FUMES ▸ **fume**
FUMET *n* liquor from cooking fish, meat, or game **fumets, fumette**
FUMETTI ▸ **fumetto**
FUMETTO *n* speech balloon in a comic or cartoon
FUMIER, fumiest, fuming, fumous ▸ **fume**
FUMS ▸ **fum**
FUMULI ▸ **fumulus**
FUMULUS *n* smokelike cloud
FUMY ▸ **fume**
FUN *n, vb*
FUNCKIA *n* type of plant resembling the lily
FUNCTOR *n* performer of a function
FUND *n, vb* **funded, funder, funders**
FUNDI *n*
FUNDIC ▸ **fundus**
FUNDIE *n* fundamentalist

Christian **fundies**
FUNDING ▸ **fund**
FUNDIS ▸ **fundi**
FUNDS *pl n* money that is readily available
FUNDUS *n* base of an organ
FUNDY *n* fundamentalist
FUNEBRE *adj* funereal or mournful
FUNERAL *n*
FUNEST *adj* lamentable
FUNFAIR *n*
FUNFEST *n* enjoyable time
FUNG = **funk**
FUNGAL *adj* of, derived from, or caused by a fungus or fungi ▹ *n* fungus or fungal infection **fungals**
FUNGI ▸ **fungus**
FUNGIC ▸ **fungus**
FUNGO *n* in baseball, act of tossing and hitting the ball ▹ *vb* toss and hit a ball **fungoes**
FUNGOID *adj* resembling a fungus
FUNGOUS *adj* appearing and spreading quickly like a fungus
FUNGS ▸ **fung**
FUNGUS *n*
FUNICLE *n* stalk that attaches an ovule to the wall of the ovary
FUNK *n, vb* **funked, funker, funkers**
FUNKIA *n* hosta **funkias**
FUNKIER ▸ **funky**
FUNKILY ▸ **funky**
FUNKING ▸ **funk**
FUNKS ▸ **funk**
FUNKY *adj* (of music) having a strong beat
FUNNED ▸ **fun**
FUNNEL *n, vb* **funnels**
FUNNER ▸ **fun**
FUNNEST ▸ **fun**
FUNNIER ▸ **funny**
FUNNIES *pl n* comic strips in a newspaper
FUNNILY ▸ **funny**
FUNNING ▸ **fun**
FUNNY *adj, n*
FUNPLEX *n* large amusement centre
FUNS ▸ **fun**
FUNSTER *n* funnyman
FUR *n, vb*
FURAL *n* furfural **furals**
FURAN *n* colourless flammable toxic liquid heterocyclic compound **furane**
FURANES ▸ **furane**
FURANS ▸ **furan**
FURBISH *vb*
FURCA *n* any forklike structure, esp in insects **furcae, furcal**
FURCATE *vb* divide into two parts ▹ *adj* forked, branching
FURCULA *n* any forklike part or organ
FURDER = **further**
FUREUR *n* rage or anger **fureurs**
FURFAIR *variant of* ▸ **furfur**
FURFUR *n* scurf or scaling of the skin **furfurs**
FURIES ▸ **fury**
FURIOSO *adv* in a frantically rushing manner ▹ *n* passage or piece to be performed in this way
FURIOUS *adj*
FURKID *n* companion animal **furkids**
FURL *vb, n*
FURLANA *variant of* ▸ **forlana**
FURLED ▸ **furl**
FURLER ▸ **furl**
FURLERS ▸ **furl**
FURLESS ▸ **fur**
FURLING ▸ **furl**
FURLONG *n*
FURLS ▸ **furl**
FURMETY = **frumenty**
FURMITY = **frumenty**
FURNACE *n, vb*
FURNISH *vb*
FUROL *variant of* > **furfural**
FUROLE *variant of* > **furfural**
FUROLES ▸ **furole**
FUROLS ▸ **furol**
FUROR = **furore**
FURORE *n* **furores**
FURORS ▸ **furor**
FURPHY *n* rumour or fictitious story
FURR *vb* furrow
FURRED = **furry**
FURRIER *n*
FURRIES ▸ **furry**
FURRILY ▸ **furry**
FURRING ▸ **fur**
FURROW *n, vb* **furrows, furrowy**
FURRS ▸ **furr**
FURRY *adj* like or covered with fur or

something furlike ▷ *n* child's fur-covered toy animal
FURS ▸ **fur**
FURTH *adv* out
FURTHER *adv, adj, vb*
FURTIVE *adj*
FURY *n*
FURZE *n* gorse **furzes, furzier, furzy**
FUSAIN *n* fine charcoal pencil **fusains**
FUSARIA > **fusarium**
FUSAROL *variant of* > **fusarole**
FUSBALL > **foosball**
FUSC *adj* dark or dark-brown
FUSCOUS *adj* of a brownish-grey colour
FUSE *n, vb* **fused**
FUSEE *n* (in early clocks and watches) a spirally grooved spindle **fusees**
FUSEL *n* mixture of amyl alcohols, propanol, and butanol **fusels**
FUSES ▸ **fuse**
FUSHION *n* spirit
FUSIBLE *adj* capable of being melted **fusibly**
FUSIDIC *adj as in* **fusidic acid** kind of acid
FUSIL *n* light flintlock musket
FUSILE *adj* easily melted
FUSILLI *n* spiral-shaped pasta
FUSILS ▸ **fusil**
FUSING ▸ **fuse**
FUSION *n, adj* **fusions**
FUSS *n, vb* **fussed, fusser, fussers, fusses**
FUSSIER ▸ **fussy**
FUSSILY ▸ **fussy**
FUSSING ▸ **fuss**
FUSSPOT *n* person who is difficult to please and complains often
FUSSY *adj*
FUST *vb* become mouldy **fusted**
FUSTET *n* wood of the Venetian sumach shrub **fustets**
FUSTIAN *n* (formerly) a hard-wearing fabric of cotton mixed with flax or wool ▷ *adj* cheap
FUSTIC *n* large tropical American tree **fustics**
FUSTIER ▸ **fusty**
FUSTILY ▸ **fusty**
FUSTING ▸ **fust**
FUSTOC = **fustic**
FUSTOCS ▸ **fustoc**
FUSTS ▸ **fust**
FUSTY *adj*
FUSUMA *n* Japanese sliding door
FUTCHEL *n* timber support in a carriage
FUTHARC = **futhark**
FUTHARK *n* phonetic alphabet consisting of runes **futhorc, futhork**
FUTILE *adj* **futiler**
FUTON *n* Japanese-style bed **futons**
FUTSAL *n* form of association football **futsals**
FUTTOCK *n* one of the ribs in the frame of a wooden vessel
FUTURAL *adj* relating to the future
FUTURE *n, adj*
FUTURES *pl n* type of commodity trading
FUTZ *vb* fritter time away **futzed, futzes, futzing**
FUZE = **fuse**
FUZED ▸ **fuze**
FUZEE = **fusee**
FUZEES ▸ **fuzee**
FUZES ▸ **fuze**
FUZIL *variant of* ▸ **fusil**
FUZILS ▸ **fuzil**
FUZING ▸ **fuze**
FUZZ *n, vb*
FUZZBOX *n* device that distorts sound
FUZZED ▸ **fuzz**
FUZZES ▸ **fuzz**
FUZZIER ▸ **fuzzy**
FUZZILY ▸ **fuzzy**
FUZZING ▸ **fuzz**
FUZZLE *vb* make drunk **fuzzled, fuzzles**
FUZZY *adj*
FY *variant of* ▸ **fie**
FYCE *variant of* ▸ **fice**
FYCES ▸ **fyce**
FYKE *n* fish trap ▷ *vb* catch fish in this manner **fyked, fykes, fyking**
FYLE *variant of* ▸ **file**
FYLES ▸ **fyle**
FYLFOT *rare word for* > **swastika**
FYLFOTS ▸ **fylfot**
FYNBOS *n* area of low-growing, evergreen vegetation
FYRD *n* militia of an Anglo-Saxon shire **fyrds**
FYTTE *n* song **fyttes**

Gg

Only three two-letter words begin with **G** (**gi, go** and **gu**). Knowing these will save you worrying about other possibilities. There are quite a few short words beginning with **G** that use **Y**, which can prove very useful. These include **gay, gey, goy** and **guy** (7 points each), as well as **gym** and **gyp** (9 points each). And don't forget the very useful **gox** for 11 points.

GAB *vb* talk or chatter ▷ *n* mechanical device
GABBA *n* type of electronic dance music
GABBARD = **gabbart**
GABBART *n* Scottish sailing barge
GABBAS ▶ **gabba**
GABBED ▶ **gab**
GABBER ▶ **gab**
GABBERS ▶ **gab**
GABBIER ▶ **gabby**
GABBING ▶ **gab**
GABBLE *vb, n* **gabbled, gabbler, gabbles**
GABBRO *n* dark basic plutonic igneous rock **gabbros**
GABBY *adj* talkative
GABELLE *n* salt tax levied until 1790
GABFEST *n* prolonged gossiping or conversation
GABIES ▶ **gaby**
GABION *n* cylindrical metal container filled with stones **gabions**
GABLE *n* **gabled, gables**
GABLET *n* small gable **gablets**
GABLING ▶ **gable**
GABNASH *n* chatter
GABOON *n* dark wood **gaboons**
GABS ▶ **gab**
GABY *n* simpleton
GAD *vb, n* **gadded, gadder, gadders**
GADDI *n* cushion on an Indian prince's throne
GADDING ▶ **gad**
GADDIS ▶ **gaddi**
GADE = **gad**
GADES ▶ **gade**
GADFLY *n* fly that bites cattle
GADGE *n* man **gadges**
GADGET *n* **gadgets, gadgety**
GADGIE *n* fellow **gadgies**
GADI *n* Indian throne
GADID *n* type of marine fish **gadids**
GADIS ▶ **gadi**
GADJE = **gadgie**
GADJES ▶ **gadje**
GADJO ▶ **gorgio**
GADLING *n* vagabond
GADOID *adj* of the cod family of marine fishes ▷ *n* gadoid fish **gadoids**
GADROON *n* type of decorative moulding
GADS ▶ **gad**
GADSMAN *n* person who uses a gad when driving animals **gadsmen**
GADSO *n* archaic expression of surprise
GADWALL *n* type of duck related to the mallard
GAE *Scot word for* ▶ **go**
GAED ▶ **gae**

GAEING ▸ **gae**
GAEN ▸ **gae**
GAES ▸ **gae**
GAFF *n* stick with an iron hook for landing large fish ▹ *vb* hook or land (a fish) with a gaff
GAFFE *n*
GAFFED ▸ **gaff**
GAFFER *n* **gaffers**
GAFFES ▸ **gaffe**
GAFFING ▸ **gaff**
GAFFS ▸ **gaff**
GAG *vb, n*
GAGA *adj*
GAGAKU *n* type of traditional Japanese music **gagakus**
GAGE *vb* gauge ▹ *n* (formerly) an object thrown down as a challenge to fight **gaged**
GAGER = **gauger**
GAGERS ▸ **gager**
GAGES ▸ **gage**
GAGGED ▸ **gag**
GAGGER *n* person or thing that gags **gaggers**
GAGGERY *n* practice of telling jokes
GAGGING ▸ **gag**
GAGGLE *n, vb* **gaggled, gaggles**
GAGING ▸ **gage**
GAGMAN *n* person who writes gags for a comedian **gagmen**
GAGS ▸ **gag**
GAGSTER *n* standup comedian
GAHNITE *n* dark green mineral
GAID = **gad**
GAIDS ▸ **gaid**
GAIETY *n*
GAIJIN *n* (in Japan) a foreigner
GAILY *adv*
GAIN *vb, n, adj* **gained**
GAINER *n* person or thing that gains **gainers**
GAINEST ▸ **gain**
GAINFUL *adj* useful or profitable
GAINING ▸ **gain**
GAINLY *adj* graceful or well-formed ▹ *adv* conveniently or suitably
GAINS *pl n* profits or winnings
GAINSAY *vb*
GAINST *short for* ▸ **against**
GAIR *n* strip of green grass on a hillside **gairs**
GAIT *n, vb*
GAITA *n* type of bagpipe **gaitas**
GAITED ▸ **gait**
GAITER *n* **gaiters**
GAITING ▸ **gait**
GAITS ▸ **gait**
GAITT *Scots word for* ▸ **gate**
GAITTS ▸ **gaitt**
GAJO = **gorgio**
GAJOS ▸ **gajo**
GAK *n* **gaks**
GAL *n* girl
GALA *n*
GALABEA = **djellaba**
GALABIA = **djellaba**
GALAGE = **galosh**
GALAGES ▸ **galage**
GALAGO *another name for* > **bushbaby**
GALAGOS ▸ **galago**
GALAH *n* **galahs**
GALANGA = **galingale**
GALANT *n* 18th-century style of music
GALANTY *n as in* **galanty show** pantomime shadow play
GALAS ▸ **gala**
GALATEA *n* strong twill-weave cotton fabric
GALAX *n* coltsfoot **galaxes**
GALAXY *n*
GALE *n*
GALEA *n* part or organ shaped like a helmet **galeae, galeas, galeate**
GALENA *n* soft bluish-grey mineral **galenas, galenic**
GALERE *n* group of people having a common interest **galeres**
GALES ▸ **gale**
GALETTE *n* type of savoury pancake
GALILEE *n* type of porch or chapel
GALIOT *n* small swift galley **galiots**
GALIPOT *n* resin obtained from several species of pine
GALL *n, vb*
GALLANT *adj, n, vb*
GALLATE *n* salt of gallic acid
GALLED ▸ **gall**

GALLEIN *n* type of dyestuff
GALLEON *n*
GALLERY *n, vb*
GALLET *vb* use mixture to support a roof-slate
GALLETA *n* low-growing, coarse grass
GALLETS ▸ **gallet**
GALLEY *n* **galleys**
GALLFLY *n* any of several small insects
GALLIC *adj* of or containing gallium in the trivalent state
GALLICA *n* variety of rose
GALLIED ▸ **gally**
GALLIES ▸ **gally**
GALLING *adj* annoying or bitterly humiliating
GALLIOT = **galiot**
GALLISE *vb* use method to increase the quantity of wine produced
GALLIUM *n* soft grey metallic element
GALLIZE = **gallise**
GALLNUT *n* type of plant gall that resembles a nut
GALLOCK *adj* left-handed
GALLON *n* **gallons**
GALLOON *n* narrow band of cord, gold braid, etc
GALLOOT = **galloot**
GALLOP *n, vb* **gallops**
GALLOUS *adj* of or containing gallium in the divalent state
GALLOW *vb* frighten
GALLOWS *n*
GALLS ▸ **gall**
GALLUS *adj* bold ▹ *n* suspender for trousers
GALLY *vb* frighten
GALOCHE = **galosh**
GALOOT *n* clumsy or uncouth person **galoots**
GALOP *n* 19th-century dance in quick duple time ▹ *vb* dance a galop **galoped**
GALOPIN *n* boy who ran errands for a cook
GALOPS ▸ **galop**
GALORE *adv, adj, n* **galores**
GALOSH *n* waterproof overshoe ▹ *vb* cover with galoshes **galoshe**
GALS ▸ **gal**
GALUMPH *vb* leap or move about clumsily
GALUT = **galuth**
GALUTH *n* exile of Jews from Palestine **galuths**
GALUTS ▸ **galut**
GALVO *n* instrument for measuring electric current **galvos**
GALYAC = **galyak**
GALYACS ▸ **galyac**
GALYAK *n* smooth glossy fur **galyaks**
GAM *n* school of whales ▹ *vb* (of whales) form a school
GAMA *n* tall perennial grass **gamas**
GAMASH *n* type of gaiter
GAMAY *n* red grape variety, or the wine made from it **gamays**
GAMB *n* in heraldry, the whole foreleg of a beast
GAMBA *n* second-largest member of the viol family
GAMBADE = **gambado**
GAMBADO *n* leap or gambol; caper ▹ *vb* perform a gambado
GAMBAS ▸ **gamba**
GAMBE = **gamb**
GAMBES ▸ **gambe**
GAMBET *n* tattler **gambets**
GAMBIA = **gambier**
GAMBIAS ▸ **gambia**
GAMBIER *n* astringent resinous substance **gambir**
GAMBIRS ▸ **gambir**
GAMBIST *n* person who plays the (viola da) gamba
GAMBIT *n, vb* **gambits**
GAMBLE *vb, n* **gambled, gambler, gambles**
GAMBO *n* farm cart **gamboes**
GAMBOGE *n* gum resin
GAMBOL *vb, n* **gambols**
GAMBREL *n* hock of a horse or similar animal
GAMBS ▸ **gamb**
GAME *n, vb, adj* **gamed**
GAMELAN *n* type of percussion orchestra
GAMELY *adv* in a brave or sporting manner
GAMER *n* person who plays computer games **gamers**

GAMES ▸ **game**
GAMEST ▸ **game**
GAMESY *adj* sporty
GAMETAL ▸ **gamete**
GAMETE *n* **gametes, gametic**
GAMEY *adj* having the smell or flavour of game
GAMGEE *n as in* **gamgee tissue** type of wound-dressing
GAMIC *adj* (esp of reproduction) requiring the fusion of gametes
GAMIER ▸ **gamey**
GAMIEST ▸ **gamey**
GAMILY ▸ **gamey**
GAMIN *n* street urchin
GAMINE *n* slim boyish young woman **gamines**
GAMING *n* gambling **gamings**
GAMINS ▸ **gamin**
GAMMA *n* third letter of the Greek alphabet **gammas**
GAMME *n* musical scale
GAMMED ▸ **gam**
GAMMES ▸ **gamme**
GAMMING ▸ **gam**
GAMMOCK *vb* clown around
GAMMON *n, vb* **gammons**
GAMONE *n* chemical used by gametes during sexual reproduction **gamones**
GAMP *n* umbrella
GAMPISH *adj* bulging
GAMPS ▸ **gamp**
GAMS ▸ **gam**
GAMUT *n* **gamuts**
GAMY = **gamey**
GAN *vb* go
GANACHE *n* rich icing or filling
GANCH *vb* impale **ganched, ganches**
GANDER *n, vb* **ganders**
GANDY *adj as in* **gandy dancer** railway track maintenance worker
GANE ▸ **gangue**
GANEF *n* unscrupulous opportunist **ganefs, ganev**
GANEVS ▸ **ganev**
GANG *n, vb* **ganged**
GANGER *n* foreman of a gang of labourers **gangers**
GANGING ▸ **gang**
GANGLIA > **ganglion**
GANGLY = **gangling**
GANGREL *n* wandering beggar
GANGS ▸ **gang**
GANGSTA *n* member of a street gang
GANGUE *n* valueless material in an ore **gangues**
GANGWAY = **gangplank**
GANJA *n* highly potent form of cannabis **ganjah**
GANJAHS ▸ **ganjah**
GANJAS ▸ **ganja**
GANNED ▸ **gan**
GANNET *n* **gannets**
GANNING ▸ **gan**
GANOF = **ganef**
GANOFS ▸ **ganof**
GANOID *adj* of the scales of certain fishes ▹ *n* ganoid fish **ganoids**
GANOIN *n* the outer layer of fish scales **ganoine, ganoins**
GANS ▸ **gan**
GANSEY *n* jersey or pullover **ganseys**
GANT *vb* yawn **ganted, ganting**
GANTLET *n* section of a railway where two tracks overlap ▹ *vb* make railway tracks form a gantlet
GANTRY *n*
GANTS ▸ **gant**
GAOL = **jail; gaoled, gaoler, gaolers, gaoling, gaols**
GAP *n*
GAPE *vb, n* **gaped**
GAPER *n* person or thing that gapes **gapers**
GAPES *n* disease of young domestic fowl **gapier, gapiest**
GAPING *adj* wide open ▹ *n* state of having a gaping mouth **gapings**
GAPLESS ▸ **gap**
GAPO *n* forest near a river, flooded in the rainy season **gapos**
GAPOSIS *n* gap between closed fastenings on a garment
GAPPED ▸ **gap**
GAPPER *n* person taking a year out of education **gappers**
GAPPIER ▸ **gap**

GAPPING *n*
GAPPY ▸ **gap**
GAPS ▸ **gap**
GAPY ▸ **gapes**
GAR = **garpike**
GARAGE *n*, *vb* **garaged, garages**
GARAGEY *adj* (of music) in a garage style
GARB *n*, *vb*
GARBAGE *n* **garbagy**
GARBE *n* in heraldry, a wheat-sheaf
GARBED ▸ **garb**
GARBES ▸ **garbe**
GARBING ▸ **garb**
GARBLE *vb* jumble (a story, quotation, etc), esp unintentionally ▷ *n* act of garbling
GARBLED *adj*
GARBLER ▸ **garble**
GARBLES ▸ **garble**
GARBO *n* dustman
GARBOIL *n* confusion or disturbance
GARBOS ▸ **garbo**
GARBS ▸ **garb**
GARBURE *n* thick soup from Bearn in France
GARCON *n* waiter **garcons**
GARDA *n* member of the Irish police force **gardai**
GARDANT = **guardant**
GARDEN *n*, *vb* **gardens**
GARE *n* filth
GARFISH = **garpike**
GARGET *n* inflammation of the mammary gland **gargets, gargety**
GARGLE *vb*, *n* **gargled, gargler, gargles**
GARI *n* thinly sliced pickled ginger
GARIAL = **gavial**
GARIALS ▸ **garial**
GARIGUE *n* open shrubby vegetation of dry Mediterranean regions
GARIS ▸ **gari**
GARISH *adj*, *vb*
GARJAN = **gurjun**
GARJANS ▸ **garjan**
GARLAND *n*, *vb*
GARLIC *n* **garlics**
GARMENT *n*, *vb*
GARNER *vb*, *n* **garners**
GARNET *n* **garnets**
GARNI *adj* garnished
GARNISH *vb*, *n*
GAROTE = **garrotte**
GAROTED ▸ **garote**
GAROTES ▸ **garote**
GAROTTE = **garrotte**
GAROUPA *in Chinese and SE Asian cookery, another name for* ▸ **groper**
GARPIKE *n* primitive freshwater bony fish
GARRAN = **garron**
GARRANS ▸ **garran**
GARRE *vb* compel
GARRED ▸ **gar**
GARRES ▸ **garre**
GARRET *n* **garrets**
GARRING ▸ **gar**
GARRON *n* small sturdy pony **garrons**
GARROT *n* goldeneye duck
GARROTE = **garrotte**
GARROTS ▸ **garrot**
GARRYA *n* catkin-bearing evergreen shrub **garryas**
GARS ▸ **gar**
GART *vb* compel
GARTER *n*, *vb* **garters**
GARTH *n* courtyard surrounded by a cloister **garths**
GARUDA *n* Hindu god **garudas**
GARUM *n* fermented fish sauce **garums**
GARVEY *n* small flat-bottomed yacht **garveys**
GARVIE *n* sprat **garvies**
GARVOCK *n* sprat
GAS *n*, *vb*
GASAHOL *n* mixture of petrol and alcohol used as fuel
GASBAG *n* person who talks too much ▷ *vb* talk in a voluble way **gasbags**
GASCON *n* boaster **gascons**
GASEITY *n* state of being gaseous
GASEOUS *adj*
GASES ▸ **gas**
GASH *vb*, *n*, *adj* **gashed, gasher, gashes, gashest**
GASHFUL *adj* full of gashes
GASHING ▸ **gash**
GASHLY *adv* wittily
GASIFY *vb* change into a gas
GASKET *n* **gaskets**
GASKIN *n* lower part of a horse's thigh
GASKING = **gasket**
GASKINS ▸ **gaskin**
GASLESS ▸ **gas**

GASLIT *adj* lit by gas
GASMAN *n* man employed by a gas company **gasmen**
GASOHOL *n* mixture of petrol and ethyl alcohol
GASP *vb, n* **gasped**
GASPER *n* person who gasps **gaspers**
GASPIER, gasping, gasps, gaspy ▸ **gasp**
GASSED ▸ **gas**
GASSER *n* drilling or well that yields natural gas **gassers**
GASSES ▸ **gas**
GASSIER ▸ **gassy**
GASSILY ▸ **gassy**
GASSING ▸ **gas**
GASSY *adj*
GAST *vb* frighten **gasted, gaster, gasters, gasting**
GASTRAL *adj* relating to the stomach
GASTREA = **gastraea**
GASTRIC *adj*
GASTRIN *n* polypeptide hormone
GASTS ▸ **gast**
GAT *n* pistol or revolver
GATE *n, vb*
GATEAU *n* **gateaus, gateaux**
GATED ▸ **gate**
GATELEG *adj* (of a table) having a hinged leg that swings out
GATEMAN *n* gatekeeper **gatemen**
GATER *variant of* ▸ **gator**
GATERS ▸ **gater**
GATES ▸ **gate**
GATEWAY *n*
GATH *n* (in Indian music) second section of a raga
GATHER *vb, n* **gathers**
GATHS ▸ **gath**
GATING ▸ **gate**
GATINGS ▸ **gate**
GATLING *n as in* **gatling gun** kind of machinegun
GATOR *shortened form of* > **alligator**
GATORS ▸ **gator**
GATS ▸ **gat**
GATVOL *adj* in South African English, fed up
GAU *n* district set up by the Nazi Party
GAUCHE *adj* **gaucher**
GAUCHO *n* S American cowboy **gauchos**
GAUCIE *variant of* ▸ **gaucy**
GAUCIER ▸ **gaucy**
GAUCY *adj* plump or jolly
GAUD *n* article of cheap finery ▹ *vb* decorate gaudily **gauded**
GAUDERY *n* cheap finery or display
GAUDGIE = **gadgie**
GAUDIER ▸ **gaudy**
GAUDIES ▸ **gaudy**
GAUDILY ▸ **gaudy**
GAUDING ▸ **gaud**
GAUDS ▸ **gaud**
GAUDY *adj, n*
GAUFER *n* wafer **gaufers**
GAUFFER = **goffer**
GAUFRE = **gaufer**
GAUFRES ▸ **gaufre**
GAUGE *vb, n, adj* **gauged**
GAUGER *n* person or thing that gauges **gaugers**
GAUGES ▸ **gauge**
GAUGING ▸ **gauge**
GAUJE = **gadgie**
GAUJES ▸ **gauje**
GAULT *n* stiff compact clay or thick heavy clayey soil
GAULTER *n* person who digs gault
GAULTS ▸ **gault**
GAUM *vb* understand **gaumed**
GAUMIER ▸ **gaumy**
GAUMING ▸ **gaum**
GAUMS ▸ **gaum**
GAUMY *adj* clogged
GAUN ▸ **go**
GAUNCH = **ganch**
GAUNT *adj, vb* **gaunted, gaunter, gauntly**
GAUNTRY = **gantry**
GAUNTS ▸ **gaunt**
GAUP = **gawp; gauped, gauper, gaupers, gauping, gaups**
GAUPUS = **gawpus**
GAUR *n* large wild member of the cattle tribe **gaurs**
GAUS ▸ **gau**
GAUSS *n* cgs unit of magnetic flux density **gausses**
GAUZE *n* **gauzes**
GAUZIER ▸ **gauzy**
GAUZILY ▸ **gauzy**
GAUZY *adj*
GAVAGE *n* forced feeding by means of a tube **gavages**

GAVE ▶ **give**
GAVEL *n, vb* **gaveled, gavels**
GAVIAL *n as in* **false gavial** small crocodile **gavials**
GAVOT = **gavotte**
GAVOTS ▶ **gavot**
GAVOTTE *n* old formal dance ▷ *vb* dance a gavotte
GAW *n as in* **weather gaw** partial rainbow
GAWCIER ▶ **gawcy**
GAWCY = **gaucy**
GAWD = **gaud**
GAWDS ▶ **gawd**
GAWK *vb* stare stupidly ▷ *n* clumsy awkward person **gawked, gawker, gawkers**
GAWKIER ▶ **gawky**
GAWKIES ▶ **gawky**
GAWKILY ▶ **gawky**
GAWKING ▶ **gawk**
GAWKISH = **gawky**
GAWKS ▶ **gawk**
GAWKY *adj, n*
GAWP *vb* **gawped, gawper, gawpers, gawping, gawps**
GAWPUS *n* silly person
GAWS ▶ **gaw**
GAWSIE = **gaucy**
GAWSIER ▶ **gawsie**
GAWSY = **gaucy**
GAY *adj, n*
GAYAL *n* type of ox **gayals**
GAYDAR *n* supposed ability of one homosexual person to know another **gaydars**
GAYER ▶ **gay**
GAYEST ▶ **gay**
GAYETY = **gaiety**
GAYLY ▶ **gay**
GAYNESS ▶ **gay**
GAYS ▶ **gay**
GAYSOME *adj* full of merriment
GAZABO *n* fellow or companion **gazabos**
GAZAL = **ghazal**
GAZALS ▶ **gazal**
GAZANIA *n* S African plant
GAZAR *n* type of silk cloth **gazars**
GAZE *vb, n*
GAZEBO *n* summerhouse with a good view **gazebos**
GAZED ▶ **gaze**
GAZEFUL *adj* gazing
GAZELLE *n*
GAZER ▶ **gaze**
GAZERS ▶ **gaze**
GAZES ▶ **gaze**
GAZETTE *n, vb*
GAZIER ▶ **gazy**
GAZIEST ▶ **gazy**
GAZING ▶ **gaze**
GAZINGS ▶ **gaze**
GAZON *n* sod used to cover a parapet in a fortification **gazons**
GAZOO *n* kazoo **gazooka**
GAZOON = **gazon**
GAZOONS ▶ **gazoon**
GAZOOS ▶ **gazoo**
GAZUMP *vb, n* **gazumps**
GAZY *adj* prone to gazing
GEAL *vb* congeal **gealed, gealing**
GEALOUS *Spenserian spelling of* ▶ **jealous**
GEALS ▶ **geal**
GEAN *n* white-flowered tree **geans**
GEAR *n, vb*
GEARBOX *n*
GEARE *Spenserian spelling of* ▶ **jeer**
GEARED ▶ **gear**
GEARES ▶ **geare**
GEARING *n* system of gears designed to transmit motion
GEARS ▶ **gear**
GEASON *adj* wonderful
GEAT *n* in casting, the channel which leads to a mould **geats**
GEBUR *n* tenant farmer **geburs**
GECK *vb* beguile **gecked, gecking**
GECKO *n* small tropical lizard **geckoes, geckos**
GECKS ▶ **geck**
GED *Scots word for* ▶ **pike**
GEDACT *n* flutelike stopped metal diapason organ pipe **gedacts**
GEDDIT *interj* exclamation meaning *do you understand it?*
GEDECKT = **gedact**
GEDS ▶ **ged**
GEE *interj* mild exclamation of surprise, admiration, etc ▷ *vb* move (an animal, esp a horse) ahead
GEEBUNG *n* Australian tree or shrub

GEECHEE *n* Black person from the southern states of the US
GEED ▸ **gee**
GEEGAW = **gewgaw**
GEEGAWS ▸ **geegaw**
GEEING ▸ **gee**
GEEK *n* **geekdom**
GEEKED *adj* highly excited
GEEKIER ▸ **geek**
GEEKS ▸ **geek**
GEEKY ▸ **geek**
GEELBEK *n* edible marine fish
GEEP *n* cross between a goat and a sheep **geeps**
GEES ▸ **gee**
GEESE ▸ **goose**
GEEST *n* area of heathland in N Germany and adjacent areas **geests**
GEEZ *interj* expression of surprise
GEEZAH *variant spelling of* ▸ **geezer**
GEEZAHS ▸ **geezah**
GEEZER *n* **geezers**
GEFILTE *adj as in* **gefilte fish** dish of fish stuffed with various ingredients
GEGGIE *Scottish, esp Glaswegian, slang word for the* ▸ **mouth**
GEGGIES ▸ **geggie**
GEISHA *n* **geishas**
GEIST *n* spirit **geists**
GEIT *n* border on clothing **geits**
GEL *n, vb*
GELABLE *adj* capable of forming a gel
GELADA *n* NE African baboon **geladas**
GELANDE *adj as in* **gelande jump** jump made in downhill skiing
GELANT = **gellant**
GELANTS ▸ **gelant**
GELATE *vb* form a gel **gelated, gelates**
GELATI *n* layered dessert
GELATIN = **gelatine**
GELATIS ▸ **gelati**
GELATO *n* Italian frozen dessert, similar to ice cream **gelatos**
GELCAP *n* medicine enclosed in gelatine **gelcaps**
GELD *vb* castrate ▷ *n* tax on land in Anglo-Saxon and Norman England **gelded, gelder, gelders, gelding, gelds**
GELEE *n* jelly **gelees**
GELID *adj* very cold, icy, or frosty **gelider, gelidly**
GELLANT *n* compound that forms a solid structure
GELLED ▸ **gel**
GELLIES ▸ **gelly**
GELLING ▸ **gel**
GELLY = **gelignite**
GELOSY *Spenserian spelling of* > **jealousy**
GELS ▸ **gel**
GELT ▸ **geld**
GELTS ▸ **geld**
GEM *n, vb*
GEMCLIP *n* paperclip
GEMEL *n* in heraldry, parallel bars **gemels**
GEMFISH *n* Australian food fish with a delicate flavour
GEMINAL *adj* occurring in pairs
GEMINI *n* expression of surprise
GEMINY *n* pair
GEMLIKE ▸ **gem**
GEMMA *n* reproductive structure in liverworts, mosses, etc **gemmae**
GEMMAN *dialect form of* > **gentleman**
GEMMATE *adj* (of some plants and animals) having gemmae ▷ *vb* produce or reproduce by gemmae
GEMMED ▸ **gem**
GEMMEN ▸ **gemman**
GEMMERY *n* gems collectively
GEMMIER ▸ **gem**
GEMMILY ▸ **gem**
GEMMING ▸ **gem**
GEMMULE *n* result of asexual reproduction by sponges
GEMMY ▸ **gem**
GEMONY = **jiminy**
GEMOT *n* (in Anglo-Saxon England) a legal or administrative assembly **gemote**
GEMOTES ▸ **gemote**
GEMOTS ▸ **gemot**
GEMS ▸ **gem**
GEMSBOK = **oryx**
GEN *n, vb*
GENA *n* cheek **genal**

GENAPPE *n* smooth worsted yarn used for braid, etc
GENAS ▸ **gena**
GENDER *n*, *vb* **genders**
GENE *n*
GENERA ▸ **genus**
GENERAL *adj*, *n*, *vb*
GENERIC *adj*, *n*
GENES ▸ **gene**
GENESES ▸ **genesis**
GENESIS *n*
GENET *n* type of agile catlike mammal
GENETIC *adj* of genes or genetics
GENETS ▸ **genet**
GENETTE = **genet**
GENEVA *n* gin **genevas**
GENIAL *adj*
GENIC *adj* of or relating to a gene or genes
GENIE *n* **genies**
GENII ▸ **genius**
GENIP = **genipap**
GENIPAP *n* evergreen Caribbean tree
GENIPS ▸ **genip**
GENISTA *n* any member of the broom family
GENITAL *adj* of the sexual organs or reproduction
GENITOR *n* biological father
GENIUS *n*
GENIZAH *n* repository for sacred objects which may not be destroyed **genizot**
GENLOCK *n* generator locking device
GENNED ▸ **gen**
GENNEL = **ginnel**
GENNELS ▸ **gennel**
GENNET *n* female donkey or ass **gennets**
GENNIES ▸ **genny**
GENNING ▸ **gen**
GENNY = **genoa**
GENOA *n* large triangular jib sail **genoas**
GENOISE *n* rich sponge cake
GENOM = **genome**
GENOME *n* **genomes, genomic**
GENOMS ▸ **genom**
GENRE *n* **genres**
GENRO *n* group of Japanese statesmen **genros**
GENS *n* (in ancient Rome) a group of aristocratic families
GENSENG = **ginseng**
GENT *n* gentleman
GENTEEL *adj*
GENTES ▸ **gens**
GENTIAN *n*
GENTIER ▸ **genty**
GENTIL *adj* gentle
GENTILE *n* non-Jewish person ▹ *adj* used to designate a place or the inhabitants of a place
GENTLE *adj*, *vb*, *n* **gentled, gentler, gentles, gently**
GENTOO *n* grey-backed penguin **gentoos**
GENTRY *n*
GENTS *n*
GENTY *adj* neat
GENU *n* any knee-like bend in a structure or part **genua**
GENUINE *adj*
GENUS *n* **genuses**
GEO *n* (esp in Shetland) a small fjord or gully
GEODE *n* cavity within a rock mass or nodule **geodes**
GEODESY *n* study of the shape and size of the earth
GEODIC ▸ **geode**
GEODUCK *n* king clam
GEOFACT *n* rock shaped by natural forces
GEOGENY = **geogony**
GEOGONY *n* science of the earth's formation
GEOID *n* hypothetical surface **geoidal, geoids**
GEOLOGY *n*
GEOMANT *n* geomancer
GEORGIC *adj* agricultural ▹ *n* poem about rural or agricultural life
GEOS ▸ **geo**
GER *n* portable Mongolian dwelling
GERAH *n* ancient Hebrew unit of weight **gerahs**
GERBE = **garbe**
GERBERA *n* type of plant
GERBES ▸ **garbe**
GERBIL *n* **gerbils**
GERE *Spenserian spelling of* ▸ **gear**
GERENT *n* person who rules or manages **gerents**
GERENUK *n* slender antelope
GERES ▸ **gear**

GERLE *Spenserian spelling of* ▸ **girl**
GERLES ▸ **gerle**
GERM *n, vb*
GERMAIN = **germen**
GERMAN *n* type of dance ▹ *adj* having the same parents as oneself
GERMANE *adj*
GERMANS ▸ **german**
GERMED ▸ **germ**
GERMEN *n* cells that gives rise to the germ cells **germens**
GERMIER ▸ **germy**
GERMIN = **germen**
GERMINA ▸ **germen**
GERMING ▸ **germ**
GERMINS ▸ **germin**
GERMS ▸ **germ**
GERMY *adj* full of germs
GERNE *vb* grin **gerned, gernes, gerning**
GERS ▸ **ger**
GERT *adv* in dialect, great or very big
GERTCHA *interj* get out of here!
GERUND *n* noun formed from a verb **gerunds**
GESSE *Spenserian spelling of* ▸ **guess**
GESSED ▸ **gesse**
GESSES ▸ **gesse**
GESSING ▸ **gesse**
GESSO *n* plaster used for painting or in sculpture ▹ *vb* apply gesso to **gessoed, gessoes**
GEST *n* notable deed or exploit
GESTALT *n* perceptual pattern or structure
GESTANT *adj* laden
GESTAPO *n* any secret state police organization
GESTATE *vb* carry (young) in the uterus during pregnancy
GESTE = **gest**
GESTES ▸ **geste**
GESTIC *adj* consisting of gestures
GESTS ▸ **gest**
GESTURE *n, vb*
GET *vb* obtain or receive
GETA *n* type of Japanese wooden sandal
GETABLE ▸ **get**
GETAS ▸ **geta**
GETAWAY *n*
GETS ▸ **get**
GETTER *n* person or thing that gets ▹ *vb* remove (a gas) by the action of a getter **getters**
GETTING ▸ **get**
GETUP *n* outfit **getups**
GEUM *n* type of herbaceous plant **geums**
GEWGAW *n* showy but valueless trinket ▹ *adj* showy and valueless **gewgaws**
GEY *adv* extremely ▹ *adj* gallant
GEYAN *adv* somewhat
GEYER ▸ **gey**
GEYEST ▸ **gey**
GEYSER *n* **geysers**
GHARIAL = **gavial**
GHARRI = **gharry**
GHARRIS ▸ **gharri**
GHARRY *n* (in India) horse-drawn vehicle
GHAST *vb* terrify **ghasted**
GHASTLY *adj, adv*
GHASTS ▸ **ghast**
GHAT *n* (in India) steps leading down to a river **ghats**
GHAUT *n* small cleft in a hill **ghauts**
GHAZAL *n* Arabic love poem **ghazals, ghazel**
GHAZELS ▸ **ghazel**
GHAZI *n* Muslim fighter against infidels **ghazies, ghazis**
GHEE *n* (in Indian cookery) clarified butter **ghees**
GHERAO *n* form of industrial action in India ▹ *vb* trap an employer in his office, to indicate the workforce's discontent **gheraos**
GHERKIN *n*
GHESSE *Spenserian spelling of* ▸ **guess**
GHESSED ▸ **ghesse**
GHESSES ▸ **ghesse**
GHEST ▸ **ghesse**
GHETTO *n, vb* **ghettos**
GHI = **ghee**
GHIBLI *n* fiercely hot wind of North Africa **ghiblis**
GHILGAI = **gilgai**
GHILLIE *n* type of tongueless shoe ▹ *vb* act as a g(h)illie
GHIS ▸ **ghi**
GHOST *n, vb* **ghosted**
GHOSTLY *adj* frightening

in appearance or effect
GHOSTS ▸ **ghost**
GHOSTY *adj* pertaining to ghosts
GHOUL *n*
GHOULIE *n* goblin
GHOULS ▸ **ghoul**
GHRELIN *n*
GHUBAR *adj as in* **ghubar numeral** type of numeral
GHYLL = **gill**
GHYLLS ▸ **ghyll**
GI *n* white suit worn in martial arts
GIANT *n, adj*
GIANTLY *adj* giantlike
GIANTRY *n* collective term for giants
GIANTS ▸ **giant**
GIARDIA *n* species of parasite
GIB *n* metal wedge, pad, or thrust bearing ▹ *vb* fasten or supply with a gib **gibbed**
GIBBER *vb, n* **gibbers**
GIBBET *n, vb* **gibbets**
GIBBING ▸ **gib**
GIBBON *n* **gibbons**
GIBBOSE = **gibbous**
GIBBOUS *adj* (of the moon) between half and fully illuminated
GIBE *vb, n* **gibed**
GIBEL *n* Prussian carp **gibels**
GIBER, gibers, gibes, gibing ▸ **gibe**
GIBLET ▸ **giblets**
GIBLETS *pl n*
GIBLI = **ghibli**
GIBLIS ▸ **gibli**
GIBS ▸ **gib**
GIBSON *n* martini garnished with onion **gibsons**
GIBUS *n* collapsible top hat **gibuses**
GID *n* disease of sheep
GIDDAP *interj* exclamation used to make a horse go faster
GIDDAY *interj*
GIDDIED, giddier, giddies, giddily ▸ **giddy**
GIDDUP = **giddyup**
GIDDY *adj, vb*
GIDDYAP = **giddyup**
GIDDYUP *interj* exclamation used to make a horse go faster
GIDGEE *n* small acacia tree **gidgees, gidjee**
GIDJEES ▸ **gidjee**
GIDS ▸ **gid**
GIE *Scot word for* ▸ **give**
GIED ▸ **give**
GIEING ▸ **give**
GIEN ▸ **give**
GIES ▸ **give**
GIF *obsolete word for* ▸ **if**
GIFT *n, vb*
GIFTED *adj*
GIFTEE *n* person given a gift **giftees**
GIFTING ▸ **gift**
GIFTS ▸ **gift**
GIG *n, vb*
GIGA = **gigue**
GIGABIT *n* unit of information in computing
GIGAS ▸ **giga**
GIGATON *n* unit of explosive force
GIGGED ▸ **gig**
GIGGING ▸ **gig**
GIGGIT *vb* move quickly **giggits**
GIGGLE *vb, n* **giggled, giggler, giggles, giggly**
GIGHE ▸ **giga**
GIGLET *n* flighty girl **giglets, giglot**
GIGLOTS ▸ **giglot**
GIGMAN *n* one who places great importance on respectability **gigmen**
GIGOLO *n* man paid by an older woman to be her escort or lover **gigolos**
GIGOT *n* leg of lamb or mutton **gigots**
GIGS ▸ **gig**
GIGUE *n* piece of music incorporated into the classical suite **gigues**
GILA *n* large venomous brightly coloured lizard **gilas**
GILBERT *n* unit of magnetomotive force
GILCUP = **giltcup**
GILCUPS ▸ **gilcup**
GILD *vb* **gilded**
GILDEN *adj* gilded
GILDER, gilders, gilding, gilds ▸ **gild**
GILET *n* waist- or hip-length garment **gilets**
GILGAI *n* natural water hole **gilgais**
GILGIE *n* type of freshwater crayfish **gilgies**
GILL *n, vb* **gilled, giller,**

gillers
GILLET *n* mare **gillets**
GILLIE *n* (in Scotland) attendant for hunting or fishing ▷ *vb* act as a gillie **gillied**
GILLIES ▸ **gilly**
GILLING ▸ **gill**
GILLION *n* (no longer in technical use) one thousand million
GILLNET *n* net designed to catch fish by the gills ▷ *vb* fish using a gillnet
GILLS *pl n* breathing organs in fish and other water creatures
GILLY *vb* act as a gillie
GILPEY *n* mischievous, frolicsome boy or girl **gilpeys, gilpies, gilpy**
GILT ▸ **gild**
GILTCUP *n* buttercup
GILTS ▸ **gild**
GIMBAL *vb* support on gimbals
GIMBALS *pl n* set of pivoted rings
GIMEL *n* third letter of the Hebrew alphabet **gimels**
GIMLET *n, adj, vb* **gimlets**
GIMMAL *n* ring composed of interlocking rings ▷ *vb* provide with gimmals **gimmals**
GIMME *interj* give me! ▷ *n* term used in shot putt
GIMMER *n* year-old ewe **gimmers**
GIMMES ▸ **gimme**
GIMMICK *n, vb*
GIMMIE *n* very short putt in golf **gimmies**
GIMMOR *n* mechanical device **gimmors**
GIN *n, vb*
GING *n* child's catapult
GINGAL *n* type of musket mounted on a swivel **gingall, gingals**
GINGE *n* person with ginger hair
GINGELI = **gingili**
GINGELY = **gingili**
GINGER *n, adj, vb* **gingers**
GINGERY *adj* like or tasting of ginger
GINGES ▸ **ginge**
GINGHAM *n*
GINGILI *n* oil obtained from sesame seeds
GINGIVA = **gum**
GINGKO = **ginkgo**
GINGKOS ▸ **gingko**
GINGLE = **jingle**
GINGLES ▸ **gingle**
GINGS ▸ **ging**
GINK *n* man or boy
GINKGO *n* ornamental Chinese tree **ginkgos**
GINKS ▸ **gink**
GINN = **jinn**
GINNED ▸ **gin**
GINNEL *n* narrow passageway between buildings **ginnels**
GINNER ▸ **gin**
GINNERS ▸ **gin**
GINNERY *another word for* ▸ **ginhouse**
GINNIER ▸ **ginny**
GINNING ▸ **gin**
GINNY *adj* relating to the spirit gin
GINS ▸ **gin**
GINSENG *n* (root of) a plant
GINSHOP *n* tavern
GIO = **geo**
GIOCOSO *adv* (of music) to be expressed joyfully or playfully
GIOS ▸ **gio**
GIP = **gyp**
GIPON *another word for* ▸ **jupon**
GIPONS ▸ **gipon**
GIPPED ▸ **gip**
GIPPER ▸ **gip**
GIPPERS ▸ **gip**
GIPPIES ▸ **gippy**
GIPPING ▸ **gip**
GIPPO = **gippy**
GIPPOES ▸ **gippo**
GIPPOS ▸ **gippo**
GIPPY *n* starling
GIPS ▸ **gip**
GIPSEN *obsolete word for* ▸ **gypsy**
GIPSENS ▸ **gipsen**
GIPSIED ▸ **gipsy**
GIPSIES ▸ **gipsy**
GIPSY *n, vb*
GIRAFFE *n*
GIRASOL *n* type of opal
GIRD *vb, n* **girded**
GIRDER *n* **girders**
GIRDING ▸ **gird**
GIRDLE *n, vb* **girdled**
GIRDLER *n* person or thing that girdles
GIRDLES ▸ **girdle**
GIRDS ▸ **gird**
GIRKIN = **gherkin**
GIRKINS ▸ **girkin**
GIRL *n*
GIRLIE *adj* (of a

magazine, etc) featuring pictures of naked women ▷ *n* little girl
GIRLIER ▶ **girly**
GIRLIES ▶ **girlie**
GIRLISH *adj* of or like a girl in looks, behaviour, innocence, etc
GIRLOND *obsolete word for* ▶ **garland**
GIRLS ▶ **girl**
GIRLY = **girlie**
GIRN *vb* snarl **girned**
GIRNEL *n* large chest for storing meal **girnels**
GIRNER ▶ **girn**
GIRNERS ▶ **girn**
GIRNIE *adj* peevish **girnier**
GIRNING ▶ **girn**
GIRNS ▶ **girn**
GIRO *n*
GIROLLE *n* chanterelle mushroom
GIRON *n* part of a heraldic shield **gironic**
GIRONNY *adj* divided into segments from the fesse point
GIRONS ▶ **giron**
GIROS ▶ **giro**
GIROSOL = **girasol**
GIRR = **gird**
GIRRS ▶ **girr**
GIRSH *n* currency unit of Saudi Arabia **girshes**
GIRT *vb* gird; bind
GIRTED ▶ **gird**
GIRTH *n*, *vb* **girthed, girths**
GIRTING ▶ **gird**
GIRTS ▶ **girt**
GIS ▶ **gi**
GISARME *n* long-shafted battle-axe
GISMO = **gizmo**
GISMOS ▶ **gismo**
GIST *n* **gists**
GIT *n* contemptible person ▷ *vb* dialect version of get
GITANA *n* female gypsy **gitanas**
GITANO *n* male gypsy **gitanos**
GITE *n* self-catering holiday cottage for let in France **gites**
GITS ▶ **git**
GITTED ▶ **git**
GITTERN *n* obsolete medieval instrument ▷ *vb* play the gittern
GITTIN *n* Jewish divorce
GITTING ▶ **git**
GIUST = **joust**
GIUSTED ▶ **giust**
GIUSTO *adv* as observed strictly
GIUSTS ▶ **giust**
GIVABLE ▶ **give**
GIVE *vb*, *n*
GIVED = **gyved**
GIVEN *n* **givens**
GIVER, givers, gives, giving, givings ▶ **give**
GIZMO *n* device **gizmos**
GIZZ *n* wig
GIZZARD *n*
GIZZEN *vb* (of wood) to warp **gizzens**
GIZZES ▶ **gizz**
GJETOST *n* type of Norwegian cheese
GJU *n* type of violin used in Shetland **gjus**

> This unusual word for a Shetland fiddle is great for disposing of awkward letters for a good score.

GLACE *adj* preserved in a thick sugary syrup ▷ *vb* ice or candy (cakes, fruits, etc) **glaceed, glaces**
GLACIAL *adj* of ice or glaciers ▷ *n* ice age
GLACIER *n*
GLACIS *n* slight incline
GLAD *adj*, *vb*, *n* **gladded**
GLADDEN *vb*
GLADDER ▶ **glad**
GLADDIE = **glad**
GLADDON *n* stinking iris
GLADE *n* **glades**
GLADFUL *adj* full of gladness
GLADIER ▶ **glade**
GLADIUS *n* short sword used by Roman legionaries
GLADLY ▶ **glad**
GLADS ▶ **glad**
GLADY ▶ **glade**
GLAIK *n* prank
GLAIKET = **glaikit**
GLAIKIT *adj* foolish
GLAIKS ▶ **glaik**
GLAIR *n* white of egg ▷ *vb* apply glair to (something) **glaire, glaired**
GLAIRES ▶ **glaire**
GLAIRIN *n* viscous mineral deposit
GLAIRS ▶ **glair**
GLAIRY ▶ **glair**
GLAIVE *archaic word for* ▶ **sword**

GLAIVED *adj* armed with a sword
GLAIVES ▸ **glaive**
GLAM *n* magical illusion ▹ *vb* make oneself look glamorous **glammed**
GLAMMY *adj* glamorous
GLAMOR = **glamour**
GLAMORS ▸ **glamor**
GLAMOUR *n, vb*
GLAMS ▸ **glam**
GLANCE *vb, n* **glanced**
GLANCER *n* log or pole used to protect trees from damage
GLANCES ▸ **glance**
GLAND *n*
GLANDES ▸ **glans**
GLANDS ▸ **gland**
GLANS *n* any small rounded body or glandlike mass
GLARE *vb, n, adj*
GLAREAL *adj* (of a plant) growing in cultivated land
GLARED ▸ **glare**
GLARES ▸ **glare**
GLARIER ▸ **glare**
GLARING *adj*
GLARY ▸ **glare**
GLASS *n, vb* **glassed**
GLASSEN *adj* glassy
GLASSES *pl n*
GLASSIE = **glassy**
GLASSY *adj, n*
GLAUM *vb* snatch **glaumed, glaums**
GLAUR *n* mud or mire **glaurs, glaury**
GLAZE *vb, n* **glazed**
GLAZEN *adj* glazed
GLAZER ▸ **glaze**
GLAZERS ▸ **glaze**
GLAZES ▸ **glaze**
GLAZIER *n*
GLAZILY ▸ **glaze**
GLAZING *n* surface of a glazed object
GLAZY ▸ **glaze**
GLEAM *n, vb* **gleamed**
GLEAMER *n* mirror used to cheat in card games
GLEAMS ▸ **gleam**
GLEAMY ▸ **gleam**
GLEAN *vb* **gleaned, gleaner, gleans**
GLEAVE = **sword**
GLEAVES ▸ **gleave**
GLEBA *n* mass of spores **glebae**
GLEBE *n* land granted to a member of the clergy **glebes**
GLEBIER ▸ **gleby**
GLEBOUS *adj* gleby
GLEBY *adj* relating to a glebe
GLED *n* kite **glede**
GLEDES ▸ **glede**
GLEDGE *vb* glance sideways **gledged, gledges**
GLEDS ▸ **gled**
GLEE *n, vb*
GLEED *n* burning ember or hot coal **gleeds**
GLEEFUL *adj* merry or joyful
GLEEING ▸ **glee**
GLEEK *vb* jeer **gleeked, gleeks**
GLEEMAN *n* minstrel **gleemen**
GLEENIE *n* guinea fowl
GLEES ▸ **glee**
GLEET *n* stage of chronic gonorrhoea ▹ *vb* discharge pus **gleeted, gleets, gleety**
GLEG *adj* quick **glegger, glegly**
GLEI = **gley**
GLEIS ▸ **glei**
GLEN *n*
GLENOID *adj* resembling or having a shallow cavity ▹ *n* shallow cavity
GLENS ▸ **glen**
GLENT = **glint**
GLENTED ▸ **glent**
GLENTS ▸ **glent**
GLEY *n* bluish-grey compact sticky soil ▹ *vb* squint **gleyed, gleying, gleys**
GLIA *n* web of tissue that supports nerve cells
GLIADIN *n* protein of cereals with a high proline content
GLIAL ▸ **glia**
GLIAS ▸ **glia**
GLIB *adj, vb* **glibbed, glibber, glibly, glibs**
GLID *adj* moving smoothly and easily **glidder**
GLIDE *vb, n* **glided**
GLIDER *n* **gliders**
GLIDES ▸ **glide**
GLIDING *n* sport of flying gliders
GLIFF *n* slap **gliffs**
GLIFT *n* moment **glifts**
GLIKE = **gleek**
GLIKES ▸ **glike**
GLIM *n* light or lamp
GLIME *vb* glance sideways **glimed,**

glimes, gliming
GLIMMER *vb, n*
GLIMPSE *n, vb*
GLIMS ▶ **glim**
GLINT *vb, n* **glinted, glints, glinty**
GLIOMA *n* tumour of the brain and spinal cord **gliomas**
GLIOSES ▶ **gliosis**
GLIOSIS *n* process leading to scarring in the nervous system
GLISK *n* glimpse **glisks**
GLISTEN *vb, n*
GLISTER *archaic word for* ▶ **glitter**
GLIT *n* slimy matter
GLITCH *n* small problem that stops something from working **glitchy**
GLITS ▶ **glit**
GLITTER *vb, n*
GLITZ *n* ostentatious showiness ▷ *vb* make something more attractive **glitzed, glitzes**
GLITZY *adj* showily attractive
GLOAM *n* dusk **gloams**
GLOAT *vb, n* **gloated, gloater, gloats**
GLOB *n* rounded mass of thick fluid
GLOBAL *adj*
GLOBATE *adj* shaped like a globe
GLOBBY *adj* thick and lumpy
GLOBE *n, vb* **globed, globes**
GLOBI ▶ **globus**
GLOBIN *n* protein component
GLOBING ▶ **globe**
GLOBINS ▶ **globin**
GLOBOID *adj* shaped approximately like a globe ▷ *n* globoid body
GLOBOSE *adj* spherical or approximately spherical ▷ *n* globose object **globous**
GLOBS ▶ **glob**
GLOBULE *n*
GLOBUS *n* any spherelike structure
GLOBY *adj* round
GLOCHID *n* barbed spine on a plant
GLODE ▶ **glide**
GLOGG *n* hot alcoholic mixed drink **gloggs**
GLOIRE *n* glory **gloires**
GLOM *vb* attach oneself to or associate oneself with
GLOMERA ▶ **glomus**
GLOMMED ▶ **glom**
GLOMS ▶ **glom**
GLOMUS *n* small anastomosis in an artery or vein
GLONOIN *n* nitroglycerin
GLOOM *n, vb* **gloomed, glooms**
GLOOMY *adj*
GLOOP *vb* cover with a viscous substance **glooped, gloops, gloopy**
GLOP *vb* cover with a viscous substance **glopped, gloppy, glops**
GLORIA *n* silk, wool, cotton, or nylon fabric **glorias**
GLORIED ▶ **glory**
GLORIES ▶ **glory**
GLORIFY *vb*
GLORY *n, vb*
GLOSS *n, vb*
GLOSSA *n* paired tonguelike lobe in the labium of an insect **glossae, glossal, glossas**
GLOSSED ▶ **gloss**
GLOSSER ▶ **gloss**
GLOSSES ▶ **gloss**
GLOSSY *adj, n*
GLOST *n* lead glaze used for pottery **glosts**
GLOTTAL *adj* of the glottis
GLOTTIC *adj* of or relating to the tongue or the glottis
GLOTTIS *n* vocal cords and the space between them
GLOUT *vb* look sullen **glouted, glouts**
GLOVE *n* **gloved**
GLOVER *n* person who makes or sells gloves **glovers**
GLOVES ▶ **glove**
GLOVING ▶ **glove**
GLOW *vb, n* **glowed**
GLOWER *n, vb* **glowers**
GLOWFLY *n* firefly
GLOWING *adj*
GLOWS ▶ **glow**
GLOZE *vb* explain away ▷ *n* flattery or deceit **glozed, glozes, glozing**
GLUCAN *n* any polysaccharide

consisting of a polymer of glucose **glucans**
GLUCINA *n* oxide of glucinum
GLUCOSE *n*
GLUE *n, vb* **glued, glueing**
GLUEPOT *n* container for holding glue
GLUER, gluers, glues, gluey ▸ **glue**
GLUG *n* word representing a gurgling sound ▹ *vb* drink noisily, taking big gulps **glugged, glugs**
GLUIER, gluiest, gluily, gluing, gluish ▸ **glue**
GLUM *adj*
GLUME *n* one of a pair of dry membranous bracts in grasses **glumes**
GLUMLY ▸ **glum**
GLUMMER ▸ **glum**
GLUMPS *n* state of sulking
GLUMPY *adj* sullen
GLUMS *n* gloomy feelings
GLUNCH *vb* look sullen
GLUON *n* hypothetical particle **gluons**
GLURGE *n* stories supposed to be true but often fabricated **glurges**
GLUT *n, vb*
GLUTAEI > **glutaeus**
GLUTE *n* = **gluteus**
GLUTEAL ▸ **gluteus**
GLUTEI ▸ **gluteus**
GLUTEN *n* **glutens**
GLUTES ▸ **glute**
GLUTEUS *n* any of the three muscles of the buttock
GLUTS ▸ **glut**
GLUTTED ▸ **glut**
GLUTTON *n*
GLYCAN *n* polysaccharide **glycans**
GLYCIN = **glycine**
GLYCINE *n* nonessential amino acid
GLYCINS ▸ **glycin**
GLYCOL *n* another name (not in technical usage) for a diol **glycols**
GLYCOSE *n* any of various monosaccharides
GLYCYL *n* radical of glycine **glycyls**
GLYPH *n* carved channel or groove **glyphic, glyphs**
GLYPTAL *n* alkyd resin
GLYPTIC *adj* of or relating to engraving or carving
GNAMMA *variant of* ▸ **namma**
GNAR = **gnarl**
GNARL *n* any knotty protuberance or swelling on a tree ▹ *vb* knot or cause to knot
GNARLED *adj*
GNARLS ▸ **gnarl**
GNARLY *adj* good
GNARR = **gnarl**
GNARRED ▸ **gnar**
GNARRS ▸ **gnarr**
GNARS ▸ **gnar**
GNASH *vb, n* **gnashed**
GNASHER *n* tooth
GNASHES ▸ **gnash**
GNAT *n*
GNATHAL = **gnathic**
GNATHIC *adj* of or relating to the jaw
GNATS ▸ **gnat**
GNATTY *adj* infested with gnats
GNAW *vb, n* **gnawed, gnawer, gnawers, gnawing, gnawn, gnaws**
GNEISS *n* coarse-grained metamorphic rock
GNOCCHI *n* dumplings
GNOMAE ▸ **gnome**
GNOME *n* **gnomes**
GNOMIC *adj* of pithy sayings
GNOMISH ▸ **gnome**
GNOMIST *n* writer of pithy sayings
GNOMON *n* stationary arm on a sundial **gnomons**
GNOSES ▸ **gnosis**
GNOSIS *n* supposedly revealed knowledge of spiritual truths
GNOSTIC *adj* of, relating to, or possessing knowledge ▹ *n* one who knows
GNOW *n* Australian wild bird **gnows**
GNU *n* **gnus**
GO *vb* move to or from a place ▹ *n* attempt
GOA *n* Tibetan gazelle
GOAD *vb, n* **goaded, goading, goads**
GOAF *n* waste left in old

mine workings **goafs**
GOAL *n, vb* **goaled**
GOALIE *n* goalkeeper **goalies**
GOALING ▸ **goal**
GOALS ▸ **goal**
GOANNA *n* **goannas**
GOARY *variant spelling of* ▸ **gory**
GOAS ▸ **goa**
GOAT *n*
GOATEE *n* pointed tuft-like beard **goateed, goatees**
GOATIER ▸ **goat**

> This means more like a goat: it may seem a silly sort of word but because it uses such common letters the chance to play it as a bonus comes up very frequently.

GOATISH *adj* of, like, or relating to a goat
GOATS ▸ **goat**
GOATY ▸ **goat**
GOB *n, vb*
GOBAN *n* board on which go is played
GOBANG *n* Japanese board-game **gobangs**
GOBANS ▸ **goban**
GOBAR *adj as in* **gobar numeral** kind of numeral
GOBBED ▸ **gob**
GOBBET *n* lump, esp of food **gobbets**
GOBBI ▸ **gobbo**
GOBBIER ▸ **gobby**
GOBBING ▸ **gob**
GOBBLE *vb, n, interj* **gobbled**
GOBBLER *n* turkey
GOBBLES ▸ **gobble**
GOBBO *n* hunchback
GOBBY *adj* loudmouthed and offensive
GOBI *n* (in Indian cookery) cauliflower
GOBIES ▸ **goby**
GOBIID *n* member of the genus Gobius **gobiids**
GOBIOID *n* type of spiny-finned fish
GOBIS ▸ **gobi**
GOBLET *n* **goblets**
GOBLIN *n* **goblins**
GOBO *n* shield placed around a microphone **goboes**
GOBONEE = **gobony**
GOBONY *adj* in heraldry, composed of a row of small, alternately-coloured, squares
GOBOS ▸ **gobo**
GOBS ▸ **gob**
GOBURRA *n* kookaburra
GOBY *n* small spiny-finned fish
GOD *n, vb*
GODDAM *vb* damn
GODDAMN *interj* oath expressing anger, surprise, etc ▹ *adj* extremely ▹ *vb* damn
GODDAMS ▸ **goddam**
GODDED ▸ **god**
GODDEN *n* evening greeting **goddens**
GODDESS *n*
GODDING ▸ **god**
GODET *n* triangular piece of material inserted into a garment
GODETIA *n* plant with showy flowers
GODETS ▸ **godet**
GODHEAD *n* essential nature and condition of being a god
GODHOOD *n* state of being divine
GODLESS *adj*
GODLIER ▸ **godly**
GODLIKE *adj* resembling or befitting a god or God
GODLILY ▸ **godly**
GODLING *n* little god
GODLY *adj*
GODOWN *n* (in East Asia and India) warehouse **godowns**
GODROON = **gadroon**
GODS ▸ **god**
GODSEND *n*
GODSHIP *n* divinity
GODSLOT *n* time in a schedule for religious broadcasts
GODSO = **gadso**
GODSON *n* male godchild **godsons**
GODWARD *adv* towards God
GODWIT *n* shore bird with long legs and an upturned bill **godwits**
GOE = **go**
GOEL *n* in Jewish law, blood-avenger **goels**
GOER *n* person who attends something regularly **goers**
GOES ▸ **go**

GOEST *vb* archaic 2nd person sing present of go
GOETH *vb* archaic 3rd person sing present of go
GOETIC ▶ **goety**
GOETIES ▶ **goety**
GOETY *n* witchcraft
GOEY *adj* go-ahead
GOFER *n* employee or assistant performing menial tasks **gofers**
GOFF *obsolete variant of* ▶ **golf**
GOFFED ▶ **goff**
GOFFER *vb* press pleats into (a frill) ▷ *n* ornamental frill made by pressing pleats **goffers**
GOFFING ▶ **goff**
GOFFS ▶ **goff**
GOGGA *n* any small insect **goggas**
GOGGLE *vb*, *n* **goggled**
GOGGLER *n* big-eyed scad
GOGGLES ▶ **goggle**
GOGGLY ▶ **goggle**
GOGLET *n* long-necked water-cooling vessel **goglets**
GOGO *n* disco **gogos**
GOIER ▶ **goey**
GOIEST ▶ **goey**
GOING ▶ **go**
GOINGS ▶ **go**
GOITER = **goitre**
GOITERS ▶ **goiter**
GOITRE *n* **goitred, goitres**
GOJI > **wolfberry**
GOJIS ▶ **goji**
GOLD *n*, *adj*
GOLDARN *euphemistic variant of* ▶ **goddamn**
GOLDBUG *n* American beetle with a bright metallic lustre
GOLDEN *adj*, *vb* **goldens**
GOLDER ▶ **gold**
GOLDEST ▶ **gold**
GOLDEYE *n* N American fish
GOLDIER ▶ **goldy**
GOLDISH ▶ **gold**
GOLDS ▶ **gold**
GOLDURN *variant of* ▶ **goddamn**
GOLDY *adj* gold-like
GOLE *obsolete spelling of* ▶ **goal**
GOLEM *n* (in Jewish legend) artificially created human **golems**
GOLES ▶ **gole**
GOLF *n*, *vb* **golfed**
GOLFER *n* person who plays golf **golfers**
GOLFING ▶ **golf**
GOLFS ▶ **golf**
GOLIARD *n* one of a number of wandering scholars
GOLIAS *vb* behave outrageously
GOLIATH *n* giant
GOLLAN *n* yellow flower **golland, gollans**
GOLLAR = **goller**
GOLLARS ▶ **gollar**
GOLLER *vb* roar **gollers**
GOLLIED ▶ **golly**
GOLLIES ▶ **golly**
GOLLOP *vb* eat or drink (something) quickly or greedily **gollops**
GOLLY *interj* exclamation of mild surprise ▷ *n* short for golliwog: used chiefly by children ▷ *vb* spit
GOLOSH = **galosh**
GOLOSHE = **galosh**
GOLP = **golpe**
GOLPE *n* in heraldry, a purple circle **golpes**
GOLPS ▶ **golp**
GOMBEEN *n* usury
GOMBO = **gumbo**
GOMBOS ▶ **gombo**
GOMBRO = **gumbo**
GOMBROS ▶ **gombro**
GOMER *n* unwanted hospital patient
GOMERAL = **gomeril**
GOMEREL = **gomeril**
GOMERIL *n* slow-witted or stupid person
GOMERS ▶ **gomer**
GOMOKU *another word for* ▶ **gobang**
GOMOKUS ▶ **gomoku**
GOMPA *n* Tibetan monastery **gompas**
GOMUTI *n* E Indian feather palm **gomutis, gomuto**
GOMUTOS ▶ **gomuto**
GON *n* geometrical grade
GONAD *n* **gonadal, gonadic, gonads**
GONDOLA *n*
GONE ▶ **go**
GONEF = **ganef**
GONEFS ▶ **gonef**
GONER *n* person or thing beyond help or recovery **goners**

GONG *n, vb* **gonged, gonging, gongs**
GONGYO *n* Buddhist ceremony **gongyos**
GONIA ▸ **gonion**
GONIDIA > **gonidium**
GONIDIC > **gonidium**
GONIF = **ganef**
GONIFF = **ganef**
GONIFFS ▸ **goniff**
GONIFS ▸ **gonif**
GONION *n* point or apex of the angle of the lower jaw
GONIUM *n* immature reproductive cell
GONK *n* stuffed toy, often used as a mascot **gonks**
GONNA *vb* going to
GONOF = **ganef**
GONOFS ▸ **ganof**
GONOPH = **ganef**
GONOPHS ▸ **gonoph**
GONOPOD *n* either of the reproductive organs of insects
GONS ▸ **gon**
GONYS *n* lower outline of a bird's bill **gonyses**
GONZO *adj* wild or crazy
GOO *n*
GOOBER *another name for* ▸ **peanut**
GOOBERS ▸ **goober**
GOOBIES ▸ **gooby**
GOOBY *n* spittle
GOOD *adj* giving pleasure ▹ *n* benefit
GOODBY = **goodbye**
GOODBYE *n, interj, sentence substitute*
GOODBYS ▸ **goodby**
GOODIE = **goody**
GOODIER ▸ **goody**
GOODIES ▸ **goody**
GOODISH ▸ **good**
GOODLY *adj* considerable
GOODMAN *n* husband **goodmen**
GOODS ▸ **good**
GOODY *n, interj, adj*
GOOEY *adj* sticky and soft
GOOF *n* mistake ▹ *vb* make a mistake **goofed**
GOOFIER ▸ **goofy**
GOOFILY ▸ **goofy**
GOOFING ▸ **goof**
GOOFS ▸ **goof**
GOOFY *adj* silly or ridiculous
GOOG *n* egg
GOOGLE *vb* search on the internet using a search engine **googled, googles**
GOOGLY *n* ball that spins unexpectedly on the bounce
GOOGOL *n* number shown as one followed by 100 zeros **googols**
GOOGS ▸ **goog**
GOOIER ▸ **gooey**
GOOIEST ▸ **gooey**
GOOILY ▸ **gooey**
GOOKY *adj* sticky and messy
GOOL *n* corn marigold
GOOLD *Scots word for* ▸ **gold**
GOOLDS ▸ **goold**
GOOLS ▸ **gool**
GOOMBAH *n* patron or mentor
GOOMBAY *n* Bahamian soft drink
GOON *n* stupid person
GOONDA *n* (in India) habitual criminal **goondas**
GOONEY *n* albatross **gooneys**
GOONIE *Scots word for a* ▸ **gown**
GOONIER ▸ **goon**
GOONIES ▸ **goonie**
GOONS ▸ **goon**
GOONY ▸ **goon**
GOOP *n* rude or ill-mannered person
GOOPED *adj as in* **gooped up** sticky with goop
GOOPIER ▸ **goop**
GOOPS ▸ **goop**
GOOPY ▸ **goop**
GOOR = **gur**
GOORAL = **goral**
GOORALS ▸ **gooral**
GOORIE ▸ **kuri**
GOORIES ▸ **goorie**
GOOROO = **guru**
GOOROOS ▸ **gooroo**
GOORS ▸ **goor**
GOORY ▸ **goor**
GOOS ▸ **goo**
GOOSE *n, vb* **goosed**
GOOSERY *n* place for keeping geese
GOOSES ▸ **goose**
GOOSEY = **goosy**
GOOSEYS ▸ **goosey**
GOOSIER ▸ **goosy**
GOOSIES ▸ **goosy**
GOOSING ▸ **goose**
GOOSY *adj* of or like a goose
GOPAK *n* Russian peasant dance **gopaks**

GOPHER *n* American burrowing rodent ▷ *vb* burrow **gophers**
GOPIK *n* money unit of Azerbaijan **gopiks**
GOPURA *n* gateway tower of an Indian temple **gopuram, gopuras**
GOR *interj* God!
GORA *n* (in Indian English) White or fair-skinned male
GORAL *n* small S Asian goat antelope **gorals**
GORAMY ▸ **gourami**
GORAS ▸ **gora**
GORCOCK *n* male of the red grouse
GORCROW *n* carrion crow
GORDITA *n* small thick tortilla
GORE *n, vb* **gored, gores**
GORGE *n, vb* **gorged, gorger, gorgers, gorges**
GORGET *n* collar-like piece of armour **gorgets**
GORGIA *n* improvised sung passage **gorgias**
GORGING ▸ **gorge**
GORGIO *n* word used by gypsies for a non-gypsy **gorgios**
GORGON *n* terrifying or repulsive woman **gorgons**
GORHEN *n* female red grouse **gorhens**
GORI *n* (in Indian English) White or fair-skinned female
GORIER ▸ **gory**
GORIEST ▸ **gory**
GORILLA *n*
GORILY ▸ **gory**
GORING ▸ **gore**
GORINGS ▸ **gore**
GORIS ▸ **gori**
GORM *n* foolish person ▷ *vb* understand
GORMAND = **gourmand**
GORMED ▸ **gorm**
GORMIER ▸ **gormy**
GORMING ▸ **gorm**
GORMS ▸ **gorm**
GORMY *adj* gormless
GORP = **gawp**
GORPED ▸ **gawp**
GORPING ▸ **gawp**
GORPS ▸ **gawp**
GORSE *n*
GORSEDD *n* meeting held daily before an eisteddfod
GORSES ▸ **gorse**
GORSIER ▸ **gorse**
GORSOON *n* young boy
GORSY ▸ **gorse**
GORY *adj*
GOS ▸ **go**
GOSH *interj* exclamation of mild surprise or wonder
GOSHAWK *n* large hawk
GOSHT *n* Indian meat dish **goshts**
GOSLET *n* pygmy goose **goslets**
GOSLING *n*
GOSPEL *n, adj, vb* **gospels**
GOSPODA > **gospodin**
GOSPORT *n* aeroplane communication device
GOSS *vb* spit
GOSSAN *n* oxidised portion of a mineral vein in rock **gossans**
GOSSE *variant of* ▸ **gorse**
GOSSED ▸ **goss**
GOSSES ▸ **gosse**
GOSSIB *n* gossip **gossibs**
GOSSING ▸ **goss**
GOSSIP *n, vb* **gossips, gossipy**
GOSSOON *n* boy, esp a servant boy
GOSTER *vb* laugh uncontrollably **gosters**
GOT ▸ **get**
GOTCHA *adj as in* **gotcha lizard** Australian name for a crocodile **gotchas**
GOTH *n* aficionado of Goth music and fashion
GOTHIC *adj* of or relating to a literary style ▷ *n* family of heavy script typefaces **gothics**
GOTHITE = **goethite**
GOTHS ▸ **goth**
GOTTA *vb* got to
GOTTEN *past participle of* ▸ **get**
GOUACHE *n* (painting using) watercolours mixed with glue
GOUCH *vb* become drowsy or lethargic under the influence of

narcotics **gouched, gouches**
GOUGE *vb, n* **gouged**
GOUGER *n* person or tool that gouges
GOUGERE *n* choux pastry flavoured with cheese
GOUGERS ▸ **gouger**
GOUGES ▸ **gouge**
GOUGING ▸ **gouge**
GOUJON *n* small strip of food **goujons**
GOUK = **gowk**
GOUKS ▸ **gouk**
GOULASH *n*
GOURA *n* large, crested ground pigeon found in New Guinea
GOURAMI *n* large SE Asian labyrinth fish
GOURAS ▸ **goura**
GOURD *n*
GOURDE *n* standard monetary unit of Haiti **gourdes**
GOURDS ▸ **gourd**
GOURDY *adj* (of horses) swollen-legged
GOURMET *n*
GOUSTY *adj* dismal
GOUT *n*
GOUTFLY *n* fly whose larvae infect crops
GOUTIER ▸ **gout**
GOUTILY ▸ **gout**
GOUTS ▸ **gout**
GOUTTE *n* heraldric device **gouttes**
GOUTY ▸ **gout**
GOV *n* boss
GOVERN *vb, n* **governs**
GOVS ▸ **gov**
GOWAN *n* any of various flowers growing in fields **gowaned, gowans, gowany**
GOWD *Scots word for* ▸ **gold**
GOWDER ▸ **gowd**
GOWDEST ▸ **gowd**
GOWDS ▸ **gowd**
GOWF *vb* strike **gowfed, gowfer, gowfers, gowfing, gowfs**
GOWK *n* stupid person **gowks**
GOWL *n* substance in the corner of the eyes after sleep ▹ *vb* howl
GOWLAN = **gollan**
GOWLAND = **gollan**
GOWLANS ▸ **gowlan**
GOWLED ▸ **gowl**
GOWLING ▸ **gowl**
GOWLS ▸ **gowl**
GOWN *n, vb*
GOWNBOY *n* foundationer schoolboy who wears a gown
GOWNED ▸ **gown**
GOWNING ▸ **gown**
GOWNMAN *n* professional person who wears a gown **gownmen**
GOWNS ▸ **gown**
GOWPEN *n* pair of cupped hands **gowpens**
GOX *n* gaseous oxygen **goxes**

> **Gox** is gaseous oxygen, especially useful if you can use it to hit a bonus square.

GOYLE *n* ravine **goyles**
GOZZAN = **gossan**
GOZZANS ▸ **gozzan**
GRAAL *n* holy grail **graals**
GRAB *vb, n* **grabbed, grabber**
GRABBLE *vb* scratch or feel about with the hands
GRABBY *adj* greedy or selfish
GRABEN *n* elongated trough of land **grabens**
GRABS ▸ **grab**
GRACE *n, vb* **graced, graces**
GRACILE *adj* gracefully thin or slender
GRACING ▸ **grace**
GRACKLE *n* American songbird with a dark iridescent plumage
GRAD *n* graduate
GRADATE *vb* change or cause to change imperceptibly
GRADDAN *vb* dress corn
GRADE *n, vb* **graded**
GRADELY *adj* fine
GRADER *n* person or thing that grades **graders**
GRADES ▸ **grade**
GRADIN *n* ledge above or behind an altar **gradine**
GRADING ▸ **grade**
GRADINI ▸ **gradino**
GRADINO *n* step above an altar
GRADINS ▸ **gradin**
GRADS ▸ **grad**
GRADUAL *adj, n*

GRADUS *n* book of études or other musical exercises
GRAFF = **graft**
GRAFFED ▸ **graff**
GRAFFS ▸ **graff**
GRAFT *n, vb* **grafted, grafter, grafts**
GRAHAM *n* made of graham flour **grahams**
GRAIL *n* any desired ambition or goal **graile**
GRAILES ▸ **graile**
GRAILS ▸ **grail**
GRAIN *n, vb*
GRAINE *n* eggs of the silkworm
GRAINED ▸ **grain**
GRAINER ▸ **grain**
GRAINES ▸ **graine**
GRAINS ▸ **grain**
GRAINY *adj*
GRAIP *n* long-handled gardening fork **graips**
GRAITH *vb* clothe **graiths**
GRAKLE = **grackle**
GRAKLES ▸ **grakle**
GRAM *n*
GRAMA *n* type of grass
GRAMARY = **gramarye**
GRAMAS ▸ **grama**
GRAMASH *n* type of gaiter
GRAME *n* sorrow **grames**
GRAMMA *n* pasture grass of the South American plains
GRAMMAR *n*
GRAMMAS ▸ **gramma**
GRAMME = **grame**
GRAMMES ▸ **gram**
GRAMP *n* grandfather
GRAMPA *variant of* ▸ **grandpa**
GRAMPAS ▸ **grampa**
GRAMPS ▸ **gramp**
GRAMPUS *n* dolphin-like mammal
GRAMS ▸ **gram**
GRAN *n*
GRANA ▸ **granum**
GRANARY *n*
GRAND *adj, n*
GRANDAD *n*
GRANDAM *n* archaic word for grandmother
GRANDE *feminine form of* ▸ **grand**
GRANDEE *n* Spanish nobleman of the highest rank
GRANDER ▸ **grand**
GRANDLY ▸ **grand**
GRANDMA *n*
GRANDPA *n* grandfather
GRANDS ▸ **grand**
GRANFER *n* grandfather
GRANGE *n* country house with farm buildings
GRANGER *n* keeper or member of a grange
GRANGES ▸ **grange**
GRANITA *n* Italian iced drink
GRANITE *n*
GRANNAM *n* old woman
GRANNIE *vb* defeat without conceding a single point
GRANNOM *n* type of caddis fly esteemed as a bait by anglers
GRANNY *n, vb*
GRANOLA *n* muesli-like breakfast cereal
GRANS ▸ **gran**
GRANT *vb, n* **granted**
GRANTEE *n* person to whom a grant is made
GRANTER ▸ **grant**
GRANTOR *n* person who makes a grant
GRANTS ▸ **grant**
GRANULE *n* small grain
GRANUM *n* membrane layers in a chloroplast
GRAPE *n, vb* **graped**
GRAPERY *n* building where grapes are grown
GRAPES *n* abnormal growth on the fetlock of a horse
GRAPEY ▸ **grape**
GRAPH *n, vb* **graphed**
GRAPHIC *adj*
GRAPHS ▸ **graph**
GRAPIER ▸ **grape**
GRAPING ▸ **grape**
GRAPLE = **grapple**
GRAPLES ▸ **graple**
GRAPLIN = **grapnel**
GRAPNEL *n* device with several hooks
GRAPPA *n* type of spirit **grappas**
GRAPPLE *vb, n*
GRAPY ▸ **grape**
GRASP *vb, n* **grasped, grasper, grasps**
GRASS *n, vb* **grassed**
GRASSER *n* police informant
GRASSES ▸ **grass**
GRASSUM *n* in Scots law, sum paid when taking a lease
GRASSY *adj* covered with, containing, or

resembling grass
GRASTE *archaic past participle of* ▸ **grace**
GRAT ▸ **greet**
GRATE *vb, n* **grated**
GRATER *n* **graters**
GRATES ▸ **grate**
GRATIFY *vb, adj*
GRATIN *n* crust of browned breadcrumbs
GRATINE *adj* cooked au gratin
GRATING *adj, n*
GRATINS ▸ **gratin**
GRATIS *adj*
GRAUNCH *vb* crush or destroy
GRAUPEL *n* soft hail or snow pellets
GRAV *n* unit of acceleration
GRAVE *n, adj, vb, adv* **graved**
GRAVEL *n, vb* **gravels**
GRAVELY ▸ **grave**
GRAVEN ▸ **grave**
GRAVER *n* any of various tools **gravers**
GRAVES ▸ **grave**
GRAVEST ▸ **grave**
GRAVID *adj* pregnant
GRAVIDA *n* pregnant woman
GRAVIES ▸ **gravy**
GRAVING ▸ **grave**
GRAVIS *adj as in* **myasthenia gravis** chronic muscle-weakening disease
GRAVITY *n*
GRAVLAX *n* dry-cured salmon
GRAVS ▸ **grav**
GRAVURE *n* method of intaglio printing
GRAVY *n*
GRAY = **grey**
GRAYED ▸ **gray**
GRAYER ▸ **gray**
GRAYEST ▸ **gray**
GRAYFLY *n* trumpet fly
GRAYING ▸ **gray**
GRAYISH ▸ **gray**
GRAYLAG = **greylag**
GRAYLE *n* holy grail **grayles**
GRAYLY ▸ **gray**
GRAYOUT *n* impairment of vision due to lack of oxygen
GRAYS ▸ **gray**
GRAZE *vb, n* **grazed, grazer, grazers, grazes**
GRAZIER *n* person who feeds cattle for market
GRAZING *n* land on which grass for livestock is grown
GREASE *n, vb* **greased**
GREASER *n* mechanic, esp of motor vehicles
GREASES ▸ **grease**
GREASY *adj* covered with or containing grease ▹ *n* shearer
GREAT *adj* large in size or number ▹ *n* distinguished person
GREATEN *vb* make or become great
GREATER ▸ **great**
GREATLY ▸ **great**
GREATS ▸ **great**
GREAVE *n* piece of armour for the shin ▹ *vb* grieve **greaved**
GREAVES *pl n* residue left after the rendering of tallow
GREBE *n* **grebes**
GREBO ▸ **greebo**
GREBOS ▸ **grebo**
GRECE *n* flight of steps **greces, grecian**
GRECISE = **graecize**
GRECIZE = **graecize**
GRECQUE *n* ornament of Greek origin
GREE *n* superiority or victory ▹ *vb* come or cause to come to agreement or harmony
GREEBO *n* unkempt or dirty-looking young man
GREECE = **grece**
GREECES ▸ **greece**
GREED *n* **greeds**
GREEDY *adj*
GREEING ▸ **gree**
GREEK *vb* represent text as grey lines on a computer screen **greeked**
GREEN *adj, n, vb* **greened**
GREENER *n* recent immigrant
GREENIE *n* conservationist
GREENLY ▸ **green**
GREENS ▸ **green**
GREENTH *n* greenness
GREENY ▸ **green**
GREES ▸ **gree**
GREESE = **grece**
GREESES ▸ **greese**
GREET *vb, n* **greete, greeted**
GREETER *n* person who

greets people
GREETES ▶ **greete**
GREETS ▶ **greet**
GREGALE *n* northeasterly wind occurring in the Mediterranean
GREGE *vb* make heavy
GREGO *n* short, thick jacket **gregos**
GREIGE *adj* (of a fabric or material) not yet dyed ▷ *n* unbleached or undyed cloth or yarn **greiges**
GREIN *vb* desire fervently **greined, greins**
GREISEN *n* light-coloured metamorphic rock
GREISLY = **grisly**
GREMIAL *n* type of cloth used in Mass
GREMLIN *n* imaginary being
GREMMIE *n* young surfer **gremmy**
GREN = **grin**
GRENADE *n*
GRENNED ▶ **gren**
GRENS ▶ **gren**
GRESE = **grece**
GRESES ▶ **grese**
GREVE = **greave**
GREVES ▶ **greve**
GREW *vb* shudder
GREWED ▶ **grow**
GREWING ▶ **grow**
GREWS ▶ **grow**
GREX *n* group of plants **grexes**
GREY *adj, n, vb* **greyed, greyer, greyest**
GREYHEN *n* female of the black grouse
GREYING ▶ **grey**
GREYISH ▶ **grey**
GREYLAG *n* large grey goose
GREYLY ▶ **grey**
GREYS ▶ **grey**
GRIBBLE *n* type of small marine crustacean
GRICE *vb* collect objects concerned with railways ▷ *n* object collected or place visited by a railway enthusiast **griced, gricer, gricers, grices, gricing**
GRID *n* **gridded**
GRIDDER *n* American football player
GRIDDLE *n* flat iron plate for cooking ▷ *vb* cook (food) on a griddle
GRIDE *vb* grate or scrape harshly ▷ *n* harsh or piercing sound **grided, grides, griding**
GRIDS ▶ **grid**
GRIECE = **grece**
GRIECED ▶ **griece**
GRIECES ▶ **griece**
GRIEF *n*
GRIEFER *n* online gamer who spoils the game for others on purpose
GRIEFS ▶ **grief**
GRIESIE = **grisy**
GRIESLY = **grisy**
GRIESY = **grisy**
GRIEVE *vb, n* **grieved, griever, grieves**
GRIFF *n* information
GRIFFE *n* carved ornament at the base of a column **griffes**
GRIFFIN *n* mythical monster **griffon**
GRIFFS ▶ **griff**
GRIFT *vb* swindle **grifted, grifter, grifts**
GRIG *n* lively person ▷ *vb* fish for grigs **grigged**
GRIGRI *n* African talisman, amulet, or charm **grigris**
GRIGS ▶ **grig**
GRIKE *n* fissure in rock **grikes**
GRILL *n, vb*
GRILLE *n*
GRILLED *adj* cooked on a grill or gridiron
GRILLER ▶ **grill**
GRILLES ▶ **grille**
GRILLS ▶ **grill**
GRILSE *n* salmon on its first return from the sea to fresh water **grilses**
GRIM *adj*
GRIMACE *n, vb*
GRIME *n, vb* **grimed, grimes, grimier, grimily, griming**
GRIMLY ▶ **grim**
GRIMMER ▶ **grim**
GRIMY ▶ **grime**
GRIN *vb, n*
GRINCH *n* person whose attitude has a depressing effect
GRIND *vb, n* **grinded**
GRINDER *n* device for grinding substances
GRINDS ▶ **grind**
GRINNED ▶ **grin**
GRINNER ▶ **grin**

GRINS ▸ **grin**
GRIOT *n* (in W Africa) member of a caste recording tribal history **griots**
GRIP *n, vb*
GRIPE *vb* complain persistently ▹ *n* complaint **griped, griper, gripers, gripes**
GRIPEY *adj* causing gripes **gripier**
GRIPING ▸ **gripe**
GRIPLE = **gripple**
GRIPMAN *n* cable-car operator **gripmen**
GRIPPE *former name for* > **influenza**
GRIPPED ▸ **grip**
GRIPPER ▸ **grip**
GRIPPES ▸ **grippe**
GRIPPLE *adj* greedy ▹ *n* hook
GRIPPY *adj* having grip
GRIPS ▸ **grip**
GRIPT *archaic variant of* ▸ **gripped**
GRIPY = **gripey**
GRIS = **grece**
GRISE *vb* shudder **grised**
GRISELY = **grisly**
GRISES ▸ **grise**
GRISING ▸ **grise**
GRISKIN *n* lean part of a loin of pork
GRISLED *another word for* > **grizzled**
GRISLY *adj, n*
GRISON *n* type of mammal **grisons**
GRIST *n*
GRISTER *n* device for grinding grain
GRISTLE *n* **gristly**
GRISTS ▸ **grist**
GRISY *adj* grim
GRIT *n, vb, adj*
GRITH *n* security or peace guaranteed for a period of time **griths**
GRITS ▸ **grit**
GRITTED ▸ **grit**
GRITTER *n* vehicle that spreads grit on the roads
GRITTY *adj* courageous and tough
GRIVET *n* E African monkey **grivets**
GRIZE = **grece**
GRIZES ▸ **grize**
GRIZZLE *vb, n*
GRIZZLY *n* large American bear ▹ *adj* somewhat grey
GROAN *n, vb* **groaned**
GROANER *n* person or thing that groans
GROANS ▸ **groan**
GROAT *n* fourpenny piece
GROATS *pl n* hulled and crushed grain of various cereals
GROCER *n* **grocers**
GROCERY *n*
GROCKED ▸ **grokked**
GROCKLE *n* tourist in SW England
GRODIER ▸ **grody**
GRODY *adj* unpleasant
GROG *n, vb* **grogged**
GROGGY *adj*
GROGRAM *n* coarse fabric
GROGS ▸ **grog**
GROIN *n, vb* **groined, groins**
GROK *vb* understand completely and intuitively
GROKED ▸ **grokked**
GROKING > **grokking**
GROKKED ▸ **grok**
GROKS ▸ **grok**
GROMA *n* Roman surveying instrument **gromas**
GROMET = **grommet**
GROMETS ▸ **gromet**
GROMMET *n* ring or eyelet
GRONE *obsolete word for* ▸ **groan**
GRONED ▸ **grone**
GRONES ▸ **grone**
GRONING ▸ **grone**
GROOF *n* face, or front of the body **groofs**
GROOLY *adj* gruesome
GROOM *n, vb* **groomed, groomer, grooms**
GROOVE *n* **grooved**
GROOVER *n* device that makes grooves
GROOVES ▸ **groove**
GROOVY *adj* attractive or exciting
GROPE *vb, n* **groped**
GROPER *n* type of large fish of warm and tropical seas **gropers**
GROPES ▸ **grope**
GROPING ▸ **grope**
GROSER *n* gooseberry **grosers, grosert, groset**
GROSETS ▸ **groset**
GROSS *adj, n, vb, interj* **grossed, grosser,**

grosses, grossly
GROSZ *n* Polish monetary unit **grosze, groszy**
GROT *n* rubbish **grots**
GROTTO *n* **grottos**
GROTTY *adj*
GROUCH *vb, n*
GROUCHY *adj* bad-tempered
GROUF = **groof**
GROUFS ▸ **grouf**
GROUGH *n* natural channel or fissure in a peat moor **groughs**
GROUND *n, adj, vb* **grounds**
GROUP *n, vb* **grouped**
GROUPER *n* large edible sea fish
GROUPIE *n* ardent fan of a celebrity or of a sport or activity
GROUPS ▸ **group**
GROUPY = **groupie**
GROUSE *n, vb, adj* **groused, grouser, grouses**
GROUT *n* thin mortar ▹ *vb* fill up with grout **grouted, grouter**
GROUTS *pl n* sediment or grounds
GROUTY *adj* sullen or surly
GROVE *n* **groved**
GROVEL *vb* **grovels**
GROVES ▸ **grove**
GROVET *n* wrestling hold **grovets**
GROW *vb*
GROWER *n* person who grows plants **growers**
GROWING ▸ **grow**
GROWL *vb, n* **growled**
GROWLER *n* person, animal, or thing that growls
GROWLS ▸ **growl**
GROWLY ▸ **growl**
GROWN ▸ **grow**
GROWNUP *n* adult
GROWS ▸ **grow**
GROWTH *n, adj* **growths**
GROWTHY *adj* rapid-growing
GROYNE *n* **groynes**
GROZING *adj as in* **grozing iron** iron for smoothing joints between lead pipes
GRRL *n as in* **riot grrl** young woman who enjoys feminist punk rock **grrls**

> This slang term for a girl who likes loud rock music can come in useful when you are short of vowels. And it can also be spelt **grrrl**.

GRRRL *n as in* **riot grrrl** young woman who enjoys feminist punk rock **grrrls**
GRUB *n, vb* **grubbed**
GRUBBER *n* person who grubs
GRUBBLE = **grabble**
GRUBBY *adj*
GRUBS ▸ **grub**
GRUDGE *vb, n, adj* **grudged, grudger, grudges**
GRUE *n* shiver or shudder ▹ *vb* shiver or shudder **grued, grueing**
GRUEL *n, vb* **grueled, grueler, gruels**
GRUES ▸ **grue**
GRUFE = **groof**
GRUFES ▸ **grufe**
GRUFF *adj, vb* **gruffed, gruffer, gruffly, gruffs**
GRUFFY *adj* gruff
GRUFTED *adj* dirty
GRUGRU *n* tropical American palm **grugrus**
GRUING ▸ **grue**
GRUM *adj* surly
GRUMBLE *vb, n* **grumbly**
GRUME *n* clot **grumes**
GRUMLY ▸ **grum**
GRUMMER ▸ **grum**
GRUMMET = **grommet**
GRUMOSE = **grumous**
GRUMOUS *adj* (esp of plant parts) consisting of granular tissue
GRUMP *n* surly or bad-tempered person ▹ *vb* complain or grumble **grumped**
GRUMPH *vb* grunt **grumphs**
GRUMPHY = **grumphie**
GRUMPS ▸ **grump**
GRUMPY *adj*
GRUND *n as in* **grund mail** payment for right of burial
GRUNGE *n* style of rock music with a fuzzy guitar sound
GRUNGER *n* fan of grunge music
GRUNGES ▸ **grunge**
GRUNGEY *adj* messy or dirty

GRUNGY *adj* squalid or seedy
GRUNION *n* Californian marine fish that spawns on beaches
GRUNT *vb, n* **grunted**
GRUNTER *n* person or animal that grunts, esp a pig
GRUNTLE *vb* grunt or groan
GRUNTS ▸ **grunt**
GRUSHIE *adj* healthy and strong
GRUTCH *vb* grudge
GRUTTEN ▸ **greet**
GRUYERE *n* hard flat whole-milk cheese with holes
GRYCE = **grice**
GRYCES ▸ **gryce**
GRYDE = **gride**
GRYDED ▸ **gryde**
GRYDES ▸ **gryde**
GRYDING ▸ **gryde**
GRYESY *adj* grey
GRYFON = **griffin**
GRYFONS ▸ **gryfon**
GRYKE = **grike**
GRYKES ▸ **gryke**
GRYPE = **gripe**
GRYPES ▸ **gripe**
GRYPHON = **griffin**
GRYPT *archaic form of* ▸ **gripped**
GRYSBOK *n* small antelope
GRYSELY = **grisly**
GRYSIE = **grisy**
GU = **gju**
GUACO *n* any of several plants used as an antidote to snakebite **guacos**
GUAIAC = **guaiacum**
GUAIACS > **guaiacum**
GUAN *n* type of bird of Central and S America
GUANA *another word for* ▸ **iguana**
GUANACO *n* S American animal related to the llama
GUANAS ▸ **guana**
GUANASE *n* type of enzyme
GUANAY *n* type of cormorant **guanays**
GUANGO *n* rain tree **guangos**
GUANIN = **guanine**
GUANINE *n* white almost insoluble compound **guanins**
GUANO *n* dried sea-bird manure **guanos**
GUANS ▸ **guan**
GUANXI *n* Chinese social concept **guanxis**
GUAR *n* Indian plant
GUARANA *n* type of shrub native to Venezuela
GUARANI *n* standard monetary unit of Paraguay
GUARD *vb, n*
GUARDED *adj*
GUARDEE *n* guardsman
GUARDER ▸ **guard**
GUARDS ▸ **guard**
GUARISH *vb* heal
GUARS ▸ **guar**
GUAVA *n* **guavas**
GUAYULE *n* bushy shrub of the southwestern US
GUB *n* white man ▹ *vb* hit or defeat **gubbah**
GUBBAHS ▸ **gubbah**
GUBBED ▸ **gub**
GUBBING ▸ **gub**
GUBBINS *n* object of little or no value
GUBS ▸ **gub**
GUCK *n* slimy matter
GUCKIER ▸ **gucky**
GUCKS ▸ **guck**
GUCKY *adj* slimy and mucky
GUDDLE *vb* catch (fish) with the hands ▹ *n* muddle **guddled, guddles**
GUDE *Scots word for* ▸ **good**
GUDEMAN *n* male householder **gudemen**
GUDES *n* goods
GUDGEON *n* small freshwater fish ▹ *vb* trick or cheat
GUE = **gju**
GUELDER *adj as in* **guelder rose** kind of shrub
GUENON *n* slender Old World monkey **guenons**
GUERDON *n* reward or payment ▹ *vb* give a guerdon to
GUEREZA *n* handsome colobus monkey
GUERITE *n* turret used by a sentry
GUES ▸ **gue**
GUESS *vb, n* **guessed, guesser, guesses**
GUEST *n, vb* **guested**
GUESTEN *vb* stay as a

guest in someone's house
GUESTS ▸ guest
GUFF *n* nonsense
GUFFAW *n, vb* **guffaws**
GUFFIE *Scots word for* **▸ pig**
GUFFIES ▸ guffie
GUFFS ▸ guff
GUGA *n* gannet chick **gugas**
GUGGLE *vb* drink making a gurgling sound **guggled, guggles**
GUGLET = **goglet**
GUGLETS ▸ guglet
GUICHET *n* grating, hatch, or small opening in a wall
GUID *Scot word for* **▸ good**
GUIDAGE *n* guidance
GUIDE *n, vb* **guided, guider, guiders, guides, guiding**
GUIDON *n* small pennant **guidons**
GUIDS *n* possessions
GUILD *n*
GUILDER *n* former monetary unit of the Netherlands
GUILDRY *n* in Scotland, corporation of merchants
GUILDS ▸ guild
GUILE *n, vb* **guiled**
GUILER *n* deceiver **guilers**
GUILES ▸ guile
GUILING ▸ guile
GUILT *n* **guilts**
GUILTY *adj*
GUIMP = **guimpe**
GUIMPE *n* short blouse worn under a pinafore dress ▹ *vb* make with gimp **guimped, guimpes**
GUIMPS ▸ guimp
GUINEA *n* **guineas**
GUIPURE *n* heavy lace
GUIRO *n* percussion instrument made from a hollow gourd **guiros**
GUISARD *n* guiser
GUISE *n, vb* **guised**
GUISER *n* mummer, esp at Christmas or Halloween revels **guisers**
GUISES ▸ guise
GUISING ▸ guise
GUITAR *n* **guitars**
GUIZER = **guiser**
GUIZERS ▸ guizer
GUL *n* design used in oriental carpets
GULA *n* gluttony
GULAG *n* forced-labour camp **gulags**
GULAR *adj* of or situated in the throat or oesophagus
GULAS ▸ gula
GULCH *n* deep narrow valley ▹ *vb* swallow fast **gulched, gulches**
GULDEN = **guilder**
GULDENS ▸ gulden
GULE *Scots word for* > **marigold**
GULES *n* red in heraldry
GULET *n* wooden Turkish sailing boat **gulets**
GULF *n, vb* **gulfed, gulfier, gulfing, gulfs, gulfy**
GULL *n, vb* **gulled**
GULLER *n* deceiver **gullers**
GULLERY *n* breeding-place for gulls
GULLET *n* **gullets**
GULLEY = **gully**
GULLEYS ▸ gulley
GULLIED ▸ gully
GULLIES ▸ gully
GULLING ▸ gull
GULLISH *adj* stupid
GULLS ▸ gull
GULLY *n, vb*
GULP *vb, n* **gulped, gulper, gulpers**
GULPH *archaic word for* **▸ gulf**
GULPHS ▸ gulph
GULPIER, gulping, gulps, gulpy ▸ gulp
GULS ▸ gul
GULY *adj* relating to gules
GUM *n, vb*
GUMBALL *n* round piece of chewing gum
GUMBO *n* mucilaginous pods of okra
GUMBOIL *n* abscess on the gum
GUMBOOT *n*
GUMBOS ▸ gumbo
GUMDROP *n* hard jelly-like sweet
GUMLESS ▸ gum
GUMLIKE ▸ gum
GUMLINE *n* line where gums meet teeth
GUMMA *n* rubbery tumour **gummas, gummata**
GUMMED ▸ gum

GUMMER *n* punch-cutting tool **gummers**
GUMMIER ▸ gummy
GUMMIES ▸ gummy
GUMMILY ▸ gummy
GUMMING ▸ gum
GUMMITE *n* orange or yellowish amorphous secondary mineral
GUMMOSE = gummous
GUMMOUS *adj* resembling or consisting of gum
GUMMY *adj* toothless ▹ *n* type of small crustacean-eating shark
GUMNUT *n* hardened seed container of the gumtree **gumnuts**
GUMP *vb* guddle **gumped, gumping, gumps**
GUMS ▸ gum
GUMSHOE *n* waterproof overshoe ▹ *vb* act stealthily
GUMTREE *n*
GUMWEED *n* any of several yellow-flowered plants
GUMWOOD = gumtree
GUN *n, vb*
GUNBOAT *n*
GUNDIES ▸ gundy
GUNDOG *n* dog trained to work with a hunter or gamekeeper **gundogs**
GUNDY *n* toffee
GUNFIRE *n*
GUNG *adj as in* **gung ho** extremely or excessively enthusiastic about something
GUNGE *n* sticky unpleasant substance ▹ *vb* block or encrust with gunge **gunged, gunges, gungier, gunging, gungy**
GUNITE *n* mortar sprayed in a very dense concrete layer **gunites**
GUNK *n* slimy or filthy substance **gunkier, gunks, gunky**
GUNLESS ▸ gun
GUNLOCK *n* mechanism in some firearms
GUNMAN *n* armed criminal **gunmen**
GUNNAGE *n* number of guns carried by a warship
GUNNED ▸ gun
GUNNEL = gunwale
GUNNELS ▸ gunnel
GUNNEN ▸ gun
GUNNER *n* artillery soldier
GUNNERA *n* type of herbaceous plant
GUNNERS ▸ gunner
GUNNERY *n* use or science of large guns
GUNNIES ▸ gunny
GUNNING ▸ gun
GUNNY *n* strong coarse fabric used for sacks
GUNPLAY *n* use of firearms, as by criminals
GUNPORT *n* porthole or other opening for a gun
GUNROOM *n* the mess allocated to junior officers
GUNS ▸ gun
GUNSEL *n* catamite **gunsels**
GUNSHIP *n* ship or helicopter armed with heavy guns
GUNSHOT *n*
GUNTER *n* type of gaffing **gunters**
GUNWALE *n*
GUNYAH *n* **gunyahs**
GUP *n* gossip
GUPPIES ▸ guppy
GUPPY *n*
GUPS ▸ gup
GUQIN *n* type of Chinese zither **guqins**
GUR *n* unrefined cane sugar
GURAMI = gourami
GURAMIS ▸ gurami
GURGE *vb* swallow up **gurged, gurges, gurging**
GURGLE *n, vb* **gurgled, gurgles**
GURGLET = goglet
GURJUN *n* S or SE Asian tree that yields a resin **gurjuns**
GURL *vb* snarl **gurled**
GURLET *n* type of pickaxe **gurlets**
GURLIER ▸ gurly
GURLING ▸ gurl
GURLS ▸ gurl
GURLY *adj* stormy
GURN *variant spelling of* **▸ girn**
GURNARD *n* spiny armour-headed sea fish
GURNED ▸ gurn

GURNET = **gurnard**
GURNETS ▶ **gurnard**
GURNEY *n* wheeled stretcher for transporting hospital patients **gurneys**
GURNING ▶ **gurn**
GURNS ▶ **gurn**
GURRAH *n* type of coarse muslin **gurrahs**
GURRIER *n* low-class tough ill-mannered person
GURRIES ▶ **gurry**
GURRY *n* dog-fight
GURS ▶ **gur**
GURSH *n* unit of currency in Saudi Arabia **gurshes**
GURU *n*
GURUDOM *n* state of being a guru
GURUISM ▶ **guru**
GURUS ▶ **guru**
GUS ▶ **gu**
GUSH *vb, n* **gushed**
GUSHER *n* spurting oil well **gushers**
GUSHES ▶ **gush**
GUSHIER ▶ **gushy**
GUSHILY ▶ **gushy**
GUSHING ▶ **gush**
GUSHY *adj* displaying excessive sentimentality
GUSLA *n* Balkan single-stringed musical instrument
GUSLAR *n* player of the gusla **guslars**
GUSLAS ▶ **gusla**
GUSLE = **gusla**
GUSLES ▶ **gusle**
GUSLI *n* Russian harp-like musical instrument **guslis**
GUSSET *n, vb* **gussets**
GUSSIE *n* young pig
GUSSIED ▶ **gussy**
GUSSIES ▶ **gussy**
GUSSY *vb* dress elaborately
GUST *n, vb* **gusted**
GUSTFUL *adj* tasty
GUSTIE *adj* tasty
GUSTIER ▶ **gusty**
GUSTILY ▶ **gusty**
GUSTING ▶ **gust**
GUSTO *n* **gustoes, gustos**
GUSTS ▶ **gust**
GUSTY *adj* blustery weather
GUT *n, vb, adj*
GUTCHER *n* grandfather
GUTFUL *n* bellyful **gutfuls**
GUTLESS *adj* cowardly
GUTLIKE ▶ **gut**
GUTROT *n* diarrhoea **gutrots**
GUTS *vb* **gutsed**
GUTSER *n as in* **come a gutser** fall heavily to the ground **gutsers**
GUTSES ▶ **guts**
GUTSFUL *n* bellyful
GUTSIER ▶ **gutsy**
GUTSILY ▶ **gutsy**
GUTSING ▶ **guts**
GUTSY *adj* courageous
GUTTA *n* small drop-like ornament **guttae, guttas**
GUTTATE *adj* covered with small drops or drop-like markings ▷ *vb* exude droplets of liquid
GUTTED ▶ **gut**
GUTTER *n, vb* **gutters, guttery**
GUTTIER ▶ **gutty**
GUTTIES ▶ **gutty**
GUTTING ▶ **gut**
GUTTLE *vb* eat greedily **guttled, guttler, guttles**
GUTTY *n* urchin or delinquent ▷ *adj* courageous
GUTZER *n* bad fall **gutzers**
GUV *informal name for* > **governor**
GUVS ▶ **guv**
GUY *n, vb* **guyed, guying**
GUYLE = **guile; guyled, guyler, guylers, guyles**
GUYLINE *n* guy rope
GUYLING ▶ **guyle**
GUYOT *n* flat-topped submarine mountain **guyots**
GUYS ▶ **guy**
GUYSE = **guise**
GUYSES ▶ **guyse**
GUZZLE *vb* **guzzled**
GUZZLER *n* person or thing that guzzles
GUZZLES ▶ **guzzle**
GWEDUC = **geoduck**
GWEDUCK = **geoduck**
GWEDUCS ▶ **gweduck**
GWINE *dialect form of* ▶ **going**
GWINIAD *n* powan
GWYNIAD *n* type of freshwater white fish

GYAL = **gayal**
GYALS ▸ **gyal**
GYBE *vb* (of a sail) swing suddenly from one side to the other ▹ *n* instance of gybing **gybed, gybes, gybing**
GYELD *n* guild **gyelds**
GYLDEN *adj* golden
GYM *n*
GYMBAL = **gimbal**
GYMBALS ▸ **gymbal**
GYMMAL = **gimmal**
GYMMALS ▸ **gymmal**
GYMNAST *n*
GYMNIC *adj* gymnastic
GYMPIE *n* tall tree with stinging hairs on its leaves **gympies**
GYMS ▸ **gym**
GYMSLIP *n* tunic or pinafore formerly worn by schoolgirls
GYNAE *adj* gynaecological ▹ *n* gynaecology **gynaes**
GYNECIA > **gynecium**
GYNECIC *adj* relating to the female sex
GYNIE *n* gynaecology **gynies**
GYNNEY *n* guinea hen **gynneys**
GYNNIES ▸ **gynny**
GYNNY = **gynney**
GYNY *n* gynaecology
GYOZA *n* Japanese fried dumpling **gyozas**
GYP *vb* swindle, cheat, or defraud ▹ *n* act of cheating

> This little word, meaning to swindle, can be useful when you are short of vowels.

GYPLURE *n* synthetic version of the gypsy moth sex pheromone
GYPPED ▸ **gyp**
GYPPER ▸ **gyp**
GYPPERS ▸ **gyp**
GYPPIE = **gippy**
GYPPIES ▸ **gyppy**
GYPPING ▸ **gyp**
GYPPY = **gippy**
GYPS ▸ **gyp**
GYPSIED ▸ **gypsy**
GYPSIES ▸ **gypsy**
GYPSTER *n* swindler
GYPSUM *n* **gypsums**
GYPSY *n, vb*
GYRAL *adj* having a circular, spiral, or rotating motion **gyrally**
GYRANT *adj* gyrating
GYRASE *n* topoisomerase enzyme **gyrases**
GYRATE *vb, adj* **gyrated, gyrates**
GYRATOR *n* electronic circuit that inverts the impedance
GYRE *n* circular or spiral movement or path ▹ *vb* whirl **gyred**
GYRENE *n* nickname for a member of the US Marine Corps **gyrenes**
GYRES ▸ **gyre**
GYRI ▸ **gyrus**
GYRING ▸ **gyre**
GYRO *n* gyrocompass
GYROCAR *n* two-wheeled car
GYRON = **giron**
GYRONIC ▸ **gyron**
GYRONNY = **gironny**
GYRONS ▸ **gyron**
GYROS ▸ **gyro**
GYROSE *adj* marked with sinuous lines
GYROUS *adj* gyrose
GYRUS *n* convolution **gyruses**
GYTE *n* spoilt child **gytes**
GYTRASH *n* spirit that haunts lonely roads
GYTTJA *n* sediment on lake bottom **gyttjas**
GYVE *vb* shackle or fetter ▹ *n* fetters **gyved, gyves, gyving**

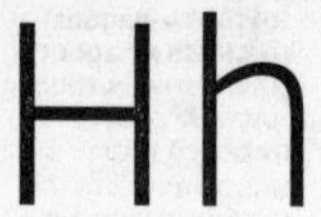

H forms a two-letter word in front of every vowel except **U** (and you can make **uh** with **U**), making it a versatile tile when you want to form words in more than one direction. It also goes with **M** to make **hm**. As **H** is worth 4 points on its own, you can earn some very high scores by doing this: even **ha, he, hi** and **ho** will give 5 points each. There are lots of good short words beginning with **H**, like **haw, hew, how, hay, hey** and **hoy** (9 each), while **hyp** can be useful if you are short of vowels. More high-scoring words with **H** include **haj, hex** and **hox** for 13 points each, and never forget the invaluable **zho** for 15 points.

HA *interj*
HAAF *n* fishing ground off the Shetland and Orkney Islands **haafs**
HAAR *n* cold sea mist or fog off the North Sea **haars**
HABDABS *n* highly nervous state
HABILE *adj* skilful
HABIT *n, vb*
HABITAN = **habitant**
HABITAT *n*
HABITED *adj* dressed in a habit
HABITS ▸ **habit**
HABITUE *n* frequent visitor to a place
HABITUS *n* general physical state
HABLE *old form of* ▸ **able**
HABOOB *n* sandstorm **haboobs**
HABU *n* large venomous snake **habus**
HACEK *n* pronunciation symbol in Slavonic language **haceks**
HACHIS *n* hash
HACHURE *n* shading drawn on a map to indicate steepness of a hill ▹ *vb* mark or show by hachures
HACK *vb, n, adj*
HACKBUT *another word for* > **arquebus**
HACKED ▸ **hack**
HACKEE *n* chipmunk **hackees**
HACKER *n* **hackers**
HACKERY *n* journalism
HACKIE *n* US word meaning cab driver **hackies**
HACKING ▸ **hack**
HACKLE = **heckle**
HACKLED ▸ **hackle**
HACKLER ▸ **hackle**
HACKLES *pl n*
HACKLET *n* kittiwake
HACKLY *adj* rough or jagged
HACKMAN *n* taxi driver **hackmen**
HACKNEY *n* taxi ▹ *vb* make commonplace and banal by too frequent use
HACKS ▸ **hack**
HACKSAW *n, vb*
HAD *vb* Scots form of hold

HADAL *adj* denoting very deep zones of the oceans
HADARIM ▸ **heder**
HADAWAY *sentence substitute* exclamation urging the hearer to refrain from delay
HADDEN ▸ **have**
HADDEST = **hadst**
HADDIE *n* finnan haddock **haddies**
HADDING ▸ **have**
HADDOCK *n*
HADE *n* angle made to the vertical by the plane of a fault or vein ▹ *vb* incline from the vertical **haded**
HADEDAH *n* large grey-green S African ibis
HADES ▸ **hade**
HADING ▸ **hade**
HADITH *n* body of legend about Mohammed and his followers **hadiths**
HADJ = **hajj**
HADJEE = **hadji**
HADJEES ▸ **hadjee**
HADJES ▸ **hadj**
HADJI = **hajji**
HADJIS ▸ **hadji**
HADROME *n* part of xylem
HADRON *n* type of elementary particle **hadrons**
HADS ▸ **have**
HADST *singular form of the past tense (indicative mood) of* ▸ **have**
HAE *Scot variant of* ▸ **have**
HAED ▸ **hae**
HAEING ▸ **hae**
HAEM *n* red organic pigment containing ferrous iron
HAEMAL *adj* of the blood
HAEMIC = **haematic**
HAEMIN *n* haematin chloride **haemins**
HAEMOID = **haematoid**
HAEMONY *n* plant mentioned in Milton's poetry
HAEMS ▸ **haem**
HAEN ▸ **hae**
HAERES = **heres**
HAES ▸ **hae**
HAET *n* whit **haets**
HAFF *n* lagoon
HAFFET *n* side of head **haffets, haffit**
HAFFITS ▸ **haffit**
HAFFLIN = **halfling**
HAFFS ▸ **haff**
HAFIZ *n* title for a person who knows the Koran by heart **hafizes**
HAFNIUM *n* metallic element found in zirconium ores
HAFT *n* handle of an axe, knife, or dagger ▹ *vb* provide with a haft
HAFTARA = **haftarah**
HAFTED, hafter, hafters, hafting, hafts ▸ **haft**
HAG *n, vb*
HAGADIC > **haggadic**
HAGBOLT = **hackbolt**
HAGBORN *adj* born of a witch
HAGBUSH = **arquebus**
HAGBUT ▸ **hagbut**
HAGBUTS ▸ **hagbut**
HAGDEN = **hackbolt**
HAGDENS ▸ **hagden**
HAGDON = **hackbolt**
HAGDONS ▸ **hagdon**
HAGDOWN = **hackbolt**
HAGFISH *n* any of various primitive eel-like vertebrates
HAGG *n* boggy place
HAGGADA = **haggadah**
HAGGARD *adj, n*
HAGGED ▸ **hag**
HAGGING ▸ **hag**
HAGGIS *n*
HAGGISH ▸ **hag**
HAGGLE *vb* **haggled, haggler, haggles**
HAGGS ▸ **hagg**
HAGLET = **hacklet**
HAGLETS ▸ **haglet**
HAGLIKE ▸ **hag**
HAGRIDE *vb* torment or obsess **hagrode**
HAGS ▸ **hag**
HAH = **ha**
HAHA *n* wall or other boundary marker that is set in a ditch **hahas**
HAHNIUM *n* transuranic element
HAHS ▸ **hah**
HAICK = **haik**
HAICKS ▸ **haick**
HAIDUK *n* rural brigand **haiduks**
HAIK *n* Arab's outer garment **haika**
HAIKAI = **haiku**
HAIKS ▸ **haik**
HAIKU *n* Japanese verse form in 17 syllables **haikus**

HAIL *n, vb, sentence substitute* **hailed, hailer, hailers, hailier, hailing, hails, haily**
HAIMISH = **heimish**
HAIN *vb* Scots word meaning save
HAINCH *Scots form of* ▸ **haunch**
HAINED ▸ **hain**
HAINING ▸ **hain**
HAINS ▸ **hain**
HAINT = **haunt**
HAINTS ▸ **haint**
HAIQUE = **haik**
HAIQUES ▸ **haik**
HAIR *n, vb*
HAIRCAP *n* type of moss
HAIRCUT *n*
HAIRDO *n* **hairdos**
HAIRED *adj* with hair
HAIRIER ▸ **hairy**
HAIRIF *another name for* > **cleavers**
HAIRIFS ▸ **hairif**
HAIRING ▸ **hair**
HAIRNET *n* any of several kinds of light netting worn over the hair
HAIRPIN *n*
HAIRS ▸ **hair**
HAIRST *Scots form of* ▸ **harvest**
HAIRSTS ▸ **hairst**
HAIRY *adj*
HAITH *interj* Scots oath
HAJ = **hadj**

A **haj** is a Muslim pilgrimage to Mecca, and one of the key words to remember for using the J. It can also be spelt **hadj** or **hajj**, and one who makes a haj is called a **hadjee, hadji, haji** or **hajji**.

HAJES ▸ **haj**
HAJI = **hajji**
HAJIS ▸ **haji**
HAJJ *n*
HAJJAH *n* Muslim woman who has made a pilgrimage to Mecca **hajjahs**
HAJJES ▸ **hajj**
HAJJI *n* Muslim who has made a pilgrimage to Mecca **hajjis**
HAKA *n*
HAKAM *n* text written by a rabbi **hakams**
HAKARI *n* Māori ritual feast **hakaris**
HAKAS ▸ **haka**
HAKE *n*
HAKEA *n* **hakeas**
HAKEEM = **hakim**
HAKEEMS ▸ **hakeem**
HAKES ▸ **hake**
HAKIM *n* Muslim judge, ruler, or administrator **hakims**
HAKU *in New Zealand English*, = **kingfish**
HAKUS ▸ **haku**
HALACHA *n* Jewish religious law **halakah, halakha**
HALAKIC ▸ **halakha**
HALAL *n* meat from animals slaughtered according to Muslim law ▹ *adj* of or relating to such meat ▹ *vb* kill (animals) in this way
HALALA *n* money unit in Saudi Arabia **halalah, halalas**
HALALS ▸ **halal**
HALAVAH = **halvah**
HALBERD *n* **halbert**
HALCYON *adj, n*
HALE *adj* healthy, robust ▹ *vb* pull or drag **haled**
HALER = **heller**
HALERS ▸ **haler**
HALERU ▸ **haler**
HALES ▸ **hale**
HALEST ▸ **hale**
HALF *n, adj, adv*
HALFA *n* African grass **halfas**
HALFEN ▸ **half**
HALFLIN = **halfling**
HALFS ▸ **half**
HALFWAY *adj*
HALFWIT *n*
HALIBUT *n*
HALID = **halide**
HALIDE *n* binary compound **halides**
HALIDOM *n* holy place or thing
HALIDS ▸ **halid**
HALIMOT *n* court held by lord
HALING ▸ **hale**
HALITE *n* colourless or white mineral **halites**
HALITUS *n* vapour
HALL *n*
HALLAH *variant spelling of* ▸ **challah**
HALLAHS ▸ **hallah**
HALLAL = **halal**
HALLALI *n* bugle call
HALLALS ▸ **hallal**
HALLAN *n* partition in

cottage **hallans**
HALLEL *n* (in Judaism) section of the liturgy **hallels**
HALLIAN = **hallion**
HALLING *n* Norwegian country dance
HALLION *n* lout
HALLO = **halloo**
HALLOA = **halloo**
HALLOAS ▸ **halloa**
HALLOED ▸ **hallo**
HALLOES ▸ **hallo**
HALLOO *interj* shout used to call hounds at a hunt ▹ *sentence substitute* shout to attract attention, esp to call hounds at a hunt ▹ *n* shout of "halloo" ▹ *vb* shout (something) to (someone) **halloos**
HALLOS ▸ **hallo**
HALLOT ▸ **hallah**
HALLOTH = **challah**
HALLOW *vb* consecrate or set apart as being holy **hallows**
HALLS ▸ **hall**
HALLUX *n* first digit on the hind foot of an animal
HALLWAY *n* entrance area
HALLYON = **hallion**
HALM = **haulm**
HALMA *n* board game **halmas**
HALMS ▸ **halm**
HALO *n*, *vb* **haloed, haloes**
HALOGEN *n*
HALOID *adj* resembling or derived from a halogen ▹ *n* compound containing halogen atoms in its molecules **haloids**
HALOING ▸ **halo**
HALON *n* any of a class of chemical compounds **halons**
HALOS ▸ **halo**
HALOUMI = **halloumi**
HALSE *vb* embrace **halsed, halser, halsers, halses, halsing**
HALT *vb*, *n*, *adj* **halted**
HALTER *n*, *vb*
HALTERE *n* one of a pair of modified hind wings in dipterous insects
HALTERS ▸ **halter**
HALTING ▸ **halt**
HALTS ▸ **halt**
HALUTZ *variant spelling of* ▸ **chalutz**
HALVA = **halvah**
HALVAH *n* E Mediterranean, Middle Eastern, or Indian sweetmeat **halvahs**
HALVAS ▸ **halva**
HALVE *vb* **halved, halver, halvers, halves, halving**
HALYARD *n*
HAM *n*, *vb*
HAMADA *n* rocky plateau in desert **hamadas**
HAMAL *n* (in Middle Eastern countries) a porter or servant **hamals**
HAMATE *adj* hook-shaped ▹ *n* small bone in the wrist **hamates**
HAMAUL = **hamal**
HAMAULS ▸ **hamaul**
HAMBLE *vb* mutilate **hambled, hambles**
HAMBONE *vb* strike body to provide percussion
HAMBURG = **hamburger**
HAME *n* Scots word for home ▹ *vb* to home **hamed, hames, haming**
HAMLET *n* **hamlets**
HAMMADA = **hamada**
HAMMAL = **hamal**
HAMMALS ▸ **hammal**
HAMMAM *n* bathing establishment **hammams**
HAMMED ▸ **ham**
HAMMER *n*, *vb* **hammers**
HAMMIER ▸ **hammy**
HAMMILY ▸ **hammy**
HAMMING ▸ **ham**
HAMMOCK = **hummock**
HAMMY *adj* (of an actor) overacting or tending to overact
HAMOSE *adj* shaped like a hook **hamous**
HAMPER *vb*, *n* **hampers**
HAMS ▸ **ham**
HAMSTER *n*
HAMULAR ▸ **hamulus**
HAMULI ▸ **hamulus**
HAMULUS *n* biological attribute
HAMZA *n* sign used in

Arabic to represent the glottal stop **hamzah**
HAMZAHS ▶ **hamzah**
HAMZAS ▶ **hamza**
HAN *archaic inflected form of* ▶ **have**
HANAP *n* medieval drinking cup
HANAPER *n* small wickerwork basket
HANAPS ▶ **hanap**
HANCE = **haunch**
HANCES ▶ **hance**
HANCH *vb* try to bite **hanched, hanches**
HAND *n, vb*
HANDAX *n* small axe held in one hand
HANDBAG *n*
HANDCAR *n* small railway vehicle
HANDED ▶ **hand**
HANDER ▶ **hand**
HANDERS ▶ **hand**
HANDFED > **handfeed**
HANDFUL *n*
HANDGUN *n* firearm such as a pistol
HANDIER ▶ **handy**
HANDILY *adv* in a handy way or manner
HANDING ▶ **hand**
HANDISM *n* discrimination against left- or right-handed people
HANDJAR *n* Persian dagger
HANDLE *n, vb* **handled**
HANDLER *n* person who controls an animal
HANDLES ▶ **handle**
HANDOFF *n* (in rugby) act of warding off an opposing player
HANDOUT *n*
HANDS ▶ **hand**
HANDSAW *n* any saw for use in one hand only
HANDSEL *n* gift for good luck ▷ *vb* give a handsel to (a person)
HANDSET *n*
HANDY *adj*
HANG *vb*
HANGAR *n, vb* **hangars**
HANGDOG *adj, n*
HANGED ▶ **hang**
HANGER *n* **hangers**
HANGI *n*
HANGING ▶ **hang**
HANGIS ▶ **hangi**
HANGMAN *n* man who executes people by hanging **hangmen**
HANGOUT *n* place where one lives or that one frequently visits
HANGS ▶ **hang**
HANGTAG *n* attached label
HANGUL *n* Korean language
HANGUP *n* emotional or psychological or problem **hangups**
HANIWA *n* Japanese funeral offering
HANJAR = **handjar**
HANJARS ▶ **hanjar**
HANK *n, vb* **hanked**
HANKER *vb* **hankers**
HANKIE = **hanky**
HANKIES ▶ **hanky**
HANKING ▶ **hank**
HANKS ▶ **hank**
HANKY *n*
HANSA = **hanse**
HANSAS ▶ **hansa**
HANSE *n* medieval guild of merchants
HANSEL = **handsel**
HANSELS ▶ **hansel**
HANSES ▶ **hanse**
HANSOM *n* two-wheeled one-horse carriage **hansoms**
HANT = **haunt**
HANTED ▶ **hant**
HANTING ▶ **hant**
HANTLE *n* good deal **hantles**
HANTS ▶ **hant**
HANUMAN *n* type of monkey
HAO *n* monetary unit of Vietnam
HAOMA *n* type of ritual drink **haomas**
HAOS ▶ **hao**
HAP *n* luck ▷ *vb* cover up
HAPAX *n* word that appears once in a work of literature **hapaxes**
HAPKIDO *n* Korean martial art
HAPLESS *adj*
HAPLITE *variant of* ▶ **aplite**
HAPLOID *adj* denoting a cell or organism with unpaired chromosomes ▷ *n* haploid cell or organism
HAPLONT *n* organism with a haploid number of chromosomes
HAPLY *archaic word for* ▶ **perhaps**

HAPPED ▸ **hap**
HAPPEN *vb* **happens**
HAPPIED ▸ **happy**
HAPPIER ▸ **happy**
HAPPIES ▸ **happy**
HAPPILY ▸ **happy**
HAPPING ▸ **hap**
HAPPY *adj* feeling or causing joy ▹ *vb* make happy
HAPS ▸ **hap**
HAPTEN *n* incomplete antigen **haptene, haptens**
HAPTIC *adj* relating to or based on the sense of touch
HAPTICS *n* science of sense of touch
HAPU *n* subtribe
HAPUKA *another name for* ▸ **groper**
HAPUKAS ▸ **hapuka**
HAPUKU = **hapuka**
HAPUKUS ▸ **hapuku**
HAPUS ▸ **hapu**
HARAM *n* anything that is forbidden by Islamic law **harams**
HARASS *vb*
HARBOR = **harbour**
HARBORS ▸ **harbor**
HARBOUR *n, vb*
HARD *adj, adv*
HARDASS *n* tough person
HARDEN *vb, n* **hardens**
HARDER ▸ **hard**
HARDEST ▸ **hard**
HARDHAT *n* hat made of a hard material for protection ▹ *adj* typical of construction workers
HARDIER ▸ **hardy**
HARDIES ▸ **hardy**
HARDILY *adv* in a hardy manner
HARDISH ▸ **hard**
HARDLY *adv*
HARDMAN *n* tough, ruthless, or violent man **hardmen**
HARDOKE *n* burdock
HARDPAN *n* hard impervious layer of clay below the soil
HARDS *pl n* coarse fibres and other refuse from flax and hemp
HARDSET *adj* in difficulties
HARDTOP *n* car equipped with a metal or plastic roof
HARDY *adj, n*
HARE *n, vb* **hared**
HAREEM = **harem**
HAREEMS ▸ **hareem**
HARELD *n* long-tailed duck **harelds**
HARELIP *n*
HAREM *n* **harems**
HARES ▸ **hare**
HARIANA *n* Indian breed of cattle
HARICOT *n* variety of French bean
HARIJAN *n* member of an Indian caste
HARIM = **harem**
HARIMS ▸ **harim**
HARING ▸ **hare**
HARIRA *n* Moroccan soup **hariras**
HARISH *adj* like hare
HARISSA *n* hot paste
HARK *vb* **harked**
HARKEN = **hearken**
HARKENS ▸ **harken**
HARKING ▸ **hark**
HARKS ▸ **hark**
HARL = **herl**
HARLED ▸ **harl**
HARLING ▸ **harl**
HARLOT *n, adj* **harlots**
HARLS ▸ **harl**
HARM *vb, n*
HARMALA *n* African plant
HARMAN *n* constable **harmans**
HARMED ▸ **harm**
HARMEL = **harmala**
HARMELS ▸ **harmel**
HARMER ▸ **harm**
HARMERS ▸ **harm**
HARMFUL *adj*
HARMIN = **harmalin**
HARMINE = **harmalin**
HARMING ▸ **harm**
HARMINS ▸ **harmin**
HARMONY *n*
HARMOST *n* Spartan governor
HARMS ▸ **harm**
HARN *n* coarse linen
HARNESS *n, vb*
HARNS ▸ **harn**
HARO *interj* cry meaning alas **haros**
HAROSET *n* Jewish dish eaten at Passover
HARP *n, vb* **harped, harper, harpers**
HARPIES ▸ **harpy**
HARPIN *n* type of protein
HARPING ▸ **harp**
HARPINS = **harpings**
HARPIST ▸ **harp**
HARPOON *n, vb*

HARPS ▸ **harp**
HARPY *n* nasty or bad-tempered woman
HARRIED ▸ **harry**
HARRIER *n* cross-country runner
HARRIES ▸ **harry**
HARROW *n* implement used to break up lumps of soil ▷ *vb* draw a harrow over **harrows**
HARRY *vb*
HARSH *adj, vb* **harshed**
HARSHEN *vb* make harsh
HARSHER ▸ **harsh**
HARSHES ▸ **harsh**
HARSHLY ▸ **harsh**
HARSLET = **haslet**
HART *n* adult male deer
HARTAL *n* (in India) closing shops or suspending work **hartals**
HARTELY *archaic spelling of* > **heartily**
HARTEN = **hearten**
HARTENS ▸ **harten**
HARTS ▸ **hart**
HARUMPH = **harrumph**
HARVEST *n, vb*
HAS ▸ **have**
HASBIAN *n* former lesbian
HASH *n, vb* **hashed, hashes, hashier, hashing**
HASHISH *n*
HASHY ▸ **hash**
HASK *n* archaic name for a basket for transporting fish **hasks**
HASLET *n* loaf of cooked minced pig's offal, eaten cold **haslets**
HASP *n, vb* **hasped, hasping, hasps**
HASS *n as in* **white hass** oatmeal pudding made with sheep's gullet
HASSAR *n* South American catfish **hassars**
HASSEL *variant of* ▸ **hassle**
HASSELS ▸ **hassel**
HASSES ▸ **hass**
HASSIUM *n* chemical element
HASSLE *n, vb* **hassled, hassles**
HASSOCK *n*
HAST *singular form of the present tense (indicative mood) of* ▸ **have**
HASTA *Spanish for* ▸ **until**
HASTATE *adj* shaped like a spear
HASTE *n, vb* **hasted**
HASTEN *vb* **hastens**
HASTES ▸ **haste**
HASTIER ▸ **hasty**
HASTILY ▸ **hasty**
HASTING ▸ **haste**
HASTY *adj*
HAT *n, vb*
HATABLE ▸ **hate**
HATBAND *n* band or ribbon around a hat
HATBOX *n* box or case for a hat or hats
HATCH *vb, n* **hatched**
HATCHEL = **heckle**
HATCHER ▸ **hatch**
HATCHES ▸ **hatch**
HATCHET *n*
HATE *vb, n* **hated**
HATEFUL *adj*
HATER ▸ **hate**
HATERS ▸ **hate**
HATES ▸ **hate**
HATFUL *n* amount a hat will hold **hatfuls**
HATH *form of the present tense (indicative mood) of* ▸ **have**
HATHA *n as in* **hatha yoga** form of yoga
HATING ▸ **hate**
HATLESS ▸ **hat**
HATLIKE ▸ **hat**
HATPEG *n* peg to hang hat on **hatpegs**
HATPIN *n* pin used to secure a woman's hat to her hair **hatpins**
HATRACK *n* rack for hanging hats on
HATRED *n* **hatreds**
HATS ▸ **hat**
HATSFUL ▸ **hatful**
HATTED ▸ **hat**
HATTER *n* person who makes and sells hats ▷ *vb* annoy **hatters**
HATTING ▸ **hat**
HATTOCK *n* small hat
HAUBERK *n* long sleeveless coat of mail
HAUBOIS = **hautboy**
HAUD *Scot word for* ▸ **hold**
HAUDING ▸ **haud**
HAUDS ▸ **haud**
HAUF *Scot word for* ▸ **half**
HAUFS ▸ **hauf**
HAUGH *n* low-lying often alluvial riverside

meadow **haughs**
HAUGHT = **haughty**
HAUGHTY *adj*
HAUL *vb, n*
HAULAGE *n*
HAULD *Scots word for* ▶ **hold**
HAULDS ▶ **hauld**
HAULED ▶ **haul**
HAULER = **haulier**
HAULERS ▶ **hauler**
HAULIER *n* firm or person that transports goods by road
HAULING ▶ **haul**
HAULM *n* stalks of beans, peas, or potatoes collectively **haulms**
HAULMY *adj* having haulms
HAULS ▶ **haul**
HAULST = **halse**
HAULT = **haughty**
HAUNCH *n* human hip or fleshy hindquarter of an animal ▷ *vb* cause (an animal) to come down on its haunches
HAUNT *vb, n*
HAUNTED *adj*
HAUNTER ▶ **haunt**
HAUNTS ▶ **haunt**
HAUSE = **halse**
HAUSED ▶ **hause**
HAUSEN *n* variety of sturgeon **hausens**
HAUSES ▶ **hause**
HAUSING ▶ **hause**
HAUT = **haughty**
HAUTBOY *n* type of strawberry
HAUTE *adj* French word meaning high
HAUTEUR *n*
HAUYNE *n* blue mineral containing calcium **hauynes**
HAVARTI *n* Danish cheese
HAVE *vb* possess, hold
HAVEN *n, vb* **havened, havens**
HAVEOUR = **havior**
HAVER *vb* talk nonsense ▷ *n* nonsense **havered**
HAVEREL *n* fool
HAVERS ▶ **haver**
HAVES ▶ **have**
HAVING ▶ **have**
HAVINGS ▶ **have**
HAVIOR = **haviour**
HAVIORS ▶ **havior**
HAVIOUR *n* possession
HAVOC *n, vb* **havocs**
HAW *n* hawthorn berry ▷ *vb* make an inarticulate utterance
HAWALA *n* Middle Eastern system of money transfer **hawalas**
HAWBUCK *n* bumpkin
HAWED ▶ **haw**
HAWING ▶ **haw**
HAWK *n, vb*
HAWKBIT *n* any of three perennial plants
HAWKED ▶ **hawk**
HAWKER *n* travelling salesman **hawkers**
HAWKEY = **hockey**
HAWKEYS ▶ **hawkey**
HAWKIE *n* cow with white stripe on face **hawkies**
HAWKING *another name for* > **falconry**
HAWKISH *adj* favouring the use of force rather than diplomacy
HAWKIT *adj* having a white streak
HAWKS ▶ **hawk**
HAWM *vb* be idle and relaxed **hawmed, hawming, hawms**
HAWS ▶ **haw**
HAWSE *vb* of boats, pitch violently when at anchor **hawsed**
HAWSER *n* **hawsers**
HAWSES ▶ **hawse**
HAWSING ▶ **hawse**
HAY *n, vb*
HAYBAND *n* rope made by twisting hay together
HAYBOX *n* airtight box used to keep partially cooked food warm
HAYCOCK *n* pile of hay left until dry enough to move
HAYED ▶ **hay**
HAYER *n* person who makes hay **hayers**
HAYEY ▶ **hay**
HAYFORK *n* long-handled fork
HAYIER ▶ **hayey**
HAYIEST ▶ **hayey**
HAYING ▶ **hay**
HAYINGS ▶ **hay**
HAYLAGE *n* type of hay for animal fodder
HAYLE *n* welfare **hayles**
HAYLOFT *n* loft for storing hay
HAYMOW *n* part of a barn where hay is

stored **haymows**
HAYRACK *n* rack for holding hay for feeding to animals
HAYRAKE *n* large rake used to collect hay
HAYRICK = **haystack**
HAYRIDE *n* pleasure trip in hay wagon
HAYS ▸ **hay**
HAYSEED *n* seeds or fragments of grass or straw
HAYSEL *n* season for making hay **haysels**
HAYWARD *n* parish officer in charge of enclosures and fences
HAYWIRE *adj* (of things) not functioning properly ▷ *n* wire for binding hay
HAZAN = **cantor**
HAZANIM ▸ **hazan**
HAZANS ▸ **hazan**
HAZARD *n*, *vb* **hazards**
HAZE *n*, *vb* **hazed**
HAZEL *n*, *adj* **hazelly, hazels**
HAZER ▸ **haze**
HAZERS ▸ **haze**
HAZES ▸ **haze**
HAZIER ▸ **hazy**
HAZIEST ▸ **hazy**
HAZILY ▸ **hazy**
HAZING ▸ **haze**
HAZINGS ▸ **haze**
HAZMAT *n* hazardous material **hazmats**
HAZY *adj*
HAZZAN = **cantor**
HAZZANS ▸ **hazzan**
HE *pron*, *n*, *interj*
HEAD *n* upper or front part of the body ▷ *adj* chief, principal ▷ *vb* be at the top or front of
HEADAGE *n* payment to farmer based on animals owned
HEADED *adj* having a head or heads
HEADEND *n* facility from which cable television is transmitted
HEADER *n* **headers**
HEADFUL *n* amount head will hold
HEADIER ▸ **heady**
HEADILY ▸ **heady**
HEADING = **head**
HEADMAN *n* chief or leader **headmen**
HEADPIN *another word for* ▸ **kingpin**
HEADRIG *n* edge of ploughed field
HEADS *adv* with the side of a coin with a head on it uppermost
HEADSET *n* pair of headphones
HEADWAY = **headroom**
HEADY *adj*
HEAL *vb*
HEALD = **heddle**
HEALDED ▸ **heald**
HEALDS ▸ **heald**
HEALED ▸ **heal**
HEALEE *n* person who is being healed **healees**
HEALER, healers, healing, heals ▸ **heal**
HEALTH *n*, *interj* **healths**
HEALTHY *adj*
HEAME *old form of* ▸ **home**
HEAP *n*, *vb* **heaped, heaper, heapers**
HEAPIER ▸ **heapy**
HEAPING *adj* (of a spoonful) heaped
HEAPS ▸ **heap**
HEAPY *adj* having many heaps
HEAR *vb*
HEARD = **herd**
HEARDS ▸ **herd**
HEARE *old form of* ▸ **hair**
HEARER ▸ **hear**
HEARERS ▸ **hear**
HEARES ▸ **heare**
HEARIE *old form of* ▸ **hairy**
HEARING ▸ **hear**
HEARKEN *vb* listen
HEARS ▸ **hear**
HEARSAY *n*
HEARSE *n*, *vb* **hearsed, hearses**
HEARSY *adj* like a hearse
HEART *n*, *vb* **hearted**
HEARTEN *vb*
HEARTH *n* **hearths**
HEARTLY *adv* vigorously
HEARTS *n* card game
HEARTY *adj*, *n*
HEAST = **hest**
HEASTE = **hest**
HEASTES ▸ **heaste**
HEASTS ▸ **heast**
HEAT *vb*, *n*
HEATED *adj* angry and excited
HEATER *n* device for supplying heat **heaters**
HEATH *n*

HEATHEN *n, adj*
HEATHER *n, adj*
HEATHS ▸ **heath**
HEATHY ▸ **heath**
HEATING *n*
HEATS ▸ **heat**
HEAUME *n* large helmet reaching the shoulders **heaumes**
HEAVE *vb, n* **heaved**
HEAVEN *n* **heavens**
HEAVER ▸ **heave**
HEAVERS ▸ **heave**
HEAVES ▸ **heave**
HEAVIER ▸ **heavy**
HEAVIES ▸ **heavy**
HEAVILY ▸ **heavy**
HEAVING ▸ **heave**
HEAVY *adj*
HEBE *n* any of various flowering shrubs
HEBEN *old form of* ▸ **ebony**
HEBENON *n* source of poison
HEBENS ▸ **heben**
HEBES ▸ **hebe**
HEBETIC *adj* of or relating to puberty
HEBONA = **hebenon**
HEBONAS ▸ **hebona**
HECH *interj* expression of surprise
HECHT = **hight**
HECHTS ▸ **hecht**
HECK *interj* mild exclamation of surprise, irritation, etc ▹ *n* frame for obstructing the passage of fish in a river
HECKLE *vb, n* **heckled, heckler, heckles**
HECKS ▸ **heck**
HECTARE *n*
HECTIC *adj, n* **hectics**
HECTOR *vb, n* **hectors**
HEDDLE *n* frame on a loom ▹ *vb* pass thread through a heddle **heddled, heddles**
HEDER *variant spelling of* ▸ **cheder**
HEDERA ▸ **ivy**
HEDERAL ▸ **hedera**
HEDERAS ▸ **hedera**
HEDERS ▸ **heder**
HEDGE *n, vb* **hedged, hedger, hedgers, hedges, hedgier, hedging, hedgy**
HEDONIC > **hedonism**
HEED *n, vb* **heeded, heeder, heeders, heedful, heeding, heeds, heedy**
HEEHAW *interj* representation of the braying sound of a donkey ▹ *vb* make braying sound **heehaws**
HEEL *n, vb*
HEELBAR *n* small shop where shoes are repaired
HEELED ▸ **heel**
HEELER *n* **heelers**
HEELING ▸ **heel**
HEELS ▸ **heel**
HEELTAP *n* layer of leather, etc, in the heel of a shoe
HEEZE *Scots word for* ▸ **hoist**
HEEZED ▸ **heeze**
HEEZES ▸ **heeze**
HEEZIE *n* act of lifting **heezies**
HEEZING ▸ **heeze**
HEFT *vb* assess the weight of (something) by lifting ▹ *n* weight
HEFTE = **heave**
HEFTED ▸ **heft**
HEFTER ▸ **heft**
HEFTERS ▸ **heft**
HEFTIER ▸ **hefty**
HEFTILY ▸ **hefty**
HEFTING ▸ **heft**
HEFTS ▸ **heft**
HEFTY *adj*
HEGARI *n* African sorghum **hegaris**
HEGEMON *n* person in authority
HEGIRA *n* emigration escape or flight **hegiras**
HEGUMEN *n* head of a monastery of the Eastern Church
HEH *interj* exclamation of surprise or inquiry **hehs**
HEID *Scot word for* ▸ **head**
HEIDS ▸ **heid**
HEIFER *n* **heifers**
HEIGH = **hey**
HEIGHT *n* **heighth, heights**
HEIL *vb* give a German greeting **heiled, heiling, heils**
HEIMISH *adj* comfortable
HEINIE *n* buttocks **heinies**
HEINOUS *adj*
HEIR *n, vb*

HEIRDOM *n* succession by right of blood
HEIRED ▸ **heir**
HEIRESS *n*
HEIRING ▸ **heir**
HEIRS ▸ **heir**
HEISHI *n* Native American shell jewellery
HEIST *n* robbery ▹ *vb* steal or burgle **heisted, heister, heists**
HEITIKI *n* Māori neck ornament of greenstone
HEJAB = **hijab**
HEJABS ▸ **hejab**
HEJIRA = **hegira**
HEJIRAS ▸ **hejira**
HEJRA = **hegira**
HEJRAS ▸ **hejra**
HEKTARE = **hectare**
HELCOID *adj* having ulcers
HELD ▸ **hold**
HELE *vb as in* **hele in** insert (cuttings, etc) into soil **heled, heles**
HELIAC = **heliacal**
HELIAST *n* ancient Greek juror
HELIBUS *n* helicopter carrying passengers
HELICAL *adj* spiral
HELICES ▸ **helix**
HELICON *n* bass tuba
HELIMAN *n* helicopter pilot **helimen**
HELING ▸ **hele**
HELIO *n* instrument for sending messages in Morse code **helios**
HELIPAD *n* place for helicopters to land and take off
HELIUM *n* **heliums**
HELIX *n* **helixes**
HELL *n, vb*
HELLBOX *n* (in printing) container for broken type
HELLCAT *n* spiteful fierce-tempered woman
HELLED ▸ **hell**
HELLER *n* monetary unit of the Czech Republic and Slovakia
HELLERI *n* Central American fish
HELLERS ▸ **heller**
HELLERY *n* wild or mischievous behaviour
HELLIER *n* slater
HELLING ▸ **hell**
HELLION *n* rough or rowdy person, esp a child
HELLISH *adj, adv*
HELLO *interj, n, sentence substitute, vb* **helloed, helloes, hellos**
HELLOVA = **helluva**
HELLS ▸ **hell**
HELLUVA *adj* (intensifier)
HELM *n, vb* **helmed**
HELMER *n* film director **helmers**
HELMET *n* **helmets**
HELMING ▸ **helm**
HELMS ▸ **helm**
HELO *n* helicopter **helos**
HELOT *n* serf or slave
HELOTRY *n* serfdom or slavery
HELOTS ▸ **helot**
HELP *vb, n* **helped, helper, helpers**
HELPFUL *adj*
HELPING *n*
HELPS ▸ **help**
HELVE *n* handle of a hand tool such as an axe or pick ▹ *vb* fit a helve to (a tool) **helved, helves, helving**
HEM *n, vb*
HEMAGOG = **hemagogue**
HEMAL = **haemal**
HEMATAL = **hemal**
HEMATIC = **haematic**
HEMATIN = **haematin**
HEME = **haem**
HEMES ▸ **heme**
HEMIC > **haematic**
HEMIN = **haemin**
HEMINA *n* old liquid measure **heminas**
HEMINS ▸ **hemin**
HEMIOLA *n* rhythmic device
HEMIONE = **hemionus**
HEMIPOD = **hemipode**
HEMLINE *n* level to which the hem of a skirt hangs
HEMLOCK *n*
HEMMED ▸ **hem**
HEMMER *n* attachment on a sewing machine for hemming **hemmers**
HEMMING ▸ **hem**
HEMOID = **haematoid**
HEMP *n* **hempen**

HEMPIE *variant of* ▸ **hempy**
HEMPIER ▸ **hempy**
HEMPIES ▸ **hempy**
HEMPS ▸ **hemp**
HEMPY *adj* of or like hemp ▹ *n* rogue
HEMS ▸ **hem**
HEN *n, vb*
HENBANE *n* poisonous plant with sticky hairy leaves
HENBIT *n* European plant with small dark red flowers **henbits**
HENCE *adv, interj*
HENCOOP *n* cage for poultry
HEND *vb* seize **hended, hending, hends**
HENGE *n* monument from the Neolithic and Bronze Ages **henges**
HENLEY *n* type of sweater **henleys**
HENLIKE ▸ **hen**
HENNA *n, vb* **hennaed, hennas**
HENNED ▸ **hen**
HENNER *n* challenge **henners**
HENNERY *n* place or farm for keeping poultry
HENNIER ▸ **henny**
HENNIES ▸ **henny**
HENNIN *n* former women's hat
HENNING ▸ **hen**
HENNINS ▸ **hennin**
HENNISH ▸ **hen**
HENNY *adj* like hen ▹ *n* cock that looks like hen
HENOTIC *adj* acting to reconcile
HENPECK *vb* (of a woman) to harass or torment (a man)
HENRIES ▸ **henry**
HENRY *n* unit of electrical inductance **henrys**
HENS ▸ **hen**
HENT *vb* seize ▹ *n* anything that has been grasped, esp by the mind **hented, henting, hents**
HEP = **hip**
HEPAR *n* compound containing sulphur
HEPARIN *n* polysaccharide present in most body tissues
HEPARS ▸ **hepar**
HEPATIC *adj* of the liver ▹ *n* any of various drugs for use in treating diseases of the liver
HEPCAT *n* person who is hep **hepcats**
HEPPER ▸ **hep**
HEPPEST ▸ **hep**
HEPS ▸ **hep**
HEPSTER = **hipster**
HEPT *archaic spelling of* ▸ **heaped**
HEPTAD *n* group or series of seven **heptads**
HEPTANE *n* alkane found in petroleum
HEPTOSE *n* any monosaccharide with seven carbon atoms per molecule
HER *pron, adj, determiner*
HERALD *n, vb* **heralds**
HERB *n*
HERBAGE *n* herbaceous plants collectively
HERBAL *adj* of or relating to herbs, usually culinary or medicinal herbs ▹ *n* book describing and listing the properties of plants **herbals**
HERBAR = **herbary**
HERBARS ▸ **herbar**
HERBARY *n* herb garden
HERBED *adj* flavoured with herbs
HERBIER ▸ **herby**
HERBIST = **herbalist**
HERBLET *n* little herb
HERBOSE = **herbous**
HERBOUS *adj* with abundance of herbs
HERBS ▸ **herb**
HERBY *adj* abounding in herbs
HERD *n, vb*
HERDBOY *n* boy who looks after herd
HERDED ▸ **herd**
HERDEN *n* type of coarse cloth **herdens**
HERDER = **herdsman**
HERDERS ▸ **herder**
HERDESS *n* female herder
HERDIC *n* small horse-drawn carriage **herdics**
HERDING ▸ **herd**
HERDMAN = **herdsman**
HERDMEN ▸ **herdman**
HERDS ▸ **herd**
HERE *adv, n*
HEREAT *adv* because of this

HEREBY *adv*
HEREDES ▸ **heres**
HEREIN *adv*
HEREOF *adv* of or concerning this
HEREON *archaic word for* > **hereupon**
HERES *pl n* ▸ **here** *n*
HERESY *n*
HERETIC *n* person who holds unorthodox opinions
HERETO *adv* this place, matter, or document
HERIED ▸ **hery**
HERIES ▸ **hery**
HERIOT *n* (in medieval England) a death duty paid to the lord **heriots**
HERISSE *adj* with bristles
HERITOR *n* person who inherits
HERL *n* barb or barbs of a feather
HERLING *n* Scots word for a type of fish
HERLS ▸ **herl**
HERM *n* (in ancient Greece) a stone head of Hermes **herma**
HERMAE ▸ **herma**
HERMAI ▸ **herma**
HERMIT *n* **hermits**
HERMS ▸ **herm**
HERN *archaic or dialect word for* ▸ **heron**
HERNIA *n* **herniae, hernial, hernias**
HERNS ▸ **hern**
HERO *n* **heroes**
HEROIC *adj*
HEROICS *pl n* extravagant behaviour
HEROIN *n*
HEROINE *n*
HEROINS ▸ **heroin**
HEROISE = **heroize**
HEROISM *n*
HEROIZE *vb* make into hero
HERON *n*
HERONRY *n* colony of breeding herons
HERONS ▸ **heron**
HEROON *n* temple or monument dedicated to hero **heroons**
HEROS ▸ **hero**
HERPES *n*
HERRIED ▸ **herry**
HERRIES ▸ **herry**
HERRING *n*
HERRY *vb* harry
HERS *pron*
HERSALL *n* rehearsal
HERSE *n* harrow
HERSED *adj* arranged like a harrow
HERSELF *pron*
HERSES ▸ **herse**
HERSHIP *n* act of plundering
HERTZ *n* **hertzes**
HERY *vb* praise **herye**
HERYED ▸ **herye**
HERYES ▸ **herye**
HERYING ▸ **hery**
HES ▸ **he**
HESP = **hasp**
HESPED ▸ **hesp**
HESPING ▸ **hesp**
HESPS ▸ **hesp**
HESSIAN *n*
HESSITE *n* black or grey metallic mineral
HEST *archaic word for* ▸ **behest**
HESTS ▸ **hest**
HET *n* short for heterosexual ▷ *adj* Scot word for hot
HETAERA *n* (esp in ancient Greece) a female prostitute **hetaira**
HETE = **hight**
HETERO *n* short for heterosexual **heteros**
HETES ▸ **hete**
HETH *n* eighth letter of the Hebrew alphabet
HETHER = **hither**
HETHS ▸ **heth**
HETING ▸ **hete**
HETMAN *another word for* ▸ **ataman**
HETMANS ▸ **hetman**
HETS ▸ **het**
HETTIE *n* **hetties**
HEUCH *Scots word for* ▸ **crag**
HEUCHS ▸ **heuch**
HEUGH = **heuch**
HEUGHS ▸ **heugh**
HEUREKA = **eureka**
HEURISM *n* use of logic
HEVEA *n* rubber-producing South American tree **heveas**
HEW *vb* **hewable, hewed, hewer, hewers**
HEWGH *interj* sound made to imitate the flight of an arrow
HEWING, hewings, hewn, hews ▸ **hew**
HEX *adj* of or relating to hexadecimal notation

▷ *n* evil spell ▷ *vb* bewitch

> This word meaning to bewitch is a really useful one for using the X.

HEXACT *n* part of a sponge with six rays **hexacts**
HEXAD *n* group or series of six **hexade**
HEXADES ▸ **hexade**
HEXADIC ▸ **hexad**
HEXADS ▸ **hexad**
HEXAGON *n*
HEXANE *n* liquid alkane existing in five isomeric forms **hexanes**
HEXAPLA *n* edition of the Old Testament
HEXAPOD *n* six-footed arthropod
HEXARCH *adj* (of plant) with six veins
HEXED ▸ **hex**
HEXENE = **hexylene**
HEXENES ▸ **hexene**
HEXER ▸ **hex**
HEXEREI *n* witchcraft
HEXERS, hexes, hexing, hexings ▸ **hex**
HEXONE *n* colourless insoluble liquid ketone **hexones**
HEXOSAN *n* form of polysaccharide
HEXOSE *n* monosaccharide, such as glucose **hexoses**
HEXYL *adj* of or consisting of a specific group of atoms **hexylic, hexyls**
HEY *interj* expression of surprise or for catching attention ▷ *vb* perform a country dance
HEYDAY *n* **heydays, heydey**
HEYDEYS ▸ **heydey**
HEYDUCK = **haiduk**
HEYED ▸ **hey**
HEYING ▸ **hey**
HEYS ▸ **hey**
HI *interj*
HIANT *adj* gaping
HIATAL ▸ **hiatus**
HIATUS *n*
HIBACHI *n* portable brazier for heating and cooking food
HIC *interj* representation of the sound of a hiccup
HICATEE = **hiccatee**
HICCUP *n*, *vb* **hiccups, hiccupy**
HICK *n* unsophisticated country person
HICKEY *n* object or gadget **hickeys, hickie**
HICKIES ▸ **hickie**
HICKISH ▸ **hick**
HICKORY *n* N American nut-bearing tree
HICKS ▸ **hick**
HID ▸ **hide**
HIDABLE ▸ **hide**
HIDAGE *n* former tax on land **hidages**
HIDALGA *n* Spanish noblewoman
HIDALGO *n* member of the lower nobility in Spain
HIDDEN ▸ **hide**
HIDDER *n* young ram **hidders**
HIDE *vb*, *n* **hided**
HIDEOUS *adj*
HIDEOUT *n*
HIDER, hiders, hides, hiding, hidings ▸ **hide**
HIDLING *n* hiding place
HIDLINS = **hidlings**
HIE *vb* hurry **hied, hieing**
HIELAND *adj* characteristic of Highlanders
HIEMAL *less common word for* > **hibernal**
HIEMS *n* winter
HIES ▸ **hie**
HIGGLE *less common word for* ▸ **haggle**
HIGGLED ▸ **higgle**
HIGGLER ▸ **higgle**
HIGGLES ▸ **higgle**
HIGH *adj* being a relatively great distance from top to bottom; tall ▷ *adv* at or to a height ▷ *n* high place or level ▷ *vb* hie
HIGHBOY *n* tall chest of drawers in two sections
HIGHED ▸ **high**
HIGHER *n* advanced level of the Scottish Certificate of Education ▷ *vb* raise up **highers**
HIGHEST ▸ **high**
HIGHING ▸ **high**
HIGHISH ▸ **high**
HIGHLY *adv*
HIGHMAN *n* dice weighted to make it

fall in particular way **highmen**
HIGHS ▶ **high**
HIGHT *vb* archaic word for name or call **highted**
HIGHTH *old form of* ▶ **height**
HIGHTHS ▶ **highth**
HIGHTOP *n* top of ship's mast
HIGHTS ▶ **hight**
HIGHWAY *n*
HIJAB *n* covering for the head and face **hijabs**
HIJACK *vb, n* **hijacks**
HIJINKS *n* lively enjoyment
HIJRA = **hijrah**
HIJRAH = **hegira**
HIJRAHS ▶ **hijrah**
HIJRAS ▶ **hijra**
HIKE *n, vb* **hiked, hiker, hikers, hikes, hiking**
HIKOI *n* walk or march, esp a Māori protest march ▷ *vb* take part in such a march **hikoied, hikois**
HILA ▶ **hilum**
HILAR ▶ **hilus**
HILCH *vb* hobble **hilched, hilches**
HILD = **hold**
HILDING *n* coward
HILI ▶ **hilus**
HILL *n, vb* **hilled, hiller, hillers, hillier, hilling**
HILLMEN = **hillfolk**
HILLO = **hello**
HILLOA = **halloa**
HILLOAS ▶ **hilloa**
HILLOCK *n*
HILLOED ▶ **hillo**
HILLOES ▶ **hillo**
HILLOS ▶ **hillo**
HILLS ▶ **hill**
HILLTOP *n* top of hill
HILLY ▶ **hill**
HILT *n, vb* **hilted, hilting, hilts**
HILUM *n* scar on a seed **hilus**
HIM *pron, n*
HIMATIA > **himation**
HIMS ▶ **him**
HIMSELF *pron*
HIN *n* Hebrew unit of capacity
HINAU *n* New Zealand tree **hinaus**
HIND *adj, n*
HINDER *vb, adj* **hinders**
HINDGUT *n* part of the vertebrate digestive tract
HINDLEG *n* back leg
HINDS ▶ **hind**
HING *n* asafoetida
HINGE *n, vb* **hinged**
HINGER *n* tool for making hinges **hingers**
HINGES ▶ **hinge**
HINGING ▶ **hinge**
HINGS ▶ **hing**
HINKIER ▶ **hinky**
HINKY *adj* strange
HINNIED ▶ **hinny**
HINNIES ▶ **hinny**
HINNY *n* offspring of a male horse and a female donkey ▷ *vb* whinny
HINS ▶ **hin**
HINT *n, vb* **hinted, hinter, hinters, hinting, hints**
HIOI *n* New Zealand plant of the mint family **hiois**
HIP *n, adj, interj*
HIPBONE *n* either of the bones that form the sides of the pelvis
HIPLESS ▶ **hip**
HIPLIKE ▶ **hip**
HIPLINE *n* widest part of a person's hips
HIPLY ▶ **hip**
HIPNESS ▶ **hip**
HIPPED *adj* having a hip or hips
HIPPEN *n* baby's nappy **hippens**
HIPPER ▶ **hip**
HIPPEST ▶ **hip**
HIPPIC *adj* of horses
HIPPIE = **hippy**
HIPPIER ▶ **hippy**
HIPPIES ▶ **hippy**
HIPPIN = **hippen**
HIPPING = **hippen**
HIPPINS ▶ **hippin**
HIPPISH *adj* in low spirits
HIPPO *n* **hippos**
HIPPUS *n* spasm of eye
HIPPY *n, adj*
HIPS ▶ **hip**
HIPSHOT *adj* having a dislocated hip
HIPSTER *n* enthusiast of modern jazz
HIPT ▶ **hip**
HIRABLE ▶ **hire**
HIRAGE *n* fee for hiring **hirages**
HIRCINE *adj* of or like a goat, esp in smell
HIRE *vb, n*

HIREAGE = **hirage**
HIRED ▶ **hire**
HIREE *n* hired person **hirees**
HIRER, hirers, hires, hiring, hirings ▶ **hire**
HIRLING *n* Scots word for a type of fish
HIRPLE *vb* limp ▷ *n* limping gait **hirpled, hirples**
HIRSEL *vb* sort into groups **hirsels**
HIRSLE *vb* wriggle or fidget **hirsled, hirsles**
HIRSTIE *adj* dry
HIRSUTE *adj*
HIRUDIN *n* anticoagulant
HIS *adj*
HISH = **hiss**
HISHED ▶ **hish**
HISHES ▶ **hish**
HISHING ▶ **hish**
HISN *dialect form of* ▶ **his**
HISPID *adj* covered with stiff hairs or bristles
HISS *n, vb, interj* **hissed**
HISSELF *dialect form of* ▶ **himself**
HISSER ▶ **hiss**
HISSERS ▶ **hiss**
HISSES ▶ **hiss**
HISSIER ▶ **hissy**
HISSIES ▶ **hissy**
HISSING ▶ **hiss**
HISSY *n* temper tantrum ▷ *adj* sound similar to a hiss
HIST *interj* exclamation used to attract attention ▷ *vb* make hist sound **histed**
HISTIE = **hirstie**
HISTING ▶ **hist**
HISTOID *adj* (esp of a tumour)
HISTONE *n* any of a group of proteins present in cell nuclei
HISTORY *n*
HISTRIO *n* actor
HISTS ▶ **hist**
HIT *vb* strike, touch forcefully ▷ *n* hitting
HITCH *n, vb* **hitched, hitcher, hitches, hitchy**
HITHE *n* small harbour
HITHER *adv, vb* **hithers**
HITHES ▶ **hithe**
HITLESS ▶ **hit**
HITMAN *n* professional killer **hitmen**
HITS ▶ **hit**
HITTER *n* boxer who has a hard punch rather than skill or finesse **hitters**
HITTING ▶ **hit**
HIVE *n, vb* **hived**
HIVER *n* person who keeps beehives **hivers**
HIVES *n* allergic reaction
HIVING ▶ **hive**
HIYA *sentence substitute* informal term of greeting
HIZEN *n* type of Japanese porcelain **hizens**
HIZZ = **hiss**
HIZZED ▶ **hizz**
HIZZES ▶ **hizz**
HIZZING ▶ **hizz**
HM *interj* sound made to express hesitation or doubt **hmm**
HOAED ▶ **hoa**
HOAGIE *n* sandwich made with long bread roll **hoagies, hoagy**
HOAING ▶ **hoa**
HOAR *adj* covered with hoarfrost ▷ *vb* make hoary
HOARD *n, vb* **hoarded, hoarder, hoards**
HOARED ▶ **hoar**
HOARIER ▶ **hoary**
HOARILY ▶ **hoary**
HOARING ▶ **hoar**
HOARS ▶ **hoar**
HOARSE *adj*
HOARSEN *vb* make or become hoarse
HOARSER ▶ **hoarse**
HOARY *adj*
HOAS ▶ **hoa**
HOAST *n* cough ▷ *vb* cough **hoasted, hoasts**
HOATZIN *n* South American bird
HOAX *n, vb* **hoaxed, hoaxer, hoaxers, hoaxes, hoaxing**
HOB *n, vb* **hobbed**
HOBBER *n* machine used in making gears **hobbers**
HOBBIES ▶ **hobby**
HOBBING ▶ **hob**
HOBBISH *adj* like a clown
HOBBIT *n* one of an imaginary race of half-size people **hobbits**
HOBBLE *vb, n* **hobbled, hobbler, hobbles**

HOBBY *n*
HOBDAY *vb* alleviate a breathing problem in certain horses **hobdays**
HOBJOB *vb* do odd jobs **hobjobs**
HOBLIKE ▶ **hob**
HOBNAIL *n* short nail with a large head for protecting soles ▷ *vb* provide with hobnails
HOBNOB *vb* **hobnobs**
HOBO *n, vb* **hobodom, hoboed, hoboes, hoboing, hoboism, hobos**
HOBS ▶ **hob**
HOC *adj* Latin for this
HOCK *n, vb* **hocked, hocker, hockers**
HOCKEY *n* **hockeys**
HOCKING ▶ **hock**
HOCKLE *vb* spit **hockled, hockles**
HOCKS ▶ **hock**
HOCUS *vb* take in **hocused, hocuses**
HOD *n, vb*
HODAD *n* person who pretends to be a surfer **hodaddy, hodads**
HODDED ▶ **hod**
HODDEN *n* coarse homespun cloth **hoddens, hoddin**
HODDING ▶ **hod**
HODDINS ▶ **hoddin**
HODDLE *vb* waddle **hoddled, hoddles**
HODJA *n* respectful Turkish form of address **hodjas**
HODMAN *n* hod carrier **hodmen**
HODS ▶ **hod**
HOE *n, vb*
HOECAKE *n* maize cake
HOED ▶ **hoe**
HOEDOWN *n* boisterous square dance
HOEING, hoelike, hoer, hoers, hoes ▶ **hoe**
HOG *n, vb*
HOGAN *n* wooden dwelling covered with earth **hogans**
HOGBACK *n* narrow ridge of steeply inclined rock strata
HOGEN *n* strong alcoholic drink **hogens**
HOGFISH *n* type of fish
HOGG = **hog**
HOGGED ▶ **hog**
HOGGER ▶ **hog**
HOGGERS ▶ **hog**
HOGGERY *n* hogs collectively
HOGGET *n* young unsheared sheep **hoggets**
HOGGIN *n* finely sifted gravel **hogging, hoggins**
HOGGISH *adj* selfish, gluttonous, or dirty
HOGGS ▶ **hogg**
HOGH *n* ridge of land
HOGHOOD *n* condition of being hog
HOGHS ▶ **hogh**
HOGLIKE ▶ **hog**
HOGMANE *n* short stiff mane
HOGNOSE *n as in* **hognose snake** puff adder
HOGNUT *another name for* ▶ **pignut**
HOGNUTS ▶ **hognut**
HOGS ▶ **hog**
HOGTIE *vb* tie together the legs or the arms and legs of **hogtied, hogties**
HOGWARD *n* person looking after hogs
HOGWASH *n* nonsense
HOGWEED *n* any of several umbelliferous plants
HOHA *adj* bored or annoyed
HOHED ▶ **hoh**
HOHING ▶ **hoh**
HOHS ▶ **hoh**
HOI = **hoy**
HOICK *vb* raise abruptly and sharply **hoicked**
HOICKS *interj* cry used to encourage hounds to hunt ▷ *vb* shout **hoicks**
HOIDEN = **hoyden**
HOIDENS ▶ **hoiden**
HOIK = **hoick**
HOIKED ▶ **hoik**
HOIKING ▶ **hoik**
HOIKS ▶ **hoik**
HOISE = **hoist**
HOISED ▶ **hoise**
HOISES ▶ **hoise**
HOISIN *n* Chinese sweet spicy sauce
HOISING ▶ **hoise**
HOISINS ▶ **hoisin**
HOIST *vb, n* **hoisted, hoister, hoists**
HOKA *n* red cod **hokas**
HOKE *vb* overplay (a part, etc) **hoked, hokes**

HOKEY *adj* corny
HOKI *n* fish of New Zealand waters
HOKIER ▸ **hokey**
HOKIEST ▸ **hokey**
HOKILY ▸ **hokey**
HOKING ▸ **hoke**
HOKIS ▸ **hoki**
HOKKU = **haiku**
HOKONUI *n* illicit whisky
HOKUM *n* rubbish, nonsense **hokums**
HOLARD *n* amount of water contained in soil **holards**
HOLD *vb, n*
HOLDALL *n*
HOLDEN *past participle of* ▸ **hold**
HOLDER *n* person or thing that holds **holders**
HOLDING ▸ **hold**
HOLDOUT *n* (in US English) someone or thing that refuses to change
HOLDS ▸ **hold**
HOLDUP *n* robbery, esp an armed one **holdups**
HOLE *n, vb* **holed, holes**
HOLESOM = **holesome**
HOLEY *adj* full of holes **holeyer**
HOLIBUT = **halibut**
HOLIDAY *n, vb*
HOLIER ▸ **holy**
HOLIES ▸ **holy**
HOLIEST ▸ **holy**
HOLILY *adv* in a holy, devout, or sacred manner
HOLING ▸ **hole**
HOLINGS ▸ **hole**
HOLISM *n* view that a whole is greater than the sum of its parts **holisms, holist, holists**
HOLK *vb* dig **holked, holking, holks**
HOLLA = **hollo**
HOLLAED ▸ **holla**
HOLLAND *n* coarse linen cloth, used esp for furnishing
HOLLAS ▸ **holla**
HOLLER *n* shout, yell ▹ *vb* shout or yell **hollers**
HOLLIES ▸ **holly**
HOLLO *interj* cry for attention, or of encouragement ▹ *vb* shout **holloa**
HOLLOAS ▸ **holloa**
HOLLOED ▸ **hollo**
HOLLOES ▸ **hollo**
HOLLOO = **halloo**
HOLLOOS ▸ **holloo**
HOLLOS ▸ **hollo**
HOLLOW *adj, n, vb* **hollows**
HOLLY *n*
HOLM *n* island in a river, lake, or estuary
HOLMIA *n* oxide of holmium **holmias**
HOLMIC *adj* of or containing holmium
HOLMIUM *n*
HOLMS ▸ **holm**
HOLON *n* autonomous self-reliant unit, esp in manufacturing **holonic, holons**
HOLP *past tense of* ▸ **help**
HOLPEN *past participle of* ▸ **help**
HOLS *pl n* holidays
HOLSTER *n, vb*
HOLT *n* otter's lair **holts**
HOLY *adj*
HOLYDAM = **halidom**
HOLYDAY *n* day on which a religious festival is observed
HOM *n* sacred plant of the Parsees and ancient Persians **homa**
HOMAGE *n, vb* **homaged, homager, homages**
HOMAS ▸ **homa**
HOMBRE *slang word for* ▸ **man**
HOMBRES ▸ **hombre**
HOMBURG *n*
HOME *n, adj, adv, vb*
HOMEBOY *n* close friend
HOMED ▸ **home**
HOMELY *adj*
HOMELYN *n* species of ray
HOMER *n* homing pigeon ▹ *vb* score a home run in baseball **homered**
HOMERIC *adj* grand or heroic
HOMERS ▸ **homer**
HOMES ▸ **home**
HOMEY = **homy**
HOMEYS ▸ **homey**
HOMIE *short for* ▸ **homeboy**
HOMIER ▸ **homy**

HOMIES ▸ **homie**
HOMIEST ▸ **homy**
HOMILY *n*
HOMINES ▸ **homo**
HOMING *adj, n* **homings**
HOMINID *n* man or any extinct forerunner of man ▹ *adj* of or belonging to this family
HOMININ *n* member of a zoological family
HOMINY *n* coarsely ground maize
HOMME *French word for* ▸ **man**
HOMMES ▸ **homme**
HOMMOCK = **hummock**
HOMMOS = **hummus**
HOMO *n* homogenized milk
HOMOLOG = **homologue**
HOMONYM *n* word that is spelt the same as another
HOMOS ▸ **homo**
HOMOSEX *n* sexual activity between homosexuals
HOMS ▸ **hom**
HOMY *adj* like a home
HON *short for* ▸ **honey**
HONAN *n* silk fabric of rough weave **honans**
HONCHO *n* person in charge ▹ *vb* supervise or be in charge of **honchos**
HOND *old form of* ▸ **hand**
HONDA *n* loop used to make a lasso **hondas**
HONDLE *vb* negotiate on price **hondled, hondles**
HONDS ▸ **hond**
HONE *vb, n* **honed, honer, honers, hones**
HONEST *adj*
HONESTY *n*
HONEY *n, vb* **honeyed, honeys**
HONG *n* (in China) a factory, warehouse, etc ▹ *vb* archaic form of hang
HONGI *n, vb* **hongied, hongies**
HONGING ▸ **hong**
HONGIS ▸ **hongi**
HONGS ▸ **hong**
HONIED ▸ **honey**
HONING ▸ **hone**
HONK *n, vb* **honked**
HONKER *n* person or thing that honks **honkers**
HONKING ▸ **honk**
HONKS ▸ **honk**
HONOR = **honour**
HONORED ▸ **honor**
HONOREE = **honorand**
HONORER ▸ **honour**
HONORS = **honours**
HONOUR *n, vb* **honours**
HONS ▸ **hon**
HOO *interj* expression of joy, excitement, etc
HOOCH *n* alcoholic drink, esp illicitly distilled spirits **hooches**
HOOCHIE *n* immoral woman
HOOD *n, vb*
HOODED *adj* (of a garment) having a hood
HOODIA *n* any of several southern African succulent plants **hoodias**
HOODIE *n* hooded sweatshirt
HOODIER ▸ **hood**
HOODIES ▸ **hoodie**
HOODING ▸ **hood**
HOODLUM *n* violent criminal, gangster
HOODMAN *n* blindfolded person in blindman's buff **hoodmen**
HOODOO *n* (cause of) bad luck ▹ *vb* bring bad luck to **hoodoos**
HOODS ▸ **hood**
HOODY ▸ **hood**
HOOEY *n* nonsense ▹ *interj* nonsense **hooeys**
HOOF *n, vb*
HOOFED *adj* having a hoof or hoofs
HOOFER *n* professional dancer **hoofers**
HOOFING ▸ **hoof**
HOOFROT *n* disease of hoof
HOOFS ▸ **hoof**
HOOK *n, vb*
HOOKA = **hookah**
HOOKAH *n* oriental pipe **hookahs**
HOOKAS ▸ **hooka**
HOOKED *adj*
HOOKER *n* prostitute **hookers**

HOOKEY = **hooky**
HOOKEYS ▸ **hookey**
HOOKIER ▸ **hooky**
HOOKIES ▸ **hooky**
HOOKING ▸ **hook**
HOOKLET *n* little hook
HOOKS ▸ **hook**
HOOKUP *n* contact of an aircraft with the hose of a tanker aircraft **hookups**
HOOKY *n* truancy, usually from school ▹ *adj* hooklike
HOOLEY *n* lively party **hooleys, hoolie**
HOOLIER ▸ **hooly**
HOOLIES ▸ **hoolie**
HOOLOCK *n* Indian gibbon
HOOLY *adj* careful or gentle
HOON *n* loutish youth who drives irresponsibly ▹ *vb* drive irresponsibly **hooned, hooning, hoons**
HOOP *n, vb* **hooped**
HOOPER *rare word for* ▸ **cooper**
HOOPERS ▸ **hooper**
HOOPING ▸ **hoop**
HOOPLA *n* fairground game **hooplas**
HOOPOE *n* bird with a pinkish-brown plumage **hoopoes, hoopoo**
HOOPOOS ▸ **hoopoo**
HOOPS ▸ **hoop**
HOOR *n* unpleasant or difficult thing
HOORAH = **hurrah**
HOORAHS ▸ **hoorah**
HOORAY = **hurrah**
HOORAYS ▸ **hooray**
HOORD = **hoard**
HOORDS ▸ **hoord**
HOOROO = **hurrah**
HOORS ▸ **hoor**
HOOSGOW ▸ **jail**
HOOSH *vb* shoo away **hooshed, hooshes**
HOOT *n, vb, interj*
HOOTCH = **hooch**
HOOTED ▸ **hoot**
HOOTER *n* **hooters**
HOOTIER ▸ **hoot**
HOOTING ▸ **hoot**
HOOTS = **hoot**
HOOTY ▸ **hoot**
HOOVE = **heave**
HOOVED ▸ **hoove**
HOOVEN ▸ **hoove**
HOOVER *vb* **hoovers**
HOOVES ▸ **hoof**
HOOVING ▸ **hoove**
HOP *vb, n*
HOPBIND *n* stalk of the hop **hopbine**
HOPDOG *n* species of caterpillar **hopdogs**
HOPE *vb, n* **hoped**
HOPEFUL *adj* having, expressing, or inspiring hope ▹ *n* person considered to be on the brink of success
HOPER ▸ **hope**
HOPERS ▸ **hope**
HOPES ▸ **hope**
HOPHEAD *n* heroin or opium addict
HOPING ▸ **hope**
HOPLITE *n* (in ancient Greece) a heavily armed infantryman
HOPPED ▸ **hop**
HOPPER *n* **hoppers**
HOPPIER ▸ **hoppy**
HOPPING ▸ **hop**
HOPPLE = **hobble**
HOPPLED ▸ **hopple**
HOPPLER ▸ **hopple**
HOPPLES ▸ **hopple**
HOPPUS *adj as in* **hoppus foot** unit of volume for round timber
HOPPY *adj* tasting of hops
HOPS ▸ **hop**
HOPSACK *n* roughly woven fabric
HOPTOAD *n* toad
HORA *n* traditional Israeli or Romanian circle dance **horah**
HORAHS ▸ **horah**
HORAL *less common word for* ▸ **hourly**
HORARY *adj* relating to the hours
HORAS ▸ **hora**
HORDE *n, vb* **horded**
HORDEIN *n* simple protein, rich in proline, that occurs in barley
HORDES ▸ **horde**
HORDING ▸ **horde**
HORDOCK = **hardoke**
HORE = **hoar**
HORIZON *n*
HORKEY = **hockey**
HORKEYS ▸ **horkey**
HORME *n* (in Jungian psychology) fundamental vital energy **hormes, hormic**
HORMONE *n*
HORN *n, vb*

HORNBUG *n* stag beetle
HORNED *adj* having a horn, horns, or hornlike parts
HORNER *n* dealer in horn **horners**
HORNET *n* **hornets**
HORNFUL *n* amount a horn will hold
HORNIER ▸ **horny**
HORNILY ▸ **horny**
HORNING ▸ **horn**
HORNISH *adj* like horn
HORNIST *n* horn player
HORNITO *n* small vent in volcano
HORNLET *n* small horn
HORNS ▸ **horn**
HORNY *adj* of or like horn
HOROEKA *n* New Zealand tree
HORRENT *adj* bristling
HORRID *adj*
HORRIFY *vb*
HORROR *n, adj*
HORRORS *pl n* fit of depression or anxiety ▹ *interj* expression of dismay, sometimes facetious
HORS *adv as in* **hors d'oeuvre** appetizer
HORSE *n, vb* **horsed, horses**
HORSEY *adj*
HORSIER ▸ **horsy**
HORSILY ▸ **horsey**
HORSING ▸ **horse**
HORSON = **whoreson**
HORSONS ▸ **horson**
HORST *n* ridge of land **horste**
HORSTES ▸ **horste**
HORSTS ▸ **horst**
HORSY = **horsey**
HOSANNA *interj, n, vb*
HOSE *n, vb* **hosed**
HOSEL *n* socket in head of golf club **hosels**
HOSEMAN *n* fireman in charge of hose **hosemen**
HOSEN ▸ **hose**
HOSER *n* person who swindles or deceives others **hosers**
HOSES ▸ **hose**
HOSEY *vb* claim possession **hoseyed, hoseys**
HOSIER *n* person who sells stockings, etc **hosiers**
HOSIERY *n*
HOSING ▸ **hose**
HOSPICE *n*
HOSS *n* horse **hosses**
HOST *n, vb*
HOSTA *n* ornamental plant
HOSTAGE *n*
HOSTAS ▸ **hosta**
HOSTED ▸ **host**
HOSTEL *n, vb* **hostels**
HOSTESS *n, vb*
HOSTIE *n* informal Australian word for an air hostess **hosties**
HOSTILE *adj, n*
HOSTING ▸ **host**
HOSTLER *another name (esp Brit) for* ▸ **ostler**
HOSTLY ▸ **host**
HOSTRY *n* lodging
HOSTS ▸ **host**
HOT *adj*
HOTBED *n* **hotbeds**
HOTBOX *n* closed room where marijuana is smoked
HOTCAKE *n* pancake
HOTCH *vb* jog **hotched, hotches**
HOTDOG *vb* perform a series of manoeuvres in skiing, etc **hotdogs**
HOTE ▸ **hight**
HOTEL *n* **hotels**
HOTEN ▸ **hight**
HOTFOOT *adv, vb*
HOTHEAD *n*
HOTLINE *n* direct telephone link for emergency use
HOTLINK *n* area on website connecting to another site
HOTLY ▸ **hot**
HOTNESS ▸ **hot**
HOTPOT *n* casserole topped with potatoes **hotpots**
HOTROD *n* car with a modified engine for increased power **hotrods**
HOTS *pl n as in* **the hots** feeling of lust
HOTSHOT *n* important person or expert, esp when showy
HOTSPOT *n* place where wireless broadband is provided
HOTSPUR *n* impetuous or fiery person
HOTTED ▸ **hot**
HOTTER *vb* simmer **hotters**
HOTTEST ▸ **hot**
HOTTIE *n* sexually

attractive person **hotties**
HOTTING *n*
HOTTISH *adj* fairly hot
HOTTY = **hottie**
HOUDAH = **howdah**
HOUDAHS ▸ **houdah**
HOUDAN *n* breed of light domestic fowl **houdans**
HOUF = **howf**
HOUFED ▸ **houf**
HOUFF = **howf**
HOUFFED ▸ **houff**
HOUFFS ▸ **houff**
HOUFING ▸ **houf**
HOUFS ▸ **houf**
HOUGH *n* in Scotland, a cut of meat corresponding to shin ▹ *vb* hamstring (cattle, horses, etc) **houghed, houghs**
HOUHERE *n* small evergreen New Zealand tree
HOUMMOS = **hummus**
HOUMOUS ▸ **hummus**
HOUMUS = **hummus**
HOUND *n, vb* **hounded, hounder, hounds**
HOUNGAN *n* voodoo priest
HOUR *n*
HOURI *n* any of the nymphs of paradise **houris**
HOURLY *adv* (happening) every hour ▹ *adj* of, occurring, or done once every hour ▹ *n* something that is done by the hour
HOURS *pl n* indefinite time
HOUSE *n, vb, adj* **housed**
HOUSEL *vb* give the Eucharist to (someone) **housels**
HOUSER ▸ **house**
HOUSERS ▸ **house**
HOUSES ▸ **house**
HOUSEY *adj* of or like house music **housier**
HOUSING *n*
HOUT = **hoot**
HOUTED ▸ **hout**
HOUTING *n* type of fish
HOUTS ▸ **hout**
HOVE ▸ **heave**
HOVEA *n* Australian plant with purple flowers **hoveas**
HOVED ▸ **heave**
HOVEL *n, vb* **hoveled, hovels**
HOVEN ▸ **heave**
HOVER *vb, n* **hovered, hoverer, hovers**
HOVES ▸ **heave**
HOVING ▸ **heave**
HOW *adv, n, sentence substitute*
HOWBE = **howbeit**
HOWBEIT *adv* in archaic usage, however
HOWDAH *n* canopied seat on an elephant's back **howdahs**
HOWDIE *n* midwife
HOWDIED ▸ **howdy**
HOWDIES ▸ **howdy**
HOWDY *vb* greet someone
HOWE *n* depression in the earth's surface **howes**
HOWEVER *adv*
HOWF *n* haunt, esp a public house ▹ *vb* visit place frequently **howfed**
HOWFF *vb* visit place frequently **howffed, howffs**
HOWFING ▸ **howf**
HOWFS ▸ **howf**
HOWK *vb* dig (out or up) **howked, howker, howkers, howking, howks**
HOWL *n, vb* **howled**
HOWLER *n* **howlers**
HOWLET *another word for* ▸ **owl**
HOWLETS ▸ **howlet**
HOWLING *adj* great
HOWLS ▸ **howl**
HOWRE = **hour**
HOWRES ▸ **howre**
HOWS ▸ **how**
HOWSO = **howsoever**
HOWZAT ▸ **how**
HOWZIT *informal word for* ▸ **hello**
HOX *vb* hamstring **hoxed, hoxes, hoxing**

> This is a word found in Shakespeare's plays, and means to cut a horse's hamstring; it's one of the many short words with X that can get you a high score.

HOY *interj* cry used to attract someone's attention ▹ *n* freight barge ▹ *vb* drive animal

with cry
HOYA *n* any of various E Asian or Australian plants **hoyas**
HOYDEN *n* wild or boisterous girl ▷ *vb* behave like a hoyden **hoydens**
HOYED ▶ **hoy**
HOYING ▶ **hoy**
HOYLE *n* archer's mark used as a target **hoyles**
HOYS ▶ **hoy**
HRYVNA *n* standard monetary unit of Ukraine **hryvnas**
HRYVNIA *n* money unit of Ukraine
HRYVNYA = **hryvna**
HUANACO = **guanaco**
HUB *n*
HUBBIES ▶ **hubby**
HUBBLY *adj* having an irregular surface
HUBBUB *n* **hubbubs**
HUBBY *n* husband
HUBCAP *n* metal disc that protects the hub of a wheel **hubcaps**
HUBRIS *n* pride, arrogance
HUBS ▶ **hub**
HUCK = **huckaback**
HUCKED ▶ **huck**
HUCKERY *adj* ugly
HUCKING ▶ **huck**
HUCKLE *n* hip or haunch ▷ *vb* force out or arrest roughly **huckled, huckles**
HUCKS ▶ **huck**
HUDDEN ▶ **haud**
HUDDLE *vb, n* **huddled, huddler, huddles**
HUDDUP *interj* get up
HUDNA *n* truce or ceasefire for a fixed duration **hudnas**
HUDUD *n* set of laws and punishments in the Koran **hududs**
HUE *n*
HUED *adj* having a hue or colour as specified
HUELESS ▶ **hue**
HUER *n* pilchard fisherman **huers**
HUES ▶ **hue**
HUFF *n, vb* **huffed**
HUFFER ▶ **huffing**
HUFFERS ▶ **huffing**
HUFFIER ▶ **huff**
HUFFILY ▶ **huff**
HUFFING *n* practice of inhaling fumes for intoxicating effects
HUFFISH ▶ **huff**
HUFFKIN *n* type of muffin
HUFFS ▶ **huff**
HUFFY ▶ **huff**
HUG *vb, n*
HUGE *adj*
HUGELY *adv* very much
HUGEOUS = **huge**
HUGER ▶ **huge**
HUGEST ▶ **huge**
HUGGED ▶ **hug**
HUGGER ▶ **hug**
HUGGERS ▶ **hug**
HUGGIER ▶ **huggy**
HUGGING ▶ **hug**
HUGGY *adj* sensitive and caring
HUGS ▶ **hug**
HUGY = **huge**
HUH *interj* exclamation of derision or inquiry
HUHU *n* type of hairy New Zealand beetle **huhus**
HUI *n*
HUIA *n* extinct bird of New Zealand **huias**
HUIC *interj* in hunting, a call to hounds
HUIPIL *n* Mayan woman's blouse **huipils**
HUIS ▶ **hui**
HUITAIN *n* verse of eighteen lines
HULA *n* swaying Hawaiian dance **hulas**
HULE = **ule**
HULES ▶ **hule**
HULK *n, vb* **hulked**
HULKIER ▶ **hulky**
HULKING *adj* bulky, unwieldy
HULKS ▶ **hulk**
HULKY = **hulking**
HULL *n, vb* **hulled, huller, hullers**
HULLIER ▶ **hully**
HULLING ▶ **hull**
HULLO = **hello**
HULLOA = **halloa**
HULLOAS ▶ **hulloa**
HULLOED ▶ **hullo**
HULLOES ▶ **hullo**
HULLOO = **halloo**
HULLOOS ▶ **hulloo**
HULLOS ▶ **hullo**
HULLS ▶ **hull**
HULLY *adj* having husks
HUM *vb, n*
HUMA *n* mythical bird
HUMAN *adj, n*
HUMANE *adj* **humaner**
HUMANLY *adv* by

human powers or means
HUMANS ▸ **human**
HUMAS ▸ **huma**
HUMATE *n* decomposed plants used as fertilizer **humates**
HUMBLE *adj, vb* **humbled, humbler, humbles, humbly**
HUMBUG *n, vb* **humbugs**
HUMBUZZ *n* type of beetle
HUMDRUM *adj, n*
HUMECT *vb* make moist **humects**
HUMEFY = **humify**
HUMERAL *adj* of or relating to the humerus ▹ *n* silk shawl worn by a priest at High Mass; humeral veil
HUMERI ▸ **humerus**
HUMERUS *n*
HUMF = **humph**
HUMFED ▸ **humf**
HUMFING ▸ **humf**
HUMFS ▸ **humf**
HUMHUM *n* Indian cotton cloth **humhums**
HUMIC *adj* of, derived from, or resembling humus
HUMID *adj* **humider**
HUMIDEX *n* system of measuring discomfort
HUMIDLY ▸ **humid**
HUMIDOR *n* humid place for storing cigars, tobacco, etc
HUMIFY *vb* convert or be converted into humus
HUMINT *n* human intelligence **humints**
HUMITE *n* mineral containing magnesium **humites**
HUMLIE *n* hornless cow **humlies**
HUMMAUM = **hammam**
HUMMED ▸ **hum**
HUMMEL *adj* (of cattle) hornless ▹ *vb* remove horns from **hummels**
HUMMER ▸ **hum**
HUMMERS ▸ **hum**
HUMMING ▸ **hum**
HUMMLE *adj as in* **hummle bonnet** type of Scottish cap
HUMMOCK *n, vb*
HUMMUM = **hammam**
HUMMUMS ▸ **hummum**
HUMMUS *n* creamy dip
HUMOGEN *n* type of fertilizer
HUMOR = **humour**
HUMORAL *adj* denoting or relating to a type of immunity
HUMORED ▸ **humor**
HUMORS ▸ **humor**
HUMOUR *n, vb* **humours**
HUMOUS = **humus**
HUMP *n, vb* **humped**
HUMPEN *n* old German drinking glass **humpens**
HUMPER ▸ **hump**
HUMPERS ▸ **hump**
HUMPH *interj* exclamation of annoyance or scepticism ▹ *vb* exclaim humph **humphed, humphs**
HUMPIER ▸ **humpy**
HUMPIES ▸ **humpy**
HUMPING ▸ **hump**
HUMPS ▸ **hump**
HUMPTY *n* low padded seat
HUMPY *adj* full of humps ▹ *n* primitive hut
HUMS ▸ **hum**
HUMUS *n* **humuses, humusy**
HUMVEE *n* military vehicle **humvees**
HUN *n* member of any of several nomadic peoples
HUNCH *n, vb* **hunched, hunches**
HUNDRED *n, adj*
HUNG ▸ **hang**
HUNGAN = **houngan**
HUNGANS ▸ **hungan**
HUNGER *n, vb* **hungers**
HUNGRY *adj*
HUNH = **huh**
HUNK *n*
HUNKER *vb* squat
HUNKERS *pl n* haunches
HUNKEY *n* person of Hungarian descent **hunkeys, hunkie**
HUNKIER ▸ **hunky**
HUNKS *n* crotchety old person **hunkses**
HUNKY *adj* excellent
HUNNISH ▸ **hun**
HUNS ▸ **hun**
HUNT *vb, n*
HUNTED *adj* harassed

and worn
HUNTER *n* person or animal that hunts wild animals **hunters**
HUNTING *n* pursuit and killing or capture of wild animals
HUNTS ▸ **hunt**
HUP *vb* cry hup to get a horse to move
HUPIRO *in New Zealand English*, = **stinkwood**
HUPIROS ▸ **hupiro**
HUPPAH *variant spelling of* ▸ **chuppah**
HUPPAHS ▸ **huppah**
HUPPED ▸ **hup**
HUPPING ▸ **hup**
HUPPOT ▸ **huppah**
HUPPOTH ▸ **huppot**
HUPS ▸ **hup**
HURDEN = **harden**
HURDENS ▸ **hurden**
HURDIES *pl n* buttocks or haunches
HURDLE *n, vb* **hurdled, hurdler, hurdles**
HURDS = **hards**
HURL *vb, n*
HURLBAT = **whirlbat**
HURLED ▸ **hurl**
HURLER ▸ **hurl**
HURLERS ▸ **hurl**
HURLEY *n* another word for the game of hurling **hurleys**
HURLIES ▸ **hurly**
HURLING *n* Irish game like hockey
HURLS ▸ **hurl**
HURLY *n* wheeled barrow
HURRA = **hurrah**
HURRAED ▸ **hurra**
HURRAH *interj* exclamation of joy or applause ▷ *n* cheer of joy or victory ▷ *vb* shout "hurrah" **hurrahs**
HURRAS ▸ **hurra**
HURRAY = **hurrah**
HURRAYS ▸ **hurray**
HURRIED *adj* done quickly or too quickly
HURRIER ▸ **hurry**
HURRIES ▸ **hurry**
HURRY *vb, n*
HURST *n* wood **hursts**
HURT *vb, n, adj* **hurter, hurters**
HURTFUL *adj* unkind
HURTING ▸ **hurt**
HURTLE *vb* **hurtled, hurtles**
HURTS ▸ **hurt**
HUSBAND *n, vb*
HUSH *vb, n, interj*
HUSHABY *interj* used in quietening a baby or child to sleep ▷ *n* lullaby ▷ *vb* quieten to sleep
HUSHED ▸ **hush**
HUSHER = **usher**
HUSHERS ▸ **husher**
HUSHES ▸ **hush**
HUSHFUL *adj* quiet
HUSHIER ▸ **hushy**
HUSHING ▸ **hush**
HUSHY *adj* secret
HUSK *n, vb* **husked, husker, huskers**
HUSKIER ▸ **husky**
HUSKIES ▸ **husky**
HUSKILY ▸ **husky**
HUSKING ▸ **husk**
HUSKS ▸ **husk**
HUSKY *adj, n*
HUSO *n* sturgeon **husos**
HUSS *n* flesh of the European dogfish
HUSSAR *n* lightly armed cavalry soldier **hussars**
HUSSES ▸ **huss**
HUSSIES ▸ **hussy**
HUSSIF *n* sewing kit **hussifs**
HUSSY *n*
HUSTLE *vb, n* **hustled, hustler, hustles**
HUSWIFE = **housewife**
HUT *n*
HUTCH *n, vb* **hutched, hutches**
HUTCHIE *n* temporary shelter
HUTIA *n* rodent of West Indies **hutias**
HUTLIKE ▸ **hut**
HUTMENT *n* number or group of huts
HUTS ▸ **hut**
HUTTED ▸ **hut**
HUTTING ▸ **hut**
HUTZPA = **hutzpah**
HUTZPAH *variant spelling of* > **chutzpah**
HUTZPAS ▸ **hutzpa**
HUZOOR *n* person of rank in India **huzoors**
HUZZA = **huzzah**
HUZZAED ▸ **huzza**
HUZZAH *archaic word for* ▸ **hurrah**
HUZZAHS ▸ **huzzah**
HUZZAS ▸ **huzza**
HUZZIES ▸ **huzzy**
HUZZY = **hussy**
HWAN *another name for* ▸ **won**

HWYL *n* emotional fervour, as in the recitation of poetry **hwyls**

This Welsh word can come in very useful for dealing with a consonant-heavy rack.

HYACINE = **hyacinth**
HYAENA = **hyena**
HYAENAS ▸ **hyaena**
HYAENIC ▸ **hyaena**
HYALIN *n* glassy translucent substance
HYALINE *adj* clear and translucent, with no fibres or granules ▷ *n* glassy transparent surface
HYALINS ▸ **hyalin**
HYALITE *n* clear and colourless variety of opal in globular form
HYALOID *adj* clear and transparent ▷ *n* delicate transparent membrane
HYBRID *n, adj* **hybrids**
HYBRIS = **hubris**
HYDATID *n* cyst containing tapeworm larvae
HYDRA *n* **hydrae**
HYDRANT *n*
HYDRAS ▸ **hydra**
HYDRASE *n* enzyme that removes water
HYDRATE *n* chemical compound of water with another substance ▷ *vb* treat or impregnate with water
HYDRIA *n* (in ancient Greece and Rome) a large water jar **hydriae**
HYDRIC *adj* of or containing hydrogen
HYDRID = **hydroid**
HYDRIDE *n*
HYDRIDS ▸ **hydrid**
HYDRO *n* hotel offering facilities for hydropathy ▷ *adj* short for hydroelectric
HYDROID *adj* of an order of colonial hydrozoan coelenterates ▷ *n* hydroid colony or individual
HYDROMA = **hygroma**
HYDROPS *n* anaemia in a fetus
HYDROS ▸ **hydro**
HYDROUS *adj* containing water
HYDROXY *adj* of a type of chemical compound
HYDYNE *n* type of rocket fuel **hydynes**
HYE = **hie**
HYED ▸ **hye**
HYEING ▸ **hye**
HYEN = **hyena**
HYENA *n* **hyenas, hyenic**
HYENINE *adj* of hyenas
HYENOID *adj* of or like hyenas
HYENS ▸ **hyen**
HYES ▸ **hye**
HYETAL *adj* of or relating to rain, rainfall, or rainy regions
HYGEIST = **hygienist**
HYGIENE *n*
HYGROMA *n* swelling soft tissue that occurs over a joint
HYING ▸ **hie**
HYKE = **haik**
HYKES ▸ **hyke**
HYLA *n* type of tropical American tree frog **hylas**
HYLDING = **hilding**
HYLE *n* wood
HYLEG *n* dominant planet when someone is born **hylegs**
HYLES ▸ **hyle**
HYLIC *adj* solid
HYLISM = **hylicism**
HYLISMS ▸ **hylism**
HYLIST ▸ **hylism**
HYLISTS ▸ **hylism**
HYLOIST *n* materialist
HYMEN *n* **hymenal**
HYMENIA > **hymenium**
HYMENS ▸ **hymen**
HYMN *n, vb*
HYMNAL *n* book of hymns ▷ *adj* of, relating to, or characteristic of hymns **hymnals, hymnary**
HYMNED ▸ **hymn**
HYMNIC ▸ **hymn**
HYMNING ▸ **hymn**
HYMNIST *n* person who composes hymns
HYMNODY *n* composition or singing of hymns
HYMNS ▸ **hymn**
HYNDE = **hind**
HYNDES ▸ **hynde**

HYOID *adj* of or relating to the hyoid bone ▷ *n* horseshoe-shaped bone
HYOIDAL *adj* of or relating to the hyoid bone
HYOIDS ▶ **hyoid**
HYP *n*
HYPATE *n* string of lyre **hypates**
HYPE *n* intensive or exaggerated publicity or sales promotion ▷ *vb* promote (a product) using intensive or exaggerated publicity **hyped, hyper**
HYPERON *n* any baryon that is not a nucleon
HYPERS ▶ **hype**
HYPES ▶ **hype**
HYPHA *n* any of the filaments in the mycelium of a fungus **hyphae, hyphal**
HYPHEN *n, vb* **hyphens**
HYPHIES ▶ **hyphy**
HYPHY *n*
HYPING ▶ **hype**
HYPINGS ▶ **hype**
HYPNIC *n* sleeping drug **hypnics**
HYPNOID *adj* of or relating to a state resembling sleep
HYPNONE *n* sleeping drug
HYPNUM *n* species of moss **hypnums**
HYPO *vb* inject with a hypodermic syringe **hypoed**
HYPOGEA > **hypogeum**
HYPOID *adj as in* **hypoid gear** type of gear
HYPOING ▶ **hypo**
HYPONEA = **hypopnea**
HYPONYM *n* word whose meaning is included as part of another
HYPOS ▶ **hypo**
HYPOXIA *n* deficiency in oxygen delivery **hypoxic**
HYPPED ▶ **hyp**
HYPPING ▶ **hyp**
HYPS ▶ **hyp**
HYPURAL *adj* below the tail
HYRACES ▶ **hyrax**
HYRAX *n* type of hoofed rodent-like animal of Africa and Asia **hyraxes**
HYSON *n* Chinese green tea **hysons**
HYSSOP *n* sweet-smelling herb used in folk medicine **hyssops**
HYTE *adj* insane
HYTHE = **hithe**
HYTHES ▶ **hythe**

The letter **I** can prove a difficult tile to use effectively in Scrabble. It's one of the most common tiles in the game, so you often end up with two or more on your rack, but it can be hard to get rid of. Where **I** does come in very useful, though, is in the number of everyday short words that can be formed from it, which are very helpful when you need to form short words in addition to the main word that you want to play. These words include **in, is, it** (2 points each), **id** (3) and **if** (5). Other handy words are **icy** (8), **ivy** (9) and **imp** (7). Don't forget the three-letter words that use **K**: **ilk, ink** and **irk** (7 each), while **iwi** for 6 points can be very useful in getting rid of a surplus of **I**s.

IAMB *n* metrical foot of two syllables
IAMBI ▸ **iambus**
IAMBIC *adj* written in a type of metrical unit ▹ *n* iambic foot, line, or stanza **iambics**
IAMBIST *n* one who writes iambs
IAMBS ▸ **iamb**
IAMBUS = **iamb**
IATRIC *adj* relating to medicine or physicians
IBADAH *n* following of Islamic beliefs and practices **ibadat**
IBERIS *n* plant with white or purple flowers
IBEX *n* wild goat **ibexes, ibices**
IBIDEM *adv* in the same place
IBIS *n* **ibises**
IBRIK ▸ **cezve**
IBRIKS ▸ **ibrik**
ICE *n, vb*
ICEBALL *n* ball of ice
ICEBERG *n*
ICEBOAT *n* boat that breaks up bodies of ice in water
ICEBOX *n*
ICECAP *n* **icecaps**
ICED *adj* covered with icing
ICEFALL *n* part of a glacier
ICELESS ▸ **ice**
ICELIKE ▸ **ice**
ICEMAN *n* person who sells or delivers ice **icemen**
ICEPACK *n* bag or folded cloth containing ice
ICER *n* person who ices cakes **icers**
ICES ▸ **ice**
ICEWINE *n* dessert wine made from grapes that have frozen before being harvested
ICH *archaic form of* ▸ **eke**

A Shakespearean spelling of **eke**, this is a useful little word worth remembering because of its unusual combination of letters and relatively high score.

ICHABOD *interj* the glory has departed
ICHED ▸ **ich**
ICHES ▸ **ich**
ICHING ▸ **ich**
ICHNITE *n* trace fossil
ICHOR *n* fluid said to flow in the veins of the gods **ichors**
ICHS ▸ **ich**
ICHTHIC = **ichthyic**
ICHTHYS *n* early Christian emblem
ICICLE *n*
ICICLED *adj* covered with icicles
ICICLES ▸ **icicle**
ICIER ▸ **icy**
ICIEST ▸ **icy**
ICILY *adv* in an icy or reserved manner
ICINESS *n* condition of being icy or very cold
ICING *n* **icings**
ICK *interj* expression of disgust

> An interjection expressing disgust, this is one of the highest-scoring three-letter words beginning with I. It does not take an S, but it does take a Y to make **icky**.

ICKER *n* ear of corn **ickers**
ICKIER ▸ **icky**
ICKIEST ▸ **icky**
ICKILY ▸ **icky**
ICKLE *ironically childish word for* ▸ **little**
ICKLER ▸ **ickle**
ICKLEST ▸ **ickle**
ICKY *adj* sticky
ICON *n* **icones**
ICONIC *adj* relating to the character of an icon
ICONIFY *vb* render as an icon
ICONISE = **iconize**
ICONIZE *vb* render as an icon
ICONS ▸ **icon**
ICTAL ▸ **ictus**
ICTERIC ▸ **icterus**
ICTERID *n* bird of the oriole family
ICTERUS *n* yellowing of plant leaves
ICTIC ▸ **ictus**
ICTUS *n* metrical or rhythmic stress in verse feet **ictuses**
ICY *adj*
ID *n*
IDANT *n* chromosome **idants**
IDE *n* silver orfe fish
IDEA *n, vb* **ideaed**
IDEAL *adj, n* **ideally, ideals**
IDEAS ▸ **idea**
IDEATA ▸ **ideatum**
IDEATE *vb* form or have an idea of **ideated, ideates**
IDEATUM *n* objective reality
IDEE *n* idea **idees**
IDEM *adj* same
IDENT *n* short visual image that works as a logo
IDENTIC *adj* having the same intention regarding another power
IDENTS ▸ **ident**
IDES *n* specific date of each month in the Roman calendar
IDIOCY *n*
IDIOM *n* **idioms**
IDIOT *n*
IDIOTCY = **idiocy**
IDIOTIC *adj*
IDIOTS ▸ **idiot**
IDLE *adj, vb* **idled**
IDLER *n* person who idles **idlers**
IDLES, idlesse, idlest, idling, idly ▸ **idle**
IDOL *n*
IDOLA ▸ **idolum**
IDOLISE = **idolize**
IDOLISM ▸ **idolize**
IDOLIST ▸ **idolize**
IDOLIZE *vb*
IDOLON *n* mental image
IDOLS ▸ **idol**
IDOLUM *n* mental picture
IDS ▸ **id**
IDYL = **idyll**
IDYLIST = **idyllist**
IDYLL *n*
IDYLLIC *adj* of or relating to an idyll
IDYLLS ▸ **idyll**
IDYLS ▸ **idyl**
IF *n*
IFF *conj* in logic, a shortened form of if and only if

> This word is one of the highest-scoring three-letter words beginning with I, and of course provides a useful extension to **if**.

IFFIER ▸ **iffy**
IFFIEST ▸ **iffy**
IFFY *adj* doubtful, uncertain
IFS ▸ **if**
IFTAR *n* meal eaten by Muslims **iftars**
IGAD = **egad**
IGAPO *n* flooded forest **igapos**
IGARAPE *n* canoe route
IGG *vb* antagonize **igged, igging, iggs**
IGLOO *n* **igloos, iglu**
IGLUS ▸ **iglu**
IGNARO *n* ignoramus **ignaros**
IGNATIA *n* dried seed
IGNEOUS *adj*
IGNIFY *vb* turn into fire
IGNITE *vb* **ignited**
IGNITER *n* person or thing that ignites
IGNITES ▸ **ignite**
IGNITOR = **igniter**
IGNOBLE *adj* **ignobly**
IGNOMY *Shakespearean variant of* > **ignominy**
IGNORE *vb, n* **ignored, ignorer, ignores**
IGUANA *n* **iguanas, iguanid**
IHRAM *n* white robes worn by Muslim pilgrims to Mecca **ihrams**
IJTIHAD *n* effort of deriving a legal ruling from the Koran
IKAN *n* (in Malaysia) fish **ikans**
IKAT *n* method of creating patterns in fabric **ikats**
IKEBANA *n* Japanese art of flower arrangement
IKON = **icon**
IKONS ▸ **ikon**
ILEA ▸ **ileum**

> This is the plural of **ileum**, part of the small intestine, and is often useful as a rack-balancing play when you have too many vowels.

ILEAC *adj* of or relating to the ileum **ileal**
ILEITIS *n* inflammation of the ileum
ILEUM *n* lowest part of the small intestine
ILEUS *n* obstruction of the intestine **ileuses**
ILEX *n* any of a genus of trees or shrubs that includes holly **ilexes**
ILIA ▸ **ilium**
ILIAC *adj* of or relating to the ilium
ILIACUS *n* iliac
ILIAD *n* epic poem **iliads**
ILIAL ▸ **ilium**
ILICES ▸ **ilex**
ILIUM *n* part of the hipbone
ILK *n* type ▹ *determiner* each **ilka**
ILKADAY *n* every day
ILKS ▸ **ilk**
ILL *adj, n, adv*
ILLAPSE *vb* slide in
ILLEGAL *adj, n*
ILLER ▸ **ill**
ILLEST ▸ **ill**
ILLIAD *n* wink **illiads**
ILLICIT *adj*
ILLIPE *n* Asian tree **illipes**
ILLITE *n* clay mineral of the mica group **illites, illitic**
ILLNESS *n*
ILLOGIC *n* reasoning characterized by lack of logic
ILLS ▸ **ill**
ILLTH *n* condition of poverty or misery **illths**
ILLUDE *vb* trick or deceive **illuded, illudes**
ILLUME *vb* illuminate **illumed, illumes**
ILLUPI = **illipe**
ILLUPIS ▸ **illupi**
ILLUVIA > **illuvium**
ILLY *adv* badly
IMAGE *n, vb* **imaged**
IMAGER *n* device that produces images **imagers**
IMAGERY *n*
IMAGES ▸ **image**
IMAGINE *vb, sentence substitute*
IMAGING ▸ **image**
IMAGISM *n* poetic movement **imagist**
IMAGO *n* sexually mature adult insect **imagoes, imagos**
IMAM *n*
IMAMATE *n* region or territory governed by an imam
IMAMS ▸ **imam**
IMARET *n* (in Turkey) a hospice for pilgrims

or travellers **imarets**
IMARI *n* Japanese porcelain **imaris**
IMAUM = **imam**
IMAUMS ▸ **imaum**
IMBALM = **embalm**
IMBALMS ▸ **imbalm**
IMBAR *vb* bar in
IMBARK *vb* cover in bark **imbarks**
IMBARS ▸ **imbar**
IMBASE *vb* degrade **imbased, imbases**
IMBATHE *vb* bathe
IMBED = **embed**
IMBEDS ▸ **imbed**
IMBIBE *vb* **imbibed, imbiber, imbibes**
IMBIZO *n* meeting in S Africa **imbizos**
IMBLAZE *vb* depict heraldically
IMBODY = **embody**
IMBOSK *vb* conceal **imbosks**
IMBOSOM *vb* hold in one's heart
IMBOSS = **emboss**
IMBOWER *vb* enclose in a bower
IMBRAST *Spenserian past participle of* ▸ **embrace**
IMBREX *n* curved tile
IMBROWN *vb* make brown
IMBRUE *vb* stain, esp with blood **imbrued, imbrues**
IMBRUTE *vb* reduce to a bestial state
IMBUE *vb* fill or inspire with (ideals or principles) **imbued, imbues, imbuing**
IMBURSE *vb* pay
IMID *n* immunomodulatory drug
IMIDE *n* any of a class of organic compounds **imides, imidic, imido**
IMIDS ▸ **imid**
IMINE *n* any of a class of organic compounds **imines, imino**
IMITANT = **imitation**
IMITATE *vb*
IMMANE *adj* monstrous
IMMASK *vb* disguise **immasks**
IMMENSE *adj*
IMMERGE *archaic word for* ▸ **immerse**
IMMERSE *vb*
IMMESH *variant of* ▸ **enmesh**
IMMEW *vb* confine **immewed, immews**
IMMIES ▸ **immy**
IMMIT *vb* insert **immits**
IMMIX *vb* mix in **immixed, immixes**
IMMORAL *adj*
IMMUNE *adj, n* **immunes**
IMMURE *vb* imprison **immured, immures**
IMMY *n* image-orthicon camera
IMP *n, vb*
IMPACT *n, vb* **impacts**
IMPAINT *vb* paint
IMPAIR *vb* **impairs**
IMPALA *n* southern African antelope **impalas**
IMPALE *vb* **impaled, impaler, impales**
IMPANEL *variant spelling (esp US) of* ▸ **empanel**
IMPARK *vb* make into a park **imparks**
IMPARL *vb* parley **imparls**
IMPART *vb* **imparts**
IMPASSE *n*
IMPASTE *vb* apply paint thickly to
IMPASTO *n, vb*
IMPAVE *vb* set in a pavement **impaved, impaves**
IMPAVID *adj* fearless
IMPAWN *vb* pawn **impawns**
IMPEACH *vb*
IMPEARL *vb* adorn with pearls
IMPED ▸ **imp**
IMPEDE *vb* **impeded, impeder, impedes**
IMPEDOR *n* component that offers impedance
IMPEL *vb* **impels**
IMPEND *vb* be about to happen **impends**
IMPERIA > **imperium**
IMPERIL *vb*
IMPETUS *n*
IMPHEE *n* African sugar cane **imphees**
IMPI *n* group of Zulu warriors **impies**
IMPIETY *n* lack of respect or religious reverence
IMPING ▸ **imp**
IMPINGE *vb*
IMPINGS ▸ **imp**
IMPIOUS *adj*

IMPIS ▸ **impi**
IMPISH *adj* mischievous
IMPLANT *n, vb*
IMPLATE *vb* sheathe
IMPLEAD *vb* sue or prosecute **impled**
IMPLETE *vb* fill
IMPLEX *n* part of an arthropod
IMPLIED *adj* hinted at or suggested
IMPLIES ▸ **imply**
IMPLODE *vb*
IMPLORE *vb*
IMPLY *vb*
IMPONE *vb* impose **imponed, impones**
IMPORT *vb, n* **imports**
IMPOSE *vb* **imposed, imposer, imposes**
IMPOSEX *n* acquisition by female organisms of male characteristics
IMPOST *n* tax, esp a customs duty ▹ *vb* classify (imported goods) according to the duty payable on them **imposts**
IMPOT *n* slang term for the act of imposing **impots**
IMPOUND *vb*
IMPOWER *less common spelling of* ▸ **empower**
IMPREGN *vb* impregnate
IMPRESA *n* heraldic device **imprese**
IMPRESS *vb, n*
IMPREST *n* fund of cash used to pay incidental expenses
IMPRINT *n, vb*
IMPROV *n* improvisational comedy
IMPROVE *vb*
IMPROVS ▸ **improv**
IMPS ▸ **imp**
IMPUGN *vb* challenge the truth or validity of **impugns**
IMPULSE *vb, n*
IMPURE *adj* **impurer**
IMPUTE *vb* **imputed, imputer, imputes**
IMSHI *interj* go away! **imshy**
IN *prep, adv, adj, n, vb*
INANE *adj, n* **inanely, inaner, inanes, inanest**
INANGA *n* common type of New Zealand grass tree **inangas**
INANITY *n* lack of intelligence or imagination
INAPT *adj* not apt or fitting **inaptly**
INARCH *vb* graft (a plant)
INARM *vb* embrace **inarmed, inarms**
INBEING *n* existence in something else
INBENT *adj* bent inwards
INBOARD *adj* (of a boat's engine) inside the hull ▹ *adv* within the sides of or towards the centre of a vessel or aircraft
INBORN *adj*
INBOUND *vb* pass into the playing area from outside it ▹ *adj* coming in
INBOX *n* **inboxes**
INBREAK *n* breaking in
INBRED *n, adj* **inbreds**
INBREED *vb*
INBRING *vb* bring in
INBUILT *adj* present from the start
INBURST *n* irruption
INBY *adv* into the house or an inner room ▹ *adj* located near or nearest to the house
INBYE *adv* near the house
INCAGE *vb* confine in or as in a cage **incaged, incages**
INCANT *vb* chant (a spell) **incants**
INCASE *variant spelling of* ▸ **encase**
INCASED ▸ **incase**
INCASES ▸ **incase**
INCAVE *vb* hide **incaved, incaves**
INCAVI ▸ **incavo**
INCAVO *n* incised part of a carving
INCEDE *vb* advance **inceded, incedes**
INCENSE *vb, n*
INCENT *vb* provide incentive **incents**
INCEPT *vb* (of organisms) to ingest (food) ▹ *n* rudimentary organ **incepts**
INCEST *n* **incests**
INCH *n, vb*
INCHASE = **enchase**
INCHED ▸ **inch**
INCHER *n* something

measuring given amount of inches **inchers**
INCHES ▶ **inch**
INCHING ▶ **inch**
INCHPIN *n* cervine sweetbread
INCIPIT *n* Latin introductory phrase
INCISAL *adj* relating to the cutting edge of incisors and cuspids
INCISE *vb* cut into with a sharp tool **incised, incises**
INCISOR *n*
INCITE *vb* **incited, inciter, incites**
INCIVIL *archaic form of* ▶ **uncivil**
INCLASP *vb* clasp
INCLE = **inkle**
INCLES ▶ **incle**
INCLINE *vb, n*
INCLIP *vb* embrace **inclips**
INCLOSE *less common spelling of* ▶ **enclose**
INCLUDE *vb*
INCOG *n* incognito **incogs**
INCOME *n*
INCOMER *n* person who comes to a place in which they were not born
INCOMES ▶ **income**
INCONIE *adj* fine or delicate
INCONNU *n* whitefish of Arctic waters
INCONY *adj* fine or delicate
INCROSS *n* variation produced by inbreeding ▷ *vb* produce by inbreeding
INCRUST = **encrust**
INCUBI ▶ **incubus**
INCUBUS *n* (in folklore) type of demon
INCUDAL ▶ **incus**
INCUDES ▶ **incus**
INCULT *adj* (of land) uncultivated
INCUR *vb* **incurs**
INCURVE *vb* curve or cause to curve inwards
INCUS *n* bone in the ear of mammals
INCUSE *n* design stamped or hammered onto a coin ▷ *vb* impress (a design) in a coin ▷ *adj* stamped or hammered onto a coin **incused, incuses**
INCUT *adj* cut or etched in
INDABA *n* (among South Africans) a meeting to discuss a serious topic **indabas**
INDAMIN = **indamine**
INDART *vb* dart in **indarts**
INDEED *adv, interj*
INDENE *n* colourless liquid hydrocarbon **indenes**
INDENT *vb* **indents**
INDEW = **indue**
INDEWED ▶ **indew**
INDEWS ▶ **indew**
INDEX *n, vb* **indexal, indexed, indexer, indexes**
INDIA *n* **indias**
INDICAN *n* compound secreted in the urine
INDICES *plural of* ▶ **index**
INDICIA > **indicium**
INDICT *vb* **indicts**
INDIE *adj* (of rock music) released by an independent record label ▷ *n* independent record company **indies**
INDIGEN = **indigene**
INDIGN *adj* undeserving
INDIGO *adj, n* **indigos**
INDITE *vb* write **indited, inditer, indites**
INDIUM *n* soft silvery-white metallic element **indiums**
INDOL = **indole**
INDOLE *n* crystalline heterocyclic compound **indoles**
INDOLS ▶ **indol**
INDOOR *adj*
INDOORS *adj*
INDORSE *variant spelling of* ▶ **endorse**
INDOW *archaic variant of* ▶ **indow**
INDOWED ▶ **indow**
INDOWS ▶ **indow**
INDOXYL *n* water-soluble crystalline compound
INDRAFT = **indraught**
INDRAWN *adj* drawn or pulled in
INDRI = **indris**
INDRIS *n* large lemuroid primate
INDUCE *vb* **induced,**

inducer, induces
INDUCT *vb* formally install (someone) in office **inducts**
INDUE *variant spelling of* ▸ **endue**
INDUED ▸ **indue**
INDUES ▸ **indue**
INDUING ▸ **indue**
INDULGE *vb*
INDULIN = **induline**
INDULT *n* type of faculty granted by the Holy See **indults**
INDUNA *n* (in South Africa) a Black African overseer **indunas**
INDUSIA > **indusium**
INDWELL *vb* (of a spirit, principle, etc) to inhabit **indwelt**
INEARTH *poetic word for* ▸ **bury**
INEDITA *pl n* unpublished writings
INEPT *adj* **inepter, ineptly**
INERM *adj* without thorns
INERT *n, adj* **inerter**
INERTIA *n*

This is not the easiest of words to see, but its combination of common letters makes it one of the most frequently played of 7-letter bonuses, while its plurals, which can be **inertiae** or **inertias**, are among the 8-letter bonus words that come up most often.

INERTLY ▸ **inert**
INERTS ▸ **inert**
INEXACT *adj* not exact or accurate
INFALL *vb* move towards (something) under the influence of gravity **infalls**
INFAME *vb* defame **infamed, infames**
INFAMY *n*
INFANCY *n* early childhood
INFANT *n, adj*
INFANTA *n* (formerly) daughter of a king of Spain or Portugal
INFANTE *n* (formerly) any son of a king of Spain or Portugal, except the heir to the throne
INFANTS ▸ **infant**
INFARCT *n* localized area of dead tissue ▹ *vb* obstruct the blood supply to part of a body
INFARE *vb* enter **infares**
INFAUNA *n* animals that live in ocean and river beds
INFAUST *adj* unlucky
INFECT *vb, adj* **infects**
INFEFT *vb* give possession of heritable property **infefts**
INFELT *adj* heartfelt
INFEOFF = **enfeoff**
INFER *vb*
INFERE *adv* together
INFERNO *n*
INFERS ▸ **infer**
INFEST *vb* **infests**
INFIDEL *n* person with no religion ▹ *adj* of unbelievers or unbelief
INFIELD *n* area of the field near the pitch
INFIGHT *vb* box at close quarters
INFILL *vb* fill in ▹ *n* act of filling or closing gaps in something **infills**
INFIMA ▸ **infimum**
INFIMUM *n* greatest lower bound
INFIRM *vb, adj* **infirms**
INFIX *vb* fix firmly in ▹ *n* affix inserted into the middle of a word **infixed, infixes**
INFLAME *vb*
INFLATE *vb*
INFLECT *vb*
INFLICT *vb*
INFLOW *n* something, such as liquid or gas, that flows in ▹ *vb* flow in **inflows**
INFLUX *n*
INFO *n* information
INFOLD *variant spelling of* ▸ **enfold**
INFOLDS ▸ **infold**
INFORCE = **enforce**
INFORM *vb, adj* **informs**
INFOS ▸ **info**
INFRA *adv* (esp in textual annotation) below
INFRACT *vb* violate or break (a law, an agreement, etc)
INFULA = **infulae**
INFULAE *pl n* two ribbons hanging from a bishop's mitre

INFUSE *vb* **infused**
INFUSER *n* any device used to make an infusion
INFUSES ▸ **infuse**
ING *n* meadow near a river
INGAN *Scots word for* ▸ **onion**
INGANS ▸ **ingan**
INGATE *n* entrance **ingates**
INGENER *Shakespearean form of* > **engineer**
INGENU *n* artless or inexperienced boy or young man
INGENUE *n* inexperienced girl or young woman
INGENUS ▸ **ingenu**
INGEST *vb* take (food or liquid) into the body
INGESTA *pl n* nourishment taken through the mouth
INGESTS ▸ **ingest**
INGINE *n* genius **ingines**
INGLE *n* fire in a room or a fireplace **ingles**
INGLOBE *vb* shape as a sphere
INGO *n* revelation **ingoes, ingoing**
INGOT *n, vb* **ingoted, ingots**
INGRAFT *variant spelling of* ▸ **engraft**
INGRAIN *vb* impress deeply on the mind or nature ▹ *adj* (of carpets) made of fibre that is dyed before being spun ▹ *n* carpet made from ingrained yarn
INGRAM *adj* ignorant
INGRATE *n* ungrateful person ▹ *adj* ungrateful
INGRESS *n* entrance
INGROSS *archaic form of* ▸ **engross**
INGROUP *n* highly cohesive and relatively closed social group
INGROWN *adj* grown abnormally into the flesh
INGRUM *adj* ignorant
INGS ▸ **ing**
INGULF *variant spelling of* ▸ **engulf**
INGULFS ▸ **ingulf**
INGULPH *archaic form of* ▸ **engulf**
INHABIT *vb*
INHALE *vb* **inhaled**
INHALER *n*
INHALES ▸ **inhale**
INHAUL *n* line for hauling in a sail **inhauls**
INHAUST *vb* drink in
INHERCE = **inhearse**
INHERE *vb* be an inseparable part (of) **inhered, inheres**
INHERIT *vb*
INHIBIN *n* peptide hormone
INHIBIT *vb*
INHOOP *vb* confine **inhoops**
INHUMAN *adj*
INHUME *vb* inter **inhumed, inhumer, inhumes**
INIA ▸ **inion**
INION *n* most prominent point at the back of the head **inions**
INISLE *vb* put on or make into an island **inisled, inisles**
INITIAL *adj, n, vb*
INJECT *vb* **injects**
INJELLY *vb* place in jelly
INJERA *n* white Ethiopian flatbread, similar to a crepe **injeras**
INJOINT *vb* join
INJUNCT *vb* issue a legal injunction against (a person)
INJURE *vb* **injured, injurer, injures**
INJURY *n*
INK *n, vb*
INKBLOT *n* abstract patch of ink
INKED ▸ **ink**
INKER ▸ **ink**
INKERS ▸ **ink**
INKHORN *n* (formerly) a small portable container for ink
INKHOSI *n* Zulu clan chief
INKIER ▸ **inky**
INKIEST ▸ **inky**
INKING ▸ **ink**
INKJET *adj* of a method of printing
INKLE *n* kind of linen tape used for trimmings ▹ *vb* hint **inkled, inkles**
INKLESS ▸ **ink**
INKLIKE ▸ **ink**

INKLING *n*
INKOSI ▸ **inkhosi**
INKOSIS ▸ **inkosi**
INKPAD *n* pad used for rubber-stamping or fingerprinting **inkpads**
INKPOT *n* ink-bottle **inkpots**
INKS ▸ **ink**
INKSPOT *n* ink stain
INKWELL *n*
INKWOOD *n* type of tree
INKY *adj* dark or black
INLACE *variant spelling of* ▸ **enlace**
INLACED ▸ **inlace**
INLACES ▸ **inlace**
INLAID ▸ **inlay**
INLAND *adv, adj, n* **inlands**
INLAY *n* inlaid substance or pattern ▹ *vb* decorate by inserting wooden pieces **inlayer, inlays**
INLET *n, vb* **inlets**
INLIER *n* outcrop of rocks surrounded by younger rocks **inliers**
INLOCK *vb* lock up **inlocks**
INLY *adv* inwardly
INLYING *adj* situated within or inside
INMATE *n* **inmates**
INMESH *variant spelling of* ▸ **enmesh**
INMOST *adj*
INN *n, vb*
INNAGE *n* type of measurement **innages**
INNARDS *pl n*
INNATE *adj*
INNED ▸ **inn**
INNER *adj, n* **innerly, inners**
INNERVE *vb* supply with nervous energy
INNING *n* division of baseball match **innings**
INNIT *interj* isn't it
INNLESS *adj* without inns
INNS ▸ **inn**
INNYARD *n* courtyard of an inn
INOCULA > **inoculum**
INORB *vb* enclose in or as if in an orb **inorbed, inorbs**
INOSINE *n* type of molecule making up cell
INOSITE = **inositol**
INPHASE *adj* in the same phase
INPOUR *vb* pour in **inpours**
INPUT *n, vb* **inputs**
INQILAB *n* (in India, Pakistan, etc) revolution
INQUERE *Spenserian form of* ▸ **inquire**
INQUEST *n*
INQUIET *vb* disturb
INQUIRE *vb*
INQUIRY *n* question
INRO *n* Japanese seal-box
INROAD *n* invasion or hostile attack **inroads**
INRUN *n* slope down which ski jumpers ski **inruns**
INRUSH *n* sudden and overwhelming inward flow
INS ▸ **in**
INSANE *adj* **insaner**
INSANIE *n* insanity
INSCAPE *n* essential inner nature of a person, etc
INSCULP *vb* engrave
INSEAM *vb* contain **inseams**
INSECT *n* **insects**
INSEEM *vb* cover with grease **inseems**
INSERT *vb, n* **inserts**
INSET *n* small picture inserted within a larger one ▹ *vb* place in or within ▹ *adj* decorated with something inserted **insets**
INSHELL *vb* retreat, as into a shell
INSHIP *vb* travel or send by ship **inships**
INSHORE *adj, adv*
INSIDE *prep, adj, adv, n*
INSIDER *n*
INSIDES ▸ **inside**
INSIGHT *n*
INSIGNE = **insignia**
INSINEW *vb* connect or strengthen, as with sinews
INSIPID *adj*
INSIST *vb* **insists**
INSNARE *less common spelling of* ▸ **ensnare**
INSOFAR *adv* to the extent

INSOLE *n* **insoles**
INSOOTH *adv* indeed
INSOUL *variant of* ▸ **ensoul**
INSOULS ▸ **insoul**
INSPAN *vb* harness (animals) to (a vehicle) **inspans**
INSPECT *vb*
INSPIRE *vb*
INSTAL = **install**
INSTALL *vb*
INSTALS ▸ **instal**
INSTANT *n, adj*
INSTAR *vb* decorate with stars ▹ *n* stage in the development of an insect **instars**
INSTATE *vb* place in a position or office
INSTEAD *adv*
INSTEP *n* **insteps**
INSTIL *vb* **instill, instils**
INSULA *n* pyramid-shaped area of the brain **insulae**
INSULAR *adj, n*
INSULIN *n*
INSULSE *adj* stupid
INSULT *vb, n* **insults**
INSURE *vb*
INSURED *adj* covered by insurance ▹ *n* those covered by an insurance policy
INSURER *n* person or company that sells insurance
INSURES ▸ **insure**
INSWEPT *adj* narrowed towards the front
INSWING *n* movement of a bowled ball
INTACT *adj*
INTAGLI > **intaglio**
INTAKE *n* **intakes**
INTEGER *n*
INTEL *n* US military intelligence **intels**
INTEND *vb* **intends**
INTENSE *adj*
INTENT *n, adj* **intents**
INTER *vb*
INTERIM *adj, n, adv*
INTERN *vb, n* **interne, interns**
INTERS ▸ **inter**
INTHRAL *archaic form of* ▸ **enthral**
INTI *n* former monetary unit of Peru
INTIL *Scot form of* ▸ **into**
INTIMA *n* innermost layer of an organ or part **intimae, intimal, intimas**
INTIME *adj* intimate
INTINE *n* inner wall of a pollen grain or a spore **intines**
INTIRE *archaic form of* ▸ **entire**
INTIS ▸ **inti**
INTITLE *archaic form of* ▸ **entitle**
INTO *prep*
INTOED *adj* having inward-turning toes
INTOMB = **entomb**
INTOMBS ▸ **intomb**
INTONE *vb* **intoned, intoner, intones**
INTORT *vb* twist inward **intorts**
INTOWN *adj* infield
INTRA *prep* within
INTRADA *n* prelude
INTRANT *n* one who enters
INTREAT *archaic spelling of* ▸ **entreat**
INTRO *n* introduction
INTROFY *vb* increase the wetting properties
INTROIT *n* short prayer said or sung
INTROLD *variant of* ▸ **entrold**
INTRON *n* stretch of DNA **introns**
INTROS ▸ **intro**
INTRUDE *vb*
INTRUST = **entrust**
INTUIT *vb* know or discover by intuition **intuits**
INTURN *n* inward turn **inturns**
INTUSE *n* contusion **intuses**
INTWINE *less common spelling of* ▸ **entwine**
INTWIST *vb* twist together
INULA *n* plant of the elecampane genus **inulas**
INULASE *n* enzyme
INULIN *n* fructose polysaccharide **inulins**
INURE *vb* **inured, inures, inuring**
INURN *vb* place (esp cremated ashes) in an urn **inurned, inurns**
INUST *adj* burnt in
INUTILE *adj* useless
INVADE *vb* **invaded, invader, invades**

INVALID *n, vb, adj*
INVAR *n* alloy made from iron and nickel **invars**
INVEIGH *vb* criticize strongly
INVENIT *sentence substitute* (he or she) designed it
INVENT *vb* **invents**
INVERSE *vb, adj, n*
INVERT *vb, n* **inverts**
INVEST *vb* **invests**
INVEXED *adj* concave
INVIOUS *adj* without paths or roads
INVITAL *adj* not vital
INVITE *vb, n* **invited**
INVITEE *n* one who is invited
INVITER ▸ **invite**
INVITES ▸ **invite**
INVOICE *n, vb*
INVOKE *vb* **invoked, invoker, invokes**
INVOLVE *vb*
INWALL *vb* surround with a wall **inwalls**
INWARD *adj, adv, n*
INWARDS *adv* towards the inside or middle of something
INWEAVE *vb* weave together
INWICK *vb* perform a type of curling stroke **inwicks**
INWIND *vb* wind or coil around **inwinds**
INWIT *n* conscience
INWITH *adv* within
INWITS ▸ **inwit**
INWORK *vb* work in **inworks**
INWORN *adj* worn in
INWOUND ▸ **inwind**
INWOVE ▸ **inweave**
INWOVEN ▸ **inweave**
INWRAP *less common spelling of* ▸ **enwrap**
INWRAPS ▸ **inwrap**
INYALA *n* antelope **inyalas**
IO *interj* an exclamation ▹ *n* cry of "io"
IODATE = **iodize**
IODATED ▸ **iodate**
IODATES ▸ **iodate**
IODIC *adj* of or containing iodine
IODID = **iodide**
IODIDE *n* chemical compound **iodides**
IODIDS ▸ **iodid**
IODIN = **iodine**
IODINE *n* **iodines**
IODINS ▸ **iodin**
IODISE = **iodize**
IODISED ▸ **iodise**
IODISER ▸ **iodise**
IODISES ▸ **iodise**
IODISM *n* poisoning caused by iodine or its compounds **iodisms**
IODIZE *vb* treat with iodine **iodized, iodizer, iodizes**
IODOUS *adj* of or containing iodine
IODURET *n* iodide
IOLITE *n* grey or violet-blue dichroic mineral **iolites**
ION *n*
IONIC *adj* of or in the form of ions
IONICS *pl n* study of ions
IONISE = **ionize**
IONISED ▸ **ionise**
IONISER = **ionizer**
IONISES ▸ **ionise**
IONIUM *n* naturally occurring radioisotope of thorium **ioniums**
IONIZE *vb* change into ions **ionized**
IONIZER *n* person or thing that ionizes
IONIZES ▸ **ionize**
IONOGEN *n* compound that exists as ions when dissolved
IONOMER *n* type of thermoplastic
IONONE *n* yellowish liquid mixture **ionones**
IONS ▸ **ion**
IOS ▸ **io**
IOTA *n* **iotas**

> This word for a Greek letter is another of those that often come in handy when you are trying to rid your rack of too many vowels.

IPECAC *n* type of S American shrub **ipecacs**
IPOMOEA *n* convolvulaceous plant
IPPON *n* winning point awarded in a judo or karate competition **ippons**
IRACUND *adj* easily angered
IRADE *n* written edict of a Muslim ruler **irades**
IRATE *adj* **irately, irater, iratest**

IRE *vb* anger ▷ *n* anger **ired, ireful, ireless**
IRENIC *adj* tending to conciliate or promote peace
IRENICS *n* branch of theology
IRES ▸ **ire**
IRID *n* type of iris **iridal, irideal**
IRIDES ▸ **iris**
IRIDIAL ▸ **irid**
IRIDIAN ▸ **irid**
IRIDIC *adj* of or containing iridium
IRIDISE *vb* make iridescent
IRIDIUM *n*
IRIDIZE *vb* make iridescent
IRIDS ▸ **irid**
IRING ▸ **ire**
IRIS *n, vb*
IRISATE *vb* make iridescent
IRISED ▸ **iris**
IRISES ▸ **iris**
IRISING ▸ **iris**
IRITIC ▸ **iritis**
IRITIS *n* inflammation of the iris of the eye

> Since a plague of Is tends to afflict every Scrabble player's rack at regular intervals, it is well worth knowing words like this one, meaning inflammation of the iris, which use several of the wretched letter!

IRK *vb* **irked, irking, irks**
IRKSOME *adj* irritating, annoying
IROKO *n* tropical African hardwood tree **irokos**
IRON *n, adj, vb*
IRONE *n* fragrant liquid

> You may surprise your opponent by adding an E to **iron** if you know this word for a kind of aromatic oil.

IRONED ▸ **iron**
IRONER ▸ **iron**
IRONERS ▸ **iron**
IRONES ▸ **irone**
IRONIC *adj* using irony
IRONIER ▸ **irony**
IRONIES ▸ **irony**
IRONING *n* clothes to be ironed
IRONISE = **ironize**
IRONIST ▸ **ironize**
IRONIZE *vb* use or indulge in irony
IRONMAN *n* very strong man **ironmen**
IRONS ▸ **iron**
IRONY *n, adj*
IRREAL *adj* unreal
IRRUPT *vb* enter forcibly or suddenly **irrupts**
IS *third person singular present tense of* ▸ **be**
ISABEL *n* brown yellow colour **isabels**
ISAGOGE *n* academic introduction
ISATIN *n* yellowish-red crystalline compound **isatine, isatins**
ISBA *n* log hut **isbas**
ISCHIA ▸ **ischium**
ISCHIAL ▸ **ischium**
ISCHIUM *n* part of the hipbone
ISH *n* issue **ishes**

> An **ish** is a word for an issue in Scots law. If you have I, S and H on your rack, remember that as well as adding **ish** to the end of many words, you can also play those letters as a word in its own right.

ISIT *sentence substitute* expression used in response to a statement
ISLAND *n, vb* **islands**
ISLE *vb, n* **isled**
ISLEMAN *n* islander **islemen**
ISLES ▸ **isle**
ISLET *n* small island
ISLETED *adj* having islets
ISLETS ▸ **islet**
ISLING ▸ **isle**
ISM *n* doctrine, system, or practice

> While **ism** can be added to the ends of many words as a suffix, it's worth remembering as a word in its own right.

ISMATIC *adj* following fashionable doctrines
ISMS ▸ **ism**
ISNA *vb* is not **isnae**
ISO *n* short segment of film that can be

replayed easily
ISOAMYL *n as in* **isoamyl acetate** colourless volatile compound
ISOBAR *n* **isobare, isobars**
ISOBASE *n* line connecting points of equal land upheaval
ISOBATH *n* line showing equal depth of water
ISOCHOR *n* line showing equal pressure and temperature
ISODICA > **isodicon**
ISODOMA > **isodomon**
ISODONT *n* animal in which the teeth are of similar size
ISODOSE *n* dose of radiation applied in radiotherapy
ISOETES *n* quillwort
ISOFORM *n* protein similar in function but not form to another
ISOGAMY *n* fusion of similar gametes
ISOGENY > **isogenous**
ISOGON *n* equiangular polygon
ISOGONE = **isogonic**
ISOGONS ▸ **isogon**
ISOGONY > **isogonic**
ISOGRAM = **isopleth**
ISOGRIV *n* line showing equal angular bearing
ISOHEL *n* line showing equal sunshine **isohels**
ISOHYET *n* line showing equal rainfall
ISOKONT = **isokontan**
ISOLATE *vb, n*
ISOLEAD *n* line on a ballistic graph
ISOLEX *n* line on map showing where a particular word is used
ISOLINE = **isopleth**
ISOLOG > **isologous**
ISOLOGS > **isologous**
ISOMER *n* compound that has the same molecular formula as another **isomere, isomers**
ISONOME *n* line on a map showing equal abundance of a species
ISONOMY *n* equality before the law of the citizens of a state
ISOPACH *n* line showing equal thickness
ISOPOD *n* type of crustacean ▷ *adj* of this type of crustacean **isopods**
ISOS ▸ **iso**
ISOSPIN *n* number used to classify elementary particles
ISOTACH *n* line showing equal wind speed
ISOTONE *n* atom with same number of neutrons as another
ISOTOPE *n* **isotopy**
ISOTRON *n* device for separating small quantities of isotopes
ISOTYPE *n* pictorial presentation of statistical information
ISOZYME *n* variant of an enzyme
ISSEI *n* first-generation Japanese immigrant **isseis**
ISSUANT *adj* emerging or issuing
ISSUE *n, vb* **issued, issuer, issuers, issues, issuing**
ISTANA *n* (in Malaysia) a royal palace **istanas**
ISTHMI ▸ **isthmus**
ISTHMIC ▸ **isthmus**
ISTHMUS *n*
ISTLE *n* fibre obtained from various agave and yucca trees **istles**
IT *pron, n*
ITA *n* type of palm
ITACISM *n* pronunciation of the Greek letter eta
ITALIC *adj* (of printing type) sloping to the right ▷ *n* style of printing type **italics**
ITAS ▸ **ita**
ITCH *n, vb* **itched, itches, itchier, itchily, itching, itchy**
ITEM *n, adv, vb* **itemed, iteming**
ITEMISE = **itemize**
ITEMIZE *vb*
ITEMS ▸ **item**
ITERANT ▸ **iterate**
ITERATE *vb* repeat
ITERUM *adv* again
ITHER *Scot word for* ▸ **other**
ITS *pron, adj*
ITSELF *pron*

IURE *adv* by law
IVIED *adj* covered with ivy
IVIES ▸ **ivy**
IVORIED ▸ **ivory**
IVORIES *pl n* keys of a piano
IVORIST *n* worker in ivory
IVORY *n, adj*
IVRESSE *n* drunkenness
IVY *n* **ivylike**
IWI *n*

This Maori word for a tribe is a great one for getting rid of an awkward combination of letters.

IWIS *archaic word for* > **certainly**
IXIA *n* southern African plant **ixias**
IXODID *n* hard-bodied tick **ixodids**
IXORA *n* flowering shrub **ixoras**
IXTLE = **istle**
IXTLES ▸ **ixtle**
IZAR *n* long garment worn by Muslim women
IZARD *n* type of goat-antelope **izards**
IZARS ▸ **izar**
IZZARD *n* letter Z **izzards**
IZZAT *n* honour or prestige **izzats**

J, being worth 8 points on its own, is a good tile for scoring well with, especially as it combines well with **Z** to make **jiz** and with **X** to make great words like **jeux, jinx** and **jynx**. However, **J** is a difficult letter when it comes to making bonus words scoring that extra 50 points, so you will normally want to play it off fairly quickly. There are two two-letter words that begin with **J**: **ja** and **jo**. As **J** has such a high value, look out for double- and triple-letter squares when playing these. There are plenty of good three-letter words starting with **J**: **jab** (12 points), **jak** (14), **jam** (12), **jar** (10), **jaw** (13), **jay** (13), **jet** (10), **jib** (12), **jig** (11), **job** (12), **jog** (11), **jot** (10), **joy** (13), **jug** (11) and **jut** (10).

JA *interj* yes ▷ *sentence substitute* yes
JAB *vb, n* **jabbed**
JABBER *vb, n* **jabbers**
JABBING ▶ **jab**
JABBLE *vb* ripple **jabbled, jabbles**
JABERS *interj* Irish exclamation
JABIRU *n* **jabirus**
JABOT *n* frill or ruffle on the front of a blouse or shirt **jabots**
JABS ▶ **jab**
JACAL *n* Mexican daub hut **jacales, jacals**
JACAMAR *n* tropical American bird with an iridescent plumage
JACANA *n* long-legged long-toed bird **jacanas**
JACARE *another name for* ▶ **cayman**
JACARES ▶ **jacare**
JACCHUS *n* small monkey
JACENT *adj* lying
JACINTH *another name for* > **hyacinth**
JACK *n, vb*
JACKAL *n, vb* **jackals**
JACKASS *n* fool
JACKDAW *n*
JACKED ▶ **jack**
JACKEEN *n* slick self-assertive lower-class Dubliner
JACKER *n* labourer **jackers**
JACKET *n, vb* **jackets**
JACKING ▶ **jack**
JACKLEG *n* unskilled worker
JACKMAN *n* retainer **jackmen**
JACKPOT *n*
JACKS *n* type of game
JACOBIN *n* variety of fancy pigeon
JACOBUS *n* English gold coin
JACONET *n* light cotton fabric
JACUZZI *n* type of bath or pool
JADE *n, adj, vb*
JADED *adj* tired and unenthusiastic **jadedly**
JADEITE *n* usually green or white mineral
JADERY *n* shrewishness
JADES, jading, jadish,

jaditic ▸ **jade**
JAEGER *n* German or Austrian marksman **jaegers**
JAFFA *n* (in cricket) well-bowled ball **jaffas**
JAG *n* period of uncontrolled indulgence in an activity ▹ *vb* cut unevenly
JAGA *n* guard ▹ *vb* guard or watch **jagaed, jagaing, jagas**
JAGER = **jaeger**
JAGERS ▸ **jager**
JAGG = **jag**
JAGGARY = **jaggery**
JAGGED ▸ **jag**
JAGGER *n* pedlar **jaggers**
JAGGERY *n* coarse brown sugar
JAGGIER ▸ **jaggy**
JAGGIES ▸ **jaggy**
JAGGING ▸ **jag**
JAGGS ▸ **jagg**
JAGGY *adj* prickly ▹ *n* jagged computer image
JAGHIR *n* Indian regional governance
JAGHIRE *n* Indian regional governance
JAGHIRS ▸ **jaghir**
JAGIR *n* Indian regional governance **jagirs**
JAGLESS ▸ **jag**
JAGRA *n* Hindu festival **jagras**
JAGS ▸ **jag**
JAGUAR *n* **jaguars**
JAI *interj* victory (to)
JAIL *n, vb* **jailed**
JAILER *n* **jailers**
JAILING ▸ **jail**
JAILOR = **jailer**
JAILORS ▸ **jailor**
JAILS ▸ **jail**
JAK ▸ **jack**
JAKE *adj* slang word meaning all right
JAKES *n* human excrement **jakeses**
JAKS ▸ **jack**
JALABIB ▸ **jilbab**
JALAP *n* Mexican convolvulaceous plant **jalapic**
JALAPIN *n* purgative resin
JALAPS ▸ **jalap**
JALOP = **jalap**
JALOPPY = **jalopy**
JALOPS ▸ **jalop**
JALOPY *n* old car
JALOUSE *vb* suspect
JAM *vb, n*
JAMAAT *n* **jamaats**
JAMADAR *n* Indian army officer
JAMB *n, vb*
JAMBART = **greave**
JAMBE = **jamb**
JAMBEAU *another word for* ▸ **greave**
JAMBED ▸ **jamb**
JAMBEE *n* light cane **jambees**
JAMBER = **greave**
JAMBERS ▸ **jamber**
JAMBES ▸ **jambe**
JAMBEUX ▸ **jambeau**
JAMBIER *n* greave
JAMBING ▸ **jamb**
JAMBIYA *n* curved dagger
JAMBO *sentence substitute* E African salutation
JAMBOK = **sjambok**
JAMBOKS ▸ **jambok**
JAMBONE *n* type of play in the card game euchre
JAMBOOL = **jambolan**
JAMBS ▸ **jamb**
JAMBU = **jambolan**
JAMBUL = **jambolan**
JAMBULS ▸ **jambul**
JAMBUS ▸ **jambu**
JAMDANI *n* patterned muslin
JAMES *n* jemmy **jameses**
JAMJAR *n* container for preserves **jamjars**
JAMLIKE, jammed, jammer, jammers ▸ **jam**
JAMMIER ▸ **jammy**
JAMMIES *informal word for* ▸ **pyjamas**
JAMMING ▸ **jam**
JAMMY *adj* lucky
JAMON *n as in* **jamon serrano** cured ham from Spain
JAMPAN *n* type of sedan chair used in India
JAMPANI = **jampanee**
JAMPANS ▸ **jampan**
JAMPOT *n* container for preserves **jampots**
JAMS ▸ **jam**
JANE *n* girl or woman **janes**
JANGLE *vb, n* **jangled, jangler, jangles**
JANGLY *adj* making a jangling sound

JANITOR *n*
JANIZAR = **janissary**

This is an old word for a Turkish soldier, combining J and Z. If your opponent plays it, remember that you can add not only an S to it to form the plural, but also a Y, making the variant spelling **janizary**.

JANKER *n* device for transporting logs **jankers**
JANN *n* lesser jinn
JANNIES ▸ **janny**
JANNOCK = **jonnock**
JANNS ▸ **jann**
JANNY *n* janitor
JANSKY *n* unit of flux density **janskys**
JANTEE *archaic version of* ▸ **jaunty**
JANTIER ▸ **janty**
JANTIES ▸ **janty**
JANTY *n* petty officer ▷ *adj* (in archaic usage) jaunty
JAP *vb* splash
JAPAN *n* very hard varnish, usu black ▷ *vb* cover with this varnish ▷ *adj* relating to or varnished with japan **japans**
JAPE *n* joke or prank ▷ *vb* joke or jest (about) **japed, japer, japers, japery, japes, japing, japings**
JAPPED ▸ **jap**
JAPPING ▸ **jap**
JAPS ▸ **jap**
JAR *n, vb* **jarful**
JARFULS ▸ **jarful**
JARGON *n, vb* **jargons, jargony, jargoon**
JARHEAD *n* US Marine
JARINA *n* South American palm tree **jarinas**
JARK *n* seal or pass
JARKMAN *n* forger of passes or licences **jarkmen**
JARKS ▸ **jark**
JARL *n* Scandinavian chieftain or noble **jarldom, jarls**
JAROOL *n* Indian tree **jarools**
JARP *vb* strike or smash **jarped, jarping, jarps**
JARRAH *n* **jarrahs**
JARRED ▸ **jar**
JARRING ▸ **jar**
JARS ▸ **jar**
JARSFUL ▸ **jarful**
JARTA *n* heart **jartas**
JARUL *variant of* ▸ **jarool**
JARULS ▸ **jarul**
JARVEY *n* hackney coachman **jarveys, jarvie**
JARVIES ▸ **jarvie**
JASEY *n* wig **jaseys, jasies**
JASMIN = **jasmine**
JASMINE *n*
JASMINS ▸ **jasmin**
JASP *another word for* ▸ **jasper**
JASPE *adj* resembling jasper ▷ *n* subtly striped woven fabric
JASPER *n* variety of quartz **jaspers, jaspery**
JASPES ▸ **jaspe**
JASPIS *archaic word for* ▸ **jasper**
JASPS ▸ **jasp**
JASS *obsolete variant of* ▸ **jazz**
JASSES ▸ **jass**
JASSID *n* leafhopper **jassids**
JASY *n* wig
JATAKA *n* text describing the birth of Buddha **jatakas**
JATO *n* jet-assisted takeoff **jatos**
JAUK *vb* dawdle **jauked, jauking, jauks**
JAUNCE *vb* prance **jaunced, jaunces, jaunse**
JAUNSED ▸ **jaunse**
JAUNSES ▸ **jaunse**
JAUNT *n, vb* **jaunted**
JAUNTEE *old spelling of* ▸ **jaunty**
JAUNTIE *old spelling of* ▸ **jaunty**
JAUNTS ▸ **jaunt**
JAUNTY *adj, n*
JAUP = **jarp**
JAUPED ▸ **jaup**
JAUPING ▸ **jaup**
JAUPS ▸ **jaup**
JAVA *n* coffee or a variety of it **javas**
JAVEL *adj as in* **javel water** bleach or disinfectant
JAVELIN *n, vb*
JAVELS ▸ **javel**
JAW *n, vb*
JAWAN *n* (in India) a soldier **jawans**

JAWARI *n* variety of sorghum **jawaris**
JAWBONE *n* lower jaw of a person or animal ▷ *vb* try to persuade by virtue of one's high office or position
JAWBOX *n* metal sink

> This Scots word for a sink combines the J and X, and of course its plural **jawboxes**, earning an extra 50 points, would be even better.

JAWED ▸ **jaw**
JAWFALL *n* depression
JAWHOLE *n* cesspit
JAWING, jawings, jawless, jawlike ▸ **jaw**
JAWLINE *n* outline of the jaw
JAWS ▸ **jaw**
JAY *n*
JAYBIRD *n* jay
JAYCEE *n* member of a Junior Chamber of Commerce **jaycees**
JAYGEE *n* lieutenant junior grade in the US army **jaygees**
JAYS ▸ **jay**
JAYVEE *n* junior varsity sports team **jayvees**
JAYWALK *vb* cross or walk in a street recklessly or illegally
JAZIES ▸ **jazy**
JAZY *n* wig

> This means a wig and is a wonderfully useful little word, combining J and Z for a high score.

JAZZ *n, vb*
JAZZBO *n* jazz musician or fan **jazzbos**
JAZZED, jazzer, jazzers, jazzes ▸ **jazz**
JAZZIER ▸ **jazzy**
JAZZILY ▸ **jazzy**
JAZZING ▸ **jazz**
JAZZMAN ▸ **jazz**
JAZZMEN ▸ **jazz**
JAZZY *adj*
JEALOUS *adj*
JEAN *n* tough twill-weave cotton fabric
JEANED *adj* wearing jeans
JEANS *pl n*
JEAT *n* jet **jeats**
JEBEL *n* hill or mountain in an Arab country **jebels**
JEDI *n* person claiming to live according to the Jedi philosophy **jedis**
JEE *variant of* ▸ **gee**
JEED ▸ **jee**
JEEING ▸ **jee**
JEEL *vb* make into jelly **jeeled**
JEELIE = **jeely**
JEELIED ▸ **jeely**
JEELIES ▸ **jeely**
JEELING ▸ **jeel**
JEELS ▸ **jeel**
JEELY *n* jelly ▷ *vb* make into jelly
JEEP *n, vb* **jeeped**
JEEPERS *interj* mild exclamation of surprise
JEEPING ▸ **jeep**
JEEPNEY *n* Filipino bus converted from a jeep
JEEPS ▸ **jeep**
JEER *vb, n* **jeered, jeerer, jeerers, jeering, jeers**
JEES ▸ **jee**
JEEZ *interj* expression of surprise or irritation
JEFE *n* (in Spanish-speaking countries) a military or political leader **jefes**
JEFF *vb* downsize or close down (an organization) **jeffed, jeffing, jeffs**
JEHAD = **jihad**
JEHADI = **jihadi**
JEHADIS ▸ **jehadi**
JEHADS ▸ **jehad**
JEHU *n* fast driver **jehus**
JEJUNA ▸ **jejunum**
JEJUNAL ▸ **jejunum**
JEJUNE *adj* simple or naive
JEJUNUM *n*
JELAB = **jellaba**
JELABS ▸ **jelab**
JELL *vb*
JELLABA *n* loose robe with a hood
JELLED ▸ **jell**
JELLIED ▸ **jelly**
JELLIES ▸ **jelly**
JELLIFY *vb* make into or become jelly
JELLING ▸ **jell**
JELLO *n* (in US English) type of dessert **jellos**
JELLS ▸ **jell**
JELLY *n, vb*
JEMADAR *n* native officer serving as a mercenary in India
JEMBE *n* hoe **jembes**

JEMIDAR = **jemadar**
JEMIMA *n* boot with elastic sides **jemimas**
JEMMIED ▸ **jemmy**
JEMMIER ▸ **jemmy**
JEMMIES ▸ **jemmy**
JEMMY *n, vb, adj*
JENNET *n* female donkey or ass **jennets**
JENNIES ▸ **jenny**
JENNY = **jennet**
JEOFAIL *n* oversight in legal pleading
JEON *n* Korean pancake
JEOPARD *vb* put in jeopardy
JERBIL *variant spelling of* ▸ **gerbil**
JERBILS ▸ **jerbil**
JERBOA *n* small mouselike rodent with long hind legs **jerboas**
JEREED = **jerid**
JEREEDS ▸ **jereed**
JERID *n* wooden javelin **jerids**
JERK *vb, n* **jerked, jerker, jerkers**
JERKIER ▸ **jerky**
JERKIES ▸ **jerky**
JERKILY ▸ **jerky**
JERKIN *n*
JERKING ▸ **jerk**
JERKINS ▸ **jerkin**
JERKS ▸ **jerk**
JERKY *adj* characterized by jerks ▹ *n* type of cured meat
JERQUE *vb* search for contraband **jerqued, jerquer, jerques**

> To **jerque** is to search a vessel for stolen goods, and if you have the right additional letters to make **jerqued, jerquer, jerques** or **jerquing**, using all your letters, you would get a really great score.

JERREED *variant spelling of* ▸ **jerid**
JERRID *n* blunt javelin **jerrids**
JERRIES ▸ **jerry**
JERRY *short for* > **jeroboam**
JERSEY *n* **jerseys**
JESS *n* short leather strap used in falconry ▹ *vb* put jesses on (a hawk or falcon)
JESSAMY *n* fop
JESSANT *adj* emerging
JESSE = **jess**
JESSED ▸ **jess**
JESSES ▸ **jess**
JESSIE *n* effeminate, weak, or cowardly boy or man **jessies**
JESSING ▸ **jess**
JEST *vb, n* **jested**
JESTEE *n* person about whom a joke is made **jestees**
JESTER *n* **jesters**
JESTFUL ▸ **jest**
JESTING ▸ **jest**
JESTS ▸ **jest**
JESUS *n* French paper size
JET *n, vb*
JETBEAD *n* ornamental shrub
JETE *n* dance step **jetes**
JETFOIL *n* type of hydrofoil that is propelled by water jets
JETLAG *n* tiredness caused by crossing timezones in jet flight **jetlags**
JETLIKE ▸ **jet**
JETON *n* gambling chip **jetons**
JETPORT *n* airport for jet planes
JETS ▸ **jet**
JETSAM *n* **jetsams, jetsom**
JETSOMS ▸ **jetsom**
JETSON *archaic form of* ▸ **jetsam**
JETSONS ▸ **jetson**
JETTED ▸ **jet**
JETTIED ▸ **jetty**
JETTIER ▸ **jetty**
JETTIES ▸ **jetty**
JETTING ▸ **jet**
JETTON *n* counter or token **jettons**
JETTY *n, adj, vb*
JETWAY *n* tradename of device used in airports **jetways**
JEU *n* game

> **Jeu** is the French word for game or play. The plural form, **jeux**, is a great little word, using both J and X, particularly if you can play it on a double- or triple-word square.

JEUNE *adj* young
JEUX ▸ **jeu**
JEWEL *n, vb* **jeweled**
JEWELER = **jeweller**
JEWELRY = **jewellery**

JEWELS ▸ **jewel**
JEWFISH *n* freshwater catfish
JEWIE *n* jewfish **jewies**
JEZAIL *n* Afghan musket **jezails**

> A **jezail** is a kind of Afghan musket, and if you have an S to go with it, earning the extra 50 points, so much the better.

JEZEBEL *n* shameless or scheming woman
JHALA *n* Indian musical style **jhalas**
JHATKA *n* slaughter of animals for food according to Sikh law **jhatkas**
JIAO *n* Chinese currency unit **jiaos**
JIB = **jibe**
JIBB = **jibe**
JIBBA *n* long, loose coat worn by Muslim men
JIBBAH = **jubbah**
JIBBAHS ▸ **jibbah**
JIBBAS ▸ **jibba**
JIBBED ▸ **jibb**
JIBBER *variant of* ▸ **gibber**
JIBBERS ▸ **jibber**
JIBBING ▸ **jibb**
JIBBONS *pl n* spring onions
JIBBOOM *n* spar forming an extension of the bowsprit
JIBBS ▸ **jibb**
JIBE *vb, n* **jibed, jiber, jibers, jibes, jibing**
JIBS ▸ **jib**
JICAMA *n* pale brown turnip **jicamas**
JIFF = **jiffy**
JIFFIES ▸ **jiffy**
JIFFS ▸ **jiff**
JIFFY *n*
JIG *n, vb*
JIGAJIG *vb* engage in sexual intercourse **jigajog**
JIGGED ▸ **jig**
JIGGER *n* small whisky glass ▹ *vb* interfere or alter **jiggers**
JIGGIER ▸ **jiggy**
JIGGING ▸ **jig**
JIGGISH ▸ **jig**
JIGGLE *vb, n* **jiggled, jiggles, jiggly**
JIGGY *adj* resembling a jig
JIGJIG *variant of* ▸ **jigajig**
JIGJIGS ▸ **jigjig**
JIGLIKE ▸ **jig**
JIGOT = **gigot**
JIGOTS ▸ **jigot**
JIGS ▸ **jig**
JIGSAW *n, vb* **jigsawn, jigsaws**
JIHAD *n*
JIHADI *n* person who takes part in a jihad **jihadis**
JIHADS ▸ **jihad**
JILBAB *n* long robe worn by Muslim women **jilbabs**
JILGIE *n* freshwater crayfish **jilgies**
JILL *variant spelling of* ▸ **gill**
JILLET *n* wanton woman **jillets**
JILLION *n* extremely large number or amount
JILLS ▸ **jill**
JILT *vb, n* **jilted, jilter, jilters, jilting, jilts**
JIMINY *interj* expression of surprise
JIMJAM ▸ **jimjams**
JIMJAMS *pl n* state of nervous tension, excitement, or anxiety
JIMMIE = **jimmy**
JIMMIED ▸ **jimmy**
JIMMIES ▸ **jimmy**
JIMMINY *interj* expression of surprise
JIMMY = **jemmy**
JIMP *adj* handsome **jimper, jimpest**
JIMPIER ▸ **jimpy**
JIMPLY *adv* neatly
JIMPSON ▸ **jimson**
JIMPY *adj* neat and tidy
JIMSON *n as in* **jimson weed** type of poisonous plant
JIN *n* Chinese unit of weight
JINGAL *n* swivel-mounted gun **jingall, jingals**
JINGKO = **gingko**
JINGLE *n, vb* **jingled, jingler, jingles**
JINGLET *n* sleigh-bell clapper
JINGLY ▸ **jingle**
JINGO *n* loud and bellicose patriot; chauvinism **jingoes**
JINJILI *n* type of sesame
JINK *vb* move quickly or jerkily in order to dodge someone ▹ *n* jinking movement **jinked**
JINKER *n* vehicle for

transporting timber ▷ *vb* carry or transport in a jinker **jinkers**
JINKING ▸ **jink**
JINKS ▸ **jink**
JINN ▸ **jinni**
JINNE *interj* South African exclamation
JINNEE = **jinni**
JINNI *n* spirit in Muslim mythology **jinnis, jinns**
JINS ▸ **jin**
JINX *n, vb* **jinxed, jinxes, jinxing**
JIPYAPA = **jipijapa**
JIRBLE *vb* pour carelessly **jirbled, jirbles**
JIRD *n* gerbil **jirds**
JIRGA *n* Afghan council **jirgas**
JIRRE = **jinne**
JITNEY *n* small cheap bus **jitneys**
JITTER *vb* be anxious or nervous **jitters**
JITTERY *adj* nervous
JIVE *n, vb*
JIVEASS *adj* misleading or phoney
JIVED, jiver, jivers, jives, jivey, jivier, jiviest, jiving, jivy ▸ **jive**
JIZ *n* wig

> When you find yourself with J and Z but nothing else that looks promising, there may well be an I on the board around which you can form **jiz**, which means a wig.

JIZZ *n* term for the characteristics that identify a particular species of bird or plant **jizzes**
JNANA *n* type of yoga **jnanas**
JO *n* Scots word for sweetheart
JOANNA *n* piano **joannas**
JOANNES = **johannes**
JOB *n, vb* **jobbed**
JOBBER *n* person who jobs **jobbers**
JOBBERY *n* practice of making private profit out of a public office
JOBBIE *n* piece of excrement **jobbies**
JOBBING *adj, n*
JOBE *vb* scold **jobed, jobes, jobing**
JOBLESS *pl n, adj*
JOBNAME *n* title of position
JOBS ▸ **job**
JOCK *n* athlete
JOCKEY *n, vb* **jockeys**
JOCKISH *adj* macho
JOCKO *n* chimpanzee **jockos**
JOCKS ▸ **jock**
JOCO *adj* relaxed
JOCOSE *adj*
JOCULAR *adj*
JOCUND *adj* merry or cheerful
JODEL = **yodel**
JODELS ▸ **jodel**
JODHPUR *n as in* **jodphur boots** ankle-length leather riding boots
JOE = **jo**
JOES ▸ **joe**
JOEY *n* **joeys**
JOG *vb, n* **jogged**
JOGGER *n* person who runs at a jog for exercise **joggers**
JOGGING ▸ **jog**
JOGGLE *vb, n* **joggled, joggler, joggles**
JOGS ▸ **jog**
JOGTROT *n* easy bouncy gait
JOHN *n* toilet
JOHNNIE = **johnny**
JOHNNY *n* chap
JOHNS ▸ **john**
JOIN *vb, n*
JOINDER *n* act of joining, esp in legal contexts
JOINED ▸ **join**
JOINER *n* **joiners**
JOINERY *n*
JOINING ▸ **join**
JOINS ▸ **join**
JOINT *adj, n, vb*
JOINTED *adj* having a joint or joints
JOINTER *n* tool for pointing mortar joints
JOINTLY ▸ **joint**
JOINTS ▸ **joint**
JOIST *n, vb* **joisted, joists**
JOJOBA *n* shrub of SW North America **jojobas**
JOKE *n, vb* **joked**
JOKER *n* **jokers**
JOKES ▸ **joke**
JOKEY *adj* intended as a joke **jokier, jokiest**
JOKILY ▸ **joke**

JOKING ▸ **joke**
JOKOL *Shetland word for* ▸ **yes**
JOKY = **jokey**
JOL *n* party ▹ *vb* have a good time
JOLE *vb* knock **joled, joles, joling, joll**
JOLLED ▸ **jol**
JOLLER *n* person who has a good time **jollers**
JOLLEY = **jolly**
JOLLEYS ▸ **jolley**
JOLLIED ▸ **jolly**
JOLLIER *n* joker
JOLLIES ▸ **jolly**
JOLLIFY *vb* be or cause to be jolly
JOLLILY ▸ **jolly**
JOLLING ▸ **jol**
JOLLITY *n*
JOLLOP *n* cream or unguent **jollops**
JOLLS ▸ **joll**
JOLLY *adj, adv, vb, n* **jollyer**
JOLS ▸ **jol**
JOLT *n, vb* **jolted, jolter, jolters, joltier, joltily, jolting, jolts, jolty**
JOMO = **zo**
JOMON *n* particular era in Japanese history
JOMOS ▸ **jomo**
JONES *vb* desire **jonesed, joneses**
JONG *n* friend, often used in direct address **jongs**
JONNOCK *adj* genuine ▹ *adv* honestly
JONQUIL *n*
JONTIES ▸ **jonty**
JONTY *n* petty officer
JOOK *vb* poke or puncture (the skin) ▹ *n* jab or the resulting wound **jooked**
JOOKERY *n* mischief
JOOKING ▸ **jook**
JOOKS ▸ **jook**
JOR *n* movement in Indian music
JORAM = **jorum**
JORAMS ▸ **joram**
JORDAN *n* chamber pot **jordans**
JORS ▸ **jor**
JORUM *n* large drinking bowl or vessel or its contents **jorums**
JOSEPH *n* woman's floor-length riding coat **josephs**
JOSH *vb* tease ▹ *n* teasing or bantering joke **joshed, josher, joshers, joshes, joshing**
JOSKIN *n* bumpkin **joskins**
JOSS *n* Chinese deity
JOSSER *n* simpleton **jossers**
JOSSES ▸ **joss**
JOSTLE *vb, n* **jostled, jostler, jostles**
JOT *vb, n*
JOTA *n* Spanish dance **jotas**
JOTS ▸ **jot**
JOTTED ▸ **jot**
JOTTER *n* **jotters**
JOTTIER ▸ **jotty**
JOTTING ▸ **jot**
JOTTY ▸ **jot**
JOTUN *n* giant **jotunn**
JOTUNNS ▸ **jotunn**
JOTUNS ▸ **jotun**
JOUAL *n* nonstandard variety of Canadian French **jouals**
JOUGS *pl n* iron ring for restraining an offender
JOUK *vb* duck or dodge ▹ *n* sudden evasive movement **jouked**
JOUKERY = **jookery**
JOUKING ▸ **jouk**
JOUKS ▸ **jouk**
JOULE *n, vb* **jouled, joules, jouling**
JOUNCE *vb* shake or jolt or cause to shake or jolt ▹ *n* jolting movement **jounced, jounces, jouncy**
JOUR *n* day
JOURNAL *n, vb*
JOURNEY *n, vb*
JOURNO *n* journalist **journos**
JOURS ▸ **jour**
JOUST *n, vb* **jousted, jouster, jousts**
JOVIAL *adj*
JOW *vb* ring (a bell)
JOWAR *n* variety of sorghum **jowari, jowaris, jowars**
JOWED ▸ **jow**
JOWING ▸ **jow**
JOWL *n, vb* **jowled**
JOWLER *n* dog with prominent jowls **jowlers**
JOWLIER, jowling, jowls, jowly
JOWS ▸ **jow**
JOY *n, vb*
JOYANCE *n* joyous feeling or festivity

JOYED ▸ **joy**
JOYFUL *adj*
JOYING ▸ **joy**
JOYLESS *adj*
JOYOUS *adj*
JOYPAD *n* computer games console **joypads**
JOYPOP *vb* take addictive drugs occasionally **joypops**
JOYRIDE *n, vb* **joyrode**
JOYS ▸ **joy**
JUBA *n* lively African-American dance **jubas**
JUBATE *adj* possessing a mane
JUBBAH *n* long loose outer garment with wide sleeves **jubbahs**
JUBE *n* **jubes**
JUBHAH = **jubbah**
JUBHAHS ▸ **jubhah**
JUBILE = **jubilee**
JUBILEE *n*
JUBILES ▸ **jubile**
JUCO *n* junior college in America **jucos**
JUD *n* large block of coal
JUDAS *n* peephole **judases**
JUDDER *vb, n* **judders**
JUDDERY *adj* shaky
JUDGE *n, vb* **judged, judger, judgers, judges, judging**
JUDIES ▸ **judy**
JUDO *n*
JUDOGI *n* white two-piece cotton costume **judogis**
JUDOIST ▸ **judo**
JUDOKA *n* competitor or expert in judo **judokas**
JUDOS ▸ **judo**
JUDS ▸ **jud**
JUDY *n* woman
JUG *n, vb*
JUGA ▸ **jugum**
JUGAL *adj* of or relating to the zygomatic bone ▹ *n* cheekbone **jugals**
JUGATE *adj* having parts arranged in pairs
JUGFUL = **jug**
JUGFULS ▸ **jugful**
JUGGED ▸ **jug**
JUGGING ▸ **jug**
JUGGINS *n* silly person
JUGGLE *vb, n* **juggled**
JUGGLER *n* person who juggles, esp a professional entertainer
JUGGLES ▸ **juggle**
JUGHEAD *n* clumsy person
JUGLET *n* small jug **juglets**
JUGS ▸ **jug**
JUGSFUL ▸ **jugful**
JUGULA ▸ **jugulum**
JUGULAR *n*
JUGULUM *n* lower throat
JUGUM *n* part of an insect's forewing **jugums**
JUICE *n, vb* **juiced**
JUICER *n* kitchen appliance **juicers**
JUICES ▸ **juice**
JUICIER ▸ **juicy**
JUICILY ▸ **juicy**
JUICING ▸ **juice**
JUICY *adj*
JUJITSU *n*
JUJU *n* W African magic charm or fetish
JUJUBE *n* chewy sweet made of flavoured gelatine **jujubes**
JUJUISM ▸ **juju**
JUJUIST ▸ **juju**
JUJUS ▸ **juju**
JUJUTSU = **jujitsu**
JUKE *vb* dance or play dance music
JUKEBOX *n*
JUKED ▸ **juke**
JUKES ▸ **juke**
JUKING ▸ **juke**
JUKSKEI *n* type of game
JUKU *n* Japanese martial art **jukus**
JULEP *n* sweet alcoholic drink **juleps**
JULIET *n* code word for the letter J **juliets**
JUMAR *n* climbing tool ▹ *vb* climb (up a fixed rope) using jumars **jumared, jumars**
JUMART *n* mythical offspring of a bull and a mare **jumarts**
JUMBAL = **jumble**
JUMBALS ▸ **jumbal**
JUMBIE *n* Caribbean ghost **jumbies**
JUMBLE *n, vb* **jumbled, jumbler, jumbles, jumbly**
JUMBO *adj, n* **jumbos**
JUMBUCK *n*
JUMBY *n* Caribbean ghost
JUMELLE *n* paired objects
JUMP *vb, n* **jumped**
JUMPER *n* **jumpers**
JUMPIER ▸ **jumpy**

JUMPILY ▸ **jumpy**
JUMPING ▸ **jump**
JUMPOFF *n* round in a showjumping contest
JUMPS ▸ **jump**
JUMPY *adj*
JUN *variant of* ▸ **chon**
JUNCATE = **junket**
JUNCO *n* North American bunting **juncoes, juncos**
JUNCUS *n* type of rush
JUNGLE *n*
JUNGLED *adj* covered with jungle
JUNGLES ▸ **jungle**
JUNGLI *n* uncultured person **junglis**
JUNGLY ▸ **jungle**
JUNIOR *adj, n* **juniors**
JUNIPER *n*
JUNK *n, vb* **junked**
JUNKER *n* (formerly) young German nobleman **junkers**
JUNKET *n, vb* **junkets**
JUNKIE *n*
JUNKIER ▸ **junky**
JUNKIES ▸ **junky**
JUNKING ▸ **junk**
JUNKMAN *n* man who trades in discarded items **junkmen**
JUNKS ▸ **junk**
JUNKY *n* drug addict ▹ *adj* of low quality
JUNTA *n* **juntas, junto**
JUNTOS ▸ **junto**
JUPATI *n* type of palm tree **jupatis**
JUPE *n* sleeveless jacket **jupes**
JUPON *n* short sleeveless padded garment **jupons**
JURA ▸ **jus**
JURAL *adj* of or relating to law or to the administration of justice **jurally**
JURANT *n* person taking oath **jurants**
JURAT *n* statement at the foot of an affidavit **jurats**
JURE *adv* by legal right
JUREL *n* edible fish **jurels**
JURIDIC = **juridical**
JURIED ▸ **jury**
JURIES ▸ **jury**
JURIST *n* **jurists**
JUROR *n* **jurors**
JURY *n, adj, vb* **jurying**
JURYMAN *n* member of a jury, esp a man **jurymen**
JUS *n* right, power, or authority
JUSSIVE *n* mood of verbs used for giving orders; imperative
JUST *adv, adj, vb* **justed, juster, justers, justest**
JUSTICE *n*
JUSTIFY *vb*
JUSTING ▸ **joust**
JUSTLE *less common word for* ▸ **jostle**
JUSTLED ▸ **justle**
JUSTLES ▸ **justle**
JUSTLY ▸ **just**
JUSTS = **joust**
JUT *vb, n*
JUTE *n* **jutes**
JUTS ▸ **jut**
JUTTED ▸ **jut**
JUTTIED ▸ **jutty**
JUTTIES ▸ **jutty**
JUTTING ▸ **jut**
JUTTY *vb* project beyond
JUVE = **juvenile**
JUVENAL *variant spelling (esp US) of* > **juvenile**
JUVES ▸ **juve**
JUVIE *n* juvenile detention centre **juvies**
JYMOLD *adj* having a hinge
JYNX *n* wryneck **jynxes**

> This unusual word, another name for the bird known as a wryneck, is unique in combining J, Y and X without using any vowels.

Kk

Worth 5 points, **K** is a valuable tile to have in your rack. However, it's not the most useful tile for forming bonus words scoring that extra 50 points, so, as with the **J**, you will normally want to play it off fairly quickly. There are four two-letter words beginning with **K**: **ka, ki, ko** and **ky**. When it comes to three-letter words, remember **keg** (8 points), **ken** (7), **key** (10), **kex** (14), **kid** (8), **kin** (7), **kip** (9) and **kit** (7). Other three-letter words with **K** well worth remembering are **jak** (14) and **zek** (16).

KA *n* (in ancient Egypt) type of spirit ▷ *vb* (in archaic usage) help
KAAL *adj* naked
KAAMA *n* large African antelope with lyre-shaped horns **kaamas**
KAAS *n* Dutch cabinet or wardrobe
KAB *variant spelling of* ▶ **cab**
KABAB = **kebab**
KABABS ▶ **kabab**
KABADDI *n* type of game
KABAKA *n* any of the former rulers of the Baganda people **kabakas**
KABALA = **kabbalah**
KABALAS ▶ **kabala**
KABAR *archaic form of* ▶ **caber**
KABARS ▶ **kabar**
KABAYA *n* tunic **kabayas**
KABBALA = **kabbalah**
KABELE = **kebele**
KABELES ▶ **kabele**
KABIKI *n* fruit tree found in India **kabikis**
KABOB = **kebab**
KABOBS ▶ **kabob**
KABS ▶ **kab**
KABUKI *n* form of Japanese drama **kabukis**
KACCHA *n* trousers worn traditionally by Sikhs **kacchas**
KACHA *adj* crude **kachcha**
KACHERI = **kachahri**
KACHINA *n* type of supernatural being
KADDISH *n* ancient Jewish liturgical prayer
KADE = **ked**
KADES ▶ **kade**
KADI *variant spelling of* ▶ **cadi**
KADIS ▶ **kadi**
KAE *n* dialect word for jackdaw or jay ▷ *vb* (in archaic usage) help **kaed, kaeing, kaes**
KAF *n* letter of the Hebrew alphabet
KAFFIR *n* **kaffirs**
KAFILA *n* caravan **kafilas**
KAFIR = **kaffir**
KAFIRS ▶ **kafir**
KAFS ▶ **kaf**
KAFTAN *n* **kaftans**
KAGO *n* Japanese sedan chair
KAGOOL *variant spelling of* ▶ **cagoule**
KAGOOLS ▶ **kagool**
KAGOS ▶ **kago**

KAGOUL *variant spelling of* ▸ **cagoule**
KAGOULE = **kagoul**
KAGOULS ▸ **kagoul**
KAGU *n* crested nocturnal bird **kagus**
KAHAL *n* Jewish community **kahals**
KAHAWAI *n* food and game fish of New Zealand
KAHUNA *n* Hawaiian priest, shaman, or expert **kahunas**
KAI *n*
KAIAK = **kayak**
KAIAKED ▸ **kaiak**
KAIAKS ▸ **kaiak**
KAID *n* North African chieftan or leader **kaids**
KAIE *archaic form of* ▸ **key**
KAIES ▸ **kaie**
KAIF = **kif**
KAIFS ▸ **kaif**
KAIK = **kainga**
KAIKA = **kainga**
KAIKAI *n* food **kaikais**
KAIKAS ▸ **kaika**
KAIKS ▸ **kaik**
KAIL = **kale**
KAILS ▸ **kail**
KAIM = **kame**
KAIMS ▸ **kaim**
KAIN *variant spelling of* ▸ **cain**
KAING ▸ **ka**
KAINGA *n* (in New Zealand) a Māori village or small settlement **kaingas**
KAINIT = **kainite**
KAINITE *n* white mineral
KAINITS ▸ **kainit**
KAINS ▸ **kain**
KAIS ▸ **kai**
KAISER *n* German or Austro-Hungarian emperor **kaisers**
KAIZEN *n* type of philosophy **kaizens**
KAJAWAH *n* type of seat or panier used on a camel
KAJEPUT *n* variety of Australian melaleuca
KAKA *n* parrot of New Zealand
KAKAPO *n* nocturnal New Zealand parrot **kakapos**
KAKAS ▸ **kaka**
KAKI *n* Asian persimmon tree **kakis**
KAKODYL *variant spelling of* ▸ **cacodyl**
KAKURO *n* crossword-style puzzle with numbers **kakuros**
KALAM *n* discussion and debate **kalams**
KALE *n*
KALENDS = **calends**
KALES ▸ **kale**
KALI *another name for* > **saltwort**
KALIAN *another name for* ▸ **hookah**
KALIANS ▸ **kalian**
KALIF *variant spelling of* ▸ **caliph**
KALIFS ▸ **kalif**
KALIMBA *n* musical instrument
KALIPH *variant spelling of* ▸ **caliph**
KALIPHS ▸ **kaliph**
KALIS ▸ **kali**
KALIUM *n* Latin for potassium **kaliums**
KALMIA *n* evergreen ericaceous shrub **kalmias**
KALONG *n* fruit bat **kalongs**
KALOOKI *n* card game
KALPA *n* period in Hindu cosmology
KALPAC = **calpac**
KALPACS ▸ **kalpac**
KALPAK *variant spelling of* ▸ **calpac**
KALPAKS ▸ **kalpak**
KALPAS ▸ **kalpa**
KALPIS *n* Greek water jar
KALUKI ▸ **kalooki**
KALUKIS ▸ **kaluki**
KAM *Shakespearean word for* ▸ **crooked**
KAMA *n* large African antelope with lyre-shaped horns
KAMAHI *n* hardwood tree **kamahis**
KAMALA *n* East Indian tree **kamalas**
KAMAS ▸ **kama**
KAME *n* irregular mound of gravel, sand, etc
KAMEES ▸ **kameez**
KAMEEZ *n* long tunic
KAMELA = **kamala**
KAMELAS ▸ **kamela**
KAMERAD *interj* shout of surrender ▷ *vb* surrender

KAMES ▸ **kame**
KAMI *n* divine being or spiritual force in Shinto
KAMICHI *n* South American bird
KAMIK *n* traditional Inuit boot **kamiks**
KAMILA = **kamala**
KAMILAS ▸ **kamila**
KAMIS = **kameez**
KAMISES ▸ **kamis**
KAMME = **kam**
KAMPONG *n* (in Malaysia) village
KAMSEEN = **khamsin**
KAMSIN = **kamseen**
KAMSINS ▸ **kamsin**
KANA *n* Japanese syllabary
KANAE *n* grey mullet **kanaes**
KANAKA *n* Australian word for any native of the South Pacific **kanakas**
KANAS ▸ **kana**
KANBAN *n* just-in-time manufacturing process **kanbans**
KANDIES ▸ **kandy**
KANDY = **candie**
KANE *n* Hawaiian man or boy
KANEH *n* 6-cubit Hebrew measure **kanehs**
KANES ▸ **kane**
KANG *n* Chinese heatable platform
KANGA *n* piece of gaily decorated thin cotton cloth **kangas**
KANGHA *n* comb traditionally worn by Sikhs **kanghas**
KANGS ▸ **kang**
KANJI *n* Japanese writing system **kanjis**
KANS *n* Indian wild sugar cane **kanses**
KANT *archaic spelling of* ▸ **cant**
KANTAR *n* unit of weight **kantars**
KANTED ▸ **kant**
KANTELA = **kantele**
KANTELE *n* Finnish stringed instrument
KANTEN = **agar**
KANTENS ▸ **kanten**
KANTHA *n* Bengali embroidered quilt **kanthas**
KANTING ▸ **kant**
KANTS ▸ **kant**
KANUKA *n* New Zealand myrtaceous tree **kanukas**
KANZU *n* long garment **kanzus**
KAOLIN *n* **kaoline, kaolins**
KAON *n* type of meson **kaonic, kaons**
KAPA *n* Hawaiian cloth made from beaten mulberry bark **kapas**
KAPH *n* 11th letter of the Hebrew alphabet **kaphs**
KAPOK *n* **kapoks**
KAPPA *n* tenth letter in the Greek alphabet **kappas**
KAPUKA = **broadleaf**
KAPUKAS ▸ **kapuka**
KAPUT *adj* ruined or broken **kaputt**
KARA *n* steel bangle traditionally worn by Sikhs
KARAISM *n* beliefs and doctrines of a Jewish sect
KARAIT = **krait**
KARAITS ▸ **krait**
KARAKA *n* New Zealand tree **karakas**
KARAKIA *n* prayer
KARAKUL *n* sheep of central Asia
KARAMU *n* small New Zealand tree **karamus**
KARANGA *n* call or chant of welcome, sung by a female elder ▹ *vb* perform a karanga
KARAOKE *n* form of entertainment
KARAS ▸ **kara**
KARAT *n* measure of the proportion of gold in an alloy
KARATE *n* **karates**
KARATS ▸ **karat**
KARENGO *n* edible type of Pacific seaweed
KARITE *n* shea tree **karites**
KARK *variant spelling of* ▸ **cark**
KARKED ▸ **kark**
KARKING ▸ **kark**
KARKS ▸ **kark**
KARMA *n* **karmas, karmic**
KARN *old word for* ▸ **cairn**
KARNS ▸ **karn**
KARO *n* small New Zealand tree or shrub

KAROO *n* high arid plateau **karoos**
KARORO *n* large seagull **karoros**
KAROS ▸ **karo**
KAROSHI *n* (in Japan) death caused by overwork
KAROSS *n* type of blanket
KARRI *n* **karris**
KARROO = **karoo**
KARROOS ▸ **karroo**
KARSEY *variant spelling of* ▸ **khazi**
KARSEYS ▸ **karsey**
KARSIES ▸ **karsy**
KARST *n* geological term **karstic, karsts**
KARSY *variant spelling of* ▸ **khazi**
KART *n* light low-framed vehicle **karter, karters, karting, karts**
KARYON *n* nucleus of a cell **karyons**
KARZIES ▸ **karzy**
KARZY *variant spelling of* ▸ **khazi**
KAS ▸ **ka**
KASBAH *n* citadel of any of various North African cities **kasbahs**
KASHA *n* dish originating in Eastern Europe **kashas**
KASHER *vb* make fit for use **kashers**
KASHMIR *variant spelling of* > **cashmere**
KASHRUS = **kashruth**
KASHRUT = **kashruth**
KASME *interj* (in Indian English) I swear
KAT = **khat**
KATA *n* form of exercise
KATAL *n* SI unit of catalytic activity **katals**
KATANA *n* Japanese samurai sword **katanas**
KATAS ▸ **kata**
KATCINA *variant spelling of* ▸ **kachina**
KATHAK *n* form of dancing **kathaks**
KATHODE *variant spelling of* ▸ **cathode**
KATI *variant spelling of* ▸ **catty**
KATION *variant spelling of* ▸ **cation**
KATIONS ▸ **kation**
KATIPO *n* **katipos**
KATIS ▸ **kati**
KATORGA *n* type of labour camp
KATS ▸ **kat**
KATSURA *n* Asian tree
KATTI *variant spelling of* ▸ **catty**
KATTIS ▸ **katti**
KATYDID *n* large green grasshopper of N America
KAUGH = **kiaugh**
KAUGHS ▸ **kaugh**
KAUPAPA *n* strategy, policy, or cause
KAURI *n*
KAURIES ▸ **kaury**
KAURIS ▸ **kauri**
KAURU *n* edible stem of the cabbage tree **kaurus**
KAURY *variant spelling of* ▸ **kauri**
KAVA *n* Polynesian shrub
KAVAL *n* type of flute played in the Balkans **kavals**
KAVAS ▸ **kava**
KAVASS *n* armed Turkish constable
KAW *variant spelling of* ▸ **caw**
KAWA *n* protocol or etiquette **kawas**
KAWAU *n* New Zealand name for black shag **kawaus**
KAWED ▸ **kaw**
KAWING ▸ **kaw**
KAWS ▸ **kaw**
KAY *n* name of the letter K
KAYAK *n, vb* **kayaked, kayaker, kayaks**
KAYLE *n* one of a set of ninepins
KAYLES *pl n* ninepins
KAYLIED *adj* (in British slang) intoxicated or drunk
KAYO *another term for* > **knockout; kayoed, kayoes, kayoing, kayos**
KAYS ▸ **kay**
KAZI *variant spelling of* ▸ **khazi**
KAZIS ▸ **kazi**
KAZOO *n* musical instrument **kazoos**
KBAR *n* kilobar **kbars**
KEA *n* **keas**
KEASAR *archaic variant of* ▸ **kaiser**
KEASARS ▸ **keasar**

KEAVIE *n* archaic or dialect word for a type of crab **keavies**
KEB *vb* Scots word meaning miscarry or reject a lamb
KEBAB *n, vb* **kebabs**
KEBAR *n* Scots word for beam or rafter **kebars**
KEBBED ▶ **keb**
KEBBIE *n* Scots word for shepherd's crook **kebbies**
KEBBING ▶ **keb**
KEBBOCK *n* Scots word for a cheese **kebbuck**
KEBELE *n* Ethiopian local council **kebeles**
KEBLAH = **kiblah**
KEBLAHS ▶ **keblah**
KEBOB = **kebab**
KEBOBS ▶ **kebob**
KEBS ▶ **keb**
KECK *vb* retch or feel nausea **kecked, kecking**
KECKLE *Scots variant of* ▶ **cackle**
KECKLED ▶ **keckle**
KECKLES ▶ **keckle**
KECKS *pl n* trousers **keckses**
KECKSY *n* dialect word meaning hollow plant stalk
KED *n as in* **sheep ked** sheep tick
KEDDAH = **kheda**
KEDDAHS ▶ **keddah**
KEDGE *vb* move (a ship) using cable attached to an anchor ▷ *n* light anchor used for kedging **kedged**
KEDGER *n* small anchor **kedgers**
KEDGES ▶ **kedge**
KEDGIER ▶ **kedgy**
KEDGING ▶ **kedge**
KEDGY *adj* dialect word for happy or lively
KEDS ▶ **ked**
KEECH *n* old word for lump of fat **keeches**
KEEF = **kif**
KEEFS ▶ **keef**
KEEK *Scot word for* ▶ **peep; keeked, keeker, keekers, keeking, keeks**
KEEL *n, vb*
KEELAGE *n* fee charged by certain ports
KEELED ▶ **keel**
KEELER *n* bargeman **keelers**
KEELIE *n* kestrel **keelies**
KEELING ▶ **keel**
KEELMAN *n* bargeman **keelmen**
KEELS ▶ **keel**
KEELSON *n* lpart of a ship
KEEMA *n* (in Indian cookery) minced meat **keemas**
KEEN *adj, vb, n* **keened, keener, keeners, keenest, keening, keenly**
KEENO = **keno**
KEENOS ▶ **keeno**
KEENS ▶ **keen**
KEEP *vb, n*
KEEPER *n* **keepers**
KEEPING ▶ **keep**
KEEPNET *n* cylindrical net used to keep fish alive
KEEPS ▶ **keep**
KEESTER = **keister**
KEET *short for* > **parakeet**
KEETS ▶ **keet**
KEEVE *n* tub or vat **keeves**
KEF = **kif**
KEFFEL *dialect word for* ▶ **horse**
KEFFELS ▶ **keffel**
KEFIR *n* effervescent drink **kefirs**
KEFS ▶ **kef**
KEG *n, vb*
KEGELER = **kegler**
KEGGED, kegger, keggers, kegging ▶ **keg**
KEGLER *n* participant in a game of tenpin bowling **keglers**
KEGLING *n* bowling
KEGS ▶ **keg**
KEHUA *n* ghost or spirit **kehuas**
KEIGHT ▶ **ketch**
KEIR = **kier**
KEIREN *n* type of track cycling event **keirens**
KEIRIN *n* **keirins**
KEIRS ▶ **keir**
KEISTER *n* rump
KEITLOA *n* type of rhinoceros
KEKENO *n* New Zealand fur seal **kekenos**
KEKS = **kecks**
KEKSYE = **kex**
KEKSYES ▶ **keksye**
KELEP *n* large ant found in Central and South America **keleps**

KELIM = **kilim**
KELIMS ▸ **kelim**
KELL *dialect word for* ▸ **hairnet**
KELLAUT = **khilat**
KELLIES ▸ **kelly**
KELLS ▸ **kell**
KELLY *n* part of a drill system
KELOID *n* type of scar tissue **keloids**
KELP *n, vb* **kelped**
KELPER *n* Falkland Islander **kelpers**
KELPIE *n*
KELPIES ▸ **kelpy**
KELPING ▸ **kelp**
KELPS ▸ **kelp**
KELPY = **kelpie**
KELSON = **keelson**
KELSONS ▸ **kelson**
KELT *n* salmon that has recently spawned
KELTER = **kilter**
KELTERS ▸ **kelter**
KELTIE *variant spelling of* ▸ **kelty**
KELTIES ▸ **kelty**
KELTS ▸ **kelt**
KELTY *n* old Scots word for a drink imposed on someone not thought to be drinking enough
KELVIN *n* **kelvins**
KEMB *old word for* ▸ **comb**
KEMBED ▸ **kemb**
KEMBING ▸ **kemb**
KEMBLA *n* small change **kemblas**
KEMBO = **kimbo**
KEMBOED ▸ **kembo**
KEMBOS ▸ **kembo**
KEMBS ▸ **kemb**
KEMP *n* coarse hair or strand of hair ▹ *vb* dialect word meaning to compete or try to come first **kemped, kemper, kempers**
KEMPIER ▸ **kempy**
KEMPING ▸ **kemp**
KEMPLE *n* variable Scottish measure for hay or straw **kemples**
KEMPS ▸ **kemp**
KEMPT *adj* (of hair) tidy
KEMPY ▸ **kemp**
KEN *vb* know ▹ *n* range of knowledge or perception
KENAF *another name for* ▸ **ambary**
KENAFS ▸ **kenaf**
KENCH *n* bin for salting and preserving fish **kenches**
KENDO *n* Japanese sport of fencing using wooden staves **kendos**
KENNED ▸ **ken**
KENNEL *n, vb* **kennels**
KENNER ▸ **ken**
KENNERS ▸ **ken**
KENNET *n* old word for a small hunting dog **kennets**
KENNETT *vb* spoil or destroy ruthlessly
KENNING ▸ **ken**
KENO *n* game of chance similar to bingo **kenos**
KENOSES ▸ **kenosis**
KENOSIS *n* Christ's renunciation of certain divine attributes **kenotic**
KENS ▸ **ken**
KENT *dialect word for* ▸ **punt**
KENTE *n* brightly coloured handwoven cloth
KENTED ▸ **kent**
KENTES ▸ **kente**
KENTIA *n* plant name **kentias**
KENTING ▸ **kent**
KENTS ▸ **kent**
KEP *vb* catch
KEPHIR = **kefir**
KEPHIRS ▸ **kephir**
KEPI *n* French military cap with a flat top and a horizontal peak **kepis**
KEPPED, keppen, kepping, keppit, keps ▸ **kep**
KEPT ▸ **keep**
KERAMIC *rare variant of* ▸ **ceramic**
KERATIN *n* fibrous protein found in the hair and nails
KERB *n, vb*
KERBAYA *n* blouse worn by Malay women
KERBED ▸ **kerb**
KERBING *n* material used for a kerb
KERBS ▸ **kerb**
KERCHOO *interj* atishoo
KEREL *n* chap or fellow **kerels**
KERERU *n* New Zealand pigeon **kererus**
KERF *n* cut made by a saw, an axe, etc ▹ *vb*

cut **kerfed, kerfing, kerfs**
KERKIER ▸ **kerky**
KERKY *adj* stupid
KERMA *n* quantity of radiation **kermas**
KERMES *n* dried bodies of female scale insects
KERMESS = **kermis**
KERMIS *n* (formerly) annual country festival or carnival
KERN *n* projection of a printed character ▹ *vb* furnish (a typeface) with a kern **kerne**
KERNED ▸ **kerne**
KERNEL *n, vb* **kernels**
KERNES ▸ **kerne**
KERNING *n* provision of kerns in printing
KERNISH *adj* resembling an armed foot soldier or peasant
KERNITE *n* light soft colourless or white mineral
KERNS ▸ **kern**
KERO *short for* > **kerosene**
KEROGEN *n* material that produces hydrocarbons when heated
KEROS ▸ **kero**
KERRIA *n* type of shrub with yellow flowers **kerrias**
KERRIES ▸ **kerry**
KERRY *n* breed of dairy cattle
KERSEY *n* smooth woollen cloth **kerseys**
KERVE *dialect word for* ▸ **carve**
KERVED ▸ **kerve**
KERVES ▸ **kerve**
KERVING ▸ **kerve**
KERYGMA *n* Christian gospel
KESAR *old variant of* ▸ **kaiser**
KESARS ▸ **kesar**
KESH *n* beard and uncut hair traditionally worn by Sikhs **keshes**
KEST *old form of* ▸ **cast**
KESTING ▸ **kest**
KESTREL *n*
KESTS ▸ **kest**
KET *n* dialect word for carrion
KETA *n* type of salmon **ketas**
KETCH *n, vb* **ketches**
KETCHUP *n*
KETE *n* basket woven from flax
KETENE *n* colourless irritating toxic gas **ketenes**
KETES ▸ **kete**
KETMIA *n as in* **bladder ketmia** plant with pale yellow flowers **ketmias**
KETO *adj as in* **keto form** form of tautomeric compounds
KETOL *n* nitrogenous substance **ketols**
KETONE *n* type of organic solvent **ketones, ketonic**
KETOSE *n* any monosaccharide that contains a ketone group
KETOSES ▸ **ketosis**
KETOSIS *n* high concentration of ketone bodies in the blood **ketotic**
KETS ▸ **ket**
KETTLE *n* **kettles**
KETUBAH *n* Jewish marriage contract **ketubot**
KEVEL *n* strong bitt or bollard for securing heavy hawsers **kevels, kevil**
KEVILS ▸ **kevil**
KEWL *nonstandard variant spelling of* ▸ **cool**
KEWLER ▸ **kewl**
KEWLEST ▸ **kewl**
KEWPIE *n* type of brightly coloured doll **kewpies**
KEX *n* any of several hollow-stemmed umbelliferous plants **kexes**

> This is another of the great high-scoring three-letter words that use X.

KEY *n, adj, vb*
KEYCARD *n* electronic card used as a key
KEYED ▸ **key**
KEYHOLE *n* opening for inserting a key into a lock
KEYING ▸ **key**
KEYINGS ▸ **key**
KEYLESS ▸ **key**
KEYLINE *n* outline image on artwork or

plans to show where it is to be placed
KEYNOTE *adj* central or dominating ▷ *n* dominant idea of a speech etc ▷ *vb* deliver a keynote address to (a political convention, etc)
KEYPAD *n* small panel with a set of buttons **keypads**
KEYPAL *n* person one regularly exchanges emails with for fun **keypals**
KEYRING *adj* of a type of computer drive
KEYS *interj* children's cry for truce
KEYSET *n* set of computer keys used for a particular purpose **keysets**
KEYSTER = **keister**
KEYWAY *n* engineering device **keyways**
KEYWORD *n* word or phrase used to find something on a computer
KGOTLA *n* (in South African English) meeting place **kgotlas**
KHADDAR *n* cotton cloth **khadi**
KHADIS ▸ **khadi**
KHAF *n* letter of the Hebrew alphabet **khafs**
KHAKI *adj*, *n* **khakis**
KHALAT = **khilat**
KHALATS ▸ **khalat**
KHALIF *variant spelling of* ▸ **caliph**
KHALIFA = **caliph**
KHALIFS ▸ **khalif**
KHAMSIN *n* hot southerly wind
KHAN *n* title of respect in Afghanistan and central Asia
KHANATE *n* territory ruled by a khan
KHANDA *n* **khandas**
KHANGA = **kanga**
KHANGAS ▸ **khanga**
KHANJAR *n* type of dagger
KHANS ▸ **khan**
KHANUM *feminine form of* ▸ **khan**
KHANUMS ▸ **khanum**
KHAPH *n* letter of the Hebrew alphabet **khaphs**
KHARIF *n* crop harvested at the beginning of winter **kharifs**
KHAT *n* white-flowered evergreen shrub **khats**
KHAYA *n* type of African tree
KHAYAL *n* kind of Indian classical vocal music **khayals**
KHAYAS ▸ **khaya**
KHAZEN = **chazan**
KHAZENS ▸ **khazen**
KHAZI *n* lavatory **khazis**
KHEDA *n* enclosure used to capture wild elephants **khedah**
KHEDAHS ▸ **khedah**
KHEDAS ▸ **kheda**
KHEDIVA *n* khedive's wife
KHEDIVE *n* viceroy of Egypt under Ottoman suzerainty
KHET *n* Thai district
KHETH = **heth**
KHETHS ▸ **kheth**
KHETS ▸ **khet**
KHI *n* letter of the Greek alphabet

> This is a letter of the Greek alphabet, also spelt **chi**. It is worth remembering as one of the higher-scoring three-letter words starting with K.

KHILAT *n* (in the Middle East) gift given to someone as a mark of honour **khilats**
KHILIM = **kilim**
KHILIMS ▸ **khilim**
KHIMAR *n* type of headscarf worn by Muslim women **khimars**
KHIRKAH *n* dervish's woollen or cotton outer garment
KHIS ▸ **khi**
KHODJA = **khoja**
KHODJAS ▸ **khodja**
KHOJA *n* teacher in a Muslim school **khojas**
KHOR *n* watercourse **khors**
KHOTBAH = **khutbah**
KHOTBEH = **khutbah**
KHOUM *n* Mauritanian monetary unit **khoums**
KHUD *n* Indian ravine **khuds**

KHURTA = **kurta**
KHURTAS ▸ **khurta**
KHUTBAH *n* sermon in a Mosque, especially on a Friday
KI *n* vital energy
KIAAT *n* tropical African leguminous tree **kiaats**
KIANG *n* variety of wild ass **kiangs**
KIAUGH *n* (in Scots) anxiety **kiaughs**
KIBBE *n* Middle Eastern dish **kibbeh**
KIBBEHS ▸ **kibbeh**
KIBBES ▸ **kibbe**
KIBBI = **kibbe**
KIBBIS ▸ **kibbi**
KIBBITZ = **kibitz**
KIBBLE *n* bucket used in wells or in mining for hoisting ▷ *vb* grind into small pieces **kibbled, kibbles**
KIBBUTZ *n*
KIBE *n* chilblain
KIBEI *n* someone of Japanese ancestry born in the US and educated in Japan **kibeis**
KIBES ▸ **kibe**
KIBITKA *n* (in Russia) covered sledge or wagon
KIBITZ *vb* interfere or offer unwanted advice
KIBLA = **kiblah**
KIBLAH *n* direction of Mecca **kiblahs**
KIBLAS ▸ **kibla**
KIBOSH *vb* put a stop to
KICK *vb, n*
KICKBOX *vb* box with hands and feet
KICKED ▸ **kick**
KICKER *n* person or thing that kicks **kickers**
KICKIER ▸ **kicky**
KICKING ▸ **kick**
KICKOFF *n* kick that starts a game of football
KICKOUT *n* (in basketball) instance of kicking the ball
KICKS ▸ **kick**
KICKUP *n* fuss **kickups**
KICKY *adj* excitingly unusual and different
KID *n, vb, adj* **kidded, kidder, kidders**
KIDDIE = **kiddy**
KIDDIED ▸ **kiddy**
KIDDIER *n* old word for a market trader
KIDDIES ▸ **kiddy**
KIDDING ▸ **kid**
KIDDISH ▸ **kid**
KIDDLE *n* device for catching fish in a river or in the sea **kiddles**
KIDDO *n* very informal term of address for a young person **kiddoes, kiddos**
KIDDUSH *n* (in Judaism) special blessing
KIDDY *n* affectionate word for a child ▷ *vb* tease or deceive
KIDEL = **kiddle**
KIDELS ▸ **kidel**
KIDGE *dialect word for* ▸ **lively**
KIDGIE *adj* dialect word for friendly and welcoming **kidgier**
KIDLET *n* humorous word for small child **kidlets**
KIDLIKE ▸ **kid**
KIDLING *n* young kid
KIDNAP *vb* **kidnaps**
KIDNEY *n* **kidneys**
KIDS ▸ **kid**
KIDSKIN *n* soft smooth leather
KIDULT *n* adult interested in entertainments intended for children ▷ *adj* aimed at or suitable for kidults, or both children and adults **kidults**
KIDVID *n* informal word for children's video or television **kidvids**
KIEF = **kif**
KIEFS ▸ **kief**
KIEKIE *n* climbing bush plant of New Zealand **kiekies**
KIER *n* vat in which cloth is bleached
KIERIE *n* South African cudgel **kieries**
KIERS ▸ **kier**
KIESTER = **keister**
KIEV *n* type of chicken dish
KIEVE = **keeve**
KIEVES ▸ **kieve**
KIEVS ▸ **kiev**
KIF *n* type of drug
KIFF *adj* South African slang for excellent

KIFS ▸ **kif**
KIGHT *n* archaic spelling of kite, the bird of prey **kights**
KIKOI *n* piece of cotton cloth **kikois**
KIKUMON *n* emblem of the imperial family of Japan
KIKUYU *n* type of grass **kikuyus**
KILD *old spelling of* ▸ **killed**
KILERG *n* 1000 ergs **kilergs**
KILEY = **kylie**
KILEYS ▸ **kiley**
KILIM *n* pileless woven rug **kilims**
KILL *vb, n*
KILLAS *n* Cornish clay slate
KILLCOW *n* important person
KILLDEE = **killdeer**
KILLED ▸ **kill**
KILLER *n* person or animal that kills, esp habitually **killers**
KILLICK *n* small anchor, esp one made of a heavy stone
KILLIE = **killifish**
KILLIES ▸ **killie**
KILLING *adj* very tiring ▹ *n* sudden financial success
KILLJOY *n* person who spoils others' pleasure
KILLOCK = **killick**
KILLS ▸ **kill**
KILLUT = **khilat**
KILLUTS ▸ **killut**
KILN *n, vb* **kilned, kilning, kilns**
KILO *n*
KILOBAR *n* 1000 bars
KILOBIT *n* 1024 bits
KILORAD *n* 1000 rads
KILOS ▸ **kilo**
KILOTON *n* one thousand tons
KILP *dialect form of* ▸ **kelp**
KILPS ▸ **kilp**
KILT *n, vb* **kilted**
KILTER *n* working order or alignment **kilters**
KILTIE *n* someone wearing a kilt **kilties**
KILTING ▸ **kilt**
KILTS ▸ **kilt**
KILTY = **kiltie**
KIMBO *vb* place akimbo **kimboed, kimbos**
KIMCHEE = **kimchi**
KIMCHI *n* Korean dish **kimchis**
KIMMER = **cummer**
KIMMERS ▸ **kimmer**
KIMONO *n* **kimonos**
KIN *n, adj*
KINA *n* standard monetary unit of Papua New Guinea
KINARA *n* African candle holder **kinaras**
KINAS ▸ **kina**
KINASE *n* type of enzyme **kinases**
KINCHIN *old slang word for* ▸ **child**
KINCOB *n* fine silk fabric **kincobs**
KIND *adj, n, vb*
KINDA *adv* very informal shortening of kind of
KINDED ▸ **kind**
KINDER *adj* more kind ▹ *n* kindergarten or nursery school
KINDERS ▸ **kind**
KINDEST ▸ **kind**
KINDIE = **kindy**
KINDIES ▸ **kindy**
KINDING ▸ **kind**
KINDLE *vb* **kindled, kindler, kindles**
KINDLY *adj* having a warm-hearted nature ▹ *adv* in a considerate way
KINDRED *adj, n*
KINDS ▸ **kind**
KINDY *n* kindergarten
KINE *pl n* cows or cattle ▹ *n* Japanese pestle
KINEMA = **cinema**
KINEMAS ▸ **kinema**
KINES *n* ▸ **kine**
KINESES ▸ **kinesis**
KINESIC *adj* of or relating to kinesics
KINESIS *n* movement of an organism
KINETIC *adj*
KINETIN *n* plant hormone
KINFOLK *another word for* > **kinsfolk**
KING *n, vb*
KINGCUP *n* yellow-flowered plant
KINGDOM *n*
KINGED ▸ **king**
KINGING ▸ **king**
KINGLE *n* Scots word for a type of hard rock **kingles**
KINGLET *n* king of a small or insignificant territory

KINGLY *adj* appropriate to a king ▷ *adv* in a manner appropriate to a king
KINGPIN *n*
KINGS ▶ **king**
KININ *n* type of polypeptide **kinins**
KINK *n, vb* **kinked**
KINKIER ▶ **kinky**
KINKILY ▶ **kinky**
KINKING ▶ **kink**
KINKLE *n* little kink **kinkles**
KINKS ▶ **kink**
KINKY *adj*
KINLESS *adj* without any relatives
KINO = **keno**
KINONE *n* benzoquinone **kinones**
KINOS ▶ **kino**
KINRED *old form of* ▶ **kindred**
KINREDS ▶ **kinred**
KINS ▶ **kin**
KINSHIP *n*
KINSMAN *n* relative **kinsmen**
KIORE *n* small brown rat native to New Zealand **kiores**
KIOSK *n* **kiosks**
KIP *vb, n*
KIPE *n* dialect word for a basket for catching fish **kipes**
KIPP *uncommon variant of* ▶ **kip**
KIPPA *n* skullcap worn by male Jews
KIPPAGE *n* Scots word for a state of anger or excitement
KIPPAS ▶ **kippa**
KIPPED ▶ **kip**
KIPPEN ▶ **kep**
KIPPER *n, vb* **kippers**
KIPPING ▶ **kip**
KIPPS ▶ **kipp**
KIPS ▶ **kip**
KIPSKIN = **kip**
KIPUNJI *n* Tanzanian species of monkey
KIR *n* drink made from dry white wine and cassis
KIRANA *n* **kiranas**
KIRBEH *n* leather bottle **kirbehs**
KIRBY *n as in* **kirby grip** type of hairgrip
KIRIMON *n* Japanese imperial crest
KIRK *Scot word for* ▶ **church**
KIRKED ▶ **kirk**
KIRKING ▶ **kirk**
KIRKMAN *n* member or strong upholder of the Kirk **kirkmen**
KIRKS ▶ **kirk**
KIRKTON *n* village or town with a parish church
KIRMESS = **kermis**
KIRN *dialect word for* ▶ **churn**
KIRNED ▶ **kirn**
KIRNING ▶ **kirn**
KIRNS ▶ **kirn**
KIRPAN *n* short sword traditionally carried by Sikhs **kirpans**
KIRRI *n* Hottentot stick **kirris**
KIRS ▶ **kir**
KIRSCH *n* cherry brandy
KIRTAN *n* devotional singing **kirtans**
KIRTLE *n* woman's skirt or dress ▷ *vb* dress with a kirtle **kirtled, kirtles**
KIS ▶ **ki**
KISAN *n* peasant or farmer **kisans**
KISH *n* graphite formed on the surface of molten iron **kishes**
KISHKA = **kishke**
KISHKAS ▶ **kishka**
KISHKE *n* stuffed beef or fowl intestine, boiled and roasted **kishkes**
KISMAT = **kismet**
KISMATS ▶ **kismat**
KISMET *n* fate or destiny **kismets**
KISS *vb, n* **kissed**
KISSEL *n* Russian dessert **kissels**
KISSER *n* mouth or face **kissers**
KISSES ▶ **kiss**
KISSIER ▶ **kissy**
KISSING ▶ **kiss**
KISSY *adj* showing exaggerated affection
KIST *n* large wooden chest ▷ *vb* place in a coffin **kisted, kistful, kisting, kists**
KIT *n, vb*
KITBAG *n* **kitbags**
KITCHEN *n, vb*
KITE *n, vb* **kited**
KITENGE *n* thick cotton cloth
KITER ▶ **kite**
KITERS ▶ **kite**
KITES ▶ **kite**

KITH *n* one's friends and acquaintances
KITHARA *variant of* ▸ **cithara**
KITHE = **kythe**
KITHED ▸ **kithe**
KITHES ▸ **kithe**
KITHING ▸ **kithe**
KITHS ▸ **kith**
KITING ▸ **kite**
KITINGS ▸ **kite**
KITLING *dialect word for* ▸ **kitten**
KITS ▸ **kit**
KITSCH *n* art or literature with popular sentimental appeal ▹ *n* object or art that is tawdry, vulgarized, oversentimental or pretentious **kitschy**
KITSET *n* **kitsets**
KITTED ▸ **kit**
KITTEL *n* white garment worn for certain Jewish rituals or burial **kittels**
KITTEN *n*, *vb* **kittens, kitteny**
KITTIES ▸ **kitty**
KITTING ▸ **kit**
KITTLE *adj* capricious and unpredictable ▹ *vb* be troublesome or puzzling to (someone) **kittled, kittler, kittles**
KITTLY *Scots word for* > **ticklish**
KITTUL *n* type of palm from which jaggery sugar comes **kittuls**
KITTY *n*
KITUL ▸ **kittul**
KITULS ▸ **kitul**
KIVA *n* large room in a Pueblo Indian village **kivas**
KIWI *n* **kiwis**
KLANG *n* (in music) kind of tone **klangs**
KLAP *vb* slap or spank **klapped, klaps**
KLATCH *n* gathering, especially over coffee **klatsch**
KLAVERN *n* local Ku Klux Klan group
KLAVIER = **clavier**
KLAXON *n* loud horn used on emergency vehicles ▹ *vb* hoot with a klaxon **klaxons**
KLEAGLE *n* person with a particular rank in the Ku Klux Klan
KLEENEX *n* tradename for a kind of tissue
KLEPHT *n* group of Greeks **klephts**
KLEPTO *n* compulsive thief **kleptos**
KLETT *n* lightweight climbing boot **kletts**
KLEZMER *n* Jewish folk musician
KLICK *n* kilometre **klicks**
KLIEG *n as in* **klieg light** intense carbon-arc light
KLIK *US military slang word for* > **kilometre**
KLIKS ▸ **klik**
KLINKER *n* type of brick used in paving
KLIPDAS *n* rock hyrax
KLISTER *n* type of ski dressing for improving grip on snow
KLONG *n* type of canal in Thailand **klongs**
KLOOCH = **kloochman**
KLOOF *n* **kloofs**
KLOOTCH = **kloochman**
KLUDGE *n* untidy solution ▹ *vb* cobble something together **kludged, kludges, kludgey, kludgy, kluge**
KLUGED ▸ **kluge**
KLUGES ▸ **kluge**
KLUGING ▸ **kluge**
KLUTZ *n* clumsy or stupid person **klutzes, klutzy**
KNACK *n*, *vb*
KNACKED *adj* broken or worn out
KNACKER *n* buyer of old horses for killing ▹ *vb* exhaust
KNACKS ▸ **knack**
KNACKY *adj* old or dialect word for cunning or artful
KNAG *n* knot in wood
KNAGGY *adj* knotty
KNAGS ▸ **knag**
KNAIDEL = **kneidel**
KNAP *n* crest of a hill ▹ *vb* hit, hammer, or chip **knapped, knapper**
KNAPPLE *old word for* ▸ **nibble**
KNAPS ▸ **knap**
KNAR *old spelling of* ▸ **gnar**
KNARL *old spelling of* ▸ **gnarl**
KNARLS ▸ **knarl**

KNARLY = gnarly
KNARRED ▸ knar
KNARRY ▸ knar
KNARS ▸ knar
KNAUR *variant form of* ▸ knur
KNAURS ▸ knaur
KNAVE *n*
KNAVERY *n* dishonest behaviour
KNAVES ▸ knave
KNAVISH ▸ knave
KNAWE = knawel
KNAWEL *n* type of Old World plant **knawels**
KNAWES ▸ knawe
KNEAD *vb* **kneaded, kneader, kneads**
KNEE *n, vb*
KNEECAP *nontechnical name for* ▸ patella
KNEED ▸ knee
KNEEING ▸ knee
KNEEL *vb, n* **kneeled, kneeler, kneels**
KNEEPAD *n* protective covering for the knee
KNEEPAN *another word for* ▸ patella
KNEES ▸ knee
KNEIDEL *n* (in Jewish cookery) small dumpling
KNELL *n, vb* **knelled, knells**
KNELT ▸ kneel
KNESSET *n* parliament or assembly
KNEVELL *vb* old Scots word meaning beat
KNEW ▸ know
KNICKER *n* woman's or girl's undergarment
KNICKS *pl n* knickers
KNIFE *n, vb* **knifed, knifer, knifers, knifes, knifing**
KNIGHT *n, vb* **knights**
KNISH *n* type of dish **knishes**
KNIT *vb, n*
KNITCH *dialect word for* ▸ bundle
KNITS ▸ knit
KNITTED ▸ knit
KNITTER ▸ knit
KNITTLE *n* old word for string or cord
KNIVE *rare variant of* ▸ knife
KNIVED ▸ knive
KNIVES ▸ knife
KNIVING ▸ knive
KNOB *n, vb* **knobbed**
KNOBBER *n* two-year-old male deer
KNOBBLE *n* small knob ▹ *vb* dialect word meaning strike
KNOBBLY *adj* covered with small bumps
KNOBBY ▸ knob
KNOBS ▸ knob
KNOCK *vb, n* **knocked**
KNOCKER *n*
KNOCKS ▸ knock
KNOLL *n, vb* **knolled, knoller, knolls, knolly**
KNOP *n* knob, esp an ornamental one **knopped, knops**
KNOSP *n* budlike architectural feature **knosps**
KNOT *n, vb* **knots, knotted, knotter**
KNOTTY *adj* full of knots
KNOUT *n* stout whip ▹ *vb* whip **knouted, knouts**
KNOW *vb* be or feel certain of the truth of (information etc)
KNOWE = knoll
KNOWER ▸ know
KNOWERS ▸ know
KNOWES ▸ knowe
KNOWHOW *n* ingenuity, knack, or skill
KNOWING, known, knowns, knows ▸ know
KNUB *dialect word for* ▸ knob
KNUBBLE *vb* dialect word for beat or pound using one's fists
KNUBBLY *adj* having small lumps or protuberances
KNUBBY *adj* knub
KNUBS ▸ knub
KNUCKLE *n* **knuckly**
KNUR *n* knot or protuberance in a tree trunk or in wood
KNURL *n* small ridge, often one of a series ▹ *vb* impress with a series of fine ridges or serrations **knurled, knurls**
KNURLY *rare word for* ▸ gnarled
KNURR = knur
KNURRS ▸ knurr
KNURS ▸ knur
KNUT *n* dandy **knuts**
KO *n* (in New Zealand) traditional digging tool

KOA *n* Hawaiian leguminous tree
KOALA *n* **koalas**
KOAN *n* (in Zen Buddhism) problem that admits no logical solution **koans**
KOAS ▸ **koa**
KOB *n* any of several species of antelope
KOBAN *n* old oval-shaped Japanese gold coin **kobang**
KOBANGS ▸ **kobang**
KOBANS ▸ **koban**
KOBO *n* Nigerian monetary unit
KOBOLD *n* mischievous household sprite **kobolds**
KOBOS ▸ **kobo**
KOBS ▸ **kob**
KOCHIA *n* any of several plants whose foliage turns dark red **kochias**
KOEKOEA *n* long-tailed cuckoo of New Zealand
KOEL *n* any of several parasitic cuckoos **koels**
KOFF *n* Dutch masted merchant vessel **koffs**
KOFTA *n* Indian dish **koftas**
KOFTGAR *n* (in India) person skilled at inlaying steel with gold
KOGAL *n* (in Japan) trendy teenage girl **kogals**
KOHA *n* gift or donation, esp of cash
KOHANIM ▸ **kohen**
KOHAS ▸ **koha**
KOHEN *n* member of the Jewish priestly caste
KOHL *n* cosmetic powder **kohls**
KOI *n* any of various ornamental forms of the common carp
KOINE *n* common language among speakers of different languages **koines**
KOIS ▸ **koi**
KOJI *n* Japanese steamed rice **kojis**
KOKA *n* former type of score in judo
KOKAKO *n* type of crow **kokakos**
KOKANEE *n* type of freshwater salmon
KOKAS ▸ **koka**
KOKER *n* Guyanese sluice **kokers**
KOKIRI *n* type of rough-skinned New Zealand triggerfish **kokiris**
KOKOBEH *adj* (of certain fruit) having a rough skin
KOKOPU *n* any of several small freshwater fish of New Zealand **kokopus**
KOKOWAI *n* type of clay
KOKRA *n* type of wood **kokras**
KOKUM *n* tropical tree **kokums**
KOLA *n as in* **kola nut** caffeine-containing seed used in medicine and soft drinks
KOLACKY *n* sweet bun with a fruit, jam, or nut filling
KOLAS ▸ **kola**
KOLBASI = **kolbassi**
KOLHOZ = **kolkhoz**
KOLHOZY = **kolkhoz**
KOLKHOS = **kolkhoz**
KOLKHOZ *n* (formerly) collective farm in the Soviet Union **kolkoz**
KOLKOZY ▸ **kolkoz**
KOLO *n* Serbian folk dance **kolos**
KOMATIK *n* type of sledge
KOMBU *n* dark brown seaweed **kombus**
KON *old word for* ▸ **know**
KONAKI = **koneke**
KONAKIS ▸ **konaki**
KONBU = **kombu**
KONBUS ▸ **konbu**
KOND ▸ **kon**
KONDO *n* (in Uganda) thief or armed robber **kondos**
KONEKE *n* type of farm vehicle **konekes**
KONFYT *n* South African fruit preserve **konfyts**
KONGONI *n* E African hartbeest
KONINI *n* edible dark purple berry **koninis**
KONK = **conk**
KONKED ▸ **konk**
KONKING ▸ **konk**
KONKS ▸ **konk**
KONNING ▸ **kon**
KONS ▸ **kon**
KOODOO = **kudu**
KOODOOS ▸ **koodoo**

KOOK *n* eccentric person ▹ *vb* dialect word for vanish **kooked**
KOOKIE = **kooky**
KOOKIER ▸ **kooky**
KOOKILY ▸ **kooky**
KOOKING ▸ **kook**
KOOKS ▸ **kook**
KOOKY *adj* crazy, eccentric, or foolish
KOOLAH *old form of* ▸ **koala**
KOOLAHS ▸ **koolah**
KOORI *n* Australian Aborigine **koories, kooris**
KOP *n* prominent isolated hill or mountain in southern Africa
KOPECK *n* former Russian monetary unit **kopecks, kopek**
KOPEKS ▸ **kopek**
KOPH *n* 19th letter in the Hebrew alphabet **kophs**
KOPIYKA *n* monetary unit of Ukraine **kopiyok**
KOPJE *n* small hill **kopjes**
KOPPA *n* consonantal letter in the Greek alphabet **koppas**
KOPPIE = **kopje**
KOPPIES ▸ **koppie**
KOPS ▸ **kop**
KOR *n* ancient Hebrew unit of capacity
KORA *n* West African instrument
KORAI ▸ **kore**
KORARI *n* native New Zealand flax plant **koraris**
KORAS ▸ **kora**
KORAT *n as in* **korat cat** rare blue-grey breed of cat **korats**
KORE *n* ancient Greek statue of a young woman wearing clothes
KORERO *n* talk or discussion ▹ *vb* speak or converse **koreros**
KORES ▸ **kore**
KORKIR *n* variety of lichen used in dyeing **korkirs**
KORMA *n* type of mild Indian dish **kormas**
KORO *n* elderly Māori man
KORORA *n* small New Zealand penguin **kororas**
KOROS ▸ **koro**
KOROWAI *n* decorative woven cloak worn by a Māori chief
KORS ▸ **kor**
KORU *n* stylized curved pattern used esp in carving
KORUN ▸ **koruna**
KORUNA *n* standard monetary unit of the Czech Republic and Slovakia **korunas, koruny**
KORUS ▸ **koru**
KOS *n* Indian unit of distance **koses**
KOSHER *adj, n, vb* **koshers**
KOSMOS *variant form of* ▸ **cosmos**
KOSS = **kos**
KOSSES ▸ **koss**
KOTARE *n* small greenish-blue kingfisher **kotares**
KOTO *n* Japanese stringed instrument **kotos**
KOTOW = **kowtow**
KOTOWED ▸ **kotow**
KOTOWER ▸ **kotow**
KOTOWS ▸ **kotow**
KOTUKU *n* type of white heron **kotukus**
KOTWAL *n* senior police officer or magistrate in an Indian town **kotwals**
KOULAN = **kulan**
KOULANS ▸ **koulan**
KOUMIS, koumiss, koumys, koumyss = **kumiss**
KOUPREY *n* large wild SE Asian ox
KOURA *n* New Zealand freshwater crayfish **kouras**
KOUROI ▸ **kouros**
KOUROS *n* ancient Greek statue of a young man
KOUSSO *n* Abyssinian tree **koussos**
KOW *old variant of* ▸ **cow**

This dialect variant of **cow** scores well for a three-letter word, and can be a good one to form when playing in more than one direction.

KOWHAI *n* **kowhais**
KOWS ▸ **kow**
KOWTOW *vb, n* **kowtows**
KRAAL *n, adj, vb* **kraaled, kraals**
KRAB = **karabiner**
KRABS ▸ **krab**
KRAFT *n* strong wrapping paper **krafts**
KRAIT *n* brightly coloured venomous snake of S and SE Asia **kraits**
KRAKEN *n* legendary sea monster **krakens**
KRANG *n* dead whale from which the blubber has been removed **krangs**
KRANS *n* sheer rock face **kranses, krantz, kranz, kranzes**
KRATER = **crater**
KRATERS ▸ **krater**
KRAUT *n* sauerkraut **krauts**
KREEP *n* lunar substance **kreeps**
KREESE = **kris**
KREESED ▸ **kreese**
KREESES ▸ **kreese**
KREMLIN *n* citadel of any Russian city
KRENG = **krang**
KRENGS ▸ **kreng**
KREUZER = **kreutzer**
KREWE *n* club taking part in New Orleans carnival parade **krewes**
KRILL *n* small shrimplike sea creature **krills**
KRIMMER *n* tightly curled light grey fur
KRIS *n* type of Malayan and Indonesian knife ▷ *vb* stab or slash with a kris **krised, krises, krising**
KRONA *n* standard monetary unit of Sweden
KRONE *n* standard monetary unit of Norway and Denmark **kronen, kroner**
KRONOR ▸ **krona**
KRONUR ▸ **krona**
KROON *n* standard monetary unit of Estonia **krooni, kroons**
KRUBI *n* aroid plant with an unpleasant smell **krubis, krubut**
KRUBUTS ▸ **krubut**
KRULLER *variant spelling of* ▸ **cruller**
KRUMPER > **krumping**
KRUNK *n* style of hip-hop music
KRUNKED ▸ **crunked**
KRUNKS ▸ **krunk**
KRYPSES ▸ **krypsis**
KRYPSIS *n* idea that Christ made secret use of his divine attributes
KRYPTON *n*
KRYTRON *n* type of fast electronic gas-discharge switch
KSAR *old form of* ▸ **tsar**
KSARS ▸ **ksar**
KUCCHA ▸ **kaccha**
KUCCHAS ▸ **kuccha**
KUCHCHA = **kacha**
KUCHEN *n* breadlike cake **kuchens**
KUDLIK *n* Inuit soapstone seal-oil lamp **kudliks**
KUDO *variant of* ▸ **kudos**
KUDOS *n* **kudoses**
KUDU *n* **kudus**
KUDZU *n* hairy leguminous climbing plant **kudzus**
KUE *n* name of the letter Q
KUEH *n* (in Malaysia) any cake of Malay, Chinese, or Indian origin
KUES ▸ **kue**
KUFI *n* cap for Muslim man **kufis**
KUFIYAH = **keffiyeh**
KUGEL *n* baked pudding in traditional Jewish cooking **kugels**
KUIA *n* Māori female elder or elderly woman **kuias**
KUKRI *n* heavy, curved knife used by Gurkhas **kukris**
KUKU *n* mussel **kukus**
KULA *n* ceremonial gift exchange among islanders in the W Pacific
KULAK *n* (formerly) property-owning Russian peasant **kulaki, kulaks**
KULAN *n* Asiatic wild ass **kulans**
KULAS ▸ **kula**

KULBASA > **kielbasa**
KULFI *n* Indian dessert **kulfis**
KULTUR *n* German civilization **kulturs**
KUMARA *n* **kumaras**
KUMARI *n* (in Indian English) maiden **kumaris**
KUMERA = **kumara**
KUMERAS ▸ **kumera**
KUMISS *n* drink made from fermented mare's or other milk
KUMITE *n* freestyle sparring or fighting **kumites**
KUMMEL *n* German liqueur **kummels**
KUMQUAT *n*
KUMYS = **kumiss**
KUMYSES ▸ **kumys**
KUNA *n* standard monetary unit of Croatia **kune**
KUNJOOS *adj* (in Indian English) mean or stingy
KUNKAR *n* type of limestone **kunkars, kunkur**
KUNKURS ▸ **kunkur**
KUNZITE *n* variety of the mineral spodumene
KURBASH *vb* whip with a hide whip
KURGAN *n* Russian burial mound **kurgans**
KURI *n* mongrel dog **kuris**
KURRE *old variant of* ▸ **cur**
KURRES ▸ **kurre**
KURSAAL *n* public room at a health resort
KURTA *n* long loose garment **kurtas**
KURU *n* degenerative disease of the nervous system **kurus**

> This word for a kind of sickness found in New Guinea can give you something to laugh about when you have two Us to dispose of.

KURVEY *vb* (in old South African English) transport goods by ox cart **kurveys**
KUSSO *variant spelling of* ▸ **kousso**
KUSSOS ▸ **kusso**
KUTA *n* (in Indian English) male dog **kutas**
KUTCH = **catechu**
KUTCHA *adj* makeshift or not solid
KUTCHES ▸ **kutch**
KUTI *n* (in Indian English) female dog or bitch **kutis**
KUTU *n* body louse **kutus**
KUVASZ *n* breed of dog from Hungary
KUZU = **kudzu**

> A Japanese climbing plant, this can be a great word for getting a high score out of a difficult rack.

KUZUS ▸ **kuzu**
KVAS = **kvass**
KVASES ▸ **kvas**
KVASS *n* alcoholic drink **kvasses**
KVELL *vb* US word meaning be happy **kvelled, kvells**
KVETCH *vb* complain or grumble
KVETCHY *adj* tending to grumble or complain
KWACHA *n* standard monetary unit of Zambia **kwachas**
KWAITO *n* type of South African pop music **kwaitos**
KWANZA *n* standard monetary unit of Angola **kwanzas**
KWELA *n* type of pop music **kwelas**
KY *pl n* Scots word for cows
KYACK *n* type of panier **kyacks**
KYAK = **kayak**
KYAKS ▸ **kyak**
KYANG = **kiang**
KYANGS ▸ **kyang**
KYANISE = **kyanize**
KYANITE *n* grey, green, or blue mineral
KYANIZE *vb* treat (timber) with corrosive sublimate
KYAR = **coir**
KYARS ▸ **kyar**
KYAT *n* standard monetary unit of Myanmar **kyats**
KYBO *n* temporary lavatory used when camping **kybos**
KYBOSH = **kibosh**
KYDST ▸ **kythe**

KYE *n* Korean fundraising meeting **kyes**

KYLE *n* narrow strait or channel **kyles**

KYLICES ▸ **kylix**

KYLIE *n* type of boomerang **kylies**

KYLIKES ▸ **kylix**

KYLIN *n* (in Chinese art) mythical animal **kylins**

KYLIX *n* drinking vessel used in ancient Greece

KYLOE *n* breed of beef cattle **kyloes**

KYND *old variant of* ▸ **kind**

KYNDE *old variant of* ▸ **kind**

KYNDED ▸ **kynd**

KYNDES ▸ **kynde**

KYNDING ▸ **kynd**

KYNDS ▸ **kynd**

KYNE *pl n* archaic word for cows

KYOGEN *n* type of Japanese drama **kyogens**

KYPE *n* hook on the lower jaw of a mature male salmon **kypes**

KYRIE *n* type of prayer **kyries**

KYTE *n* belly **kytes**

KYTHE *vb* appear **kythed, kythes, kything**

KYU *n* (in judo) one of the five student grades **kyus**

This means a novice grade in judo, and its unusual combination of letters makes it a useful word to remember when you have an unpromising set of letters on your rack.

L can be a difficult letter to use well, especially when you need to play short words. Just three two-letter words begin with **L**: **la, li** and **lo**. Knowing this will save you valuable time in a game, especially when you are trying to fit words into a crowded board. There aren't very many three-letter words either, but don't forget common words like **lab** (5 points), **law** (6), **lay** (6), **low** (6) and **lye** (6). Try to remember the three-letter words that combine **L** with **X**: **lax, lex, lox** and **lux** (10 points each). These are particularly useful towards the end of a game if you have an **X** but little opportunity to play it. There is also the very useful **luz** for 12 points.

LA *n* exclamation of surprise or emphasis ▷ *n* the sixth note of the musical scale
LAAGER *n* (in Africa) a camp defended by a circular formation of wagons ▷ *vb* form (wagons) into a laager **laagers**
LAARI = **lari**
LAARIS ▶ **laari**
LAB *n*
LABARA ▶ **labarum**
LABARUM *n* standard carried in Christian processions
LABDA = **lambda**
LABDAS ▶ **labda**
LABEL *n, vb* **labeled, labeler**
LABELLA > **labellum**
LABELS ▶ **label**
LABIA ▶ **labium**
LABIAL *adj* of the lips ▷ *n* speech sound that involves the lips **labials**
LABIATE *n* plant with square stems, aromatic leaves, and a two-lipped flower ▷ *adj* of this family
LABILE *adj* (of a compound) prone to chemical change
LABIS *n* cochlear **labises**
LABIUM *n* lip or liplike structure
LABLAB *n* twining leguminous plant **lablabs**
LABOR = **labour**
LABORED = **laboured**
LABORER = **labourer**
LABORS ▶ **labor**
LABOUR *n, vb* **labours**
LABRA ▶ **labrum**
LABRAL *adj* of or like a lip
LABRET *n* piece of bone or shell **labrets**
LABRID = **labroid**
LABRIDS ▶ **labrid**
LABROID *n* type of fish ▷ *adj* of or relating to such fish
LABROSE *adj* thick-lipped
LABRUM *n* lip or liplike part **labrums**
LABRYS *n* type of axe

LABS ▸ **lab**
LAC = **lakh**
LACE *n, vb* **laced, lacer, lacers, laces**
LACET *n* braidwork **lacets**
LACEY = **lacy**
LACHES *n* unreasonable delay in pursuing a legal remedy
LACIER ▸ **lacy**
LACIEST ▸ **lacy**
LACILY ▸ **lacy**
LACING ▸ **lace**
LACINGS ▸ **lace**
LACINIA *n* narrow fringe on petal
LACK *n, vb* **lacked**
LACKER *variant spelling of* ▸ **lacquer**
LACKERS ▸ **lacker**
LACKEY *n, vb* **lackeys**
LACKING ▸ **lack**
LACKS ▸ **lack**
LACMUS *n* old form of litmus
LACONIC *adj*
LACQUER *n, vb*
LACQUEY = **lackey**
LACS ▸ **lac**
LACTAM *n* any of a group of inner amides **lactams**
LACTARY *adj* relating to milk
LACTASE *n* any of a group of enzymes that hydrolyse lactose to glucose and galactose
LACTATE *vb, n*
LACTEAL *adj* of or like milk ▹ *n* any of the lymphatic vessels that convey chyle from the small intestine to the blood
LACTEAN *another word for* > **lacteous**
LACTIC *adj* of or derived from milk
LACTONE *n* any of a class of organic compounds
LACTOSE *n*
LACUNA *n* gap or missing part, esp in a document or series **lacunae, lacunal**
LACUNAR *n* ceiling, soffit, or vault having coffers ▹ *adj* having a lacuna
LACUNAS ▸ **lacuna**
LACUNE *n* hiatus **lacunes**
LACY *adj* fine, like lace
LAD *n*
LADANUM = **labdanum**
LADDER *n, vb* **ladders, laddery**
LADDIE *n* **laddies**
LADDISH *adj* behaving in a macho or immature manner
LADDISM *n* laddish attitudes and behaviour
LADE *vb* put cargo on board ▹ *n* watercourse **laded**
LADEN *adj, vb* **ladened, ladens**
LADER ▸ **lade**
LADERS ▸ **lade**
LADES ▸ **lade**
LADETTE *n* young woman who behaves like a young man
LADHOOD ▸ **lad**
LADIES *n* women's public toilet
LADIFY = **ladyfy**
LADING ▸ **lade**
LADINGS ▸ **lade**
LADINO *n* Italian variety of white clover **ladinos**
LADLE *n, vb* **ladled**
LADLER *n* person who serves with a ladle **ladlers**
LADLES ▸ **ladle**
LADLING ▸ **ladle**
LADRON = **ladrone**
LADRONE *n* thief
LADRONS ▸ **ladron**
LADS ▸ **lad**
LADY *n, adj*
LADYBOY *n* transvestite or transsexual from the Far East
LADYBUG = **ladybird**
LADYCOW *another word for* > **ladybird**
LADYFLY *another word for* > **ladybird**
LADYFY *vb* make a lady of (someone)
LADYISH ▸ **lady**
LADYISM ▸ **lady**
LADYKIN *n* endearing form of lady
LAER *another word for* ▸ **laager**
LAERED ▸ **laer**
LAERING ▸ **laer**
LAERS ▸ **laer**
LAESIE *old form of* ▸ **lazy**
LAETARE *n* fourth Sunday of Lent
LAEVO *adj* on the left
LAG *vb, n*

LAGAN *n* goods or wreckage on the sea bed **lagans**
LAGENA *n* bottle with a narrow neck **lagenas**
LAGEND = **lagan**
LAGENDS ▸ **lagend**
LAGER *n, vb* **lagered, lagers**
LAGGARD *n, adj*
LAGGED ▸ **lag**
LAGGEN *n* spar of a barrel **laggens**
LAGGER *n* person who lags pipes **laggers**
LAGGIN = **laggen**
LAGGING ▸ **lag**
LAGGINS ▸ **laggin**
LAGOON *n* **lagoons**
LAGS ▸ **lag**
LAGUNA *n* lagoon **lagunas**
LAGUNE = **lagoon**
LAGUNES ▸ **lagune**
LAH *n* (in tonic sol-fa) sixth degree of any major scale
LAHAR *n* landslide of volcanic debris and water **lahars**
LAHS ▸ **lah**
LAIC *adj* laical ▹ *n* layman
LAICAL *adj* secular
LAICH *n* low-lying piece of land **laichs**
LAICISE = **laicize**
LAICISM ▸ **laic**
LAICITY *n* state of being laical
LAICIZE *vb* remove ecclesiastical status from
LAICS ▸ **laic**
LAID *Scots form of* ▸ **load**
LAIDED ▸ **laid**
LAIDING ▸ **laid**
LAIDLY *adj* very ugly
LAIDS ▸ **laid**
LAIGH *adj* low-lying ▹ *n* area of low-lying ground **laigher, laighs**
LAIK *vb* play (a game, etc)
LAIKA *n* type of small dog **laikas**
LAIKED, laiker, laikers, laiking, laiks ▸ **laik**
LAIN ▸ **lie**
LAIPSE *vb* beat soundly **laipsed, laipses**
LAIR *n, vb*
LAIRAGE *n* accommodation for farm animals
LAIRD *n*
LAIRDLY *adj* pertaining to laird(s)
LAIRDS ▸ **laird**
LAIRED ▸ **lair**
LAIRIER ▸ **lairy**
LAIRING ▸ **lair**
LAIRISE = **lairize**
LAIRIZE *vb* show off
LAIRS ▸ **lair**
LAIRY *adj* gaudy or flashy
LAISSE *n* type of rhyme scheme **laisses**
LAITH *Scots form of* ▸ **loath**
LAITHLY = **laidly**
LAITIES ▸ **laity**
LAITY *n*
LAKE *n, vb*
LAKEBED *n* bed of lake
LAKED ▸ **lake**
LAKELET *n* small lake
LAKER *n* lake cargo vessel **lakers**
LAKES ▸ **lake**
LAKH *n* (in India) 100 000, esp referring to this sum of rupees **lakhs**
LAKIER ▸ **laky**
LAKIEST ▸ **laky**
LAKIN *short form of* ▸ **ladykin**
LAKING ▸ **lake**
LAKINGS ▸ **lake**
LAKINS ▸ **lakin**
LAKISH *adj* similar to poetry of Lake poets
LAKSA *n* (in Malaysia) Chinese dish of rice noodles in curry or hot soup **laksas**
LAKY *adj* of the reddish colour of the pigment lake
LALANG *n* coarse weedy Malaysian grass **lalangs**
LALDIE *n* great gusto **laldies, laldy**
LALIQUE *n* ornamental glass
LALL *vb* make bad 'l' or 'r' sounds
LALLAN *n* literary version of the English spoken in Lowland Scotland **lalland, lallans**
LALLED ▸ **lall**
LALLING ▸ **lall**
LALLS ▸ **lall**
LAM *vb* attack vigorously
LAMA *n* **lamas**
LAMB *n, vb*

LAMBADA *n* erotic Brazilian dance
LAMBAST *vb* beat or thrash
LAMBDA *n* 11th letter of the Greek alphabet **lambdas**
LAMBED ▸ **lamb**
LAMBENT *adj* (of a flame) flickering softly
LAMBER *n* person that attends to lambing ewes **lambers**
LAMBERT *n* cgs unit of illumination, equal to 1 lumen per square centimetre
LAMBIE = **lambkin**
LAMBIER ▸ **lamby**
LAMBIES ▸ **lambie**
LAMBING *n* birth of lambs at the end of winter
LAMBKIN *n* young lamb
LAMBOYS *n* skirt-like piece of armour made from metal strips
LAMBS ▸ **lamb**
LAMBY *adj* lamb-like
LAME *adj, vb, n*
LAMED *n* 12th letter in the Hebrew alphabet **lamedh**
LAMEDHS ▸ **lamedh**
LAMEDS ▸ **lamed**
LAMELLA *n* thin layer, plate, etc, like the calcified layers of which bone is formed
LAMELY ▸ **lame**
LAMENT *vb, n* **laments**
LAMER ▸ **lame**
LAMES ▸ **lame**
LAMEST ▸ **lame**
LAMETER *Scots form of* ▸ **lamiger**
LAMIA *n* female monster with a snake's body and a woman's head and breasts **lamiae, lamias**
LAMIGER *n* disabled person
LAMINA *n* thin plate, esp of bone or mineral **laminae**
LAMINAL *n* consonant articulated with blade of tongue
LAMINAR ▸ **lamina**
LAMINAS ▸ **lamina**
LAMING ▸ **lame**
LAMININ *n* type of protein
LAMISH *adj* rather lame
LAMITER = **lameter**
LAMMED ▸ **lam**
LAMMER *Scots word for* ▸ **amber**
LAMMERS ▸ **lammer**
LAMMIE = **lammy**
LAMMIES ▸ **lammy**
LAMMING ▸ **lam**
LAMMY *n* thick woollen jumper
LAMP *n, vb*
LAMPAD *n* candlestick **lampads**
LAMPAS *n* swelling of the mucous membrane of the hard palate of horses
LAMPED ▸ **lamp**
LAMPER *n* lamprey
LAMPERN *n* migratory European lamprey
LAMPERS ▸ **lamper**
LAMPING ▸ **lamp**
LAMPION *n* oil-burning lamp
LAMPLIT *adj* lit by lamps
LAMPOON *n, vb*
LAMPREY *n*
LAMPS ▸ **lamp**
LAMPUKA = **lampuki**
LAMPUKI *n* type of fish
LAMS ▸ **lam**
LAMSTER *n* fugitive
LANA *n* wood from genipap tree
LANAI *Hawaiian word for* ▸ **veranda**
LANAIS ▸ **lanai**
LANAS ▸ **lana**
LANATE *adj* having or consisting of a woolly covering of hairs **lanated**
LANCE *n, vb* **lanced**
LANCER *n* formerly, cavalry soldier armed with a lance
LANCERS *n* quadrille for eight or sixteen couples
LANCES ▸ **lance**
LANCET *n* **lancets**
LANCH *obsolete form of* ▸ **launch**
LANCHED ▸ **lanch**
LANCHES ▸ **lanch**
LANCING ▸ **lance**
LAND *n, vb*
LANDAU *n* **landaus**
LANDE *n* type of moorland in SW France
LANDED *adj*
LANDER *n* spacecraft which lands on a planet or other body **landers**
LANDES ▸ **lande**

LANDING *n*
LANDLER *n* Austrian country dance
LANDMAN *n* person who lives and works on land **landmen**
LANDS *pl n* holdings in land
LANE *n*
LANELY *Scots form of* ▸ **lonely**
LANES ▸ **lane**
LANEWAY *n* lane
LANG *Scot word for* ▸ **long**
LANGAHA *n* type of Madagascan snake
LANGAR *n* dining hall in a gurdwara **langars**
LANGEST ▸ **lang**
LANGLEY *n* unit of solar radiation
LANGREL = **langrage**
LANGUE *n* language considered as an abstract system
LANGUED *adj* having a tongue
LANGUES ▸ **langue**
LANGUET *n* anything resembling a tongue
LANGUID *adj*
LANGUOR *n*
LANGUR *n* type of arboreal Old World monkey **langurs**
LANIARD = **lanyard**
LANIARY *adj* adapted for tearing ▹ *n* tooth adapted for tearing
LANITAL *n* fibre used in production of synthetic wool
LANK *adj*, *vb* **lanked, lanker, lankest**
LANKIER ▸ **lanky**
LANKILY ▸ **lanky**
LANKING ▸ **lank**
LANKLY ▸ **lank**
LANKS ▸ **lank**
LANKY *adj*
LANNER *n* large falcon **lanners**
LANOLIN *n*
LANOSE = **lanate**
LANT *n* stale urine
LANTANA *n*
LANTERN *n*, *vb*
LANTS ▸ **lant**
LANUGO *n* layer of fine hairs, esp the covering of the human fetus before birth **lanugos**
LANX *n* dish; plate
LANYARD *n*
LAOGAI *n* forced labour camp in China **laogais**
LAP *n*, *vb*
LAPDOG *n* **lapdogs**
LAPEL *n* **lapeled, lapels**
LAPFUL = **lap**
LAPFULS ▸ **lapful**
LAPHELD *adj* small enough to be used on one's lap
LAPIDES ▸ **lapis**
LAPILLI > **lapillus**
LAPIN *n* castrated rabbit **lapins**
LAPIS *n as in* **lapis lazuli** brilliant blue mineral gemstone **lapises**
LAPJE = **lappie**
LAPJES ▸ **lapje**
LAPPED ▸ **lap**
LAPPEL = **lapel**
LAPPELS ▸ **lappel**
LAPPER *n* one that laps ▹ *vb* curdle **lappers**
LAPPET *n* small hanging flap **lappets**
LAPPIE *n* rag **lappies**
LAPPING ▸ **lap**
LAPS ▸ **lap**
LAPSANG *n* Chinese tea
LAPSE *n*, *vb* **lapsed, lapser, lapsers, lapses, lapsing**
LAPSUS *n* lapse or error
LAPTOP *adj* small enough to fit on a user's lap ▹ *n* small computer **laptops**
LAPTRAY *n* tray with a cushioned underside
LAPWING *n*
LAPWORK *n* work with lapping edges
LAR *n* boy or young man
LARCENY *n*
LARCH *n*
LARCHEN *adj* of larch
LARCHES ▸ **larch**
LARD *n*, *vb* **larded**
LARDER *n* **larders**
LARDIER ▸ **lardy**
LARDING ▸ **lard**
LARDON *n* strip or cube of fat or bacon used in larding meat **lardons, lardoon**
LARDS ▸ **lard**
LARDY *adj* fat
LARE *another word for* ▸ **lore**
LAREE *n* Asian fish-hook **larees**
LARES ▸ **lare**
LARGE *adj* great in size, number ▹ *n* formerly, musical note
LARGELY *adv*

LARGEN *another word for* ▶ **enlarge**
LARGENS ▶ **largen**
LARGER ▶ **large**
LARGES ▶ **large**
LARGESS = **largesse**
LARGEST ▶ **large**
LARGISH *adj* fairly large
LARGO *adv* in a slow and dignified manner ▷ *n* performance piece in a slow manner **largos**
LARI *n* monetary unit of Georgia
LARIAT *n* lasso ▷ *vb* tether with lariat **lariats**
LARINE *adj* of, relating to, or resembling a gull
LARIS ▶ **lari**
LARK *n, vb* **larked, larker, larkers**
LARKIER ▶ **larky**
LARKING ▶ **lark**
LARKISH ▶ **lark**
LARKS ▶ **lark**
LARKY *adj* frolicsome
LARMIER *n* pouch under lower eyelid of deer
LARN *vb* learn
LARNAX *n* terracotta coffin
LARNED ▶ **larn**
LARNEY *n* white person ▷ *adj* (of clothes) smart **larneys, larnier**
LARNING ▶ **larn**
LARNS ▶ **larn**
LAROID *adj* relating to Larus genus of gull family
LARRUP *vb* beat or flog **larrups**
LARS ▶ **lar**
LARUM *archaic word for* ▶ **alarm**
LARUMS ▶ **larum**
LARVA *n* **larvae, larval, larvas**
LARVATE *adj* masked; concealed
LARYNX *n*
LAS ▶ **la**
LASAGNA = **lasagne**
LASAGNE *n*
LASCAR *n* East Indian seaman **lascars**
LASE *vb* to be capable of acting as a laser **lased**
LASER *n* **lasers**
LASES ▶ **lase**
LASH *n, vb* **lashed, lasher, lashers, lashes, lashing**
LASHINS *variant of* > **lashings**
LASHKAR *n* troop of Indian men with weapons
LASING ▶ **lase**
LASINGS ▶ **lase**
LASKET *n* loop at the foot of a sail onto which an extra sail may be fastened **laskets**
LASQUE *n* flat-cut diamond **lasques**
LASS *n* **lasses**
LASSI *n* cold drink made of yoghurt or buttermilk, flavoured with sugar, salt, or spice
LASSIE *n* **lassies**
LASSIS ▶ **lassi**
LASSO *n, vb*
LASSOCK *another word for* ▶ **lass**
LASSOED, lassoer, lassoes, lassos ▶ **lasso**
LASSU *n* slow part of csárdás folk dance **lassus**
LAST *adv* coming at the end or after all others ▷ *adj* only remaining ▷ *n* last person or thing ▷ *vb* continue
LASTAGE *n* space for storing goods in ship
LASTED ▶ **last**
LASTER ▶ **last**
LASTERS ▶ **last**
LASTING *adj* remaining effective for a long time ▷ *n* strong durable fabric used for shoe uppers, etc
LASTLY *adv* at the end or at the last point
LASTS ▶ **last**
LAT *n* former coin of Latvia
LATAH *n* psychological condition **latahs**
LATAKIA *n* Turkish tobacco
LATCH *n, vb* **latched, latches**
LATCHET *n* shoe fastening
LATE *adj, adv*
LATED *archaic word for* ▶ **belated**
LATEEN *adj* of a rig with a triangular sail bent to a yard hoisted to the

head of a low mast **lateens**
LATELY *adv*
LATEN *vb* become or cause to become late
LATENCE ▸ **latent**
LATENCY ▸ **latent**
LATENED ▸ **laten**
LATENS ▸ **laten**
LATENT *adj, n* **latents**
LATER *adv* afterwards
LATERAD *adv* towards the side
LATERAL *adj, n, vb*
LATEST *n* the most recent news **latests**
LATEX *n* **latexes**
LATH *n, vb*
LATHE *n, vb* **lathed**
LATHEE = **lathi**
LATHEES ▸ **lathee**
LATHEN *adj* covered with laths
LATHER *n, vb* **lathers, lathery**
LATHES ▸ **lathe**
LATHI *n* long heavy wooden stick used as a weapon in India
LATHIER ▸ **lathy**
LATHING ▸ **lathe**
LATHIS ▸ **lathi**
LATHS ▸ **lath**
LATHY *adj* resembling a lath, esp in being tall and thin
LATI ▸ **lat**
LATICES ▸ **latex**
LATIGO *n* strap on horse's saddle **latigos**
LATILLA *n* stick making up part of ceiling
LATINA *n* US female of Latin American origin **latinas**
LATINO *n* US male of Latin American origin **latinos**
LATISH *adv* rather late ▹ *adj* rather late
LATITAT *n* writ presuming that person accused was hiding
LATKE *n* crispy Jewish pancake **latkes**
LATOSOL *n* type of deep, well-drained soil
LATRANT *adj* barking
LATRIA *n* adoration that may be offered to God alone **latrias**
LATRINE *n*
LATRON *n* bandit **latrons**
LATS ▸ **lat**
LATTE *n* coffee with hot milk
LATTEN *n* metal or alloy, esp brass, made in thin sheets **lattens**
LATTER *adj*
LATTES ▸ **latte**
LATTICE *n, vb*
LATTIN *n* brass alloy beaten into a thin sheet **lattins**
LATU ▸ **lat**
LAUAN *n* type of wood used in furniture-making **lauans**
LAUCH *Scots form of* ▸ **laugh**
LAUCHS ▸ **lauch**
LAUD *vb, n* **lauded, lauder, lauders, lauding**
LAUDS *n* traditional morning prayer of the Western Church
LAUF *n* run in bobsleighing **laufs**
LAUGH *vb* make sounds with the voice expressing amusement ▹ *n* act of laughing **laughed, laugher, laughs**
LAUGHY *adj* laughing a lot
LAUNCE *old form of* ▸ **lance**
LAUNCED ▸ **launce**
LAUNCES ▸ **launce**
LAUNCH *vb, n*
LAUND *n* open grassy space
LAUNDER *vb, n*
LAUNDRY *n*
LAUNDS ▸ **laund**
LAURA *n* group of monastic cells **laurae, lauras**
LAUREL *n, vb* **laurels**
LAURIC *adj as in* **lauric acid** dodecanoic acid
LAURYL *n as in* **lauryl alcohol** crystalline solid used to make detergents **lauryls**
LAUWINE *n* avalanche
LAV *short for* > **lavatory**
LAVA *n*
LAVABO *n* ritual washing of priest's hands at Mass **lavabos**
LAVAGE *n* washing out of a hollow organ **lavages**
LAVAS ▸ **lava**
LAVASH *n* Armenian flat bread

LAVE *archaic word for* ▸ **wash**
LAVED ▸ **lave**
LAVEER *vb* (in sailing) tack **laveers**
LAVER *n* priest's waterbasin for ritual ablutions **lavers**
LAVES ▸ **lave**
LAVING ▸ **lave**
LAVISH *adj, vb*
LAVOLT = **lavolta**
LAVOLTA *n* old Italian dance ▹ *vb* dance the lavolta
LAVOLTS ▸ **lavolt**
LAVRA = **laura**
LAVRAS ▸ **lavra**
LAVROCK = **laverock**
LAVS ▸ **lav**
LAVVIES ▸ **lavvy**
LAVVY *n* lavatory
LAW *n, vb, adj*
LAWBOOK *n* book on subject of law
LAWED ▸ **law**
LAWER ▸ **law**
LAWEST ▸ **law**
LAWFARE *n* use of the law by a country against its enemies
LAWFUL *adj* allowed by law
LAWIN *n* bill or reckoning
LAWINE *n* avalanche **lawines**
LAWING = **lawin**
LAWINGS ▸ **lawing**
LAWINS ▸ **lawin**
LAWK *interj* used to show surprise **lawks**
LAWLAND = **lowland**
LAWLESS *adj*
LAWLIKE ▸ **law**
LAWMAN *n* officer of the law **lawmen**
LAWN *n*
LAWNED *adj* having a lawn
LAWNIER ▸ **lawn**
LAWNS ▸ **lawn**
LAWNY ▸ **lawn**
LAWS ▸ **law**
LAWSUIT *n*
LAWYER *n, vb* **lawyers**
LAX *adj, n*
LAXATOR *n* muscle that loosens body part
LAXER ▸ **lax**
LAXES ▸ **lax**
LAXEST ▸ **lax**
LAXISM ▸ **laxist**
LAXISMS ▸ **laxist**
LAXIST *n* lenient or tolerant person **laxists**
LAXITY ▸ **lax**
LAXLY ▸ **lax**
LAXNESS ▸ **lax**
LAY ▸ **lie**
LAYAWAY *n* merchandise reserved for future delivery
LAYBACK *n* technique for climbing cracks ▹ *vb* use layback technique
LAYDEEZ *pl n* jocular spelling of ladies
LAYED ▸ **lay**
LAYER *n, vb* **layered, layers**
LAYETTE *n*
LAYIN *n* basketball score
LAYING ▸ **lay**
LAYINGS ▸ **lay**
LAYINS ▸ **layin**
LAYLOCK *old form of* ▸ **lilac**
LAYMAN *n* **laymen**
LAYOFF *n* act of suspending employees **layoffs**
LAYOUT *n* **layouts**
LAYOVER *n* break in a journey
LAYS ▸ **lie**
LAYTIME *n* time allowed for loading cargo
LAYUP *n* period of incapacity through illness **layups**
LAZAR *archaic word for* ▸ **leper**
LAZARET = **lazaretto**
LAZARS ▸ **lazar**
LAZE *vb, n* **lazed, lazes**
LAZIED, lazier, lazies, laziest, lazily ▸ **lazy**
LAZING ▸ **laze**
LAZO *another word for* ▸ **lasso; lazoed, lazoes, lazoing, lazos**
LAZULI *n* lapis lazuli **lazulis**
LAZY *vb, adj* **lazying, lazyish**
LAZZI ▸ **lazzo**
LAZZO *n* comic routine in the commedia dell'arte
LEA *n* meadow
LEACH *vb, n* **leached, leacher, leaches**
LEACHY *adj* porous
LEAD *vb, n, adj*
LEADED *adj* (of windows) made from many small panes of glass held together by lead strips
LEADEN *adj, vb* **leadens**

LEADER *n* **leaders**
LEADIER ▸ **leady**
LEADING ▸ **lead**
LEADMAN *n* man who leads **leadmen**
LEADOFF *n* initial move
LEADS ▸ **lead**
LEADY *adj* like lead
LEAF *n, vb*
LEAFAGE *n* leaves of plants
LEAFBUD *n* bud producing leaves rather than flowers
LEAFED ▸ **leaf**
LEAFERY *n* foliage
LEAFIER ▸ **leafy**
LEAFING ▸ **leaf**
LEAFLET *n, vb*
LEAFS ▸ **leaf**
LEAFY *adj* covered with leaves
LEAGUE *n* **leagued**
LEAGUER *vb* harass; beset ▹ *n* encampment, esp of besiegers
LEAGUES ▸ **league**
LEAK *n, vb*
LEAKAGE *n*
LEAKED ▸ **leak**
LEAKER ▸ **leak**
LEAKERS ▸ **leak**
LEAKIER ▸ **leaky**
LEAKILY ▸ **leaky**
LEAKING ▸ **leak**
LEAKS ▸ **leak**
LEAKY *adj* leaking
LEAL *adj* loyal **lealer, lealest, leally, lealty**
LEAM *vb* shine **leamed, leaming, leams**
LEAN *vb, adj, n* **leaned, leaner, leaners, leanest, leaning, leanly, leans, leant, leany**
LEAP *vb, n* **leaped, leaper, leapers, leaping, leaps, leapt**
LEAR *vb* instruct **leare, leared**
LEARES ▸ **leare**
LEARIER ▸ **leary**
LEARING ▸ **lear**
LEARN *vb* **learned**
LEARNER *n* someone who is learning something
LEARNS ▸ **learn**
LEARNT ▸ **learn**
LEARS ▸ **lear**
LEARY = **leery**
LEAS ▸ **lea**
LEASE *n, vb* **leased, leaser, leasers, leases**
LEASH *n, vb* **leashed, leashes**
LEASING ▸ **lease**
LEASOW *vb* pasture **leasowe, leasows**
LEAST *n, adj, adv* **leasts**
LEASURE *old form of* ▸ **leisure**
LEAT *n* trench or ditch that conveys water to a mill wheel
LEATHER *n, adj, vb*
LEATS ▸ **leat**
LEAVE *vb, n*
LEAVED *adj* with leaves
LEAVEN *n, vb* **leavens**
LEAVER ▸ **leave**
LEAVERS ▸ **leave**
LEAVES ▸ **leaf**
LEAVIER ▸ **leavy**
LEAVING ▸ **leave**
LEAVY = **leafy**
LEAZE = **lease**
LEAZES ▸ **leaze**
LEBBEK *n* type of timber tree **lebbeks**
LEBEN *n* semiliquid food made from curdled milk **lebens**
LECCIES ▸ **leccy**
LECCY *n* electricity
LECH *vb* behave lecherously ▹ *n* lecherous act
LECHAIM *interj* drinking toast ▹ *n* drink for a toast
LECHED ▸ **lech**
LECHER *n* man who has or shows excessive sexual desire ▹ *vb* behave lecherously **lechers**
LECHERY *n* unrestrained and promiscuous sexuality
LECHES ▸ **lech**
LECHING ▸ **lech**
LECHWE *n* African antelope **lechwes**
LECTERN *n*
LECTIN *n* type of protein **lectins**
LECTION *n* variant reading of a passage in a text
LECTOR *n* university lecturer **lectors**
LECTURE *n, vb*
LECTURN *old form of* ▸ **lectern**
LECYTHI > **lecythus**
LED ▸ **lead**
LEDDEN *n* language; speech **leddens**
LEDGE *n* **ledged**

LEDGER *n, vb* **ledgers**
LEDGES ▸ **ledge**
LEDGIER ▸ **ledge**
LEDGY ▸ **ledge**
LEDUM *n* evergreen shrub **ledums**
LEE *n, vb*
LEEAR *Scots form of* ▸ **liar**
LEEARS ▸ **leear**
LEECH *n, vb* **leeched**
LEECHEE = **litchi**
LEECHES ▸ **leech**
LEED ▸ **lee**
LEEING ▸ **lee**
LEEK *n* **leeks**
LEEP *vb* boil; scald **leeped, leeping, leeps**
LEER *vb, n* **leered**
LEERIER ▸ **leery**
LEERILY ▸ **leery**
LEERING ▸ **leer**
LEERS ▸ **leer**
LEERY *adj*
LEES *pl n*
LEESE *old form of* ▸ **loose**
LEESES ▸ **leese**
LEESING ▸ **leese**
LEET *n* shortlist
LEETLE *form of* ▸ **little**
LEETS ▸ **leet**
LEEWARD *n, adv, adj*
LEEWAY *n* **leeways**
LEEZE *adj as in* **leeze me** Scots for lief is me, an expression of affection
LEFT *adj, n*
LEFTE *old past tense of* ▸ **lift**
LEFTER ▸ **left**
LEFTEST ▸ **left**
LEFTIE = **lefty**
LEFTIES ▸ **lefty**
LEFTISH ▸ **left**
LEFTISM ▸ **leftist**
LEFTIST *adj, n*
LEFTS ▸ **left**
LEFTY *n* left-winger
LEG *n*
LEGACY *n*
LEGAL *adj, n* **legally, legals**
LEGATE *n, vb* **legated**
LEGATEE *n* recipient of a legacy
LEGATES ▸ **legate**
LEGATO *adv* smoothly ▹ *n* playing with no gaps between notes
LEGATOR *n* person who gives a legacy or makes a bequest
LEGATOS ▸ **legato**
LEGEND *n* **legends**
LEGER *variant of* ▸ **ledger**
LEGERS ▸ **leger**
LEGES ▸ **lex**
LEGGE *vb* lighten or lessen
LEGGED ▸ **leg**
LEGGER *n* man who moves barge through tunnel using legs **leggers**
LEGGES ▸ **legge**
LEGGIE *n* leg spin bowler
LEGGIER ▸ **leggy**
LEGGIES ▸ **leggie**
LEGGIN = **legging**
LEGGING *n* extra outer covering for the lower leg
LEGGINS ▸ **leggin**
LEGGISM *n* blacklegging
LEGGY *adj*
LEGHORN *n* talian wheat straw woven into hats
LEGIBLE *adj* **legibly**
LEGION *n, adj* **legions**
LEGIST *n* legal mind **legists**
LEGIT *n* legitimate drama ▹ *adj* legitimate
LEGITIM *n* inheritance due to children from father
LEGITS ▸ **legit**
LEGLAN = **leglin**
LEGLANS ▸ **leglan**
LEGLEN = **leglin**
LEGLENS ▸ **leglen**
LEGLESS *adj* without legs
LEGLET *n* leg jewellery **leglets**
LEGLIKE ▸ **leg**
LEGLIN *n* milk-pail **leglins**
LEGMAN *n* newsman who reports from the scene **legmen**
LEGONG *n* Indonesian dance **legongs**
LEGROOM *n* space to move one's legs comfortably
LEGS ▸ **leg**
LEGSIDE *n* part of a cricket field to the left of a right-handed batsman as he faces the bowler
LEGUAAN *n* S African lizard **leguan**
LEGUANS ▸ **leguan**
LEGUME *n* **legumes**
LEGUMIN *n* protein from leguminous plants
LEGWEAR *n* clothing for legs

LEGWORK *n* work that involves travelling on foot or as if on foot
LEHAIM = **lechaim**
LEHAIMS ▸ **lehaim**
LEHAYIM = **lehaim**
LEHR *n* long tunnel-shaped oven used for annealing glass **lehrs**
LEHUA *n* flower of Hawaii **lehuas**
LEI ▸ **leu**
LEIDGER = **ledger**
LEIGER = **ledger**
LEIGERS ▸ **leiger**
LEIPOA *n* Australian bird **leipoas**
LEIR = **lear**
LEIRED ▸ **leir**
LEIRING ▸ **leir**
LEIRS ▸ **leir**
LEIS ▸ **leu**
LEISH *adj* agile **leisher**
LEISLER *n* small bat
LEISTER *n* pronged fishing spear ▹ *vb* spear with a leister
LEISURE *n*, *vb*
LEK *n* bird display area ▹ *vb* gather at lek
LEKE *old form of* ▸ **leak**
LEKKED ▸ **lek**
LEKKER *adj*
LEKKING ▸ **lek**
LEKS ▸ **lek**
LEKU ▸ **lek**
LEKVAR *n* prune or apricot pie filling **lekvars**
LEKYTHI > **lekythos**
LEMAN *n* beloved **lemans**
LEME = **leam**
LEMED ▸ **leme**
LEMEL *n* metal filings **lemels**
LEMES ▸ **leme**
LEMING ▸ **leme**
LEMMA *n* word in its citation form **lemmas, lemmata**
LEMMING *n*
LEMON *n, adj, vb* **lemoned, lemons**
LEMONY *adj* like a lemon
LEMPIRA *n* monetary unit of Honduras
LEMUR *n*
LEMURES *pl n* spirits of the dead
LEMURS ▸ **lemur**
LEND *vb* **lender, lenders, lending, lends**
LENES ▸ **lenis**
LENG *vb* linger ▹ *adj* long **lenged, lenger, lengest, lenging, lengs**
LENGTH *n* **lengths**
LENGTHY *adj*
LENIENT *adj, n*
LENIFY *vb* make lenient
LENIS *adj* pronounced with little muscular tension ▹ *n* consonant like this
LENITE *vb* undergo lenition **lenited, lenites**
LENITY *n* mercy or clemency
LENO *n* weave in which the warp yarns are twisted in pairs between the weft **lenos**
LENS *n* **lense**
LENSED *adj* incorporating a lens
LENSES ▸ **lens**
LENSING *n* materials which colour and diffuse light
LENSMAN *n* camera operator **lensmen**
LENT ▸ **lend**
LENTEN *adj* of or relating to Lent
LENTI ▸ **lento**
LENTIC *adj* of, relating to, or inhabiting still water
LENTIGO *technical name for a* ▸ **freckle**
LENTIL *n* **lentils**
LENTISC ▸ **lentisk**
LENTISK *n* mastic tree
LENTO *adv* slowly ▹ *n* movement or passage performed slowly
LENTOID *adj* lentiform ▹ *n* lentiform object
LENTOR *n* lethargy **lentors**
LENTOS ▸ **lento**
LENTOUS *adj* lethargic
LENVOY *another word for* ▸ **envoy**
LENVOYS ▸ **lenvoy**
LEONE *n* monetary unit of Sierra Leone **leones**
LEONINE *adj*
LEOPARD *n*
LEOTARD *n*
LEP *dialect word for* ▸ **leap**
LEPER *n* **lepers**
LEPID *adj* amusing
LEPORID *adj* of the family of mammals including rabbits and

hares ▷ *n* any animal belonging to this family
LEPPED ▸ **lep**
LEPPING ▸ **lep**
LEPRA *n* leprosy **lepras**
LEPROSE *adj* having or denoting a whitish scurfy surface
LEPROSY *n*
LEPROUS *adj* having leprosy
LEPS ▸ **lep**
LEPT ▸ **leap**
LEPTA ▸ **lepton**
LEPTIN *n* protein that regulates the amount of fat in the body **leptins**
LEPTOME *n* tissue of plant conducting food
LEPTON *n* any of a group of elementary particles with weak interactions **leptons**
LEQUEAR = **lacunar**
LERE = **lear**
LERED ▸ **lere**
LERES ▸ **lere**
LERING ▸ **lere**
LERP *n* crystallized honeydew **lerps**
LESBIAN *n, adj*
LESBIC *adj* relating to lesbians
LESION *n, vb* **lesions**
LESS *n, adj, pron, adv, prep*
LESSEE *n* **lessees**
LESSEN *vb* **lessens**
LESSER *adj*
LESSES ▸ **less**
LESSON *n, vb* **lessons**
LESSOR *n* **lessors**
LEST *conj, vb* **lested, lesting, lests**
LET *n, vb*
LETCH = **lech**
LETCHED ▸ **letch**
LETCHES ▸ **letch**
LETDOWN *n*
LETHAL *adj, n* **lethals**
LETHE *n* forgetfulness **lethean**
LETHEE *n* life-blood **lethees**
LETHES ▸ **lethe**
LETHIED *adj* forgetful
LETS ▸ **let**
LETTED ▸ **let**
LETTER *n, vb*
LETTERN *another word for* ▸ **lectern**
LETTERS *pl n* literary knowledge
LETTING ▸ **let**
LETTRE *n* letter **lettres**
LETTUCE *n*
LETUP *n* lessening or abatement **letups**
LEU *n* monetary unit of Romania
LEUCH ▸ **lauch**
LEUCHEN ▸ **lauch**
LEUCIN = **leucine**
LEUCINE *n* essential amino acid
LEUCINS ▸ **leucin**
LEUCITE *n* grey or white mineral
LEUCO *n as in* **leuco base** colourless compound
LEUCOMA *n* white opaque scar of the cornea
LEUD *Scots word for* ▸ **breadth**
LEUDES ▸ **leud**
LEUDS ▸ **leud**
LEUGH ▸ **lauch**
LEUGHEN ▸ **lauch**
LEUKOMA = **leucoma**
LEUKON *n* white blood cell count **leukons**
LEV *n* monetary unit of Bulgaria **leva**
LEVANT *n* leather made from the skins of goats, sheep, or seals ▷ *vb* bolt or abscond **levants**
LEVATOR *n* muscle that raises a part of the body
LEVE *adj* darling ▷ *adv* gladly
LEVEE *n, vb* **leveed, levees**
LEVEL *adj, vb, n* **leveled**
LEVELER = **leveller**
LEVELLY ▸ **level**
LEVELS ▸ **level**
LEVER *n, vb* **levered**
LEVERET *n*
LEVERS ▸ **lever**
LEVES ▸ **leve**
LEVIED, levier, leviers, levies ▸ **levy**
LEVIN *archaic word for* > **lightning**
LEVINS ▸ **levin**
LEVIS *n* jeans
LEVITE *n* Christian clergyman **levites, levitic**
LEVITY *n*
LEVO *adj* anticlockwise
LEVULIN *n* substance obtained from certain bulbs
LEVY *vb, n* **levying**
LEW *adj* tepid

LEWD *adj* **lewder, lewdest, lewdly**
LEWDSBY *another word for* > **lewdster**
LEWIS *n* lifting device for heavy stone or concrete blocks **lewises**
LEWISIA *n* type of herb
LEX *n* system or body of laws
LEXEME *n* minimal meaningful unit of language **lexemes, lexemic**
LEXES ▸ **lex**
LEXICA ▸ **lexicon**
LEXICAL *adj* relating to the vocabulary of a language
LEXICON *n*
LEXIS *n* totality of vocabulary in a language **lexises**
LEY *n* land under grass **leys**
LI *n* Chinese measurement of distance
LIABLE *adj*
LIAISE *vb* **liaised, liaises**
LIAISON *n*
LIANA *n* **lianas, liane**
LIANES ▸ **liane**
LIANG *n* Chinese unit of weight **liangs**
LIANOID ▸ **liana**
LIAR *n*
LIARD *adj* grey ▹ *n* former small coin **liards**
LIARS ▸ **liar**
LIART *Scots form of* ▸ **liard**
LIAS *n* lowest series of rocks of the Jurassic system **liases**
LIATRIS *n* North American plant with white flowers
LIB *n* informal word for liberation ▹ *vb* geld
LIBANT *adj* touching lightly
LIBATE *vb* offer as gift to the gods **libated, libates**
LIBBARD *another word for* ▸ **leopard**
LIBBED ▸ **lib**
LIBBING ▸ **lib**
LIBEL *n, vb* **libeled**
LIBELEE = **libellee**
LIBELER ▸ **libel**
LIBELS ▸ **libel**
LIBER *n* tome or book
LIBERAL *adj, n*
LIBERO *another name for* ▸ **sweeper**
LIBEROS ▸ **libero**
LIBERS ▸ **liber**
LIBERTY *n*
LIBIDO *n* **libidos**
LIBKEN *n* lodging **libkens**
LIBLAB *n* 19th century British liberal **liblabs**
LIBRA *n* ancient Roman unit of weight **librae**
LIBRARY *n*
LIBRAS ▸ **libra**
LIBRATE *vb* oscillate or waver
LIBRI ▸ **liber**
LIBS ▸ **lib**
LICE ▸ **louse**
LICENCE *n, vb*
LICENSE *vb*
LICENTE *adj* permitted; allowed
LICH *n* dead body
LICHEE = **litchi**
LICHEES ▸ **lichee**
LICHEN *n, vb* **lichens**
LICHES ▸ **lich**
LICHI = **litchi**
LICHIS ▸ **lichi**
LICHT *Scot word for* ▸ **light**
LICHTED ▸ **licht**
LICHTER ▸ **licht**
LICHTLY *vb* treat discourteously
LICHTS ▸ **licht**
LICHWAY *n* path used to carry coffin into church
LICIT *adj* lawful, permitted **licitly**
LICK *vb, n* **licked, licker, lickers**
LICKING *n* beating
LICKS ▸ **lick**
LICTOR *n* one of a group of ancient Roman officials **lictors**
LID *n*
LIDAR *n* radar-type instrument **lidars**
LIDDED ▸ **lid**
LIDDING *n* lids
LIDGER *variant form of* ▸ **ledger**
LIDGERS ▸ **ledger**
LIDLESS *adj* having no lid or top
LIDO *n* open-air centre for swimming and water sports **lidos**
LIDS ▸ **lid**
LIE *vb, n*
LIED *n* setting for solo

voice and piano of a poem **lieder**
LIEF *adv* gladly ▷ *adj* ready ▷ *n* beloved person **liefer, liefest, liefly, liefs**
LIEGE *adj, n*
LIEGER = **ledger**
LIEGERS ▸ **lieger**
LIEGES ▸ **liege**
LIEN *n* right to hold another's property until a debt is paid
LIENAL *adj* of or relating to the spleen
LIENS ▸ **lien**
LIER *n* person who lies down
LIERNE *n* short secondary rib that connects intersections of the primary ribs **liernes**
LIERS ▸ **lier**
LIES ▸ **lie**
LIEU *n* **lieus**
LIEVE = **leve**
LIEVER ▸ **lieve**
LIEVES ▸ **lieve**
LIEVEST ▸ **lieve**
LIFE *n*
LIFEFUL *adj* full of life
LIFER *n* **lifers**
LIFES *pl n as in* **still lifes** paintings or drawings of inanimate objects
LIFEWAY *n* way of life
LIFT *vb, n*
LIFTBOY *n* person who operates a lift
LIFTED, lifter, lifters, lifting ▸ **lift**
LIFTMAN = **liftboy**
LIFTMEN ▸ **liftman**
LIFTOFF *n, vb*
LIFTS ▸ **lift**
LIFULL *obsolete form of* ▸ **lifeful**
LIG *n* function with free entertainment and refreshments ▷ *vb* attend such a function
LIGAN = **lagan**
LIGAND *n* atom, molecule, radical, or ion forming a complex with a central atom **ligands**
LIGANS ▸ **ligan**
LIGASE *n* any of a class of enzymes **ligases**
LIGATE *vb* tie up or constrict (something) with a ligature **ligated, ligates**
LIGER *n* hybrid offspring of a female tiger and a male lion **ligers**
LIGGE *obsolete form of* ▸ **lie**
LIGGED ▸ **lig**
LIGGER ▸ **lig**
LIGGERS ▸ **lig**
LIGGES ▸ **ligge**
LIGGING ▸ **lig**
LIGHT *n, adj, vb, adv* **lighted**
LIGHTEN *vb*
LIGHTER *n, vb*
LIGHTLY *adv* in a light way ▷ *vb* belittle
LIGHTS ▸ **light**
LIGNAGE *another word for* ▸ **lineage**
LIGNAN *n* beneficial substance found in plants **lignans**
LIGNE *n* unit of measurement **lignes**
LIGNIFY *vb* become woody with the deposition of lignin in cell walls
LIGNIN *n* complex polymer occurring in certain plant cell walls making the plant rigid **lignins**
LIGNITE *n*
LIGNOSE *n* explosive compound
LIGNUM *n* wood **lignums**
LIGROIN *n* volatile fraction of petroleum
LIGS ▸ **lig**
LIGULA = **ligule**
LIGULAE ▸ **ligula**
LIGULAR ▸ **ligula**
LIGULAS ▸ **ligula**
LIGULE *n* membranous outgrowth between the leaf blade and sheath **ligules**
LIGURE *n* any of the 12 precious stones used in the breastplates of high priests **ligures**
LIKABLE *adj* **likably**
LIKE *adj* similar ▷ *vb* find enjoyable ▷ *n* favourable feeling, desire, or preference **liked**
LIKELY *adj, adv*
LIKEN *vb* **likened, likens**
LIKER, likers, likes, likest ▸ **like**
LIKIN *n* historically, Chinese tax
LIKING *n* **likings**

LIKINS ▶ **likin**
LIKUTA *n* coin in Zaïre
LILAC *n, adj* **lilacs**
LILIED *adj* decorated with lilies
LILIES ▶ **lily**
LILL *obsolete form of* ▶ **loll**
LILLED ▶ **lill**
LILLING ▶ **lill**
LILLS ▶ **lill**
LILO *n* inflatable mattress **lilos**
LILT *n, vb* **lilted, lilting, lilts**
LILY *n*
LIMA *n* type of edible bean
LIMACEL *n* small shell inside some kinds of slug
LIMACES ▶ **limax**
LIMACON *n* heart-shaped curve
LIMAIL = **lemel**
LIMAILS ▶ **limail**
LIMAN *n* lagoon **limans**
LIMAS ▶ **lima**
LIMAX *n* slug
LIMB *n, vb*
LIMBA *n* type of African tree **limbas**
LIMBATE *adj* having an edge or border of a different colour from the rest
LIMBEC *obsolete form of* ▶ **alembic**
LIMBECK *obsolete form of* ▶ **alembic**
LIMBECS ▶ **limbec**
LIMBED ▶ **limb**
LIMBER *vb, adj, n* **limbers**
LIMBI ▶ **limbus**
LIMBIC ▶ **limbus**
LIMBIER ▶ **limby**
LIMBING ▶ **limb**
LIMBO *n* **limbos**
LIMBOUS *adj* with overlapping edges
LIMBS ▶ **limb**
LIMBUS *n* border
LIMBY *adj* with long legs, stem, branches, etc
LIME *n, vb, adj*
LIMEADE *n* drink made from sweetened lime juice and plain or carbonated water
LIMED ▶ **lime**
LIMELIT > **limelight**
LIMEN *another term for* > **threshold**
LIMENS ▶ **limen**
LIMEPIT *n* pit containing lime in which hides are placed to remove the hair
LIMES *n* fortified boundary of the Roman Empire
LIMEY *n, adj* **limeys**
LIMIER ▶ **limy**
LIMIEST ▶ **limy**
LIMINA ▶ **limen**
LIMINAL *adj* relating to the point (or threshold) beyond which a sensation becomes too faint to be experienced
LIMING ▶ **lime**
LIMINGS ▶ **lime**
LIMIT *n, vb*
LIMITED *adj, n*
LIMITER *n* electronic circuit whose amplitude is limited to some fixed value above which the peaks become flattened
LIMITES ▶ **limes**
LIMITS ▶ **limit**
LIMMA *n* semitone **limmas**
LIMMER *n* scoundrel **limmers**
LIMN *vb* represent in drawing or painting **limned, limner, limners**
LIMNIC *adj* relating to lakes
LIMNING ▶ **limn**
LIMNS ▶ **limn**
LIMO *short for* > **limousine**
LIMOS ▶ **limo**
LIMOSES ▶ **limosis**
LIMOSIS *n* excessive hunger
LIMOUS *adj* muddy
LIMP *vb, n, adj*
LIMPA *n* type of rye bread **limpas**
LIMPED, limper, limpers, limpest ▶ **limp**
LIMPET *n, adj* **limpets**
LIMPID *adj*
LIMPING ▶ **limp**
LIMPKIN *n* rail-like wading bird
LIMPLY ▶ **limp**
LIMPS ▶ **limp**
LIMPSEY = **limpsy**
LIMPSY *adj* limp
LIMULI ▶ **limulus**
LIMULUS *n* horseshoe crab
LIMY *adj* of, like, or smeared with birdlime

LIN *vb* cease
LINABLE ▸ **line**
LINAC *n* linear accelerator **linacs**
LINAGE *n* number of lines in written or printed matter **linages**
LINALOL = **linalool**
LINCH *n* ledge **linches, linchet**
LINCTUS *n*
LIND *variant of* ▸ **linden**
LINDANE *n* white poisonous crystalline powder
LINDEN *n* large tree with heart-shaped leaves and fragrant yellowish flowers **lindens**
LINDIES ▸ **lindy**
LINDS ▸ **lind**
LINDY *n* lively dance
LINE *n, vb*
LINEAGE *n*
LINEAL *adj* in direct line of descent
LINEAR *adj*
LINEATE *adj* marked with lines
LINECUT *n* method of relief printing
LINED ▸ **line**
LINEMAN = **linesman**
LINEMEN ▸ **lineman**
LINEN *n* **linens, lineny**
LINER *n* **liners**
LINES ▸ **line**
LINEUP *n* row or arrangement of people or things **lineups**
LINEY ▸ **line**
LING *n* slender food fish
LINGA = **lingam**
LINGAM *n* (in Sanskrit) masculine gender **lingams**
LINGAS ▸ **linga**
LINGCOD *n* type of food fish
LINGEL *n* shoemaker's thread **lingels**
LINGER *vb* **lingers**
LINGIER ▸ **lingy**
LINGLE = **lingel**
LINGLES ▸ **lingle**
LINGO *n* **lingoes**
LINGOT *n* ingot **lingots**
LINGS ▸ **ling**
LINGUA *n* any tongue-like structure **linguae**
LINGUAL *adj* of the tongue ▹ *n* lingual consonant
LINGUAS ▸ **lingua**
LINGULA *n* small tongue
LINGY *adj* heather-covered
LINHAY *n* farm building with an open front **linhays**
LINIER ▸ **line**
LINIEST ▸ **line**
LININ *n* network of viscous material in the nucleus of a cell that connects the chromatin granules
LINING *n* **linings**
LININS ▸ **linin**
LINISH *vb* polish metal
LINK *n, vb*
LINKAGE *n* act of linking or the state of being linked
LINKBOY *n* (formerly) a boy who carried a torch for pedestrians in dark streets
LINKED ▸ **link**
LINKER *n* person or thing that links **linkers**
LINKIER ▸ **linky**
LINKING ▸ **link**
LINKMAN = **linkboy**
LINKMEN ▸ **linkman**
LINKROT *n*
LINKS ▸ **link**
LINKUP *n* establishing of a union between objects, groups, organizations, etc **linkups**
LINKY *adj* (of countryside) consisting of links
LINN *n* waterfall or a pool at the foot of it
LINNED ▸ **lin**
LINNET *n* **linnets**
LINNEY = **linhay**
LINNEYS ▸ **linney**
LINNIES ▸ **linny**
LINNING ▸ **lin**
LINNS ▸ **linn**
LINNY = **linhay**
LINO = **linoleum**
LINOCUT *n*
LINOS ▸ **lino**
LINS ▸ **lin**
LINSANG *n* any of several forest-dwelling viverrine mammals
LINSEED *n* seed of the flax plant
LINSEY *n* type of cloth **linseys**
LINT *n, vb*
LINTED *adj* having lint
LINTEL *n* **lintels**
LINTER *n* machine for stripping the short

fibres of ginned cotton seeds **linters**
LINTIE *Scot word for* ▸ **linnet**
LINTIER ▸ **lint**
LINTIES ▸ **lintie**
LINTING ▸ **lint** *vb*
LINTOL = **lintel**
LINTOLS ▸ **lintel**
LINTS ▸ **lint**
LINTY ▸ **lint**
LINUM *n* type of plant of temperate regions **linums**
LINURON *n* type of herbicide
LINUX *n* nonproprietary computer operating system **linuxes**
LINY ▸ **line**
LION *n*
LIONCEL *n* (in heraldry) small lion **lionel**
LIONELS ▸ **lionel**
LIONESS *n* female lion
LIONET *n* young lion **lionets**
LIONISE = **lionize**
LIONISM *n* lion-like appearance of leprosy
LIONIZE *vb*
LIONLY ▸ **lion**
LIONS ▸ **lion**
LIP *n, vb*
LIPA *n* monetary unit of Croatia **lipas**
LIPASE *n* any of a group of enzymes that digest fat **lipases**
LIPE ▸ **lipa**
LIPEMIA = **lipaemia**
LIPID *n* any of a group of organic compounds including fats, oils, waxes, and sterols **lipide**
LIPIDES ▸ **lipide**
LIPIDIC ▸ **lipid**
LIPIDS ▸ **lipid**
LIPIN *n* family of nuclear proteins **lipins**
LIPLESS ▸ **lip**
LIPLIKE ▸ **lip**
LIPO *n* liposuction
LIPOIC *adj as in* **lipoic acid** sulphur-containing fatty acid
LIPOID *n* fatlike substance, such as wax **lipoids**
LIPOMA *n* benign tumour composed of fatty tissue **lipomas**
LIPOS ▸ **lipo**
LIPPED ▸ **lip**
LIPPEN *vb* trust **lippens**
LIPPER *Scots word for* ▸ **ripple**
LIPPERS ▸ **lipper**
LIPPIE *variant of* ▸ **lippy**
LIPPIER ▸ **lippy**
LIPPIES ▸ **lippie**
LIPPING ▸ **lip**
LIPPY *adj* insolent or cheeky ▹ *n* lipstick
LIPREAD *vb* follow what someone says by watching their lips
LIPS ▸ **lip**
LIPURIA *n* presence of fat in the urine
LIQUATE *vb* separate one component of by heating until the more fusible part melts
LIQUEFY *vb*
LIQUEUR *n, vb*
LIQUID *n, adj* **liquids**
LIQUIFY = **liquefy**
LIQUOR *n, vb* **liquors**
LIRA *n* **liras, lire, liri**
LIRIOPE *n* grasslike plant
LIRK *vb* wrinkle **lirked, lirking, lirks**
LIROT ▸ **lira**
LIROTH ▸ **lira**
LIS *n* fleur-de-lis
LISENTE ▸ **sente**
LISK *Yorkshire dialect for* ▸ **groin**
LISKS ▸ **lisk**
LISLE *n* strong fine cotton thread or fabric **lisles**
LISP *n, vb* **lisped, lisper, lispers, lisping, lisps**
LISPUND = **lispound**
LISSES ▸ **lis**
LISSOM *adj* **lissome**
LIST *n, vb* **listed**
LISTEE *n* person on list **listees**
LISTEL *another name for* ▸ **fillet**
LISTELS ▸ **listel**
LISTEN *vb* **listens**
LISTER *n* plough with a double mouldboard to throw soil to sides of a central furrow **listers**
LISTETH ▸ **list**
LISTFUL *adj* paying attention
LISTING *n* list or an entry in a list
LISTS *pl n* field of combat in a tournament
LIT *n* archaic word for dye or colouring
LITAI ▸ **litas**

LITANY *n*
LITAS *n* monetary unit of Lithuania
LITCHI *n* Chinese tree with round edible fruits **litchis**
LITE = **light**
LITED ▸ **light**
LITER = **litre**
LITERAL *adj, n*
LITERS ▸ **liter**
LITES ▸ **lite**
LITH *n* limb or joint
LITHATE *n* salt of uric acid
LITHE *adj, vb* **lithed, lithely, lither, lithes, lithest**
LITHIA *n* lithium present in mineral waters as lithium salts **lithias**
LITHIC *adj* of stone
LITHIFY *vb* turn into rock
LITHING ▸ **lithe**
LITHITE *n* part of cell with sensory element
LITHIUM *n*
LITHO *n* lithography ▷ *vb* print using lithography **lithoed**
LITHOID *adj* resembling rock
LITHOPS *n* fleshy-leaved plant
LITHOS ▸ **litho**
LITHS ▸ **lith**
LITING ▸ **lite**
LITMUS *n*
LITORAL = **littoral**
LITOTES *n* ironical understatement used for effect **litotic**
LITRE *n* **litres**
LITS ▸ **lit**
LITTEN *adj* lighted
LITTER *n, vb* **litters**
LITTERY *adj* covered in litter
LITTLE *adj* small ▷ *adv* not a lot ▷ *n* small amount, extent, or duration **littler, littles**
LITTLIE *n* young child
LITTLIN = **littling**
LITU ▸ **litas**
LITURGY *n*
LITUUS *n* curved trumpet
LIVABLE *adj* tolerable or pleasant to live (with)
LIVE *vb, adj, adv* **lived**
LIVEDO *n* reddish discoloured patch on the skin **livedos**
LIVELOD *n* livelihood
LIVELY *adj*
LIVEN *vb* **livened, livener, livens**
LIVER *n*
LIVERED *adj* having liver
LIVERS ▸ **liver**
LIVERY *n, adj*
LIVES ▸ **life**
LIVEST ▸ **live**
LIVEYER *n* (in Newfoundland) a full-time resident
LIVID *adj* **livider, lividly**
LIVIER = **liveyer**
LIVIERS ▸ **livier**
LIVING *adj, n* **livings**
LIVOR *another word for* > **lividity**
LIVORS ▸ **livor**
LIVRE *n* former French unit of money of account **livres**
LIVYER = **liveyer**
LIVYERS ▸ **livyer**
LIXIVIA > **lixivium**
LIZARD *n* **lizards**
LIZZIE *n as in* **tin lizzie** old or decrepit car **lizzies**
LLAMA *n* **llamas**
LLANERO *n* native of llanos
LLANO *n* extensive grassy treeless plain **llanos**
LO *interj* look!
LOACH *n* carplike fish **loaches**
LOAD *n, vb*
LOADED *adj*
LOADEN *vb* load **loadens**
LOADER *n* person who loads a gun or other firearm **loaders**
LOADING *n* load or burden
LOADS *pl n* lots or a lot
LOAF *n, vb* **loafed**
LOAFER *n* idler **loafers**
LOAFING ▸ **loaf**
LOAFS ▸ **loaf**
LOAM *n, vb* **loamed, loamier, loaming, loams, loamy**
LOAN *n, vb* **loaned**
LOANEE *n* **loanees**
LOANER, loaners, loaning, loans ▸ **loan**
LOAST ▸ **loose**
LOATH *adj*
LOATHE *vb* **loathed, loather, loathes**
LOATHLY *adv* with reluctance
LOATHY *obsolete form of*

> **loathsome**
LOAVE *vb* form a loaf **loaved**
LOAVES ▸ loaf
LOAVING ▸ loave
LOB *n, vb*
LOBAR *adj* of or affecting a lobe
LOBATE *adj* with or like lobes **lobated**
LOBBED ▸ lob
LOBBER *n* one who lobs **lobbers**
LOBBIED ▸ lobby
LOBBIES ▸ lobby
LOBBING ▸ lob
LOBBY *n, vb* **lobbyer**
LOBE *n* **lobed**
LOBEFIN *n* type of fish
LOBELET *n* small lobe
LOBELIA *n*
LOBES ▸ lobe
LOBI ▸ lobus
LOBING *n* formation of lobes **lobings**
LOBIPED *adj* with lobed toes
LOBO *n* timber wolf
LOBOLA *n* (in African custom) price paid by a bridegroom's family to his bride's family **lobolas, lobolo**
LOBOLOS ▸ lobolo
LOBOS ▸ lobo
LOBOSE *another word for* **▸ lobate**
LOBS ▸ lob
LOBSTER *n, vb*
LOBULAR ▸ lobule
LOBULE *n* small lobe or a subdivision of a lobe **lobules**
LOBULI ▸ lobulus
LOBULUS *n* small lobe
LOBUS *n* lobe
LOBWORM = **lugworm**
LOCA ▸ locus
LOCAL *adj, n*
LOCALE *n* scene of an event **locales**
LOCALLY *adv* within a particular area or place
LOCALS ▸ local
LOCATE *vb* **located, locater, locates**
LOCATOR *n* part of index that shows where to find information
LOCH *n*
LOCHAN *n* small inland loch **lochans**
LOCHIA *n* vaginal discharge following childbirth **lochial**
LOCHS ▸ loch
LOCI ▸ locus
LOCK *n, vb*
LOCKAGE *n* system of locks in a canal
LOCKBOX *n* system of collecting funds from companies by banks
LOCKED ▸ lock
LOCKER *n* **lockers**
LOCKET *n* **lockets**
LOCKFUL *n* sufficient to fill a canal lock
LOCKING ▸ lock
LOCKJAW *n* tetanus
LOCKMAN *n* lock-keeper **lockmen**
LOCKNUT *n* nut screwed down on a primary nut to stop it from loosening
LOCKOUT *n*
LOCKRAM *n* type of linen cloth
LOCKS ▸ lock
LOCKSET *n* hardware used to lock door
LOCKUP *n* prison **lockups**
LOCO *n* locomotive ▹ *adj* insane ▹ *vb* poison with locoweed **locoed, locoes, locoing**
LOCOISM *n* disease of cattle, sheep, and horses caused by eating locoweed
LOCOMAN *n* railwayman **locomen**
LOCOS ▸ loco
LOCULAR *adj* divided into compartments by septa
LOCULE *n* any of the chambers of an ovary or anther
LOCULED *adj* having locules
LOCULES ▸ locule
LOCULI ▸ loculus
LOCULUS = **locule**
LOCUM *n* **locums**
LOCUS *n* area or place where something happens
LOCUST *n, vb*
LOCUSTA *n* flower cluster unit in grasses
LOCUSTS ▸ locust
LOD *n* type of logarithm
LODE *n* vein of ore
LODEN *n* thick waterproof, woollen cloth **lodens**
LODES ▸ lode

LODGE *n, vb* **lodged**
LODGER *n* **lodgers**
LODGES ▸ **lodge**
LODGING *n* temporary residence
LODS ▸ **lod**
LOERIE = **lourie**
LOERIES ▸ **loerie**
LOESS *n* fine-grained soil **loessal, loesses**
LOESSIC *adj* relating to or consisting of loess
LOFT *n, vb* **lofted**
LOFTER *n* type of golf club **lofters**
LOFTIER ▸ **lofty**
LOFTILY ▸ **lofty**
LOFTING ▸ **loft**
LOFTS ▸ **loft**
LOFTY *adj*
LOG *n, vb*
LOGAN *another name for* ▸ **bogan**
LOGANIA *n* type of Australian plant
LOGANS ▸ **logan**
LOGBOOK *n*
LOGE *n* small enclosure or box in a theatre or opera house **loges**
LOGGAT *n* small piece of wood **loggats**
LOGGED ▸ **log**
LOGGER *n* tractor or crane for handling logs **loggers**
LOGGETS *n* old-fashioned game played with sticks
LOGGIA *n* covered gallery at the side of a building **loggias, loggie**
LOGGIER ▸ **loggy**
LOGGING ▸ **log**
LOGGISH ▸ **log**
LOGGY *adj* sluggish
LOGIA ▸ **logion**
LOGIC *n*
LOGICAL *adj*
LOGICS ▸ **logic**
LOGIE *n* fire-place of a kiln
LOGIER ▸ **logy**
LOGIES ▸ **logie**
LOGIEST ▸ **logy**
LOGILY ▸ **logy**
LOGIN *n* process by which a computer user logs on **logins**
LOGION *n* saying of Christ regarded as authentic **logions**
LOGJAM *n* blockage of logs in a river ▹ *vb* cause a logjam **logjams**
LOGLINE *n* synopsis of screenplay
LOGLOG *n* logarithm of a logarithm (in equations, etc) **loglogs**
LOGO = **logotype**
LOGOFF *n* process by which a computer user logs out **logoffs**
LOGOI ▸ **logos**
LOGON *variant of* ▸ **login**
LOGONS ▸ **logon**
LOGOS *n* reason expressed in words and things, argument, or justification
LOGOUT *variant of* ▸ **logoff**
LOGOUTS ▸ **logout**
LOGROLL *vb* use logrolling in order to procure the passage of (legislation)
LOGS ▸ **log**
LOGWAY *another name for* ▸ **gangway**
LOGWAYS ▸ **logway**
LOGWOOD *n* tree of the Caribbean and Central America
LOGY *adj* dull or listless
LOHAN *another word for* ▸ **arhat**
LOHANS ▸ **lohan**
LOID *vb* open (a lock) using a celluloid strip **loided, loiding, loids**
LOIN *n*
LOINS *pl n* hips and the inner surface of the legs
LOIPE *n* cross-country skiing track **loipen**
LOIR *n* large dormouse **loirs**
LOITER *vb* **loiters**
LOKE *n* track **lokes**
LOKSHEN *pl n* noodles
LOLIGO *n* type of squid **loligos**
LOLIUM *n* type of grass **loliums**
LOLL *vb, n* **lolled, loller, lollers**
LOLLIES ▸ **lolly**
LOLLING ▸ **loll**
LOLLOP *vb* move clumsily **lollops, lollopy**
LOLLS ▸ **loll**
LOLLY *n*
LOLOG = **loglog**
LOLOGS ▸ **lolog**
LOMA *n* lobe **lomas, lomata**

LOME *vb* cover with lome **lomed**
LOMEIN *n* Chinese dish **lomeins**
LOMENT *n* pod of certain leguminous plants
LOMENTA > **lomentum**
LOMENTS ▸ **loment**
LOMES ▸ **lome**
LOMING ▸ **lome**
LOMPISH *another word for* ▸ **lumpish**
LONE *adj*
LONELY *adj*
LONER *n* **loners**
LONG *adj* having length ▹ *adv* for a certain time ▹ *vb* have a strong desire (for)
LONGA *n* long note
LONGAN *n* sapindaceous tree of tropical and subtropical Asia **longans**
LONGAS ▸ **longa**
LONGBOW *n*
LONGE *n* rope used in training a horse ▹ *vb* train using a longe
LONGED ▸ **long**
LONGER *n* line of barrels on a ship **longers**
LONGES ▸ **longe**
LONGEST ▸ **long**
LONGIES *n* long johns
LONGING *n, adj*
LONGISH *adj* rather long
LONGLY ▸ **long**
LONGS *pl n* full-length trousers
LOO *n, vb*
LOOBIER ▸ **looby**
LOOBIES ▸ **looby**
LOOBILY ▸ **looby**
LOOBY *adj* foolish ▹ *n* foolish or stupid person
LOOED ▸ **loo**
LOOEY *n* lieutenant **looeys**
LOOF *n* part of ship's side
LOOFA = **loofah**
LOOFAH *n* **loofahs**
LOOFAS ▸ **loofa**
LOOFFUL *n* handful
LOOFS ▸ **loof**
LOOIE = **looey**
LOOIES ▸ **looie**
LOOING ▸ **loo**
LOOK *vb* direct the eyes or attention (towards) ▹ *n* instance of looking **looked**
LOOKER *n* person who looks **lookers**
LOOKING ▸ **look**
LOOKISM *n* discrimination because of appearance **lookist**
LOOKOUT *n, vb*
LOOKS ▸ **look**
LOOKUP *n* act of looking up informatiion **lookups**
LOOM *n, vb* **loomed, looming, looms**
LOON *n* diving bird
LOONEY = **loony**
LOONEYS ▸ **loony**
LOONIE *n* Canadian dollar coin
LOONIER ▸ **loony**
LOONIES ▸ **loony**
LOONILY ▸ **loony**
LOONING *n* cry of the loon
LOONS ▸ **loon**
LOONY *adj, n*
LOOP *n, vb* **looped**
LOOPER *n* person or thing that loops or makes loops **loopers**
LOOPIER ▸ **loopy**
LOOPILY ▸ **loopy**
LOOPING ▸ **loop**
LOOPS ▸ **loop**
LOOPY *adj* slightly mad or crazy
LOOR ▸ **lief**
LOORD *obsolete word for* ▸ **lout**
LOORDS ▸ **loord**
LOOS ▸ **loo**
LOOSE *adj, adv, vb* **loosed, loosely**
LOOSEN *vb* **loosens**
LOOSER ▸ **loose**
LOOSES ▸ **loose**
LOOSEST ▸ **loose**
LOOSIE *n* informal word for loose forward
LOOSIES *pl n* cigarettes sold individually
LOOSING *n* celebration of one's 21st birthday
LOOT *vb, n* **looted**
LOOTEN *Scots past form of* ▸ **let**
LOOTER, looters, looting, loots ▸ **loot**
LOOVES ▸ **loof**
LOP *vb, n*
LOPE *vb, n* **loped, loper, lopers, lopes, loping**
LOPPED ▸ **lop**
LOPPER *n* tool for lopping ▹ *vb* curdle **loppers**
LOPPIER ▸ **loppy**
LOPPIES ▸ **loppy**

LOPPING ▸ **lop**
LOPPY *adj* floppy ▹ *n* ranch hand
LOPS ▸ **lop**
LOQUAT *n* ornamental evergreen rosaceous tree **loquats**
LOR *interj* exclamation of surprise or dismay
LORAL *adj* of part of side of bird's head
LORAN *n* radio navigation system operating over long distances **lorans**
LORATE *adj* like a strap
LORCHA *n* junk-rigged vessel **lorchas**
LORD *n, vb* **lorded**
LORDING *n* gentleman
LORDKIN *n* little lord
LORDLY *adj, adv*
LORDOMA = **lordosis**
LORDS ▸ **lord**
LORDY *interj* exclamation of surprise or dismay
LORE *n*
LOREAL *adj* concerning or relating to lore
LOREL *another word for* ▸ **losel**
LORELS ▸ **lorel**
LORES ▸ **lore**
LORETTE *n* concubine
LORGNON *n* monocle or pair of spectacles
LORIC ▸ **lorica**
LORICA *n* hard outer covering of rotifers, ciliate protozoans, and similar organisms **loricae, lorics**
LORIES ▸ **lory**
LORIMER *n* (formerly) a person who made bits and spurs **loriner**
LORING *n* teaching **lorings**
LORIOT *n* golden oriole (bird) **loriots**
LORIS *n* any of several prosimian primates **lorises**
LORN *adj* forsaken or wretched
LORRELL *obsolete word for* ▸ **losel**
LORRIES ▸ **lorry**
LORRY *n*
LORY *n*
LOS *n* approval
LOSABLE ▸ **loose**
LOSE *vb* **losed**
LOSEL *n* worthless person ▹ *adj* worthless **losels**
LOSEN ▸ **loose**
LOSER *n* person or thing that loses **losers**
LOSES ▸ **loose**
LOSH *interj* lord
LOSING ▸ **lose**
LOSINGS *pl n* losses
LOSS *n* **losses**
LOSSIER ▸ **lossy**
LOSSY *adj* designed to have a high attenuation
LOST *adj*
LOT *pron, n, vb*
LOTA *n* globular water container **lotah**
LOTAHS ▸ **lotah**
LOTAS ▸ **lota**
LOTE *another word for* ▸ **lotus**
LOTES ▸ **lote**
LOTH = **loath**
LOTHER ▸ **loth**
LOTHEST ▸ **loth**
LOTI *n* monetary unit of Lesotho
LOTIC *adj* of communities living in rapidly flowing water
LOTION *n* **lotions**
LOTO = **lotto**
LOTOS = **lotus**
LOTOSES ▸ **lotos**
LOTS ▸ **lot**
LOTTE *n* type of fish
LOTTED ▸ **lot**
LOTTER *n* someone who works an allotment **lotters**
LOTTERY *n*
LOTTES ▸ **lotte**
LOTTING ▸ **lot**
LOTTO *n* game of chance **lottos**
LOTUS *n* **lotuses**
LOU *Scot word for* ▸ **love**
LOUCHE *adj* shifty **loucher**
LOUD *adj*
LOUDEN *vb* make louder **loudens**
LOUDER ▸ **loud**
LOUDEST ▸ **loud**
LOUDISH *adj* fairly loud
LOUDLY ▸ **loud**
LOUED ▸ **lou**
LOUGH *n* **loughs**
LOUIE = **looey**
LOUIES ▸ **louie**
LOUING ▸ **lou**
LOUIS *n* former French gold coin
LOUMA *n* market in developing countries **loumas**
LOUN = **lown**

LOUND = **loun**
LOUNDED ▸ **lound**
LOUNDER *vb* beat severely
LOUNDS ▸ **lound**
LOUNED ▸ **loun**
LOUNGE *n, vb* **lounged**
LOUNGER *n* comfortable sometimes adjustable couch or extending chair designed for someone to relax on
LOUNGES ▸ **lounge**
LOUNGEY *n* suggestive of a lounge bar or easy-listening music
LOUNGY *adj* casual; relaxed
LOUNING ▸ **loun**
LOUNS ▸ **loun**
LOUP *Scot word for* ▸ **leap**
LOUPE *n* magnifying glass used by jewellers, horologists, etc
LOUPED, loupen ▸ **loup**
LOUPES ▸ **loupe**
LOUPING, loupit, loups ▸ **loup**
LOUR *vb, n*
LOURE *n* slow, former French dance
LOURED ▸ **lour**
LOURES ▸ **loure**
LOURIE *n*
LOURIER ▸ **loury**
LOURIES ▸ **lourie**
LOURING ▸ **lour**
LOURS ▸ **lour**
LOURY *adj* sombre
LOUS ▸ **lou**
LOUSE *n, vb* **loused**
LOUSER *n* mean nasty person **lousers**
LOUSES ▸ **louse**
LOUSIER ▸ **lousy**
LOUSILY ▸ **lousy**
LOUSING ▸ **louse**
LOUSY *adj*
LOUT *n, vb* **louted, louting**
LOUTISH *adj* of a lout
LOUTS ▸ **lout**
LOUVAR *n* large silvery whalelike scombroid fish **louvars**
LOUVER = **louvre**
LOUVERS ▸ **louver**
LOUVRE *n*
LOUVRED *adj* having louvres
LOUVRES ▸ **louvre**
LOVABLE *adj* **lovably**
LOVAGE *n* European plant used for flavouring food **lovages**
LOVAT *n* yellowish-or bluish-green mixture in tweeds **lovats**
LOVE *vb, n*
LOVEBUG *n* small US flying insect
LOVED ▸ **love**
LOVELY *adj, n*
LOVER *n*
LOVERED *adj* having a lover
LOVERLY *adj* loverlike
LOVERS ▸ **lover**
LOVES ▸ **love**
LOVEY *another word for* ▸ **love**
LOVEYS ▸ **lovey**
LOVING *adj* **lovings**
LOW *adj, adv, n, vb*
LOWAN *n* type of Australian bird **lowans**
LOWBALL *vb* deliberately under-charge
LOWBORN *adj* of ignoble or common parentage
LOWBOY *n* **lowboys**
LOWBRED = **lowborn**
LOWBROW *adj, n*
LOWDOWN *n* inside info
LOWE *variant of* ▸ **low**
LOWED ▸ **low**
LOWER *adj, vb* **lowered, lowers**
LOWERY *adj* sombre
LOWES ▸ **lowe**
LOWEST, lowing, lowings, lowish ▸ **low**
LOWLAND *n* low-lying country ▹ *adj* of a lowland or lowlands
LOWLIER ▸ **lowly**
LOWLIFE *n* member or members of the underworld
LOWLILY ▸ **lowly**
LOWLY *adj, adv*
LOWN *vb* calm **lownd**
LOWNDED ▸ **lownd**
LOWNDS ▸ **lownd**
LOWNE = **loon**
LOWNED ▸ **lown**
LOWNES ▸ **lowne**
LOWNESS ▸ **low**
LOWNING ▸ **lown**
LOWNS ▸ **lown**
LOWP = **loup**
LOWPED ▸ **lowp**
LOWPING ▸ **lowp**
LOWPS ▸ **lowp**
LOWRIE *another name for* ▸ **lory**
LOWRIES ▸ **lowry**

LOWRY *another name for* ▶ **lory**
LOWS ▶ **low**
LOWSE *vb* release or loose ▷ *adj* loose **lowsed, lowser, lowses, lowsest, lowsing, lowsit**
LOWT = **lout**
LOWTED ▶ **lowt**
LOWTING ▶ **lowt**
LOWTS ▶ **lowt**
LOWVELD *n* low ground in S Africa
LOX *vb* load fuel tanks of spacecraft with liquid oxygen ▷ *n* kind of smoked salmon **loxed, loxes, loxing**

> A good word when you have an X to dispose of.

LOXYGEN *n* liquid oxygen
LOY *n* narrow spade with a single footrest
LOYAL *adj* **loyaler, loyally**
LOYALTY *n* quality of being loyal
LOYS ▶ **loy**
LOZELL *obsolete form of* ▶ **losel**
LOZELLS ▶ **lozell**
LOZEN *n* window pane
LOZENGE *n*
LOZENGY *adj* divided by diagonal lines to form a lattice
LOZENS ▶ **lozen**
LUACH *n* Jewish calendar
LUAU *n* feast of Hawaiian food **luaus**
LUBBARD = **lubber**
LUBBER *n* big, awkward, or stupid person **lubbers**
LUBE *n* lubricating oil ▷ *vb* lubricate with oil **lubed, lubes**
LUBFISH *n* type of fish
LUBING ▶ **lube**
LUBRA *n* **lubras**
LUBRIC *adj* slippery
LUCARNE *n* type of dormer window
LUCE *another name for* ▶ **pike**
LUCENCE ▶ **lucent**
LUCENCY ▶ **lucent**
LUCENT *adj* brilliant
LUCERN = **lucerne**
LUCERNE *n*
LUCERNS ▶ **lucern**
LUCES ▶ **luce**
LUCHOT ▶ **luach**
LUCHOTH ▶ **luach**
LUCID *adj* **lucider, lucidly**
LUCIFER *n* friction match
LUCIGEN *n* type of lamp
LUCITE *n* type of transparent acrylic-based plastic **lucites**
LUCK *n, vb* **lucked**
LUCKEN *adj* shut
LUCKIE = **lucky**
LUCKIER ▶ **lucky**
LUCKIES ▶ **luckie**
LUCKILY ▶ **lucky**
LUCKING ▶ **luck**
LUCKS ▶ **luck**
LUCKY *adj, n*
LUCRE *n* **lucres**
LUCUMA *n* S American tree **lucumas**
LUCUMO *n* Etruscan king **lucumos**
LUD *n* lord ▷ *interj* exclamation of dismay or surprise
LUDE *n* slang word for drug for relieving anxiety **ludes**
LUDIC *adj* playful
LUDO *n* game played with dice and counters on a board **ludos**
LUDS ▶ **lud**
LUDSHIP ▶ **lud**
LUES *n* any venereal disease **luetic, luetics**
LUFF *vb* sail (a ship) towards the wind ▷ *n* leading edge of a fore-and-aft sail
LUFFA = **loofah**
LUFFAS ▶ **luffa**
LUFFED ▶ **luff**
LUFFING ▶ **luff**
LUFFS ▶ **luff**
LUG *vb, n*
LUGE *n* racing toboggan ▷ *vb* ride on a luge **luged, lugeing**
LUGER *n* pistol **lugers**
LUGES ▶ **luge**
LUGGAGE *n*
LUGGED ▶ **lug**
LUGGER *n* small working boat with an oblong sail **luggers**
LUGGIE *n* wooden bowl **luggies**
LUGGING ▶ **lug**
LUGHOLE *informal word for* ▶ **ear**
LUGING ▶ **luge**
LUGINGS ▶ **luge**
LUGS ▶ **lug**
LUGSAIL *n* four-sided sail

LUGWORM *n* large worm used as bait
LUIT *Scots past form of* ▸ **let**
LUITEN ▸ **let**
LUKE *variant of* > **lukewarm**
LULIBUB *obsolete form of* > **lollipop**
LULL *vb, n*
LULLABY *n, vb*
LULLED, luller, lullers, lulling, lulls ▸ **lull**
LULU *n* person or thing deemed to be outstanding **lulus**
LUM *n* chimney
LUMA *n* monetary unit of Armenia **lumas**
LUMBAGO *n*
LUMBANG *n* type of tree
LUMBAR *adj, n* **lumbars**
LUMBER *n, vb* **lumbers**
LUMEN *n* **lumenal, lumens, lumina, luminal**
LUMINE *vb* illuminate **lumined, lumines**
LUMME *interj* exclamation of surprise or dismay
LUMMIER ▸ **lummy**
LUMMOX *n* clumsy person
LUMMY *interj* exclamation of surprise ▷ *adj* excellent
LUMP *n, vb* **lumped**
LUMPEN *adj* stupid or unthinking ▷ *n* member of underclass **lumpens**
LUMPER *n* stevedore **lumpers**
LUMPIER ▸ **lumpy**
LUMPILY ▸ **lumpy**
LUMPING ▸ **lump**
LUMPISH *adj* stupid or clumsy
LUMPKIN *n* lout
LUMPS ▸ **lump**
LUMPY *adj* full of lumps
LUMS ▸ **lum**
LUNA *n* large American moth
LUNACY *n*
LUNAR *adj, n* **lunars**
LUNARY *n* moonwort herb
LUNAS ▸ **luna**
LUNATE *adj* shaped like a crescent ▷ *n* crescent-shaped bone forming part of the wrist **lunated, lunates**
LUNATIC *adj, n*
LUNCH *n, vb* **lunched, luncher, lunches**
LUNE = **lunette**
LUNES ▸ **lune**
LUNET *n* small moon or satellite **lunets**
LUNETTE *n* anything that is shaped like a crescent
LUNG *n*
LUNGAN = **longan**
LUNGANS ▸ **lungan**
LUNGE *n, vb* **lunged**
LUNGEE = **lungi**
LUNGEES ▸ **lungee**
LUNGER ▸ **lunge**
LUNGERS ▸ **lunge**
LUNGES ▸ **lunge**
LUNGFUL ▸ **lung**
LUNGI *n* cotton cloth worn as a loincloth, sash, or turban
LUNGIE *n* guillemot **lungies**
LUNGING ▸ **lunge**
LUNGIS ▸ **lungi**
LUNGS ▸ **lung**
LUNGYI = **lungi**
LUNGYIS ▸ **lungyi**
LUNIER ▸ **luny**
LUNIES ▸ **luny**
LUNIEST ▸ **luny**
LUNK *n* awkward person
LUNKER *n* very large fish **lunkers**
LUNKS ▸ **lunk**
LUNT *vb* produce smoke **lunted, lunting, lunts**
LUNULA *n* white area at base of the fingernail **lunulae**
LUNULAR = **lunulate**
LUNULE = **lunula**
LUNULES ▸ **lunule**
LUNY = **loony**
LUNYIE = **lungie**
LUNYIES ▸ **lunyie**
LUPANAR *n* brothel
LUPIN *n*
LUPINE *adj* like a wolf ▷ *n* lupin **lupines**
LUPINS ▸ **lupin**
LUPOID *adj* suffering from lupus
LUPOUS *adj* relating to lupus
LUPPEN *Scots past form of* ▸ **leap**
LUPULIN *n* resinous powder extracted from the female flowers of the hop plant
LUPUS *n* ulcerous skin disease **lupuses**

LUR *n* large bronze musical horn
LURCH *vb, n* **lurched**
LURCHER *n* crossbred dog trained to hunt silently
LURCHES ▶ **lurch**
LURDAN *n* stupid or dull person ▷ *adj* dull or stupid **lurdane, lurdans, lurden**
LURDENS ▶ **lurden**
LURE *vb, n* **lured, lurer, lurers, lures**
LUREX *n* thin glittery thread **lurexes**
LURGI = **lurgy**
LURGIES ▶ **lurgy**
LURGIS ▶ **lurgi**
LURGY *n* any undetermined illness
LURID *adj* **lurider, luridly**
LURING ▶ **lure**
LURINGS ▶ **luring**
LURK *vb* **lurked, lurker, lurkers**
LURKING *adj* lingering
LURKS ▶ **lurk**
LURRIES ▶ **lurry**
LURRY *n* confused jumble
LURS ▶ **lur**
LURVE *n* love **lurves**
LUSER *n* humorous term for computer user **lusers**
LUSH *adj, n, vb* **lushed**
LUSHER *adj* more lush ▷ *n* drunkard **lushers**
LUSHES ▶ **lush**
LUSHEST ▶ **lush**
LUSHIER ▶ **lushy**
LUSHING ▶ **lush**
LUSHLY ▶ **lush**
LUSHY *adj* slightly intoxicated
LUSK *vb* lounge around **lusked, lusking**
LUSKISH *adj* lazy
LUSKS ▶ **lusk**
LUST *n, vb* **lusted**
LUSTER = **lustre**
LUSTERS ▶ **luster**
LUSTFUL *adj*
LUSTICK *obsolete word for* ▶ **lusty**
LUSTIER ▶ **lusty**
LUSTILY ▶ **lusty**
LUSTING ▶ **lust**
LUSTRA ▶ **lustrum**
LUSTRAL *adj* of or relating to a ceremony of purification
LUSTRE *n, vb* **lustred, lustres**
LUSTRUM *n* period of five years
LUSTS ▶ **lust**
LUSTY *adj*
LUSUS *n* freak, mutant **lususes**
LUTE *n, vb*
LUTEA *adj* yellow
LUTEAL *adj* relating to the development of the corpus luteum
LUTED ▶ **lute**
LUTEIN *n* xanthophyll pigment **luteins**
LUTEOUS *adj* of a greenish-yellow colour
LUTER *n* lute player **luters**
LUTES ▶ **lute**
LUTEUM *adj* yellow
LUTFISK = **lutefisk**
LUTHERN *another name for* ▶ **dormer**
LUTHIER *n* lute-maker
LUTING *n* cement and clay **lutings**
LUTIST = **lutenist**
LUTISTS ▶ **lutist**
LUTITE *another name for* ▶ **pelite**
LUTITES ▶ **lutite**
LUTTEN ▶ **loot**
LUTZ *n* skating jump **lutzes**
LUV *n* love
LUVS ▶ **love**
LUVVIE *n* person who is involved in acting or the theatre
LUVVIES ▶ **luvvy**
LUVVY= **luvvie**
LUX *n* unit of illumination

> One of the key words using X.

LUXATE *vb* put (a shoulder, knee, etc) out of joint **luxated, luxates**
LUXE *n as in* **de luxe** rich **luxes**
LUXURY *n, adj*
LUZ *n* supposedly indestructible bone of the human body

> This very unusual word is very useful for playing the Z.

LUZERN *n* alfalfa **luzerns**
LUZZES ▶ **luz**
LWEI *n* Angolan monetary unit **lweis**
LYAM *n* leash **lyams**
LYARD = **liard**

LYART = **liard**
LYASE *n* any enzyme that catalyses the separation of two parts of a molecule **lyases**
LYCEA ▶ **lyceum**
LYCEE *n* secondary school **lycees**
LYCEUM *n* public building for concerts **lyceums**
LYCH = **lich**
LYCHEE = **litchi**
LYCHEES ▶ **lychee**
LYCHES ▶ **lych**
LYCHNIS *n* plant with red, pink, or white flowers
LYCOPOD *n* type of moss
LYCRA *n* type of elastic fabric used for tight-fitting garments **lycras**
LYDDITE *n* explosive consisting chiefly of fused picric acid
LYE *n* caustic solution **lyes**
LYFULL *obsolete form of* ▶ **lifeful**
LYING ▶ **lie**
LYINGLY ▶ **lie**
LYINGS ▶ **lie**
LYM *obsolete form of* ▶ **lyam**
LYME *n as in* **lyme grass** type of perennial dune grass **lymes**
LYMITER = **limiter**
LYMPH *n*
LYMPHAD *n* ancient rowing boat
LYMPHS *n* lymph
LYMS ▶ **lym**
LYNAGE *obsolete form of* ▶ **lineage**
LYNAGES ▶ **lynage**
LYNCEAN *adj* of a lynx
LYNCH *vb* **lynched, lyncher, lynches**
LYNCHET *n* ridge formed by ploughing a hillside
LYNE *n* flax **lynes**
LYNX *n* **lynxes**
LYOPHIL = **lyophilic**
LYRA *n as in* **lyra viol** lutelike musical instrument
LYRATE *adj* shaped like a lyre **lyrated**
LYRE *n* **lyres**
LYRIC *adj, n* **lyrical**
LYRICON *n* wind synthesizer
LYRICS ▶ **lyric**
LYRISM *n* art or technique of playing the lyre **lyrisms**
LYRIST = **lyricist**
LYRISTS ▶ **lyrist**
LYSATE *n* material formed by lysis **lysates**
LYSE *vb* undergo lysis **lysed**
LYSES ▶ **lysis**
LYSIN *n* antibodies that dissolute cells against which they are directed
LYSINE *n* essential amino acid that occurs in proteins **lysines**
LYSING ▶ **lyse**
LYSINS ▶ **lysin**
LYSIS *n* destruction of cells by a lysin
LYSOGEN *n* lysis-inducing agent
LYSOL *n* antiseptic solution **lysols**
LYSSA *less common word for* ▶ **rabies**
LYSSAS ▶ **lyssa**
LYTE *vb* dismount **lyted, lytes**
LYTHE *n* type of fish **lythes**
LYTIC *adj* relating to, causing, or resulting from lysis
LYTING ▶ **lyte**
LYTTA *n* mass of cartilage under the tongue in carnivores **lyttae, lyttas**

Mm

M is a very useful letter when you need to form short words as it starts a two-letter word with every vowel, as well as with **Y** and with another **M**. Remembering this allows you to use **M** effectively when you're forming a word parallel to, and in contact with, a word that is already on the board. **M** also combines well with **X** and **Z**, so there is a lot of potential for high-scoring words. Keep **max, mix** and **mux** (12 points each) in mind, as well as **miz** and **muz** (14 each). It's also worth remembering the three-letter words ending in **W**: **maw, mew** and **mow** (8 points each). **Myc** is another useful word to remember when you are short of vowels.

MA *n* mother
MAA *vb* (of goats) bleat **maaed, maaing**
MAAR *n* coneless volcanic crater **maare, maars**
MAAS *n* thick soured milk **maases**
MAATJES *n* pickled herring
MABE *n* type of pearl
MABELA *n* ground kaffir corn **mabelas**
MABES ▸ **mabe**
MAC *n*
MACABER = **macabre**
MACABRE *adj*
MACACO *n* type of lemur **macacos**
MACADAM *n* road surface
MACAQUE *n* monkey of Asia and Africa
MACAW *n* large tropical American parrot **macaws**
MACCHIA *n* thicket in Italy **macchie**
MACE *n, vb* **maced**
MACER *n* macebearer, esp (in Scotland) an official who acts as usher in a court of law
MACERAL *n* any of the organic units that constitute coal
MACERS ▸ **macer**
MACES ▸ **mace**
MACH *n* ratio of the speed of a body in a particular medium to the speed of sound in that medium
MACHAIR *n* (in the western Highlands of Scotland) a strip of sandy, grassy, land
MACHAN *n* (in India) a raised platform used in tiger hunting **machans**
MACHE *n* papier-mâché
MACHER *n* important or influential person **machers**
MACHES ▸ **mache**
MACHETE *n*
MACHI *n as in* **machi chips** in Indian English, fish and chips
MACHINE *n, vb*
MACHO *adj, n* **machos**

MACHREE *n* Irish form of address meaning my dear
MACHS ▸ **mach**
MACHZOR *n* Jewish prayer book
MACING ▸ **mace**
MACK = **mac**
MACKLE *n* blurred impression ▹ *vb* mend hurriedly or in a makeshift way **mackled, mackles**
MACKS ▸ **mack**
MACLE *n* crystal consisting of two parts **macled, macles**
MACON *n* wine from the Mâcon area **macons**
MACOYA *n* South American tree **macoyas**
MACRAME *n* ornamental work of knotted cord **macrami**
MACRO *n* close-up lens
MACRON *n* mark placed over a letter to represent a long vowel **macrons**
MACROS ▸ **macro**
MACS ▸ **mac**
MACULA *n* small spot like a freckle **maculae, macular, maculas**
MACULE = **mackle**
MACULED ▸ **macule**
MACULES ▸ **macule**
MACUMBA *n* religious cult in Brazil
MAD *adj, vb*
MADAFU *n* coconut milk **madafus**
MADAM *n, vb*
MADAME *n* French title equivalent to *Mrs*
MADAMED ▸ **madam**
MADAMES ▸ **madame**
MADAMS ▸ **madam**
MADCAP *adj* foolish or reckless ▹ *n* impulsive or reckless person **madcaps**
MADDED ▸ **mad**
MADDEN *vb* **maddens**
MADDER *n* type of rose
MADDERS ▸ **madam**
MADDEST ▸ **mad**
MADDING ▸ **mad**
MADDISH ▸ **mad**
MADDOCK = **mattock**
MADE ▸ **make**
MADEFY *vb* make moist
MADEIRA *n* kind of rich sponge cake
MADGE *n* type of hammer **madges**
MADID *adj* wet
MADISON *n* type of cycle relay race
MADLING *n* insane person
MADLY *adv*
MADMAN *n* person who is insane **madmen**
MADNESS *n* insanity
MADONNA *n* picture or statue of the Virgin Mary
MADOQUA *n* Ethiopian antelope
MADRAS *n* medium-hot curry
MADRASA = **madrasah**
MADRE *Spanish word for* ▸ **mother**
MADRES ▸ **madre**
MADRONA *n* N American evergreen tree or shrub **madrone, madrono**
MADS ▸ **mad**
MADTOM *n* species of catfish **madtoms**
MADURO *adj* (of cigars) dark and strong ▹ *n* cigar of this type **maduros**
MADWORT *n* low-growing Eurasian plant with small blue flowers
MADZOON = **matzoon**
MAE *adj* more
MAELID *n* mythical spirit of apple **maelids**
MAENAD *n* female disciple of Dionysus, the Greek god of wine **maenads**
MAERL *n* type of red coralline algae **maerls**
MAES ▸ **mae**
MAESTRI ▸ **maestro**
MAESTRO *n* outstanding musician or conductor
MAFFIA = **mafia**
MAFFIAS ▸ **maffia**
MAFFICK *vb* celebrate extravagantly and publicly
MAFFLED *adj* baffled
MAFFLIN *n* half-witted person
MAFIA *n* international secret organization founded in Sicily **mafias**
MAFIC *n* minerals present in igneous rock **mafics**

MAFIOSI ▸ **mafioso**
MAFIOSO *n* member of the Mafia
MAFTED *adj* suffering under oppressive heat
MAFTIR *n* final section of the weekly Torah reading **maftirs**
MAG *vb* talk ▷ *n* talk
MAGALOG = **magalogue**
MAGE *archaic word for* > **magician**
MAGENTA *adj, n*
MAGES ▸ **mage**
MAGG = **mag**
MAGGED ▸ **mag**
MAGGIE *n* magpie **maggies**
MAGGING ▸ **mag**
MAGGOT *n* **maggots**
MAGGOTY *adj* relating to, resembling, or ridden with maggots
MAGGS ▸ **magg**
MAGI ▸ **magus**
MAGIAN ▸ **magus**
MAGIANS ▸ **magus**
MAGIC *n, vb, adj* **magical, magics**
MAGILP = **megilp**
MAGILPS ▸ **magilp**
MAGISM ▸ **magus**
MAGISMS ▸ **magus**
MAGLEV *n* type of high-speed train **maglevs**
MAGMA *n* **magmas, magmata**
MAGNATE *n*
MAGNES *n* magnetic iron ore
MAGNET *n*
MAGNETO *n*
MAGNETS ▸ **magnet**
MAGNIFY *vb*
MAGNON *n* short for Cro-Magnon **magnons**
MAGNOX *n* alloy used in fuel elements of some nuclear reactors
MAGNUM *n* large wine bottle holding about 1.5 litres **magnums**
MAGNUS *adj as in* **magnus hitch** knot similar to a clove hitch but having one more turn
MAGOT *n* Chinese or Japanese figurine in a crouching position, usually grotesque **magots**
MAGPIE *n* **magpies**
MAGS ▸ **mag**
MAGSMAN *n* raconteur **magsmen**
MAGUEY *n* tropical American agave plant **magueys**
MAGUS *n* Zoroastrian priest of the ancient Medes and Persians
MAGYAR *adj* of or relating to a style of sleeve
MAHA *n as in* **maha yoga** form of yoga
MAHATMA *n* person revered for holiness and wisdom
MAHEWU *n* (in South Africa) fermented liquid mealie-meal porridge **mahewus**
MAHJONG *n* game of Chinese origin, using tiles
MAHMAL *n* litter used in Muslim ceremony **mahmals**
MAHOE *n* New Zealand tree **mahoes**
MAHONIA *n* Asian and American evergreen shrub
MAHOUT *n* (in India and the East Indies) elephant driver or keeper **mahouts**
MAHSEER *n* large freshwater Indian fish **mahsir**
MAHSIRS ▸ **mahsir**
MAHUA *n* Indian tree
MAHUANG *n* herbal medicine from shrub
MAHUAS ▸ **mahua**
MAHWA = **mahua**
MAHWAS ▸ **mahwa**
MAHZOR = **machzor**
MAHZORS ▸ **mahzor**
MAID *n, vb*
MAIDAN *n* (in Pakistan, India, etc) open area **maidans**
MAIDED ▸ **maid**
MAIDEN *n, adj* **maidens**
MAIDING ▸ **maid**
MAIDISH ▸ **maid**
MAIDISM *n* pellagra
MAIDS ▸ **maid**
MAIGRE *adj* not containing meat ▷ *n* species of fish **maigres**
MAIHEM = **mayhem**
MAIHEMS ▸ **maihem**
MAIK *n* old halfpenny

MAIKO *n* apprentice geisha **maikos**
MAIKS ▶ **maik**
MAIL *n, vb*
MAILBAG *n* large bag for transporting or delivering mail
MAILBOX *n* box into which letters and parcels are delivered
MAILCAR = **mailcoach**
MAILE *n* halfpenny
MAILED ▶ **mail**
MAILER *n* person who addresses or mails letters, etc **mailers**
MAILES ▶ **maile**
MAILING ▶ **mail**
MAILL *n* Scots word meaning rent
MAILLOT *n* tights worn for ballet, gymnastics, etc
MAILLS ▶ **maill**
MAILMAN *n* postman **mailmen**
MAILS ▶ **mail**
MAILVAN *n* vehicle used to transport post
MAIM *vb, n* **maimed, maimer, maimers, maiming, maims**
MAIN *adj, n, vb* **mained, mainer, mainest, maining**
MAINLY *adv*
MAINOR *n* act of doing something **mainors, mainour**
MAINS ▶ **main**
MAINTOP *n* top or platform at the head of the mainmast
MAIR *Scots form of* ▶ **more**
MAIRE *n* New Zealand tree **maires**
MAIRS ▶ **mair**
MAISE *n* measure of herring **maises**
MAIST *Scot word for* ▶ **most**
MAISTER *Scots word for* ▶ **master**
MAISTRY ▶ **maister**
MAISTS ▶ **maist**
MAIZE *n* **maizes**
MAJAGUA = **mahoe**
MAJESTY *n*
MAJLIS *n* (in Arab countries) an assembly
MAJOR *adj, n, vb*
MAJORAT *n* estate, the right to which is that of the first born child of a family
MAJORED ▶ **major**
MAJORLY *adv* very
MAJORS ▶ **major**
MAK *Scot word for* ▶ **make**
MAKABLE ▶ **make**
MAKAR = **maker**
MAKARS ▶ **makar**
MAKE *vb, n*
MAKER *n* person or company that makes something **makers**
MAKES ▶ **make**
MAKEUP *n* cosmetics applied to the face **makeups**
MAKI *n* in Japanese cuisine, rice and other ingredients wrapped in a short seaweed roll
MAKING ▶ **make**
MAKINGS *pl n* potentials, qualities, or materials
MAKIS ▶ **maki**
MAKO *n* powerful shark of the Atlantic and Pacific Oceans **makos**
MAKS ▶ **mak**
MAKUTA *plural of* ▶ **likuta**
MAKUTU *n* Polynesian witchcraft ▷ *vb* cast a spell on **makutus**
MAL *n* illness
MALA *n* string of beads or knots, used in praying and meditating
MALACCA *n* stem of the rattan palm
MALACIA *n* softening of an organ or tissue
MALADY *n*
MALAISE *n*
MALAM = **mallam**
MALAMS ▶ **malam**
MALANGA = **cocoyam**
MALAR *n* cheekbone ▷ *adj* of or relating to the cheek or cheekbone
MALARIA *n*
MALARKY = **malarkey**
MALARS ▶ **malar**
MALAS ▶ **mala**
MALATE *n* any salt or ester of malic acid **malates**
MALAX *vb* soften **malaxed, malaxes**
MALE *adj, n*
MALEATE *n* any salt or ester of maleic acid

MALEFIC *adj* causing evil
MALEIC *adj as in* **maleic acid** colourless soluble crystalline substance
MALES ▶ **male**
MALFED *adj* having malfunctioned
MALGRE = **maugre**
MALGRED ▶ **malgre**
MALGRES ▶ **malgre**
MALI *n* member of an Indian caste
MALIBU *n as in* **malibu board** lightweight surfboard
MALIC *adj as in* **malic acid** colourless crystalline compound occurring in apples
MALICE *n, vb* **maliced, malices**
MALICHO *n* mischief
MALIGN *vb, adj* **maligns**
MALIK *n* person of authority in India **maliks**
MALINE *n* stiff net **malines**
MALIS ▶ **mali**
MALISM *n* belief that evil dominates world **malisms**
MALISON *archaic or poetic word for* ▶ **curse malist**
MALKIN *archaic or dialect name for a* ▶ **cat**
MALKINS ▶ **malkin**
MALL *n* street or shopping area closed to vehicles ▷ *vb* maul
MALLAM *n* (in W Africa) expert in the Koran **mallams**
MALLARD *n*
MALLED ▶ **mall**
MALLEE *n* **mallees**
MALLEI ▶ **malleus**
MALLET *n* **mallets**
MALLEUS *n* small bone in the middle ear
MALLING ▶ **mall**
MALLOW *n* plant with pink or purple flowers **mallows**
MALLS ▶ **mall**
MALM *n* soft greyish limestone that crumbles easily
MALMAG *n* Asian monkey **malmags**
MALMIER ▶ **malmy**
MALMS ▶ **malm**
MALMSEY *n* sweet Madeira wine
MALMY *adj* looking like malm
MALODOR = **malodour**
MALONIC *adj as in* **malonic acid** colourless crystalline compound
MALOTI *plural of* ▶ **loti**
MALS ▶ **mal**
MALT *n, vb*
MALTASE *n* enzyme that hydrolyses maltose to glucose
MALTED ▶ **malt**
MALTEDS ▶ **malt**
MALTESE *adj as in* **maltese cross** cross-shaped part of a film projector
MALTHA *n* any of various naturally occurring mixtures of hydrocarbons **malthas**
MALTIER ▶ **malty**
MALTING *n* building in which malt is made or stored
MALTMAN = **maltster**
MALTMEN ▶ **maltman**
MALTOL *n* food additive **maltols**
MALTOSE *n* sugar formed by the action of enzymes on starch
MALTS ▶ **malt**
MALTY *adj* of, like, or containing malt
MALVA *n* mallow plant **malvas**
MALWA *n* Ugandan drink brewed from millet
MALWARE *n* computer program designed to cause damage to a system
MALWAS ▶ **malwa**
MAM = **mother**
MAMA *n* mother
MAMAGUY *vb* deceive or tease ▷ *n* deception or flattery
MAMAKAU = **mamaku**
MAMAKO = **mamaku**
MAMAKOS ▶ **mamako**
MAMAKU *n* tall edible New Zealand tree fern **mamakus**
MAMAS ▶ **mama**
MAMBA *n* deadly S African snake **mambas**

MAMBO *n* Latin American dance resembling the rumba ▷ *vb* perform this dance **mamboed, mamboes, mambos**
MAMEE = **mamey**
MAMEES ▸ **mamee**
MAMELON *n* small rounded hillock
MAMEY *n* tropical tree **mameyes, mameys**
MAMIE *n* tropical tree **mamies**
MAMILLA *n* nipple or teat
MAMLUK = **mameluke**
MAMLUKS ▸ **mamluk**
MAMMA *n* buxom and voluptuous woman **mammae**
MAMMAL *n* **mammals**
MAMMARY *adj*
MAMMAS ▸ **mamma**
MAMMATE *adj* having breasts
MAMMATI > **mammatus**
MAMMEE = **mamey**
MAMMEES ▸ **mammee**
MAMMER *vb* hesitate **mammers**
MAMMET = **maumet**
MAMMETS ▸ **mammet**
MAMMEY = **mamey**
MAMMEYS ▸ **mammey**
MAMMIE = **mammy**
MAMMIES ▸ **mammy**
MAMMOCK *n* fragment ▷ *vb* tear or shred
MAMMON *n* wealth regarded as a source of evil **mammons**
MAMMOTH *n*, *adj*
MAMMY *n* Black woman employed as a nurse or servant to a White family
MAMPARA *n* foolish person, idiot
MAMPOER *n* home-distilled brandy
MAMS ▸ **mam**
MAMZER *n* child of an incestuous or adulterous union **mamzers**
MAN *n*, *vb*
MANA *n*
MANACLE *vb*, *n*
MANAGE *vb* **managed**
MANAGER *n*
MANAGES ▸ **manage**
MANAIA *n* figure in Māori carving **manaias**
MANAKIN = **manikin**
MANANA *n* tomorrow ▷ *adv* tomorrow **mananas**
MANAS ▸ **mana**
MANAT *n* standard monetary unit of Azerbaijan
MANATEE *n* large tropical plant-eating aquatic mammal **manati**
MANATIS ▸ **manati**
MANATS ▸ **manat**
MANATU *n* large flowering deciduous New Zealand tree **manatus**
MANAWA *in New Zealand*, = **mangrove**
MANAWAS ▸ **manawa**
MANCALA *n* African and Asian board game
MANCHE *n* long sleeve **manches**
MANCHET *n* type of bread
MANCUS *n* former English coin
MAND ▸ **man**
MANDALA *n* circular design symbolizing the universe
MANDATE *n*, *vb*
MANDI *n* (in India) a big market
MANDIOC = **manioc**
MANDIR *n* **mandira, mandirs**
MANDIS ▸ **mandi**
MANDOLA *n* early type of mandolin
MANDOM *n* mankind **mandoms**
MANDORA *n* ancestor of mandolin
MANDREL *n* shaft on which work is held in a lathe **mandril**
MANE *n* **maned**
MANEGE *n* art of training horses and riders ▷ *vb* train horse **maneged, maneges**
MANEH = **mina**
MANEHS ▸ **maneh**
MANENT ▸ **manet**
MANES *pl n* spirits of the dead, often revered as minor deities
MANET *vb* theatre direction, remain on stage
MANFUL *adj* determined and brave

MANG *vb* speak
MANGA *n* type of Japanese comic book
MANGABY = **mangabey**
MANGAL *n* Turkish brazier **mangals**
MANGAS ▸ **manga**
MANGE *n* skin disease of domestic animals
MANGEAO *n* small New Zealand tree with glossy leaves
MANGED ▸ **mang**
MANGEL *n* Eurasian variety of the beet plant **mangels**
MANGER *n* **mangers**
MANGES ▸ **mange**
MANGEY = **mangy**
MANGIER ▸ **mangy**
MANGILY ▸ **mangy**
MANGING ▸ **mang**
MANGLE *vb, n* **mangled, mangler, mangles**
MANGO *n* **mangoes**
MANGOLD *n* type of root vegetable
MANGOS ▸ **mango**
MANGS ▸ **mang**
MANGY *adj*
MANHOLE *n*
MANHOOD *n*
MANHUNT *n* organized search, usu by police, for a wanted man
MANI *n* place to pray
MANIA *n*
MANIAC *n* **maniacs**
MANIAS ▸ **mania**
MANIC *adj, n* **manics**
MANIES ▸ **many**
MANIHOC *variation of* ▸ **manioc**
MANIHOT *n* tropical American plant
MANIKIN *n* little man or dwarf
MANILA *n* strong brown paper used for envelopes **manilas**
MANILLA *n* early currency in W Africa in the form of a small bracelet
MANILLE *n* (in ombre and quadrille) the second best trump
MANIOC = **cassava**
MANIOCA = **manioc**
MANIOCS ▸ **manioc**
MANIPLE *n* (in ancient Rome) a unit of 120 to 200 foot soldiers
MANIS *n* pangolin
MANITO = **manitou**
MANITOS ▸ **manito**
MANITOU *n* (among the Algonquian Indians) a deified spirit or force **manitu**
MANITUS ▸ **manitu**
MANJACK *n* single individual
MANKIER ▸ **manky**
MANKIND *n*
MANKINI *n*
MANKY *adj* worthless, rotten, or in bad taste
MANLESS ▸ **man**
MANLIER ▸ **manly**
MANLIKE *adj* resembling or befitting a man
MANLILY ▸ **manly**
MANLY *adj*
MANMADE *adj* made or produced by man
MANNA *n*
MANNAN *n* drug derived from mannose **mannans**
MANNAS ▸ **manna**
MANNED ▸ **man**
MANNER *n*
MANNERS *pl n* person's social conduct
MANNING ▸ **man**
MANNISH *adj* (of a woman) like a man
MANNITE = **mannitol**
MANNOSE *n* hexose sugar
MANO *n* stone for grinding grain
MANOAO *n* New Zealand shrub **manoaos**
MANOR *n* **manors**
MANOS ▸ **mano**
MANPACK *n* load carried by one person
MANQUE *adj* would-be
MANRED *n* homage **manreds, manrent**
MANROPE *n* rope railing
MANS ▸ **man**
MANSARD *n* type of sloping roof
MANSE *n* house provided for a minister in some religious denominations **manses**
MANSION *n*
MANTA *n* type of large ray with very wide winglike pectoral fins **mantas**

MANTEAU *n* cloak or mantle
MANTEEL *n* cloak
MANTEL *n* structure round a fireplace ▷ *vb* construct a mantel **mantels**
MANTES ▸ **mantis**
MANTIC *adj* of or relating to divination and prophecy
MANTID = **mantis**
MANTIDS ▸ **mantid**
MANTIES ▸ **manty**
MANTIS *n* carnivorous insect like a grasshopper
MANTLE = **mantel**
MANTLED ▸ **mantle**
MANTLES ▸ **mantle**
MANTLET = **mantelet**
MANTO = **manteau**
MANTOES ▸ **manto**
MANTOS ▸ **manto**
MANTRA *n* **mantram**
MANTRAP *n* snare for catching people, esp trespassers
MANTRAS ▸ **mantra**
MANTRIC ▸ **mantra**
MANTUA *n* loose gown of the 17th and 18th centuries **mantuas, manty**
MANUAL *adj*, *n* **manuals, manuary**
MANUKA *n* New Zealand tree **manukas**
MANUL *n* Asian wildcat **manuls**
MANUMEA *n* pigeon of Samoa
MANUMIT *vb* free from slavery
MANURE *n*, *vb* **manured, manurer, manures**
MANUS *n* wrist and hand
MANWARD *adv* towards humankind
MANWISE *adv* in human way
MANY *adj*, *n*
MANYATA = **manyatta**
MAOMAO *n* fish of New Zealand seas **maomaos**
MAORMOR = **mormaor**
MAP *n*, *vb*
MAPAU *n* small New Zealand tree **mapaus**
MAPLE *n* **maples**
MAPLESS, maplike, mapped, mapper, mappers ▸ **map**
MAPPERY *n* making of maps
MAPPING ▸ **map**
MAPPIST ▸ **map**
MAPS ▸ **map**
MAPWISE *adv* like map
MAQUI *n* Chilean shrub
MAQUILA *n* US-owned factory in Mexico
MAQUIS *n* French underground movement in World War II
MAR *vb*, *n*
MARA *n* harelike S American rodent
MARABI *n* kind of music popular in S African townships in the 1930s **marabis**
MARABOU *n* large black-and-white African stork
MARACA *n* shaken percussion instrument **maracas**
MARAE *n* **maraes**
MARAH *n* bitterness **marahs**
MARANTA *n* tropical American plant
MARARI *n* eel-like blennoid food fish **mararis**
MARAS ▸ **mara**
MARASCA *n* European cherry tree with red acid-tasting fruit
MARAUD *vb* wander or raid in search of plunder **marauds**
MARBLE *n*, *vb* **marbled, marbler**
MARBLES *n* game in which marble balls are rolled at one another
MARBLY ▸ **marble**
MARC *n* remains of grapes or other fruit that have been pressed for wine-making
MARCATO *adj* (of notes) heavily accented ▷ *adv* with each note heavily accented ▷ *n* heavily accented note
MARCEL *n* hairstyle characterized by repeated regular waves ▷ *vb* make such waves in (the hair) **marcels**
MARCH *vb*, *n* **marched**
MARCHEN *n* German story

MARCHER *n* person who marches
MARCHES ▸ **march**
MARCONI *vb* communicate by wireless
MARCS ▸ **marc**
MARD ▸ **mar**
MARDIED ▸ **mardy**
MARDIER ▸ **mardy**
MARDIES ▸ **mardy**
MARDY *adj* (of a child) spoilt ▹ *vb* behave in mardy way
MARE *n*
MAREMMA *n* marshy unhealthy region near the shore, esp in Italy **maremme**
MARENGO *adj* browned in oil and cooked with tomatoes, mushrooms, garlic, wine, etc
MARERO *n* **mareros**
MARES ▸ **mare**
MARG *short for* > **margarine**
MARGAY *n* feline mammal of Central and S America **margays**
MARGE *n* margarine
MARGENT = **margin**
MARGES ▸ **marge**
MARGIN *n*, *vb* **margins**
MARGOSA *n* Indian tree
MARGS ▸ **marg**
MARIA ▸ **mare**
MARID *n* spirit in Muslim mythology **marids**
MARIES ▸ **mary**
MARIMBA *n* Latin American percussion instrument
MARINA *n* **marinas**
MARINE *adj*, *n*
MARINER *n*
MARINES ▸ **marine**
MARISH *n* marsh
MARITAL *adj*
MARK *n* line, dot, scar, etc visible on a surface ▹ *vb* make a mark on
MARKA *n* unit of currency introduced as an interim currency in Bosnia-Herzegovina **markas**
MARKED *adj*
MARKER *n* object used to show the position of something **markers**
MARKET *n*, *vb* **markets**
MARKHOR *n* large wild Himalayan goat
MARKING *n* arrangement of colours on an animal or plant
MARKKA *n* former standard monetary unit of Finland **markkaa, markkas**
MARKMAN *n* person owning land **markmen**
MARKS ▸ **mark**
MARKUP *n* percentage or amount added to the cost of a commodity to provide the seller with a profit and to cover overheads, costs, etc **markups**
MARL *n* soil formed of clay and lime, used as fertilizer ▹ *vb* fertilize (land) with marl
MARLE = **marvel**
MARLED ▸ **marl**
MARLES ▸ **marle**
MARLIER ▸ **marly**
MARLIN = **marline**
MARLINE *n* light rope, usually tarred, made of two strands laid left-handed **marling**
MARLINS ▸ **marlin**
MARLITE *n* type of marl that contains clay and calcium carbonate
MARLS ▸ **marl**
MARLY *adj* marl-like
MARM = **madam**
MARMEM *n as in* **marmem alloy** type of alloy
MARMITE *n* large cooking pot
MARMOSE *n* South American opossum
MARMOT *n* burrowing rodent **marmots**
MARMS ▸ **marm**
MARON *n* freshwater crustacean **marons**
MAROON *adj*, *vb*, *n* **maroons**
MAROR *n* Jewish ceremonial dish of bitter herbs **marors**
MARPLOT *n* person interfering with plot
MARQUE *n* brand of product, esp of a car
MARQUEE *n*
MARQUES ▸ **marque**
MARQUIS *n*

MARRAM *n as in* **marram grass** any of several grasses that grow on sandy shores **marrams**
MARRANO *n* Spanish or Portuguese Jew of the late Middle Ages who was converted to Christianity
MARRED ▶ **mar**
MARRELS = **merils**
MARRER ▶ **mar**
MARRERS ▶ **mar**
MARRI *n* W Australian eucalyptus
MARRIED ▶ **marry**
MARRIER ▶ **marry**
MARRIES ▶ **marry**
MARRING ▶ **mar**
MARRIS ▶ **marri**
MARRON *n* large edible sweet chestnut **marrons**
MARROW *n, vb* **marrows, marrowy**
MARRUM = **marram**
MARRUMS ▶ **marrum**
MARRY *vb, interj*
MARS ▶ **mar**
MARSALA *n* dark sweet dessert wine made in Sicily
MARSE = **master**
MARSES ▶ **marse**
MARSH *n*
MARSHAL *n, vb*
MARSHES ▶ **marsh**
MARSHY *adj* of, involving, or like a marsh
MART *n* market ▷ *vb* sell or trade **marted**
MARTEL *n* hammer-shaped weapon ▷ *vb* use such a weapon **martels**
MARTEN *n* weasel-like animal **martens**
MARTEXT *n* preacher who makes many mistakes
MARTIAL *adj*
MARTIAN *n* inhabitant of Mars
MARTIN *n* bird with a slightly forked tail
MARTING ▶ **mart**
MARTINI *n* cocktail of vermouth and gin
MARTINS ▶ **martin**
MARTLET *n* footless bird often found in coats of arms
MARTS ▶ **mart**
MARTYR *n, vb* **martyrs**
MARTYRY *n* shrine or chapel erected in honour of a martyr
MARVEL *vb, n* **marvels**
MARVER *vb* roll molten glass on slab **marvers**
MARVIER ▶ **marvy**
MARVY *shortened form of* > **marvelous**
MARY *n* woman
MARYBUD *n* bud of marigold
MAS ▶ **ma**
MASA *n* Mexican maize dough
MASALA *n* mixture of spices ground into a paste ▷ *adj* spicy **masalas**
MASAS ▶ **masa**
MASCARA *n*
MASCLE *n* charge consisting of a lozenge with a lozenge-shaped hole in the middle **mascled, mascles**
MASCON *n* any of several lunar regions of high gravity **mascons**
MASCOT *n* **mascots**
MASCULY ▶ **mascle**
MASE *vb* function as maser **mased**
MASER *n* device for amplifying microwaves **masers**
MASES ▶ **mase**
MASH *n, vb* **mashed, masher, mashers, mashes**
MASHIE *n* former golf club, used for approach shots
MASHIER ▶ **mashy**
MASHIES ▶ **mashie**
MASHING ▶ **mash**
MASHLAM = **maslin**
MASHLIM = **maslin**
MASHLIN = **maslin**
MASHLUM = **maslin**
MASHMAN *n* brewery worker **mashmen**
MASHUA *n* South American plant **mashuas**
MASHUP *n* piece of music in which a producer or DJ blends together two or more tracks **mashups**
MASHY *adj* like mash
MASING ▶ **mase**
MASJID = **mosque**
MASJIDS ▶ **masjid**
MASK *n, vb*

MASKED *adj* disguised or covered by or as if by a mask
MASKEG *n* North American bog **maskegs**
MASKER *n* person who wears a mask or takes part in a masque **maskers**
MASKING *n* act or practice of masking
MASKS ▶ **mask**
MASLIN *n* mixture of wheat, rye or other grain **maslins**
MASON *n, vb* **masoned**
MASONIC *adj*
MASONRY *n*
MASONS ▶ **mason**
MASQUE *n* 16th–17th-century form of dramatic entertainment
MASQUER = **masker**
MASQUES ▶ **masque**
MASS *n, adj, vb*
MASSA *old fashioned variant of* ▶ **master**
MASSAGE *n, vb*
MASSAS ▶ **massa**
MASSE *n* billiard stroke that makes the ball move in a curve around another ball
MASSED ▶ **mass**
MASSES *pl n* body of common people
MASSEUR *n*
MASSIER ▶ **massy**
MASSIF *n* **massifs**
MASSING ▶ **mass**
MASSIVE *adj, n* **massy**
MAST *n*
MASTABA *n* mud-brick superstructure above tombs in ancient Egypt
MASTED ▶ **mast**
MASTER *n, vb* **masters**
MASTERY *n*
MASTFUL ▶ **mast**
MASTIC *n* gum obtained from certain trees **mastich, mastics**
MASTIER ▶ **mast**
MASTIFF *n* large dog
MASTING ▶ **mast**
MASTIX *n* type of gum
MASTOID *n* projection of the bone behind the ear ▷ *adj* shaped like a nipple or breast
MASTS ▶ **mast**
MASTY ▶ **mast**
MASU *n* Japanese salmon
MASULA = **masoolah**
MASULAS ▶ **masula**
MASUS ▶ **masu**
MAT *n, vb, adj*
MATADOR *n*
MATAI *n* New Zealand tree, the wood of which is used for timber for building **matais**
MATATA = **fernbird**
MATATAS ▶ **matata**
MATATU *n* type of shared taxi used in Kenya **matatus**
MATCH *n, vb* **matched, matcher, matches**
MATCHET = **machete**
MATCHUP *n* sports match
MATE *n, vb* **mated**
MATELOT *n* sailor
MATER *n* mother: often used facetiously **maters**
MATES ▶ **mate**
MATEY *adj* friendly or intimate ▷ *n* friend or fellow: usually used in direct address **mateys**
MATH = **mathematics**
MATHS = **mathematics**
MATICO *n* Peruvian shrub **maticos**
MATIER ▶ **maty**
MATIES ▶ **maty**
MATIEST ▶ **maty**
MATILDA *n* bushman's swag
MATILY ▶ **maty**
MATIN *adj* of or relating to matins **matinal**
MATINEE *n*
MATING ▶ **mate**
MATINGS ▶ **mate**
MATINS *pl n*
MATIPO *n* New Zealand shrub **matipos**
MATJES = **maatjes**
MATLESS ▶ **mat**
MATLO = **matelot**
MATLOS ▶ **matlo**
MATLOW = **matelot**
MATLOWS ▶ **matlow**
MATOKE *n* (in Uganda) the flesh of bananas, boiled and mashed as a food **matokes, matooke**
MATRASS *n* long-necked glass flask
MATRES ▶ **mater**
MATRIC *n* matriculation

MATRICE = **matrix**
MATRICS ▸ **matric**
MATRIX *n*
MATRON *n* **matrons**
MATROSS *n* gunner's assistant
MATS ▸ **mat**
MATSAH = **matzo**
MATSAHS ▸ **matsah**
MATSURI *n* Japanese religious ceremony
MATT *adj* **matte**
MATTED ▸ **mat**
MATTER *n, vb* **matters**
MATTERY *adj* discharging pus
MATTES ▸ **matte**
MATTIE *n* young herring **matties**
MATTIFY *vb* make (the skin of the face) less oily or shiny using cosmetics
MATTIN = **matin**
MATTING ▸ **mat**
MATTINS = **matins**
MATTOCK *n* large pick with one of its blade ends flattened for loosening soil
MATTOID *n* person displaying eccentric behaviour and mental characteristics
MATTS ▸ **matt**
MATURE *adj, vb* **matured, maturer, matures**
MATWEED *n* grass found on moors
MATY = **matey**
MATZA = **matzo**
MATZAH = **matzo**
MATZAHS ▸ **matzah**
MATZAS ▸ **matza**
MATZO *n* large very thin biscuit of unleavened bread **matzoh**
MATZOHS ▸ **matzoh**
MATZOON *n* fermented milk product similar to yogurt
MATZOS ▸ **matzo**
MATZOT ▸ **matzo**
MATZOTH ▸ **matzoh**
MAUBIES ▸ **mauby**
MAUBY *n* Caribbean bittersweet drink
MAUD *n* shawl or rug of grey wool plaid
MAUDLIN *adj*
MAUDS ▸ **maud**
MAUGER = **maugre**
MAUGRE *prep* in spite of ▹ *vb* behave spitefully towards **maugred, maugres**
MAUL *vb, n* **mauled, mauler**
MAULERS *pl n* hands
MAULGRE = **maugre**
MAULING ▸ **maul**
MAULS ▸ **maul**
MAULVI *n* expert in Islamic law **maulvis**
MAUMET *n* false god **maumets**
MAUN *dialect word for* ▸ **must**
MAUND *n* unit of weight used in Asia ▹ *vb* beg **maunded**
MAUNDER *vb* talk or act aimlessly or idly
MAUNDS ▸ **maund**
MAUNDY *n* ceremonial washing of the feet of poor people
MAUNGY *adj* (esp of a child) sulky, bad-tempered, or peevish
MAUNNA *vb* Scots term meaning must not
MAURI *n* soul **mauris**
MAUT = **mahout**
MAUTHER *n* girl
MAUTS ▸ **maut**
MAUVAIS *adj* bad
MAUVE *adj, n*
MAUVEIN = **mauveine**
MAUVER ▸ **mauve**
MAUVES ▸ **mauve**
MAUVEST ▸ **mauve**
MAUVIN = **mauveine**
MAUVINE = **mauveine**
MAUVINS ▸ **mauvin**
MAVEN *n* expert or connoisseur **mavens**
MAVIE *n* type of thrush **mavies**
MAVIN = **maven**
MAVINS ▸ **mavin**
MAVIS *n* song thrush **mavises**
MAW *n* animal's mouth, throat, or stomach ▹ *vb* eat or bite **mawed**
MAWGER *adj* (of persons or animals) thin or lean
MAWING ▸ **maw**
MAWK *n* maggot **mawkier**
MAWKIN *n* slovenly woman **mawkins**
MAWKISH *adj*
MAWKS ▸ **mawk**
MAWKY ▸ **mawk**
MAWMET = **maumet**
MAWMETS ▸ **mawmet**
MAWN ▸ **maw**

MAWPUS = **mopus**
MAWR = **mauther**
MAWRS ▸ **mawr**
MAWS ▸ **maw**
MAWSEED *n* poppy seed
MAWTHER = **mauther**
MAX *vb* reach the full extent **maxed, maxes**

> **Max** is a short form of **maximum**, and can also be a verb giving **maxed, maxes** and **maxing**. Another of the key words using X, and it can be extended to **maxi**.

MAXI *adj* (of a garment) very long ▹ *n* type of large racing yacht
MAXILLA *n* upper jawbone of a vertebrate
MAXIM *n*
MAXIMA ▸ **maximum**
MAXIMAL *adj* maximum ▹ *n* maximum
MAXIMIN *n* highest of a set of minimum values
MAXIMS ▸ **maxim**
MAXIMUM *n, adj*
MAXIMUS *n* method rung on twelve bells
MAXING ▸ **max**
MAXIS ▸ **maxi**
MAXIXE *n* Brazilian dance in duple time **maxixes**
MAXWELL *n* cgs unit of magnetic flux
MAY *vb*
MAYA *n* illusion, esp the material world of the senses regarded as illusory **mayan, mayas**
MAYBE *adv, sentence substitute* **maybes**
MAYBIRD *n* American songbird
MAYBUSH *n* flowering shrub
MAYDAY *n* international radiotelephone distress signal **maydays**
MAYED ▸ **may**
MAYEST = **mayst**
MAYFLY *n* short-lived aquatic insect
MAYHAP *archaic word for* ▸ **perhaps**
MAYHEM *n* **mayhems**
MAYING ▸ **may**
MAYINGS ▸ **maying**
MAYO *n* mayonnaise
MAYOR *n* **mayoral, mayors**
MAYOS ▸ **mayo**
MAYPOLE *n* pole set up for dancing round on the first day of May to celebrate spring
MAYPOP *n* American wild flower **maypops**
MAYS ▸ **may**
MAYST *singular form of the present tense of* ▸ **may**
MAYSTER = **master**
MAYVIN = **maven**
MAYVINS ▸ **mayvin**
MAYWEED *n* widespread Eurasian weedy plant
MAZARD = **mazer**
MAZARDS ▸ **mazard**
MAZE *n* **mazed**
MAZEDLY *adv* in a bewildered way
MAZEFUL ▸ **maze**
MAZER *n* large hardwood drinking bowl **mazers**
MAZES ▸ **maze**
MAZEY *adj* dizzy
MAZHBI *n* low-caste Sikh **mazhbis**
MAZIER ▸ **mazy**
MAZIEST ▸ **mazy**
MAZILY ▸ **mazy**
MAZING ▸ **maze**
MAZOUT = **mazut**
MAZOUTS ▸ **mazout**
MAZUMA *n* money **mazumas**
MAZURKA *n* lively Polish dance
MAZUT *n* residue left after distillation of petrol **mazuts**
MAZY *adj* of or like a maze
MAZZARD = **mazard**
MBIRA *n* African musical instrument **mbiras**
ME *n, pron*
MEACOCK *n* timid person
MEAD *n* alcoholic drink made from honey
MEADOW *n* **meadows, meadowy**
MEADS ▸ **mead**
MEAGER = **meagre**
MEAGRE *adj, n* **meagrer, meagres**
MEAL *n, vb* **mealed**
MEALER *n* person eating but not lodging

at boarding house **mealers**
MEALIE *n*
MEALIER ▸ **mealy**
MEALIES *South African word for* ▸ **maize**
MEALING ▸ **meal**
MEALS ▸ **meal**
MEALY *adj* resembling meal
MEAN *vb, adj, n*
MEANDER *vb, n*
MEANE *vb* moan **meaned**
MEANER ▸ **mean**
MEANERS ▸ **mean**
MEANES ▸ **meane**
MEANEST ▸ **mean**
MEANIE *n* unkind or miserly person
MEANIES ▸ **meany**
MEANING *n* what something means
MEANLY ▸ **mean**
MEANS ▸ **mean**
MEANT ▸ **mean**
MEANY = **meanie**
MEARE = **mere**
MEARES ▸ **meare**
MEARING *adj* forming boundary
MEASE *vb* assuage **meased, meases, measing**
MEASLE *vb* infect with measles
MEASLED *adj* (of cattle, sheep, or pigs) infested with tapeworm larvae
MEASLES *n*
MEASLY *adj*
MEASURE *n, vb*
MEAT *n*
MEATAL ▸ **meatus**
MEATAXE *n* meat cleaver
MEATED *adj* fattened
MEATH = **mead**
MEATHE = **mead**
MEATHES ▸ **meathe**
MEATHS ▸ **meath**
MEATIER ▸ **meaty**
MEATILY ▸ **meaty**
MEATMAN *n* meat seller **meatmen**
MEATS ▸ **meat**
MEATUS *n* natural opening or channel
MEATY *adj* (tasting) of or like meat
MEAWES = **mews**
MEAZEL = **mesel**
MEAZELS ▸ **meazel**
MEBOS *n* South African dish of dried apricots **meboses**
MECCA *n* place that attracts many visitors **meccas**
MECK = **maik**
MECKS ▸ **meck**
MECONIC *adj* derived from poppies
MECONIN *n* substance found in opium
MED *n* doctor
MEDACCA *n* Japanese freshwater fish **medaka**
MEDAKAS ▸ **medaka**
MEDAL *n, vb* **medaled**
MEDALET *n* small medal
MEDALS ▸ **medal**
MEDDLE *vb* **meddled, meddler, meddles**
MEDEVAC *n* evacuation of casualties ▹ *vb* transport (a wounded or sick person) to hospital
MEDFLY *n* Mediterranean fruit fly
MEDIA *n*
MEDIACY *n* quality or state of being mediate
MEDIAD *adj* situated near the median line or plane of an organism
MEDIAE ▸ **medium**
MEDIAL *adj* of or in the middle ▹ *n* speech sound between being fortis and lenis **medials**
MEDIAN *n, adj* **medians**
MEDIANT *n* third degree of a major or minor scale
MEDIAS ▸ **medium**
MEDIATE *vb, adj*
MEDIC *n*
MEDICAL *adj, n*
MEDICK *n* type of small leguminous plant with yellow or purple flowers **medicks**
MEDICO *n* doctor or medical student **medicos**
MEDICS ▸ **medic**
MEDIGAP *n* private health insurance
MEDII ▸ **medius**
MEDINA *n* ancient quarter of North African city **medinas**
MEDIUM *adj, n*
MEDIUMS *pl n* medium-dated gilt-edged securities
MEDIUS *n* middle finger

MEDIVAC *variant spelling of* ▸ **medevac**
MEDLAR *n* apple-like fruit of a small tree **medlars**
MEDLE = **meddle**
MEDLED ▸ **medle**
MEDLES ▸ **medle**
MEDLEY *n, adj* **medleys**
MEDLING ▸ **medle**
MEDRESA > **madrasah**
MEDRESE = **madrasah**
MEDS ▸ **med**
MEDULLA *n* marrow, pith, or inner tissue
MEDUSA *n* jellyfish **medusae, medusal, medusan, medusas**
MEE *n* Malaysian noodle dish
MEED *n* recompense **meeds**
MEEK *adj*
MEEKEN *vb* make meek **meekens**
MEEKER ▸ **meek**
MEEKEST ▸ **meek**
MEEKLY ▸ **meek**
MEEMIE *n* hysterical person **meemies**
MEER = **mere**
MEERCAT = **meerkat**
MEERED ▸ **meer**
MEERING ▸ **meer**
MEERKAT *n* S African mongoose
MEERS ▸ **meer**
MEES ▸ **mee**
MEET *vb, n, adj* **meeter, meeters, meetest, meeting, meetly, meets**
MEFF *dialect word for* ▸ **tramp**
MEFFS ▸ **meff**
MEG *short for* > **megabyte**
MEGA *adj* extremely good, great, or successful
MEGABAR *n* unit of million bars
MEGABIT *n* one million bits
MEGAFOG *n* amplified fog signal
MEGAHIT *n* great success
MEGAPOD = **megapode**
MEGARA ▸ **megaron**
MEGARAD *n* unit of million rads
MEGARON *n* tripartite rectangular room, found in Bronze Age Greece and Asia Minor
MEGASS *another name for* ▸ **bagasse**
MEGASSE = **megass**
MEGATON *n*
MEGILLA = **megillah**
MEGILP *n* oil-painting medium of linseed oil mixed with mastic varnish or turpentine **megilph, megilps**
MEGOHM *n* one million ohms **megohms**
MEGRIM *n* caprice
MEGRIMS *n* fit of depression
MEGS ▸ **meg**
MEH *interj*
MEHNDI *n* (esp in India) the practice of painting designs on the hands, feet, etc using henna **mehndis**
MEIKLE *adj* Scots word meaning large
MEIN *Scots word for* ▸ **moan**
MEINED ▸ **mein**
MEINEY = **meiny**
MEINEYS ▸ **meiney**
MEINIE = **meiny**
MEINIES ▸ **meiny**
MEINING ▸ **mein**
MEINS ▸ **mein**
MEINT = **ming**
MEINY *n* retinue or household
MEIOSES ▸ **meiosis**
MEIOSIS *n* **meiotic**
MEISHI *n* business card in Japan **meishis**
MEISTER *n* person who excels at a particular activity
MEITH *n* landmark **meiths**
MEJLIS = **majlis**
MEKKA = **mecca**
MEKKAS ▸ **mekka**
MEL *n* pure form of honey
MELA *n* Asian cultural or religious fair or festival
MELAMED *n* Hebrew teacher
MELANGE *n* mixture
MELANIC *adj* relating to melanism or melanosis ▹ *n* darker form of creature
MELANIN *n* dark pigment found in the hair, skin, and eyes

MELANO *n* person with abnormally dark skin **melanos**
MELAS ▸ **mela**
MELBA *adj* relating to a type of dessert sauce or toast
MELD *vb* merge or blend ▹ *n* act of melding **melded, melder, melders, melding, melds**
MELEE *n* noisy confused fight or crowd **melees**
MELENA *n* excrement or vomit stained by blood **melenas**
MELIC *adj* (of poetry, esp ancient Greek lyric poems) intended to be sung ▹ *n* type of grass
MELICK *n* either of two pale green perennial grasses **melicks**
MELICS ▸ **melic**
MELIK = **malik**
MELIKS ▸ **melik**
MELILOT *n* plant with small white or yellow fragrant flowers
MELISMA *n* expressive vocal phrase or passage consisting of several notes sung to one syllable
MELL *vb* mix
MELLAY = **melee**
MELLAYS ▸ **mellay**
MELLED ▸ **mell**
MELLING ▸ **mell**
MELLITE *n* soft yellow mineral
MELLOW *adj, vb* **mellows, mellowy**
MELLS ▸ **mell**
MELODIA = **melodica**
MELODIC *adj*
MELODY *n*
MELOID *n* type of long-legged beetle **meloids**
MELON *n* **melons**
MELS ▸ **mel**
MELT *vb, n*
MELTAGE *n* process or result of melting or the amount melted
MELTED ▸ **melt**
MELTEMI *n* northerly wind in the northeast Mediterranean
MELTER ▸ **melt**
MELTERS ▸ **melt**
MELTIER ▸ **melty**
MELTING ▸ **melt**
MELTITH *n* meal
MELTON *n* heavy smooth woollen fabric with a short nap, used esp for overcoats **meltons**
MELTS ▸ **melt**
MELTY *adj* tending to melt
MEM *n* 13th letter in the Hebrew alphabet, transliterated as *m*
MEMBER *n, adj* **members**
MEMBRAL *adj* of limbs
MEME *n* idea or element of social behaviour
MEMENTO *n*
MEMES ▸ **meme**
MEMETIC *adj* of or relating to a meme
MEMO *n*
MEMOIR *n* biography or historical account based on personal knowledge
MEMOIRS *pl n*
MEMORY *n*
MEMOS ▸ **memo**
MEMS ▸ **mem**
MEN ▸ **man**
MENACE *n, vb* **menaced, menacer, menaces**
MENAD = **maenad**
MENADS ▸ **menad**
MENAGE *old form of* ▸ **manage**
MENAGED ▸ **menage**
MENAGES ▸ **menage**
MENAZON *n* type of insecticide
MEND *vb, n* **mended, mender, menders**
MENDIGO *n* Spanish beggar or vagrant
MENDING *n* something to be mended, esp clothes
MENDS ▸ **mend**
MENE *Scots form of* ▸ **moan**
MENED ▸ **mene**
MENEER *n* S African title of address **meneers**
MENES ▸ **mene**
MENFOLK *pl n* men collectively, esp the men of a particular family
MENG *vb* mix **menge, menged**
MENGES ▸ **menge**
MENGING ▸ **meng**
MENGS ▸ **meng**

MENHIR *n* single upright prehistoric stone **menhirs**
MENIAL *adj, n* **menials**
MENING ▶ **mene**
MENINX *n* one of three membranes that envelop the brain and spinal cord
MENISCI > **meniscus**
MENO *adv* musical instruction indicating 'less'
MENORAH *n*
MENSA *n* faint constellation in the S hemisphere
MENSAE *n* star of the mensa constellation
MENSAL *adj* monthly
MENSAS ▶ **mensa**
MENSCH *n* decent person **menschy**
MENSE *vb* grace **mensed**
MENSES *n* menstruation
MENSH *vb* mention **menshed**
MENSHEN *n* Chinese door god
MENSHES ▶ **mensh**
MENSING ▶ **mense**
MENSUAL = **mensal**
MENT = **ming**
MENTA ▶ **mentum**
MENTAL *adj*
MENTEE *n* person trained by mentor **mentees**
MENTHOL *n*
MENTION *vb, n*
MENTO *n* Jamaican song
MENTOR *n, vb* **mentors**
MENTOS ▶ **mento**
MENTUM *n* chin
MENU *n*
MENUDO *n* Mexican soup **menudos**
MENUS ▶ **menu**
MENYIE = **meinie**
MENYIES ▶ **menyie**
MEOU = **meow**
MEOUED ▶ **meou**
MEOUING ▶ **meou**
MEOUS ▶ **meou**
MEOW *vb* (of a cat) to make a characteristic crying sound ▷ *interj* imitation of this sound **meowed, meowing, meows**
MERANTI *n* wood from any of several Malaysian trees
MERC *n* mercenary
MERCAT *Scots word for* ▶ **market**
MERCATS ▶ **mercat**
MERCER *n* dealer in textile fabrics and fine cloth **mercers, mercery**
MERCES ▶ **merc**
MERCH *n* merchandise **merches**
MERCHET *n* (in feudal England) fine paid by tenant to his lord for allowing the marriage of his daughter
MERCIES ▶ **mercy**
MERCIFY *vb* show mercy to
MERCS ▶ **merc**
MERCURY *n*
MERCY *n*
MERDE *French word for* > **excrement**
MERDES ▶ **merde**
MERE *adj, n, vb*
MERED *adj* forming a boundary
MEREL = **meril**
MERELL = **meril**
MERELLS = **merils**
MERELS ▶ **merils**
MERELY *adv* only
MERER ▶ **mere**
MERES ▶ **mere**
MEREST ▶ **mere**
MERFOLK *n* mermaids and mermen
MERGE *vb* **merged**
MERGEE *n* business taken over by merger **mergees**
MERGER *n* combination of business firms into one **mergers**
MERGES ▶ **merge**
MERGING ▶ **merge**
MERI *n* Māori war club
MERIL *n* counter used in merils
MERILS *n* old board game
MERING ▶ **mere**
MERINGS ▶ **mering**
MERINO *n* **merinos**
MERIS ▶ **meri**
MERISES ▶ **merisis**
MERISIS *n* growth by division of cells
MERISM *n* duplication of biological parts **merisms**
MERIT *n, vb* **merited, merits**
MERK *n* old Scots coin

MERKIN *n* artificial hairpiece for the pudendum **merkins**
MERKS ▸ **merk**
MERL = **merle**
MERLE *adj* (of a dog, esp a collie) having a bluish-grey coat with speckles or streaks of black **merles**
MERLIN *n* small falcon
MERLING *n* whiting
MERLINS ▸ **merlin**
MERLON *n* solid upright section in a crenellated battlement **merlons**
MERLOT *n* type of black grape **merlots**
MERLS ▸ **merl**
MERMAID *n*
MERMAN *n* male counterpart of the mermaid **mermen**
MEROME = **merosome**
MEROMES ▸ **merome**
MERONYM *n* part of something used to refer to the whole
MEROPIA *n* partial blindness **meropic**
MERRIER ▸ **merry**
MERRIES ▸ **merry**
MERRILY ▸ **merry**
MERRY *adj, n*
MERSE *n* low level ground by a river or shore **merses**
MERSION *n* dipping in water
MES ▸ **me**
MESA *n* flat-topped hill found in arid regions
MESAIL *n* visor **mesails**
MESAL = **mesial**
MESALLY ▸ **mesal**
MESARCH *adj* (of a xylem strand) having the first-formed xylem surrounded by that formed later, as in fern stems
MESAS ▸ **mesa**
MESCAL *n* spineless globe-shaped cactus **mescals**
MESCLUM = **mesclun**
MESCLUN *n* type of green salad
MESE *n* middle string on lyre
MESEEMS *vb* it seems to me
MESEL *n* leper
MESELED *adj* afflicted by leprosy
MESELS ▸ **mesel**
MESES ▸ **mese**
MESETA *n* plateau in Spain **mesetas**
MESH *n, vb, adj* **meshed, meshes, meshier, meshing**
MESHUGA *adj* crazy
MESHY ▸ **mesh**
MESIAD *adj* relating to or situated at the middle or centre
MESIAL *another word for* ▸ **medial**
MESIAN = **mesial**
MESIC ▸ **meson**
MESNE *adj* (in law) intermediate or intervening **mesnes**
MESON *n* elementary atomic particle **mesonic, mesons**
MESQUIN *adj* mean
MESQUIT = **mesquite**
MESS *n, vb*
MESSAGE *n, vb*
MESSAN *Scots word for* ▸ **dog**
MESSANS ▸ **messan**
MESSED ▸ **mess**
MESSES ▸ **mess**
MESSIAH *n* exceptional or hoped for liberator **messias**
MESSIER ▸ **messy**
MESSILY ▸ **messy**
MESSING ▸ **mess**
MESSMAN *n* sailor working in ship's mess **messmen**
MESSY *adj* dirty, confused, or untidy
MESTEE = **mustee**
MESTEES ▸ **mestee**
MESTER *n* master: used as a term of address for a man who is the head of a house **mesters**
MESTESO *n* Spanish music genre
MESTINO *n* person of mixed race
MESTIZA ▸ **mestizo**
MESTIZO *n* person of mixed parentage
MESTO *adj* sad
MESTOM = **mestome**
MESTOME *n* conducting tissue associated with parenchyma
MESTOMS ▸ **mestom**
MET *n* meteorology
META *adj* in a self-parodying style

METAGE *n* official measuring of weight or contents **metages**
METAL *n, adj, vb* **metaled**
METALLY *adj* like metal
METALS ▶ **metal**
METAMER *n* any of two or more isomeric compounds exhibiting metamerism
METATAG *n* element of HTML code used by search engines to index pages
METATE *n* stone for grinding grain on **metates**
METAYER *n* farmer who pays rent in kind
METAZOA > **metazoan**
METCAST *n* weather forecast
METE *vb, n* **meted**
METEOR *n* **meteors**
METEPA *n* type of pesticide **metepas**
METER = **metre**
METERED ▶ **meter**
METERS ▶ **meter**
METES ▶ **mete**
METH *n* variety of amphetamine
METHANE *n*
METHINK = **methinks**
METHO *n* methylated spirits
METHOD *n* **methods**
METHOS ▶ **metho**
METHOXY *n* steroid drug
METHS *n*
METHYL *n* compound containing a saturated hydrocarbon group of atoms **methyls**
METIC *n* (in ancient Greece) alien having some rights of citizenship
METICAL *n* money unit in Mozambique
METICS ▶ **metic**
METIER *n* profession or trade **metiers**
METIF *n* person of mixed race **metifs**
METING ▶ **mete**
METIS *n* person of mixed parentage **metisse**
METOL *n* organic substance used as a photographic developer **metols**
METONYM *n* word used in a metonymy
METOPAE ▶ **metope**
METOPE *n* square space between two triglyphs in a Doric frieze **metopes**
METOPIC *adj* of or relating to the forehead
METOPON *n* painkilling drug
METRE *n, vb* **metred, metres**
METRIC *adj*
METRICS *n* art of using poetic metre
METRIFY *vb* render into poetic metre
METRING ▶ **metre**
METRIST *n* person skilled in the use of poetic metre
METRO *n* **metros**
METS ▶ **met**
METTLE *n*
METTLED *adj* spirited, courageous, or valiant
METTLES ▶ **mettle**
METUMP *n* band for carrying a load or burden **metumps**
MEU *another name for* ▶ **spignel**
MEUS ▶ **meu**
MEUSE *n* gap through which an animal passed ▷ *vb* go through this gap **meused, meuses, meusing**
MEVE = **move**
MEVED ▶ **meve**
MEVES ▶ **meve**
MEVING ▶ **meve**
MEVROU *n* S African title of address **mevrous**
MEW *n, vb* **mewed, mewing**
MEWL *vb* (esp of a baby) to cry weakly ▷ *n* weak or whimpering cry **mewled, mewler, mewlers, mewling, mewls**
MEWS = **meuse**
MEWSED ▶ **mews**
MEWSES ▶ **mews**
MEWSING ▶ **mews**
MEYNT ▶ **ming**
MEZAIL = **mesail**
MEZAILS ▶ **mezail**
MEZCAL *variant spelling of* ▶ **mescal**
MEZCALS ▶ **mezcal**
MEZE *n* type of hors d'oeuvre **mezes**
MEZQUIT = **mesquite**

> A **mezquit** is a kind of American tree, and makes a great bonus

to play. Remember also that it takes an E to form the variant spelling **mezquite**.

MEZUZA = **mezuzah**
MEZUZAH *n* piece of parchment inscribed with biblical passages
MEZUZAS ▸ **mezuza**
MEZUZOT ▸ **mezuzah**
MEZZ = **mezzanine**
MEZZE = **meze**
MEZZES ▸ **mezze**
MEZZO *adv* moderately **mezzos**
MGANGA *n* witch doctor **mgangas**
MHO *former name for* ▸ **siemens**
MHORR *n* African gazelle **mhorrs**
MHOS ▸ **mho**
MI *n* (in tonic sol-fa) the third degree of any major scale
MIAOU = **meow**
MIAOUED ▸ **miaou**

These 7-letter words using all of the vowels are not easy to see on your rack, but they come in useful so often that it's well worth paying them special attention.

MIAOUS ▸ **miaou**
MIAOW = **meow**
MIAOWED ▸ **miaow**
MIAOWS ▸ **miaow**
MIASM = **miasma**
MIASMA *n* **miasmal, miasmas, miasmic**
MIASMS ▸ **miasm**
MIAUL = **meow**
MIAULED ▸ **miaul**
MIAULS ▸ **miaul**
MIB *n* marble used in games **mibs**
MIBUNA *n* type of Japanese leafy vegetable **mibunas**
MIC *n* microphone
MICA *n* **micas**
MICATE *vb* add mica to **micated, micates**
MICE ▸ **mouse**
MICELL = **micelle**
MICELLA = **micelle**
MICELLE *n* charged aggregate of molecules of colloidal size in a solution
MICELLS ▸ **micell**
MICH = **mitch; miched, micher, michers, miches, miching**
MICHAEL *n as in* **take the michael** teasing
MICHE = **mich**
MICHT *n* Scots word for might **michts**
MICKERY *n* waterhole, esp in a dry riverbed
MICKEY *n* young bull ▹ *vb* drug person's drink **mickeys**
MICKIES ▸ **micky**
MICKLE *adj* large or abundant ▹ *adv* much ▹ *n* great amount **mickler, mickles**
MICKY = **mickey**
MICO *n* marmoset **micos**
MICRA ▸ **micron**
MICRIFY *vb* make very small
MICRO *n* small computer
MICROBE *n*
MICROHM *n* millionth of ohm
MICRON *n* **microns**
MICROS ▸ **micro**
MICS ▸ **mic**
MICTION *n* urination
MID *adj* intermediate, middle ▹ *n* middle ▹ *prep* amid
MIDAIR *n* some point above ground level, in the air **midairs**
MIDBAND *adj* using a range of frequencies between narrowband and broadband
MIDCAP *adj* (of investments) involving medium-sized amounts of capital
MIDCULT *n* middlebrow culture
MIDDAY *n* **middays**
MIDDEN *n* dunghill or rubbish heap **middens**
MIDDEST *adj* in middle
MIDDIE *n* glass or bottle containing 285ml of beer
MIDDIES ▸ **middy**
MIDDLE *adj, n, vb* **middled**
MIDDLER *n* pupil in middle years at school
MIDDLES ▸ **middle**
MIDDY *n* middle-sized glass of beer
MIDGE *n* **midges**
MIDGET *n, adj* **midgets**
MIDGIE *n* informal word for a small winged

biting insect such as the midge or sandfly
MIDGIER ▸ **midge**
MIDGIES ▸ **midgie**
MIDGUT *n* middle part of the digestive tract **midguts**
MIDGY ▸ **midge**
MIDI *adj* (of a skirt, coat, etc) reaching to below the knee or midcalf ▹ *n* skirt, coat, etc reaching to below the knee or midcalf
MIDIRON *n* golf club used for medium-length approach shots
MIDIS ▸ **midi**
MIDLAND *n* middle part of a country
MIDLEG *n* middle of leg **midlegs**
MIDLIFE *n* middle age
MIDLINE *n* line at middle of something
MIDLIST *n* books in publisher's range that sell reasonably well
MIDMOST *adv* in the middle or midst ▹ *n* the middle or midst
MIDNOON *n* noon
MIDRASH *n* homily on a Jewish scriptural passage
MIDRIB *n* main vein of a leaf **midribs**
MIDRIFF *n*
MIDS ▸ **mid**
MIDSHIP *adj* in, of, or relating to the middle of a vessel ▹ *n* middle of a vessel
MIDSIZE *adj* medium-sized
MIDSOLE *n* layer between the inner and the outer sole of a shoe
MIDST *See* ▸ **amid**
MIDSTS ▸ **midst**
MIDTERM *n* middle of a term in a school, university, etc
MIDTOWN *n* centre of a town
MIDWAY *adv, adj, n* **midways**
MIDWEEK *n* middle of the week
MIDWIFE *n, vb*
MIDWIVE *vb* act as midwife
MIDYEAR *n* middle of the year
MIELIE = **mealie**
MIELIES ▸ **mielie**
MIEN *n* person's bearing, demeanour, or appearance **miens**
MIEVE = **move**
MIEVED ▸ **mieve**
MIEVES ▸ **mieve**
MIEVING ▸ **mieve**
MIFF *vb* take offence or offend ▹ *n* petulant mood **miffed**
MIFFIER ▸ **miffy**
MIFFILY ▸ **miffy**
MIFFING ▸ **miff**
MIFFS ▸ **miff**
MIFFY *adj* easily upset **mifty**
MIG *n* marble used in games **migg**
MIGGLE *n* US word for playing marble **miggles**
MIGGS ▸ **migg**
MIGHT ▸ **may**
MIGHTS ▸ **may**
MIGHTST ▸ **may**
MIGHTY *adj, adv*
MIGNON *adj* small and pretty ▹ *n* tender boneless cut of meat **mignons**
MIGRANT *n* person or animal that moves from one place to another ▹ *adj* moving from one place to another
MIGRATE *vb*
MIGS ▸ **mig**
MIHA *n* young fern frond which has not yet opened **mihas**
MIHI *n* Māori ceremonial greeting ▹ *vb* greet **mihied, mihiing, mihis**
MIHRAB *n* niche in a mosque showing the direction of Mecca **mihrabs**
MIKADO *n* Japanese emperor **mikados**
MIKE *n* **miked, mikes, miking**
MIKRA ▸ **mikron**
MIKRON = **micron**
MIKRONS ▸ **mikron**
MIKVAH *n* pool used for ritual purification **mikvahs, mikveh**
MIKVEHS ▸ **mikveh**
MIKVOS ▸ **mikveh**
MIKVOT ▸ **mikveh** **mikvoth**
MIL *n* unit of length equal to one thousandth of an inch

MILADI = **milady**
MILADIS ▸ **miladi**
MILADY *n* (formerly) a continental title for an English gentlewoman
MILAGE = **mileage**
MILAGES ▸ **milage**
MILCH *adj* (of a cow) giving milk
MILCHIG = **milchik**
MILCHIK *adj* containing or used in the preparation of milk products
MILD *adj, n, vb* **milded**
MILDEN *vb* make or become mild or milder **mildens**
MILDER ▸ **mild**
MILDEST ▸ **mild**
MILDEW = **mould**
MILDEWS ▸ **mildew**
MILDEWY ▸ **mildew**
MILDING ▸ **mild**
MILDLY ▸ **mild**
MILDS ▸ **mild**
MILE *n*
MILEAGE *n*
MILER *n* athlete, horse, etc, that specializes in races of one mile **milers**
MILES ▸ **mile**
MILFOIL = **yarrow**
MILIA ▸ **milium**
MILIARY *adj* resembling or relating to millet seeds
MILIEU *n* **milieus, milieux**
MILITAR = **military**
MILITIA *n*
MILIUM *n* pimple
MILK *n, vb* **milked**
MILKEN *adj* of or like milk
MILKER *n* cow, goat, etc, that yields milk **milkers**
MILKIER ▸ **milky**
MILKILY ▸ **milky**
MILKING ▸ **milk**
MILKMAN *n* man who delivers milk to people's houses **milkmen, milko**
MILKOS ▸ **milko**
MILKS ▸ **milk**
MILKSOP *n* feeble man
MILKY *adj*
MILL *n, vb*
MILLAGE *adj* American tax rate calculated in thousandths per dollar
MILLDAM *n* dam built to raise the water level to turn a millwheel
MILLE *French word for* > **thousand**
MILLED *adj* crushed or ground in a mill
MILLER *n* **millers**
MILLES ▸ **mille**
MILLET *n* **millets**
MILLIER *n* metric weight of million grams
MILLIME = **millieme**
MILLINE *n* measurement of advertising space
MILLING *n* act or process of grinding, cutting, pressing, or crushing in a mill
MILLION *n*
MILLRUN = **millrace**
MILLS ▸ **mill**
MILNEB *n* type of pesticide **milnebs**
MILO *n* variety of sorghum with heads of yellow or pinkish seeds
MILOR = **milord**
MILORD *n* (formerly) a continental title used for an English gentleman **milords**
MILORS ▸ **milor**
MILOS ▸ **milo**
MILPA *n* form of subsistence agriculture in Mexico **milpas**
MILREIS *n* former monetary unit of Portugal and Brazil
MILS ▸ **mil**
MILSEY *n* milk strainer **milseys**
MILT *n* sperm of fish ▹ *vb* fertilize (the roe of a female fish) with milt, esp artificially **milted**
MILTER *n* male fish that is mature and ready to breed **milters**
MILTIER ▸ **milty**
MILTING ▸ **milt**
MILTS ▸ **milt**
MILTY *adj* full of milt
MILTZ = **milt**
MILTZES ▸ **miltz**
MILVINE *adj* of kites and related birds
MIM *adj* prim, modest, or demure
MIMBAR *n* pulpit in mosque **mimbars**
MIME *n, vb* **mimed**
MIMEO *vb* mimeograph **mimeoed, mimeos**

MIMER ▸ **mime**
MIMERS ▸ **mime**
MIMES ▸ **mime**
MIMESES ▸ **mimesis**
MIMESIS *n* imitative representation of nature or human behaviour
MIMETIC *adj* imitating or representing something
MIMIC *vb, n, adj* **mimical**
MIMICRY *n* act or art of copying or imitating closely
MIMICS ▸ **mimic**
MIMING ▸ **mime**
MIMMER ▸ **mim**
MIMMEST ▸ **mim**
MIMMICK = **minnick**
MIMOSA *n* shrub with fluffy yellow flowers and sensitive leaves **mimosae, mimosas**
MIMSEY = **mimsy**
MIMSIER ▸ **mimsy**
MIMSY *adj* prim, underwhelming, and ineffectual
MIMULUS *n* plants cultivated for their yellow or red flowers
MINA *n* ancient unit of weight and money, used in Asia Minor
MINABLE ▸ **mine**
MINAE ▸ **mina**
MINAR *n* tower
MINARET *n*
MINARS ▸ **minar**
MINAS ▸ **mina**
MINBAR = **mimbar**
MINBARS ▸ **minbar**
MINCE *vb, n* **minced**
MINCER *n* **mincers**
MINCES ▸ **mince**
MINCEUR *adj* (of food) low-fat
MINCIER ▸ **mincy**
MINCING *adj* affected in manner
MINCY *adj* effeminate
MIND *n, vb*
MINDED *adj* having an inclination as specified
MINDER *n* aide or bodyguard **minders**
MINDFUL *adj*
MINDING ▸ **mind**
MINDS ▸ **mind**
MINDSET *n* ideas and attitudes with which a person approaches a situation
MINE *pron, n, vb* **mined**
MINEOLA = **minneola**
MINER *n* person who works in a mine
MINERAL *n, adj*
MINERS ▸ **miner**
MINES ▸ **mine**
MINETTE *n* type of rock
MINEVER = **miniver**
MING *vb* mix **minged**
MINGIER ▸ **mingy**
MINGING *adj* unattractive or unpleasant
MINGLE *vb* **mingled, mingler, mingles**
MINGS ▸ **ming**
MINGY *adj* miserly
MINI = **minidress**
MINIATE *vb* paint with minium
MINIBAR *n* selection of drinks and confectionery provided in a hotel room
MINIBUS *n*
MINICAB *n* ordinary car used as a taxi
MINICAM *n* portable television camera
MINICAR *n* small car
MINICOM *n* device allowing typed telephone messages to be sent and received
MINIER ▸ **miny**
MINIEST ▸ **miny**
MINIFY *vb* minimize or lessen the size or importance of (something)
MINIKIN *n* small, dainty, or affected person or thing ▹ *adj* dainty, prim, or affected
MINILAB *n* equipment for processing photographic film
MINIM *n, adj*
MINIMA ▸ **minimum**
MINIMAL *adj, n*
MINIMAX *n* lowest of a set of maximum values ▹ *vb* make maximum as low as possible
MINIMS ▸ **minim**
MINIMUM *n, adj*
MINIMUS *adj* youngest: used after the surname of a schoolboy with elder brothers at the same school
MINING *n* act, process, or industry of extracting coal or ores from the earth **minings**

MINION *n, adj* **minions**
MINIS ▸ **mini**
MINISH *vb* diminish
MINISKI *n* short ski
MINIUM *n* bright red poisonous insoluble oxide of lead **miniums**
MINIVAN *n* small van, esp one with seats in the back for carrying passengers
MINIVER *n* white fur, used in ceremonial costumes
MINIVET *n* brightly coloured tropical Asian cuckoo shrike
MINK *n*
MINKE *n as in* **minke whale** type of small whalebone whale or rorqual **minkes**
MINKS ▸ **mink**
MINNICK *vb* behave in fussy way
MINNIE *n* mother **minnies**
MINNOCK = **minnick**
MINNOW *n* **minnows**
MINNY = **minnie**
MINO = **mynah**
MINOR *adj, n, vb*
MINORCA *n* breed of light domestic fowl
MINORED ▸ **minor**
MINORS ▸ **minor**
MINOS ▸ **mino**
MINSTER *n* cathedral or large church
MINT *n, vb*
MINTAGE *n* process of minting
MINTED, minter, minters, mintier, minting, mints, minty ▸ **mint**
MINUEND *n* number from which another number is to be subtracted
MINUET *n* **minuets**
MINUS *adj, n, prep* **minuses**
MINUTE *n, vb, adj* **minuted, minuter**
MINUTES *pl n* official record of the proceedings of a meeting or conference
MINUTIA *singular noun of* > **minutiae**
MINX *n* bold or flirtatious girl **minxes, minxish**
MINY *adj* of or like mines
MINYAN *n* number of persons required by Jewish law to be present for a religious service **minyans**
MIOCENE *adj* of, denoting, or formed in the fourth epoch of the Tertiary period
MIOMBO *n* (in E Africa) a dry wooded area with sparse deciduous growth **miombos**
MIOSES ▸ **miosis**
MIOSIS *n* excessive contraction of the pupil of the eye, as in response to drugs **miotic, miotics**
MIPS *n* unit used to express the speed of a computer's central processing unit
MIR *n* peasant commune in prerevolutionary Russia
MIRABLE *adj* wonderful
MIRACLE *n*
MIRADOR *n* window, balcony, or turret
MIRAGE *n* **mirages**
MIRBANE *n* substance used in perfumes
MIRCHI *Indian English word for* ▸ **hot**
MIRE *n, vb* **mired, mires**
MIREX *n* type of insecticide **mirexes**
MIRI ▸ **mir**
MIRIER ▸ **mire**
MIRIEST ▸ **mire**
MIRIFIC *adj* achieving wonderful things
MIRIN *n* Japanese rice wine
MIRING ▸ **mire**
MIRINS ▸ **mirin**
MIRITI *n* South American palm **miritis**
MIRK = **murk; mirker, mirkest, mirkier, mirkily, mirks, mirky**
MIRLIER ▸ **mirly**
MIRLY = **marly**
MIRO *n* tall New Zealand tree **miros**
MIRROR *n, vb* **mirrors**
MIRS ▸ **mir**
MIRTH *n* **mirths**
MIRV *n* missile that has several warheads, each one being directed to different enemy targets ▹ *vb* arm with

mirvs **mirved, mirving, mirvs**
MIRY ▶ mire
MIRZA *n* title of respect placed before the surname of a distinguished man **mirzas**
MIS ▶ mi
MISACT *vb* act wrongly **misacts**
MISADD *vb* add badly **misadds**
MISAIM *vb* aim badly **misaims**
MISALLY *vb* form unsuitable alliance
MISATE ▶ miseat
MISAVER *vb* claim wrongly
MISBIAS *vb* prejudice wrongly
MISBILL *vb* present inaccurate bill
MISBIND *vb* bind wrongly
MISBORN *adj* abortive
MISCALL *vb* call by the wrong name
MISCAST *vb* cast (a role or actor) inappropriately
MISCH *adj as in* **misch metal** alloy of cerium and other rare earth metals
MISCITE *vb* cite wrongly
MISCODE *vb* code wrongly
MISCOIN *vb* coin wrongly
MISCOOK *vb* cook badly
MISCOPY *vb* copy badly
MISCUE *n* faulty stroke in snooker, etc ▷ *vb* make a miscue **miscued, miscues**
MISCUT *n* cut wrongly **miscuts**
MISDATE *vb* date (a letter, event, etc) wrongly
MISDEAL *vb* deal out cards incorrectly ▷ *n* faulty deal
MISDEED *n*
MISDEEM *vb* form bad opinion of
MISDIAL *vb* dial telephone number incorrectly
MISDID ▶ misdo
MISDIET *n* wrong diet
MISDO *vb* do badly or wrongly **misdoer, misdoes**
MISDONE *adj* done badly
MISDRAW *vb* draw poorly **misdrew**
MISE *n* issue in the obsolete writ of right
MISEASE *n* unease
MISEAT *vb* eat unhealthy food **miseats**
MISEDIT *vb* edit badly
MISER *n*
MISERE *n* call in solo whist and other card games declaring a hand that will win no tricks **miseres**
MISERLY *adj* of or resembling a miser
MISERS ▶ miser
MISERY *n*
MISES ▶ mise
MISFALL *vb* happen as piece of bad luck
MISFARE *vb* get on badly
MISFED ▶ misfeed
MISFEED *vb* feed wrongly
MISFELL ▶ misfall
MISFILE *vb* file (papers, records, etc) wrongly
MISFIRE *vb, n*
MISFIT *n, vb* **misfits**
MISFORM *vb* form badly
MISGAVE ▶ misgive
MISGIVE *vb* make or be apprehensive or suspicious
MISGO *vb* go wrong way **misgoes, misgone**
MISGREW ▶ misgrow
MISGROW *vb* grow in unsuitable way
MISHAP *n, vb* **mishaps**
MISHAPT = **misshapen**
MISHEAR *vb* hear (what someone says) wrongly
MISHIT *n* faulty shot, kick, or stroke ▷ *vb* hit or kick a ball with a faulty stroke **mishits**
MISHMEE *n* root of Asian plant
MISHMI *n* evergreen perennial plant **mishmis**
MISJOIN *vb* join badly
MISKAL *n* unit of weight in Iran **miskals**
MISKEEP *vb* keep wrongly
MISKEN *vb* be unaware of **miskens, miskent**

MISKEPT ▸ **miskeep**
MISKEY *vb* key wrongly **miskeys**
MISKICK *vb* fail to kick properly
MISKNEW *vb* ▸ **misknow**
MISKNOW *vb* have wrong idea about
MISLAID ▸ **mislay**
MISLAIN ▸ **mislay**
MISLAY *vb* **mislays**
MISLEAD *vb* **misled**
MISLIE *vb* lie wrongly **mislies**
MISLIKE *vb* dislike ▹ *n* dislike or aversion
MISLIT > **mislight**
MISLIVE *vb* live wickedly
MISLUCK *vb* have bad luck
MISMADE ▸ **mismake**
MISMAKE *vb* make badly
MISMARK *vb* mark wrongly
MISMATE *vb* mate wrongly
MISMEET *vb* fail to meet **mismet**
MISMOVE *vb* move badly
MISNAME *vb* name badly
MISO *n* thick brown salty paste made from soya beans **misos**
MISPAGE *vb* page wrongly
MISPART *vb* part wrongly
MISPEN *vb* write wrongly **mispens**
MISPLAN *vb* plan badly or wrongly
MISPLAY *vb* play badly or wrongly in games or sports ▹ *n* wrong or unskilful play
MISPLED > **misplead**
MISRATE *vb* rate wrongly
MISREAD *vb* misinterpret (a situation etc)
MISRELY *vb* rely wrongly
MISRULE *vb* govern inefficiently or unjustly ▹ *n* inefficient or unjust government
MISS *vb*, *n*
MISSA *n* Roman Catholic mass **missae**
MISSAID ▸ **missay**
MISSAL *n* book containing the prayers and rites of the Mass **missals**
MISSAW ▸ **missee**
MISSAY *vb* say wrongly **missays**
MISSEAT *vb* seat wrongly
MISSED ▸ **miss**
MISSEE *vb* see wrongly
MISSEEM *vb* be unsuitable for
MISSEEN ▸ **missee**
MISSEES ▸ **missee**
MISSEL *adj as in* **missel thrush** large European thrush
MISSELL *vb* sell (a product, esp a financial one) misleadingly
MISSELS ▸ **missel**
MISSEND *vb* send wrongly **missent**
MISSES ▸ **miss**
MISSET *vb* set wrongly **missets**
MISSHOD *adj* badly shod
MISSIER ▸ **missy**
MISSIES ▸ **missy**
MISSILE *n*
MISSING *adj*
MISSION *n*, *vb*
MISSIS = **missus**
MISSISH *adj* like a schoolgirl
MISSIVE *n*, *adj*
MISSOLD ▸ **missell**
MISSORT *vb* sort wrongly
MISSOUT *n* someone who has been overlooked
MISSTEP *n* false step ▹ *vb* take a false step
MISSTOP *vb* stop wrongly
MISSUIT *vb* be unsuitable for
MISSUS *n* one's wife or the wife of the person addressed or referred to
MISSY *n* affectionate or disparaging form of address to a girl ▹ *adj* missish
MIST *n*, *vb*
MISTAKE *n*, *vb*
MISTAL *n* cow shed **mistals**
MISTBOW = **fogbow**
MISTED ▸ **mist**
MISTELL *vb* tell wrongly
MISTEND *vb* tend wrongly

MISTER *n, vb*
MISTERM *vb* term badly
MISTERS ▸ **mister**
MISTERY = **mystery**
MISTEUK *Scots variant of* ▸ **mistook**
MISTFUL ▸ **mist**
MISTICO *n* small Mediterranean sailing ship
MISTIER ▸ **misty**
MISTILY ▸ **misty**
MISTIME *vb* do (something) at the wrong time
MISTING *n* application of a fake suntan by spray
MISTLE = **mizzle**
MISTLED ▸ **mistle**
MISTLES ▸ **mistle**
MISTOLD ▸ **mistell**
MISTOOK *past tense of* ▸ **mistake**
MISTRAL *n* strong dry northerly wind of S France
MISTS ▸ **mist**
MISTUNE *vb* fail to tune properly
MISTY *adj*
MISTYPE *vb* type badly
MISUSE *n, vb* **misused**
MISUSER *n* abuse of some right, privilege, office, etc
MISUSES ▸ **misuse**
MISUST ▸ **misuse**
MISWEEN *vb* assess wrongly
MISWEND *vb* become lost **miswent**
MISWORD *vb* word badly
MISWRIT > **miswrite**
MISYOKE *vb* join wrongly
MITCH *vb* play truant from school **mitched, mitches**
MITE *n*
MITER = **mitre**
MITERED ▸ **miter**
MITERER ▸ **miter**
MITERS ▸ **miter**
MITES ▸ **mite**
MITHER *vb* fuss over or moan about something **mithers**
MITIER ▸ **mity**
MITIEST ▸ **mity**
MITIS *n* malleable iron **mitises**
MITOGEN *n* any agent that induces mitosis
MITOSES ▸ **mitosis**
MITOSIS *n* **mitotic**
MITRAL *adj* of or like a mitre
MITRE *n, vb* **mitred, mitres, mitring**
MITSVAH = **mitzvah**
MITT = **mitten**
MITTEN *n* **mittens**
MITTS ▸ **mitt**
MITUMBA *n* used clothes imported for sale in African countries
MITY *adj* having mites
MITZVAH *n* commandment or precept, esp one found in the Bible
MIURUS *n* type of rhythm in poetry
MIX *vb, n* **mixable**
MIXDOWN *n* (in sound recording) the transfer of a multitrack master mix to two-track stereo tape
MIXED *adj* **mixedly**
MIXEN *n* dunghill **mixens**
MIXER *n* **mixers**
MIXES ▸ **mix**
MIXIBLE ▸ **mix**
MIXIER ▸ **mix**
MIXIEST ▸ **mix**
MIXING ▸ **mix**
MIXT ▸ **mix**
MIXTE *adj* of or denoting a type of bicycle frame in which angled twin lateral tubes run back to the rear axle
MIXTION *n* amber-based mixture used in making gold leaf
MIXTURE *n*
MIXUP *n* something that is mixed up **mixups**
MIXY *adj* mixed
MIZ *shortened form of* ▸ **misery**

> **Miz** is an informal short form of **misery**, very useful as a Z word. But you'll need a blank tile for the second Z if you want to form the plural **mizzes**.

MIZEN = **mizzen**
MIZENS ▸ **mizen**
MIZMAZE *n* maze
MIZUNA *n* Japanese variety of lettuce **mizunas**

MIZZ = **miz**
MIZZEN *n* sail set on a mizzenmast ▷ *adj* of or relating to any kind of gear used with a mizzenmast **mizzens**
MIZZES ▶ **miz**
MIZZLE *vb* decamp **mizzled, mizzles, mizzly**
MIZZY *adj as in* **mizzy maze** dialect expression meaning state of confusion
MM *interj*
MNA = **mina**
MNAS ▶ **mna**
MNEME *n* ability to retain memory **mnemes, mnemic**
MNEMON *n* unit of memory **mnemons**
MO *n* moment
MOA *n*
MOAI *n* any of the gigantic carved stone figures found on Easter Island (Rapa Nui)
MOAN *n, vb* **moaned, moaner, moaners, moanful, moaning, moans**
MOAS ▶ **moa**
MOAT *n, vb* **moated, moating, moats**
MOB *n, vb* **mobbed, mobber, mobbers**
MOBBIE = **mobby**
MOBBIES ▶ **mobby**
MOBBING ▶ **mob**
MOBBISH ▶ **mob**
MOBBISM *n* behaviour as mob
MOBBLE = **moble**
MOBBLED ▶ **mobble**
MOBBLES ▶ **mobble**
MOBBY *n* West Indian drink
MOBCAP *n* woman's 18th-century cotton cap **mobcaps**
MOBCAST *vb*
MOBE *n* mobile phone **mobes**
MOBEY ▶ **moby**
MOBEYS ▶ **mobey**
MOBIE *n* mobile phone
MOBIES ▶ **moby**
MOBILE *adj, n* **mobiles**
MOBLE *vb* muffle **mobled, mobles, mobling**
MOBLOG *n* blog recorded in the form of mobile phone calls, text messages, and photographs **moblogs**
MOBS ▶ **mob**
MOBSMAN *n* person in mob **mobsmen**
MOBSTER *n* member of a criminal organization
MOBY *n* mobile phone
MOC *shortening of* > **moccasin**
MOCCIES *pl n* informal Australian word for moccasins
MOCH *n* spell of humid weather
MOCHA *n* kind of strong dark coffee **mochas**
MOCHELL = **much**
MOCHIE *adj* damp or humid **mochier**
MOCHILA *n* South American shoulder bag
MOCHS ▶ **moch**
MOCHY = **mochie**
MOCK *vb, adj, n*
MOCKADO *n* imitation velvet
MOCKAGE = **mockery**
MOCKED ▶ **mock**
MOCKER *vb* dress up **mockers**
MOCKERY *n*
MOCKING ▶ **mock**
MOCKNEY *n* person who affects a cockney accent ▷ *adj* denoting an affected cockney accent or a person who has one
MOCKS ▶ **mock**
MOCKUP *n* working full-scale model of a machine, apparatus, etc, for testing, research, etc **mockups**
MOCOCK *n* Native American birchbark container **mococks**
MOCS ▶ **moc**
MOCUCK = **mocock**
MOCUCKS ▶ **mocuck**
MOD *n* member of a group of fashionable young people, orig. in the 1960s ▷ *vb* modify (a piece of software or hardware)
MODAL *adj* of or relating to mode or manner ▷ *n* modal word **modally, modals**
MODDED ▶ **mod** *vb*

MODDER *n* person who modifies a piece of hardware or software **modders**
MODDING *n*
MODE *n*
MODEL *n, adj, vb* **modeled, modeler**
MODELLI ▶ **modello**
MODELLO *n* artist's preliminary sketch or model
MODELS ▶ **model**
MODEM *n, vb* **modemed, modems**
MODENA *n* popular variety of domestic fancy pigeon **modenas**
MODER *n* intermediate layer in humus
MODERN *adj, n*
MODERNE *n* style of architecture and design of the late 1920s and 1930s ▷ *adj* of or relating to this style of architecture and design
MODERNS ▶ **modern**
MODERS ▶ **moder**
MODES ▶ **mode**
MODEST *adj*
MODESTY *n* quality or condition of being modest
MODGE *vb* do shoddily **modged, modges, modging**
MODI ▶ **modus**
MODICA ▶ **modicum**
MODICUM *n*
MODIFY *vb*
MODII ▶ **modius**
MODIOLI > **modiolus**
MODISH *adj* in fashion
MODIST *n* follower of fashion
MODISTE *n* fashionable dressmaker or milliner
MODISTS ▶ **modist**
MODIUS *n* ancient Roman quantity measure
MODS ▶ **mod**
MODULAR *adj* of, consisting of, or resembling a module or modulus ▷ *n* thing comprised of modules
MODULE *n* **modules**
MODULI ▶ **modulus**
MODULO *adv* with reference to modulus
MODULUS *n* coefficient expressing a specified property
MODUS *n* way of doing something
MOE *adv, n*
MOELLON *n* rubble
MOER *n* in South Africa, slang word for the womb ▷ *vb* in South Africa, attack (someone or something) violently **moered, moering, moers**
MOES ▶ **moe**
MOFETTE *n* opening in a region of nearly extinct volcanic activity, through which gases pass
MOFFIE *n* homosexual ▷ *adj* homosexual **moffies**
MOG *vb* go away
MOGGAN *n* stocking without foot **moggans**
MOGGED ▶ **mog**
MOGGIE = **moggy**
MOGGIES ▶ **moggy**
MOGGING ▶ **mog**
MOGGY *n* cat
MOGHUL = **mogul**
MOGHULS ▶ **moghul**
MOGS ▶ **mog**
MOGUL *n* important or powerful person
MOGULED *adj* having moguls
MOGULS ▶ **mogul**
MOHAIR *n* **mohairs**
MOHALIM = **mohelim**
MOHAWK *n* half turn from either edge of either skate to the corresponding edge of the other skate **mohawks**
MOHEL *n* man qualified to conduct circumcisions **mohelim, mohels**
MOHICAN *n* punk hairstyle
MOHR = **mhorr**
MOHRS ▶ **mohr**
MOHUA *n* small New Zealand bird **mohuas**
MOHUR *n* former Indian gold coin worth 15 rupees **mohurs**
MOI ▶ **me**
MOIDER = **moither**
MOIDERS ▶ **moider**
MOIDORE *n* former Portuguese gold coin
MOIETY *n* half
MOIL *vb* moisten or soil or become moist,

soiled, etc ▷ *n* toil **moiled, moiler, moilers, moiling, moils**

MOINEAU *n* small fortification

> Meaning part of a fortification, this is another of those very useful 7-letter vowel dumps.

MOIRA *n* fate **moirai**

MOIRE *adj* having a watered or wavelike pattern ▷ *n* any fabric that has such a pattern **moires**

MOISER *n* informer **moisers**

MOIST *adj*, *vb* **moisted**

MOISTEN *vb*

MOISTER ▶ **moist**

MOISTLY ▶ **moist**

MOISTS ▶ **moist**

MOIT = **mote**

MOITHER *vb* bother or bewilder

MOITS ▶ **moit**

MOJARRA *n* tropical American sea fish

MOJITO *n* rum-based cocktail **mojitos**

MOJO *n* charm or magic spell **mojoes, mojos**

MOKE *n* donkey **mokes**

MOKI *n* edible sea fish of New Zealand

MOKIHI *n* Māori raft **mokihis**

MOKIS ▶ **moki**

MOKO *n* Māori tattoo or tattoo pattern

MOKORO *n* (in Botswana) the traditional dugout canoe of the people of the Okavango Delta **mokoros**

MOKOS ▶ **moko**

MOKSHA *n* freedom from the endless cycle of transmigration into a state of bliss **mokshas**

MOL *n*

MOLA *another name for* ▶ **sunfish**

MOLAL *adj* of or consisting of a solution containing one mole of solute per thousand grams of solvent

MOLAR *n*, *adj* **molars**

MOLAS ▶ **mola**

MOLASSE *n* soft sediment produced by the erosion of mountain ranges after the final phase of mountain building

MOLD = **mould**

MOLDED ▶ **mold**

MOLDER = **moulder**

MOLDERS ▶ **molder**

MOLDIER ▶ **moldy**

MOLDING = **moulding**

MOLDS ▶ **mold**

MOLDY = **mouldy**

MOLE *n* **moles**

MOLEST *vb* **molests**

MOLIES ▶ **moly**

MOLIMEN *n* effort needed to perform bodily function

MOLINE *adj* (of a cross) having arms of equal length, forked and curved back at the ends ▷ *n* moline cross **molines**

MOLINET *n* stick for whipping chocolate

MOLL *n* gangster's female accomplice

MOLLA = **mollah**

MOLLAH = **mullah**

MOLLAHS ▶ **mollah**

MOLLAS ▶ **molla**

MOLLIE = **molly**

MOLLIES ▶ **molly**

MOLLIFY *vb*

MOLLS ▶ **moll**

MOLLUSC *n* **mollusk**

MOLLY *n* American freshwater fish

MOLOCH *n* spiny Australian desert-living lizard **molochs**

MOLOSSI > **molossus**

MOLS ▶ **mol**

MOLT = **moult**

MOLTED ▶ **molt**

MOLTEN ▶ **melt**

MOLTER ▶ **molt**

MOLTERS ▶ **molt**

MOLTING ▶ **molt**

MOLTO *adv* very

MOLTS ▶ **molt**

MOLY *n* mythical magic herb

MOM = **mother**

MOME *n* fool

MOMENT *n*

MOMENTA > **momentum**

MOMENTO = **memento**

MOMENTS ▶ **moment**

MOMES ▶ **mome**

MOMI = **mom**

MOMISM *n* excessive domination of a child

by his or her mother **momisms**
MOMMA = **mamma**
MOMMAS ▸ **momma**
MOMMET = **mammet**
MOMMETS ▸ **mommet**
MOMMIES ▸ **mommy**
MOMMY = **mom**
MOMS ▸ **mom**
MOMSER = **momzer**
MOMSERS ▸ **momser**
MOMUS *n* person who ridicules **momuses**
MOMZER = **mamzer**
MOMZERS ▸ **momzer**
MON *dialect variant of* ▸ **man**
MONA *n* W African guenon monkey
MONACID = **monoacid**
MONACT *adj* (of sponge) with single-spiked structures in skeleton
MONAD *n* any fundamental singular metaphysical entity **monadal**
MONADES ▸ **monas**
MONADIC *adj* being or relating to a monad
MONADS ▸ **monad**
MONAL *n* S Asian pheasant **monals**
MONARCH *n*
MONARDA *n* mintlike N American plant
MONAS = **monad**
MONASES ▸ **monas**
MONAUL = **monal**
MONAULS ▸ **monaul**
MONAXON *n* type of sponge
MONDAIN *n* man who moves in fashionable society ▹ *adj* characteristic of fashionable society
MONDE *n* French word meaning world or society **mondes**
MONDIAL *adj* of or involving the whole world
MONDO *n* Buddhist questioning technique **mondos**
MONEME *less common word for* > **morpheme**
MONEMES ▸ **moneme**
MONER *n* hypothetical simple organism **monera**
MONERAN *n* type of bacterium
MONERON = **moner**
MONETH = **month**
MONETHS ▸ **moneth**
MONEY *n*
MONEYED *adj*
MONEYER *n* person who coins money
MONEYS ▸ **money**
MONGED *adj* under the influence of drugs
MONGER *n* trader or dealer ▹ *vb* deal in **mongers, mongery**
MONGO = **mungo**
MONGOE = **mongo**
MONGOES ▸ **mongoe**
MONGOS ▸ **mongo**
MONGREL *n, adj*
MONGST *short for* ▸ **amongst**
MONIAL *n* mullion **monials**
MONIE *Scots word for* ▸ **many**
MONIED = **moneyed**
MONIES ▸ **money**
MONIKER *n* person's name or nickname
MONILIA *n* type of fungus
MONISH = **admonish**
MONISM *n* doctrine that reality consists of only one basic substance or element **monisms, monist, monists**
MONITOR *n, vb*
MONK *n*
MONKEY *n, vb* **monkeys**
MONKISH *adj* of, relating to, or resembling a monk or monks
MONKS ▸ **monk**
MONO *n*
MONOAO *n* New Zealand plant with rigid leaves **monoaos**
MONOCLE *n*
MONOCOT *n* type of flowering plant with a single embryonic seed leaf
MONODIC ▸ **monody**
MONODY *n* (in Greek tragedy) an ode sung by a single actor
MONOECY = **monoecism**
MONOFIL *n* synthetic thread or yarn composed of a single strand rather than twisted fibres
MONOLOG = **monologue**

MONOMER *n* compound whose molecules can join together to form a polymer
MONONYM *n* person who is famous enough to be known only by one name
MONOPOD = **monopode**
MONOS ▶ **mono**
MONOSES ▶ **monosis**
MONOSIS *n* abnormal separation
MONOSKI *n* wide ski on which the skier stands with both feet ▷ *vb* ski on a monoski
MONOSY = **monosis**
MONS ▶ **mon**
MONSOON *n*
MONSTER *n, adj, vb*
MONTAGE *n, vb*
MONTAN *adj as in* **montan wax** hard wax obtained from lignite and peat
MONTANE *n* area of mountain dominated by vegetation ▷ *adj* of or inhabiting mountainous regions
MONTANT *n* vertical part in woodwork
MONTE *n* gambling card game of Spanish origin
MONTEM *n* former money-raising practice at Eton school **montems**
MONTERO *n* round cap with a flap at the back worn by hunters
MONTES ▶ **monte**
MONTH *n*
MONTHLY *adj, adv, n*
MONTHS ▶ **month**
MONTIES ▶ **monty**
MONTRE *n* pipes of organ **montres**
MONTURE *n* mount or frame
MONTY *n* complete form of something
MONURON *n* type of weedkiller
MONY *Scot word for* ▶ **many**
MOO *n, vb, interj*
MOOBS *pl n*
MOOCH *vb* **mooched, moocher, mooches**
MOOD *n*
MOODIED, moodier, moodies, moodily ▶ **moody**
MOODS ▶ **mood**
MOODY *adj, vb*
MOOED ▶ **moo**
MOOI *adj* pleasing or nice
MOOING ▶ **moo**
MOOKTAR = **mukhtar**
MOOL = **mould**
MOOLA = **moolah**
MOOLAH *slang word for* ▶ **money**
MOOLAHS ▶ **moolah**
MOOLAS ▶ **moola**
MOOLED ▶ **mool**
MOOLEY = **mooly**
MOOLEYS ▶ **mooley**
MOOLI *n* type of large white radish
MOOLIES ▶ **mooly**
MOOLING ▶ **mool**
MOOLIS ▶ **mooli**
MOOLOO *n* person from the Waikato **mooloos**
MOOLS ▶ **mool**
MOOLVI = **moolvie**
MOOLVIE *n* (esp in India) Muslim learned man
MOOLVIS ▶ **moolvi**
MOOLY = **muley**
MOON *n, vb*
MOONBOW *n* rainbow made by moonlight
MOONED *adj* decorated with a moon
MOONER ▶ **moon**
MOONERS ▶ **moon**
MOONEYE *n* N American large-eyed freshwater fish
MOONG *n as in* **moong bean** kind of bean
MOONIER ▶ **moony**
MOONIES ▶ **moony**
MOONILY ▶ **moony**
MOONING ▶ **moon**
MOONISH ▶ **moon**
MOONLET *n* small moon
MOONLIT *adj* illuminated by the moon
MOONS ▶ **moon**
MOONSET *n* moment when the moon disappears below the horizon
MOONY *adj* dreamy or listless ▷ *n* crazy or foolish person
MOOP = **moup**
MOOPED ▶ **moop**
MOOPING ▶ **moop**
MOOPS ▶ **moop**

MOOR *n, vb*
MOORAGE *n* place for mooring a vessel
MOORED ▸ **moor**
MOORHEN *n*
MOORIER ▸ **moor**
MOORILL *n* disease of cattle on moors
MOORING *n*
MOORISH *adj* of or relating to the Moor people of North Africa
MOORLOG *n* rotted wood below the surface of a moor
MOORMAN *n* person living on a moor **moormen**
MOORS ▸ **moor**
MOORVA = **murva**
MOORVAS ▸ **moorva**
MOORY ▸ **moor**
MOOS ▸ **moo**
MOOSE *n*
MOOT *adj, vb, n* **mooted, mooter, mooters, mootest, mooting**
MOOTMAN *n* person taking part in a moot **mootmen**
MOOTS ▸ **moot**
MOOVE = **move**
MOOVED ▸ **moove**
MOOVES ▸ **moove**
MOOVING ▸ **moove**
MOP *n, vb*
MOPANE = **mopani**
MOPANES ▸ **mopane**
MOPANI *n* S African tree that is highly resistant to drought **mopanis**
MOPE *vb, n*
MOPED *n* **mopeds**
MOPER ▸ **mope**
MOPERS ▸ **mope**
MOPERY *n* gloominess
MOPES ▸ **mope**
MOPEY ▸ **mope**
MOPHEAD *n* person with shaggy hair
MOPIER ▸ **mope**
MOPIEST ▸ **mope**
MOPILY ▸ **mopy**
MOPING ▸ **mope**
MOPISH ▸ **mope**
MOPOKE *n* **mopokes**
MOPPED ▸ **mop**
MOPPER ▸ **mop**
MOPPERS ▸ **mop**
MOPPET = **poppet**
MOPPETS ▸ **moppet**
MOPPIER ▸ **moppy**
MOPPING ▸ **mop**
MOPPY *adj* drunk
MOPS ▸ **mop**
MOPSIES ▸ **mopsy**
MOPSY *n* untidy or dowdy person
MOPUS *n* person who mopes **mopuses**
MOPY ▸ **mope**
MOR *n* layer of acidic humus formed in cool moist areas
MORA *n* quantity of a short syllable in verse **morae**
MORAINE *n* accumulated mass of debris deposited by a glacier
MORAL *adj, n, vb*
MORALE *n* **morales**
MORALL = **mural**
MORALLS ▸ **morall**
MORALLY ▸ **moral**
MORALS ▸ **moral**
MORAS ▸ **mora**
MORASS *n* **morassy**
MORAT *n* drink containing mulberry juice **morats**
MORAY *n* large voracious eel **morays**
MORBID *adj*
MORBUS *n* disease
MORCEAU *n* fragment or morsel
MORCHA *n* (in India) hostile demonstration **morchas**
MORDANT *adj, n, vb*
MORDENT *n* melodic ornament in music
MORE *adj, adv, pron*
MOREEN *n* heavy, usually watered, fabric of wool or wool and cotton **moreens**
MOREISH *adj* (of food) causing a desire for more
MOREL *n* edible mushroom with a pitted cap
MORELLE *n* nightshade
MORELLO *n* variety of small very dark sour cherry
MORELS ▸ **morel**
MORENDO *adv* (in music) dying away
MORES *pl n*
MORGAN *n* American breed of small compact saddle horse **morgans**
MORGAY *n* small dogfish **morgays**
MORGEN *n* South African unit of area **morgens**

MORGUE = **mortuary**
MORGUES ▸ **morgue**
MORIA *n* folly **morias**
MORICHE = **miriti**
MORION *n* 16th-century helmet with a brim and wide comb **morions**
MORISCO *n* morris dance
MORISH = **moreish**
MORKIN *n* animal dying in accident **morkins**
MORLING *n* sheep killed by disease
MORMAOR *n* former high-ranking Scottish nobleman
MORN *n* morning
MORNAY *adj* served with a cheese sauce **mornays**
MORNE = **mourn**
MORNED ▸ **morne**
MORNES ▸ **morne**
MORNING *n*
MORNS ▸ **morn**
MOROCCO *n* goatskin leather
MORON *n* **moronic, morons**
MOROSE *adj* **moroser**
MORPH *n* phonological representation of a morpheme ▹ *vb* undergo or cause to undergo morphing **morphed**
MORPHEW *n* blemish on skin
MORPHIA = **morphine**
MORPHIC *adj as in* **morphic resonance** idea that an event can lead to similar events in the future through a telepathic effect
MORPHIN *variant form of* > **morphine**
MORPHO *n* type of butterfly **morphos**
MORPHS ▸ **morph**
MORRA = **mora**
MORRAS ▸ **morra**
MORRELL *n* tall SW Australian eucalyptus with pointed buds
MORRHUA *n* cod
MORRICE = **morris**
MORRION = **morion**
MORRIS *vb* perform morris dance
MORRO *n* rounded hill or promontory **morros**
MORROW *n* next day **morrows**
MORS ▸ **mor**
MORSAL ▸ **morsure**
MORSE *n* clasp or fastening on a cope
MORSEL *n, vb* **morsels**
MORSES ▸ **morse**
MORSURE *n* bite
MORT *n* call blown on a hunting horn to signify the death of the animal hunted
MORTAL *adj, n* **mortals**
MORTAR *n, vb* **mortars**
MORTARY *adj* of or like mortar
MORTICE = **mortise**
MORTIFY *vb*
MORTISE *n* slot cut into a piece of wood, stone, etc ▹ *vb* cut a slot in (a piece of wood, stone, etc)
MORTS ▸ **mort**
MORULA *n* solid ball of cells resulting from cleavage of a fertilized ovum **morulae, morular, morulas**
MORWONG *n* food fish of Australasian coastal waters
MORYAH *interj* exclamation of annoyance, disbelief, etc
MOS ▸ **mo**
MOSAIC *n* **mosaics**
MOSE *vb* have glanders **mosed**
MOSELLE *n* German white wine from the Moselle valley
MOSES ▸ **mose**
MOSEY *vb* walk in a leisurely manner **moseyed, moseys**
MOSH *n* dance performed to loud rock music ▹ *vb* dance in this manner
MOSHAV *n* cooperative settlement in Israel
MOSHED, mosher, moshers, moshes, moshing ▸ **mosh**
MOSING ▸ **mose**
MOSK = **mosque**
MOSKS ▸ **mosk**
MOSQUE *n* **mosques**
MOSS *n, vb* **mossed, mosser, mossers, mosses**
MOSSIE *n* common sparrow

MOSSIER ▸ **moss**
MOSSIES ▸ **mossie**
MOSSING ▸ **moss**
MOSSO *adv* to be performed with rapidity
MOSSY ▸ **moss**
MOST *n, adj, adv*
MOSTE ▸ **mote**
MOSTEST ▸ **most**
MOSTLY *adv*
MOSTS ▸ **most**
MOT *n* girl or young woman, esp one's girlfriend
MOTE *n* tiny speck ▹ *vb* may or might
MOTED *adj* containing motes
MOTEL *n* **motels**
MOTEN ▸ **mote**
MOTES ▸ **mote**
MOTET *n* short sacred choral song **motets, motett, motetts**
MOTEY *adj* containing motes
MOTH *n*
MOTHED *adj* damaged by moths
MOTHER *n, adj, vb* **mothers, mothery**
MOTHIER ▸ **mothy**
MOTHS ▸ **moth**
MOTHY *adj* ragged
MOTIER ▸ **motey**
MOTIEST ▸ **motey**
MOTIF *n*
MOTIFIC *adj* causing motion
MOTIFS ▸ **motif**
MOTILE *adj* capable of independent movement ▹ *n* person whose mental imagery strongly reflects movement **motiles**
MOTION *n, vb* **motions**
MOTIVE *n, adj, vb* **motived, motives**
MOTIVIC *adj* of musical motif
MOTLEY *adj, n* **motleys, motlier**
MOTMOT *n* tropical American bird with a long tail and blue and brownish-green plumage **motmots**
MOTOR *n, vb, adj* **motored, motoric, motors, motory**
MOTS ▸ **mot**
MOTSER *n* large sum of money, esp a gambling win **motsers**
MOTT *n* clump of trees
MOTTE *n* mound on which a castle was built **mottes**
MOTTIER ▸ **motty**
MOTTIES ▸ **motty**
MOTTLE *vb* colour with streaks or blotches of different shades ▹ *n* mottled appearance, as of the surface of marble **mottled**
MOTTLER *n* paintbrush for mottled effects
MOTTLES ▸ **mottle**
MOTTO *n*
MOTTOED *adj* having motto
MOTTOES ▸ **motto**
MOTTOS ▸ **motto**
MOTTS ▸ **mott**
MOTTY *n* target at which coins are aimed in pitch-and-toss ▹ *adj* containing motes
MOTUCA *n* Brazilian fly **motucas**
MOTZA = **motser**
MOTZAS ▸ **motza**
MOU *Scots word for* ▸ **mouth**
MOUCH = **mooch**
MOUCHED ▸ **mouch**
MOUCHER ▸ **mouch**
MOUCHES ▸ **mouch**
MOUE *n* disdainful or pouting look **moues**
MOUFLON *n* wild mountain sheep of Corsica and Sardinia
MOUGHT ▸ **mote**
MOUILLE *adj* palatalized, as in the sounds represented by Spanish *ll* or *ñ*
MOUJIK = **muzhik**
MOUJIKS ▸ **moujik**
MOULAGE *n* mould making
MOULD *n, vb* **moulded**
MOULDER *vb* decay into dust ▹ *n* person who moulds or makes moulds
MOULDS ▸ **mould**
MOULDY *adj* stale or musty
MOULIN *n* vertical shaft in a glacier **moulins**
MOULS *Scots word for* ▸ **mould**
MOULT *vb, n* **moulted**
MOULTEN *adj* having moulted
MOULTER ▸ **moult**
MOULTS ▸ **moult**
MOUND *n, vb*

mounded, mounds
MOUNT *vb, n*
MOUNTED *adj* riding horses
MOUNTER ▸ **mount**
MOUNTS ▸ **mount**
MOUP *n* nibble **mouped, mouping, moups**
MOURN *vb* **mourned**
MOURNER *n*
MOURNS ▸ **mourn**
MOUS ▸ **mou**
MOUSAKA = **moussaka**
MOUSE *n, vb* **moused**
MOUSER *n* cat used to catch mice **mousers**
MOUSERY *n* place infested with mice
MOUSES ▸ **mouse**
MOUSEY = **mousy**
MOUSIE *n* little mouse
MOUSIER ▸ **mousy**
MOUSIES ▸ **mousie**
MOUSILY ▸ **mousy**
MOUSING *n* device for closing off a hook
MOUSLE *vb* handle roughly **mousled, mousles**
MOUSME *n* Japanese girl **mousmee, mousmes**
MOUSSE *n, vb* **moussed, mousses**
MOUST = **must**
MOUSTED ▸ **moust**
MOUSTS ▸ **moust**
MOUSY *adj*
MOUTAN *n* variety of peony **moutans**
MOUTER = **multure**
MOUTERS ▸ **mouter**
MOUTH *n, vb* **mouthed, mouther, mouths**
MOUTHY *adj* bombastic
MOUTON *n* sheepskin processed to resemble the fur of another animal **moutons**
MOVABLE *adj, n* **movably**
MOVE *vb* change in place or position ▷ *n* moving **moved**
MOVER *n* person or animal that moves in a particular way **movers**
MOVES ▸ **move**
MOVIE *n* cinema film **movies**
MOVING *adj*
MOVIOLA *n* viewing machine used in cutting and editing film
MOW *vb, n*
MOWA = **mahua**
MOWAS ▸ **mowa**
MOWBURN *vb* heat up in mow
MOWDIE *Scot words for* ▸ **mole**
MOWDIES ▸ **mowdie**
MOWED ▸ **mow**
MOWER ▸ **mow**
MOWERS ▸ **mow**
MOWING ▸ **mow**
MOWINGS ▸ **mow**
MOWN ▸ **mow**
MOWRA = **mahua**
MOWRAS ▸ **mowra**
MOWS ▸ **mow**
MOXA *n* downy material obtained from various plants **moxas**
MOXIE *n* courage, nerve, or vigour **moxies**
MOY *n* coin
MOYA *n* mud emitted from a volcano **moyas**
MOYITY = **moiety**
MOYL = **moyle**
MOYLE *vb* toil **moyled, moyles, moyling**
MOYLS ▸ **moyl**
MOYS ▸ **moy**
MOZ *n* hex

> This unusual word, Australian slang for bad luck, is another of the very useful short words that use the Z, and it can be extended to **moze** or **mozo**.

MOZE *vb* give nap to **mozed**
MOZES ▸ **moz**
MOZETTA = **mozzetta**
MOZETTE ▸ **mozetta**
MOZING ▸ **moze**
MOZO *n* porter in southwest USA **mozos**
MOZZ = **moz**
MOZZES ▸ **mozz**
MOZZIE = **mossie**
MOZZIES ▸ **mozzie**
MOZZLE *n* luck **mozzles**
MPRET *n* former Albanian ruler **mprets**
MRIDANG *n* drum used in Indian music
MU *n* 12th letter in the Greek alphabet
MUCATE *n* salt of mucic acid **mucates**
MUCH *adj, n, adv* **muchel, muchell**
MUCHELS ▸ **muchel**

MUCHES ▸ **much**
MUCHLY ▸ **much**
MUCHO *adv* Spanish for very
MUCIC *adj as in* **mucic acid** colourless crystalline solid carboxylic acid
MUCID *adj* mouldy, musty, or slimy
MUCIGEN *n* substance present in mucous cells that is converted into mucin
MUCIN *n* any of a group of nitrogenous mucoproteins occurring in saliva, skin, tendon, etc **mucins**
MUCK *n* **mucked**
MUCKER *n* person who shifts broken rock or waste ▹ *vb* hoard **muckers**
MUCKIER ▸ **mucky**
MUCKILY ▸ **mucky**
MUCKING ▸ **muck**
MUCKLE = **mickle**
MUCKLES ▸ **muckle**
MUCKS ▸ **muck**
MUCKY *adj* dirty or muddy
MUCLUC = **mukluk**
MUCLUCS ▸ **mucluc**
MUCOID *adj* of the nature of or resembling mucin ▹ *n* substance like mucin **mucoids**
MUCOR *n* type of fungus **mucors**
MUCOSA *n* mucus-secreting membrane that lines body cavities **mucosae, mucosal, mucosas**
MUCOSE = **mucous**
MUCOUS *adj* of, resembling, or secreting mucus
MUCRO *n* short pointed projection from certain parts or organs **mucros**
MUCUS *n* **mucuses**
MUD *n, vb*
MUDBATH *n* medicinal bath in heated mud
MUDBUG *n* crayfish **mudbugs**
MUDCAP *vb* use explosive charge in blasting **mudcaps**
MUDCAT *n* any of several large North American catfish **mudcats**
MUDDED ▸ **mud**
MUDDER *n* horse that runs well in mud **mudders**
MUDDIED ▸ **muddy**
MUDDIER ▸ **muddy**
MUDDIES ▸ **muddy**
MUDDILY ▸ **muddy**
MUDDING ▸ **mud**
MUDDLE *vb, n* **muddled**
MUDDLER *n* person who muddles or muddles through
MUDDLES ▸ **muddle**
MUDDLY ▸ **muddle**
MUDDY *adj, vb*
MUDEJAR *n* Spanish Moor ▹ *adj* of or relating to a style of architecture
MUDEYE *n* larva of the dragonfly **mudeyes**
MUDFISH *n* fish that lives at the muddy bottoms of rivers, lakes, etc
MUDFLAP *n* flap above wheel to deflect mud
MUDFLAT *n* tract of low muddy land
MUDFLOW *n* flow of soil mixed with water down a steep unstable slope
MUDGE *vb* speak vaguely **mudged, mudger, mudgers, mudges, mudging**
MUDHEN *n* water bird living in muddy place **mudhens**
MUDHOLE *n* hole with mud at bottom
MUDHOOK *n* anchor
MUDIR *n* local governor
MUDIRIA *n* province of mudir
MUDIRS ▸ **mudir**
MUDLARK *n* street urchin ▹ *vb* play in mud
MUDPACK *n* cosmetic paste applied to the face
MUDRA *n* hand movement in Hindu religious dancing **mudras**
MUDROCK *n* type of sedimentary rock
MUDROOM *n* room where muddy shoes may be left
MUDS ▸ **mud**

MUDSCOW *n* boat for travelling over mudflats
MUDSILL *n* support for building at or below ground
MUDWORT *n* plant growing in mud
MUEDDIN = **muezzin**
MUESLI *n* **mueslis**
MUEZZIN *n* official who summons Muslims to prayer
MUFF *n* tube-shaped covering to keep the hands warm ▷ *vb* bungle (an action) **muffed**
MUFFIN *n*
MUFFING ▸ **muff**
MUFFINS ▸ **muffin**
MUFFISH ▸ **muff**
MUFFLE *vb, n* **muffled**
MUFFLER *n* scarf
MUFFLES ▸ **muffle**
MUFFS ▸ **muff**
MUFLON = **moufflon**
MUFLONS ▸ **muflon**
MUFTI *n* **muftis**
MUG *n, vb* **mugful**
MUGFULS ▸ **mugful**
MUGG = **mug**
MUGGA *n* Australian eucalyptus tree
MUGGAR = **mugger**
MUGGARS ▸ **muggar**
MUGGAS ▸ **mugga**
MUGGED ▸ **mug**
MUGGEE *n* mugged person **muggees**
MUGGER *n* person who commits robbery with violence **muggers**
MUGGIER ▸ **muggy**
MUGGILY ▸ **muggy**
MUGGING ▸ **mug**
MUGGINS *n* stupid or gullible person
MUGGISH = **muggy**
MUGGS ▸ **mug**
MUGGUR = **mugger**
MUGGURS ▸ **muggur**
MUGGY *adj*
MUGHAL = **mogul**
MUGHALS ▸ **mughal**
MUGS ▸ **mug**
MUGSHOT *n* police photograph of person's face
MUGWORT *n* N temperate herbaceous plant with aromatic leaves
MUGWUMP *n* neutral or independent person
MUHLIES ▸ **muhly**
MUHLY *n* American grass
MUID *n* former French measure of capacity **muids**
MUIL = **mule**
MUILS ▸ **muil**
MUIR = **moor**
MUIRS ▸ **muir**
MUIST = **must**
MUISTED ▸ **muist**
MUISTS ▸ **muist**
MUJIK = **muzhik**
MUJIKS ▸ **mujik**
MUKHTAR *n* lawyer in India
MUKLUK *n* soft boot, usually of sealskin **mukluks**
MUKTUK *n* thin outer skin of the beluga, used as food **muktuks**
MULATTA *n* female mulatto
MULATTO *n* child of one Black and one White parent ▷ *adj* of a light brown colour
MULCH *n, vb* **mulched, mulches**
MULCT *vb* cheat or defraud ▷ *n* fine or penalty **mulcted, mulcts**
MULE *n, vb* **muled**
MULES *vb* surgically remove folds of skin from a sheep **mulesed, muleses**
MULETA *n* small cape attached to a stick used by a matador **muletas**
MULEY *adj* (of cattle) having no horns ▷ *n* any hornless cow **muleys**
MULGA *n* **mulgas**
MULING ▸ **mule**
MULISH *adj*
MULL *vb, n*
MULLA = **mullah**
MULLAH *n* Muslim scholar, teacher, or religious leader **mullahs**
MULLAS ▸ **mulla**
MULLED ▸ **mull**
MULLEIN *n* type of European plant **mullen**
MULLENS ▸ **mullen**
MULLER *n* flat heavy implement used to grind material ▷ *vb* beat up or defeat thoroughly **mullers**

MULLET *n* **mullets**
MULLEY = **muley**
MULLEYS ▶ **mulley**
MULLING ▶ **mull**
MULLION *n* vertical dividing bar in a window ▷ *vb* furnish with mullions
MULLITE *n* colourless mineral
MULLOCK *n* waste material from a mine
MULLS ▶ **mull**
MULMUL *n* muslin **mulmull, mulmuls**
MULSE *n* drink containing honey **mulses**
MULSH = **mulch**
MULSHED ▶ **mulsh**
MULSHES ▶ **mulsh**
MULTUM *n* substance used in brewing **multums**
MULTURE *n* fee formerly paid to a miller for grinding grain ▷ *vb* take multure
MUM *n, vb*
MUMBLE *vb, n* **mumbled, mumbler, mumbles, mumbly**
MUMM = **mum**
MUMMED ▶ **mum**
MUMMER *n* actor in a traditional English folk play **mummers**
MUMMERY *n* performance by mummers
MUMMIA *n* mummified flesh used as medicine **mummias**
MUMMIED ▶ **mummy**
MUMMIES ▶ **mummy**
MUMMIFY *vb* preserve a body as a mummy
MUMMING ▶ **mum**
MUMMOCK = **mammock**
MUMMS ▶ **mumm**
MUMMY *n, vb*
MUMP *vb* be silent **mumped, mumper, mumpers, mumping**
MUMPISH ▶ **mumps**
MUMPS *n*
MUMS ▶ **mum**
MUMSIER ▶ **mumsy**
MUMSY *adj* out of fashion
MUMU *n* oven in Papua New Guinea **mumus**
MUN = **maun**
MUNCH *vb* **munched, muncher, munches**
MUNDANE *adj*
MUNDIC *n* iron pyrites **mundics**
MUNDIFY *vb* cleanse
MUNG *vb* process (computer data)
MUNGA *n* army canteen **mungas**
MUNGE *vb* modify a password into an unguessable state
MUNGED ▶ **mung**
MUNGES ▶ **mung**
MUNGING ▶ **mung**
MUNGO *n* cheap felted fabric made from waste wool **mungoes, mungos**
MUNGS ▶ **mung**
MUNI *n* municipal radio broadcast
MUNIFY *vb* fortify
MUNIS ▶ **muni**
MUNITE *vb* strengthen **munited, munites**
MUNNION *archaic word for* ▶ **mullion**
MUNS ▶ **mun**
MUNSHI *n* secretary in India **munshis**
MUNSTER *variant of* > **muenster**
MUNTIN *n* supporting or strengthening bar **munting, muntins**
MUNTJAC *n* small Asian deer **muntjak**
MUNTRIE *n* Australian shrub with green-red edible berries
MUON *n* elementary particle with a mass 207 times that of an electron **muonic**
MUONIUM *n* form of hydrogen
MUONS ▶ **muon**
MUPPET *n* stupid person **muppets**
MURA *n* group of people living together in Japanese countryside
MURAENA *n* moray eel
MURAGE *n* tax levied for the construction or maintenance of town walls **murages**
MURAL *n, adj*
MURALED = **muralled**
MURALS ▶ **mural**
MURAS ▶ **mura**
MURDER *n, vb* **murders**
MURE *archaic or literary word for* ▶ **immure**
MURED ▶ **mure**

MUREIN *n* polymer found in cells **mureins**
MURENA = **muraena**
MURENAS ▸ **murena**
MURES ▸ **mure**
MUREX *n* marine gastropod formerly used as a source of purple dye **murexes**
MURGEON *vb* grimace at
MURIATE *obsolete name for a* > **chloride**
MURICES ▸ **murex**
MURID *n* animal of mouse family **murids**
MURINE *n* animal belonging to the family that includes rats and mice **murines**
MURING ▸ **mure**
MURK *n* thick darkness ▹ *adj* dark or gloomy **murker, murkest**
MURKIER ▸ **murky**
MURKILY ▸ **murky**
MURKISH ▸ **murk**
MURKLY ▸ **murk**
MURKS ▸ **murk**
MURKY *adj*
MURL *vb* crumble
MURLAIN *n* type of basket **murlan**
MURLANS ▸ **murlan**
MURLED ▸ **murl**
MURLIER ▸ **murl**
MURLIN = **murlain**
MURLING ▸ **murl**
MURLINS ▸ **murlin**
MURLS ▸ **murl**
MURLY ▸ **murl**
MURMUR *vb, n* **murmurs**
MURPHY *dialect or informal word for* ▸ **potato**
MURR *n* former name for a cold
MURRA = **murrhine**
MURRAGH *n* type of large caddis fly
MURRAIN *n* cattle plague
MURRAM *n* type of gravel **murrams**
MURRAS ▸ **murra**
MURRAY *n* large Australian freshwater fish **murrays**
MURRE *n* type of guillemot
MURREE *n* native Australian **murrees**
MURREN = **murrain**
MURRENS ▸ **murren**
MURRES ▸ **murre**
MURREY *adj* mulberry colour **murreys**
MURRHA = **murra**
MURRHAS ▸ **murrha**
MURRI = **murree**
MURRIES ▸ **murry**
MURRIN = **murrain**
MURRINE = **murrhine**
MURRINS ▸ **murrin**
MURRION = **murrain**
MURRIS ▸ **murri**
MURRS ▸ **murr**
MURRY = **moray**
MURTHER = **murder**
MURTI *n* image of a deity, which itself is considered divine **murtis**
MURVA *n* type of hemp **murvas**
MUS ▸ **mu**
MUSANG *n* catlike animal of Malaysia **musangs**
MUSAR *n* rabbinic literature concerned with ethics **musars**
MUSCA *n* small constellation in the S hemisphere **muscae**
MUSCAT = **muscatel**
MUSCATS ▸ **muscat**
MUSCID *n* type of fly **muscids**
MUSCLE *n, vb* **muscled, muscles, muscly**
MUSCOID *adj* of family of plants
MUSCONE = **muskone**
MUSCOSE *adj* like moss
MUSCOVY *adj as in* **muscovy duck** a kind of duck
MUSE *vb, n* **mused, museful, muser, musers, muses**
MUSET = **musit**
MUSETS ▸ **muset**
MUSETTE *n* type of bagpipe formerly popular in France
MUSEUM *n* **museums**
MUSH *n, interj, vb*
MUSHA *interj* Irish exclamation of surprise
MUSHED, musher, mushers, mushes ▸ **mush**
MUSHIER ▸ **mushy**
MUSHILY ▸ **mushy**
MUSHING ▸ **mush**
MUSHY *adj*
MUSIC *n, vb*
MUSICAL *adj, n*

MUSICK = **music**
MUSICKS ▸ **musick**
MUSICS ▸ **music**
MUSIMON = **moufflon**
MUSING ▸ **muse**
MUSINGS ▸ **muse**
MUSIT *n* gap in fence **musits**
MUSIVE *adj* mosaic
MUSJID = **masjid**
MUSJIDS ▸ **musjid**
MUSK *n, vb* **musked**
MUSKEG *n* area of undrained boggy land **muskegs**
MUSKET *n* **muskets**
MUSKIE *n* large North American freshwater game fish **muskier, muskies**
MUSKILY ▸ **musky**
MUSKING ▸ **musk**
MUSKIT = **mesquite**
MUSKITS ▸ **muskit**
MUSKLE = **mussel**
MUSKLES ▸ **muskle**
MUSKONE *n* substance in musk
MUSKOX *n* large Canadian mammal
MUSKRAT *n*
MUSKS ▸ **musk**
MUSKY = **muskie**
MUSLIN *n* **muslins**
MUSMON = **musimon**
MUSMONS ▸ **musmon**
MUSO *n* musician who is concerned with technique rather than content or expression **musos**
MUSPIKE *n* Canadian freshwater fish
MUSROL *n* part of bridle **musrols**
MUSS *vb* make untidy ▹ *n* state of disorder **musse, mussed**
MUSSEL *n* **mussels**
MUSSES ▸ **muss**
MUSSIER ▸ **mussy**
MUSSILY ▸ **mussy**
MUSSING ▸ **muss**
MUSSY *adj* untidy or disordered
MUST *vb, n*
MUSTANG *n*
MUSTARD *n, adj*
MUSTED ▸ **must**
MUSTEE *n* offspring of a White and a quadroon **mustees**
MUSTER *vb, n* **musters**
MUSTH *n* state of frenzied sexual excitement in the males of certain large mammals **musths**
MUSTIER ▸ **musty**
MUSTILY ▸ **musty**
MUSTING ▸ **must**
MUSTS ▸ **must**
MUSTY *adj*
MUT *another word for* ▸ **em**
MUTABLE *adj* liable to change **mutably**
MUTAGEN *n* any substance that can induce genetic mutation
MUTANDA > **mutandum**
MUTANT *n* mutated animal, plant, etc ▹ *adj* of or resulting from mutation **mutants**
MUTASE *n* type of enzyme **mutases**
MUTATE *vb* **mutated, mutates**
MUTCH *n* close-fitting linen cap ▹ *vb* cadge **mutched, mutches**
MUTE *adj, n, vb*
MUTED *adj* **mutedly**
MUTELY, muter, mutes, mutest ▸ **mute**
MUTI *n*
MUTINE *vb* mutiny **mutined, mutines**
MUTING ▸ **mute**
MUTINY *n, vb*
MUTIS ▸ **muti**
MUTISM *n* state of being mute **mutisms**
MUTON *n* part of gene **mutons**
MUTS ▸ **mut**
MUTT *n* mongrel dog
MUTTER *vb, n* **mutters**
MUTTON *n* **muttons, muttony**
MUTTS ▸ **mutt**
MUTUAL *adj, n* **mutuals**
MUTUCA = **motuca**
MUTUCAS ▸ **mutuca**
MUTUEL *n* system of betting **mutuels**
MUTULAR ▸ **mutule**
MUTULE *n* flat block in a Doric cornice **mutules**
MUTUUM *n* contract for loan of goods **mutuums**
MUUMUU *n* loose brightly-coloured dress worn by women in Hawaii **muumuus**

MUX *vb* spoil **muxed, muxes, muxing**

This word meaning to spoil or botch is very useful not only because it contains an X, but because its verb forms can enable you to clear your rack of unpromising letters.

MUZAKY *adj* having a bland sound
MUZHIK *n* Russian peasant, esp under the tsars **muzhiks, muzjik**
MUZJIKS ▸ **muzjik**
MUZZ *vb* make (something) muzzy **muzzed, muzzes**
MUZZIER ▸ **muzzy**
MUZZILY ▸ **muzzy**
MUZZING ▸ **muzz**
MUZZLE *n, vb* **muzzled, muzzler, muzzles**
MUZZY *adj*
MVULE *n* tropical African tree **mvules**
MWAH *interj*
MWALIMU *n* teacher
MY *adj, interj*
MYAL ▸ **myalism**
MYALGIA *n* pain in a muscle or a group of muscles **myalgic**
MYALISM *n* kind of witchcraft **myalist**
MYALL *n* Australian acacia with hard scented wood **myalls**
MYASES ▸ **myasis**
MYASIS = **myiasis**
MYC *n* oncogene that aids the growth of tumorous cells
MYCELE *n* microscopic spike-like structure in mucus **myceles**
MYCELIA > **mycelium**
MYCELLA *n* blue-veined Danish cream cheese
MYCETES *n* fungus
MYCOSES ▸ **mycosis**
MYCOSIS *n* any infection or disease caused by fungus **mycotic**
MYCS ▸ **myc**
MYELIN *n* white tissue forming an insulating sheath around certain nerve fibres **myeline, myelins**
MYELOID *adj* of or relating to the spinal cord or the bone marrow
MYELOMA *n* tumour of the bone marrow
MYELON *n* spinal cord **myelons**
MYGALE *n* large American spider **mygales**
MYIASES ▸ **myiasis**
MYIASIS *n* infestation of the body by the larvae of flies
MYLAR *n* tradename for a kind of strong polyester film **mylars**
MYLODON *n* prehistoric giant sloth
MYNA = **mynah**
MYNAH *n* tropical Asian starling which can mimic human speech **mynahs**
MYNAS ▸ **myna**
MYNHEER *n* Dutch title of address
MYOGEN *n* albumin found in muscle **myogens**
MYOGRAM *n* tracings of muscular contractions
MYOID *adj* like muscle
MYOLOGY *n* study of the structure and diseases of muscles
MYOMA *n* benign tumour composed of muscle tissue **myomas, myomata**
MYOPE *n* any person afflicted with myopia **myopes**
MYOPIA *n* **myopias**
MYOPIC *n* shortsighted person **myopics**
MYOPIES ▸ **myopy**
MYOPS = **myope**
MYOPSES ▸ **myops**
MYOPY = **myopia**
MYOSES ▸ **myosis**
MYOSIN *n* protein found in muscle **myosins**
MYOSIS = **miosis**
MYOSOTE = **myosotis**
MYOTIC ▸ **miosis**
MYOTICS ▸ **miosis**
MYOTOME *n* any segment of embryonic mesoderm that develops into skeletal muscle
MYOTUBE *n* cylindrical cell in muscle
MYRBANE = **mirbane**
MYRIAD *adj, n* **myriads**
MYRICA *n* dried root bark of the wax myrtle, used as a tonic

and to treat diarrhoea **myricas**
MYRINGA *n* eardrum
MYRRH *n* **myrrhic**
MYRRHOL *n* oil of myrrh
MYRRHS ▸ **myrrh**
MYRTLE *n* flowering evergreen shrub **myrtles**
MYSELF *pron*
MYSID *n* small shrimplike crustacean **mysids**
MYSOST *n* Norwegian cheese **mysosts**
MYSPACE *vb*
MYSTERY *n*
MYSTIC *n, adj* **mystics**
MYSTIFY *vb*
MYTH *n*
MYTHI ▸ **mythus**
MYTHIC = **mythical**
MYTHIER ▸ **mythy**
MYTHISE = **mythize**
MYTHISM = **mythicism**
MYTHIST ▸ **mythism**
MYTHIZE = **mythicize**
MYTHOI ▸ **mythos**
MYTHOS *n* beliefs of a specific group or society
MYTHS ▸ **myth**
MYTHUS = **mythos**
MYTHY *adj* of or like myth
MYXO *n* viral disease of rabbits
MYXOID *adj* containing mucus
MYXOMA *n* tumour composed of mucous connective tissue **myxomas**
MYXOS ▸ **myxo**
MZEE *n* old person ▷ *adj* advanced in years **mzees**
MZUNGU *n* White person **mzungus**

Nn

Along with **R** and **T**, **N** is one of the most common consonants in Scrabble. As you'll often have it on your rack, it's well worth learning what **N** can do in different situations. **N** is useful when you need short words, as it begins two-letter words with every vowel except **I**, and with **Y** as well. There are plenty of three-letter words starting with **N**, but there aren't many high-scoring ones apart from **nix** and **nox** for 10 points each and **nek** for 7 points. Remember words like **nab** (5 points), **nag** (4), **nap** (5), **nay** (6), **new** (6), **nib** (5), **nob** (5), **nod** (4) and **now** (6).

NA = **nae**
NAAM = **nam**
NAAMS ▸ **naam**
NAAN *n* slightly leavened flat Indian bread **naans**
NAARTJE = **naartjie**
NAB *vb* arrest (someone) **nabbed**
NABBER *n* thief **nabbers**
NABBING ▸ **nab**
NABE *n* Japanese hotpot **nabes**
NABIS *n* Parisian art movement
NABK *n* edible berry **nabks**
NABLA *another name for* ▸ **del**
NABLAS ▸ **nabla**
NABOB = **nawab**
NABOBS ▸ **nabob**
NABS ▸ **nab**
NACARAT *n* red-orange colour
NACELLE *n* streamlined enclosure on an aircraft
NACH *n* Indian dance
NACHAS *n* pleasure
NACHE *n* rump **naches**
NACHO *n* snack of a piece of tortilla with a topping **nachos**
NACKET *n* light lunch, snack **nackets**
NACRE *n* mother of pearl **nacred, nacres**
NACRITE *n* mineral
NACROUS ▸ **nacre**
NADA *n* nothing **nadas**
NADIR *n* **nadiral, nadirs**
NADORS *n* thirst brought on by excess of alcohol
NAE *Scot word for* ▸ **no**
NAEBODY *Scots variant of* ▸ **nobody**
NAEVE *n* birthmark
NAEVES ▸ **naevus**
NAEVI ▸ **naevus**
NAEVOID ▸ **naevus**
NAEVUS *n* birthmark or mole
NAFF *adj* lacking quality or taste ▹ *vb* go away **naffed, naffer, naffest, naffing, naffly, naffs**
NAG *vb, n*
NAGA *n* cobra
NAGANA *n* disease of all domesticated animals of central and

southern Africa **naganas**
NAGAPIE *n* bushbaby
NAGARI *n* scripts for writing several languages of India **nagaris**
NAGAS ▸ **naga**
NAGGED ▸ **nag**
NAGGER ▸ **nag**
NAGGERS ▸ **nag**
NAGGIER ▸ **nag**
NAGGING ▸ **nag**
NAGGY ▸ **nag**
NAGMAAL *n* Communion
NAGOR *another name for* > **reedbuck**
NAGORS ▸ **nagor**
NAGS ▸ **nag**
NAH = **no**
NAHAL *n* agricultural settlement run by an Israeli military youth organization **nahals**
NAIAD *n* nymph living in a lake or river **naiades, naiads**
NAIANT *adj* swimming
NAIF *less common word for* ▸ **naive**
NAIFER ▸ **naif**
NAIFEST ▸ **naif**
NAIFLY ▸ **naive**
NAIFS ▸ **naif**
NAIK *n* chief **naiks**
NAIL *n, vb* **nailed, nailer, nailers**
NAILERY *n* nail factory
NAILING ▸ **nail**
NAILS ▸ **nail**
NAILSET *n* punch for driving down the head of a nail
NAIN *adj* own
NAIRA *n* standard monetary unit of Nigeria, divided into 100 kobo **nairas**
NAIRU *n* Non-Accelerating Inflation Rate of Unemployment **nairus**
NAIVE *adj, n* **naively, naiver, naives, naivest**
NAIVETE *variant of* ▸ **naivety**
NAIVETY *n* state or quality of being naive
NAIVIST ▸ **naive**
NAKED *adj* **nakeder, nakedly**
NAKER *n* small kettledrum used in medieval music **nakers**
NAKFA *n* standard currency unit of Eritrea **nakfas**
NALA *n* ravine **nalas**
NALED *n* type of insecticide **naleds**
NALLA *n* ravine **nallah**
NALLAHS ▸ **nallah**
NALLAS ▸ **nalla**
NAM *n* distraint
NAMABLE ▸ **name**
NAMASTE *n* Indian greeting
NAME *n, vb* **named**
NAMELY *adv*
NAMER ▸ **name**
NAMERS ▸ **name**
NAMES ▸ **name**
NAMETAG *n* identification badge
NAMING ▸ **name**
NAMINGS ▸ **name**
NAMMA *adj as in* **namma hole** Australian word for a natural well in rock
NAMS ▸ **nam**
NAMU *n* black New Zealand sandfly **namus**
NAN *n* grandmother **nana**
NANAS ▸ **nana**
NANDIN *n* type of shrub
NANDINA *n* type of shrub
NANDINE *n* African palm civet
NANDINS ▸ **nandin**
NANDOO ▸ **nandu**
NANDOOS ▸ **nandoo**
NANDU *n* type of ostrich **nandus**
NANE *Scot word for* ▸ **none**
NANG *adj*
NANISM *n* dwarfism **nanisms**
NANITE *n* microscopically small machine or robot **nanites**
NANKEEN *n* hard-wearing buff-coloured cotton fabric **nankin**
NANKINS ▸ **nankin**
NANNA = **nan**
NANNAS ▸ **nanna**
NANNIE = **nanny**
NANNIED ▸ **nanny**
NANNIES ▸ **nanny**
NANNY *n, vb*

NANOBE *n* microbe that is smaller than the smallest known bacterium **nanobes**
NANOBOT *n* microscopically small robot
NANODOT *n* microscopic cluster of atoms used to store data in a computer chip
NANOOK *n* polar bear **nanooks**
NANS ▸ **nan**
NANUA = **moki**
NANUAS ▸ **nanua**
NAOI ▸ **naos**

The plural of **naos**, the inner cell of a temple. A very useful word for ridding your rack of unwanted vowels.

NAOS *n* ancient classical temple **naoses**
NAP *n, vb*
NAPA *n* type of leather
NAPALM *n, vb* **napalms**
NAPAS ▸ **napa**
NAPE *n, vb* **naped**
NAPERY *n* household linen, esp table linen
NAPES ▸ **nape**
NAPHTHA *n* liquid mixture used as a solvent and in petrol
NAPHTOL = **naphthol**
NAPING ▸ **nape**
NAPKIN = **nappy**
NAPKINS ▸ **napkin**
NAPLESS *adj* threadbare
NAPOO *vb* kill **napooed, napoos**
NAPPA *n* soft leather **nappas**
NAPPE *n* mass of rock that has been thrust from its original position by earth movements
NAPPED ▸ **nap**
NAPPER *n* person or thing that raises the nap on cloth **nappers**
NAPPES ▸ **nappe**
NAPPIE = **nappy**
NAPPIER ▸ **nappy**
NAPPIES ▸ **nappy**
NAPPING ▸ **nap**
NAPPY *n, adj*
NAPRON = **apron**
NAPRONS ▸ **napron**
NAPS ▸ **nap**
NARAS = **narras**
NARASES ▸ **naras**
NARC *n* narcotics agent
NARCEEN = **narceine**
NARCEIN = **narceine**
NARCISM *n* exceptional admiration for oneself
NARCIST *n* narcissist
NARCO *n* officer working in the area of anti-drug operations
NARCOMA *n* coma caused by intake of narcotic drugs
NARCOS *n* drug smugglers
NARCOSE = **narcosis**
NARCS ▸ **narc**
NARD *n* any of several plants with aromatic roots ▹ *vb* anoint with nard oil **narded, nardine, narding**
NARDOO *n* cloverlike fern which grows in swampy areas **nardoos**
NARDS ▸ **nard**
NARE *n* nostril
NARES *pl n* nostrils
NARGILE = **narghile**
NARGILY = **narghile**
NARIAL *adj* of or relating to the nares
NARIC ▸ **nare**
NARINE = **narial**
NARIS ▸ **nares**
NARK *vb* annoy ▹ *n* informer or spy **narked**
NARKIER ▸ **narky**
NARKING ▸ **nark**
NARKS ▸ **nark**
NARKY *adj* irritable or complaining
NARRAS *n* type of shrub
NARRATE *vb*
NARRE *adj* nearer
NARROW *adj, vb*
NARROWS *pl n* narrow part of a strait, river, or current
NARTHEX *n* portico at the west end of a basilica or church
NARTJIE = **naartjie**

This word for a small sweet orange is one to look out for when you have the J with the good letters of 'retain'. And it has alternative spellings **naartje** and **naartjie**.

NARWAL = **narwhal**
NARWALS ▸ **narwal**
NARWHAL *n* arctic whale with a long spiral tusk

NARY *adv* not
NAS *vb* has not
NASAL *adj, n* **nasally, nasals**
NASARD *n* organ stop **nasards**
NASCENT *adj* starting to grow or develop
NASHGAB *n* chatter
NASHI *n* fruit of the Japanese pear **nashis**
NASIAL ▸ **nasion**
NASION *n* craniometric point where the top of the nose meets the ridge of the forehead **nasions**
NASTIC *adj* (of movement of plants) independent of the direction of the external stimulus
NASTIER ▸ **nasty**
NASTIES ▸ **nasty**
NASTILY ▸ **nasty**
NASTY *adj, n*
NASUTE *n* type of termite **nasutes**
NAT *n* supporter of nationalism
NATAL *adj*
NATANT *adj* (of aquatic plants) floating on the water
NATCH *sentence substitute* naturally ▹ *n* notch **natches**
NATES *pl n* buttocks
NATHEMO = **nathemore**
NATION *n* **nations**
NATIS ▸ **nates**
NATIVE *adj, n* **natives**
NATRIUM *obsolete name for* ▸ **sodium**
NATRON *n* whitish or yellow mineral **natrons**
NATS ▸ **nat**
NATTER *vb, n* **natters**
NATTERY *adj* irritable
NATTIER ▸ **natty**
NATTILY ▸ **natty**
NATTY *adj* smart and spruce
NATURA *n* nature **naturae**
NATURAL *adj, n*
NATURE *n*
NATURED *adj* having a certain disposition
NATURES ▸ **nature**
NAUCH = **nautch**
NAUCHES ▸ **nauch**
NAUGHT *n, adv* **naughts**
NAUGHTY *adj, n*
NAUNT *n* aunt **naunts**
NAUPLII > **nauplius**
NAUSEA *n* **nauseas**
NAUTCH *n* intricate traditional Indian dance
NAUTIC = **nautical**
NAUTICS ▸ **nautic**
NAUTILI > **nautilus**
NAVAID *n* navigational aid **navaids**
NAVAL *adj* **navally**
NAVAR *n* system of air navigation
NAVARCH *n* admiral
NAVARHO *n* aircraft navigation system
NAVARIN *n* stew of mutton or lamb with root vegetables
NAVARS ▸ **navar**
NAVE *n*
NAVEL *n* **navels**
NAVES ▸ **nave**
NAVETTE *n* gem cut
NAVEW *another name for* ▸ **turnip**
NAVEWS ▸ **navew**
NAVIES ▸ **navy**
NAVVIED ▸ **navvy**
NAVVIES ▸ **navvy**
NAVVY *n, vb*
NAVY *n, adj*
NAW = **no**
NAWAB *n* (formerly) a Muslim ruler or landowner in India **nawabs**
NAY *interj, n, adv, sentence substitute* **nays**
NAYSAID ▸ **naysay**
NAYSAY *vb* say no **naysays**
NAYWARD *n* towards denial
NAYWORD *n* proverb
NAZE *n* flat marshy headland **nazes**
NAZI *n* person who thinks or acts in a brutal or dictatorial way
NAZIFY *vb* make nazi in character
NAZIR *n* Muslim official **nazirs**
NAZIS ▸ **nazi**
NE *conj* nor
NEAFE = **nieve**
NEAFES ▸ **neafe**
NEAFFE = **nieve**
NEAFFES ▸ **neaffe**
NEAL = **anneal**
NEALED ▸ **neal**
NEALING ▸ **neal**

NEALS ▸ **neal**
NEANIC *adj* of or relating to the early stages in a life cycle
NEAP *adj* of, relating to, or constituting a neap tide ▹ *vb* be grounded by a neap tide **neaped, neaping, neaps**
NEAR *adj, vb, prep, adv, n*
NEARBY *adj, adv*
NEARED, nearer, nearest, nearing ▸ **near**
NEARLY *adv*
NEARS ▸ **near**
NEAT *adj, n*
NEATEN *vb* make neat **neatens**
NEATER ▸ **neat**
NEATEST ▸ **neat**
NEATH *short for* ▸ **beneath**
NEATLY ▸ **neat**
NEATNIK *n* very neat and tidy person
NEATS ▸ **neat**
NEB *n* beak of a bird or the nose of an animal ▹ *vb* look around nosily **nebbed**
NEBBICH = **nebbish**
NEBBING ▸ **neb**
NEBBISH *n* unfortunate simpleton
NEBBUK *n* type of shrub **nebbuks, nebeck**
NEBECKS ▸ **nebeck**
NEBEK = **nebbuk**
NEBEKS ▸ **nebek**
NEBEL *n* Hebrew musical instrument **nebels**
NEBISH = **nebbish**
NEBRIS *n* fawn-skin
NEBS ▸ **neb**
NEBULA *n* **nebulae, nebular, nebulas**
NEBULE *n* cloud **nebules**
NEBULY *adj* wavy
NECK *n, vb* **necked, necker, neckers**
NECKING *n* activity of kissing and embracing passionately
NECKLET *n* ornament worn round the neck
NECKS ▸ **neck**
NECKTIE = **tie**
NECROSE *vb* cause or undergo necrosis
NECTAR *n* **nectars**
NECTARY *n* structure secreting nectar in a plant
NEDDIER ▸ **neddy**
NEDDIES ▸ **neddy**
NEDDISH ▸ **neddy**
NEDDY *n* donkey ▹ *adj* of or relating to neds
NEE *prep* indicating the maiden name of a married woman ▹ *adj* indicating the maiden name of a married woman
NEED *vb, n* **needed, needer, needers**
NEEDFUL *adj* necessary or required
NEEDIER ▸ **needy**
NEEDILY ▸ **needy**
NEEDING ▸ **need**
NEEDLE *n, vb* **needled**
NEEDLER *n* needle maker
NEEDLES ▸ **needle**
NEEDLY ▸ **needle**
NEEDS *adv* necessarily ▹ *pl n* what is required
NEEDY *adj*
NEELD = **needle**
NEELDS ▸ **neeld**
NEELE = **needle**
NEELES ▸ **neele**
NEEM *n* type of large Indian tree **neemb**
NEEMBS ▸ **neemb**
NEEMS ▸ **neem**
NEEP *dialect name for* ▸ **turnip**
NEEPS ▸ **neep**
NEESE = **neeze**
NEESED ▸ **neese**
NEESES ▸ **neese**
NEESING ▸ **neese**
NEEZE *vb* sneeze **neezed, neezes, neezing**
NEF *n* church nave
NEFAST *adj* wicked
NEFS ▸ **nef**
NEG *n* photographic negative
NEGATE *vb* **negated, negater, negates**
NEGATON = **negatron**
NEGATOR ▸ **negate**
NEGLECT *vb, n*
NEGLIGE *variant of* > **negligee**
NEGRONI *n* type of cocktail
NEGS ▸ **neg**
NEGUS *n* hot drink of port and lemon juice **neguses**
NEIF = **nieve**
NEIFS ▸ **neif**
NEIGH *n, vb* **neighed, neighs**

NEINEI *n* type of plant **neineis**
NEIST *Scots variant of* ▸ **next**
NEITHER *pron, adj*
NEIVE = **nieve**
NEIVES ▸ **neive**
NEK *n* mountain pass **neks**
NEKTON *n* free-swimming animals in the middle depths of a sea or lake **nektons**
NELIES = **nelis**
NELIS *n* type of pear
NELLIE *n* effeminate man **nellies**
NELLY *n as in* **not on your nelly** not under any circumstances
NELSON *n* type of wrestling hold **nelsons**
NELUMBO *n* type of aquatic plant
NEMA *n* filament **nemas**
NEMATIC *adj* having a mesomorphic state in which a linear orientation of the molecules causes anisotropic properties
NEMESES ▸ **nemesis**
NEMESIA *n* type of southern African plant
NEMESIS *n* retribution or vengeance
NEMN *vb* name **nemned, nemning, nemns**
NEMORAL *adj* of a wood
NEMPT *adj* named
NENE *n* rare black-and-grey short-winged Hawaiian goose **nenes**
NEOCON *n* supporter of conservative politics **neocons**
NEOGENE *adj* of, denoting, or formed during the Miocene and Pliocene epochs
NEOLITH *n* Neolithic stone implement
NEOLOGY = **neologism**
NEON *n, adj*
NEONATE *n* newborn child
NEONED *adj* lit with neon
NEONS ▸ **neon**
NEOSOUL *n* soul music combined with other genres
NEOTENY *n* persistence of larval or fetal features in the adult form of an animal
NEOTYPE *n* specimen selected to replace a type specimen that has been lost or destroyed
NEP *n* catmint
NEPER *n* unit expressing the ratio of two quantities **nepers**
NEPETA = **catmint**
NEPETAS ▸ **nepeta**
NEPHEW *n* **nephews**
NEPHRIC *adj* renal
NEPHRON *n* urine-secreting tubule in the kidney
NEPIT *n* **nepits**
NEPOTIC > **nepotism**
NEPS ▸ **nep**
NERAL *n* isomer of citral **nerals**
NERD *n* boring person obsessed with a particular subject
NERDIC > **geekspeak**
NERDICS ▸ **nerdic**
NERDIER, nerdish, nerds, nerdy ▸ **nerd**
NEREID *n* sea nymph in Greek mythology **nereids**
NEREIS *n* type of marine worm
NERINE *n* type of S African plant related to the amaryllis **nerines**
NERITE *n* type of sea snail **nerites**
NERITIC *adj* of or formed in shallow seas near a coastline
NERK *n* fool
NERKA *n* type of salmon **nerkas**
NERKS ▸ **nerk**
NEROL *n* scented liquid
NEROLI *n* brown oil used in perfumery **nerolis**
NEROLS ▸ **nerol**
NERTS *interj* nuts **nertz**
NERVAL ▸ **nerve**
NERVATE *adj* (of leaves) with veins
NERVE *n, vb* **nerved, nerver, nervers, nerves**

NERVIER ▸ **nervy**
NERVILY ▸ **nervy**
NERVINE *adj* having a soothing effect upon the nerves ▹ *n* nervine drug or agent
NERVING ▸ **nerve**
NERVOUS *adj*
NERVULE *n* small vein
NERVURE *n* stiff rod in an insect's wing
NERVY *adj* excitable or nervous
NESH *adj* sensitive to the cold **nesher, neshest**
NESS *n* headland, cape **nesses**
NEST *n, vb* **nested, nester, nesters, nestful, nesting**
NESTLE *vb* **nestled, nestler, nestles**
NESTOR *n* wise old man **nestors**
NESTS ▸ **nest**
NET *n, vb, adj*
NETBALL *n*
NETE *n* lyre string **netes**
NETFUL ▸ **net**
NETFULS ▸ **net**
NETHEAD *n* expert on the internet
NETHER *adj* lower
NETIZEN *n* person who regularly uses the internet
NETLESS ▸ **net**
NETLIKE ▸ **net**
NETOP *n* friend **netops**
NETROOT *n*
NETS ▸ **net**
NETSUKE *n* (in Japan) a carved ornamental toggle
NETT = **net**
NETTED ▸ **net**
NETTER *n* person that makes nets **netters**
NETTIE *n* enthusiastic user of the internet
NETTIER ▸ **net**
NETTIES ▸ **netty**
NETTING ▸ **net**
NETTLE *n, vb* **nettled, nettler, nettles, nettly**
NETTS ▸ **nett**
NETTY *n* lavatory, originally an earth closet
NETWORK *n, vb*
NEUK *Scot word for* ▸ **nook**
NEUKS ▸ **neuk**
NEUM = **neume**
NEUME *n* notational symbol **neumes, neumic**
NEUMS ▸ **neum**
NEURAL *adj* of a nerve or the nervous system
NEURINE *n* poisonous alkaloid
NEURISM *n* nerve force
NEURITE *n* biological cell component
NEUROID *adj* nervelike
NEUROMA *n* any tumour composed of nerve tissue
NEURON = **neurone**
NEURONE *n*
NEURONS ▸ **neuron**
NEURULA *n* stage of embryonic development
NEUSTIC ▸ **neuston**
NEUSTON *n* organisms that float on the surface of open water
NEUTER *adj, vb, n* **neuters**
NEUTRAL *adj, n*
NEUTRON *n*
NEVE *n* mass of porous ice, formed from snow
NEVEL *vb* beat with the fists **nevels**
NEVER *adv, sentence substitute, interj*
NEVES ▸ **neve**
NEVI ▸ **nevus**
NEVOID ▸ **naevus**
NEVUS = **naevus**
NEW *adj* not existing before ▹ *adv* recently ▹ *vb* make new
NEWBIE *n* person new to a job, club, etc **newbies**
NEWBORN *adj, n*
NEWCOME > **newcomer**
NEWED ▸ **new**
NEWEL *n* post at the top or bottom of a flight of stairs
NEWELL *n* new thing **newells**
NEWELS ▸ **newel**
NEWER ▸ **new**
NEWEST ▸ **new**
NEWIE *n* fresh idea or thing **newies**
NEWING ▸ **new**
NEWISH *adj* fairly new
NEWLY *adv*
NEWMOWN *adj* freshly cut
NEWNESS ▸ **new**
NEWS *n, vb*

NEWSBOY *n* boy who sells or delivers newspapers
NEWSED ▸ **news**
NEWSES ▸ **news**
NEWSIE = **newsy**
NEWSIER ▸ **newsy**
NEWSIES ▸ **newsie**
NEWSING ▸ **news**
NEWSMAN *n* male newsreader or reporter **newsmen**
NEWSY *adj* full of news ▹ *n* newsagent
NEWT *n*
NEWTON *n* **newtons**
NEWTS ▸ **newt**
NEXT *adv* immediately following ▹ *n* next person or thing **nextly, nexts**
NEXUS *n* connection or link **nexuses**
NGAI *n*
NGAIO *n* small New Zealand tree **ngaios**
NGANA = **nagana**
NGANAS ▸ **ngana**
NGARARA *n* lizard found in New Zealand
NGATI *n* (occurring as part of the tribe name) a tribe or clan **ngatis**
NGOMA *n* type of drum **ngomas**
NGWEE *n* Zambian monetary unit
NHANDU *n* type of spider **nhandus**
NIACIN *n* **niacins**
NIB *n, vb* **nibbed, nibbing**
NIBBLE *vb, n* **nibbled**
NIBBLER *n* person, animal, or thing that nibbles
NIBBLES ▸ **nibble**
NIBLICK *n* former golf club giving a great deal of lift
NIBLIKE ▸ **nib**
NIBS ▸ **nib**
NICAD *n* rechargeable dry-cell battery **nicads**
NICE *adj* pleasant **niceish, nicely, nicer, nicest**
NICETY *n*
NICHE *n, adj, vb* **niched**
NICHER *vb* snigger **nichers**
NICHES ▸ **niche**
NICHING ▸ **niche**
NICHT *Scot word for* ▸ **night**
NICHTS ▸ **nicht**
NICISH ▸ **nice**
NICK *vb, n*
NICKAR *n* hard seed **nickars**
NICKED ▸ **nick**
NICKEL *n, vb* **nickels**
NICKER *n* pound sterling ▹ *vb* (of a horse) to neigh softly **nickers**
NICKING ▸ **nick**
NICKLE = **nickel**
NICKLED ▸ **nickle**
NICKLES ▸ **nickle**
NICKS ▸ **nick**
NICKUM *n* mischievous person **nickums**
NICOISE *adj* prepared with tomatoes, black olives, garlic and anchovies
NICOL *n* device for producing plane-polarized light **nicols**
NICOTIN = **nicotine**
NICTATE = **nictitate**
NID = **nide**
NIDAL ▸ **nidus**
NIDATE *vb* undergo nidation **nidated, nidates**
NIDDICK *n* nape of the neck
NIDE *vb* nest **nided, nides**
NIDGET *n* fool **nidgets**
NIDI ▸ **nidus**
NIDIFY *vb* (of a bird) to make or build a nest
NIDING *n* coward **nidings**
NIDOR *n* cooking smell **nidors**
NIDS ▸ **nid**
NIDUS *n* nest in which insects or spiders deposit their eggs **niduses**
NIE *archaic spelling of* ▸ **nigh**
NIECE *n* **nieces**
NIED ▸ **nie**
NIEF = **nieve**
NIEFS ▸ **nief**
NIELLI ▸ **niello**
NIELLO *n* black compound of sulphur and silver, lead, or copper ▹ *vb* decorate or treat with niello **niellos**
NIES ▸ **nie**
NIEVE *n* closed hand **nieves**
NIFE *n* earth's core **nifes**
NIFF *n* stink ▹ *vb* stink **niffed**

NIFFER *vb* barter **niffers**
NIFFIER ▸ niff
NIFFING ▸ niff
NIFFS ▸ niff
NIFFY ▸ niff
NIFTIER ▸ nifty
NIFTIES ▸ nifty
NIFTILY ▸ nifty
NIFTY *adj, n*
NIGELLA *n* type of Mediterranean plant
NIGGARD *n* stingy person ▹ *adj* miserly ▹ *vb* act in a niggardly way
NIGGLE *vb, n* **niggled, niggler, niggles, niggly**
NIGH *prep* near ▹ *adv* nearly ▹ *adj* near ▹ *vb* approach **nighed, nigher, nighest, nighing, nighly, nighs**
NIGHT *n, adj*
NIGHTED *adj* darkened
NIGHTIE = **nightgown**
NIGHTLY *adv, adj*
NIGHTS *adv* at night or on most nights
NIGHTY = **nightie**
NIGIRI *n* small oval block of cold rice, wasabi and fish **nigiris**
NIGRIFY *vb* blacken
NIHIL *n* nil **nihils**
NIHONGA *n* Japanese form of painting
NIKAB = **niqab**
NIKABS ▸ nikab
NIKAH *n* Islamic marriage contract **nikahs**
NIKAU *n* palm tree native to New Zealand **nikaus**
NIL *n*
NILGAI *n* large Indian antelope **nilgais**
NILGAU = **nilghau**
NILGAUS ▸ nilgau
NILGHAI = **nilgai**
NILGHAU = **nilgai**
NILL *vb* be unwilling **nilled, nilling, nills**
NILS ▸ nil
NIM *n* game involving removing one or more small items from several rows or piles ▹ *vb* steal
NIMB *n* halo **nimbed**
NIMBI ▸ nimbus
NIMBLE *adj* **nimbler, nimbly**
NIMBS ▸ nimb
NIMBUS *n*
NIMIETY *rare word for* **▸ excess**
NIMIOUS ▸ nimiety
NIMMED ▸ nim
NIMMER ▸ nim
NIMMERS ▸ nim
NIMMING ▸ nim
NIMONIC *adj as in* **nimonic alloy** type of nickel-based alloy
NIMPS *adj* easy
NIMROD *n* hunter **nimrods**
NIMS ▸ nim
NINCOM = **nicompoop**
NINCOMS ▸ nincom
NINCUM = **nicompoop**
NINCUMS ▸ nincum
NINE *n*
NINEPIN *n* skittle used in ninepins
NINES ▸ nine
NINETY *n, determiner*
NINJA *n* person skilled in ninjutsu **ninjas**
NINNIES ▸ ninny
NINNY *n* stupid person
NINON *n* fine strong silky fabric **ninons**
NINTH *n* (of) number nine in a series ▹ *adj* coming after the eighth ▹ *adv* after the eighth **ninthly, ninths**
NIOBATE *n* type of salt crystal
NIOBIC *adj* of or containing niobium in the pentavalent state
NIOBITE *another name for* > **columbite**
NIOBIUM *n* white metallic element
NIOBOUS *adj* of or containing niobium in the trivalent state
NIP *vb, n*
NIPA *n* palm tree of S and SE Asia **nipas**
NIPPED ▸ nip
NIPPER *n, vb*
NIPPERS *pl n* instrument or tool for pinching or squeezing
NIPPIER ▸ nippy
NIPPILY ▸ nippy
NIPPING ▸ nip
NIPPLE *n, vb* **nippled, nipples**
NIPPY *adj*
NIPS ▸ nip
NIPTER *n* type of religious ceremony **nipters**

NIQAB *n* type of veil worn by some Muslim women **niqabs**

> One of those invaluable words allowing you to play the Q without a U. It can also be spelt **nikab**.

NIRL *vb* shrivel **nirled**
NIRLIE *variant of* ▸ **nirly**
NIRLIER ▸ **nirly**
NIRLING ▸ **nirl**
NIRLIT ▸ **nirl**
NIRLS ▸ **nirl**
NIRLY *adj* shrivelled
NIRVANA *n*
NIS *n* friendly goblin
NISEI *n* native-born citizen of the US or Canada whose parents were Japanese **niseis**
NISGUL *n* smallest and weakest bird in a brood of chickens **nisguls**
NISH *n* nothing **nishes**
NISI *adj* (of a court order) coming into effect on a specified date
NISSE = **nis**
NISSES ▸ **nisse**
NISUS *n* impulse towards or striving after a goal
NIT *n*
NITE *variant of* ▸ **night**
NITER = **nitre**
NITERIE *n* nightclub
NITERS ▸ **niter**
NITERY ▸ **niter**
NITES ▸ **nite**
NITHER *vb* shiver **nithers**
NITHING *n* coward
NITID *adj* bright
NITINOL *n* metal alloy
NITON *less common name for* ▸ **radon**
NITONS ▸ **niton**
NITPICK *vb* criticize unnecessarily
NITRATE *n*, *vb*
NITRE *n* potassium nitrate **nitres**
NITRIC *adj* of or containing nitrogen
NITRID = **nitride**
NITRIDE *n* compound of nitrogen ▹ *vb* make into a nitride
NITRIDS ▸ **nitrid**
NITRIFY *vb* treat or cause to react with nitrogen
NITRIL = **nitrile**
NITRILE *n* any one of a particular class of organic compounds
NITRILS ▸ **nitril**
NITRITE *n* salt or ester of nitrous acid
NITRO *n* nitrogylcerine **nitros**
NITROSO *adj* of a particular monovalent group
NITROUS *adj* derived from or containing nitrogen in a low valency state
NITROX *n* mixture of nitrogen and oxygen used in diving
NITRY *adj* nitrous
NITRYL *n* chemical compound **nitryls**
NITS ▸ **nit**
NITTIER ▸ **nitty**
NITTY *adj* infested with nits
NITWIT *n* stupid person **nitwits**
NIVAL *adj* of or growing in or under snow
NIVEOUS *adj* resembling snow, esp in colour
NIX *sentence substitute* be careful! watch out! ▹ *n* rejection or refusal ▹ *vb* veto, deny, reject, or forbid (plans, suggestions, etc)

> This is a handy little word, combining X with two of the most common tiles in the game.

NIXE *n* water sprite
NIXED ▸ **nix**
NIXER *n* spare-time job **nixers**
NIXES ▸ **nix**
NIXIE *n* female water sprite, usually unfriendly to humans **nixies**
NIXING ▸ **nix**
NIXY = **nixie**
NIZAM *n* (formerly) a Turkish regular soldier **nizams**
NKOSI *n* term of address to a superior **nkosis**
NO *interj*, *adj*, *adv*, *n*
NOAH *n* shark **noahs**
NOB *n* person of wealth or social distinction **nobbier, nobbily**
NOBBLE *vb* attract the attention of **nobbled, nobbler, nobbles**

NOBBUT *adv* nothing but
NOBBY ▸ **nob**
NOBLE *adj, n* **nobler, nobles, noblest, nobly**
NOBODY *pron, n*
NOBS ▸ **nob**
NOCAKE *n* Indian meal made from dried corn **nocakes**
NOCENT *n* guilty person **nocents**
NOCHEL ▸ **notchel**
NOCHELS ▸ **nochel**
NOCK *n* notch on an arrow or a bow for the bowstring ▹ *vb* fit (an arrow) on a bowstring **nocked**
NOCKET = **nacket**
NOCKETS ▸ **nocket**
NOCKING ▸ **nock**
NOCKS ▸ **nock**
NOCTUA *n* type of moth **noctuas**
NOCTUID *n* type of nocturnal moth ▹ *adj* of or relating to this type of moth
NOCTULE *n* any of several large Old World insectivorous bats
NOCTURN *n* any of the main sections of the office of matins
NOCUOUS *adj* harmful
NOD *vb, n*
NODAL *adj* of or like a node **nodally**
NODATED *adj* knotted
NODDED ▸ **nod**
NODDER ▸ **nod**
NODDERS ▸ **nod**
NODDIER ▸ **noddy**
NODDIES ▸ **noddy**
NODDING ▸ **nod**
NODDLE *n* head ▹ *vb* nod (the head), as through drowsiness **noddled, noddles**
NODDY *n* tropical tern with a dark plumage ▹ *adj* very easy to use or understand
NODE *n* **nodes**
NODI ▸ **nodus**
NODICAL *adj* of or relating to the nodes of a celestial body
NODOSE *adj* having nodes or knotlike swellings **nodous**
NODS ▸ **nod**
NODULAR ▸ **nodule**
NODULE *n* **noduled, nodules**
NODUS *n* problematic idea, situation, etc
NOEL *n* Christmas **noels**
NOES ▸ **no**
NOESES ▸ **noesis**
NOESIS *n* exercise of reason
NOETIC *adj* of or relating to the mind
NOG = **nogging**
NOGAKU *n* Japanese style of drama
NOGG = **nog**
NOGGED *adj* built with timber and brick
NOGGIN *n* head
NOGGING *n* short horizontal timber member
NOGGINS ▸ **noggin**
NOGGS ▸ **nogg**
NOGS ▸ **nog**
NOH *n* stylized classic drama of Japan
NOHOW *adv* under any conditions
NOIL *n* short or knotted fibres that are separated from the long fibres by combing
NOILIER ▸ **noily**
NOILS ▸ **noil**
NOILY ▸ **noil**
NOINT *vb* anoint **nointed**
NOINTER *n* mischievous child
NOINTS ▸ **noint**
NOIR *adj* (of a film) showing characteristics of a *film noir*, in plot or style ▹ *n* film noir **noirish, noirs**
NOISE *n* **noised, noises**
NOISIER ▸ **noisy**
NOISILY ▸ **noisy** **noising**
NOISOME *adj* (of smells) offensive
NOISY *adj*
NOLE = **noll**
NOLES ▸ **nole**
NOLL *n* head **nolls**
NOLO *vb as in* **nolo contendere** plea indicating that the defendant does not wish to contest the case **nolos**
NOM *n* name
NOMA *n* gangrenous inflammation of the mouth

NOMAD *n* **nomade**
NOMADES ▸ **nomade**
NOMADIC *adj* relating to or characteristic of nomads
NOMADS ▸ **nomad**
NOMADY *n* practice of living like nomads
NOMARCH *n* head of an ancient Egyptian nome
NOMAS ▸ **noma**
NOMBLES *variant spelling of* ▸ **numbles**
NOMBRIL *n* point on a shield
NOME *n* any of the former provinces of modern Greece
NOMEN *n* ancient Roman's second name
NOMES ▸ **nome**
NOMIC *adj* normal or habitual
NOMINA ▸ **nomen**
NOMINAL *adj, n*
NOMINEE *n* candidate
NOMISM *n* adherence to laws as a primary exercise of religion **nomisms**
NOMOI ▸ **nomos**
NOMOS *n* convention
NOMS ▸ **nom**
NON *adv* not
NONA *n* sleeping sickness
NONACID *adj* not acid ▹ *n* nonacid substance
NONAGE *n* state of being under full legal age **nonaged, nonages**
NONAGON *n* geometric figure with nine sides
NONANE *n* type of chemical compound **nonanes**
NONART *n* something that does not constitute art **nonarts**
NONARY *adj* based on the number nine
NONAS ▸ **nones**
NONBANK *n* business or institution that is not a bank but provides similar services
NONBODY *n* nonphysical nature of a person
NONBOOK *n* book with little substance
NONCASH *adj* other than cash
NONCE *n* present time or occasion **nonces**
NONCOLA *n* soft drink other than cola
NONCOM *n* person not involved in combat **noncoms**
NONCORE *adj* not central or essential
NONDRIP *adj* (of paint) specially formulated to minimize dripping during application
NONDRUG *adj* not involving the use of drugs
NONE *pron*
NONEGO *n* everything that is outside one's conscious self **nonegos**
NONES *n* (in the Roman calendar) the ninth day before the ides of each month
NONET *n* piece of music composed for a group of nine instruments **nonets, nonette, nonetti, nonetto**
NONFACT *n* event or thing not provable
NONFAN *n* person who is not a fan **nonfans**
NONFARM *adj* not connected with a farm
NONFAT *adj* fat free
NONFOOD *n* item that is not food
NONFUEL *adj* not relating to fuel
NONG *n* stupid or incompetent person
NONGAME *adj* not pursued for competitive sport purposes
NONGAY *n* person who is not gay **nongays**
NONGS ▸ **nong**
NONHEME *adj* of dietary iron, obtained from vegetable foods
NONHERO *n* person who is not a hero
NONHOME *adj* not of the home
NONI *n* tree of SE Asia and the Pacific islands
NONIRON *adj* not requiring ironing
NONIS ▸ **noni**
NONJURY *n* trial without a jury
NONLIFE *n* matter which is not living

NONMAN *n* being that is not a man
NONMEAT *n* not containing meat
NONMEN ▸ **nonman**
NONNEWS *adj* not concerned with news
NONNIES ▸ **nonny**
NONNY *n* meaningless word
NONOILY *adj* not oily
NONORAL *adj* not oral
NONPAID *adj* without payment
NONPAR *adj* nonparticipating
NONPAST *n* grammatical term
NONPEAK *n* period of low demand
NONPLAY *n* social behaviour that is not classed as play
NONPLUS *vb* put at a loss ▹ *n* state of utter perplexity prohibiting action or speech
NONPOOR *adj* not poor
NONPROS *vb* enter a judgment of non prosequitur
NONSELF *n* foreign molecule in the body
NONSKED *n* non-scheduled aeroplane
NONSKID *adj* designed to reduce skidding
NONSLIP *adj* designed to prevent slipping
NONSTOP *adv, adj, n*
NONSUCH = **nonesuch**
NONSUIT *n* order of a judge dismissing a suit ▹ *vb* order the dismissal of the suit of (a person)
NONTAX *n* tax that has little real effect
NONUPLE *adj* ninefold ▹ *n* ninefold number
NONUSE *n* failure to use **nonuser, nonuses**
NONWAGE *adj* not part of wages
NONWAR *n* state of nonviolence **nonwars**
NONWOOL *adj* not wool
NONWORD *n* series of letters not recognised as a word
NONWORK *adj* not involving work
NONYL *n* type of chemical **nonyls**
NONZERO *adj* not equal to zero
NOO *n* type of Japanese musical drama
NOOB ▸ **newbie**
NOOBS ▸ **noob**
NOODGE *vb* annoy persistently **noodged, noodges**
NOODLE *n, vb* **noodled, noodles**
NOOGIE *n* act of inflicting pain by rubbing head hard **noogies**
NOOIT *interj* South African exclamation of surprise
NOOK *n* **nooks**
NOOLOGY *n* study of intuition
NOON *n, vb*
NOONDAY *adj* happening at noon ▹ *n* middle of the day
NOONED ▸ **noon**
NOONER *n* sexual encounter during a lunch hour **nooners**
NOONING *n* midday break for rest or food
NOONS ▸ **noon**
NOOP *n* point of the elbow **noops**
NOOSE *n* **noosed**
NOOSER *n* person who uses a noose **noosers**
NOOSES ▸ **noose**
NOOSING ▸ **noose**
NOPAL *n* type of cactus **nopales, nopals**
NOPE *interj* no
NOPLACE = **nowhere**
NOR *prep*
NORDIC *adj* of competitions in cross-country racing and ski-jumping
NORI *n* edible seaweed
NORIA *n* water wheel with buckets attached to its rim **norias**
NORIMON *n* Japanese passenger vehicle
NORIS ▸ **nori**
NORITE *n* variety of gabbro **norites, noritic**
NORK *n* female breast **norks**
NORLAND *n* north part of a country or the earth
NORM *n*
NORMA *n* norm or standard
NORMAL *adj, n* **normals**

NORMAN *n* post used for winding on a ship **normans**
NORMAS ▸ **norma**
NORMED *n* mathematical term
NORMS ▸ **norm**
NORSEL *vb* fit with short lines for fastening hooks **norsels**
NORTENA = **norteno**
NORTENO *n* type of Mexican music
NORTH *n, adj, adv, vb* **northed**
NORTHER *n* wind or storm from the north ▹ *vb* move north
NORTHS ▸ **north**
NORWARD = **northward**
NOS ▸ **no**
NOSE *n, vb*
NOSEAN *n* type of mineral **noseans**
NOSEBAG *n* bag containing feed fastened round a horse's head
NOSED ▸ **nose**
NOSEGAY *n* small bunch of flowers
NOSER *n* strong headwind **nosers**
NOSES ▸ **nose**
NOSEY *adj* prying or inquisitive ▹ *n* nosey person **noseys**
NOSH *n* food ▹ *vb* eat **noshed, nosher, noshers**
NOSHERY *n* restaurant or other place where food is served
NOSHES ▸ **nosh**
NOSHING ▸ **nosh**
NOSIER, nosies, nosiest, nosily ▸ **nosy**
NOSING *n* edge of a step or stair tread **nosings**
NOSODE *n* homeopathic remedy **nosodes**
NOSTOC *n* type of bacterium occurring in moist places **nostocs**
NOSTOI ▸ **nostos**
NOSTOS *n* story of a return home
NOSTRIL *n*
NOSTRO *adj as in* **nostro account** bank account conducted by a British bank with a foreign bank
NOSTRUM *n* quack medicine
NOSY *adj*
NOT *adv*
NOTA ▸ **notum**
NOTABLE *adj, n*
NOTABLY *adv* particularly or especially
NOTAEUM *n* back of a bird's body
NOTAIRE *n*
NOTAL ▸ **notum**
NOTANDA > **notandum**
NOTARY *n*
NOTATE *vb* write (esp music) in notation **notated, notates**
NOTCH *n, vb* **notched**
NOTCHEL *vb* refuse to pay another person's debts
NOTCHER *n* person who cuts notches
NOTCHES ▸ **notch**
NOTCHY *adj* (of a motor vehicle gear mechanism) requiring careful gear-changing
NOTE *n, vb*
NOTED *adj* **notedly**
NOTELET *n* small folded card with a design on the front
NOTEPAD *n* number of sheets of paper fastened together
NOTER *n* person who takes notes **noters**
NOTES *pl n* short descriptive or summarized jottings
NOTHER = **other**
NOTHING *pron, adv, n*
NOTICE *n, vb* **noticed**
NOTICER *n* person who takes notice
NOTICES ▸ **notice**
NOTIFY *vb*
NOTING ▸ **note**
NOTION *n*
NOTIONS *pl n* pins, cotton, ribbon, and similar wares used for sewing
NOTITIA *n* register or list, esp of ecclesiastical districts
NOTOUR *adj* notorious
NOTT = **not**
NOTUM *n* cuticular plate on an insect
NOUGAT *n* **nougats**
NOUGHT *n* **noughts**
NOUL = **noll**
NOULD *vb* would not **noulde**

NOULE = **noll**
NOULES ▶ **noule**
NOULS ▶ **noul**
NOUMENA
> **noumenon**
NOUN *n* **nounal**
NOUNIER ▶ **nouny**
NOUNS ▶ **noun**
NOUNY *adj* nounlike
NOUP *n* steep headland **noups**
NOURICE *n* nurse
NOURISH *vb*
NOURSLE *vb* nurse
NOUS *n* common sense
NOUSELL *vb* foster
NOUSES ▶ **nous**
NOUSLE *vb* nuzzle **nousled, nousles**
NOUT = **nought**
NOUVEAU *adj* having recently become the thing specified
NOVA *n* **novae**
NOVALIA *n* newly reclaimed land
NOVAS ▶ **nova**
NOVATE *vb* substitute one thing in place of another
NOVATED *adj as in* **novated lease** Australian system of employer-aided car purchase
NOVATES ▶ **novate**
NOVEL *n, adj*
NOVELLA *n* short novel **novelle**
NOVELLY ▶ **novel**
NOVELS ▶ **novel**
NOVELTY *n*
NOVENA *n* set of prayers or services on nine consecutive days **novenae, novenas**
NOVICE *n* **novices**
NOVITY *n* novelty
NOVUM *n* game played with dice **novums**
NOW *adv*
NOWAY *adv* in no manner ▷ *sentence substitute* used to make an emphatic refusal, denial etc **noways**
NOWED *adj* knotted
NOWHERE *adv, n*
NOWISE *another word for* ▶ **noway**
NOWL *n* crown of the head **nowls**
NOWN = **own**
NOWNESS ▶ **nown**
NOWS ▶ **now**
NOWT *n* nothing
NOWTIER ▶ **nowty** **nowts**
NOWTY *adj* bad-tempered
NOWY *adj* having a small projection at the centre (of a cross)
NOX *n* nitrogen oxide

> Meaning nitrogen oxide, this is another of those very useful short words containing X.

NOXAL *adj* relating to damage done by something belonging to another
NOXES ▶ **nox**
NOXIOUS *adj*
NOY *vb* harrass
NOYADE *n* execution by drowning **noyades**
NOYANCE *n* nuisance
NOYAU *n* brandy-based liqueur **noyaus**
NOYED ▶ **noy**
NOYES *archaic form of* ▶ **noise**
NOYESES ▶ **noyes**
NOYING ▶ **noy**
NOYOUS ▶ **noy**
NOYS ▶ **noy**
NOYSOME ▶ **noy**
NOZZER *n* new recruit (in the Navy) **nozzers**
NOZZLE *n* **nozzles**
NTH *adj* of an unspecified number

> A good word to remember for awkward situations on the board, as it's one of very few three-letter words that doesn't contain a vowel.

NU *n* 13th letter in the Greek alphabet
NUANCE *n, vb* **nuanced, nuances**
NUB *n, vb* **nubbed**
NUBBIER ▶ **nubby**
NUBBIN *n* something small or undeveloped, esp a fruit or ear of corn
NUBBING ▶ **nub**
NUBBINS ▶ **nubbin**
NUBBLE *n* small lump **nubbled, nubbles, nubbly**
NUBBY *adj* having small lumps or protuberances
NUBIA *n* fleecy scarf for the head, worn by women **nubias**

NUBILE *adj*
NUBS ▸ **nub**
NUBUCK *n* type of leather with a velvety finish **nubucks**
NUCELLI > **nucellus**
NUCHA *n* back or nape of the neck **nuchae**
NUCHAL *n* scale on a reptile's neck **nuchals**
NUCLEAL ▸ **nucleus**
NUCLEAR *adj*
NUCLEI ▸ **nucleus**
NUCLEIC *adj as in* **nucleic acid** type of complex compound that is a vital constituent of living cells
NUCLEIN *n* protein that occurs in the nuclei of living cells
NUCLEON *n* proton or neutron
NUCLEUS *n*
NUCLIDE *n* species of atom characterized by its atomic number and its mass number
NUCULE *n* small seed **nucules**
NUDDIES ▸ **nuddy**
NUDDY *n as in* **in the nuddy** in the nude
NUDE *adj, n* **nudely, nuder, nudes, nudest**
NUDGE *vb, n* **nudged, nudger, nudgers, nudges, nudging**
NUDIE *n* film, show, or magazine depicting nudity **nudies**
NUDISM *n* practice of not wearing clothes **nudisms, nudist, nudists**
NUDITY *n* state or fact of being nude
NUDNICK = **nudnik**
NUDNIK *n* boring person **nudniks**
NUDZH = **nudge**
NUDZHED ▸ **nudzh**
NUDZHES ▸ **nudzh**
NUFF *slang form of* ▸ **enough**
NUFFIN *slang form of* ▸ **nothing**
NUFFINS ▸ **nuffin**
NUFFS ▸ **nuff**
NUGAE *n* jests
NUGGAR *n* sailing boat used to carry cargo on the Nile **nuggars**
NUGGET *n, vb* **nuggets**
NUGGETY *adj* of or resembling a nugget
NUKE *vb* attack with nuclear weapons ▹ *n* nuclear weapon **nuked, nukes, nuking**
NULL *adj, vb*
NULLA = **nullah**
NULLAH *n* stream or drain **nullahs**
NULLAS ▸ **nulla**
NULLED ▸ **null**
NULLIFY *vb*
NULLING *n* knurling
NULLITY *n* state of being null
NULLS ▸ **null**
NUMB *adj, vb*
NUMBAT *n* **numbats**
NUMBED ▸ **numb**
NUMBER *n, vb* **numbers**
NUMBEST ▸ **numb**
NUMBING ▸ **numb**
NUMBLES *pl n* animal organs, cooked for food
NUMBLY ▸ **numb**
NUMBS ▸ **numb**
NUMDAH *n* coarse felt made esp in India **numdahs**
NUMEN *n* deity or spirit presiding over a thing or place
NUMERAL *n, adj*
NUMERIC *n* number or numeral
NUMINA *plural of* ▸ **numen**
NUMMARY *adj* of or relating to coins
NUMNAH = **numdah**
NUMNAHS ▸ **numnah**
NUMPTY *n* stupid person
NUN *n*
NUNATAK *n* isolated mountain peak projecting through glacial ice
NUNCIO *n* pope's ambassador **nuncios**
NUNCLE *archaic or dialect word for* ▸ **uncle**
NUNCLES ▸ **nuncle**
NUNDINE *n* market day
NUNHOOD *n* condition, practice, or character of a nun
NUNLIKE ▸ **nun**
NUNNERY *n* convent
NUNNISH ▸ **nun**
NUNNY *n as in* **nunny bag** small sealskin haversack used in Canada
NUNS ▸ **nun**
NUNSHIP ▸ **nun**

NUPTIAL *adj* relating to marriage
NUR *n* wooden ball
NURAGHE *n* Sardinian round tower **nuraghi**
NURD = **nerd**
NURDIER ▸ **nerd**
NURDISH ▸ **nerd**
NURDLE *vb* score runs in cricket by soft deflections **nurdled, nurdles**
NURDS ▸ **nurd**
NURDY ▸ **nurd**
NURHAG *n* Sardinian round tower **nurhags**
NURL *variant of* ▸ **knurl**
NURLED ▸ **nurl**
NURLING ▸ **nurl**
NURLS ▸ **nurl**
NURR *n* wooden ball **nurrs**
NURS ▸ **nur**
NURSE *n*, *vb* **nursed**
NURSER *n* person who treats something carefully **nursers**
NURSERY *n*
NURSES ▸ **nurse**
NURSING *n*
NURSLE *vb* nuzzle **nursled, nursles**
NURTURE *n*, *vb*
NUS ▸ **nu**
NUT *n*, *vb*
NUTANT *adj* having the apex hanging down
NUTATE *vb* nod **nutated, nutates**
NUTGALL *n* nut-shaped gall caused by gall wasps on the oak and other trees
NUTJOB *n* crazy person **nutjobs**
NUTLET *n* portion of a fruit that fragments when mature **nutlets**
NUTLIKE ▸ **nut**
NUTMEAL *n* type of grain
NUTMEAT *n* kernel of a nut
NUTMEG *n*, *vb* **nutmegs**
NUTPICK *n* tool used to dig the meat from nuts
NUTRIA *n* fur of the coypu **nutrias**
NUTS ▸ **nut**
NUTTED ▸ **nut**
NUTTERY *n* place where nut trees grow
NUTTIER ▸ **nutty**
NUTTILY ▸ **nutty**
NUTTING *n* act of gathering nuts
NUTTY *adj*
NUTWOOD *n* any of various nut-bearing trees, such as walnut
NUZZER *n* present given to a superior in India **nuzzers**
NUZZLE *vb* **nuzzled**
NUZZLER *n* person or thing that nuzzles
NUZZLES ▸ **nuzzle**
NY = **nigh**
NYAFF *n* small or contemptible person ▹ *vb* yelp like a small dog **nyaffed, nyaffs**
NYALA *n* spiral-horned southern African antelope **nyalas**
NYANZA *n* (in E Africa) a lake **nyanzas**
NYAS *n* young hawk **nyases**
NYBBLE *n* small byte **nybbles**
NYE *n* flock of pheasants ▹ *vb* near **nyed, nyes, nying**
NYLGHAI = **nilgai**
NYLGHAU = **nilgai**
NYLON *n*
NYLONS *pl n* stockings made of nylon
NYMPH *n*
NYMPHA *n* either one of the labia minora **nymphae**
NYMPHAL ▸ **nymph**
NYMPHET *n* sexually precocious young girl
NYMPHIC ▸ **nymph**
NYMPHLY ▸ **nymph**
NYMPHO *n* nymphomaniac **nymphos**
NYMPHS ▸ **nymph**
NYS ▸ **ny**
NYSSA *n* type of tree **nyssas**

Oo

With eight **O**s in the bag, you're likely to have at least one on your rack during a game. There are plenty of good two-letter words starting with **O**. It's worth knowing that **O** will form a two-letter word in front of every other vowel except **A**, as well as in front of **Y**. **O** also combines well with **X**, with **ox** (9 points) as the obvious starting point, and several words that refer to **oxygen** (17), including **oxo** (10) and **oxy** (13). Don't forget the short everyday words that begin with **O**. While **on** and **or** (2 each) won't earn you many points, they can be very helpful when you are trying to score in more than one direction at a time. **Of** and **oh** (5 each) can also prove very useful.

OAF *n* **oafish, oafs**
OAK *n*
OAKED *adj* relating to wine that is stored for a time in oak barrels prior to bottling
OAKEN *adj* made of the wood of the oak
OAKER = **ochre**
OAKERS ▶ **oaker**
OAKIER ▶ **oaky**
OAKIES ▶ **oaky**
OAKIEST ▶ **oaky**
OAKLIKE ▶ **oak**
OAKLING *n* young oak
OAKMOSS *n* type of lichen
OAKS ▶ **oak**
OAKUM *n* fibre obtained by unravelling old rope **oakums**
OAKY *adj* hard like the wood of an oak ▷ *n* ice cream
OAR *n, vb*
OARAGE *n* use or number of oars **oarages**
OARED *adj* equipped with oars
OARFISH *n* very long ribbonfish with long slender ventral fins
OARIER ▶ **oary**
OARIEST ▶ **oary**
OARING ▶ **oar**
OARLESS ▶ **oar**
OARLIKE ▶ **oar**
OARLOCK *n* swivelling device that holds an oar in place
OARS ▶ **oar**
OARSMAN *n* person who rows **oarsmen**
OARWEED *n* type of brown seaweed
OARY *adj* of or like an oar
OASES ▶ **oasis**
OASIS *n*
OAST *n* oven for drying hops **oasts**
OAT *n*
OATCAKE *n* thin flat biscuit of oatmeal
OATEN *adj* made of oats or oat straw
OATER *n* film about the American Wild West **oaters**
OATH *n* **oaths**
OATIER ▶ **oaty**
OATIEST ▶ **oaty**

OATLIKE ▶ **oat**
OATMEAL *n, adj*
OATS ▶ **oat**
OATY *adj* of, like, or containing oats
OAVES ▶ **oaf**
OB *n* expression of opposition
OBA *n* (in W Africa) a Yoruba chief or ruler
OBANG *n* former Japanese coin **obangs**
OBAS ▶ **oba**
OBCONIC *adj* shaped like a cone and attached at the pointed end
OBDURE *vb* make obdurate **obdured, obdures**
OBE *n* ancient Laconian village
OBEAH *vb* cast spell on **obeahed, obeahs**
OBECHE *n* African tree **obeches**
OBEISM *n* belief in obeah **obeisms**
OBELI ▶ **obelus**
OBELIA *n* type of jellyfish **obelias**
OBELION *n* area of skull
OBELISE = **obelize**
OBELISK *n*
OBELISM *n* practice of marking passages in text
OBELIZE *vb* mark (a word or passage) with an obelus
OBELUS *n* mark used to indicate spurious words or passages
OBENTO *n* Japanese lunch box **obentos**
OBES ▶ **obe**
OBESE *adj* **obesely, obeser, obesest, obesity**
OBEY *vb* **obeyed, obeyer, obeyers, obeying, obeys**
OBI *n* broad sash tied in a large flat bow at the back ▷ *vb* bewitch
OBIA = **obeah**
OBIAS ▶ **obia**
OBIED, obiing, obiism, obiisms ▶ **obi**
OBIIT *vb* died
OBIS ▶ **obi**
OBIT *n* memorial service
OBITAL *adj* of obits
OBITER *adv* by the way
OBITS ▶ **obit**
OBITUAL *adj* of obits
OBJECT *n, vb* **objects**
OBJET *n* object **objets**
OBJURE *vb* put on oath **objured, objures**
OBLAST *n* administrative division of the constituent republics of Russia **oblasti, oblasts**
OBLATE *adj* (of a sphere) flattened at the poles ▷ *n* person dedicated to a monastic or religious life **oblates**
OBLIGE *vb* **obliged**
OBLIGEE *n* person in whose favour an obligation, contract, or bond is created
OBLIGER ▶ **oblige**
OBLIGES ▶ **oblige**
OBLIGOR *n* person who binds himself by contract
OBLIQUE *adj, n, vb*
OBLONG *adj, n* **oblongs**
OBLOQUY *n* verbal abuse
OBO *n* ship carrying oil and ore
OBOE *n* **oboes, oboist, oboists**
OBOL = **obolus**
OBOLARY *adj* very poor
OBOLE *n* former weight unit in pharmacy **oboles**
OBOLI ▶ **obolus**
OBOLS ▶ **obol**
OBOLUS *n* Greek unit of weight
OBOS ▶ **obo**
OBOVATE *adj* (of a leaf) shaped like the longitudinal section of an egg with the narrower end at the base
OBOVOID *adj* (of a fruit) egg-shaped with the narrower end at the base
OBS ▶ **ob**
OBSCENE *adj*
OBSCURE *adj, vb*
OBSEQUY *singular of* > **obsequies**
OBSERVE *vb*
OBSESS *vb* preoccupy (someone) compulsively
OBSIGN *vb* confirm **obsigns**
OBTAIN *vb* **obtains**

OBTECT *adj* (of a pupa) encased in a hardened secretion
OBTEND *vb* put forward **obtends**
OBTEST *vb* beg (someone) earnestly **obtests**
OBTRUDE *vb* push oneself or one's ideas on others
OBTUND *vb* deaden or dull **obtunds**
OBTUSE *adj* **obtuser**
OBVERSE *n, adj*
OBVERT *vb* deduce the obverse of (a proposition) **obverts**
OBVIATE *vb*
OBVIOUS *adj*
OCA *n* any of various South American herbaceous plants
OCARINA *n* small oval wind instrument
OCAS ▸ **oca**
OCCAM *n* computer programming language **occams**
OCCAMY *n* type of alloy
OCCIES ▸ **occy**
OCCIPUT *n* back of the head
OCCLUDE *vb* obstruct
OCCULT *adj, vb* **occults**
OCCUPY *vb*
OCCUR *vb* **occurs**
OCCY *n as in* **all over the occy** dialect expression meaning in every direction
OCEAN *n*
OCEANIC *adj* of or relating to the ocean
OCEANID *n* ocean nymph in Greek mythology
OCEANS ▸ **ocean**
OCELLAR ▸ **ocellus**
OCELLI ▸ **ocellus**
OCELLUS *n* simple eye of insects and some other invertebrates
OCELOID *adj* of or like an ocelot
OCELOT *n* **ocelots**
OCH *interj* expression of surprise, annoyance, or disagreement
OCHE *n* (in darts) mark behind which a player must stand
OCHER = **ochre**
OCHERED ▸ **ocher**
OCHERS ▸ **ocher**
OCHERY ▸ **ocher**
OCHES ▸ **oche**
OCHONE *interj* expression of sorrow or regret
OCHRE *n, adj, vb*
OCHREA *n* cup-shaped structure that sheathes the stems of certain plants **ochreae**
OCHRED, ochres, ochrey, ochring, ochroid, ochrous, ochry ▸ **ochre**
OCICAT *n* breed of cat with a spotted coat **ocicats**
OCKER *n* uncultivated or boorish Australian **ockers**
OCREA = **ochrea**
OCREAE ▸ **ocrea**
OCREATE *adj* possessing an ocrea
OCTA = **okta**
OCTAD *n* group or series of eight **octadic, octads**
OCTAGON *n*
OCTAL *n* number system with a base 8 **octals**
OCTAN *n* illness that occurs weekly
OCTANE *n* **octanes**
OCTANOL *n* alcohol containing eight carbon atoms
OCTANS ▸ **octan**
OCTANT *n* any of the eight parts into which the three planes containing the Cartesian coordinate axes divide space **octants**
OCTAPLA *n* book with eight texts
OCTAS ▸ **octa**
OCTAVAL ▸ **octave**
OCTAVE *n, adj* **octaves**
OCTAVO *n* book size in which the sheets are folded into eight leaves **octavos**
OCTET *n* **octets, octett, octette**
OCTETTS ▸ **octett**
OCTOFID *adj* divided into eight
OCTOPI ▸ **octopus**
OCTOPOD *n* type of mollusc ▹ *adj* of these molluscs
OCTOPUS *n*
OCTROI *n* duty on various goods brought

into certain European towns **octrois**
OCTUOR *n* octet **octuors**
OCTUPLE *n* quantity or number eight times as great as another ▷ *adj* eight times as much or as many ▷ *vb* multiply by eight
OCTUPLY *adv* by eight times
OCTYL *n* group of atoms **octyls**
OCULAR *adj* relating to the eyes or sight ▷ *n* lens in an optical instrument **oculars**
OCULATE *adj* possessing eyes
OCULI ▸ **oculus**
OCULIST *n*
OCULUS *n* round window
OD *n* hypothetical force
ODA *n* room in a harem **odah**
ODAHS ▸ **odah**
ODAL = **udal**
ODALISK = **odalisque**
ODALLER ▸ **odal**
ODALS ▸ **odal**
ODAS ▸ **oda**
ODD *adj*
ODDBALL *n* eccentric person ▷ *adj* strange or peculiar
ODDER ▸ **odd**
ODDEST ▸ **odd**
ODDISH ▸ **odd**
ODDITY *n*
ODDLY ▸ **odd**
ODDMENT *n* odd piece or thing
ODDNESS ▸ **odd**
ODDS *pl n* probability of something happening
ODDSMAN *n* umpire **oddsmen**
ODE *n*
ODEA ▸ **odeum**
ODEON = **odeum**
ODEONS ▸ **odeon**
ODES ▸ **ode**
ODEUM *n* ancient building for musical performances **odeums**
ODIC ▸ **od**
ODIOUS *adj*
ODISM ▸ **od**
ODISMS ▸ **od**
ODIST ▸ **od**
ODISTS ▸ **od**
ODIUM *n* widespread dislike **odiums**
ODONATE *n* dragonfly or related insect
ODONTIC *adj* of teeth
ODOR = **odour**
ODORANT *n* something with a strong smell
ODORATE *adj* having a strong smell
ODORED = **odoured**
ODORFUL = **odourful**
ODORISE = **odorize**
ODORIZE *vb* give an odour to
ODOROUS *adj* having or emitting a characteristic smell
ODORS ▸ **odor**
ODOUR *n*
ODOURED *adj* having odour
ODOURS ▸ **odour**
ODS ▸ **od**
ODSO *n* cry of suprise
ODYL = **od**
ODYLE = **od**
ODYLES ▸ **odyle**
ODYLISM ▸ **odyl**
ODYLS ▸ **odyl**
ODYSSEY *n*
ODZOOKS *interj* cry of surprise
OE *n* grandchild
OECIST *n* colony founder **oecists**
OEDEMA *n* **oedemas**
OEDIPAL *adj* relating to a complex whereby a male child wants to replace his father
OENOMEL *n* drink made of wine and honey
OERSTED *n* cgs unit of magnetic field strength
OES ▸ **oe**
OESTRAL ▸ **oestrus**
OESTRIN *obsolete term for* > **oestrogen**
OESTRUM = **oestrus**
OESTRUS *n* regularly occurring period of fertility in female mammals
OEUVRE *n* work of art, literature, music, etc **oeuvres**
OF *prep*
OFF *prep, adv, adj, n, vb*
OFFAL *n* **offals**
OFFBEAT *adj* unusual or eccentric ▷ *n* any of the normally unaccented beats in a bar
OFFCAST *n* cast-off
OFFCUT *n* piece remaining after the required parts have been cut out **offcuts**

OFFED ▸ **off**
OFFENCE *n*
OFFEND *vb* **offends**
OFFENSE = **offence**
OFFER *vb, n* **offered**
OFFEREE *n* person to whom an offer is made
OFFERER ▸ **offer**
OFFEROR ▸ **offer**
OFFERS ▸ **offer**
OFFHAND *adj, adv*
OFFICE *n*
OFFICER *n, vb*
OFFICES ▸ **office**
OFFIE *n* off-licence **offies**
OFFING *n* **offings**
OFFISH *adj* aloof or distant in manner
OFFKEY *adj* out of tune
OFFLINE *adj*
OFFLOAD *vb* pass responsibilty to someone else
OFFPEAK *adj* relating to times outside periods of intensive use
OFFPUT *n* act of putting off **offputs**
OFFRAMP *n* road allowing traffic to leave a motorway
OFFS ▸ **off**
OFFSCUM *n* scum
OFFSET *vb, n* **offsets**
OFFSIDE *adv, n*
OFFTAKE *n* act of taking off
OFFY ▸ **offie**
OFLAG *n* prisoner-of-war camp for officers in World War II **oflags**
OFT *adv* often
OFTEN *adv* **oftener**
OFTER ▸ **oft**
OFTEST ▸ **oft**
OGAM = **ogham**
OGAMIC ▸ **ogam**
OGAMS ▸ **ogam**
OGDOAD *n* group of eight **ogdoads**
OGEE *n* moulding having a cross section in the form of a letter S
OGEED *adj* (of an arch or moulding) having an ogee
OGEES ▸ **ogee**
OGGIN *n* sea **oggins**
OGHAM *n* ancient writing system used by the Celts **oghamic, oghams**
OGIVAL ▸ **ogive**
OGIVE *n* diagonal rib or groin of a Gothic vault **ogives**
OGLE *vb, n* **ogled, ogler, oglers, ogles, ogling, oglings**
OGMIC ▸ **ogam**
OGRE *n* **ogreish, ogreism, ogres, ogress, ogrish, ogrism, ogrisms**
OH *interj* exclamation of surprise, pain, etc ▹ *vb* say oh **ohed**
OHIA *n* Hawaiian plant **ohias**
OHING ▸ **oh**
OHM *n*
OHMAGE *n* electrical resistance in ohms **ohmages**
OHMIC *adj* of or relating to a circuit element
OHMS ▸ **ohm**
OHO *n* exclamation expressing surprise, exultation, or derision
OHONE = **ochone**
OHS ▸ **oh**
OI *interj* shout to attract attention ▹ *n* grey-faced petrel
OIDIA ▸ **oidium**
OIDIOID ▸ **oidium**
OIDIUM *n* type of fungal spore
OIKIST = **oecist**
OIKISTS ▸ **oikist**
OIL *n, vb*
OILBIRD *n* type of nocturnal gregarious cave-dwelling bird
OILCAMP *n* camp for oilworkers
OILCAN *n* container with a long nozzle for applying oil to machinery **oilcans**
OILCUP *n* cup-shaped oil reservoir in a machine providing continuous lubrication for a bearing **oilcups**
OILED ▸ **oil**
OILER *n* person, device, etc, that lubricates or supplies oil **oilers**
OILERY *n* oil business
OILGAS *n* gaseous mixture of hydrocarbons used as a fuel
OILHOLE *n* hole for oil
OILIER ▸ **oily**
OILIEST ▸ **oily**
OILILY ▸ **oily**
OILING ▸ **oil**

OILLET = **eyelet**
OILLETS ▸ **oillet**
OILMAN *n* person who owns or operates oil wells **oilmen**
OILNUT *n* nut from which oil is extracted **oilnuts**
OILS ▸ **oil**
OILSEED *n* seed from which oil is extracted
OILSKIN *n*
OILWAY *n* channel for oil **oilways**
OILY *adj*
OINK *n* grunt of a pig or an imitation of this ▹ *interj* imitation or representation of the grunt of a pig ▹ *vb* make noise of pig **oinked, oinking, oinks**
OINOMEL = **oenomel**
OINT *vb* anoint **ointed, ointing, oints**
OIS ▸ **oi**
OJIME *n* Japanese bead used to secure cords **ojimes**
OKA *n* unit of weight used in Turkey
OKAPI *n* African animal related to the giraffe but with a shorter neck **okapis**
OKAS ▸ **oka**
OKAY *adj, vb, n, interj* **okayed, okaying, okays**
OKE = **oka**
OKEH = **okay**
OKEHS ▸ **okeh**
OKES ▸ **oke**
OKIMONO *n* Japanese ornamental item
OKRA *n* **okras**
OKTA *n* unit used in meteorology to measure cloud cover **oktas**
OLD *adj* having lived or existed for a long time ▹ *n* earlier or past time
OLDE *adj* old-world or quaint, used facetiously
OLDEN *adj, vb* **oldened, oldens**
OLDER *adj* having lived or existed longer
OLDEST ▸ **old**
OLDIE *n* old but popular song or film **oldies**
OLDISH ▸ **old**
OLDNESS ▸ **old**
OLDS ▸ **old**
OLDSTER *n* older person
OLDWIFE *n* any of various fishes, esp the menhaden or the alewife
OLDY = **oldie**
OLE *interj* exclamation of approval or encouragement customary at bullfights ▹ *n* cry of olé
OLEA ▸ **oleum**
OLEARIA *n* daisy bush
OLEATE *n* any salt or ester of oleic acid **oleates**
OLEFIN = **olefine**
OLEFINE *another name for* ▸ **alkene**
OLEFINS ▸ **olefin**
OLEIC *adj as in* **oleic acid** colourless oily liquid used in making soap
OLEIN *another name for* > **triolein**
OLEINE = **olein**
OLEINES ▸ **oleine**
OLEINS ▸ **olein**
OLENT *adj* having smell
OLEO *n as in* **oleo oil** oil extracted from beef fat **oleos**
OLES ▸ **ole**
OLESTRA *n* trademark term for an artificial fat
OLEUM *n* type of sulphuric acid **oleums**
OLFACT *vb* smell something **olfacts**
OLICOOK *n* doughnut
OLID *adj* foul-smelling
OLIGIST *n* type of iron ore
OLINGO *n* South American mammal **olingos**
OLIO *n* dish of many different ingredients **olios**
OLITORY *n* kitchen garden
OLIVARY *adj* shaped like an olive
OLIVE *n, adj*
OLIVER *n as in* **Bath oliver** type of unsweetened biscuit **olivers**
OLIVES ▸ **olive**
OLIVET *n* button shaped like olive **olivets**

OLIVINE *n* olive-green mineral of the olivine group
OLLA *n* cooking pot
OLLAMH *n* old Irish term for a wise man **ollamhs**
OLLAS ▸ **olla**
OLLAV = **ollamh**
OLLAVS ▸ **ollav**
OLLER *n* waste ground **ollers**
OLLIE *n* type of skateboarding jump **ollies**
OLM *n* pale blind eel-like salamander **olms**
OLOGIES ▸ **ology**
OLOGIST *n* scientist
OLOGOAN *vb* complain loudly without reason
OLOGY *n* science or other branch of knowledge
OLOROSO *n* golden-coloured sweet sherry
OLPAE ▸ **olpe**
OLPE *n* ancient Greek jug **olpes**
OLYCOOK = **olykoek**
OLYKOEK *n* American type of doughnut
OM *n* sacred syllable in Hinduism
OMASA ▸ **omasum**
OMASAL ▸ **omasum**
OMASUM *n* compartment in the stomach of a ruminant animal
OMBER = **ombre**
OMBERS ▸ **omber**
OMBRE *n* 18th-century card game **ombres**
OMBU *n* South American tree **ombus**
OMEGA *n* last letter in the Greek alphabet **omegas**
OMELET = **omelette**
OMELETS ▸ **omelet**
OMEN *n*, *vb* **omened, omening, omens**
OMENTA ▸ **omentum**
OMENTAL ▸ **omentum**
OMENTUM *n* double fold of the peritoneum
OMER *n* ancient Hebrew unit of dry measure **omers**
OMERTA *n* conspiracy of silence **omertas**
OMICRON *n* 15th letter in the Greek alphabet
OMIGOD *interj* exclamation of surprise, pleasure, dismay, etc
OMIKRON = **omicron**
OMINOUS *adj*
OMIT *vb* **omits, omitted, omitter**
OMLAH *n* staff team in India **omlahs**
OMMATEA > **ommateum**
OMNEITY *n* state of being all
OMNIANA *n* miscellaneous collection
OMNIBUS *n*, *adj*
OMNIETY = **omneity**
OMNIFIC *adj* creating all things
OMNIFY *vb* make something universal
OMNIUM *n* total value **omniums**
OMOV *n* voting system in which each voter has one vote to cast **omovs**
OMPHALI > **omphalos**
OMRAH *n* Muslim noble **omrahs**
OMS ▸ **om**
ON *prep*, *adv*, *adj*, *n*, *vb*
ONAGER *n* wild ass of Persia **onagers, onagri**
ONANISM *n* withdrawal in sexual intercourse before ejaculation **onanist**
ONBEAT *n* first and third beats in a bar of four-four time **onbeats**
ONBOARD *adj* on a ship or other craft
ONCE *adv*, *n*
ONCER *n* (formerly) a one-pound note **oncers**
ONCES ▸ **once**
ONCET *dialect form of* ▸ **once**
ONCOGEN *n* substance causing tumours to form
ONCOME *n* act of coming on **oncomes**
ONCOST = **overheads**
ONCOSTS ▸ **oncost**
ONCUS = **onkus**
ONDATRA = **musquash**
ONDINE = **undine**
ONDINES ▸ **ondine**
ONDING *Scots word for* ▸ **onset**

ONDINGS ▶ **onding**
ONE *adj, n, pron*
ONEFOLD *adj* simple
ONEIRIC *adj* of or relating to dreams
ONELY = **only**
ONENESS *n*
ONER *n* single continuous action
ONERIER ▶ **onery**
ONEROUS *adj*
ONERS ▶ **oner**
ONERY = **ornery**
ONES ▶ **one**
ONESELF *pron*
ONETIME *adj* at some time in the past
ONEYER *old form of* ▶ **one**
ONEYERS ▶ **oneyer**
ONEYRE = **oneyer**
ONEYRES ▶ **oneyre**
ONFALL *n* attack or onset **onfalls**
ONFLOW *n* flowing on **onflows**
ONGOING *adj*
ONIE *variant spelling of* ▶ **ony**
ONION *n, vb* **onioned, onions, oniony**
ONIRIC = **oneiric**
ONIUM *n as in* **onium compound** type of chemical salt **oniums**
ONKUS *adj* bad
ONLAY *n* artificial veneer for a tooth **onlays**
ONLIEST = **only**
ONLINE *adj*
ONLINER *n* person who uses the internet regularly
ONLOAD *vb* load files on to a computer **onloads**
ONLY *adj, adv*
ONNED ▶ **on**
ONNING ▶ **on**
ONO *n* Hawaiian fish **onos**
ONRUSH *n* forceful forward rush or flow
ONS ▶ **on**
ONSET *n* **onsets**
ONSHORE *adv* towards the land
ONSIDE *adv* (of a player in various sports) in a legal position ▷ *adj* taking one's part or side ▷ *n* part of cricket field where a batsman stands **onsides**
ONST = **once**
ONSTAGE *adj* visible by audience
ONSTEAD *Scots word for* > **farmstead**
ONTIC *adj* having real existence
ONTO *prep*
ONUS *n* **onuses**
ONWARD = **onwards**
ONWARDS *adv*
ONY *Scots word for* ▶ **any**
ONYCHA *n* part of mollusc **onychas**
ONYCHIA *n* inflammation of the nails or claws of animals
ONYMOUS *adj* (of a book) bearing its author's name
ONYX *n* **onyxes**
OO *Scots word for* ▶ **wool**
OOBIT *n* hairy caterpillar **oobits**
OOCYST *n* type of zygote **oocysts**
OOCYTE *n* immature female germ cell that gives rise to an ovum **oocytes**
OODLES *pl n* great quantities **oodlins**
OOF *n* money **oofier, oofiest, oofs**
OOFTISH *n* money
OOFY ▶ **oof**
OOGAMY *n* type of sexual reproduction
OOGENY = **oogenesis**
OOGONIA > **oogonium**
OOH *interj* exclamation of surprise, pleasure, pain, etc ▷ *vb* say ooh **oohed, oohing, oohs**
OOIDAL *adj* shaped like egg
OOLAKAN = **eulachon**
OOLITE *n* limestone made up of tiny grains of calcium carbonate **oolites**
OOLITH *n* tiny spherical grain of sedimentary rock **ooliths**
OOLITIC ▶ **oolite**
OOLOGIC ▶ **oology**
OOLOGY *n* study of birds' eggs
OOLONG *n* kind of dark tea **oolongs**
OOM *n* title of respect used to refer to an elderly man
OOMIAC = **umiak**

OOMIACK = **umiak**
OOMIACS ▸ **oomiac**
OOMIAK = **umiak**
OOMIAKS ▸ **oomiak**
OOMPAH *n* representation of the sound made by a deep brass instrument ▹ *vb* make the noise of a brass instrument **oompahs**
OOMPH *n* enthusiasm, vigour, or energy **oomphs**
OOMS ▸ **oom**
OON *Scots word for* ▸ **oven**
OONS ▸ **oon**
OONT *n* camel **oonts**
OOP *vb* Scots word meaning to bind **ooped**
OOPHYTE *n* gametophyte in mosses, liverworts, and ferns
OOPING ▸ **oop**
OOPS *interj* exclamation of surprise or apology
OOR *Scots form of* ▸ **our**
OORALI *n* member of Indian people **ooralis**
OORIAL *n* Himalayan sheep **oorials**
OORIE *adj* Scots word meaning shabby **oorier, ooriest**

> This Scots word is one of the classic 5-letter vowel dumps. It has almost equally useful variants **ourie** and **owrie**.

OOS ▸ **oo**
OOSE *n* dust **ooses, oosier, oosiest**
OOSPERM *n* fertilized ovum
OOSPORE *n* thick-walled sexual spore
OOSY ▸ **oose**
OOT *Scots word for* ▸ **out**
OOTHECA *n* capsule containing eggs
OOTID *n* immature female gamete that develops into an ovum **ootids**
OOTS ▸ **oot**
OOZE *vb, n* **oozed, oozes**
OOZIER ▸ **oozy**
OOZIEST ▸ **oozy**
OOZILY ▸ **oozy**
OOZING ▸ **ooze**
OOZY *adj* moist or dripping
OP *n* operation
OPACIFY *vb* become or make opaque
OPACITY *n* state or quality of being opaque
OPACOUS = **opaque**
OPAH *n* large soft-finned deep-sea fish **opahs**
OPAL *n*
OPALED *adj* made like opal
OPALINE *adj* opalescent ▹ *n* opaque or semiopaque whitish glass
OPALS ▸ **opal**
OPAQUE *adj, n, vb* **opaqued, opaquer, opaques**

OPCODE *n* computer code containing operating instructions **opcodes**
OPE *archaic or poetic word for* ▸ **open**
OPED ▸ **ope**
OPEN *adj, vb, n* **opened**
OPENER *n* tool for opening cans and bottles **openers**
OPENEST ▸ **open**
OPENING *n, adj*
OPENLY ▸ **open**
OPENS ▸ **open**
OPEPE *n* African tree **opepes**
OPERA *n*
OPERAND *n* quantity, variable, or function upon which an operation is performed
OPERANT *adj* producing effects ▹ *n* person or thing that operates
OPERAS ▸ **opera**
OPERATE *vb*
OPERON *n* group of adjacent genes in bacteria **operons**
OPEROSE *adj* laborious
OPES ▸ **ope**
OPHITE *n* any of several greenish mottled rocks **ophites**
OPHITIC *adj* having small elongated feldspar crystals enclosed
OPHIURA *n* sea creature like a starfish
OPIATE *n, adj, vb* **opiated, opiates**

OPINE *vb* express an opinion **opined, opines**
OPING ▸ **ope**
OPINING ▸ **opine**
OPINION *n*
OPIOID *n* substance that resembles morphine **opioids**
OPIUM *n* **opiums**
OPORICE *n* former medicine made from fruit
OPOSSUM *n*
OPPIDAN *adj* of a town ▷ *n* person living in a town
OPPO *n* counterpart in another organization **oppos**
OPPOSE *vb* **opposed, opposer, opposes**
OPPRESS *vb* control by cruelty or force
OPPUGN *vb* call into question **oppugns**
OPS ▸ **op**
OPSIN *n* type of protein **opsins**
OPSONIC ▸ **opsonin**
OPSONIN *n* constituent of blood serum
OPT *vb*
OPTANT *n* person who opts **optants**
OPTED ▸ **opt**
OPTER ▸ **opt**
OPTERS ▸ **opt**
OPTIC *adj*
OPTICAL *adj*
OPTICS *n*
OPTIMA ▸ **optimum**
OPTIMAL *adj* best or most favourable
OPTIME *n* mathematics student at Cambridge University **optimes**
OPTIMUM *n, adj*
OPTING ▸ **opt**
OPTION *n, vb* **options**
OPTS ▸ **opt**
OPULENT *adj*
OPULUS *n* flowering shrub
OPUNTIA *n* type of cactus
OPUS *n*
OPUSCLE = **opuscule**
OPUSES ▸ **opus**
OQUASSA *n* American trout
OR *prep, adj, n*
ORA ▸ **os**
ORACH = **orache**
ORACHE *n* type of plant **oraches**
ORACIES ▸ **oracy**
ORACLE *n, vb* **oracled, oracles**
ORACY *n* capacity to use speech
ORAD *adv* towards the mouth
ORAL *adj, n*
ORALISM *n* oral method of communicating with deaf people **oralist**
ORALITY *n* state of being oral
ORALLY ▸ **oral**
ORALS ▸ **oral**
ORANG *n* orangutan
ORANGE *n, adj* **oranger, oranges, orangey**
ORANGS ▸ **orang**
ORANGY ▸ **orange**
ORANT *n* artistic representation of worshipper **orants**
ORARIA ▸ **orarium**
ORARIAN *n* person who lives on the coast
ORARION *n* garment worn by Greek clergyman
ORARIUM *n* handkerchief
ORATE *vb* make or give an oration **orated, orates, orating**
ORATION *n*
ORATOR *n* **orators**
ORATORY *n*
ORATRIX *n* female orator
ORB *n, vb* **orbed**
ORBIER ▸ **orby**
ORBIEST ▸ **orby**
ORBING ▸ **orb**
ORBIT *n, vb* **orbita**
ORBITAL *adj, n*
ORBITAS ▸ **orbita**
ORBITED ▸ **orbit**
ORBITER *n* spacecraft or satellite designed to orbit a planet without landing on it
ORBITS ▸ **orbit**
ORBITY *n* bereavement
ORBLESS ▸ **orb**
ORBS ▸ **orb**
ORBY *adj* orb-shaped
ORC *n* any of various whales, such as the killer and grampus
ORCA *n* killer whale **orcas**
ORCEIN *n* brown crystalline material **orceins**
ORCHARD *n* **orchat**
ORCHATS ▸ **orchat**

ORCHEL = **orchil**
ORCHELS ▶ **orchel**
ORCHID *n* **orchids**
ORCHIL *n* any of various lichens **orchils**
ORCHIS *n* type of orchid
ORCIN = **orcinol**
ORCINE = **orcinol**
ORCINES ▶ **orcine**
ORCINOL *n* colourless crystalline water-soluble solid
ORCINS ▶ **orcin**
ORCS ▶ **orc**
ORD *n* pointed weapon
ORDAIN *vb* **ordains**
ORDEAL *n* **ordeals**
ORDER *n, vb* **ordered, orderer**
ORDERLY *adj, n, adv*
ORDERS ▶ **order**
ORDINAL *adj* denoting a certain position in a sequence of numbers ▷ *n* book containing the forms of services for the ordination of ministers
ORDINAR *Scots word for* > **ordinary**
ORDINEE *n* person being ordained
ORDINES ▶ **ordo**
ORDO *n* religious order **ordos**
ORDS ▶ **ord**
ORDURE *n* **ordures**
ORE *n*
OREAD *n* mountain nymph **oreades, oreads**
ORECTIC *adj* of or relating to the desires
OREGANO *n*
OREIDE = **oroide**
OREIDES ▶ **oreide**
ORES ▶ **ore**
OREWEED *n* seaweed
OREXIN *n* hormone that promotes wakefulness and stimulates the appetite **orexins**
OREXIS *n* appetite
ORF *n* infectious disease of sheep
ORFE *n* small slender European fish **orfes**
ORFRAY = **orphrey**
ORFRAYS ▶ **orfray**
ORFS ▶ **orf**
ORGAN *n*
ORGANA ▶ **organon**
ORGANDY = **organdie**
ORGANIC *adj, n*
ORGANON *n* system of logical or scientific rules
ORGANS ▶ **organ**
ORGANUM = **organon**
ORGANZA *n*
ORGASM *n, vb* **orgasms**
ORGEAT *n* drink made with orange flower water **orgeats**
ORGIA = **orgy**
ORGIAC ▶ **orgy**
ORGIAS ▶ **orgia**
ORGIAST *n* participant in orgy
ORGIC ▶ **orgy**
ORGIES ▶ **orgy**
ORGONE *n* substance claimed to be needed for sexual activity and mental health **orgones**
ORGUE *n* number of stakes lashed together **orgues**
ORGY *n*
ORIBI *n* small African antelope **oribis**
ORIEL *n* **oriels**
ORIENCY *n* state of being orient
ORIENT *vb, n, adj* **orients**
ORIFEX = **orifice**
ORIFICE *n*
ORIGAMI *n*
ORIGAN *another name for* > **marjoram**
ORIGANE = **origan**
ORIGANS ▶ **origan**
ORIGIN *n* **origins**
ORIHOU *n* small New Zealand tree **orihous**
ORIOLE *n* tropical or American songbird **orioles**
ORISHA *n* any of the minor gods or spirits of traditional Yoruba religion **orishas**
ORISON *another word for* ▶ **prayer**
ORISONS ▶ **orison**
ORIXA = **orisha**
ORIXAS ▶ **orixa**
ORLE *n* border around a shield
ORLEANS *n* type of fabric
ORLES ▶ **orle**
ORLON *n* crease-resistant acrylic fibre or fabric **orlons**
ORLOP *n* (in a vessel with four or more decks) the lowest deck **orlops**

ORMER *n* edible marine mollusc **ormers**
ORMOLU *n* **ormolus**
ORNATE *adj* **ornater**
ORNERY *adj* stubborn or vile-tempered
ORNIS *less common word for* > **avifauna**
ORNISES ▸ **ornis**
OROGEN *n* part of earth subject to orogeny **orogens**
OROGENY *n* formation of mountain ranges
OROIDE *n* alloy containing copper, tin, and other metals **oroides**
OROLOGY = **orography**
OROPESA *n* float used in minesweeping
OROTUND *adj* (of the voice) resonant and booming
ORPHAN *n*, *vb* **orphans**
ORPHIC *adj* mystical or occult
ORPHISM *n* style of abstract art
ORPHREY *n* richly embroidered band or border
ORPIN = **orpine**
ORPINE *n* type of plant **orpines**
ORPINS ▸ **orpin**
ORRA *adj* odd or unmatched
ORRAMAN *n* man who does odd jobs **orramen**
ORRERY *n* mechanical model of the solar system
ORRICE = **orris**
ORRICES ▸ **orrice**
ORRIS *n* kind of iris **orrises**
ORS ▸ **or**
ORT *n* fragment
ORTHIAN *adj* having high pitch
ORTHO *n* type of photographic plate **orthos**
ORTHROS *n* canonical hour in the Greek Church
ORTOLAN *n* small European songbird eaten as a delicacy
ORTS *pl n* scraps or leavings
ORVAL *n* plant of sage family **orvals**
ORYX *n* **oryxes**
ORZO *n* pasta in small grain shapes **orzos**
OS *n* mouth or mouthlike part or opening **osar**
OSCAR *n* cash **oscars**
OSCHEAL *adj* of scrotum
OSCINE *n* songbird ▹ *adj* of songbirds **oscines**
OSCULA ▸ **osculum**
OSCULAR *adj* of or relating to an osculum
OSCULE *n* small mouth or opening **oscules**
OSCULUM *n* mouthlike aperture
OSE = **esker**
OSES ▸ **ose**
OSETRA *n* type of caviar **osetras**
OSHAC *n* plant smelling of ammonia **oshacs**
OSIER *n*
OSIERED *adj* covered with osiers
OSIERS ▸ **osier**
OSIERY *n* work done with osiers
OSMATE *n* salt of osmic acid **osmates**
OSMATIC *adj* relying on sense of smell
OSMIATE = **osmate**
OSMIC *adj* of or containing osmium in a high valence state
OSMICS *n* science of smell
OSMIOUS = **osmous**
OSMIUM *n* heaviest known metallic element **osmiums**
OSMOL = **osmole**
OSMOLAL ▸ **osmole**
OSMOLAR *adj* containing one osmole per litre
OSMOLE *n* unit of osmotic pressure **osmoles**
OSMOLS ▸ **osmol**
OSMOSE *vb* undergo or cause to undergo osmosis **osmosed, osmoses**
OSMOSIS *n* **osmotic**
OSMOUS *adj* of or containing osmium in a low valence state
OSMUND = **osmunda**
OSMUNDA *n* type of fern
OSMUNDS ▸ **osmund**
OSPREY *n* **ospreys**
OSSA ▸ **os**

OSSEIN *n* protein that forms the organic matrix of bone **osseins**
OSSELET *n* growth on knee of horse
OSSEOUS *adj* consisting of or like bone
OSSETER *n* sturgeon
OSSETRA = **osetra**
OSSIA *conj* (in music) or
OSSICLE *n* small bone, esp one of those in the middle ear
OSSIFIC *adj* making something turn to bone
OSSIFY *vb*
OSSUARY *n* any container for the burial of human bones, such as an urn or vault
OSTEAL *adj* of or relating to bone or to the skeleton
OSTENT *n* appearance **ostents**
OSTEOID *adj* of or resembling bone ▷ *n* bony deposit
OSTEOMA *n* tumour composed of bone or bonelike tissue
OSTIA ▸ **ostium**
OSTIAL ▸ **ostium**
OSTIARY *another word for* ▸ **porter**
OSTIATE *adj* having ostium
OSTIOLE *n* pore in the reproductive bodies of certain algae and fungi
OSTIUM *n* pore in sponges through which water enters the body
OSTLER *n* stableman at an inn **ostlers**
OSTMARK *n* currency of the former East Germany
OSTOMY *n* surgically made opening
OSTOSES ▸ **ostosis**
OSTOSIS *n* formation of bone
OSTRACA > **ostracon**
OSTRAKA > **ostrakon**
OSTRICH *n*
OTAKU *n* Japanese computer geeks
OTALGIA *technical name for* ▸ **earache**
OTALGIC ▸ **otalgia**
OTALGY = **otalgia**
OTARIES ▸ **otary**
OTARINE ▸ **otary**

> This means like an otary or eared seal, and is perhaps the most commonly played of all 7-letter bonus words, so well worth learning for that extra 50 points it can give you.

OTARY *n* seal with ears
OTHER *adj, n* **others**
OTIC *adj* of or relating to the ear
OTIOSE *adj* not useful
OTITIC ▸ **otitis**
OTITIS *n* inflammation of the ear
OTOCYST *n* embryonic structure in vertebrates that develops into the inner ear
OTOLITH *n* granule of calcium carbonate in the inner ear of vertebrates
OTOLOGY *n* branch of medicine concerned with the ear
OTTAR *variant of* ▸ **attar**
OTTARS ▸ **ottar**
OTTAVA *n* interval of an octave **ottavas**
OTTER *n, vb* **ottered, otters**
OTTO *another name for* ▸ **attar**
OTTOMAN *n*
OTTOS ▸ **otto**
OU *interj* expressing concession ▷ *n* man, bloke, or chap
OUABAIN *n* poisonous white crystalline glycoside
OUAKARI *n* South American monkey
OUBAAS *n* man in authority
OUBIT *n* hairy caterpillar **oubits**
OUCH *interj, n, vb* **ouched, ouches, ouching**
OUCHT *Scots word for* > **anything**
OUCHTS ▸ **oucht**
OUD *n* Arabic stringed musical instrument **ouds**
OUENS ▸ **ou**
OUGHLY *variant of* ▸ **ugly**
OUGHT *vb, n* **oughted, oughts**
OUGLIE *variant of* ▸ **ugly**
OUGLIED ▸ **ouglie**
OUGLIES ▸ **ouglie**

OUGUIYA *n* standard monetary unit of Mauritania
OUIJA *n* tradename for a board through which spirits supposedly answer questions **ouijas**
OUK *Scots word for* ▸ **week**
OUKS ▸ **ouk**
OULAKAN = **eulachon**
OULD *Scots or Irish form of* ▸ **old**
OULDER ▸ **ould**
OULDEST ▸ **ould**
OULK *Scots form of* ▸ **week**
OULKS ▸ **oulk**
OULONG = **oolong**
OULONGS ▸ **oulong**
OUMA *n* grandmother, often as a title with a surname **oumas**
OUNCE *n* **ounces**
OUNDY *adj* wavy
OUP = **oop**
OUPA *n* grandfather, often as a title with a surname **oupas**
OUPED ▸ **oup**
OUPH = **oaf**
OUPHE = **oaf**
OUPHES ▸ **ouphe**
OUPHS ▸ **ouph**
OUPING ▸ **oup**
OUPS ▸ **oup**
OUR *adj, determiner*
OURALI *n* plant from which curare comes **ouralis**
OURANG = **orang**
OURANGS ▸ **ourang**
OURARI = **ourali**
OURARIS ▸ **ourari**
OUREBI = **oribi**
OUREBIS ▸ **ourebi**
OURIE = **oorie**
OURIER ▸ **ourie**
OURIEST ▸ **ourie**
OURN *dialect form of* ▸ **our**
OURS *pron*
OURSELF *pron* formal word for *myself* used by monarchs
OUS ▸ **ou**
OUSEL = **ouzel**
OUSELS ▸ **ousel**
OUST *vb* **ousted**
OUSTER *n* act of forcing someone out of a position **ousters**
OUSTING ▸ **oust**
OUSTITI *n* device for opening locked door
OUSTS ▸ **oust**
OUT *adj, vb*
OUTACT *vb* surpass in acting **outacts**
OUTADD *vb* beat or surpass at adding **outadds**
OUTAGE *n* period of power failure **outages**
OUTASK *vb* declare wedding banns **outasks**
OUTATE ▸ **outeat**
OUTBACK *n*
OUTBAKE *vb* bake more or better than
OUTBAR *vb* keep out
OUTBARK *vb* bark more or louder than
OUTBARS ▸ **outbar**
OUTBAWL *vb* bawl more or louder than
OUTBEAM *vb* beam more or brighter than
OUTBEG *vb* beg more or better than **outbegs**
OUTBID *vb* **outbids**
OUTBOX *vb* surpass in boxing
OUTBRAG *vb* brag more or better than
OUTBRED > **outbreed**
OUTBULK *vb* exceed in bulk
OUTBURN *vb* burn longer or brighter than
OUTBUY *vb* buy more than **outbuys**
OUTBY *adv* outside **outbye**
OUTCALL *n* visit to customer's home by professional
OUTCAST *n, adj*
OUTCHID > **outchide**
OUTCITY *n* anywhere outside a city's confines
OUTCOME *n*
OUTCOOK *vb* cook more or better than
OUTCROP *n, vb*
OUTCROW *vb* exceed in crowing
OUTCRY *n, vb*
OUTDARE *vb* be more brave than
OUTDATE *vb* make or become old-fashioned or obsolete
OUTDID ▸ **outdo**
OUTDO *vb* **outdoer, outdoes, outdone**
OUTDOOR *adj*
OUTDRAG *vb* beat in drag race

OUTDRAW *vb* draw (a gun) faster than **outdrew**
OUTDROP = **outcrop**
OUTDUEL *vb* defeat in duel
OUTDURE *vb* last longer than
OUTEARN *vb* earn more than
OUTEAT *vb* eat more than **outeats**
OUTECHO *vb* echo more than
OUTED ▸ **out**
OUTEDGE *n* furthest limit
OUTER *adj*, *n* **outers**
OUTFACE *vb* subdue or disconcert by staring
OUTFALL *n* mouth of a river or drain
OUTFAST *vb* fast longer than
OUTFAWN *vb* exceed in fawning
OUTFEEL *vb* exceed in feeling **outfelt**
OUTFIND *vb* exceed in finding
OUTFIRE *vb* exceed in firing
OUTFISH *vb* catch more fish than
OUTFIT *n*, *vb* **outfits**
OUTFLEW ▸ **outfly**
OUTFLOW *n* anything that flows out, such as liquid or money ▹ *vb* flow faster than
OUTFLY *vb* fly better or faster than
OUTFOOL *vb* be more foolish than
OUTFOOT *vb* (of a boat) to go faster than (another boat)
OUTFOX *vb* defeat or foil by being more cunning
OUTGAIN *vb* gain more than
OUTGAS *vb* undergo the removal of adsorbed or absorbed gas from solids
OUTGATE *n* way out
OUTGAVE ▸ **outgive**
OUTGAZE *vb* gaze beyond
OUTGIVE *vb* exceed in giving
OUTGLOW *vb* glow more than
OUTGNAW *vb* exceed in gnawing
OUTGO *vb* exceed or outstrip ▹ *n* cost **outgoer, outgoes, outgone**
OUTGREW ▸ **outgrow**
OUTGRIN *vb* exceed in grinning
OUTGROW *vb*
OUTGUN *vb* surpass in fire power **outguns**
OUTGUSH *vb* gush out
OUTHAUL *n* line or cable for tightening the foot of a sail
OUTHEAR *vb* exceed in hearing
OUTHER = **other**
OUTHIRE *vb* hire out
OUTHIT *vb* hit something further than (someone else) **outhits**
OUTHOWL *vb* exceed in howling
OUTHUNT *vb* exceed in hunting
OUTHYRE = **outhire**
OUTING *n* **outings**
OUTJEST *vb* exceed in jesting
OUTJET *n* projecting part **outjets**
OUTJINX *vb* exceed in jinxing

> If someone else plays **jinx**, you can outjinx them by adding O, U and T! And if you can form the whole word using all of your letters, you'll get a 50-point bonus.

OUTJUMP *vb* jump higher or farther than
OUTJUT *vb* jut out ▹ *n* projecting part **outjuts**
OUTKEEP *vb* beat or surpass at keeping **outkept**
OUTKICK *vb* exceed in kicking
OUTKILL *vb* exceed in killing
OUTKISS *vb* exceed in kissing
OUTLAID ▸ **outlay**
OUTLAIN ▸ **outlay**
OUTLAND *adj* outlying or distant ▹ *n* outlying areas of a country or region
OUTLASH *n* sudden attack
OUTLAST *vb*
OUTLAW *n*, *vb* **outlaws**
OUTLAY *n*, *vb* **outlays**

OUTLEAD *vb* be better leader than
OUTLEAP *vb* leap higher or farther than
OUTLED ▸ **outlead**
OUTLER *n* farm animal kept out of doors **outlers**
OUTLET *n* **outlets**
OUTLIE *vb* lie outside a particular place **outlied**
OUTLIER *n* outcrop of rocks that is entirely surrounded by older rocks
OUTLIES ▸ **outlie**
OUTLINE *n, vb*
OUTLIVE *vb*
OUTLOOK *n, vb*
OUTLOVE *vb* exceed in loving
OUTMAN *vb* surpass in manpower **outmans**
OUTMODE *vb* make unfashionable
OUTMOST *another word for* > **outermost**
OUTMOVE *vb* move faster or better than
OUTNAME *vb* be more notorious than
OUTNESS *n* state or quality of being external
OUTPACE *vb*
OUTPART *n* remote region
OUTPASS *vb* exceed in passing
OUTPEEP *vb* peep out
OUTPEER *vb* surpass
OUTPITY *vb* exceed in pitying
OUTPLAN *vb* exceed in planning
OUTPLAY *vb*
OUTPLOD *vb* exceed in plodding
OUTPLOT *vb* exceed in plotting
OUTPOLL *vb* win more votes than
OUTPORT *n* isolated fishing village, esp in Newfoundland
OUTPOST *n*
OUTPOUR *n* act of flowing or pouring out ▷ *vb* pour or cause to pour out freely or rapidly
OUTPRAY *vb* exceed in praying
OUTPULL *vb* exceed in pulling
OUTPUSH *vb* exceed in pushing
OUTPUT *n, vb* **outputs**
OUTRACE *vb* surpass in racing
OUTRAGE *n, vb*
OUTRAN ▸ **outrun**
OUTRANG ▸ **outring**
OUTRANK *vb* be of higher rank than (someone)
OUTRATE *vb* offer better rate than
OUTRAVE *vb* outdo in raving
OUTRE *adj* shockingly eccentric
OUTREAD *vb* outdo in reading
OUTRED *vb* be redder than **outreds**
OUTRIDE *vb* outdo by riding faster, farther, or better than ▷ *n* extra unstressed syllable within a metrical foot
OUTRIG *vb* supply with outfit **outrigs**
OUTRING *vb* exceed in ringing
OUTRO *n* instrumental passage that concludes a piece of music
OUTROAR *vb* roar louder than
OUTROCK *vb* outdo in rocking
OUTRODE ▸ **outride**
OUTROLL *vb* exceed in rolling
OUTROOP *n* auction
OUTROOT *vb* root out
OUTROPE = **outroop**
OUTROS ▸ **outro**
OUTROW *vb* outdo in rowing **outrows**
OUTRUN *vb* run faster than
OUTRUNG ▸ **outring**
OUTRUNS ▸ **outrun**
OUTRUSH *n* flowing or rushing out ▷ *vb* rush out
OUTS ▸ **out**
OUTSAID ▸ **outsay**
OUTSAIL *vb* sail better than
OUTSANG ▸ **outsing**
OUTSAT ▸ **outsit**
OUTSAW ▸ **outsee**
OUTSAY *vb* say something out loud **outsays**
OUTSEE *vb* exceed in seeing **outseen, outsees**

OUTSELL *vb* be sold in greater quantities than
OUTSERT *another word for* > **wrapround**
OUTSET *n* **outsets**
OUTSHOT *n* projecting part
OUTSIDE *adv, adj, n*
OUTSIN *vb* sin more than
OUTSING *vb* sing better or louder than
OUTSINS ▸ **outsin**
OUTSIT *vb* sit longer than **outsits**
OUTSIZE *adj, n*
OUTSOAR *vb* fly higher than
OUTSOLD ▸ **outsell**
OUTSOLE *n* outermost sole of a shoe
OUTSPAN *vb*
OUTSPED > **outspeed**
OUTSTAY *vb*
OUTSTEP *vb* step farther than
OUTSULK *vb* outdo in sulking
OUTSUM *vb* add up to more than **outsums**
OUTSUNG ▸ **outsing**
OUTSWAM ▸ **outswim**
OUTSWIM *vb* outdo in swimming **outswum**
OUTTAKE *n* unreleased take from a recording session, film, or TV programme ▹ *vb* take out
OUTTALK *vb* talk more, longer, or louder than (someone)
OUTTASK *vb* assign task to staff outside organization
OUTTELL *vb* make known **outtold**
OUTTOOK ▸ **outtake**
OUTTOP *vb* rise higher than **outtops**
OUTTROT *vb* exceed at trotting
OUTTURN = **output**
OUTVIE *vb* outdo in competition **outvied, outvies**
OUTVOTE *vb* defeat by getting more votes than
OUTWAIT *vb* wait longer than
OUTWALK *vb* walk farther or longer than
OUTWAR *vb* surpass or exceed in warfare
OUTWARD = **outwards**
OUTWARS ▸ **outwar**
OUTWASH *n* gravel carried and deposited by water from melting glaciers
OUTWEAR *vb* use up or destroy by wearing
OUTWEED *vb* root out
OUTWEEP *vb* outdo in weeping
OUTWELL *vb* pour out
OUTWENT ▸ **outgo**
OUTWEPT ▸ **outweep**
OUTWICK *vb* move one curling stone by striking with another
OUTWILE *vb* surpass in cunning
OUTWILL *vb* demonstrate stronger will than
OUTWIN *vb* get out of
OUTWIND *vb* unwind
OUTWING *vb* surpass in flying
OUTWINS ▸ **outwin**
OUTWISH *vb* surpass in wishing
OUTWIT *vb*
OUTWITH *prep* outside
OUTWITS ▸ **outwit**
OUTWON ▸ **outwin**
OUTWORE ▸ **outwear**
OUTWORK *n* defences which lie outside main defensive works ▹ *vb* work better, harder, etc, than
OUTWORN *adj*
OUTWRIT > **outwrite**
OUTYELL *vb* outdo in yelling
OUTYELP *vb* outdo in yelping
OUVERT *adj* open **ouverte**
OUVRAGE *n* work
OUVRIER *n* worker
OUZEL *n* type of bird **ouzels**
OUZO *n* strong aniseed-flavoured spirit from Greece **ouzos**
OVA ▸ **ovum**
OVAL *adj, n* **ovality, ovally, ovals**
OVARIAL ▸ **ovary**
OVARIAN ▸ **ovary**
OVARIES ▸ **ovary**
OVARY *n*
OVATE *adj* shaped like an egg ▹ *vb* give ovation **ovated, ovately, ovates, ovating**
OVATION *n*

OVATOR ▶ **ovate**
OVATORS ▶ **ovate**
OVEL *n* mourner, esp during the first seven days after a death **ovels**
OVEN *n, vb* **ovened, ovening, ovens**
OVER *adv, adj, n, vb*
OVERACT *vb*
OVERAGE *adj, n*
OVERALL *adv, n, adj*
OVERAPT *adj* tending excessively
OVERARM *adv, adj, vb*
OVERATE ▶ **overeat**
OVERAWE *vb*
OVERBED *adj* fitting over bed
OVERBET *vb* bet too much
OVERBID *vb* bid for more tricks than one can expect to win ▷ *n* bid higher than someone else's bid
OVERBIG *adj* too big
OVERBUY *vb* buy too much or too many
OVERBY *adv* Scots expression meaning over the road or across the way
OVERCOY *adj* too modest
OVERCUT *vb* cut too much
OVERDID ▶ **overdo**
OVERDO *vb*
OVERDOG *n* person or side in an advantageous position
OVERDRY *vb* dry too much
OVERDUB *vb* add (new sounds) to a tape so that the old and the new sounds can be heard ▷ *n* sound or series of sounds added by this method
OVERDUE *adj*
OVERDYE *vb* dye (a fabric, yarn, etc) excessively
OVEREAT *vb* eat more than is necessary or healthy
OVERED ▶ **over**
OVEREGG *vb* exaggerate absurdly
OVEREYE *vb* survey
OVERFAR *adv* too far
OVERFAT *adj* too fat
OVERFED > **overfeed**
OVERFIT *adj* too fit
OVERFLY *vb* fly over (a territory) or past (a point)
OVERGET *vb* overtake
OVERGO *vb* go beyond
OVERGOT ▶ **overget**
OVERHIT *vb* hit too strongly
OVERHOT *adj* too hot
OVERING ▶ **over**
OVERJOY *vb* give great delight to
OVERLAP *vb, n*
OVERLAX *adj* too lax
OVERLAY *vb, n*
OVERLET *vb* let to too many
OVERLIE *vb* lie on or cover (something or someone)
OVERLIT > **overlight**
OVERLY *adv*
OVERMAN *vb* provide with too many staff ▷ *n* man who oversees others **overmen**
OVERMIX *vb* mix too much
OVERNET *vb* cover with net
OVERNEW *adj* too new
OVERPAY *vb* pay (someone) at too high a rate
OVERPLY *vb* ply too much
OVERRAN ▶ **overrun**
OVERRED *vb* paint over in red
OVERREN = **overrun**
OVERRUN *vb, n*
OVERS ▶ **over**
OVERSAD *adj* too sad
OVERSAW ▶ **oversee**
OVERSEA = **overseas**
OVERSEE *vb*
OVERSET *vb* disturb or upset
OVERSEW *vb* sew (two edges) with stitches that pass over them both
OVERSOW *vb* sow again after first sowing
OVERSUP *vb* sup too much
OVERT *adj*
OVERTAX *vb*
OVERTIP *vb* give too much money as a tip
OVERTLY ▶ **overt**
OVERTOP *vb* exceed in height
OVERUSE *vb* use excessively ▷ *n* excessive use

OVERWET *vb* make too wet
OVIBOS *n* type of ox
OVICIDE *n* killing of sheep
OVIDUCT *n*
OVIFORM *adj* shaped like an egg
OVINE *adj* of or like a sheep ▷ *n* member of sheep family **ovines**
OVIPARA *n* all oviparous animals
OVISAC *n* capsule or sac in which egg cells are produced **ovisacs**
OVIST *n* person believing ovum contains all subsequent generations **ovists**
OVOID *adj* egg-shaped ▷ *n* something that is ovoid
OVOIDAL *adj* ovoid ▷ *n* something that is ovoid
OVOIDS ▸ **ovoid**
OVOLI ▸ **ovolo**
OVOLO *n* type of convex moulding **ovolos**

> Two Os on your rack can normally be dealt with; three is a bit much, but this word for a moulding can handle them. Note that the plural can be **ovolos** or **ovoli**.

OVONIC *adj* using particular electronic storage batteries
OVONICS *n* science of ovonic equipment
OVULAR ▸ **ovule**
OVULARY ▸ **ovule**
OVULATE *vb*
OVULE *n* plant part that contains the egg cell **ovules**
OVUM *n*
OW *interj* exclamation of pain
OWCHE = **ouch**
OWCHES ▸ **owche**
OWE *vb* **owed**
OWELTY *n* equality, esp in financial transactions
OWER *Scots word for* ▸ **over**
OWERBY *adv* over there
OWES ▸ **owe**
OWING ▸ **owe**
OWL *n, vb* **owled**
OWLER *vb* smuggler **owlers**
OWLERY *n* place where owls live
OWLET *n* young or nestling owl **owlets**
OWLIER ▸ **owly**
OWLIEST ▸ **owly**
OWLING ▸ **owl**
OWLISH *adj* like an owl
OWLLIKE ▸ **owl**
OWLS ▸ **owl**
OWLY = **owlish**
OWN *adj* used to emphasize possession ▷ *pron* thing(s) belonging to a particular person ▷ *vb* possess
OWNABLE *adj* able to be owned
OWNED ▸ **own**
OWNER *n* **owners**
OWNING ▸ **own**
OWNS ▸ **own**
OWRE = **ower**
OWRELAY *Scots form of* ▸ **overlay**
OWRES ▸ **owre**
OWRIE = **oorie**
OWRIER ▸ **owrie**
OWRIEST ▸ **owrie**
OWSE *Scots form of* ▸ **ox**
OWSEN *Scots word for* ▸ **oxen**
OWT *dialect word for* ▸ **anything**
OWTS ▸ **owt**
OX *n*
OXALATE *n* salt or ester of oxalic acid ▷ *vb* treat with oxalate
OXALIC *adj as in* **oxalic acid** poisonous acid found in many plants
OXALIS *n* type of plant
OXAZINE *n* type of chemical compound
OXBLOOD *n* dark reddish-brown colour ▷ *adj* of this colour
OXBOW *n* piece of wood fitted around the neck of a harnessed ox **oxbows**
OXCART *n* cart pulled by ox **oxcarts**
OXEN ▸ **ox**
OXER *n* high fence **oxers**
OXES ▸ **ox**
OXEYE *n* daisy-like flower **oxeyes**
OXFORD *n* type of stout laced shoe with a low heel **oxfords**
OXGANG *n* old measure of farmland **oxgangs, oxgate**

OXGATES ▶ **oxgate**
OXHEAD *n* head of an ox **oxheads**
OXHEART *n* heart-shaped cherry
OXHIDE *n* leather made from the hide of an ox **oxhides**
OXID = **oxide**
OXIDANT *n*
OXIDASE *n* enzyme that brings about oxidation
OXIDATE *another word for* ▶ **oxidize**
OXIDE *n* **oxides, oxidic**
OXIDISE = **oxidize**
OXIDIZE *vb*
OXIDS ▶ **oxid**
OXIES ▶ **oxy**
OXIM = **oxime**
OXIME *n* type of chemical compound **oximes**
OXIMS ▶ **oxim**
OXLAND = **oxgang**
OXLANDS ▶ **oxland**
OXLIKE ▶ **ox**
OXLIP *n* type of woodland plant **oxlips**
OXO *n as in* **oxo acid** acid that contains oxygen
OXONIUM *n as in* **oxonium compound** type of salt derived from an organic ether
OXSLIP = **oxlip**
OXSLIPS ▶ **oxslip**
OXTAIL *n* **oxtails**
OXTER *n* armpit ▷ *vb* grip under arm **oxtered, oxters**
OXY ▶ **ox**
OXYACID *n* any acid that contains oxygen
OXYGEN *n* **oxygens**
OXYMEL *n* mixture of vinegar and honey **oxymels**
OXYMORA > **oxymoron**
OXYNTIC *adj* of or denoting stomach cells that secrete acid
OXYPHIL *n* type of cell found in glands
OXYSALT *n* any salt of an oxyacid
OXYSOME *n* group of molecules
OXYTONE *adj* having an accent on the final syllable ▷ *n* oxytone word
OY *n* grandchild **oye**
OYER *n* (in the 13th century) an assize **oyers**
OYES = **oyez**
OYESES ▶ **oyes**
OYESSES ▶ **oyes**
OYEZ *interj* shouted three times by a public crier calling for attention ▷ *n* such a cry **oyezes**
OYS ▶ **oy**
OYSTER *n, vb* **oysters**
OZAENA *n* inflammation of nasal mucous membrane **ozaenas**
OZALID *n* method of duplicating writing or illustrations **ozalids**
OZEKI *n* sumo wrestling champion **ozekis**
OZONATE *vb* add ozone to
OZONE *n* **ozones, ozonic**
OZONIDE *n* type of unstable explosive compound
OZONISE = **ozonize**
OZONIZE *vb* convert (oxygen) into ozone
OZONOUS ▶ **ozone**
OZZIE *n* hospital **ozzies**

Pp

P forms a two-letter word in front of every vowel except **U**, which makes it very useful for joining a new word to one already on the board. It also forms several three-letter words with **X**: **pax, pix, pox** (12 points each) and **pyx** (15). Other three-letter words with **P** well worth remembering are **zap, zep** and **zip** for 14 points each and **jap** for 12 points.

PA *n*
PAAL *n* stake driven into the ground **paals**
PAAN *n* leaf of the betel tree **paans**
PABLUM = **pabulum**
PABLUMS ▸ **pablum**
PABULAR ▸ **pabulum**
PABULUM *n* food
PAC *n* soft shoe
PACA *n* large burrowing rodent
PACABLE *adj* easily appeased
PACAS ▸ **paca**
PACE *n, vb, prep* **paced**
PACEMAN *n* **pacemen**
PACER *n* horse trained to move at a special gait, esp for racing **pacers**
PACES ▸ **pace**
PACEWAY *n* racecourse for trotting and pacing
PACEY *adj* fast-moving, quick, lively
PACHA = **pasha**
PACHAK *n* fragrant roots of Asian plant **pachaks**
PACHAS ▸ **pacha**
PACHISI *n* Indian game resembling backgammon
PACHUCO *n* young Mexican living in the US
PACIER ▸ **pacy**
PACIEST ▸ **pacy**
PACIFIC *adj* tending to bring peace
PACIFY *vb*
PACING ▸ **pace**
PACK *vb, n*
PACKAGE = **packet**
PACKED *adj*
PACKER *n* person or company who packs goods **packers**
PACKET *n, vb* **packets**
PACKING *n* material, such as paper or plastic, used to protect packed goods
PACKLY ▸ **pack**
PACKMAN *n* person carrying pack **packmen**
PACKS ▸ **pack**
PACKWAX *n* neck ligament
PACKWAY *n* path for pack animals
PACO *n* S American mammal **pacos**
PACS ▸ **pac**
PACT *n*
PACTA ▸ **pactum**
PACTION *vb* concur with
PACTS ▸ **pact**
PACTUM *n* pact
PACY = **pacey**
PAD *n, vb*
PADANG *n* (in Malaysia) playing field **padangs**
PADAUK *n* tropical African or Asian tree **padauks**

PADDED ▸ **pad**
PADDER *n* highwayman who robs on foot **padders**
PADDIES ▸ **paddy**
PADDING ▸ **pad**
PADDLE *n, vb* **paddled, paddler, paddles**
PADDOCK *n, vb*
PADDY *n*
PADELLA *n* type of candle
PADI = **paddy**
PADIS ▸ **padi**
PADKOS *n* snacks and provisions for a journey
PADLE *another name for* > **lumpfish**
PADLES ▸ **padle**
PADLOCK *n, vb*
PADMA *n* type of lotus **padmas**
PADNAG *n* ambling horse **padnags**
PADOUK = **padauk**
PADOUKS ▸ **padouk**
PADRE *n* **padres, padri**
PADRONE *n* owner or proprietor of an inn, esp in Italy **padroni**
PADS ▸ **pad**
PADSAW *n* small narrow saw used for cutting curves **padsaws**
PADSHAH = **padishah**
PAEAN *n* song of triumph or thanksgiving **paeans**
PAEDO *n* **paedos**
PAELLA *n* Spanish dish of rice, chicken, shellfish, and vegetables **paellas**
PAENULA *n* ancient Roman cloak
PAEON *n* metrical foot of four syllables **paeonic, paeons**
PAEONY = **peony**
PAESAN *n* fellow countryman
PAESANI ▸ **paesano**
PAESANO *n* Italian-American man
PAESANS ▸ **paesan**
PAGAN *adj, n* **pagans**
PAGE *n, vb*
PAGEANT *n*
PAGEBOY *n* type of hairstyle
PAGED ▸ **page**
PAGEFUL *n* amount (of text, etc) that a page will hold
PAGER *n* small electronic device, capable of receiving short messages **pagers**
PAGES ▸ **page**
PAGINAL *adj* page-for-page
PAGING ▸ **page**
PAGINGS ▸ **page**
PAGLE = **paigle**
PAGLES ▸ **pagle**
PAGOD *n* oriental idol
PAGODA *n* **pagodas**
PAGODS ▸ **pagod**
PAGRI *n* type of turban **pagris**
PAGURID = **pagurian**
PAH = **pa**
PAHLAVI *n* Iranian coin
PAHS ▸ **pah**
PAID ▸ **pay**
PAIDLE *Scots variant of* ▸ **paddle**
PAIDLES ▸ **paidle**
PAIGLE *n* cowslip **paigles**
PAIK *vb* thump or whack **paiked, paiking, paiks**
PAIL *n* **pailful**
PAILLON *n* thin leaf of metal
PAILS ▸ **pail**
PAIN *n, vb*
PAINCH *Scots variant of* ▸ **paunch**
PAINED *adj* having or suggesting pain or distress
PAINFUL *adj*
PAINIM *n* heathen or pagan **painims**
PAINING ▸ **pain**
PAINS *pl n* care or trouble
PAINT *n, vb* **painted**
PAINTER *n*
PAINTS ▸ **paint**
PAINTY ▸ **paint**
PAIOCK *obsolete word for* ▸ **peacock**
PAIOCKE *obsolete word for* ▸ **peacock**
PAIOCKS ▸ **paiock**
PAIR *n, vb* **paire, paired, pairer**
PAIRES ▸ **paire**
PAIREST ▸ **pair**
PAIRIAL *variant of* ▸ **prial**
PAIRING ▸ **pair**
PAIRS ▸ **pair**
PAIS *n* country
PAISA *n* monetary unit of Bangladesh, Bhutan, India, Nepal, and Pakistan
PAISAN *n* fellow countryman

PAISANA *n* female peasant
PAISANO *n* friend
PAISANS ▸ **paisan**
PAISAS ▸ **paisa**
PAISE ▸ **paisa**
PAISLEY *n* pattern of small curving shapes with intricate detailing
PAJAMA = **pyjama**
PAJAMAS ▸ **pajama**
PAJOCK *obsolete word for* ▸ **peacock**
PAJOCKE *obsolete word for* ▸ **peacock**
PAJOCKS ▸ **pajock**
PAKAHI *n* acid land that is unsuitable for cultivation **pakahis**
PAKAPOO *n* Chinese lottery
PAKEHA *n* **pakehas**
PAKFONG = **packfong**
PAKIHI *n* area of swampy infertile land **pakihis**
PAKKA *variant of* ▸ **pukka**
PAKOKO *n* small freshwater fish **pakokos**
PAKORA *n* fried battered pieces of vegetable, chicken, etc **pakoras**
PAKTONG = **pakthong**
PAL *n, vb*
PALABRA *n* word
PALACE *n*
PALACED *adj* having palaces
PALACES ▸ **palace**
PALADIN *n* knight who did battle for a monarch
PALAGI *n* **palagis**
PALAIS *n* dance hall
PALAMA *n* webbing on bird's feet **palamae**
PALAPA *n* open-sided tropical building **palapas**
PALAS *n* East Indian tree **palases**
PALATAL *adj* of or relating to the palate ▹ *n* bony plate that forms the palate
PALATE *n, vb* **palated, palates**
PALAVER *n, vb*
PALAY *n* type of rubber **palays**
PALAZZI ▸ **palazzo**
PALAZZO *n* Italian palace
PALE *adj, vb, n*
PALEA *n* bract in a grass spikelet **paleae, paleal**
PALEATE *adj* having scales
PALED, palely, paler, pales, palest ▸ **pale**
PALET *n* perpendicular band on escutcheon
PALETOT *n* loose outer garment
PALETS ▸ **palet**
PALETTE *n*
PALFREY *n* light saddle horse, esp ridden by women
PALIER ▸ **paly**
PALIEST ▸ **paly**
PALIKAR *n* Greek soldier
PALING *n* wooden or metal post used in fences **palings**
PALINKA *n* type of apricot brandy
PALISH *adj* rather pale
PALKEE *n* covered Oriental litter **palkees, palki**
PALKIS ▸ **palki**
PALL *n, vb*
PALLA *n* ancient Roman cloak **pallae**
PALLAH *n* S African antelope **pallahs**
PALLED ▸ **pall**
PALLET = **palette**
PALLETS ▸ **pallet**
PALLIA ▸ **pallium**
PALLIAL *adj* relating to cerebral cortex
PALLID *adj*
PALLIED ▸ **pally**
PALLIER ▸ **pally**
PALLIES ▸ **pally**
PALLING ▸ **pall**
PALLIUM *n* garment worn by men in ancient Greece or Rome
PALLONE *n* Italian ball game
PALLOR *n* **pallors**
PALLS ▸ **pall**
PALLY *adj* on friendly terms ▹ *vb as in* **pally up** become friends with
PALM *n, vb*
PALMAR *adj* of or relating to the palm of the hand
PALMARY *adj* worthy of praise
PALMATE *adj*
PALMED ▸ **palm**
PALMER *n* medieval pilgrim **palmers**
PALMFUL *n* amount that can be held in the palm of a hand

PALMIE *n* palmtop computer
PALMIER ▸ **palmy**
PALMIES ▸ **palmie**
PALMIET *n* South African rush
PALMING ▸ **palm**
PALMIST > **palmistry**
PALMS ▸ **palm**
PALMTOP *adj* small enough to be held in the hand ▹ *n* computer small enough to be held in the hand
PALMY *adj* successful, prosperous and happy
PALMYRA *n* tall tropical Asian palm
PALOLO *n* polychaete worm of the S Pacific Ocean **palolos**
PALOOKA *n* stupid or clumsy boxer or other person
PALP *n* sensory appendage in crustaceans and insects ▹ *vb* feel **palpal**
PALPATE *vb* examine (an area of the body) by touching ▹ *adj* of, relating to, or possessing a palp or palps
PALPED ▸ **palp**
PALPI ▸ **palpus**
PALPING ▸ **palp**
PALPS ▸ **palp**
PALPUS = **palp**
PALS ▸ **pal**
PALSHIP *n* state of being pals
PALSIED ▸ **palsy**
PALSIER ▸ **palsy**
PALSIES ▸ **palsy**
PALSY *n, vb, adj*
PALTER *vb* act or talk insincerely **palters**
PALTRY *adj*
PALUDAL *adj* of, relating to, or produced by marshes
PALUDIC *adj* of malaria
PALY *adj* vertically striped
PAM *n* knave of clubs
PAMPA *n* grassland area
PAMPAS *pl n* **pampean**
PAMPER *vb*
PAMPERO *n* dry cold wind in South America
PAMPERS ▸ **pamper**
PAMPOEN *n* pumpkin
PAMS ▸ **pam**
PAN *n, vb*
PANACEA *n*
PANACHE *n*
PANADA *n* mixture used as a thickening in cookery **panadas**
PANAMA *n* hat made of plaited leaves **panamas**
PANARY *n* storehouse for bread
PANAX *n* genus of perennial herbs **panaxes**
PANCAKE *n, vb*
PANCE *n* pansy **pances**
PANCHAX *n* brightly coloured tropical Asian cyprinodont fish
PAND *n* valance
PANDA *n*
PANDANI *n* tropical tree
PANDAR *vb* act as a pimp **pandars**
PANDAS ▸ **panda**
PANDECT *n* treatise covering all aspects of a particular subject
PANDER *vb, n* **panders**
PANDIED ▸ **pandy**
PANDIES ▸ **pandy**
PANDIT = **pundit**
PANDITS ▸ **pandit**
PANDOOR = **pandour**
PANDORA *n* handsome red sea bream
PANDORE *another word for* ▸ **bandore**
PANDOUR *n* one of an 18th-century force of Croatian soldiers
PANDS ▸ **pand**
PANDURA *n* ancient stringed instrument
PANDY *n* (in schools) stroke on the hand with a strap as a punishment ▹ *vb* punish with such strokes
PANE *n, adj* **paned**
PANEER *n* soft white cheese, used in Indian cookery **paneers**
PANEITY *n* state of being bread
PANEL *n, vb, adj* **paneled, panels**
PANES ▸ **pane**
PANFISH *n* small food fish
PANFRY *vb* fry in a pan
PANFUL ▸ **pan**
PANFULS ▸ **pan**
PANG *n, vb*
PANGA *n* broad heavy knife of E Africa, used as a tool or weapon

PANGAMY *n* unrestricted mating
PANGAS ▸ panga
PANGED ▸ pang
PANGEN = pangene
PANGENE *n* hypothetical particle of protoplasm
PANGENS ▸ pangen
PANGING ▸ pang
PANGRAM *n* sentence incorporating all the letters of the alphabet
PANGS ▸ pang
PANIC *n, vb, adj* **panick**
PANICKS ▸ panick
PANICKY ▸ panic
PANICLE *n* loose, irregularly branched cluster of flowers
PANICS ▸ panic
PANICUM *n* type of grass
PANIER = pannier
PANIERS ▸ panier
PANIM *n* heathen or pagan **panims**
PANING ▸ pane
PANINI ▸ panino
PANINIS ▸ panini
PANINO *n* Italian sandwich
PANISC *n* faun; attendant of Pan **paniscs, panisk**
PANISKS ▸ panisk
PANKO *n* flaky breadcrumbs used in Japanese cookery **pankos**
PANNAGE *n* pasturage for pigs, esp in a forest
PANNE *n* lightweight velvet fabric
PANNED ▸ pan
PANNER ▸ pan
PANNERS ▸ pan
PANNES ▸ panne
PANNICK *old spelling of the noun* **▸ panic**
PANNIER *n*
PANNING ▸ pan
PANNOSE *adj* like felt
PANNUS *n* inflammatory fleshy lesion on the surface of the eye
PANOCHA *n* coarse grade of sugar made in Mexico
PANOCHE *n* type of dark sugar
PANOPLY *n*
PANPIPE *n* wind instrument
PANS ▸ pan
PANSIED *adj* covered with pansies
PANSIES ▸ pansy
PANSY *n*
PANT *vb, n* **panted**
PANTER *n* person who pants **panters**
PANTHER *n*
PANTIE = panty
PANTIES *pl n* women's underpants
PANTILE *n* roofing tile with an S-shaped cross section ▹ *vb* tile roof with pantiles
PANTINE *n* pasteboard puppet
PANTING ▸ pant
PANTLER *n* pantry servant
PANTO = pantomime
PANTON *n* type of horseshoe **pantons**
PANTOS ▸ panto
PANTOUM *n* verse form
PANTRY *n*
PANTS *pl n*
PANTUN *n* Malayan poetry **pantuns**
PANTY *n* woman's undergarment
PANZER *n* German tank **panzers**
PAOLI ▸ paolo
PAOLO *n* Italian silver coin
PAP *n, vb*
PAPA *n* father
PAPABLE *adj* suitable for papacy
PAPACY *n*
PAPADAM *variant of* > **poppadom**
PAPADOM *variant of* > **poppadom**
PAPADUM *variant of* > **poppadom**
PAPAIN *n* enzyme in the unripe fruit of the papaya **papains**
PAPAL *adj* of the pope **papally**
PAPAS ▸ papa
PAPAUMA *n* New Zealand word for broadleaf
PAPAW = papaya
PAPAWS ▸ papaw
PAPAYA *n* **papayan, papayas**
PAPE *n* spiritual father
PAPER *n, vb* **papered, paperer, papers**
PAPERY *adj* like paper, esp in thinness, flimsiness, or dryness

PAPES ▸ pape
PAPHIAN *n* prostitute
PAPILIO *n* butterfly
PAPILLA *n* small projection of tissue
PAPOOSE *n* Native American child
PAPPED ▸ pap
PAPPI ▸ pappus
PAPPIER ▸ pappy
PAPPIES ▸ pappy
PAPPING ▸ pap
PAPPOSE ▸ pappus
PAPPOUS ▸ pappus
PAPPUS *n* ring of hairs surrounding the fruit in composite plants
PAPPY *adj* resembling pap
PAPRICA = paprika
PAPRIKA *n*
PAPS ▸ pap
PAPULA = papule
PAPULAE ▸ papula
PAPULAR ▸ papule
PAPULE *n* small solid usually round elevation of the skin **papules**
PAPYRAL ▸ papyrus
PAPYRI ▸ papyrus
PAPYRUS *n*
PAR *n, vb*
PARA *n* paratrooper
PARABEN *n*
PARABLE *n, vb*
PARACME *n* phase where fever lessens
PARADE *n, vb* **paraded, parader, parades**
PARADOR *n* state-run hotel in Spain
PARADOS *n* bank behind a trench or other fortification
PARADOX *n*
PARAE *n* type of fish
PARAFLE = paraffle
PARAGE *n* type of feudal land tenure **parages**
PARAGON *n, vb*
PARAMO *n* high plateau in the Andes **paramos**
PARANG *n* knife used by the Dyaks of Borneo **parangs**
PARANYM *n* euphemism
PARAPET *n, vb*
PARAPH *n* flourish after a signature ▹ *vb* embellish signature **paraphs**
PARAS ▸ para
PARASOL *n*
PARATHA *n* (in Indian cookery) flat unleavened bread
PARAZOA > parazoan
PARBAKE *vb* partially bake
PARBOIL *vb*
PARCEL *n, vb* **parcels**
PARCH *vb* make very hot and dry **parched, parches**
PARD *n* leopard or panther
PARDAH = purdah
PARDAHS ▸ pardah
PARDAL *variant spelling of* ▸ **pardale**
PARDALE *n* leopard
PARDALS ▸ pardal
PARDED *adj* having spots
PARDEE *adv* certainly **pardi, pardie**
PARDINE *adj* spotted
PARDNER *n* friend or partner: used as a term of address
PARDON *vb, n, interj, sentence substitute* **pardons**
PARDS ▸ pard
PARDY = pardee
PARE *vb* **pared**
PAREIRA *n* root of a South American climbing plant
PARELLA *n* type of lichen **parelle**
PARENT *n, vb* **parents**
PAREO = pareu
PAREOS ▸ pareu
PARER ▸ pare
PARERA *n* New Zealand duck **pareras**
PARERGA > parergon
PARERS ▸ pare
PARES ▸ pare
PARESES ▸ paresis
PARESIS *n* incomplete or slight paralysis of motor functions **paretic**
PAREU *n* Polynesian skirt or loincloth **pareus**
PAREV *adj* containing neither meat nor milk products **pareve**
PARFAIT *n* dessert consisting of layers of ice cream, fruit, and sauce
PARGANA *n* Indian sub-district
PARGE *vb* coat with plaster **parged, parges**
PARGET *n* plaster, mortar, etc, used to

line chimney flues or cover walls ▷ *vb* cover or decorate with parget **pargets**
PARGING ▶ **parge**
PARGO *n* sea bream **pargos**
PARIAH *n* **pariahs**
PARIAL *n* pair royal of playing cards **parials**
PARIAN *n* type of marble or porcelain **parians**
PARIES *n* wall of an organ or bodily cavity
PARING *n* piece pared off **parings**
PARIS *n* type of herb **parises**
PARISH *n*
PARISON *n* unshaped mass of glass
PARITOR *n* official who summons witnesses
PARITY *n*
PARK *n*, *vb*
PARKA *n*
PARKADE *n* building used as a car park
PARKAS ▶ **parka**
PARKED ▶ **park**
PARKEE *n* Eskimo outer garment **parkees**
PARKER ▶ **park**
PARKERS ▶ **park**
PARKI *variant of* ▶ **parka**
PARKIE *n* park keeper
PARKIER ▶ **parky**
PARKIES ▶ **parkie**
PARKIN *n* moist spicy ginger cake
PARKING ▶ **park**
PARKINS ▶ **parkin**
PARKIS ▶ **parki**
PARKISH *adj* like a park
PARKLY *adj* having many parks or resembling a park
PARKOUR *n* sport of running in urban areas over obstacles
PARKS ▶ **park**
PARKWAY *n* wide road planted with trees, turf, etc
PARKY *adj* (of the weather) chilly
PARLAY *vb* stake (winnings from one bet) on a subsequent wager ▷ *n* bet in which winnings are parlayed **parlays**
PARLE *vb* speak **parled, parles**
PARLEY *n* meeting between opponents to discuss terms ▷ *vb* have a parley **parleys**
PARLIES *pl n* small Scottish biscuits
PARLING ▶ **parle**
PARLOR = **parlour**
PARLORS ▶ **parlor**
PARLOUR *n*
PARLOUS *adj*, *adv*
PARLY *n* short form of parliament
PARODIC ▶ **parody**
PARODOI *n* path leading to Greek theatre
PARODOS *n* ode sung by Greek chorus
PARODY *n*, *vb*
PAROL *n* (formerly) pleadings in an action when presented by word of mouth ▷ *adj* (of a contract, lease, etc) not made under seal
PAROLE *n*, *vb* **paroled, parolee, paroles**
PAROLS ▶ **parol**
PARONYM *n* cognate word
PARORE *n* type of fish found around Australia and New Zealand **parores**
PAROTIC *adj* situated near the ear
PAROTID *adj* relating to or situated near the parotid gland ▷ *n* parotid gland
PAROTIS *n* parotid gland
PAROUS *adj* having given birth
PARP *vb* make a honking sound
PARPANE *n* parapet on bridge
PARPED ▶ **parp**
PARPEN = **parpend**
PARPEND = **perpend**
PARPENS ▶ **parpen**
PARPENT *n* parapet on bridge
PARPING ▶ **parp**
PARPS ▶ **parp**
PARQUET *n*, *vb*
PARR *n* salmon up to two years of age
PARRA *n* tourist or non-resident on a beach
PARRAL = **parrel**
PARRALS ▶ **parral**
PARRAS ▶ **parra**

PARRED ▸ **par**
PARREL *n* ring that holds the jaws of a boom to the mast **parrels**
PARRIED ▸ **parry**
PARRIER ▸ **parry**
PARRIES ▸ **parry**
PARRING ▸ **par**
PARROCK *vb* put (an animal) in a small field
PARROT *n*, *vb* **parrots**
PARROTY *adj* like a parrot; chattering
PARRS ▸ **parr**
PARRY *vb*, *n*
PARS ▸ **par**
PARSE *vb*
PARSEC *n* unit of astronomical distance **parsecs**
PARSED ▸ **parse**
PARSER *n* program that interprets input to a computer **parsers**
PARSES ▸ **parse**
PARSING ▸ **parse**
PARSLEY *n*, *vb*
PARSNEP = **parsnip**
PARSNIP *n*
PARSON *n* **parsons**
PART *n*, *vb*
PARTAKE *vb*
PARTAN *Scottish word for* ▸ **crab**
PARTANS ▸ **partan**
PARTED *adj* divided almost to the base
PARTER *n* thing that parts **parters**
PARTI *n* concept of architectural design
PARTIAL *adj*, *n*, *vb*
PARTIED ▸ **party**
PARTIER *n* person who parties
PARTIES ▸ **party**
PARTIM *adv* in part
PARTING = **part**
PARTIS ▸ **parti**
PARTITA *n* type of suite
PARTITE *adj* composed of or divided into a specified number of parts
PARTLET *n* woman's garment
PARTLY *adv*
PARTNER *n*, *vb*
PARTON *n* hypothetical elementary particle **partons**
PARTOOK ▸ **partake**
PARTS *pl n* abilities or talents
PARTURE *n* departure
PARTWAY *adv* some of the way
PARTY *n*, *vb*, *adj*
PARTYER *n* person who parties
PARULIS *another name for* ▸ **gumboil**
PARURA = **parure**
PARURAS ▸ **parura**
PARURE *n* set of jewels or other ornaments **parures**
PARVE = **parev**
PARVENU *n* person newly risen to a position of power or wealth ▹ *adj* of or characteristic of a parvenu
PARVIS *n* court or portico in front of a building, esp a church **parvise**
PARVO *n* disease of cattle and dogs **parvos**
PAS *n* dance step or movement, esp in ballet
PASCAL *n* unit of pressure **pascals**
PASCHAL *adj* of the Passover or Easter ▹ *n* Passover or Easter
PASCUAL *adj* relating to pasture
PASE *n* movement of the cape or muleta by a matador
PASEAR *vb* go for a rambling walk **pasears**
PASELA = **bonsela**
PASELAS ▸ **pasela**
PASEO *n* bullfighters' procession **paseos**
PASES ▸ **pase**
PASH *n* infatuation ▹ *vb* throw or be thrown and break or be broken to bits
PASHA *n* high official of the Ottoman Empire **pashas**
PASHED ▸ **pash**
PASHES ▸ **pash**
PASHIM = **pashm**
PASHIMS ▸ **pashm**
PASHING ▸ **pash**
PASHKA *n* rich Russian dessert **pashkas**
PASHM *n* underfur of various Tibetan animals, esp goats, used for cashmere shawls **pashms**
PASPIES ▸ **paspy**

PASPY *n* piece of music in triple time
PASQUIL *n* abusive lampoon or satire ▷ *vb* ridicule with pasquil
PASS *vb, n*
PASSADE *n* act of moving back and forth in the same place
PASSADO *n* forward thrust with sword
PASSAGE *n, vb*
PASSANT *adj* (of a heraldic beast) walking
PASSATA *n* sauce made from sieved tomatoes
PASSE *adj* out-of-date
PASSED ▸ **pass**
PASSEE *adj* out of fashion
PASSEL *n* group or quantity of no fixed number **passels**
PASSER *n* person or thing that passes **passers**
PASSES ▸ **pass**
PASSIM *adv* everywhere, throughout
PASSING *adj, n*
PASSION *n, vb*
PASSIVE *adj, n*
PASSKEY *n* private key
PASSMAN *n* student who passes without honours **passmen**
PASSOUT *n* (in ice hockey) pass by an attacking player from behind the opposition goal line
PASSUS *n* division or section of a poem, story, etc
PAST *adj, n, adv, prep*
PASTA *n* **pastas**
PASTE *n, vb* **pasted**
PASTEL *n, adj* **pastels**
PASTER *n* person or thing that pastes
PASTERN *n* part of a horse's foot
PASTERS ▸ **paster**
PASTES ▸ **paste**
PASTEUP *n* material pasted on a sheet of paper or board
PASTIE *n* decorative cover for nipple
PASTIER ▸ **pasty**
PASTIES ▸ **pasty**
PASTIL = **pastille**
PASTILS ▸ **pastil**
PASTILY ▸ **pasty**
PASTIME *n*
PASTINA *n* small pieces of pasta
PASTING *n* heavy defeat
PASTIS *n* anise-flavoured alcoholic drink
PASTOR *n, vb* **pastors**
PASTRY *n*
PASTS ▸ **past**
PASTURE *n, vb*
PASTY *adj, n*
PAT *vb, n, adj*
PATACA *n* monetary unit of Macao **patacas**
PATAGIA > **patagium**
PATAKA *n* building on stilts, used for storing provisions **patakas**
PATAMAR *n* type of boat
PATBALL *n* game like squash but using hands
PATCH *n, vb* **patched, patcher, patches**
PATCHY *adj*
PATE *n* head **pated**
PATELLA *n*
PATEN *n* plate used for the bread at Communion
PATENCY *n* condition of being obvious
PATENS ▸ **paten**
PATENT *n, adj, vb* **patents**
PATER *n* father
PATERA *n* shallow ancient Roman bowl **paterae**
PATERS ▸ **pater**
PATES ▸ **pate**
PATH *n, vb* **pathed**
PATHIC *n* catamite ▷ *adj* of or relating to a catamite **pathics**
PATHING ▸ **path**
PATHOS *n*
PATHS ▸ **path**
PATHWAY *n*
PATIBLE *adj* endurable
PATIENT *adj, n, vb*
PATIKI *n* New Zealand sand flounder or dab **patikis**
PATIN = **paten**
PATINA *n* **patinae, patinas**
PATINE *vb* cover with patina **patined, patines**
PATINS ▸ **patin**
PATIO *n* **patios**
PATKA *n* head covering worn by Sikh men **patkas**
PATLY *adv* fitly
PATNESS *n* appropriateness
PATOIS *n*

PATONCE *adj* (of cross) with limbs which broaden from centre
PATRIAL *n* (in Britain, formerly) person with a right to live in the United Kingdom
PATRICK *n* former Irish coin
PATRICO *n* fraudulent priest
PATRIOT *n*
PATROL *n, vb* **patrols**
PATRON *n* **patrons**
PATROON *n* Dutch land-holder in New Netherland and New York
PATS ▸ **pat**
PATSIES ▸ **patsy**
PATSY *n* person who is easily cheated, victimized, etc
PATTE *n* band keeping belt in place
PATTED ▸ **pat**
PATTEE *adj* (of a cross) having triangular arms widening outwards
PATTEN *n* wooden clog or sandal ▹ *vb* wear pattens **pattens**
PATTER *vb, n*
PATTERN *n, vb*
PATTERS ▸ **patter**
PATTES ▸ **patte**
PATTIE = **patty**
PATTIES ▸ **patty**
PATTING ▸ **pat**
PATTLE *dialect for* ▸ **paddle**
PATTLES ▸ **pattle**
PATTY *n* small flattened cake of minced food
PATU *n* short Māori club, now used ceremonially
PATULIN *n* toxic antibiotic
PATUS ▸ **patu**
PATY *adj* (of cross) having arms of equal length
PATZER *n* novice chess player **patzers**
PAUA *n* edible shellfish of New Zealand **pauas**
PAUCAL *n* grammatical number for words in contexts where a few of their referents are described ▹ *adj* relating to or inflected for this number **paucals**
PAUCITY *n*
PAUGHTY *Scots word for* ▸ **haughty**
PAUL = **pawl**
PAULIN *n* tarpaulin **paulins**
PAULS ▸ **paul**
PAUNCE *n* pansy **paunces**
PAUNCH *n, vb*
PAUNCHY *adj* having a protruding belly or abdomen
PAUPER *n, vb* **paupers**
PAUSAL ▸ **pause**
PAUSE *vb, n* **paused, pauser, pausers, pauses, pausing**
PAV *short for* ▸ **pavlova**
PAVAGE *n* tax towards paving streets **pavages**
PAVAN = **pavane**
PAVANE *n* slow and stately dance **pavanes**
PAVANS ▸ **pavan**
PAVE *vb, n* **paved**
PAVEED *adj* (of jewels) set close together
PAVEN = **pavane**
PAVENS ▸ **paven**
PAVER ▸ **pave**
PAVERS ▸ **pave**
PAVES ▸ **pave**
PAVID *adj* fearful
PAVIN = **pavane**
PAVING *n* paved surface ▹ *adj* of or for a paved surface or pavement **pavings**
PAVINS ▸ **pavin**
PAVIOR = **paviour**
PAVIORS ▸ **pavior**
PAVIOUR *n* person who lays paving
PAVIS *n* large square shield **pavise**
PAVISER *n* soldier holding pavise
PAVISES ▸ **pavise**
PAVISSE = **pavis**
PAVLOVA *n* meringue cake topped with whipped cream and fruit
PAVONE *n* peacock **pavones**
PAVS ▸ **pav**
PAW *n, vb*
PAWA *old word for* ▸ **peacock**
PAWAS ▸ **pawa**
PAWAW *vb* recite N American incantation **pawawed, pawaws**
PAWED ▸ **paw**
PAWER *n* person or animal that paws **pawers**

PAWING ▸ **paw**
PAWK *Scots word for* ▸ **trick**
PAWKIER ▸ **pawky**
PAWKILY ▸ **pawky**
PAWKS ▸ **pawk**
PAWKY *adj* having or characterized by a dry wit
PAWL *n* pivoted lever shaped to engage with a ratchet **pawls**
PAWN *vb, n* **pawnage**
PAWNCE *old word for* ▸ **pansy**
PAWNCES ▸ **pawnce**
PAWNED ▸ **pawn**
PAWNEE *n* one who accepts goods in pawn **pawnees**
PAWNER *n* one who pawns his or her possessions **pawners**
PAWNING ▸ **pawn**
PAWNOR = **pawner**
PAWNORS ▸ **pawnor**
PAWNS ▸ **pawn**
PAWPAW = **papaw**
PAWPAWS ▸ **pawpaw**
PAWS ▸ **paw**
PAX *n* peace ▹ *interj* call signalling a desire to end hostilities **paxes**

> Latin for peace, this is yet another of those very useful short words containing X.

PAXIUBA *n* tropical tree
PAXWAX *n* strong ligament in the neck of many mammals
PAY *vb, n*
PAYABLE *adj* **payably**
PAYBACK *n* return on an investment
PAYDAY *n* day on which wages or salaries are paid **paydays**
PAYED ▸ **pay**
PAYEE *n* **payees**
PAYER *n* person who pays **payers**
PAYFONE *US spelling of* > **payphone**
PAYING ▸ **pay**
PAYINGS ▸ **pay**
PAYLIST *n* list of people to be paid
PAYLOAD *n*
PAYMENT *n*
PAYNIM *n* heathen or pagan **paynims**
PAYOFF *n* final settlement, esp in retribution **payoffs**
PAYOLA *n* bribe to promote a commercial product **payolas**
PAYOR = **payer**
PAYORS ▸ **payor**
PAYOUT *n* sum of money paid out **payouts**
PAYROLL *n*
PAYS ▸ **pay**
PAYSAGE *n* landscape
PAYSD *Spenserian form of* ▸ **poised**
PAYSLIP *n* note of payment given to employee
PAZAZZ = **pizzazz**
PAZZAZZ = **pizzazz**
PE *n* 17th letter of the Hebrew alphabet, transliterated as *p*
PEA *n*
PEACE *n* **peaced, peaces**
PEACH *n, adj, vb* **peached, peacher, peaches**
PEACHY *adj* of or like a peach, esp in colour or texture
PEACING ▸ **peace**
PEACOAT *n* woollen jacket
PEACOCK *n, vb*
PEACOD = **peapod**
PEACODS ▸ **peacod**
PEAFOWL *n* peacock or peahen
PEAG *n* (formerly) money used by North American Indians **peage**
PEAGES ▸ **peage**
PEAGS ▸ **peag**
PEAHEN ▸ **peacock**
PEAHENS ▸ **peacock**
PEAK *n, vb, adj*
PEAKED *adj* having a peak
PEAKIER ▸ **peak**
PEAKING ▸ **peak**
PEAKISH *adj* sickly
PEAKS ▸ **peak**
PEAKY ▸ **peak**
PEAL *n, vb* **pealed**
PEALIKE ▸ **pea**
PEALING ▸ **peal**
PEALS ▸ **peal**
PEAN = **peen**
PEANED ▸ **pean**
PEANING ▸ **pean**
PEANS ▸ **pean**
PEANUT *n* **peanuts**
PEAPOD *n* pod of the pea plant **peapods**
PEAR *n*

PEARCE *old spelling of* ▸ **pierce**
PEARCED ▸ **pearce**
PEARCES ▸ **pearce**
PEARE *obsolete spelling of* ▸ **pear**
PEARES ▸ **peare**
PEARL = **purl**
PEARLED ▸ **pearl**
PEARLER *n* person who dives for or trades in pearls ▹ *adj* excellent
PEARLIN *n* type of lace used to trim clothes
PEARLS ▸ **pearl**
PEARLY *adj* resembling a pearl, esp in lustre ▹ *n* London costermonger who wears pearl buttons
PEARS ▸ **pear**
PEARST *archaic variant of* ▸ **pierced**
PEART *adj* lively **pearter, peartly**
PEAS ▸ **pea**
PEASANT *n*
PEASCOD = **cod**
PEASE *n* archaic or dialect word for pea ▹ *vb* appease **peased, peasen, peases, peasing, peason**
PEAT *n*
PEATARY *n* area covered with peat **peatery**
PEATIER ▸ **peat**
PEATMAN *n* person who collects peat **peatmen**
PEATS ▸ **peat**
PEATY ▸ **peat**
PEAVEY *n* wooden lever used for handling logs **peaveys**
PEAVIES ▸ **peavy**
PEAVY = **peavey**
PEAZE = **pease**
PEAZED ▸ **peaze**
PEAZES ▸ **peaze**
PEAZING ▸ **peaze**
PEBA *n* type of armadillo **pebas**
PEBBLE *n, vb* **pebbled, pebbles, pebbly**
PEBRINE *n* disease of silkworms
PEC *n* pectoral muscle
PECAN *n* **pecans**
PECCANT *adj* guilty of an offence
PECCARY *n* piglike animal of American forests
PECCAVI *n* confession of guilt
PECH *Scottish word for* ▸ **pant**
PECHAN *Scots word for* ▸ **stomach**
PECHANS ▸ **pechan**
PECHED ▸ **pech**
PECHING ▸ **pech**
PECHS ▸ **pech**
PECK *vb, n*
PECKE *n* quarter of bushel
PECKED ▸ **peck**
PECKES ▸ **pecke**
PECKIER ▸ **pecky**
PECKING ▸ **peck**
PECKISH *adj*
PECKS ▸ **peck**
PECKY *adj* discoloured
PECS *pl n* pectoral muscles
PECTASE *n* enzyme occurring in certain ripening fruits
PECTATE *n* salt or ester of pectic acid
PECTEN *n* comblike structure in the eye of birds and reptiles **pectens**
PECTIC ▸ **pectin**
PECTIN *n* **pectins**
PECTISE = **pectize**
PECTIZE *vb* change into a jelly
PECTOSE *n* insoluble carbohydrate found in unripe fruit
PECULIA > **peculium**
PED *n* pannier
PEDAGOG = **pedagogue**
PEDAL *n, vb, adj* **pedaled, pedaler**
PEDALO *n* pedal-operated pleasure craft **pedalos**
PEDALS ▸ **pedal**
PEDANT *n* **pedants**
PEDATE *adj* (of a plant leaf) divided into several lobes arising at a common point
PEDDER *old form of* ▸ **pedlar**
PEDDERS ▸ **pedder**
PEDDLE *vb* **peddled**
PEDDLER = **pedlar**
PEDDLES ▸ **peddle**
PEDES ▸ **pes**
PEDESES ▸ **pedesis**
PEDESIS *n* random motion of small particles
PEDETIC *adj* of feet
PEDICAB *n* pedal-operated tricycle, available for hire

PEDICEL *n* stalk bearing a single flower of an inflorescence
PEDICLE *n* any small stalk
PEDLAR *n* person who sells goods from door to door **pedlars**
PEDLARY = **pedlery**
PEDLER = **pedlar**
PEDLERS ▸ **pedler**
PEDLERY *n* business of pedler
PEDOCAL *n* type of soil that is rich in lime
PEDRAIL *n* device replacing wheel on rough surfaces
PEDRERO *n* type of cannon
PEDRO *n* card game **pedros**
PEDS ▸ **ped**
PEEBEEN *n* type of large evergreen
PEECE *obsolete variant of* ▸ **piece**
PEECES ▸ **peece**
PEEK *n*, *vb*
PEEKABO = **peekaboo**
PEEKED ▸ **peek**
PEEKING ▸ **peek**
PEEKS ▸ **peek**
PEEL *vb*, *n* **peeled**
PEELER *n* device for peeling vegetables, fruit, etc **peelers**
PEELING *n* strip that has been peeled off
PEELS ▸ **peel**
PEEN *n* end of a hammer head opposite the striking face ▹ *vb* strike with the peen of a hammer **peened**
PEENGE *vb* complain **peenged, peenges**
PEENING ▸ **peen**
PEENS ▸ **peen**
PEEOY *n* homemade firework **peeoys**
PEEP *vb*, *n*
PEEPE *old spelling of* ▸ **pip**
PEEPED ▸ **peep**
PEEPER *n* person who peeps **peepers**
PEEPES *archaic spelling of* ▸ **peeps**
PEEPING ▸ **peep**
PEEPS ▸ **peep**
PEEPUL *n* Indian moraceous tree **peepuls**
PEER *n*, *vb*
PEERAGE *n*
PEERED ▸ **peer**
PEERESS *n* (in Britain) woman holding the rank of a peer
PEERIE *n* spinning top ▹ *adj* small **peerier, peeries**
PEERING ▸ **peer**
PEERS ▸ **peer**
PEERY *n* child's spinning top
PEEVE *vb* irritate or annoy ▹ *n* something that irritates **peeved**
PEEVER *n* hopscotch **peevers**
PEEVES ▸ **peeve**
PEEVING ▸ **peeve**
PEEVISH *adj*
PEEWEE = **pewee**
PEEWEES ▸ **peewee**
PEEWIT = **lapwing**
PEEWITS ▸ **peewit**
PEG *n*, *vb*
PEGASUS *n* winged horse
PEGBOX *n* part of stringed instrument that holds tuning pegs
PEGGED ▸ **peg**
PEGGIES ▸ **peggy**
PEGGING ▸ **peg**
PEGGY *n* type of small warbler
PEGH *variant of* ▸ **pech**
PEGHED ▸ **pegh**
PEGHING ▸ **pegh**
PEGHS ▸ **pegh**
PEGLESS ▸ **peg**
PEGLIKE ▸ **peg**
PEGS ▸ **peg**
PEH ▸ **pe**
PEHS ▸ **peh**
PEIN = **peen**
PEINCT *vb* paint **peincts**
PEINED ▸ **pein**
PEINING ▸ **pein**
PEINS ▸ **pein**
PEISE = **peize**
PEISED ▸ **peise**
PEISES ▸ **peise**
PEISHWA *n* Indian leader
PEISING ▸ **peise**
PEIZE *vb* weight or poise **peized, peizes, peizing**
PEKAN *n* large North American marten **pekans**
PEKE *n* Pekingese dog
PEKEPOO = **peekapoo**
PEKES ▸ **peke**
PEKIN *n* silk fabric **pekins**
PEKOE *n* high-quality

tea **pekoes**
PEL *n* pixel
PELA *n* insect living on wax
PELAGE *n* coat of a mammal, consisting of hair, wool, fur, etc **pelages**
PELAGIC *adj* of or relating to the open sea ▷ *n* any pelagic creature
PELAS ▸ **pela**
PELE *Spenserian variant of* ▸ **peal**
PELES ▸ **pele**
PELF *n* money or wealth **pelfs**
PELHAM *n* horse's bit for a double bridle **pelhams**
PELICAN *n*
PELISSE *n* cloak or loose coat which is usually fur-trimmed
PELITE *n* any argillaceous rock such as shale **pelites, pelitic**
PELL *n* hide of an animal
PELLACH = **pellack**
PELLACK *n* porpoise
PELLET *n, vb* **pellets**
PELLOCK *n* porpoise
PELLS ▸ **pell**
PELLUM *n* dust **pellums**
PELMA *n* sole of the foot **pelmas**
PELMET *n* **pelmets**
PELOID *n* mud used therapeutically **peloids**
PELON *adj* hairless
PELORIA *n* abnormal production of flowers in a plant **peloric**
PELORUS *n* sighting device
PELORY *n* floral mutation
PELOTA *n* game where players propel a ball against a wall **pelotas**
PELOTON *n* main field of riders in a road race
PELS ▸ **pel**
PELT *vb, n*
PELTA *n* small ancient shield **peltae, peltas**
PELTAST *n* (in ancient Greece) lightly armed foot soldier
PELTATE *adj* (of leaves) having the stalk attached to the centre of the lower surface
PELTED ▸ **pelt**
PELTER *vb*
PELTERS ▸ **pelt**
PELTING ▸ **pelt**
PELTRY *n* pelts of animals collectively
PELTS ▸ **pelt**
PELVES ▸ **pelvis**
PELVIC *adj* of, near, or relating to the pelvis ▷ *n* pelvic bone **pelvics**
PELVIS *n*
PEMBINA *n* type of cranberry
PEMICAN = **pemmican**
PEMPHIX *n* type of crustacean
PEN *n, vb*
PENAL *adj* **penally**
PENALTY *n*
PENANCE *n, vb*
PENANG *variant of* ▸ **pinang**
PENANGS ▸ **penang**
PENATES *pl n* household gods
PENCE ▸ **penny**
PENCEL *n* small pennon **pencels**
PENCES ▸ **penny**
PENCIL *n, vb* **pencils**
PEND *vb* await judgment or settlement ▷ *n* archway or vaulted passage
PENDANT *n*
PENDED ▸ **pend**
PENDENT *adj* hanging ▷ *n* pendant
PENDING *prep, adj*
PENDS ▸ **pend**
PENDU *adj* in informal Indian English, culturally backward
PENDULE *n* type of climbing manoeuvre
PENE *variant of* ▸ **peen**
PENED ▸ **pene**
PENES ▸ **penis**
PENFOLD = **pinfold**
PENFUL *n* contents of pen **penfuls**
PENGO *n* former monetary unit of Hungary **pengos**
PENGUIN *n*
PENI *old spelling of* ▸ **penny**
PENIAL ▸ **penis**
PENICIL *n* small pad for wounds
PENIE *old spelling of* ▸ **penny**
PENIES ▸ **penie**

PENILE *adj* of or relating to the penis
PENILL > **penillion**
PENING ▸ **pene**
PENIS *n* **penises**
PENK *n* small fish **penks**
PENLITE = **penlight**
PENMAN *n* person skilled in handwriting **penmen**
PENNA *n* large feather **pennae**
PENNAL *n* first-year student of Protestant university **pennals**
PENNAME *n* author's pseudonym
PENNANT = **pendant**
PENNATE *adj* having feathers, wings, or winglike structures
PENNE *n* pasta in the form of short tubes
PENNED ▸ **pen**
PENNER *n* person who writes **penners**
PENNES ▸ **penne**
PENNI *n* former Finnish monetary unit **pennia**
PENNIED *adj* having money
PENNIES ▸ **penny**
PENNILL *n* stanza in a Welsh poem
PENNINE *n* mineral found in the Pennine Alps
PENNING ▸ **pen**
PENNIS ▸ **penni**
PENNON *n* triangular or tapering flag **pennons**
PENNY *n*
PENOCHE *n* type of fudge
PENS ▸ **pen**
PENSEE *n* thought put down on paper **pensees**
PENSEL = **pencel**
PENSELS ▸ **pensel**
PENSIL = **pencel**
PENSILE *adj* designating or building a hanging nest
PENSILS ▸ **pensil**
PENSION *n*, *vb*
PENSIVE *adj*
PENSTER *n* writer
PENSUM *n* school exercise **pensums**
PENT *n* penthouse
PENTACT *n* sponge spicule with five rays
PENTAD *n* group or series of five **pentads**
PENTANE *n* alkane hydrocarbon with three isomers
PENTENE *n* colourless flammable liquid alkene
PENTHIA *n* child born fifth
PENTICE *vb* accommodate in a penthouse **pentise**
PENTITI ▸ **pentito**
PENTITO *n* criminal who offers information to the police
PENTODE *n* electronic valve having five electrodes
PENTOSE *n* monosaccharide containing five atoms of carbon per molecule
PENTS ▸ **pent**
PENTYL *n* one of a particular chemical group **pentyls**
PENUCHE = **panocha**
PENUCHI = **panocha**
PENULT *n* last syllable but one in a word **penults**
PENURY *n*
PEON *n* Spanish-American farm labourer or unskilled worker
PEONAGE *n* state of being a peon
PEONES ▸ **peon**
PEONIES ▸ **peony**
PEONISM = **peonage**
PEONS ▸ **peon**
PEONY *n*
PEOPLE *pl n*, *vb* **peopled**
PEOPLER *n* settler
PEOPLES ▸ **people**
PEP *n* high spirits, energy, or enthusiasm ▹ *vb* liven by imbuing with new vigour
PEPFUL *adj* full of vitality
PEPINO *n* purple-striped yellow fruit **pepinos**
PEPLA ▸ **peplum**
PEPLOS *n* part of a woman's attire in ancient Greece **peplum**
PEPLUMS ▸ **peplum**
PEPLUS = **peplos**
PEPO *n* fruit such as the melon, squash, cucumber, or pumpkin **pepos**
PEPPED ▸ **pep**
PEPPER *n*, *vb* **peppers**
PEPPERY *adj* tasting of pepper

PEPPIER ▸ **peppy**
PEPPILY ▸ **peppy**
PEPPING ▸ **pep**
PEPPY *adj* full of vitality
PEPS ▸ **pep**
PEPSIN *n* enzyme produced in the stomach **pepsine, pepsins**
PEPTALK *n* talk meant to inspire ▹ *vb* give a peptalk to
PEPTIC *adj* relating to digestion or the digestive juices ▹ *n* substance that aids digestion **peptics**
PEPTID *variant of* ▸ **peptide**
PEPTIDE *n* organic chemical compound
PEPTIDS ▸ **peptid**
PEPTISE = **peptize**
PEPTIZE *vb* disperse into a colloidal state
PEPTONE *n* any of a group of organic compounds
PER *prep*
PERACID *n* acid in which the element forming the acid radical exhibits its highest valency
PERAEA ▸ **peraeon**
PERAEON = **pereion**
PERAI *another name for* ▸ **piranha**
PERAIS ▸ **perai**
PERCALE *n* close-textured woven cotton fabric
PERCASE *adv* perchance
PERCE *obsolete word for* ▸ **pierce**
PERCED ▸ **perce**
PERCEN ▸ **perce**
PERCENT *n* percentage or proportion
PERCEPT *n* concept that depends on recognition of some external object or phenomenon
PERCES ▸ **perce**
PERCH *n, vb* **perched, percher, perches**
PERCINE *adj* of perches
PERCING ▸ **perce**
PERCOCT *adj* well-cooked
PERCOID *n* type of spiny-finned teleost fish
PERCUSS *vb* strike sharply, rapidly, or suddenly
PERDIE *adv* certainly
PERDU *adj* (of a soldier) placed on hazardous sentry duty ▹ *n* soldier placed on hazardous sentry duty **perdue**
PERDUES ▸ **perdue**
PERDURE *vb* last for long time
PERDUS ▸ **perdu**
PERDY *adv* certainly
PERE *n* addition to a French surname to specify the father
PEREA ▸ **pereon**
PEREGAL *adj* equal ▹ *n* equal
PEREIA ▸ **pereion**
PEREION *n* thorax of some crustaceans
PEREIRA *n* bark of a South American apocynaceous tree
PERENTY = **perentie**
PEREON = **pereion**
PEREONS ▸ **pereon**
PERES ▸ **pere**
PERFAY *interj* by my faith
PERFECT *adj, n, vb* **perfet**
PERFIDY *n* perfidious act
PERFIN *former name for* ▸ **spif**
PERFING *n* practice of taking early retirement from the police force
PERFINS ▸ **perfin**
PERFORM *vb*
PERFUME *n, vb*
PERFUMY *adj* like perfume
PERFUSE *vb* permeate through or over
PERGOLA *n* framework of trellis supporting climbing plants
PERHAPS *adv, sentence substitute, n*
PERI *n* (in Persian folklore) one of a race of beautiful supernatural beings
PERIAPT *n* charm or amulet
PERICON *n* Argentinian dance
PERIDIA > **peridium**
PERIDOT *n* pale green transparent gemstone
PERIGEE *n* point in the orbit of the moon or a satellite that is nearest the earth
PERIGON *n* angle of 360°
PERIL *n, vb* **periled**

PERILLA *n* type of mint
PERILS ▸ **peril**
PERINEA > **perineum**
PERIOD *n, adj, vb* **periods**
PERIOST *n* thick fibrous two-layered membrane covering the surface of bones
PERIQUE *n* strong highly-flavoured tobacco
PERIS ▸ **peri**
PERISH *vb*
PERITI ▸ **peritus**
PERITUS *n* Catholic theology consultant
PERIWIG = **peruke**
PERJINK *adj* prim or finicky
PERJURE *vb* render (oneself) guilty of perjury
PERJURY *n*
PERK *n, adj, vb* **perked**
PERKIER ▸ **perky**
PERKILY ▸ **perky**
PERKIN = **parkin**
PERKING ▸ **perk**
PERKINS ▸ **perkin**
PERKISH *adj* perky
PERKS ▸ **perk**
PERKY *adj* lively or cheerful
PERLITE *n* variety of obsidian
PERLOUS = **perilous**
PERM *n, vb* **permed**
PERMIAN *adj* of, denoting, or formed in the last period of the Palaeozoic era
PERMIE *n* person, esp an office worker, employed by a firm on a permanent basis **permies**
PERMING ▸ **perm**
PERMIT *vb, n* **permits**
PERMS ▸ **perm**
PERMUTE *vb* change the sequence of
PERN *n* type of buzzard
PERNIO *n* chilblain
PERNOD *n* aniseed-flavoured aperitif from France **pernods**
PERNS ▸ **pern**
PEROGI *n* type of Polish dumpling
PERONE *n* fibula **perones**
PERORAL *adj* administered through mouth
PEROXID *variant of* > **peroxide**
PEROXO *n* type of acid
PEROXY *adj* containing the peroxide group
PERP *n* someone who has committed a crime
PERPEND *n* large stone that passes through a wall from one side to the other ▹ *vb* ponder **perpent**
PERPLEX *vb*
PERPS ▸ **perp**
PERRIER *n* short mortar
PERRIES ▸ **perry**
PERRON *n* external flight of steps **perrons**
PERRY *n* alcoholic drink made from fermented pears
PERSALT *n* any salt of a peracid
PERSANT *adj* piercing
PERSE *old variant of* ▸ **pierce**
PERSES ▸ **perse**
PERSICO = **persicot**
PERSING ▸ **perse**
PERSIST *vb*
PERSON *n*
PERSONA *n*
PERSONS ▸ **person**
PERSPEX *n* any of various clear acrylic resins
PERST *adj* perished
PERSUE *obsolete form of* ▸ **pursue**
PERSUED ▸ **persue**
PERSUES ▸ **persue**
PERT *adj, n*
PERTAIN *vb*
PERTAKE *obsolete form of* ▸ **partake**
PERTER ▸ **pert**
PERTEST ▸ **pert**
PERTLY ▸ **pert**
PERTOOK ▸ **pertake**
PERTS ▸ **pert**
PERTURB *vb*
PERTUSE *adj* having holes
PERUKE *n* wig for men worn in the 17th and 18th centuries
PERUKED *adj* wearing wig
PERUKES ▸ **peruke**
PERUSAL ▸ **peruse**
PERUSE *vb* **perused, peruser, peruses**
PERV *n* pervert ▹ *vb* give a person an erotic look
PERVADE *vb*
PERVE = **perv**
PERVED ▸ **perv**
PERVERT *vb, n*

PERVES ▸ **perv**
PERVIER ▸ **pervy**
PERVING ▸ **perv**
PERVS ▸ **perv**
PERVY *adj* perverted
PES *n* animal part corresponding to the foot
PESADE *n* position in which the horse stands on the hind legs with the forelegs in the air **pesades**
PESANT *obsolete spelling of* ▸ **peasant**
PESANTE *adv* to be performed clumsily
PESANTS ▸ **pesant**
PESAUNT *obsolete spelling of* ▸ **peasant**
PESETA *n* **pesetas**
PESEWA *n* Ghanaian monetary unit **pesewas**
PESHWA = **peishwa**
PESHWAS ▸ **peshwa**
PESKIER ▸ **pesky**
PESKILY ▸ **pesky**
PESKY *adj* troublesome
PESO *n* **pesos**
PESSARY *n*
PESSIMA *n* lowest point
PEST *n*
PESTER *vb* **pesters**
PESTFUL *adj* causing annoyance
PESTIER ▸ **pesty**
PESTLE *n, vb* **pestled, pestles**
PESTO *n* sauce for pasta **pestos**
PESTS ▸ **pest**
PESTY *adj* persistently annoying
PET *n, adj, vb*
PETAL *n* **petaled, petals**
PETAR *obsolete variant of* ▸ **petard**
PETARA *n* clothes basket **petaras**
PETARD *n* **petards**
PETARS ▸ **petar**
PETARY *n* weapon for hurling stones
PETASOS = **petasus**
PETASUS *n* broad-brimmed hat worn by the ancient Greeks
PETCOCK *n* small valve
PETER *vb* fall (off) in volume, intensity, etc, and finally cease ▹ *n* act of petering **petered, peters**
PETHER *old variant of* ▸ **pedlar**
PETHERS ▸ **pether**
PETIOLE *n* stalk which attaches a leaf to a plant
PETIT *adj* of little or lesser importance
PETITE *adj, n* **petites**
PETNAP *vb* steal pet **petnaps**
PETRALE *n* type of sole
PETRARY *n* weapon for hurling stones
PETRE = **saltpetre**
PETREL *n* **petrels**
PETRES ▸ **petre**
PETRI *n as in* **petri dish** shallow glass dish used for cultures of bacteria
PETRIFY *vb*
PETROL *n, vb* **petrols**
PETROUS *adj* denoting the dense part of the temporal bone around the inner ear
PETS ▸ **pet**
PETSAI *n* Chinese cabbage **petsais**
PETTED ▸ **pet**
PETTER ▸ **pet**
PETTERS ▸ **pet**
PETTI ▸ **petto**
PETTIER ▸ **petty**
PETTIES ▸ **petti**
PETTILY ▸ **petty**
PETTING ▸ **pet**
PETTISH *adj* peevish or fretful
PETTLE *vb* pat animal **pettled, pettles**
PETTO *n* breast of animal
PETTY *adj*
PETUNIA *n*
PEW *n*
PEWEE *n* small N American flycatcher **pewees**
PEWIT *another name for* ▸ **lapwing**
PEWITS ▸ **pewit**
PEWS ▸ **pew**
PEWTER *n* **pewters**
PEYOTE *another name for* ▸ **mescal**
PEYOTES ▸ **peyote**
PEYOTL = **peyote**
PEYOTLS ▸ **peyotl**
PEYSE *vb* weight or poise **peysed, peyses, peysing**
PEYTRAL = **peytrel**
PEYTREL *n* breastplate of horse's armour

PEZANT *obsolete spelling of* ▸ **peasant**
PEZANTS ▸ **pezant**
PFENNIG *n*
PFFT *interj* sound indicating sudden disappearance of something
PFUI *interj* phooey
PHACOID *adj* lentil- or lens-shaped
PHAEIC *adj* (of animals) having dusky coloration **phaeism**
PHAETON *n* light four-wheeled horse-drawn carriage
PHAGE *n* parasitic virus that destroys its host **phages**
PHALANX *n*
PHALLI ▸ **phallus**
PHALLIC *adj* of or resembling a phallus
PHALLIN *n* poisonous substance from mushroom
PHALLUS *n*
PHANG *old variant spelling of* ▸ **fang**
PHANGED ▸ **phang**
PHANGS ▸ **phang**
PHANTOM *n, adj*
PHARAOH *n*
PHARE *n* beacon tower **phares**
PHARM *vb* redirect (a website user) to another, bogus website
PHARMA *n* pharmaceutical companies considered together as an industry **pharmas**
PHARMED ▸ **pharm**
PHARMS ▸ **pharm**
PHAROS *n* lighthouse
PHARYNX *n*
PHASE *n, vb* **phaseal, phased, phases, phasic**
PHASING *n* effect achieved by varying the phase relationship of two similar audio signals
PHASIS *another word for* ▸ **phase**
PHASMID *n* stick insect or leaf insect
PHASOR *n* rotating vector representing a quantity that varies sinusoidally **phasors**
PHAT *adj* terrific
PHATIC *adj* (of speech) used to express sociability rather than specific meaning
PHATTER ▸ **phat**
PHEAZAR *old variant of* ▸ **vizier**
PHEER = **fere**
PHEERE = **fere**
PHEERES ▸ **pheere**
PHEERS ▸ **pheer**
PHEESE *vb* worry **pheesed, pheeses, pheeze**
PHEEZED ▸ **pheeze**
PHEEZES ▸ **pheeze**
PHELLEM *technical name for* ▸ **cork**
PHENATE *n* ester or salt of phenol
PHENE *n* genetically determined characteristic of organism **phenes**
PHENIC *adj* of phenol
PHENIX = **phoenix**
PHENOL *n* chemical used in disinfectants and antiseptics **phenols**
PHENOM *n* person or thing of outstanding abilities **phenoms**
PHENOXY *modifier as in* **phenoxy resin** any of a class of resins derived from polyhydroxy ethers
PHENYL *n* chemical substance **phenyls**
PHEON *n* barbed iron head of dart **pheons**
PHESE = **pheese**
PHESED ▸ **phese**
PHESES ▸ **phese**
PHESING ▸ **phese**
PHEW *interj* exclamation of relief, surprise, etc
PHI *n* 21st letter in the Greek alphabet
PHIAL *n, vb* **phials**
PHILTER *n* drink supposed to arouse love, desire, etc ▹ *vb* arouse sexual or romantic feelings by means of a philter
PHILTRA > **philtrum**
PHILTRE *n* magic drink supposed to arouse love in the person who drinks it ▹ *vb* mix with love potion

PHIS ▸ **phi**
PHIZ *n* face or a facial expression **phizes, phizog**
PHIZOGS ▸ **phizog**
PHIZZES ▸ **phiz**
PHLEGM *n* **phlegms, phlegmy**
PHLOEM *n* plant tissue that acts as a path for the distribution of food **phloems**
PHLOMIS *n* plant of Phlomis genus
PHLOX *n* **phloxes**
PHO *n* Vietnamese noodle soup
PHOBIA *n* **phobias**
PHOBIC *adj* of, relating to, or arising from a phobia ▹ *n* person suffering from a phobia **phobics**
PHOBISM *n* phobia **phobist**
PHOCA *n* genus of seals **phocae, phocas**
PHOCINE *adj* of, relating to, or resembling a seal
PHOEBE *n* greyish-brown North American flycatcher **phoebes**
PHOEBUS *n* sun
PHOENIX *n*
PHOH *variant of* ▸ **foh**
PHOLAS *n* type of bivalve mollusc
PHON *n* unit of loudness
PHONAL *adj* relating to voice
PHONATE *vb* articulate speech sounds
PHONE *vb, n* **phoned**
PHONEME *n* one of the set of speech sounds in a language
PHONER *n* person making a telephone call **phoners**
PHONES ▸ **phone**
PHONEY *adj, n, vb* **phoneys**
PHONIC ▸ **phonics**
PHONICS *n* method of teaching people to read
PHONIED, phonier, phonies, phonily ▸ **phony**
PHONING ▸ **phone**
PHONO *n* phonograph
PHONON *n* quantum of vibrational energy **phonons**
PHONOS ▸ **phono**
PHONS ▸ **phon**
PHONY *vb* fake
PHOOEY *interj* exclamation of scorn or contempt
PHORATE *n* type of insecticide
PHORESY *n* association in which one animal clings to another to ensure movement from place to place
PHOS ▸ **pho**
PHOSSY *adj as in* **phossy jaw** gangrenous condition of the lower jawbone
PHOT *n* unit of illumination
PHOTIC *adj* of or concerned with light
PHOTICS *n* science of light
PHOTISM *n* sensation of light or colour caused by stimulus of another sense
PHOTO *n, vb* **photoed**
PHOTOG *n* photograph **photogs**
PHOTON *n* quantum of electromagnetic radiation energy **photons**
PHOTOS ▸ **photo**
PHOTS ▸ **phot**
PHPHT *interj* expressing irritation or reluctance
PHRASAL *adj* of, relating to, or composed of phrases
PHRASE *n, vb* **phrased, phraser, phrases**
PHRASY *adj* containing phrases
PHRATRY *n* group of people within a tribe who have a common ancestor
PHREAK *vb* hack into a telecommunications system **phreaks**
PHRENIC *adj* of or relating to the diaphragm ▹ *n* (a nerve, blood vessel, etc) located in the diaphragm
PHRENSY *obsolete spelling of* ▸ **frenzy**

PHT = **phpht**

> It is easy to overlook this little word, that may offer a way out when your rack seems hopelessly clogged with consonants.

PHUT *vb* make muffled explosive sound **phuts, phutted**
PHWOAH ▸ **phwoar**
PHWOAR *interj* expression of sexual interest or attraction
PHYLA ▸ **phylum**
PHYLAE ▸ **phyle**
PHYLAR ▸ **phylum**
PHYLE *n* tribe or clan of an ancient Greek people **phylic**
PHYLLID *n* leaf of a liverwort or moss
PHYLLO *variant of* ▸ **filo**
PHYLLOS ▸ **phyllo**
PHYLON *n* tribe
PHYLUM *n* major taxonomic division of animals and plants
PHYSED *n* physical education **physeds**
PHYSES ▸ **physis**
PHYSIC *n* medicine or drug, esp a cathartic or purge ▹ *vb* treat (a patient) with medicine
PHYSICS *n*
PHYSIO *n* physiotherapy **physios**
PHYSIS *n* part of bone responsible for lengthening
PHYTANE *n* hydrocarbon found in fossilised plant remains
PHYTIN *n* substance from plants used as an energy supplement **phytins**
PHYTOID *adj* resembling plant
PHYTOL *n* alcohol used to synthesize some vitamins **phytols**
PHYTON *n* unit of plant structure **phytons**
PI *n, vb*
PIA *n* innermost of the three membranes that cover the brain and the spinal cord
PIAFFE *n* passage done on the spot ▹ *vb* strut on the spot **piaffed, piaffer, piaffes**
PIAL *adj* relating to pia mater
PIAN *n* contagious tropical skin disease
PIANI ▸ **piano**
PIANIC *adj* of piano
PIANINO *n* small upright piano
PIANISM *n* technique, skill, or artistry in playing the piano
PIANIST *n* person who plays the piano
PIANO *n, adv* **pianos**
PIANS ▸ **pian**
PIARIST *n* member of a Roman religious order
PIAS ▸ **pia**
PIASABA = **piassava**
PIASAVA = **piassava**
PIASTER = **piastre**
PIASTRE *n* standard monetary unit of South Vietnam
PIAZZA *n* **piazzas, piazze**
PIBAL *n* method of measuring wind **pibals**
PIBROCH *n* form of bagpipe music
PIC *n* photograph or illustration
PICA *n* abnormal craving to ingest substances
PICACHO *n* pointed solitary mountain
PICADOR *n* mounted bullfighter with a lance
PICAL *adj* relating to pica
PICAMAR *n* hydrocarbon extract of beechwood tar
PICANTE *adj* spicy
PICARA *n* female adventurer **picaras**
PICARO *n* roguish adventurer **picaros**
PICAS ▸ **pica**
PICCATA *adj* sautéed and served in a lemon sauce
PICCIES ▸ **piccy**
PICCOLO *n*
PICCY *n* picture or photograph
PICE *n* former Indian coin worth one sixty-fourth of a rupee
PICENE *n* type of hydrocarbon **picenes**
PICEOUS *adj* of, relating to, or resembling pitch
PICINE *adj* relating to woodpeckers
PICK *vb, n*

PICKAX = **pickaxe**
PICKAXE *n, vb*
PICKED ▸ **pick**
PICKEER *vb* make raid for booty
PICKER *n* person or thing that picks **pickers**
PICKERY *n* petty theft
PICKET *n, vb* **pickets**
PICKIER ▸ **picky**
PICKILY ▸ **picky**
PICKIN *n* small child
PICKING ▸ **pick**
PICKINS ▸ **pickin**
PICKLE *n, vb*
PICKLED *adj*
PICKLER ▸ **pickle**
PICKLES ▸ **pickle**
PICKMAW *n* type of gull
PICKOFF *n* baseball play
PICKS ▸ **pick**
PICKUP *n* small truck with an open body and low sides **pickups**
PICKY *adj* fussy
PICNIC *n, vb* **picnics**
PICOLIN *variant of* > **picoline**
PICONG *n* any teasing or satirical banter **picongs**
PICOT *n* any of pattern of small loops, as on lace ▹ *vb* decorate material with small loops
PICOTE *adj* (of material) picoted
PICOTED ▸ **picot**
PICOTEE *n* type of carnation
PICOTS ▸ **picot**
PICQUET *vb* provide early warning of attack
PICRA *n* powder of aloes and canella **picras**
PICRATE *n* any salt or ester of picric acid
PICRIC *adj as in* **picric acid** toxic sparingly soluble crystalline yellow acid
PICRITE *n* coarse-grained ultrabasic igneous rock
PICS ▸ **pic**
PICTURE *n, vb*
PICUL *n* unit of weight, used in China, Japan, and SE Asia
PICULET *n* small tropical woodpecker with a short tail
PICULS ▸ **picul**
PIDDLE *vb* urinate **piddled, piddler, piddles**
PIDDLY *adj* trivial
PIDDOCK *n* marine bivalve that bores into rock, clay, or wood
PIDGEON *variant of* ▸ **pidgin**
PIDGIN *n* **pidgins**
PIE *n*
PIEBALD *adj, n*
PIECE *n* **pieced**
PIECEN *vb* join broken threads **piecens**
PIECER *n* person who mends, repairs, or joins something **piecers**
PIECES ▸ **piece**
PIECING ▸ **piece**
PIED ▸ **pi**
PIEDISH *n* container for baking pies
PIEFORT = **piedfort**
PIEHOLE *n* person's mouth
PIEING ▸ **pie**
PIEMAN *n* seller of pies **piemen**
PIEND *n* salient angle **piends**
PIER *n*
PIERAGE *n* accommodation for ships at piers
PIERCE *vb* **pierced, piercer, pierces**
PIERID *n* type of butterfly **pierids**
PIERIS *n* American or Asiatic shrub
PIEROGI *n* Polish dumpling
PIERROT *n* clown or masquerader with a whitened face
PIERS ▸ **pier**
PIERST *archaic spelling of* ▸ **pierced**
PIERT *n* small plant with small greenish flowers **pierts**
PIES ▸ **pie**
PIET *n* magpie
PIETA *n* sculpture, painting, or drawing of the dead Christ, supported by the Virgin Mary **pietas**
PIETIES ▸ **piety**
PIETISM *n* exaggerated piety **pietist**
PIETS ▸ **piet**
PIETY *n*
PIEZO *adj* piezoelectric
PIFFERO *n* small rustic flute

PIFFLE *n*, *vb* **piffled**
PIFFLER *n* talker of nonsense
PIFFLES ▶ **piffle**
PIG *n*, *vb*
PIGBOAT *n* submarine
PIGEON *n*, *vb* **pigeons**
PIGFACE *n* creeping succulent plant
PIGFEED *n* food for pigs
PIGFISH *n* grunting fish of the North American Atlantic coast
PIGGED ▶ **pig**
PIGGERY *n* place for keeping and breeding pigs
PIGGIE = **piggy**
PIGGIER ▶ **piggy**
PIGGIES ▶ **piggy**
PIGGIN *n* small wooden bucket or tub
PIGGING ▶ **pig**
PIGGINS ▶ **piggin**
PIGGISH *adj* like a pig, esp in appetite or manners
PIGGY *n* child's word for a pig ▷ *adj* like a pig
PIGHT *vb* pierce **pighted**
PIGHTLE *n* small enclosure
PIGHTS ▶ **pight**
PIGLET *n* **piglets**
PIGLIKE ▶ **pig**
PIGLING *n* young pig
PIGMEAN = **pygmaean**
PIGMEAT *less common name for* ▶ **pork**
PIGMENT *n*, *vb*
PIGMIES ▶ **pigmy**
PIGMOID *adj* of pygmies
PIGMY = **pygmy**
PIGNOLI = **pignolia**
PIGNORA ▶ **pignus**
PIGNUS *n* pawn or pledge
PIGNUT *n* bitter nut of hickory trees **pignuts**
PIGOUT *n* binge **pigouts**
PIGPEN = **pigsty**
PIGPENS ▶ **pigpen**
PIGS ▶ **pig**
PIGSKIN *n* skin of the domestic pig ▷ *adj* made of pigskin
PIGSNEY = **pigsny**
PIGSNIE = **pigsny**
PIGSNY *n* former pet name for girl
PIGSTY = **pigpen**
PIGTAIL *n*
PIGWASH *n* wet feed for pigs
PIGWEED *n* coarse North American weed
PIING ▶ **pi**
PIKA *n* burrowing mammal
PIKAKE *n* type of Asian vine **pikakes**
PIKAS ▶ **pika**
PIKAU *n* pack, knapsack, or rucksack **pikaus**
PIKE *n*, *vb*, *adj* **piked**
PIKELET *n* small thick pancake
PIKEMAN *n* (formerly) soldier armed with a pike **pikemen**
PIKER *n* shirker **pikers**
PIKES ▶ **pike**
PIKI *n* bread made from blue cornmeal
PIKING ▶ **pike**
PIKINGS ▶ **pike**
PIKIS ▶ **piki**
PIKUL = **picul**
PIKULS ▶ **pikul**
PILA *n* pillar-like anatomical structure
PILAF = **pilau**
PILAFF = **pilau**
PILAFFS ▶ **pilaff**
PILAFS ▶ **pilaf**
PILAO = **pilau**
PILAOS ▶ **pilao**
PILAR *adj* relating to hair
PILAU *n* Middle Eastern dish **pilaus, pilaw**
PILAWS ▶ **pilaw**
PILCH *n* outer garment, originally one made of skin
PILCHER *n* scabbard for sword
PILCHES ▶ **pilch**
PILCORN *n* type of oat
PILCROW *n* paragraph mark
PILE *n*, *vb*
PILEA *n* plant which releases a cloud of pollen when shaken **pileas**
PILEATE *adj* (of birds) having a crest
PILED ▶ **pile**
PILEI ▶ **pileus**
PILEOUS *adj* hairy
PILER *n* placer of things on pile **pilers**
PILES *pl n* swollen veins in the rectum, haemorrhoids
PILEUM *n* top of a bird's head
PILEUP *n* multiple collision of vehicles **pileups**

PILEUS *n* upper cap-shaped part of a mushroom
PILFER *vb* **pilfers**
PILFERY *n* theft
PILGRIM *n*
PILI *n* Philippine tree with edible seeds resembling almonds
PILING *n* act of driving piles **pilings**
PILINUT *n* type of nut found in the Philippines
PILIS ▶ **pili**
PILL *n, vb*
PILLAGE *vb, n*
PILLAR *n, vb* **pillars**
PILLAU = **pilau**
PILLAUS ▶ **pillau**
PILLBOX *n* small box for pills
PILLED ▶ **pill**
PILLIE *n* pilchard **pillies**
PILLING ▶ **pill**
PILLION *n, adv, vb*
PILLOCK *n* stupid or annoying person
PILLORY *n, vb*
PILLOW *n, vb* **pillows, pillowy**
PILLS ▶ **pill**
PILOSE *adj* covered with fine soft hairs
PILOT *n, adj, vb* **piloted**
PILOTIS *pl n* posts raising a building up from the ground
PILOTS ▶ **pilot**
PILOUS = **pilose**
PILOW = **pilau**
PILOWS ▶ **pilow**
PILSNER *n* type of pale beer with a strong flavour of hops
PILULA *n* pill **pilulae**
PILULAR ▶ **pilule**
PILULAS ▶ **pilula**
PILULE *n* small pill **pilules**
PILUM *n* ancient Roman javelin
PILUS ▶ **pili**
PILY *adj* like wool or pile
PIMA *n* type of cotton **pimas**
PIMENT *n* wine flavoured with spices
PIMENTO = **pimiento**
PIMENTS ▶ **piment**
PIMP *n, vb* **pimped, pimping**
PIMPLE *n* **pimpled, pimples, pimply**
PIMPS ▶ **pimp**
PIN *n, vb*
PINA *n* cone of silver amalgam
PINANG *n* areca tree **pinangs**
PINAS ▶ **pina**
PINATA *n* papier-mâché party decoration filled with sweets **pinatas**
PINBALL *vb*
PINBONE *n* part of sirloin
PINCASE *n* case for holding pins
PINCER *vb* grip with pincers
PINCERS *pl n*
PINCH *vb, n* **pinched, pincher, pinches**
PINDAN *n* desert region of Western Australia **pindans**
PINDARI *n* former irregular Indian horseman
PINDER *n* person who impounds **pinders**
PINDOWN *n* wrestling manoeuvre
PINE *n, vb*
PINEAL *adj* resembling a pine cone ▷ *n* pineal gland **pineals**
PINED ▶ **pine**
PINENE *n* isomeric terpene found in many essential oils **pinenes**
PINERY *n* place, esp a hothouse, where pineapples are grown
PINES ▶ **pine**
PINESAP *n* red herb of N America
PINETA ▶ **pinetum**
PINETUM *n* area of land where pine trees are grown
PINEY ▶ **pine**
PINFALL *another name for* ▶ **fall**
PINFISH *n* small porgy of the Atlantic
PINFOLD *n* pound for stray cattle ▷ *vb* gather or confine in or as if in a pinfold
PING *n* short high-pitched sound ▷ *vb* make such a noise **pinged**
PINGER *n* device, esp a timer, that makes a pinging sound **pingers**
PINGING ▶ **ping**
PINGLE *vb* enclose small area of ground **pingled, pingler, pingles**

PINGO *n* mound of earth or gravel formed in Arctic regions **pingoes, pingos**
PINGS ▸ **ping**
PINGUID *adj* fatty, oily, or greasy
PINGUIN = **penguin**
PINHEAD *n* head of a pin
PINHOLE *n* small hole made with or as if with a pin
PINIER ▸ **piny**
PINIES ▸ **piny**
PINIEST ▸ **piny**
PINING ▸ **pine**
PINION *n, vb* **pinions**
PINITE *n* greyish-green or brown mineral **pinites**
PINITOL *n* compound found in pinewood
PINK *n, adj, vb* **pinked**
PINKEN *vb* turn pink **pinkens**
PINKER *n* something that pinks **pinkers**
PINKEST ▸ **pink**
PINKEY *n* type of ship
PINKEYE *n* acute inflammation of the conjunctiva of the eye
PINKEYS ▸ **pinkey**
PINKIE *n* little finger
PINKIER ▸ **pinky**
PINKIES ▸ **pinkie**
PINKING ▸ **pink**
PINKISH ▸ **pink**
PINKLY ▸ **pink**
PINKO *n* person regarded as mildly left-wing **pinkoes, pinkos**
PINKS ▸ **pink**
PINKY *adj* of a pink colour
PINNA *n* external part of the ear
PINNACE *n* ship's boat
PINNAE ▸ **pinna**
PINNAL ▸ **pinna**
PINNAS ▸ **pinna**
PINNATE *adj* (of compound leaves) having leaflets growing opposite each other in pairs
PINNED ▸ **pin**
PINNER *n* person or thing that pins **pinners**
PINNET *n* pinnacle **pinnets**
PINNIE = **pinny**
PINNIES ▸ **pinnie**
PINNING ▸ **pin**
PINNOCK *n* small bird
PINNOED *adj* held or bound by the arms
PINNULA = **pinnule**
PINNULE *n* lobe of a leaflet of a pinnate compound leaf
PINNY *informal or child's name for* > **pinafore**
PINOCLE = **pinochle**
PINOLE *n* flour made in the southwestern United States **pinoles**
PINON *n* low-growing pine **pinones, pinons**
PINOT *n* any of several grape varieties **pinots**
PINS ▸ **pin**
PINT *n*
PINTA *n* pint of milk
PINTADA = **pintado**
PINTADO *n* species of seagoing petrel
PINTAIL *n* greyish-brown duck with a pointed tail
PINTANO *n* tropical reef fish
PINTAS ▸ **pinta**
PINTLE *n* pin or bolt forming the pivot of a hinge **pintles**
PINTO *adj* marked with patches of white ▹ *n* pinto horse **pintoes, pintos**
PINTS ▸ **pint**
PINUP *n* picture of a sexually attractive person **pinups**
PINWALE *n* fabric with narrow ridges
PINWEED *n* herb with tiny flowers
PINWORK *n* (in needlepoint lace) fine raised stitches
PINWORM *n* parasitic nematode worm
PINXIT *vb* (he or she) painted (it)
PINY *variant of* ▸ **peony**
PINYIN *n* system of romanized spelling for the Chinese language
PINYON *n* low-growing pine **pinyons**
PIOLET *n* type of ice axe **piolets**
PION *n* type of subatomic particle
PIONED *adj* abounding in marsh marigolds
PIONEER *n, vb* **pioner**

PIONERS ▸ **pioner**
PIONEY = **peony**
PIONEYS ▸ **pioney**
PIONIC ▸ **pion**
PIONIES ▸ **piony**
PIONING *n* work of pioneers
PIONS ▸ **pion**
PIONY = **peony**
PIOPIO *n* New Zealand thrush, thought to be extinct **piopios**
PIOSITY *n* grandiose display of piety
PIOTED *adj* pied
PIOUS *adj* **piously**
PIOY *variant of* ▸ **peeoy**
PIOYE *variant of* ▸ **peeoy**
PIOYES ▸ **pioye**
PIOYS ▸ **pioy**
PIP *n*, *vb*
PIPA *n* tongueless S American toad
PIPAGE *n* pipes collectively **pipages**
PIPAL = **peepul**
PIPALS ▸ **pipal**
PIPAS ▸ **pipa**
PIPE *n*, *vb*
PIPEAGE = **pipage**
PIPED ▸ **pipe**
PIPEFUL ▸ **pipe**
PIPER *n*
PIPERIC > **piperine**
PIPERS ▸ **piper**
PIPES ▸ **pipe**
PIPET = **pipette**
PIPETS ▸ **pipet**
PIPETTE *n*, *vb*
PIPI *n* edible mollusc often used as bait
PIPIER ▸ **pipe**
PIPIEST ▸ **pipe**
PIPING *n* **pipings**
PIPIS ▸ **pipi**
PIPIT *n* **pipits**
PIPKIN = **piggin**
PIPKINS ▸ **pipkin**
PIPLESS ▸ **pip**
PIPPED ▸ **pip**
PIPPIER ▸ **pippy**
PIPPIN *n*
PIPPING ▸ **pip**
PIPPINS ▸ **pippin**
PIPPY *adj* containing many pips
PIPS ▸ **pip**
PIPUL *n* Indian fig tree **pipuls**
PIPY ▸ **pipe**
PIQUANT *adj*
PIQUE *n*, *vb* **piqued, piques**
PIQUET *n* card game for two ▹ *vb* play game of piquet **piquets**
PIQUING ▸ **pique**
PIR *n* Sufi master
PIRACY *n*
PIRAGUA = **pirogue**
PIRAI *n* large S American fish **pirais**
PIRANA = **piranha**
PIRANAS ▸ **pirana**
PIRANHA *n*
PIRATE *n*, *vb* **pirated, pirates, piratic**
PIRAYA = **pirai**
PIRAYAS ▸ **piraya**
PIRL *n* ripple in water **pirls**
PIRN *n* reel or bobbin
PIRNIE *n* stripy nightcap **pirnies**
PIRNIT *adj* striped
PIRNS ▸ **pirn**
PIROG *n* large pie filled with meat, vegetables, etc
PIROGEN *n* turnovers made from kneaded dough
PIROGHI ▸ **pirog**
PIROGI ▸ **pirog**
PIROGUE *n* any of various kinds of dugout canoes
PIROJKI = **piroshki**
PIROQUE = **pirogue**
PIRS ▸ **pir**
PIS ▸ **pi**
PISCARY *n* place where fishing takes place
PISCINA *n* stone basin where water used at Mass is poured away
PISCINE *n* pond or pool
PISCO *n* S American brandy **piscos**
PISE *n* rammed earth or clay used to make floors or walls **pises**
PISH *interj* exclamation of impatience or contempt ▹ *vb* make this exclamation at (someone or something) **pished**
PISHEOG > **pishogue**
PISHER *n* Yiddish term for small boy **pishers**
PISHES ▸ **pish**
PISHING ▸ **pish**
PISHOGE = **pishogue**
PISKIES ▸ **pisky**
PISKY *n* Cornish fairy
PISMIRE *archaic or dialect word for* ▸ **ant**
PISO *n* peso of the Philippines **pisos**
PISTE *n* ski slope **pistes**

PISTIL *n* **pistils**
PISTOL *n, vb*
PISTOLE *n* gold coin formerly used in Europe
PISTOLS ▸ **pistol**
PISTON *n* **pistons**
PISTOU *n* French sauce **pistous**
PIT *n, vb*
PITA *n* any of several agave plants yielding a strong fibre
PITAPAT *adv* with quick light taps ▹ *n* such taps ▹ *vb* make quick light taps or beats
PITARA *variant of* ▸ **petara**
PITARAH *variant of* ▸ **petara**
PITARAS ▸ **pitara**
PITAS ▸ **pita**
PITAYA = **pitahaya**
PITAYAS ▸ **pitaya**
PITCH *vb, n* **pitched**
PITCHER *n*
PITCHES ▸ **pitch**
PITCHY *adj* full of or covered with pitch
PITEOUS *adj*
PITFALL *n*
PITH *n, vb*
PITHEAD *n* top of a mine shaft and the buildings and hoisting gear around it
PITHED ▸ **pith**
PITHFUL ▸ **pith**
PITHIER ▸ **pithy**
PITHILY ▸ **pithy**
PITHING ▸ **pith**
PITHOI ▸ **pithos**
PITHOS *n* large ceramic container for oil or grain
PITHS ▸ **pith**
PITHY *adj*
PITIED, pitier, pitiers, pities ▸ **pity**
PITIETH *vb as in* **it pitieth me** archaic inflection of 'pity'
PITIFUL *adj*
PITMAN *n* coal miner ▹ *n* connecting rod (in a machine) **pitmans, pitmen**
PITON *n* metal spike used in climbing to secure a rope **pitons**
PITPROP *n* support beam in mine shaft
PITS ▸ **pit**
PITSAW *n* large saw formerly used for cutting logs into planks **pitsaws**
PITTA *n* small brightly coloured ground-dwelling tropical bird **pittas**
PITTED ▸ **pit**
PITTEN *adj* having been put
PITTER *vb* make pattering sound **pitters**
PITTING ▸ **pit**
PITTITE *n* occupant of a theatre pit
PITUITA *n* thick nasal secretion
PITUITE *n* mucus
PITURI *n* Australian solanaceous shrub **pituris**
PITY *n, vb* **pitying**
PIU *adv* more (quickly, softly, etc)
PIUM *n* stinging insect **piums**
PIUPIU *n* skirt worn by Māoris on ceremonial occasions **piupius**
PIVOT *n, vb*
PIVOTAL *adj* of crucial importance
PIVOTED ▸ **pivot**
PIVOTER ▸ **pivot**
PIVOTS ▸ **pivot**
PIX *less common spelling of* ▸ **pyx**
PIXEL *n* any of a number of very small picture elements **pixels**
PIXES ▸ **pix**
PIXIE *n*
PIXIES ▸ **pixy**
PIXY = **pixie**
PIXYISH ▸ **pixy**
PIZAZZ = **pizzazz**
PIZAZZY ▸ **pizazz**
PIZE *vb* strike (someone a blow) **pized, pizes, pizing**
PIZZA *n* **pizzas**
PIZZAZ = **pzazz**
PIZZAZZ *n* attractive combination of energy and style
PIZZLE *n* penis of an animal, esp a bull **pizzles**
PLAAS *n* farm **plaases**
PLACARD *n, vb*
PLACATE *vb*
PLACCAT *variant of* ▸ **placket**
PLACE *n, vb*
PLACEBO *n*
PLACED ▸ **place**

PLACER *n* surface sediment containing particles of gold or some other valuable mineral **placers**
PLACES ▶ **place**
PLACET *n* vote or expression of assent **placets**
PLACID *adj*
PLACING *n* method of issuing securities to the public using an intermediary
PLACIT *n* decree or dictum
PLACITA > **placitum**
PLACITS ▶ **placit**
PLACK *n* small former Scottish coin
PLACKET *n* opening at the waist of a dress or skirt for buttons or zips or for access to a pocket
PLACKS ▶ **plack**
PLACOID *adj* platelike or flattened ▷ *n* fish with placoid scales
PLAFOND *n* ceiling, esp one having ornamentation
PLAGAL *adj* (of a cadence) progressing from the subdominant to the tonic chord
PLAGE *n* bright patch in the sun's chromosphere **plages**
PLAGIUM *n* crime of kidnapping
PLAGUE *n, vb* **plagued, plaguer, plagues**
PLAGUEY = **plaguy**
PLAGUY *adj* disagreeable or vexing ▷ *adv* disagreeably or annoyingly
PLAICE *n* **plaices**
PLAID *n, vb* **plaided, plaids**
PLAIN *adj, n, adv, vb* **plained, plainer, plainly**
PLAINS *pl n* extensive tracts of flat treeless countryside
PLAINT *n* complaint or lamentation **plaints**
PLAIT *n, vb* **plaited, plaiter, plaits**
PLAN *n, vb*
PLANAR *adj* of or relating to a plane
PLANATE *adj* having been flattened
PLANCH *vb* cover with planks **planche**
PLANE *n, adj, vb* **planed**
PLANER *n* machine with a cutting tool that makes repeated horizontal strokes **planers**
PLANES ▶ **plane**
PLANET *n* **planets**
PLANING ▶ **plane**
PLANISH *vb* give a smooth surface to (a metal)
PLANK *n, vb* **planked, planks**
PLANNED ▶ **plan**
PLANNER *n* person who makes plans
PLANS ▶ **plan**
PLANT *n, vb*
PLANTA *n* sole of foot **plantae**
PLANTAR *adj* of, relating to, or occurring on the sole of the foot
PLANTAS ▶ **planta**
PLANTED ▶ **plant**
PLANTER *n* owner of a plantation
PLANTS ▶ **plant**
PLANULA *n* free-swimming larva of hydrozoan coelenterates
PLANURY *another name for* ▶ **planury**
PLANXTY *n* Celtic melody for harp
PLAP = **plop**
PLAPPED ▶ **plap**
PLAPS ▶ **plap**
PLAQUE *n* **plaques**
PLASH = **pleach**
PLASHED ▶ **plash**
PLASHER *n* type of farm tool
PLASHES ▶ **plash**
PLASHET *n* small pond
PLASHY *adj* wet or marshy
PLASM = **plasma**
PLASMA *n* **plasmas, plasmic**
PLASMID *n* small circle of bacterial DNA
PLASMIN *n* proteolytic enzyme that causes fibrinolysis in blood clots
PLASMON *n* sum total of plasmagenes in a cell
PLASMS ▶ **plasm**
PLAST *archaic past participle of* ▶ **place**

PLASTE *archaic past participle of* ▶ **place**
PLASTER *n, vb*
PLASTIC *n, adj*
PLASTID *n* small particle in the cells of plants and some animals
PLAT *n* small area of ground
PLATAN *n* plane tree **platane, platans**
PLATE *n, vb*
PLATEAU *n, vb*
PLATED *adj*
PLATEN *n* roller of a typewriter, against which the paper is held **platens**
PLATER *n* person or thing that plates **platers**
PLATES ▶ **plate**
PLATIER ▶ **platy**
PLATIES ▶ **platy**
PLATINA *n* alloy of platinum and several other metals
PLATING *n* coating of metal
PLATOON *n, vb*
PLATS ▶ **plat**
PLATTED ▶ **plat**
PLATTER *n*
PLATY *adj* of, relating to, or designating rocks the constituents of which occur in flaky layers ⊳ *n* brightly coloured freshwater fish
PLATYPI > **platypus**
PLATYS ▶ **platy**
PLAUDIT *n* expression of enthusiastic approval
PLAY *vb, n*
PLAYA *n* (in the US) temporary lake in a desert basin
PLAYACT *vb* pretend or make believe
PLAYAS ▶ **playa**
PLAYBOY *n*
PLAYDAY *n* day given to play
PLAYED ▶ **play**
PLAYER *n* person who plays a game or sport **players**
PLAYFUL *adj*
PLAYING ▶ **play**
PLAYLET *n* short play
PLAYOFF *n* extra contest to decide the winner when two or more competitors are tied
PLAYPEN *n*
PLAYS ▶ **play**
PLAZA *n* **plazas**
PLEA *n, vb*
PLEACH *vb* interlace the stems or boughs of (a tree or hedge)
PLEAD *vb* **pleaded, pleader, pleads**
PLEAED ▶ **plea**
PLEAING ▶ **plea**
PLEAS ▶ **plea**
PLEASE *vb, adv* **pleased, pleaser, pleases**
PLEAT *n, vb* **pleated**
PLEATER *n* attachment on a sewing machine that makes pleats
PLEATS ▶ **pleat**
PLEB *n* common vulgar person
PLEBBY *adj* common or vulgar
PLEBE *n* member of the lowest class at the US Naval Academy or Military Academy
PLEBEAN *old variant of* > **plebeian**
PLEBES ▶ **plebe**
PLEBIFY *vb* make plebeian
PLEBS *n* common people
PLECTRA > **plectrum**
PLECTRE *variant of* > **plectrum**
PLED ▶ **plead**
PLEDGE *n, vb* **pledged**
PLEDGEE *n* person to whom a pledge is given
PLEDGER = **pledgor**
PLEDGES ▶ **pledge**
PLEDGET *n* small flattened pad of wool, cotton, etc
PLEDGOR *n* person who gives or makes a pledge
PLEIAD *n* brilliant or talented group, esp one with seven members **pleiads**
PLENA ▶ **plenum**
PLENARY *adj, n*
PLENCH *n* tool combining wrench and pliers
PLENIPO *n* plenipotentiary diplomat
PLENISH *vb* fill, stock, or resupply
PLENISM *n* philosophical theory **plenist**

PLENTY *n, adj, adv*
PLENUM *n* enclosure containing gas at a high pressure **plenums**
PLEON *n* abdomen of crustacean
PLEONAL *adj* of the abdomen of a crustacean
PLEONIC ▸ **pleon**
PLEONS ▸ **pleon**
PLEOPOD *another name for* > **swimmeret**
PLERION *n* filled-centre supernova remnant
PLEROMA *n* abundance
PLEROME *n* central column in growing stem or root
PLESH *n* small pool **pleshes**
PLESSOR = **plexor**
PLEUCH = **pleugh**
PLEUCHS ▸ **pleuch**
PLEUGH *Scottish word for* ▸ **plough**
PLEUGHS ▸ **pleugh**
PLEURA, pleurae, pleural, pleuras ▸ **pleuron**
PLEURON *n* part of the cuticle of arthropods
PLEW *n* (formerly in Canada) beaver skin used as a standard unit of value in the fur trade **plews**
PLEX *n* shortening of multiplex
PLEXAL ▸ **plexus**
PLEXES ▸ **plex**
PLEXOR *n* small hammer with a rubber head **plexors**
PLEXURE *n* act of weaving together
PLEXUS *n* complex network of nerves or blood vessels
PLIABLE *adj* **pliably**
PLIANCY ▸ **pliant**
PLIANT *adj*
PLICA *n* folding over of parts, such as a fold of skin, muscle, peritoneum, etc **plicae, plical**
PLICATE *adj* having or arranged in parallel folds or ridges ▹ *vb* arrange into parallel folds
PLIE *n* classic ballet practice posture with back erect and knees bent
PLIED ▸ **ply**
PLIER *n* person who plies a trade
PLIERS *pl n*
PLIES ▸ **ply**
PLIGHT *n* **plights**
PLIM *vb* swell with water **plimmed, plims**
PLIMSOL = **plimsole**
PLING *n* (in computer jargon) an exclamation mark **plings**
PLINK *n* short sharp often metallic sound ▹ *vb* make such a noise **plinked, plinker, plinks**
PLINKY *adj* (of a sound) short, sharp, and often metallic
PLINTH *n* **plinths**
PLISKIE *n* practical joke **plisky**
PLISSE *n* fabric with a wrinkled finish, achieved by treatment involving caustic soda **plisses**
PLOAT *vb* thrash **ploated, ploats**
PLOD *vb, n* **plodded**
PLODDER *n* person who plods
PLODGE *vb* wade in water, esp the sea ▹ *n* act of wading **plodged, plodges**
PLODS ▸ **plod**
PLOIDY *n* number of copies of set of chromosomes in cell
PLONG *obsolete variant of* ▸ **plunge**
PLONGD ▸ **plong**
PLONGE ▸ **plunge**
PLONGED ▸ **plonge**
PLONGES ▸ **plonge**
PLONGS ▸ **plong**
PLONK *vb, n, interj* **plonked**
PLONKER *n* stupid person
PLONKO *n* alcoholic, esp one who drinks wine **plonkos**
PLONKS ▸ **plonk**
PLONKY ▸ **plonk**
PLOOK = **plouk**
PLOOKIE = **plouky**
PLOOKS ▸ **plook**
PLOOKY ▸ **plook**
PLOP *n, vb, interj* **plopped, plops**

PLOSION *n* sound of an abrupt break or closure, esp the audible release of a stop
PLOSIVE *adj* pronounced with a sudden release of breath ▷ *n* plosive consonant
PLOT *n, vb* **plotful, plots, plotted**
PLOTTER = **plouter**
PLOTTIE *n* hot spiced drink
PLOTTY *adj* intricately plotted
PLOTZ *vb* faint or collapse **plotzed, plotzes**
PLOUGH *n, vb* **ploughs**
PLOUK *n* pimple **ploukie, plouks, plouky**
PLOUTER = **plowter**
PLOVER *n* **plovers, plovery**
PLOW = **plough**
PLOWBOY = **ploughboy**
PLOWED, plower, plowers, plowing ▸ **plow**
PLOWMAN = **ploughman**
PLOWMEN ▸ **plowman**
PLOWS ▸ **plow**
PLOWTER *vb* work or play in water or mud ▷ *n* act of plowtering
PLOY *n, vb* **ployed, ploying, ploys**
PLU = **plew**
PLUCK *vb, n* **plucked, plucker, plucks**
PLUCKY *adj* brave
PLUE = **plew**
PLUES ▸ **plue**
PLUFF *vb* expel in puffs **pluffed, pluffs, pluffy**
PLUG *n, vb* **plugged, plugger**
PLUGOLA *n* plugging of products on television
PLUGS ▸ **plug**
PLUM *n, adj*
PLUMAGE *n*
PLUMATE *adj* of, relating to, or possessing one or more feathers or plumes
PLUMB *vb, adv, n* **plumbed**
PLUMBER *n*
PLUMBIC *adj* of or containing lead in the tetravalent state
PLUMBS ▸ **plumb**
PLUMBUM *n* obsolete name for lead (the metal)
PLUMCOT *n* hybrid of apricot and plum
PLUME *n, vb* **plumed**
PLUMERY *n* plumes collectively
PLUMES ▸ **plume**
PLUMIER ▸ **plumy**
PLUMING ▸ **plume**
PLUMIST *n* person who makes plumes
PLUMMER ▸ **plum**
PLUMMET *vb, n*
PLUMMY *adj* of, full of, or like plums
PLUMOSE = **plumate**
PLUMOUS *adj* having plumes or feathers
PLUMP *adj, vb, n, adv* **plumped**
PLUMPEN *vb* make or become plump
PLUMPER *n* pad carried in the mouth by actors to round out the cheeks
PLUMPIE = **plumpy**
PLUMPLY ▸ **plump**
PLUMPS ▸ **plump**
PLUMPY *adj* plump
PLUMS ▸ **plum**
PLUMULA *n* down feather
PLUMULE *n* embryonic shoot of seed-bearing plants
PLUMY *adj* like a feather
PLUNDER *vb, n*
PLUNGE *vb, n* **plunged**
PLUNGER *n*
PLUNGES ▸ **plunge**
PLUNK *vb* pluck the strings of (a banjo etc) to produce a twanging sound ▷ *n* act or sound of plunking ▷ *interj* exclamation imitative of the sound of something plunking ▷ *adv* exactly **plunked, plunker, plunks**
PLUNKY *adj* sounding like plucked banjo string
PLURAL *adj, n* **plurals**
PLURRY *euphemism for* ▸ **bloody**
PLUS *vb*
PLUSAGE = **plussage**
PLUSED ▸ **plus**
PLUSES ▸ **plus**
PLUSH *n, adj* **plusher, plushes, plushly, plushy**
PLUSING ▸ **plus**

PLUSSED ▸ **plus**
PLUSSES ▸ **plus**
PLUTEAL ▸ **pluteus**
PLUTEI ▸ **pluteus**
PLUTEUS *n* larva of sea urchin
PLUTON *n* any mass of igneous rock that has solidified below the surface of the earth **plutons**
PLUVIAL *adj* of or caused by the action of rain ▹ *n* of or relating to rainfall or precipitation
PLUVIAN *n* crocodile bird
PLUVIUS *adj as in* **pluvius insurance** insurance against rain
PLY *vb, n*
PLYER *n* person who plies trade **plyers**
PLYING ▸ **ply**
PLYWOOD *n*
PNEUMA *n* person's vital spirit, soul, or creative energy **pneumas**
PO *n* chamber pot
POA *n* type of grass
POACH *vb* **poached**
POACHER *n* person who catches animals illegally on someone else's land
POACHES ▸ **poach**
POACHY *adj* (of land) wet and soft
POAKA *n* type of stilt (bird) native to New Zealand **poakas**
POAKE *n* waste matter from tanning of hides **poakes**
POAS ▸ **poa**
POBLANO *n* variety of chilli pepper
POBOY *n* New Orleans sandwich **poboys**
POCHARD *n* European diving duck
POCHAY *n* closed horse-drawn four-wheeled coach **pochays**
POCHOIR *n* print made from stencils
POCK *n* pus-filled blister resulting from smallpox ▹ *vb* mark with scars
POCKARD *variant of* ▸ **pochard**
POCKED ▸ **pock**
POCKET *n, vb, adj* **pockets**
POCKIER ▸ **pock**
POCKIES *pl n* woollen mittens
POCKILY ▸ **pock**
POCKING ▸ **pock**
POCKPIT *n* mark left on skin after a pock has gone
POCKS ▸ **pock**
POCKY ▸ **pock**
POCO *adv* little
POCOSEN = **pocosin**
POCOSIN *n* swamp in US upland coastal region **pocoson**
POD *n, vb*
PODAGRA *n* gout of the foot or big toe
PODAL *adj* relating to feet
PODALIC *adj* relating to feet
PODCAST *n* audio file able to be downloaded and listened to on a computer or MP3 player ▹ *vb* make available in this format
PODDED ▸ **pod**
PODDIE *n* user of or enthusiast for the iPod, a portable digital music player
PODDIER ▸ **poddy**
PODDIES ▸ **poddy**
PODDING ▸ **pod**
PODDLE *vb* move or travel in a leisurely manner **poddled, poddles**
PODDY *n, adj*
PODESTA *n* (in modern Italy) subordinate magistrate in some towns
PODEX *n* posterior **podexes**
PODGE *n* short chubby person **podges**
PODGIER ▸ **podgy**
PODGILY ▸ **podgy**
PODGY *adj*
PODIA ▸ **podium**
PODIAL ▸ **podium**
PODITE *n* crustacean leg **podites**
PODITIC *adj* similar to the limb segment of an arthropod
PODIUM *n* **podiums**
PODLEY *n* young coalfish **podleys**
PODLIKE ▸ **pod**
PODS ▸ **pod**

PODSOL = **podzol**
PODSOLS ▸ **podsol**
PODZOL *n* type of soil characteristic of coniferous forest regions **podzols**
POEM *n* **poems**
POEP *n* emission of gas from the anus **poeps**
POESIED ▸ **poesy**
POESIES ▸ **poesy**
POESY *n* poetry ▹ *vb* write poems
POET *n*
POETESS *n* female poet
POETIC *adj*
POETICS *n* principles and forms of poetry or the study of these
POETISE = **poeticize**
POETIZE = **poeticize**
POETRY *n*
POETS ▸ **poet**
POFFLE *n* small piece of land **poffles**
POGEY *n* financial or other relief given to the unemployed by the government **pogeys**
POGGE *n* European marine scorpaenoid fish **pogges**
POGIES ▸ **pogy**
POGO *vb* jump up and down in one spot **pogoed, pogoer, pogoers, pogoing**
POGONIA *n* orchid with pink or white fragrant flowers
POGONIP *n* icy winter fog
POGOS ▸ **pogo**
POGROM *n* organized persecution and massacre ▹ *vb* carry out a pogrom **pogroms**
POGY = **pogey**
POH *interj* exclamation expressing contempt or disgust
POHIRI *variant spelling of* ▸ **powhiri**
POHIRIS ▸ **pohiri**
POI *n* ball of woven flax swung rhythmically by Māori women during poi dances
POILU *n* infantryman in the French Army **poilus**
POINADO *old variant of* ▸ **poniard**
POIND *vb* take (property of a debtor) in execution or by way of distress **poinded, poinder, poinds**
POINT *n, vb*
POINTE *n* tip of the toe
POINTED *adj*
POINTEL *n* engraver's tool
POINTER *n*
POINTES ▸ **pointe**
POINTS ▸ **point**
POINTY *adj* having a sharp point or points
POIS ▸ **poi**
POISE *n, vb*
POISED *adj*
POISER *n* balancing organ of some insects **poisers**
POISES ▸ **poise**
POISHA *n* monetary unit of Bangladesh
POISING ▸ **poise**
POISON *n, vb* **poisons**
POISSON *n* fish
POITIN *variant spelling of* ▸ **poteen**
POITINS ▸ **poitin**
POITREL *n* breastplate of horse's armour
POKABLE ▸ **poke**
POKAL *n* tall drinking cup **pokals**
POKE *vb, n* **poked**
POKEFUL *n* contents of small bag
POKER *n* **pokers**
POKES ▸ **poke**
POKEY = **pokie**
POKEYS ▸ **pokey**
POKIE *n* poker machine
POKIER, pokies, pokiest, pokily ▸ **poky**
POKING ▸ **poke**
POKY *adj*
POL *n* political campaigner
POLACCA = **polacre**
POLACRE *n* three-masted sailing vessel
POLAR *adj, n*
POLARON *n* kind of electron
POLARS ▸ **polar**
POLDER *n, vb* **polders**
POLE *n, vb*
POLEAX = **poleaxe**
POLEAXE *vb, n*
POLECAT *n*
POLED ▸ **pole**
POLEIS ▸ **polis**
POLEMIC *n, adj*
POLENTA *n* thick porridge made in Italy, usually from maize

POLER *n* person or thing that poles, esp a punter **polers**
POLES ▸ **pole**
POLEY *adj* (of cattle) hornless or polled ▹ *n* animal with horns removed
POLEYN *n* piece of armour for protecting the knee **poleyns**
POLEYS ▸ **poley**
POLICE *n*, *vb* **policed**
POLICER *n* computer device controlling use
POLICES ▸ **police**
POLICY *n*
POLIES ▸ **poly**
POLING ▸ **pole**
POLINGS ▸ **pole**
POLIO *n* **polios**
POLIS *n* ancient Greek city-state **polises**
POLISH *vb*, *n*
POLITE *adj* **politer**
POLITIC *adj*
POLITY *n* politically organized state, church, or society
POLJE *n* large elliptical depression in karst regions **poljes**
POLK *vb* dance a polka
POLKA *n*, *vb* **polkaed, polkas**
POLKED ▸ **polk**
POLKING ▸ **polk**
POLKS ▸ **polk**
POLL *n*, *vb*
POLLACK *n* food fish related to the cod, found in northern seas
POLLAN *n* whitefish that occurs in lakes in Northern Ireland **pollans**
POLLARD *n* animal that has shed its horns or has had them removed ▹ *vb* cut off the top of (a tree) to make it grow bushy
POLLAXE = **poleaxe**
POLLED *adj* (of animals, esp cattle) having the horns cut off or being naturally hornless
POLLEE ▸ **poll**
POLLEES ▸ **poll**
POLLEN *n*, *vb* **pollens**
POLLENT *adj* strong
POLLER ▸ **poll**
POLLERS ▸ **poll**
POLLEX *n* first digit of the forelimb of amphibians, reptiles, birds, and mammals
POLLICY *obsolete spelling of* ▸ **policy**
POLLIES ▸ **polly**
POLLING *n* casting or registering of votes at an election
POLLIST *n* one advocating the use of polls
POLLMAN *n* one passing a degree without honours **pollmen**
POLLOCK = **pollack**
POLLS ▸ **poll**
POLLUTE *vb*
POLLY *n* politician
POLO *n*
POLOIST *n* devotee of polo
POLONIE = **polony**
POLONY *n* bologna sausage
POLOS ▸ **polo**
POLS ▸ **pol**
POLT *n* thump or blow ▹ *vb* strike **polted, polting, polts**
POLY *n* polytechnic
POLYACT *adj* (of a sea creature) having many tentacles or limb-like protrusions
POLYCOT *n* plant that has or appears to have more than two cotyledons
POLYENE *n* organic chemical compound
POLYGAM *n* plant of the Polygamia class
POLYGON *n*
POLYMER *n*
POLYNIA = **polynya**
POLYNYA *n* stretch of open water surrounded by ice **polynyi**
POLYOL *n* type of alcohol **polyols**
POLYOMA *n* type of tumour caused by virus
POLYP *n* **polype**
POLYPED = **polypod**
POLYPES ▸ **polype**
POLYPI ▸ **polypus**
POLYPOD *adj* (esp of insect larvae) having many legs or similar appendages ▹ *n* animal of this type
POLYPS ▸ **polyp**
POLYPUS = **polyp**
POLYS ▸ **poly**

POLYZOA *n* small mosslike aquatic creatures
POMACE *n* apple pulp left after pressing for juice **pomaces**
POMADE *n* perfumed oil put on the hair to make it smooth and shiny ▷ *vb* put pomade on **pomaded, pomades**
POMATO *n* hybrid of tomato and potato
POMATUM = **pomade**
POMBE *n* any alcoholic drink **pombes**
POME *n* fleshy fruit of the apple and related plants
POMELO *n* edible yellow fruit, like a grapefruit **pomelos**
POMEROY *n* bullet used to down airships
POMES ▸ **pome**
POMFRET *n* small black rounded liquorice sweet
POMMEE *adj* (of cross) having end of each arm ending in disk
POMMEL = **pummel**
POMMELE *adj* having a pommel
POMMELS ▸ **pommel**
POMO *n* postmodernism **pomos**
POMP *n*
POMPANO *n* deep-bodied carangid food fish
POMPELO *n* large Asian citrus fruit
POMPEY *vb* mollycoddle **pompeys**
POMPIER *adj* slavishly conventional
POMPION *n* pumpkin
POMPOM *n* decorative ball of tufted wool, silk, etc **pompoms, pompon**
POMPONS ▸ **pompon**
POMPOON = **pompom**
POMPOUS *adj*
POMPS ▸ **pomp**
POMROY *variant of* ▸ **pomeroy**
POMROYS ▸ **pomroy**
POMS ▸ **pom**
PONCEAU *n* scarlet red
PONCHO *n* loose circular cloak with a hole for the head **ponchos**
POND *n, vb*
PONDAGE *n* water held in reservoir
PONDED ▸ **pond**
PONDER *vb* **ponders**
PONDING ▸ **pond**
PONDOK *n* (in southern Africa) crudely made house or shack **pondoks**
PONDS ▸ **pond**
PONE *n* bread made of maize
PONENT *adj* westerly
PONES ▸ **pone**
PONEY = **pony**
PONEYS ▸ **poney**
PONG *n, vb*
PONGA *n* tall New Zealand tree fern **pongas**
PONGED ▸ **pong**
PONGEE *n* thin plain-weave silk fabric **pongees**
PONGID *n* primate of the family which includes the gibbons and the great apes **pongids**
PONGIER ▸ **pong**
PONGING ▸ **pong**
PONGO *n* anthropoid ape, esp an orang-utan or (formerly) a gorilla **pongoes, pongos**
PONGS ▸ **pong**
PONGY ▸ **pong**
PONIARD *n* small slender dagger ▷ *vb* stab with a poniard
PONIED ▸ **pony**
PONIES ▸ **pony**
PONK *n* evil spirit ▷ *vb* stink **ponked, ponking, ponks**
PONS *n* bridge of connecting tissue
PONT *n* (in South Africa) river ferry
PONTAGE *n* tax paid for repairing bridge
PONTAL *adj* of or relating to the pons
PONTES ▸ **pons**
PONTIC *adj* of or relating to the pons
PONTIE = **ponty**
PONTIES ▸ **ponty**
PONTIFF *n*
PONTIFY *vb* speak or behave in a pompous or dogmatic manner
PONTIL = **punty**
PONTILE *adj* relating to pons ▷ *n* metal bar used in glass-making
PONTILS ▸ **pontil**

PONTINE *adj* of or relating to bridges
PONTON *variant of* ▸ **pontoon**
PONTONS ▸ **ponton**
PONTOON *n, vb*
PONTS ▸ **pont**
PONTY *n* rod used for shaping molten glass
PONY *n, vb* **ponying**
PONZU *n* type of Japanese dipping sauce **ponzus**
POO *vb* defecate
POOCH *n* slang word for dog ▹ *vb* bulge or protrude **pooched, pooches**
POOD *n* unit of weight, used in Russia
POODLE *n* **poodles**
POODS ▸ **pood**
POOED ▸ **poo**
POOGYE *n* Hindu nose-flute **poogyes**
POOH *interj* exclamation of disdain, contempt, or disgust ▹ *vb* make such an exclamation **poohed, poohing, poohs**
POOING ▸ **poo**
POOJA *variant of* ▸ **puja**
POOJAH *variant of* ▸ **puja**
POOJAHS ▸ **poojah**
POOJAS ▸ **pooja**
POOK *vb* pluck
POOKA *n* malevolent Irish spirit **pookas**
POOKING ▸ **pook**
POOKIT ▸ **pook**
POOKS ▸ **pook**
POOL *n, vb* **pooled**
POOLER *n* person taking part in pool **poolers**
POOLING ▸ **pool**
POOLS *pl n* organized nationwide gambling pool
POON *n* SE Asian tree
POONAC *n* coconut residue **poonacs**
POONS ▸ **poon**
POOP *n* raised part at the back of a sailing ship ▹ *vb* (of a wave or sea) break over the stern of (a vessel) **pooped**
POOPER *n as in* **party pooper** person who spoils other people's enjoyment **poopers**
POOPING ▸ **poop**
POOPS ▸ **poop**
POOR *adj* **poorer, poorest**
POORI *n* unleavened Indian bread **pooris**
POORISH ▸ **poor**
POORLY *adv, adj*
POORT *n* (in South Africa) steep narrow mountain pass **poorts**
POOS ▸ **poo**
POOT *vb* break wind **pooted, pooter, pooters, pooting**
POOTLE *vb* travel or go in a relaxed or leisurely manner **pootled, pootles**
POOTS ▸ **poot**
POP *vb, n, adj*
POPADUM = **poppadom**
POPCORN *n*
POPE *n* bishop of Rome as head of the Roman Catholic Church
POPEDOM *n* office or dignity of a pope
POPERA *n* music drawing on opera or classical music and aiming for popular appeal **poperas**
POPERIN *n* kind of pear
POPES ▸ **pope**
POPETTE *n* young female fan or performer of pop music
POPEYED *adj* staring in astonishment
POPGUN *n* toy gun that fires a pellet or cork by means of compressed air **popguns**
POPJOY *vb* amuse oneself **popjoys**
POPLAR *n* **poplars**
POPLIN *n* ribbed cotton material **poplins**
POPOVER *n* individual Yorkshire pudding, often served with roast beef
POPPA = **papa**
POPPAS ▸ **poppa**
POPPED ▸ **pop**
POPPER *n* **poppers**
POPPET *n* term of affection for a small child or sweetheart **poppets**
POPPIED *adj* covered with poppies
POPPIER ▸ **poppy**
POPPIES ▸ **poppy**

POPPING ▸ **pop**
POPPISH *adj* like pop music
POPPIT *n* bead used to form necklace **poppits**
POPPLE *vb* (of boiling water or a choppy sea) to heave or toss **poppled, popples**
POPPLY *adj* covered in small bumps
POPPY *n, adj*
POPRIN = **poperin**
POPS ▸ **pop**
POPSIE = **popsy**
POPSIES ▸ **popsy**
POPSOCK *n* women's knee-length nylon stocking
POPSTER *n* pop star
POPSY *n* attractive young woman
POPULAR *adj, n*
PORAE *n* large edible sea fish of New Zealand waters **poraes**
PORAL *adj* relating to pores
PORANGI *adj* crazy
PORCH *n* **porches**
PORCINE *adj* of or like a pig
PORCINI ▸ **porcino**
PORCINO *n* edible woodland fungus
PORE *n, vb* **pored**
PORER *n* person who pores
PORERS ▸ **pore**
PORES ▸ **pore**
PORGE *vb* cleanse (slaughtered animal) ceremonially **porged, porges**
PORGIE = **porgy**
PORGIES ▸ **porgy**
PORGING ▸ **porge**
PORGY *n* any of various sparid fishes
PORIER ▸ **pory**
PORIEST ▸ **pory**
PORIFER *n* type of invertebrate
PORINA *n* larva of a moth which causes damage to grassland **porinas**
PORING ▸ **pore**
PORISM *n* type of mathematical proposition **porisms**
PORK *vb, n* **porked**
PORKER *n* pig raised for food **porkers**
PORKIER ▸ **porky**
PORKIES ▸ **porky**
PORKING ▸ **pork**
PORKPIE *n* hat with a round flat crown and a brim that can be turned up or down
PORKS ▸ **pork**
PORKY *adj* of or like pork ▹ *n* lie
PORLOCK *vb* interrupt or intrude at an awkward moment
PORN *n* pornography
PORNIER ▸ **porny**
PORNO = **porn**
PORNOS ▸ **porno**
PORNS ▸ **porn**
PORNY *adj* pornographic
POROSE *adj* pierced with small pores
POROSES ▸ **porosis**
POROSIS *n* porous condition of bones
POROUS *adj*
PORPESS *n* type of fish
PORRECT *adj* extended forwards ▹ *vb* stretch forward
PORRIGO *n* disease of the scalp
PORT = **porthole**
PORTA *n* aperture in an organ
PORTAGE *n* (route for) transporting boats overland ▹ *vb* transport (boats) in this way
PORTAL *n* **portals**
PORTAS ▸ **porta**
PORTATE *adj* diagonally athwart escutcheon
PORTED ▸ **port**
PORTEND *vb* be a sign of
PORTENT *n*
PORTER *n, vb* **porters**
PORTESS *variant of* > **portesse**
PORTHOS = **portesse**
PORTICO *n*
PORTIER ▸ **port**
PORTING ▸ **port**
PORTION *n, vb*
PORTLY *adj*
PORTMAN *n* inhabitant of port **portmen**
PORTOUS *variant of* > **portesse**
PORTRAY *vb*
PORTS ▸ **port**
PORTY *adj* like port
PORY *adj* containing pores
POS ▸ **po**
POSABLE ▸ **pose**

POSADA *n* inn in a Spanish-speaking country **posadas**
POSAUNE *n* organ chorus reed
POSE *vb, n* **posed**
POSER *n* **posers**
POSES ▸ **pose**
POSEUR *n* person who behaves in an affected way to impress others **poseurs**
POSEUSE *n* female poseur
POSEY *adj* (of a place) for, characteristic of, or full of posers
POSH *adj, adv, vb* **poshed, posher, poshes, poshest, poshing, poshly**
POSHO *n* corn meal **poshos**
POSIER ▸ **posy**
POSIES ▸ **posy**
POSIEST ▸ **posy**
POSING ▸ **pose**
POSINGS ▸ **pose**
POSIT *vb* lay down as a basis for argument ▷ *n* fact, idea, etc, that is posited **posited**
POSITIF *n* (on older organs) manual controlling soft stops
POSITON *n* part of chromosome
POSITS ▸ **posit**
POSNET *n* small basin or dish **posnets**
POSOLE *n* hominy **posoles**
POSS *vb* wash (clothes) by agitating them with a long rod, pole, etc
POSSE *n* group of men organized to maintain law and order
POSSED ▸ **poss**
POSSER *n* short stick used for stirring clothes in a washtub **possers**
POSSES ▸ **posse**
POSSESS *vb*
POSSET *n* drink of hot milk curdled with ale, beer, etc, flavoured with spices ▷ *vb* treat with a posset **possets**
POSSIE *n* place **possies**
POSSING ▸ **poss**
POSSUM *vb* **possums**
POST *n, vb*
POSTAGE *n*
POSTAL *adj* of a Post Office or the mail-delivery service ▷ *n* postcard **postals**
POSTBAG *n* postman's bag
POSTBOX *n*
POSTBOY *n* man or boy who brings the post round to offices
POSTBUS *n* vehicle carrying the mail that also carries passengers
POSTDOC *n* postdoctoral degree
POSTED ▸ **post**
POSTEEN *n* Afghan leather jacket
POSTER *n, vb*
POSTERN *n* small back door or gate ▷ *adj* situated at the rear or the side
POSTERS ▸ **poster**
POSTFIX *vb* add or append at the end of something
POSTIE *n* postman **posties**
POSTIL *n* commentary or marginal note, as in a Bible ▷ *vb* annotate (a biblical passage) **postils**
POSTIN *variant of* ▸ **posteen**
POSTING *n* job to which someone is assigned
POSTINS ▸ **postin**
POSTMAN *n* **postmen**
POSTOP *n* person recovering from surgery **postops**
POSTS ▸ **post**
POSTTAX *adj* of the period after tax is paid
POSTURE *n, vb*
POSTWAR *adj* occurring or existing after a war
POSY *n*
POT *n, vb*
POTABLE *adj* drinkable ▷ *n* something fit to drink
POTAE *n* hat **potaes**
POTAGE *n* thick soup
POTAGER *n* small kitchen garden
POTAGES ▸ **potage**
POTALE *n* residue from a grain distillery, used as animal feed **potales**
POTAMIC *adj* of or relating to rivers
POTASH *n, vb*
POTASS *abbreviated form of* > **potassium**

POTASSA *n* potassium oxide
POTATO *n*
POTBOIL *vb* boil in a pot
POTBOY *n* (esp formerly) youth or man employed at a public house to serve beer, etc **potboys**
POTCH *n* inferior quality opal used in jewellery for mounting precious opals
POTCHE *vb* stab **potched, potcher**
POTCHES ▸ **potch**
POTE *vb* push **poted**
POTEEN *n* (in Ireland) illegally made alcoholic drink **poteens**
POTENCE = **potency**
POTENCY *n* state or quality of being potent
POTENT *adj, n* **potents**
POTES ▸ **pote**
POTFUL *n* amount held by a pot **potfuls**
POTGUN *n* pot-shaped mortar **potguns**
POTHEAD *n* habitual user of cannabis
POTHEEN *rare variant of* ▸ **poteen**
POTHER *n* fuss or commotion ▷ *vb* make or be troubled or upset
POTHERB *n* plant whose leaves, flowers, or stems are used in cooking
POTHERS ▸ **pother**
POTHERY *adj* stuffy
POTHOLE *n*
POTHOOK *n* S-shaped hook for suspending a pot over a fire
POTHOS *n* climbing plant
POTICHE *n* tall vase or jar that narrows towards the neck
POTIN *n* bronze alloy with high tin content
POTING ▸ **pote**
POTINS ▸ **potin**
POTION *n* **potions**
POTJIE *n* **potjies**
POTLACH = **potlatch**
POTLIKE ▸ **pot**
POTLINE *n* row of electrolytic cells for reducing metals
POTLUCK *n*
POTMAN = **potboy**
POTMEN ▸ **potman**
POTOO *n* nocturnal tropical bird **potoos**
POTOROO *n* Australian leaping rodent
POTPIE *n* meat and vegetable stew with a pie crust on top **potpies**
POTS ▸ **pot**
POTSHOP *n* public house
POTSHOT *n* shot taken without careful aim
POTSIE = **potsy**
POTSIES ▸ **potsy**
POTSY *n* hopscotch
POTT *old variant of* ▸ **pot**
POTTAGE *n* thick soup or stew
POTTED ▸ **pot**
POTTEEN = **poteen**
POTTER = **putter**
POTTERS ▸ **potter**
POTTERY *n*
POTTIER ▸ **potty**
POTTIES ▸ **potty**
POTTING ▸ **pot**
POTTLE *n* liquid measure equal to half a gallon **pottles**
POTTO *n* short-tailed prosimian primate **pottos**
POTTS ▸ **pott**
POTTY *adj, n*
POTZER = **patzer**
POTZERS ▸ **potzer**
POUCH *n, vb* **pouched, pouches, pouchy**
POUDER *obsolete spelling of* ▸ **powder**
POUDERS ▸ **pouder**
POUDRE *old spelling of* ▸ **powder**
POUDRES ▸ **poudre**
POUF *n* large solid cushion used as a seat ▷ *vb* pile up hair into rolled puffs **poufed, pouff, pouffe**
POUFFED ▸ **pouffe**
POUFFES ▸ **pouffe**
POUFFS ▸ **pouff**
POUFING ▸ **pouf**
POUFS ▸ **pouf**
POUK *Scots variant of* ▸ **poke**
POUKE *n* mischievous spirit **poukes**
POUKING ▸ **pouk**
POUKIT ▸ **pouk**
POUKS ▸ **pouk**
POULARD *n* hen that has been spayed for fattening

POULDER *obsolete spelling of* ▸ **powder**
POULDRE *archaic spelling of* ▸ **powder**
POULE *n* fowl suitable for slow stewing **poules**
POULP *n* octopus **poulpe**
POULPES ▸ **poulpe**
POULPS ▸ **poulp**
POULT *n* young of a gallinaceous bird
POULTER *n* poultry dealer
POULTRY *n*
POULTS ▸ **poult**
POUNCE *vb, n* **pounced, pouncer, pounces**
POUNCET *n* box with a perforated top used for perfume
POUND *n, vb*
POUNDAL *n* fps unit of force
POUNDED ▸ **pound**
POUNDER ▸ **pound**
POUNDS ▸ **pound**
POUPE *vb* make sudden blowing sound **pouped, poupes, pouping, poupt**
POUR *vb* **poured, pourer, pourers**
POURIE *n* jug **pouries**
POURING ▸ **pour**
POURS ▸ **pour**
POURSEW *obsolete spelling of* ▸ **pursue**
POURSUE *obsolete spelling of* ▸ **pursue**
POUSADA *n* traditional Portuguese hotel
POUSSE = **pease**
POUSSES ▸ **pousse**
POUSSIE *old variant of* ▸ **pussy**
POUSSIN *n* young chicken reared for eating
POUT *vb, n* **pouted**
POUTER *n* pigeon that can puff out its crop **pouters**
POUTFUL *adj* tending to pout
POUTHER *Scots variant of* ▸ **powder**
POUTIER ▸ **pout**
POUTINE *n* dish of chipped potatoes topped with cheese and sauce
POUTING ▸ **pout**
POUTS ▸ **pout**
POUTY ▸ **pout**
POVERTY *n*
POW *interj* exclamation to indicate that a collision or explosion has taken place ▹ *n* head or a head of hair
POWAN *n* type of freshwater whitefish occurring in some Scottish lakes **powans**
POWDER *n, vb* **powders, powdery**
POWER *n, vb* **powered, powers**
POWHIRI *n* Māori ceremony of welcome, esp to a marae
POWIN *n* peacock **powins, pown**
POWND *obsolete spelling of* ▸ **pound**
POWNDED ▸ **pownd**
POWNDS ▸ **pownd**
POWNEY *old Scots spelling of* ▸ **pony**
POWNEYS ▸ **powney**
POWNIE *old Scots spelling of* ▸ **pony**
POWNIES ▸ **pownie**
POWNS ▸ **pown**
POWNY *old Scots spelling of* ▸ **pony**
POWRE *obsolete spelling of* ▸ **power**
POWRED ▸ **powre**
POWRES ▸ **powre**
POWRING ▸ **powre**
POWS ▸ **pow**
POWTER *vb* scrabble about **powters**
POWWAW *interj* expression of disbelief or contempt
POWWOW *n* talk or conference ▹ *vb* hold a powwow **powwows**
POX *n* disease in which skin pustules form ▹ *vb* infect with pox **poxed, poxes**
POXIER ▸ **poxy**
POXIEST ▸ **poxy**
POXING ▸ **pox**
POXY *adj* having or having had syphilis
POYNANT *old variant of* > **poignant**
POYNT *obsolete spelling of* ▸ **point**
POYNTED ▸ **poynt**
POYNTS ▸ **poynt**
POYOU *n* type of armadillo **poyous**
POYSE *obsolete variant of* ▸ **poise**

POYSED ▸ **poyse**
POYSES ▸ **poyse**
POYSING ▸ **poyse**
POYSON *obsolete spelling of* ▸ **poison**
POYSONS ▸ **poyson**
POZ *adj* positive

> **Poz** is an old-fashioned short form of **positive**, and one of the most frequently played short Z words.

POZOLE = **posole**
POZOLES ▸ **pozole**
POZZ *adj* positive
POZZIES ▸ **pozzy**
POZZY = **possie**
PRAAM = **pram**
PRAAMS ▸ **praam**
PRABBLE *variant of* ▸ **brabble**
PRACTIC *adj* practical ▷ *n* practice
PRAD *n* horse **prads**
PRAESES *n* Roman governor
PRAETOR *n* (in ancient Rome) senior magistrate ranking just below the consuls
PRAHU = **proa**
PRAHUS ▸ **prahu**
PRAIRIE *n*
PRAISE *vb, n* **praised, praiser, praises**
PRAJNA *n* wisdom or understanding **prajnas**
PRALINE *n* sweet made of nuts and caramelized sugar
PRAM *n* **prams**
PRANA *n* cosmic energy believed to come from the sun **pranas**
PRANCE *vb, n* **pranced, prancer, prances**
PRANCK *obsolete variant of* ▸ **prank**
PRANCKE *obsolete variant of* ▸ **prank**
PRANCKS ▸ **pranck**
PRANG *n* crash in a car or aircraft ▷ *vb* crash or damage (an aircraft or car) **pranged, prangs**
PRANK *n, vb* **pranked**
PRANKLE *obsolete variant of* ▸ **prance**
PRANKS ▸ **prank**
PRANKY ▸ **prank**
PRAO = **proa**
PRAOS ▸ **prao**
PRASE *n* light green translucent variety of chalcedony **prases**
PRAT *n* stupid person
PRATE *vb* talk idly and at length ▷ *n* chatter **prated, prater, praters, prates**
PRATIE *n* potato **praties**
PRATING ▸ **prate**
PRATS ▸ **prat**
PRATT *n* buttocks ▷ *vb* hit on the buttocks **pratted**
PRATTLE *vb, n*
PRATTS ▸ **pratt**
PRATY *obsolete variant of* ▸ **pretty**
PRAU = **proa**
PRAUNCE *obsolete variant of* ▸ **prance**
PRAUS ▸ **prau**
PRAVITY *n* moral degeneracy
PRAWLE *n* Shakespearian spelling of "brawl" **prawles**
PRAWLIN *variant of* ▸ **praline**
PRAWN *n, vb* **prawned, prawner, prawns**
PRAXES ▸ **praxis**
PRAXIS *n* practice as opposed to theory
PRAY *vb, adv, interj* **prayed**
PRAYER *n* **prayers**
PRAYING ▸ **pray**
PRAYS ▸ **pray**
PRE *prep* before
PREACE *obsolete variant of* ▸ **press**
PREACED ▸ **preace**
PREACES ▸ **preace**
PREACH *vb*
PREACHY *adj* inclined to or marked by preaching
PREACT *vb* act beforehand **preacts**
PREAGED *adj* treated to appear older
PREAMP *n* electronic amplifier **preamps**
PREANAL *adj* situated in front of anus
PREARM *vb* arm beforehand **prearms**
PREASE *vb* crowd or press **preased, preases**
PREASSE *obsolete spelling of* ▸ **press**
PREAVER *vb* aver in advance
PREBADE ▸ **prebid**
PREBAKE *vb* bake

before further cooking
PREBEND *n* allowance paid to a canon or member of the cathedral chapter
PREBID *vb* bid beforehand **prebids**
PREBILL *vb* issue an invoice before the service has been provided
PREBIND *vb* bind a book in a hard-wearing binding
PREBOIL *vb* boil beforehand
PREBOOK *vb* book well in advance
PREBOOM *adj* of the period before an economic boom
PREBORN *adj* unborn
PREBUY *vb* buy in advance **prebuys**
PRECAST *adj* cast in a particular form before being used ▷ *vb* cast (concrete) in a particular form before use
PRECAVA *n* superior vena cava
PRECEDE *vb*
PRECENT *vb* issue a command or law
PRECEPT *n*
PRECES *pl n* prayers
PRECESS *vb* undergo or cause to undergo precession
PRECIPE *n* type of legal document
PRECIS *n* short written summary of a longer piece ▷ *vb* make a precis of
PRECISE *adj*
PRECODE *vb* code beforehand
PRECOOK *vb* cook (food) beforehand
PRECOOL *vb* cool in advance
PRECOUP *adj* of the period before a coup
PRECURE *vb* cure in advance
PRECUT *vb* cut in advance **precuts**
PREDATE *vb* occur at an earlier date than
PREDAWN *n* period before dawn
PREDIAL = **praedial**
PREDICT *vb*
PREDIED ▸ **predy**
PREDIES ▸ **predy**
PREDIVE *adj* happening before a dive
PREDOOM *vb* pronounce (someone or something's) doom beforehand
PREDRY *vb* dry beforehand
PREDUSK *n* period before dawn
PREDY *vb* prepare for action
PREE *vb* try or taste **preed**
PREEDIT *vb* edit beforehand
PREEING ▸ **pree**
PREEMIE *n* premature infant
PREEMPT *vb* acquire in advance of or to the exclusion of others
PREEN *vb*, *n* **preened, preener, preens**
PREES ▸ **pree**
PREEVE *old form of* ▸ **prove**
PREEVED ▸ **preeve**
PREEVES ▸ **preeve**
PREFAB *n*, *vb* **prefabs**
PREFACE *n*, *vb*
PREFADE *vb* fade beforehand
PREFARD *vb* old form of preferred
PREFECT *n*
PREFER *vb* **prefers**
PREFILE *vb* file beforehand
PREFIRE *vb* fire beforehand
PREFIX *n*, *vb*
PREFORM *vb* form beforehand
PREFUND *vb* pay for in advance
PREGAME *adj* of the period before a sports match ▷ *n* such a period
PREGGY *informal word for* > **pregnant**
PREHEAT *vb* heat (an oven, grill, pan, etc) beforehand
PREHEND *vb* take hold of
PREIF *old form of* ▸ **proof**
PREIFE *old form of* ▸ **proof**
PREIFES ▸ **preife**
PREIFS ▸ **preif**
PREJINK *variant of* ▸ **perjink**

PRELACY *n* office or status of a prelate
PRELATE *n*
PRELATY *n* prelacy
PRELAW *adj* before taking up study of law
PRELECT *vb* lecture or discourse in public
PRELIFE *n* life lived before one's life on earth
PRELIM *n* event which precedes another
PRELIMS *pl n* pages of a book which come before the main text
PRELOAD *vb* load beforehand
PRELUDE *n, vb*
PRELUDI > **preludio**
PREM *n* informal word for a premature infant
PREMADE *adj* made in advance
PREMAN *n* hominid
PREMEAL *adj* of the period before a meal
PREMED *n* premedical student **premeds**
PREMEET *adj* happening before a meet
PREMEN ▸ **preman**
PREMIA ▸ **premium**
PREMIE = **preemie**
PREMIER *n, adj*
PREMIES ▸ **premie**
PREMISE *n, vb* **premiss**
PREMIUM *n*
PREMIX *vb* mix beforehand **premixt**
PREMOLD *vb* mold in advance
PREMOLT *adj* happening in the period before an animal molts
PREMOVE *vb* prompt to action
PREMS ▸ **prem**
PREMUNE *adj* having immunity to a disease as a result of latent infection
PREMY *variant of* ▸ **preemie**
PRENAME *n* forename
PRENEED *adj*
PRENOON *adj* of the period before noon
PRENT *Scots variant of* ▸ **print**
PRENTED ▸ **prent**
PRENTS ▸ **prent**
PRENUP *n* prenuptial agreement **prenups**
PRENZIE *adj* Shakespearian word supposed by some to mean "princely"
PREON *n* (in particle physics) hypothetical subcomponent of a quark **preons**
PREOP *n* patient being prepared for surgery **preops**
PREORAL *adj* situated in front of mouth
PREP *vb* prepare
PREPACK *vb* pack in advance of sale
PREPAID ▸ **prepay**
PREPARE *vb*
PREPAVE *vb* pave beforehand
PREPAY *vb* pay for in advance **prepays**
PREPILL *adj* of the period before the contraceptive pill became available
PREPLAN *vb* plan beforehand
PREPONE *vb* bring forward to an earlier time
PREPOSE *vb* place before
PREPPED ▸ **prep**
PREPPIE = **preppy**
PREPPY *adj* denoting a fashion style of neat, understated clothes ▷ *n* person exhibiting such style
PREPREG *n* material already impregnated with synthetic resin
PREPS ▸ **prep**
PREPUCE *n* foreskin
PREPUPA *n* insect in stage of life before pupa
PREQUEL *n* film or book about an earlier stage of a story
PRERACE *adj* of the period before a race
PRERIOT *adj* of the period before a riot
PREROCK *adj* of the era before rock music
PRERUPT *adj* abrupt
PRESA *n* musical sign or symbol to indicate the entry of a part
PRESAGE *vb, n*
PRESALE *n* practice of arranging the sale of a product before it is available
PRESE ▸ **presa**
PRESELL *vb* promote in advance of appearance

PRESENT *adj, n, vb*
PRESES *variant of* ▶ **praeses**
PRESET *vb* set a timer so that equipment starts to work at a specific time ▷ *adj* (of equipment) with the controls set in advance ▷ *n* control that is used to set initial conditions **presets**
PRESHIP *vb* ship in advance
PRESHOW *vb* show in advance
PRESIDE *vb*
PRESIFT *vb* sift beforehand
PRESOAK *vb* soak beforehand
PRESOLD ▶ **presell**
PRESONG *adj* of the period before a song is sung
PRESORT *vb* sort in advance
PRESS *vb, n* **pressed, presser, presses**
PRESSIE *informal word for* ▶ **present**
PRESSOR *n* something that produces an increase in blood pressure
PREST *adj* prepared for action or use ▷ *n* loan of money ▷ *vb* give as a loan **prested, prester**
PRESTO *adv* very quickly ▷ *n* passage to be played very quickly **prestos**
PRESTS ▶ **prest**
PRESUME *vb*
PRETAPE *vb* tape in advance
PRETAX *adj* before tax
PRETEEN *n* boy or girl approaching his or her teens
PRETELL *vb* predict
PRETEND *vb, adj*
PRETERM *n* premature baby
PRETEST *vb* test (something) before presenting it to its intended public or client ▷ *n* act or instance of pretesting
PRETEXT *n, vb*
PRETOLD ▶ **pretell**
PRETOR = **praetor**
PRETORS ▶ **pretor**
PRETRIM *vb* trim in advance
PRETTY *adj, adv, vb*
PRETYPE *vb* type in advance
PRETZEL *n* brittle salted biscuit
PREVAIL *vb*
PREVE *vb* prove **preved**
PREVENE *vb* come before
PREVENT *vb*
PREVERB *n* particle preceding root of verb
PREVES ▶ **preve**
PREVIEW *n, vb*
PREVING ▶ **preve**
PREVISE *vb* predict or foresee
PREVUE = **preview**
PREVUED ▶ **prevue**
PREVUES ▶ **prevue**
PREWAR *adj* relating to the period before a war, esp before World War I or II
PREWARM *vb* warm beforehand
PREWARN *vb* warn in advance
PREWASH *vb* give a preliminary wash to (clothes) ▷ *n* preliminary wash
PREWIRE *vb* wire beforehand
PREWORK *vb* work in advance
PREWORN *adj* (of clothes) second-hand
PREWRAP *vb* wrap in advance
PREWYN *obsolete spelling of* ▶ **prune**
PREWYNS ▶ **prewyn**
PREX = **prexy**
PREXES ▶ **prex**
PREXIES ▶ **prexy**
PREXY *n* US college president
PREY *n, vb* **preyed, preyer, preyers**
PREYFUL *adj* rich in prey
PREYING ▶ **prey**
PREYS ▶ **prey**
PREZ *n* president **prezes**
PREZZIE = **pressie**
PRIAL *n* pair royal of cards **prials**
PRIAPI ▶ **priapus**
PRIAPIC *adj* phallic
PRIAPUS *n* representation of the penis

PRIBBLE *variant of* ▸ **prabble**
PRICE *n, vb* **priced, pricer, pricers, prices**
PRICEY *adj*
PRICIER ▸ **pricy**
PRICILY ▸ **pricey**
PRICING ▸ **price**
PRICK *vb, n* **pricked**
PRICKER *n* person or thing that pricks
PRICKET *n* male deer in the second year of life
PRICKLE *n, vb*
PRICKLY *adj* having prickles
PRICKS ▸ **prick**
PRICKY *adj* covered with pricks
PRICY = **pricey**
PRIDE *n* **prided, prides**
PRIDIAN *adj* relating to yesterday
PRIDING ▸ **pride**
PRIED ▸ **pry**
PRIEF *obsolete variant of* ▸ **proof**
PRIEFE *obsolete variant of* ▸ **proof**
PRIEFES ▸ **priefe**
PRIEFS ▸ **prief**
PRIER *n* person who pries **priers**
PRIES ▸ **pry**
PRIEST *n, vb* **priests**
PRIEVE *obsolete variant of* ▸ **proof**
PRIEVED ▸ **prieve**
PRIEVES ▸ **prieve**
PRIG *n* **prigged**
PRIGGER *n* thief
PRIGS ▸ **prig**
PRILL *vb* convert (a material) into a granular free-flowing form ▹ *n* prilled material **prilled, prills**
PRIM *adj, vb*
PRIMA = **primo**
PRIMACY *n*
PRIMAGE *n* tax added to customs duty
PRIMAL *adj*
PRIMARY *adj, n*
PRIMAS ▸ **prima**
PRIMATE *n*
PRIME *adj, n, vb* **primed, primely**
PRIMER *n*
PRIMERO *n* 16th- and 17th-century card game
PRIMERS ▸ **primer**
PRIMES ▸ **prime**
PRIMEUR *n* anything (esp fruit) produced early
PRIMI ▸ **primo**
PRIMINE *n* integument surrounding an ovule or the outer of two such integuments
PRIMING = **primer**
PRIMLY ▸ **prim**
PRIMMED ▸ **prim**
PRIMMER ▸ **prim**
PRIMO *n* upper or right-hand part in a piano duet **primos**
PRIMP *vb* tidy (one's hair or clothes) fussily **primped, primps**
PRIMS ▸ **prim**
PRIMSIE *Scots variant of* ▸ **prim**
PRIMULA *n* type of primrose with brightly coloured flowers
PRIMUS *n* presiding bishop in the Synod
PRIMY *adj* prime
PRINCE *vb* **princed, princes**
PRINCOX *n* pert youth
PRINK *vb* dress (oneself) finely **prinked, prinker, prinks**
PRINT *vb, n* **printed**
PRINTER *n* person or company engaged in printing
PRINTS ▸ **print**
PRION *n* dovelike petrel with a serrated bill **prions**
PRIOR *adj, n* **priorly, priors**
PRIORY *n*
PRISAGE *n* customs duty levied until 1809 upon wine imported into England
PRISE = **pry**
PRISED ▸ **prise**
PRISER ▸ **prise**
PRISERE *n* primary sere or succession from bare ground to the community climax
PRISERS ▸ **prise**
PRISES ▸ **prise**
PRISING ▸ **prise**
PRISM *n* **prisms, prismy**
PRISON *n, vb* **prisons**
PRISS *n* prissy person ▹ *vb* act prissily **prissed, prisses**
PRISSY *adj* prim, correct, and easily shocked ▹ *n* prissy person

PRITHEE *interj* pray thee
PRIVACY *n* condition of being private
PRIVADO *n* close friend
PRIVATE *adj, n*
PRIVET *n* **privets**
PRIVIER ▶ **privy**
PRIVIES ▶ **privy**
PRIVILY *adv* in a secret way
PRIVITY *n* legally recognized relationship between two parties
PRIVY *adj, n*
PRIZE *n, adj, vb* **prized**
PRIZER *n* contender for prize **prizers**
PRIZES ▶ **prize**
PRIZING ▶ **prize**
PRO *prep, n, adv*
PROA *n* canoe-like boat used in the South Pacific **proas**
PROB *n* problem
PROBALL *adj* believable
PROBAND *n* first patient to be investigated in a family study
PROBANG *n* long flexible rod used to apply medication
PROBATE *n* process of proving the validity of a will ▷ *vb* establish officially the authenticity and validity of (a will)
PROBE *vb, n* **probed, prober, probers, probes, probing**
PROBIT *n* statistical measurement **probits**
PROBITY *n* honesty, integrity
PROBLEM *n, adj*
PROBS ▶ **prob**
PROCARP *n* female reproductive organ in red algae
PROCEED *vb*
PROCESS *n, vb*
PROCTAL *adj* relating to the rectum
PROCTOR *n* university worker who enforces discipline ▷ *vb* invigilate (an examination)
PROCURE *vb*
PROD *vb, n* **prodded, prodder**
PRODIGY *n*
PRODRUG *n* compound that is metabolized in the body to produce an active drug
PRODS ▶ **prod**
PRODUCE *vb, n*
PRODUCT *n*
PROEM *n* introduction or preface **proems**
PROETTE *n* female golfing professional
PROF *short for* > **professor**
PROFACE *interj* much good may it do you
PROFANE *adj, vb*
PROFESS *vb*
PROFFER *vb, n*
PROFILE *n, vb*
PROFIT *n, vb* **profits**
PROFS ▶ **prof**
PROFUSE *adj*
PROG *vb* prowl about for or as if for food or plunder ▷ *n* food obtained by begging
PROGENY *n*
PROGGED ▶ **prog**
PROGGER *n* fan of progressive rock
PROGRAM = **programme**
PROGS ▶ **prog**
PROGUN *adj* in favour of public owning firearms
PROIGN = **proin**
PROIGNS ▶ **proign**
PROIN *vb* trim or prune **proine, proined**
PROINES ▶ **proine**
PROINS ▶ **proin**
PROJECT *n, vb*
PROJET *n* draft of a proposed treaty **projets**
PROKE *vb* thrust or poke **proked, proker, prokers, prokes, proking**
PROLAN *n* constituent of human pregnancy urine **prolans**
PROLATE *adj* having a polar diameter which is longer than the equatorial diameter ▷ *vb* pronounce or utter
PROLE *old form of* ▶ **prowl**
PROLED ▶ **prole**
PROLEG *n* appendage on abdominal segment of a caterpillar **prolegs**
PROLER *n* prowler **prolers**

PROLES ▸ **prole**
PROLINE *n* nonessential amino acid that occurs in protein
PROLING ▸ **prole**
PROLIX *adj* (of speech or a piece of writing) overlong and boring
PROLL *vb* prowl or search **prolled, proller, prolls**
PROLOG = **prologue**
PROLOGS ▸ **prolog**
PROLONG *vb*
PROM *n*
PROMINE *n* substance promoting cell growth
PROMISE *vb, n*
PROMMER *n* spectator at promenade concert
PROMO *vb* promote (something) **promoed, promos**
PROMOTE *vb*
PROMPT *vb, adj, adv, n* **prompts**
PROMS ▸ **prom**
PRONAOI ▸ **pronaos**
PRONAOS *n* inner area of the portico of a classical temple
PRONATE *vb* turn (a limb, hand, or foot) so that the palm or sole is directed downwards
PRONE *n* **pronely, proner, prones, pronest**
PRONEUR *n* flatterer
PRONG *n, vb* **pronged, prongs**
PRONK *vb* jump straight up **pronked, pronks**
PRONOTA > **pronotum**
PRONOUN *n*
PRONTO *adv* at once
PROO *interj* (to a horse) stop!
PROOF *n, adj, vb* **proofed**
PROOFER *n* reader of proofs
PROOFS ▸ **proof**
PROOTIC *n* bone in front of ear
PROP *vb, n*
PROPAGE *vb* propagate
PROPALE *vb* publish (something)
PROPANE *n*
PROPEL *vb* **propels**
PROPEND *vb* be inclined or disposed
PROPENE *n* colourless gaseous alkene obtained by cracking petroleum
PROPER *adj, n* **propers**
PROPHET *n*
PROPINE *vb* drink a toast to
PROPJET *another name for* > **turboprop**
PROPMAN *n* member of the stage crew in charge of the stage props **propmen**
PROPONE *vb* propose or put forward, esp before a court
PROPOSE *vb*
PROPPED ▸ **prop**
PROPRIA > **proprium**
PROPS ▸ **prop**
PROPYL *n* of, consisting of, or containing the monovalent group of atoms C_3H_7-
PROPYLA > **propylon**
PROPYLS ▸ **propyl**
PRORATE *vb* divide, assess, or distribute (something) proportionately
PRORE *n* forward part of ship **prores**
PROS ▸ **pro**
PROSAIC *adj*
PROSE *n, vb*
PROSECT *vb* dissect a cadaver for a public demonstration
PROSED ▸ **prose**
PROSER *n* writer of prose **prosers**
PROSES ▸ **prose**
PROSIER ▸ **prosy**
PROSIFY *vb* write prose
PROSILY ▸ **prosy**
PROSING ▸ **prose**
PROSIT *interj* good health! cheers!
PROSO *n* millet
PROSODY *n* study of poetic metre and techniques
PROSOMA *n* head and thorax of an arachnid
PROSOS ▸ **proso**
PROSPER *vb*
PROSS *n* prostitute **prosses**
PROSSIE *n* prostitute
PROST = **prosit**
PROSTIE *n* prostitute
PROSY *adj* dull and long-winded
PROTEA *n*
PROTEAN *adj* constantly changing ▷ *n* creature that can change shape

PROTEAS ▸ **protea**
PROTECT *vb*
PROTEGE *n* person who is protected and helped by another
PROTEI ▸ **proteus**
PROTEID *n* protein
PROTEIN *n*
PROTEND *vb* hold out or stretch
PROTEST *n, vb*
PROTEUS *n* aerobic bacterium
PROTHYL *variant of* ▸ **protyle**
PROTIST *n* organism belonging to the protozoans, unicellular algae, and simple fungi
PROTIUM *n* most common isotope of hydrogen
PROTO *n as in* **proto team** relating to a team of people trained to deal with underground rescues, etc
PROTON *n* **protons**
PROTORE *n* primary mineral deposit
PROTYL = **protyle**
PROTYLE *n* hypothetical primitive substance
PROTYLS ▸ **protyl**
PROUD *adj* **prouder, proudly**
PROUL *variant of* ▸ **prowl**
PROULED ▸ **proul**
PROULER *Scots variant of* ▸ **prowler**
PROULS ▸ **proul**
PROVAND *n* food
PROVANT *adj* supplied with provisions
PROVE *vb* **proved, proven**
PROVEND = **provand**
PROVER ▸ **prove**
PROVERB *n, vb*
PROVERS ▸ **prove**
PROVES ▸ **prove**
PROVIDE *vb*
PROVINE *vb* plant branch of vine in ground for propagation
PROVING ▸ **prove**
PROVISO *n*
PROVOKE *vb*
PROVOST *n*
PROW *n, adj*
PROWAR *adj* in favour of or supporting war
PROWER ▸ **prow**
PROWESS *n*
PROWEST ▸ **prow**
PROWL *vb, n* **prowled, prowler, prowls**
PROWS ▸ **prow**
PROXIES ▸ **proxy**
PROXIMO *adv* in or during the next or coming month
PROXY *n*
PROYN *obsolete spelling of* ▸ **prune**
PROYNE *obsolete spelling of* ▸ **prune**
PROYNED ▸ **proyn**
PROYNES ▸ **proyne**
PROYNS ▸ **proyn**
PRUDE *n*
PRUDENT *adj*
PRUDERY ▸ **prude**
PRUDES ▸ **prude**
PRUDISH ▸ **prude**
PRUH *variant of* ▸ **proo**
PRUINA *n* woolly white covering on some lichens **pruinas**
PRUINE *obsolete spelling of* ▸ **prune**
PRUINES ▸ **pruine**
PRUNE *n, vb* **pruned, pruner, pruners, prunes, pruning**
PRUNT *n* glass ornamentation **prunted, prunts**
PRUNUS *n* type of ornamental tree or shrub
PRURIGO *n* chronic inflammatory disease of the skin
PRUSIK *n* sliding knot used in climbing ▷ *vb* climb (up a rope) using prusiks **prusiks**
PRUSSIC *adj as in* **prussic acid** weakly acidic extremely poisonous aqueous solution of hydrogen cyanide
PRUTA = **prutah**
PRUTAH *n* former Israeli coin **prutot, prutoth**
PRY *vb, n*
PRYER = **prier**
PRYERS ▸ **pryer**
PRYING ▸ **pry**
PRYINGS ▸ **pry**
PRYS *old variant of* ▸ **price**
PRYSE *old variant of* ▸ **price**
PRYSED ▸ **pryse**
PRYSES ▸ **pryse**
PRYSING ▸ **pryse**

PRYTHEE = **prithee**
PSALM *n*, *vb* **psalmed, psalmic, psalms**
PSALTER *n* book containing a version of Psalms
PSALTRY = **psaltery**
PSAMMON *n* microscopic life forms living between grains of sand
PSCHENT *n* ancient Egyptian crown
PSEUD *n* pretentious person
PSEUDO *n* pretentious person **pseudos**
PSEUDS ▸ **pseud**
PSHAW *n* exclamation of disgust, impatience, disbelief, etc ▹ *vb* make this exclamation **pshawed, pshaws**
PSI *n* 23rd letter of the Greek alphabet
PSION *n* type of elementary particle
PSIONIC > **psionics**
PSIONS ▸ **psion**
PSIS ▸ **psi**
PSOAE ▸ **psoas**
PSOAI ▸ **psoas**
PSOAS *n* either of two muscles of the loins that aid in flexing and rotating the thigh **psoases, psoatic**
PSOCID *n* tiny wingless insect **psocids**
PSORA *n* itching skin complaint **psoras, psoric**
PSST *interj* sound made to attract someone's attention, esp without others noticing
PST *interj* sound made to attract someone's attention

> You would need to be fairly desperate to use good letters to play this exclamation, but sometimes with no vowels on your rack things can be that desperate.

PSYCH *vb* psychoanalyse **psyche, psyched, psyches**
PSYCHIC *adj*, *n*
PSYCHS ▸ **psych**
PSYLLA = **psyllid**
PSYLLAS ▸ **psylla**
PSYLLID *n* type of insect of the family which comprises the jumping plant lice
PSYOP *n* psychological operation **psyops**
PSYWAR *n* psychological warfare **psywars**
PTARMIC *n* material that causes sneezing
PTERIA ▸ **pterion**
PTERIN *n* compound such as folic acid **pterins**
PTERION *n* point on the side of the skull where a number of bones meet
PTEROIC *adj as in* **pteroic acid** a kind of acid found in spinach
PTERYLA *n* any of the tracts of skin that bear contour feathers
PTISAN *n* grape juice drained off without pressure **ptisans**
PTOMAIN = **ptomaine**
PTOOEY *interj* imitation of the sound of spitting
PTOSES ▸ **ptosis**
PTOSIS *n* prolapse or drooping of a part, esp the eyelid **ptotic**
PTUI = **ptooey**
PTYALIN *n* amylase secreted in the saliva of man and other animals
PTYXES ▸ **ptyxis**
PTYXIS *n* folding of a leaf in a bud
PUB *n*, *vb* **pubbed, pubbing**
PUBCO *n* company operating a chain of pubs **pubcos**
PUBE *n* pubic hair
PUBERAL *adj* relating to puberty
PUBERTY *n*
PUBES ▸ **pube**
PUBIC *adj*
PUBIS *n* one of the three sections of the hipbone that forms part of the pelvis **pubises**
PUBLIC *adj* of or concerning the people as a whole ▹ *n* community, people in general **publics**
PUBLISH *vb*

PUBS ▸ **pub**
PUCAN *n* traditional Connemara open sailing boat **pucans**
PUCCOON *n* N American plant that yields a red dye
PUCE *adj, n*
PUCELLE *n* maid or virgin
PUCER ▸ **puce**
PUCES ▸ **puce**
PUCEST ▸ **puce**
PUCK *n* mischievous or evil spirit ▹ *vb* strike (the ball) in hurling
PUCKA = **pukka**
PUCKED ▸ **puck**
PUCKER *vb, n* **puckers**
PUCKERY *adj* (of wine) high in tannins
PUCKING ▸ **puck**
PUCKISH ▸ **puck**
PUCKLE *n* early type of machine gun **puckles**
PUCKOUT *n*
PUCKS ▸ **puck**
PUD *short for* ▸ **pudding**
PUDDEN *dialect spelling of* ▸ **pudding**
PUDDENS ▸ **pudden**
PUDDER *vb* make bother or fuss **pudders**
PUDDIES ▸ **puddy**
PUDDING *n*
PUDDLE *n, vb* **puddled, puddler, puddles, puddly**
PUDDOCK = **paddock**
PUDDY *n* paw
PUDENCY *n* modesty, shame, or prudishness
PUDENDA > **pudendum**
PUDENT *adj* lacking in ostentation; humble
PUDGE = **podge**
PUDGES ▸ **pudge**
PUDGIER ▸ **pudgy**
PUDGILY ▸ **pudgy**
PUDGY *adj* podgy
PUDIC > **pudendum**
PUDOR *n* sense of shame **pudors**
PUDS ▸ **pud**
PUDSEY *variant of* ▸ **pudsy**
PUDSIER ▸ **pudsy**
PUDSY *adj* plump
PUDU *n* diminutive Andean antelope **pudus**
PUEBLO *n* communal village of flat-roofed houses **pueblos**
PUER *vb* steep hides in an alkaline substance from the dung of dogs **puered**
PUERILE *adj*
PUERING ▸ **puer**
PUERS ▸ **puer**
PUFF *n, vb* **puffed**
PUFFER *n* person or thing that puffs **puffers**
PUFFERY *n* exaggerated praise, esp in publicity or advertising
PUFFIER ▸ **puffy**
PUFFILY ▸ **puffy**
PUFFIN *n*
PUFFING ▸ **puff**
PUFFINS ▸ **puffin**
PUFFS ▸ **puff**
PUFFY *adj* short of breath
PUG *n, vb*
PUGAREE = **puggree**
PUGGED ▸ **pug**
PUGGERY = **puggree**
PUGGIE *n* Scottish word for fruit machine
PUGGIER ▸ **puggy**
PUGGIES ▸ **puggie**
PUGGING ▸ **pug**
PUGGISH ▸ **pug**
PUGGLE *vb* stir up by poking **puggled, puggles**
PUGGREE *n* scarf, usually pleated, around the crown of some hats, esp sun helmets **puggry**
PUGGY *adj* sticky, claylike ▹ *n* term of endearment
PUGH *interj* exclamation of disgust
PUGIL *n* pinch or small handful **pugils**
PUGMARK *n* trail of an animal
PUGREE = **puggree**
PUGREES ▸ **pugree**
PUGS ▸ **pug**
PUH *interj* exclamation expressing contempt or disgust
PUHA *n* sow thistle **puhas**
PUIR *Scottish word for* ▸ **poor**
PUIRER ▸ **puir**
PUIREST ▸ **puir**
PUISNE *adj* (esp of a subordinate judge) of lower rank ▹ *n* judge of lower rank **puisnes**
PUISNY *adj* younger or inferior
PUJA *n* **pujah**
PUJAHS ▸ **pujah**

PUJARI *n* Hindu priest **pujaris**
PUJAS ▸ **puja**
PUKA *in New Zealand English*, = **broadleaf**
PUKAS ▸ **puka**
PUKATEA *n* aromatic New Zealand tree
PUKE *vb, n* **puked**
PUKEKO *n* brightly coloured New Zealand wading bird **pukekos**
PUKER *n* person who vomits **pukers**
PUKES ▸ **puke**
PUKEY *adj* of or like vomit **pukier, pukiest**
PUKING ▸ **puke**
PUKKA *adj* properly done, constructed, etc
PUKU *n* belly or stomach **pukus**
PUKY ▸ **pukey**
PUL *n* Afghan monetary unit
PULA *n* standard monetary unit of Botswana
PULAO = **pilau**
PULAOS ▸ **pulao**
PULAS ▸ **pula**
PULDRON = **pauldron**
PULE *vb* whine or whimper **puled, puler, pulers, pules**
PULI ▸ **pul**
PULIER ▸ **puly**
PULIEST ▸ **puly**
PULIK ▸ **pul**
PULING ▸ **pule**
PULINGS ▸ **pule**
PULIS ▸ **pul**
PULK = **pulka**
PULKA *n* reindeer-drawn sleigh **pulkas, pulkha**
PULKHAS ▸ **pulkha**
PULKS ▸ **pulk**
PULL *vb, n* **pulled, puller, pullers**
PULLET *n* **pullets**
PULLEY *n* **pulleys**
PULLI ▸ **pullus**
PULLING ▸ **pull**
PULLMAN *n* luxurious railway coach, esp a sleeping car
PULLOUT *n* removable section of a magazine, etc
PULLS ▸ **pull**
PULLUP *n* exercise in which the body is raised by the arms pulling on a horizontal bar **pullups**
PULLUS *n* technical term for a chick or young bird
PULMO *n* lung
PULP *n, vb* **pulpal, pulped, pulper, pulpers**
PULPIER ▸ **pulpy**
PULPIFY *vb* reduce to pulp
PULPILY ▸ **pulpy**
PULPING ▸ **pulp**
PULPIT *n* **pulpits**
PULPOUS *n* soft and yielding
PULPS ▸ **pulp**
PULPY *adj* having a soft or soggy consistency
PULQUE *n* light alcoholic drink from Mexico **pulques**
PULS ▸ **pul**
PULSANT *adj* vibrant
PULSAR *n* **pulsars**
PULSATE *vb*
PULSE *n, vb* **pulsed**
PULSER *n* thing that pulses **pulsers**
PULSES ▸ **pulse**
PULSING ▸ **pulse**
PULSION *n* act of driving forward
PULTAN *n* native Indian regiment **pultans, pulton**
PULTONS ▸ **pulton**
PULTOON = **pultan**
PULTUN = **pultan**
PULTUNS ▸ **pultun**
PULTURE *n* food and drink claimed by foresters
PULU *n* substance used for stuffing cushions **pulus**
PULVER *vb* make into powder **pulvers**
PULVIL *vb* apply perfumed powder **pulvils**
PULVINI > **pulvinus**
PULWAR *n* light Indian river boat **pulwars**
PULY *adj* whiny
PUMA *n* **pumas**
PUMELO = **pomelo**
PUMELOS ▸ **pumelo**
PUMICE *n, vb* **pumiced, pumicer, pumices**
PUMIE *n* small stone **pumies**
PUMMEL *vb*
PUMMELO = **pomelo**
PUMMELS ▸ **pummel**
PUMP *n, vb* **pumped, pumper, pumpers, pumping**

PUMPION *archaic word for* ▸ **pumpkin**
PUMPKIN *n*
PUMPS ▸ **pump**
PUMY *adj* large and round
PUN *n, vb*
PUNA *n* high cold dry plateau, esp in the Andes
PUNALUA *n* marriage between the sisters of one family to the brothers of another
PUNAS ▸ **puna**
PUNCE *n* kick ▹ *vb* kick **punced, punces**
PUNCH *vb, n* **punched, puncher, punches**
PUNCHY *adj*
PUNCING ▸ **punce**
PUNCTA ▸ **punctum**
PUNCTO *n* tip of a fencing sword **punctos**
PUNCTUM *n* tip or small point
PUNDIT *n* **pundits**
PUNG *n* horse-drawn sleigh with a boxlike body on runners
PUNGA *variant spelling of* ▸ **ponga**
PUNGAS ▸ **punga**
PUNGENT *adj*
PUNGLE *vb* make payment **pungled, pungles**
PUNGS ▸ **pung**
PUNIER ▸ **puny**
PUNIEST ▸ **puny**
PUNILY ▸ **puny**
PUNISH *vb*
PUNJI *n* sharpened bamboo stick **punjis**
PUNK *n, adj*
PUNKA *n* fan made of a palm leaf or leaves **punkah**
PUNKAHS ▸ **punkah**
PUNKAS ▸ **punka**
PUNKER ▸ **punk**
PUNKERS ▸ **punk**
PUNKEST ▸ **punk**
PUNKEY *n* small winged insect **punkeys, punkie**
PUNKIER ▸ **punky**
PUNKIES ▸ **punkie**
PUNKIN = **pumpkin**
PUNKINS ▸ **punkin**
PUNKISH ▸ **punk**
PUNKS ▸ **punk**
PUNKY *adj* of punk music
PUNNED ▸ **pun**
PUNNER ▸ **pun**
PUNNERS ▸ **pun**
PUNNET *n* **punnets**
PUNNIER ▸ **punny**
PUNNING ▸ **pun**
PUNNY *adj* of puns
PUNS ▸ **pun**
PUNSTER *n* person who is fond of making puns
PUNT *n, vb* **punted**
PUNTEE = **punty**
PUNTEES ▸ **puntee**
PUNTER *n* **punters**
PUNTIES ▸ **punty**
PUNTING ▸ **punt**
PUNTO *n* hit in fencing **puntos**
PUNTS ▸ **punt**
PUNTY *n* long iron rod used in the finishing process of glass-blowing
PUNY *adj*
PUP *n, vb*
PUPA *n* **pupae, pupal**
PUPARIA > **puparium**
PUPAS ▸ **pupa**
PUPATE *vb* (of an insect larva) to develop into a pupa **pupated, pupates**
PUPFISH *n* type of small fish
PUPIL *n* **pupilar, pupils**
PUPPED ▸ **pup**
PUPPET *n* **puppets**
PUPPIED ▸ **puppy**
PUPPIES ▸ **puppy**
PUPPING ▸ **pup**
PUPPY *n, vb*
PUPS ▸ **pup**
PUPU *n* Hawaiian dish
PUPUNHA *n* fruit of a type of palm tree
PUPUS ▸ **pupu**
PUR = **purr**
PURANA *n* type of Sanskrit sacred writing **puranas, puranic**
PURDA = **purdah**
PURDAH *n* **purdahs**
PURDAS ▸ **purda**
PURE *adj, vb* **pured**
PUREE *n* smooth thick pulp of cooked and sieved fruit, vegetables, meat, or fish ▹ *vb* make (cooked foods) into a puree **pureed, purees**
PURELY *adv*
PURER ▸ **pure**
PURES ▸ **pure**
PUREST ▸ **pure**
PURFLE *n* ruffled or curved ornamental band ▹ *vb* decorate

with such a band or bands **purfled, purfler, purfles, purfly**
PURGE *vb, n* **purged, purger, purgers, purges, purging**
PURI *n* unleavened flaky Indian bread, that is deep-fried in ghee and served hot
PURIFY *vb*
PURIN = **purine**
PURINE *n* colourless crystalline solid that can be prepared from uric acid **purines**
PURING ▸ **pure**
PURINS ▸ **purin**
PURIRI *n* forest tree of New Zealand **puriris**
PURIS ▸ **puri**
PURISM *n* strict insistence on the correct usage or style **purisms, purist, purists**
PURITAN *n, adj*
PURITY *n* state or quality of being pure
PURL *n, vb* **purled**
PURLER *n* headlong or spectacular fall **purlers**
PURLIEU *n* land on the edge of a royal forest
PURLIN *n* horizontal beam that supports the rafters of a roof **purline**
PURLING ▸ **purl**
PURLINS ▸ **purlin**
PURLOIN *vb*
PURLS ▸ **purl**
PURPIE *old Scots word for* > **purslane**
PURPIES ▸ **purpie**
PURPLE *n, adj, vb* **purpled, purpler, purples, purply**
PURPORT *vb, n*
PURPOSE *n*
PURPURA *n* blood disease causing purplish spots
PURPURE *n* purple
PURPY *variant of* ▸ **purpie**
PURR *vb, n* **purred, purring, purrs**
PURS ▸ **pur**
PURSE *n, vb* **pursed**
PURSER *n* **pursers**
PURSES ▸ **purse**
PURSEW *archaic spelling of* ▸ **pursue**
PURSEWS ▸ **pursew**
PURSIER ▸ **pursy**
PURSILY ▸ **pursy**
PURSING ▸ **purse**
PURSUAL *n* act of pursuit
PURSUE *vb* **pursued, pursuer, pursues**
PURSUIT *n* pursuing
PURSY *adj* short-winded
PURTIER ▸ **purty**
PURTY *adj* pretty
PURVEY *vb* supply (provisions) ▹ *n* food and drink laid on at a wedding reception, etc **purveys**
PURVIEW *n* scope or range of activity or outlook
PUS *n* **puses**
PUSH *vb, n*
PUSHED *adj* short of
PUSHER *n* **pushers**
PUSHES ▸ **push**
PUSHFUL ▸ **push**
PUSHIER ▸ **pushy**
PUSHILY ▸ **pushy**
PUSHING *prep, adj, adv*
PUSHPIN *n* pin with a small ball-shaped head
PUSHPIT *n* safety rail at the stern of a boat
PUSHROD *n* metal rod transmitting motion in an engine
PUSHUP *n* exercise in which the body is alternately raised from and lowered to the floor by the arms **pushups**
PUSHY *adj*
PUSLE *old spelling of* ▸ **puzzle**
PUSLED ▸ **pusle**
PUSLES ▸ **pusle**
PUSLEY = **purslane**
PUSLEYS ▸ **pusley**
PUSLIKE ▸ **pus**
PUSLING ▸ **pusle**
PUSS = **pussy**
PUSSEL *n* slatternly woman **pussels**
PUSSER *n* naval purser **pussers**
PUSSES ▸ **puss**
PUSSIER ▸ **pussy**
PUSSIES ▸ **pussy**
PUSSLEY *n* weedy trailing herb **pussly**
PUSSY *n, adj*
PUSTULE *n* pimple containing pus

PUT *vb, n*
PUTAMEN *n* hard endocarp or stone of fruit
PUTCHER *n* trap for catching salmon
PUTCHUK = **pachak**
PUTDOWN *n* snub or insult
PUTEAL *n* enclosure around a well **puteals**
PUTELI *n* (in India) type of boat **putelis**
PUTID *adj* having an unpleasant odour
PUTLOCK = **putlog**
PUTLOG *n* short horizontal beam that with others supports the floor planks of a scaffold **putlogs**
PUTOFF *n* pretext or delay **putoffs**
PUTOIS *n* brush to paint pottery
PUTON *n* hoax or piece of mockery **putons**
PUTOUT *n* baseball play in which the batter or runner is put out **putouts**
PUTREFY *vb*
PUTRID *adj*
PUTS ▶ **put**
PUTSCH *n* sudden violent attempt to remove a government from power
PUTT *n, vb* **putted**
PUTTEE *n* strip of cloth worn wound around the leg **puttees**
PUTTEN *old Scots past participle of* ▶ **put**
PUTTER *n* golf club for putting ▷ *vb* busy oneself in a desultory though agreeable manner **putters**
PUTTI ▶ **putto**
PUTTIE = **puttee**
PUTTIED ▶ **putty**
PUTTIER *n* glazier
PUTTIES ▶ **putty**
PUTTING ▶ **put**
PUTTO *n* representation of a small boy
PUTTOCK *n* type of bird of prey
PUTTS ▶ **putt**
PUTTY *n, vb*
PUTURE *n* claim of foresters for food **putures**
PUTZ *n* despicable or stupid person ▷ *vb* waste time **putzed, putzes, putzing**
PUY *n* small volcanic cone **puys**
PUZEL = **pucelle**
PUZELS ▶ **puzel**
PUZZEL *n* prostitute **puzzels**
PUZZLE *vb, n* **puzzled**
PUZZLER *n* person or thing that puzzles
PUZZLES ▶ **puzzle**
PYA *n* monetary unit of Myanmar worth one hundredth of a kyat
PYAEMIA *n* blood poisoning with pus-forming microorganisms in the blood **pyaemic**
PYAS ▶ **pya**
PYAT *n* magpie ▷ *adj* pied **pyats**
PYCNIC = **pyknic**
PYCNITE *n* variety of topaz
PYCNON *old word for* > **semitone**
PYCNONS ▶ **pycnon**
PYE = **pie**
PYEBALD = **piebald**
PYEING ▶ **pye**
PYEMIA = **pyaemia**
PYEMIAS ▶ **pyemia**
PYEMIC ▶ **pyaemia**
PYES ▶ **pye**
PYET = **pyat**
PYETS ▶ **pyet**
PYGAL *n* rear part **pygals**
PYGARG *n* type of horned mammal **pygargs**
PYGIDIA > **pygidium**
PYGMEAN ▶ **pygmy**
PYGMIES ▶ **pygmy**
PYGMOID *adj* of or like pygmies
PYGMY *n, adj*
PYIC *adj* relating to pus
PYIN *n* constituent of pus **pyins**
PYJAMA = **pyjamas**
PYJAMAS *pl n*
PYKNIC *adj* (of a physical type) characterized by a broad squat fleshy physique with a large chest and abdomen ▷ *n* person with this physical type **pyknics**
PYLON *n* **pylons**
PYLORI ▶ **pylorus**
PYLORIC ▶ **pylorus**

PYLORUS *n* small circular opening at the base of the stomach
PYNE *archaic variant of* ▶ **pine**
PYNED ▶ **pyne**
PYNES ▶ **pyne**
PYNING ▶ **pyne**
PYOID *adj* resembling pus
PYONER *old variant of* ▶ **pioneer**
PYONERS ▶ **pyoner**
PYOSES ▶ **pyosis**
PYOSIS *n* formation of pus
PYOT = **pyat**
PYOTS ▶ **pyot**
PYRAL ▶ **pyre**
PYRALID *n* tropical moth **pyralis**
PYRAMID *n, vb*
PYRAMIS *n* pyramid-shaped structure
PYRAN *n* unsaturated heterocyclic organic compound **pyrans**
PYRE *n*
PYRENE *n* solid polynuclear aromatic hydrocarbon extracted from coal tar **pyrenes**
PYRES ▶ **pyre**
PYRETIC *adj* of, relating to, or characterized by fever
PYREX *n* tradename for glass used in cookery and chemical apparatus **pyrexes**
PYREXIA *technical name for* ▶ **fever**
PYREXIC ▶ **pyrexia**
PYRIC *adj* of or relating to burning
PYRIDIC > **pyridine**
PYRITE *n* yellow mineral consisting of iron sulphide in cubic crystalline form **pyrites, pyritic**
PYRO *n* pyromaniac
PYROGEN *n* any of a group of substances that cause a rise in temperature in an animal body
PYROLA *n* evergreen perennial **pyrolas**
PYRONE *n* type of heterocyclic compound **pyrones**
PYROPE *n* deep yellowish-red garnet used as a gemstone **pyropes, pyropus**
PYROS ▶ **pyro**
PYROSES ▶ **pyrosis**
PYROSIS *technical name for* > **heartburn**
PYRRHIC *n* metrical foot of two short or unstressed syllables ▷ *adj* of or relating to such a metrical foot
PYRROL = **pyrrole**
PYRROLE *n* colourless insoluble toxic liquid
PYRROLS ▶ **pyrrol**
PYRUVIC *adj as in* **pyruvic acid** colourless pleasant-smelling liquid
PYTHIUM *n* type of fungi
PYTHON *n* **pythons**
PYURIA *n* any condition characterized by the presence of pus in the urine **pyurias**
PYX *n* any receptacle for the Eucharistic Host ▷ *vb* put (something) in a pyx **pyxed, pyxes**

> This word can also be spelt **pix**. It's a great word to know as it can earn a good score from a rack that is short of vowels.

PYXIDES ▶ **pyxis**
PYXIDIA > **pyxidium**
PYXIE *n* creeping evergreen shrub of the eastern US **pyxies**
PYXING ▶ **pyx**
PYXIS = **pyxidium**
PZAZZ = **pizzazz**
PZAZZES ▶ **pzazz**

Qq

With a value of 10 points, **Q** can help you to some good scores, but it can also be a very awkward tile, making it difficult to get bonus words scoring that extra 50 points, and you will normally want to play it off quickly. Often you will not have a **U** to go with it, so it's a good idea to remember the short words beginning with **Q** that don't need a **U**. This is easy, as there's only one two-letter word starting with **Q**: **qi** (11 points). There are four three-letter words, only one of which needs a **U**: **qua** (12). The other three are **qat, qin** and **qis** (12 each). If you do have a **U**, remember **quiz** (22), which is a very useful word, and can take an **S** at the front to make **squiz**. Don't forget **quartz** (24) either, while the useful **suq** (12 points) is easily overlooked.

QABALA = **kabbalah**
QABALAH = **kabbalah**
QABALAS ▸ **qabala**
QADI *variant spelling of* ▸ **cadi**
QADIS ▸ **qadi**
QAID *n* chief **qaids**

> An Arabic word, this and its variant **qadi** are two of the most frequently played words in Scrabble. There are also alternative spellings **cadi, caid, kadi** and **kaid**.

QANAT *n* underground irrigation channel **qanats**

> This word comes up many times as one of the words allowing you to play the Q without a U.

QASIDA *n* Arabic verse form **qasidas**
QAT *variant spelling of* ▸ **khat**

> The leaves of this shrub are chewed as a stimulant, and it's certainly been a stimulus for Scrabble, being one of the three three-letter words that can be played without a U: the others are **qin** and **qis**.

QATS ▸ **qat**
QAWWAL *n* qawwali singer
QAWWALI *n* Islamic religious song, esp in Asia
QAWWALS ▸ **qawwal**
QI *variant of* ▸ **chi**
QIBLA *variant of* ▸ **kiblah**

> The direction in which Muslims turn to pray, a useful word allowing the Q to be played without the U. It can also be spelt **keblah, kibla** and **kiblah**.

QIBLAS ▸ **qibla**
QIGONG *n* system of breathing and exercise **qigongs**
QIN *n* Chinese stringed

instrument related to the zither

This Chinese musical instrument is another indispensable word as, like **qat**, it combines Q with two of the most common letters in the game.

QINDAR *n* Albanian monetary unit **qindars**
QINS ▸ **qin**
QINTAR = **qindar**
QINTARS ▸ **qintar**
QIS ▸ **qi**
QIVIUT *n* soft muskox wool **qiviuts**
QOPH *variant of* ▸ **koph**

A letter of the Hebrew alphabet, also spelt **koph**. The Hebrew alphabet, like the Greek alphabet, is well worth studying from the Scrabble point of view, as it gives us many other useful short words like **ayin, beth, heth, kaph** and **lamedh**.

QOPHS ▸ **qoph**
QORMA *variant spelling of* ▸ **korma**
QORMAS ▸ **qorma**
QUA *prep* in the capacity of

This is the only three-letter word beginning with Q that needs a U. It is played so often that it is well worth mastering all the hooks to this: it takes A at the front to make **aqua** and D, G, I, T and Y at the back to make **quad, quag, quai, quat** and **quay**.

QUACK *vb, n* **quacked, quacker, quackle, quacks, quacky**
QUAD *n*
QUADDED *adj* formed of multiple quads
QUADRAT *n* area marked out for study of the plants in the surrounding area
QUADRIC *adj* having or characterized by an equation of the second degree ▹ *n* quadric curve, surface, or function
QUADS ▸ **quad**
QUAERE *n* query or question ▹ *interj* ask or inquire ▹ *vb* ask **quaered, quaeres**
QUAFF *vb* **quaffed, quaffer, quaffs**
QUAG *another word for* > **quagmire**
QUAGGA *n* recently extinct zebra **quaggas**
QUAGGY *adj* resembling a marsh or quagmire
QUAGS ▸ **quag**
QUAHAUG = **quahog**
QUAHOG *n* edible clam **quahogs**
QUAI = **quay**
QUAICH *n* small shallow drinking cup **quaichs, quaigh**
QUAIGHS ▸ **quaigh**
QUAIL *n, vb* **quailed, quails**
QUAINT *adj*
QUAIR *n* book **quairs**
QUAIS ▸ **quai**
QUAKE *vb, n* **quaked, quaker, quakers, quakes**
QUAKIER ▸ **quaky**
QUAKILY ▸ **quaky**
QUAKING ▸ **quake**
QUAKY *adj* inclined to quake
QUALE *n* essential property or quality **qualia**
QUALIFY *vb*
QUALITY *n, adj*
QUALM *n* **qualms, qualmy**
QUAMASH *another name for* ▸ **camass**
QUANGO *n* **quangos**
QUANNET *n* flat file with handle at one end
QUANT *n* long pole for propelling a boat ▹ *vb* propel (a boat) with a quant
QUANTA ▸ **quantum**
QUANTAL *adj* of or relating to a quantum or an entity that is quantized
QUANTED ▸ **quant**
QUANTIC *n* mathematical function
QUANTS ▸ **quant**
QUANTUM *n, adj*
QUARE *adj* remarkable or strange **quarer, quarest**
QUARK *n* **quarks**

This subatomic particle appears in the Scrabble cloud-chamber fairly often, and when it does, remember that you can put an S on the front of it to make **squark**.

QUARREL *n, vb*
QUARRY *n, vb*
QUART *n*
QUARTAN *adj* (esp of a malarial fever) occurring every third day ▷ *n* quartan malaria
QUARTE *n* fourth of eight basic positions from which a parry or attack can be made in fencing
QUARTER *n, vb, adj*
QUARTES ▶ **quarte**
QUARTET *n*
QUARTIC *n* biquadratic equation
QUARTO *n* book size in which the sheets are folded into four leaves **quartos**
QUARTS ▶ **quart**
QUARTZ *n* **quartzy**
QUASAR *n* **quasars**
QUASH *vb* **quashed, quasher, quashes**
QUASI *adv* as if
QUASS *variant of* ▶ **kvass**
QUASSES ▶ **quass**
QUASSIA *n* tropical American tree
QUASSIN *n* bitter crystalline substance
QUAT *n* spot
QUATCH *vb* move
QUATE *n* fortune
QUATRE *n* playing card with four pips **quatres**
QUATS ▶ **quat**
QUAVER *vb, n* **quavers, quavery**
QUAY *n*
QUAYAGE *n* system of quays
QUAYD *archaic past participle of* ▶ **quail**

a Spenserian word meaning daunted, that makes a surprising hook for **quay**.

QUAYS ▶ **quay**
QUAZZY *adj* unwell
QUBIT *n* quantum bit **qubits**
QUBYTE *n* unit of eight qubits **qubytes**
QUEACH *n* thicket
QUEACHY *adj* unwell
QUEAN *n* boisterous, impudent, or disreputable woman **queans**
QUEASY *adj* **queazy**
QUEBEC *n* **quebecs**
QUEECHY = **queachy**
QUEEN *n, vb* **queened**
QUEENIE *n* scallop
QUEENLY *adj* resembling or appropriate to a queen ▷ *adv* in a manner appropriate to a queen
QUEENS ▶ **queen**
QUEENY *adj* effeminate
QUEER *adj, n, vb* **queered, queerer, queerly, queers**
QUEEST *n* wood pigeon **queests**
QUEINT = **quaint**
QUELCH = **squelch**
QUELEA *n* East African weaver bird **queleas**
QUELL *vb* **quelled, queller, quells**
QUEME *vb* please **quemed, quemes, queming**
QUENA *n* Andean flute **quenas**
QUENCH *vb*
QUEP *interj* expression of derision
QUERIDA *n* sweetheart
QUERIED ▶ **query**
QUERIER ▶ **query**
QUERIES ▶ **query**
QUERIST *n* person who makes inquiries or queries
QUERN *n* stone hand mill for grinding corn **querns**
QUERY *n, vb*
QUEST *n, vb* **quested, quester**
QUESTOR = **quaestor**
QUESTS ▶ **quest**
QUETCH *vb* move
QUETHE *vb* say **quethes**
QUETSCH *n* plum brandy
QUETZAL *n* crested bird of Central and N South America

This is a great word if you can get the tiles for it, so it's well worth remembering both spellings – it can also be **quezal** – and the four plural forms, which are **quetzals** or **quetzales** and **quezals** or **quezales**.

QUEUE *n, vb* **queued, queuer, queuers, queues, queuing**

QUEY *n* young cow
QUEYN *n* girl **queynie, queyns**
QUEYS ▸ **quey**
QUEZAL = **quetzal**
QUEZALS ▸ **quezal**
QUIBBLE *vb, n* **quiblin**
QUICH *vb* move
QUICHE *n*
QUICHED ▸ **quich**
QUICHES ▸ **quiche**
QUICK *adj, n, adv*
QUICKEN *vb* make or become faster ▹ *n* rowan tree
QUICKER ▸ **quick**
QUICKIE *n* anything done or made hurriedly ▹ *adj* made or done rapidly
QUICKLY ▸ **quick**
QUICKS ▸ **quick**
QUICKY *n* hastily arranged divorce
QUID *n*
QUIDAM *n* specified person **quidams**
QUIDDIT = **quiddity**
QUIDDLE *vb* waste time
QUIDS ▸ **quid**
QUIESCE *vb* quieten
QUIET *adj, n, vb* **quieted**
QUIETEN *vb*
QUIETER ▸ **quiet**
QUIETLY ▸ **quiet**
QUIETS ▸ **quiet**
QUIETUS *n* release from life
QUIFF *n* tuft of hair brushed up above the forehead **quiffs**
QUIGHT *vb* quit **quights**
QUILL *n, vb*
QUILLAI *another name for* > **soapbark**
QUILLED ▸ **quill**
QUILLET *n* quibble or subtlety
QUILLON *n* either half of the extended crosspiece of a sword or dagger
QUILLS ▸ **quill**
QUILT *n, vb* **quilted, quilter, quilts**
QUIN *short for* > **quintuplet**
QUINA *n* quinine
QUINARY *adj* consisting of fives or by fives ▹ *n* set of five
QUINAS ▸ **quina**
QUINATE *adj* arranged in or composed of five parts
QUINCE *n* **quinces**
QUINCHE *vb* move
QUINE *variant of* ▸ **quean**
QUINELA = **quinella**
QUINES ▸ **quine**
QUINIC *adj as in* **quinic acid** white crystalline soluble optically active carboxylic acid
QUINIE *n* girl **quinies**
QUININ = **quinine**
QUININA = **quinine**
QUININE *n*
QUININS ▸ **quinin**
QUINNAT *n* Pacific salmon
QUINO = **keno**
QUINOA *n* type of grain high in nutrients **quinoas**
QUINOID = **quinonoid**
QUINOL *n* white crystalline soluble phenol used as a photographic developer **quinols**
QUINONE *n* yellow crystalline water-soluble unsaturated ketone
QUINOS ▸ **quino**
QUINS ▸ **quin**
QUINSY *n* inflammation of the throat or tonsils
QUINT = **quin**
QUINTA *n* Portuguese vineyard where grapes for wine or port are grown
QUINTAL *n* unit of weight
QUINTAN *adj* (of a fever) occurring every fourth day ▹ *n* quintan fever
QUINTAR *n* Albanian unit of currency
QUINTAS ▸ **quinta**
QUINTE *n* fifth of eight basic positions from which a parry or attack can be made in fencing **quintes**
QUINTET *n*
QUINTIC *adj* of or relating to the fifth degree ▹ *n* mathematical function
QUINTIN = **quintain**
QUINTS ▸ **quint**
QUINZE *n* card game where players aim to score 15 **quinzes**

> Deriving from the French word for fifteen, this makes a high-scoring word that you may well

get to play, and if you can use all your tiles to form the plural, you'll get a 50-point bonus.

QUIP *n, vb*
QUIPO = **quipu**
QUIPOS ▸ **quipo**
QUIPPED ▸ **quip**
QUIPPER ▸ **quip**
QUIPPU = **quipu**
QUIPPUS ▸ **quippu**
QUIPPY ▸ **quip**
QUIPS ▸ **quip**
QUIPU *n* device of the Incas used to record information using knotted cords **quipus**
QUIRE *n* set of 24 or 25 sheets of paper ▹ *vb* arrange in quires **quired, quires, quiring**
QUIRK *n, vb* **quirked, quirks, quirky**
QUIRT *n* whip with a leather thong at one end ▹ *vb* strike with a quirt **quirted, quirts**
QUIST *n* wood pigeon **quists**
QUIT *vb, adj*
QUITCH *vb* move
QUITE *archaic form of* ▸ **quit**
QUITED ▸ **quite**
QUITES ▸ **quite**
QUITING ▸ **quite**
QUITS ▸ **quit**
QUITTAL *n* repayment of an action with a similar action
QUITTED ▸ **quit**
QUITTER *n* person who lacks perseverance
QUITTOR *n* infection of the cartilages on the side of a horse's foot
QUIVER *vb, n* **quivers, quivery**
QUIXOTE *n* impractical idealist

Using the Q and X, this word for an impractical dreamer has a reasonable chance of coming up, so keeping an eye open for it is not that quixotic!

QUIZ *n, vb* **quizzed, quizzer, quizzes**
QUOAD *adv* as far as
QUOD *n* jail ▹ *vb* say **quodded**
QUODLIN *n* cooking apple
QUODS ▸ **quod**
QUOHOG *n* edible clam **quohogs**
QUOIF *vb* arrange (the hair) **quoifed, quoifs**
QUOIN *n* external corner of a building ▹ *vb* wedge **quoined, quoins**
QUOIST *n* wood pigeon **quoists**
QUOIT *n* large ring used in the game of quoits ▹ *vb* throw as a quoit **quoited, quoiter**
QUOITS *n* game in which quoits are tossed at a stake in the ground
QUOKKA *n* small Australian wallaby **quokkas**
QUOLL *n* Australian catlike carnivorous marsupial **quolls**
QUOMODO *n* manner
QUONDAM *adj* of an earlier time
QUONK *vb* make an accidental noise while broadcasting **quonked, quonks**
QUOOKE *archaic past participle of* ▸ **quake**
QUOP *vb* pulsate or throb **quopped, quops**
QUORATE *adj* having or being a quorum
QUORUM *n* **quorums**
QUOTA *n* **quotas**
QUOTE *vb, n, interj* **quoted, quoter, quoters, quotes**
QUOTH *vb*
QUOTHA *interj* expression of mild sarcasm, used in picking up a word or phrase used by someone else
QUOTING ▸ **quote**
QUOTUM = **quota**
QUOTUMS ▸ **quotum**
QURSH = **qurush**
QURSHES ▸ **qurush**
QURUSH *n* Saudi Arabian currency unit
QUYTE = **quit**
QUYTED ▸ **quyte**
QUYTES ▸ **quyte**
QUYTING ▸ **quyte**
QWERTY *n* standard English-language typewriter or computer keyboard **qwertys**

Rr

R is one of the most common consonants in Scrabble, along with **N** and **T**. Despite this, however, there is only one two-letter word beginning with **R**: **re** (2 points). This is worth remembering, as you won't need to waste time trying to think of others. There are some good three-letter words with **R**, however, some of which are quite unusual: **raj, rax, rex** (10 each), **rez** and **riz** (12 each). Also, don't forget common words like **raw, ray** and **row** (6 each).

RABANNA *n* Madagascan woven raffia
RABAT *vb* rotate so that the plane rotated coincides with another
RABATO *n* wired or starched collar **rabatos**
RABATS ▸ **rabat**
RABATTE = **rabat**
RABBET *n* recess cut into a surface ▹ *vb* cut or form a rabbet in (timber) **rabbets**
RABBI *n* **rabbies, rabbin**
RABBINS ▸ **rabbin**
RABBIS ▸ **rabbi**
RABBIT *n, vb*
RABBITO = **rabbitoh**
RABBITS ▸ **rabbit**
RABBITY *adj* rabbitlike
RABBLE *n, vb* **rabbled**
RABBLER *n* device for stirring, mixing, or skimming a molten charge in a furnace
RABBLES ▸ **rabble**
RABBONI *n* very respectful Jewish title or form of address
RABI *n* (in Pakistan, India, etc) a crop that is harvested at the end of winter
RABIC ▸ **rabies**
RABID *adj* **rabider, rabidly**
RABIES *n*
RABIS ▸ **rabi**
RACA *adj* biblical word meaning worthless or empty-headed
RACCOON *n*
RACE *n, vb* **raced**
RACEME *n* cluster of flowers along a central stem, as in the foxglove
RACEMED *adj* with or in racemes
RACEMES ▸ **raceme**
RACEMIC *adj* being a mixture of equal amounts of enantiomers
RACER *n* person, animal, or machine that races **racers**
RACES ▸ **race**
RACEWAY *n* racetrack, esp one for banger racing
RACH *n* scent hound **rache, raches**
RACHET = **ratchet**
RACHETS ▸ **rachet**
RACHIAL ▸ **rachis**
RACHIS *n* main axis or stem of an inflorescence or compound leaf
RACIAL *adj*
RACIER ▸ **racy**

RACIEST ▸ **racy**
RACILY ▸ **racy**
RACING *adj* denoting or associated with horse races ▹ *n* practice of engaging in contests of speed **racings**
RACINO *n* combined racetrack and casino **racinos**
RACISM *n* **racisms, racist, racists**
RACK *n, vb* **racked, racker, rackers**
RACKET *n, vb*
RACKETS *n* ball game played in a paved walled court
RACKETT *n* early double-reeded wind instrument
RACKETY *adj* involving noise, commotion and excitement
RACKFUL ▸ **rack**
RACKING ▸ **rack**
RACKLE *adj* dialect word meaning rash
RACKS ▸ **rack**
RACLOIR *n* scraper
RACON *n* radar beacon **racons**
RACOON = **raccoon**
RACOONS ▸ **racoon**
RACQUET = **racket**
RACY *adj*
RAD *n, vb, adj*
RADAR *n* **radars**
RADDED, radder, raddest, radding ▸ **rad**
RADDLE = **ruddle**
RADDLED *adj* (of a person) unkempt or run-down in appearance
RADDLES ▸ **raddle**
RADE *(in Scots dialect) past tense of* ▸ **ride**
RADGE *adj* angry or uncontrollable ▹ *n* person acting in such a way **radger, radges, radgest**
RADIAL *adj, n*
RADIALE *n* bone in the wrist
RADIALS ▸ **radial**
RADIAN *n* **radians**
RADIANT *adj, n*
RADIATA *adj as in* **radiata pine** type of pine tree
RADIATE *vb, adj*
RADICAL *adj, n*
RADICEL *n* very small root
RADICES ▸ **radix**
RADICLE *n*
RADII ▸ **radius**
RADIO *n, vb, adj* **radioed, radios**
RADISH *n*
RADIUM *n* **radiums**
RADIUS *n*
RADIX *n* any number that is the base of a number system or of a system of logarithms **radixes**
RADOME *n* protective housing for a radar antenna **radomes**
RADON *n* **radons**
RADS ▸ **rad**
RADULA *n* horny tooth-bearing strip on the tongue of molluscs **radulae, radular, radulas**
RAFALE *n* burst of artillery fire **rafales**
RAFF *n* rubbish
RAFFIA *n* **raffias**
RAFFISH *adj*
RAFFLE *n, vb* **raffled, raffler, raffles**
RAFFS ▸ **raff**
RAFT *n, vb* **rafted**
RAFTER *n, vb* **rafters**
RAFTING ▸ **raft**
RAFTMAN = **raftsman**
RAFTMEN ▸ **raftman**
RAFTS ▸ **raft**
RAG *n, vb, adj*
RAGA *n* pattern of melody and rhythm in Indian music **ragas**
RAGBAG *n* confused assortment, jumble **ragbags**
RAGBOLT *n* bolt that has angled projections on it
RAGDE *archaic past form of* ▸ **rage**
RAGE *n, vb* **raged**
RAGEE = **ragi**
RAGEES ▸ **ragee**
RAGEFUL, rager, ragers, rages ▸ **rage**
RAGG = **ragstone**
RAGGA *n* dance-oriented style of reggae **raggas**
RAGGED ▸ **rag**
RAGGEDY *adj* somewhat ragged
RAGGEE = **ragi**
RAGGEES ▸ **raggee**

RAGGERY *n* rags
RAGGIER ▸ **raggy**
RAGGIES ▸ **raggy**
RAGGING ▸ **rag**
RAGGLE *n* thin groove cut in stone or brickwork ▹ *vb* cut a raggle in **raggled, raggles**
RAGGS ▸ **ragg**
RAGGY *adj* raglike ▹ *n* cereal grass cultivated in Africa and Asia for its edible grain
RAGI *n* cereal grass cultivated in Africa and Asia for its edible grain
RAGING ▸ **rage**
RAGINGS ▸ **rage**
RAGINI *n* Indian musical form related to a raga **raginis**
RAGIS ▸ **ragi**
RAGLAN *adj*, *n* **raglans**
RAGMAN *n* rag-and-bone man **ragmans, ragmen**
RAGMENT *n* statute, roll, or list
RAGOUT *n* richly seasoned stew of meat and vegetables ▹ *vb* make into a ragout **ragouts**
RAGS ▸ **rag**
RAGTAG *n* disparaging term for common people **ragtags**
RAGTIME *n*
RAGTOP *n* informal word for a car with a folding or removable roof **ragtops**
RAGU *n* Italian meat and tomato sauce
RAGULED = **raguly**
RAGULY *adj* (in heraldry) having toothlike or stublike projections
RAGUS ▸ **ragu**
RAGWEED *n* any of several plants
RAGWORK *n* weaving or needlework using rags
RAGWORM *n* type of worm that lives chiefly in burrows in sand or mud
RAGWORT *n* plant with ragged leaves and yellow flowers
RAH *informal US word for* ▸ **cheer**
RAHED ▸ **rah**
RAHING ▸ **rah**
RAHS ▸ **rah**
RAHUI *n* Māori prohibition **rahuis**
RAI *n* type of Algerian popular music
RAIA = **rayah**
RAIAS ▸ **raia**
RAID *n*, *vb* **raided, raider, raiders, raiding, raids**
RAIK *n* wander ▹ *vb* wander **raiked, raiking, raiks**
RAIL *n*, *vb*
RAILAGE *n* cost of transporting goods by rail
RAILBED *n* ballast layer supporting the sleepers of a railway track
RAILBUS *n* buslike vehicle for use on railway lines
RAILCAR *n* passenger-carrying railway vehicle consisting of a single coach
RAILE *archaic spelling of* ▸ **rail**
RAILED ▸ **rail**
RAILER ▸ **rail**
RAILERS ▸ **rail**
RAILES ▸ **raile**
RAILING *n*
RAILLY *old word for* ▸ **mock**
RAILMAN *n* railway employee **railmen**
RAILS ▸ **rail**
RAILWAY *n*
RAIMENT *n*
RAIN *n*, *vb*
RAINBOW *n*
RAINE *archaic spelling of* ▸ **reign**
RAINED ▸ **rain**
RAINES ▸ **raine**
RAINIER ▸ **rainy**
RAINILY ▸ **rainy**
RAINING ▸ **rain**
RAINOUT *n* radioactive fallout or atmospheric pollution carried to the earth by rain
RAINS ▸ **rain**
RAINY *adj* characterized by a large rainfall
RAIRD = **reird**
RAIRDS ▸ **raird**
RAIS ▸ **rai**
RAISE *vb*, *n* **raised, raiser, raisers, raises**
RAISIN *n*

RAISING *n* rule that moves a constituent from an embedded clause into the main clause
RAISINS ▸ **raisin**
RAISINY ▸ **raisin**
RAIT = **ret**
RAITA *n* Indian dish of chopped cucumber, mint, etc, in yogurt **raitas**
RAITED ▸ **rait**
RAITING ▸ **rait**
RAITS ▸ **rait**
RAIYAT = **ryot**
RAIYATS ▸ **raiyat**
RAJ *n* (in India) government

> This Indian word for rule or empire is one of the essential short words that use a J. Remember that it can extended to **raja**.

RAJA = **rajah**
RAJAH *n* **rajahs**
RAJAS ▸ **raja**
RAJES ▸ **raj**
RAKE *n, vb* **raked**
RAKEE = **raki**
RAKEES ▸ **rakee**
RAKEOFF *n* share of profits, esp one that is illegal or given as a bribe
RAKER *n* person who rakes **rakers**
RAKERY *n* rakish behaviour
RAKES ▸ **rake**
RAKI *n* strong spirit distilled from grain
RAKIA *n* strong fruit-based alcoholic drink popular in the Balkans **rakias, rakija**
RAKIJAS ▸ **rakija**
RAKING *n* (in rugby) offence of scraping an opponent with the studs **rakings**
RAKIS ▸ **raki**
RAKISH *adj*
RAKSHAS = **rakshasa**
RAKU *n* type of Japanese pottery **rakus**
RALE *n* abnormal coarse crackling sound heard on auscultation of the chest **rales**
RALLIED ▸ **rally**
RALLIER ▸ **rally**
RALLIES ▸ **rally**
RALLINE *adj* relating to a family of birds that includes the rails, crakes, and coots
RALLY *n, vb* **rallye**
RALLYES ▸ **rallye**
RAM *n, vb*
RAMADA *n* outdoor eating area with roof but open sides **ramadas**
RAMAKIN = **ramekin**
RAMAL *adj* relating to a branch or branches
RAMATE *adj* with branches
RAMBLA *n* dried-up riverbed **ramblas**
RAMBLE *vb, n* **rambled**
RAMBLER *n* person who rambles
RAMBLES ▸ **ramble**
RAMCAT *n* dialect word for a male cat **ramcats**
RAMEAL = **ramal**
RAMEE = **ramie**
RAMEES ▸ **ramee**
RAMEKIN *n* small ovenproof dish for a single serving of food
RAMEN *n* Japanese dish consisting of a clear broth containing thin white noodles **ramens**
RAMENTA > **ramentum**
RAMEOUS = **ramal**
RAMET *n* any of the individuals in a group of clones **ramets**
RAMI = **ramie**
RAMIE *n* woody Asian shrub with broad leaves **ramies**
RAMIFY *vb* become complex
RAMILIE = **ramillie**
RAMIN *n* swamp-growing tree found in Malaysia and Indonesia **ramins**
RAMIS ▸ **rami**
RAMJET *n* type of jet engine **ramjets**
RAMMED ▸ **ram**
RAMMEL *n* discarded or waste matter **rammels**
RAMMER ▸ **ram**
RAMMERS ▸ **ram**
RAMMIER ▸ **rammish**
RAMMIES ▸ **rammish**
RAMMING ▸ **ram**
RAMMISH *adj* like a ram, esp in being lustful or foul-smelling

RAMMLE *n* collection of items saved in case they become useful **rammles**
RAMMY *n* noisy disturbance or free-for-all ▷ *vb* make a rammy
RAMONA = **sagebrush**
RAMONAS ▸ **ramona**
RAMOSE *adj* having branches **ramous**
RAMP *n*, *vb*
RAMPAGE *vb*
RAMPANT *adj*
RAMPART *n*, *vb*
RAMPED ▸ **ramp**
RAMPER ▸ **ramp**
RAMPERS ▸ **ramp**
RAMPICK = **rampike**
RAMPIKE *n* US or dialect word for a dead tree
RAMPING ▸ **ramp**
RAMPION *n* European and Asian plant
RAMPIRE *archaic variant of* ▸ **rampart**
RAMPOLE = **rampike**
RAMPS ▸ **ramp**
RAMROD *n*, *adj*, *vb* **ramrods**
RAMS ▸ **ram**
RAMSON *n* type of garlic **ramsons**
RAMSTAM *adv* headlong ▷ *adj* headlong
RAMTIL *n* African plant grown in India esp for its oil **ramtils**
RAMULAR *adj* relating to a branch or branches
RAMULI ▸ **ramulus**
RAMULUS *n* small branch
RAMUS *n* barb of a bird's feather
RAN ▸ **run**
RANA *n* genus of frogs **ranas**
RANCE *Scots word for* ▸ **prop**
RANCED ▸ **rance**
RANCEL *vb* (in Shetland and Orkney) carry out a search **rancels**
RANCES ▸ **rance**
RANCH *n*, *vb* **ranched**
RANCHER *n* person who owns, manages, or works on a ranch
RANCHES ▸ **ranch**
RANCHO *n* hut or group of huts for housing ranch workers **ranchos**
RANCID *adj*
RANCING ▸ **rance**
RANCOR = **rancour**
RANCORS ▸ **rancor**
RANCOUR *n*
RAND *n*, *vb*
RANDAN *n* boat rowed by three people **randans**
RANDED ▸ **rand**
RANDEM *adv* with three horses harnessed together as a team ▷ *n* carriage or team of horses so driven **randems**
RANDIE = **randy**
RANDIER ▸ **randy**
RANDIES ▸ **randy**
RANDILY ▸ **randy**
RANDING ▸ **rand**
RANDOM *adj*, *n* **randoms, randon**
RANDONS ▸ **randon**
RANDS ▸ **rand**
RANDY *adj* sexually aroused ▷ *n* rude or reckless person
RANEE = **rani**
RANEES ▸ **ranee**
RANG ▸ **ring**
RANGE *n*, *vb* **ranged**
RANGER *n* **rangers**
RANGES ▸ **range**
RANGI *n* sky
RANGIER ▸ **rangy**
RANGILY ▸ **rangy**
RANGING ▸ **range**
RANGIS ▸ **rangi**
RANGOLI *n* traditional Indian ground decoration
RANGY *adj* having long slender limbs
RANI *n* wife or widow of a rajah
RANID *n* frog **ranids**
RANINE *adj* relating to frogs
RANIS ▸ **rani**
RANK *n*, *vb*, *adj* **ranke, ranked**
RANKER *n* soldier in the ranks **rankers**
RANKES ▸ **ranke**
RANKEST ▸ **rank**
RANKING *adj* prominent ▷ *n* position on a scale
RANKISH *adj* old word meaning rather rank
RANKISM *n* discrimination against people on the grounds of rank

RANKLE *vb* **rankled, rankles**
RANKLY ▸ **rank**
RANKS ▸ **rank**
RANPIKE = **rampike**
RANSACK *vb*
RANSEL = **rancel**
RANSELS ▸ **ransel**
RANSOM *n, vb* **ransoms**
RANT *vb, n* **ranted, ranter, ranters, ranting, rants**
RANULA *n* saliva-filled cyst that develops under the tongue
RANULAR *adj* of a cyst under the tongue
RANULAS ▸ **ranula**
RANZEL = **rancel**
RANZELS ▸ **ranzel**
RAOULIA *n* flowering plant of New Zealand
RAP *vb, n*
RAPE *vb, n* **raped, raper, rapers, rapes**
RAPHAE ▸ **raphe**
RAPHE *n* elongated ridge of conducting tissue along the side of certain seeds **raphes**
RAPHIA = **raffia**
RAPHIAS ▸ **raphia**
RAPHIDE *n* needle-shaped crystal that occurs in many plant cells **raphis**
RAPID *adj* **rapider, rapidly**
RAPIDS *pl n* part of a river with a fast turbulent current
RAPIER *n* **rapiers**
RAPINE *n* pillage or plundering **rapines**
RAPING ▸ **rape**
RAPINI *pl n* type of leafy vegetable
RAPIST *n* person who commits rape **rapists**
RAPLOCH *n* Scots word for homespun woollen material ▹ *adj* Scots word meaning coarse or homemade
RAPPE *n* Arcadian dish of grated potatoes and pork or chicken
RAPPED ▸ **rap**
RAPPEE *n* moist English snuff of the 18th and 19th centuries **rappees**
RAPPEL *n* (formerly) a drumbeat to call soldiers to arms ▹ *vb* abseil **rappels**
RAPPEN *n* Swiss coin equal to one hundredth of a franc
RAPPER *n* something used for rapping, such as a knocker on a door **rappers**
RAPPES ▸ **rappe**
RAPPING ▸ **rap**
RAPPINI = **rapini**
RAPPORT *n*
RAPS ▸ **rap**
RAPT *adj* **raptly**
RAPTOR *n* any bird of prey **raptors**
RAPTURE *n, vb*
RARE *adj, vb*
RAREBIT *n as in* **Welsh rarebit** dish made from melted cheese served on toast
RARED ▸ **rare**
RAREE *n as in* **raree show** street show or carnival
RAREFY *vb* make or become rarer or less dense
RARELY *adv* seldom
RARER ▸ **rare**
RARES ▸ **rare**
RAREST ▸ **rare**
RARIFY = **rarefy**
RARING *adj*
RARITY *n*
RARK *vb as in* **rark up** informal New Zealand expression meaning reprimand severely **rarked, rarking, rarks**
RAS *n* headland
RASBORA *n* often brightly coloured tropical fish
RASCAL *n, adj* **rascals**
RASCHEL *n* type of loosely knitted fabric
RASE = **raze; rased, raser, rasers, rases**
RASH *adj, n, vb* **rashed**
RASHER *n* **rashers**
RASHES ▸ **rash**
RASHEST ▸ **rash**
RASHIE *n* protective shirt worn by surfers **rashies**
RASHING ▸ **rash**
RASHLY ▸ **rash**
RASING ▸ **rase**
RASP *n, vb* **rasped, rasper, raspers**
RASPIER ▸ **raspy**
RASPING *adj* (esp of a noise) harsh or grating
RASPISH ▸ **rasp**
RASPS ▸ **rasp**

RASPY = **rasping**
RASSE *n* small S Asian civet **rasses**
RASSLE *dialect variant of* ▶ **wrestle**
RASSLED ▶ **rassle**
RASSLES ▶ **rassle**
RAST *archaic past form of* ▶ **race**
RASTA *adj* of a member of a particular Black religious movement
RASTER *n* image consisting of rows of pixel information ▷ *vb* turn a digital image into a large picture **rasters**
RASTRUM *n* pen for drawing the five lines of a musical stave simultaneously
RASURE *n* scraping **rasures**
RAT *n, vb*
RATA *n* New Zealand hard-wood forest tree
RATABLE *adj* able to be rated or evaluated **ratably**
RATAFEE = **ratafia**
RATAFIA *n*
RATAL *n* amount on which rates are assessed ▷ *adj* of or relating to rates (local taxation) **ratals**
RATAN = **rattan**
RATANS ▶ **ratan**
RATANY *n* flowering desert shrub
RATAS ▶ **rata**
RATATAT *n* sound of knocking on a door
RATBITE *n as in* **ratbite fever** acute infectious disease that can be caught from rats
RATCH = **ratchet**
RATCHED ▶ **ratch**
RATCHES ▶ **ratch**
RATCHET *n, vb*
RATE *n, vb* **rated**
RATEEN = **ratine**
RATEENS ▶ **rateen**
RATEL *n* large African and S Asian musteline mammal **ratels**
RATER ▶ **rate**
RATERS ▶ **rate**
RATES *pl n* (in some countries) a tax on property levied by a local authority
RATFINK *n* contemptible or undesirable person
RATFISH *n* deep-sea fish with a whiplike tail
RATH = **rathe**
RATHA *n* (in India) a four-wheeled carriage drawn by horses or bullocks **rathas**
RATHE *adj* blossoming or ripening early in the season
RATHER *adv, interj, sentence substitute*
RATHEST *adv* dialect or archaic word meaning soonest
RATHOLE *n* rat's hiding place or burrow
RATHS ▶ **rath**
RATIFY *vb*
RATINE *n* coarse loosely woven cloth **ratines**
RATING *n* **ratings**
RATIO *n*
RATION *n, vb*
RATIONS *pl n* fixed daily allowance of food
RATIOS ▶ **ratio**
RATITE *adj* (of flightless birds) having a breastbone that lacks a keel ▷ *n* bird that belongs to this group **ratites**
RATLIKE ▶ **rat**
RATLIN = **ratline**
RATLINE *n* light line tied across the shrouds of a sailing vessel
RATLING *n* young rat
RATLINS ▶ **ratlin**
RATO *n* rocket-assisted take-off
RATOO = **ratu**
RATOON *n* new shoot that grows from near the root or crown of crop plants ▷ *vb* propagate by such a growth **ratoons**
RATOOS ▶ **ratoo**
RATOS ▶ **rato**
RATPACK *n* members of the press who pursue celebrities
RATS ▶ **rat**
RATTAIL *n* type of fish
RATTAN *n* climbing palm with jointed stems used for canes **rattans**
RATTED ▶ **rat**
RATTEEN = **ratine**
RATTEN *vb* sabotage or steal tools in order to disrupt the work of **rattens**

RATTER *n* dog or cat that catches and kills rats **ratters**
RATTERY *n* rats' dwelling area
RATTIER ▸ **ratty**
RATTILY ▸ **ratty**
RATTING ▸ **rat**
RATTISH *adj* of, resembling, or infested with rats
RATTLE *vb, n* **rattled**
RATTLER *n* something that rattles
RATTLES ▸ **rattle**
RATTLIN = **ratline**
RATTLY *adj* having a rattle
RATTON *n* dialect word for a little rat **rattons**
RATTOON = **ratoon**
RATTRAP *n* device for catching rats
RATTY *adj*
RATU *n* title used by Fijian chiefs or nobles **ratus**
RAUCID *adj* raucous
RAUCITY ▸ **raucous**
RAUCLE *adj* Scots word for rough or tough **raucler**
RAUCOUS *adj*
RAUGHT *archaic past form of* ▸ **reach**
RAUN *n* fish roe or spawn
RAUNCH *n* lack of polish or refinement ▹ *vb* behave in a raunchy manner
RAUNCHY *adj* earthy, sexy
RAUNGE *archaic word for* ▸ **range**
RAUNGED ▸ **raunge**
RAUNGES ▸ **raunge**
RAUNS ▸ **raun**
RAUPATU *n* confiscation or seizure of land
RAUPO *n* New Zealand bulrush **raupos**
RAURIKI *n* any of various plants with prickly leaves
RAV *n* Hebrew word for rabbi
RAVAGE *vb, n* **ravaged, ravager, ravages**
RAVE *vb, n* **raved**
RAVEL *vb* tangle or become entangled ▹ *n* tangle or complication **raveled, raveler**
RAVELIN *n* outwork having two embankments at a salient angle
RAVELLY ▸ **ravel**
RAVELS ▸ **ravel**
RAVEN *n, adj, vb* **ravened, ravener, ravens**
RAVER *n* person who leads a wild or uninhibited social life **ravers**
RAVES ▸ **rave**
RAVIN *archaic spelling of* ▸ **raven**
RAVINE *n*
RAVINED ▸ **ravin**
RAVINES ▸ **ravine**
RAVING *adj, n* **ravings**
RAVINS ▸ **ravin**
RAVIOLI *n*
RAVISH *vb*
RAVS ▸ **rav**
RAW *as in* **in the raw** *adj*
RAWARU *n* New Zealand name for blue cod **rawarus**
RAWBONE *archaic variant of* > **rawboned**
RAWER ▸ **raw**
RAWEST ▸ **raw**
RAWHEAD *n* bogeyman
RAWHIDE *n* untanned hide ▹ *vb* whip
RAWIN *n* monitoring of winds in the upper atmosphere using radar and a balloon
RAWING *(in dialect)* = **rowen**
RAWINGS ▸ **rawing**
RAWINS ▸ **rawin**
RAWISH ▸ **raw**
RAWLY ▸ **raw**
RAWN *(in dialect)* = **rowen**
RAWNESS ▸ **raw**
RAWNS ▸ **rawn**
RAWS ▸ **raw**
RAX *vb* stretch or extend ▹ *n* act of stretching or straining **raxed, raxes, raxing**

> A dialect word meaning to stretch or strain, and one of the essential short words to know for using the X.

RAY *n, vb*
RAYA = **rayah**
RAYAH *n* (formerly) a non-Muslim subject of the Ottoman Empire **rayahs**
RAYAS ▸ **raya**
RAYED ▸ **ray**

RAYING ▸ **ray**
RAYLE *archaic spelling of* ▸ **rail**
RAYLED ▸ **rayle**
RAYLES ▸ **rayle**
RAYLESS *adj* dark
RAYLET *n* small ray **raylets**
RAYLIKE *adj* resembling a ray
RAYLING ▸ **rayle**
RAYNE *archaic spelling of* ▸ **reign**
RAYNES ▸ **rayne**
RAYON *n* **rayons**
RAYS ▸ **ray**
RAZE *vb* **razed**
RAZEE *n* sailing ship that has had its upper deck or decks removed ▹ *vb* remove the upper deck or decks of (a sailing ship) **razeed, razees**
RAZER, razers, razes, razing ▸ **raze**
RAZOO *n* imaginary coin **razoos**
RAZOR *n, vb* **razored, razors**
RAZURE = **rasure**
RAZURES ▸ **razure**
RAZZ *vb* make fun of **razzed, razzes**
RAZZIA *n* raid for plunder or slaves **razzias**
RAZZING ▸ **razz**
RAZZLE *n as in* **on the razzle** out enjoying oneself or celebrating **razzles**
RE *prep* concerning ▹ *n* the second note of the musical scale
REACH *vb, n* **reached, reacher, reaches**
REACT *vb* **reacted**
REACTOR *n*
REACTS ▸ **react**
READ *vb, n*
READAPT *vb* adapt again
READD *vb* add again **readded, readds**
READER *n* **readers**
READIED ▸ **ready**
READIER ▸ **ready**
READIES *pl n* ready money
READILY *adv*
READING ▸ **read**
README *n* document which accompanies computer files or software
READMIT *vb* let (a person, country, etc) back in to a place or organization
READOPT *vb* adopt again
READORN *vb* adorn again
READOUT *n* act of retrieving information from a computer memory or storage device
READS ▸ **read**
READY *adj, vb*
REAFFIX *vb* affix again
REAGENT *n*
REAGIN *n* type of antibody that is formed against an allergen **reagins**
REAK = **reck**
REAKED ▸ **reak**
REAKING ▸ **reak**
REAKS ▸ **reak**
REAL *adj, n* **realer, reales, realest**
REALGAR *n* rare orange-red soft mineral
REALIA *pl n* real-life facts and material used in teaching
REALIGN *vb* change or put back to a new or former place or position
REALISE = **realize**
REALISM *n*
REALIST *n* person who accepts events, etc, as they are
REALITY *n*
REALIZE *vb*
REALLIE *old or dialect variant of* ▸ **really**
REALLOT *vb* allot again
REALLY *adv, interj, vb*
REALM *n* **realms**
REALO *n* member of the German Green party with moderate views **realos**

> A **realo** is a member of the less radical section of the German Green party. It is important to know not because it scores well, but because it provides an easily overlooked 'hook', by allowing you to add O to **real**.

REALS ▸ **real**
REALTER *vb* alter again

REALTIE *n* archaic word meaning sincerity
REALTOR *n* estate agent
REALTY *n* immovable property
REAM *n, vb*
REAME *archaic variant of* ▸ **realm**
REAMED ▸ **ream**
REAMEND *vb* amend again
REAMER *n* tool used for smoothing the bores of holes accurately to size **reamers**
REAMES ▸ **reame**
REAMIER ▸ **reamy**
REAMING ▸ **ream**
REAMS ▸ **ream**
REAMY *Scots for* ▸ **creamy**
REAN = **reen**
REANNEX *vb* annex again
REANS ▸ **rean**
REAP *vb* **reaped**
REAPER *n* person who reaps or machine for reaping **reapers**
REAPING ▸ **reap**
REAPPLY *vb* put or spread (something) on again
REAPS ▸ **reap**
REAR *n, vb* **reared, rearer, rearers**
REARGUE *vb* argue again
REARING ▸ **rear**
REARISE *vb* arise again
REARLY *old word for* ▸ **early**
REARM *vb* **rearmed, rearms**
REAROSE ▸ **rearise**
REARS ▸ **rear**
REASON *n, vb* **reasons**
REAST = **reest**
REASTED ▸ **reast**
REASTS ▸ **reast**
REASTY *adj* (in dialect) rancid
REATA *n* lasso **reatas**
REATE *n* type of crowfoot **reates**
REAVAIL *vb* avail again
REAVE *vb* carry off (property, prisoners, etc) by force **reaved, reaver, reavers, reaves, reaving**
REAVOW *vb* avow again **reavows**
REAWAKE *vb* awake again **reawoke**
REB *n* Confederate soldier in the American Civil War
REBACK *vb* provide with a new back, backing, or lining **rebacks**
REBADGE *vb* relaunch (a product) under a new name, brand, or logo
REBAIT *vb* bait again **rebaits**
REBAR *n* rod providing reinforcement in concrete structures **rebars**
REBATE *n, vb* **rebated, rebater, rebates**
REBATO = **rabato**
REBATOS ▸ **rebato**
REBBE *n* individual's chosen spiritual mentor **rebbes**
REBEC *n* medieval stringed instrument resembling the violin **rebeck**
REBECKS ▸ **rebeck**
REBECS ▸ **rebec**
REBEGAN ▸ **rebegin**
REBEGIN *vb* begin again **rebegun**
REBEL *vb, n, adj* **rebels**
REBID *vb* bid again **rebids**
REBILL *vb* bill again **rebills**
REBIND *vb* bind again **rebinds**
REBIRTH *n* revival or renaissance
REBIT ▸ **rebite**
REBITE *vb* (in printing) to give another application of acid **rebites**
REBLEND *vb* blend again **reblent**
REBLOOM *vb* bloom again
REBOANT *adj* resounding or reverberating
REBOARD *vb* board again
REBODY *vb* give a new body to
REBOIL *vb* boil again **reboils**
REBOOK *vb* book again **rebooks**
REBOOT *vb* shut down and then restart (a computer system) **reboots**
REBOP = **bebop**
REBOPS ▸ **rebop**

REBORE *n* boring of a cylinder to restore its true shape ▷ *vb* carry out this process **rebored, rebores**
REBORN *adj* active again after a period of inactivity
REBOUND *vb, n*
REBOZO *n* long scarf covering the shoulders and head **rebozos**
REBRACE *vb* brace again
REBRAND *vb* change or update the image of (an organization or product)
REBRED ▶ **rebreed**
REBREED *vb* breed again
REBS ▶ **reb**
REBUFF *vb, n* **rebuffs**
REBUILD *vb* **rebuilt**
REBUKE *vb, n* **rebuked, rebuker, rebukes**
REBURY *vb* bury again
REBUS *n* puzzle consisting of pictures and symbols representing words or syllables **rebuses**
REBUT *vb* **rebuts**
REBUY *vb* buy again **rebuys**
REC *n* short for recreation
RECAL = **recall**
RECALL *vb, n* **recalls, recals**
RECANE *vb* cane again **recaned, recanes**
RECANT *vb* **recants**
RECAP *vb, n* **recaps**
RECARRY *vb* carry again
RECAST *vb* organize or set out in a different way **recasts**
RECATCH *vb* catch again
RECCE *vb* reconnoitre ▷ *n* reconnaissance **recced, recceed, recces**
RECCIED ▶ **reccy**
RECCIES ▶ **reccy**
RECCO = **recce**
RECCOS ▶ **recco**
RECCY = **recce**
RECEDE *vb* **receded, recedes**
RECEIPT *n, vb*
RECEIVE *vb*
RECENCY ▶ **recent**
RECENSE *vb* revise
RECENT *adj*
RECEPT *n* idea or image formed in the mind by repeated experience **recepts**
RECESS *n, vb*
RECHART *vb* chart again
RECHATE = **recheat**
RECHEAT *n* (in a hunt) sounding of the horn to call back the hounds ▷ *vb* sound the horn to call back the hounds
RECHECK *vb* check again
RECHEW *vb* chew again **rechews**
RECHIE *adj* smoky
RECHIP *vb* put a new chip into (a stolen mobile phone) so it can be reused **rechips**
RECHOSE > **rechoose**
RECIPE *n* **recipes**
RECIT *n* narrative
RECITAL *n*
RECITE *vb* **recited, reciter, recites**
RECITS ▶ **recit**
RECK *vb* mind or care about (something)
RECKAN *adj* strained, tormented, or twisted
RECKED ▶ **reck**
RECKING ▶ **reck**
RECKON *vb* **reckons**
RECKS ▶ **reck**
RECLAD *vb* cover in a different substance **reclads**
RECLAIM *vb, n*
RECLAME *n* public acclaim or attention
RECLASP *vb* clasp again
RECLEAN *vb* clean again
RECLIMB *vb* climb again
RECLINE *vb*
RECLOSE *vb* close again
RECLUSE *n, adj*
RECOAL *vb* supply or be supplied with fresh coal **recoals**
RECOAT *vb* coat again **recoats**
RECOCK *vb* cock again **recocks**
RECODE *vb* put into a new code **recoded, recodes**
RECOIL *vb, n* **recoils**
RECOIN *vb* coin again **recoins**
RECOLOR *vb* give a new colour to
RECOMB *vb* comb again **recombs**

RECON *vb* make a preliminary survey **recons**
RECOOK *vb* cook again **recooks**
RECOPY *vb* copy again
RECORD *n, vb* **records**
RECORK *vb* cork again **recorks**
RECOUNT *vb*
RECOUP *vb*
RECOUPE *vb* (in law) keep back or withhold
RECOUPS ▸ **recoup**
RECOURE *archaic variant of* ▸ **recover**
RECOVER *vb* **recower**
RECOYLE *archaic spelling of* ▸ **recoil**
RECRATE *vb* crate again
RECROSS *vb* move or go across (something) again
RECROWN *vb* crown again
RECRUIT *vb, n*
RECS ▸ **rec**
RECTA ▸ **rectum**
RECTAL *adj* of the rectum
RECTI ▸ **rectus**
RECTIFY *vb*
RECTION *n* (in grammar) the determination of the form of one word by another word
RECTO *n* right-hand page of a book
RECTOR *n* **rectors**
RECTORY *n*
RECTOS ▸ **recto**
RECTRIX *n* any of the large stiff feathers of a bird's tail
RECTUM *n* **rectums**
RECTUS *n* straight muscle
RECUILE *archaic variant of* ▸ **recoil**
RECULE *archaic variant of* ▸ **recoil**
RECULED ▸ **recule**
RECULES ▸ **recule**
RECUR *vb*
RECURE *vb* archaic word for cure or recover **recured, recures**
RECURS ▸ **recur**
RECURVE *vb* curve or bend (something) back or down
RECUSAL *n* withdrawal of a judge from a case
RECUSE *vb* (in law) object to or withdraw (a judge) **recused, recuses**
RECUT *vb* cut again **recuts**
RECYCLE *vb, n*
RED *adj, n*
REDACT *vb* compose or draft (an edict, proclamation, etc) **redacts**
REDAN *n* fortification of two parapets at a salient angle **redans**
REDATE *vb* change date of **redated, redates**
REDBACK *n*
REDBAIT *vb* harass those with leftwing leanings
REDBAY *n* type of tree **redbays**
REDBIRD *n* type of bird, the male of which has bright red plumage
REDBONE *n* type of American dog
REDBUD *n* American tree with heart-shaped leaves **redbuds**
REDBUG *another name for* ▸ **chigger**
REDBUGS ▸ **redbug**
REDCAP *n* military policeman **redcaps**
REDCOAT *n* British soldier
REDD *vb* bring order to ▹ *n* act or an instance of redding **redded**
REDDEN *vb* **reddens**
REDDER ▸ **redd**
REDDERS ▸ **redd**
REDDEST ▸ **red**
REDDIER ▸ **reddy**
REDDING ▸ **redd**
REDDISH *adj* somewhat red
REDDLE = **ruddle**
REDDLED ▸ **reddle**
REDDLES ▸ **reddle**
REDDS ▸ **redd**
REDDY *adj* reddish
REDE *n* advice or counsel ▹ *vb* advise
REDEAL *vb* deal again **redeals, redealt**
REDEAR *n* variety of sunfish with a red flash above the gills **redears**
REDED ▸ **rede**
REDEEM *vb* **redeems**
REDEFY *vb* defy again
REDENY *vb* deny again
REDES ▸ **rede**

REDEYE *n* inferior whiskey **redeyes**
REDFIN *n* any of various small fishes with reddish fins that are popular aquarium fishes **redfins**
REDFISH *n* male salmon that has recently spawned
REDFOOT *n* fatal disease of newborn lambs
REDHEAD *n* person with reddish hair
REDIA *n* parasitic larva of flukes **rediae**
REDIAL *vb* dial (a telephone number) again **redials**
REDIAS ▸ **redia**
REDID ▸ **redo**
REDING ▸ **rede**
REDIP *vb* dip again **redips, redipt**
REDLINE *vb* refuse a loan to (a person or country) because of the presumed risks involved
REDLY ▸ **red**
REDNESS ▸ **red**
REDO *vb* do over again in order to improve ▹ *n* instance of redoing something
REDOCK *vb* dock again **redocks**
REDOES ▸ **redo**
REDOING ▸ **redo**
REDON *vb* don again
REDONE ▸ **redo**
REDONS ▸ **redon**
REDOS ▸ **redo**
REDOUBT *n* small fort defending a hilltop or pass ▹ *vb* fear
REDOUND *vb* cause advantage or disadvantage (to)
REDOUT *n* reddened vision caused by a rush of blood to the head **redouts**
REDOWA *n* Bohemian folk dance similar to the waltz **redowas**
REDOX *n* chemical reaction in which one substance is reduced and the other is oxidized **redoxes**
REDPOLL *n* mostly grey-brown finch with a red crown and pink breast
REDRAFT *vb* write a second copy of (a letter, proposal, essay, etc) ▹ *n* second draft
REDRAW *vb* draw or draw up (something) again or differently **redrawn, redraws**
REDREAM *vb* dream again
REDRESS *vb, n*
REDREW ▸ **redraw**
REDRIED ▸ **redry**
REDRIES ▸ **redry**
REDRILL *vb* drill again
REDRIVE *vb* drive again
REDROOT *n* yellow-flowered bog plant whose roots yield a red dye
REDROVE ▸ **redrive**
REDRY *vb* dry again
REDS ▸ **red**
REDSEAR = **redshort**
REDTAIL *n* variety of bird with red colouring on its tail
REDTOP *n* sensationalist tabloid newspaper **redtops**
REDUB *vb* fix or repair **redubs**
REDUCE *vb* **reduced**
REDUCER *n* chemical solution used to lessen the density of a negative or print
REDUCES ▸ **reduce**
REDUIT *n* fortified part from which a garrison may fight on once an enemy has taken outworks **reduits**
REDUX *adj* brought back or returned
REDWARE *another name for* ▸ **kelp**
REDWING *n* small European thrush
REDWOOD *n*
REDYE *vb* dye again **redyed, redyes**
REE *n* Scots word for walled enclosure
REEARN *vb* earn again **rearns**
REEBOK = **rhebok**
REEBOKS ▸ **reebok**
REECH *vb* (in dialect) smoke **reeched, reeches**
REECHIE = **reechy**
REECHO *vb* echo again
REECHY *adj* (in dialect) smoky
REED *n*

REEDBED *n* area of wetland with reeds growing in it
REEDE *obsolete variant of* ▸ **red**
REEDED ▸ **reed**
REEDEN *adj* of or consisting of reeds
REEDER *n* thatcher **reeders**
REEDES ▸ **reede**
REEDIER ▸ **reedy**
REEDIFY *vb* edify again or rebuild
REEDILY ▸ **reedy**
REEDING *n* set of small semicircular architectural mouldings
REEDIT *vb* edit again **reedits**
REEDMAN *n* musician who plays a wind instrument that has a reed **reedmen**
REEDS ▸ **reed**
REEDY *adj* harsh and thin in tone
REEF *n, vb* **reefed**
REEFER *n* **reefers**
REEFIER ▸ **reefy**
REEFING ▸ **reef**
REEFS ▸ **reef**
REEFY *adj* with reefs
REEJECT *vb* eject again
REEK *vb, n* **reeked, reeker, reekers**
REEKIE = **reeky**
REEKIER ▸ **reek**
REEKING ▸ **reek**
REEKS ▸ **reek**
REEKY *adj* steamy or smoky
REEL *n, vb*
REELECT *vb* elect again
REELED, reeler, reelers, reeling ▸ **reel**
REELMAN *n* (formerly) member of a beach life-saving team operating a winch **reelmen**
REELS ▸ **reel**
REEMIT *vb* emit again **reemits**
REEN *n* ditch, esp a drainage channel
REENACT *vb* enact again
REENDOW *vb* endow again
REENJOY *vb* enjoy again
REENS ▸ **reen**
REENTER *vb* enter again
REENTRY *n* return of a spacecraft into the earth's atmosphere
REEQUIP *vb* equip again
REERECT *vb* erect again
REES ▸ **ree**
REEST *vb* (esp of horses) to be noisily uncooperative **reested, reests**
REESTY = **reasty**
REEVE *n* local representative of the king in a shire until the early 11th century ▹ *vb* pass (a rope or cable) through an eye or other narrow opening **reeved, reeves, reeving**
REEVOKE *vb* evoke again
REEXPEL *vb* expel again
REF *n* referee in sport ▹ *vb* referee
REFACE *vb* repair or renew the facing of (a wall) **refaced, refaces**
REFALL *vb* fall again **refalls**
REFECT *vb* archaic word for restore or refresh with food and drink **refects**
REFED ▸ **refeed**
REFEED *vb* feed again **refeeds**
REFEEL *vb* feel again **refeels**
REFEL *vb* refute
REFELL ▸ **refall**
REFELS ▸ **refel**
REFELT ▸ **refeel**
REFENCE *vb* fence again
REFER *vb*
REFEREE *n, vb*
REFERS ▸ **refer**
REFFED ▸ **ref**
REFFING ▸ **ref**
REFIGHT *vb* fight again ▹ *n* second or new fight
REFILE *vb* file again **refiled, refiles**
REFILL *vb* fill again ▹ *n* second or subsequent filling **refills**
REFILM *vb* film again **refilms**
REFIND *vb* find again **refinds**
REFINE *vb*
REFINED *adj*
REFINER *n* person, device, or substance that removes impurities, etc
REFINES ▸ **refine**

REFIRE *vb* fire again **refired, refires**
REFIT *vb* make ready for use again by repairing or re-equipping ▷ *n* repair or re-equipping for further use **refits**
REFIX *vb* fix again **refixed, refixes**
REFLAG *vb* flag again **reflags**
REFLATE *vb* inflate or be inflated again
REFLECT *vb*
REFLET *n* iridescent glow or lustre, as on ceramic ware **reflets**
REFLEW ▸ refly
REFLEX *n, adj, vb*
REFLIES ▸ refly
REFLOAT *vb* float again
REFLOOD *vb* flood again
REFLOW *vb* flow again
REFLOWN ▸ refly
REFLOWS ▸ reflow
REFLUX *vb* boil in a vessel attached to a condenser, so that the vapour condenses and flows back in ▷ *n* act of refluxing
REFLY *vb* fly again
REFOCUS *vb* focus again or anew
REFOLD *vb* fold again **refolds**
REFOOT *vb* foot again **refoots**
REFORGE *vb* forge again
REFORM *n, vb* **reforms**
REFOUND *vb* found again
REFRACT *vb* change the course of (light etc) passing from one medium to another
REFRAIN *n, vb*
REFRAME *vb* support or enclose (a picture, photograph, etc) in a new or different frame
REFRESH *vb*
REFRIED ▸ refry
REFRIES ▸ refry
REFRONT *vb* put a new front on
REFROZE > **refreeze**
REFRY *vb* fry again
REFS ▸ ref
REFT ▸ reave
REFUEL *vb* **refuels**
REFUGE *n, vb* **refuged**
REFUGEE *n*
REFUGES ▸ refuge
REFUGIA > **refugium**
REFUND *vb, n* **refunds**
REFUSAL *n*
REFUSE *vb, n* **refused, refuser, refuses**
REFUTAL *n* act or process of refuting
REFUTE *vb* **refuted, refuter, refutes**
REG *n* large expanse of stony desert terrain
REGAIN *vb, n* **regains**
REGAL *adj, n*
REGALE *vb, n* **regaled, regaler, regales**
REGALIA *pl n*
REGALLY ▸ regal
REGALS ▸ regal
REGAR = **regur**
REGARD *vb, n* **regards**
REGARS ▸ regar
REGATTA *n*
REGAUGE *vb* gauge again
REGAVE ▸ regive
REGEAR *vb* readjust **regears**
REGENCE *old variant of* **▸ regency**
REGENCY *n*
REGENT *n, adj* **regents**
REGES ▸ rex
REGEST *n* archaic word for register **regests**
REGGAE *n* **reggaes**
REGGO = **rego**
REGGOS ▸ reggo
REGIE *n* government-directed management or government monopoly **regies**
REGIFT *vb* give (a previously received gift) to someone else **regifts**
REGILD *vb* gild again **regilds, regilt**
REGIME *n*
REGIMEN *n* prescribed system of diet etc
REGIMES ▸ regime
REGINA *n* queen **reginae**
REGINAL *adj* queenly
REGINAS ▸ regina
REGION *n* **regions**
REGIUS *adj as in* **regius professor** Crown-appointed holder of a university chair
REGIVE *vb* give again or back **regiven, regives**
REGLAZE *vb* glaze again
REGLET *n* flat narrow architectural moulding **reglets**

REGLOSS *vb* gloss again or give a new gloss to
REGLOW *vb* glow again **reglows**
REGLUE *vb* glue again **reglued, reglues**
REGMA *n* type of fruit with cells that break open and break away when ripe **regmata**
REGNA ▸ **regnum**
REGNAL *adj* of a sovereign, reign, or kingdom
REGNANT *adj* reigning
REGNUM *n* reign or rule
REGO *n* registration of a motor vehicle
REGORGE *vb* vomit up
REGOS ▸ **rego**
REGOSOL *n* type of azonal soil
REGRADE *vb* grade again
REGRAFT *vb* graft again
REGRANT *vb* grant again
REGRATE *vb* buy up (commodities) in advance so as to raise their price for resale
REGREDE *vb* go back
REGREEN *vb* green again
REGREET *vb* greet again or return greetings of
REGRESS *vb, n*
REGRET *vb, n* **regrets**
REGREW ▸ **regrow**
REGRIND *vb* grind again
REGROOM *vb* groom again
REGROUP *vb* reorganize (military forces) after an attack or a defeat
REGROW *vb* grow or be grown again after having been cut or having died or withered **regrown, regrows**
REGS ▸ **reg**
REGULA *n* rule **regulae**
REGULAR *adj, n*
REGULI ▸ **regulus**
REGULO *n* any of a number of temperatures to which a gas oven may be set **regulos**
REGULUS *n* impure metal forming beneath the slag during the smelting of ores
REGUR *n* black loamy Indian soil **regurs**
REH *n* (in India) salty surface crust on the soil
REHAB *vb* help (a person) to readapt to society or a new job ▷ *n* treatment or help given to an addict, etc **rehabs**
REHANG *vb* hang again **rehangs**
REHASH *vb, n*
REHEAR *vb* hear again **reheard, rehears**
REHEAT *vb* heat or be heated again **reheats**
REHEEL *vb* put a new heel or new heels on **reheels**
REHEM *vb* hem again **rehems**
REHINGE *vb* put a new hinge or new hinges on
REHIRE *vb* hire again **rehired, rehires**
REHOME *vb* find a new home for (esp a pet) **rehomed, rehomes**
REHOUSE *vb*
REHS ▸ **reh**
REHUNG ▸ **rehang**
REI *n* name for a former Portuguese coin
REIF *n* Scots word meaning robbery or plunder
REIFIED ▸ **reify**
REIFIER ▸ **reify**
REIFIES ▸ **reify**
REIFS ▸ **reif**
REIFY *vb* consider or make (an abstract idea or concept) real or concrete
REIGN *n, vb* **reigned, reigns**
REIK *Scots word for* ▸ **smoke**
REIKI *n* form of therapy to encourage healing or restore wellbeing **reikis**
REIKS ▸ **reik**
REIMAGE *vb* image again
REIN *vb*
REINCUR *vb* incur again
REINDEX *vb* index again
REINED ▸ **rein**
REINING ▸ **rein**
REINK *vb* ink again **reinked, reinks**
REINS *pl n* narrow straps attached to a bit to guide a horse

REINTER *vb* inter again
REIRD *Scots word for* ▶ **din**
REIRDS ▶ **reird**
REIS ▶ **rei**
REISES ▶ **rei**
REISSUE *n* book, record, etc, that is released again after being unavailable ▷ *vb* release (a book, record, etc) again after a period of unavailability
REIST = **reest**
REISTED ▶ **reist**
REISTS ▶ **reist**
REITBOK = **reedbuck**
REITER *n* soldier in the German cavalry **reiters**
REIVE *vb* go on a plundering raid **reived, reiver, reivers, reives, reiving**
REJECT *vb, n* **rejects**
REJIG *vb* re-equip (a factory or plant) ▷ *n* act or process of rejigging **rejigs**
REJOICE *vb*
REJOIN *vb* **rejoins**
REJON *n* bullfighting lance
REJONEO *n* bullfighting activity in which a mounted bullfighter spears the bull with lances
REJONES ▶ **rejon**
REJOURN *vb* archaic word meaning postpone or adjourn
REJUDGE *vb* judge again
REKE = **reck**
REKED ▶ **reke**
REKES ▶ **reke**
REKEY *vb* key again **rekeyed, rekeys**
REKING ▶ **reke**
REKNIT *vb* knit again **reknits**
REKNOT *vb* knot again **reknots**
RELABEL *vb* label again
RELACE *vb* lace again **relaced, relaces**
RELACHE *n* break
RELAID ▶ **relay**
RELAND *vb* land again **relands**
RELAPSE *vb, n*
RELATA ▶ **relatum**
RELATE *vb*
RELATED *adj*
RELATER ▶ **relate**
RELATES ▶ **relate**
RELATOR *n* person who relates a story
RELATUM *n* one of the objects between which a relation is said to hold
RELAX *vb* **relaxed**
RELAXER *n* person or thing that relaxes
RELAXES ▶ **relax**
RELAXIN *n* hormone secreted during pregnancy
RELAY *n, vb* **relayed, relays**
RELEARN *vb* learn (something previously known) again
RELEASE *vb, n*
RELEND *vb* lend again **relends**
RELENT *vb* **relents**
RELET *vb* let again **relets**
RELEVE *n* dance move in which heels are off the ground **releves**
RELIANT > **reliance**
RELIC *n* **relics**
RELICT *n* relic **relicts**
RELIDE *archaic past form of* ▶ **rely**
RELIE *archaic spelling of* ▶ **rely**
RELIED ▶ **rely**
RELIEF *n* **reliefs**
RELIER ▶ **rely**
RELIERS ▶ **rely**
RELIES ▶ **rely**
RELIEVE *vb*
RELIEVO = **relief**
RELIGHT *vb* ignite or cause to ignite again
RELINE *vb* line again or anew **relined, relines**
RELINK *vb* link again **relinks**
RELIQUE *archaic spelling of* ▶ **relic**
RELISH *vb, n*
RELIST *vb* list again **relists**
RELIT ▶ **relight**
RELIVE *vb* **relived**
RELIVER *vb* deliver up again
RELIVES ▶ **relive**
RELLENO *n* Mexican dish of stuffed vegetable
RELLIE *n* relative
RELLIES *pl n* relatives or relations
RELLISH *(in music) variant of* ▶ **relish**

RELOAD *vb* put fresh ammunition into (a firearm) **reloads**
RELOAN *vb* loan again **reloans**
RELOCK *vb* lock again **relocks**
RELOOK *vb* look again **relooks**
RELUCT *vb* struggle or rebel **relucts**
RELUME *vb* light or brighten again **relumed, relumes**
RELY *vb* **relying**
REM *n* dose of ionizing radiation
REMADE *n* object that has been reconstructed from original materials **remades**
REMAIL *vb* mail again **remails**
REMAIN *vb*
REMAINS *pl n* relics, esp of ancient buildings
REMAKE *vb* make again in a different way ▷ *n* new version of an old film **remaker, remakes**
REMAN *vb* man again or afresh
REMAND *vb* **remands**
REMANET *n* something left over
REMANIE *n* fragments and fossils of older origin found in a more recent deposit
REMANS ▸ **reman**
REMAP *vb* map again **remaps**
REMARK *vb, n* **remarks**
REMARRY *vb*
REMATCH *n* second or return game or contest between two players ▷ *vb* match (two contestants) again
REMATE *vb* mate again ▷ *n* finishing pass in bullfighting **remated, remates**
REMBLAI *n* earth used for an embankment or rampart
REMBLE *dialect word for* ▸ **remove**
REMBLED ▸ **remble**
REMBLES ▸ **remble**
REMEAD *archaic or dialect word for* ▸ **remedy**
REMEADS ▸ **remead**
REMEDE *archaic or dialect word for* ▸ **remedy**
REMEDED ▸ **remede**
REMEDES ▸ **remede**
REMEDY *n, vb*
REMEET *vb* meet again **remeets**
REMEID *archaic or dialect word for* ▸ **remedy**
REMEIDS ▸ **remeid**
REMELT *vb* melt again **remelts**
REMEN *n* ancient Egyptian measurement unit
REMEND *vb* mend again **remends**
REMENS ▸ **remen**
REMERCY *vb* archaic word for thank
REMERGE *vb* merge again
REMET ▸ **remeet**
REMEX *n* any of the large flight feathers of a bird's wing **remiges**
REMIND *vb* **reminds**
REMINT *vb* mint again **remints**
REMISE *vb* give up or relinquish (a right, claim, etc) ▷ *n* second thrust made on the same lunge after the first has missed **remised, remises**
REMISS *adj*
REMIT *vb, n* **remits**
REMIX *vb* change the relative prominence of each performer's part of (a recording) ▷ *n* remixed version of a recording **remixed, remixes, remixt**
REMNANT *n, adj*
REMODEL *vb* give a different shape or form to ▷ *n* something that has been remodelled
REMOLD *US spelling of* ▸ **remould**
REMOLDS ▸ **remold**
REMORA *n* spiny-finned fish **remoras, remorid**
REMORSE *n*
REMOTE *adj, n* **remoter, remotes**
REMOUD *Spenserian variant of* ▸ **removed**
REMOULD *vb, n*
REMOUNT *vb* get on (a horse, bicycle, etc) again ▷ *n* fresh horse

REMOVAL *n*
REMOVE *vb, n*
REMOVED *adj*
REMOVER ▸ **remove**
REMOVES ▸ **remove**
REMS ▸ **rem**
REMUAGE *n* process of turning wine bottles to let the sediment out
REMUDA *n* stock of horses enabling riders to change mounts **remudas**
REMUEUR *n* person carrying out remuage
REN *archaic variant of* ▸ **run**
RENAGUE = **renege**
RENAIL *vb* nail again **renails**
RENAL *adj*
RENAME *vb* **renamed, renames**
RENAY *vb* archaic word meaning renounce **renayed, renays**
REND *vb* tear or wrench apart **rended**
RENDER *vb, n* **renders**
RENDING ▸ **rend**
RENDS ▸ **rend**
RENEGE *vb* **reneged, reneger, reneges, renegue**
RENEST *vb* nest again or form a new nest **renests**
RENEW *vb*
RENEWAL *n* act of renewing or state of being renewed
RENEWED ▸ **renew**
RENEWER ▸ **renew**
RENEWS ▸ **renew**
RENEY = **renay**
RENEYED ▸ **reney**
RENEYS ▸ **reney**
RENGA *n* type of collaborative poetry found in Japan **rengas**
RENIED ▸ **reny**
RENIES ▸ **reny**
RENIG = **renege**
RENIGS ▸ **renig**
RENIN *n* enzyme secreted by the kidneys **renins**
RENK *adj* unpleasant **renker, renkest**
RENNASE = **rennin**
RENNE *archaic variant of* ▸ **run**
RENNED ▸ **ren**
RENNES ▸ **renne**
RENNET *n* **rennets**
RENNIN *n* enzyme that occurs in gastric juice
RENNING ▸ **ren**
RENNINS ▸ **rennin**
RENOWN *n* widespread good reputation ▹ *vb* make famous **renowns**
RENS ▸ **ren**
RENT *n* payment made by a tenant to a landlord or owner of a property ▹ *vb* grant the right to use one's property for payment
RENTAL *n, adj* **rentals**
RENTE *n* annual income from capital investment
RENTED ▸ **rent**
RENTER *n* person who lets his property in return for rent **renters**
RENTES ▸ **rente**
RENTIER *n* person who lives off unearned income such as rents or interest
RENTING ▸ **rent**
RENTS ▸ **rent**
RENVOI *n* referring of a dispute to a jurisdiction other than that in which it arose **renvois, renvoy**
RENVOYS ▸ **renvoy**
RENY = **renay**
RENYING ▸ **reny**
REO *n* New Zealand language
REOCCUR *vb* happen, take place, or come about again
REOFFER *vb* offer again
REOIL *vb* oil again **reoiled, reoils**
REOPEN *vb* open again after a period of being closed or suspended **reopens**
REORDER *vb* change the order of
REOS ▸ **reo**
REP *n, vb*
REPACK *vb* place or arrange (articles) in (a container) again or in a different way **repacks**
REPAID ▸ **repay**
REPAINT *vb* apply a new or fresh coat of paint
REPAIR *vb, n* **repairs**
REPAND *adj* having a wavy margin
REPANEL *vb* panel again or anew

REPAPER *vb* paper again or afresh
REPARK *vb* park again **reparks**
REPASS *vb* pass again
REPAST *n, vb* **repasts**
REPATCH *vb* patch again
REPAVE *vb* pave again **repaved, repaves**
REPAY *vb* **repays**
REPEAL *vb, n* **repeals**
REPEAT *vb, n* **repeats**
REPEG *vb* peg again **repegs**
REPEL *vb* **repels**
REPENT *vb, adj* **repents**
REPERK *vb* perk again **reperks**
REPIN *vb* pin again
REPINE *vb* fret or complain **repined, repiner, repines**
REPINS ▸ **repin**
REPIQUE *n* score of 30 in the card-game piquet ▹ *vb* score a repique against (someone)
REPLA ▸ **replum**
REPLACE *vb*
REPLAN *vb* plan again **replans**
REPLANT *vb* plant again
REPLATE *vb* plate again
REPLAY *n, vb* **replays**
REPLEAD *vb* plead again **repled**
REPLETE *adj, vb*
REPLEVY *vb* recover possession of (goods) by replevin
REPLICA *n*
REPLIED ▸ **reply**
REPLIER ▸ **reply**
REPLIES ▸ **reply**
REPLOT *vb* plot again **replots**
REPLOW *vb* plow again **replows**
REPLUM *n* internal separating wall in some fruits
REPLUMB *vb* plumb again
REPLY *vb, n*
REPO *n* act of repossessing
REPOINT *vb* repair the joints of (brickwork, masonry, etc) with mortar or cement
REPOLL *vb* poll again **repolls**
REPOMAN *n* man employed to repossess goods in cases of non-payment **repomen**
REPONE *vb* restore (someone) to his former status, office, etc **reponed, repones**
REPORT *vb, n* **reports**
REPOS ▸ **repo**
REPOSAL *n* repose
REPOSE *n, vb* **reposed, reposer, reposes**
REPOSIT *vb* put away, deposit, or store up
REPOST *vb* post again **reposts**
REPOT *vb* put (a house plant) into a new usually larger pot **repots**
REPOUR *vb* pour back or again **repours**
REPOWER *vb* put new engine in
REPP = **rep**
REPPED ▸ **rep**
REPPING ▸ **rep**
REPPS ▸ **repp**
REPRESS *vb*
REPRICE *vb* price again
REPRIME *vb* prime again
REPRINT *vb, n*
REPRISE *n* repeating of an earlier theme ▹ *vb* repeat an earlier theme
REPRIVE *archaic spelling of* > **reprieve**
REPRIZE *archaic spelling of* ▸ **reprise**
REPRO *n* imitation or facsimile of a work of art; reproduction
REPROBE *vb* probe again
REPROOF *n, vb*
REPROS ▸ **repro**
REPROVE *vb*
REPRYVE *archaic spelling of* > **reprieve**
REPS ▸ **rep**
REPTANT *adj* creeping, crawling, or lying along the ground
REPTILE *n, adj*
REPUGN *vb* oppose or conflict (with) **repugns**
REPULP *vb* pulp again **repulps**
REPULSE *vb, n*
REPUMP *vb* pump again **repumps**
REPUNIT *n* any number that consists entirely

of the same repeated digits
REPURE *vb* archaic word meaning make pure again **repured, repures**
REPUTE *n, vb*
REPUTED *adj*
REPUTES ▸ **repute**
REQUERE *archaic variant of* ▸ **require**
REQUEST *vb, n*
REQUIEM *n*
REQUIN *n* type of shark **requins**
REQUIRE *vb*
REQUIT *vb* quit again
REQUITE *vb* return to someone (the same treatment or feeling as received)
REQUITS ▸ **requit**
REQUOTE *vb* quote again
RERACK *vb* rack again **reracks**
RERAIL *vb* put back on a railway line **rerails**
RERAISE *vb* raise again
RERAN ▸ **rerun**
REREAD *vb* read (something) again **rereads**
REREDOS *n* ornamental screen behind an altar
REREMAI *n* New Zealand word for the basking shark
RERENT *vb* rent again **rerents**
RERIG *vb* rig again **rerigs**
RERISE *vb* rise again **rerisen, rerises**
REROLL *vb* roll again **rerolls**
REROOF *vb* put a new roof or roofs on **reroofs**
REROSE ▸ **rerise**
REROUTE *vb*
RERUN *n* film or programme that is broadcast again, repeat ▹ *vb* put on (a film or programme) again **reruns**
RES *informal word for* > **residence**
RESAID ▸ **resay**
RESAIL *vb* sail again **resails**
RESALE *n* selling of something purchased earlier **resales**
RESAT ▸ **resit**
RESAW *vb* saw again **resawed, resawn, resaws**
RESAY *vb* say again or in response **resays**
RESCALE *vb* resize
RESCIND *vb*
RESCORE *vb* score afresh
RESCUE *vb, n* **rescued, rescuer, rescues**
RESEAL *vb* close or secure tightly again **reseals**
RESEAT *vb* show (a person) to a new seat **reseats**
RESEAU *n* mesh background to a lace or other pattern **reseaus, reseaux**
RESECT *vb* cut out part of (a bone, an organ, or other structure or part) **resects**
RESEDA *n* plant that has small spikes of grey-green flowers ▹ *adj* of a greyish-green colour **resedas**
RESEE *vb* see again
RESEED *vb* form seed and reproduce naturally, forming a constant plant population **reseeds**
RESEEK *vb* seek again **reseeks**
RESEEN ▸ **resee**
RESEES ▸ **resee**
RESEIZE *vb* seize again
RESELL *vb* sell (something) one has previously bought **resells**
RESEND *vb* send again **resends**
RESENT *vb* **resents**
RESERVE *vb, n*
RESES ▸ **res**
RESET *vb* set again (a broken bone, matter in type, a gemstone, etc) ▹ *n* act or an instance of setting again **resets**
RESEW *vb* sew again **resewed, resewn, resews**
RESH *n* 20th letter of the Hebrew alphabet
RESHAPE *vb* shape (something) again or differently
RESHAVE *vb* shave again
RESHES ▸ **resh**
RESHINE *vb* shine again

RESHIP *vb* ship again **reships**
RESHOD ▸ **reshoe**
RESHOE *vb* put a new shoe or shoes on **reshoed, reshoes**
RESHONE ▸ **reshine**
RESHOOT *vb* shoot again **reshot**
RESHOW *vb* show again **reshown, reshows**
RESIANT *archaic word for* > **resident**
RESID *n* residual oil left over from the petroleum distillation process
RESIDE *vb* **resided, resider, resides**
RESIDS ▸ **resid**
RESIDUA > **residuum**
RESIDUE *n*
RESIFT *vb* sift again **resifts**
RESIGHT *vb* sight again
RESIGN *vb* **resigns**
RESILE *vb* spring or shrink back **resiled, resiles**
RESILIN *n* substance found in insect bodies
RESIN *n, vb* **resined**
RESINER *n* applier or collector of resin
RESINS ▸ **resin**
RESINY *adj* resembling, containing or covered with resin
RESIST *vb, n* **resists**
RESIT *vb* take (an exam) again ▹ *n* exam that has to be taken again
RESITE *vb* move to a different site **resited, resites**
RESITS ▸ **resit**
RESIZE *vb* change size of **resized, resizes**
RESKEW *archaic spelling of* ▸ **rescue**
RESKEWS ▸ **reskew**
RESKILL *vb* train (workers) to acquire new skills
RESKUE *archaic spelling of* ▸ **rescue**
RESKUED ▸ **reskue**
RESKUES ▸ **reskue**
RESLATE *vb* slate again
RESMELT *vb* smelt again
RESOAK *vb* soak again **resoaks**
RESOD *vb* returf **resods**
RESOJET *n* type of jet engine
RESOLD ▸ **resell**
RESOLE *vb* put a new sole or new soles on **resoled, resoles**
RESOLVE *vb, n*
RESORB *vb* absorb again **resorbs**
RESORT *vb, n* **resorts**
RESOUND *vb*
RESOW *vb* sow again **resowed, resown, resows**
RESPACE *vb* change the spacing of
RESPADE *vb* dig over
RESPEAK *vb* speak further
RESPECT *n, vb*
RESPELL *vb* spell again **respelt**
RESPIRE *vb*
RESPITE *n, vb*
RESPLIT *vb* split again
RESPOKE ▸ **respeak**
RESPOND *vb, n*
RESPOOL *vb* rewind onto spool
RESPOT *vb* (in billiards) replace on one of the spots **respots**
RESPRAY *n* new coat of paint applied to a car, van, etc ▹ *vb* spray (a car, wheels, etc) with a new coat of paint
REST *n, vb*
RESTACK *vb* stack again
RESTAFF *vb* staff again
RESTAGE *vb* produce or perform a new production of (a play)
RESTAMP *vb* stamp again
RESTART *vb* commence (something) or set (something) in motion again ▹ *n* act or an instance of starting again
RESTATE *vb* state or affirm (something) again or in a different way
RESTED ▸ **rest**
RESTEM *vb* stem again **restems**
RESTER ▸ **rest**
RESTERS ▸ **rest**
RESTFUL *adj*
RESTIER ▸ **resty**
RESTIFF = **restive**
RESTING ▸ **rest**
RESTIVE *adj*
RESTO *n* restored antique, vintage car, etc
RESTOCK *vb* replenish stores or supplies

RESTOKE *vb* stoke again
RESTORE *vb*
RESTOS ▸ **resto**
RESTS ▸ **rest**
RESTUDY *vb* study again
RESTUFF *vb* put new stuffing in
RESTUMP *vb* provide with new stumps
RESTY *adj* restive
RESTYLE *vb* style again
RESULT *n, vb* **results**
RESUME *vb, n* **resumed, resumer, resumes**
RESURGE *vb* rise again from or as if from the dead
RET *vb* moisten or soak (flax, hemp, jute, etc) to facilitate separation of fibres
RETABLE *n* ornamental screenlike structure above and behind an altar
RETACK *vb* tack again **retacks**
RETAG *vb* tag again **retags**
RETAIL *n, adj, adv, vb* **retails**
RETAIN *vb* **retains**

Perhaps the most important word in Scrabble, because its letters combine with every other letter apart from A, Q, V, X, Y and Z to form a 7-letter bonus word that will score you an extra 50 points, so if you have these six letters on your rack you know that a bonus is either available or very close. And if you have an S as well, so much the better, because not only does this rack offer you 11 different words to choose from, but if none of those can be fitted in then RETAINS combines with every other letter except for Q, V, X, Y and Z to form at least one eight-letter word.

RETAKE *vb* recapture ▷ *n* act of rephotographing a scene **retaken, retaker, retakes**
RETALLY *vb* count up again
RETAMA *n* type of shrub **retamas**
RETAPE *vb* tape again **retaped, retapes**
RETARD *vb, n* **retards**
RETASTE *vb* taste again
RETAX *vb* tax again **retaxed, retaxes**
RETCH *vb, n* **retched, retches**
RETE *n* any network of nerves or blood vessels
RETEACH *vb* teach again
RETEAM *vb* team up again **reteams**
RETEAR *vb* tear again **retears**
RETELL *vb* relate (a story, etc) again or differently **retells**
RETEM *n* type of shrub **retems**
RETENE *n* yellow crystalline hydrocarbon found in tar oils **retenes**
RETEST *vb* test (something) again or differently **retests**
RETHINK *vb, n*
RETIA ▸ **rete**
RETIAL ▸ **rete**
RETIARY *adj* of, relating to, or resembling a net or web
RETICLE *n* network of fine lines, wires, etc, used in optical instruments
RETIE *vb* tie again **retied, reties**
RETILE *vb* put new tiles in or on **retiled, retiles**
RETIME *vb* time again or alter time of **retimed, retimes**
RETINA *n* **retinae**
RETINAL *adj* of or relating to the retina ▷ *n* aldehyde form of the polyene retinol
RETINAS ▸ **retina**
RETINE *n* chemical found in body cells that slows cell growth and division **retines**
RETINOL *n* another name for vitamin A and rosin oil

RETINT *vb* tint again or change tint of **retints**
RETINUE *n*
RETIRAL *n* act of retiring from office, one's work, etc
RETIRE *vb*
RETIRED *adj* having retired from work etc
RETIREE *n* person who has retired from work
RETIRER ▸ **retire**
RETIRES ▸ **retire**
RETITLE *vb* give a new title to
RETOLD ▸ **retell**
RETOOK ▸ **retake**
RETOOL *vb* replace, re-equip, or rearrange the tools in (a factory, etc) **retools**
RETORE ▸ **retear**
RETORN ▸ **retear**
RETORT *vb, n* **retorts**
RETOTAL *vb* add up again
RETOUCH *vb, n*
RETOUR *vb* (in Scottish law) to return as heir **retours**
RETRACE *vb*
RETRACK *vb* track again
RETRACT *vb*
RETRAIN *vb* train to do a new or different job
RETRAIT *archaic form of* ▸ **retreat**
RETRAL *adj* at, near, or towards the back
RETRATE *archaic form of* ▸ **retreat**
RETREAD *n, vb*
RETREAT *vb, n*
RETREE *n* imperfectly made paper **retrees**
RETRIAL *n* second trial of a case or defendant in a court of law
RETRIED ▸ **retry**
RETRIES ▸ **retry**
RETRIM *vb* trim again **retrims**
RETRO *adj* associated with or revived from the past ▹ *n* a retro style of art
RETROD ▸ **retread**
RETROS ▸ **retro**
RETRY *vb* try again (a case already determined)
RETS ▸ **ret**
RETSINA *n* Greek wine flavoured with resin
RETTED ▸ **ret**
RETTERY *n* flax-retting place
RETTING ▸ **ret**
RETUND *vb* weaken or blunt **retunds**
RETUNE *vb* tune (a musical instrument) differently or again **retuned, retunes**
RETURF *vb* turf again **returfs**
RETURN *vb, n, adj* **returns**
RETUSE *adj* having a rounded apex and a central depression
RETWIST *vb* twist again
RETYING ▸ **retie**
RETYPE *vb* type again **retyped, retypes**
REUNIFY *vb* bring together again something previously divided
REUNION *n*
REUNITE *vb*
REURGE *vb* urge again **reurged, reurges**
REUSE *vb* use again ▹ *n* act of using something again **reused, reuses, reusing**
REUTTER *vb* utter again
REV *n, vb*
REVALUE *vb*
REVAMP *vb, n* **revamps**
REVEAL *vb, n* **reveals**
REVEL *vb, n* **reveled, reveler**
REVELRY *n* festivity
REVELS ▸ **revel**
REVENGE *n, vb*
REVENUE *n*
REVERB *n* electronic device that creates artificial acoustics ▹ *vb* reverberate **reverbs**
REVERE *vb* **revered, reverer, reveres**
REVERIE *n*
REVERS *n*
REVERSE *vb, n, adj*
REVERSI *n* game played on a draughtboard
REVERSO *another name for* ▸ **verso**
REVERT *vb* **reverts**
REVERY = **reverie**
REVEST *vb* restore (former power, authority, status, etc, to a person) **revests**
REVET *vb* face (a wall or embankment) with stones **revets**
REVEUR *n* daydreamer **reveurs**

REVEUSE *n* female daydreamer
REVIE *vb* archaic cards term meaning challenge by placing a larger stake **revied, revies**
REVIEW *n, vb* **reviews**
REVILE *vb* be abusively scornful of **reviled, reviler, reviles**
REVISAL ▶ **revise**
REVISE *vb, n* **revised, reviser, revises**
REVISIT *vb* visit again
REVISOR ▶ **revise**
REVIVAL *n* reviving or renewal
REVIVE *vb* **revived, reviver, revives**
REVIVOR *n* means of reviving a lawsuit that has been suspended
REVOICE *vb* utter again
REVOKE *vb, n* **revoked, revoker, revokes**
REVOLT *n, vb* **revolts**
REVOLVE *vb, n*
REVOTE *vb* decide or grant again by a new vote **revoted, revotes**
REVS ▶ **rev**
REVUE *n* **revues, revuist**
REVVED ▶ **rev**
REVVING ▶ **rev**
REVYING ▶ **revie**
REW *archaic spelling of* ▶ **rue**
REWAKE *vb* awaken again **rewaked**
REWAKEN *vb* awaken again
REWAKES ▶ **rewake**
REWAN *archaic past form of* ▶ **rewin**
REWARD *n, vb* **rewards**
REWARM *vb* warm again **rewarms**
REWASH *vb* wash again
REWATER *vb* water again
REWAX *vb* wax again **rewaxed, rewaxes**
REWEAR *vb* wear again **rewears**
REWEAVE *vb* weave again
REWED *vb* wed again **reweds**
REWEIGH *vb* weigh again
REWELD *vb* weld again **rewelds**
REWET *vb* wet again **rewets**
REWIDEN *vb* widen again
REWIN *vb* win again
REWIND *vb* **rewinds**
REWINS ▶ **rewin**
REWIRE *vb* provide (a house, engine, etc) with new wiring **rewired, rewires**
REWOKE ▶ **rewake**
REWOKEN ▶ **rewake**
REWON ▶ **rewin**
REWORD *vb* alter the wording of **rewords**
REWORE ▶ **rewear**
REWORK *vb* improve or bring up to date **reworks**
REWORN ▶ **rewear**
REWOUND ▶ **rewind**
REWOVE ▶ **reweave**
REWOVEN ▶ **reweave**
REWRAP *vb* wrap again **rewraps, rewrapt**
REWRITE *vb, n* **rewrote**
REWS ▶ **rew**
REWTH *archaic variant of* ▶ **ruth**
REWTHS ▶ **rewth**
REX *n* king **rexes**

> **Rex** is a Latin word for **king**, a very commonly played X word.

REXINE *n* tradename for a form of artificial leather **rexines**
REYNARD *n* fox
REZ *n* informal word for an instance of reserving; reservation

> **Rez** is a short informal word for **reservation**, and is one of the most commonly played Z words.

REZERO *vb* reset to zero **rezeros**
REZONE *vb* zone again **rezoned, rezones**
REZZES ▶ **rez**
RHABDOM *n* rodlike structures found in the eye of insects
RHABDUS *n* sponge spicule
RHACHIS = **rachis**
RHAMNUS *n* buckthorn
RHANJA *n* Indian English word for a male lover **rhanjas**
RHAPHAE ▶ **rhaphe**
RHAPHE = **raphe**
RHAPHES ▶ **rhaphe**
RHAPHIS = **raphide**

RHATANY *n* South American leguminous shrub
RHEA *n* **rheas**
RHEBOK *n* woolly brownish-grey southern African antelope **rheboks**
RHEME *n* constituent of a sentence that adds most new information **rhemes**
RHENIUM *n* silvery-white metallic element with a high melting point
RHESUS *n*
RHETOR *n* teacher of rhetoric **rhetors**
RHEUM *n* watery discharge from the eyes or nose
RHEUMED *adj* rheumy
RHEUMIC *adj* of or relating to rheum
RHEUMS ▶ **rheum**
RHEUMY *adj* of the nature of rheum
RHEXES ▶ **rhexis**
RHEXIS *n* rupture
RHIES ▶ **rhy**
RHIME *old spelling of* ▶ **rhyme**
RHIMES ▶ **rhime**
RHINAL *adj* of or relating to the nose
RHINE *n* dialect word for a ditch **rhines**
RHINO *n* **rhinos**
RHIZIC *adj* of or relating to the root of an equation
RHIZINE = **rhizoid**
RHIZOID *n* hairlike structure in mosses, ferns, and related plants
RHIZOMA = **rhizome**
RHIZOME *n*
RHIZOPI > **rhizopus**
RHO *n* 17th letter in the Greek alphabet

> It's useful to remember words that start with RH, as they can come in useful. If you or someone else plays rho, which is a Greek letter, remember that it can be expanded to, for example, **rhody, rhomb, rhodium, rhombus** or **rhomboid**.

RHODIC *adj* of or containing rhodium, esp in the tetravalent state
RHODIE = **rhody**
RHODIES ▶ **rhody**
RHODIUM *n*
RHODORA *n* type of shrub
RHODOUS *adj* of or containing rhodium (but proportionally more than a rhodic compound)
RHODY *n* rhododendron
RHOMB = **rhombus**
RHOMBI ▶ **rhombus**
RHOMBIC *adj* relating to or having the shape of a rhombus
RHOMBOI ▶ **rhombos**
RHOMBOS *n* wooden slat attached to a thong that makes a roaring sound when the thong is whirled
RHOMBS ▶ **rhomb**
RHOMBUS *n*
RHONCHI > **rhonchus**
RHONE = **rone**
RHONES ▶ **rhone**
RHOS ▶ **rho**
RHOTIC *adj* denoting or speaking a dialect of English in which postvocalic *r* s are pronounced
RHUBARB *n, interj, vb*
RHUMB *n as in* **rhumb line** imaginary line on the surface of a sphere that intersects all meridians at the same angle
RHUMBA = **rumba**
RHUMBAS ▶ **rhumba**
RHUMBS ▶ **rhumb**
RHUS *n* genus of shrubs and small trees **rhuses**
RHY *archaic spelling of* ▶ **rye**

> This alternative spelling of **rye** can come in useful when you are short of vowels.

RHYME *n, vb* **rhymed**
RHYMER = **rhymester**
RHYMERS ▶ **rhymer**
RHYMES ▶ **rhyme**
RHYMING ▶ **rhyme**
RHYMIST ▶ **rhyme**
RHYNE = **rhine**
RHYNES ▶ **rhyne**
RHYTA ▶ **rhyton**
RHYTHM *n*

RHYTHMI > **rhythmus**
RHYTHMS ▶ **rhythm**
RHYTINA *n* type of sea cow
RHYTON *n* (in ancient Greece) horn-shaped drinking vessel **rhytons**
RIA *n* long narrow inlet of the seacoast
RIAD *n* traditional Moroccan house with an interior garden **riads**
RIAL *n* standard monetary unit of Iran **rials**
RIALTO *n* market or exchange **rialtos**
RIANCY ▶ **riant**
RIANT *adj* laughing **riantly**
RIAS ▶ **ria**
RIATA = **reata**
RIATAS ▶ **riata**
RIB *n*, *vb*
RIBA *n* (in Islam) interest or usury
RIBALD *adj*, *n* **ribalds**
RIBAND *n* ribbon awarded for some achievement **ribands**
RIBAS ▶ **riba**
RIBAUD *archaic variant of* ▶ **ribald**
RIBAUDS ▶ **ribaud**
RIBBAND = **riband**
RIBBED ▶ **rib**
RIBBER *n* someone who ribs **ribbers**
RIBBIER ▶ **ribby**
RIBBING ▶ **rib**
RIBBON *n*, *vb* **ribbons, ribbony**
RIBBY *adj* with noticeable ribs
RIBCAGE *n*
RIBES *n* genus of shrubs that includes currants
RIBEYE *n* beefsteak cut from the outer side of the rib section **ribeyes**
RIBIBE *n* rebeck **ribibes, ribible**
RIBIER *n* variety of grape **ribiers**
RIBLESS ▶ **rib**
RIBLET *n* small rib **riblets**
RIBLIKE ▶ **rib**
RIBOSE *n* pentose sugar that occurs in RNA and riboflavin **riboses**
RIBS ▶ **rib**
RIBSTON *n* variety of apple
RIBWORK *n* work or structure involving ribs
RIBWORT *n* Eurasian plant with lancelike ribbed leaves
RICE *n*, *vb* **riced**
RICER *n* kitchen utensil through which soft foods are pressed to form a coarse mash **ricers**
RICES ▶ **rice**
RICEY *adj* resembling or containing rice
RICH *adj*, *vb* **riched**
RICHEN *vb* enrich **richens**
RICHER ▶ **rich**
RICHES *pl n* wealth
RICHEST ▶ **rich**
RICHING ▶ **rich**
RICHLY *adv*
RICHT *adj*, *adv*, *n*, *vb* right **richted, richter, richts**
RICIER ▶ **ricy**
RICIEST ▶ **ricy**
RICIN *n* highly toxic protein, a lectin, derived from castor-oil seeds
RICING ▶ **rice**
RICINS ▶ **ricin**
RICINUS *n* genus of plants
RICK *n*, *vb* **ricked**
RICKER *n* young kauri tree of New Zealand **rickers**
RICKET *n* mistake
RICKETS *n*
RICKETY *adj*
RICKEY *n* cocktail consisting of gin or vodka, lime juice, and soda water, served iced **rickeys**
RICKING ▶ **rick**
RICKLE *n* unsteady or shaky structure **rickles**
RICKLY *adj* archaic word for run-down or rickety
RICKS ▶ **rick**
RICKSHA = **rickshaw**
RICOTTA *n* soft white unsalted Italian cheese made from sheep's milk
RICRAC = **rickrack**
RICRACS ▶ **ricrac**
RICTAL ▶ **rictus**
RICTUS *n* gape or cleft of an open mouth or beak
RICY = **ricey**
RID *vb*

RIDABLE ▸ **ride**
RIDDED ▸ **rid**
RIDDEN ▸ **ride**
RIDDER ▸ **rid**
RIDDERS ▸ **rid**
RIDDING ▸ **rid**
RIDDLE *n, vb* **riddled, riddler, riddles**
RIDE *vb, n*
RIDENT *adj* laughing, smiling, or gay
RIDER *n* **ridered, riders**
RIDES ▸ **ride**
RIDGE *n, vb* **ridged**
RIDGEL = **ridgeling**
RIDGELS ▸ **ridgel**
RIDGER *n* plough used to form furrows and ridges **ridgers**
RIDGES ▸ **ridge**
RIDGIER ▸ **ridge**
RIDGIL = **ridgeling**
RIDGILS ▸ **ridgil**
RIDGING ▸ **ridge**
RIDGY ▸ **ridge**
RIDING ▸ **ride**
RIDINGS ▸ **ride**
RIDLEY *n* marine turtle **ridleys**
RIDOTTO *n* entertainment with music and dancing, often in masquerade
RIDS ▸ **rid**
RIEL *n* standard monetary unit of Cambodia **riels**
RIEM *n* strip of hide
RIEMPIE *n* leather thong or lace used mainly to make chair seats
RIEMS ▸ **riem**
RIEVE *n* archaic word for rob or plunder
RIEVER *n* archaic word for robber or plunderer **rievers**
RIEVES ▸ **rieve**
RIEVING ▸ **rieve**
RIF *vb* lay off
RIFE *adj* **rifely, rifer, rifest**
RIFF *n* short repeated melodic figure ▹ *vb* play or perform riffs in jazz or rock music
RIFFAGE *n* (in jazz or rock music) act or an instance of playing a short series of chords
RIFFED ▸ **riff**
RIFFING ▸ **riff**
RIFFLE *vb, n* **riffled**
RIFFLER *n* file with a curved face for filing concave surfaces
RIFFLES ▸ **riffle**
RIFFOLA *n* use of an abundance of dominant riffs
RIFFS ▸ **riff**
RIFLE *n, vb* **rifled, rifler, riflers**
RIFLERY *n* rifle shots
RIFLES ▸ **rifle**
RIFLING *n* cutting of spiral grooves on the inside of a firearm's barrel
RIFLIP *n* genetic difference between two individuals **riflips**
RIFS ▸ **rif**
RIFT *n, vb* **rifte, rifted, riftier, rifting, rifts, rifty**
RIG *vb, n*
RIGG *n* type of fish
RIGGALD = **ridgeling**
RIGGED ▸ **rig**
RIGGER *n* workman who rigs vessels, etc **riggers**
RIGGING ▸ **rig**
RIGGISH *adj* dialect word meaning wanton
RIGGS ▸ **rigg**
RIGHT *adj* just ▹ *adv* correctly ▹ *n* claim, title, etc allowed or due ▹ *vb* bring or come back to a normal or correct state **righted**
RIGHTEN *vb* set right
RIGHTER ▸ **right**
RIGHTLY *adv* in accordance with the true facts or justice
RIGHTO *interj* expression of agreement or compliance
RIGHTS ▸ **right**
RIGHTY *n* informal word for a right-winger
RIGID *adj, adv, n* **rigider, rigidly, rigids**
RIGLIN = **ridgeling**
RIGLING = **ridgeling**
RIGLINS ▸ **riglin**
RIGOL *n* (in dialect) ditch or gutter **rigoll**
RIGOLLS ▸ **rigoll**
RIGOLS ▸ **rigol**
RIGOR = **rigour**
RIGORS ▸ **rigor**
RIGOUR *n* **rigours**
RIGOUT *n* person's clothing **rigouts**

RIGS ▸ **rig**
RIKISHA = **rickshaw**
RIKISHI *n* sumo wrestler
RIKSHAW = **rickshaw**
RILE *vb* **riled, riles**
RILEY *adj* cross or irritable **rilier, riliest**
RILIEVI ▸ **rilievo**
RILIEVO = **relief**
RILING ▸ **rile**
RILL *n* small stream ▹ *vb* trickle **rille, rilled**
RILLES ▸ **rille**
RILLET *n* little rill **rillets**
RILLING ▸ **rill**
RILLS ▸ **rill**
RIM *n, vb*
RIMA *n* long narrow opening **rimae**
RIMAYE *n* crevasse at the head of a glacier **rimayes**
RIME = **rhyme**
RIMED ▸ **rime**
RIMER = **rhymester**
RIMERS ▸ **rimer**
RIMES ▸ **rime**
RIMFIRE *adj* (of a cartridge) having the primer in the rim of the base ▹ *n* cartridge of this type
RIMIER ▸ **rimy**
RIMIEST ▸ **rimy**
RIMING ▸ **rime**
RIMLAND *n* area situated on the outer edges of a region
RIMLESS ▸ **rim**
RIMMED ▸ **rim**
RIMMER *n* tool for shaping the edge of something **rimmers**
RIMMING ▸ **rim**
RIMOSE *adj* (esp of plant parts) having the surface marked by a network of intersecting cracks **rimous**
RIMPLE *vb* crease or wrinkle **rimpled, rimples**
RIMROCK *n* rock forming the boundaries of a sandy or gravelly alluvial deposit
RIMS ▸ **rim**
RIMSHOT *n* deliberate simultaneous striking of skin and rim of drum
RIMU *n* **rimus**
RIMY *adj* coated with rime
RIN *Scots variant of* ▸ **run**
RIND *n, vb* **rinded**
RINDIER ▸ **rindy**
RINDING ▸ **rind**
RINDS ▸ **rind**
RINDY *adj* with a rind or rindlike skin
RINE *archaic variant of* ▸ **rind**
RINES ▸ **rine**
RING *vb, n*
RINGBIT *n* type of bit worn by a horse
RINGED ▸ **ring**
RINGENT *adj* (of the corolla of plants) consisting of two gaping lips
RINGER *n* **ringers**
RINGGIT *n* standard monetary unit of Malaysia
RINGING ▸ **ring**
RINGLET *n*
RINGMAN *n* (in dialect) ring finger **ringmen**
RINGS ▸ **ring**
RINGTAW *n* game in which the aim is to knock marbles out of a ring
RINGWAY *n* bypass
RINK *n, vb* **rinked, rinking, rinks**
RINNING ▸ **rin**
RINS ▸ **rin**
RINSE *vb, n* **rinsed, rinser, rinsers, rinses, rinsing**
RIOJA *n* red or white Spanish wine with a vanilla bouquet and flavour **riojas**
RIOT *n, vb* **rioted, rioter, rioters, rioting**
RIOTISE *n* archaic word for riotous behaviour and excess **riotize**
RIOTOUS *adj*
RIOTRY *n* riotous behaviour
RIOTS ▸ **riot**
RIP *vb, n*
RIPCORD *n*
RIPE *adj, vb*
RIPECK = **ryepeck**
RIPECKS ▸ **ripeck**
RIPED ▸ **ripe**
RIPELY ▸ **ripe**
RIPEN *vb* **ripened, ripener, ripens**
RIPER *adj* more ripe ▹ *n* old Scots word meaning plunderer **ripers**
RIPES ▸ **ripe**

RIPEST ▸ **ripe**
RIPIENI ▸ **ripieno**
RIPIENO *n* (in baroque concertos and concerti grossi) the full orchestra
RIPING ▸ **ripe**
RIPOFF *n* grossly overpriced article **ripoffs**
RIPOST = **riposte**
RIPOSTE *n, vb*
RIPOSTS ▸ **ripost**
RIPP *n* old Scots word for a handful of grain
RIPPED ▸ **rip**
RIPPER *n* **rippers**
RIPPIER *n* archaic word for fish seller
RIPPING ▸ **rip**
RIPPLE *n, vb* **rippled, rippler, ripples**
RIPPLET *n* tiny ripple
RIPPLY ▸ **ripple**
RIPPS ▸ **ripp**
RIPRAP *vb* deposit broken stones in or on **ripraps**
RIPS ▸ **rip**
RIPSAW *n* handsaw for cutting along the grain of timber ▹ *vb* saw with a ripsaw **ripsawn, ripsaws**
RIPSTOP *n* tear-resistant cloth
RIPT *archaic past form of* ▸ **rip**
RIPTIDE *n* stretch of turbulent water in the sea
RISE *vb, n* **risen**
RISER *n* **risers**
RISES ▸ **rise**
RISHI *n* Indian seer or sage **rishis**
RISIBLE *adj* causing laughter, ridiculous **risibly**
RISING ▸ **rise**
RISINGS ▸ **rise**
RISK *n, vb* **risked, risker, riskers, riskful**
RISKIER ▸ **risky**
RISKILY ▸ **risky**
RISKING ▸ **risk**
RISKS ▸ **risk**
RISKY *adj* full of risk, dangerous
RISORII > **risorius**
RISOTTO *n*
RISP *vb* Scots word meaning rasp **risped, risping, risps**
RISQUE *n* risk **risques**
RISSOLE *n*
RISTRA *n* string of dried chilli peppers **ristras**
RISUS *n* involuntary grinning expression **risuses**
RIT *vb* Scots word for cut or slit
RITARD *n* (in music) a slowing down **ritards**
RITE *n* **rites**
RITS ▸ **rit**
RITT = **rit**
RITTED ▸ **rit**
RITTER *n* knight or horseman **ritters**
RITTING ▸ **rit**
RITTS ▸ **ritt**
RITUAL *n, adj* **rituals**
RITZ *modifier as in* **put on the ritz** assume a superior air or make an ostentatious display **ritzes**
RITZIER ▸ **ritzy**
RITZILY ▸ **ritzy**
RITZY *adj* luxurious or elegant
RIVA *n* rock cleft
RIVAGE *n* bank, shore, or coast **rivages**
RIVAL *n, adj, vb* **rivaled**
RIVALRY *n*
RIVALS ▸ **rival**
RIVAS ▸ **riva**
RIVE *vb* split asunder **rived**
RIVEL *vb* archaic word meaning wrinkle **rivels**
RIVEN ▸ **rive**
RIVER *n*
RIVERED *adj* with a river or rivers
RIVERET *n* archaic word for rivulet or stream
RIVERS ▸ **river**
RIVERY *adj* riverlike
RIVES ▸ **rive**
RIVET *n, vb* **riveted, riveter, rivets**
RIVIERA *n* coastline resembling the Meditteranean Riviera
RIVIERE *n* necklace of diamonds which gradually increase in size
RIVING ▸ **rive**
RIVLIN *n* Scots word for rawhide shoe **rivlins**
RIVO *interj* (in the past) an informal toast
RIVULET *n*
RIYAL *n* standard monetary unit of Qatar, divided into 100 dirhams **riyals**

RIZ *(in some dialects) past form of* ▸ **rise**

> This unusual past tense of **rise** is one of the essential Z words.

RIZA *n* partial icon cover made from precious metal
RIZARD *n* redcurrant **rizards**
RIZAS ▸ **riza**
RIZZAR *n* Scots word for red currant ▹ *vb* Scots word for sun-dry **rizzars**
RIZZART *n* Scots word for red currant
RIZZER = **rizzar**
RIZZERS ▸ **rizzer**
RIZZOR *vb* dry **rizzors**
ROACH *n, vb*
ROACHED *adj* arched convexly, as the back of certain breeds of dog, such as the whippet
ROACHES ▸ **roach**
ROAD *n*
ROADBED *n* material used to make a road
ROADEO *n* competition testing driving skills **roadeos**
ROADIE *n* person who transports and sets up equipment for a band **roadies**
ROADING *n* road building
ROADMAN *n* someone involved in road repair or construction **roadmen**
ROADS ▸ **road**
ROADWAY *n* part of a road used by vehicles
ROAM *vb, n* **roamed, roamer, roamers, roaming, roams**
ROAN *adj, n* **roans**
ROAR *vb, n* **roared, roarer, roarers**
ROARIE *Scots word for* ▸ **noisy**
ROARIER ▸ **roary**
ROARING ▸ **roar**
ROARS ▸ **roar**
ROARY *adj* roarlike or tending to roar
ROAST *vb, n, adj* **roasted**
ROASTER *n* person or thing that roasts
ROASTS ▸ **roast**
ROATE *archaic form of* ▸ **rote**
ROATED ▸ **roate**
ROATES ▸ **roate**
ROATING ▸ **roate**
ROB *vb*
ROBALO *n* tropical fish **robalos**
ROBAND *n* piece of marline used for fastening a sail to a spar **robands**
ROBBED ▸ **rob**
ROBBER ▸ **rob**
ROBBERS ▸ **rob**
ROBBERY *n* stealing of property from a person by using or threatening to use force
ROBBIN = **roband**
ROBBING ▸ **rob**
ROBBINS ▸ **robbin**
ROBE *n, vb* **robed, robes**
ROBIN *n*
ROBING ▸ **robe**
ROBINGS ▸ **robe**
ROBINIA *n* type of leguminous tree
ROBINS ▸ **robin**
ROBLE *n* oak tree **robles**
ROBOT *n* **robotic, robotry, robots**
ROBS ▸ **rob**
ROBUST *adj*
ROBUSTA *n* species of coffee tree
ROC *n* monstrous bird of Arabian mythology
ROCH = **rotch**
ROCHES ▸ **rotch**
ROCHET *n* white surplice with tight sleeves, worn by Church dignitaries **rochets**
ROCK *n, vb, adj*
ROCKABY = **rockabye**
ROCKED ▸ **rock**
ROCKER *n* **rockers**
ROCKERY *n*
ROCKET *n, vb* **rockets**
ROCKIER *n*
ROCKILY ▸ **rocky**
ROCKING ▸ **rock**
ROCKLAY = **rokelay**
ROCKOON *n* rocket fired from a balloon at high altitude
ROCKS ▸ **rock**
ROCKY *adj*
ROCOCO *adj* (of furniture, architecture, etc) having much elaborate decoration ▹ *n* style of architecture and decoration

characterized by elaborate ornamentation **rococos**
ROCQUET *n* another name for the salad plant rocket
ROCS ▸ **roc**
ROD *n*, *vb* **rodded, rodding**
RODE *vb* (of the male woodcock) to perform a display flight **roded**
RODENT *n* **rodents**
RODEO *n*, *vb* **rodeoed, rodeos**
RODES ▸ **rode**
RODEWAY *archaic spelling of* ▸ **roadway**
RODING ▸ **rode**
RODINGS ▸ **rode**
RODLESS ▸ **rod**
RODLIKE ▸ **rod**
RODMAN *n* someone who uses or fishes with a rod **rodmen**
RODS ▸ **rod**
RODSMAN = **rodman**
RODSMEN ▸ **rodsman**
RODSTER *n* angler
ROE *n*
ROEBUCK *n* male of the roe deer
ROED *adj* with roe inside
ROEMER *n* drinking glass, typically having an ovoid bowl on a short stem **roemers**
ROES ▸ **roe**
ROESTI ▸ **rosti**
ROESTIS ▸ **roesti**
ROGALLO *n* flexible fabric delta wing
ROGNON *n* isolated rock outcrop on a glacier **rognons**
ROGUE *n*, *adj*, *vb* **rogued**
ROGUER *n* rogue **roguers**
ROGUERY *n* dishonest or immoral behaviour
ROGUES ▸ **rogue**
ROGUING ▸ **rogue**
ROGUISH *adj* **roguy**
ROIL *vb* make (a liquid) cloudy or turbid by stirring up dregs or sediment **roiled**
ROILIER ▸ **roily**
ROILING ▸ **roil**
ROILS ▸ **roil**
ROILY *adj* cloudy or muddy
ROIN = **royne**
ROINED ▸ **roin**
ROINING ▸ **roin**
ROINISH = **roynish**
ROINS ▸ **roin**
ROIST *archaic variant of* ▸ **roister**
ROISTED ▸ **roist**
ROISTER *vb* make merry noisily or boisterously
ROISTS ▸ **roist**
ROJAK *n* (in Malaysia) a salad dish served in chilli sauce **rojaks**
ROJI *n* Japanese tea garden or its path of stones **rojis**
ROK = **roc**

> **Rok** is an alternative spelling of **roc**, the mythical bird. Other spellings are **ruc** and **rukh**.

ROKE *vb* (in dialect) steam or smoke **roked**
ROKELAY *n* type of cloak
ROKER *n* variety of ray **rokers**
ROKES ▸ **roke**
ROKIER ▸ **roky**
ROKIEST ▸ **roky**
ROKING ▸ **roke**
ROKKAKU *n* hexagonal Japanese kite
ROKS ▸ **rok**
ROKY *adj* (in dialect) steamy or smoky
ROLAG *n* roll of carded wool ready for spinning **rolags**
ROLE *n* **roles**
ROLF *vb* massage following a particular technique **rolfed, rolfer, rolfers, rolfing, rolfs**
ROLL *vb*, *n*
ROLLBAR *n* bar that reinforces the frame of a car
ROLLED ▸ **roll**
ROLLER *n* **rollers**
ROLLICK *vb* behave in a boisterous manner ▹ *n* boisterous or carefree escapade
ROLLING ▸ **roll**
ROLLMOP *n* herring fillet rolled round onion slices and pickled
ROLLOCK = **rowlock**
ROLLOUT *n* presentation to the public of a new aircraft, product, etc; launch

ROLLS ▸ **roll**
ROLLTOP *n as in* **rolltop desk** desk having a slatted wooden panel that can be pulled down over the writing surface
ROLLWAY *n* incline down which logs are rolled
ROM *n* male gypsy
ROMA *n* gypsy
ROMAGE *archaic variant of* ▸ **rummage**
ROMAGES ▸ **romage**
ROMAIKA *n* Greek dance
ROMAINE *n* usual US and Canadian name for 'cos' (lettuce)
ROMAJI *n* Roman alphabet as used to write Japanese **romajis**
ROMAL = **rumal**
ROMALS ▸ **romal**
ROMAN *adj* in or relating to the vertical style of printing type used for most printed matter ▷ *n* roman type
ROMANCE *n, vb*
ROMANO *n* hard light-coloured sharp-tasting cheese **romanos**
ROMANS ▸ **roman**
ROMANZA *n* short instrumental piece of song-like character
ROMAUNT *n* verse romance
ROMCOM *n* comedy based around the romantic relationships of the characters **romcoms**
ROMEO *n* ardent male lover **romeos**
ROMNEYA *n* bushy type of poppy
ROMP *vb, n* **romped**
ROMPER *n* playful or boisterous child
ROMPERS *pl n*
ROMPING ▸ **romp**
ROMPISH ▸ **romp**
ROMPS ▸ **romp**
ROMS ▸ **rom**
RONDE *n* round dance
RONDEAU *n* poem with the opening words of the first line used as a refrain
RONDEL *n* rondeau with a two-line refrain appearing twice or three times **rondels**
RONDES ▸ **ronde**
RONDINO *n* short rondo
RONDO *n* **rondos**
RONDURE *n* circle or curve
RONE *n* drainpipe or gutter for carrying rainwater from a roof
RONEO *vb* duplicate (a document) from a stencil ▷ *n* document reproduced by this process **roneoed, roneos**
RONES ▸ **rone**
RONG *archaic past participle of* ▸ **ring**
RONIN *n* lordless samurai, esp one whose feudal lord had been deprived of his territory **ronins**
RONIONS ▸ **ronion**
RONNE *archaic form of* ▸ **run**
RONNEL *n* type of pesticide **ronnels**
RONNIE *n* Dublin slang word for moustache **ronnies**
RONNING ▸ **ronne**
RONT *archaic variant of* ▸ **runt**
RONTE *archaic variant of* ▸ **runt**
RONTES ▸ **ronte**
RONTGEN *variant spelling of* > **roentgen**
RONTS ▸ **ront**
RONZ *n* rest of New Zealand
RONZER *n* New Zealand word for a New Zealander not from Auckland **ronzers**
ROO *n*
ROOD *n* Cross **roods**
ROOF *n, vb* **roofed, roofer, roofers**
ROOFIE *n* tablet of sedative drug
ROOFIER ▸ **roofy**
ROOFIES ▸ **roofie**
ROOFING *n*
ROOFS ▸ **roof**
ROOFTOP *n*
ROOFY *adj* with roofs
ROOIBOS *n* tea prepared from the dried leaves of an African plant
ROOIKAT *n* South African lynx
ROOK *n, vb* **rooked**

ROOKERY *n*
ROOKIE *n* new recruit
ROOKIER ▸ **rooky**
ROOKIES ▸ **rookie**
ROOKING ▸ **rook**
ROOKISH ▸ **rook**
ROOKS ▸ **rook**
ROOKY *adj* abounding in rooks
ROOM *n*, *vb* **roomed, roomer, roomers**
ROOMFUL *n* number or quantity sufficient to fill a room
ROOMIE *n* roommate
ROOMIER ▸ **roomy**
ROOMIES ▸ **roomie**
ROOMILY ▸ **roomy**
ROOMING ▸ **room**
ROOMS ▸ **room**
ROOMY *adj* spacious
ROON *n* Scots word for shred or strip **roons**
ROOP = **roup**
ROOPED ▸ **roop**
ROOPIER ▸ **roopy**
ROOPING ▸ **roop**
ROOPIT = **roopy**
ROOPS ▸ **roop**
ROOPY *adj* (in dialect) hoarse
ROOS ▸ **roo**
ROOSA *n* type of grass **roosas**
ROOSE *vb* flatter **roosed, rooser, roosers, rooses, roosing**
ROOST *n*, *vb* **roosted**
ROOSTER *n*
ROOSTS ▸ **roost**
ROOT *n*, *vb*
ROOTAGE *n* root system
ROOTCAP *n* layer of cells at root tip
ROOTED, rooter, rooters, rootier ▸ **root**
ROOTIES ▸ **rooty**
ROOTING ▸ **root**
ROOTKIT *n*
ROOTLE = **root**
ROOTLED ▸ **rootle**
ROOTLES ▸ **rootle**
ROOTLET *n* small root or branch of a root
ROOTS *adj* (of popular music) going back to the origins of a style **rootsy**
ROOTY *adj* rootlike ▹ *n* (in military slang) bread
ROPABLE *adj* capable of being roped
ROPE *n* **roped**
ROPER *n* someone who makes ropes **ropers**
ROPERY *n* place where ropes are made
ROPES ▸ **rope**
ROPEWAY *n* type of aerial lift
ROPEY *adj*
ROPIER ▸ **ropy**
ROPIEST ▸ **ropy**
ROPILY ▸ **ropey**
ROPING ▸ **rope**
ROPINGS ▸ **rope**
ROPY = **ropey**
ROQUE *n* game developed from croquet **roques**
ROQUET *vb* drive one's ball against (another person's ball) in croquet ▹ *n* act of roqueting **roquets**
RORAL *archaic word for* ▸ **dewy**
RORE *archaic spelling of* ▸ **roar**
RORES ▸ **rore**
RORIC = **roral**
RORID = **roral**
RORIE = **roary**
RORIER ▸ **rory**
RORIEST ▸ **rory**
RORQUAL *n* toothless whale with a dorsal fin
RORT *n* dishonest scheme ▹ *vb* take unfair advantage of something **rorted**
RORTER *n* small-scale confidence trickster **rorters**
RORTIER, rorting, rorts, rorty ▸ **rort**
RORY *adj* dewy
ROSACE *another name for* ▸ **rosette**
ROSACEA *n* chronic inflammatory disease affecting the skin of the face
ROSACES ▸ **rosace**
ROSAKER *archaic word for* ▸ **realgar**
ROSALIA *n* melody which is repeated but at a higher pitch each time
ROSARIA > **rosarium**
ROSARY *n*
ROSBIF *n* term used in France for an English person **rosbifs**
ROSCID *adj* dewy
ROSCOE *slang word for* ▸ **gun**
ROSCOES ▸ **roscoe**
ROSE ▸ **rise**

ROSEAL *adj* rosy or roselike
ROSEATE *adj* rose-coloured
ROSEBAY *n as in* **rosebay willowherb** perennial plant with spikes of deep pink flowers
ROSEBUD *n* rose which has not yet fully opened
ROSED ▸ **rise**
ROSEHIP *n* berry-like fruit of a rose plant
ROSELLA *n*
ROSELLE *n* Indian flowering plant
ROSEOLA *n* feverish condition of young children caused by the human herpes virus
ROSERY *n* bed or garden of roses
ROSES ▸ **rise**
ROSET *n* Scots word meaning rosin ▹ *vb* rub rosin on **roseted, rosets**
ROSETTE *n*
ROSETTY ▸ **roset**
ROSETY ▸ **roset**
ROSHI *n* teacher of Zen Buddhism **roshis**
ROSIED ▸ **rosy**
ROSIER *archaic word for* > **rosebush**
ROSIERE *archaic word for* > **rosebush**
ROSIERS ▸ **rosier**
ROSIES ▸ **rosy**
ROSIEST ▸ **rosy**
ROSILY ▸ **rosy**
ROSIN *n* resin used for treating the bows of violins etc ▹ *vb* apply rosin to **rosined**
ROSINER *n* strong alcoholic drink
ROSING ▸ **rise**
ROSINOL *n* yellowish fluorescent oily liquid obtained from certain resins
ROSINS ▸ **rosin**
ROSINY ▸ **rosin**
ROSIT = **roset**
ROSITED ▸ **rosit**
ROSITS ▸ **rosit**
ROSOLIO *n* type of cordial
ROSSER *n* bark-removing machine **rossers**
ROST *archaic spelling of* ▸ **roast**
ROSTED ▸ **rost**
ROSTER *n, vb* **rosters**
ROSTI *n* cheese-topped fried Swiss dish of grated potato
ROSTING ▸ **rost**
ROSTIS ▸ **rosti**
ROSTRA ▸ **rostrum**
ROSTRAL *adj* of or like a beak or snout
ROSTRUM *n*
ROSTS ▸ **rost**
ROSULA *n* rosette **rosulas**
ROSY *adj, vb* **rosying**
ROT *vb, n*
ROTA *n*
ROTAL *adj* of or relating to wheels or rotation
ROTAN *another name for* ▸ **rattan**
ROTANS ▸ **rotan**
ROTARY *adj, n*
ROTAS ▸ **rota**
ROTATE *vb, adj* **rotated, rotates**
ROTATOR *n* person, device, or part that rotates or causes rotation
ROTCH *n* little auk **rotche, rotches, rotchie**
ROTE *n, vb* **roted, rotes**
ROTGUT *n* alcoholic drink of inferior quality **rotguts**
ROTHER *dialect word for* ▸ **ox**
ROTHERS ▸ **rother**
ROTI *n* (in India and the Caribbean) a type of unleavened bread
ROTIFER *n* minute aquatic multicellular invertebrate
ROTING ▸ **rote**
ROTIS ▸ **roti**
ROTL *n* unit of weight used in Muslim countries **rotls**
ROTO *n* printing process using a cylinder etched with many small recesses in a rotary press
ROTOLO *n* (in Italian cuisine) a roll **rotolos**
ROTON *n* quantum of vortex motion **rotons**
ROTOR *n* **rotors**
ROTOS ▸ **roto**
ROTS ▸ **rot**
ROTTAN *n* (in dialect) a rat **rottans**
ROTTE *n* ancient stringed instrument

ROTTED ▶ **rot**
ROTTEN *adj, adv, n* **rottens**
ROTTER *n* despicable person **rotters**
ROTTES ▶ **rotte**
ROTTING ▶ **rot**
ROTULA *n* kneecap **rotulae, rotulas**
ROTUND *adj, vb*
ROTUNDA *n* circular building or room, esp with a dome
ROTUNDS ▶ **rotund**
ROUBLE *n* **roubles**
ROUCHE = **ruche**
ROUCHES ▶ **rouche**
ROUCOU *another name for* ▶ **annatto**
ROUCOUS ▶ **roucou**
ROUE *n* man given to immoral living
ROUEN *n* breed of duck **rouens**
ROUES ▶ **roue**
ROUGE *n, vb* **rouged, rouges**
ROUGH *adj, vb, n* **roughed**
ROUGHEN *vb*
ROUGHER *n* person that does the rough preparatory work on something ▷ *adj* more rough
ROUGHIE *n* small food fish found in Australian waters
ROUGHLY *adv* without being exact or fully authenticated
ROUGHS ▶ **rough**
ROUGHT *archaic past form of* ▶ **reach**
ROUGHY *spelling variant of* ▶ **roughie**
ROUGING ▶ **rouge**
ROUILLE *n* kind of sauce
ROUL *archaic form of* ▶ **roll**
ROULADE *n* slice of meat rolled and cooked
ROULE *archaic form of* ▶ **roll**
ROULEAU *n* roll of paper containing coins
ROULES ▶ **roule**
ROULS ▶ **roul**
ROUM *archaic spelling of* ▶ **room**
ROUMING *n* pasture given for an animal
ROUMS ▶ **roum**
ROUNCE *n* handle that is turned to move paper and plates on a printing press **rounces**
ROUNCY *archaic word for* ▶ **horse**
ROUND *adj, prep, vb, n*
ROUNDED *adj*
ROUNDEL = **roundelay**
ROUNDER *n* run round all four bases after one hit in rounders
ROUNDLE = **roundel**
ROUNDLY *adv*
ROUNDS ▶ **round**
ROUNDUP *n*
ROUP *n* any of various chronic respiratory diseases of birds, esp poultry ▷ *vb* sell by auction **rouped**
ROUPET *adj* Scots word meaning hoarse or croaky
ROUPIER, roupily, rouping ▶ **roup**
ROUPIT = **roupet**
ROUPS, roupy ▶ **roup**
ROUSANT *adj* (in heraldry) rising
ROUSE = **reveille**
ROUSED ▶ **rouse**
ROUSER *n* person or thing that rouses people **rousers**
ROUSES ▶ **rouse**
ROUSING *adj* lively, vigorous
ROUST *vb* rout or stir, as out of bed **rousted**
ROUSTER *n* unskilled labourer on an oil rig
ROUSTS ▶ **roust**
ROUT *n, vb*
ROUTE *n, vb* **routed**
ROUTER *n* device that allows data to be moved between points on a network **routers**
ROUTES ▶ **route**
ROUTH *n* abundance ▷ *adj* abundant
ROUTHIE *adj* abundant, plentiful, or well filled
ROUTHS ▶ **routh**
ROUTINE *n, adj*
ROUTING ▶ **rout**
ROUTOUS ▶ **rout**
ROUTS ▶ **rout**
ROUX *n*
ROVE ▶ **reeve**
ROVED ▶ **reeve**
ROVEN ▶ **reeve**
ROVER *n* wanderer, traveller **rovers**
ROVES ▶ **reeve**
ROVING ▶ **rove**
ROVINGS ▶ **rove**
ROW *n, vb* **rowable**

ROWAN *n* **rowans**
ROWBOAT *n* small boat propelled by one or more pairs of oars
ROWDIER ▶ **rowdy**
ROWDIES ▶ **rowdy**
ROWDILY ▶ **rowdy**
ROWDY *adj, n*
ROWED ▶ **row**
ROWEL *n* small spiked wheel on a spur ▷ *vb* goad (a horse) using a rowel **roweled, rowels**
ROWEN *another word for* > **aftermath**
ROWENS ▶ **rowen**
ROWER, rowers, rowing, rowings ▶ **row**
ROWLOCK *n*
ROWME *archaic variant of* ▶ **room**
ROWMES ▶ **rowme**
ROWND *archaic variant of* ▶ **round**
ROWNDED ▶ **rownd**
ROWNDS ▶ **rownd**
ROWOVER *n* act of winning a rowing race unopposed
ROWS ▶ **row**
ROWT *archaic variant of* ▶ **rout**
ROWTED ▶ **rowt**
ROWTH = **routh**
ROWTHS ▶ **rowth**
ROWTING ▶ **rowt**
ROWTS ▶ **rowt**
ROYAL *adj, n*
ROYALET *n* minor king
ROYALLY ▶ **royal**
ROYALS ▶ **royal**
ROYALTY *n*
ROYNE *archaic word for* ▶ **gnaw**
ROYNED ▶ **royne**
ROYNES ▶ **royne**
ROYNING ▶ **royne**
ROYNISH *archaic word for* ▶ **mangy**
ROYST = **roist**
ROYSTED ▶ **royst**
ROYSTER = **roister**
ROYSTS ▶ **royst**
ROZELLE = **roselle**
ROZET = **roset**
ROZETED ▶ **rozet**
ROZETS ▶ **rozet**
ROZIT = **roset**
ROZITED ▶ **rozit**
ROZITS ▶ **rozit**
ROZZER *n* policeman **rozzers**
RUANA *n* woollen wrap resembling a poncho **ruanas**
RUB *vb, n*
RUBABOO *n* soup or stew made by boiling pemmican with, if available, flour and vegetables
RUBACE = **rubasse**
RUBACES ▶ **rubace**
RUBAI *n* verse form of Persian origin consisting of four-line stanzas
RUBASSE *n* type of quartz containing red haematite
RUBATI ▶ **rubato**
RUBATO *n* (with) expressive flexibility of tempo ▷ *adv* be played with a flexible tempo **rubatos**
RUBBED ▶ **rub**
RUBBER *n, adj, vb* **rubbers**
RUBBERY *adj*
RUBBET *old Scots past form of* ▶ **rob**
RUBBIDY = **rubbity**
RUBBIES ▶ **rubby**
RUBBING ▶ **rub**
RUBBISH *n, vb*
RUBBIT *old Scots past form of* ▶ **rob**
RUBBITY *n* pub
RUBBLE *n, vb* **rubbled, rubbles, rubbly**
RUBBY *n* rubbing alcohol, esp when mixed with cheap wine for drinking
RUBDOWN *n* act of drying or cleaning vigorously
RUBEFY *vb* make red
RUBEL *n* currency unit of Belarus
RUBELLA *n*
RUBELS ▶ **rubel**
RUBEOLA *technical name for* ▶ **measles**
RUBICON *n* point of no return ▷ *vb* (in bezique) to beat before the loser has managed to gain as many as 1000 points
RUBIDIC > **rubidium**
RUBIED, rubier, rubies, rubiest ▶ **ruby**
RUBIFY = **rubefy**
RUBIGO *old Scots word for* ▶ **penis**
RUBIGOS ▶ **rubigo**
RUBIN *archaic word for* ▶ **ruby**
RUBINE *archaic word for* ▶ **ruby**

RUBINES ▸ **rubine**
RUBINS ▸ **rubin**
RUBIOUS *adj* of the colour ruby
RUBLE = **rouble**
RUBLES ▸ **ruble**
RUBOFF *n* resulting effect on something else; consequences **ruboffs**
RUBOUT *n* killing or elimination **rubouts**
RUBRIC *n, adj* **rubrics**
RUBS ▸ **rub**
RUBUS *n* fruit-bearing genus of shrubs
RUBY *n, adj, vb* **rubying**
RUC = **roc**
RUCHE *n* pleat or frill of lace etc as a decoration ▹ *vb* put a ruche on **ruched, ruches**
RUCHING *n* material used for a ruche
RUCK *n* rough crowd of common people ▹ *vb* wrinkle or crease **rucked, rucking, ruckle**
RUCKLED ▸ **ruckle**
RUCKLES ▸ **ruckle**
RUCKMAN *n* person who plays in the ruck **ruckmen**
RUCKS ▸ **ruck**
RUCKUS *n* uproar
RUCOLA *n* another name for the salad plant rocket **rucolas**
RUCS ▸ **ruc**
RUCTION *n*
RUD *n* red or redness ▹ *vb* redden
RUDAS *n* Scots word for a coarse, rude old woman **rudases**
RUDD *n* European freshwater fish
RUDDED ▸ **rud**
RUDDER *n* **rudders**
RUDDIED, ruddier, ruddies, ruddily ▸ **ruddy**
RUDDING ▸ **rud**
RUDDLE *n* red ochre, used esp to mark sheep ▹ *vb* mark (sheep) with ruddle **ruddled, ruddles**
RUDDOCK *dialect name for the* ▸ **robin**
RUDDS ▸ **rudd**
RUDDY *adj, adv, vb*
RUDE *archaic spelling of* ▸ **rood**
RUDELY ▸ **rude**
RUDER ▸ **rude**
RUDERAL *n* plant that grows on waste ground ▹ *adj* growing in waste places
RUDERY ▸ **rude**
RUDES ▸ **rude**
RUDESBY *n* archaic word for rude person
RUDEST ▸ **rude**
RUDIE *n* member of a youth movement originating in the 1960s **rudies**
RUDISH *adj* somewhat rude
RUDS ▸ **rud**
RUE *vb* feel regret for ▹ *n* plant with evergreen bitter leaves **rued**
RUEDA *n* type of Cuban round dance **ruedas**
RUEFUL *adj*
RUEING ▸ **rue**
RUEINGS ▸ **rue**
RUELLE *n* area between bed and wall **ruelles**
RUELLIA *n* genus of plants
RUER ▸ **rue**
RUERS ▸ **rue**
RUES ▸ **rue**
RUFF *n, vb*
RUFFE *n* European freshwater fish
RUFFED ▸ **ruff**
RUFFES ▸ **ruffe**
RUFFIAN *n, vb*
RUFFIN *archaic name for* ▸ **ruffe**
RUFFING ▸ **ruff**
RUFFINS ▸ **ruffin**
RUFFLE *vb, n* **ruffled**
RUFFLER *n* person or thing that ruffles
RUFFLES ▸ **ruffle**
RUFFLY *adj* ruffled
RUFFS ▸ **ruff**
RUFIYAA *n* standard monetary unit of the Maldives
RUFOUS *adj* reddish-brown
RUG *n, vb*
RUGA *n* fold, wrinkle, or crease **rugae**
RUGAL *adj* (in anatomy) with ridges or folds
RUGATE = **rugose**
RUGBIES ▸ **rugby**
RUGBY *n*
RUGGED *adj*
RUGGER = **rugby**
RUGGERS ▸ **rugger**

RUGGIER ▸ **ruggy**
RUGGING ▸ **rug**
RUGGY *adj* (in dialect) rough or rugged
RUGLIKE ▸ **rug**
RUGOLA *n* another name for the salad plant rocket **rugolas**
RUGOSA *n* any of various shrubs descended from a particular type of wild rose **rugosas**
RUGOSE *adj* wrinkled **rugous**
RUGS ▸ **rug**
RUIN *vb, n*
RUINATE *vb* archaic word for bring or come to ruin
RUINED ▸ **ruin**
RUINER ▸ **ruin**
RUINERS ▸ **ruin**
RUING ▸ **rue**
RUINGS ▸ **rue**
RUINING ▸ **ruin**
RUINOUS *adj*
RUINS ▸ **ruin**
RUKH = **roc**
RUKHS ▸ **rukh**
RULABLE ▸ **rule**
RULE *n, vb* **ruled**
RULER *n, vb* **rulered, rulers**
RULES ▸ **rule**
RULESSE *adj* archaic word meaning ruleless or without rules
RULIER ▸ **ruly**
RULIEST ▸ **ruly**
RULING *n* formal decision ▹ *adj* controlling or exercising authority **rulings**
RULLION *n* Scots word for rawhide shoe
RULLOCK = **rowlock**
RULY *adj* orderly
RUM *n, adj*
RUMAKI *n* savoury of chicken liver and sliced water chestnut wrapped in bacon **rumakis**
RUMAL *n* handkerchief or type of cloth **rumals**
RUMBA *n* lively ballroom dance of Cuban origin ▹ *vb* dance the rumba **rumbaed, rumbas**
RUMBLE *vb, n* **rumbled, rumbler, rumbles**
RUMBLY *adj* rumbling or liable to rumble
RUMBO *n* rum-based cocktail **rumbos**
RUME *archaic form of* ▸ **rheum**
RUMEN *n* first compartment of the stomach of ruminants **rumens**
RUMES ▸ **rume**
RUMINA ▸ **rumen**
RUMINAL ▸ **rumen**
RUMKIN *n* archaic term for a drinking vessel **rumkins**
RUMLY ▸ **rum**
RUMMAGE *vb, n*
RUMMER ▸ **rum**
RUMMERS ▸ **rum**
RUMMEST ▸ **rum**
RUMMIER ▸ **rummy**
RUMMIES ▸ **rummy**
RUMMILY ▸ **rummy**
RUMMISH *adj* rather strange, peculiar or odd
RUMMY *n, adj*
RUMNESS ▸ **rum**
RUMOR = **rumour**
RUMORED ▸ **rumor**
RUMORS ▸ **rumor**
RUMOUR *n, vb* **rumours**
RUMP *n, vb* **rumped**
RUMPIES ▸ **rumpy**
RUMPING ▸ **rump**
RUMPLE *vb, n* **rumpled, rumples, rumply**
RUMPS ▸ **rump**
RUMPUS *n*
RUMPY *n* tailless Manx cat ▹ *adj* with a large or noticeable rump
RUMS ▸ **rum**
RUN *vb* move with a more rapid gait than walking ▹ *n* act or spell of running
RUNANGA *n* Māori assembly or council
RUNAWAY *n*
RUNBACK *n* (in tennis) the areas behind the baselines of the court
RUNCH *n* another name for white charlock **runches**
RUND = **roon**
RUNDALE *n* system of land tenure in Ireland
RUNDLE *n* rung of a ladder
RUNDLED *adj* rounded
RUNDLES ▸ **rundle**
RUNDLET *n* liquid measure, generally about 15 gallons
RUNDOWN *adj, n*

RUNDS ▸ **rund**
RUNE *n* any character of the earliest Germanic alphabet
RUNED *n* with runes on
RUNES ▸ **rune**
RUNFLAT *adj* having a safety feature that prevents tyres becoming dangerous when flat
RUNG ▸ **ring**
RUNGS ▸ **ring**
RUNIC ▸ **rune**
RUNKLE *vb* (in dialect) crease or wrinkle **runkled, runkles**
RUNLESS ▸ **run**
RUNLET *n* cask for wine, beer, etc **runlets**
RUNNEL *n* small brook **runnels**
RUNNER *n* **runners**
RUNNET *dialect word for* ▸ **rennet**
RUNNETS ▸ **runnet**
RUNNIER ▸ **runny**
RUNNING ▸ **run**
RUNNY *adj*
RUNOFF *n* extra race to decide the winner after a tie **runoffs**
RUNOUT *n* dismissal of a batsman by running him out **runouts**
RUNOVER *n* incident in which someone is run over by a vehicle
RUNRIG = **rundale**
RUNRIGS ▸ **runrig**
RUNS ▸ **run**
RUNT *n*
RUNTED *adj* stunted
RUNTIER ▸ **runt**
RUNTISH ▸ **runt**
RUNTS ▸ **runt**
RUNTY ▸ **runt**
RUNWAY *n* **runways**
RUPEE *n* **rupees**
RUPIA *n* type of skin eruption
RUPIAH *n* standard monetary unit of Indonesia **rupiahs**
RUPIAS ▸ **rupia**
RUPTURE *n, vb*
RURAL *adj, n* **rurally, rurals**
RURBAN *adj* part country, part urban
RURP *n* very small piton **rurps**
RURU *another name for* ▸ **mopoke**
RURUS ▸ **ruru**
RUSA *n* type of deer with a mane
RUSALKA *n* water nymph or spirit
RUSAS ▸ **rusa**
RUSCUS *n* type of shrub
RUSE *n* **ruses**
RUSH *vb, n, adj* **rushed**
RUSHEE *n* someone interested in gaining fraternity or sorority membership **rushees**
RUSHEN *adj* made of rushes
RUSHER ▸ **rush**
RUSHERS ▸ **rush**
RUSHES *pl n* (in film-making) the initial prints of a scene or scenes before editing
RUSHIER ▸ **rushy**
RUSHING ▸ **rush**
RUSHY *adj* full of rushes
RUSINE *adj* of or relating to rusa deer
RUSK *n* **rusks**
RUSMA *n* Turkish depilatory **rusmas**
RUSSE *adj as in* **charlotte russe** cold dessert made from cream, etc, surrounded by sponge fingers
RUSSEL *n* type of woollen fabric **russels**
RUSSET *adj, n, vb* **russets, russety**
RUSSIA *n* Russia leather **russias**
RUSSIFY *vb* cause to become Russian in character
RUSSULA *n* type of fungus, typically of toadstool shape
RUST *n, adj, vb* **rusted**
RUSTIC *adj, n* **rustics**
RUSTIER ▸ **rusty**
RUSTILY ▸ **rusty**
RUSTING ▸ **rust**
RUSTLE *n, vb* **rustled**
RUSTLER *n* cattle thief
RUSTLES ▸ **rustle**
RUSTRE *n* (in heraldry) lozenge with a round hole in the middle showing the background colour **rustred, rustres**
RUSTS ▸ **rust**
RUSTY *adj*
RUT *n, vb*
RUTH *n* pity
RUTHFUL *adj* full of or causing sorrow or pity
RUTHS ▸ **ruth**

RUTILE *n* black, yellowish, or reddish-brown mineral **rutiles**

RUTIN *n* bioflavonoid found in various plants including rue **rutins**

RUTS ▸ **rut**

RUTTED ▸ **rut**

RUTTER *n* (in history) type of cavalry soldier **rutters**

RUTTIER ▸ **rutty**

RUTTILY ▸ **rutty**

RUTTING ▸ **rut**

RUTTISH *adj* (of an animal) in a condition of rut

RUTTY *adj* full of ruts or holes

RYA *n* type of rug originating in Scandinavia

RYAL *n* one of several old coins **ryals**

RYAS ▸ **rya**

RYBAT *n* polished stone piece forming the side of a window or door **rybats**

RYE *n*

RYEPECK *n* punt-mooring pole

RYES ▸ **rye**

RYFE *archaic variant of* ▸ **rife**

RYKE *Scots variant of* ▸ **reach**

RYKED ▸ **ryke**

RYKES ▸ **ryke**

RYKING ▸ **ryke**

RYMME = **rim**

RYMMED ▸ **rymme**

RYMMES ▸ **rymme**

RYMMING ▸ **rymme**

RYND *n* (in milling) crossbar piece forming part of the support structure of the upper millstone **rynds**

RYOKAN *n* traditional Japanese inn **ryokans**

RYOT *n* (in India) a peasant or tenant farmer **ryots**

RYPE *n* ptarmigan

RYPECK = **ryepeck**

RYPECKS ▸ **rypeck**

RYPER ▸ **rype**

Ss

S begins only four two-letter words, **sh** (5 points), **si, so** and **st** (2 each). These are easy to remember, and it's worth noting that two of them, **sh** and **st**, don't use any vowels. Interestingly, there are quite a few three-letter words beginning with **S** that don't contain vowels, some of which give good scores. These are **shh** (9), **shy** (9), **sky** (10), **sly** (6), **sny** (6), **spy** (8), **sty** (6), **swy** (9) and **syn** (6). **S** also forms a number of three-letter words with **X**. These are easy to remember as they use every vowel except **U**: **sax, sex, six** and **sox** (10 each). When it comes to **Z**, you will find **saz, sez** and **soz** (12 each) very useful, and the same applies to **suq** (12 points).

SAAG *n* (in Indian cookery) spinach **saags**
SAB *n* person engaged in direct action to prevent a targeted activity taking place ▷ *vb* take part in such action
SABAL *n* variety of palm tree **sabals**
SABATON *n* foot covering in suit of armour
SABAYON *n* dessert or sweet sauce made with egg yolks, sugar, and wine
SABBAT *n* midnight meeting of witches
SABBATH *n* period of rest
SABBATS ▶ **sabbat**
SABBED ▶ **sab**
SABBING ▶ **sab**
SABE *n* very informal word meaning sense or savvy ▷ *vb* very informal word meaning know or savvy **sabed, sabeing**
SABELLA *n* marine worm
SABER = **sabre**
SABERED ▶ **saber**
SABERS ▶ **saber**
SABES ▶ **sabe**
SABHA *n* set of Muslim prayer beads **sabhas**
SABIN *n* unit of acoustic absorption
SABINE *variant of* ▶ **savin**
SABINES ▶ **sabine**
SABINS ▶ **sabin**
SABIR *n* member of ancient Turkic people **sabirs**
SABKHA *n* flat coastal plain with a salt crust, common in Arabia
SABKHAH *n* sabkha
SABKHAS ▶ **sabkha**
SABKHAT *n* sabkha
SABLE *n*, *adj* **sabled, sables, sabling**
SABOT *n* wooden shoe traditionally worn by peasants in France **sabots**
SABRA *n* native-born Israeli Jew **sabras**
SABRE *n*, *vb* **sabred, sabres**

SABREUR *n* person wielding sabre
SABRING ▸ **sabre**
SABS ▸ **sab**
SABURRA *n* granular deposit
SAC *n*
SACATON *n* coarse grass of the southwestern US and Mexico
SACBUT *n* medieval trombone **sacbuts**
SACCADE *n* movement of the eye when it makes a sudden change of fixation, as in reading
SACCATE *adj* in the form of a sac
SACCOI ▸ **saccos**
SACCOS *n* bishop's garment in the Orthodox Church
SACCULE *n* small sac
SACCULI > **sacculus**
SACELLA > **sacellum**
SACHEM = **sagamore**
SACHEMS ▸ **sachem**
SACHET *n* **sachets**
SACK *n*, *vb*
SACKAGE *n* act of sacking a place
SACKBUT *n* medieval form of trombone
SACKED, sacker, sackers, sackful ▸ **sack**
SACKING *n* rough woven material used for sacks
SACKS ▸ **sack**
SACLESS *adj* old word meaning unchallengeable
SACLIKE ▸ **sac**
SACQUE = **sack**
SACQUES ▸ **sacque**
SACRA ▸ **sacrum**
SACRAL *adj* of or associated with sacred rites ▹ *n* sacral vertebra **sacrals**
SACRED *adj*
SACRIFY *vb* old form of sacrifice
SACRING *n* act or ritual of consecration
SACRIST = **sacristan**
SACRUM *n* wedge-shaped bone at the base of the spine **sacrums**
SACS ▸ **sac**
SAD *adj*, *vb* **sadded**
SADDEN *vb* **saddens**
SADDER ▸ **sad**
SADDEST ▸ **sad**
SADDHU = **sadhu**
SADDHUS ▸ **saddhu**
SADDIE ▸ **saddo** *n*
SADDIES ▸ **saddie**
SADDING ▸ **sad**
SADDISH ▸ **sad**
SADDLE *n*, *vb* **saddled**
SADDLER *n*
SADDLES ▸ **saddle**
SADDO *vb* make sad ▹ *n* socially inadequate or pathetic person **saddoes, saddos**
SADE = **sadhe**
SADES ▸ **sade**
SADHANA *n* one of a number of spiritual practices which lead to perfection
SADHE *n* 18th letter in the Hebrew alphabet **sadhes**
SADHU *n* Hindu wandering holy man **sadhus**
SADI *variant of* ▸ **sadhe**
SADIRON *n* heavy iron pointed at both ends, for pressing clothes
SADIS ▸ **sadi**
SADISM *n* **sadisms, sadist, sadists**
SADLY ▸ **sad**
SADNESS ▸ **sad**
SADO *variant of* ▸ **chado**
SADOS ▸ **sado**
SADS ▸ **sad**
SADZA *n* southern African porridge **sadzas**
SAE *Scot word for* ▸ **so**
SAETER *n* upland pasture in Norway **saeters**
SAFARI *n*, *vb* **safaris**
SAFE *adj*, *n*, *vb* **safed, safely, safer, safes, safest**
SAFETY *n*, *vb*
SAFFIAN *n* leather tanned with sumach and usually dyed a bright colour
SAFFRON *n*, *adj*
SAFING ▸ **safe**
SAFROL *n* oily liquid obtained from sassafras
SAFROLE *n* colourless or yellowish oily water-insoluble liquid
SAFROLS ▸ **safrol**
SAFT *Scot word for* ▸ **soft**
SAFTER ▸ **saft**
SAFTEST ▸ **saft**
SAG *vb*, *n*
SAGA *n*

SAGAMAN *n* person reciting Norse sagas **sagamen**
SAGAS ▸ **saga**
SAGATHY *n* type of light fabric
SAGBUT *n* medieval trombone **sagbuts**
SAGE *n*, *adj* **sagely**
SAGENE *n* fishing net **sagenes**
SAGER ▸ **sage**
SAGES ▸ **sage**
SAGEST ▸ **sage**
SAGGAR *n* box in which fragile ceramic wares are placed for protection ▹ *vb* put in a saggar
SAGGARD *n* saggar
SAGGARS ▸ **saggar**
SAGGED ▸ **sag**
SAGGER = **saggar**
SAGGERS ▸ **sagger**
SAGGIER ▸ **saggy**
SAGGING ▸ **sag**
SAGGY *adj* tending to sag
SAGIER ▸ **sagy**
SAGIEST ▸ **sagy**
SAGITTA *n* sine of an arc
SAGO *n*
SAGOIN *n* South American monkey **sagoins**
SAGOS ▸ **sago**
SAGOUIN *n* South American monkey
SAGRADA *adj as in* **cascara sagrada** dried bark of the cascara buckthorn
SAGS ▸ **sag**
SAGUARO *n* giant cactus of desert regions
SAGUIN *n* South American monkey **saguins**
SAGUM *n* Roman soldier's cloak
SAGY *adj* like or containing sage
SAHEB = **sahib**
SAHEBS ▸ **saheb**
SAHIB *n* Indian term of address placed after a man's name as a mark of respect
SAHIBA *n* respectful Indian term of address for woman
SAHIBAH *n* sahiba
SAHIBAS ▸ **sahiba**
SAHIBS ▸ **sahib**
SAHIWAL *n* breed of cattle in India
SAHUARO = **saguaro**
SAI *n* South American monkey
SAIC *n* boat of eastern Mediterranean
SAICE = **syce**
SAICES ▸ **saice**
SAICK *n* boat of eastern Mediterranean **saicks**
SAICS ▸ **saic**
SAID = **sayyid**
SAIDEST ▸ **say**
SAIDS ▸ **said**
SAIDST ▸ **say**
SAIGA *n* either of two antelopes of the plains of central Asia **saigas**
SAIKEI *n* Japanese ornamental miniature landscape **saikeis**
SAIL *n*, *vb* **sailed**
SAILER *n* vessel, esp one equipped with sails, with specified sailing characteristics **sailers**
SAILING *n* practice, art, or technique of sailing a vessel
SAILOR *n* **sailors**
SAILS ▸ **sail**
SAIM *Scots word for* ▸ **lard**
SAIMIN *n* Hawaiian dish of noodles **saimins**
SAIMIRI *n* South American monkey
SAIMS ▸ **saim**
SAIN *vb* make the sign of the cross over so as to bless or protect from evil or sin
SAINE *vb* old form of say
SAINED ▸ **sain**
SAINING ▸ **sain**
SAINS ▸ **sain**
SAINT *n*, *vb*
SAINTED *adj* formally recognized by a Christian Church as a saint
SAINTLY *adj*
SAINTS ▸ **saint**
SAIQUE *n* boat in eastern Mediterranean **saiques**
SAIR *Scot word for* ▸ **sore; saired, sairer, sairest, sairing, sairs**
SAIS ▸ **sai**
SAIST ▸ **say**
SAITH *form of the present tense (indicative mood) of* ▸ **say**

SAITHE *n* dark-coloured food fish found in northern seas **saithes**
SAITHS ▸ **saith**
SAIYID *n* Muslim descended from Mohammed's grandson **saiyids**
SAJOU *n* South American monkey **sajous**
SAKAI *n* Malaysian aborigine **sakais**
SAKE *n*
SAKER *n* large falcon of E Europe and central Asia
SAKERET *n* male saker
SAKERS ▸ **saker**
SAKES ▸ **sake**
SAKI = **sake**
SAKIA *n* water wheel in Middle East **sakias**
SAKIEH *n* water wheel in Middle East **sakiehs**
SAKIS ▸ **saki**
SAKIYEH *n* water wheel in Middle East
SAKKOI ▸ **sakkos**
SAKKOS *n* bishop's garment in Orthodox Church
SAKSAUL *n* Asian tree
SAL *pharmacological term for* ▸ **salt**
SALAAM *n* low bow of greeting among Muslims ▹ *vb* make a salaam **salaams**
SALABLE = **saleable**
SALABLY > **saleably**
SALAD *n*
SALADE = **sallet**
SALADES ▸ **salade**
SALADS ▸ **salad**
SALAL *n* North American shrub **salals**
SALAMI *n* **salamis**
SALAMON *n* word used in old oaths
SALARY *n, vb*
SALBAND *n* coating of mineral
SALCHOW *n* type of figure-skating jump
SALE *n*
SALEP *n* dried ground starchy tubers of various orchids **saleps**
SALES ▸ **sale**
SALET = **sallet**
SALETS ▸ **salet**
SALEWD ▸ **salue**
SALFERN *n* plant of borage family
SALIC *adj* (of rocks and minerals) having a high content of silica and alumina
SALICES ▸ **salix**
SALICET *n* soft-toned organ stop
SALICIN *n* colourless or white crystalline water-soluble glucoside
SALIENT *adj, n*
SALIFY *vb* treat, mix with, or cause to combine with a salt
SALIGOT *n* water chestnut
SALINA *n* salt marsh, lake, or spring **salinas**
SALINE *adj, n* **salines**
SALIVA *n* **salival, salivas**
SALIX *n* plant or tree of willow family
SALL *archaic form of* ▸ **shall**
SALLAD *old spelling of* ▸ **salad**
SALLADS ▸ **sallad**
SALLAL *n* North American shrub **sallals**
SALLE *n* hall
SALLEE *n* SE Australian eucalyptus **sallees**
SALLES ▸ **salle**
SALLET *n* light round helmet **sallets**
SALLIED ▸ **sally**
SALLIER ▸ **sally**
SALLIES ▸ **sally**
SALLOW *adj, vb, n* **sallows, sallowy**
SALLY *n, vb*
SALMI *n* ragout of game stewed in a rich brown sauce **salmis**
SALMON *n, adj* **salmons**
SALMONY *adj* of or like a salmon
SALOL *n* white sparingly soluble crystalline compound **salols**
SALON *n* **salons**
SALOON *n* **saloons**
SALOOP *n* infusion of aromatic herbs or other plant parts formerly used as a tonic or cure **saloops, salop**
SALOPS ▸ **salop**
SALP *n* minute animal floating in sea
SALPA *n* any of various minute floating

animals of warm oceans **salpae, salpas**
SALPIAN *n* minute animal floating in sea
SALPID *n* minute animal floating in sea **salpids**
SALPINX *n* Fallopian tube or Eustachian tube
SALPS ▶ **salp**
SALS ▶ **sal**
SALSA *n* lively Puerto Rican dance ▷ *vb* dance the salsa **salsaed, salsas**
SALSE *n* volcano expelling mud **salses**
SALSIFY *n* Mediterranean plant with a long white edible root
SALT *n, vb*
SALTANT *adj* (of an organism) differing from others of its species because of a saltation ▷ *n* saltant organism
SALTATE *vb* go through saltation
SALTATO *n* saltando
SALTBOX *n* box for salt with a sloping lid
SALTCAT *n* salty medicine for pigeons
SALTED *adj* seasoned, preserved, or treated with salt
SALTER *n* person who deals in or manufactures salt
SALTERN *n* place where salt is obtained from pools of evaporated sea water
SALTERS ▶ **salter**
SALTEST ▶ **salt**
SALTIE *n* saltwater crocodile
SALTIER ▶ **saltire**
SALTIES ▶ **saltie**
SALTILY ▶ **salty**
SALTINE *n* salty biscuit
SALTING *n* area of low ground regularly inundated with salt water
SALTIRE *n* diagonal cross on a shield
SALTISH ▶ **salt**
SALTLY ▶ **salt**
SALTO *n* daring jump ▷ *vb* perform a daring jump **saltoed, saltos**
SALTPAN *n* shallow basin containing salt from an evaporated salt lake
SALTS ▶ **salt**
SALTUS *n* break in the continuity of a sequence
SALTY *adj*
SALUE *vb* old word meaning salute **salued, salues, saluing**
SALUKI *n* type of tall hound with a smooth coat **salukis**
SALUTE *n, vb* **saluted, saluter, salutes**
SALVAGE *n, vb*
SALVE *n, vb* **salved**
SALVER = **salvor**
SALVERS ▶ **salver**
SALVES ▶ **salve**
SALVETE *n* Latin greeting
SALVIA *n* plant with blue or red flowers **salvias**
SALVING ▶ **salve**
SALVO *n, vb* **salvoed, salvoes**
SALVOR *n* person instrumental in salvaging a vessel or its cargo **salvors**
SALVOS ▶ **salvo**
SALWAR *n as in* **salwar kameez** long tunic worn over a pair of baggy trousers **salwars**
SAM *vb* collect
SAMA *n* Japanese title of respect
SAMAAN *n* South American tree **samaans**
SAMADHI *n* state of deep meditative contemplation
SAMAN *n* South American tree **samans**
SAMARA *n* dry indehiscent one-seeded fruit **samaras**
SAMAS ▶ **sama**
SAMBA *n, vb* **sambaed**
SAMBAL *n* Malaysian dish **sambals**
SAMBAR *n* S Asian deer with three-tined antlers **sambars**
SAMBAS ▶ **samba**
SAMBHAR *n* Indian dish
SAMBHUR *n* Asian deer

SAMBUCA *n* Italian liqueur
SAMBUKE *n* ancient Greek stringed instrument
SAMBUR = **sambar**
SAMBURS ▸ **sambur**
SAME *adj, n*
SAMECH *n* letter in Hebrew alphabet **samechs**
SAMEK *variant of* ▸ **samekh**
SAMEKH *n* 15th letter in the Hebrew alphabet **samekhs**
SAMEKS ▸ **samek**
SAMEL *adj* of brick, not sufficiently fired
SAMELY *adj* the same
SAMEN *old Scots form of* ▸ **same**
SAMES ▸ **same**
SAMEY *adj* monotonous
SAMFOO *n* style of casual dress worn by Chinese women **samfoos**
SAMFU *n* Chinese female outfit **samfus**
SAMIEL = **simoom**
SAMIELS ▸ **samiel**
SAMIER ▸ **samey**
SAMIEST ▸ **samey**
SAMISEN *n* Japanese plucked stringed instrument with a long neck
SAMITE *n* heavy fabric of silk used in the Middle Ages **samites**
SAMITHI = **samiti**
SAMITI *n* (in India) an association, esp one formed to organize political activity **samitis**
SAMLET *n* young salmon **samlets**
SAMLOR *n* motor vehicle in Thailand **samlors**
SAMMED ▸ **sam**
SAMMIES ▸ **sammy**
SAMMING ▸ **sam**
SAMMY *n* (in South Africa) an Indian fruit and vegetable vendor
SAMOSA *n* **samosas**
SAMOVAR *n*
SAMOYED *n* Siberian breed of dog with a tightly curled tail
SAMP *n* crushed maize used for porridge
SAMPAN *n* **sampans**
SAMPI *n* old Greek number character
SAMPIRE *n* samphire
SAMPIS ▸ **sampi**
SAMPLE *n, vb* **sampled**
SAMPLER *n*
SAMPLES ▸ **sample**
SAMPS ▸ **samp**
SAMS ▸ **sam**
SAMSARA *n* endless cycle of birth, death, and rebirth
SAMSHOO *n* Chinese alcoholic drink
SAMSHU *n* alcoholic drink made from fermented rice **samshus**
SAMURAI *n*
SAN *n* sanatorium
SANCAI *n* glaze in Chinese pottery **sancais**
SANCHO *n* African stringed instrument **sanchos**
SANCTA ▸ **sanctum**
SANCTUM *n* sacred place
SAND *n, vb*
SANDAL *n, vb* **sandals**
SANDBAG *n, vb*
SANDBAR *n* ridge of sand in a river or sea, often exposed at low tide
SANDBOX *n* container on a locomotive from which sand is released onto the rails
SANDBOY *n as in* **happy as a sandboy** very happy or high-spirited
SANDBUR *n* variety of wild grass
SANDDAB *n* type of small Pacific flatfish
SANDED ▸ **sand**
SANDEK *n* man who holds a baby being circumcised **sandeks**
SANDER *n* power tool for smoothing surfaces **sanders**
SANDFLY *n* any of various small mothlike flies
SANDHI *n* modification of a word under the influence of an adjacent word **sandhis**
SANDHOG *n* person who works in underground or underwater construction projects

SANDIER ▸ **sandy**
SANDING ▸ **sand**
SANDLOT *n* area of vacant ground used for children's games
SANDMAN *n* (in folklore) a magical person supposed to put children to sleep **sandmen**
SANDPIT *n* shallow pit or container holding sand for children to play in
SANDS ▸ **sand**
SANDY *adj*
SANE *adj, vb* **saned, sanely, saner, sanes, sanest**
SANG *Scots word for* ▸ **song**
SANGA *n* Ethiopian ox
SANGAR *n* breastwork of stone or sods **sangars**
SANGAS ▸ **sanga**
SANGEET *n* Indian pre-wedding celebration
SANGER *n* sandwich **sangers**
SANGH *n* Indian union or association
SANGHA *n* Buddhist monastic order or community **sanghas**
SANGHAT *n* local Sikh community or congregation
SANGHS ▸ **sangh**
SANGO = **sanger**
SANGOMA *n* witch doctor or herbalist
SANGOS ▸ **sango**
SANGRIA *n* Spanish drink of red wine and fruit
SANGS ▸ **sang**
SANICLE *n* type of plant with clusters of small white flowers
SANIES *n* thin greenish foul-smelling discharge from a wound, etc
SANIFY *vb* make healthy
SANING ▸ **sane**
SANIOUS ▸ **sanies**
SANITY *n*
SANJAK *n* (in the Turkish Empire) a subdivision of a vilayet **sanjaks**
SANK ▸ **sink**
SANKO *n* African stringed instrument **sankos**
SANNIE *Scots word for* > **sandshoe**
SANNIES ▸ **sannie**
SANNOP *n* Native American married man **sannops**
SANNUP *n* Native American married man **sannups**
SANPAN *n* sampan **sanpans**
SANPRO *n* sanitary-protection products, collectively **sanpros**
SANS *archaic word for* ▸ **without**
SANSA *n* African musical instrument
SANSAR *n* name of a wind that blows in Iran **sansars**
SANSAS ▸ **sansa**
SANSEI *n* American whose parents were Japanese immigrants **sanseis**
SANT *n* devout person in India
SANTAL *n* sandalwood **santals**
SANTERA *n* priestess of santeria
SANTERO *n* priest of santeria
SANTIMI ▸ **santims**
SANTIMS *n* money unit in Latvia **santimu**
SANTIR *n* Middle Eastern stringed instrument **santirs**
SANTO *n* saint or representation of one
SANTOL *n* fruit from Southeast Asia **santols**
SANTON *n* French figurine **santons**
SANTOOR = **santir**
SANTOS ▸ **santo**
SANTOUR *n* Middle Eastern stringed instrument
SANTS ▸ **sant**
SANTUR *n* Middle Eastern stringed instrument **santurs**
SANYASI = **sannyasi**
SAOLA *n* small, very rare bovine mammal of Vietnam and Laos **saolas**
SAOUARI *n* tropical American tree
SAP *n, vb*

SAPAJOU *n* capuchin monkey
SAPAN *n* tropical tree **sapans**
SAPEGO *n* skin disease
SAPELE *n* type of W African tree **sapeles**
SAPFUL *adj* full of sap
SAPHEAD *n* simpleton, idiot, or fool
SAPHENA *n* either of two large superficial veins of the legs
SAPID *adj* having a pleasant taste
SAPIENS *adj* relating to or like modern human beings
SAPIENT *adj* wise, shrewd ▷ *n* wise person
SAPLESS ▸ **sap**
SAPLING *n*
SAPONIN *n* any of a group of plant glycosides
SAPOR *n* quality in a substance that is perceived by the sense of taste **sapors**
SAPOTA = **sapodilla**
SAPOTAS ▸ **sapota**
SAPOTE *n* Central American tree **sapotes**
SAPOUR *variant of* ▸ **sapor**
SAPOURS ▸ **sapour**
SAPPAN *n* tropical tree **sappans**
SAPPED ▸ **sap**
SAPPER *n* soldier in an engineering unit **sappers**
SAPPHIC *adj* lesbian ▷ *n* verse written in a particular form
SAPPIER ▸ **sappy**
SAPPILY ▸ **sappy**
SAPPING ▸ **sap**
SAPPLE *vb* Scots word meaning wash in water **sappled, sapples**
SAPPY *adj* (of plants) full of sap
SAPROBE *n* organism that lives on decaying organisms
SAPS ▸ **sap**
SAPSAGO *n* hard greenish Swiss cheese
SAPWOOD *n* soft wood, just beneath the bark in tree trunks, that consists of living tissue
SAR *n* marine fish ▷ *vb* Scots word meaning savour
SARAFAN *n* Russian woman's cloak
SARAN *n* any one of a class of thermoplastic resins
SARANGI *n* stringed instrument of India played with a bow
SARANS ▸ **saran**
SARAPE *n* serape **sarapes**
SARCASM *n* (use of) bitter or wounding ironic language
SARCINA *n* type of bacterium
SARCODE *n* material making up living cell
SARCOID *adj* of, relating to, or resembling flesh ▷ *n* tumour resembling a sarcoma
SARCOMA *n* malignant tumour beginning in connective tissue
SARCOUS *adj* (of tissue) muscular or fleshy
SARD *n* orange, red, or brown variety of chalcedony
SARDANA *n* Catalan dance
SARDAR *n* title used before the name of Sikh men **sardars**
SARDEL *n* small fish **sardels**
SARDINE *n*, *vb*
SARDIUS = **sard**
SARDS ▸ **sard**
SARED ▸ **sar**
SAREE = **sari**
SAREES ▸ **saree**
SARGE *n* sergeant **sarges**
SARGO = **sargus**
SARGOS *variant of* ▸ **sargus**
SARGUS *n* species of sea fish
SARI *n*
SARIN *n* chemical used in warfare as a lethal nerve gas producing asphyxia
SARING ▸ **sar**
SARINS ▸ **sarin**
SARIS ▸ **sari**
SARK *n* shirt or (formerly) chemise
SARKIER ▸ **sarky**
SARKILY ▸ **sarky**
SARKING *n* flat

planking supporting the roof cladding of a building
SARKS ▸ sark
SARKY *adj* sarcastic
SARMENT *n* thin twig
SARMIE *n* **sarmies**
SARNEY *n* sandwich **sarneys**
SARNIE *n* sandwich **sarnies**
SAROD *n* Indian stringed musical instrument
SARODE *n* Indian stringed instrument **sarodes**
SARODS ▸ sarod
SARONG *n* **sarongs**
SARONIC ▸ saros
SAROS *n* cycle in which eclipses of the sun and moon occur in the same sequence **saroses**
SARS ▸ sar
SARSAR = **sansar**
SARSARS ▸ sarsar
SARSDEN *n* sarsen
SARSEN *n* boulder of silicified sandstone **sarsens**
SARSNET *n* type of silk
SARTOR *humorous or literary word for* **▸ tailor**
SARTORS ▸ sartor
SARUS *n* Indian bird of crane family **saruses**
SASER *n* device for amplifying ultrasound **sasers**
SASH *n, vb*
SASHAY *vb* move or walk in a casual or a showy manner **sashays**
SASHED ▸ sash
SASHES ▸ sash
SASHIMI *n* Japanese dish of thin fillets of raw fish
SASHING ▸ sash
SASIN *another name for* > **blackbuck**
SASINE *n* granting of legal possession of feudal property **sasines**
SASINS ▸ sasin
SASS *n* insolent or impudent talk or behaviour ▹ *vb* talk or answer back in such a way
SASSABY *n* African antelope of grasslands and semideserts
SASSE *n* old word meaning canal lock
SASSED ▸ sass
SASSES ▸ sass
SASSIER ▸ sassy
SASSIES ▸ sassy
SASSILY ▸ sassy
SASSING ▸ sass
SASSY *adj* insolent, impertinent ▹ *n* W African leguminous tree with poisonous bark
SASTRA = **shastra**
SASTRAS ▸ sastra
SAT ▸ sit
SATAI = **satay**
SATAIS ▸ satai
SATANG *n* monetary unit of Thailand worth one hundredth of a baht **satangs**
SATANIC *adj*
SATARA *n* type of cloth **sataras**
SATAY *n* Indonesian and Malaysian dish **satays**
SATCHEL *n*
SATE *vb* satisfy (a desire or appetite) fully **sated**
SATEEN *n* glossy linen or cotton fabric, woven in such a way that it resembles satin **sateens**
SATEM *adj* denoting or belonging to a particular group of Indo-European languages
SATES ▸ sate
SATI *n* Indian widow suicide
SATIATE *vb*
SATIETY *n* feeling of having had too much
SATIN *n, adj, vb* **satined**
SATINET *n* thin or imitation satin
SATING ▸ sate
SATINS ▸ satin
SATINY ▸ satin
SATIRE *n* **satires**
SATIRIC = **satirical**
SATIS ▸ sati
SATISFY *vb*
SATIVE *adj* old word meaning cultivated
SATORI *n* state of sudden indescribable intuitive enlightenment **satoris**
SATRAP *n* (in ancient Persia) a provincial governor or subordinate ruler **satraps**

SATRAPY *n* province, office, or period of rule of a satrap
SATSUMA *n*
SATYR *n* woodland god, part man, part goat
SATYRA *n* female satyr
SATYRAL *n* mythical beast in heraldry
SATYRAS ▸ **satyra**
SATYRIC ▸ **satyr**
SATYRID *n* butterfly with typically brown or dark wings with paler markings
SATYRS ▸ **satyr**
SAU *archaic past tense of* ▸ **see**
SAUBA *n* South American ant **saubas**
SAUCE *n*, *vb* **sauced**
SAUCER *n* **saucers**
SAUCES ▸ **sauce**
SAUCH *n* sallow or willow **sauchs**
SAUCIER *n* chef who makes sauces
SAUCILY ▸ **saucy**
SAUCING ▸ **sauce**
SAUCY *adj*
SAUGER *n* small North American pikeperch **saugers**
SAUGH = **sauch**
SAUGHS ▸ **saugh**
SAUGHY *adj* Scots word meaning made of willow
SAUL *Scots word for* ▸ **soul**
SAULGE *n* old word for sage plant **saulges**
SAULIE *n* Scots word meaning professional mourner **saulies**
SAULS ▸ **saul**
SAULT *n* waterfall in Canada **saults**
SAUNA *n*, *vb* **saunaed, saunas**
SAUNT *Scots form of* ▸ **saint**
SAUNTED ▸ **saunt**
SAUNTER *vb*, *n*
SAUNTS ▸ **saunt**
SAUREL *n* type of mackerel **saurels**
SAURIAN *n*
SAURIES ▸ **saury**
SAUROID *adj* like a lizard
SAURY *n* type of fish of tropical and temperate seas
SAUSAGE *n*
SAUT *Scot word for* ▸ **salt**
SAUTE *vb* fry quickly in a little fat ▹ *n* dish of sautéed food ▹ *adj* sautéed until lightly brown
SAUTED ▸ **saut**
SAUTEED ▸ **saute**
SAUTES ▸ **saute**
SAUTING ▸ **saut**
SAUTOIR *n* long necklace or pendant
SAUTS ▸ **saut**
SAV *short for* ▸ **saveloy**
SAVABLE ▸ **save**
SAVAGE *adj*, *n*, *vb* **savaged, savager, savages**
SAVANNA *n*
SAVANT *n* learned person **savante, savants**
SAVARIN *n* type of cake
SAVATE *n* form of boxing in which blows may be delivered with the feet **savates**
SAVE *vb*, *n*, *prep* **saved**
SAVELOY *n* spicy smoked sausage
SAVER ▸ **save**
SAVERS ▸ **save**
SAVES ▸ **save**
SAVEY *vb* understand **saveyed, saveys**
SAVIN *n* small spreading juniper bush of Europe, N Asia, and North America **savine**
SAVINES ▸ **savine**
SAVING *n*, *prep*, *adj* **savings**
SAVINS ▸ **savin**
SAVIOR = **saviour**
SAVIORS ▸ **savior**
SAVIOUR *n*
SAVOR = **savour**
SAVORED ▸ **savor**
SAVORER ▸ **savor**
SAVORS ▸ **savor**
SAVORY = **savoury**
SAVOUR *vb*, *n* **savours**
SAVOURY *adj*, *n*
SAVOY *n* variety of cabbage **savoys**
SAVS ▸ **sav**
SAVVEY *vb* understand **savveys**
SAVVIED, savvier, savvies, savvily ▸ **savvy**
SAVVY *vb* understand ▹ *n* understanding, intelligence ▹ *adj* shrewd
SAW *n*, *vb*

SAWAH *n* paddyfield **sawahs**
SAWBILL *n* type of hummingbird
SAWBUCK *n* sawhorse, esp one having an X-shaped supporting structure
SAWDER *n* flattery ▷ *vb* flatter **sawders**
SAWDUST *n, vb*
SAWED ▸ **saw**
SAWER ▸ **saw**
SAWERS ▸ **saw**
SAWFISH *n* fish with a long toothed snout
SAWFLY *n* any of various hymenopterous insects
SAWING ▸ **saw**
SAWINGS ▸ **saw**
SAWLIKE ▸ **saw**
SAWLOG *n* log suitable for sawing **sawlogs**
SAWMILL *n*
SAWN *past participle of* ▸ **saw**
SAWPIT *n* pit above which a log is sawn into planks **sawpits**
SAWS ▸ **saw**
SAWYER *n* person who saws timber for a living **sawyers**
SAX = **saxophone**
SAXAUL *n* Asian tree **saxauls**
SAXE *adj as in* **saxe blue** light greyish-blue colour
SAXES ▸ **sax**
SAXHORN *n* valved brass instrument used chiefly in brass and military bands
SAXONY *n* fine 3-ply yarn used for knitting and weaving
SAXTUBA *n* bass saxhorn
SAY *vb* speak or utter ▷ *n* right or chance to speak **sayable**
SAYED = **sayyid**
SAYEDS ▸ **sayed**
SAYER ▸ **say**
SAYERS ▸ **say**
SAYEST ▸ **say**
SAYID = **sayyid**
SAYIDS ▸ **sayid**
SAYING ▸ **say**
SAYINGS ▸ **say**
SAYNE ▸ **say**
SAYON *n* type of tunic **sayons**
SAYS ▸ **say**
SAYST ▸ **say**
SAYYID *n* Muslim claiming descent from Mohammed's grandson Husain **sayyids**
SAZ *n* Middle Eastern stringed instrument

> This musical instrument is one of the most frequently played Z words.

SAZERAC *n* mixed drink of whisky, Pernod, syrup, bitters, and lemon
SAZES ▸ **saz**
SAZHEN *n* Russian measure of length **sazhens**
SAZZES ▸ **saz**
SBIRRI ▸ **sbirro**
SBIRRO *n* Italian police officer
SCAB *n, vb* **scabbed**
SCABBLE *vb* shape (stone) roughly
SCABBY *adj* covered with scabs
SCABIES *n*
SCABRID *adj* having a rough or scaly surface
SCABS ▸ **scab**
SCAD *n* any of various carangid fishes
SCADS *pl n* large amount or number
SCAFF *n* Scots word meaning food
SCAFFIE *n* Scots word meaning street cleaner
SCAFFS ▸ **scaff**
SCAG *n* tear in a garment or piece of cloth ▷ *vb* make a tear in (cloth) **scagged**
SCAGLIA *n* type of limestone
SCAGS ▸ **scag**
SCAIL *vb* Scots word meaning disperse **scailed, scails**
SCAITH *vb* old word meaning injure **scaiths**
SCALA *n* passage inside the cochlea
SCALADE *short for* > **escalade**
SCALADO = **scalade**
SCALAE ▸ **scala**
SCALAGE *n* percentage deducted from the price of goods liable to shrink or leak

SCALAR *adj* having magnitude but no direction ▷ *n* quantity that has magnitude but not direction
SCALARE *another name for* > **angelfish**
SCALARS ▶ **scalar**
SCALD = **skald**
SCALDED ▶ **scald**
SCALDER ▶ **scald**
SCALDIC ▶ **skald**
SCALDS ▶ **scald**
SCALE *n, vb* **scaled**
SCALENE *adj*
SCALENI > **scalenus**
SCALER *n* person or thing that scales **scalers**
SCALES ▶ **scale**
SCALEUP *n* increase
SCALIER ▶ **scaly**
SCALING ▶ **scaling**
SCALL *n* disease of the scalp characterized by itching and scab formation **scalled**
SCALLOP *n, vb*
SCALLS ▶ **scall**
SCALLY *n* rascal
SCALP *n, vb* **scalped**
SCALPEL *n*
SCALPER ▶ **scalp**
SCALPS ▶ **scalp**
SCALY *adj*
SCAM *n* dishonest scheme ▷ *vb* swindle (someone) by means of a trick
SCAMBLE *vb* scramble
SCAMEL *n* Shakespearian word of uncertain meaning **scamels**
SCAMMED ▶ **scam**
SCAMMER *n* person who perpetrates a scam
SCAMP *n* mischievous child ▷ *vb* perform without care **scamped**
SCAMPER *vb, n*
SCAMPI *pl n* **scampis**
SCAMPS ▶ **scamp**
SCAMS ▶ **scam**
SCAMTO *n* argot of urban South African Blacks **scamtos**
SCAN *vb, n* **scand**
SCANDAL *n, vb*
SCANDIA *n* scandium oxide
SCANDIC *adj* of or containing scandium
SCANNED ▶ **scan**
SCANNER *n*
SCANS ▶ **scan**
SCANT *adj, vb, adv* **scanted, scanter**
SCANTLE *vb* stint
SCANTLY ▶ **scant**
SCANTS ▶ **scant**
SCANTY *adj*
SCAPA *variant of* ▶ **scarper**
SCAPAED ▶ **scapa**
SCAPAS ▶ **scapa**
SCAPE *n* leafless stalk in plants ▷ *vb* archaic word for escape **scaped, scapes**
SCAPI ▶ **scapus**
SCAPING ▶ **scape**
SCAPOSE ▶ **scape**
SCAPPLE *vb* shape roughly
SCAPULA *n*
SCAPUS *n* flower stalk
SCAR *n, vb*
SCARAB *n* sacred beetle of ancient Egypt **scarabs**
SCARCE *adj* **scarcer**
SCARE *vb, n, adj* **scared, scarer, scarers, scares**
SCAREY *adj* frightening
SCARF *n, vb* **scarfed, scarfer, scarfs**
SCARIER ▶ **scary**
SCARIFY *vb* scratch or cut slightly all over
SCARILY ▶ **scary**
SCARING ▶ **scare**
SCARLET *n, adj, vb*
SCARP *n, vb*
SCARPA *vb* run away **scarpas**
SCARPED ▶ **scarp**
SCARPER *vb, n*
SCARPH *vb* join with scarf joint **scarphs**
SCARPS ▶ **scarp**
SCARRE *n* Shakespearian word of unknown meaning
SCARRED ▶ **scar**
SCARRES ▶ **scarre**
SCARRY ▶ **scar**
SCARS ▶ **scar**
SCART *vb* scratch or scrape ▷ *n* scratch or scrape **scarted**
SCARTH *Scots word for* > **cormorant**
SCARTHS ▶ **scarth**
SCARTS ▶ **scart**
SCARVES ▶ **scarf**
SCARY *adj*
SCAT *vb* go away ▷ *n* jazz singing using improvised vocal

sounds instead of words
SCATCH = **stilt**
SCATH *vb* old word meaning injure
SCATHE *vb* attack with severe criticism ▷ *n* harm **scathed, scathes**
SCATHS ▸ **scath**
SCATOLE *n* substance found in coal
SCATS ▸ **scat**
SCATT *n* old word meaning tax ▷ *vb* tax
SCATTED ▸ **scat**
SCATTER *vb, n*
SCATTS ▸ **scatt**
SCATTY *adj*
SCAUD *Scot word for* ▸ **scald**
SCAUDED ▸ **scaud**
SCAUDS ▸ **scaud**
SCAUP *variant of* ▸ **scalp**
SCAUPED ▸ **scaup**
SCAUPER = **scorper**
SCAUPS ▸ **scaup**
SCAUR = **scar**
SCAURED ▸ **scaur**
SCAURS ▸ **scaur**
SCAURY *n* young seagull
SCAVAGE *n* old word meaning toll
SCAW *n* headland **scaws**
SCAZON *n* metre in poetry **scazons**
SCEAT *n* Anglo-Saxon coin
SCEATT *n* Anglo-Saxon coin
SCEDULE *old spelling of* > **schedule**
SCENA *n* scene in an opera, usually longer than a single aria
SCENARY *n* scenery
SCENAS ▸ **scena**
SCEND *vb* (of a vessel) to surge upwards in a heavy sea ▷ *n* upward heaving of a vessel pitching **scended, scends**
SCENE *n, vb* **scened**
SCENERY *n*
SCENES ▸ **scene**
SCENIC *adj, n* **scenics**
SCENING ▸ **scene**
SCENT *n, vb* **scented, scents**
SCEPSIS *n* doubt
SCEPTER = **sceptre**
SCEPTIC *n, adj*
SCEPTRE *n, vb*
SCEPTRY *adj* having sceptre
SCERNE *vb* old word meaning discern **scerned, scernes**
SCHANSE *n* stones heaped to shelter soldier in battle
SCHANZE *n* stones heaped to shelter soldier in battle
SCHAPPE *n* yarn or fabric made from waste silk
SCHAV *n* Polish soup **schavs**
SCHELLY *n* freshwater whitefish of the English Lake District
SCHELM *n* South African word meaning rascal **schelms**
SCHEMA *n* **schemas**
SCHEME *n, vb* **schemed, schemer, schemes**
SCHERZI ▸ **scherzo**
SCHERZO *n* brisk lively piece of music
SCHISM *n*
SCHISMA *n* musical term
SCHISMS ▸ **schism**
SCHIST *n* crystalline rock which splits into layers **schists**
SCHLEP *vb* drag or lug (oneself or an object) with difficulty ▷ *n* stupid or clumsy person
SCHLEPP *vb* schlep
SCHLEPS ▸ **schlep**
SCHLICH *n* finely crushed ore
SCHLOCK *n* goods or produce of cheap or inferior quality ▷ *adj* cheap, inferior, or trashy
SCHLOSS *n* castle
SCHLUB *n* coarse or contemptible person **schlubs**
SCHLUMP *vb* move in lazy way
SCHMALZ = **schmaltz**
SCHMEAR *n* situation, matter, or affair ▷ *vb* spread or smear
SCHMECK *n* taste
SCHMEER = **schmear**
SCHMELZ *n* ornamental glass
SCHMICK *adj* (in Australia) excellent, elegant, or stylish
SCHMO *n* dull, stupid, or boring person

SCHMOCK *n* stupid person
SCHMOE *n* stupid person
SCHMOES ▸ **schmo**
SCHMOOS *variant of* > **schmoose**
SCHMOOZ *n* chat
SCHMOS ▸ **schmo**
SCHMUCK *n* stupid or contemptible person
SCHNAPS = **schnapps**
SCHNELL *adj* German word meaning quick
SCHNOOK *n* stupid or gullible person
SCHNORR *vb* beg
SCHNOZ *n* nose
SCHNOZZ *n* nose
SCHOLAR *n*
SCHOLIA > **scholium**
SCHOOL *n, vb*
SCHOOLE *n* old form of shoal
SCHOOLS ▸ **school**
SCHORL *n* type of black tourmaline **schorls**
SCHOUT *n* council officer in Netherlands **schouts**
SCHRIK *variant of* ▸ **skrik**
SCHRIKS ▸ **schrik**
SCHROD *n* young cod **schrods**
SCHTICK = **shtick**
SCHTIK *n* schtick **schtiks**
SCHTOOK *n* trouble
SCHTOOM *adj* silent
SCHTUCK *n* trouble
SCHTUM *adj* silent or dumb
SCHUIT *n* Dutch boat with flat bottom **schuits**
SCHUL = **shul**
SCHULN ▸ **schul**
SCHULS ▸ **schul**
SCHUSS *n* straight high-speed downhill run ▹ *vb* perform a schuss
SCHUYT *n* Dutch boat with flat bottom **schuyts**
SCHWA *n* vowel representing the sound in unstressed syllables **schwas**
SCIARID *n* small fly
SCIATIC *adj* of the hip ▹ *n* sciatic part of the body
SCIENCE *n*
SCIENT *adj* old word meaning scientific
SCILLA *n* plant with small bell-shaped flowers **scillas**
SCIOLTO *adv* musical direction meaning freely
SCION *n* **scions**
SCIROC *n* hot Mediterranean wind **scirocs**
SCIRRHI > **scirrhus**
SCISSEL *n* waste metal left over from sheet metal after discs have been punched out of it
SCISSIL *n* scissel
SCISSOR *vb* cut (an object) with scissors
SCIURID *n* squirrel or related rodent
SCLAFF *vb* cause (the club) to hit (the ground behind the ball) when making a stroke ▹ *n* sclaffing stroke or shot **sclaffs**
SCLATE *vb* Scots word meaning slate **sclates**
SCLAVE *n* old form of slave **sclaves**
SCLERA *n* tough white substance that forms the outer covering of the eyeball **sclerae, scleral, scleras**
SCLERE *n* supporting anatomical structure **scleres**
SCLIFF *n* Scots word for small piece **scliffs**
SCLIM *vb* Scots word meaning climb **sclims**
SCODIER ▸ **scody**
SCODY *adj* unkempt
SCOFF *vb, n* **scoffed, scoffer, scoffs**
SCOG *vb* shelter **scogged, scogs**
SCOLD *vb, n* **scolded, scolder, scolds**
SCOLEX *n* headlike part of a tapeworm
SCOLIA ▸ **scolion**
SCOLION *n* ancient Greek drinking song
SCOLLOP *variant of* ▸ **scallop**
SCONCE *n* bracket on a wall for holding candles or lights ▹ *vb* challenge (a fellow student) to drink a large quantity of beer **sconced, sconces**

SCONE *n* **scones**
SCOOBY *n* clue; notion
SCOOCH *vb* compress one's body into smaller space
SCOOG *vb* shelter **scooged, scoogs**
SCOOP *n, vb* **scooped, scooper, scoops**
SCOOSH *vb* squirt ▷ *n* squirt or rush of liquid
SCOOT *vb* leave or move quickly ▷ *n* act of scooting
SCOOTCH = **scooch**
SCOOTED ▸ **scoot**
SCOOTER *n*
SCOOTS ▸ **scoot**
SCOP *n* (in Anglo-Saxon England) a bard or minstrel
SCOPA *n* tuft of hairs on the abdomen or hind legs of bees **scopae**
SCOPATE *adj* having tuft
SCOPE *n, vb* **scoped, scopes, scoping**
SCOPS ▸ **scop**
SCOPULA *n* small tuft of dense hairs on the legs and chelicerae of some spiders
SCORCH *vb* burn on the surface ▷ *n* slight burn
SCORE *n, vb* **scored, scorer, scorers, scores**
SCORIA *n* mass of solidified lava containing many cavities **scoriac, scoriae**
SCORIFY *vb* remove (impurities) from metals by forming scoria
SCORING *n* act or practice of scoring
SCORN *n, vb* **scorned, scorner, scorns**
SCORPER *n* kind of fine chisel with a square or curved tip
SCORSE *vb* exchange **scorsed, scorser, scorses**
SCOT *n* payment or tax
SCOTCH *vb, n*
SCOTER *n* type of sea duck **scoters**
SCOTIA *n* deep concave moulding **scotias**
SCOTOMA *n* blind spot
SCOTOMY *n* dizziness
SCOTS ▸ **scot**
SCOTTIE *n* type of small sturdy terrier
SCOUG *vb* shelter **scouged, scougs**
SCOUP *vb* Scots word meaning jump **scouped, scoups**
SCOUR *vb, n* **scoured, scourer**
SCOURGE *n, vb*
SCOURIE *n* young seagull
SCOURS ▸ **scour**
SCOURSE *vb* exchange
SCOUSE *n* stew made from left-over meat
SCOUSER *n* inhabitant of Liverpool
SCOUSES ▸ **scouse**
SCOUT *n, vb* **scouted, scouter**
SCOUTH *n* Scots word meaning plenty of scope **scouths**
SCOUTS ▸ **scout**
SCOW *n* unpowered barge used for carrying freight ▷ *vb* transport by scow
SCOWDER *vb* Scots word meaning scorch
SCOWED ▸ **scow**
SCOWING ▸ **scow**
SCOWL *n, vb* **scowled**
SCOWLER *n* person who scowls
SCOWLS ▸ **scowl**
SCOWP *vb* Scots word meaning jump **scowped, scowps**
SCOWRER *n* old word meaning hooligan
SCOWRIE *n* young seagull
SCOWS ▸ **scow**
SCOWTH *n* Scots word meaning plenty of scope **scowths**
SCOZZA *n* rowdy person, esp one who drinks a lot of alcohol **scozzas**
SCRAB *vb* scratch **scrabs**
SCRAE *Scots word for* ▸ **scree**
SCRAES ▸ **scrae**
SCRAG *n* thin end of a neck of mutton ▷ *vb* wring the neck of
SCRAGGY *adj*
SCRAGS ▸ **scrag**
SCRAICH *vb* Scots word meaning scream
SCRAIGH *vb* Scots word meaning scream
SCRAM *vb, n*

SCRAMB *vb* scratch with nails or claws **scrambs**
SCRAMS ▸ **scram**
SCRAN *n* food
SCRANCH *vb* crunch
SCRANNY *adj* scrawny
SCRANS ▸ **scran**
SCRAP *n, vb*
SCRAPE *vb, n* **scraped, scraper, scrapes**
SCRAPIE *n* disease of sheep and goats
SCRAPPY *adj*
SCRAPS ▸ **scrap**
SCRAT *vb* scratch
SCRATCH *vb, n, adj*
SCRATS ▸ **scrat**
SCRAUCH *vb* squawk
SCRAUGH *vb* squawk
SCRAW *n* sod from the surface of a peat bog or from a field
SCRAWL *vb, n* **scrawls, scrawly**
SCRAWM *vb* dialect word meaning scratch **scrawms**
SCRAWNY *adj*
SCRAWP *vb* scratch (the skin) to relieve itching **scrawps**
SCRAWS ▸ **scraw**
SCRAY *n* tern
SCRAYE *n* tern **scrayes**
SCRAYS ▸ **scray**
SCREAK *vb* screech or creak ▷ *n* screech or creak **screaks, screaky**
SCREAM *vb, n*
SCREAMO *n*
SCREAMS ▸ **scream**
SCREE *n*
SCREECH *n, vb*
SCREED *n* long tedious piece of writing ▷ *vb* rip **screeds**
SCREEN *n, vb* **screens**
SCREES ▸ **scree**
SCREET *vb* shed tears ▷ *n* act or sound of crying **screets**
SCREEVE *vb* write
SCREICH = **screigh**
SCREIGH *Scot word for* ▸ **screech**
SCREW *n, vb*
SCREWED *adj* fastened by a screw or screws
SCREWER ▸ **screw**
SCREWS ▸ **screw**
SCREWUP *n* something done badly
SCREWY *adj* crazy or eccentric
SCRIBAL ▸ **scribe**
SCRIBE *n, vb* **scribed**
SCRIBER *n* pointed steel tool used to score materials as a guide to cutting, etc
SCRIBES ▸ **scribe**
SCRIECH *vb* Scots word meaning screech
SCRIED ▸ **scry**
SCRIENE *n* old form of screen
SCRIES ▸ **scry**
SCRIEVE *vb* Scots word meaning write
SCRIKE *vb* old word meaning shriek **scriked, scrikes**
SCRIM *n* open-weave muslin or hessian fabric
SCRIMP *vb* **scrimps, scrimpy**
SCRIMS ▸ **scrim**
SCRINE *n* old form of shrine **scrines**
SCRIP *n* certificate representing a claim to stocks or shares **scrips**
SCRIPT *n, vb* **scripts**
SCRITCH *vb* screech
SCRIVE *Scots word for* ▸ **write**
SCRIVED ▸ **scrive**
SCRIVES ▸ **scrive**
SCROBE *n* groove **scrobes**
SCROD *n* young cod or haddock **scrods**
SCROG *n* Scots word meaning small tree
SCROGGY *variant of* > **scroggie**
SCROGS ▸ **scrog**
SCROLL *n, vb* **scrolls**
SCROME *vb* crawl or climb **scromed, scromes**
SCROOCH *vb* scratch (the skin) to relieve itching
SCROOGE *variant of* ▸ **scrouge**
SCROOP *vb* emit a grating or creaking sound ▷ *n* such a sound **scroops**
SCRORP *n* deep scratch or weal **scrorps**
SCROTA ▸ **scrotum**
SCROTAL ▸ **scrotum**
SCROTUM *n*
SCROUGE *vb* crowd or press
SCROW *n* scroll
SCROWL *vb* old form of scroll

SCROWLE *vb* old form of scroll
SCROWLS ▸ **scrowl**
SCROWS ▸ **scrow**
SCROYLE *n* old word meaning wretch
SCRUB *vb, n, adj*
SCRUBBY *adj* covered with scrub
SCRUBS ▸ **scrub**
SCRUFF = **scum**
SCRUFFS ▸ **scruff**
SCRUFFY *adj*
SCRUM *n, vb*
SCRUMMY *adj* delicious
SCRUMP *vb* steal (apples) from an orchard or garden **scrumps**
SCRUMPY *n* rough dry cider
SCRUMS ▸ **scrum**
SCRUNCH *vb* crumple or crunch or be crumpled or crunched ▷ *n* act or sound of scrunching
SCRUNT *n* Scots word meaning stunted thing **scrunts, scrunty**
SCRUPLE *n, vb*
SCRUTO *n* trapdoor on stage **scrutos**
SCRUZE *vb* old word meaning squeeze **scruzed, scruzes**
SCRY *vb* divine, esp by crystal gazing **scryde, scryer, scryers, scrying**
SCRYNE *n* old form of shrine **scrynes**
SCUBA *n* apparatus used in diving ▷ *vb* dive using scuba equipment **scubaed, scubas**
SCUCHIN *n* old form of scutcheon
SCUD *vb, n* **scudded, scudder**
SCUDDLE *vb* scuttle
SCUDI ▸ **scudo**
SCUDLER *n* Scots word meaning leader of festivities
SCUDO *n* any of several former Italian coins
SCUDS ▸ **scud**
SCUFF *vb, n* **scuffed**
SCUFFER *n* type of sandal
SCUFFLE *vb, n*
SCUFFS ▸ **scuff**
SCUFT *n* dialect word meaning nape of neck **scufts**
SCUG *vb* shelter **scugged, scugs**
SCUL *n* old form of school
SCULCH *n* rubbish
SCULK *vb* old form of skulk **sculked, sculker, sculks**
SCULL *n, vb*
SCULLE *n* old form of school
SCULLED ▸ **scull**
SCULLER ▸ **scull**
SCULLES ▸ **sculle**
SCULLS ▸ **scull**
SCULP *variant of* > **sculpture**
SCULPED ▸ **sculp**
SCULPIN *n* type of fish of the family which includes bullheads and sea scorpions
SCULPS ▸ **sculp**
SCULPT = **sculpture**
SCULPTS ▸ **sculpt**
SCULS ▸ **scul**
SCULTCH = **sculch**
SCUM *n, vb*
SCUMBER *vb* old word meaning defecate
SCUMBLE *vb* soften or blend (an outline or colour) with a thin upper coat of opaque colour ▷ *n* upper layer of colour applied in this way
SCUMMED ▸ **scum**
SCUMMER ▸ **scum**
SCUMMY *adj* of, resembling, consisting of, or covered with scum
SCUMS ▸ **scum**
SCUNGE *vb* borrow ▷ *n* dirty or worthless person **scunged, scunges**
SCUNGY *adj*
SCUNNER *vb* feel aversion ▷ *n* strong aversion
SCUP *n* common sparid fish of American coastal regions of the Atlantic
SCUPPER *vb, n*
SCUPS ▸ **scup**
SCUR *n* small unattached growth of horn at the site of a normal horn in cattle
SCURF *n* **scurfs, scurfy**
SCURRED ▸ **scur**

SCURRIL *adj* old word meaning vulgar
SCURRY *vb, n*
SCURS ▶ **scur**
SCURVY *n, adj*
SCUSE *shortened form of* ▶ **excuse**
SCUSED ▶ **scuse**
SCUSES ▶ **scuse**
SCUSING ▶ **scuse**
SCUT *n* short tail of the hare, rabbit, or deer
SCUTA ▶ **scutum**
SCUTAGE *n* payment to a lord from his vassal in lieu of military service
SCUTAL ▶ **scute**
SCUTATE *adj* (of animals) having or covered with large bony or horny plates
SCUTCH *vb* separate the fibres from the woody part of (flax) by pounding ▷ *n* tool used for this
SCUTE *n* horny or chitinous plate that makes up part of the exoskeleton in armadillos, etc **scutes**
SCUTS ▶ **scut**
SCUTTER *informal word for* ▶ **scurry**
SCUTTLE *n, vb*
SCUTUM *n* middle of three plates into which the notum of an insect's thorax is divided
SCUZZ *n* dirt **scuzzes**
SCUZZY *adj* unkempt, dirty, or squalid
SCYBALA > **scybalum**
SCYE *n* Scots word meaning sleeve-hole **scyes**
SCYPHI ▶ **scyphus**
SCYPHUS *n* ancient Greek two-handled drinking cup
SCYTALE *n* coded message in ancient Sparta
SCYTHE *n, vb* **scythed, scyther, scythes**
SDAINE *vb* old form of disdain **sdained, sdaines**
SDAYN *vb* old form of disdain **sdayned, sdayns**
SDEIGN *vb* old form of disdain
SDEIGNE *vb* old form of disdain
SDEIGNS ▶ **sdeign**
SDEIN *vb* old form of disdain **sdeined, sdeins**
SEA *n*
SEABAG *n* canvas bag for holding a sailor's belongings **seabags**
SEABANK *n* sea shore
SEABED *n* bottom of sea **seabeds**
SEABIRD *n* bird that lives on the sea
SEABOOT *n* sailor's waterproof boot
SEACOCK *n* valve in the hull of a vessel below the water line
SEADOG *another word for* ▶ **fogbow**
SEADOGS ▶ **seadog**
SEAFOLK *n* people who sail sea
SEAFOOD *n* edible saltwater fish or shellfish
SEAFOWL *n* seabird
SEAGIRT *adj* surrounded by the sea
SEAGULL *n*
SEAHAWK *n* skua
SEAHOG *n* porpoise **seahogs**
SEAKALE *n* European coastal plant
SEAL *n, vb*
SEALANT *n* any substance used for sealing
SEALCH *Scots word for* ▶ **seal**
SEALCHS ▶ **sealch**
SEALED *adj* (of a road) having a hard surface
SEALER *n* person or thing that seals **sealers**
SEALERY *n* occupation of hunting seals
SEALGH *Scots word for* ▶ **seal**
SEALGHS ▶ **sealgh**
SEALIFT *vb* transport by ship
SEALINE *n* company running regular sailings
SEALING ▶ **seal**
SEALS ▶ **seal**
SEALWAX *n* sealing wax
SEAM *n, vb*
SEAMAID *n* mermaid
SEAMAN *n*
SEAMARK *n* conspicuous object on a shore used as a guide

SEAME *n* old word meaning grease
SEAMED ▸ **seam**
SEAMEN ▸ **seaman**
SEAMER *n* bowler who makes the ball bounce on its seam **seamers**
SEAMES ▸ **seame**
SEAMIER ▸ **seamy**
SEAMING ▸ **seam**
SEAMS ▸ **seam**
SEAMSET *n* tool for flattening seams in metal
SEAMY *adj*
SEAN *vb* fish with seine net
SEANCE *n* **seances**
SEANED ▸ **sean**
SEANING ▸ **sean**
SEANS ▸ **sean**
SEAPORT *n* town or city with a harbour for boats and ships
SEAR *vb, n, adj*
SEARAT *n* pirate **searats**
SEARCE *vb* sift **searced, searces**
SEARCH *vb, n*
SEARE *adj* old word meaning dry and withered
SEARED, searer, searest, searing, sears ▸ **sear**
SEAS ▸ **sea**
SEASE *vb* old form of seize **seased, seases**
SEASICK *adj*
SEASIDE *n*
SEASING ▸ **sease**
SEASON *n, vb* **seasons**
SEASURE *n* old form of seizure
SEAT *n, vb* **seated**
SEATER *n* person or thing that seats **seaters**
SEATING *n, adj*
SEATS ▸ **seat**
SEAWALL *n* wall built to prevent encroachment or erosion by the sea
SEAWAN *n* shell beads used by certain North American Indians as money **seawans**
SEAWANT *n* Native American name for silver coins
SEAWARD = **seawards**
SEAWARE *n* any of numerous large coarse seaweeds
SEAWAY *n* waterway giving access to an inland port **seaways**
SEAWEED *n*
SEAWIFE *n* variety of sea fish
SEAWORM *n* marine worm
SEAZE *vb* old form of seize **seazed, seazes, seazing**
SEBACIC *adj* derived from sebacic acid, a white crystalline acid **sebasic**
SEBATE *n* salt of sebacic acid **sebates**
SEBIFIC *adj* producing fat
SEBUM *n* oily substance secreted by the sebaceous glands **sebums**
SEBUNDY *n* irregular soldier in India
SEC = **secant**
SECANT *n* (in trigonometry) the ratio of the length of the hypotenuse to the length of the adjacent side **secants**
SECCO *n* wall painting done on dried plaster with tempera **seccos**
SECEDE *vb* **seceded, seceder, secedes**
SECERN *vb* (of a gland or follicle) to secrete **secerns**
SECESH *n* secessionist in US Civil War
SECH *n* hyperbolic secant **sechs**
SECKEL *variant of* ▸ **seckle**
SECKELS ▸ **seckel**
SECKLE *n* type of pear **seckles**
SECLUDE *vb* keep (a person) from contact with others
SECO *adj* (of wine) dry
SECONAL *n* tradename for secobarbitol
SECOND *adj, n, vb*
SECONDE *n* second of eight positions from which a parry or attack can be made in fencing
SECONDI ▸ **secondo**
SECONDO *n* left-hand part in a piano duet
SECONDS ▸ **second**
SECPAR *n* distance unit in astronomy **secpars**

SECRECY *n* state of being secret
SECRET *adj, n*
SECRETA *n* secretions
SECRETE *vb*
SECRETS ▸ **secret**
SECS ▸ **sec**
SECT *n*
SECTARY *n* member of a sect
SECTILE *adj* able to be cut smoothly
SECTION *n, vb*
SECTOR *n, vb* **sectors**
SECTS ▸ **sect**
SECULAR *adj, n*
SECULUM *n* age in astronomy
SECUND *adj* having or designating parts arranged on or turned to one side of the axis
SECURE *adj, vb* **secured, securer, secures**
SED *old spelling of* ▸ **said**
SEDAN = **saloon**
SEDANS ▸ **sedan**
SEDARIM ▸ **seder**
SEDATE *adj, vb* **sedated, sedater, sedates**
SEDENT *adj* seated
SEDER *n* Jewish ceremonial meal held on the first night or first two nights of Passover **seders**
SEDES *Latin word for* ▸ **seat**
SEDGE *n*
SEDGED *adj* having sedge
SEDGES ▸ **sedge**
SEDGIER ▸ **sedge**
SEDGY ▸ **sedge**
SEDILE *n* seat for clergy in church
SEDILIA *n* group of three seats where the celebrant and ministers sit during High Mass
SEDUCE *vb* **seduced**
SEDUCER *n* person who entices, allures, or seduces
SEDUCES ▸ **seduce**
SEDUM *n* rock plant **sedums**
SEE *vb* perceive with the eyes or mind ▹ *n* diocese of a bishop **seeable**
SEED *n, vb*
SEEDBED *n* area of soil prepared for the growing of seedlings before they are transplanted
SEEDBOX *n* part of plant that contains seeds
SEEDED ▸ **seed**
SEEDER *n* person or thing that seeds **seeders**
SEEDIER ▸ **seedy**
SEEDILY ▸ **seedy**
SEEDING ▸ **seed**
SEEDLIP *n* basket holding seeds to be sown
SEEDMAN *n* seller of seeds **seedmen**
SEEDPOD *n* carpel enclosing the seeds of a flowering plant
SEEDS ▸ **seed**
SEEDY *adj*
SEEING ▸ **see**
SEEINGS ▸ **see**
SEEK *vb* **seeker, seekers, seeking, seeks**
SEEL *vb* sew up the eyelids of (a hawk or falcon) so as to render it quiet and tame
SEELD *adj* old word meaning rare
SEELED ▸ **seel**
SEELIE *pl n* good benevolent fairies
SEELIER ▸ **seely**
SEELING ▸ **seel**
SEELS ▸ **seel**
SEELY *adj* old word meaning happy
SEEM *vb* **seemed, seemer, seemers**
SEEMING *adj, n*
SEEMLY *adj, adv*
SEEMS ▸ **seem**
SEEN ▸ **see**
SEEP *vb, n*
SEEPAGE *n* act or process of seeping
SEEPED ▸ **seep**
SEEPIER ▸ **seepy**
SEEPING ▸ **seep**
SEEPS ▸ **seep**
SEEPY *adj* tending to seep
SEER *n* **seeress, seers**
SEES ▸ **see**
SEESAW *n, vb* **seesaws**
SEETHE *vb, n* **seethed, seether, seethes**
SEEWING *n* suing
SEFER *n* scrolls of the Law

SEG *n* metal stud on shoe sole
SEGAR *n* cigar **segars**
SEGETAL *adj* (of weeds) growing amongst crops
SEGGAR *n* box in which pottery is baked **seggars**
SEGHOL *n* pronunciation mark in Hebrew **seghols**
SEGMENT *n, vb*
SEGNI ▸ **segno**
SEGNO *n* sign at the beginning or end of a section directed to be repeated **segnos**
SEGO *n* American variety of lily
SEGOL *variant of* ▸ **seghol**
SEGOLS ▸ **segol**
SEGOS ▸ **sego**
SEGS ▸ **seg**
SEGUE *vb* proceed from one section or piece of music to another without a break ▹ *n* practice or an instance of playing music in this way **segued, segues**
SEHRI *n* meal eaten before sunrise by Muslims fasting during Ramadan **sehris**
SEI *n* type of rorqual
SEICHE *n* periodic oscillation of the surface of an enclosed or semienclosed body of water **seiches**
SEIDEL *n* vessel for drinking beer **seidels**
SEIF *n* long ridge of blown sand in a desert **seifs**
SEIK *Scot word for* ▸ **sick**
SEIKER ▸ **seik**
SEIKEST ▸ **seik**
SEIL *vb* dialect word meaning strain **seiled, seiling, seils**
SEINE *n* large fishing net that hangs vertically from floats ▹ *vb* catch (fish) using this net **seined, seiner, seiners, seines, seining**
SEIR *n* fish of Indian seas **seirs**
SEIS ▸ **sei**
SEISE *vb* put into legal possession of (property, etc) **seised, seiser, seisers, seises**
SEISIN *n* feudal possession of an estate in land
SEISING ▸ **seise**
SEISINS ▸ **seisin**
SEISM *n* earthquake
SEISMAL *adj* of earthquakes
SEISMIC *adj*
SEISMS ▸ **seism**
SEISOR *n* person who takes seisin **seisors**
SEISURE *n* act of seisin
SEITAN = **seiten**
SEITANS ▸ **seitan**
SEITEN *n* gluten from wheat **seitens**
SEITIES ▸ **seity**
SEITY *n* selfhood
SEIZE *vb* **seized, seizer, seizers, seizes**
SEIZIN = **seisin**
SEIZING *n* binding used for holding together two ropes, two spars, etc
SEIZINS ▸ **seizin**
SEIZOR *n* person who takes seisin **seizors**
SEIZURE *n*
SEJANT *adj* (of a beast) shown seated **sejeant**
SEKOS *n* holy place **sekoses**
SEKT *n* German sparkling wine **sekts**
SEL *Scot word for* ▸ **self**
SELAH *n* Hebrew word of unknown meaning occurring in the Old Testament psalms **selahs**
SELD *adj* old word meaning rare
SELDOM *adv*
SELE *n* old word meaning happiness
SELECT *vb, adj*
SELECTA *n* disc jockey
SELECTS ▸ **select**
SELENIC *adj* of or containing selenium, esp in the hexavalent state
SELES ▸ **sele**
SELF *n, pron, vb*
SELFDOM *n* selfhood
SELFED ▸ **self**
SELFING ▸ **self**
SELFISH *adj*
SELFISM *n* emphasis on self **selfist**
SELFS ▸ **self**
SELKIE = **silkie**
SELKIES ▸ **selkie**

SELL *vb, n*
SELLA *n* area of bone in body **sellae, sellas**
SELLE *n* old word meaning seat
SELLER *n* person who sells **sellers**
SELLES ▸ **selle**
SELLING *n*
SELLOFF *n* act of selling cheaply
SELLOUT *n*
SELLS ▸ **sell**
SELS ▸ **sel**
SELSYN = **synchro**
SELSYNS ▸ **selsyn**
SELTZER *n* natural effervescent water containing minerals
SELVA *n* dense equatorial forest
SELVAGE *n, vb*
SELVAS ▸ **selva**
SELVES ▸ **self**
SEMATIC *adj* acting as a warning, esp to potential predators
SEMBLE *vb* seem **sembled, sembles**
SEME *adj* dotted (with) **semee**
SEMEED *adj* seme
SEMEIA ▸ **semeion**
SEMEION *n* unit of metre in ancient poetry
SEMEME *n* meaning of a morpheme **sememes, sememic**
SEMEN *n* **semens**
SEMES ▸ **seme**
SEMI *n* semidetached house
SEMIDRY *adj* partly dry
SEMIE *n* historical name for a student in second year at a Scottish university **semies**
SEMIFIT *adj* not fully fit
SEMILOG *adj* semilogarithmic
SEMIMAT *adj* semimatt
SEMINA ▸ **semen**
SEMINAL *adj*
SEMINAR *n*
SEMIPED *n* measure in poetic metre
SEMIPRO *n* semiprofessional
SEMIRAW *adj* not fully cooked or processed
SEMIS ▸ **semi**
SEMISES ▸ **semi**
SEMITAR *old spelling of* > **scimitar**
SEMMIT *n* vest **semmits**
SEMPER *adv* Latin word meaning always
SEMPLE *adj* Scots word meaning simple **sempler**
SEMPRE *adv* (preceding a tempo or dynamic marking) always
SEMSEM *n* sesame **semsems**
SEN *n* monetary unit of Brunei, Cambodia, Indonesia, Malaysia, and formerly of Japan
SENA *n* (in India) the army
SENARII > **senarius**
SENARY *adj* of or relating to the number six
SENAS ▸ **sena**
SENATE *n* main governing body at some universities **senates**
SENATOR *n*
SEND *vb*
SENDAL *n* fine silk fabric used for ceremonial clothing, etc **sendals**
SENDED *vb* old word meaning sent
SENDER ▸ **send**
SENDERS ▸ **send**
SENDING ▸ **send**
SENDOFF *n* demonstration of good wishes at a person's departure ▹ *vb* dispatch (something, such as a letter)
SENDS ▸ **send**
SENDUP *n* parody or imitation **sendups**
SENE *n* money unit in Samoa
SENECA *variant of* ▸ **senega**
SENECAS ▸ **seneca**
SENECIO *n* type of plant of the genus which includes groundsels and ragworts
SENEGA *n* milkwort plant of the eastern US **senegas**
SENES ▸ **sene**
SENGI *n* African shrew
SENHOR *n* Portuguese term of address for man
SENHORA *n* Portuguese term of address for woman
SENHORS ▸ **senhor**
SENILE *adj, n* **seniles**

SENIOR *adj, n* **seniors**
SENITI *n* money unit in Tonga
SENNA *n* tropical plant **sennas**
SENNET *n* fanfare: used as a stage direction in Elizabethan drama **sennets**
SENNIT *n* flat braided cordage used on ships **sennits**
SENOPIA *n* short-sightedness in old age
SENOR *n* Spanish term of address equivalent to *sir* or *Mr*
SENORA *n* Spanish term of address equivalent to *madam* or *Mrs* **senoras**
SENORES ▸ **senor**
SENORS ▸ **senor**
SENRYU *n* Japanese short poem
SENS ▸ **sen**
SENSA ▸ **sensum**
SENSATE *adj* perceived by the senses ▹ *vb* make sensate
SENSE *n, vb* **sensed**
SENSEI *n* martial arts teacher **senseis**
SENSES ▸ **sense**
SENSI = **sensei**
SENSILE *adj* capable of feeling
SENSING ▸ **sense**
SENSIS ▸ **sensi**
SENSISM *n* theory that ideas spring from senses **sensist**
SENSOR *n* **sensors**
SENSORY *adj*
SENSUAL *adj*
SENSUM *n* sensation detached from the information it conveys
SENT *n* former monetary unit of Estonia
SENTE *n* money unit in Lesotho
SENTED ▸ **send**
SENTI ▸ **sent**
SENTIMO *n* money unit in Philippines
SENTING ▸ **send**
SENTRY *n*
SENTS ▸ **sent**
SENVIES ▸ **senvy**
SENVY *n* mustard
SENZA *prep* without
SEPAD *vb* suppose **sepads**
SEPAL *n* leaflike division of the calyx of a flower **sepaled, sepals**
SEPHEN *n* stingray **sephens**
SEPIA *n, adj* **sepias**
SEPIC *adj* of sepia
SEPIOST *n* cuttlefish bone
SEPIUM *n* cuttlefish bone **sepiums**
SEPMAG *adj* designating a film, etc for which the sound is recorded on separate magnetic material
SEPOY *n* (formerly) Indian soldier in the service of the British **sepoys**
SEPPUKU *n* Japanese ritual suicide
SEPS *n* species of lizard
SEPSES ▸ **sepsis**
SEPSIS *n* poisoning caused by pus-forming bacteria
SEPT *n* clan, esp in Ireland or Scotland
SEPTA ▸ **septum**
SEPTAGE *n* waste removed from septic tank
SEPTAL *adj* of or relating to a septum
SEPTATE *adj* divided by septa
SEPTET *n* group of seven performers **septets**
SEPTIC *adj, n* **septics**
SEPTIME *n* seventh of eight basic positions from which a parry can be made in fencing
SEPTS ▸ **sept**
SEPTUM *n* dividing partition between two cavities in the body **septums**
SEPTUOR *n* group of seven musicians
SEQUEL *n*
SEQUELA *n* disease related to or arising from a pre-existing disease
SEQUELS ▸ **sequel**
SEQUENT *adj* following in order or succession ▹ *n* something that follows
SEQUIN *n, vb* **sequins**
SEQUOIA *n* giant Californian coniferous tree

> This word for a redwood tree is one of the most

frequently played bonuses using the Q, a great one to remember as it also clears out a surplus of vowels.

SER *n* unit of weight used in India
SERA ▸ **serum**
SERAC *n* pinnacle of ice among crevasses on a glacier, usually on a steep slope **seracs**
SERAFIN *n* old silver coin of Goa
SERAI *n* (in the East) a caravanserai or inn
SERAIL = **seraglio**
SERAILS ▸ **serail**
SERAIS ▸ **serai**
SERAL ▸ **sere**
SERANG *n* native captain of a crew of sailors in the East Indies **serangs**
SERAPE *n* blanket-like shawl often of brightly-coloured wool **serapes**
SERAPH *n* **seraphs**
SERDAB *n* secret chamber in an ancient Egyptian tomb **serdabs**
SERE *adj* dried up or withered ▹ *n* series of changes occurring in the ecological succession of a particular community ▹ *vb* sear **sered**
SEREIN *n* fine rain falling from a clear sky after sunset **sereins**
SERENE *adj*, *vb* **serened, serener, serenes**
SERER ▸ **sere**
SERES ▸ **sere**
SEREST ▸ **sere**
SERF *n* **serfage, serfdom, serfish, serfs**
SERGE *n*
SERGED *adj* with sewn seam
SERGER *n* sewing machine attachment for finishing seams **sergers**
SERGES ▸ **serge**
SERGING *n* type of sewing
SERIAL *n*, *adj* **serials**
SERIATE *adj* forming a series ▹ *vb* form into a series
SERIC *adj* of silk
SERICIN *n* gelatinous protein found on the fibres of raw silk
SERICON *n* solution used in alchemy
SERIEMA *n* either of two cranelike South American birds
SERIES *n*
SERIF *n* small line at the extremities of a main stroke in a type character
SERIFED *adj* having serifs
SERIFS ▸ **serif**
SERIN *n* any of various small yellow-and-brown finches
SERINE *n* sweet-tasting amino acid **serines**
SERING ▸ **sere**
SERINGA *n* any of several trees that yield rubber
SERINS ▸ **serin**
SERIOUS *adj* giving cause for concern
SERIPH = **serif**
SERIPHS ▸ **seriph**
SERK *Scots word for* ▸ **shirt**
SERKALI *n* government in Africa
SERKS ▸ **serk**
SERMON *n*, *vb* **sermons**
SERON *n* crate **serons**
SEROON *n* crate **seroons**
SEROPUS *n* liquid consisting of serum and pus
SEROSA *n* one of the thin membranes surrounding the embryo in an insect's egg **serosae, serosal, serosas**
SEROUS *adj* of, containing, or like serum
SEROVAR *n* subdivision of species
SEROW *n* either of two antelopes of mountainous regions of S and SE Asia **serows**
SERPENT *n*
SERPIGO *n* any progressive skin eruption
SERR *vb* press close together
SERRA *n* sawlike part or organ **serrae**

SERRAN *n* species of fish
SERRANO *n* type of Spanish ham
SERRANS ▸ **serran**
SERRAS ▸ **serra**
SERRATE *adj* (of leaves) having a margin of forward pointing teeth ▹ *vb* make serrate
SERRATI > **serratus**
SERRE *vb* press close together **serred, serres**
SERRIED *adj*
SERRIES ▸ **serry**
SERRING ▸ **serre**
SERRS ▸ **serr**
SERRY *vb* close together
SERS ▸ **ser**
SERUEWE *vb* old word meaning survey
SERUM *n* **serumal, serums**
SERVAL *n* feline African mammal **servals**
SERVANT *n, vb*
SERVE *vb, n* **served**
SERVER *n* **servers**
SERVERY *n* room from which food is served
SERVES ▸ **serve**
SERVEWE *vb* old word meaning survey
SERVICE *n, adj, vb*
SERVILE *adj, n*
SERVING *n*
SERVLET *n* small program that runs on a web server
SERVO *n* servomechanism ▹ *adj* of a servomechanism **servos**
SESAME *n* **sesames**
SESE *interj* exclamation found in Shakespeare
SESELI *n* garden plant **seselis**
SESEY *interj* exclamation found in Shakespeare
SESH *short for* ▸ **session**
SESHES ▸ **sesh**
SESS *n* old word meaning tax
SESSA *interj* exclamation found in Shakespeare
SESSES ▸ **sess**
SESSILE *adj* (of flowers or leaves) having no stalk
SESSION *n*
SESTET *n* last six lines of a sonnet **sestets**
SESTETT *n* group of six
SESTINA *n* elaborate verse form of Italian origin
SESTINE *n* poem of six lines
SESTON *n* type of plankton **sestons**
SET *vb, n, adj*
SETA *n* bristle or bristle-like appendage **setae, setal**
SETBACK *n*
SETLINE *n* any of various types of fishing line
SETNESS ▸ **set**
SETOFF *n* counterbalance **setoffs**
SETON *n* surgical thread inserted below the skin **setons**
SETOSE *adj* covered with setae
SETOUS ▸ **seta**
SETOUT *n* beginning or outset **setouts**
SETS ▸ **set**
SETT *n* badger's burrow
SETTEE *n* **settees**
SETTER *n, vb* **setters**
SETTING ▸ **set**
SETTLE *vb, n* **settled**
SETTLER *n*
SETTLES ▸ **settle**
SETTLOR *n* person who settles property on someone
SETTS ▸ **sett**
SETUALE *n* valerian
SETULE *n* small bristle **setules**
SETUP *n* way in which anything is organized or arranged **setups**
SETWALL *n* valerian
SEVEN *n, adj, determiner*
SEVENS *n* Rugby Union match or series of matches played with seven players on each side
SEVENTH *n, adj, adv*
SEVENTY *n, adj, determiner*
SEVER *vb*
SEVERAL *adj, n*
SEVERE *adj*
SEVERED ▸ **sever**
SEVERER ▸ **severe**
SEVERS ▸ **sever**
SEVERY *n* part of vaulted ceiling
SEVICHE *n* Mexican fish dish

SEVRUGA *n* species of sturgeon
SEW *vb* **sewable**
SEWAGE *n* **sewages**
SEWAN = **seawan**
SEWANS ▸ **sewan**
SEWAR *n* Asian dagger **sewars**
SEWED ▸ **sew**
SEWEL *n* scarecrow **sewels**
SEWEN = **sewin**
SEWENS ▸ **sewen**
SEWER *n*, *vb* **sewered, sewers**
SEWIN *n* sea trout
SEWING ▸ **sew**
SEWINGS ▸ **sew**
SEWINS ▸ **sewin**
SEWN ▸ **sew**
SEWS ▸ **sew**
SEX *n*, *vb*, *adj*
SEXED *adj* having a specified degree of sexuality
SEXER *n* person checking sex of chickens **sexers**
SEXES ▸ **sex**
SEXFID *adj* split into six
SEXFOIL *n* flower with six petals or leaves
SEXIER ▸ **sexy**
SEXIEST ▸ **sexy**
SEXILY ▸ **sexy**
SEXING ▸ **sex**
SEXINGS ▸ **sexing**
SEXISM *n* **sexisms, sexist, sexists**
SEXLESS *adj*
SEXPERT *n* person who professes a knowledge of sexual matters
SEXPOT *n* person considered as sexually very attractive **sexpots**
SEXT *n* fourth of the seven canonical hours of the divine office
SEXTAIN = **sestina**
SEXTAN *adj* (of a fever) marked by paroxysms that recur after an interval of five days
SEXTANS *n* Roman coin
SEXTANT *n*
SEXTET *n* **sextets**
SEXTETT *n* sextet
SEXTILE *n* value of a variable dividing its distribution into six groups with equal frequencies
SEXTO = **sixmo**
SEXTON *n* **sextons**
SEXTOS ▸ **sexto**
SEXTS ▸ **sext**
SEXTUOR *n* sextet
SEXUAL *adj*
SEXY *adj*
SEY *n* Scots word meaning part of cow carcase
SEYEN *n* old form of scion **seyens**
SEYS ▸ **sey**
SEYSURE *n* old form of seizure
SEZ *vb* informal spelling of 'says'

> **Sez** is a short informal form of **says**, very useful for disposing of the Z.

SFERICS = **spherics**
SFUMATO *n* gradual transition between areas of different colour in painting
SH *interj*
SHA *interj* be quiet
SHABASH *interj* (in Indian English) bravo or well done
SHABBLE *n* Scots word meaning old sword
SHABBY *adj*
SHACK *n*, *vb* **shacked**
SHACKLE *n*, *vb*
SHACKO = **shako**
SHACKOS ▸ **shacko**
SHACKS ▸ **shack**
SHAD *n* herring-like fish
SHADE *n*, *vb* **shaded, shader, shaders**
SHADES *pl n* gathering darkness at nightfall
SHADFLY *American name for* ▸ **mayfly**
SHADIER ▸ **shady**
SHADILY ▸ **shady**
SHADING *n* graded areas of tone indicating light and dark in a painting or drawing
SHADOOF *n* mechanism for raising water
SHADOW *n*, *vb* **shadows**
SHADOWY *adj*
SHADS ▸ **shad**
SHADUF = **shadoof**
SHADUFS ▸ **shaduf**
SHADY *adj*
SHAFT *n*, *vb* **shafted, shafter, shafts**
SHAGGY *adj*
SHAH *n* formerly, ruler of Iran

SHAHADA *n* Islamic declaration of faith
SHAHDOM ▸ **shah**
SHAHEED ▸ **shahid**
SHAHID *n* Muslim martyr **shahids**
SHAHS ▸ **shah**
SHAIKH *n* sheikh **shaikhs**
SHAIRD *n* Scots word meaning shred **shairds**
SHAIRN *Scots word for* ▸ **dung**
SHAIRNS ▸ **shairn**
SHAITAN *n* (in Muslim countries) an evil spirit
SHAKE *vb, n*
SHAKED *vb* old form of shook
SHAKEN ▸ **shake**
SHAKER *n* container in which drinks are mixed or from which powder is shaken **shakers**
SHAKES ▸ **shake**
SHAKEUP *n* radical reorganization
SHAKIER ▸ **shaky**
SHAKILY ▸ **shaky**
SHAKING ▸ **shake**
SHAKO *n* tall cylindrical peaked military hat with a plume **shakoes, shakos**
SHAKT *vb* old form of shook
SHAKUDO *n* Japanese alloy of copper and gold
SHAKY *adj*
SHALE *n* **shaled, shales, shaley, shalier, shaling**
SHALL *vb*
SHALLI *n* type of fabric **shallis**
SHALLON *n* American shrub
SHALLOP *n* light boat used for rowing in shallow water
SHALLOT *n*
SHALLOW *adj, n, vb*
SHALM *n* old woodwind instrument **shalms**
SHALOM *n* Jewish greeting meaning 'peace be with you' **shaloms**
SHALOT *n* shallot **shalots**
SHALT *singular form of the present tense (indicative mood) of* ▸ **shall**
SHALWAR *n* pair of loose-fitting trousers tapering to a narrow fit around the ankles
SHALY ▸ **shale**
SHAM *n, adj, vb*
SHAMA *n* Indian songbird
SHAMAL *n* hot northwesterly wind **shamals**
SHAMAN *n* priest of shamanism **shamans**
SHAMAS ▸ **shama**
SHAMBA *n* (in E Africa) any field used for growing crops **shambas**
SHAMBLE *vb, n* **shambly**
SHAME *n, vb* **shamed**
SHAMER *n* cause of shame
SHAMERS ▸ **shame**
SHAMES ▸ **shame**
SHAMINA *n* wool blend of pashm and shahtoosh
SHAMING ▸ **shame**
SHAMMAS = **shammes**
SHAMMED ▸ **sham**
SHAMMER ▸ **sham**
SHAMMES *n* official acting as the beadle, sexton, and caretaker of a synagogue **shammos**
SHAMMY *n* piece of chamois leather ▹ *vb* rub with a shammy
SHAMOIS *n* chamois
SHAMOS = **shammes**
SHAMOY *n* chamois ▹ *vb* rub with a shamoy **shamoys**
SHAMPOO *n, vb*
SHAMS ▸ **sham**
SHAMUS *n* police or private detective
SHAN *variant of* ▸ **shand**
SHAND *n* old word meaning fake coin
SHANDRY *n* light horse-drawn cart
SHANDS ▸ **shand**
SHANDY *n*
SHANK *n, vb* **shanked, shanks**
SHANNY *n* European blenny of rocky coastal waters
SHANS ▸ **shan**
SHANTEY = **shanty**
SHANTI *n* peace **shantih, shantis**
SHANTY *n*

SHAPE *n, vb* **shaped**
SHAPELY *adj*
SHAPEN *vb* old form of shaped
SHAPER ▸ **shape**
SHAPERS ▸ **shape**
SHAPES ▸ **shape**
SHAPEUP *n* system of hiring dockers for a day's work
SHAPING ▸ **shape**
SHAPS *n* leather over-trousers worn by cowboys
SHARD *n*
SHARDED *adj* old word meaning hidden under dung
SHARDS ▸ **shard**
SHARE *n, vb* **shared, sharer, sharers, shares**
SHARIA *n* body of doctrines that regulate the lives of Muslims **shariah, sharias**
SHARIAT *n* Islamic religious law
SHARIF = **sherif**
SHARIFS ▸ **sharif**
SHARING ▸ **share**
SHARK *n, vb* **sharked**
SHARKER *n* shark hunter
SHARKS ▸ **shark**
SHARN *Scots word for* ▸ **dung**
SHARNS ▸ **sharn**
SHARNY ▸ **sharn**
SHARON *n as in* **sharon fruit** persimmon
SHARP *adj, adv, n, vb* **sharped**
SHARPEN *vb*
SHARPER *n* person who cheats
SHARPIE *n* member of a teenage group having short hair and distinctive clothes
SHARPLY ▸ **sharp**
SHARPS ▸ **sharp**
SHARPY *n* swindler
SHASH *vb* old form of sash **shashed, shashes**
SHASLIK *n* type of kebab
SHASTER = **shastra**
SHASTRA *n* any of the sacred writings of Hinduism
SHATTER *vb, n*
SHAUGH *n* old word meaning small wood **shaughs**
SHAUL *vb* old form of shawl **shauled, shauls**
SHAVE *vb, n* **shaved**
SHAVEN *adj*
SHAVER *n* **shavers**
SHAVES ▸ **shaul**
SHAVIE *n* Scots word meaning trick **shavies**
SHAVING ▸ **shave**
SHAW *n* small wood ▹ *vb* show **shawed, shawing**
SHAWL *n, vb* **shawled, shawls**
SHAWM *n* medieval form of the oboe with a conical bore and flaring bell **shawms, shawn**
SHAWS ▸ **shaw**
SHAY *dialect word for* ▸ **chaise**
SHAYA *n* Indian plant **shayas**
SHAYS ▸ **shay**
SHAZAM *interj* magic slogan
SHCHI *n* Russian cabbage soup **shchis**
SHE *pron, n*
SHEA *n* tropical African tree
SHEAF *n, vb* **sheafed, sheafs, sheafy**
SHEAL *vb* old word meaning shell **shealed, sheals**
SHEAR *vb, n* **sheared, shearer, shears**
SHEAS ▸ **shea**
SHEATH *n*
SHEATHE *vb*
SHEATHS ▸ **sheath**
SHEATHY ▸ **sheathe**
SHEAVE *vb* gather or bind into sheaves ▹ *n* wheel with a grooved rim **sheaved**
SHEAVES ▸ **sheaf**
SHEBANG *n* situation, matter, or affair
SHEBEAN = **shebeen**
SHEBEEN *n* place where alcohol is sold illegally ▹ *vb* run a shebeen
SHED *n, vb* **shedded**
SHEDDER *n* person or thing that sheds
SHEDFUL *n* quantity or amount contained in a shed
SHEDS ▸ **shed**
SHEEL *vb* old word meaning shell **sheeled, sheels**

SHEEN *n, adj, vb* **sheened, sheens**
SHEEP *n*
SHEEPLE *pl n* people who follow the majority in matters of opinion, taste, etc
SHEEPO *n* person employed to bring sheep to the catching pen in a shearing shed **sheepos**
SHEEPY ▸ **sheep**
SHEER *adj, adv, vb, n* **sheered, sheerer, sheerly, sheers**
SHEESH *interj* exclamation of surprise or annoyance
SHEESHA *n* Oriental water-pipe for smoking tobacco
SHEET *n, vb* **sheeted, sheeter, sheets, sheety**
SHEEVE *n* part of mine winding gear **sheeves**
SHEHITA *n* slaughter of animal according to Jewish religious law
SHEIK = **sheikh**
SHEIKH *n* Arab chief
SHEIKHA *n* chief wife of sheikh
SHEIKHS ▸ **sheikh**
SHEIKS ▸ **sheik**
SHEILA *n* girl or woman **sheilas**
SHEITAN *n* Muslim demon
SHEKEL *n* monetary unit of Israel **shekels**
SHELF *n, vb* **shelfed, shelfs, shelfy**
SHELL *n, vb*
SHELLAC *n* resin used in varnishes ▷ *vb* coat with shellac
SHELLED, sheller, shells, shelly ▸ **shell**
SHELTA *n* secret language used by some traveling people in Britain and Ireland **sheltas**
SHELTER *n, vb*
SHELTIE *n* small dog similar to a collie **shelty**
SHELVE *vb* **shelved, shelver**
SHELVES ▸ **shelf**
SHELVY *adj* having shelves
SHEMALE *n* male who has acquired female physical characteristics through surgery
SHEND *vb* put to shame **shends, shent**
SHEOL *n* hell **sheols**
SHEQEL = **shekel**
SHEQELS ▸ **sheqel**
SHERANG *n* person in charge
SHERBET *n*
SHERD = **shard**
SHERDS ▸ **sherd**
SHERE *old spelling of* ▸ **sheer**
SHEREEF = **sherif**
SHERIA = **sharia**
SHERIAS ▸ **sheria**
SHERIAT *n* Muslim religious law
SHERIF *n* descendant of Mohammed through his daughter Fatima
SHERIFF *n*
SHERIFS ▸ **sherif**
SHEROOT *n* cheroot
SHERPA *n* official who assists at a summit meeting **sherpas**
SHERRIS *n* old form of sherry
SHERRY *n*
SHES ▸ **she**
SHET *vb* old form of shut **shets**
SHEUCH *n* ditch or trough ▷ *vb* dig **sheuchs, sheugh**
SHEUGHS ▸ **sheugh**
SHEVA *n* mark in Hebrew writing **shevas**
SHEW *archaic spelling of* ▸ **show**
SHEWED ▸ **shew**
SHEWEL *n* old word meaning scarecrow **shewels**
SHEWER, shewers, shewing, shewn, shews ▸ **shew**
SHH *interj* sound made to ask for silence
SHIAI *n* judo contest **shiais**
SHIATSU *n* type of massage
SHIATZU *n* shiatzu
SHIBAH *n* Jewish period of mourning **shibahs**
SHICKER *n* alcoholic drink
SHIDDER *n* old word meaning female animal

SHIED ▸ **shy**
SHIEL *vb* sheal
SHIELD *n, vb* **shields**
SHIELED ▸ **shiel**
SHIELS ▸ **shiel**
SHIER *n* horse that shies habitually **shiers**
SHIES ▸ **shy**
SHIEST ▸ **shy**
SHIFT *vb, n* **shifted, shifter, shifts**
SHIFTY *adj*
SHIKAR *n* hunting, esp big-game hunting ▹ *vb* hunt (game, esp big game)
SHIKARI *n* (in India) a hunter
SHIKARS ▸ **shikar**
SHIKKER *n* Yiddish term for drunk person
SHILL *n* confidence trickster's assistant ▹ *vb* act as a shill **shilled, shills**
SHILPIT *adj* puny
SHILY ▸ **shy**
SHIM *n* thin strip of material placed between two close surfaces to fill a gap ▹ *vb* fit or fill up with a shim
SHIMAAL *n* hot Middle Eastern wind
SHIMMED ▸ **shim**
SHIMMER *n, vb*
SHIMMEY *n* chemise
SHIMMY *n* American ragtime dance ▹ *vb* dance the shimmy
SHIMS ▸ **shim**
SHIN *n, vb*
SHINDIG *n*
SHINDY *n* quarrel or commotion **shindys**
SHINE *vb, n* **shined**
SHINER *n* black eye **shiners**
SHINES ▸ **shine**
SHINESS ▸ **shy**
SHINGLE *n, vb* **shingly**
SHINIER ▸ **shiny**
SHINIES ▸ **shiny**
SHINILY ▸ **shiny**
SHINING ▸ **shine**
SHINJU *n* (formerly, in Japan) a ritual double suicide of lovers **shinjus**
SHINKIN *n* worthless person
SHINNE *n* old form of chin
SHINNED ▸ **shin**
shinnes
SHINNEY *vb* climb with hands and legs
SHINNY = **shinty**
SHINS ▸ **shin**
SHINTY *n* game like hockey ▹ *vb* play shinty
SHINY *adj*
SHIP *n, vb*
SHIPFUL *n* amount carried by ship
SHIPLAP *n* method of constructing ship hull
SHIPMAN *n* master or captain of a ship **shipmen**
SHIPPED ▸ **ship**
SHIPPEN *n* dialect word for cattle shed
SHIPPER *n* person or company that ships
SHIPPIE *n* prostitute who solicits at a port
SHIPPO *n* Japanese enamel work
SHIPPON *n* dialect word for cattle shed
SHIPPOS ▸ **shippo**
SHIPS ▸ **ship**
SHIPWAY *n* structure on which a vessel is built, then launched
SHIR *n* gathering in material
SHIRE *n, vb* **shired, shires, shiring**
SHIRK *vb, n* **shirked, shirker, shirks**
SHIRR *vb* gather (fabric) into parallel rows to decorate a dress, etc ▹ *n* series of gathered rows decorating a dress, etc
SHIRRA *old Scots word for* ▸ **sheriff**
SHIRRAS ▸ **shirra**
SHIRRED ▸ **shirr**
SHIRRS ▸ **shirr**
SHIRS ▸ **shir**
SHIRT *n, vb* **shirted, shirts**
SHIRTY *adj*
SHISH *adj as in* **shish kebab** dish of meat and vegetables grilled on skewers
SHISHA = **hookah**
SHISHAS ▸ **shisha**
SHISO *n* Asian plant with aromatic leaves **shisos**
SHIST *n* schist **shists**
SHITAKE = **shiitake**
SHITTAH *n* tree mentioned in the Old Testament **shittim**

SHITZU *n* breed of small dog with long, silky fur **shitzus**
SHIUR *n* lesson in which a passage of the Talmud is studied **shiurim**
SHIV *variant spelling of* ▸ **chiv**
SHIVA *variant of* ▸ **shivah**
SHIVAH *n* Jewish period of formal mourning **shivahs**
SHIVAS ▸ **shiva**
SHIVE *n* flat cork or bung for wide-mouthed bottles
SHIVER *vb, n* **shivers**
SHIVERY *adj*
SHIVES ▸ **shive**
SHIVITI *n* Jewish decorative plaque with religious message
SHIVOO *n* Australian word meaning rowdy party **shivoos**
SHIVS ▸ **shiv**
SHIVVED ▸ **shiv**
SHLEP *vb* schlep
SHLEPP *vb* schlep **shlepps**
SHLEPS ▸ **shlep**
SHLOCK *n* something of poor quality **shlocks, shlocky**
SHLUB = **schlub**
SHLUBS ▸ **shlub**
SHLUMP *vb* move in lazy way **shlumps, shlumpy**
SHMALTZ *n* schmaltz
SHMATTE *n* rag
SHMEAR *n* set of things **shmears**
SHMEK *n* smell **shmeks**
SHMO = **schmo**
SHMOCK *n* despicable person **shmocks**
SHMOES ▸ **shmo**
SHMOOSE *variant of* > **schmooze**
SHMOOZE *variant of* > **schmooze**
SHMOOZY *adj* talking casually, gossipy
SHMUCK *n* despicable person
SHMUCKS ▸ **schmuck**
SHNAPPS = **schnapps**
SHNAPS *n* schnaps
SHNOOK *n* stupid person **shnooks**
SHOAL *n, vb, adj* **shoaled, shoaler, shoals**
SHOALY *adj* shallow
SHOAT *n* piglet that has recently been weaned **shoats**
SHOCHET *n* (in Judaism) a person licensed to slaughter animals and birds
SHOCK *vb, n, adj* **shocked**
SHOCKER *n* person or thing that shocks or horrifies
SHOCKS ▸ **shock**
SHOD ▸ **shoe**
SHODDEN *vb* old form of shod
SHODDY *adj, n*
SHODER *n* skins used in making gold leaf **shoders**
SHOE *n, vb*
SHOEBOX *n* cardboard box for shoes
SHOED ▸ **shoe**
SHOEING ▸ **shoe**
SHOEPAC *n* waterproof boot
SHOER *n* person who shoes horses **shoers**
SHOES ▸ **shoe**
SHOFAR *n* ram's horn sounded in Jewish synagogue **shofars**
SHOG *vb* shake **shogged**
SHOGGLE *vb* shake **shoggly**
SHOGI *n* Japanese chess **shogis**
SHOGS ▸ **shog**
SHOGUN *n* Japanese chief military commander **shoguns**
SHOJI *n* Japanese rice-paper screen in a sliding wooden frame **shojis**
SHOLA *n* Indian plant **sholas**
SHOLOM *n* Hebrew greeting **sholoms**
SHONE ▸ **shine**
SHONEEN *n* Irishman who imitates English ways
SHONKY *adj* unreliable or unsound
SHOO *interj, vb* **shooed**
SHOOFLY *n as in* **shoofly pie** US dessert similar to treacle tart
SHOOGIE *vb* Scots word meaning swing

SHOOGLE *vb* shake, sway, or rock back and forth ▷ *n* rocking motion **shoogly**
SHOOING ▶ **shoo**
SHOOK *n* set of parts ready for assembly **shooks**
SHOOL *dialect word for* ▶ **shovel**
SHOOLE *dialect word for* ▶ **shovel**
SHOOLED ▶ **shool**
SHOOLES ▶ **shoole**
SHOOLS ▶ **shool**
SHOON *plural of* ▶ **shoe**
SHOORA = **shura**
SHOORAS ▶ **shoora**
SHOOS ▶ **shoo**
SHOOT *vb, n*
SHOOTER *n* person or thing that shoots
SHOOTS ▶ **shoot**
SHOP *n, vb*
SHOPBOT *n*
SHOPBOY *n* boy working in shop
SHOPE *n* old form of shape
SHOPFUL *n* amount stored in shop
SHOPHAR = **shofar**
SHOPMAN *n* man working in shop **shopmen**
SHOPPE *old-fashioned spelling of* ▶ **shop**
SHOPPED ▶ **shop**
SHOPPER *n* person who buys goods in a shop
SHOPPES ▶ **shoppe**
SHOPPY *adj* of a shop
SHOPS ▶ **shop**
SHORAN *n* short-range radar system **shorans**
SHORE *n, vb* **shored, shorer, shorers, shores, shoring**
SHORL *n* black mineral **shorls**
SHORN *past participle of* ▶ **shear**
SHORT *adj* not long ▷ *adv* abruptly ▷ *n* drink of spirits ▷ *vb* short-circuit **shorted**
SHORTEN *vb*
SHORTER ▶ **short**
SHORTIA *n* American flowering plant
SHORTIE *n* person or thing that is extremely short
SHORTLY *adv*
SHORTS *pl n* trousers reaching the top of the thigh or partway to the knee
SHORTY = **shortie**
SHOT *vb* load with shot
SHOTE = **shoat**
SHOTES ▶ **shote**
SHOTGUN *n, adj, vb*
SHOTS ▶ **shot**
SHOTT *n* shallow temporary salt lake or marsh in the North African desert
SHOTTE *n* old form of shoat
SHOTTED ▶ **shot**
SHOTTEN *adj* (of fish, esp herring) having recently spawned
SHOTTES ▶ **shotte**
SHOTTLE *n* small drawer
SHOTTS ▶ **shott**
SHOUGH *n* old word meaning lapdog **shoughs**
SHOULD ▶ **shall**
SHOUSE *n* toilet ▷ *adj* unwell or in poor spirits **shouses**
SHOUT *n, vb* **shouted, shouter, shouts**
SHOUTY *adj* characterized by or involving shouting
SHOVE *vb, n* **shoved**
SHOVEL *n, vb* **shovels**
SHOVER ▶ **shove**
SHOVERS ▶ **shove**
SHOVES ▶ **shove**
SHOVING *n* act of pushing hard
SHOW *vb* make, be, or become noticeable or visible ▷ *n* public exhibition
SHOWBIZ *n* entertainment industry including theatre, films, and TV
SHOWBOX *n* box containing showman's material
SHOWD *vb* rock or sway to and fro ▷ *n* rocking motion **showded, showds**
SHOWED ▶ **show**
SHOWER *n, vb* **showers, showery**
SHOWGHE *n* old word meaning lapdog
SHOWIER ▶ **showy**
SHOWILY ▶ **showy**
SHOWING ▶ **show**
SHOWMAN *n* man skilled at presenting

anything spectacularly **showmen**
SHOWN ▸ **show**
SHOWOFF *n* person who makes a vain display of himself or herself
SHOWS ▸ **show**
SHOWY *adj*
SHOYU *n* Japanese variety of soy sauce **shoyus**
SHRANK ▸ **shrink**
SHRED *n, vb* **shreddy, shreds**
SHREEK *old spelling of* ▸ **shriek**
SHREEKS ▸ **shreek**
SHREIK *old spelling of* ▸ **shriek**
SHREIKS ▸ **shreik**
SHREW *n, vb*
SHREWD *adj*
SHREWED ▸ **shrew**
SHREWS ▸ **shrew**
SHRI *n* Indian title of respect
SHRIECH *old spelling of* ▸ **shriek**
SHRIEK *n, vb* **shrieks, shrieky**
SHRIEVE *archaic word for* ▸ **sheriff**
SHRIFT *n* **shrifts**
SHRIGHT *n* old word meaning shriek
SHRIKE *n* songbird with a heavy hooked bill ▹ *vb* archaic word for shriek **shriked, shrikes**
SHRILL *adj, vb* **shrills, shrilly**
SHRIMP *n, vb* **shrimps, shrimpy**
SHRINAL ▸ **shrine**
SHRINE *n, vb* **shrined, shrines**
SHRINK *vb, n* **shrinks**
SHRIS ▸ **shri**
SHRITCH *vb* old word meaning shriek
SHRIVE *vb* hear the confession of (a penitent) **shrived**
SHRIVEL *vb*
SHRIVEN ▸ **shrive**
SHRIVER ▸ **shrive**
SHRIVES ▸ **shrive**
SHROFF *n* (in China and Japan) expert employed to identify counterfeit money ▹ *vb* test (money) and separate out the counterfeit and base **shroffs**
SHROOM *n* slang for magic mushroom ▹ *vb* take magic mushrooms **shrooms**
SHROUD *n, vb* **shrouds, shroudy**
SHROVE *vb* dialect word meaning to observe Shrove-tide **shroved, shroves**
SHROW *vb* old form of shrew
SHROWD *adj* old form of shrewd
SHROWED ▸ **shrow**
SHROWS ▸ **shrow**
SHRUB *n, vb*
SHRUBBY *adj* consisting of, planted with, or abounding in shrubs
SHRUBS ▸ **shrub**
SHRUG *vb, n* **shrugs**
SHRUNK ▸ **shrink**
SHTCHI *n* Russian cabbage soup **shtchis**
SHTETEL *n* Jewish community in Eastern Europe
SHTETL *n* Jewish community in Eastern Europe **shtetls**
SHTICK *n* comedian's routine **shticks, shticky**
SHTIK *n* shtick **shtiks**
SHTOOK *n* trouble **shtooks**
SHTOOM *adj* silent
SHTUCK *n* trouble **shtucks**
SHTUM *adj* silent
SHTUMM *adj* silent
SHTUP *vb* have sex (with) **shtups**
SHUCK *n* outer covering of something ▹ *vb* remove the shucks from **shucked, shucker**
SHUCKS *pl n* something of little value ▹ *interj* exclamation of disappointment, annoyance, etc
SHUDDER *vb, n*
SHUFFLE *vb, n*
SHUFTI = **shufty**
SHUFTIS ▸ **shufti**
SHUFTY *n* look
SHUGGY *n* swing, as at a fairground
SHUL *Yiddish word for* > **synagogue**
SHULE *vb* saunter **shuled, shules, shuling**

SHULN ▸ **shul**
SHULS ▸ **shul**
SHUN *vb* **shunned, shunner, shuns**
SHUNT *vb, n* **shunted**
SHUNTER *n* small railway locomotive used for manoeuvring coaches
SHUNTS ▸ **shunt**
SHURA *n* consultative council or assembly **shuras**
SHUSH *interj* be quiet! ▹ *vb* quiet by saying 'shush' **shushed, shusher, shushes**
SHUT *vb*
SHUTE *variant of* ▸ **chute**
SHUTED ▸ **shute**
SHUTES ▸ **shute**
SHUTEYE *n* sleep
SHUTING ▸ **shute**
SHUTOFF *n* device that shuts something off
SHUTOUT *n* game in which the opposing team does not score
SHUTS ▸ **shut**
SHUTTER *n, vb*
SHUTTLE *n, vb*
SHWA = **schwa**
SHWAS ▸ **shwa**
SHY *adj, vb, n* **shyer, shyers, shyest, shying, shyish**
SHYLOCK *vb* lend money at an exorbitant rate of interest
SHYLY ▸ **shy**
SHYNESS ▸ **shy**
SHYPOO *n* liquor of poor quality **shypoos**
SHYSTER *n* person who uses discreditable or unethical methods
SI = **te**
SIAL *n* silicon-rich and aluminium-rich rocks of the earth's continental upper crust **sialic**
SIALID *n* species of fly **sialids**
SIALOID *adj* resembling saliva
SIALON *n* type of ceramic **sialons**
SIALS ▸ **sial**
SIAMANG *n* large black gibbon
SIAMESE *variant of* ▸ **siameze**
SIAMEZE *vb* join together
SIB *n* blood relative
SIBB *n* sib **sibbs**
SIBLING *n*
SIBS ▸ **sib**
SIBSHIP *n* group of children of the same parents
SIBYL *n* (in ancient Greece and Rome) prophetess **sibylic, sibyls**
SIC *adv, vb*
SICCAN *adj* Scots word meaning such
SICCAR *adj* sure
SICCED ▸ **sic**
SICCING ▸ **sic**
SICCITY *n* dryness
SICE = **syce**
SICES ▸ **sice**
SICH *adj* old form of such
SICHT *Scot word for* ▸ **sight**
SICHTED ▸ **sicht**
SICHTS ▸ **sicht**
SICK *adj, n, vb*
SICKBAY *n* room for the treatment of sick people
SICKBED *n*
SICKED ▸ **sick**
SICKEE *n* person off work through illness **sickees**
SICKEN *vb* **sickens**
SICKER ▸ **sick**
SICKEST ▸ **sick**
SICKIE *n* day of sick leave from work **sickies**
SICKING ▸ **sick**
SICKISH ▸ **sick**
SICKLE *n, vb* **sickled, sickles**
SICKLY *adj, adv, vb*
SICKO *n* person who is mentally disturbed or perverted ▹ *adj* perverted or in bad taste **sickos**
SICKOUT *n* industrial action in which all workers report sick simultaneously
SICKS ▸ **sick**
SICLIKE *adj* Scots word meaning suchlike
SICS ▸ **sic**
SIDA *n* Australian hemp plant **sidas**
SIDDHA *n* (in Hinduism) person who has achieved perfection **siddhas**

SIDDHI *n* (in Hinduism) power attained with perfection **siddhis**
SIDDUR *n* Jewish prayer book **siddurs**
SIDE *n, adj*
SIDEARM *n* weapon worn on belt
SIDEBAR *n* small newspaper article beside larger one
SIDECAR *n*
SIDED ▸ **side**
SIDEMAN *n* member of a dance band or a jazz group other than the leader **sidemen**
SIDER *n* one who sides with another
SIDERAL *adj* from the stars
SIDERS ▸ **sider**
SIDES ▸ **side**
SIDEWAY *variant of* > **sideways**
SIDH *pl n* fairy people
SIDHA *n* (in Hinduism) person who has achieved perfection **sidhas**
SIDHE *pl n* inhabitants of fairyland
SIDING *n* **sidings**
SIDLE *vb, n* **sidled, sidler, sidlers, sidles, sidling**
SIECLE *n* century, period, or era **siecles**
SIEGE *n, vb* **sieged**
SIEGER *n* person who besieges **siegers**
SIEGES ▸ **siege**
SIEGING ▸ **siege**
SIELD *adj* provided with a ceiling
SIEMENS *n* SI unit of electrical conductance
SIEN *n* old word meaning scion
SIENITE *n* type of igneous rock
SIENNA *n* reddish- or yellowish-brown pigment made from natural earth **siennas**
SIENS ▸ **sien**
SIENT *n* old word meaning scion **sients**
SIERRA *n* range of mountains in Spain or America with jagged peaks **sierran, sierras**
SIES *interj*
SIESTA *n* **siestas**
SIETH *n* old form of scythe **sieths**
SIEUR *n* French word meaning lord **sieurs**
SIEVE *n, vb* **sieved**
SIEVERT *n* derived SI unit of dose equivalent, equal to 1 joule per kilogram
SIEVES ▸ **sieve**
SIEVING ▸ **sieve**
SIF *adj* South African slang for disgusting
SIFAKA *n* either of two large rare arboreal lemuroid primates **sifakas**
SIFFLE *vb* whistle **siffled, siffles**
SIFREI ▸ **sefer**
SIFT *vb* **sifted, sifter, sifters, sifting, sifts**
SIGANID *n* tropical fish
SIGH *n, vb* **sighed, sigher, sighers, sighful, sighing, sighs**
SIGHT *n, vb*
SIGHTED *adj*
SIGHTER *n* any of six practice shots allowed to each competitor in a tournament
SIGHTLY *adj* pleasing or attractive to see
SIGHTS ▸ **sight**
SIGIL *n* seal or signet **sigils**
SIGLA *n* list of symbols used in a book **siglas**
SIGLOI ▸ **siglos**
SIGLOS *n* silver coin of ancient Persia
SIGLUM *n* symbol used in book
SIGMA *n* 18th letter in the Greek alphabet **sigmas**
SIGMATE *adj* shaped like the Greek letter sigma or the Roman *S* ▹ *n* sigmate thing ▹ *vb* add a sigma
SIGMOID *adj* shaped like the letter S ▹ *n* S-shaped bend in the final portion of the large intestine
SIGN *n, vb*
SIGNA *pl n* symbols
SIGNAGE *n* signs collectively
SIGNAL *n, adj, vb* **signals**
SIGNARY *n* set of symbols
SIGNED ▸ **sign**
SIGNEE *n* person signing document **signees**

SIGNER *n* person who signs something **signers**
SIGNET *n* small seal used to authenticate documents ▷ *vb* stamp or authenticate with a signet **signets**
SIGNEUR *old spelling of* ▸ **senior**
SIGNIFY *vb*
SIGNING *n* system of communication using hand and arm movements
SIGNIOR = **signor**
SIGNOR *n* Italian term of address equivalent to *sir* or *Mr*
SIGNORA *n* Italian term of address equivalent to *madam* or *Mrs*
SIGNORE *n* Italian man: a title of respect equivalent to *sir* **signori**
SIGNORS ▸ **signor**
SIGNORY = **seigniory**
SIGNS ▸ **sign**
SIJO *n* Korean poem **sijos**
SIK *adj* excellent
SIKA *n* Japanese forest-dwelling deer **sikas**
SIKE *n* small stream
SIKER *adj* old spelling of sicker
SIKES ▸ **sike**
SILAGE *n, vb* **silaged, silages**
SILANE *n* gas containing silicon **silanes**
SILD *n* any of various small young herrings **silds**
SILE *vb* pour with rain **siled**
SILEN *n* god of woodland
SILENCE *n, vb*
SILENE *n* type of plant with mostly red or pink flowers, often grown as a garden plant **silenes**
SILENI ▸ **silenus**
SILENS ▸ **silen**
SILENT *adj, n* **silents**
SILENUS *n* woodland deity
SILER *n* strainer **silers**
SILES ▸ **sile**
SILESIA *n* twill-weave fabric of cotton or other fibre
SILEX *n* type of heat-resistant glass made from fused quartz **silexes**
SILICA *n* **silicas**
SILICIC *adj* of, concerned with, or containing silicon or an acid obtained from silicon
SILICLE = **silicula**
SILICON *n, adj*
SILING ▸ **sile**
SILIQUA *n* long dry dehiscent fruit of cruciferous plants such as the wallflower **silique**
SILK *n, vb* **silked**
SILKEN *adj, vb* **silkens**
SILKIE *n* Scots word for a seal
SILKIER ▸ **silky**
SILKIES ▸ **silkie**
SILKILY ▸ **silky**
SILKING ▸ **silk**
SILKS ▸ **silk**
SILKY *adj*
SILL *n*
SILLER *n* silver ▷ *adj* silver **sillers**
SILLIER ▸ **silly**
SILLIES ▸ **silly**
SILLILY ▸ **silly**
SILLOCK *n* young coalfish
SILLS ▸ **sill**
SILLY *adj, n*
SILO *n, vb* **siloed, siloing, silos**
SILPHIA > **silphium**
SILT *n, vb* **silted, siltier, silting, silts, silty**
SILURID *n* type of freshwater fish of the family which includes catfish
SILVA = **sylva**
SILVAE ▸ **silva**
SILVAN = **sylvan**
SILVANS ▸ **silvan**
SILVAS ▸ **silva**
SILVER *n, adj, vb*
SILVERN *adj* silver
SILVERS ▸ **silver**
SILVERY *adj*
SILVEX *n* type of weedkiller
SILVICS *n* study of trees
SIM *n* computer game that simulates an activity
SIMA *n* silicon-rich and magnesium-rich rocks of the earth's oceanic crust
SIMAR *variant spelling of* ▸ **cymar**

SIMARRE *n* woman's loose gown
SIMARS ▸ **simar**
SIMAS ▸ **sima**
SIMATIC ▸ **sima**
SIMBA *E African word for* ▸ **lion**
SIMBAS ▸ **simba**
SIMI *n* East African sword
SIMIAL *adj* of apes
SIMIAN *n, adj* **simians**
SIMILAR *adj*
SIMILE *n* **similes**
SIMILOR *n* alloy used in cheap jewellery
SIMIOID *adj* of apes
SIMIOUS *adj* of apes
SIMIS ▸ **simi**
SIMITAR = **scimitar**
SIMKIN *word used in India for* > **champagne**
SIMKINS ▸ **simkin**
SIMLIN *n* American variety of squash plant **simlins**
SIMMER *vb, n* **simmers**
SIMNEL *n as in* **simnel cake** fruit cake with marzipan eaten at Easter **simnels**
SIMONY *n* practice of buying or selling Church benefits
SIMOOM *n* hot suffocating sand-laden desert wind **simooms, simoon**
SIMOONS ▸ **simoon**
SIMORG *n* bird in Persian myth **simorgs**
SIMP *short for* > **simpleton**
SIMPAI *n* Indonesian monkey **simpais**
SIMPER *vb, n* **simpers**
SIMPKIN *word used in India for* > **champagne**
SIMPLE *adj, n, vb* **simpled, simpler, simples**
SIMPLEX *adj* permitting the transmission of signals in only one direction in a radio circuit ▹ *n* simple not a compound word
SIMPLY *adv*
SIMPS ▸ **simp**
SIMS ▸ **sim**
SIMUL *adj* simultaneous ▹ *n* simultaneous broadcast
SIMULAR *n* person or thing that simulates or imitates ▹ *adj* fake
SIMULS ▸ **simul**
SIMURG *n* bird in Persian myth
SIMURGH *n* bird in Persian myth
SIMURGS ▸ **simurg**
SIN *n, vb*
SINCE *prep, adv*
SINCERE *adj*
SIND *variant of* ▸ **syne**
SINDED ▸ **sind**
SINDING ▸ **sind**
SINDON *n* type of cloth **sindons**
SINDS ▸ **sind**
SINE ▸ **syne**
SINED ▸ **sine**
SINES ▸ **sine**
SINEW *n, vb*
SINEWED *adj* having sinews
SINEWS ▸ **sinew**
SINEWY *adj*
SINFUL *adj*
SING *vb, n*
SINGE *vb, n* **singed**
SINGER *n* person who sings, esp professionally **singers**
SINGES ▸ **singe**
SINGING ▸ **sing**
SINGLE *adj, n, vb* **singled**
SINGLES *pl n* match played with one person on each side
SINGLET *n*
SINGLY *adv*
SINGS ▸ **sing**
SINGULT *n* old word meaning sob
SINH *n* hyperbolic sine **sinhs**
SINICAL ▸ **sine**
SINING ▸ **sine**
SINK *vb, n*
SINKAGE *n* act of sinking or degree to which something sinks or has sunk
SINKER *n* weight for a fishing line **sinkers**
SINKIER ▸ **sinky**
SINKING ▸ **sink**
SINKS ▸ **sink**
SINKY *adj* giving underfoot
SINLESS *adj* free from sin or guilt
SINNED ▸ **sin**
SINNER *n, vb*
SINNERS ▸ **sin**
SINNET *n* braided rope **sinnets**
SINNING ▸ **sin**
SINOPIA *n* pigment made from iron ore **sinopie**

SINOPIS *n* pigment made from iron ore
SINS ▸ **sin**
SINSYNE *adv* Scots word meaning since
SINTER *n* whitish porous incrustation deposited from hot springs ▹ *vb* form large particles from (powders) by heating or pressure **sinters, sintery**
SINUATE *vb* wind
SINUOSE *adj* sinuous
SINUOUS *adj*
SINUS *n* **sinuses**
SIP *vb, n*
SIPE *vb* soak **siped, sipes**
SIPHON *n, vb* **siphons**
SIPING ▸ **sipe**
SIPPED ▸ **sip**
SIPPER ▸ **sip**
SIPPERS ▸ **sip**
SIPPET *n* small piece of toast eaten with soup or gravy **sippets**
SIPPING ▸ **sip**
SIPPLE *vb* sip **sippled, sipples**
SIPPY *adj as in* **sippy cup** infant's drinking cup with a tight-fitting lid and perforated spout
SIPS ▸ **sip**
SIR *n, vb*
SIRCAR *n* government in India **sircars**
SIRDAR = **sardar**
SIRDARS ▸ **sirdar**
SIRE *n, vb* **sired**
SIREE *emphasized form of* ▸ **sir**
SIREES ▸ **siree**
SIREN *n* **sirenic, sirens**
SIRES ▸ **sire**
SIRGANG *n* Asian bird
SIRI *n* betel
SIRIH *n* betel **sirihs**
SIRING ▸ **sire**
SIRINGS ▸ **siring**
SIRIS ▸ **siri**
SIRKAR *n* government in India **sirkars**
SIRLOIN *n*
SIRNAME *vb* old form of surname
SIROC *n* sirocco
SIROCCO *n* hot wind blowing from N Africa into S Europe
SIROCS ▸ **siroc**
SIROSET *adj* of the chemical treatment of woollen fabrics to give a permanent-press effect
SIRRA *disrespectful form of* ▸ **sir**
SIRRAH *n* contemptuous term used in addressing a man or boy **sirrahs**
SIRRAS ▸ **sirra**
SIRRED ▸ **sir**
SIRREE *n* form of 'sir' used for emphasis **sirrees**
SIRRING ▸ **sir**
SIRS ▸ **sir**
SIRTUIN *n* protein that regulates cell metabolism and ageing
SIRUP = **syrup**
SIRUPED ▸ **sirup**
SIRUPS ▸ **sirup**
SIRUPY ▸ **sirup**
SIS *n*
SISAL *n* **sisals**
SISES ▸ **sis**
SISKIN *n* yellow-and-black finch **siskins**
SISS *shortening of* ▸ **sister**
SISSES ▸ **siss**
SISSIER ▸ **sissy**
SISSIES ▸ **sissy**
SISSOO *n* Indian tree **sissoos**
SISSY *n, adj*
SIST *vb* Scottish law term meaning stop **sisted**
SISTER *n, adj, vb* **sisters**
SISTING ▸ **sist**
SISTRA ▸ **sistrum**
SISTRUM *n* musical instrument of ancient Egypt consisting of a metal rattle
SISTS ▸ **sist**
SIT *vb*
SITAR *n* **sitars**
SITCOM *n* **sitcoms**
SITE *n, vb* **sited**
SITELLA *n* type of small generally black-and-white bird
SITES ▸ **site**
SITFAST *n* sore on a horse's back caused by rubbing of the saddle
SITH *archaic word for* ▸ **since**
SITHE *vb* old form of scythe **sithed**
SITHEE *interj* look here! listen!
SITHEN *adv* old word meaning since

SITHENS *adv* old word meaning since
SITHES ▸ **sithe**
SITHING ▸ **sithe**
SITING ▸ **site**
SITKA *modifier as in* **sitka spruce** tall North American spruce tree
SITREP *n* military situation report **sitreps**
SITS ▸ **sit**
SITTAR *n* sitar **sittars**
SITTEN *adj* dialect word for in the saddle
SITTER *n* baby-sitter **sitters**
SITTINE *adj* of nuthatch bird family
SITTING ▸ **sit**
SITUATE *vb* place ▹ *adj* (now used esp in legal contexts) situated
SITULA *n* bucket-shaped container **situlae**
SITUP *n* exercise in which the body is brought into a sitting position **situps**
SITUS *n* position or location **situses**
SITZ *n as in* **sitz bath** bath in which the buttocks and hips are immersed in hot water
SIVER = **syver**
SIVERS ▸ **siver**
SIWASH *vb* (in the Pacific Northwest) to camp out with only natural shelter
SIX *n*
SIXAIN *n* stanza or poem of six lines
SIXAINE *n* six-line stanza of poetry
SIXAINS ▸ **sixain**
SIXER = **six**
SIXERS ▸ **sixer**
SIXES ▸ **six**
SIXFOLD *adj* having six times as many or as much ▹ *adv* by six times as many or as much
SIXMO *n* book size resulting from folding a sheet of paper into six leaves **sixmos**
SIXTE *n* sixth of eight basic positions from which a parry or attack can be made in fencing
SIXTEEN *n, adj, determiner*
SIXTES ▸ **sixte**
SIXTH *n, adj, adv* **sixthly, sixths**
SIXTIES ▸ **sixty**
SIXTY *n, adj*
SIZABLE *adj* **sizably**
SIZAR *n* undergraduate receiving a maintenance grant from the college **sizars**
SIZE *n, vb*
SIZED *adj* of a specified size
SIZEISM *n* discrimination on the basis of a person's size **sizeist**
SIZEL *n* scrap metal clippings **sizels**
SIZER, sizers, sizes, sizier, siziest, sizing, sizings ▸ **size**
SIZISM *n* discrimination against people because of weight **sizisms, sizist, sizists**
SIZY ▸ **size**
SIZZLE *vb, n* **sizzled**
SIZZLER *n* something that sizzles
SIZZLES ▸ **sizzle**
SJAMBOK *n, vb*
SJOE *interj* South African exclamation of surprise, admiration, exhaustion, etc
SKA *n* type of West Indian pop music of the 1960s
SKAG = **scag**
SKAGS ▸ **skag**
SKAIL *vb* Scots word meaning disperse **skailed, skails**
SKAITH *vb* Scots word meaning injure **skaiths**
SKALD *n* (in ancient Scandinavia) a bard or minstrel **skaldic, skalds**
SKANK *n* fast dance to reggae music ▹ *vb* perform this dance **skanked, skanker, skanks**
SKANKY *adj* dirty or unattractive
SKART *Scots word for* > **cormorant**
SKARTH *Scots word for* > **cormorant**
SKARTHS ▸ **skarth**
SKARTS ▸ **skart**
SKAS ▸ **ska**

SKAT *n* three-handed card game using 32 cards
SKATE *n, vb* **skated**
SKATER *n* person who skates **skaters**
SKATES ▸ **skate**
SKATING ▸ **skate**
SKATOL *n* skatole
SKATOLE *n* white or brownish crystalline solid
SKATOLS ▸ **skatol**
SKATS ▸ **skat**
SKATT *n* dialect word meaning throw **skatts**
SKAW *variant of* ▸ **scaw**
SKAWS ▸ **skaw**
SKEAN *n* kind of double-edged dagger
SKEANE = **skein**
SKEANES ▸ **skeane**
SKEANS ▸ **skean**
SKEAR *dialect form of* ▸ **scare**
SKEARED ▸ **skear**
SKEARS ▸ **skear**
SKEARY *dialect form of* ▸ **scary**
SKEE *variant spelling of* ▸ **ski**
SKEED ▸ **skee**
SKEEF *adj, adv* South African slang for at an oblique angle
SKEEING ▸ **skee**
SKEELY *adj* Scots word meaning skilful
SKEEN *n* type of ibex **skeens**
SKEER *dialect form of* ▸ **scare**
SKEERED ▸ **skeer**
SKEERS ▸ **skeer**
SKEERY *dialect form of* ▸ **scary**
SKEES ▸ **skee**
SKEET *n* form of clay-pigeon shooting
SKEETER *informal word for* > **mosquito**
SKEETS ▸ **skeet**
SKEG *n* reinforcing brace between the after end of a keel and the rudderpost
SKEGG *n* skeg
SKEGGER *n* young salmon
SKEGGS ▸ **skegg**
SKEGS ▸ **skeg**
SKEIGH *adj* Scots word meaning shy
SKEIN *n, vb* **skeined, skeins**
SKELDER *vb* beg
SKELF *n* splinter of wood, esp when embedded accidentally in the skin **skelfs**
SKELL *n* homeless person
SKELLIE *adj* skelly
SKELLS ▸ **skell**
SKELLUM *n* rogue
SKELLY *n* whitefish of certain lakes in the Lake District ▹ *vb* look sideways or squint ▹ *adj* cross-eyed
SKELM *n* villain or crook **skelms**
SKELP *vb* slap ▹ *n* slap **skelped**
SKELPIT *vb* Scots word meaning skelped
SKELPS ▸ **skelp**
SKELTER *vb* scurry
SKELUM *n* Scots word meaning rascal **skelums**
SKEN *vb* squint or stare
SKENE *n* Scots word meaning dagger **skenes**
SKENNED ▸ **sken**
SKENS ▸ **sken**
SKEO *n* Scots dialect word meaning hut **skeos**
SKEP *n* beehive, esp one constructed of straw ▹ *vb* gather into a hive
SKEPFUL *n* amount skep will hold
SKEPPED ▸ **skep**
SKEPS ▸ **skep**
SKEPSIS *n* doubt
SKEPTIC = **sceptic**
SKER *vb* scour **skerred**
SKERRY *n* rocky island or reef
SKERS ▸ **sker**
SKET *vb* splash (water)
SKETCH *n, vb*
SKETCHY *adj*
SKETS ▸ **sket**
SKETTED ▸ **sket**
SKEW *vb, adj, n* **skewed**
SKEWER *n, vb* **skewers**
SKEWEST ▸ **skew**
SKEWING ▸ **skew**
SKEWS ▸ **skew**
SKI *n, vb* **skiable**
SKIBOB *n* vehicle made of two short skis for gliding down snow slopes **skibobs**
SKID *vb, n* **skidded, skidder**

SKIDDOO *vb* go away quickly
SKIDDY ▸ **skid**
SKIDLID *n* crash helmet
SKIDOO *n* snowmobile ▹ *vb* travel on a skidoo **skidoos**
SKIDPAN *n* area made slippery so that vehicle drivers can practise controlling skids
SKIDS ▸ **skid**
SKIDWAY *n* platform on which logs ready for sawing are piled
SKIED ▸ **sky**
SKIER ▸ **ski**
SKIERS ▸ **ski**
SKIES ▸ **sky**
SKIEY *adj* of the sky **skieyer**
SKIFF *n, vb* **skiffed**
SKIFFLE *n* style of popular music of the 1950s ▹ *vb* play this style of music
SKIFFS ▸ **skiff**
SKIING ▸ **ski**
SKIINGS ▸ **ski**
SKILFUL *adj*
SKILL *n*
SKILLED *adj*
SKILLET *n*
SKILLS ▸ **skill**
SKILLY *n* thin soup or gruel ▹ *adj* skilled
SKIM *vb, n* **skimmed**
SKIMMER *n* person or thing that skims
SKIMMIA *n* shrub of S and SE Asia
SKIMP *vb* **skimped, skimps**
SKIMPY *adj*
SKIMS ▸ **skim**
SKIN *n, vb*
SKINFUL *n* sufficient alcoholic drink to make one drunk
SKINK *n* type of lizard with reduced limbs and smooth scales ▹ *vb* serve a drink **skinked, skinker, skinks**
SKINNED ▸ **skin**
SKINNER *n* person who prepares or deals in animal skins
SKINNY *adj, n*
SKINS ▸ **skin**
SKINT *adj* **skinter**
SKIO *n* Scots dialect word meaning hut **skios**
SKIP *vb, n* **skipped**
SKIPPER *vb, n*
SKIPPET *n* small round box for preserving a document or seal
SKIPPY *adj* in high spirits
SKIPS ▸ **skip**
SKIRL *n* sound of bagpipes ▹ *vb* (of bagpipes) to give out a shrill sound **skirled, skirls**
SKIRR *vb* move, run, or fly rapidly ▹ *n* whirring or grating sound, as of the wings of birds in flight **skirred**
SKIRRET *n* umbelliferous Old World plant
SKIRRS ▸ **skirr**
SKIRT *n, vb* **skirted**
SKIRTER *n* man who skirts fleeces
SKIRTS ▸ **skirt**
SKIS ▸ **ski**
SKIT *n*
SKITCH *vb* (of a dog) to attack
SKITE *n, vb* **skited, skites, skiting**
SKITS ▸ **skit**
SKITTER *vb* move or run rapidly or lightly
SKITTLE *n, vb*
SKIVE *vb* **skived**
SKIVER *n* tanned outer layer split from a skin ▹ *vb* cut leather **skivers**
SKIVES ▸ **skive**
SKIVIE *adj* old Scots word meaning disarranged **skivier**
SKIVING ▸ **skive**
SKIVVY *n* female servant who does menial work ▹ *vb* work as a skivvy
SKIVY ▸ **skive**
SKIWEAR *n* clothes for skiing in
SKLATE *Scots word for* ▸ **slate**
SKLATED ▸ **sklate**
SKLATES ▸ **sklate**
SKLENT *Scots word for* ▸ **slant**
SKLENTS ▸ **sklent**
SKLIFF *n* Scots word meaning little piece **skliffs**
SKLIM *vb* Scots word meaning climb **sklims**
SKOAL = **skol**
SKOALED ▸ **skoal**
SKOALS ▸ **skoal**
SKOFF *vb* eat greedily **skoffed, skoffs**

SKOL *sentence substitute* good health! (a drinking toast) ▷ *vb* down (an alcoholic drink) in one go
SKOLIA ▸ **skolion**
SKOLION *n* ancient Greek drinking song
SKOLLED ▸ **skol**
SKOLLIE = **skolly**
SKOLLY *n* hooligan, usually one of a gang
SKOLS ▸ **skol**
SKOOKUM *adj* strong or brave
SKOOL *ironically illiterate or childish spelling of* ▸ **school**
SKOOLS ▸ **skool**
SKOOSH *vb* Scots word meaning squirt
SKORT *n* pair of shorts with a front panel which gives the appearance of a skirt **skorts**
SKOSH *n* little bit **skoshes**
SKRAN *n* food **skrans**
SKREEGH *vb* Scots word meaning screech
SKREEN *n* screen **skreens**
SKREIGH *vb* Scots word meaning screech
SKRIECH *vb* Scots word meaning screech
SKRIED ▸ **skry**
SKRIEGH *vb* Scots word meaning screech
SKRIES ▸ **skry**
SKRIK *n* South African word meaning fright
SKRIKE *vb* cry **skriked, skrikes**
SKRIKS ▸ **skrik**
SKRIMP *vb* steal apples **skrimps**
SKRONK *n* type of dissonant, grating popular music **skronks**
SKRUMP *vb* steal apples **skrumps**
SKRY *vb* try to tell future **skryer, skryers, skrying**
SKUA *n* large predatory gull **skuas**
SKUDLER *n* Scots word meaning leader of festivities
SKUG *vb* shelter **skugged, skugs**
SKULK *vb, n* **skulked, skulker, skulks**
SKULL *n, vb* **skulled, skulls**
SKULPIN *n* North American fish
SKUMMER *vb* defecate
SKUNK *n, vb* **skunked, skunks, skunky**
SKURRY *vb* scurry
SKUTTLE *vb* scuttle
SKY *n, vb*
SKYBORN *adj* born in heaven
SKYBOX *n* luxurious suite high up in the stand of a sports stadium
SKYCAP *n* luggage porter at American airport **skycaps**
SKYCLAD *adj* naked
SKYDIVE *vb* take part in skydiving **skydove**
SKYED ▸ **sky**
SKYER *n* cricket ball hit up into air **skyers**
SKYEY *adj* of the sky
SKYF *n* South African slang for a cigarette or substance for smoking ▷ *vb* smoke a cigarette **skyfed, skyfing, skyfs**
SKYHOME *n* Australian slang for a sub-penthouse flat in a tall building
SKYHOOK *n* hook hung from helicopter
SKYIER ▸ **skyey**
SKYIEST ▸ **skyey**
SKYING ▸ **sky**
SKYISH ▸ **sky**
SKYJACK *vb* hijack (an aircraft)
SKYLAB *n* orbiting space station **skylabs**
SKYLARK *n* lark that sings while soaring at a great height ▷ *vb* play or frolic
SKYLESS *adj* having no sky
SKYLIKE ▸ **sky**
SKYLINE *n*
SKYLIT *adj* having skylight
SKYMAN *n* paratrooper **skymen**
SKYPHOI ▸ **skyphos**
SKYPHOS *n* ancient Greek drinking cup
SKYR *n* Scandinavian cheese
SKYRE *vb* Scots word meaning shine **skyred, skyres, skyring**
SKYRS ▸ **skyr**

SKYSAIL *n* square sail set above the royal on a square-rigger
SKYSURF *vb* perform freefall aerobatics
SKYTE *vb* Scots word meaning slide **skyted, skytes, skyting**
SKYWALK *n* tightrope walk at great height
SKYWARD *adj* towards the sky ▷ *adv* towards the sky
SKYWAY *n* air route **skyways**
SLAB *n, vb* **slabbed**
SLABBER *vb* dribble from the mouth
SLABBY ▶ **slab**
SLABS ▶ **slab**
SLACK = **slake**
SLACKED ▶ **slack**
SLACKEN *vb*
SLACKER *n* person who evades work or duty
SLACKLY ▶ **slack**
SLACKS *pl n* casual trousers
SLADANG *n* Malayan tapir
SLADE *n* little valley **slades**
SLAE *Scots word for* ▶ **sloe**
SLAES ▶ **slae**
SLAG *n, vb* **slagged, slaggy, slags**
SLAID *vb* Scots word for 'slid'
SLAIN ▶ **slay**
SLAINTE *interj* cheers!
SLAIRG *Scots word for* ▶ **spread**
SLAIRGS ▶ **slairg**
SLAKE *vb* **slaked, slaker, slakers, slakes, slaking**
SLALOM *n, vb* **slaloms**
SLAM *vb, n* **slammed**
SLAMMER *n* prison
SLAMS ▶ **slam**
SLANDER *n, vb*
SLANE *n* spade for cutting turf **slanes**
SLANG *n, vb* **slanged**
SLANGER *n* street vendor
SLANGS ▶ **slang**
SLANGY ▶ **slang**
SLANK *dialect word for* ▶ **lank**
SLANT *vb, n* **slanted**
SLANTER = **slinter**
SLANTLY ▶ **slant**
SLANTS ▶ **slant**
SLANTY *adj* slanting
SLAP *n, vb* **slapped, slapper, slaps**
SLART *vb* spill (something) **slarted, slarts**
SLASH *vb, n* **slashed**
SLASHER *n* machine used for cutting scrub or undergrowth in the bush
SLASHES ▶ **slash**
SLAT *n, vb*
SLATCH *n* slack part of rope
SLATE *n, vb, adj* **slated**
SLATER *n* person trained in laying roof slates **slaters**
SLATES ▶ **slate**
SLATEY *adj* slightly mad
SLATHER *vb* spread quickly or lavishly
SLATIER ▶ **slaty**
SLATING *n* act or process of laying slates
SLATS ▶ **slat**
SLATTED ▶ **slat**
SLATTER *vb* be slovenly
SLATY *adj* consisting of or resembling slate
SLAVE *n, vb* **slaved**
SLAVER *n, vb* **slavers**
SLAVERY *n* state or condition of being a slave
SLAVES ▶ **slave**
SLAVEY *n* female general servant **slaveys**
SLAVING ▶ **slave**
SLAVISH *adj*
SLAW *short for* > **coleslaw**
SLAWS ▶ **slaw**
SLAY *vb* **slayed, slayer, slayers, slaying, slays**
SLEAVE *n* tangled thread ▷ *vb* disentangle (twisted thread, etc) **sleaved, sleaves**
SLEAZE *n* behaviour considered dishonest or disreputable **sleazes**
SLEAZO *n* sleazy person
SLEAZY *adj*
SLEB *n* celebrity **slebs**
SLED = **sledge**
SLEDDED ▶ **sled**
SLEDDER ▶ **sled**
SLEDED ▶ **sled**
SLEDGE *n, vb* **sledged, sledger, sledges**
SLEDS ▶ **sled**
SLEE *Scots word for* ▶ **sly**
SLEECH *n* slippery mud **sleechy**

SLEEK *adj, vb* **sleeked**
SLEEKEN *vb* make sleek
SLEEKER ▸ **sleek**
SLEEKIT *adj* smooth
SLEEKLY ▸ **sleek**
SLEEKS ▸ **sleek**
SLEEKY ▸ **sleek**
SLEEP *n, vb*
SLEEPER *n*
SLEEPRY *Scots word for* ▸ **sleepy**
SLEEPS ▸ **sleep**
SLEEPY *adj*
SLEER ▸ **slee**
SLEEST ▸ **slee**
SLEET *n, vb* **sleeted, sleets, sleety**
SLEEVE *n* **sleeved**
SLEEVER *n* old beer measure
SLEEVES ▸ **sleeve**
SLEEZY *adj* sleazy
SLEIDED *adj* old word meaning separated
SLEIGH = **sledge**
SLEIGHS ▸ **sleigh**
SLEIGHT *n* skill or cunning
SLENDER *adj*
SLENTER = **slinter**
SLEPT ▸ **sleep**
SLEUTH *n, vb* **sleuths**
SLEW *vb* **slewed, slewing, slews**
SLEY *n* weaver's tool for separating threads **sleys**
SLICE *n, vb* **sliced, slicer, slicers, slices, slicing**
SLICK *adj, n, vb* **slicked**
SLICKEN *vb* make smooth
SLICKER *n* sly or untrustworthy person
SLICKLY ▸ **slick**
SLICKS ▸ **slick**
SLID ▸ **slide**
SLIDDEN ▸ **slide**
SLIDDER *vb* slip
SLIDE *vb, n* **slided, slider, sliders, slides, sliding**
SLIER ▸ **sly**
SLIEST ▸ **sly**
SLIEVE *n* Irish mountain **slieves**
SLIGHT *adj, n, vb* **slights**
SLILY ▸ **sly**
SLIM *adj, vb*
SLIME *n, vb* **slimed, slimes**
SLIMIER ▸ **slimy**
SLIMILY ▸ **slimy**
SLIMING ▸ **slime**
SLIMLY ▸ **slim**
SLIMMED ▸ **slim**
SLIMMER ▸ **slim**
SLIMPSY *adj* thin and flimsy
SLIMS ▸ **slim**
SLIMSY *adj* frail
SLIMY *adj*
SLING *n, vb* **slinger, slings**
SLINK *vb, n* **slinked, slinker, slinks**
SLINKY *adj*
SLINTER *n* dodge, trick, or stratagem
SLIOTAR *n* ball used in hurling
SLIP *vb, n*
SLIPE *n* wool removed from the pelt of a slaughtered sheep ▷ *vb* remove skin **sliped, slipes, sliping**
SLIPOUT *n* instance of slipping out
SLIPPED ▸ **slip**
SLIPPER *n, vb*
SLIPPY *adj* slippery
SLIPS ▸ **slip**
SLIPT *vb* old form of slipped
SLIPUP *n* mistake or mishap **slipups**
SLIPWAY *n*
SLISH *n* old word meaning cut **slishes**
SLIT *n, vb*
SLITHER *vb, n*
SLITS, slitted, slitter, slitty ▸ **slit**
SLIVE *vb* slip **slived, sliven**
SLIVER *n, vb* **slivers**
SLIVES ▸ **slive**
SLIVING ▸ **slive**
SLOAN *n* severe telling-off **sloans**
SLOB *n*
SLOBBER *vb, n*
SLOBBY ▸ **slob**
SLOBS ▸ **slob**
SLOCKEN *vb* Scots word meaning slake
SLOE *n* **sloes**
SLOG *vb, n*
SLOGAN *n* **slogans**
SLOGGED ▸ **slog**
SLOGGER ▸ **slog**
SLOGS ▸ **slog**
SLOID *n* Swedish woodwork **sloids**
SLOJD *n* Swedish woodwork **slojds**
SLOKEN *vb* Scots word meaning slake **slokens**
SLOOM *vb* slumber **sloomed, slooms, sloomy**

SLOOP *n* **sloops**
SLOOSH *vb* wash with water
SLOOT *n* ditch for irrigation or drainage **sloots**
SLOP *vb, n*
SLOPE *vb, n* **sloped, sloper, slopers, slopes, slopier, sloping**
SLOPPED ▸ slop
SLOPPY *adj*
SLOPS ▸ slop
SLOPY ▸ slope
SLORM *vb* wipe carelessly **slormed, slorms**
SLOSH *vb, n* **sloshed, sloshes, sloshy**
SLOT *n, vb*
SLOTH *n, vb* **slothed, sloths**
SLOTS ▸ slot
SLOTTED ▸ slot
SLOTTER ▸ slot
SLOUCH *vb, n*
SLOUCHY *adj* slouching
SLOUGH *n, vb*
SLOUGHI *n* N African breed of dog resembling a greyhound
SLOUGHS ▸ slough
SLOUGHY ▸ slough
SLOVE ▸ slive
SLOVEN *n* habitually dirty or untidy person **slovens**
SLOW *adj, adv, vb* **slowed, slower, slowest, slowing, slowish, slowly, slows**
SLOYD *n* Swedish woodwork **sloyds**
SLUB *n* lump in yarn or fabric ▷ *vb* draw out and twist (a sliver of fibre) before spinning ▷ *adj* (of material) having an irregular appearance **slubb, slubbed**
SLUBBER *vb* smear
SLUBBS ▸ slubb
SLUBBY ▸ slub
SLUBS ▸ slub
SLUDGE *n, vb* **sludged, sludges**
SLUDGY *adj* consisting of, containing, or like sludge
SLUE = slew
SLUED ▸ slue
SLUEING ▸ slue
SLUES ▸ slue
SLUFF = slough
SLUFFED ▸ sluff
SLUFFS ▸ sluff
SLUG *n, vb* **slugged**
SLUGGER *n* (esp in boxing, baseball, etc) a person who strikes hard
SLUGS ▸ slug
SLUICE *n, vb* **sluiced, sluices, sluicy**
SLUING ▸ slue
SLUIT *n* water channel in South Africa **sluits**
SLUM *n, vb*
SLUMBER *n, vb*
SLUMBRY = slumbery
SLUMGUM *n* material left after wax is extracted from honeycomb
SLUMISM *n* existence of slums
SLUMMED ▸ slum
SLUMMER ▸ slum
SLUMMY ▸ slum
SLUMP *vb, n* **slumped, slumps**
SLUMPY *adj* boggy
SLUMS ▸ slum
SLUNG ▸ sling
SLUNK ▸ slink
SLUR *vb, n*
SLURB *n* suburban slum **slurban, slurbs**
SLURP *vb, n* **slurped, slurper, slurps**
SLURPY *adj* making a slurping noise
SLURRED ▸ slur
SLURRY *n, vb*
SLURS ▸ slur
SLUSE = sluice
SLUSES ▸ sluice
SLUSH *n, vb* **slushed, slushes**
SLUSHY *adj* of, resembling, or consisting of slush ▷ *n* unskilled kitchen assistant
SLUTCH *n* mud **slutchy**
SLY *adj* **slyer, slyest, slyish, slyly, slyness**
SLYPE *n* covered passageway in a church **slypes**
SMA *Scots word for* **▸ small**
SMAAK *vb* South African slang for like or love **smaaked, smaaks**
SMACK *vb, n, adv* **smacked**
SMACKER *n* loud kiss

SMACKS ▶ **smack**
SMAIK *n* Scots word meaning rascal **smaiks**
SMALL *adj* not large in size, number, or amount ▷ *n* narrow part of the lower back ▷ *adv* into small pieces ▷ *vb* make small **smalled, smaller, smalls**
SMALM = **smarm**
SMALMED ▶ **smalm**
SMALMS ▶ **smalm**
SMALMY = **smarmy**
SMALT *n* type of silica glass coloured deep blue with cobalt oxide
SMALTI ▶ **smalto**
SMALTO *n* coloured glass, etc, used in mosaics **smaltos**
SMALTS ▶ **smalt**
SMARAGD *n* any green gemstone, such as the emerald
SMARM *vb* bring (oneself) into favour (with) ▷ *n* obsequious flattery **smarmed, smarms**
SMARMY *adj*
SMART *adj, vb, n, adv* **smarted**
SMARTEN *vb*
SMARTER ▶ **smart**
SMARTIE = **smarty**
SMARTLY ▶ **smart**
SMARTS *pl n* know-how, intelligence, or wits
SMARTY *n* would-be clever person
SMASH *vb, n, adv*
SMASHED *adj*
SMASHER *n* attractive person or thing
SMASHES ▶ **smash**
SMASHUP *n* bad collision of cars
SMATCH *less common word for* ▶ **smack**
SMATTER *n* smattering ▷ *vb* prattle
SMAZE *n* smoky haze, less damp than fog **smazes**
SMEAR *vb, n* **smeared, smearer, smears**
SMEARY *adj* smeared, dirty
SMEATH *n* duck **smeaths**
SMECTIC *adj* (of a substance) existing in state in which the molecules are oriented in layers
SMEDDUM *n* any fine powder
SMEE *n* duck
SMEECH *Southwest English dialect form of* ▶ **smoke**
SMEEK *vb* smoke **smeeked**
SMEEKS ▶ **smeech**
SMEES ▶ **smee**
SMEETH *n* duck **smeeths**
SMEGMA *n* whitish sebaceous secretion that accumulates beneath the prepuce **smegmas**
SMEIK ▶ **smeke**
SMEIKED ▶ **smeked**
SMEIKS ▶ **smeik**
SMEKE *n* smoke ▷ *vb* smoke **smeked, smekes, smeking**
SMELL *vb, n* **smelled, smeller, smells**
SMELLY *adj*
SMELT *vb* extract metal from an ore
SMELTED ▶ **smell**
SMELTER *n* industrial plant where smelting is carried out
SMELTS ▶ **smell**
SMERK = **smirk**
SMERKED ▶ **smerk**
SMERKS ▶ **smerk**
SMEUSE *n* way through hedge **smeuses**
SMEW *n* duck of N Europe and Asia **smews**
SMICKER *vb* look at someone amorously
SMICKET *n* smock
SMICKLY *adv* amorously
SMIDDY *Scots word for* ▶ **smithy**
SMIDGE *n* very small amount or part
SMIDGEN *n* very small amount or part
SMIDGES ▶ **smidge**
SMIDGIN = **smidgen**
SMIGHT = **smite**
SMIGHTS ▶ **smight**
SMILAX *n* type of climbing shrub
SMILE *n, vb* **smiled, smiler, smilers, smiles**
SMILET *n* little smile **smilets**
SMILEY *n* symbol depicting a smile or

other facial expression, used in e-mail ▷ *adj* cheerful **smileys, smilier**
SMILING ▸ smile
SMIR *n* drizzly rain ▷ *vb* drizzle lightly
SMIRCH *n* stain ▷ *vb* disgrace
SMIRK *n, vb* **smirked, smirker, smirks, smirky**
SMIRR = **smir**
SMIRRED ▸ smirr
SMIRRS ▸ smirr
SMIRRY ▸ smirr
SMIRS ▸ smir
SMIT ▸ smite
SMITE *vb* **smiter, smiters, smites**
SMITH *n, vb* **smithed, smiths**
SMITHY *n, vb*
SMITING ▸ smite
SMITS ▸ smit
SMITTED ▸ smit
SMITTEN ▸ smite
SMITTLE *adj* infectious
SMOCK *n, vb* **smocked, smocks**
SMOG *n* **smoggy, smogs**
SMOILE = **smile**
SMOILED ▸ smoile
SMOILES ▸ smoile
SMOKE *n, vb* **smoked**
SMOKEHO = **smoko**
SMOKER *n* person who habitually smokes tobacco **smokers**
SMOKES ▸ smoke
SMOKEY = **smoky**
SMOKIE *n* smoked haddock
SMOKIER ▸ smoky
SMOKIES ▸ smoky
SMOKILY ▸ smoky
SMOKING ▸ smoke
SMOKO *n* short break from work for tea or a cigarette **smokos**
SMOKY *adj, n*
SMOLDER = **smoulder**
SMOLT *n* young salmon at the stage when it migrates to the sea **smolts**
SMOOCH *vb* kiss and cuddle ▷ *n* smooching
SMOOCHY *adj* romantic
SMOODGE = **smooch**
SMOOGE = **smooch**
SMOOGED ▸ smooge
SMOOGES ▸ smooge
SMOOR *vb* Scots word meaning put out fire **smoored, smoors**
SMOOSH *vb* paint to give softened look
SMOOT *vb* work as printer **smooted**
SMOOTH *adj, vb, adv, n* **smooths**
SMOOTHY = **smoothie**
SMOOTS ▸ smoot
SMORE = **smoor**
SMORED ▸ smore
SMORES ▸ smore
SMORING ▸ smore
SMOTE ▸ smite
SMOTHER *vb, n*
SMOUCH *vb* kiss
SMOUSE *vb* South African word meaning peddle **smoused, smouser, smouses**
SMOUT *n* child or undersized person ▷ *vb* creep or sneak **smouted, smouts, smowt**
SMOWTS ▸ smowt
SMOYLE = **smile**
SMOYLED ▸ smoyle
SMOYLES ▸ smoyle
SMRITI *n* class of Hindu sacred literature **smritis**
SMUDGE *vb, n* **smudged, smudger, smudges**
SMUDGY *adj* smeared, blurred, or soiled, or likely to become so
SMUG *adj, vb* **smugged, smugger**
SMUGGLE *vb*
SMUGLY ▸ smug
SMUGS ▸ smug
SMUR = **smir**
SMURRED ▸ smur
SMURRY ▸ smur
SMURS ▸ smur
SMUSH *vb* crush **smushed, smushes**
SMUT *n, vb*
SMUTCH *vb* smudge ▷ *n* mark **smutchy**
SMUTS ▸ smut
SMUTTED ▸ smut
SMUTTY ▸ smut
SMYTRIE *n* Scots word meaning collection
SNAB = **snob**
SNABBLE = **snaffle**
SNABS ▸ snab
SNACK *n, vb* **snacked, snacker, snacks**
SNAFFLE *n* jointed bit for a horse ▷ *vb* steal
SNAFU *n* confusion or chaos regarded as the

normal state ▷ *adj* confused or muddled up, as usual ▷ *vb* throw into chaos **snafued, snafus**
SNAG *n, vb* **snagged**
SNAGGY *adj* having sharp protuberances
SNAGS ▸ **snag**
SNAIL *n, vb* **snailed, snails, snaily**
SNAKE *n, vb* **snaked, snakes**
SNAKEY = **snaky**
SNAKIER ▸ **snaky**
SNAKILY ▸ **snaky**
SNAKING ▸ **snake**
SNAKISH ▸ **snake**
SNAKY *adj* twisted or winding
SNAP *vb, n, adj, adv* **snapped**
SNAPPER *n, vb*
SNAPPY *adj*
SNAPS ▸ **snap**
SNAPTIN *n* container for food
SNAR = **snarl**
SNARE *n, vb* **snared, snarer, snarers, snares**
SNARF *vb* eat or drink greedily **snarfed, snarfs**
SNARIER ▸ **snare**
SNARING ▸ **snare**
SNARK *n* imaginary creature in Lewis Carroll's poetry **snarks**
SNARKY *adj* unpleasant and scornful
SNARL *vb, n* **snarled, snarler, snarls, snarly**
SNARRED ▸ **snar**
SNARS ▸ **snar**
SNARY ▸ **snare**
SNASH *vb* Scots word meaning speak cheekily **snashed, snashes**
SNASTE *n* candle wick **snastes**
SNATCH *vb, n*
SNATCHY *adj* disconnected or spasmodic
SNATH *n* handle of a scythe **snathe**
SNATHES ▸ **snathe**
SNATHS ▸ **snath**
SNAW *Scots variant of* ▸ **snow**
SNAWED ▸ **snaw**
SNAWING ▸ **snaw**
SNAWS ▸ **snaw**
SNAZZY *adj*
SNEAD *n* scythe handle **sneads**
SNEAK *vb, n, adj* **sneaked**
SNEAKER *n*
SNEAKS ▸ **sneak**
SNEAKY ▸ **sneak**
SNEAP *vb* nip **sneaped, sneaps**
SNEATH = **snath**
SNEATHS ▸ **sneath**
SNEB = **snib**
SNEBBE = **snub**
SNEBBED ▸ **sneb**
SNEBBES ▸ **snebbe**
SNEBS ▸ **sneb**
SNECK *n* small squared stone used in a rubble wall to fill spaces between stones ▷ *vb* fasten (a latch) **snecked, snecks**
SNED *vb* prune or trim **snedded, sneds**
SNEE *vb* cut **sneed, sneeing**
SNEER *n, vb* **sneered, sneerer, sneers**
SNEERY *adj* contemptuous or scornful
SNEES ▸ **snee**
SNEESH *n* Scots word meaning pinch of snuff
SNEEZE *vb, n* **sneezed, sneezer, sneezes, sneezy**
SNELL *adj* biting ▷ *vb* attach hook to fishing line **snelled, sneller, snells, snelly**
SNIB *n* catch of a door or window ▷ *vb* bolt or fasten (a door) **snibbed, snibs**
SNICK *n* (make) a small cut or notch ▷ *vb* make a small cut or notch in (something) **snicked**
SNICKER = **snigger**
SNICKET *n* passageway between walls or fences
SNICKS ▸ **snick**
SNIDE *adj, n, vb* **snided, snidely, snider, snides, snidest, snidey**
SNIDIER ▸ **snidey**
SNIDING ▸ **snide**
SNIES ▸ **sny**
SNIFF *vb, n* **sniffed**
SNIFFER *n* device for detecting hidden substances such as drugs

SNIFFLE *vb, n* **sniffly**
SNIFFS ▸ **sniff**
SNIFFY *adj* contemptuous or scornful
SNIFT = **sniff**
SNIFTED ▸ **snift**
SNIFTER *n* small quantity of alcoholic drink ▹ *vb* sniff
SNIFTS ▸ **snift**
SNIFTY *adj* slang word meaning excellent
SNIG *vb* drag (a felled log) by a chain or cable **snigged**
SNIGGER *n, vb*
SNIGGLE *vb* fish for eels by dangling or thrusting a baited hook into cavities ▹ *n* baited hook used for sniggling eels
SNIGLET *n* invented word
SNIGS ▸ **snig**
SNIP *vb, n, interj*
SNIPE *n, vb* **sniped**
SNIPER *n* person who shoots at someone from cover **snipers**
SNIPES ▸ **snipe**
SNIPIER ▸ **snipy**
SNIPING ▸ **snipe**
SNIPPED ▸ **snip**
SNIPPER ▸ **snip**
SNIPPET *n*
SNIPPY *adj* scrappy
SNIPS ▸ **snip**
SNIPY *adj* like a snipe
SNIRT *n* Scots word meaning suppressed laugh
SNIRTLE *vb* Scots word meaning snicker
SNIRTS ▸ **snirt**
SNIT *n* fit of temper
SNITCH *vb* act as an informer ▹ *n* informer
SNITCHY *adj* bad-tempered or irritable
SNITS ▸ **snit**
SNIVEL *vb, n* **snivels**
SNOB *n* **snobby, snobs**
SNOD *vb* Scots word meaning make tidy **snodded, snodder, snoddit, snods**
SNOEK *n* edible marine fish **snoeks**
SNOEP *adj* mean or tight-fisted
SNOG *vb* kiss and cuddle ▹ *n* act of kissing and cuddling **snogged, snogs**
SNOKE = **snook**
SNOKED ▸ **snoke**
SNOKES ▸ **snoke**
SNOKING ▸ **snoke**
SNOOD *n* pouch loosely holding a woman's hair at the back ▹ *vb* hold (the hair) in a snood **snooded, snoods**
SNOOK *n* any of several large game fishes ▹ *vb* lurk **snooked**
SNOOKER *n, vb*
SNOOKS ▸ **snook**
SNOOL *vb* Scots word meaning dominate **snooled, snools**
SNOOP *vb, n* **snooped**
SNOOPER *n*
SNOOPS ▸ **snoop**
SNOOPY ▸ **snoop**
SNOOT *n* nose ▹ *vb* look contemptuously at **snooted, snoots**
SNOOTY *adj*
SNOOZE *vb, n* **snoozed, snoozer, snoozes**
SNOOZLE *vb* cuddle and sleep
SNOOZY ▸ **snooze**
SNORE *vb, n* **snored, snorer, snorers, snores, snoring**
SNORKEL *n, vb*
SNORT *vb, n* **snorted**
SNORTER *n* person or animal that snorts
SNORTS ▸ **snort**
SNORTY ▸ **snort**
SNOT *n, vb*
SNOTRAG *n* handkerchief
SNOTS ▸ **snot**
SNOTTED ▸ **snot**
SNOTTER *vb* breathe through obstructed nostrils
SNOTTIE *n* midshipman
SNOTTY *adj* covered with mucus from the nose
SNOUT *n, vb* **snouted, snouts, snouty**
SNOW *n, vb*
SNOWCAP *n* cap of snow on top of a mountain
SNOWCAT *n* tracked vehicle for travelling over snow
SNOWED *adj* under the influence of narcotic drugs
SNOWIER ▸ **snowy**
SNOWILY ▸ **snowy**

SNOWING ▸ **snow**
SNOWISH *adj* like snow
SNOWK = **snook**
SNOWKED ▸ **snowk**
SNOWKS ▸ **snowk**
SNOWMAN *n* **snowmen**
SNOWS ▸ **snow**
SNOWY *adj* covered with or abounding in snow
SNUB *vb, n, adj*
SNUBBE *n* stub
SNUBBED ▸ **snub**
SNUBBER ▸ **snub**
SNUBBES ▸ **snubbe**
SNUBBY ▸ **snub**
SNUBFIN *adj as in* **snubfin dolphin** Australian dolphin with a small dorsal fin
SNUBS ▸ **snub**
SNUCK *past tense and past participle of* ▸ **sneak**
SNUDGE *vb* be miserly **snudged, snudges**
SNUFF *n, vb* **snuffed, snuffer**
SNUFFLE *vb, n* **snuffly**
SNUFFS ▸ **snuff**
SNUFFY *adj* of, relating to, or resembling snuff
SNUG *adj, n, vb* **snugged, snugger**
SNUGGLE *vb, n*
SNUGLY ▸ **snug**
SNUGS ▸ **snug**
SNUSH *vb* take snuff **snushed, snushes**
SNUZZLE *vb* root in ground
SNY = **snye**

> A side channel of a river, that can be useful when you are short of vowels. And note that it can be extended to form **snye**.

SNYE *n* side channel of a river **snyes**
SO *adv, interj, n*
SOAK *vb, n*
SOAKAGE *n* process or a period in which a permeable substance is soaked in a liquid
SOAKED, soaken, soaker, soakers, soaking, soaks ▸ **soak**
SOAP *n, vb*
SOAPBOX *n* crate used as a platform for speech-making ▹ *vb* deliver a speech from a soapbox
SOAPED ▸ **soap**
SOAPER *n* soap opera **soapers**
SOAPIE *n* soap opera
SOAPIER ▸ **soapy**
SOAPIES ▸ **soapie**
SOAPILY ▸ **soapy**
SOAPING ▸ **soap**
SOAPS ▸ **soap**
SOAPY *adj* covered with soap
SOAR *vb, n*
SOARE *n* young hawk
SOARED, soarer, soarers ▸ **soar**
SOARES ▸ **soare**
SOARING, soars ▸ **soar**
SOAVE *n* dry white Italian wine **soaves**
SOB *vb, n*
SOBA *n* (in Japanese cookery) noodles made from buckwheat flour **sobas**
SOBBED, sobber, sobbers, sobbing ▸ **sob**
SOBEIT *conj* provided that
SOBER *adj, vb* **sobered, soberer, soberly, sobers**
SOBFUL *adj* tearful
SOBOLE *n* creeping underground stem that produces roots and buds **soboles**
SOBS ▸ **sob**
SOC *n* feudal right to hold court
SOCA *n* mixture of soul and calypso music
SOCAGE *n* tenure of land by certain services **socager, socages**
SOCAS ▸ **soca**
SOCCAGE = **socage**
SOCCER *n* **soccers**
SOCIAL *adj, n* **socials**
SOCIATE *n* associate
SOCIETY *n*
SOCK *n, vb* **socked**
SOCKET *n, vb* **sockets**
SOCKEYE *n* Pacific salmon with red flesh
SOCKING ▸ **sock**
SOCKMAN = **socman**
SOCKMEN ▸ **sockman**
SOCKO *adj* excellent
SOCKS ▸ **sock**
SOCLE *another name for* ▸ **plinth**
SOCLES ▸ **socle**
SOCMAN *n* tenant holding land by socage **socmen**

SOCS ▶ **soc**
SOD *n, vb*
SODA *n*
SODAIC *adj* containing soda
SODAIN = **sudden**
SODAINE = **sudden**
SODAS ▶ **soda**
SODDED ▶ **sod**
SODDEN *adj, vb* **soddens**
SODDIER ▶ **soddy**
SODDIES ▶ **soddy**
SODDING ▶ **sod**
SODDY *adj* covered with turf
SODGER *dialect variant of* ▶ **soldier**
SODGERS ▶ **sodger**
SODIC *adj* containing sodium
SODIUM *n* **sodiums**
SODOM *n* person who performs sodomy **sodoms**
SODOMY *n* anal intercourse
SODS ▶ **sod**
SOEVER *adv* in any way at all
SOFA *n*
SOFABED *n* sofa that converts into a bed
SOFAR *n* system for determining a position at sea **sofars**
SOFAS ▶ **sofa**
SOFFIT *n* underside of a part of a building or a structural component **soffits**
SOFT *adj, adv, vb*
SOFTA *n* Muslim student of divinity and jurisprudence **softas**
SOFTED ▶ **soft**
SOFTEN *vb* **softens**
SOFTER ▶ **soft**
SOFTEST ▶ **soft**
SOFTIE *n* person who is easily upset
SOFTIES ▶ **softy**
SOFTING ▶ **soft**
SOFTISH ▶ **soft**
SOFTLY ▶ **soft**
SOFTS ▶ **soft**
SOFTY = **softie**
SOG *vb* soak
SOGER = **sodger**
SOGERS ▶ **soger**
SOGGED ▶ **sog**
SOGGIER ▶ **soggy**
SOGGILY ▶ **soggy**
SOGGING ▶ **sog**
SOGGY *adj*
SOGS ▶ **sog**
SOH *n* (in tonic sol-fa) fifth degree of any major scale
SOHO *interj* exclamation announcing the sighting of a hare
SOHS ▶ **soh**
SOHUR ▶ **suhur**
SOHURS ▶ **sohur**
SOIGNE *adj* well-groomed, elegant **soignee**
SOIL *n, vb*
SOILAGE *n* green fodder
SOILED, soilier, soiling, soils ▶ **soil**
SOILURE *n* act of soiling or the state of being soiled
SOILY ▶ **soil**
SOIREE *n* **soirees**
SOJA = **soya**
SOJAS ▶ **soja**
SOJOURN *n, vb*
SOKAH = **soca**
SOKAHS ▶ **sokah**
SOKAIYA *n* Japanese extortionist
SOKE *n* right to hold a local court
SOKEMAN = **socman**
SOKEMEN ▶ **sokeman**
SOKEN *n* feudal district **sokens**
SOKES ▶ **soke**
SOKOL *n* Czech gymnastic association **sokols**
SOL *n* liquid colloidal solution
SOLA ▶ **solum**
SOLACE *vb, n* **solaced, solacer, solaces**
SOLAH *n* Indian plant **solahs**
SOLAN *archaic name for* ▶ **gannet**
SOLAND *n* solan goose **solands**
SOLANIN = **solanine**
SOLANO *n* hot wind in Spain **solanos**
SOLANS ▶ **solan**
SOLANUM *n* any plant of the genus that includes the potato
SOLAR *adj*
SOLARIA > **solarium**
SOLARS ▶ **solum**
SOLAS ▶ **solum**
SOLATE *vb* change from gel to liquid **solated, solates**
SOLATIA > **solatium**

SOLD *n* obsolete word for salary
SOLDADO *n* soldier
SOLDAN *archaic word for* ▶ **sultan**
SOLDANS ▶ **soldan**
SOLDE *n* wages
SOLDER *n*, *vb* **solders**
SOLDES ▶ **solde**
SOLDI ▶ **soldo**
SOLDIER *n*, *vb*
SOLDO *n* former Italian copper coin
SOLDS ▶ **sold**
SOLE *adj*, *n*, *vb* **soled**
SOLEI ▶ **soleus**
SOLEIN = **sullen**
SOLELY *adv*
SOLEMN *adj*
SOLER = **sole**
SOLERA *n* system for aging sherry and other fortified wines **soleras**
SOLERET *n* armour for foot
SOLERS ▶ **soler**
SOLES ▶ **sole**
SOLEUS *n* muscle in calf of leg
SOLFEGE *variant of* > **solfeggio**
SOLGEL *adj* changing between sol and gel
SOLI *adv* to be performed by or with soloists
SOLICIT *vb*
SOLID *adj*, *n* **solider**
SOLIDI ▶ **solidus**
SOLIDLY ▶ **solid**
SOLIDS ▶ **solid**
SOLIDUM *n* part of pedestal
SOLIDUS = **slash**
SOLING ▶ **sole**
SOLION *n* amplifier used in chemistry **solions**
SOLIPED *n* animal whose hooves are not cloven
SOLITO *adv* musical instruction meaning play in usual manner
SOLITON *n* type of isolated particle-like wave
SOLIVE *n* type of joist **solives**
SOLLAR *n* archaic word meaning attic **sollars, soller**
SOLLERS ▶ **soller**
SOLO *n*, *adj*, *adv*, *vb* **soloed, soloing**
SOLOIST *n*
SOLON *n* US congressman **solons**
SOLOS ▶ **solo**
SOLS ▶ **sol**
SOLUBLE *adj*, *n* **solubly**
SOLUM *n* upper layers of the soil profile **solums**
SOLUNAR *adj* relating to sun and moon
SOLUS *adj* alone
SOLUTAL *adj* relating to a solute
SOLUTE *n*, *adj* **solutes**
SOLVATE *vb* undergo, cause to undergo, or partake in solvation
SOLVE *vb* **solved**
SOLVENT *adj*, *n*
SOLVER, solvers, solves, solving ▶ **solve**
SOM *n* currency of Kyrgyzstan and Uzbekistan
SOMA *n* body of an organism as distinct from the germ cells
SOMAN *n* compound developed as a nerve gas **somans**
SOMAS ▶ **soma**
SOMATA ▶ **soma**
SOMATIC *adj* of the body, as distinct from the mind
SOMBER *adj* (in the US) sombre ▷ *vb* (in the US) make sombre **sombers**
SOMBRE *adj*, *vb* **sombred, sombrer, sombres**
SOME *adj*, *pron*, *adv*, *determiner*
SOMEDAY *adv* at some unspecified time in the future
SOMEHOW *adv*
SOMEONE *pron*, *n*
SOMEWAY *adv* in some unspecified manner
SOMEWHY *adv* for some reason
SOMITAL ▶ **somite**
SOMITE *n* segment of mesoderm in vertebrate embryos **somites, somitic**
SOMNIAL *adj* of dreams
SOMONI *n* monetary unit of Tajikistan
SOMS ▶ **som**
SOMY ▶ **som**
SON *n*
SONANCE ▶ **sonant**

SONANCY ▸ **sonant**
SONANT *n* voiced sound able to form a syllable or syllable nucleus ▹ *adj* denoting a voiced sound like this **sonants**
SONAR *n* **sonars**
SONATA *n* **sonatas**
SONCE *n* Scots word meaning good luck **sonces**
SONDAGE *n* deep trial trench for inspecting stratigraphy
SONDE *n* rocket, balloon, or probe used for observing in the upper atmosphere
SONDELI *n* Indian shrew
SONDER *n* yacht category **sonders**
SONDES ▸ **sonde**
SONE *n* subjective unit of loudness
SONERI *n* Indian cloth of gold **soneris**
SONES ▸ **sone**
SONG *n*
SONGFUL *adj* tuneful
SONGKOK *n* (in Malaysia and Indonesia) a kind of oval brimless hat, resembling a skull
SONGMAN *n* singer **songmen**
SONGS ▸ **song**
SONHOOD ▸ **son**
SONIC *adj*
SONICS *n* study of mechanical vibrations in matter
SONLESS ▸ **son**
SONLIKE ▸ **son**
SONLY *adj* like a son
SONNE = **son**
SONNES ▸ **sonne**
SONNET *n*, *vb* **sonnets**
SONNIES ▸ **sonny**
SONNY *n* term of address to a boy
SONOVOX *n* device used to alter sound of human voice in music recordings
SONS ▸ **son**
SONSE = **sonce**
SONSES ▸ **sonse**
SONSHIP ▸ **son**
SONSIE = **sonsy**
SONSIER ▸ **sonsy**
SONSY *adj* plump
SONTAG *n* type of knitted women's cape **sontags**
SONTIES *n* Shakespearian oath
SOOEY *interj* call used to summon pigs
SOOGEE *vb* clean ship using a special solution **soogeed, soogees, soogie**
SOOGIED ▸ **soogie**
SOOGIES ▸ **soogie**
SOOJEY = **soogee**
SOOJEYS ▸ **soojey**
SOOK *n* baby ▹ *vb* suck **sooked, sooking, sooks**
SOOL *vb* incite (a dog) to attack **soole, sooled**
SOOLES ▸ **soole**
SOOLING ▸ **sool**
SOOLS ▸ **sool**
SOOM *Scots word for* ▸ **swim**
SOOMED ▸ **soom**
SOOMING ▸ **soom**
SOOMS ▸ **soom**
SOON *adv*
SOONER *adv* rather ▹ *n* idler or shirker **sooners**
SOONEST *adv* as soon as possible
SOOP *Scots word for* ▸ **sweep**
SOOPED ▸ **soop**
SOOPING ▸ **soop**
SOOPS ▸ **soop**
SOOT *n*, *vb*
SOOTE *n* sweet
SOOTED ▸ **soot**
SOOTES ▸ **soot**
SOOTH *n* truth or reality ▹ *adj* true or real
SOOTHE *vb* **soothed**
SOOTHER *vb*
SOOTHES ▸ **soothe**
SOOTHLY ▸ **sooth**
SOOTHS ▸ **sooth**
SOOTIER ▸ **sooty**
SOOTILY ▸ **sooty**
SOOTING ▸ **soot**
SOOTS ▸ **soot**
SOOTY *adj* covered with soot
SOP *n*, *vb*
SOPH *shortened form of* > **sophomore**
SOPHIES ▸ **sophy**
SOPHISM *n* argument that seems reasonable but is actually false and misleading
SOPHIST *n* person who uses clever but invalid arguments
SOPHS ▸ **soph**

SOPHY *n* title of the Persian monarchs
SOPITE *vb* lull to sleep **sopited, sopites**
SOPOR *n* abnormally deep sleep **sopors**
SOPPED ▸ **sop**
SOPPIER ▸ **soppy**
SOPPILY ▸ **soppy**
SOPPING ▸ **sop**
SOPPY *adj*
SOPRA *adv* musical instruction meaning above
SOPRANI ▸ **soprano**
SOPRANO *n, adj*
SOPS ▸ **sop**
SORA *n* North American rail with a yellow bill
SORAGE *n* first year in hawk's life **sorages**
SORAL ▸ **sorus**
SORAS ▸ **sora**
SORB *n* any of various related trees, esp the mountain ash ▹ *vb* absorb or adsorb
SORBATE *n* salt of sorbic acid
SORBED ▸ **sorb**
SORBENT ▸ **sorb**
SORBET = **sherbet**
SORBETS ▸ **sorbet**
SORBIC ▸ **sorb**
SORBING ▸ **sorb**
SORBITE *n* mineral found in steel
SORBO *n as in* **sorbo rubber** spongy form of rubber
SORBOSE *n* sugar derived from the berries of the mountain ash
SORBS ▸ **sorb**
SORBUS *n* rowan or related tree
SORCERY *n*
SORD *n* flock of mallard ducks
SORDA *n* deaf woman
SORDES *pl n* dark incrustations on the lips and teeth of patients with prolonged fever
SORDID *adj*
SORDINE = **sordino**
SORDINI ▸ **sordino**
SORDINO *n* mute for a stringed or brass musical instrument
SORDO *n* deaf man
SORDOR *n* sordidness **sordors**
SORDS ▸ **sord**
SORE *adj, n, adv, vb* **sored**
SOREDIA > **soredium**

> This is the plural of **soredium**, a reproductive body in lichens. It is a very frequently played bonus, and it has a 'twin' **roadies**. It is a good idea to become familiar with at least the higher probability twin sevens and eights, since the thought of one will often prompt the other, and it may well be that one twin will fit on the board where the other would not.

SOREE = **sora**
SOREES ▸ **soree**
SOREHON *n* old Irish feudal right
SOREL *variant of* ▸ **sorrel**
SORELL = **sorrel**
SORELLS ▸ **sorell**
SORELS ▸ **sorel**
SORELY *adv* greatly
SORER ▸ **sore**
SORES ▸ **sore**
SOREST ▸ **sore**
SOREX *n* shrew or related animal **sorexes**
SORGHO = **sorgo**
SORGHOS ▸ **sorgho**
SORGHUM *n*
SORGO *n* any of several varieties of sorghum that have watery sweet juice **sorgos**
SORI ▸ **sorus**
SORING ▸ **sore**
SORINGS ▸ **sore**
SORITES *n* type of syllogism in which only the final conclusion is stated **soritic**
SORN *vb* obtain food, etc, from another person by presuming on his or her generosity **sorned, sorner**
SORNERS ▸ **sore**
SORNING ▸ **sorn**
SORNS ▸ **sorn**
SOROBAN *n* Japanese abacus
SOROCHE *n* altitude sickness

SORORAL *adj* of sister
SOROSES ▸ **sorosis**
SOROSIS *n* fleshy multiple fruit
SORRA *Irish word for* ▸ **sorrow**
SORRAS ▸ **sorra**
SORREL *n* **sorrels**
SORRIER ▸ **sorry**
SORRILY ▸ **sorry**
SORROW *n, vb* **sorrows**
SORRY *adj, interj*
SORT *n, vb*
SORTA *adv* phonetic representation of 'sort of'
SORTAL *n* type of logical or linguistic concept **sortals**
SORTED *interj* exclamation of satisfaction, approval, etc ▷ *adj* possessing the desired recreational drugs
SORTER ▸ **sort**
SORTERS ▸ **sort**
SORTES *n* divination by opening book at random
SORTIE *n, vb* **sortied, sorties**
SORTING ▸ **sort**
SORTS ▸ **sort**
SORUS *n* cluster of sporangia on the undersurface of certain fern leaves
SOS ▸ **so**
SOSATIE *n* skewer of curried meat pieces
SOSS *vb* make dirty or muddy **sossed, sosses, sossing**
SOT *n* habitual drunkard ▷ *adv* indeed: used to contradict a negative statement ▷ *vb* be a drunkard
SOTH *archaic variant of* ▸ **sooth**
SOTHS ▸ **soth**
SOTOL *n* American plant related to agave **sotols**
SOTS, sotted, sotting, sottish ▸ **sot**
SOU *n* former French coin
SOUARI *n* tree of tropical America **souaris**
SOUBISE *n* purée of onions mixed into a thick white sauce and served over eggs, fish, etc
SOUCAR *n* Indian banker **soucars**
SOUCE = **souse; souced, souces, soucing, souct**
SOUDAN *obsolete variaint of* ▸ **sultan**
SOUDANS ▸ **soudan**
SOUFFLE *n* light fluffy dish made with beaten egg whites ▷ *adj* made light and puffy
SOUGH *vb* (of the wind) make a sighing sound ▷ *n* soft continuous murmuring sound **soughed, soughs**
SOUGHT ▸ **seek**
SOUK = **sook**
SOUKED ▸ **souk**
SOUKING ▸ **souk**
SOUKOUS *n* style of African popular music
SOUKS ▸ **souk**
SOUL *n*
SOULDAN = **soldan**
SOULED *adj* having soul
SOULFUL *adj*
SOULS ▸ **soul**
SOUM *vb* decide how many animals can graze particular pasture **soumed, souming, soums**
SOUND *n* something heard, noise ▷ *vb* make or cause to make a sound ▷ *adj* in good condition ▷ *adv* soundly **sounded**
SOUNDER *n* device formerly used to convert electric signals into sounds
SOUNDLY ▸ **sound**
SOUNDS ▸ **sound**
SOUP *n, vb*
SOUPCON *n* small amount
SOUPED ▸ **soup**
SOUPER *n* person dispensing soup **soupers**
SOUPFIN *n* Pacific requiem shark valued for its fins
SOUPIER ▸ **soupy**
SOUPING ▸ **soup**
SOUPLE = **supple**
SOUPLED ▸ **souple**
SOUPLES ▸ **souple**
SOUPS ▸ **soup**

SOUPY *adj* having the appearance or consistency of soup
SOUR *adj, vb*
SOURCE *n, vb* **sourced, sources**
SOURED, sourer, sourest, souring, sourish, sourly ▸ **sour**
SOUROCK *n* Scots word for sorrel plant
SOURS ▸ **sour**
SOURSE = **source**
SOURSES ▸ **sourse**
SOURSOP *n* small West Indian tree
SOUS ▸ **sou**
SOUSE *vb, n* **soused, souses, sousing**
SOUSLIK = **suslik**
SOUT = **soot**
SOUTANE *n* Roman Catholic priest's cassock
SOUTAR = **souter**
SOUTARS ▸ **soutar**
SOUTER *n* shoemaker or cobbler **souters**
SOUTH *n, adj, adv, vb* **southed**
SOUTHER *n* strong wind or storm from the south ▷ *vb* turn south
SOUTHS ▸ **south**
SOUTS ▸ **sout**
SOV *shortening of* > **sovereign**
SOVIET *n* formerly, elected council in the USSR ▷ *adj* of the former USSR **soviets**
SOVKHOZ *n* large mechanized farm in former USSR
SOVRAN *literary word for* > **sovereign**
SOVRANS ▸ **sovran**
SOVS ▸ **sov**
SOW *vb, n* **sowable**
SOWANS = **sowens**
SOWAR *n* Indian cavalryman
SOWARRY = **sowarree**
SOWARS ▸ **sowar**
SOWBACK *another name for* ▸ **hogback**
SOWCAR = **soucar**
SOWCARS ▸ **sowcar**
SOWCE = **souse**
SOWCED ▸ **sowce**
SOWCES ▸ **sowce**
SOWCING ▸ **sowce**
SOWDER ▸ **sawder** *n*
SOWDERS ▸ **sowder**
SOWED ▸ **sow**
SOWENS *n* pudding made from oatmeal husks steeped and boiled
SOWER ▸ **sow**
SOWERS ▸ **sow**
SOWF = **sowth**
SOWFED ▸ **sowf**
SOWFF = **sowth**
SOWFFED ▸ **sowff**
SOWFFS ▸ **sowff**
SOWFING ▸ **sowf**
SOWFS ▸ **sowf**
SOWING ▸ **sow**
SOWINGS ▸ **sow**
SOWL = **sole**
SOWLE = **sole**
SOWLED ▸ **sowl**
SOWLES ▸ **sowle**
SOWLING ▸ **sowl**
SOWLS ▸ **sowl**
SOWM = **soum**
SOWMED ▸ **sowm**
SOWMING ▸ **sowm**
SOWMS ▸ **sowm**
SOWN ▸ **sow**
SOWND *vb* wield **sownded, sownds**
SOWNE = **sound**
SOWNES ▸ **sowne**
SOWP *n* spoonful **sowps**
SOWS ▸ **sow**
SOWSE = **souse**
SOWSED ▸ **sowse**
SOWSES ▸ **sowse**
SOWSING ▸ **sowse**
SOWSSE = **souse**
SOWSSED ▸ **sowsse**
SOWSSES ▸ **sowsse**
SOWTER = **souter**
SOWTERS ▸ **sowter**
SOWTH *vb* Scots word meaning whistle **sowthed, sowths**
SOX *pl n* informal spelling of 'socks'

> This informal word for **socks** is one of the key short words to remember for using the X.

SOY *n as in* **soy sauce** salty dark brown sauce made from soya beans
SOYA *n* **soyas**
SOYBEAN *n* soya bean
SOYLE *n* body **soyles**
SOYMILK *n* milk substitute made from soya
SOYS ▸ **soy**
SOYUZ *n* Russian spacecraft **soyuzes**
SOZ *interj*
SOZIN *n* form of protein **sozine**

SOZINES ▶ **sozine**
SOZINS ▶ **sozin**
SOZZLE *vb* make wet
SOZZLED *adj* drunk
SOZZLES ▶ **sozzle**
SOZZLY *adj* wet
SPA *n*, *vb*
SPACE *n*, *vb* **spaced**
SPACER *n* piece of material used to create or maintain a space between two things **spacers**
SPACES ▶ **space**
SPACEY *adj* vague and dreamy, as if under the influence of drugs
SPACIAL = **spatial**
SPACIER ▶ **spacey**
SPACING *n* arrangement of letters, words, etc, on a page in order to achieve legibility
SPACKLE *vb* fill holes in plaster
SPACY = **spacey**
SPADE *n* **spaded, spader, spaders, spades**
SPADGER *n* sparrow
SPADING ▶ **spade**
SPADIX *n* spike of small flowers on a fleshy stem
SPADO *n* neutered animal **spadoes, spados**
SPAE *vb* foretell (the future) **spaed, spaeing**
SPAEMAN *n* man who foretells future **spaemen**
SPAER ▶ **spae**
SPAERS ▶ **spae**
SPAES ▶ **spae**
SPAG *vb* (of a cat) to scratch (a person) with the claws ▷ *n* Australian offensive slang for an Italian **spagged, spags**
SPAHEE = **spahi**
SPAHEES ▶ **spahee**
SPAHI *n* (formerly) an irregular cavalryman in the Turkish armed forces **spahis**
SPAIL *Scots word for* ▶ **spall**
SPAILS ▶ **spail**
SPAIN *variant of* ▶ **spane**
SPAINED ▶ **spain**
SPAING ▶ **spa**
SPAINGS ▶ **spa**
SPAINS ▶ **spain**
SPAIRGE *Scots word for* ▶ **sparge**
SPAIT = **spate**
SPAITS ▶ **spait**
SPAKE *past tense of* ▶ **speak**
SPALD = **spauld**
SPALDS ▶ **spald**
SPALE *Scots word for* ▶ **spall**
SPALES ▶ **spale**
SPALL *n* splinter or chip of ore, rock, or stone ▷ *vb* split or cause to split into such fragments
SPALLE = **spauld**
SPALLED ▶ **spall**
SPALLER ▶ **spall**
SPALLES ▶ **spalle**
SPALLS ▶ **spall**
SPALT *vb* split **spalted, spalts**
SPAM *vb*, *n*
SPAMBOT *n* computer program that sends spam
SPAMMED ▶ **spam**
SPAMMER ▶ **spam**
SPAMMIE *n* love bite
SPAMMY *adj* bland
SPAMS ▶ **spam**
SPAN *n*, *vb*
SPANCEL *n* length of rope for hobbling an animal ▷ *vb* hobble (an animal) with a loose rope
SPANDEX *n* type of synthetic stretch fabric made from polyurethane fibre
SPANE *vb* Scots word meaning wean **spaned, spanes**
SPANG *adv* exactly, firmly, or straight ▷ *vb* dash **spanged**
SPANGLE *n*, *vb* **spangly**
SPANGS ▶ **spang**
SPANIEL *n*
SPANING ▶ **spane**
SPANK *vb*, *n* **spanked**
SPANKER *n* fore-and-aft sail or a mast that is aftermost in a sailing vessel
SPANKS ▶ **spank**
SPANNED ▶ **span**
SPANNER *n*
SPANS ▶ **span**
SPAR *n*, *vb*
SPARD ▶ **spare**
SPARE *adj*, *n*, *vb* **spared, sparely, sparer,**

sparers, spares, sparest
SPARGE *vb* sprinkle or scatter (something) **sparged, sparger, sparges**
SPARID *n* type of marine percoid fish ▷ *adj* of or belonging to this family of fish **sparids**
SPARING *adj*
SPARK *n, vb*
SPARKE *n* weapon
SPARKED ▶ **spark**
SPARKER ▶ **spark**
SPARKES ▶ **sparke**
SPARKIE *n* electrician
SPARKLE *vb, n*
SPARKLY *adj* sparkling ▷ *n* sparkling thing
SPARKS *n* electrician
SPARKY *adj* lively
SPAROID = **sparid**
SPARRE = **spar**
SPARRED ▶ **spar**
SPARRER ▶ **spar**
SPARRES ▶ **sparre**
SPARROW *n*
SPARRY *adj* (of minerals) containing, relating to, or resembling spar
SPARS ▶ **spar**
SPARSE *adj* **sparser**
SPART *n* esparto
SPARTAN *adj, n*
SPARTH *n* type of battle-axe **sparthe, sparths**
SPARTS ▶ **spart**
SPAS ▶ **spa**
SPASM *n, vb* **spasmed, spasmic, spasms**
SPAT *vb* have a quarrel
SPATE *n* **spates**
SPATHAL ▶ **spathe**
SPATHE *n* large sheathlike leaf enclosing a flower cluster **spathed, spathes**
SPATHIC *adj* (of minerals) resembling spar
SPATIAL *adj*
SPATS ▶ **spat**
SPATTED ▶ **spat**
SPATTEE *n* type of gaiter
SPATTER *vb, n*
SPATULA *n*
SPATULE *n* spatula
SPATZLE = **spaetzle**
SPAUL = **spauld**
SPAULD *n* shoulder **spaulds**
SPAULS ▶ **spaul**
SPAVIE *Scots variant of* ▶ **spavin**
SPAVIES ▶ **spavie**
SPAVIET *adj* Scots word meaning spavined
SPAVIN *n* enlargement of the hock of a horse by a bony growth **spavins**
SPAW = **spa**
SPAWL *vb* spit **spawled, spawls**
SPAWN *n, vb* **spawned, spawner, spawns**
SPAWNY *adj* like spawn
SPAWS ▶ **spaw**
SPAY *vb*
SPAYAD *n* male deer **spayads, spayd**
SPAYDS ▶ **spayd**
SPAYED ▶ **spay**
SPAYING ▶ **spay**
SPAYS ▶ **spay**
SPAZA *adj as in* **spaza shop** South African slang for a small shop in a township
SPEAK *vb*
SPEAKER *n*
SPEAKS ▶ **speak**
SPEAL = **spule**
SPEALS ▶ **speal**
SPEAN = **spane**
SPEANED ▶ **spean**
SPEANS ▶ **spean**
SPEAR *n, vb* **speared, spearer, spears, speary**
SPEAT = **spate**
SPEATS ▶ **speat**
SPEC *vb* **specced**
SPECCY *n* person wearing spectacles
SPECIAL *adj, n, vb*
SPECIE *n* coins as distinct from paper money
SPECIES *n*
SPECIFY *vb*
SPECK *n, vb* **specked**
SPECKLE *n, vb*
SPECKS ▶ **speck**
SPECKY = **speccy**
SPECS *pl n* spectacles
SPECTER = **spectre**
SPECTRA > **spectrum**
SPECTRE *n*
SPECULA > **speculum**
SPED ▶ **speed**
SPEECH *n, vb*
SPEED *n, vb* **speeded, speeder**
SPEEDO *n* speedometer **speedos**
SPEEDS ▶ **speed**

SPEEDUP *n* acceleration
SPEEDY *adj*
SPEEL *n* splinter of wood ▷ *vb* Scots word meaning climb **speeled, speeler, speels**
SPEER = **speir**
SPEERED ▶ **speer**
SPEERS ▶ **speer**
SPEIL *dialect word for* ▶ **climb**
SPEILED ▶ **speil**
SPEILS ▶ **speil**
SPEIR *vb* ask **speired, speirs**
SPEISE = **speiss**
SPEISES ▶ **speise**
SPEISS *n* compounds formed when ores containing arsenic or antimony are smelted
SPEK *n* bacon, fat, or fatty pork used for larding venison or other game **speks**
SPELD *vb* Scots word meaning spread **spelded, spelder**
SPELDIN *n* fish split and dried
SPELDS ▶ **speld**
SPELEAN = **spelaean**
SPELK *n* splinter of wood **spelks**
SPELL *vb, n* **spelled**
SPELLER *n* person who spells words in the manner specified
SPELLS ▶ **spell**
SPELT ▶ **spell**
SPELTER *n* impure zinc, usually containing about 3 per cent of lead and other impurities
SPELTS ▶ **spell**
SPELTZ *n* wheat variety
SPELUNK *vb* explore caves
SPENCE *n* larder or pantry
SPENCER *n* short fitted coat or jacket
SPENCES ▶ **spence**
SPEND *vb*
SPENDER *n* person who spends money in a manner specified
SPENDS ▶ **spend**
SPENDY *adj* expensive
SPENSE = **spence**
SPENSES ▶ **spense**
SPENT ▶ **spend**
SPEOS *n* (esp in ancient Egypt) a temple or tomb cut into a rock face **speoses**
SPERM *n*
SPERMIC = **spermatic**
SPERMS ▶ **sperm**
SPERRE *vb* bolt **sperred, sperres**
SPERSE *vb* disperse **spersed, sperses, sperst**
SPERTHE = **sparth**
SPET = **spit**
SPETCH *n* piece of animal skin
SPETS ▶ **spet**
SPEUG *n* sparrow **speugs**
SPEW *vb, n* **spewed, spewer, spewers**
SPEWIER ▶ **spewy**
SPEWING ▶ **spew**
SPEWS ▶ **spew**
SPEWY *adj* marshy
SPHAER = **sphere**
SPHAERE = **sphere**
SPHAERS ▶ **sphaere**
SPHEAR = **sphere**
SPHEARE = **sphere**
SPHEARS ▶ **sphear**
SPHENE *n* brown, yellow, green, or grey lustrous mineral **sphenes**
SPHENIC *adj* having the shape of a wedge
SPHERAL *adj* of or shaped like a sphere
SPHERE *n, vb* **sphered, spheres**
SPHERIC = **spherical**
SPHERY *adj* resembling a sphere
SPHINX *n*
SPHYNX *n* breed of cat
SPIAL *n* observation **spials**
SPICA *n* spiral bandage formed by a series of overlapping figure-of-eight turns **spicae, spicas**
SPICATE *adj* having, arranged in, or relating to spikes
SPICE *n, vb* **spiced, spicer, spicers**
SPICERY *n* spices collectively
SPICES ▶ **spice**
SPICEY = **spicy**
SPICIER ▶ **spicy**
SPICILY ▶ **spicy**
SPICING ▶ **spice**
SPICULA > **spiculum**
SPICULE *n* small slender pointed structure or crystal

SPICY *adj*
SPIDER *n* **spiders**
SPIDERY *adj*
SPIE = **spy**
SPIED ▸ **spy**
SPIEGEL *n* manganese-rich pig iron
SPIEL *n* speech made to persuade someone to do something ▹ *vb* deliver a prepared spiel **spieled, spieler, spiels**
SPIER *variant of* ▸ **speir**
SPIERED ▸ **spier**
SPIERS ▸ **spier**
SPIES ▸ **spy**
SPIF *n* postage stamp perforated with the initials of a firm to avoid theft by employees
SPIFF *vb* make smart **spiffed, spiffs**
SPIFFY *adj* smart ▹ *n* smart thing or person ▹ *vb* smarten
SPIFS ▸ **spif**
SPIGHT = **spite**
SPIGHTS ▸ **spight**
SPIGNEL *n* European umbelliferous plant
SPIGOT *n* stopper for, or tap fitted to, a cask **spigots**
SPIKE *n, vb* **spiked, spiker, spikers**
SPIKERY *n* High-Church Anglicanism
SPIKES ▸ **spike**
SPIKEY = **spiky**
SPIKIER ▸ **spiky**
SPIKILY ▸ **spiky**
SPIKING ▸ **spike**
SPIKY *adj*
SPILE *n* heavy timber stake or pile ▹ *vb* provide or support with a spile **spiled, spiles, spiling**
SPILITE *n* type of igneous rock
SPILL *vb, n* **spilled, spiller, spills, spilt**
SPILTH *n* something spilled **spilths**
SPIM *n* unsolicited communications received via an instant-messaging system **spims**
SPIN *vb, n*
SPINA *n* spine
SPINACH *n*
SPINAE ▸ **spina**
SPINAGE = **spinach**
SPINAL *adj, n* **spinals**
SPINAR *n* fast-spinning star **spinars**
SPINAS ▸ **spina**
SPINATE *adj* having a spine
SPINDLE *n, vb*
SPINDLY *adj*
SPINE *n* **spined**
SPINEL *n* any of a group of hard glassy minerals of variable colour **spinels**
SPINES ▸ **spine**
SPINET *n* **spinets**
SPINIER ▸ **spiny**
SPINK *n* finch **spinks**
SPINNER *n* bowler who makes the ball change direction when it bounces
SPINNET = **spinet**
SPINNEY *n* **spinny**
SPINODE *another name for* ▸ **cusp**
SPINOFF *n* development derived incidentally from an existing enterprise
SPINONE *n as in* **Italian spinone** wiry-coated gun dog **spinoni**
SPINOR *n* type of mathematical object **spinors**
SPINOSE *adj* (esp of plants) bearing many spines
SPINOUS *adj* resembling a spine or thorn
SPINOUT *n* spinning skid that causes a car to run off the road
SPINS ▸ **spin**
SPINTO *n* lyrical singing voice **spintos**
SPINULA *n* small spine
SPINULE *n* very small spine, thorn, or prickle
SPINY *adj*
SPIRAEA *n* plant with small white or pink flowers
SPIRAL *n, vb, adj* **spirals**
SPIRANT *n* fricative consonant
SPIRE *n, vb*
SPIREA = **spiraea**
SPIREAS ▸ **spirea**
SPIRED ▸ **spire**
SPIREM = **spireme**
SPIREME *n* tangled mass of chromatin threads

SPIREMS ▶ **spirem**
SPIRES ▶ **spire**
SPIRIC *n* type of curve **spirics**
SPIRIER ▶ **spire**
SPIRING ▶ **spire**
SPIRIT *n*, *vb* **spirits**
SPIRITY *adj* spirited
SPIROID *adj* resembling a spiral or displaying a spiral form
SPIRT = **spurt**
SPIRTED ▶ **spirt**
SPIRTLE = **spurtle**
SPIRTS ▶ **spirt**
SPIRULA *n* tropical cephalopod mollusc
SPIRY ▶ **spire**
SPIT *vb*, *n*
SPITAL *n* hospital, esp for the needy sick **spitals**
SPITE *n*, *vb* **spited, spites, spiting**
SPITS, spitted, spitten, spitter ▶ **spit**
SPITTLE *n*
SPITZ *n* stockily built dog with a tightly curled tail **spitzes**
SPIV *n* smartly dressed man who makes a living by shady dealings **spivs, spivvy**
SPLAKE *n* type of hybrid trout bred by Canadian zoologists **splakes**
SPLASH *vb*, *n*
SPLASHY *adj* having irregular marks
SPLAT *n* wet slapping sound ▷ *vb* make wet slapping sound
SPLATCH *vb* splash
SPLATS ▶ **splat**
SPLAY *vb*, *adj*, *n* **splayed, splays**
SPLEEN *n* **spleens, spleeny**
SPLENIA > **splenium**
SPLENIC *adj* of, relating to, or in the spleen
SPLENII > **splenius**
SPLENT = **splint**
SPLENTS ▶ **splent**
SPLICE *vb* **spliced, splicer, splices**
SPLIFF *n* cannabis, used as a drug **spliffs**
SPLINE *n* type of narrow key around a shaft that fits into a corresponding groove ▷ *vb* provide (a shaft, part, etc) with splines **splined, splines**
SPLINT *n*, *vb* **splints**
SPLISH *vb* splash
SPLIT *vb*, *n* **splits**
SPLODGE *n*, *vb* **splodgy**
SPLOG *n* spam blog **splogs**
SPLOOSH *vb* splash or cause to splash about uncontrollably ▷ *n* instance or sound of splooshing
SPLORE *n* revel **splores**
SPLOSH *vb* scatter (liquid) vigorously about in blobs ▷ *n* instance or sound of sploshing
SPLOTCH *vb* splash, daub
SPLURGE *vb*, *n* **splurgy**
SPOD *adj* boring, unattractive, or overstudious **spoddy**
SPODE *n* type of English china or porcelain **spodes**
SPODIUM *n* black powder
SPODS ▶ **spod**
SPOFFY = **spoffish**
SPOIL *vb* **spoiled**
SPOILER *n* device on an aircraft or car to increase drag
SPOILS ▶ **spoil**
SPOILT ▶ **spoil**
SPOKE *n* radial member of a wheel ▷ *vb* equip with spokes **spoked**
SPOKEN ▶ **speak**
SPOKES ▶ **spoke**
SPOKING ▶ **spoke**
SPONDEE *n* metrical foot of two long syllables
SPONDYL *n* vertebra
SPONGE *n*, *vb* **sponged**
SPONGER *n* person who sponges on others
SPONGES ▶ **sponge**
SPONGIN *n* fibrous horny protein in sponges
SPONGY *adj*
SPONSAL *n* marriage
SPONSON *n* outboard support for a gun enabling it to fire fore and aft
SPONSOR *n*, *vb*
SPOOF *n*, *vb* **spoofed, spoofer, spoofs, spoofy**
SPOOK *n*, *vb* **spooked, spooks**

SPOOKY *adj*
SPOOL *n, vb* **spooled, spooler, spools**
SPOOM *vb* sail fast before wind **spoomed, spooms**
SPOON *n, vb* **spooned**
SPOONEY = **spoony**
SPOONS ▶ **spoon**
SPOONY *adj* foolishly or stupidly amorous ▷ *n* fool or silly person, esp one in love
SPOOR *n, vb* **spoored, spoorer, spoors**
SPOOT *n* razor shell **spoots**
SPORAL ▶ **spore**
SPORE *n, vb* **spored, spores, sporing**
SPORK *n* spoon-shaped piece of cutlery with tines like a fork **sporks**
SPOROID *adj* of or like a spore
SPORRAN *n*
SPORT *n, vb* **sported, sporter**
SPORTIF *adj* sporty
SPORTS *adj* of or used in sports ▷ *n* meeting held at a school or college for competitions in athletic events
SPORTY *adj, n*
SPORULE *n* spore, esp a very small spore
SPOSH *n* slush **sposhes, sposhy**
SPOT *n, vb*
SPOTLIT > **spotlight**
SPOTS ▶ **spot**
SPOTTED ▶ **spot**
SPOTTER *n*
SPOTTIE *n* young deer of up to three months of age
SPOTTY *adj*
SPOUSAL *n* marriage ceremony ▷ *adj* of or relating to marriage
SPOUSE *n, vb* **spoused, spouses**
SPOUT *vb, n* **spouted, spouter, spouts, spouty**
SPRACK *adj* vigorous
SPRAD ▶ **spread**
SPRAG *n* device used to prevent a vehicle from running backwards on an incline ▷ *vb* use sprag to prevent vehicle from moving **sprags**
SPRAID *vb* chapped
SPRAIN *vb, n* **sprains**
SPRAINT *n* piece of otter's dung
SPRANG *n* branch **sprangs**
SPRAT *n* **sprats**
SPRAWL *vb, n* **sprawls, sprawly**
SPRAY *n, vb* **sprayed, sprayer, sprayey, sprays**
SPREAD *vb, n, adj* **spreads**
SPREAGH *n* cattle raid
SPREAZE = **spreathe**
SPRED = **spread**
SPREDD = **spread**
SPREDDE = **spread**
SPREDDS ▶ **spredd**
SPREDS ▶ **spred**
SPREE *n, vb* **spreed, sprees**
SPREEZE = **spreathe**
SPRENT > **sprinkle**
SPREW = **sprue**
SPREWS ▶ **sprew**
SPRIER ▶ **spry**
SPRIEST ▶ **spry**
SPRIG *n, vb* **spriggy**
SPRIGHT = **sprite**
SPRIGS ▶ **sprig**
SPRING *vb, n*
SPRINGE *n* type of snare for catching small wild animals or birds ▷ *vb* set such a snare
SPRINGS ▶ **spring**
SPRINGY *adj*
SPRINT *n, vb* **sprints**
SPRIT *n* small spar set diagonally across a sail to extend it
SPRITE *n* **sprites**
SPRITS ▶ **sprit**
SPRITZ *vb* spray liquid
SPROD *n* young salmon **sprods**
SPROG *n* child **sprogs**
SPRONG ▶ **spring**
SPROUT *vb, n* **sprouts**
SPRUCE *n, adj* **spruced, sprucer, spruces, sprucy**
SPRUE *n* vertical channel in a mould **sprues**
SPRUG *n* sparrow **sprugs**
SPRUIK *vb* speak in public (used esp of a showman or salesman) **spruiks**
SPRUIT *n* small tributary stream or

watercourse **spruits**
SPRUNG ▸ **spring**
SPRUSH *Scots form of* ▸ **spruce**
SPRY *adj* **spryer, spryest, spryly**
SPUD *n, vb* **spudded, spudder**
SPUDDLE *n* feeble movement
SPUDDY *adj* short and fat
SPUDS ▸ **spud**
SPUE = **spew; spued, spueing, spuer, spuers, spues**
SPUG = **spuggy**
SPUGGY *n* house sparrow
SPUGS ▸ **spug**
SPUING ▸ **spue**
SPULE *Scots word for* > **shoulder**
SPULES ▸ **spule**
SPULYE = **spuilzie**
SPULYED ▸ **spulye**
SPULYES ▸ **spulye**
SPULYIE = **spuilzie**
SPULZIE = **spuilzie**
SPUME *vb, n* **spumed, spumes**
SPUMIER ▸ **spumy**
SPUMING ▸ **spume**
SPUMONE *n* creamy Italian ice cream **spumoni**
SPUMOUS ▸ **spume**
SPUMY ▸ **spume**
SPUN ▸ **spin**
SPUNGE = **sponge**
SPUNGES ▸ **spunge**
SPUNK *n, vb* **spunked**
SPUNKIE *n* will-o'-the-wisp
SPUNKS ▸ **spunk**
SPUNKY ▸ **spunk**
SPUR *n, vb*
SPURGE *n* plant with milky sap **spurges**
SPURIAE *n* type of bird feathers
SPURN *vb, n*
SPURNE *vb* spur
SPURNED ▸ **spurn**
SPURNER ▸ **spurn**
SPURNES ▸ **spurne**
SPURNS ▸ **spurn**
SPURRED ▸ **spur**
SPURRER ▸ **spur**
SPURREY *n* any of several low-growing European plants
SPURRY *n* spurrey ▹ *adj* resembling a spur
SPURS ▸ **spur**
SPURT *vb, n* **spurted, spurter**
SPURTLE *n* wooden spoon for stirring porridge
SPURTS ▸ **spurt**
SPURWAY *n* path used by riders
SPUTA ▸ **sputum**
SPUTNIK *n*
SPUTTER *n, vb*
SPUTUM *n*
SPY *n, vb*
SPYAL *n* spy **spyals**
SPYCAM *n* camera used for covert surveillance **spycams**
SPYHOLE *n* small hole in a door, etc through which one may watch secretly
SPYING ▸ **spy**
SPYINGS ▸ **spy**
SPYRE = **spire**
SPYRES ▸ **spyre**
SPYWARE *n* software used to gain information about a computer user
SQUAB *n* young bird yet to leave the nest ▹ *adj* (of birds) recently hatched and still unfledged ▹ *vb* fall **squabby, squabs**
SQUACCO *n* S European heron
SQUAD *n, vb*
SQUADDY = **squaddie**
SQUADS ▸ **squad**
SQUAIL *vb* throw sticks at **squails**
SQUALID *adj*
SQUALL *n, vb* **squalls, squally**
SQUALOR *n*
SQUAMA *n* scale or scalelike structure **squamae, squame**
SQUAMES ▸ **squame**
SQUARE *n, adj, vb, adv* **squared, squarer, squares**
SQUARK *n* hypothetical boson partner of a quark **squarks**
SQUASH *vb, n*
SQUASHY *adj*
SQUAT *vb, n, adj* **squatly, squats**
SQUATTY *adj* short and broad
SQUAWK *n, vb* **squawks, squawky**
SQUEAK *n, vb* **squeaks, squeaky**
SQUEAL *n, vb* **squeals**

SQUEEZE *vb, n* **squeezy**
SQUEG *vb* oscillate **squegs**
SQUELCH *vb, n*
SQUIB *n* **squibs**
SQUID *n, vb*
SQUIDGE *vb* squash
SQUIDGY *adj* soft, moist, and squashy
SQUIDS ▸ **squid**
SQUIER = **squire**
SQUIERS ▸ **squier**
SQUIFF = **squiffy**
SQUIFFY *adj* slightly drunk
SQUILL *n* Mediterranean plant of the lily family
SQUILLA *n* type of mantis shrimp
SQUILLS ▸ **squill**
SQUINCH *n* small arch across an internal corner of a tower ▹ *vb* squeeze
SQUINNY *vb* squint ▹ *adj* squint
SQUINT *vb, n, adj* **squints, squinty**
SQUINY = **squinny**
SQUIRE *n, vb* **squired, squires**
SQUIRM *vb, n* **squirms**
SQUIRMY *adj* moving with a wriggling motion
SQUIRR = **skirr**
SQUIRRS ▸ **squirr**
SQUIRT *vb, n* **squirts**
SQUISH *n* a soft squelching sound ▹ *vb* crush (something) with a soft squelching sound
SQUISHY *adj* soft and yielding to the touch
SQUIT *n* insignificant person
SQUITCH *n* couch grass
SQUITS ▸ **squit**
SQUIZ *n* look or glance, esp an inquisitive one

> The word **quiz** comes up surprisingly often, so it is useful to remember that you can put an S on the front of it to form this Australian slang word for a quick look.

SQUOOSH *vb* squash **squush**
SRADDHA *n* Hindu offering to ancestor
SRADHA = **sradha**
SRADHAS ▸ **sradha**
SRI *n* title of respect used when addressing a Hindu **sris**
ST *interj* exclamation to attract attention
STAB *vb, n* **stabbed, stabber**
STABILE *n* stationary abstract construction, usually of wire, metal, wood, etc ▹ *adj* fixed
STABLE *n, vb, adj* **stabled**
STABLER *n* stable owner
STABLES ▸ **stable**
STABLY ▸ **stable**
STABS ▸ **stab**
STACHYS *n* type of plant of the genus which includes lamb's ears and betony
STACK *n, vb* **stacked, stacker**
STACKET *n* fence of wooden posts
STACKS ▸ **stack**
STACKUP *n* number of aircraft waiting to land
STACTE *n* one of several sweet-smelling spices used in incense **stactes**
STADDA *n* type of saw **staddas**
STADDLE *n* type of support or prop
STADE = **stadium**
STADES ▸ **stade**
STADIA *n* instrument used in surveying
STADIAL *n* stage in development of glacier
STADIAS ▸ **stadia**
STADIUM *n*
STAFF *n, vb* **staffed**
STAFFER *n* member of staff, esp. in journalism, of editorial staff
STAFFS ▸ **staff**
STAG *n, adv, vb*
STAGE *n, vb* **staged**
STAGER *n* person of experience **stagers**
STAGERY *n* theatrical effects or techniques
STAGES ▸ **stage**
STAGEY = **stagy**
STAGGED ▸ **stag**
STAGGER *vb, n*
STAGGIE *n* little stag
STAGGY ▸ **stag**
STAGIER ▸ **stagy**

STAGILY ▸ stagy
STAGING *n* temporary support used in building
STAGS ▸ stag
STAGY *adj* too theatrical or dramatic
STAID *adj* **staider, staidly**
STAIG *Scots variant of* **▸ stag**
STAIGS ▸ staig
STAIN *vb, n* **stained, stainer, stains**
STAIR *n*
STAIRED *adj* having stairs
STAIRS *pl n* flight of steps between floors, usu indoors
STAITH = staithe
STAITHE *n* wharf
STAITHS ▸ staith
STAKE *n, vb* **staked, stakes, staking**
STALAG *n* German prisoner-of-war camp **stalags**
STALE *adj, vb, n* **staled, stalely, staler, stales, stalest, staling**
STALK *n, vb* **stalked, stalker**
STALKO *n* idle gentleman
STALKS ▸ stalk
STALKY *adj* like a stalk
STALL *n, vb* **stalled, stalls**
STAMEN *n* **stamens**
STAMINA *n*
STAMMEL *n* coarse woollen cloth in former use for undergarments
STAMMER *vb, n*
STAMNOI ▸ stamnos
STAMNOS *n* ancient Greek jar
STAMP *n, vb* **stamped, stamper, stamps**
STANCE *n* **stances**
STANCH *vb* stem the flow of (a liquid, esp blood) ▹ *adj* loyal and dependable
STANCK *adj* faint
STAND *vb, n*
STANDBY *n* person or thing that is ready for use
STANDEE *n* person who stands
STANDEN ▸ stand
STANDER ▸ stand
STANDS ▸ stand
STANDUP *n* comedian who performs solo
STANE *Scot word for* **▸ stone**
STANED ▸ stane
STANES ▸ stane
STANG *vb* sting **stanged, stangs**
STANIEL *n* kestrel
STANINE *n* scale of nine levels
STANING ▸ stane
STANK *vb* dam
STANKED ▸ stink
STANKS ▸ stink
STANNEL = staniel
STANNIC *adj* of or containing tin, esp in the tetravalent state
STANNUM *n* tin (the metal)
STANOL *n* drug taken to prevent heart disease **stanols**
STANYEL = staniel
STANZA *n* **stanzas**
STANZE = stanza
STANZES ▸ stanze
STANZO = stanza
STANZOS ▸ stanzo
STAP = stop
STAPES *n* stirrup-shaped bone in the middle ear of mammals
STAPH *n* staphylococcus **staphs**
STAPLE *n, vb, adj* **stapled**
STAPLER *n*
STAPLES ▸ staple
STAPPED ▸ stap
STAPPLE = stopple
STAPS ▸ stap
STAR *n, vb, adj*
STARCH *n, vb, adj*
STARCHY *adj* containing starch
STARDOM *n* status of a star in the entertainment or sports world
STARE *vb, n* **stared, starer, starers, stares**
STARETS *n* Russian holy man
STARETZ = staretz
STARING ▸ stare
STARK *adj, adv, vb* **starked**
STARKEN *vb* become or make stark
STARKER ▸ stark
STARKLY ▸ stark
STARKS ▸ stark

STARLET *n* young actress presented as a future star
STARLIT = **starlight**
STARN = **stern**
STARNED ▸ **starn**
STARNIE *n* Scots word for little star
STARNS ▸ **starn**
STARR *n* (in Judaism) release from a debt
STARRED ▸ **star**
STARRS ▸ **starr**
STARRY *adj*
STARS ▸ **star**
START *vb* take the first step, begin ▹ *n* first part of something **started**
STARTER *n*
STARTLE *vb*
STARTLY = **startlish**
STARTS ▸ **start**
STARTSY ▸ **starets**
STARTUP *n* business enterprise that has been launched recently
STARVE *vb* **starved, starver, starves**
STASES ▸ **stasis**
STASH *vb*, *n* **stashed, stashes**
STASHIE = **stushie**
STASIMA > **stasimon**
STASIS *n* stagnation in the normal flow of bodily fluids
STAT *n* statistic
STATAL *adj* of a federal state
STATANT *adj* (of an animal) in profile with all four feet on the ground
STATE *n*, *adj*, *vb*
STATED *adj* (esp of a sum) determined by agreement
STATELY *adj*, *adv*
STATER *n* any of various usually silver coins of ancient Greece **staters**
STATES ▸ **state**
STATIC *adj*, *n*
STATICE *n* plant name formerly used for both thrift and sea lavender
STATICS *n* study of the forces producing a state of equilibrium
STATIM *adv* right away
STATIN *n* type of drug that lowers the levels of low-density lipoproteins in the blood
STATING ▸ **state**
STATINS ▸ **statin**
STATION *n*, *vb*
STATISM *n* theory or practice of concentrating economic and political power in the state
STATIST *n* advocate of statism ▹ *adj* of, characteristic of, advocating, or relating to statism
STATIVE *adj* denoting a verb describing a state rather than an activity, act, or event ▹ *n* stative verb
STATOR *n* stationary part of a rotary machine or device **stators**
STATS ▸ **stat**
STATTO *n* person preoccupied with the facts and figures of a subject **stattos**
STATUA = **statue**
STATUAS ▸ **statua**
STATUE *n*
STATUED *adj* decorated with or portrayed in a statue or statues
STATUES ▸ **statue**
STATURE *n*
STATUS *n*
STATUSY *adj* conferring or having status
STATUTE *n*
STAUN *Scot word for* ▸ **stand**
STAUNCH = **stanch**
STAUNS ▸ **staun**
STAVE = **staff**
STAVED ▸ **stave**
STAVES ▸ **stave**
STAVING ▸ **stave**
STAW *Scots form of* ▸ **stall**
STAWED ▸ **staw**
STAWING ▸ **staw**
STAWS ▸ **staw**
STAY *vb*, *n* **stayed**
STAYER *n* person or thing that stays **stayers**
STAYING ▸ **stay**
STAYNE = **stain**
STAYNED ▸ **stayne**
STAYNES ▸ **stayne**
STAYRE = **stair**
STAYRES ▸ **stayre**
STAYS *pl n* old-fashioned corsets with bones in them
STEAD *n*, *vb* **steaded, steads**

STEADY *adj, vb, adv*
STEAK *n* steaks
STEAL *vb*
STEALE *n* handle
STEALED ▸ **steal**
STEALER *n* person who steals something
STEALES ▸ **steale**
STEALS ▸ **steal**
STEALT ▸ **steal**
STEALTH *n, adj, vb*
STEAM *n, vb* **steamed**
STEAMER *n, vb*
STEAMIE *n* public wash house
STEAMS ▸ **steam**
STEAMY *adj* full of steam
STEAN *n* earthenware vessel
STEANE = **steen**
STEANED ▸ **steane**
STEANES ▸ **steane**
STEANS ▸ **stean**
STEAR = **steer**
STEARD ▸ **stear**
STEARE = **steer**
STEARED ▸ **steare**
STEARES ▸ **steare**
STEARIC *adj* of or relating to suet or fat
STEARIN *n* colourless crystalline ester of glycerol and stearic acid
STEARS ▸ **stear**
STED = **stead**
STEDD = **stead**
STEDDE = **stead**
STEDDED ▸ **sted**
STEDDES ▸ **stedde**
STEDDS ▸ **stedd**
STEDDY = **steady**
STEDE = **stead**
STEDED ▸ **stede**
STEDES ▸ **stede**
STEDING ▸ **stede**
STEDS ▸ **sted**
STEED = **stead**
STEEDED ▸ **steed**
STEEDS ▸ **steed**
STEEDY = **steady**
STEEK *vb* Scots word meaning shut **steeked, steekit, steeks**
STEEL *n, vb* **steeld, steeled**
STEELIE *n* steel ball bearing used as marble
STEELS *pl n* shares and bonds of steel companies
STEELY ▸ **steel**
STEEM *variant of* ▸ **esteem**
STEEMED ▸ **steem**
STEEMS ▸ **steem**
STEEN *vb* line with stone **steened, steens**
STEEP *adj, vb, n* **steeped**
STEEPEN *vb* become steep or steeper
STEEPER ▸ **steep**
STEEPLE = **spire**
STEEPLY ▸ **steep**
STEEPS ▸ **steep**
STEEPUP *adj* very steep
STEEPY = **steep**
STEER *vb, n* **steered, steerer, steers**
STEERY *n* commotion
STEEVE *n* spar having a pulley block at one end ▹ *vb* stow (cargo) securely in the hold of a ship **steeved, steever, steeves**
STEIL = **steal**
STEILS ▸ **steil**
STEIN = **steen**
STEINED ▸ **stein**
STEINS ▸ **stein**
STELA = **stele**
STELAE ▸ **stele**
STELAI ▸ **stele**
STELAR ▸ **stele**
STELE *n* upright stone slab or column decorated with figures or inscriptions **stelene, steles, stelic**
STELL *n* shelter for cattle or sheep built on moorland or hillsides ▹ *vb* position or place
STELLA *n* star or something star-shaped
STELLAR *adj*
STELLAS ▸ **stella**
STELLED ▸ **stell**
STELLIO *n as in* **stellio lizard** denoting type of lizard
STELLS ▸ **stell**
STEM *vb, n*
STEMBOK = **steenbok**
STEME = **steam**
STEMED ▸ **steme**
STEMES ▸ **steme**
STEMING ▸ **steme**
STEMLET *n* little stem
STEMMA *n* family tree **stemmas**
STEMME *archaic variant of* ▸ **stem**
STEMMED ▸ **stem**
STEMMER ▸ **stem**
STEMMES ▸ **stemme**

STEMMY *adj* (of wine) young and raw
STEMPEL *n* timber support **stemple**
STEMS ▸ **stem**
STEMSON *n* curved timber at the bow of a wooden vessel
STEN *vb* stride
STENCH *n, vb* **stenchy**
STENCIL *n, vb*
STEND *vb* Scots word meaning bound **stended, stends**
STENGAH = **stinger**
STENNED ▸ **sten**
STENO *n* stenographer
STENOKY *n* survival dependent on conditions remaining within a narrow range of variables
STENOS ▸ **steno**
STENS ▸ **sten**
STENT *n* surgical implant used to keep an artery open ▹ *vb* assess **stented**
STENTOR *n* person with an unusually loud voice
STENTS ▸ **stent**
STEP *vb, n*
STEPNEY *n* spare wheel
STEPPE *n*
STEPPED ▸ **step**
STEPPER *n* person who or animal that steps, esp a horse or a dancer
STEPPES ▸ **steppe**
STEPS ▸ **step**
STEPSON *n*
STEPT ▸ **step**
STERE *n* unit used to measure volumes of stacked timber
STEREO *n, adj, vb* **stereos**
STERES ▸ **stere**
STERIC *adj* of or caused by the spatial arrangement of atoms in a molecule
STERILE *adj*
STERLET *n* small sturgeon of N Asia and E Europe
STERN *adj, n, vb*
STERNA ▸ **sternum**
STERNAL ▸ **sternum**
STERNED, sterner, sternly, sterns ▸ **stern**
STERNUM *n*
STEROID *n*
STEROL *n* natural insoluble alcohol such as cholesterol and ergosterol **sterols**
STERTOR *n* laborious or noisy breathing
STERVE = **starve**
STERVED ▸ **sterve**
STERVES ▸ **sterve**
STET *interj* instruction to ignore an alteration previously made ▹ *vb* indicate to a printer that deleted matter is to be kept ▹ *n* mark indicating that deleted matter is to be kept **stets**
STETSON *n* cowboy hat
STETTED ▸ **stet**
STEVEN *n* voice **stevens**
STEW *n, vb*
STEWARD *n, vb*
STEWBUM *n* drunkard
STEWED *adj* (of food) cooked by stewing
STEWER, stewers, stewier, stewing ▸ **stew**
STEWPAN *n* pan used for making stew
STEWPOT *n* pot used for making stew
STEWS ▸ **stew**
STEWY ▸ **stew**
STEY *adj* Scots word meaning steep **steyer, steyest**
STHENIA *n* abnormal strength
STHENIC *adj* abounding in energy or bodily strength
STIBBLE *Scots form of* ▸ **stubble**
STIBIAL ▸ **stibium**
STIBINE *n* colourless slightly soluble poisonous gas
STIBIUM *obsolete name for* > **antimony**
STICH *n* line of poetry **stichic**
STICHOI ▸ **stichos**
STICHOS *n* line of poem
STICHS ▸ **stich**
STICK *n, vb* **sticked**
STICKER *n, vb*
STICKIT *Scots form of* ▸ **stuck**
STICKLE *vb* dispute stubbornly, esp about minor points
STICKS ▸ **stick**
STICKUM *n* adhesive
STICKUP *n* robbery at gun-point

STICKY *adj, vb, n*
STIDDIE = **stithy**
STIE = **sty**
STIED ▸ **sty**
STIES ▸ **sty**
STIEVE = **steeve**
STIEVER ▸ **stieve**
STIFF *adj, n, adv, vb* **stiffed**
STIFFEN *vb*
STIFFER ▸ **stiff**
STIFFLY ▸ **stiff**
STIFFS ▸ **stiff**
STIFFY *n* erection of the penis
STIFLE *vb, n* **stifled, stifler, stifles**
STIGMA *n*
STIGMAL *adj* of part of insect wing
STIGMAS ▸ **stigma**
STIGME *n* dot in Greek punctuation **stigmes**
STILB *n* unit of luminance **stilbs**
STILE = **style**
STILED ▸ **stile**
STILES ▸ **stile**
STILET = **stylet**
STILETS ▸ **stilet**
STILING ▸ **stile**
STILL *adv, adj, n, vb* **stilled, stiller, stills**
STILLY *adv* quietly or calmly ▹ *adj* still, quiet, or calm
STILT *n, vb*
STILTED *adj*
STILTER ▸ **stilt**
STILTS ▸ **stilt**
STILTY ▸ **stilt**
STIM *n* very small amount
STIME = **styme**
STIMED ▸ **stime**
STIMES ▸ **stime**
STIMIE = **stymie**
STIMIED ▸ **stimie**
STIMIES ▸ **stimie**
STIMING ▸ **stime**
STIMS ▸ **stim**
STIMULI > **stimulus**
STIMY = **stymie**
STING *vb, n* **stinged**
STINGER *n* person, plant, animal, etc, that stings or hurts
STINGO *n* strong alcohol **stingos**
STINGS ▸ **sting**
STINGY *adj, n*
STINK *n, vb*
STINKER *n* difficult or unpleasant person or thing
STINKO *adj* drunk
STINKS ▸ **stink**
STINKY *adj* having a foul smell
STINT *vb, n* **stinted, stinter, stints, stinty**
STIPA *n* variety of grass **stipas**
STIPE *n* stalk in plants that bears reproductive structures
STIPED = **stipitate**
STIPEL *n* small paired leaflike structure at the base of certain leaflets **stipels**
STIPEND *n*
STIPES *n* second maxillary segment in insects and crustaceans
STIPPLE *vb* paint, draw, or engrave using dots ▹ *n* technique of stippling
STIPULE *n* small paired usually leaflike outgrowth occurring at the base of a leaf or its stalk
STIR *vb, n*
STIRE = **steer**
STIRED ▸ **stire**
STIRES ▸ **stire**
STIRING ▸ **stire**
STIRK *n* heifer of 6 to 12 months old **stirks**
STIRP = **stirps**
STIRPES ▸ **stirps**
STIRPS *n* line of descendants from an ancestor
STIRRA = **sirra**
STIRRAH = **sirrah**
STIRRAS ▸ **stirra**
STIRRE = **steer**
STIRRED ▸ **stir**
STIRRER *n* person who deliberately causes trouble
STIRRES ▸ **stirre**
STIRRUP *n*
STIRS ▸ **stir**
STISHIE = **stushie**
STITCH *n, vb*
STITHY *n* forge or anvil ▹ *vb* forge on an anvil
STIVE *vb* stifle **stived**
STIVER *n* former Dutch coin worth **stivers**
STIVES ▸ **stive**
STIVIER ▸ **stivy**
STIVING ▸ **stive**
STIVY *adj* stuffy
STOA *n* covered walk that has a colonnade on one or both sides

stoae, stoai, stoas
STOAT *n* **stoats**
STOB = **stab**
STOBBED ▸ **stob**
STOBIE *adj as in* **stobie pole** steel and concrete pole for supporting electricity wires
STOBS ▸ **stob**
STOCK *n, adj, vb* **stocked, stocker**
STOCKS *pl n* instrument of punishment in which an offender was locked
STOCKY *adj*
STODGE *n* heavy starchy food ▹ *vb* stuff (oneself or another) with food **stodged**
STODGER *n* dull person
STODGES ▸ **stodge**
STODGY *adj*
STOEP *n* verandah **stoeps**
STOGEY = **stogy**
STOGEYS ▸ **stogey**
STOGIE = **stogy**
STOGIES ▸ **stogy**
STOGY *n* any long cylindrical inexpensive cigar
STOIC *n, adj*
STOICAL *adj* suffering great difficulties without showing one's feelings
STOICS ▸ **stoic**
STOIT *vb* bounce **stoited**
STOITER *vb* stagger
STOITS ▸ **stoit**
STOKE *vb*
STOKED *adj* very pleased
STOKER *n* person employed to tend a furnace on a ship or train powered by steam **stokers**
STOKES *n* cgs unit of kinematic viscosity
STOKING ▸ **stoke**
STOKVEL *n* (in S Africa) informal savings pool or syndicate
STOLE *n* long scarf or shawl
STOLED *adj* wearing a stole
STOLEN ▸ **steal**
STOLES ▸ **stole**
STOLID *adj*
STOLLEN *n* rich sweet bread containing nuts, raisins, etc
STOLN ▸ **steal**
STOLON *n* long horizontal stem that grows along the surface of the soil **stolons**
STOMA *n*
STOMACH *n, vb*
STOMACK *n as in* **have a stomack** (in E Africa) be pregnant
STOMAL ▸ **stoma**
STOMAS ▸ **stoma**
STOMATA ▸ **stoma**
STOMATE *n* opening on leaf through which water evaporates
STOMIA ▸ **stomium**
STOMIUM *n* part of the sporangium of ferns that ruptures to release the spores
STOMP *vb, n* **stomped**
STOMPER *n* song with a strong beat
STOMPIE *n* cigarette butt
STOMPS ▸ **stomp**
STOND = **stand**
STONDS ▸ **stond**
STONE *n, vb*
STONED *adj*
STONEN *adj* of stone
STONER *n* device for removing stones from fruit
STONERN = **stonen**
STONERS ▸ **stoner**
STONES ▸ **stone**
STONEY = **stony**
STONG ▸ **sting**
STONIED, stonier, stonies, stonily ▸ **stony**
STONING ▸ **stone**
STONISH = **astonish**
STONK *vb* bombard (soldiers, buildings, etc) with artillery ▹ *n* concentrated bombardment **stonked**
STONKER *vb* destroy
STONKS ▸ **stonk**
STONN = **stun**
STONNE = **stun**
STONNED ▸ **stonne**
STONNES ▸ **stonne**
STONNS ▸ **stonn**
STONY *adj, vb*
STOOD ▸ **stand**
STOODEN ▸ **stand**
STOOGE *n, vb* **stooged, stooges**
STOOK *n* number of

sheaves set upright in a field to dry ▷ *vb* set up (sheaves) in stooks **stooked, stooker**
STOOKIE *n* stucco
STOOKS ▸ stook
STOOL *n, vb* **stooled**
STOOLIE *n* police informer
STOOLS ▸ stool
STOOP *vb*
STOOPE = stoup
STOOPED ▸ stoop
STOOPER ▸ stoop
STOOPES ▸ stoope
STOOPS ▸ stoop
STOOR = stour
STOORS ▸ stoor
STOOZE *vb* borrow money cheaply and invest it to make a profit **stoozed**
STOOZER *n* person who stoozes
STOOZES ▸ stooze
STOP *vb, n*
STOPE *n* steplike excavation made in a mine to extract ore ▷ *vb* mine (ore, etc) by cutting stopes **stoped**
STOPER *n* drill used in mining **stopers**
STOPES ▸ stope
STOPGAP *n*
STOPING *n* process by which country rock is broken up and engulfed by magma
STOPOFF *n* break in a journey
STOPPED ▸ stop
STOPPER *n, vb* **stopple**
STOPS ▸ stop
STOPT ▸ stop
STORAGE *n*
STORAX *n* type of tree or shrub with white flowers
STORE *vb, n* **stored, storer, storers**
STORES *pl n* supply of food and essentials for a journey
STOREY *n* **storeys**
STORGE *n* affection **storges**
STORIED ▸ story
STORIES ▸ story
STORING ▸ store
STORK *n* **storks**
STORM *n, vb* **stormed**
STORMER *n* outstanding example of its kind
STORMS ▸ storm
STORMY *adj* characterized by storms
STORY *n, vb*
STOSS *adj* (of the side of a hill) facing the onward flow of a glacier ▷ *n* hillside facing glacier flow **stosses**
STOT *n* bullock ▷ *vb* bounce or cause to bounce
STOTIN *n* monetary unit of Slovenia **stotins**
STOTS ▸ stot
STOTT = stot
STOTTED ▸ stot
STOTTER = stot
STOTTIE *n* wedge of bread cut from a flat round loaf
STOTTS ▸ stott
STOTTY *n* type of flat, round loaf made in NE England
STOUN = stun
STOUND *n* short while ▷ *vb* ache **stounds**
STOUNS ▸ stoun
STOUP *n* small basin for holy water **stoups**
STOUR *n* turmoil or conflict **stoure**
STOURES ▸ stoure
STOURIE = stoury
STOURS ▸ stour
STOURY *adj* dusty
STOUSH *vb* hit or punch (someone) ▷ *n* fighting or violence
STOUT *adj, n*
STOUTEN *vb* make or become stout
STOUTER ▸ stout
STOUTH *n* Scots word meaning theft **stouths**
STOUTLY ▸ stout
STOUTS ▸ stout
STOVE *n, vb* **stoved**
STOVER *n* fodder **stovers**
STOVES ▸ stove
STOVIES *pl n* potatoes stewed with onions
STOVING ▸ stove
STOW *vb*
STOWAGE *n* space or charge for stowing goods
STOWED, stower, stowers, stowing ▸ stow
STOWN ▸ steal
STOWND = stound
STOWNDS ▸ stownd

STOWP = **stoup**
STOWPS ▸ **stowp**
STOWRE = **stour**
STOWRES ▸ **stowre**
STOWS ▸ **stow**
STRACK *vb* archaic past tense form of strike
STRAD *n* violin made by Stradivarius **strads**
STRAE *Scots form of* ▸ **straw**
STRAES ▸ **strae**
STRAFE *vb* attack (an enemy) with machine guns from the air ▹ *n* act or instance of strafing **strafed, strafer, strafes, straff**
STRAFFS ▸ **straff**
STRAG *n* straggler **strags**
STRAIK *Scots word for* ▸ **stroke**
STRAIKS ▸ **straik**
STRAIN *vb, n* **strains**
STRAINT *n* pressure
STRAIT *n, adj, vb* **straits**
STRAK *vb* archaic past tense form of strike
STRAKE *n* curved metal plate forming part of the metal rim on a wooden wheel
STRAKED *adj* having a strake
STRAKES ▸ **strake**
STRAMP *Scots variant of* ▸ **tramp**
STRAMPS ▸ **stramp**
STRAND *vb, n* **strands**
STRANG *dialect variant of* ▸ **strong**
STRANGE *adj, n*
STRAP *n, vb*
STRAPPY *adj* having straps
STRAPS ▸ **strap**
STRASS *another word for* ▸ **paste**
STRATA ▸ **stratum**
STRATAL ▸ **stratum**
STRATAS ▸ **stratum**
STRATH *n* flat river valley **straths**
STRATI ▸ **stratus**
STRATUM *n*
STRATUS *n* grey layer cloud
STRAW *n, vb* **strawed**
STRAWEN *adj* of straw
STRAWN ▸ **strew**
STRAWS ▸ **straw**
STRAWY *adj* containing straw, or like straw in colour or texture
STRAY *vb, adj, n* **strayed, strayer, strays**
STRAYVE *vb* wander aimlessly
STREAK *n, vb* **streaks**
STREAKY *adj* marked with streaks
STREAM *n, vb* **streams**
STREAMY *adj* (of an area, land, etc) having many streams
STREEK *Scots word for* ▸ **stretch**
STREEKS ▸ **streek**
STREEL *n* slovenly woman ▹ *vb* trail **streels**
STREET *n, vb* **streets**
STREETY *adj* of streets
STRENE = **strain**
STRENES ▸ **strene**
STREP *n* streptococcus **streps**
STRESS *n, vb*
STRETCH *vb, n*
STRETTA = **stretto**
STRETTE ▸ **stretta**
STRETTI ▸ **stretto**
STRETTO *n* (in a fugue) the close overlapping of two parts or voices
STREW *vb* **strewed, strewer, strewn, strews**
STREWTH *interj* expression of surprise or alarm
STRIA *n* scratch or groove on the surface of a rock crystal **striae**
STRIATA > **striatum**
STRIATE *adj* marked with striae ▹ *vb* mark with striae
STRICH *n* screech owl
STRICK *n* any bast fibres preparatory to being made into slivers **stricks**
STRICT *adj*
STRIDE *vb, n* **strider, strides**
STRIDOR *n* high-pitched whistling sound made during respiration
STRIFE *n* **strifes**
STRIFT *n* struggle **strifts**
STRIG *vb* remove stalk from
STRIGA = **stria**
STRIGAE ▸ **striga**
STRIGIL *n* curved blade used to scrape the body after bathing
STRIGS ▸ **strig**

STRIKE *vb, n*
STRIKER *n*
STRIKES ▸ **strike**
STRIM *vb* cut (grass) using a strimmer **strims**
STRING *n, vb* **strings**
STRINGY *adj*
STRIP *vb, n*
STRIPE *n, vb*
STRIPED *adj* marked or decorated with stripes
STRIPER *n* officer who has a stripe or stripes on his uniform
STRIPES ▸ **stripe**
STRIPEY = **stripy**
STRIPS ▸ **strip**
STRIPT ▸ **strip**
STRIPY *adj* marked by or with stripes
STRIVE *vb* **strived, striven, striver, strives**
STROAM *vb* wander **stroams**
STROBE *n* high intensity flashing beam of light ▹ *vb* give the appearance of slow motion by using a strobe **strobed, strobes**
STROBIC *adj* spinning or appearing to spin
STROBIL *n* scaly multiple fruit
STRODE ▸ **stride**
STRODLE = **straddle**
STROKE *vb, n* **stroked**
STROKEN ▸ **strike**
STROKER ▸ **stroke**
STROKES ▸ **stroke**
STROLL *vb, n* **strolls**
STROMA *n* gel-like matrix of chloroplasts and certain cells **stromal**
STROMB *n* shellfish like a whelk **strombs**
STROND = **strand**
STRONDS ▸ **strond**
STRONG *adj* having physical power
STROOK ▸ **strike**
STROOKE *n* stroke
STROP *n* leather strap for sharpening razors ▹ *vb* sharpen (a razor, etc) on a strop
STROPHE *n* movement made by chorus during a choral ode
STROPPY *adj*
STROPS ▸ **strop**
STROUD *n* coarse woollen fabric **strouds**
STROUP *Scots word for* ▸ **spout**
STROUPS ▸ **stroup**
STROUT *vb* bulge **strouts**
STROVE ▸ **strive**
STROW *archaic variant of* ▸ **strew; strowed, strower, strown, strows**
STROY *archaic variant of* ▸ **destroy**
STROYED ▸ **stroy**
STROYER ▸ **stroy**
STROYS ▸ **stroy**
STRUCK ▸ **strike**
STRUDEL *n* thin sheet of filled dough rolled up and baked
STRUM *vb*
STRUMA *n* abnormal enlargement of the thyroid gland **strumae, strumas**
STRUMS ▸ **strum**
STRUNG ▸ **string**
STRUNT *Scots word for* ▸ **strut**
STRUNTS ▸ **strunt**
STRUT *vb, n* **struts**
STUB *n, vb* **stubbed**
STUBBIE = **stubby**
STUBBLE *n* **stubbly**
STUBBY *adj, n*
STUBS ▸ **stub**
STUCCO *n, vb* **stuccos**
STUCK *n* **stucks**
STUD *n, vb* **studded**
STUDDEN ▸ **stand**
STUDDIE *Scots word for* ▸ **anvil**
STUDDLE *n* post
STUDE *vb* past tense and past participle of staun (Scots form of stand)
STUDENT *n*
STUDIED *adj* carefully practised
STUDIER ▸ **study**
STUDIES ▸ **study**
STUDIO *n* **studios**
STUDLY *adj* strong and virile
STUDS ▸ **stud**
STUDY *vb, n*
STUFF *n, vb* **stuffed, stuffer, stuffs**
STUFFY *adj*
STUGGY *adj* stout
STUIVER = **stiver**
STULL *n* timber prop or platform in a stope **stulls**
STULM *n* shaft **stulms**
STUM *n* partly

fermented wine added to fermented wine as a preservative ▷ *vb* preserve (wine) by adding stum
STUMBLE *vb, n*
STUMBLY *adj* tending to stumble
STUMER *n* forgery or cheat **stumers**
STUMM = **shtoom**
STUMMED ▸ **stum**
STUMMEL *n* bowl of pipe
STUMP *n, vb* **stumped, stumper, stumps**
STUMPY *adj, n*
STUMS ▸ **stum**
STUN *vb, n*
STUNG ▸ **sting**
STUNK ▸ **stink**
STUNNED ▸ **stun**
STUNNER *n* beautiful person or thing
STUNS ▸ **stun**
STUNT *vb, n* **stunted, stunts**
STUPA *n* domed edifice housing Buddhist or Jain relics **stupas**
STUPE *n* hot damp cloth applied to the body to relieve pain ▷ *vb* treat with a stupe **stuped**
STUPEFY *vb* make insensitive or lethargic
STUPENT *adj* astonished
STUPES ▸ **stupe**
STUPID *adj, n* **stupids**
STUPING ▸ **stupe**
STUPOR *n* **stupors**
STURDY *adj, n*
STURE = **stoor**
STURMER *n* type of eating apple with pale green skin
STURNUS *n* bird of starling family
STURT *vb* bother **sturted, sturts**
STUSHIE *n* commotion, rumpus, or row
STUTTER *vb, n*
STY *vb*
STYE *n* **styed, styes**
STYGIAN *adj* dark, gloomy, or hellish
STYING ▸ **sty**
STYLAR ▸ **stylus**
STYLATE *adj* having style
STYLE *n, vb* **styled, stylee**
STYLEES ▸ **stylee**
STYLER ▸ **style**
STYLERS ▸ **style**
STYLES ▸ **style**
STYLET *n* wire to stiffen a flexible cannula or catheter **stylets**
STYLI ▸ **stylus**
STYLIE *adj* fashion-conscious **stylier**
STYLING ▸ **style**
STYLISE = **stylize**
STYLISH *adj*
STYLIST *n* hairdresser
STYLITE *n* one of a class of recluses who in ancient times lived on the top of high pillars
STYLIZE *vb* cause to conform to an established stylistic form
STYLO *n* type of fountain pen
STYLOID *adj* resembling a stylus ▷ *n* spiny growth
STYLOPS *n* type of insect that lives as a parasite in other insects
STYLOS ▸ **stylo**
STYLUS *n*
STYME *vb* peer **stymed, stymes**
STYMIE *vb*
STYMIED ▸ **stymy**
STYMIES ▸ **stymy**
STYMING ▸ **styme stymy**
STYMY = **stymie**
STYPSIS *n* action, application, or use of a styptic
STYPTIC *adj* (drug) used to stop bleeding ▷ *n* styptic drug
STYRAX *n* type of tropical or subtropical tree
STYRE = **stir**
STYRED ▸ **styre**
STYRENE *n* colourless oily volatile flammable water-insoluble liquid
STYRES ▸ **styre**
STYRING ▸ **styre**
STYTE *vb* bounce **styted, stytes, styting**
SUABLE *adj* liable to be sued in a court **suably**
SUASION *n* persuasion **suasive, suasory**
SUAVE *adj* **suavely, suaver, suavest, suavity**
SUB *n* subeditor ▷ *vb* act

as a substitute
SUBA *n* shepherd's cloak
SUBACID *adj* (esp of some fruits) moderately acid or sour
SUBACT *vb* subdue **subacts**
SUBADAR *n* chief native officer of a company of Indian soldiers in the British service **subah**
SUBAHS ▶ **subah**
SUBALAR *adj* below a wing
SUBAQUA *adj* of or relating to underwater sport
SUBAREA *n* area within a larger area
SUBARID *adj* receiving slightly more rainfall than arid regions
SUBAS ▶ **suba**
SUBATOM *n* part of an atom
SUBBASE = **subbass**
SUBBASS *another name for* ▶ **bourdon**
SUBBED ▶ **sub**
SUBBIE *n* subcontractor **subbies**
SUBBING ▶ **sub**
SUBBY = **subbie**
SUBCELL *n* cell within a larger cell
SUBCLAN *n* clan within a larger clan
SUBCODE *n* computer tag identifying data
SUBCOOL *vb* make colder
SUBCULT *n* cult within larger cult
SUBDEAN *n* deputy of dean
SUBDEB *n* young woman who is not yet a debutante **subdebs**
SUBDEW = **subdue**
SUBDEWS ▶ **subdew**
SUBDUAL ▶ **subdue**
SUBDUCE *vb* withdraw
SUBDUCT *vb* draw or turn (the eye, etc) downwards
SUBDUE *vb*
SUBDUED *adj*
SUBDUER ▶ **subdue**
SUBDUES ▶ **subdue**
SUBECHO *n* echo resonating more quietly than another echo
SUBEDAR = **subadar**
SUBEDIT *vb* edit and correct (written or printed material)
SUBER *n* cork
SUBERIC = **suberose**
SUBERIN *n* fatty or waxy substance that is present in the walls of cork cells
SUBERS ▶ **suber**
SUBFEU *vb* grant feu to vassal **subfeus**
SUBFILE *n* file within another file
SUBFIX *n* suffix
SUBFUSC *adj* devoid of brightness or appeal ▷ *n* (at Oxford University) formal academic dress **subfusk**
SUBGOAL *n* secondary goal
SUBGUM *n* Chinese dish **subgums**
SUBHA *n* string of beads used in praying and meditating **subhas**
SUBHEAD *n* heading of a subsection in a printed work
SUBIDEA *n* secondary idea
SUBITEM *n* item that is less important than another item
SUBITO *adv* (preceding or following a dynamic marking, etc) suddenly
SUBJECT *n, adj, vb*
SUBJOIN *vb* add or attach at the end of something spoken, written, etc
SUBLATE *vb* deny
SUBLET *vb, n* **sublets**
SUBLIME *adj, vb*
SUBLINE *n* secondary headline
SUBLOT *n* subdivision of a lot **sublots**
SUBMAN *n* primitive form of human **submen**
SUBMENU *n* further list of options within computer menu
SUBMISS *adj* docile
SUBMIT *vb* **submits**
SUBNET *n* part of network **subnets**
SUBORAL *adj* not quite oral
SUBORN *vb* bribe or incite (a person) to commit a wrongful act **suborns**
SUBOVAL *adj* not quite oval
SUBPAR *adj* not up to

standard
SUBPART *n* part within another part
SUBPENA = **subpoena**
SUBPLOT *n* secondary plot in a novel, play, or film
SUBRACE *n* race of people considered to be inferior
SUBRENT *n* rent paid to renter who rents to another
SUBRING *n* mathematical ring that is a subset of another ring
SUBRULE *n* rule within another rule
SUBS ▶ **sub**
SUBSALE *n* sale carried out within the process of a larger sale
SUBSEA *adj* undersea
SUBSECT *n* sect within a larger sect
SUBSERE *n* secondary sere arising when the progress of a sere has been interrupted
SUBSET *n* **subsets**
SUBSIDE *vb*
SUBSIDY *n*
SUBSIST *vb*
SUBSITE *n* location within a website
SUBSOIL *n, vb*
SUBSONG *n* subdued form of birdsong modified from the full territorial song
SUBSUME *vb*
SUBTACK *Scots word for* > **sublease**
SUBTASK *n* task that is part of a larger task
SUBTAXA > **subtaxon**
SUBTEEN *n* young person who has not yet become a teenager
SUBTEND *vb* be opposite (an angle or side)
SUBTEST *n* test that is part of larger test
SUBTEXT *n* underlying theme in a piece of writing
SUBTIL = **subtle**
SUBTILE *rare spelling of* ▶ **subtle**
SUBTLE *adj* **subtler, subtly**
SUBTONE *n* subdivision of a tone
SUBTYPE *n* secondary or subordinate type or genre
SUBUNIT *n* distinct part or component of something larger
SUBURB *n* **suburbs**
SUBVENE *vb* happen in such a way as to be of assistance
SUBVERT *vb*
SUBWAY *n, vb* **subways**
SUBZERO *adj* lower than zero
SUBZONE *n* subdivision of a zone
SUCCADE *n* piece of candied fruit
SUCCAH = **sukkah**
SUCCAHS ▶ **succah**
SUCCEED *vb*
SUCCES *French word for* ▶ **success**
SUCCESS *n*
SUCCI ▶ **succus**
SUCCISE *adj* ending abruptly, as if cut off
SUCCOR = **succour**
SUCCORS ▶ **succor**
SUCCORY *another name for* ▶ **chicory**
SUCCOS = **succoth**
SUCCOSE ▶ **succus**
SUCCOT = **sukkoth**
SUCCOTH *variant of* ▶ **sukkoth**
SUCCOUR *n, vb*
SUCCOUS ▶ **succus**
SUCCUBA = **succubus**
SUCCUBI > **succubus**
SUCCUMB *vb*
SUCCUS *n* fluid
SUCCUSS *vb* shake (a patient) to detect the sound of fluid in a cavity
SUCH *adj, pron*
SUCK *vb, n* **sucked**
SUCKEN *Scots word for* > **district**
SUCKENS ▶ **sucken**
SUCKER *n, vb* **suckers**
SUCKET = **succade**
SUCKETS ▶ **sucket**
SUCKIER ▶ **sucky**
SUCKING *adj* not yet weaned
SUCKLE *vb* **suckled, suckler, suckles**
SUCKS *interj* expression of disappointment
SUCKY *adj* despicable
SUCRASE *another name for* > **invertase**
SUCRE *n* former standard monetary unit of Ecuador **sucres**
SUCRIER *n* small

container for sugar at table
SUCROSE = **sugar**
SUCTION *n, vb*
SUD *singular of* ▸ **suds**
SUDAMEN *n* small cavity in the skin
SUDARIA > **sudarium**
SUDARY = **sudarium**
SUDATE *vb* sweat **sudated, sudates**
SUDD *n* floating masses of reeds and weeds on the White Nile
SUDDEN *adj* **suddens**
SUDDER *n* supreme court in India **sudders**
SUDDS ▸ **sudd**
SUDOR *technical name for* ▸ **sweat**
SUDORAL ▸ **sudor**
SUDORS ▸ **sudor**
SUDS *pl n, vb* **sudsed**
SUDSER *n* soap opera **sudsers**
SUDSES, sudsier, sudsing, sudsy ▸ **suds**
SUE *vb* **sueable, sued**
SUEDE *n, vb* **sueded, suedes, sueding**
SUENT *adj* smooth
SUER ▸ **sue**
SUERS ▸ **sue**
SUES ▸ **sue**
SUET *n* **suetier, suets, suetty, suety**
SUFFARI = **safari**
SUFFECT *adj* additional
SUFFER *vb* **suffers**
SUFFETE *n* official in ancient Carthage
SUFFICE *vb*
SUFFIX *n, vb*
SUFFUSE *vb*
SUG *vb* sell a product while pretending to conduct market research
SUGAN *n* straw rope **sugans**
SUGAR *n, vb*
SUGARED *adj* made sweeter or more appealing with or as with sugar
SUGARER ▸ **sugar**
SUGARS ▸ **sugar**
SUGARY *adj* of, like, or containing sugar
SUGGED ▸ **sug**
SUGGEST *vb*
SUGGING *n* practice of selling products under the pretence of conducting market research
SUGH = **sough**
SUGHED ▸ **sugh**
SUGHING ▸ **sugh**
SUGHS ▸ **sugh**
SUGO *n* Italian pasta sauce **sugos**
SUGS ▸ **sug**
SUHUR *n* meal eaten before sunrise by Muslims fasting during Ramadan **suhurs**
SUI *adj* of itself
SUICIDE *n, vb*
SUID *n* pig or related animal **suidian, suids**
SUING ▸ **sue**
SUINGS ▸ **sue**
SUINT *n* water-soluble substance found in the fleece of sheep **suints**
SUIPLAP *n* South African slang for a drunkard
SUIT *n, vb*
SUITE *n*
SUITED ▸ **suit**
SUITER *n* piece of luggage for carrying suits and dresses **suiters**
SUITES ▸ **suite**
SUITING *n* fabric used for suits
SUITOR *n, vb* **suitors**
SUITS ▸ **suit**
SUIVEZ *vb* musical direction meaning follow
SUJEE = **soogee**
SUJEES ▸ **sujee**
SUK = **souk**
SUKH = **souk**
SUKHS ▸ **sukh**
SUKKAH *n* structure in which orthodox Jews eat and sleep during Sukkoth **sukkahs**
SUKKOS = **sukkoth**
SUKKOT = **sukkoth**
SUKKOTH *n* eight-day Jewish harvest festival
SUKS ▸ **suk**
SUKUK *n* **sukuks**
SULCAL ▸ **sulcus**
SULCATE *adj* marked with longitudinal parallel grooves
SULCI ▸ **sulcus**
SULCUS *n* linear groove, furrow, or slight depression
SULDAN = **sultan**
SULDANS ▸ **suldan**
SULFA = **sulpha**
SULFAS ▸ **sulfa**
SULFATE = **sulphate**
SULFID = **sulphide**

SULFIDE = **sulphide**
SULFIDS ▸ **sulfid**
SULFITE = **sulphite**
SULFO = **sulphonic**
SULFONE = **sulphone**
SULFUR *variant of* ▸ **sulphur**
SULFURS ▸ **sulfur**
SULFURY ▸ **sulfur**
SULK *vb, n* **sulked, sulker**
SULKERS ▸ **sulker**
SULKIER ▸ **sulky**
SULKIES ▸ **sulky**
SULKILY ▸ **sulky**
SULKING ▸ **sulk**
SULKS ▸ **sulk**
SULKY *adj, n*
SULLAGE *n* filth or waste, esp sewage
SULLEN *adj, n* **sullens**
SULLIED ▸ **sully**
SULLIES ▸ **sully**
SULLY *vb, n*
SULPH *n* amphetamine sulphate
SULPHA *n* any of a group of sulphonamides that prevent the growth of bacteria **sulphas**
SULPHID = **sulphide**
SULPHS ▸ **sulph**
SULPHUR *n, vb*
SULTAN *n*
SULTANA *n*
SULTANS ▸ **sultan**
SULTRY *adj*
SULU *n* type of sarong worn in Fiji **sulus**
SUM *n, vb*
SUMAC = **sumach**
SUMACH *n* type of temperate or subtropical shrub or small tree **sumachs**
SUMACS ▸ **sumac**
SUMATRA *n* violent storm blowing from the direction of Sumatra
SUMLESS *adj* uncountable
SUMMA *n* compendium of theology, philosophy, or canon law **summae**
SUMMAND *n* number or quantity forming part of a sum
SUMMAR *Scots variant of* ▸ **summer**
SUMMARY *n, adj*
SUMMAS ▸ **summa**
SUMMAT *pron* something ▹ *n* impressive or important person or thing
SUMMATE *vb* add up
SUMMATS ▸ **summat**
SUMMED ▸ **sum**
SUMMER *n, vb* **summers, summery**
SUMMING ▸ **sum**
SUMMIST *n* writer of summae
SUMMIT *n, vb* **summits**
SUMMON *vb*
SUMMONS *n, vb*
SUMO *n* Japanese style of wrestling **sumoist, sumos**
SUMP *n*
SUMPH *n* stupid person **sumphs**
SUMPIT *n* Malay blowpipe **sumpits**
SUMPS ▸ **sump**
SUMPTER *n* packhorse, mule, or other beast of burden
SUMS ▸ **sum**
SUMY *pl n* the monetary units of Uzbekistan
SUN *n, vb*
SUNBACK *adj* (of dress) cut low at back
SUNBAKE *vb* sunbathe, esp in order to become tanned ▹ *n* period of sunbaking
SUNBATH *n* exposure of the body to the sun to get a suntan
SUNBEAM *n*
SUNBEAT *adj* exposed to sun
SUNBED *n* machine for giving an artificial tan **sunbeds**
SUNBELT *n* southern states of the US
SUNBIRD *n* type of small songbird with a bright plumage in the males
SUNBOW *n* bow of colours produced when sunlight shines through spray **sunbows**
SUNBURN *n, vb*
SUNDAE *n* **sundaes**
SUNDARI *n* Indian tree
SUNDECK *n* upper open deck on a passenger ship
SUNDER *vb* break apart **sunders**
SUNDEW *n* type of bog plant with leaves covered in sticky hairs **sundews**

SUNDIAL *n*
SUNDOG *n* small rainbow or halo near the horizon **sundogs**
SUNDOWN = **sunset**
SUNDRA = **sundari**
SUNDRAS ▸ **sundra**
SUNDRI = **sundari**
SUNDRIS ▸ **sundri**
SUNDRY *adj*
SUNFAST *adj* not fading in sunlight
SUNFISH *n* large sea fish with a rounded body
SUNG ▸ **sing**
SUNGAR = **sangar**
SUNGARS ▸ **sungar**
SUNGLOW *n* pinkish glow often seen in the sky before sunrise or after sunset
SUNHAT *n* hat that shades the face and neck from the sun **sunhats**
SUNI *n* S African dwarf antelope **sunis**
SUNK *n* bank or pad
SUNKEN *adj*
SUNKET *n* something good to eat **sunkets**
SUNKIE *n* little stool **sunkies**
SUNKS ▸ **sunk**
SUNLAMP *n* lamp that generates ultraviolet rays
SUNLAND *n* sunny area
SUNLESS *adj* without sun or sunshine
SUNLIKE ▸ **sun**
SUNLIT > **sunlight**
SUNN *n* leguminous plant of the East Indies
SUNNA *n* body of traditional Islamic law **sunnah**
SUNNAHS ▸ **sunnah**
SUNNAS ▸ **sunna**
SUNNED ▸ **sun**
SUNNIER ▸ **sunny**
SUNNIES *pl n* pair of sunglasses
SUNNILY ▸ **sunny**
SUNNING ▸ **sun**
SUNNS ▸ **sunn**
SUNNY *adj*
SUNRAY *n* ray of light from the sun **sunrays**
SUNRISE *n*
SUNROOF *n*
SUNROOM *n* room or glass-enclosed porch designed to display beautiful views
SUNS ▸ **sun**
SUNSET *n* **sunsets**
SUNSPOT *n*
SUNSTAR *n* type of starfish with up to 13 arms
SUNSUIT *n* child's outfit consisting of a brief top and shorts or a short skirt
SUNTAN *n* **suntans**
SUNTRAP *n* very sunny sheltered place
SUNUP = **sunrise**
SUNUPS ▸ **sunup**
SUNWARD = **sunwards**
SUNWISE *adv* moving in the same direction as the sun
SUP = **supine**
SUPAWN = **suppawn**
SUPAWNS ▸ **supawn**
SUPE *n* superintendent
SUPER *adj, n, interj, vb*
SUPERB *adj*
SUPERED ▸ **super**
SUPERS ▸ **super**
SUPES ▸ **supe**
SUPINE *adj, n* **supines**
SUPLEX *n* type of wrestling hold
SUPPAWN *n* kind of porridge
SUPPED ▸ **sup**
SUPPER *n, vb* **suppers**
SUPPING ▸ **sup**
SUPPLE *adj, vb* **suppled, suppler, supples**
SUPPLY *vb, n, adj, adv*
SUPPORT *vb, n*
SUPPOSE *vb*
SUPRA *adv* above, esp referring to earlier parts of a book etc
SUPREMA > **supremum**
SUPREME *adj, n*
SUPREMO *n* person in overall authority
SUPS ▸ **sup**
SUQ = **souk**

> This unusual word for an Arab market-place is easy to overlook because we tend not to think of words ending in Q. It can also be spelt **sook, souk, suk** or **sukh**.

SUQS ▸ **suq**
SUR *prep* above
SURA *n* any of the 114 chapters of the Koran
SURAH *n* twill-weave fabric of silk or rayon, used for dresses,

blouses, etc **surahs**
SURAL *adj* of or relating to the calf of the leg
SURAMIN *n* drug used in treating sleeping sickness
SURANCE = **assurance**
SURAS ▸ **sura**
SURAT *n* cotton fabric from Surat in India **surats**
SURBASE *n* uppermost part, such as a moulding, of a pedestal, base, or skirting
SURBATE *vb* make feet sore through walking
SURBED *vb* put something on its edge **surbeds**
SURBET ▸ **surbate**
SURCOAT *n* tunic worn by a knight over his armour
SURCULI > **surculus**
SURD *n* number that cannot be expressed in whole numbers ▹ *adj* of or relating to a surd
SURDITY *n* deafness
SURDS ▸ **surd**
SURE *adj, interj, vb* **sured**
SURELY *adv*
SURER ▸ **sure**
SURES ▸ **sure**
SUREST ▸ **sure**
SURETY *n, vb*
SURF *n, vb*
SURFACE *n, vb*
SURFED ▸ **surf**
SURFEIT *n, vb*
SURFER ▸ **surfing**
SURFERS ▸ **surfing**
SURFIE *n* young person whose main interest is in surfing
SURFIER ▸ **surf**
SURFIES ▸ **surfie**
SURFING *n*
SURFMAN *n* sailor skilled in sailing through surf **surfmen**
SURFS ▸ **surf**
SURFY ▸ **surf**
SURGE *n, vb* **surged, surgent**
SURGEON *n*
SURGER ▸ **surge**
SURGERS ▸ **surge**
SURGERY *n*
SURGES, surgier, surging, surgy ▸ **surge**
SURIMI *n* blended seafood product made from precooked fish **surimis**
SURING ▸ **sure**
SURLIER ▸ **surly**
SURLILY ▸ **surly**
SURLOIN = **sirloin**
SURLY *adj*
SURMISE *n, vb*
SURNAME *n, vb*
SURPASS *vb*
SURPLUS *n, adj, vb*
SURRA *n* tropical febrile disease of animals **surras**
SURREAL *adj, n*
SURREY *n* light four-wheeled horse-drawn carriage **surreys**
SURTAX *n, vb*
SURTOUT *n* man's overcoat resembling a frock coat
SURVEIL = **surveille**
SURVEY *vb, n* **surveys**
SURVIEW *vb* survey
SURVIVE *vb*
SUS = **suss**
SUSES ▸ **sus**
SUSHI *n* Japanese dish of small cakes of cold rice with a topping of raw fish **sushis**
SUSLIK *n* central Eurasian ground squirrel **susliks**
SUSPECT *vb, adj, n*
SUSPEND *vb*
SUSPENS = **suspense**
SUSPIRE *vb* sigh or utter with a sigh
SUSS *vb* attempt to work out (a situation, etc), using one's intuition ▹ *n* sharpness of mind **sussed, susses, sussing**
SUSTAIN *vb, n*
SUSU *n* (in the Caribbean) savings fund shared by friends **susus**
SUTILE *adj* involving sewing
SUTLER *n* merchant who accompanied an army in order to sell provisions **sutlers, sutlery**
SUTOR *n* cobbler **sutors**
SUTRA *n* Sanskrit sayings or collections of sayings **sutras**
SUTTA *n* Buddhist scripture **suttas**

SUTTEE *n* custom whereby a widow burnt herself on her husband's funeral pyre **suttees**
SUTTLE *vb* work as sutler **suttled, suttles**
SUTTLY ▶ **subtle**
SUTURAL ▶ **suture**
SUTURE *n, vb* **sutured, sutures**
SVARAJ = **swaraj**
SVELTE *adj* **svelter**
SWAB *n, vb* **swabbed**
SWABBER *n* person who uses a swab
SWABBIE = **swabby**
SWABBY *n* seaman
SWABS ▶ **swab**
SWACK *adj* flexible
SWACKED *adj* in a state of intoxication, stupor, or euphoria induced by drugs or alcohol
SWAD *n* loutish person
SWADDIE = **swaddy**
SWADDLE *vb* wrap (a baby) in swaddling clothes ▷ *n* swaddling clothes
SWADDY *n* private soldier
SWADS ▶ **swaddle**
SWAG *n, vb*
SWAGE *n* shaped tool or die used in forming cold metal by hammering ▷ *vb* form (metal) with a swage **swaged, swager, swagers, swages**
SWAGGED ▶ **swag**
SWAGGER *vb, n, adj* **swaggie**
SWAGING ▶ **swage**
SWAGMAN *n* **swagmen**
SWAGS ▶ **swag**
SWAIL = **swale**
SWAILS ▶ **swail**
SWAIN *n* suitor **swains**
SWALE *n* moist depression in a tract of land ▷ *vb* sway **swaled, swales, swalier, swaling**
SWALLET *n* hole where water goes underground
SWALLOW *vb, n*
SWALY ▶ **swale**
SWAM ▶ **swim**
SWAMI *n* Hindu religious teacher **swamies, swamis**
SWAMP *n, vb* **swamped**
SWAMPER *n* person who lives or works in a swampy region
SWAMPS ▶ **swamp**
SWAMPY ▶ **swamp**
SWAMY = **swami**
SWAN *n, vb*
SWANG ▶ **swing**
SWANK *vb* show off or boast ▷ *n* showing off or boasting **swanked, swanker**
SWANKEY = **swanky**
SWANKIE = **swanky**
SWANKS ▶ **swank**
SWANKY *adj, n*
SWANNED ▶ **swan**
SWANNIE *n* (in NZ) type of all-weather heavy woollen shirt
SWANNY *adj* swanlike
SWANPAN *n* Chinese abacus
SWANS ▶ **swan**
SWAP *vb, n* **swapped, swapper, swaps, swapt**
SWARAJ *n* (in British India) self-government
SWARD *n* stretch of short grass ▷ *vb* cover or become covered with grass **swarded, swards**
SWARDY *adj* covered with sward
SWARE ▶ **swear**
SWARF *n* material removed by cutting tools in the machining of metals, stone, etc ▷ *vb* faint **swarfed, swarfs**
SWARM *n, vb* **swarmed, swarmer, swarms**
SWART *adj* swarthy **swarth**
SWARTHS ▶ **swarth**
SWARTHY *adj*
SWARTY ▶ **swart**
SWARVE = **swarf**
SWARVED ▶ **swarf**
SWARVES ▶ **swarf**
SWASH *n* rush of water up a beach following each break of the waves ▷ *vb* wash or move with noisy splashing **swashed**
SWASHER *n* braggart
SWASHES ▶ **swash**
SWASHY *adj* slushy
SWAT *vb, n*
SWATCH *n* sample of cloth
SWATH *n* width of one sweep of a scythe or of the blade of a mowing

machine
SWATHE *vb, n* **swathed, swather, swathes**
SWATHS ▸ **swath**
SWATHY ▸ **swath**
SWATS ▸ **swat**
SWATTED ▸ **swat**
SWATTER *n* device for killing insects ▹ *vb* splash
SWATTY ▸ **swotty**
SWAY *vb, n* **swayed, swayer, swayers, swayful, swaying**
SWAYL = **sweal**
SWAYLED ▸ **swayl**
SWAYLS ▸ **swayl**
SWAYS ▸ **sway**
SWAZZLE *n* small metal instrument used to produce a shrill voice
SWEAL *vb* scorch **swealed, sweals**
SWEAR *vb*
SWEARD = **sword**
SWEARDS ▸ **sweard**
SWEARER ▸ **swear**
SWEARS ▸ **swear**
SWEARY *adj* using swear-words
SWEAT *n, vb*
SWEATED *adj* made by exploited labour
SWEATER *n*
SWEATS ▸ **sweat**
SWEATY *adj*
SWEDE *n* **swedes**
SWEDGER *n* Scots dialect word for sweet
SWEE *vb* sway **sweed, sweeing**
SWEEL = **sweal**
SWEELED ▸ **sweel**
SWEELS ▸ **sweel**
SWEENEY *n* police flying squad
SWEENY *n* wasting of the shoulder muscles of a horse
SWEEP *vb, n*
SWEEPER *n* device used to sweep carpets
SWEEPS ▸ **sweep**
SWEEPY ▸ **sweep**
SWEER *variant of* ▸ **sweir**
SWEERED ▸ **sweer**
SWEERS ▸ **sweer**
SWEERT ▸ **sweer**
SWEES ▸ **swee**
SWEET *adj, n, vb* **sweeted**
SWEETEN *vb*
SWEETER ▸ **sweet**
SWEETIE *n* lovable person
SWEETLY ▸ **sweet**
SWEETS ▸ **sweet**
SWEETY = **sweetie**
SWEIR *vb* swear ▹ *adj* lazy **sweired, sweirer, sweirs, sweirt**
SWELL *vb, n, adj* **swelled, sweller, swells**
SWELT *vb* die **swelted**
SWELTER *vb, n*
SWELTRY *adj* sultry
SWELTS ▸ **swelt**
SWEPT ▸ **sweep**
SWERF = **swarf**
SWERFED ▸ **swerf**
SWERFS ▸ **swerf**
SWERVE *vb, n* **swerved, swerver, swerves**
SWEVEN *n* vision or dream **swevens**
SWEY = **swee**
SWEYED ▸ **swey**
SWEYING ▸ **swey**
SWEYS ▸ **swey**
SWIDDEN *n* area of land where slash-and-burn techniques have been used
SWIES ▸ **swy**
SWIFT *adj, n, adv, vb* **swifted**
SWIFTER *n* line run around the ends of capstan bars
SWIFTIE *n* trick, ruse, or deception
SWIFTLY ▸ **swift**
SWIFTS ▸ **swift**
SWIFTY = **swiftie**
SWIG *n, vb* **swigged, swigger, swigs**
SWILER *n* (in Newfoundland) a seal hunter **swilers**
SWILL *vb, n* **swilled, swiller, swills**
SWIM *vb, n* **swimmer**
SWIMMY *adj* dizzy
SWIMS ▸ **swim**
SWINDGE = **swinge**
SWINDLE *vb, n*
SWINE *n*
SWINERY *n* pig farm
SWINES ▸ **swine**
SWING *vb, n*
SWINGBY *n* act of spacecraft passing close to planet
SWINGE *vb* beat, flog, or punish **swinged**
SWINGER *n* person regarded as being modern and lively
SWINGES ▸ **swinge**

SWINGLE *n* flat-bladed wooden instrument used for beating and scraping flax ▷ *vb* use a swingle on
SWINGS ▶ **swing**
SWINGY *adj* lively and modern
SWINISH ▶ **swine**
SWINK *vb* toil or drudge ▷ *n* toil or drudgery **swinked, swinker, swinks**
SWINNEY *variant of* ▶ **sweeny**
SWIPE *vb, n* **swiped, swiper, swipers**
SWIPES *pl n* beer, esp when poor or weak
SWIPEY *adj* drunk **swipier**
SWIPING ▶ **swipe**
SWIPLE = **swipple**
SWIPLES ▶ **swiple**
SWIPPLE *n* part of a flail that strikes the grain
SWIRE *n* neck **swires**
SWIRL *vb, n* **swirled, swirls, swirly**
SWISH *vb, n, adj* **swished, swisher, swishes**
SWISHY *adj* moving with a swishing sound
SWISS *n* type of muslin **swisses**
SWITCH *n, vb* **switchy**
SWITH *adv* swiftly **swithe**
SWITHER *vb* hesitate or be indecisive ▷ *n* state of hesitation or uncertainty
SWITHLY ▶ **swith**
SWITS = **switch**
SWITSES ▶ **swits**
SWIVE *vb* have sexual intercourse with (a person) **swived**
SWIVEL *vb, n* **swivels**
SWIVES ▶ **swive**
SWIVET *n* nervous state **swivets**
SWIVING ▶ **swive**
SWIZ *n* swindle or disappointment **swizz**
SWIZZED ▶ **swizz**
SWIZZES ▶ **swizz**
SWIZZLE *n* unshaken cocktail ▷ *vb* stir a swizzle stick in (a drink)
SWOB *less common word for* ▶ **swab**
SWOBBED ▶ **swob**
SWOBBER ▶ **swob**
SWOBS ▶ **swob**
SWOFFER > **swoffing**
SWOLLEN ▶ **swell**
SWOLN ▶ **swell**
SWOON *n, vb* **swooned, swooner, swoons**
SWOONY *adj* romantic or sexy
SWOOP *vb, n* **swooped, swooper, swoops, swoopy**
SWOOSH *vb* make a swirling or rustling sound when moving or pouring out ▷ *n* swirling or rustling sound or movement
SWOP = **swap; swopped, swopper, swops, swopt**
SWORD *n, vb* **sworded**
SWORDER *n* fighter with sword
SWORDS ▶ **sword**
SWORE ▶ **swear**
SWORN ▶ **swear**
SWOT *vb, n* **swots, swotted, swotter**
SWOTTY *adj* given to studying hard, esp to the exclusion of other activities
SWOUN = **swoon**
SWOUND = **swoon**
SWOUNDS *less common spelling of* ▶ **zounds**
SWOUNE = **swoon**
SWOUNED ▶ **swoune**
SWOUNES ▶ **swoune**
SWOUNS ▶ **swoun**
SWOWND = **swoon**
SWOWNDS ▶ **swownd**
SWOWNE = **swoon**
SWOWNES ▶ **swowne**
SWOZZLE = **swazzle**
SWUM ▶ **swim**
SWUNG ▶ **swing**
SWY *n* Australian gambling game involving two coins

> A type of card-game, that can be useful in helping you to clear a difficult rack.

SYBBE = **sib**
SYBBES ▶ **sybbe**
SYBIL = **sibyl**
SYBILS ▶ **sybil**
SYBO *n* spring onion **syboe**
SYBOES ▶ **syboe**
SYBOTIC *adj* of a swineherd
SYBOW = **sybo**
SYBOWS ▶ **sybow**
SYCE *n* (formerly, in

India) a servant employed to look after horses, etc
SYCEE *n* silver ingots formerly used as a medium of exchange in China **sycees**
SYCES ▸ **syce**
SYCONIA > **syconium**
SYCOSES ▸ **sycosis**
SYCOSIS *n* chronic inflammation of the hair follicles
SYE *vb* strain **syed, syeing**
SYEN = **scion**
SYENITE *n* light-coloured coarse-grained plutonic igneous rock
SYENS ▸ **syen**
SYES ▸ **sye**
SYKE = **sike**
SYKER *adv* surely
SYKES ▸ **syke**
SYLI *n* Finnish unit of volume **sylis**
SYLLABI > **syllabus**
SYLLOGE *n* collection or summary
SYLPH *n* **sylphic**
SYLPHID *n* little sylph
SYLPHS ▸ **sylph**
SYLPHY ▸ **sylph**
SYLVA *n* trees growing in a particular region **sylvae**
SYLVAN *adj*, *n* **sylvans**
SYLVAS ▸ **sylva**
SYLVIA *n* songbird **sylvias**
SYLVIN = **sylvite**
SYLVINE = **sylvite**
SYLVINS ▸ **sylvin**
SYLVITE *n* soluble colourless, white, or coloured mineral
SYMAR = **cymar**
SYMARS ▸ **symar**
SYMBION = **symbiont**
SYMBIOT = **symbiont**
SYMBOL *n*, *vb*
SYMBOLE = **cymbal**
SYMBOLS ▸ **symbol**
SYMITAR = **scimitar**
SYMPTOM *n*
SYN *Scots word for* ▸ **since**
SYNAGOG = **synagogue**
SYNANON *n* type of therapy given to drug addicts
SYNAPSE *n*, *vb*
SYNAPTE *n* litany in Greek Orthodox Church
SYNAXES ▸ **synaxis**
SYNAXIS *n* early Christian meeting
SYNC *n* synchronization ▷ *vb* synchronize
SYNCARP *n* fleshy multiple fruit
SYNCED ▸ **sync**
SYNCH = **sync**
SYNCHED ▸ **synch**
SYNCHRO *n* type of electrical device
SYNCHS ▸ **synch**
SYNCING ▸ **sync**
SYNCOM *n* communications satellite in stationary orbit **syncoms**
SYNCOPE *n* omission of one or more sounds or letters from the middle of a word
SYNCS ▸ **sync**
SYND = **syne**
SYNDED ▸ **synd**
SYNDET *n* synthetic detergent **syndets**
SYNDIC *n* business or legal agent of some institutions **syndics**
SYNDING ▸ **synd**
SYNDS ▸ **synd**
SYNE *vb* rinse ▷ *n* rinse ▷ *adv* since **syned**
SYNERGY *n*
SYNES ▸ **syne**
SYNESES ▸ **synesis**
SYNESIS *n* grammatical construction in which the form of a word is conditioned by the meaning
SYNFUEL *n* synthetic fuel
SYNGAMY *n* sexual reproduction
SYNGAS *n* mixture of carbon monoxide and hydrogen
SYNING ▸ **syne**
SYNOD *n*
SYNODAL *adj* of or relating to a synod ▷ *n* money paid to a bishop by less senior members of the clergy at a synod
SYNODIC *adj* involving conjunction of the same star, planet, or satellite
SYNODS ▸ **synod**
SYNONYM *n*
SYNOVIA *n* clear thick fluid that lubricates the body joints
SYNROC *n*

titanium-ceramic substance that can incorporate nuclear waste in its crystals **synrocs**
SYNTAGM = **syntagma**
SYNTAN *n* synthetic tanning substance **syntans**
SYNTAX *n*
SYNTENY *n* presence of two or more genes on the same chromosome
SYNTH *n* type of electrophonic musical instrument operated by a keyboard and pedals
SYNTHON *n* molecule used in synthesis
SYNTHS ▶ **synth**
SYNTONY *n* matching of frequencies
SYNURA *n* variety of microbe **synurae**
SYPE = **sipe**
SYPED ▶ **sype**
SYPES ▶ **sype**
SYPH *shortening of* > **syphilis**
SYPHER *vb* lap (a chamfered edge) in order to form a flush surface **syphers**
SYPHON = **siphon**
SYPHONS ▶ **syphon**
SYPHS ▶ **syph**
SYPING ▶ **sype**
SYRAH *n* type of French red wine **syrahs**
SYREN = **siren**
SYRENS ▶ **syren**
SYRETTE *n* small disposable syringe
SYRINGA *n* mock orange or lilac
SYRINGE *n, vb*
SYRINX *n* vocal organ of a bird
SYRPHID *n* type of fly
SYRTES ▶ **syrtis**
SYRTIS *n* area of quicksand
SYRUP *n, vb* **syruped, syrups**
SYRUPY *adj* thick and sweet
SYSOP *n* person who runs a system or network **sysops**
SYSTEM *n* **systems**
SYSTOLE *n* regular contraction of the heart as it pumps blood
SYSTYLE *n* building with different types of columns
SYTHE = **sith**
SYTHES ▶ **sythe**
SYVER *n* street drain or the grating over it **syvers**
SYZYGAL ▶ **syzygy**
SYZYGY *n* position of a celestial body when sun, earth, and the body are in line

Tt

T is one of the most common consonants in Scrabble. There are only four two-letter words that begin with **T**, but they are easy to remember as there is one for every vowel except **U**. Like **S**, **T** begins a number of three-letter words that don't use vowels, which are well worth remembering. These are: **thy** (6 points), **try** (6), **tsk** (7), **twp** (8) and **tyg** (7). There are also some useful three-letter words using **X**: **tax, tex, tix** and **tux** (10 each). If you have an **X** during a game, remember words like **text** (11), **texts** (12), **textile** (14), **textual** (14) and **texture** (14). The last three of these have seven letters, and so will earn you 50-point bonuses if you use all your tiles to form them. Other threes well worth remembering are **taj** (10) and **tik** (7).

TA *interj* thank you ▷ *n* thank you

TAAL *n* language: usually, by implication, Afrikaans **taals**

TAATA *child's word for* ▸ **father**

> This East African word for a father is one of those short words that can help you dispose of a surplus of As.

TAATAS ▸ **taata**

TAB *n, vb*

TABANID *n* stout-bodied fly

TABARD *n* short sleeveless tunic decorated with a coat of arms, worn in medieval times **tabards**

TABARET *n* hard-wearing fabric of silk or similar cloth with stripes of satin or moire

TABBED ▸ **tab**

TABBIED ▸ **tabby**

TABBIES ▸ **tabby**

TABBING ▸ **tab**

TABBIS *n* silken cloth

TABBY *vb, n*

TABEFY *vb* emaciate or become emaciated

TABER *old variant of* ▸ **tabor**

TABERD = **tabard**

TABERDS ▸ **taberd**

TABERED ▸ **taber**

TABERS ▸ **taber**

TABES *n* wasting of a bodily organ or part **tabetic**

TABI *n* thick-soled Japanese sock, worn with sandals

TABID *adj* emaciated

TABINET *n* type of tabbied fabric

TABLA *n* one of a pair of Indian drums played with the hands **tablas**

TABLE *n, vb*

TABLEAU *n*

TABLED ▸ **table**

TABLES ▸ **table**

TABLET *n, vb* **tablets**

TABLIER *n* (formerly) part of a dress resembling an apron
TABLING ▸ **table**
TABLOID *n*
TABOO *n, adj, vb* **tabooed, taboos**
TABOR *vb* **tabored, taborer**
TABORET *n* low stool, originally in the shape of a drum **taborin**
TABORS ▸ **tabor**
TABOULI = **tabbouleh**
TABOUR = **tabor**
TABOURS ▸ **tabour**
TABRERE = **tabor**
TABRET *n* smaller version of a tabor **tabrets**
TABS ▸ **tab**
TABU = **taboo**
TABUED ▸ **tabu**
TABUING ▸ **tabu**
TABULA *n* tablet for writing on **tabulae**
TABULAR *adj*
TABULI *variant of* > **tabbouleh**
TABULIS ▸ **tabuli**
TABUN *n* organic compound used as a lethal nerve gas **tabuns**
TABUS ▸ **tabu**
TACAN *n* electronic ultrahigh-frequency navigation system for aircraft **tacans**
TACE = **tasset**
TACES ▸ **tace**
TACET *n* musical direction indicating that an instrument or singer does not take part
TACH *n* device for measuring speed
TACHE *n* buckle, clasp, or hook **taches**
TACHINA *n as in* **tachina fly** bristly fly
TACHISM = **tachisme**
TACHIST ▸ **tachism**
TACHO = **tachogram**
TACHOS ▸ **tacho**
TACHS ▸ **tach**
TACHYON *n* hypothetical elementary particle
TACIT *adj* **tacitly**
TACK *n, vb* **tacked, tacker, tackers**
TACKET *n* nail, esp a hobnail **tackets, tackety**
TACKEY = **tacky**
TACKIER ▸ **tacky**
TACKIES *pl n*
TACKIFY *vb* give (eg rubber) a sticky feel
TACKILY ▸ **tacky**
TACKING ▸ **tack**
TACKLE *vb, n* **tackled, tackler, tackles**
TACKS ▸ **tack**
TACKY *adj*
TACNODE *n* point at which two branches of a curve have a common tangent
TACO *n* tortilla fried until crisp, served with a filling **tacos**
TACRINE *n* drug used to treat Alzheimer's disease
TACT *n* **tactful**
TACTIC *n*
TACTICS *n* art of directing military forces in battle
TACTILE *adj*
TACTION *n* act of touching
TACTISM *another word for* ▸ **taxis**
TACTS ▸ **tact**
TACTUAL *adj* caused by touch
TAD *n* small bit or piece
TADDIE *short for* ▸ **tadpole**
TADDIES ▸ **taddie**
TADPOLE *n*
TADS ▸ **tad**
TAE *Scots form of the verb* ▸ **toe**
TAED ▸ **tae**
TAEDIUM *archaic spelling of* ▸ **tedium**
TAEING ▸ **tae**
TAEL *n* unit of weight, used in the Far East **taels**
TAENIA *n* (in ancient Greece) a narrow fillet or headband for the hair **taeniae, taenias**
TAES ▸ **tae**
TAFFETA *n* **taffety**
TAFFIA = **tafia**
TAFFIAS ▸ **taffia**
TAFFIES ▸ **taffy**
TAFFY = **toffee**
TAFIA *n* type of rum, esp from Guyana or the Caribbean **tafias**
TAG *n, vb*
TAGETES *n* any of a genus of plants with yellow or orange flowers

TAGGANT *n* microscopic material added to substance to identify it
TAGGED ▸ **tag**
TAGGEE *n* one who has been made to wear a tag **taggees**
TAGGER *n* one who marks with a tag **taggers**
TAGGIER ▸ **taggy**
TAGGING ▸ **tag**
TAGGY *adj* (of wool, hair, etc) matted
TAGINE *n* large, heavy N African cooking pot with a conical lid **tagines**
TAGLESS *adj* having no tag
TAGLIKE *adj* resembling a tag
TAGLINE *n* funny line of joke
TAGMA *n* distinct region of the body of an arthropod **tagmata**
TAGMEME *n* class of speech elements all of which may fulfil the same grammatical role
TAGRAG = **ragtag**
TAGRAGS ▸ **tagrag**
TAGS ▸ **tag**
TAGUAN *n* nocturnal flying squirrel of the East Indies **taguans**
TAHA *n* type of South African bird **tahas**
TAHINA = **tahini**
TAHINAS ▸ **tahina**
TAHINI *n* paste made from ground sesame seeds **tahinis**
TAHR *n* goatlike mammal of mountainous regions of S and SW Asia **tahrs**
TAHSIL *n* administrative division of a zila in certain states in India **tahsils**
TAI *n* type of sea bream
TAIAHA *n* carved weapon in the form of a staff, now used in Māori ceremonial oratory **taiahas**
TAIGA *n* belt of coniferous forest **taigas**
TAIGLE *vb* entangle or impede **taigled, taigles**
TAIHOA *interj* hold on! no hurry!
TAIKO *n* large Japanese drum **taikos**
TAIL *n, adj, vb*
TAILARD *n* one having a tail
TAILED ▸ **tail**
TAILER *n* one that tails **tailers**
TAILFAN *n* fanned structure at the hind end of a lobster
TAILFIN *n* decorative projection at back of car
TAILFLY *n* in angling, the lowest fly on a wet-fly cast
TAILING *n* part of a beam, rafter, projecting brick or stone, etc, embedded in a wall
TAILLE *n* (in France before 1789) a tax levied by a king or overlord on his subjects **tailles**
TAILLIE *n* (in law) the limitation of an estate or interest to a person and the heirs of his body
TAILOR *n, vb* **tailors**
TAILS *adv* with the side of a coin that does not have a portrait of a head on it uppermost
TAILYE = **taillie**
TAILYES ▸ **tailye**
TAILZIE = **taillie**
TAIN *n* tinfoil used in backing mirrors **tains**
TAINT *vb, n* **tainted, taints**
TAIPAN *n* **taipans**
TAIRA = **tayra**
TAIRAS ▸ **taira**
TAIS ▸ **tai**
TAISCH *n* (in Scotland) apparition of a person whose death is imminent **taish**
TAISHES ▸ **taish**
TAIT = **tate**
TAITS ▸ **tait**
TAIVER = **taver**
TAIVERS ▸ **taiver**
TAIVERT *adj* Scots word meaning confused or bewildered
TAJ *n* tall conical cap worn as a mark of distinction by Muslims **tajes**

This word for a Muslim's cap is one

of the key words to remember for using the J.

TAJINE = **tagine**
TAJINES ▸ **tajine**
TAK *Scots variant spelling of* ▸ **take**
TAKA *n* standard monetary unit of Bangladesh, divided into 100 paise
TAKABLE ▸ **take**
TAKAHE *n* very rare flightless New Zealand bird **takahes**
TAKAS ▸ **taka**
TAKE *vb* remove from a place ▹ *n* one of a series of recordings from which the best will be used **taken**
TAKEOFF *n* act or process of making an aircraft airborne
TAKEOUT *n* shop or restaurant that sells such food
TAKER *n* person who agrees to take something that is offered **takers**
TAKES ▸ **take**
TAKEUP *n* claiming or acceptance of something that is due or available **takeups**
TAKHI *n* type of wild Mongolian horse **takhis, taki**
TAKIER ▸ **taky**
TAKIEST ▸ **taky**
TAKIN *n* bovid mammal of mountainous regions of S Asia
TAKING ▸ **take**
TAKINGS ▸ **take**
TAKINS ▸ **takin**
TAKIS ▸ **taki**
TAKKIES = **tackies**
TAKS ▸ **tak**
TAKY *adj* appealing
TALA *n* standard monetary unit of Samoa, divided into 100 sene
TALAK = **talaq**
TALAKS ▸ **talak**
TALANT *old variant of* ▸ **talon**
TALANTS ▸ **talant**
TALAQ *n* Muslim form of divorce **talaqs**

In Islamic law, a word for divorce: easy to miss because one tends not to think of words ending in Q.

TALAR *n* ankle-length robe
TALARIA *pl n* winged sandals, such as those worn by Hermes
TALARS ▸ **talar**
TALAS ▸ **tala**
TALAUNT *old variant of* ▸ **talon**
TALAYOT *n* ancient Balearic stone tower
TALBOT *n* ancient breed of large hound **talbots**
TALC *n, vb, adj* **talced**
TALCIER ▸ **talcy**
TALCING ▸ **talc**
TALCKED ▸ **talcky**
TALCKY = **talcy**
TALCOSE ▸ **talc**
TALCOUS ▸ **talc**
TALCS ▸ **talc**
TALCUM *n* white, grey, brown, or pale green mineral **talcums**
TALCY *adj* like, containing, or covered in talc
TALE *n*
TALEA *n* rhythmic pattern in certain mediaeval choral compositions **taleae**
TALEFUL *adj* having many tales
TALENT *n* **talents**
TALER = **thaler**
TALERS ▸ **taler**
TALES *n* group of persons summoned to fill vacancies on a jury panel
TALI ▸ **talus**
TALION *n* principle of making punishment correspond to the crime **talions**
TALIPAT = **talipot**
TALIPED *adj* having a club foot ▹ *n* club-footed person
TALIPES *n* congenital deformity of the foot by which it is twisted in any of various positions
TALIPOT *n* palm tree of the East Indies
TALK *vb, n*
TALKBOX *n* voice box
TALKED ▸ **talk**
TALKER ▸ **talk**
TALKERS ▸ **talk**
TALKIE *n* early film with a soundtrack

TALKIER ▸ **talky**
TALKIES ▸ **talkie**
TALKING *n* speech; the act of speaking
TALKS ▸ **talk**
TALKY *adj* containing too much dialogue or inconsequential talk
TALL *adj*
TALLAGE *n* tax levied on Crown lands and royal towns ▹ *vb* levy a tax (upon)
TALLAT = **tallet**
TALLATS ▸ **tallat**
TALLBOY *n*
TALLENT *n* plenty
TALLER ▸ **tall**
TALLEST ▸ **tall**
TALLET *n* loft **tallets**
TALLIED ▸ **tally**
TALLIER ▸ **tally**
TALLIES ▸ **tally**
TALLIS *variant of* ▸ **tallith**
TALLISH *adj* quite tall
TALLIT *variant of* ▸ **tallith**
TALLITH *n* shawl worn by Jewish males during religious services
TALLITS ▸ **tallit**
TALLOL *n* oily liquid used for making soaps, lubricants, etc **tallols**
TALLOT = **tallet**
TALLOTS ▸ **tallot**
TALLOW *n, vb* **tallows, tallowy**
TALLS ▸ **tall**
TALLY *vb, n*
TALLYHO *n* cry to encourage hounds when the quarry is sighted ▹ *vb* make the cry of tallyho
TALMA *n* short cloak **talmas**
TALMUD *n* primary source of Jewish religious law, consisting of the Mishnah and the Gemara **talmuds**
TALON *n* **taloned, talons**
TALOOKA = **taluk**
TALPA *n* sebaceous cyst **talpae, talpas**
TALUK *n* subdivision of a district **taluka**
TALUKAS ▸ **taluka**
TALUKS ▸ **taluk**
TALUS *n* bone of the ankle that articulates with the leg bones to form the ankle joint **taluses**
TALWEG = **thalweg**
TALWEGS ▸ **talweg**
TAM *n* type of hat
TAMABLE ▸ **tame**
TAMAL = **tamale**
TAMALE *n* Mexican dish of minced meat wrapped in maize husks and steamed **tamales**
TAMALS ▸ **tamal**
TAMANDU = **tamandua**
TAMANU *n* poon tree **tamanus**
TAMARA *n* powder consisting of cloves, cinnamon, fennel, coriander, etc
TAMARAO = **tamarau**
TAMARAS ▸ **tamara**
TAMARAU *n* small rare member of a cattle tribe in the Philippines
TAMARI *n* Japanese variety of soy sauce
TAMARIN *n* small monkey of South and Central America
TAMARIS ▸ **tamari**
TAMASHA *n* (in India) a show
TAMBAC = **tombac**
TAMBACS ▸ **tambac**
TAMBAK = **tombac**
TAMBAKS ▸ **tambak**
TAMBALA *n* unit of Malawian currency
TAMBER = **timbre**
TAMBERS ▸ **tamber**
TAMBOUR *n* embroidery frame consisting of two hoops ▹ *vb* embroider (fabric or a design) on a tambour
TAMBUR *n* old Turkish stringed instrument
TAMBURA *n* Middle-Eastern stringed instrument with a long neck
TAMBURS ▸ **tambur**
TAME *adj, vb* **tamed**
TAMEIN *n* Burmese skirt **tameins**
TAMELY, tamer, tamers, tames, tamest ▸ **tame**
TAMIN *n* thin woollen fabric **tamine**
TAMINES ▸ **tamine**
TAMING *n* act of making

(something) tame **tamings**
TAMINS ▸ **tamin**
TAMIS = **tammy**
TAMISE *n* type of thin cloth
TAMISES ▸ **tamis**
TAMMAR *n* small scrub wallaby **tammars**
TAMMIE *n* short for tam-o'shanter, a traditional Scottish hat
TAMMIED ▸ **tammy**
TAMMIES ▸ **tammy**
TAMMY *n* glazed woollen or mixed fabric ▹ *vb* strain (sauce, soup, etc) through a tammy
TAMP *vb* pack down by repeated taps
TAMPALA *n* Asian plant, eaten as food
TAMPAN *n* biting mite **tampans**
TAMPED ▸ **tamp**
TAMPER *vb*, *n* **tampers**
TAMPING *adj* very angry ▹ *n* act or instance of tamping
TAMPION *n* plug placed in a gun's muzzle to keep out moisture and dust
TAMPON *n*, *vb* **tampons**
TAMPS ▸ **tamp**
TAMS ▸ **tam**
TAN *n*, *vb*, *adj*
TANA *n* small Madagascan lemur
TANADAR *n* commanding officer of an Indian police station
TANAGER *n* American songbird with a short thick bill
TANAGRA *n* type of tanager
TANAS ▸ **tana**
TANBARK *n* bark of certain trees, esp the oak and hemlock, used as a source of tannin
TANDEM *n* **tandems**
TANDOOR *n* type of Indian clay oven
TANE *old Scottish variant of* ▸ **taken**
TANG *n*, *vb*
TANGA *n* triangular loincloth worn by indigenous peoples in tropical America **tangas**
TANGED ▸ **tang**
TANGELO *n* hybrid produced by crossing a tangerine tree with a grapefruit tree
TANGENT *n*
TANGHIN *n* poison formerly used in Madagascar to determine the guilt of crime suspects
TANGI *n* Māori funeral ceremony
TANGIE *n* water spirit of Orkney, appearing as a figure draped in seaweed, or as a seahorse
TANGIER ▸ **tangy**
TANGIES ▸ **tangie**
TANGING ▸ **tang**
TANGIS ▸ **tangi**
TANGLE *n*, *vb* **tangled, tangler, tangles, tangly**
TANGO *n*, *vb* **tangoed, tangos**
TANGRAM *n* type of Chinese puzzle
TANGS ▸ **tang**
TANGUN *n* small and sturdy Tibetan pony **tanguns**
TANGY *adj* having a pungent, fresh, or briny flavour or aroma
TANH *n* hyperbolic tangent **tanhs**
TANIST *n* heir apparent of a Celtic chieftain **tanists**
TANIWHA *n*
TANK *n*, *vb*
TANKA *n* Japanese verse form consisting of five lines
TANKAGE *n* capacity or contents of a tank or tanks
TANKARD *n*
TANKAS ▸ **tanka**
TANKED ▸ **tank**
TANKER *n* **tankers**
TANKFUL *n* quantity contained in a tank
TANKIA *n* type of boat used in Canton **tankias**
TANKIES ▸ **tanky**
TANKING *n* heavy defeat
TANKINI *n* swimming costume consisting of a camisole top and bikini briefs
TANKS ▸ **tank**
TANKY *n* die-hard communist

TANLING *n* suntanned person
TANNA *n* Indian police station or army base
TANNAGE *n* act or process of tanning
TANNAH = **tanna**
TANNAHS ▸ tannah
TANNAS ▸ tanna
TANNATE *n* any salt or ester of tannic acid
TANNED ▸ tan
TANNER ▸ tan
TANNERS ▸ tan
TANNERY *n*
TANNEST ▸ tan
TANNIC *adj* of, containing, or produced from tannin or tannic acid
TANNIE *n* in S Africa, title of respect used to refer to an elderly woman **tannies**
TANNIN *n*
TANNING ▸ tan
TANNINS ▸ tannin
TANNISH ▸ tan
TANNOY *n* sound-amplifying apparatus used as a public-address system ▹ *vb* announce (something) using a Tannoy system **tannoys**
TANREC = **tenrec**
TANRECS ▸ tanrec
TANS ▸ tan
TANSIES ▸ tansy
TANSY *n* yellow-flowered plant
TANTARA *n* blast, as on a trumpet or horn
TANTI *adj* old word for worthwhile
TANTIVY *adv* at full speed ▹ *interj* hunting cry, esp at full gallop
TANTO *adv* too much
TANTONY *n* runt
TANTRA *n* sacred books of Tantrism **tantras, tantric**
TANTRUM *n*
TANUKI *n* animal similar to a raccoon, found in Japan **tanukis**
TANYARD *n* part of a tannery
TAO *n* (in Confucian philosophy) the correct course of action
TAONGA *n* treasure **taongas**
TAOS ▸ tao
TAP *vb, n*
TAPA *n* inner bark of the paper mulberry
TAPALO *n* Latin American scarf, often patterned and brightly coloured **tapalos**
TAPAS *pl n* (in Spanish cookery) light snacks or appetizers
TAPE *n, vb* **taped**
TAPEN *adj* made of tape
TAPER, tapered, taperer, tapers, tapes ▸ tape
TAPET *n* example of tapestry
TAPETA ▸ tapetum
TAPETAL ▸ tapetum
TAPETI *n* forest rabbit of Brazil **tapetis**
TAPETS ▸ tapet
TAPETUM *n* layer of nutritive cells that surrounds developing spore cells
TAPHOLE *n* hole in a furnace for running off molten metal or slag
TAPING ▸ tape
TAPIOCA *n*
TAPIR *n* **tapirs**
TAPIS *n* tapestry or carpeting **tapises**
TAPIST *n* person who records read out printed matter in an audio format **tapists**
TAPLASH *n* dregs of beer
TAPPA = **tapa**
TAPPAS ▸ tappa
TAPPED ▸ tap
TAPPER *n* person who taps **tappers**
TAPPET *n* **tappets**
TAPPICE *vb* hide
TAPPING ▸ tap
TAPPIT *adj* crested; topped
TAPROOM *n* public bar in a hotel or pub
TAPROOT *n*
TAPS ▸ tap
TAPSMAN *n* old word for a barman **tapsmen**
TAPSTER *n* barman
TAPSTRY *adj* relating to tapestry
TAPU *adj* sacred ▹ *n* Māori religious or superstitious restriction on something ▹ *vb* put a tapu on something

tapued, tapuing, tapus
TAR *n, vb*
TARA = **taro**
TARAIRE *n* type of New Zealand tree
TARAMA *n* cod roe **taramas**
TARAMEA *n* variety of New Zealand speargrass
TARAND *n* northern animal of legend, now supposed to have been the reindeer **tarands**
TARAS ▸ **tara**
TARBOY *n* boy who applies tar to the skin of sheep cut during shearing **tarboys**
TARBUSH = **tarboosh**
TARCEL = **tarcel**
TARCELS ▸ **tarcel**
TARDIED, tardier, tardies, tardily ▸ **tardy**
TARDIVE *adj* tending to develop late
TARDO *adj* (of music) slow; to be played slowly
TARDY *adj, vb*
TARDYON *n* particle travelling slower than the speed of light
TARE *n* weight of the wrapping or container of goods ▹ *vb* weigh (a package, etc) in order to calculate the amount of tare **tared, tares**
TARGA *n as in* **targa top** denotes removable hard roof on a car
TARGE *vb* interrogate **targed, targes**
TARGET *n, vb* **targets**
TARGING ▸ **targe**
TARIFF *n, vb* **tariffs**
TARING ▸ **tare**
TARINGS ▸ **tare**
TARMAC *See also* ▸ **macadam**
TARMACS ▸ **tarmac**
TARN *n*
TARNAL *adj* damned ▹ *adv* extremely
TARNISH *vb, n*
TARNS ▸ **tarn**
TARO *n* plant with a large edible rootstock
TAROC *old variant of* ▸ **tarot**
TAROCS ▸ **taroc**
TAROK *old variant of* ▸ **tarot**
TAROKS ▸ **tarok**
TAROS ▸ **taro**
TAROT *n, adj* **tarots**
TARP *informal word for* > **tarpaulin**
TARPAN *n* European wild horse common in prehistoric times **tarpans**
TARPON *n* large silvery clupeoid game fish found in warm Atlantic waters **tarpons**
TARPS ▸ **tarp**
TARRAS = **trass**
TARRE *vb* old word meaning to provoke or goad
TARRED ▸ **tar**
TARRES ▸ **tarre**
TARRIED ▸ **tarry**
TARRIER ▸ **tarry**
TARRIES ▸ **tarry**
TARRING ▸ **tar**
TARROCK *n* seabird
TARROW *vb* exhibit reluctance **tarrows**
TARRY *vb, n, adj*
TARS ▸ **tar**
TARSAL *adj* of the tarsus or tarsi ▹ *n* tarsal bone **tarsals**
TARSEAL *n*
TARSEL = **tercel**
TARSELS ▸ **tarsel**
TARSI ▸ **tarsus**
TARSIA *another term for* > **intarsia**
TARSIAS ▸ **tarsia**
TARSIER *n* small nocturnal primate of the E Indies, which has very large eyes
TARSUS *n*
TART *n, adj, vb*
TARTAN *n*
TARTANA *n* small Mediterranean sailing boat **tartane**
TARTANS ▸ **tartan**
TARTAR *n*
TARTARE *n* mayonnaise sauce mixed with hard-boiled egg yolks, herbs, etc
TARTARS ▸ **tartar**
TARTED ▸ **tart**
TARTER ▸ **tart**
TARTEST ▸ **tart**
TARTIER ▸ **tarty**
TARTILY ▸ **tarty**
TARTINE *n* slice of bread with butter or jam spread on it
TARTING ▸ **tart**

TARTISH ▸ **tart**
TARTLET *n* individual pastry case with a filling of fruit or other sweet or savoury mixture
TARTLY ▸ **tart**
TARTS ▸ **tart**
TARTUFE = **tartuffe**
TARTUFO *n* Italian mousse-like chocolate dessert
TARTY *adj* provocative in a cheap and bawdy way
TARWEED *n* resinous Californian plant
TARZAN *n* man with great physical strength **tarzans**
TAS ▸ **tass**
TASAR = **tussore**
TASARS ▸ **tasar**
TASBIH *n* form of Islamic prayer **tasbihs**
TASER *vb* use a Taser stun gun on (someone) **tasered, tasers**
TASH *vb* stain or besmirch **tashed, tashes, tashing**
TASK *n, vb*
TASKBAR *n* area of computer screen showing what programs are running
TASKED, tasker, taskers, tasking, tasks ▸ **task**
TASLET = **tasset**
TASLETS ▸ **taslet**
TASS *n* cup, goblet, or glass
TASSE = **tasset**
TASSEL *n, vb* **tassell, tassels**
TASSES ▸ **tasse**
TASSET *n* piece of armour to protect the thigh **tassets**
TASSIE = **tass**
TASSIES ▸ **tassie**
TASTE *n, vb* **tasted**
TASTER *n* person employed to test the quality of food or drink by tasting it **tasters**
TASTES ▸ **taste**
TASTIER ▸ **tasty**
TASTILY ▸ **tasty**
TASTING ▸ **taste**
TASTY *adj*
TAT *n* tatty or tasteless article(s) ▹ *vb* make (something) by tatting
TATAMI *n* thick rectangular mat of woven straw **tatamis**
TATAR *n* brutal person **tatars**
TATE *n* small tuft of fibre
TATER *n* potato **taters**
TATES ▸ **tate**
TATH *vb* (of cattle) to defecate **tathed, tathing, taths**
TATIE = **tattie**
TATIES ▸ **tatie**
TATLER *old variant of* ▸ **tattler**
TATLERS ▸ **tatler**
TATOU *n* armadillo
TATOUAY *n* large armadillo of South America
TATOUS ▸ **tatou**
TATS ▸ **tat**
TATSOI *n* variety of Chinese cabbage **tatsois**
TATT = **tat**
TATTED ▸ **tat**
TATTER *vb* make or become torn **tatters**
TATTERY = **tattered**
TATTIE *Scot or dialect word for* ▸ **potato**
TATTIER ▸ **tatty**
TATTIES ▸ **tattie**
TATTILY ▸ **tatty**
TATTING ▸ **tat**
TATTLE *n, vb* **tattled**
TATTLER *n* person who tattles
TATTLES ▸ **tattle**
TATTOO *n, vb* **tattoos, tattow**
TATTOWS ▸ **tattow**
TATTS ▸ **tatt**
TATTY *adj*
TATU *old variant of* ▸ **tattoo**
TATUED ▸ **tatu**
TATUING ▸ **tatu**
TATUS ▸ **tatu**
TAU *n* 19th letter in the Greek alphabet
TAUBE *n* type of German aeroplane **taubes**
TAUGHT ▸ **teach**
TAUHINU *New Zealand name for* ▸ **poplar**
TAUHOU = **silvereye**
TAUHOUS ▸ **tauhou**
TAUIWI *n* Māori term for the non-Māori people of New Zealand **tauiwis**
TAULD *vb* old Scots variant of told

TAUNT *vb, n, adj* **taunted, taunter, taunts**
TAUON *n* negatively charged elementary particle **tauons**
TAUPATA *n* New Zealand shrub or tree
TAUPE *adj* brownish-grey ▷ *n* brownish-grey colour **taupes**
TAUPIE = **tawpie**
TAUPIES ▶ **taupie**
TAUREAN *adj* born under or characteristic of Taurus **tauric**
TAURINE *adj* of, relating to, or resembling a bull ▷ *n* substance obtained from the bile of animals
TAUS ▶ **tau**
TAUT *adj, vb*
TAUTAUG = **tautog**
TAUTED ▶ **taut**
TAUTEN *vb* **tautens**
TAUTER ▶ **taut**
TAUTEST ▶ **taut**
TAUTING ▶ **taut**
TAUTIT *adj* Scots word meaning tangled
TAUTLY ▶ **taut**
TAUTOG *n* large dark-coloured wrasse, used as a food fish **tautogs**
TAUTS ▶ **taut**
TAV *n* 23rd and last letter in the Hebrew alphabet
TAVA *n* thick Indian frying pan **tavah**
TAVAHS ▶ **tavah**
TAVAS ▶ **tava**
TAVER *vb* wander about **tavered**
TAVERN *n*
TAVERNA *n* (in Greece) a guesthouse that has its own bar
TAVERNS ▶ **tavern**
TAVERS ▶ **taver**
TAVERT *adj* bewildered or confused
TAVS ▶ **tav**
TAW *vb* convert skins into leather
TAWA *n* tall timber tree from New Zealand
TAWAI *n* New Zealand beech **tawais**
TAWAS ▶ **tawa**
TAWDRY *adj, n*
TAWED ▶ **taw**
TAWER ▶ **taw**
TAWERS ▶ **taw**
TAWERY *n* place where tawing is carried out
TAWHAI = **tawai**
TAWHAIS ▶ **tawhai**
TAWHIRI *n* small New Zealand tree with wavy green glossy leaves
TAWIE *adj* easily persuaded or managed **tawier, tawiest**
TAWING ▶ **taw**
TAWINGS ▶ **taw**
TAWNEY = **tawny**
TAWNEYS ▶ **tawney**
TAWNIER ▶ **tawny**
TAWNIES ▶ **tawny**
TAWNILY ▶ **tawny**
TAWNY *adj, n*
TAWPIE *n* foolish or maladroit girl **tawpies**
TAWS = **tawse**
TAWSE *n* leather strap with one end cut into thongs ▷ *vb* punish (someone) with or as if with a tawse **tawsed, tawses, tawsing**
TAWT = **taut; tawted, tawtie, tawtier, tawting, tawts**
TAX *n, vb*
TAXA ▶ **taxon**
TAXABLE *adj* capable of being taxed ▷ *n* person, income, property, etc, that is subject to tax **taxably**
TAXED ▶ **tax**
TAXEME *n* any element of speech that may differentiate meaning **taxemes, taxemic**
TAXER ▶ **tax**
TAXERS ▶ **tax**
TAXES ▶ **tax**
TAXI *n, vb* **taxicab, taxied**
TAXIES ▶ **taxis**
TAXIING ▶ **taxi**
TAXIMAN *n* taxi driver **taximen**
TAXING *adj* demanding, onerous
TAXINGS ▶ **tax**
TAXIS *n* movement of a cell or organism in response to an external stimulus ▷ *n* ancient Greek army unit
TAXITE *n* type of volcanic rock **taxites, taxitic**

TAXIWAY *n* marked path along which aircraft taxi to or from a runway, parking area, etc
TAXLESS ▶ **tax**
TAXMAN *n* collector of taxes **taxmen**
TAXOL *n* trademarked anti-cancer drug **taxols**
TAXON *n* any taxonomic group or rank **taxons**
TAXOR ▶ **tax**
TAXORS ▶ **tax**
TAXPAID *adj* (of taxable products, esp wine) having had the applicable tax paid already
TAXUS *n* genus of conifers
TAXWISE *adv* regarding tax
TAXYING ▶ **taxi**
TAY *Irish dialect word for* ▶ **tea**
TAYRA *n* large arboreal mammal of Central and South America **tayras**
TAYS ▶ **tay**
TAZZA *n* wine cup with a shallow bowl and a circular foot **tazzas, tazze**
TCHICK *vb* make a clicking noise with the tongue **tchicks**
TE *n* (in tonic sol-fa) seventh degree of any major scale
TEA *n, vb*
TEABAG *n* porous bag of tea leaves for infusion **teabags**
TEABOWL *n* small bowl used (instead of a teacup) for serving tea
TEABOX *n* box for storing tea
TEACAKE *n*
TEACART *n* trolley from which tea is served
TEACH *vb*
TEACHER *n*
TEACHES ▶ **teach**
TEACHIE *old form of* ▶ **tetchy**
TEACUP *n* cup out of which tea may be drunk **teacups**
TEAD *old word for* ▶ **torch**
TEADE = **tead**
TEADES ▶ **teade**
TEADS ▶ **tead**
TEAED ▶ **tea**
TEAGLE *vb* raise or hoist using a tackle **teagled, teagles**
TEAING ▶ **tea**
TEAK *n* **teaks**
TEAL *n*
TEALIKE *adj* resembling tea
TEALS ▶ **teal**
TEAM *n, vb* **teamed, teamer, teamers, teaming, teams**
TEAPOT *n* **teapots**
TEAPOY *n* small table or stand with a tripod base **teapoys**
TEAR *n, vb* **teared, tearer, tearers**
TEARFUL *adj*
TEARGAS *n* gas or vapour that makes the eyes smart and water ▷ *vb* deploy teargas against
TEARIER ▶ **teary**
TEARILY ▶ **teary**
TEARING ▶ **tear**
TEAROOM = **teashop**
TEARS ▶ **tear**
TEARY *adj* characterized by, covered with, or secreting tears
TEAS ▶ **tea**
TEASE *vb, n* **teased**
TEASEL *n* plant with prickly leaves and flowers ▷ *vb* tease (a fabric) **teasels**
TEASER *n* annoying or difficult problem **teasers**
TEASES ▶ **tease**
TEASHOP *n* restaurant where tea and light refreshments are served
TEASING ▶ **tease**
TEAT *n* **teated**
TEATIME *n* late afternoon
TEATS ▶ **teat**
TEAWARE *n* implements for brewing and serving tea
TEAZE *old variant of* ▶ **tease**
TEAZED ▶ **teaze**
TEAZEL = **teasel**
TEAZELS ▶ **teazel**
TEAZES ▶ **teaze**
TEAZING ▶ **teaze**
TEAZLE = **teasel**
TEAZLED ▶ **teazle**
TEAZLES ▶ **teazle**
TEBBAD *n* sandstorm **tebbads**

TEC *short for* > **detective**
TECH *n*
TECHED *adj* showing slight insanity
TECHIE *n* person who is skilled in the use of technology ▷ *adj* relating to or skilled in the use of technology
TECHIER ▶ **techy**
TECHIES ▶ **techie**
TECHILY ▶ **techy**
TECHNIC *another word for* > **technique**
TECHNO *n* type of electronic dance music with a very fast beat **technos**
TECHS ▶ **tech**
TECHY = **techie**
TECKEL *n* dachshund **teckels**
TECS ▶ **tec**
TECTA ▶ **tectum**
TECTAL ▶ **tectum**
TECTITE = **tektite**
TECTRIX *another name for* ▶ **covert**
TECTUM *n* any roof-like structure in the body **tectums**
TED *vb* shake out (hay), so as to dry it **tedded**
TEDDER *n* machine equipped with a series of small rotating forks for tedding hay **tedders**
TEDDIE = **teddy**
TEDDIES ▶ **teddy**
TEDDING ▶ **ted**
TEDDY *n*
TEDIER ▶ **tedy**
TEDIEST ▶ **tedy**
TEDIOUS *adj*
TEDIUM *n* **tediums**
TEDS ▶ **ted**
TEDY = **tedious**
TEE *n, vb* **teed, teeing**
TEEK *adj* in Indian English, well
TEEL = **sesame**
TEELS ▶ **teel**
TEEM *vb* **teemed, teemer, teemers, teemful, teeming, teems**
TEEN *n* affliction or woe ▷ *n* teenager ▷ *vb* set alight
TEENAGE *adj, n*
TEEND = **tind**
TEENDED ▶ **teend**
TEENDS ▶ **teend**
TEENE = **teen**
TEENED ▶ **teen**
TEENER ▶ **teen**
TEENERS ▶ **teen**
TEENES ▶ **teene**
TEENFUL ▶ **teen**
TEENIER ▶ **teeny**
TEENING ▶ **teen**
TEENS ▶ **teen**
TEENSY = **teeny**
TEENTSY = **teeny**
TEENTY = **teeny**
TEENY *adj* extremely small
TEEPEE = **tepee**
TEEPEES ▶ **teepee**
TEER *vb* smear; daub **teered, teering, teers**
TEES ▶ **tee**
TEETER *vb* **teeters**
TEETH ▶ **tooth**
TEETHE *vb* **teethed**
TEETHER *n* object for an infant to bite on during teething
TEETHES ▶ **teethe**
TEF *n* annual grass, of NE Africa, grown for its grain **teff**
TEFFS ▶ **teff**
TEFLON *n* substance used in nonstick cooking vessels **teflons**
TEFS ▶ **tef**
TEG *n* two-year-old sheep **tegg**
TEGGS ▶ **tegg**
TEGMEN *n* either of the leathery forewings of the cockroach and related insects **tegmina**
TEGS ▶ **teg**
TEGU *n* large South American lizard
TEGUA *n* type of moccasin **teguas**
TEGULA *n* one of a pair of coverings of the forewings of certain insects **tegulae**
TEGULAR *adj* of, relating to, or resembling a tile or tiles
TEGUMEN = **tegmen**
TEGUS ▶ **tegu**
TEHR = **tahr**
TEHRS ▶ **tehr**
TEHSIL *n* administrative region in some S Asian countries **tehsils**
TEIID *n* member of the Teiidae family of lizards **teiids**

TEIL *n* lime tree **teils**
TEIN *n* monetary unit of Kazakhstan
TEIND *Scot and northern English word for* ▸ **tithe**
TEINDED ▸ **teind**
TEINDS ▸ **teind**
TEINS ▸ **tein**
TEKKIE *variant of* ▸ **techie**
TEKKIES ▸ **tekkie**
TEKTITE *n* small dark glassy object found in several areas around the world
TEL = **tell**
TELA *n* any delicate tissue or weblike structure **telae**
TELAMON *n* column in the form of a male figure
TELARY *adj* capable of spinning a web
TELCO *n* telecommunications company **telcos**
TELD = **tauld**
TELE = **telly**
TELECOM *n* telecommunications
TELEDU *n* badger of SE Asia and Indonesia **teledus**
TELEFAX *another word for* ▸ **fax**
TELEGA *n* rough four-wheeled cart used in Russia **telegas**
TELEMAN *n* noncommissioned officer in the US navy **telemen**
TELEOST *n* bony fish with rayed fins and a swim bladder ▹ *adj* of, relating to, or belonging to this type of fish
TELEPIC *n* feature-length film made for television
TELERAN *n* electronic navigational aid
TELERGY *n* name for the form of energy supposedly transferred during telepathy
TELES ▸ **tele**
TELESES ▸ **telesis**
TELESIS *n* purposeful use of natural and social processes to obtain specific social goals
TELESM *n* talisman **telesms**
TELETEX *n* international means of communicating text between a variety of terminals
TELEX *n*, *vb* **telexed, telexes**
TELFER *n* overhead transport system **telfers**
TELFORD *n* road built using a method favoured by Thomas Telford
TELIA ▸ **telium**
TELIAL ▸ **telium**
TELIC *adj* directed or moving towards some goal
TELIUM *n* spore-producing body of some rust fungi in which the teliospores are formed
TELL *vb* make known in words ▹ *n* large mound resulting from the accumulation of rubbish
TELLAR = **tiller**
TELLARS ▸ **tellar**
TELLEN = **tellin**
TELLENS ▸ **tellen**
TELLER *n*, *vb* **tellers**
TELLIES ▸ **telly**
TELLIN *n* slim marine bivalve molluscs that live in intertidal sand
TELLING ▸ **tell**
TELLINS ▸ **tellin**
TELLS ▸ **tell**
TELLUS *n* earth
TELLY *n* **tellys**
TELNET *n* system allowing remote access to other computers on the same network ▹ *vb* use a telnet system **telnets**
TELOI ▸ **telos**
TELOME *n* fundamental unit of a plant's structure **telomes, telomic**
TELOS *n* objective; ultimate purpose
TELPHER = **telferage**
TELS ▸ **tel**
TELSON *n* segment of the body of crustaceans and arachnids **telsons**
TELT = **tauld**

TEMBLOR *n* earthquake or earth tremor
TEME *old variant of* ▶ **team**
TEMED ▶ **teme**
TEMENE ▶ **temenos**
TEMENOS *n* sacred area, esp one surrounding a temple
TEMES ▶ **teme**
TEMP = **temporary**
TEMPED ▶ **temp**
TEMPEH *n* fermented soya beans **tempehs**
TEMPER *n, vb*
TEMPERA *n*
TEMPERS ▶ **temper**
TEMPEST *n, vb*
TEMPI ▶ **tempo**
TEMPING ▶ **temp**
TEMPLAR *n* lawyer who has chambers in the Inner or Middle Temple in London
TEMPLE *n* **templed, temples**
TEMPLET = **template**
TEMPO *n*
TEMPORE *adv* in the time of
TEMPOS ▶ **tempo**
TEMPS ▶ **temp**
TEMPT *vb* **tempted, tempter, tempts**
TEMPURA *n* Japanese dish of seafood or vegetables dipped in batter and deep-fried
TEMS = **temse**
TEMSE *vb* sieve **temsed, temses, temsing**
TEN *n, adj*
TENABLE *adj* **tenably**
TENACE *n* holding of two nonconsecutive high cards of a suit, such as the ace and queen **tenaces**
TENAIL = **tenaille**
TENAILS ▶ **tenail**
TENANCY *n* temporary possession of property owned by somebody else
TENANT *n, vb* **tenants**
TENCH *n* **tenches**
TEND *vb* **tended**
TENDENZ = **tendency**
TENDER *adj, vb, n* **tenders**
TENDING ▶ **tend**
TENDON *n* **tendons**
TENDRE *n* care **tendres**
TENDRIL *n*
TENDRON *n* shoot
TENDS ▶ **tend**
TENDU *n* position in ballet **tendus**
TENE = **teen**
TENES ▶ **tene**
TENET *n* **tenets**
TENFOLD *n* one tenth
TENGE *n* standard monetary unit of Kazakhstan **tenges**
TENIA = **taenia**
TENIAE ▶ **tenia**

> This plural of **tenia**, a kind of hair-ribbon, is another of those 6-letter words which come in useful for dumping a surplus of vowels.

TENIAS ▶ **tenia**
TENIOID ▶ **tenia**
TENNE *n* tawny colour
TENNER *n* **tenners**
TENNES ▶ **tenne**
TENNIES ▶ **tenny**
TENNIS *n*
TENNIST *n* tennis player
TENNO *n* formal title of the Japanese emperor **tennos**
TENNY = **tenne**
TENON *n, vb* **tenoned, tenoner, tenons**
TENOR *n, adj* **tenors, tenour**
TENOURS ▶ **tenour**
TENPIN *n* one of the pins used in tenpin bowling **tenpins**
TENREC *n* small mammal resembling hedgehogs or shrews **tenrecs**
TENS ▶ **ten**
TENSE *adj, vb, n* **tensed, tensely, tenser, tenses, tensest**
TENSILE *adj*
TENSING ▶ **tense**
TENSION *n, vb* **tensity**
TENSIVE *adj* of or causing tension or strain
TENSON *n* type of French lyric poem **tensons**
TENSOR *n* any muscle that can cause a part to become firm or tense **tensors**
TENT *n, vb*
TENTAGE *n* tents collectively
TENTED ▶ **tent**
TENTER ▶ **tent**
TENTERS ▶ **tent**

TENTFUL *n* number of people or objects that can fit in a tent
TENTH *n* (of) number ten in a series ▷ *adj* coming after the ninth in numbering or counting order, position, time, etc ▷ *adv* after the ninth person, position, event, etc **tenthly, tenths**
TENTIE *adj* wary **tentier**
TENTIGO *n* morbid preoccupation with sex
TENTING ▶ **tent**
TENTS ▶ **tent**
TENTY = **tentie**
TENUE *n* deportment
TENUES ▶ **tenuis**
TENUIS *n* (in the grammar of classical Greek) any of the voiceless stops
TENUITY ▶ **tenuous**
TENUOUS *adj*
TENURE *n*, *vb*
TENURED *adj* having tenure of office
TENURES ▶ **tenure**
TENUTI ▶ **tenuto**
TENUTO *adv* (of a note) to be held for or beyond its full time value ▷ *vb* note sustained thus **tenutos**
TENZON = **tenson**
TENZONS ▶ **tenzon**
TEOPAN *n* enclosure surrounding a teocalli **teopans**
TEPA *n* type of tree native to South America
TEPAL *n* subdivisions of a perianth **tepals**
TEPAS ▶ **tepa**
TEPEE *n* **tepees**
TEPEFY *vb* make or become tepid
TEPHRA *n* solid matter ejected during a volcanic eruption **tephras**
TEPID *adj* **tepider, tepidly**
TEPOY = **teapoy**
TEPOYS ▶ **tepoy**
TEQUILA *n*
TERAI *n* felt hat with a wide brim worn in subtropical regions **terais**
TERAOHM *n* unit of resistance equal to 10^{12} ohms
TERAPH *n* household god or image venerated by ancient Semitic peoples
TERAS *n* monstrosity; teratism **terata**
TERBIA *n* amorphous white insoluble powder **terbias**
TERBIC ▶ **terbium**
TERBIUM *n* rare metallic element
TERCE *n* third of the seven canonical hours of the divine office
TERCEL *n* male falcon or hawk, esp as used in falconry **tercels**
TERCES ▶ **terce**
TERCET *n* group of three lines of verse that rhyme together **tercets**
TERCIO *n* regiment of Spanish or Italian infantry **tercios**
TEREBIC *adj as in* **terebic acid** white crystalline carboxylic acid produced by the action of nitric acid on turpentine
TEREBRA *n* ancient Roman device used for boring holes in defensive walls
TEREDO *n* marine mollusc that bores into and destroys submerged timber **teredos**
TEREFA = **tref**
TEREFAH = **tref**
TEREK *n* type of sandpiper **tereks**
TERES *n* shoulder muscle
TERETE *adj* (esp of plant parts) smooth and usually cylindrical and tapering **teretes**
TERF *old variant of* ▶ **turf**
TERFE *old variant of* ▶ **turf**
TERFES ▶ **terfe**
TERFS ▶ **terf**
TERGA ▶ **tergum**
TERGAL ▶ **tergum**
TERGITE *n* constituent part of a tergum
TERGUM *n* cuticular plate covering the

dorsal surface of a body segment of an arthropod
TERM *n*, *vb* **termed**
TERMER = **termor**
TERMERS ▸ **termer**
TERMING ▸ **term**
TERMINI > **terminus**
TERMITE *n*
TERMLY *n* publication issued once a term
TERMOR *n* person who holds an estate for a term of years or until he dies **termors**
TERMS ▸ **term**
TERN *n* **ternal**
TERNARY *adj*, *n*
TERNATE *adj* (esp of a leaf) consisting of three leaflets or other parts
TERNE *n* alloy of lead containing tin and antimony ▹ *vb* coat with this alloy **terned, ternes, terning**
TERNION *n* group of three
TERNS ▸ **tern**
TERPENE *n* unsaturated hydrocarbon found in the essential oils of many plants
TERRA *n* (in legal contexts) earth or land
TERRACE *n*, *vb*
TERRAE ▸ **terra**
TERRAIN = **terrane**
TERRANE *n* series of rock formations
TERRAS = **trass**
TERREEN *old variant of* ▸ **tureen**
TERRENE *adj* of or relating to the earth ▹ *n* land
TERRET *n* ring on a harness saddle through which the reins are passed **terrets**
TERRIER *n*
TERRIES ▸ **terry**
TERRIFY *vb*
TERRINE *n* earthenware dish with a lid
TERRIT = **terret**
TERRITS ▸ **territ**
TERROIR *n* combination of factors that gives a wine its distinctive character
TERROR *n* **terrors**
TERRY *n*
TERSE *adj* **tersely, terser, tersest**
TERSION *n* action of rubbing off or wiping
TERTIA = **tercio**
TERTIAL = **tertiary**
TERTIAN *adj* (of a fever or the symptoms of a disease) occurring every other day ▹ *n* tertian fever or symptoms
TERTIAS ▸ **tertia**
TERTIUM *adj as in* **tertium quid** unknown or indefinite thing related in some way to two known or definite things, but distinct from both
TERTIUS *n* third (in a group)
TERTS *n* card game using 32 cards
TES ▸ **te**
TESLA *n* derived SI unit of magnetic flux density **teslas**
TESSERA *n* small square tile used in mosaics
TEST *vb*, *n*
TESTA *n* hard outer layer of a seed
TESTACY ▸ **testate**
TESTAE ▸ **testa**
TESTATE *adj* having left a valid will ▹ *n* person who dies and leaves a legally valid will
TESTE *n* witness
TESTED ▸ **test**
TESTEE *n* person subjected to a test **testees**
TESTER *n* person or thing that tests or is used for testing
TESTERN *vb* give (someone) a teston
TESTERS ▸ **tester**
TESTES ▸ **testis**
TESTIER ▸ **testy**
TESTIFY *vb*
TESTILY ▸ **testy**
TESTING ▸ **test**
TESTIS = **testicle**
TESTON *n* French silver coin of the 16th century **testons, testoon**
TESTRIL = **testrill**
TESTS ▸ **test**
TESTUDO *n* protective cover used by the ancient Roman army
TESTY *adj*
TET = **teth**
TETANAL ▸ **tetanus**

TETANIC *adj* of, relating to, or producing tetanus or the spasms of tetanus ▷ *n* tetanic drug or agent
TETANUS *n*
TETANY *n* abnormal increase in the excitability of nerves and muscles
TETCHED = **teched**
TETCHY *adj*
TETE *n* elaborate hairstyle **tetes**
TETH *n* ninth letter of the Hebrew alphabet
TETHER *n, vb* **tethers**
TETHS ▸ **teth**
TETOTUM = **teetotum**
TETRA *n* brightly coloured tropical freshwater fish
TETRACT *n* sponge spicule with four rays
TETRAD *n* group or series of four **tetrads**
TETRAS ▸ **tetra**
TETRI *n* currency unit of Georgia **tetris**
TETRODE *n* electronic valve having four electrodes
TETRYL *n* yellow crystalline explosive solid used in detonators **tetryls**
TETS ▸ **tet**
TETTER *n* blister or pimple ▷ *vb* cause a tetter to erupt (on) **tetters**
TETTIX *n* cicada
TEUCH *Scots variant of* ▸ **tough**
TEUCHAT *Scots variant of* ▸ **tewit**
TEUCHER ▸ **teuch**
TEUGH = **teuch**
TEUGHER ▸ **teugh**
TEUGHLY ▸ **teugh**
TEW *vb* work hard
TEWART = **tuart**
TEWARTS ▸ **tewart**
TEWED ▸ **tew**
TEWEL *n* horse's rectum **tewels**
TEWHIT = **tewit**
TEWHITS ▸ **tewhit**
TEWING ▸ **tew**
TEWIT *n* lapwing **tewits**
TEWS ▸ **tew**
TEX *n* unit of weight used to measure yarn density
TEXAS *n* structure on the upper deck of a paddle-steamer **texases**
TEXES ▸ **tex**
TEXT *n, vb* **texted**
TEXTER *n* person who communicates by text messaging **texters**
TEXTILE *n, adj*
TEXTING ▸ **text**
TEXTS ▸ **text**
TEXTUAL *adj* of, based on, or relating to, a text or texts
TEXTURE *n, vb*
THACK *Scots word for* ▸ **thatch**
THACKED ▸ **thack**
THACKS ▸ **thack**
THAE *Scots word for* ▸ **those**
THAGI = **thuggee**
THAGIS ▸ **thagi**
THAIM *Scots variant of* ▸ **them**
THAIRM *n* catgut **thairms**
THALAMI > **thalamus**
THALE *n as in* **thale cress** cruciferous wall plant
THALER *n* former German, Austrian, or Swiss silver coin **thalers**
THALI *n* meal consisting of several small dishes accompanied by rice, bread, etc
THALIAN *adj* of or relating to comedy
THALIS ▸ **thali**
THALLI ▸ **thallus**
THALLIC *adj* of or containing thallium
THALLUS *n* undifferentiated vegetative body of algae, fungi, and lichens
THALWEG *n* longitudinal outline of a riverbed from source to mouth
THAN *prep, n*
THANA = **tana**
THANAGE *n* state of being a thane
THANAH = **tana**
THANAHS ▸ **thanah**
THANAS ▸ **thana**
THANE *n* Anglo-Saxon or medieval Scottish nobleman **thanes**
THANG *n* thing
THANGKA *n* (in Tibetan Buddhism) a religious painting on a scroll

THANGS ▸ **thang**
THANK *vb* **thanked**
THANKEE *interj* thank you
THANKER ▸ **thank**
THANKIT *adj as in* **be thankit** thank God
THANKS *pl n, interj*
THANNA = **tana**
THANNAH = **tana**
THANNAS ▸ **thanna**
THANS ▸ **than**
THAR = **tahr**
THARM *n* stomach **tharms**
THARS ▸ **thar**
THAT *pron*
THATCH *n, vb*
THATCHT *old variant of* > **thatched**
THATCHY ▸ **thatch**
THAW *vb, n* **thawed, thawer, thawers**
THAWIER ▸ **thawy**
THAWING ▸ **thaw**
THAWS ▸ **thaw**
THAWY *adj* tending to thaw
THE *determiner*
THEATER = **theatre**
THEATRE *n*
THEAVE *n* young ewe **theaves**
THEBE *n* inner satellite of Jupiter discovered in 1979 **thebes**
THECA *n* enclosing organ, cell, or spore case **thecae, thecal, thecate**
THEE *pron, vb* **theed, theeing**
THEEK *Scots variant of* ▸ **thatch**
THEEKED ▸ **theek**
THEEKS ▸ **theek**
THEELIN *trade name for* ▸ **estrone**
THEELOL *n* estriol
THEES ▸ **thee**
THEFT *n* **thefts**
THEGN = **thane**
THEGNLY ▸ **thegn**
THEGNS ▸ **thegn**
THEIC *n* person who drinks excessive amounts of tea **theics**
THEIN *old variant of* ▸ **thane**
THEINE *another name for* > **caffeine**
THEINES ▸ **theine**
THEINS ▸ **thein**
THEIR *determiner*
THEIRS *pron*
THEISM *n* belief in a God or gods **theisms, theist, theists**
THELF *n* old contraction of "the element" **thelves**
THEM *pron*
THEMA *n* theme **themata**
THEME *n, vb* **themed, themes, theming**
THEN *adv, pron, adj, n*
THENAGE *old variant of* ▸ **thanage**
THENAL *adj* of or relating to the thenar
THENAR *n* palm of the hand ▷ *adj* of or relating to the palm or the region at the base of the thumb **thenars**
THENCE *adv*
THENS ▸ **then**
THEOCON *n*
THEOLOG = **theologue**
THEORBO *n* obsolete form of the lute, having two necks
THEOREM *n*
THEORIC *n* theory; conjecture
THEORY *n*
THEOW *n* slave in Anglo-Saxon Britain **theows**
THERAPY *n*
THERE *adv, n*
THEREAT *adv* at that point or time
THEREBY *adv*
THEREIN *adv* in or into that place or thing
THEREOF *adv* of or concerning that or it
THEREON *archaic word for* > **thereupon**
THERES ▸ **there**
THERETO *adv* that or it
THERIAC *n* ointment or potion used as an antidote to a poison
THERIAN *n* animal of the class Theria, a subclass of mammals
THERM *n*
THERMAE *pl n* public baths or hot springs, esp in ancient Greece or Rome
THERMAL *adj, n*
THERME *old variant of* ▸ **therm**
THERMEL *n* type of thermometer using thermoelectric current
THERMES ▸ **therme**
THERMIC = **thermal**

THERMIT *variant of* > **thermite**
THERMOS *n* trademark for a stoppered vacuum flask
THERMS ▸ **therm**
THEROID *adj* of, relating to, or resembling a beast
THESE *determiner*
THESES ▸ **thesis**
THESIS *n*
THESP *short for* > **thespian**
THESPS ▸ **thesp**
THETA *n* eighth letter of the Greek alphabet **thetas**
THETCH *old variant spelling of* ▸ **thatch**
THETE *n* member of the lowest order of freeman in ancient Athens **thetes**
THETHER *old variant of* ▸ **thither**
THETIC *adj* (in classical prosody) of, bearing, or relating to a metrical stress
THEURGY *n* intervention of a divine or supernatural agency in the affairs of man
THEW *n* muscle, esp if strong or well-developed
THEWED *adj* strong; muscular
THEWES, thewier, thews, thewy ▸ **thew**
THEY *pron*
THIAMIN = **thiamine**
THIASUS *n* people gathered to sing and dance in honour of a god
THIAZIN = **thiazine**
THIAZOL = **thiazole**
THIBET *n* coloured woollen cloth **thibets**
THIBLE *n* stick for stirring porridge **thibles**
THICK *adj, vb* **thicked**
THICKEN *vb*
THICKER ▸ **thick**
THICKET *n*
THICKLY ▸ **thick**
THICKS ▸ **thick**
THIEF *n*
THIEVE *vb* steal **thieved, thieves**
THIG *vb* beg **thigger, thiggit**
THIGH *n*
THIGHED *adj* having thighs
THIGHS ▸ **thigh**
THIGS ▸ **thig**
THILK *pron* that same
THILL *another word for* ▸ **shaft**
THILLER *n* horse that goes between the thills of a cart
THILLS ▸ **thill**
THIMBLE *n, vb*
THIN *adj* not thick ▷ *vb* make or become thin ▷ *adv* in order to produce something thin
THINE *adj* (something) of or associated with you (thou) ▷ *pron* something belonging to you (thou) ▷ *determiner* of, belonging to, or associated in some way with you (thou)
THING *n* **things**
THINGY *adj* existing in reality; actual
THINK *vb* consider, judge, or believe **thinker, thinks**
THINLY, thinned, thinner, thins ▸ **thin**
THIO *adj* of, or relating to, sulphur
THIOL *n* any of a class of sulphur-containing organic compounds **thiolic, thiols**
THIONIC *adj* of, relating to, or containing sulphur
THIONIN = **thionine**
THIONYL *n* of, consisting of, or containing the divalent group SO
THIR *Scots word for* ▸ **these**
THIRAM *n* antifungal agent **thirams**
THIRD *adj, n, adv, vb* **thirded, thirdly, thirds**
THIRL *vb* bore or drill **thirled, thirls**
THIRST *n, vb* **thirsts**
THIRSTY *adj* feeling a desire to drink
THIRTY *n, adj, determiner*
THIS *pron, adj*
THISTLE *n* **thistly**
THITHER *adv* or towards that place

THIVEL = **thible**
THIVELS ▸ **thivel**
THO *short for* ▸ **though**
THOFT *n* bench (in a boat) upon which a rower sits **thofts**
THOLE *n* wooden pin set in the side of a rowing boat to serve as a fulcrum for rowing ▹ *vb* bear or put up with **tholed, tholes**
THOLI ▸ **tholus**
THOLING ▸ **thole**
THOLOI ▸ **tholos**
THOLOS *n* beehive-shaped tomb associated with Mycenaean Greece
THOLUS *n* domed tomb
THON *Scot word for* ▸ **yon**
THONDER *Scot word for* ▸ **yonder**
THONG *n*
THONGED *adj* fastened with a thong
THONGS ▸ **thong**
THORAX *n*
THORIA ▸ **thorium**
THORIAS ▸ **thorium**
THORIC ▸ **thorium**
THORITE *n* yellow, brownish, or black radioactive mineral
THORIUM *n*
THORN *n, vb* **thorned, thorns**
THORNY *adj*
THORO *(nonstandard) variant spelling of* > **thorough**
THORON *n* radioisotope of radon that is a decay product of thorium **thorons**
THORP *n* small village **thorpe**
THORPES ▸ **thorpe**
THORPS ▸ **thorp**
THOSE *determiner*
THOTHER *pron* old contraction of *the other*
THOU *pron, n, vb* **thoued**
THOUGH *adv*
THOUGHT ▸ **think**
THOUING ▸ **thou**
THOUS ▸ **thou**
THOWEL *old variant of* ▸ **thole**
THOWELS ▸ **thowel**
THOWL *old variant of* ▸ **thole**
THOWLS ▸ **thowel**
THRAE = **frae**
THRALL *n* state of being in the power of another person ▹ *vb* enslave or dominate **thralls**
THRANG *n* throng ▹ *vb* throng ▹ *adj* crowded **thrangs**
THRASH *vb, n*
THRAVE *n* twenty-four sheaves of corn **thraves**
THRAW *vb* twist (something); make something thrawn **thrawed**
THRAWN *adj* crooked or twisted
THRAWS ▸ **thraw**
THREAD *n, vb*
THREADS *slang word for* ▸ **clothes**
THREADY *adj* of, relating to, or resembling a thread or threads
THREAP *vb* scold **threaps**
THREAT *n* **threats**
THREAVE = **thrave**
THREE *n, adj, determiner*
THREEP = **threap**
THREEPS ▸ **threep**
THREES ▸ **three**
THRENE *n* dirge; threnody **threnes**
THRENOS *n* threnody; lamentation
THRESH *vb, n*
THRETTY *nonstandard variant of* ▸ **thirty**
THREW ▸ **throw**
THRICE *adv*
THRID *old variant of* ▸ **thread**
THRIDS ▸ **thrid**
THRIFT *n* **thrifts**
THRIFTY *adj*
THRILL *n, vb* **thrills**
THRILLY *adj* causing thrills
THRIMSA = **thrymsa**
THRIP = **thrips**
THRIPS *n* small slender-bodied insect with piercing mouthparts that feeds on plant sap
THRIST *old variant of* ▸ **thirst**
THRISTS ▸ **thrist**
THRISTY ▸ **thrist**
THRIVE *vb* **thrived, thriven, thriver, thrives**
THRO = **through**
THROAT *n, vb* **throats**

THROATY *adj*
THROB *vb, n* **throbs**
THROE *n* pang or pain ▷ *n* endure throes **throed**
THROES *pl n*
THROMBI > **thrombus**
THRONE *n, vb* **throned, thrones**
THRONG *vb, n, adj* **throngs**
THROUGH *prep, adj*
THROVE ▶ **thrive**
THROW *vb, n*
THROWE *old variant of* ▶ **throe**
THROWER ▶ **throw**
THROWES ▶ **throwe**
THROWN ▶ **throw**
THROWS ▶ **throw**
THRU = **through**
THRUM *vb* strum rhythmically but without expression ▷ *n* in textiles, unwoven ends of wap thread
THRUMMY *adj* made of thrums
THRUMS ▶ **thrum**
THRUPUT *n* quantity of raw material or information processed in a given period
THRUSH *n*
THRUST *vb, n* **thrusts**
THRUTCH *n* narrow, fast-moving stream ▷ *vb* thrust
THRUWAY *n* thoroughfare
THRYMSA *n* gold coin used in Anglo-Saxon England
THUD *n, vb* **thudded, thuds**
THUG *n*
THUGGEE *n* methods and practices of the thugs of India
THUGGO *n* tough and violent person **thuggos**
THUGS ▶ **thug**
THUJA *n* coniferous tree of North America and East Asia **thujas**
THULIA *n* oxide of thulium **thulias**
THULITE *n* rose-coloured zoisite sometimes incorporated into jewellery
THULIUM *n* malleable ductile silvery-grey element
THUMB *n, vb* **thumbed, thumbs**
THUMBY *adj* clumsy; uncoordinated
THUMP *n, vb* **thumped, thumper, thumps**
THUNDER *n, vb*
THUNK *another word for* ▶ **thud**
THUNKED ▶ **thunk**
THUNKS ▶ **thunk**
THURIFY *vb* burn incense near or before an altar, shrine, etc
THURL = **thirl**
THURLS ▶ **thurl**
THUS *adv, n* **thuses**
THUSLY *adv* in such a way; thus
THUYA = **thuja**
THUYAS ▶ **thuya**
THWACK *n, vb, interj* **thwacks**
THWAITE *n* piece of land cleared from forest or reclaimed from wasteland
THWART *vb, n, adj, adv* **thwarts**
THY *adj, determiner*
THYINE *adj* of or relating to the sandarac tree
THYLOSE *old variant of* ▶ **tylosis**
THYME *n* **thymes, thymey**
THYMI ▶ **thymus**
THYMIC *adj* of or relating to the thymus
THYMIER ▶ **thyme**
THYMINE *n* white crystalline pyrimidine base found in DNA
THYMOL *n* substance obtained from thyme **thymols**
THYMUS *n*
THYMY ▶ **thyme**
THYROID *n* (of) a gland in the neck controlling body growth ▷ *adj* of or relating to the thyroid gland
THYRSE *n* type of inflorescence, occurring in the lilac and grape **thyrses**
THYRSI ▶ **thyrsus**
THYRSUS = **thyrse**
THYSELF *pron* reflexive form of thou
TI = **te**
TIAN *n* traditional French vegetable stew or earthenware dish it is cooked in **tians**

TIAR = **tiara**
TIARA *n* **tiaraed, tiaras**
TIARS ▸ **tiar**
TIBIA *n* **tibiae, tibial, tibias**
TIC *n*
TICAL *n* former standard monetary unit of Thailand **ticals**
TICCA *adj* acquired for temporary use in exchange for payment
TICCED ▸ **tic**
TICCING ▸ **tic**
TICE *vb* tempt or allure; entice **ticed, tices**
TICH = **titch**
TICHES ▸ **tich**
TICHIER ▸ **tichy**
TICHY = **titchy**
TICING ▸ **tice**
TICK *n, vb* **ticked**
TICKEN = **ticking**
TICKENS ▸ **ticken**
TICKER *n* heart **tickers**
TICKET *n, vb*
TICKETS *pl n* death or ruin
TICKEY *n* South African threepenny piece **tickeys**
TICKIES ▸ **ticky**
TICKING *n*
TICKLE *vb, n* **tickled**
TICKLER *n* difficult or delicate problem
TICKLES ▸ **tickle**
TICKLY ▸ **tickle**
TICKS ▸ **tick**
TICKY = **tickey**
TICS ▸ **tic**
TICTAC = **ticktack**
TICTACS ▸ **tictac**
TICTOC = **ticktock**
TICTOCS ▸ **tictoc**
TID *n* girl
TIDAL *adj* **tidally**
TIDBIT = **titbit**
TIDBITS ▸ **tidbit**
TIDDIER ▸ **tiddy**
TIDDIES ▸ **tiddy**
TIDDLE *vb* busy oneself with inconsequential tasks **tiddled**
TIDDLER *n*
TIDDLES ▸ **tiddle**
TIDDLEY = **tiddly**
TIDDLY *adj, n*
TIDDY *n* four of trumps in the card game gleek
TIDE *n, vb* **tided**
TIDERIP = **riptide**
TIDES ▸ **tide**
TIDEWAY *n* strong tidal current or its channel, esp the tidal part of a river
TIDIED, tidier, tidiers, tidies, tidiest, tidily ▸ **tidy**
TIDING ▸ **tide**
TIDINGS *pl n*
TIDS ▸ **tid**
TIDY *adj, vb, n* **tidying**
TIE *vb, n*
TIEBACK *n* length of cord, ribbon, or other fabric used for tying a curtain to one side
TIED ▸ **tie**
TIEING = **tie**
TIELESS ▸ **tie**
TIEPIN *n* ornamental pin used to pin the two ends of a tie to a shirt **tiepins**
TIER *n, vb*
TIERCE = **terce**
TIERCED *adj* (of a shield) divided into three sections of similar size but different colour
TIERCEL = **tercel**
TIERCES ▸ **tierce**
TIERCET = **tercet**
TIERED ▸ **tier**
TIERING ▸ **tier**
TIERS ▸ **tier**
TIES ▸ **tie**
TIETAC *n* fastener for holding a tie in place **tietack, tietacs**
TIFF *n, vb*
TIFFANY *n* sheer fine gauzy fabric
TIFFED ▸ **tiff**
TIFFIN *n* (in India) a light meal, esp at midday ▹ *vb* take tiffin
TIFFING ▸ **tiff**
TIFFINS ▸ **tiffin**
TIFFS ▸ **tiff**
TIFOSI ▸ **tifoso**
TIFOSO *n* fanatical fan (esp an Italian F1 fan)
TIFT *Scots variant of* ▸ **tiff**
TIFTED ▸ **tift**
TIFTING ▸ **tift**
TIFTS ▸ **tift**
TIG *n* child's game
TIGE *n* trunk of an architectural column
TIGER *n*
TIGERLY *adj* of or like a tiger
TIGERS ▸ **tiger**
TIGERY ▸ **tiger**
TIGES ▸ **tige**
TIGGED ▸ **tig**
TIGGING ▸ **tig**

TIGHT *adj, adv*
TIGHTEN *vb*
TIGHTER ▸ **tight**
TIGHTLY ▸ **tight**
TIGHTS *pl n*
TIGLIC *adj as in* **tiglic acid** syrupy liquid or crystalline colourless unsaturated carboxylic acid
TIGLON = **tigon**
TIGLONS ▸ **tiglon**
TIGON *n* hybrid offspring of a male tiger and a female lion **tigons**
TIGRESS *n* female tiger
TIGRINE *adj* of, characteristic of, or resembling a tiger
TIGRISH ▸ **tiger**
TIGROID *adj* resembling a tiger
TIGS ▸ **tig**
TIK *n* South African slang term for crystal meth
TIKA = **tikka**
TIKANGA *n* Māori ways or customs
TIKAS ▸ **tika**
TIKI *n, vb* **tikied, tikiing, tikis**
TIKKA *adj* marinated in spices and dry-roasted ▹ *n* act of marking a tikka on the forehead **tikkas**
TIKS ▸ **tik**
TIL *another name for* ▸ **sesame**
TILAK *n* coloured spot or mark worn by Hindus **tilaks**
TILAPIA *n* type of fish
TILBURY *n* light two-wheeled horse-drawn open carriage
TILDE *n* **tildes**
TILE *n, vb* **tiled, tiler, tilers**
TILERY *n* place where tiles are produced
TILES ▸ **tile**
TILING *n* tiles collectively **tilings**
TILL *prep, vb, n*
TILLAGE *n* act, process, or art of tilling
TILLED ▸ **till**
TILLER *n, vb*
TILLERS ▸ **till**
TILLIER ▸ **till**
TILLING ▸ **till**
TILLITE *n* rock formed from hardened till
TILLS ▸ **till**
TILLY ▸ **till**
TILS ▸ **til**
TILT *vb, n* **tilted, tilter, tilters**
TILTH *n* (condition of) land that has been tilled **tilths**
TILTING ▸ **tilt**
TILTS ▸ **tilt**
TIMARAU = **tamarau**
TIMBAL *n* type of kettledrum
TIMBALE *n* mixture of meat, fish, etc, in a rich sauce
TIMBALS ▸ **timbal**
TIMBER *n, adj, vb, interj* **timbers, timbery**
TIMBO *n* Amazonian vine from which a useful insecticide can be derived **timbos**
TIMBRAL *adj* relating to timbre
TIMBRE *n*
TIMBREL *n* tambourine
TIMBRES ▸ **timbre**
TIME *n* past, present, and future as a continuous whole ▹ *vb* note the time taken by **timed**
TIMELY *adj, adv*
TIMEOUS *adj* in good time
TIMEOUT *n* in sport, interruption in play during which players rest, etc
TIMER *n* **timers**
TIMES ▸ **time**
TIMID *adj* **timider, timidly**
TIMING *n* **timings**
TIMIST *n* one concerned with time **timists**
TIMOLOL *n* relaxant medicine used (for example) to reduce blood pressure
TIMON *n* apparatus by which a vessel is steered **timons**
TIMOTHY *n as in* **timothy grass** perennial grass of temperate regions
TIMOUS = **timeous**
TIMPANA *n* traditional Maltese baked pasta and pastry dish
TIMPANI *pl n*
TIMPANO *n* kettledrum

TIMPS = **timpani**
TIN *n, vb*
TINA *n*
TINAJA *n* large jar for cooling water **tinajas**
TINAMOU *n* type of bird of Central and S America
TINAS ▸ **tina**
TINCAL *another name for* ▸ **borax**
TINCALS ▸ **tincal**
TINCHEL *n* in Scotland, a circle of deer hunters who gradually close in on their quarry
TINCT *vb* tint ▹ *adj* tinted or coloured **tincted, tincts**
TIND *vb* set alight
TINDAL *n* petty officer **tindals**
TINDED ▸ **tind**
TINDER *n* **tinders, tindery**
TINDING ▸ **tind**
TINDS ▸ **tind**
TINE *n, vb*
TINEA *n* any fungal skin disease, esp ringworm **tineal, tineas**
TINED ▸ **tine**
TINEID *n* type of moth of the family which includes the clothes moths **tineids**
TINES ▸ **tine**
TINFOIL *n*
TINFUL *n* contents of a tin or the amount a tin will hold **tinfuls**
TING = **thing**
TINGE *n, vb* **tinged, tinges, tinging**
TINGLE *n, vb* **tingled, tingler, tingles, tingly**
TINGS ▸ **ting**
TINHORN *n* cheap pretentious person, esp a gambler with extravagant claims ▹ *adj* cheap and showy
TINIER ▸ **tiny**
TINIES *pl n* small children
TINIEST ▸ **tiny**
TINILY ▸ **tiny**
TINING ▸ **tine**
TINK *shortened form of* ▸ **tinker**
TINKED ▸ **tink**
TINKER *n, vb* **tinkers**
TINKING ▸ **tink**
TINKLE *vb, n* **tinkled**
TINKLER = **tinker**
TINKLES ▸ **tinkle**
TINKLY ▸ **tinkle**
TINKS ▸ **tink**
TINLIKE ▸ **tin**
TINMAN *n* one who works with tin or tin plate **tinmen**
TINNED ▸ **tin**
TINNER *n* tin miner **tinners**
TINNIE = **tinny**
TINNIER ▸ **tinny**
TINNIES ▸ **tinny**
TINNILY ▸ **tinny**
TINNING ▸ **tin**
TINNY *adj, n*
TINPOT *adj, n* **tinpots**
TINS ▸ **tin**
TINSEL *n, adj, vb* **tinsels, tinsey**
TINSEYS ▸ **tinsey**
TINT *n, vb*
TINTACK *n* tin-plated tack
TINTED ▸ **tint**
TINTER ▸ **tint**
TINTERS ▸ **tint**
TINTIER ▸ **tinty**
TINTING ▸ **tint**
TINTS ▸ **tint**
TINTY *adj* having many tints
TINTYPE *another name for* > **ferrotype**
TINWARE *n* objects made of tin plate
TINWORK *n* objects made of tin
TINY *adj*
TIP *n, vb*
TIPCART *n* cart that can be tipped to empty out its contents
TIPCAT *n* game in which a piece of wood is tipped in the air with a stick **tipcats**
TIPI *variant spelling of* ▸ **tepee**
TIPIS ▸ **tipi**
TIPLESS ▸ **tip**
TIPOFF *n* warning or hint, esp given confidentially **tipoffs**
TIPPED ▸ **tip**
TIPPEE *n* person who receives a tip, esp regarding share prices **tippees**
TIPPER *n* person who gives or leaves a tip **tippers**
TIPPET *n* scarflike piece of fur **tippets**
TIPPIER ▸ **tippy**
TIPPING ▸ **tip**
TIPPLE *vb, n* **tippled, tippler, tipples**

TIPPY *adj* extremely fashionable or stylish
TIPS ▸ **tip**
TIPSIER ▸ **tipsy**
TIPSIFY *vb* make tipsy
TIPSILY ▸ **tipsy**
TIPSTER *n* person who sells tips about races
TIPSY *adj*
TIPT ▸ **tip**
TIPTOE *vb* **tiptoed, tiptoes**
TIPTOP *adj* of the highest quality or condition ▷ *adv* of the highest quality or condition ▷ *n* best in quality **tiptops**
TIPULA *n* crane fly **tipulas**
TIPUNA *n* ancestor **tipunas**
TIRADE *n* **tirades**
TIRAGE *n* drawing of wine from a barrel prior to bottling **tirages**
TIRASSE *n* mechanism in an organ connecting two pedals
TIRE *vb*
TIRED *adj* **tireder, tiredly**
TIRES ▸ **tire**
TIRING ▸ **tire**
TIRINGS ▸ **tire**
TIRITI *n* another name for the Treaty of Waitangi

> A Maori word for treaty. Any 6-letter word that lets you get rid of three Is can't be bad! **tiritis**

TIRL *vb* turn **tirled, tirling, tirls**
TIRO = **tyro**
TIROES ▸ **tiro**
TIRONIC *variant of* ▸ **tyronic**
TIROS ▸ **tiro**
TIRR *vb* strip or denude **tirred, tirring**
TIRRIT *n* panic; scare **tirrits**
TIRRS ▸ **tirr**
TIS ▸ **ti**
TISANE *n* infusion of dried or fresh leaves or flowers **tisanes**
TISICK *n* splutter; cough **tisicks**
TISSUAL *adj* relating to tissue
TISSUE *n, vb* **tissued, tissues, tissuey**
TISWAS *n* state of anxiety or excitement
TIT *n, vb*
TITAN *n* person who is huge, strong, or very important
TITANIA > **titanium**
TITANIC *adj*
TITANIS *n* large predatory flightless prehistoric bird
TITANS ▸ **titan**
TITBIT *n* **titbits**
TITCH *n* small person **titches**
TITCHY *adj* very small
TITE *adj* immediately
TITELY *adv* immediately
TITER = **titre**
TITERS ▸ **titer**
TITFER *n* hat **titfers**
TITHE *n, vb* **tithed, tither, tithers, tithes, tithing**
TITI *n* small omnivorous monkey
TITIAN *n* **titians**
TITIS ▸ **titi**
TITLARK *another name for* ▸ **pipit**
TITLE *n, vb*
TITLED *adj*
TITLER *n* one who writes titles
TITLERS ▸ **title**
TITLES ▸ **title**
TITLING ▸ **title**
TITLIST *n* titleholder
TITMAN *n* (of pigs) the runt of a litter **titmen**
TITMICE > **titmouse**
TITMOSE *old spelling of* > **titmouse**
TITOKI *n* New Zealand evergreen tree with a spreading crown and glossy green leaves **titokis**
TITRANT *n* solution in a titration that is added to a measured quantity of another solution
TITRATE *vb* measure the volume or concentration of (a solution) by titration
TITRE *n* concentration of a solution as determined by titration **titres**
TITS ▸ **tit**
TITTED ▸ **tit**
TITTER *vb, n* **titters**
TITTIE *n* sister; young woman **titties**
TITTING ▸ **tit**

TITTISH *adj* testy
TITTLE *n* very small amount ▷ *vb* chatter; tattle **tittled, tittles**
TITTUP *vb* prance or frolic ▷ *n* caper **tittups**
TITTUPY *adj* spritely; lively
TITTY = **tittie**
TITULAR *adj, n*
TITULE = **title**
TITULED ▶ **titule**
TITULES ▶ **titule**
TITULI ▶ **titulus**
TITULUS *n* sign attached to the top of the cross during crucifixion
TITUP = **tittup**
TITUPED ▶ **titup**
TITUPS ▶ **titup**
TITUPY = **tittupy**
TIVY = **tantivy**
TIX *pl n* tickets

> **Tix** is an informal word for **tickets**, and one of the key short words for using the X.

TIYIN *n* monetary unit of Uzbekistan and Kyrgyzstan **tiyins**
TIZWAS = **tiswas**
TIZZ = **tizzy**
TIZZES ▶ **tizz**
TIZZIES ▶ **tizzy**
TIZZY *n* confused or agitated state
TMESES ▶ **tmesis**
TMESIS *n* interpolation of a word between the parts of a compound word
TO *prep, adv*
TOAD *n*
TOADIED ▶ **toady**
TOADIES ▶ **toady**
TOADISH ▶ **toad**
TOADS ▶ **toad**
TOADY *n, vb*
TOAST *n, vb* **toasted, toaster**
TOASTIE = **toasty**
TOASTS ▶ **toast**
TOASTY *n* toasted sandwich ▷ *adj* tasting or smelling like toast
TOAZE *variant spelling of* ▶ **toze**
TOAZED ▶ **toaze**
TOAZES ▶ **toaze**
TOAZING ▶ **toaze**
TOBACCO *n*
TOBIES ▶ **toby**
TOBY *n* water stopcock at the boundary of a street and house section
TOC *n* in communications code, signal for letter t
TOCCATA *n* rapid piece of music for a keyboard instrument **toccate**
TOCHER *n* dowry ▷ *vb* give a dowry to **tochers**
TOCK *n* sound made by a clock ▷ *vb* (of a clock) make such a sound **tocked**
TOCKIER ▶ **tocky**
TOCKING ▶ **tock**
TOCKS ▶ **tock**
TOCKY *adj* muddy
TOCO *n* punishment **tocos**
TOCS ▶ **toc**
TOCSIN *n* warning signal **tocsins**
TOD *n* unit of weight, used for wool, etc ▷ *vb* produce a tod
TODAY *n, adv* **todays**
TODDE = **tod**
TODDED ▶ **tod**
TODDES ▶ **todde**
TODDIES ▶ **toddy**
TODDING ▶ **tod**
TODDLE *vb, n* **toddled**
TODDLER *n*
TODDLES ▶ **toddle**
TODDY *n*
TODIES ▶ **tody**
TODS ▶ **tod**
TODY *n* small bird of the Caribbean
TOE *n, vb*
TOEA *n* monetary unit of Papua New Guinea **toeas**

> This monetary unit of Papua New Guinea is very often played to rid the rack of a surplus of vowels.

TOEBIE *n* South African slang for sandwich **toebies**
TOECAP *n* strengthened covering for the toe of a shoe **toecaps**
TOECLIP *n* clip on a bicycle pedal into which the toes are inserted to prevent the foot from slipping
TOED ▶ **toe**
TOEHOLD *n*

TOEIER ▸ **toey**

> This is the comparative of **toey**, Australian slang for nervous or edgy, and can come in useful for dumping a surplus of vowels.

TOEIEST ▸ **toey**
TOEING ▸ **toe**
TOELESS *adj* not having toes
TOELIKE ▸ **toe**
TOENAIL *n* thin hard clear plate covering part of the upper surface of the end of each toe ▹ *vb* join (beams) by driving nails obliquely
TOES ▸ **toe**
TOESHOE *n* ballet pump with padded toes
TOETOE = **toitoi**
TOETOES ▸ **toetoe**
TOEY *adj* (of a person) nervous or anxious
TOFF *n*
TOFFEE *n* **toffees**
TOFFIER ▸ **toffy**
TOFFIES ▸ **toffy**
TOFFISH *adj* belonging to or characteristic of the upper class
TOFFS *adj* like a toff
TOFFY = **toffee**
TOFORE *prep* before
TOFT *n* homestead **tofts**
TOFU *n* soft food made from soya-bean curd **tofus**
TOFUTTI *n* tradename for nondairy, soya-based food products
TOG *n* unit for measuring the insulating power of duvets ▹ *vb* dress oneself
TOGA *n*, *vb* **togae, togaed, togas**
TOGATE *adj* clad in a toga **togated**
TOGE *old variant of* ▸ **toga**
TOGED ▸ **toge**
TOGES ▸ **toge**
TOGGED ▸ **tog**
TOGGER *vb* play football ▹ *n* football player **toggers**
TOGGERY *n* clothes
TOGGING ▸ **tog**
TOGGLE *n*, *vb* **toggled, toggler, toggles**
TOGS ▸ **tog**
TOGUE *n* large North American freshwater game fish **togues**
TOHEROA *n* large edible mollusc of New Zealand
TOHO *n* (to a hunting dog) an instruction to stop
TOHUNGA *n* Māori priest
TOIL *n*, *vb*
TOILE *n* transparent linen or cotton fabric
TOILED ▸ **toil**
TOILER ▸ **toil**
TOILERS ▸ **toil**
TOILES ▸ **toile**
TOILET *n*, *vb* **toilets**
TOILFUL = **toilsome**
TOILING ▸ **toil**
TOILS ▸ **toil**
TOING *n as in* **toing and froing** state of going back and forth **toings**
TOISE *n* obsolete French unit of length roughly equal to 2m
TOISECH = **toiseach**
TOISES ▸ **toise**
TOISON *n* fleece **toisons**
TOIT *vb* walk or move in an unsteady manner, as from old age **toited, toiting**
TOITOI *n* tall grasses with feathery fronds **toitois**
TOITS ▸ **toit**
TOKAMAK *n* reactor used in thermonuclear experiments
TOKAY *n* small gecko of S and SE Asia, having a retractile claw at the tip of each digit **tokays**
TOKE *n* draw on a cannabis cigarette ▹ *vb* take a draw on a cannabis cigarette **toked**
TOKEN *n*, *adj* **tokened, tokens**
TOKER, tokers, tokes, toking ▸ **toke**
TOKO = **toco**
TOKOMAK *variant spelling of* ▸ **tokamak**
TOKOS ▸ **toko**
TOLA *n* unit of weight, used in India
TOLAN *n* white crystalline derivative of acetylene **tolane**

TOLANES ▸ **tolane**
TOLANS ▸ **tolan**
TOLAR *n* standard monetary unit of Slovenia **tolarji, tolars**
TOLAS ▸ **tola**
TOLD ▸ **tell**
TOLE = **toll**
TOLED ▸ **tole**
TOLEDO *n* type of sword originally made in Toledo **toledos**
TOLES ▸ **tole**
TOLIDIN = **tolidine**
TOLING ▸ **tole**
TOLINGS ▸ **tole**
TOLL *vb, n* **tollage**
TOLLBAR *n* bar blocking passage of a thoroughfare, raised on payment of a toll
TOLLED ▸ **toll**
TOLLER ▸ **toll**
TOLLERS ▸ **toller**
TOLLEY *n* large shooting marble used in a game of marbles **tolleys**
TOLLIE = **tolly**
TOLLIES ▸ **tolly**
TOLLING ▸ **toll**
TOLLMAN *n* man who collects tolls **tollmen**
TOLLS ▸ **toll**
TOLLWAY *n* road on which users must pay tolls to travel
TOLLY *n* castrated calf
TOLSEL *n* tolbooth **tolsels**
TOLSEY *n* tolbooth
TOLSEYS > **tolbooth**
TOLT *n* type of obsolete English writ
TOLTER *vb* struggle or move with difficulty, as in mud **tolters**
TOLTS ▸ **tolt**
TOLU *n* sweet-smelling balsam obtained from a South American tree
TOLUATE *n* any salt or ester of any of the three isomeric forms of toluic acid
TOLUENE *n* colourless volatile flammable liquid obtained from petroleum and coal tar
TOLUIC *adj as in* **toluic acid** white crystalline derivative of toluene
TOLUID *n* white crystalline derivative of glycocoll **toluide, toluids**
TOLUOL *another name for* ▸ **toluene**
TOLUOLE *another name for* ▸ **toluene**
TOLUOLS ▸ **toluol**
TOLUS ▸ **tolu**
TOLUYL *n* of, consisting of, or containing any of three groups derived from a toluic acid **toluyls**
TOLYL *n* of, consisting of, or containing any of three isomeric groups, $CH_3C_6H_4$-, derived from toluene **tolyls**
TOLZEY *n* tolbooth **tolzeys**
TOM *n, adj, vb*
TOMAN *n* gold coin formerly issued in Persia **tomans**
TOMATO *n*
TOMB *n*
TOMBAC *n* any of various brittle alloys containing copper and zinc **tomback, tombacs, tombak**
TOMBAKS ▸ **tombak**
TOMBAL *adj* like or relating to a tomb
TOMBED ▸ **tomb**
TOMBIC *adj* of or relating to tombs
TOMBING ▸ **tomb**
TOMBOC *n* weapon **tombocs**
TOMBOLA *n*
TOMBOLO *n* narrow bar linking a small island with another island or the mainland
TOMBOY *n* **tomboys**
TOMBS ▸ **tomb**
TOMCAT *vb* (of a man) to be promiscuous **tomcats**
TOMCOD *n* small fish resembling the cod **tomcods**
TOME *n*
TOMENTA > **tomentum**
TOMES ▸ **tome**
TOMFOOL *n* fool ▹ *vb* act the fool
TOMIA ▸ **tomium**
TOMIAL ▸ **tomium**
TOMIUM *n* sharp edge of a bird's beak
TOMMIED ▸ **tommy**
TOMMIES ▸ **tommy**
TOMMY *n, vb*
TOMO *n* shaft formed by the action of water on limestone or volcanic rock **tomos**

TOMPION = **tampion**
TOMPON = **tampon**
TOMPONS ▶ **tompon**
TOMS ▶ **tom**
TOMTIT *n* small European bird that eats insects and seeds **tomtits**
TON *n*
TONAL *adj* **tonally**
TONANT *adj* very loud
TONDI ▶ **tondo**
TONDINI ▶ **tondino**
TONDINO *n* small tondo
TONDO *n* circular easel painting or relief carving **tondos**
TONE *n, vb*
TONEARM = **pickup**
TONED ▶ **tone**
TONEME *n* phoneme that is distinguished from another phoneme only by its tone **tonemes, tonemic**
TONEPAD *n* keypad used to transmit information
TONER *n* cosmetic applied to the skin to reduce oiliness **toners**
TONES ▶ **tone**
TONETIC *adj* (of a language) distinguishing words by tone as well as by other sounds
TONETTE *n* small musical instrument resembling a recorder
TONEY *variant spelling of* ▶ **tony**
TONG *vb* gather or seize with tongs ▷ *n* (formerly) a Chinese secret society
TONGA *n* light two-wheeled vehicle used in rural areas of India **tongas**
TONGED ▶ **tong**
TONGER *n* one who uses tongs to gather oysters **tongers**
TONGING ▶ **tong**
TONGMAN *another word for* ▶ **tonger**
TONGMEN ▶ **tongman**
TONGS *pl n*
TONGUE *n, vb* **tongued, tongues**
TONIC *n, adj* **tonics**
TONIER ▶ **tony**
TONIES ▶ **tony**
TONIEST ▶ **tony**
TONIGHT *n, adv*
TONING ▶ **tone**
TONINGS ▶ **tone**
TONISH ▶ **ton**
TONITE *n* explosive used in quarrying **tonites**
TONK *vb* strike with a heavy blow ▷ *n* effete or effeminate man
TONKA *n as in* **tonka bean** tall leguminous tree of tropical America
TONKED, tonker, tonkers, tonking, tonks ▶ **tonk**
TONLET *n* skirt of a suit of armour, consisting of overlapping metal bands **tonlets**
TONNAG *n* type of (usually tartan) shawl
TONNAGE *n*
TONNAGS ▶ **tonnag**
TONNE = **ton**
TONNEAU *n* detachable cover to protect the rear part of an open car
TONNELL *old spelling of* ▶ **tunnel**
TONNER *n* something that weighs one ton
TONNERS ▶ **tonne**
TONNES ▶ **tonne**
TONNISH ▶ **ton**
TONS ▶ **ton**
TONSIL *n* **tonsils**
TONSOR *n* barber **tonsors**
TONSURE *n, vb*
TONTINE *n* type of annuity scheme
TONUS *n* normal tension of a muscle at rest **tonuses**
TONY *adj* stylish or distinctive ▷ *n* stylish or distinctive person
TOO *adv*
TOOART *variant spelling of* ▶ **tuart**
TOOARTS ▶ **tooart**
TOOK ▶ **take**
TOOL *n, vb*
TOOLBAG *n* bag for storing or carrying tools
TOOLBAR *n* row or column of selectable buttons displayed on a computer screen
TOOLBOX *n* box for storing or carrying tools
TOOLED ▶ **tool**
TOOLER ▶ **tool**
TOOLERS ▶ **tool**
TOOLIE *n* **toolies**

TOOLING *n* any decorative work done with a tool
TOOLKIT *n* set of tools designed to be used together or for a particular purpose
TOOLMAN *n* person who works with tools **toolmen**
TOOLS ▸ **tool**
TOOLSET *n* set of tools associated with a computer application
TOOM *vb* empty (something) ▹ *adj* empty **toomed, toomer, toomest, tooming, tooms**
TOON *n* large tree of the East Indies and Australia
TOONIE *n* Canadian two-dollar coin **toonies**
TOONS ▸ **toon**
TOORIE *n* tassel or bobble on a bonnet **toories**
TOOSHIE *adj* angry
TOOT *n, vb* **tooted, tooter, tooters**
TOOTH *n*
TOOTHED *adj* having a tooth or teeth
TOOTHS ▸ **tooth**
TOOTHY *adj* having or showing numerous, large, or prominent teeth
TOOTING ▸ **toot**
TOOTLE *vb* hoot softly or repeatedly ▹ *n* soft hoot or series of hoots **tootled, tootler, tootles**
TOOTS *Scots version of* ▸ **tut**
TOOTSED ▸ **toots**
TOOTSES ▸ **toots**
TOOTSIE = **tootsy**
TOOTSY = **toots**
TOP *n, adj, vb*
TOPARCH *n* ruler of a small state or realm
TOPAZ *n* semiprecious stone in various colours **topazes**
TOPCOAT *n* overcoat
TOPE *vb* drink alcohol regularly ▹ *n* small European shark **toped**
TOPEE *n* lightweight hat worn in tropical countries **topees**
TOPEK = **tupik**
TOPEKS ▸ **topek**
TOPER ▸ **tope**
TOPERS ▸ **tope**
TOPES ▸ **tope**
TOPFUL *variant spelling of* ▸ **topfull**
TOPFULL *adj* full to the top
TOPH *n* variety of sandstone **tophe**
TOPHES ▸ **tophe**
TOPHI ▸ **tophus**
TOPHS ▸ **toph**
TOPHUS *n* deposit of sodium urate in the helix of the ear or surrounding a joint
TOPI = **topee**
TOPIARY *n, adj*
TOPIC *n*
TOPICAL *adj*
TOPICS ▸ **topic**
TOPING ▸ **tope**
TOPIS ▸ **topi**
TOPKICK *n* (formerly) sergeant
TOPKNOT *n* crest, tuft, decorative bow, etc, on the top of the head
TOPLESS *adj* (of a costume or woman) with no covering for the breasts
TOPLINE *vb* headline; be the main focus of a newspaper story
TOPMAN *n* sailor positioned in the rigging of the topsail
TOPMAST *n* mast next above a lower mast on a sailing vessel
TOPMEN ▸ **topman**
TOPMOST *adj*
TOPO *n* picture of a mountain with details of climbing routes superimposed on it **topoi**
TOPONYM *n* name of a place
TOPOS ▸ **topo**
TOPPED ▸ **top**
TOPPER *n* top hat **toppers**
TOPPIER ▸ **toppy**
TOPPING ▸ **top**
TOPPLE *vb* **toppled, topples**
TOPPY *adj* (of audio reproduction) having too many high-frequency sounds
TOPS ▸ **top**
TOPSAIL *n* square sail carried on a yard set on a topmast

TOPSIDE *n* lean cut of beef from the thigh containing no bone
TOPSMAN *n* chief drover **topsmen**
TOPSOIL *n, vb*
TOPSPIN *n* spin imparted to make a ball bounce or travel exceptionally far, high, or quickly
TOPWORK *vb* graft shoots or twigs onto the main branches of (a tree)
TOQUE = **tuque**
TOQUES ▸ **toque**
TOQUET = **toque**
TOQUETS ▸ **toquet**
TOR *n*
TORA *variant spelling of* ▸ **torah**
TORAH *n* whole body of traditional Jewish teaching **torahs**
TORAN *n* (in Indian architecture) an archway **torana**
TORANAS ▸ **torana**
TORANS ▸ **toran**
TORAS ▸ **tora**
TORC = **torque**
TORCH *n, vb* **torched, torcher, torches**
TORCHON *n as in* **torchon lace** coarse linen or cotton lace with a simple openwork pattern
TORCHY *adj* sentimental; maudlin; characteristic of a torch song
TORCS ▸ **torc**
TORDION *n* old triple-time dance for two people
TORE = **torus**
TORERO *n* bullfighter, esp one on foot **toreros**
TORES ▸ **tore**
TORGOCH *n* type of char
TORI ▸ **torus**
TORIC *adj* of, relating to, or having the form of a torus **torics**
TORIES ▸ **tory**
TORII *n* gateway, esp one at the entrance to a Japanese Shinto temple
TORMENT *vb, n*
TORMINA *n* complaints
TORN ▸ **tear**
TORNADE = **tornado**
TORNADO *n*
TORO *n* bull
TOROID *n* surface generated by rotating a closed plane curve about a coplanar line that does not intersect it **toroids**
TOROS ▸ **toro**
TOROSE *adj* (of a cylindrical part) having irregular swellings
TOROT ▸ **torah**
TOROTH ▸ **torah**
TOROUS = **torose**
TORPEDO *n, vb*
TORPEFY *n* make torpid
TORPID *adj*
TORPIDS *n* series of boat races held at Oxford University
TORPOR *n* **torpors**
TORQUE *n* force causing rotation ▹ *vb* apply torque to (something) **torqued, torquer**
TORQUES *n* distinctive band of hair, feathers, skin, or colour around the neck of an animal
TORR *n* unit of pressure
TORREFY *vb* dry (drugs, ores, etc) by subjection to intense heat
TORRENT *n, adj*
TORRET = **terret**
TORRETS ▸ **torret**
TORRID *adj*
TORRIFY = **torrefy**
TORRS ▸ **torr**
TORS ▸ **tor**
TORSADE *n* ornamental twist or twisted cord, as on hats
TORSE = **torso**
TORSEL *n* wooden beam along the top of a wall **torsels**
TORSES ▸ **torse**
TORSI ▸ **torso**
TORSION *n* twisting of a part by equal forces being applied at both ends but in opposite directions
TORSIVE *adj* twisted
TORSK *n* fish with a single long dorsal fin **torsks**
TORSO *n* **torsos**
TORT *n* civil wrong or injury for which damages may be claimed
TORTA *n* (in mining) a flat circular pile of

silver ore **tortas**
TORTE *n* rich cake, originating in Austria **torten, tortes**
TORTILE *adj* twisted or coiled
TORTIVE *adj* twisted
TORTONI *n* rich ice cream often flavoured with sherry
TORTRIX *n* type of moth
TORTS ▸ **tort**
TORTURE *vb, n*
TORULA *n* species of fungal microorganisms **torulae, torulas**
TORULI ▸ **torulus**
TORULIN *n* vitamin found in yeast
TORULUS *n* socket in an insect's head in which its antenna is attached
TORUS *n* large convex moulding approximately semicircular in cross section, esp one used on the base of a classical column
TORY *n* ultraconservative or reactionary person ▹ *adj* ultraconservative or reactionary
TOSA *n* large reddish dog, originally bred for fighting **tosas**
TOSE = **toze**
TOSED ▸ **tose**
TOSES ▸ **tose**
TOSH *n* nonsense ▹ *vb* tidy or trim
TOSHACH *n* military leader of a clan
TOSHED, tosher, toshers, toshes ▸ **tosh**
TOSHIER ▸ **toshy**
TOSHING ▸ **tosh**
TOSHY *adj* neat; trim
TOSING ▸ **tose**
TOSS *vb, n* **tossed, tossen, tosses**
TOSSIER ▸ **tossy**
TOSSILY ▸ **tossy**
TOSSING ▸ **toss**
TOSSUP *n* instance of tossing up a coin **tossups**
TOSSY *adj* impudent
TOST *old past participle of* ▸ **toss**
TOSTADA *n* crispy deep-fried tortilla topped with meat, cheese, and refried beans **tostado**
TOT *n, vb*
TOTABLE ▸ **tote**
TOTAL *n, adj, vb* **totaled, totally, totals**
TOTANUS *another name for* > **redshank**
TOTARA *n* tall coniferous forest tree of New Zealand **totaras**
TOTE *vb, n* **toted**
TOTEM *n* **totemic, totems**
TOTER ▸ **tote**
TOTERS ▸ **tote**
TOTES ▸ **tote**
TOTHER *n* other
TOTIENT *n* quantity of numbers less than, and sharing no common factors with, a number
TOTING ▸ **tote**
TOTS ▸ **tot**
TOTTED ▸ **tot**
TOTTER *vb, n* **totters, tottery**
TOTTIE *adj* very small
TOTTIER ▸ **totty**
TOTTIES ▸ **totty**
TOTTING ▸ **tot**
TOTTY *n* people, esp women, collectively considered as sexual objects ▹ *adj* very small
TOUCAN *n* **toucans**
TOUCH *vb, n, adj*
TOUCHE *interj* acknowledgment of a remark or witty reply
TOUCHED *adj* emotionally moved
TOUCHER ▸ **touch**
TOUCHES ▸ **touch**
TOUCHUP *n* renovation or retouching, as of a painting
TOUCHY *adj*
TOUGH *adj, n* **toughed**
TOUGHEN *vb* make or become tough or tougher
TOUGHER ▸ **tough**
TOUGHIE *n* person who is tough
TOUGHLY ▸ **tough**
TOUGHS ▸ **tough**
TOUGHY = **toughie**
TOUK = **tuck**
TOUKED ▸ **touk**
TOUKING ▸ **touk**
TOUKS ▸ **touk**
TOUN *n* town **touns**

TOUPEE *n*
TOUPEED *adj* wearing a toupee
TOUPEES ▸ **toupee**
TOUPET = **toupee**
TOUPETS ▸ **toupet**
TOUR *n, vb*
TOURACO *n* brightly coloured crested arboreal African bird
TOURED ▸ **tour**
TOURER *n* large open car with a folding top **tourers**
TOURIE = **toorie**
TOURIES ▸ **tourie**
TOURING ▸ **tour**
TOURISM *n*
TOURIST *n, adj*
TOURNEY *n* knightly tournament ▹ *vb* engage in a tourney
TOURS ▸ **tour**
TOUSE *vb* tangle, ruffle, or disarrange; treat roughly **toused, touser, tousers, touses**
TOUSIER ▸ **tousy**
TOUSING ▸ **touse**
TOUSLE *vb* make (hair or clothes) ruffled and untidy ▹ *n* disorderly, tangled, or rumpled state **tousled, tousles**
TOUSTIE *adj* irritable; testy
TOUSY *adj* tousled
TOUT *vb, n* **touted, touter, touters**
TOUTIE *adj* childishly irritable or sullen **toutier**
TOUTING ▸ **tout**
TOUTS ▸ **tout**
TOUZE *variant spelling of* ▸ **touse**
TOUZED ▸ **touze**
TOUZES ▸ **touze**
TOUZIER ▸ **touzy**
TOUZING ▸ **touze**
TOUZLE *rare spelling of* ▸ **tousle**
TOUZLED ▸ **touzle**
TOUZLES ▸ **touzle**
TOUZY *variant spelling of* ▸ **tousy**
TOW *vb, n* **towable**
TOWAGE *n* charge made for towing **towages**
TOWARD = **towards**
TOWARDS *prep*
TOWAWAY *n* vehicle which has been towed away
TOWBAR *n* **towbars**
TOWBOAT *n* another word for tug (the boat)
TOWED ▸ **tow**
TOWEL *n, vb* **toweled, towels**
TOWER *n, vb*
TOWERED *adj* having a tower or towers
TOWERS ▸ **tower**
TOWERY *adj* with towers
TOWHEAD *n* often disparaging term for a person with blond or yellowish hair
TOWHEE *n* N American brownish-coloured sparrow **towhees**
TOWIE *n* truck used for towing
TOWIER ▸ **tow**
TOWIES ▸ **towie**
TOWIEST, towing, towings ▸ **tow**
TOWKAY *n* sir **towkays**
TOWLINE = **towrope**
TOWMON = **towmond**
TOWMOND *n* old word for year
TOWMONS ▸ **towmon**
TOWMONT = **towmond**
TOWN *n*
TOWNEE = **townie**
TOWNEES ▸ **townee**
TOWNIE *n* often disparaging term for a resident in a town
TOWNIER ▸ **towny**
TOWNIES ▸ **towny**
TOWNISH ▸ **town**
TOWNLET *n* small town
TOWNLY *adj* characteristic of a town
TOWNS ▸ **town**
TOWNY *adj* characteristic of a town
TOWPATH *n*
TOWROPE *n* rope or cable used for towing a vehicle or vessel
TOWS ▸ **tow**
TOWSACK *n* sack made from tow
TOWSE = **touse; towsed, towser, towsers, towses**
TOWSIER ▸ **towsy**
TOWSING ▸ **towse**
TOWSY = **tousy**
TOWT *vb* sulk **towted, towting, towts**
TOWY ▸ **tow**
TOWZE = **touse**
TOWZED ▸ **towze**

TOWZES ▶ **towze**
TOWZIER ▶ **towzy**
TOWZING ▶ **towze**
TOWZY = **tousy**
TOXEMIA = **toxaemia**
TOXEMIC > **toxaemia**
TOXIC *adj, n*
TOXICAL *adj* toxic
TOXICS ▶ **toxic**
TOXIN *n* toxine
TOXINES ▶ **toxine**
TOXINS ▶ **toxin**
TOXOID *n* toxin that has been treated to reduce its toxicity **toxoids**
TOY *n, adj, vb* **toyed, toyer, toyers**
TOYETIC *adj*
TOYING ▶ **toy**
TOYINGS ▶ **toy**
TOYISH *adj* resembling a toy
TOYLESS ▶ **toy**
TOYLIKE ▶ **toy**
TOYLSOM *old spelling of* > **toilsome**
TOYMAN *n* man who sells toys **toymen**
TOYO *n* Japanese straw-like material made out of rice paper and used to make hats
TOYON *n* shrub related to the rose **toyons**
TOYOS ▶ **toyo**
TOYS ▶ **toy**
TOYSHOP *n* shop selling toys
TOYSOME *adj* playful
TOYTOWN *adj* having an unreal and picturesque appearance
TOZE *vb* tease out; (of wool, etc) card **tozed, tozes**
TOZIE *n* type of shawl **tozies**
TOZING ▶ **toze**
TRABS *pl n* training shoes
TRACE *vb, n* **traced**
TRACER *n* projectile which leaves a visible trail **tracers**
TRACERY *n*
TRACES ▶ **trace**
TRACEUR *n* parkour participant
TRACHEA *n*
TRACHLE *vb* (of hair, clothing, etc) make untidy
TRACING *n* traced copy
TRACK *n, vb* **tracked, tracker, tracks**
TRACT *n, vb* **tracted**
TRACTOR *n*
TRACTS ▶ **tract**
TRACTUS *n* anthem sung in some RC masses
TRAD *n* traditional jazz, as revived in the 1950s
TRADE *n, vb, adj* **traded**
TRADER *n* **traders**
TRADES ▶ **trade**
TRADING ▶ **trade**
TRADS ▶ **trad**
TRADUCE *vb*
TRAFFIC *n, vb*
TRAGAL ▶ **tragus**
TRAGEDY *n*
TRAGI ▶ **tragus**
TRAGIC *adj, n* **tragics**
TRAGULE *n* mouse deer
TRAGUS *n* fleshy projection that partially covers the entrance to the external ear
TRAIK *vb* trudge; trek with difficulty **traiked, traikit, traiks**
TRAIL *n, vb* **trailed**
TRAILER *n, vb*
TRAILS ▶ **trail**
TRAIN *vb, n* **trained**
TRAINEE *n, adj*
TRAINER *n* person who trains an athlete or sportsman
TRAINS ▶ **train**
TRAIPSE *vb, n*
TRAIT *n*
TRAITOR *n*
TRAITS ▶ **trait**
TRAJECT *vb* transport or transmit
TRAM = **trammel**
TRAMCAR = **tram**
TRAMEL *variant spelling of* ▶ **trammel**
TRAMELL *variant spelling of* ▶ **trammel**
TRAMELS ▶ **tramel**
TRAMMED ▶ **tram**
TRAMMEL *n, vb*
TRAMMIE *n* conductor or driver of a tram
TRAMP *vb, n* **tramped**
TRAMPER *n* person who tramps
TRAMPET *variant spelling of* > **trampette**
TRAMPLE *vb, n*
TRAMPS ▶ **tramp**
TRAMPY *adj* (of woman) disreputable
TRAMS ▶ **tram**

TRAMWAY = **tramline**
TRANCE *n, vb* **tranced, trances**
TRANCEY *adj* (of music) characteristic of the trance sub-genre
TRANCHE *n* portion of something large
TRANECT *n* ferry
TRANGAM *n* bauble or trinket
TRANGLE *n* (in heraldry) a small fesse
TRANK *n* short form of tranquillizer: drug that calms a person **tranks**
TRANKUM = **trangam**
TRANNIE *n* transistor radio **tranny**
TRANQ = **trank**

Short for tranquilliser; another of those useful words allowing you to play the Q without a U.

TRANQS ▸ **tranq**
TRANS *n* short from of translation
TRANSE *n* way through; passage **transes**
TRANSIT *n, vb*
TRANSOM *n* horizontal bar across a window
TRANT *vb* travel from place to place selling goods **tranted, tranter, trants**
TRAP *n, vb*
TRAPAN = **trepan**
TRAPANS ▸ **trapan**
TRAPE = **traipse**
TRAPED ▸ **trape**
TRAPES = **traipse**
TRAPEZE *n, vb*
TRAPING ▸ **trape**
TRAPPED ▸ **trap**
TRAPPER *n*
TRAPPY *adj* having many traps
TRAPS ▸ **trap**
TRAPT *old past participle of* ▸ **trap**
TRASH *n, vb*
TRASHED *adj* drunk
TRASHER ▸ **trash**
TRASHES ▸ **trash**
TRASHY *adj*
TRASS *n* variety of the volcanic rock tuff **trasses**
TRAT *n* type of fishing line holding a series of baited hooks **trats**
TRATT *short for* > **trattoria**
TRATTS ▸ **tratt**
TRAUMA *n* **traumas**
TRAVAIL *n, vb*
TRAVE *n* stout wooden cage in which difficult horses are shod
TRAVEL *vb, n* **travels**
TRAVES ▸ **trave**
TRAVIS = **treviss**
TRAVOIS *n* sled used for dragging logs
TRAWL *n, vb* **trawled**
TRAWLER *n*
TRAWLEY = **trolley**
TRAWLS ▸ **trawl**
TRAY *n*
TRAYBIT *n* threepenny bit
TRAYFUL *n* as many or as much as will fit on a tray
TRAYNE *old spelling of* ▸ **train**
TRAYNED ▸ **train**
TRAYNES ▸ **trayne**
TRAYS ▸ **tray**
TREACLE *n, vb* **treacly**
TREAD *vb, n* **treaded, treader**
TREADLE *n, vb*
TREADS ▸ **tread**
TREAGUE *n* agreement to stop fighting
TREASON *n*
TREAT *vb, n* **treated, treater, treats**
TREATY *n*
TREBLE *adj, n, vb* **trebled, trebles, trebly**
TRECK = **trek**
TRECKED ▸ **treck**
TRECKS ▸ **treck**
TREDDLE *variant spelling of* ▸ **treadle**
TREE *n* **treed, treeing**
TREEN *adj* made of wood ▹ *n* art of making treenware **treens**
TREES ▸ **tree**
TREETOP *n* top of a tree
TREEWAX *n* yellowish wax secreted by an oriental scale insect
TREF *adj* in Judaism, ritually unfit to be eaten **trefa, trefah**
TREFOIL *n*
TREHALA *n* edible sugary substance from the cocoon of an Asian weevil
TREIF = **tref**
TREIFA = **tref**
TREILLE *another word for* ▸ **trellis**

TREK *n, vb* **trekked, trekker, treks**
TRELLIS *n, vb*
TREMA *n* mark placed over vowel to indicate it is to be pronounced separately **tremas**
TREMBLE *vb, n* **trembly**
TREMIE *n* metal hopper and pipe used to distribute freshly mixed concrete underwater **tremies**
TREMOLO *n*
TREMOR *n, vb* **tremors**
TRENAIL = **treenail**
TRENCH *n, adj, vb*
TREND *n, vb* **trended, trends**
TRENDY *n, adj*
TRENISE *n* one of the figures in a quadrille
TRENTAL *n* mass said in remembrance of a person 30 days after his or her death
TREPAN = **trephine**
TREPANG *n* any of various large sea cucumbers
TREPANS ▸ **trepan**
TREPID *adj* trembling
TRES *adj* very
TRESS *n* lock of hair, esp a long lock of woman's hair ▷ *vb* arrange in tresses
TRESSED *adj* having a tress or tresses as specified
TRESSEL *variant spelling of* ▸ **trestle**
TRESSES ▸ **tress**
TRESSY ▸ **tress**
TREST *old variant of* ▸ **trestle**
TRESTLE *n*
TRESTS ▸ **trest**
TRET *n* (formerly) allowance granted for waste due to transportation **trets**
TREVET = **trivet**
TREVETS ▸ **trevet**
TREVIS *variant spelling of* ▸ **treviss**
TREVISS *n* partition in a stable for keeping animals apart
TREW *old variant spelling of* ▸ **true**
TREWS *pl n* close-fitting tartan trousers
TREY *n* any card or dice throw with three spots
TREYBIT = **traybit**
TREYS ▸ **trey**
TREZ = **trey**
TREZES ▸ **trez**
TRIABLE *adj* liable to be tried judicially
TRIAC *n* device for regulating the amount of electric current allowed to reach a circuit
TRIACID *adj* (of a base) capable of reacting with three molecules of a monobasic acid
TRIACS ▸ **triac**
TRIACT *adj* having three rays
TRIAD *n*
TRIADIC *n* something that has the characteristics of a triad
TRIADS ▸ **triad**
TRIAGE *n* sorting emergency patients into categories of priority ▷ *vb* sort (patients) into categories of priority **triaged, triages**
TRIAL *n* **trials**
TRIARCH *n* one of three rulers of a triarchy
TRIATIC *n* rope between a ship's mastheads
TRIAXON *another name for* > **triaxial**
TRIAZIN = **triazine**
TRIBADE *n* lesbian, esp one who practises tribadism
TRIBAL *adj* of or denoting a tribe or tribes ▷ *n* member of a tribal community **tribals**
TRIBBLE *n* frame for drying paper
TRIBE *n* **tribes**
TRIBLET *n* spindle or mandrel used in making rings, tubes, etc
TRIBUNE *n*
TRIBUTE *n*
TRICAR *n* car with three wheels **tricars**
TRICE *n, vb* **triced**
TRICEP = **triceps**
TRICEPS *n*
TRICES ▸ **trice**
TRICING ▸ **trice**
TRICK *n, vb* **tricked, tricker**
TRICKIE *Scots form of* ▸ **tricky**

TRICKLE *vb, n* **trickly**
TRICKS ▸ **trick**
TRICKSY *adj* playing tricks habitually
TRICKY *adj*
TRICLAD *n* type of worm having a tripartite intestine
TRICORN *n* cocked hat with opposing brims turned back and caught in three places ▹ *adj* having three horns or corners
TRICOT *n* thin rayon or nylon fabric knitted or resembling knitting, used for dresses, etc **tricots**
TRIDARN *n* sideboard with three levels
TRIDE *old spelling of the past tense of* ▸ **try**
TRIDENT *n, adj*
TRIDUAN *adj* three days long
TRIDUUM *n* period of three days for prayer before a feast
TRIE *old spelling of* ▸ **try**
TRIED ▸ **try**
TRIELLA *n* bet on the winners of three nominated horse races
TRIENE *n* chemical compound containing three double bonds **trienes**
TRIENS *n* Byzantine gold coin worth one third of a solidus
TRIER *n* person or thing that tries **triers**
TRIES ▸ **try**
TRIFF *adj* terrific; very good indeed **triffer**
TRIFFIC *adj* terrific; very good indeed
TRIFFID *n* fictional plant that could kill humans
TRIFID *adj* divided or split into three parts or lobes
TRIFLE *n, vb* **trifled, trifler, trifles**
TRIFOLD *less common word for* ▸ **triple**
TRIFOLY = **trefoil**
TRIFORM *adj* having three parts
TRIG *adj* neat or spruce ▹ *vb* make or become spruce
TRIGAMY *n* condition of having three spouses
TRIGGED ▸ **trig**
TRIGGER *n, vb*
TRIGLOT *n* person who can speak three languages
TRIGLY ▸ **trig**
TRIGO *n* wheat field
TRIGON *n* (in classical Greece or Rome) a triangular harp or lyre **trigons**
TRIGOS ▸ **trigo**
TRIGRAM *n* three-letter inscription
TRIGS ▸ **trig**
TRIJET *n* jet with three engines **trijets**
TRIKE *n* tricycle **trikes**
TRILBY *n* **trilbys**
TRILD *old past tense of* ▸ **trill**
TRILITH = **trilithon**
TRILL *n, vb* **trilled, triller**
TRILLO *n* (in music) a trill
TRILLS ▸ **trill**
TRILOBE *n* three-lobed thing
TRILOGY *n*
TRIM *adj, vb, n*
TRIMER *n* polymer or a molecule of a polymer consisting of three identical monomers **trimers**
TRIMIX *n* gas mixture of nitrogen, helium and oxygen used by deep-sea divers
TRIMLY, trimmed, trimmer, trims ▸ **trim**
TRIMTAB *n* small control surface to enable the pilot to balance an aircraft
TRIN *n* triplet
TRINAL ▸ **trine**
TRINARY *adj* made up of three parts
TRINDLE *vb* move heavily on (or as if on) wheels
TRINE *n* aspect of 120° between two planets, an orb of 8° being allowed ▹ *adj* of or relating to a trine ▹ *vb* put in a trine aspect **trined, trines**
TRINGLE *n* slim rod
TRINING ▸ **trine**
TRINITY *n*
TRINKET *n, vb*
TRINKUM *n* trinket or bauble

TRINS ▸ **trin**
TRIO *n*
TRIODE *n* electronic valve having three electrodes, a cathode, an anode, and a grid **triodes**
TRIOL *n* any of a class of alcohols that have three hydroxyl groups per molecule
TRIOLET *n* verse form of eight lines
TRIOLS ▸ **triol**
TRIONES *n* seven stars of the constellation Ursa Major
TRIONYM *another name for* > **trinomial**
TRIOR *old form of* ▸ **trier**
TRIORS ▸ **trior**
TRIOS ▸ **trio**
TRIOSE *n* simple monosaccharide produced by the oxidation of glycerol **trioses**
TRIOXID = **trioxide**
TRIP *n*, *vb*
TRIPACK *n* pack of three
TRIPART *adj* composed of three parts
TRIPE *n*
TRIPERY *n* place where tripe is prepared
TRIPES ▸ **tripe**
TRIPEY ▸ **tripe**
TRIPIER ▸ **tripe**
TRIPLE *adj*, *vb*, *n* **tripled, triples**
TRIPLET *n*
TRIPLEX *n* building divided into three separate dwellings
TRIPLY *vb* give a reply to a duply
TRIPOD *n* **tripods**
TRIPODY *n* metrical unit consisting of three feet
TRIPOLI *n* lightweight porous siliceous rock
TRIPOS *n* final examinations for an honours degree at Cambridge University
TRIPPED ▸ **trip**
TRIPPER *n*
TRIPPET *n* any mechanism that strikes or is struck at regular intervals, as by a cam
TRIPPLE *vb* canter
TRIPPY *adj* suggestive of or resembling the effect produced by a hallucinogenic drug
TRIPS ▸ **trip**
TRIPSES ▸ **tripsis**
TRIPSIS *n* act of kneading the body to promote circulation, suppleness, etc
TRIPTAN *n* drug used to treat migraine
TRIPY ▸ **tripe**
TRIREME *n* ancient Greek warship with three rows of oars on each side
TRISECT *vb* divide into three parts, esp three equal parts
TRISEME *n* metrical foot of a length equal to three short syllables
TRISHAW *another name for* > **rickshaw**
TRISMIC ▸ **trismus**
TRISMUS *n* state of being unable to open the mouth
TRISOME *n* chromosome occurring three times (rather than twice) in a cell
TRISOMY *n* condition of having one chromosome represented three times
TRIST *variant spelling of* ▸ **triste**
TRISTE *adj* sad
TRISUL *n* trident symbol of Siva **trisula, trisuls**
TRITE *adj*, *n* **tritely, triter, trites, tritest**
TRITIDE *n* tritium compound
TRITIUM *n* radioactive isotope of hydrogen
TRITOMA *another name for* > **kniphofia**
TRITON *n* any of various chiefly tropical marine gastropod molluscs
TRITONE *n* musical interval consisting of three whole tones
TRITONS ▸ **triton**
TRIUMPH *n*, *vb*
TRIUNE *adj* constituting three things in one ▹ *n* group of three **triunes**
TRIVET *n* **trivets**
TRIVIA *pl n*
TRIVIAL *adj*

TRIVIUM *n* (in medieval learning) the lower division of the seven liberal arts
TRIZONE *n* area comprising three zones
TROAD = **trod**
TROADE = **trod**
TROADES ▶ **troade**
TROADS ▶ **troad**
TROAK *old form of* ▶ **truck**
TROAKED ▶ **troak**
TROAKS ▶ **troak**
TROAT *vb* (of a rutting buck) to call or bellow **troated, troats**
TROCAR *n* surgical instrument for removing fluid from bodily cavities **trocars**
TROCHAL *adj* shaped like a wheel
TROCHAR *old variant spelling of* ▶ **trocar**
TROCHE *another name for* ▶ **lozenge**
TROCHEE *n* metrical foot of one long and one short syllable
TROCHES ▶ **troche**
TROCHI ▶ **trochus**
TROCHIL = **trochilus**
TROCHUS *n* hoop (used in exercise)
TROCK = **truck**
TROCKED ▶ **trock**
TROCKEN *adj* dry (used of wine)
TROCKS ▶ **trock**
TROD *vb* past participle of tread ▷ *n* path
TRODDEN ▶ **tread**
TRODE = **trod**
TRODES ▶ **trode**
TRODS ▶ **trod**
TROELIE = **troolie**
TROELY = **troolie**
TROFFER *n* fixture for holding and reflecting light from a fluorescent tube
TROG *vb* walk, esp aimlessly or heavily **trogged**
TROGGS *n* loyalty; fidelity
TROGON *n* bird of tropical and subtropical America, Africa, and Asia **trogons**
TROGS ▶ **trog**
TROIKA *n* **troikas**
TROILUS *n* type of large butterfly
TROIS *Scots form of* ▶ **troy**
TROKE = **truck**
TROKED ▶ **troke**
TROKES ▶ **troke**
TROKING ▶ **troke**
TROLAND *n* unit of light intensity in the eye
TROLL *n, vb* **trolled, troller**
TROLLEY *n, vb*
TROLLS ▶ **troll**
TROLLY = **trolley**
TROMINO *n* shape made from three squares, each joined to the next along one full side
TROMMEL *n* revolving cylindrical sieve used to screen crushed ore
TROMP *vb* trample
TROMPE *n* apparatus for supplying the blast of air in a forge
TROMPED ▶ **tromp**
TROMPES ▶ **trompe**
TROMPS ▶ **tromp**
TRON *n* public weighing machine
TRONA *n* greyish mineral that occurs in salt deposits **tronas**
TRONC *n* pool into which waiters, waitresses, hotel workers, etc, pay their tips **troncs**
TRONE = **tron**
TRONES ▶ **trone**
TRONK *n* jail **tronks**
TRONS ▶ **tron**
TROOLIE *n* large palm leaf
TROOP *n, vb* **trooped**
TROOPER *n*
TROOPS ▶ **troop**
TROOZ = **trews**
TROP *adv* too, too much
TROPE *n* figure of speech ▷ *vb* use tropes (in speech or writing) **troped, tropes**
TROPHI *pl n* collective term for the mandibles and other parts of an insect's mouth
TROPHIC *adj* of or relating to nutrition
TROPHY *n, adj, vb*
TROPIC *n* either of two lines of latitude at 23½°N (tropic of Cancer) or 23½°S (tropic of Capricorn) **tropics**

TROPIN *n* andrenal androgen
TROPINE *n* white crystalline poisonous alkaloid
TROPING ▸ **trope**
TROPINS ▸ **tropin**
TROPISM *n* **tropist**
TROPPO *adv* too much ▹ *adj* mentally affected by a tropical climate
TROT *vb, n*
TROTH *n, vb* **trothed, troths**
TROTS ▸ **trot**
TROTTED ▸ **trot**
TROTTER *n*
TROTYL *n* yellow solid used chiefly as a high explosive **trotyls**
TROUBLE *n, vb*
TROUCH *n* rubbish
TROUGH *n, vb* **troughs**
TROULE *old variant of* ▸ **troll**
TROULED ▸ **troule**
TROULES ▸ **troule**
TROUNCE *vb*
TROUPE *n, vb* **trouped**
TROUPER *n* member of a troupe
TROUPES ▸ **troupe**
TROUSE *pl n* close-fitting breeches worn in Ireland
TROUSER *adj* of trousers ▹ *vb* take (something, esp money), often surreptitiously or unlawfully ▹ *n* of or relating to trousers
TROUSES ▸ **trouse**
TROUT *n, vb* **trouter, trouts, trouty**
TROVE *n as in* **treasure-trove** valuable articles found hidden in the earth
TROVER *n* act of assuming proprietary rights over goods or property belonging to another **trovers**
TROVES ▸ **trove**
TROW *vb* think, believe, or trust **trowed**
TROWEL *n, vb* **trowels**
TROWING ▸ **trow**
TROWS ▸ **trow**
TROWTH *variant spelling of* ▸ **troth**
TROWTHS ▸ **trowth**
TROY *n as in* **troy weight** system of weights used for precious metals and gemstones, based on the grain, which is identical to the avoirdupois grain **troys**
TRUANCY ▸ **truant**
TRUANT *n, adj, vb* **truants**
TRUCAGE *n* art forgery
TRUCE *n, vb* **truced, truces, trucial, trucing**
TRUCK *n, vb* **trucked**
TRUCKER *n* truck driver
TRUCKIE *n* truck driver
TRUCKLE *vb* yield weakly or give in ▹ *n* small wheel
TRUCKS ▸ **truck**
TRUDGE *vb, n* **trudged**
TRUDGEN *n* type of swimming stroke
TRUDGER ▸ **trudge**
TRUDGES ▸ **trudge**
TRUE *adj* **trued, trueing**
TRUEMAN *n* honest person **truemen**
TRUER ▸ **true**
TRUES ▸ **true**
TRUEST ▸ **true**
TRUFFE *rare word for* ▸ **truffle**
TRUFFES ▸ **truffe**
TRUFFLE *n, vb*
TRUG *n* long shallow basket used by gardeners
TRUGO *n* game similar to croquet **trugos**
TRUGS ▸ **trug**
TRUING ▸ **true**
TRUISM *n* **truisms**
TRULL *n* prostitute **trulls**
TRULY *adv* in a true manner
TRUMEAU *n* section of a wall or pillar between two openings
TRUMP *adj, vb, pl n* **trumped**
TRUMPET *n, vb*
TRUMPS ▸ **trump**
TRUNCAL *adj* of or relating to the trunk
TRUNDLE *vb, n*
TRUNK *n, vb* **trunked**
TRUNKS *pl n* shorts worn by a man for swimming
TRUNNEL = **treenail**
TRUSS *vb, n* **trussed, trusser, trusses**

TRUST *vb, n, adj* **trusted**
TRUSTEE *n, vb*
TRUSTER ▸ **trust**
TRUSTOR *n* person who sets up a trust
TRUSTS ▸ **trust**
TRUSTY *adj, n*
TRUTH *n* **truths**
TRUTHY *adj* truthful
TRY *vb, n*
TRYE *adj* very good; select
TRYER *variant of* ▸ **trier**
TRYERS ▸ **tryer**
TRYING ▸ **try**
TRYINGS ▸ **try**
TRYKE *variant spelling of* ▸ **trike**
TRYKES ▸ **tryke**
TRYMA *n* drupe produced by the walnut and similar plants **trymata**
TRYOUT *n* trial or test, as of an athlete or actor **tryouts**
TRYP *n* parastitic protozoan
TRYPAN *modifier as in* **trypan blue** dye used for staining cells in biological research
TRYPS ▸ **tryp**
TRYPSIN *n* enzyme occurring in pancreatic juice **tryptic**
TRYSAIL *n* small fore-and-aft sail on a sailing vessel
TRYST *n, vb* **tryste, trysted, tryster**
TRYSTES ▸ **tryste**
TRYSTS ▸ **tryst**
TSADDIK *variant of* ▸ **zaddik**
TSADDIQ *variant of* ▸ **zaddik**
TSADE *variant spelling of* ▸ **sadhe**
TSADES ▸ **tsade**
TSADI *variant of* ▸ **sadhe**
TSADIS ▸ **tsadi**
TSAMBA *n* Tibetan dish made from roasted barley and tea **tsambas**
TSANTSA *n* shrunken head of an enemy kept as a trophy
TSAR *n* **tsardom**
TSARINA *n*
TSARISM *n* system of government by a tsar **tsarist**
TSARS ▸ **tsar**
TSATSKE *variant of* > **tchotchke**
TSETSE *n* any of various bloodsucking African flies **tsetses**
TSIGANE *variant of* ▸ **tzigane**
TSIMMES *variant spelling of* ▸ **tzimmes**
TSK *vb* utter the sound "tsk", usu in disapproval **tsked, tsking, tsks, tsktsk**

> This can occasionally be useful because it enables you to play K without using vowels.

TSKTSKS ▸ **tsktsk**
TSOORIS *variant of* ▸ **tsuris**
TSORES *variant of* ▸ **tsuris**
TSORIS *variant of* ▸ **tsuris**
TSOTSI *n* Black street thug or gang member **tsotsis**
TSOURIS *variant of* ▸ **tsuris**
TSUBA *n* sword guard of a Japanese sword **tsubas**
TSUNAMI *n*
TSURIS *n* grief or strife
TUAN *n* lord **tuans**
TUART *n* eucalyptus tree of Australia **tuarts**
TUATARA *n* **tuatera**
TUATH *n* territory of an ancient Irish tribe **tuaths**
TUATUA *n* edible marine bivalve of New Zealand waters **tuatuas**
TUB *n, vb*
TUBA *n* **tubae**
TUBAGE *n* insertion of a tube **tubages**
TUBAIST ▸ **tuba**
TUBAL *adj* of or relating to a tube
TUBAR *another word for* ▸ **tubular**
TUBAS ▸ **tuba**
TUBATE *less common word for* ▸ **tubular**
TUBBED ▸ **tub**
TUBBER ▸ **tub**
TUBBERS ▸ **tub**
TUBBIER ▸ **tubby**
TUBBING ▸ **tub**
TUBBISH *adj* fat
TUBBY *adj*
TUBE *n* **tubed**

TUBEFUL *n* quantity (of something) that a tube can hold
TUBER *n* **tubers**
TUBES ▸ **tube**
TUBFAST *n* period of fasting and sweating in a tub, intended as a cure for disease
TUBFISH *another name for* ▸ **gurnard**
TUBFUL *n* amount a tub will hold **tubfuls**
TUBIFEX *n* type of small reddish freshwater worm
TUBING *n* length of tube **tubings**
TUBIST ▸ **tuba**
TUBISTS ▸ **tuba**
TUBLIKE ▸ **tub**
TUBS ▸ **tub**
TUBULAR *adj*
TUBULE *n* any small tubular structure **tubules**
TUBULIN *n* protein forming the basis of microtubules
TUCHUN *n* (formerly) a Chinese military governor or warlord **tuchuns**
TUCK *vb, n* **tucked**
TUCKER *n, vb* **tuckers**
TUCKET *n* flourish on a trumpet **tuckets**
TUCKING ▸ **tuck**
TUCKS ▸ **tuck**
TUFA *n* **tufas**
TUFF *n* porous rock formed from volcanic dust or ash
TUFFE *old form of* ▸ **tuft**
TUFFES ▸ **tuffe**
TUFFET *n* small mound or seat **tuffets**
TUFFS ▸ **tuff**
TUFOLI *n* type of tubular pasta
TUFT *n, vb*
TUFTED *adj* having a tuft or tufts
TUFTER, tufters, tuftier, tuftily, tufting, tufts, tufty ▸ **tuft**
TUG *vb, n* **tugboat, tugged, tugger, tuggers, tugging**
TUGHRA *n* Turkish Sultan's official emblem **tughras**
TUGHRIK = **tugrik**
TUGLESS ▸ **tug**
TUGRA = **tughra**
TUGRAS ▸ **tugra**
TUGRIK *n* standard monetary unit of Mongolia **tugriks**
TUGS ▸ **tug**
TUI *n* New Zealand honeyeater that mimics human speech and the songs of other birds
TUILLE *n* (in a suit of armour) hanging plate protecting the thighs **tuilles**
TUILYIE *vb* fight **tuilzie**
TUINA *n* form of massage originating in China **tuinas**
TUIS ▸ **tui**
TUISM *n* practice of putting the interests of another before one's own **tuisms**
TUITION *n*
TUKTOO = **tuktu**
TUKTOOS ▸ **tuktoo**
TUKTU *(in Canada) another name for* ▸ **caribou**
TUKTUS ▸ **tuktu**
TULADI *n* large trout found in Canada and northern US **tuladis**
TULBAN *old form of* ▸ **turban**
TULBANS ▸ **tulban**
TULCHAN *n* skin of a calf placed next to a cow to induce it to give milk
TULE *n* type of bulrush found in California **tules**
TULIP *n* **tulips**
TULLE *n* **tulles**
TULPA *n* being or object created through willpower and visualization techniques **tulpas**
TULWAR *n* Indian sabre **tulwars**
TUM *informal or childish word for* ▸ **stomach**
TUMBLE *vb, n* **tumbled**
TUMBLER *n*
TUMBLES ▸ **tumble**
TUMBREL *n* **tumbril**
TUMEFY *vb* make or become tumid
TUMESCE *vb* swell
TUMID *adj* (of an organ or part of the body) enlarged or swollen **tumidly**
TUMMIES ▸ **tummy**

TUMMLER *n* entertainer employed to encourage audience participation
TUMMY *n*
TUMOR = **tumour**
TUMORAL ▸ **tumour**
TUMORS ▸ **tumor**
TUMOUR *n* **tumours**
TUMP *n* small mound or clump ▷ *vb* make a tump around **tumped**
TUMPHY *n* dolt; fool
TUMPIER, tumping, tumps, tumpy ▸ **tump**
TUMS ▸ **tum**
TUMSHIE *n* turnip
TUMULAR *adj* of, relating to, or like a mound
TUMULI ▸ **tumulus**
TUMULT *n, vb* **tumults**
TUMULUS *n*
TUN *n, vb*
TUNA *n*
TUNABLE *adj* able to be tuned **tunably**
TUNAS ▸ **tuna**
TUND *vb* beat; strike **tunded, tunding**
TUNDISH *n* type of funnel
TUNDRA *n* **tundras**
TUNDS ▸ **tund**
TUNDUN *n* wooden instrument used by Native Australians in religious rites **tunduns**
TUNE *n, vb* **tuned**
TUNEFUL *adj*
TUNER *n* **tuners**
TUNES ▸ **tune**
TUNEUP *n* adjustments made to an engine to improve its performance **tuneups**
TUNG *n as in* **tung oil** fast-drying oil obtained from the seeds of a central Asian tree **tungs**
TUNIC *n*
TUNICA *n* tissue forming a layer or covering of an organ or part **tunicae**
TUNICIN *n* cellulose-like substance found in tunicates
TUNICLE *n* vestment worn at High Mass and other religious ceremonies
TUNICS ▸ **tunic**
TUNIER ▸ **tuny**
TUNIEST ▸ **tuny**
TUNING *n* set of pitches to which the open strings of a guitar, violin, etc, are tuned **tunings**
TUNNAGE = **tonnage**
TUNNED ▸ **tun**
TUNNEL *n, vb* **tunnels**
TUNNIES ▸ **tunny**
TUNNING ▸ **tun**
TUNNY = **tuna**
TUNS ▸ **tun**
TUNY *adj* having an easily discernable melody
TUP *n* male sheep ▷ *vb* cause (a ram) to mate with a ewe
TUPEK = **tupik**
TUPEKS ▸ **tupek**
TUPELO *n* large tree of deep swamps and rivers of the southern US **tupelos**
TUPIK *n* tent of seal or caribou skin used for shelter by the Inuit in summer **tupiks**
TUPLE *n* row of values in a relational database **tuples**
TUPPED ▸ **tup**
TUPPING ▸ **tup**
TUPS ▸ **tup**
TUPUNA = **tipuna**
TUPUNAS ▸ **tupuna**
TUQUE *n* knitted cap with a long tapering end **tuques**
TURACIN *n* red pigment found in touraco feathers
TURACO = **touraco**
TURACOS ▸ **turaco**
TURACOU *variant of* ▸ **touraco**
TURBAN *n* **turband, turbans, turbant**
TURBARY *n* land where peat or turf is cut or has been cut
TURBETH *variant of* ▸ **turpeth**
TURBID *adj*
TURBINE *n*
TURBIT *n* crested breed of domestic pigeon
TURBITH *variant of* ▸ **turpeth**
TURBITS ▸ **turbit**
TURBO *n*
TURBOND *old variant of* ▸ **turban**
TURBOS ▸ **turbo**

TURBOT *n* **turbots**
TURDINE *adj* of, relating to, or characteristic of thrushes
TURDION *variant of* ▸ **tordion**
TURDOID = **turdine**
TUREEN *n* **tureens**
TURF *n, vb* **turfed**
TURFEN *adj* made of turf
TURFIER ▸ **turfy**
TURFING ▸ **turf**
TURFITE = **turfman**
TURFMAN *n* person devoted to horse racing **turfmen**
TURFS ▸ **turf**
TURFSKI *n* ski down a grassy hill on skis modified with integral wheels
TURFY *adj* of, covered with, or resembling turf
TURGENT *obsolete word for* ▸ **turgid**
TURGID *adj*
TURGITE *n* red or black mineral consisting of hydrated ferric oxide
TURGOR *n* normal rigid state of a cell **turgors**
TURION *n* perennating bud produced by many aquatic plants **turions**
TURISTA *n* traveller's diarrhoea
TURKEY *n* **turkeys**
TURKIES *old form of* > **turquoise**
TURKIS *old form of* > **turquoise**
TURKOIS *old form of* > **turquoise**
TURM *n* troop of horsemen **turme**
TURMES ▸ **turme**
TURMOIL *n, vb*
TURMS ▸ **turm**
TURN *vb, n*
TURNDUN *another name for* ▸ **tundun**
TURNED ▸ **turn**
TURNER *n* person or thing that turns **turners**
TURNERY *n* objects made on a lathe
TURNING *n*
TURNIP *n, vb* **turnips**
TURNIPY *adj* like a turnip
TURNKEY *n, adj*
TURNOFF *n* road or other way branching off from the main
TURNON *n* something sexually exciting **turnons**
TURNOUT *n*
TURNS ▸ **turn**
TURNUP *n* the turned-up fold at the bottom of some trouser legs **turnups**
TURPETH *n* convolvulaceous plant of the East Indies, having roots with purgative properties
TURPS *n*
TURRET *n* **turrets**
TURTLE *n* **turtled, turtler, turtles**
TURVES ▸ **turf**
TUSCHE *n* substance used in lithography for drawing the design **tusches**
TUSH *interj* exclamation of disapproval or contempt ▹ *n* small tusk ▹ *vb* utter the interjection "tush" **tushed**
TUSHERY *n* use of affectedly archaic language in novels, etc
TUSHES ▸ **tush**
TUSHIE *n* pair of buttocks **tushies**
TUSHING ▸ **tush**
TUSHKAR *variant of* ▸ **tuskar**
TUSHKER *variant of* ▸ **tuskar**
TUSHY = **tushie**
TUSK *n, vb*
TUSKAR *n* peat-cutting spade **tuskars**
TUSKED ▸ **tusk**
TUSKER *n* any animal with prominent tusks, esp a wild boar or elephant **tuskers**
TUSKIER, tusking, tusks, tusky ▸ **tusk**
TUSSAC *modifier as in* **tussac grass** kind of grass
TUSSAH = **tussore**
TUSSAHS ▸ **tussah**
TUSSAL ▸ **tussis**
TUSSAR *variant of* ▸ **tussore**
TUSSARS ▸ **tussar**
TUSSEH *variant of* ▸ **tussore**
TUSSEHS ▸ **tusseh**

TUSSER = **tussore**
TUSSERS ▸ **tusser**
TUSSES ▸ **tussis**
TUSSIS *technical name for a* ▸ **cough**
TUSSIVE ▸ **tussis**
TUSSLE *vb, n* **tussled, tussles**
TUSSOCK *n*
TUSSOR *variant of* ▸ **tussore**
TUSSORE *n* strong coarse brownish Indian silk obtained from the cocoons of an Oriental saturniid silkworm
TUSSORS ▸ **tussor**
TUSSUCK *variant of* ▸ **tussock**
TUSSUR = **tussore**
TUSSURS ▸ **tussur**
TUT *interj* an exclamation of mild disapproval, or surprise ▹ *vb* express disapproval by the exclamation of "tut-tut." ▹ *n* payment system based on measurable work done
TUTANIA *n* alloy of low melting point used mostly for decorative purposes
TUTEE *n* one who is tutored, esp in a university **tutees**
TUTELAR = **tutelary**
TUTENAG *n* zinc alloy
TUTMAN *n* one who does tutwork **tutmen**
TUTOR *n, vb* **tutored, tutors**
TUTOYED *adj* addressed in a familiar way
TUTOYER *vb* speak to someone on familiar terms
TUTRESS = **tutoress**
TUTRIX *n* female tutor; tutoress
TUTS *Scots version of* ▸ **tut**
TUTSAN *n* woodland shrub of Europe and W Asia **tutsans**
TUTSED ▸ **tuts**
TUTSES ▸ **tuts**
TUTSING ▸ **tuts**
TUTTED ▸ **tut**
TUTTI *adv* be performed by the whole orchestra or choir ▹ *n* piece of tutti music
TUTTIES ▸ **tutty**
TUTTING ▸ **tut**
TUTTIS ▸ **tutti**
TUTTY *n* finely powdered impure zinc oxide
TUTU *n*
TUTUED *adj* wearing tutu
TUTUS ▸ **tutu**
TUTWORK *n* work paid using a tut system
TUX *short for* ▸ **tuxedo**

> **Tux** is a short form of **tuxedo**, and is a very commonly played X word.

TUXEDO *n* **tuxedos**
TUXES ▸ **tux**
TUYER *variant of* ▸ **tuyere**
TUYERE *n* water-cooled nozzle through which air is blown into a cupola, blast furnace, or forge **tuyeres**
TUYERS ▸ **tuyer**
TUZZ *n* tuft or clump of hair **tuzzes**
TWA *Scots word for* ▸ **two**
TWADDLE *n, vb* **twaddly**
TWAE = **twa**
TWAES ▸ **twae**
TWAFALD *Scots variant of* ▸ **twofold**
TWAIN *n* **twains**
TWAITE *n* herring-like food fish **twaites**
TWAL *n* twelve **twals**
TWANG *n, vb* **twanged, twanger**
TWANGLE *vb* make a continuous loose twanging sound
TWANGS ▸ **twang**
TWANGY ▸ **twang**
TWANK *vb* make a sharply curtailed twang
TWANKAY *n* variety of Chinese green tea
TWANKS ▸ **twank**
TWANKY = **twankay**
TWAS ▸ **twa**
TWASOME = **twosome**
TWATTLE *rare word for* ▸ **twaddle**
TWAY *old variant of* ▸ **twain**
TWAYS ▸ **tway**
TWEAK *vb, n* **tweaked**
TWEAKER *n* engineer's small screwdriver
TWEAKS ▸ **tweak**
TWEAKY ▸ **tweak**

TWEE *adj*
TWEED *n*
TWEEDLE *vb* improvise aimlessly on a musical instrument
TWEEDS ▸ **tweed**
TWEEDY *adj* of or made of tweed
TWEEL *variant of* ▸ **twill**
TWEELED ▸ **tweel**
TWEELS ▸ **tweel**
TWEELY ▸ **twee**
TWEEN = **between**
TWEENER = **tweenager**
TWEENIE = **tweeny**
TWEENS ▸ **tween**
TWEENY *n* maid who assists both cook and housemaid
TWEER *variant of* ▸ **twire**
TWEERED ▸ **tweer**
TWEERS ▸ **tweer**
TWEEST ▸ **twee**
TWEET *vb, interj* **tweeted**
TWEETER *n* loudspeaker reproducing high-frequency sounds
TWEETS ▸ **tweet**
TWEEZE *vb* take hold of or pluck (hair, small objects, etc) with or as if with tweezers **tweezed**
TWEEZER = **tweezers** **tweezes**
TWELFTH *n* (of) number twelve in a series ▷ *adj* of or being number twelve in a series
TWELVE *n, adj, determiner* **twelves**
TWENTY *n, adj, determiner*
TWERP *n* silly person **twerps, twerpy**
TWIBIL = **twibill**
TWIBILL *n* mattock with a blade shaped like an adze at one end and like an axe at the other
TWIBILS ▸ **twibil**
TWICE *adv*
TWICER *n* someone who does something twice **twicers**
TWIDDLE *vb, n* **twiddly**
TWIER *variant of* ▸ **tuyere**
TWIERS ▸ **twier**
TWIFOLD *variant of* ▸ **twofold**
TWIG *n, vb* **twigged**
TWIGGEN *adj* made of twigs
TWIGGER ▸ **twig**
TWIGGY *adj* of or relating to a twig or twigs
TWIGHT *old variant of* ▸ **twit**
TWIGHTS ▸ **twight**
TWIGLET *n* small twig
TWIGLOO *n* temporary shelter made from twigs, branches, leaves, etc
TWIGS ▸ **twig**
TWILIT > **twilight**
TWILL *n, adj, vb* **twilled, twills**
TWILLY *n* machine having revolving spikes for opening and cleaning raw textile fibres
TWILT *variant of* ▸ **quilt**
TWILTED ▸ **twilt**
TWILTS ▸ **twilt**
TWIN *n, vb*
TWINE *n, vb* **twined, twiner, twiners, twines**
TWINGE *n, vb* **twinged, twinges**
TWINIER ▸ **twine**
TWINING ▸ **twine**
TWINJET *n* jet aircraft with two engines
TWINK *n* white correction fluid for deleting written text ▷ *vb* twinkle **twinked**
TWINKIE *n* stupid person
TWINKLE *vb, n* **twinkly**
TWINKS ▸ **twink**
TWINNED ▸ **twin**
TWINS ▸ **twin**
TWINSET *n*
TWINTER *n* animal that is 2 years old
TWINY ▸ **twine**
TWIRE *vb* look intently at with (or as if with) difficulty **twired, twires, twiring**
TWIRL *vb, n* **twirled, twirler, twirls, twirly**
TWIRP = **twerp**
TWIRPS ▸ **twirp**
TWIRPY ▸ **twirp**
TWISCAR *variant of* ▸ **tuskar**
TWIST *vb, n* **twisted**
TWISTER *n*
TWISTOR *n* variable corresponding to the coordinates of a point in space and time

TWISTS ▸ **twist**
TWISTY ▸ **twist**
TWIT *vb, n*
TWITCH *vb, n*
TWITCHY *adj* nervous, worried, and ill-at-ease
TWITE *n* N European finch with a brown streaked plumage **twites**
TWITS ▸ **twit**
TWITTED ▸ **twit**
TWITTEN *n* narrow alleyway
TWITTER *vb, n*
TWIXT = **betwixt**
TWIZZLE *vb* spin around
TWO *n*
TWOCCER > **twoccing**
TWOCKER > **twoccing**
TWOER *n* (in a game) something that scores two **twoers**
TWOFER *n* single ticket allowing the buyer entrance to two events **twofers**
TWOFOLD *adj, adv, n*
TWONESS *n* state or condition of being two
TWONIE = **toonie**
TWONIES ▸ **twonie**
TWOONIE *variant of* ▸ **toonie**
TWOS ▸ **two**
TWOSOME *n*
TWP *adj* stupid

> This Welsh word for stupid is useful because it contains no vowels, and can thus help when you have an awkward rack full of consonants.

TWYER = **tuyere**
TWYERE *variant of* ▸ **tuyere**
TWYERES ▸ **twyere**
TWYERS ▸ **twyer**
TWYFOLD *adj* twofold
TYCHISM *n* theory that chance is an objective reality at work in the universe
TYCOON *n* **tycoons**
TYDE *old variant of the past participle of* ▸ **tie**
TYE *n* trough used in mining to separate valuable material from dross ▹ *vb* (in mining) isolate valuable material from dross using a tye **tyed**
TYEE *n* large northern Pacific salmon **tyees**
TYEING, tyer, tyers, tyes ▸ **tye**
TYG *n* mug with two handles **tygs**

> This old word for a two-handled drinking cup is another key word to know for situations when you are short of vowels.

TYIN *variant of* ▸ **tyiyn**
TYING ▸ **tie**
TYIYN *n* money unit of Kyrgyzstan **tyiyns**
TYLER *variant of* ▸ **tiler**
TYLERS ▸ **tyler**
TYLOPOD *n* mammal with padded feet, such as a camel or llama
TYLOSES ▸ **tylosis**
TYLOSIN *n* broad spectrum antibiotic
TYLOSIS *n* bladder-like outgrowth from certain cells in woody tissue
TYLOTE *n* knobbed sponge spicule **tylotes**
TYMBAL = **timbal**
TYMBALS ▸ **tymbal**
TYMP *n* blast furnace outlet through which molten metal flows
TYMPAN = **tympanum**
TYMPANA > **tympanum**
TYMPANI = **timpani**
TYMPANO ▸ **tympani**
TYMPANS ▸ **tympan**
TYMPANY *n* distention of the abdomen
TYMPS ▸ **tymp**
TYND *variant of* ▸ **tind**
TYNDE *variant of* ▸ **tind**
TYNE *variant of* ▸ **tine**
TYNED *variant of* ▸ **tyne**
TYNES ▸ **tyne**
TYNING ▸ **tyne**
TYPABLE ▸ **type**
TYPAL *rare word for* ▸ **typical**
TYPE *n, vb*
TYPEBAR *n* one of the bars in a typewriter that carry the type and are operated by keys
TYPED ▸ **type**
TYPES ▸ **type**
TYPESET *vb*
TYPEY *variant of* ▸ **typy**
TYPHOID *adj*
TYPHON *n* whirlwind **typhons**

TYPHOON *n*
TYPHOSE *adj* relating to typhoid
TYPHOUS ▸ **typhus**
TYPHUS *n*
TYPIC = **typical**
TYPICAL *adj*
TYPIER ▸ **typy**
TYPIEST ▸ **typy**
TYPIFY *vb*
TYPING *n* **typings**
TYPIST *n* **typists**
TYPO *n* typographical error **typos**
TYPP *n* unit of thickness of yarn **typps**
TYPTO *vb* learn Greek conjugations **typtoed, typtos**
TYPY *adj* (of an animal) typifying the breed
TYRAN *vb* act as a tyrant **tyraned, tyranne**
TYRANNY *n*
TYRANS ▸ **tyran**
TYRANT *n, vb* **tyrants**
TYRE *n, vb* **tyred, tyres, tyring**
TYRO *n* **tyroes, tyrones, tyronic, tyros**
TYSTIE *n* black guillemot **tysties**
TYTE *variant spelling of* ▸ **tite**
TYTHE *variant of* ▸ **tithe**
TYTHED ▸ **tythe**
TYTHES ▸ **tythe**
TYTHING ▸ **tythe**
TZADDI ▸ **sadhe**
TZADDIK *variant of* ▸ **zaddik**
TZADDIQ *variant of* ▸ **zaddik**

An unlikely word from Judaism, meaning a person of great piety, but offering a great score played as a bonus.

TZADDIS ▸ **tzaddi**
TZAR = **tsar**
TZARDOM ▸ **tzar**
TZARINA *variant of* ▸ **tsarina**
TZARISM *variant of* ▸ **tsarism**
TZARIST ▸ **tzarism**
TZARS ▸ **tzar**
TZETSE *variant of* ▸ **tsetse**
TZETSES ▸ **tzetse**
TZETZE *variant of* ▸ **tsetse**
TZETZES ▸ **tzetze**
TZIGANE *n* type of Gypsy music **tzigany**
TZIMMES *n* traditional Jewish stew
TZITZIS *variant of* > **tsitsith**
TZITZIT *variant of* ▸ **tzitzit**
TZURIS *variant of* ▸ **tsuris**

Uu

U can be a difficult tile to use effectively. Although there are quite a few two -letter words beginning with **U**, most of them are quite unusual, and so difficult to remember. Only **up** (4 points) and **us** (2) are immediately obvious, so it's well worth learning words like **ug** (3), **uh** (5), **um** (4), and **un, ur** and **ut** (2 each). Three-letter words beginning with **U** can also be difficult to remember. If you are trying to use a **Q, X** or **Z**, bear in mind that there aren't any valid three-letter words with these letters that start with **U**. Knowing this can save you valuable time. It's also helpful to remember that there aren't any particularly high-scoring two- or three-letter words starting with **U**, the best being **uke** (7 points) and **uva** (6 points). If you have a surplus of **U**s, it is well worth remembering **ulu, umu** and **utu**, which score only 3 points but should improve your rack.

UAKARI *n* type of monkey **uakaris**
UBEROUS *adj* abundant
UBERTY *n* abundance
UBIETY *n* condition of being in a particular place
UBIQUE *adv* everywhere
UBUNTU *n* quality of compassion and humanity **ubuntus**
UCKERS *n* type of naval game
UDAL *n* form of freehold possession of land used in Orkney and Shetland
UDALLER *n* person possessing a udal
UDALS ▸ **udal**
UDDER *n* **uddered, udders**
UDO *n* stout perennial plant of Japan and China
UDON *n* (in Japanese cookery) large noodles made of wheat flour **udons**
UDOS ▸ **udo**
UDS *interj* God's or God save
UEY *n* u-turn **ueys**
UFO *n* flying saucer
UFOLOGY *n* study of UFOs
UFOS ▸ **ufo**
UG *vb* hate
UGALI *n* type of stiff porridge **ugalis**
UGGED ▸ **ug**
UGGING ▸ **ug**
UGH *interj* exclamation of disgust ▹ *n* sound made to indicate disgust **ughs**

> Together with **uke**, this is the highest-scoring three-letter word starting with U.

UGLIED, uglier, uglies, ugliest ▸ **ugly**
UGLIFY *vb* make or become ugly or more ugly
UGLILY ▸ **ugly**
UGLY *adj, vb* **uglying**
UGS ▸ **ug**
UGSOME *adj* loathsome
UH *interj* used to express hesitation
UHLAN *n* member of a body of lancers first employed in the Polish army **uhlans**
UHURU *n* national independence **uhurus**

> You won't often have three Us on your rack, but when you do this Swahili word for freedom may get you out of trouble. The only other 5-letter word containing three Us is **urubu**, a kind of vulture.

UILLEAN *adj as in* **uillean pipes** bagpipes developed in Ireland
UJAMAA *n as in* **ujamaa village** communally organized village in Tanzania **ujamaas**
UKASE *n* (in imperial Russia) a decree from the tsar **ukases**
UKE *short form of* ▸ **ukulele**

> Together with ugh, this is the highest-scoring three-letter word starting with U.

UKELELE = **ukulele**
UKES ▸ **uke**
UKULELE *n*
ULAMA *n* body of Muslim scholars or religious leaders **ulamas**
ULAN = **uhlan**
ULANS ▸ **ulan**
ULCER *n, vb* **ulcered, ulcers**
ULE *n* rubber tree
ULEMA = **ulama**
ULEMAS ▸ **ulema**
ULES ▸ **ule**
ULEX *n* variety of shrub **ulexes**
ULEXITE *n* type of mineral
ULICES ▸ **ulex**
ULICON = **eulachon**
ULICONS ▸ **ulicon**
ULIKON = **eulachon**
ULIKONS ▸ **ulikon**
ULITIS *n* gingivitis
ULLAGE *n* volume by which a liquid container falls short of being full ▹ *vb* create ullage in **ullaged, ullages**
ULLING *n* process of filling **ullings**
ULMIN *n* substance found in decaying vegetation **ulmins**
ULNA *n*
ULNAD *adv* towards the ulna
ULNAE ▸ **ulna**
ULNAR ▸ **ulna**
ULNARE *n* bone in the wrist **ulnaria**
ULNAS ▸ **ulna**
ULOSES ▸ **ulosis**
ULOSIS *n* formation of a scar
ULPAN *n* Israeli study centre **ulpanim**
ULSTER *n* man's heavy double-breasted overcoat **ulsters**
ULTIMA *n* final syllable of a word **ultimas**
ULTIMO *adv* in or during the previous month
ULTION *n* vengeance **ultions**
ULTRA *n* person who has extreme or immoderate beliefs or opinions ▹ *adj* extreme or immoderate, esp in beliefs or opinions **ultras**
ULU *n* type of knife
ULULANT ▸ **ululate**
ULULATE *vb* howl or wail
ULUS ▸ **ulu**
ULVA *n* genus of seaweed **ulvas**
ULYIE *Scots variant of* ▸ **oil**
ULYIES ▸ **ulyie**
ULZIE *Scots variant of* ▸ **oil**
ULZIES ▸ **ulzie**
UM *interj* representation of a common sound made when hesitating in speech ▹ *vb* hesitate while speaking
UMAMI *n* savoury flavour **umamis**
UMBEL *n* umbrella-like flower cluster
UMBELED = **umbelled**
UMBELS ▸ **umbel**

UMBER *adj, n, vb* **umbered, umbers, umbery**
UMBLE *adj as in* **umble pie** (formerly) a pie made from the heart, entrails, etc, of a deer
UMBLES *another term for* ▸ **numbles**
UMBO *n* small hump projecting from the centre of the cap in certain mushrooms **umbonal, umbones, umbonic, umbos**
UMBRA *n* shadow, esp the shadow cast by the moon onto the earth during a solar eclipse **umbrae**
UMBRAGE *n, vb*
UMBRAL ▸ **umbra**
UMBRAS ▸ **umbra**
UMBRE = **umbrette**
UMBREL *n* umbrella **umbrels**
UMBRERE *n* helmet visor
UMBRES ▸ **umbre**
UMBRIL = **umbrere**
UMBRILS ▸ **umbril**
UMBROSE = **umbrous**
UMBROUS *adj* shady
UMFAZI *n* African married woman **umfazis**
UMIAC *variant of* ▸ **umiak**
UMIACK *variant of* ▸ **umiak**
UMIACKS ▸ **umiack**
UMIACS ▸ **umiac**
UMIAK *n* Inuit boat made of skins **umiaks, umiaq**
UMIAQS ▸ **umiaq**
UMLAUT *n, vb* **umlauts**
UMLUNGU *n* White man: used esp as a term of address
UMM = **um**
UMMA *n* Muslim community **ummah**
UMMAHS ▸ **ummah**
UMMAS ▸ **umma**
UMMED ▸ **um**
UMMING ▸ **um** *vb*
UMP *short for* ▸ **umpire**
UMPED ▸ **ump**
UMPH = **humph**
UMPIE *informal word for* ▸ **umpire**
UMPIES ▸ **umpy**
UMPING ▸ **ump**
UMPIRE *n, vb* **umpired, umpires**
UMPS ▸ **ump**
UMPTEEN *adj, determiner* **umpty**
UMPY = **umpie**
UMRA *n* pilgrimage to Mecca that can be made at any time of the year **umrah**
UMRAHS ▸ **umrah**
UMRAS ▸ **umra**
UMS ▸ **um**
UMU *n* type of oven **umus**
UMWELT *n* environmental factors affecting the behaviour of an animal or individual **umwelts**
UMWHILE = **umquhile**
UN *pron* spelling of 'one' intended to reflect a dialectal or informal pronunciation
UNABLE *adj*
UNACTED *adj* not acted or performed
UNADDED *adj* not added
UNADEPT *adj* not adept
UNADULT *adj* not mature
UNAGED *adj* not old
UNAGILE *adj* not agile
UNAGING = **unageing**
UNAI = **unau**
UNAIDED *adv, adj*
UNAIMED *adj* not aimed or specifically targeted
UNAIRED *adj* not aired
UNAIS ▸ **unai**
UNAKIN *adj* not related
UNAKING *Shakespearean form of* > **unaching**
UNAKITE *n* type of mineral
UNALIKE *adj* not similar
UNALIST *n* priest holding only one benefice
UNALIVE *adj* unaware
UNAPT *adj* not suitable or qualified **unaptly**
UNARM *less common word for* ▸ **disarm**
UNARMED *adj*
UNARMS ▸ **unarm**
UNARY *adj* consisting of, or affecting, a single element or component
UNASKED *adv* without being asked to do something ▷ *adj* (of a question) not asked, although sometimes implied

UNAU *n* two-toed sloth **unaus**
UNAWAKE *adj* not awake
UNAWARE *adj, adv*
UNAWED *adj* not awed
UNAXED *adj* not axed
UNBAG *vb* take out of a bag **unbags**
UNBAKED *adj* not having been baked
UNBALE *vb* remove from bale **unbaled, unbales**
UNBAN *vb* stop banning or permit again **unbans**
UNBAR *vb* take away a bar or bars from
UNBARE *vb* expose **unbared, unbares**
UNBARK *vb* strip bark from **unbarks**
UNBARS ▸ **unbar**
UNBASED *adj* not having a base
UNBATED *adj* (of a sword, lance, etc) not covered with a protective button
UNBE *vb* make non-existent
UNBEAR *vb* release (horse) from the bearing rein **unbears**
UNBED *vb* remove from bed **unbeds**
UNBEEN ▸ **unbe**
UNBEGET *vb* deprive of existence
UNBEGOT *adj* unbegotten
UNBEGUN *adj* not commenced
UNBEING *n* non-existence
UNBELT *vb* unbuckle the belt of (a garment) **unbelts**
UNBEND *vb* become less strict or more informal in one's attitudes or behaviour **unbends**
UNBENT *adj* not bent or bowed
UNBIAS *vb* free from prejudice
UNBID = **unbidden**
UNBIND *vb* set free from bonds or chains **unbinds**
UNBITT *vb* remove (cable) from the bitts **unbitts**
UNBLENT = **unblended**
UNBLESS *vb* deprive of a blessing
UNBLEST = **unblessed**
UNBLIND *vb* rid of blindness
UNBLOCK *vb* remove a blockage from
UNBLOWN *adj* (of a flower) still in the bud
UNBOLT *vb* unfasten a bolt of (a door) **unbolts**
UNBONE *vb* remove bone from
UNBONED *adj* (of meat, fish, etc) not having had the bones removed
UNBONES ▸ **unbone**
UNBOOT *vb* remove boots from **unboots**
UNBORE *adj* unborn
UNBORN *adj*
UNBORNE *adj* not borne
UNBOSOM *vb* relieve (oneself) of (secrets or feelings) by telling someone
UNBOUND *adj* (of a book) not bound within a cover
UNBOWED *adj* not giving in or submitting
UNBOX *vb* empty a box **unboxed, unboxes**
UNBRACE *vb* remove tension or strain from
UNBRAID *vb* remove braids from
UNBRAKE *vb* stop reducing speed by releasing brake
UNBRED *adj* not taught or instructed
UNBROKE = **unbroken**
UNBUILD *vb* destroy **unbuilt**
UNBULKY *adj* not bulky
UNBURNT *adj* not burnt
UNBURY *vb* unearth
UNBUSY *adj* not busy
UNCAGE *vb* release from a cage
UNCAGED *adj* at liberty
UNCAGES ▸ **uncage**
UNCAKE *vb* remove compacted matter from **uncaked, uncakes**
UNCANNY *adj*
UNCAP *vb* remove a cap or top from (a container)
UNCAPE *vb* remove the cape from **uncaped, uncapes**

UNCAPS ▶ **uncap**
UNCARED *adj as in* **uncared for** not cared (for)
UNCART *vb* remove from a cart **uncarts**
UNCASE *vb* display **uncased, uncases**
UNCAST *adj* not cast
UNCATE = **uncinate**
UNCE = **ounce**
UNCEDED *adj* not ceded
UNCES ▶ **unce**
UNCHAIN *vb* remove a chain or chains from
UNCHAIR *vb* unseat from chair
UNCHARM *vb* disenchant
UNCHARY *adj* not cautious
UNCHECK *vb* remove check mark from
UNCHIC *adj* not chic
UNCHILD *vb* deprive of children
UNCHOKE *vb* unblock
UNCI ▶ **uncus**
UNCIA *n* twelfth part **unciae**
UNCIAL *adj* of a writing style used in manuscripts of the third to ninth centuries ▷ *n* uncial letter or manuscript **uncials**
UNCINAL = **uncinate**
UNCINI ▶ **uncinus**
UNCINUS *n* small hooked structure
UNCITED *adj* not quoted
UNCIVIL *adj*
UNCLAD *adj* having no clothes on
UNCLAMP *vb* remove clamp from
UNCLASP *vb* unfasten the clasp of (something)
UNCLE *n, vb*
UNCLEAN *adj*
UNCLEAR *adj*
UNCLED ▶ **uncle**
UNCLEFT *adj* not cleft
UNCLES ▶ **uncle**
UNCLEW *vb* undo **unclews**
UNCLING ▶ **uncle**
UNCLIP *vb* remove clip from **unclips, unclipt**
UNCLOAK *vb* remove cloak from
UNCLOG *vb* remove an obstruction from (a drain, etc) **unclogs**
UNCLOSE *vb* open or cause to open
UNCLOUD *vb* clear clouds from
UNCO *adj* awkward ▷ *n* awkward or clumsy person
UNCOCK *vb* remove from a cocked position **uncocks**
UNCODED *adj* not coded
UNCOER ▶ **unco**
UNCOES ▶ **unco**
UNCOEST ▶ **unco**
UNCOIL *vb* unwind or untwist **uncoils**
UNCOLT *vb* divest of a horse **uncolts**
UNCOMFY *adj* not comfortable
UNCOMIC *adj* not comical
UNCOOL *adj* unsophisticated
UNCOPE *vb* unmuzzle **uncoped, uncopes**
UNCORD *vb* release from cords **uncords**
UNCORK *vb* remove the cork from (a bottle) **uncorks**
UNCOS ▶ **unco**
UNCOUTH *adj*
UNCOVER *vb*
UNCOWL *vb* remove hood from **uncowls**
UNCOY *adj* not modest
UNCRATE *vb* remove from a crate
UNCRAZY *adj* not crazy
UNCROSS *vb* cease to cross
UNCROWN *vb* take the crown from
UNCTION *n*
UNCUFF *vb* remove handcuffs from **uncuffs**
UNCURB *vb* remove curbs from (a horse) **uncurbs**
UNCURED *adj* not cured
UNCURL *vb* move or cause to move out of a curled or rolled up position **uncurls**
UNCURSE *vb* remove curse from
UNCUS *n* hooked part or process, as in the human cerebrum
UNCUT *adj* not shortened or censored
UNCUTE *adj* not cute
UNDAM *vb* free from a dam **undams**

UNDATE *vb* remove date from
UNDATED *adj* (of a manuscript, letter, etc) not having an identifying date
UNDE = **undee**
UNDEAD *adj* alive
UNDEAF *vb* restore hearing to **undeafs**
UNDEALT *adj* not dealt (with)
UNDEAR *adj* not dear
UNDECK *vb* remove decorations from **undecks**
UNDEE *adj* wavy
UNDEIFY *vb* strip of the status of a deity
UNDER *adv, prep*
UNDERDO *vb* do (something) inadequately
UNDERGO *vb*
UNDERN *n* time between sunrise and noon **underns**
UNDID ▶ **undo**
UNDIES *pl n* underwear, esp women's
UNDIGHT *vb* remove
UNDINE *n* female water spirit **undines**
UNDO *vb*
UNDOCK *vb* take out of a dock **undocks**
UNDOER ▶ **undo**
UNDOERS ▶ **undo**
UNDOES ▶ **undo**
UNDOING *n*
UNDONE *adj* not done or completed
UNDRAPE *vb* remove drapery from
UNDRAW *vb* open (curtains) **undrawn, undraws**
UNDRESS *vb, n, adj*
UNDREST = **undressed**
UNDREW ▶ **undraw**
UNDRIED *adj* not dried
UNDRUNK *adj* not drunk
UNDUE *adj*
UNDUG *adj* not having been dug
UNDULAR > **undulate**
UNDULY *adv* excessively
UNDY = **undee**
UNDYED *adj* not dyed
UNDYING *adj*
UNEAGER *adj* nonchalant
UNEARED *adj* not ploughed
UNEARTH *vb*
UNEASE ▶ **uneasy**
UNEASES ▶ **uneasy**
UNEASY *adj*
UNEATEN *adj* (of food) not having been consumed
UNEATH *adv* not easily
UNEDGE *vb* take the edge off **unedged, unedges**
UNENDED *adj* without end
UNEQUAL *adj, n*
UNETH = **uneath**
UNEVEN *adj*
UNEYED *adj* unseen
UNFACT *n* event or thing not provable **unfacts**
UNFADED *adj* not faded
UNFAIR *adj, vb* **unfairs**
UNFAITH *n* lack of faith
UNFAKED *adj* not faked
UNFAMED *adj* not famous
UNFANCY *vb* consider (a sportsperson or team) unlikely to win or succeed
UNFAZED *adj* not disconcerted
UNFED *adj* not fed
UNFEED *adj* unpaid
UNFELT *adj* not felt
UNFENCE *vb* remove a fence from
UNFEUED *adj* not feued
UNFILDE *archaic form of* ▶ **unfiled**
UNFILED *adj* not filed
UNFINE *adj* not fine
UNFIRED *adj* not fired
UNFIRM *adj* soft or unsteady
UNFIT *adj, vb*
UNFITLY *adv* in an unfit way
UNFITS ▶ **unfit**
UNFIX *vb* unfasten, detach, or loosen
UNFIXED *adj* not fixed
UNFIXES ▶ **unfix**
UNFIXT = **unfixed**
UNFLESH *vb* remove flesh from
UNFLUSH *vb* lose the colour caused by flushing
UNFOLD *vb* **unfolds**
UNFOND *adj* not fond
UNFOOL *vb* undeceive **unfools**
UNFORM *vb* make formless **unforms**
UNFOUND *adj* not found

UNFREE *vb* remove freedom from **unfreed, unfrees**
UNFROCK *vb* deprive (a priest in holy orders) of his or her priesthood
UNFROZE > **unfreeze**
UNFUMED *adj* not fumigated
UNFUNNY *adj* not funny
UNFURL *vb* unroll or unfold **unfurls**
UNFUSED *adj* not fused
UNFUSSY *adj* not characterized by overelaborate detail
UNGAG *vb* restore freedom of speech to **ungags**
UNGAIN *adj* inconvenient
UNGATED *adj* without gate
UNGAZED *adj as in* **ungazed at/ungazed upon** not gazed (at or upon)
UNGEAR *vb* disengage **ungears**
UNGET *vb* get rid of **ungets**
UNGILD *vb* remove gilding from **ungilds, ungilt**
UNGIRD *vb* remove belt from **ungirds**
UNGIRT *adj* not belted
UNGIRTH *vb* release from a girth
UNGLAD *adj* not glad
UNGLOVE *vb* remove glove(s)
UNGLUE *vb* remove adhesive from **unglued, unglues**
UNGOD *vb* remove status of being a god from
UNGODLY *adj*
UNGODS ▸ **ungod**
UNGORD = **ungored**
UNGORED *adj* not gored
UNGOT = **ungotten**
UNGOWN *vb* remove gown (from) **ungowns**
UNGREEN *adj* not environmentally friendly
UNGROWN *adj* not fully developed
UNGUAL *adj* of, relating to, or affecting the fingernails or toenails
UNGUARD *vb* expose (to attack)
UNGUENT *n* ointment
UNGUES ▸ **unguis**
UNGUIS *n* nail, claw, or hoof, or the part of the digit giving rise to it
UNGULA *n* truncated cone, cylinder, etc **ungulae, ungular**
UNGULED *adj* hoofed
UNGUM *vb* remove adhesive from **ungums**
UNGYVE *vb* release from shackles **ungyved, ungyves**
UNHABLE = **unable**
UNHAIR *vb* remove the hair from (a hide) **unhairs**
UNHAND *vb* release from one's grasp **unhands**
UNHANDY *adj* not skilful with one's hands
UNHANG *vb* take down from hanging position **unhangs**
UNHAPPY *adj, vb*
UNHARDY *adj* fragile
UNHASP *vb* unfasten **unhasps**
UNHASTY *adj* not speedy
UNHAT *vb* doff one's hat **unhats**
UNHEAD *vb* remove the head from **unheads**
UNHEAL *vb* expose **unheals**
UNHEARD *adj* not listened to
UNHEART *vb* discourage
UNHEEDY *adj* not heedful
UNHELE = **unheal**
UNHELED ▸ **unhele**
UNHELES ▸ **unhele**
UNHELM *vb* remove the helmet of (oneself or another) **unhelms**
UNHERST *archaic past form of* > **unhearse**
UNHEWN *adj* not hewn
UNHINGE *vb*
UNHIP *adj* not at all fashionable or up to date
UNHIRED *adj* not hired
UNHITCH *vb* unfasten or detach
UNHIVE *vb* remove from a hive **unhived, unhives**

UNHOARD *vb* remove from a hoard
UNHOLY *adj* immoral or wicked
UNHOOD *vb* remove hood from **unhoods**
UNHOOK *vb* unfasten the hooks of (a garment) **unhooks**
UNHOOP *vb* remove hoop(s) from **unhoops**
UNHOPED *adj* unhoped-for
UNHORSE *vb* knock or throw from a horse
UNHOUSE *vb* remove from a house
UNHUMAN *adj* inhuman or not human
UNHUNG ▶ **unhang**
UNHURT *adj* not injured in an accident, attack, etc
UNHUSK *vb* remove the husk from **unhusks**
UNI *n* (in informal English) university
UNIBODY *adj* of a vehicle in which frame and body are one unit
UNIBROW *n* informal word for eyebrows that meet above the nose
UNICITY *n* oneness
UNICORN *n*
UNIDEAL *adj* not ideal
UNIFACE *n* type of tool
UNIFIC *adj* unifying
UNIFIED ▶ **unify**
UNIFIER ▶ **unify**
UNIFIES ▶ **unify**
UNIFORM *n, adj, vb*
UNIFY *vb*
UNION *n, adj* **unions**
UNIPED *n* person or thing with one foot **unipeds**
UNIPOD *n* one-legged support, as for a camera **unipods**
UNIQUE *n* **uniquer, uniques**
UNIS ▶ **uni**
UNISEX *adj, n*
UNISIZE *adj* in one size only
UNISON *n* **unisons**
UNIT *n* **unitage, unital**
UNITARD *n* all-in-one skintight suit
UNITARY *adj* consisting of a single undivided whole
UNITE *vb, n*
UNITED *adj* produced by two or more people or things in combination
UNITER ▶ **unite**
UNITERS ▶ **unite**
UNITES ▶ **unite**
UNITIES ▶ **unity**
UNITING ▶ **unite**
UNITION *n* joining
UNITISE = **unitize**
UNITIVE *adj* tending to unite or capable of uniting
UNITIZE *vb* convert (an investment trust) into a unit trust
UNITS ▶ **unit**
UNITY *n*
UNJADED *adj* not jaded
UNJAM *vb* remove blockage from **unjams**
UNJOINT *vb* disjoint
UNJUST *adj*
UNKED *adj* alien
UNKEMPT *adj*
UNKEND = **unkenned**
UNKENT = **unkenned**
UNKEPT *adj* not kept
UNKET = **unked**
UNKID = **unked**
UNKIND *adj*
UNKING *vb* strip of sovereignty **unkings**
UNKINK *vb* straighten out **unkinks**
UNKISS *vb* cancel (a previous action) with a kiss
UNKNIT *vb* make or become undone, untied, or unravelled **unknits**
UNKNOT *vb* disentangle or undo a knot or knots in **unknots**
UNKNOWN *adj, n*
UNLACE *vb* loosen or undo the lacing of (shoes, garments, etc)
UNLACED *adj* not laced
UNLACES ▶ **unlace**
UNLADE *less common word for* ▶ **unload**
UNLADED ▶ **unlade**
UNLADEN *adj* not laden
UNLADES ▶ **unlade**
UNLAID ▶ **unlay**
UNLASH *vb* untie or unfasten
UNLAST *archaic variant of* ▶ **unlaced**
UNLASTE *archaic variant of* ▶ **unlaced**
UNLATCH *vb* open or unfasten or come open or unfastened by

the lifting or release of a latch
UNLAW *vb* penalize **unlawed, unlaws**
UNLAY *vb* untwist (a rope or cable) to separate its strands **unlays**
UNLEAD *vb* strip off lead **unleads**
UNLEAL *adj* treacherous
UNLEARN *vb* try to forget something learnt or to discard accumulated knowledge
UNLEASH *vb*
UNLED *adj* not led
UNLESS *conj, prep*
UNLET *adj* not rented
UNLEVEL *adj* not level ▷ *vb* make unbalanced
UNLICH *Spenserian form of* ▸ **unlike**
UNLID *vb* remove lid from **unlids**
UNLIKE *adj, prep, n*
UNLIKED *adj* not liked
UNLIKES ▸ **unlike**
UNLIME *vb* detach **unlimed, unlimes**
UNLINE *vb* remove the lining from
UNLINED *adj* not having any lining
UNLINES ▸ **unline**
UNLINK *vb* undo the link or links between **unlinks**
UNLIT *adj*
UNLIVE *vb* live so as to nullify, undo, or live down (past events or times) **unlived, unlives**
UNLOAD *vb* **unloads**
UNLOBED *adj* without lobes
UNLOCK *vb* **unlocks**
UNLOOSE *vb* set free or release
UNLORD *vb* remove from position of being lord **unlords**
UNLOST *adj* not lost
UNLOVE *vb* stop loving
UNLOVED *adj* not loved by anyone
UNLOVES ▸ **unlove**
UNLUCKY *adj*
UNMACHO *adj* not macho
UNMADE *adj*
UNMAKE *vb* undo or destroy **unmaker, unmakes**
UNMAN *vb* cause to lose courage or nerve
UNMANLY *adj*
UNMANS ▸ **unman**
UNMARD = **unmarred**
UNMARRY *vb* divorce
UNMASK *vb* remove the mask or disguise from **unmasks**
UNMATED *adj* not mated
UNMEANT *adj* unintentional
UNMEEK *adj* not submissive
UNMEET *adj* not meet
UNMERRY *adj* not merry
UNMESH *vb* release from mesh
UNMET *adj* unfulfilled
UNMETED *adj* unmeasured
UNMEW *vb* release from confinement **unmewed, unmews**
UNMINED *adj* not mined
UNMIRY *adj* not swampy
UNMITER = **unmitre**
UNMITRE *vb* divest of a mitre
UNMIX *vb* separate **unmixed, unmixes, unmixt**
UNMOLD = **unmould**
UNMOLDS ▸ **unmold**
UNMOOR *vb* weigh the anchor or drop the mooring of (a vessel) **unmoors**
UNMORAL *adj* outside morality
UNMOULD *vb* change shape of
UNMOUNT *vb* dismount
UNMOVED *adj*
UNMOWN *adj* not mown
UNNAIL *vb* unfasten by removing nails **unnails**
UNNAMED *adj* not mentioned by name
UNNEATH *adj* archaic word for underneath
UNNERVE *vb*
UNNEST *vb* remove from a nest **unnests**
UNNOBLE *vb* strip of nobility
UNNOISY *adj* quiet
UNNOTED *adj* not noted
UNOAKED *adj* (of wine) not matured in an oak barrel

UNOFTEN *adv* infrequently
UNOILED *adj* not lubricated with oil
UNOPEN *adj* not open
UNORDER *vb* cancel an order
UNOWED = **unowned**
UNOWNED *adj* not owned
UNPACED *adj* without the aid of a pacemaker
UNPACK *vb* **unpacks**
UNPAGED *adj* (of a book) having no page numbers
UNPAID *adj*
UNPAINT *vb* remove paint from
UNPANEL *vb* unsaddle
UNPAPER *vb* remove paper from
UNPARED *adj* not pared
UNPAVED *adj* not covered in paving
UNPAY *vb* undo **unpays**
UNPEG *vb* remove the peg or pegs from, esp to unfasten **unpegs**
UNPEN *vb* release from a pen **unpens, unpent**
UNPERCH *vb* remove from a perch
UNPICK *vb* **unpicks**
UNPILE *vb* remove from a pile **unpiled, unpiles**
UNPIN *vb* remove a pin or pins from
UNPINKT = **unpinked**
UNPINS ▸ **unpin**
UNPLACE = **displace**
UNPLAIT *vb* remove plaits from
UNPLUG *vb* **unplugs**
UNPLUMB *vb* remove lead from
UNPLUME *vb* remove feathers from
UNPOPE *vb* strip of popedom **unpoped, unpopes**
UNPOSED *adj* not posed
UNPRAY *vb* withdraw (a prayer) **unprays**
UNPROP *vb* remove support from **unprops**
UNPURE = **impure**
UNPURSE *vb* relax (lips) from pursed position
UNQUEEN *vb* depose from the position of queen
UNQUIET *adj, n, vb*
UNQUOTE *interj* expression used to indicate the end of a quotation ▹ *vb* close (a quotation), esp in printing
UNRACED *adj* not raced
UNRAKE *vb* unearth through raking
UNRAKED *adj* not raked
UNRAKES ▸ **unrake**
UNRATED *adj* not rated
UNRAVEL *vb*
UNRAZED *adj* not razed
UNREAD *adj* (of a book or article) not yet read
UNREADY *adj* not ready or prepared
UNREAL *adj*
UNREAVE *vb* unwind
UNRED = **unread**
UNREDY = **unready**
UNREEL *vb* unwind from a reel **unreels**
UNREEVE *vb* withdraw (a rope) from a block, thimble, etc
UNREIN *vb* free from reins **unreins**
UNRENT *adj* not torn
UNREST *n* **unrests**
UNRID *adj* unridden
UNRIG *vb* strip (a vessel) of standing and running rigging
UNRIGHT *n* wrong
UNRIGS ▸ **unrig**
UNRIMED = **unrhymed**
UNRIP *vb* rip open
UNRIPE *adj* not fully matured **unriper**
UNRIPS ▸ **unrip**
UNRISEN *adj* not risen
UNRIVEN *adj* not torn apart
UNRIVET *vb* remove rivets from
UNROBE = **disrobe**
UNROBED ▸ **unrobe**
UNROBES ▸ **unrobe**
UNROLL *vb* **unrolls**
UNROOF *vb* remove the roof from **unroofs**
UNROOST *vb* remove from a perch
UNROOT *less common word for* ▸ **uproot**
UNROOTS ▸ **unroot**
UNROPE *vb* release from a rope **unroped, unropes**
UNROUGH *adj* not rough
UNROUND *vb* release (lips) from a rounded position
UNROVE ▸ **unreeve**
UNROVEN ▸ **unreeve**
UNROYAL *adj* not royal
UNRUDE *adj* not rude

UNRUFFE = **unrough**
UNRULE *n* lack of authority
UNRULED *adj* not ruled
UNRULES ▸ **unrule**
UNRULY *adj*
UNS ▸ **un**
UNSAFE *adj* dangerous **unsafer**
UNSAID *adj* not said or expressed
UNSAINT *vb* remove status of being a saint from
UNSATED *adj* not sated
UNSAVED *adj* not saved
UNSAWED = **unsawn**
UNSAWN *adj* not cut with a saw
UNSAY *vb* retract or withdraw (something said or written) **unsays**
UNSCALE = **descale**
UNSCARY *adj* not scary
UNSCREW *vb*
UNSEAL *vb* **unseals**
UNSEAM *vb* open or undo the seam of **unseams**
UNSEAT *vb* **unseats**
UNSEEL *vb* undo seeling **unseels**
UNSEEN *adj, adv, n* **unseens**
UNSELF *vb* remove self-centredness from ▹ *n* lack of self **unselfs**
UNSELL *vb* speak unfavourably and off-puttingly of (something or someone) **unsells**
UNSENSE *vb* remove sense from
UNSENT *adj* not sent
UNSET *adj* not yet solidified or firm ▹ *vb* displace **unsets**
UNSEW *vb* undo stitching of **unsewed, unsewn, unsews**
UNSEX *vb* deprive (a person) of the attributes of his or her sex **unsexed, unsexes**
UNSEXY *adj* not sexually attractive
UNSHALE *vb* expose
UNSHAPE *vb* make shapeless
UNSHARP *adj* not sharp
UNSHED *adj* not shed
UNSHELL *vb* remove from a shell
UNSHENT *adj* undamaged
UNSHEWN *adj* unshown
UNSHIFT *vb* release the shift key on a keyboard
UNSHIP *vb* be or cause to be unloaded, discharged, or disembarked from a ship **unships**
UNSHOD *adj* not wearing shoes
UNSHOE *vb* remove shoes from
UNSHOED = **unshod**
UNSHOES ▸ **unshoe**
UNSHOOT *Shakespearean variant of* ▸ **unshout**
UNSHORN *adj* not cut
UNSHOT *adj* not shot
UNSHOUT *vb* revoke (an earlier statement) by shouting a contrary one
UNSHOWN *adj* not shown
UNSHOWY *adj* not showy
UNSHUT *vb* open **unshuts**
UNSIGHT *vb* obstruct vision of
UNSINEW *vb* weaken
UNSIZED *adj* not made or sorted according to size
UNSLAIN *adj* not killed
UNSLICK *adj* not slick
UNSLING *vb* remove or release from a slung position **unslung**
UNSMART *adj* not smart
UNSMOTE = **unsmitten**
UNSNAG *vb* remove snags from **unsnags**
UNSNAP *vb* unfasten (the snap or catch) of (something) **unsnaps**
UNSNARL *vb* free from a snarl or tangle
UNSNECK *vb* unlatch
UNSOBER *adj* not sober
UNSOD = **unsodden**
UNSOFT *adj* hard
UNSOLD *adj* not sold
UNSOLID *adj* not solid
UNSONCY = **unsonsy**
UNSONSY *adj* unfortunate
UNSOOTE *adj* not sweet
UNSOUL *vb* cause to be soulless **unsouls**
UNSOUND *adj*
UNSOWED = **unsown**

UNSOWN *adj* not sown
UNSPAR *vb* open **unspars**
UNSPEAK *obsolete word for* ▸ **unsay**
UNSPED *adj* not achieved
UNSPELL *vb* release from a spell
UNSPENT *adj* not spent
UNSPIDE = **unspied**
UNSPIED *adj* unnoticed
UNSPILT *adj* not spilt
UNSPLIT *adj* not split
UNSPOKE ▸ **unspeak**
UNSPOOL *vb* unwind from spool
UNSPUN *adj* not spun
UNSTACK *vb* remove from a stack
UNSTAID *adj* not staid
UNSTATE *vb* deprive of state
UNSTEEL *vb* make (the heart, feelings, etc) more gentle or compassionate
UNSTEP *vb* remove (a mast) from its step **unsteps**
UNSTICK *vb* free or loosen (something stuck)
UNSTOCK *vb* remove stock from
UNSTOP *vb* remove the stop or stopper from **unstops**
UNSTOW *vb* remove from storage **unstows**
UNSTRAP *vb* undo the straps fastening (something) in position
UNSTRIP *vb* strip
UNSTUCK *adj*
UNSTUFT = **unstuffed**
UNSTUNG *adj* not stung
UNSUIT *vb* make unsuitable **unsuits**
UNSUNG *adj*
UNSUNK *adj* not sunken
UNSUNNY *adj* not sunny
UNSURE *adj*
UNSURED *adj* not assured
UNSURER ▸ **unsure**
UNSWEAR *vb* retract or revoke (a sworn oath)
UNSWEET *adj* not sweet
UNSWEPT *adj* not swept
UNSWORE ▸ **unswear**
UNSWORN ▸ **unswear**
UNTACK *vb* remove saddle and harness, etc, from **untacks**
UNTAKEN *adj* not taken
UNTAME *vb* undo the taming of
UNTAMED *adj* not brought under human control
UNTAMES ▸ **untame**
UNTAX *vb* stop taxing
UNTAXED *adj* not subject to taxation
UNTAXES ▸ **untax**
UNTEACH *vb* cause to disbelieve (teaching)
UNTEAM *vb* disband a team **unteams**
UNTENT *vb* remove from a tent **untents**
UNTENTY *adj* inattentive
UNTHAW = **thaw**
UNTHAWS ▸ **unthaw**
UNTHINK *vb* reverse one's opinion about
UNTIDY *adj*, *vb*
UNTIE *vb* **untied, unties**
UNTIL *prep*
UNTILE *vb* strip tiles from **untiled, untiles**
UNTIMED *adj* not timed
UNTIN *vb* remove tin from **untins**
UNTIRED *adj* not tired
UNTO *prep*
UNTOLD *adj*
UNTOMB *vb* exhume **untombs**
UNTONED *adj* not toned
UNTORN *adj* not torn
UNTRACE *vb* remove traces from
UNTRACK *vb* remove from track
UNTREAD *vb* retrace (a course, path, etc)
UNTRIDE = **untried**
UNTRIED *adj*
UNTRIM *vb* deprive of elegance or adornment **untrims**
UNTROD ▸ **untread**
UNTRUE *adj* **untruer, untruly**
UNTRUSS *vb* release from or as if from a truss
UNTRUST *n* mistrust
UNTRUTH *n*
UNTUCK *vb* become or cause to become loose or not tucked in **untucks**
UNTUNE *vb* make out of tune **untuned, untunes**

UNTURF *vb* remove turf from **unturfs**
UNTURN *vb* turn in a reverse direction **unturns**
UNTWINE *vb* untwist, unravel, and separate
UNTWIST *vb* twist apart and loosen
UNTYING ▸ **untie**
UNURGED *adj* not urged
UNUSED *adj*
UNUSUAL *adj*
UNVAIL = **unveil**
UNVAILE = **unveil**
UNVAILS ▸ **unvail**
UNVEIL *vb* **unveils**
UNVEXED *adj* not annoyed **unvext**
UNVISOR *vb* remove visor from
UNVITAL *adj* not vital
UNVOCAL *adj* not vocal
UNVOICE *vb* pronounce without vibration of the vocal cords
UNWAGED *adj* (of a person) not having a paid job
UNWAKED = **unwakened**
UNWARE = **unaware**
UNWARES = **unawares**
UNWARIE = **unwary**
UNWARY *adj*
UNWATER *vb* dry out
UNWAXED *adj* not treated with wax
UNWAYED *adj* having no routes
UNWEAL *n* ill or sorrow **unweals**
UNWEARY *adj* not weary
UNWEAVE *vb* undo (weaving)
UNWED *adj* not wed
UNWELDY = **unwieldy**
UNWELL *adj*
UNWEPT *adj* not wept for or lamented
UNWET *adj* not wet
UNWHIPT = **unwhipped**
UNWHITE *adj* not white
UNWILL *vb* will the reversal of (something that has already occurred) **unwills**
UNWIND *vb* **unwinds**
UNWIPED *adj* not wiped
UNWIRE *vb* remove wiring from **unwired, unwires**
UNWISE *adj* **unwiser**
UNWISH *vb* retract or revoke (a wish)
UNWIST *adj* unknown
UNWIT *vb* divest of wit
UNWITCH *vb* release from witchcraft
UNWITS ▸ **unwit**
UNWITTY *adj* not clever and amusing
UNWIVE *vb* remove a wife from **unwived, unwives**
UNWOMAN *vb* remove womanly qualities from
UNWON *adj* not won
UNWONT *adj* unaccustomed
UNWOOED *adj* not wooed
UNWORK *vb* destroy (work previously done) **unworks**
UNWORN *adj* not having deteriorated through use or age
UNWORTH *n* lack of value
UNWOUND *past tense and past participle of* ▸ **unwind**
UNWOVE ▸ **unweave**
UNWOVEN ▸ **unweave**
UNWRAP *vb* **unwraps**
UNWRITE *vb* cancel (what has been written) **unwrote**
UNWRUNG *adj* not twisted
UNYOKE *vb* release (an animal, etc) from a yoke **unyoked, unyokes**
UNYOUNG *adj* not young
UNZIP *vb* unfasten the zip of (a garment) **unzips**
UNZONED *adj* not divided into zones
UP *adv, adj, vb*
UPAS *n* large Javan tree with whitish bark and poisonous milky sap **upases**
UPBEAR *vb* sustain **upbears**
UPBEAT *adj* cheerful and optimistic ▷ *n* unaccented beat **upbeats**
UPBIND *vb* bind up **upbinds**
UPBLEW ▸ **upblow**
UPBLOW *vb* inflate **upblown, upblows**
UPBOIL *vb* boil up **upboils**

UPBORE ▸ **upbear**
UPBORNE *adj* held up
UPBOUND *adj* travelling upwards
UPBOW *n* stroke of the bow from its tip to its nut on a stringed instrument **upbows**
UPBRAID *vb* scold or reproach
UPBRAST = **upburst**
UPBRAY *vb* shame **upbrays**
UPBREAK *vb* escape upwards
UPBRING *vb* rear
UPBROKE ▸ **upbreak**
UPBUILD *vb* build up **upbuilt**
UPBURST *vb* burst upwards
UPBY = **upbye**
UPBYE *adv* yonder
UPCAST *n* material cast or thrown up ▹ *adj* directed or thrown upwards ▹ *vb* throw or cast up **upcasts**
UPCATCH *vb* catch up
UPCHEER *vb* cheer up
UPCHUCK *vb* vomit
UPCLIMB *vb* ascend
UPCLOSE *vb* close up
UPCOAST *adv* up the coast
UPCOIL *vb* make into a coil **upcoils**
UPCOME *vb* come up **upcomes**
UPCOURT *adv* up basketball court
UPCURL *vb* curl up **upcurls**
UPCURVE *vb* curve upwards
UPDART *vb* dart upwards **updarts**
UPDATE *vb, n* **updated, updater, updates**
UPDIVE *vb* leap upwards **updived, updives**
UPDO *n* type of hairstyle **updos**
UPDOVE ▸ **updive**
UPDRAFT *n* upwards air current
UPDRAG *vb* drag up **updrags**
UPDRAW *vb* draw up **updrawn, updraws, updrew**
UPDRIED ▸ **updry**
UPDRIES ▸ **updry**
UPDRY *vb* dry up
UPEND *vb* **upended, upends**
UPFIELD *adj* in sport, away from the defending team's goal
UPFILL *vb* fill up **upfills**
UPFLING *vb* throw upwards
UPFLOW *vb* flow upwards **upflows**
UPFLUNG ▸ **upfling**
UPFOLD *vb* fold up **upfolds**
UPFRONT *adj* open and frank ▹ *adv* (of money) paid out at the beginning of a business arrangement
UPFURL *vb* roll up **upfurls**
UPGANG *n* climb **upgangs**
UPGAZE *vb* gaze upwards **upgazed, upgazes**
UPGIRD *vb* belt up **upgirds, upgirt**
UPGO *vb* ascend **upgoes, upgoing, upgone**
UPGRADE *vb*
UPGREW ▸ **upgrow**
UPGROW *vb* grow up **upgrown, upgrows**
UPGUSH *vb* flow upwards
UPHAND *adj* lifted by hand
UPHANG *vb* hang up **uphangs**
UPHAUD *Scots variant of* ▸ **uphold**
UPHAUDS ▸ **uphaud**
UPHEAP *vb* computing term **upheaps**
UPHEAVE *vb* heave or rise upwards
UPHELD ▸ **uphold**
UPHILD *archaic past form of* ▸ **uphold**
UPHILL *adj, adv, n* **uphills**
UPHOARD *vb* hoard up
UPHOIST *vb* raise
UPHOLD *vb* **upholds**
UPHOORD *vb* heap up
UPHOVE ▸ **upheave**
UPHROE *variant spelling of* ▸ **euphroe**
UPHROES ▸ **uphroe**
UPHUNG ▸ **uphang**
UPHURL *vb* throw upwards **uphurls**
UPJET *vb* stream upwards **upjets**
UPKEEP *n* **upkeeps**
UPKNIT *vb* bind **upknits**

UPLAID ▸ **uplay**
UPLAND *adj, n* **uplands**
UPLAY *vb* stash **uplays**
UPLEAD *vb* lead upwards **upleads**
UPLEAN *vb* lean on something **upleans, upleant**
UPLEAP *vb* jump upwards **upleaps, upleapt**
UPLED ▸ **uplead**
UPLIFT *vb* raise or lift up ▹ *n* act or process of improving moral, social, or cultural conditions ▹ *adj* (of a bra) designed to lift and support the breasts **uplifts**
UPLIGHT *n* lamp or wall light designed or positioned to cast its light upwards ▹ *vb* light in an upward direction
UPLINK *n* transmitter that sends signals up to a communications satellite ▹ *vb* send (data) to a communications satellite **uplinks**
UPLIT ▸ **uplight**
UPLOAD *vb* **uploads**
UPLOCK *vb* lock up **uplocks**
UPLOOK *vb* look up **uplooks**
UPLYING *adj* raised
UPMAKE *vb* make up **upmaker, upmakes**
UPMOST *another word for* > **uppermost**
UPO *prep* upon
UPON *prep*
UPPED ▸ **up**
UPPER *adj, n* **uppers**
UPPILE *vb* pile up **uppiled, uppiles**
UPPING ▸ **up**
UPPINGS ▸ **up**
UPPISH *adj* snobbish, arrogant, or presumptuous
UPPITY *adj* snobbish, arrogant, or presumptuous
UPPROP *vb* support **upprops**
UPRAISE *vb* lift up
UPRAN ▸ **uprun**
UPRATE *vb* raise the value, rate, or size of, upgrade **uprated, uprates**
UPREACH *vb* reach up
UPREAR *vb* lift up **uprears**
UPREST *n* uprising **uprests**
UPRIGHT *adj, adv, n, vb*
UPRISAL ▸ **uprise**
UPRISE *vb* rise up **uprisen, upriser, uprises**
UPRIST = **uprest**
UPRISTS ▸ **uprist**
UPRIVER *adv* towards or near the source of a river ▹ *n* area located upstream
UPROAR *n, vb* **uproars**
UPROLL *vb* roll up **uprolls**
UPROOT *vb* **uproots**
UPROSE ▸ **uprise**
UPROUSE *vb* rouse or stir up
UPRUN *vb* run up **upruns**
UPRUSH *n* upward rush, as of consciousness ▹ *vb* rush upwards
UPRYST = **uprest**
UPS ▸ **up**
UPSCALE *adj* of or for the upper end of an economic or social scale ▹ *vb* upgrade
UPSEE *n* drunken revel **upsees**
UPSELL *vb* persuade a customer to buy a more expensive or additional item **upsells**
UPSEND *vb* send up **upsends, upsent**
UPSET *adj, vb, n* **upsets**
UPSEY = **upsee**
UPSEYS ▸ **upsey**
UPSHIFT *vb* move up (a gear)
UPSHOOT *vb* shoot upwards
UPSHOT *n* **upshots**
UPSIDE *n* upper surface or part **upsides**
UPSIES ▸ **upsy**
UPSILON *n* 20th letter in the Greek alphabet
UPSIZE *vb* increase in size **upsized, upsizes**
UPSKILL *vb* improve the aptitude for work of (a person)
UPSLOPE *adv* up a or the slope
UPSOAR *vb* soar up **upsoars**

UPSOLD ▸ **upsell**
UPSPAKE ▸ **upspeak**
UPSPEAK *vb* speak with rising intonation
UPSPEAR *vb* grow upwards in a spear-like manner
UPSPOKE ▸ **upspeak**
UPSTAGE *adj*, *vb*, *adv*, *n*
UPSTAIR = **upstairs**
UPSTAND *vb* rise
UPSTARE *vb* stare upwards
UPSTART *n*, *vb*
UPSTATE *adv* towards, in, from, or relating to the outlying or northern sections of a state ▹ *n* outlying, esp northern, sections of a state
UPSTAY *vb* support **upstays**
UPSTEP *n* type of vocal intonation **upsteps**
UPSTIR *vb* stir up ▹ *n* commotion **upstirs**
UPSTOOD ▸ **upstand**
UPSURGE *n*, *vb*
UPSWAY *vb* swing in the air **upsways**
UPSWEEP *n* curve or sweep upwards ▹ *vb* sweep, curve, or brush or be swept, curved, or brushed upwards
UPSWELL *vb* swell up or cause to swell up
UPSWEPT ▸ **upsweep**
UPSWING *n* recovery period in the trade cycle ▹ *vb* swing or move up **upswung**
UPSY = **upsee**
UPTA = **upter**
UPTAK = **uptake**
UPTAKE *n*, *vb* **uptaken, uptakes**
UPTAKS ▸ **uptak**
UPTALK *n* style of speech in which every sentence ends with a rising tone ▹ *vb* talk in this manner **uptalks**
UPTEAR *vb* tear up **uptears**
UPTEMPO *adj* fast ▹ *n* uptempo piece
UPTER *adj* of poor quality
UPTHREW ▸ **upthrow**
UPTHROW *n* upward movement of rocks on one side of a fault plane relative to rocks on the other side ▹ *vb* throw upwards
UPTICK *n* rise or increase **upticks**
UPTIE *vb* tie up **uptied, upties**
UPTIGHT *adj*
UPTILT *vb* tilt up **uptilts**
UPTIME *n* time during which a machine, such as a computer, actually operates **uptimes**
UPTOOK ▸ **uptake**
UPTORE ▸ **uptear**
UPTORN ▸ **uptear**
UPTOSS *vb* throw upwards
UPTOWN *adv* towards, in, or relating to some part of a town that is away from the centre ▹ *n* such a part of town, esp a residential part **uptowns**
UPTRAIN *vb* train up
UPTREND *n* upward trend
UPTURN *n*, *vb* **upturns**
UPTYING ▸ **uptie**
UPVALUE *vb* raise the value of
UPWAFT *vb* waft upwards **upwafts**
UPWARD = **upwards**
UPWARDS *adv*
UPWELL *vb* well up **upwells**
UPWENT ▸ **upgo**
UPWHIRL *vb* spin upwards
UPWIND *adv* into or against the wind ▹ *adj* going against the wind ▹ *vb* wind up **upwinds, upwound**
UPWRAP *vb* wrap up **upwraps**
UR *interj* hesitant utterance used to fill gaps in talking
URACHI ▸ **urachus**
URACHUS *n* cord of tissue connected to the bladder
URACIL *n* pyrimidine present in all living cells **uracils**
URAEI ▸ **uraeus**

> This plural of **uraeus**, an Egyptian symbol of kingship, is very useful for dumping a surplus of vowels.

URAEMIA *n* accumulation of waste products in the blood **uraemic**

URAEUS *n* sacred serpent of ancient Egypt
URALI *n* type of plant **uralis**
URALITE *n* mineral that replaces pyroxene in some rocks
URANIA *n* uranium dioxide
URANIAN *adj* heavenly
URANIAS ▸ **urania**
URANIC *adj* of or containing uranium, esp in a high valence state
URANIDE *n* any element having an atomic number greater than that of protactinium
URANIN *n* type of alkaline substance **uranins**
URANISM *n* homosexuality
URANITE *n* any of various minerals containing uranium, esp torbernite or autunite
URANIUM *n*
URANOUS *adj* of or containing uranium, esp in a low valence state
URANYL *n* of, consisting of, or containing the divalent ion UO_2^{2+} or the group $-UO_2$ **uranyls**
URAO *n* type of mineral **uraos**
URARE = **urali**
URARES ▸ **urare**
URARI = **urali**
URARIS ▸ **urari**
URASE = **urease**
URASES ▸ **urase**
URATE *n* any salt or ester of uric acid **urates, uratic**
URB *n* urban area
URBAN *adj*
URBANE *adj* **urbaner**
URBIA *n* urban area **urbias**
URBS ▸ **urb**
URCEOLI > **urceolus**
URCHIN *n* **urchins**
URD *n* type of plant with edible seeds
URDE *adj* (in heraldry) having points **urdee**
URDS ▸ **urd**
URDY *n* heraldic line pattern
URE = **aurochs**
UREA *n* white soluble crystalline compound found in urine **ureal, ureas**
UREASE *n* enzyme that converts urea to ammonium carbonate **ureases**
UREDIA ▸ **uredium**
UREDIAL ▸ **uredium**
UREDINE ▸ **uredo**
UREDIUM *n* spore-producing body of some rust fungi in which uredospores are formed
UREDO *less common name for* > **urticaria**
UREDOS ▸ **uredo**
UREIC ▸ **urea**
UREIDE *n* any of a class of organic compounds derived from urea **ureides**
UREMIA = **uraemia**
UREMIAS ▸ **uremia**
UREMIC ▸ **uremia**
URENA *n* plant genus **urenas**
URENT *adj* burning
URES ▸ **ure**
URESES ▸ **uresis**
URESIS *n* urination
URETER *n* **ureters**
URETHAN = **urethane**
URETHRA *n*
URETIC *adj* of or relating to the urine
URGE *n, vb* **urged**
URGENCE ▸ **urgent**
URGENCY ▸ **urgent**
URGENT *adj*
URGER, urgers, urges, urging, urgings ▸ **urge**
URIAL *n* type of sheep **urials**
URIC *adj* of or derived from urine
URICASE *n* type of enzyme
URIDINE *n* nucleoside present in all living cells in a combined form, esp in RNA
URINAL *n* **urinals**
URINANT *adj* having the head downwards
URINARY *adj* of urine or the organs that secrete and pass urine ▹ *n* reservoir for urine
URINATE *vb*
URINE *n, vb* **urined, urines, urining**
URINOSE = **urinous**

URINOUS *adj* of, resembling, or containing urine
URITE *n* part of the abdomen **urites**
URMAN *n* forest **urmans**
URN *n, vb* **urnal, urned**
URNFUL *n* capacity of an urn **urnfuls**
URNING *n* homosexual man **urnings**
URNLIKE ▸ **urn**
URNS ▸ **urn**
URODELE *n* amphibian of the order which includes the salamanders and newts
UROLITH *n* calculus in the urinary tract
UROLOGY *n* branch of medicine concerned with the urinary system and its diseases
UROMERE *n* part of the abdomen
UROPOD *n* paired appendage forming part of the tailfan in lobsters **uropods**
UROSES ▸ **urosis**
UROSIS *n* urinary disease
UROSOME *n* abdomen of arthropods
URP *dialect word for* ▸ **vomit**
URPED ▸ **urp**
URPING ▸ **urp**
URPS ▸ **urp**
URSA *n* she-bear **ursae**
URSID *n* meteor **ursids**
URSINE *adj* of or like a bear
URSON *n* type of porcupine **ursons**
URTEXT *n* earliest form of a text **urtexts**
URTICA *n* type of nettle **urticas**
URUBU *n* type of bird **urubus**
URUS *another name for the* ▸ **aurochs**
URUSES ▸ **urus**
URVA *n* Indian mongoose **urvas**
US *pron*
USABLE *adj* able to be used **usably**
USAGE *n*
USAGER *n* person who has the use of something in trust **usagers**
USAGES ▸ **usage**
USANCE *n* period of time permitted for the redemption of foreign bills of exchange **usances, usaunce**
USE *vb, n*
USEABLE = **usable**
USEABLY ▸ **usable**
USED *adj*
USEFUL *adj, n* **usefuls**
USELESS *adj*
USER *n* continued exercise, use, or enjoyment of a right, esp in property **users**
USES ▸ **use**
USHER *n, vb* **ushered, ushers**
USING ▸ **use**
USNEA *n* type of lichen **usneas**
USQUE *n* whisky **usques**
USTION *n* burning **ustions**
USUAL *adj, n*
USUALLY *adv* most often, in most cases
USUALS ▸ **usual**
USUCAPT > **usucapion**
USURE *vb* be involved in usury **usured**
USURER *n* person who lends funds at an exorbitant rate of interest **usurers**
USURES ▸ **usure**
USURESS *n* female usurer
USURIES ▸ **usury**
USURING ▸ **usure**
USUROUS ▸ **usury**
USURP *vb* **usurped, usurper, usurps**
USURY *n* practice of lending money at an extremely high rate of interest
USWARD *adv* towards us **uswards**
UT *n* syllable used in the fixed system of solmization for the note C
UTA *n* side-blotched lizard
UTAS *n* eighth day of a festival **utases**
UTE = **utility**
UTENSIL *n*
UTERI ▸ **uterus**
UTERINE *adj* of or affecting the womb

UTERUS *n*
UTES ▸ **ute**
UTILE *obsolete word for* ▸ **useful**
UTILISE = **utilize**
UTILITY *n, adj*
UTILIZE *vb*
UTIS *n* uproar **utises**
UTMOST *n, adj* **utmosts**
UTOPIA *n* real or imaginary society, place, state, etc, considered to be perfect or ideal
UTOPIAN *adj* of or relating to a perfect or ideal existence ▹ *n* idealistic social reformer
UTOPIAS ▸ **utopia**
UTOPISM ▸ **utopia**
UTOPIST ▸ **utopia**
UTRICLE *n* larger of the two parts of the membranous labyrinth of the internal ear
UTS ▸ **ut**
UTTER *vb, adj* **uttered, utterer**
UTTERLY *adv* extrremely
UTTERS ▸ **utter**
UTU *n* reward **utus**
UVA *n* grape or fruit resembling this **uvae, uvas**
UVEA *n* part of the eyeball consisting of the iris, ciliary body, and choroid **uveal, uveas**
UVEITIC ▸ **uveitis**
UVEITIS *n* inflammation of the uvea
UVEOUS ▸ **uvea**
UVULA *n* **uvulae**
UVULAR *adj* of or relating to the uvula ▹ *n* uvular consonant **uvulars**
UVULAS ▸ **uvula**
UXORIAL *adj* of or relating to a wife

Vv

If you have a **V** on your rack, the first thing to remember is that there are no valid two-letter words beginning with **V**. In fact, there are no two-letter words that end in **V** either, so you can't form any two-letter words using **V**. Remembering this will stop you wasting time trying to think of some. While **V** is useless for two-letter words, it does start some good three-letter words. **Vex** and **vox** (13 points each) are the best of these, while **vaw, vow** and **vly** (9 each) are also useful.

VAC *vb* clean with a vacuum cleaner

> Meaning to clean with a vacuum cleaner, this can be a useful short word for dealing with that awkward letter V.

VACANCE *n* vacant period
VACANCY *n* unfilled job
VACANT *adj*
VACATE *vb* **vacated, vacates**
VACATUR *n* annulment
VACCINA = **vaccinia**
VACCINE *n*
VACKED ▶ **vac**
VACKING ▶ **vac**
VACS ▶ **vac**
VACUA ▶ **vacuum**
VACUATE *vb* empty
VACUIST *n* person believing in the existence of vacuums in nature
VACUITY *n* absence of intelligent thought or ideas
VACUOLE *n*
VACUOUS *adj*
VACUUM *n, vb* **vacuums**
VADE *vb* fade **vaded, vades, vading**
VADOSE *adj* of or derived from water occurring above the water table
VAE = **voe**
VAES ▶ **vae**
VAG *n* vagrant
VAGAL *adj* of, relating to, or affecting the vagus nerve **vagally**
VAGARY *n*
VAGGED ▶ **vag**
VAGGING ▶ **vag**
VAGI ▶ **vagus**
VAGILE *adj* able to move freely
VAGINA *n* **vaginae, vaginal, vaginas**
VAGITUS *n* new-born baby's cry
VAGRANT *n, adj* **vagrom**
VAGS ▶ **vag**
VAGUE *adj, vb* **vagued, vaguely, vaguer, vagues, vaguest, vaguing**
VAGUS *n* tenth cranial nerve, which supplies the heart, lungs, and viscera
VAHANA *n* vehicle **vahanas**
VAHINE *n* Polynesian woman **vahines**
VAIL *vb* lower (something, such as a weapon), esp as a sign of deference or

submission **vailed, vailing, vails**
VAIN *adj* **vainer, vainest, vainly**
VAIR *n* fur used to trim robes in the Middle Ages
VAIRE *adj* of Russian squirrel fur
VAIRIER ▸ **vair**
VAIRS ▸ **vair**
VAIRY ▸ **vair**
VAIVODE *n* European ruler
VAKAS *n* Armenian priestly garment **vakases**
VAKEEL *n* ambassador **vakeels, vakil**
VAKILS ▸ **vakil**
VALANCE *n* piece of drapery round the edge of a bed ▹ *vb* provide with a valance
VALE *n, sentence substitute*
VALENCE = **valency**
VALENCY *n*
VALERIC *adj* of, relating to, or derived from valerian
VALES ▸ **vale**
VALET *n, vb*
VALETA *n* old-time dance in triple time **valetas**
VALETE *n* farewell
VALETED ▸ **valet**
VALETES ▸ **valete**
VALETS ▸ **valet**
VALGOID ▸ **valgus**
VALGOUS = **valgus**
VALGUS *adj* denoting a deformity of a limb ▹ *n* abnormal position of a limb
VALI *n* Turkish civil governor
VALIANT *adj, n*
VALID *adj* **valider, validly**
VALINE *n* essential amino acid **valines**
VALIS ▸ **vali**
VALISE *n* **valises**
VALIUM *n as in* **valium picnic** refers to a day on the New York Stock Exchange when business is slow
VALKYR *variant of* > **valkyrie**
VALKYRS ▸ **valkyr**
VALLAR *adj* pertaining to a rampart **vallary**
VALLATE *adj* surrounded with a wall
VALLEY *n* **valleys**
VALLUM *n* Roman rampart or earthwork **vallums**
VALONEA = **valonia**
VALONIA *n* acorn cups and unripe acorns of a particular oak
VALOR = **valour**
VALORS ▸ **valor**
VALOUR *n* **valours**
VALSE *another word for* ▸ **waltz**
VALSED ▸ **valse**
VALSES ▸ **valse**
VALSING ▸ **valse**
VALUATE *vb* value or evaluate
VALUE *n, vb* **valued, valuer, valuers, values, valuing**
VALUTA *n* value of one currency in terms of its exchange rate with another **valutas**
VALVAL = **valvular**
VALVAR = **valvular**
VALVATE *adj* furnished with a valve or valves
VALVE *n, vb* **valved, valves, valving**
VALVULA = **valvule**
VALVULE *n* small valve or a part resembling one
VAMOOSE *vb* leave a place hurriedly **vamose**
VAMOSED ▸ **vamose**
VAMOSES ▸ **vamose**
VAMP *n, vb* **vamped, vamper, vampers, vampier, vamping**
VAMPIRE *n, vb*
VAMPISH ▸ **vamp**
VAMPS ▸ **vamp**
VAMPY ▸ **vamp**
VAN *n, vb*
VANADIC *adj* of or containing vanadium, esp in a trivalent or pentavalent state
VANDA *n* type of orchid
VANDAL *n* **vandals**
VANDAS ▸ **vanda**
VANDYKE *n* short pointed beard ▹ *vb* cut with deep zigzag indentations
VANE *n* **vaned, vanes**
VANESSA *n* type of butterfly
VANG *n* type of rope or tackle on a sailing ship **vangs**

VANILLA *n, adj*
VANISH *vb, n*
VANITAS *n* type of Dutch painting
VANITY *n*
VANLOAD *n* amount van will carry
VANMAN *n* man in control of a van **vanmen**
VANNED ▸ **van**
VANNER *n* horse used to pull delivery vehicles **vanners**
VANNING ▸ **van**
VANPOOL *n* van-sharing group
VANS ▸ **van**
VANT *archaic word for* > **vanguard**
VANTAGE *n* state, position, or opportunity offering advantage ▹ *vb* benefit
VANTS ▸ **vant**
VANWARD *adv* in or towards the front
VAPID *adj* **vapider, vapidly**
VAPOR = **vapour**
VAPORED ▸ **vapor**
VAPORER ▸ **vapor**
VAPORS ▸ **vapor**
VAPORY ▸ **vapour**
VAPOUR *n, vb* **vapours, vapoury**
VAQUERO *n* cattlehand
VAR *n* unit of reactive power of an alternating current
VARA *n* unit of length used in Spain, Portugal, and South America
VARAN *n* type of lizard **varans**
VARAS ▸ **vara**
VARDIES ▸ **vardy**
VARDY *n* verdict
VARE *n* rod
VAREC *n* ash obtained from kelp **varech**
VARECHS ▸ **varech**
VARECS ▸ **varec**
VARES ▸ **vare**
VAREUSE *n* type of coat
VARIA *n* collection or miscellany, esp of literary works
VARIANT *adj, n*
VARIAS ▸ **varia**
VARIATE *n* random variable or a numerical value taken by it ▹ *vb* vary
VARICES ▸ **varix**
VARIED ▸ **vary**
VARIER *n* person who varies **variers**
VARIES ▸ **vary**
VARIETY *n*
VARIOLA *n* smallpox
VARIOLE *n* any of the rounded masses that make up the rock variolite
VARIOUS *adj*
VARIX *n* tortuous dilated vein
VARLET *n* menial servant **varlets**
VARMENT = **varmint**
VARMINT *n* irritating or obnoxious person or animal
VARNA *n* any of the four Hindu castes **varnas**
VARNISH *n, vb*
VAROOM = **vroom**
VAROOMS = **varoom**
VARROA *n* small parasite **varroas**
VARS ▸ **var**
VARSAL *adj* universal
VARSITY *n* university
VARUS *adj* denoting a deformity of a limb ▹ *n* abnormal position of a limb **varuses**
VARVE *n* typically thin band of sediment deposited annually in glacial lakes
VARVED *adj* having layers of sedimentary deposit
VARVEL *n* piece of falconry equipment **varvels**
VARVES ▸ **varve**
VARY *vb* **varying**
VAS *n* vessel or tube that carries a fluid **vasa, vasal**
VASCULA > **vasculum**
VASE *n* **vases**
VASSAIL *archaic variant of* ▸ **vassal**
VASSAL *n, adj, vb* **vassals**
VAST *adj, n* **vaster, vastest**
VASTIER ▸ **vasty**
VASTITY ▸ **vast**
VASTLY ▸ **vast**
VASTS ▸ **vast**
VASTY *archaic or poetic word for* ▸ **vast**
VAT *n, vb*
VATABLE *adj* subject to VAT

VATFUL *n* amount enough to fill a vat **vatfuls**
VATIC *adj* of, relating to, or characteristic of a prophet **vatical**
VATMAN *n* Customs and Excise employee **vatmen**
VATS ▸ vat
VATTED ▸ vat
VATTER *n* person who works with vats; blender **vatters**
VATTING ▸ vat
VATU *n* standard monetary unit of Vanuatu **vatus**
VAU = **vav**
VAUCH *vb* move fast **vauched, vauches**
VAUDOO = **voodoo**
VAUDOOS ▸ vaudoo
VAUDOUX = **voodoo**
VAULT *n, vb* **vaulted, vaulter, vaults**
VAULTY *adj* arched
VAUNCE ▸ advance
VAUNCED ▸ vaunce
VAUNCES ▸ vaunce
VAUNT *vb* describe or display (success or possessions) boastfully ▹ *n* boast **vaunted, vaunter**
VAUNTIE = **vaunty**
VAUNTS ▸ vaunt
VAUNTY *adj* proud
VAURIEN *n* rascal
VAUS ▸ vau
VAUT = **vault**
VAUTE = **vault**
VAUTED ▸ vaute
VAUTES ▸ vaute
VAUTING ▸ vaut
VAUTS ▸ vaut
VAV *n* sixth letter of the Hebrew alphabet

> It is surprising how often one wants to get rid of two Vs, and when one does, this word, the name of a Hebrew letter, fits the bill nicely. It has an equally useful variant **vaw**.

VAVASOR *n* (in feudal society) vassal who also has vassals himself
VAVS ▸ vav
VAW *n* Hebrew letter
VAWARD *n* vanguard **vawards**
VAWNTIE ▸ vaunt
VAWS ▸ vaw
VAWTE = **vault**
VAWTED ▸ vawte
VAWTES ▸ vawte
VAWTING ▸ vawte
VEAL *n, vb*
VEALE = **veil**
VEALED ▸ veal
VEALER *n* young bovine animal of up to 14 months old grown for veal **vealers**
VEALES ▸ veale
VEALIER, vealing, veals, vealy ▸ veal
VECTOR *n, vb* **vectors**
VEDALIA *n* Australian ladybird which is a pest of citrus fruits
VEDETTE *n* small patrol vessel
VEDUTA *n* painting of a town or city **vedute**
VEE *n* letter 'v'
VEEJAY *n* video jockey **veejays**
VEENA = **vina**
VEENAS ▸ veena
VEEP *n* vice president
VEEPEE *n* vice president **veepees**
VEEPS ▸ veep
VEER *vb, n* **veered**
VEERIES ▸ veery
VEERING ▸ veer
VEERS ▸ veer
VEERY *n* tawny brown North American thrush
VEES ▸ vee
VEG *n* vegetable or vegetables ▹ *vb* relax

> **Veg** is a short form of **vegetable**. If someone plays this, remember that you can add an A or O to it to form **vega** or **vego**.

VEGA *n* tobacco plantation
VEGAN *n, adj*
VEGANIC *adj* farmed without the use of animal products or byproducts
VEGANS ▸ vegan
VEGAS ▸ vega
VEGES ▸ veg
VEGETAL *adj* of or relating to plant life ▹ *n* vegetable
VEGETE *adj* lively
VEGGED ▸ veg
VEGGES ▸ veg

VEGGIE *n* vegetable ▷ *adj* vegetarian **veggies**
VEGGING ▶ **veg**
VEGIE = **veggie**
VEGIES ▶ **vegie**
VEGO *adj* vegetarian ▷ *n* vegetarian **vegos**
VEHICLE *n*
VEHM *n* type of medieval German court **vehme, vehmic**
VEIL *n, vb*
VEILED *adj* disguised
VEILER ▶ **veil**
VEILERS ▶ **veil**
VEILIER ▶ **veil**
VEILING *n* veil or the fabric used for veils
VEILS ▶ **veil**
VEILY ▶ **veil**
VEIN *n, vb* **veinal, veined**
VEINER *n* wood-carving tool **veiners**
VEINIER ▶ **vein**
VEINING *n* pattern or network of veins or streaks
VEINLET *n* any small vein or venule
VEINOUS ▶ **vein**
VEINS ▶ **vein**
VEINULE *less common spelling of* ▶ **venule**
VEINY ▶ **vein**
VELA ▶ **velum**
VELAMEN *n* thick layer of dead cells that covers the aerial roots of certain orchids
VELAR *adj* of, relating to, or attached to a velum ▷ *n* velar sound
VELARIA > **velarium**
VELARIC ▶ **velar**
VELARS ▶ **velar**
VELATE *adj* having or covered with velum **velated**
VELCRO *n* tradename for a fastening consisting of two strips of nylon fabric that are pressed together **velcros**
VELD *n* **velds, veldt**
VELDTS ▶ **veldt**
VELE = **veil**
VELES ▶ **vele**
VELETA = **valeta**
VELETAS ▶ **veleta**
VELIGER *n* free-swimming larva of many molluscs
VELITES *pl n* light-armed troops in ancient Rome, drawn from the poorer classes
VELL *vb* cut turf
VELLET *n* velvet **vellets**
VELLON *n* silver and copper alloy used in old Spanish coins **vellons**
VELLS ▶ **vell**
VELLUM *n, adj* **vellums**
VELLUS *n as in* **vellus hair** short fine unpigmented hair covering the human body
VELOCE *adv* be played rapidly
VELOUR *n* **velours**
VELOUTE *n* rich white sauce or soup made from stock, egg yolks, and cream
VELUM *n* any of various membranous structures
VELURE *n* velvet or a similar fabric ▷ *vb* cover with velure **velured, velures**
VELVET *n, vb* **velvets, velvety**
VENA *n* vein in the body **venae**
VENAL *adj* **venally**
VENATIC *adj* of, relating to, or used in hunting
VENATOR *n* hunter
VEND *vb* sell
VENDACE *n* either of two small whitefish occurring in lakes in Scotland and NW England
VENDAGE *n* vintage
VENDED ▶ **vend**
VENDEE *n* person to whom something, esp real property, is sold **vendees**
VENDER = **vendor**
VENDERS ▶ **vender**
VENDING ▶ **vend**
VENDIS = **vendace**
VENDISS = **vendace**
VENDOR *n* **vendors**
VENDS ▶ **vend**
VENDUE *n* public sale **vendues**
VENEER *n, vb* **veneers**
VENEFIC *adj* having poisonous effects
VENENE *n* medicine from snake venom **venenes**
VENERER *n* hunter

VENERY *n* pursuit of sexual gratification
VENEWE = **venue**
VENEWES ▸ **venewe**
VENEY *n* thrust **veneys**
VENGE *vb* avenge **venged, venger, vengers, venges, venging**
VENIAL *adj*
VENIN *n* any of the poisonous constituents of animal venoms **venine**
VENINES ▸ **venine**
VENINS ▸ **venin**
VENIRE *n* list from which jurors are selected **venires**
VENISON *n*
VENITE *n* musical setting for the 95th psalm **venites**
VENNEL *n* lane **vennels**
VENOM *n, vb* **venomed, venomer, venoms**
VENOSE *adj* having veins
VENOUS *adj*
VENT *n, vb*
VENTAGE *n* small opening
VENTAIL *n* (in medieval armour) a covering for the lower part of the face
VENTANA *n* window
VENTED ▸ **vent**
VENTER ▸ **vent**
VENTERS ▸ **vent**
VENTIGE = **ventage**
VENTIL *n* valve on a musical instrument **ventils**
VENTING ▸ **vent**
VENTOSE *adj* full of wind
VENTRAL *adj* relating to the front of the body ▹ *n* ventral fin
VENTRE = **venture**
VENTRED ▸ **ventre**
VENTRES ▸ **ventre**
VENTS ▸ **vent**
VENTURE *n, vb*
VENTURI *n* tube used to control the flow of fluid
VENUE *n* **venues**
VENULAR ▸ **venule**
VENULE *n* any of the small branches of a vein **venules**
VENUS *n* type of marine bivalve mollusc **venuses**
VERA *adj as in* **aloe vera** plant substance used in skin and hair preparations
VERANDA *n*
VERB *n*
VERBAL *adj, n, vb* **verbals**
VERBENA *n* plant with sweet-smelling flowers
VERBID *n* any nonfinite form of a verb or any nonverbal word derived from a verb **verbids**
VERBIFY *another word for* > **verbalize**
VERBILE *n* person who is best stimulated by words
VERBING *n* use of nouns as verbs
VERBOSE *adj*
VERBS ▸ **verb**
VERD *adj as in* **verd antique** dark green mottled impure variety of serpentine marble
VERDANT *adj*
VERDET *n* type of verdigris **verdets**
VERDICT *n*
VERDIN *n* small W North American tit having grey plumage with a yellow head **verdins**
VERDIT = **verdict**
VERDITE *n* type of rock used in jewellery
VERDITS ▸ **verdit**
VERDOY *n* floral or leafy shield decoration
VERDURE *n* flourishing green vegetation
VERGE *n, vb* **verged**
VERGER *n* **vergers**
VERGES ▸ **verge**
VERGING ▸ **verge**
VERGLAS *n* thin film of ice on rock
VERIDIC = **veridical**
VERIER ▸ **very**
VERIEST ▸ **very**
VERIFY *vb*
VERILY *adv* in truth
VERISM *n* extreme naturalism in art or literature
VERISMO *n* school of composition that originated in Italian opera
VERISMS ▸ **verism**
VERIST ▸ **verism**
VERISTS ▸ **verism**
VERITAS *n* truth

VERITE *adj* involving a high degree of realism or naturalism ▷ *n* this kind of realism in film **verites**
VERITY *n*
VERLAN *n* variety of French slang in which the syllables are inverted **verlans**
VERLIG *adj* enlightened
VERMAL ▶ **vermis**
VERMEIL *n* gilded silver, bronze, or other metal, used esp in the 19th century ▷ *vb* decorate with vermeil ▷ *adj* vermilion **vermell**
VERMES ▶ **vermis**
VERMIAN ▶ **vermis**
VERMIL = **vermeil**
VERMILS ▶ **vermil**
VERMILY ▶ **vermeil**
VERMIN *pl n* **vermins, verminy**
VERMIS *n* middle lobe connecting the two halves of the cerebellum
VERMUTH = **vermouth**
VERNAL *adj* occurring in spring **vernant**
VERNIER *n* movable scale on a measuring instrument for taking readings in fractions
VERNIX *n* white substance covering the skin of a foetus
VERONAL *n* long-acting barbiturate used medicinally
VERRA *Scot word for* ▶ **very**
VERREL *n* ferrule **verrels**
VERREY = **vair**
VERRUCA *n* **verruga**
VERRY = **vair**
VERS *n* verse
VERSAL *n* embellished letter **versals**
VERSANT *n* side or slope of a mountain or mountain range
VERSE *n, vb*
VERSED *adj*
VERSER *n* versifier **versers**
VERSES ▶ **verse**
VERSET *n* short, often sacred, verse **versets**
VERSIFY *vb* write in verse
VERSIN = **versine**
VERSINE *n* mathematical term
VERSING ▶ **verse**
VERSINS ▶ **versin**
VERSION *n*
VERSO *n* left-hand page of a book **versos**
VERST *n* unit of length used in Russia **verste**
VERSTES ▶ **verste**
VERSTS ▶ **verst**
VERSUS *prep*
VERSUTE *adj* cunning
VERT *n* right to cut green wood in a forest ▷ *vb* turn **verted**
VERTEX *n*
VERTIGO *n*
VERTING ▶ **vert**
VERTS ▶ **vert**
VERTU = **virtu**
VERTUE = **virtu**
VERTUES ▶ **vertue**
VERTUS ▶ **vertu**
VERVAIN *n* plant with spikes of blue, purple, or white flowers
VERVE *n*
VERVEL = **varvel**
VERVELS ▶ **vervel**
VERVEN = **vervain**
VERVENS ▶ **verven**
VERVES ▶ **verve**
VERVET *n* variety of a South African guenon monkey **vervets**
VERY *adv, adj*
VESICA *n* bladder **vesicae**
VESICAL *adj* of or relating to a vesica, esp the urinary bladder
VESICLE *n* sac or small cavity, esp one containing fluid
VESPA *n* type of wasp **vespas**
VESPER *n* evening prayer, service, or hymn
VESPERS *pl n*
VESPID *n* insect of the family that includes the common wasp and hornet ▷ *adj* of or belonging to this family **vespids**
VESPINE *adj* of, relating to, or resembling a wasp or wasps
VESPOID *adj* like a wasp
VESSAIL *archaic variant of* ▶ **vessel**
VESSEL *n, adj* **vessels**
VEST *n, vb*

VESTA *n* short friction match, usually of wood
VESTAL *adj* pure, chaste ▷ *n* chaste woman **vestals**
VESTAS ▸ vesta
VESTED *adj* having an existing right to the immediate or future possession of property
VESTEE *n* person having a vested interest in something **vestees**
VESTIGE *n*
VESTING ▸ vest
VESTRAL ▸ vestry
VESTRY *n*
VESTS ▸ vest
VESTURE *n* garment or something that seems like a garment ▷ *vb* clothe
VET *vb, n*
VETCH *n* **vetches**
VETCHY *adj* consisting of vetches
VETERAN *n, adj*
VETIVER *n* tall hairless grass of tropical and subtropical Asia
VETKOEK *n* South African cake
VETO *n, vb* **vetoed, vetoer, vetoers, vetoes, vetoing**
VETS, vetted, vetter, vetters ▸ vet
VETTING *n as in* **positive vetting**
VETTURA *n* Italian mode of transport
VEX *vb*
VEXED *adj* **vexedly**
VEXER ▸ vex
VEXERS ▸ vex
VEXES ▸ vex
VEXIL = vexillum
VEXILLA > vexillum
VEXILS ▸ vexil
VEXING ▸ vex
VEXINGS ▸ vex
VEXT = vexed
VEZIR = vizier
VEZIRS ▸ vezir
VIA *prep, n*
VIABLE *adj* **viably**
VIADUCT *n*
VIAE ▸ via
VIAL *n, vb* **vialed, vialful, vialing, vialled, vials**
VIAND *n* type of food, esp a delicacy **viands**
VIAS ▸ via
VIATIC = viatical
VIATICA > viaticum
VIATOR *n* traveller **viators**
VIBE *n* feeling or flavour of the kind specified
VIBES *pl n*
VIBEX *n* mark under the skin
VIBEY *adj* lively and vibrant
VIBICES ▸ vibex
VIBIER ▸ vibey
VIBIEST ▸ vibey
VIBIST *n* person who plays a vibraphone in a jazz band or group **vibists**
VIBRANT *adj, n*
VIBRATE *vb*
VIBRATO *n*
VIBRIO *n* curved or spiral rodlike bacterium **vibrion, vibrios**
VIBS *pl n* type of climbing shoes
VICAR *n* **vicarly, vicars**
VICARY *n* office of a vicar
VICE *n, adj, vb, prep* **viced**
VICEROY *n*
VICES ▸ vice
VICHIES ▸ vichy
VICHY *n* French mineral water
VICIATE = vitiate
VICINAL *adj* neighbouring
VICING ▸ vice
VICIOUS *adj*
VICOMTE *n* French nobleman
VICTIM *n* **victims**
VICTOR *n* **victors**
VICTORY *n*
VICTRIX = victress
VICTUAL *vb* supply with or obtain victuals
VICUGNA = vicuna
VICUNA *n* S American animal like the llama **vicunas**
VID = video
VIDAME *n* French nobleman **vidames**
VIDE *interj* look
VIDENDA > videndum
VIDEO *vb, adj, n* **videoed, videos**
VIDETTE = vedette
VIDICON *n* small television camera tube used in closed-circuit television

VIDIMUS *n* inspection
VIDS ▸ **vid**
VIDUAGE *n* widows collectively
VIDUAL *adj* widowed
VIDUITY *n* widowhood
VIDUOUS *adj* empty
VIE *vb* **vied**
VIELLE *n* stringed musical instrument **vielles**
VIENNA *n as in* **vienna loaf, vienna steak** associated with Vienna
VIER ▸ **vie**
VIERS ▸ **vie**
VIES ▸ **vie**
VIEW *n, vb* **viewed**
VIEWER *n* **viewers**
VIEWIER ▸ **viewy**
VIEWING *n* act of watching television
VIEWLY *adj* pleasant on the eye
VIEWS ▸ **view**
VIEWY *adj* having fanciful opinions or ideas
VIFDA = **vivda**
VIFDAS ▸ **vifda**
VIG *n* interest on a loan that is paid to a moneylender
VIGA *n* rafter **vigas**
VIGIA *n* navigational hazard whose existence has not been confirmed **vigias**
VIGIL *n* **vigils**
VIGOR = **vigour**
VIGORO *n* women's game similar to cricket **vigoros**
VIGORS ▸ **vigor**
VIGOUR *n* physical or mental energy **vigours**
VIGS ▸ **vig**
VIHARA *n* type of Buddhist temple **viharas**
VIHUELA *n* obsolete plucked stringed instrument of Spain
VIKING *n* Dane, Norwegian, or Swede who raided by sea between the 8th and 11th centuries **vikings**
VILAYET *n* major administrative division of Turkey
VILD = **vile**
VILDE = **vile**
VILDLY ▸ **vild**
VILE *adj* **vilely, viler, vilest**
VILIACO *n* scoundrel **viliago**
VILIFY *vb*
VILL *n* township
VILLA *n* **villae**
VILLAGE *n*
VILLAIN *n*
VILLAN = **villein**
VILLANS ▸ **villan**
VILLANY = **villainy**
VILLAR ▸ **vill**
VILLAS ▸ **villa**
VILLEIN *n* peasant bound in service to his lord
VILLI ▸ **villus**
VILLOSE = **villous**
VILLOUS *adj* (of plant parts) covered with long hairs
VILLS ▸ **vill**
VILLUS *n*
VIM *n* force, energy

> This word can be helpful when you're stuck with unpromising letters, and gives a reasonable score for a three-letter word.

VIMANA *n* Indian mythological chariot of the gods **vimanas**
VIMEN *n* long flexible shoot that occurs in certain plants **vimina, viminal**
VIMS ▸ **vim**
VIN *n* French wine
VINA *n* stringed musical instrument related to the sitar
VINAL *n* type of manmade fibre **vinals**
VINAS ▸ **vina**
VINASSE *n* residue left in a still after distilling spirits, esp brandy
VINCA *n* type of trailing plant with blue flowers **vincas**
VINCULA > **vinculum**
VINE *n, vb*
VINEAL *adj* relating to wines
VINED ▸ **vine**
VINEGAR *n, vb*
VINER *n* vinedresser **viners**
VINERY *n* hothouse for growing grapes
VINES ▸ **vine**
VINEW *vb* become mouldy **vinewed, vinews**

VINIC *adj* of, relating to, or contained in wine
VINIER ▸ **vine**
VINIEST ▸ **vine**
VINIFY *vb* convert into wine
VINING ▸ **vine**
VINO *n* wine **vinos**
VINOUS *adj* of or characteristic of wine
VINS ▸ **vin**
VINT *vb* sell (wine)
VINTAGE *n, adj, vb*
VINTED ▸ **vint**
VINTING ▸ **vint**
VINTNER *n* dealer in wine
VINTRY *n* place where wine is sold
VINTS ▸ **vint**
VINY ▸ **vine**
VINYL *n, adj* **vinylic, vinyls**
VIOL *n*
VIOLA *n* **violas**
VIOLATE *vb, adj*
VIOLD *archaic or poetic past form of* ▸ **vial**
VIOLENT *adj, vb*
VIOLER *n* person who plays the viol **violers**
VIOLET *n, adj* **violets**
VIOLIN *n* **violins**
VIOLIST *n* person who plays the viola
VIOLONE *n* double-bass member of the viol family
VIOLS ▸ **viol**
VIPER *n* **vipers**
VIRAGO *n* aggressive woman **viragos**
VIRAL *adj* of or caused by a virus **virally**
VIRANDA = **veranda**
VIRANDO = **veranda**
VIRE *vb* turn **vired**
VIRELAI = **virelay**
VIRELAY *n* old French verse form
VIREMIA = **viraemia**
VIREMIC ▸ **viremia**
VIRENT *adj* green
VIREO *n* American songbird **vireos**
VIRES ▸ **vire**
VIRETOT *n as in* **on the viretot** in a rush
VIRGA *n* wisps of rain or snow that evaporate before reaching the earth **virgas**
VIRGATE *adj* long, straight, and thin ▹ *n* obsolete measure of land area
VIRGE *n* rod
VIRGER *n* rod-bearer **virgers**
VIRGES ▸ **virge**
VIRGIN *n, adj, vb* **virgins**
VIRGULE *another name for* ▸ **slash**
VIRID *adj* verdant
VIRILE *adj*
VIRING ▸ **vire**
VIRINO *n* entity postulated to be the causative agent of BSE **virinos**
VIRION *n* virus in infective form, consisting of an RNA particle within a protein covering **virions**
VIRL = **ferrule**
VIRLS ▸ **virl**
VIROID *n* any of various infective RNA particles **viroids**
VIROSE *adj* poisonous
VIROSES ▸ **virosis**
VIROSIS *n* viral disease
VIROUS = **virose**
VIRTU *n* taste or love for curios or works of fine art
VIRTUAL *adj*
VIRTUE *n* **virtues**
VIRTUS ▸ **virtu**
VIRUS *n* **viruses**
VIS *n* power, force, or strength
VISA *n, vb* **visaed**
VISAGE *n* **visaged, visages**
VISAING ▸ **visa**
VISARD = **vizard**
VISARDS ▸ **visard**
VISAS ▸ **visa**
VISCERA *pl n*
VISCID *adj* sticky
VISCIN *n* sticky substance found on plants **viscins**
VISCOID *adj* (of a fluid) somewhat viscous
VISCOSE = **viscous**
VISCOUS *adj*
VISCUM *n* shrub genus **viscums**
VISCUS *n* internal organ
VISE *vb* advise or award a visa to ▹ *n* (in US English) vice **vised, viseed, viseing, vises**
VISHING *n* telephone scam used to gain access to credit card numbers or bank details

VISIBLE *adj, n* **visibly**
VISIE = **vizy; visied, visier, visiers, visies**
VISILE *n* person best stimulated by vision **visiles**
VISING ▸ **vise**
VISION *n, vb* **visions**
VISIT *vb, n*
VISITE *n* type of cape
VISITED ▸ **visit**
VISITEE *n* person who is visited
VISITER *variant of* ▸ **visitor**
VISITES ▸ **visite**
VISITOR *n* person who visits a person or place
VISITS ▸ **visit**
VISIVE *adj* visual
VISNE *n* neighbourhood **visnes**
VISNOMY *n* method of judging character from facial features
VISON *n* type of mink **visons**
VISOR *n, vb* **visored, visors**
VISTA *n, vb* **vistaed, vistal, vistas, visto**
VISTOS ▸ **visto**
VISUAL *adj, n* **visuals**
VITA *n* curriculum vitae **vitae**
VITAL *adj, n* **vitally, vitals**
VITAMER *n* type of chemical
VITAMIN *n*
VITAS ▸ **vita**
VITE *adv* musical direction
VITELLI > **vitellus**
VITESSE *n* speed
VITEX *n* type of herb **vitexes**
VITIATE *vb*
VITIOUS *adj* mistaken
VITRAGE *n* light fabric
VITRAIL *n* stained glass
VITRAIN *n* type of coal
VITRAUX ▸ **vitrail**
VITREUM *n* vitreous body
VITRIC *adj* of, relating to, resembling, or having the nature of glass
VITRICS *n* glassware
VITRIFY *vb* change or be changed into glass or a glassy substance
VITRINE *n* glass display case or cabinet for works of art, curios, etc
VITRIOL *n, vb*
VITTA *n* tubelike cavity containing oil that occurs in the fruits of certain plants **vittae, vittate**
VITTLE *obsolete or dialect spelling of* ▸ **victual**
VITTLED ▸ **vittle**
VITTLES *obsolete or dialect spelling of* > **victuals**
VITULAR = **vituline**
VIVA *interj, n, vb*
VIVACE *adj, adv* (to be performed) in a lively manner ▹ *n* piece of music to be performed in this way **vivaces**
VIVAED ▸ **viva**
VIVAING ▸ **viva**
VIVARIA > **vivarium**
VIVARY = **vivarium**
VIVAS ▸ **viva**
VIVAT *interj* long live ▹ *n* expression of acclamation **vivats**
VIVDA *n* method of drying meat **vivdas**
VIVE *interj* long live
VIVELY *adv* in a lively manner
VIVENCY *n* physical or mental energy
VIVER *n* fish pond
VIVERRA *n* civet genus
VIVERS ▸ **viver**
VIVES *n* disease found in horses
VIVID *adj* **vivider, vividly**
VIVIFIC *adj* giving life
VIVIFY *vb* animate, inspire
VIVO *adv* with life and vigour
VIVRES *n* provisions
VIXEN *n* **vixenly, vixens**
VIZARD *n* means of disguise ▹ *vb* conceal by means of a disguise **vizards**
VIZIED ▸ **vizy**
VIZIER *n* high official in certain Muslim countries **viziers**
VIZIES ▸ **vizy**
VIZIR = **vizier**
VIZIRS ▸ **vizir**
VIZOR = **visor**
VIZORED ▸ **vizor**
VIZORS ▸ **vizor**
VIZSLA *n* breed of Hungarian hunting dog **vizslas**
VIZY *vb* look **vizying, vizzie**

VIZZIED ▸ **vizzie**
VIZZIES ▸ **vizzie**
VLEI *n* area of low marshy ground **vleis**
VLIES ▸ **vly**
VLOG *n*
VLOGGER *n* person who keeps a video blog
VLOGS ▸ **vlog**
VLY = **vlei**

> This word for low-lying wet ground can be useful when you are short of vowels. It can also be spelt **vlei**.

VOAR *n* spring **voars**
VOCAB *n* vocabulary
VOCABLE *n* word regarded simply as a sequence of letters or spoken sounds ▹ *adj* capable of being uttered **vocably**
VOCABS ▸ **vocab**
VOCAL *adj, n*
VOCALIC *adj* of, relating to, or containing a vowel or vowels
VOCALLY ▸ **vocal**
VOCALS ▸ **vocal**
VOCES ▸ **vox**
VOCODER *n* type of synthesizer that uses the human voice as an oscillator
VOCULAR ▸ **vocule**
VOCULE *n* faint noise made when articulating certain sounds **vocules**
VODCAST *vb*
VODDIES ▸ **voddy**
VODDY *n* vodka
VODKA *n* **vodkas**
VODOU *variant of* ▸ **voodoo**

> This West Indian word for a kind of black magic may indeed work magic on an unpromising rack. And it has a host of variants, though few people will remember them all: **vaudoo, vaudoux, vodoun, vodun, voudon, voudou** and **voudoun**!

VODOUN = **vodun**
VODOUNS ▸ **vodoun**
VODOUS ▸ **vodou**
VODUN *n* voodoo **voduns**
VOE *n* (in Orkney and Shetland) a small bay or narrow creek
VOEMA *n* vigour or energy **voemas**
VOES ▸ **voe**
VOGIE *adj* conceited **vogier, vogiest**
VOGUE *n, adj, vb* **vogued, voguer, voguers, vogues, voguey, voguier**
VOGUING = **vogueing**
VOGUISH ▸ **vogue**
VOICE *n, vb*
VOICED *adj* articulated with accompanying vibration of the vocal cords
VOICER, voicers, voices, voicing ▸ **voice**
VOID *adj, n, vb*
VOIDED *adj* (of a design) with a hole in the centre of the same shape as the design
VOIDEE *n* light meal eaten before bed **voidees**
VOIDER, voiders, voiding, voids ▸ **void**
VOILA *interj* word used to express satisfaction
VOILE *n* light semitransparent fabric **voiles**
VOIP *n* **voips**
VOITURE *n* type of vehicle
VOIVODE *n* type of military leader
VOL *n* heraldic wings
VOLA *n* palm of hand or sole of foot
VOLABLE *adj* quick-witted
VOLAE ▸ **vola**
VOLAGE *adj* changeable
VOLANT *adj* in a flying position
VOLANTE *n* Spanish horse carriage
VOLAR *adj* of or relating to the palm of the hand or the sole of the foot
VOLARY *n* large bird enclosure
VOLATIC *adj* flying
VOLCANO *n*
VOLE *n, vb* **voled**
VOLENS *adj as in* **nolens volens** whether willing or unwilling
VOLERY = **volary**
VOLES ▸ **vole**

VOLET *n* type of veil **volets**
VOLING ▸ vole
VOLK *n* people or nation, esp the nation of Afrikaners **volks**
VOLLEY *n, vb* **volleys**
VOLOST *n* (in the former Soviet Union) a rural soviet **volosts**
VOLPINO *n* Italian breed of dog
VOLS ▸ vol
VOLT *n, vb*
VOLTA *n* quick-moving Italian dance
VOLTAGE *n*
VOLTAIC *adj* producing an electric current
VOLTE = **volt**
VOLTED ▸ volt *vb*
VOLTES ▸ volte
VOLTI *adv* musical direction
VOLTING ▸ volt *vb*
VOLTS ▸ volt
VOLUBIL = **voluble**
VOLUBLE *adj* **volubly**
VOLUME *n, vb* **volumed, volumes**
VOLUSPA *n* Icelandic mythological poem
VOLUTE *n* spiral or twisting turn, form, or object ▹ *adj* having the form of a volute **voluted, volutes**
VOLUTIN *n* granular substance found in cells
VOLVA *n* cup-shaped structure that sheathes the base of the stalk of certain mushrooms **volvae, volvas, volvate**
VOLVE *vb* turn over **volved, volves, volving**
VOLVOX *n* freshwater protozoan
VOLVULI > **volvulus**
VOMER *n* thin flat bone separating the nasal passages in mammals **vomers**
VOMICA *n* pus-containing cavity **vomicae, vomicas**
VOMIT *vb, n* **vomited, vomiter**
VOMITO *n* form of yellow fever **vomitos**
VOMITS ▸ vomit
VOMITUS *n* matter that has been vomited
VONGOLE *pl n* (in Italian cookery) clams
VOODOO *n, adj, vb* **voodoos**
VOR *vb* (in dialect) warn
VORAGO *n* chasm
VORANT *adj* devouring
VORLAGE *n* skiing position
VORPAL *adj* sharp
VORRED ▸ vor
VORRING ▸ vor
VORS ▸ vor
VORTEX *n*
VOSTRO *adj as in* **vostro account** bank account held by a foreign bank with a British bank
VOTABLE ▸ vote
VOTARY *n* person dedicated to religion or to a cause ▹ *adj* ardently devoted to the services or worship of God
VOTE *n, vb* **voted**
VOTEEN *n* devotee **voteens**
VOTER *n* person who can or does vote **voters**
VOTES ▸ vote
VOTING ▸ vote
VOTINGS ▸ vote
VOTIVE *adj* done or given to fulfil a vow ▹ *n* votive offering **votives**
VOTRESS > **votaress**
VOUCH *vb, n* **vouched**
VOUCHEE *n* person summoned to court to defend a title
VOUCHER *n, vb*
VOUCHES ▸ vouch
VOUDON *variant of* **▸ voodoo**
VOUDONS ▸ voudon
VOUDOU = **voodoo**
VOUDOUN *variant of* **▸ voodoo**
VOUDOUS ▸ voudou
VOUGE *n* form of pike used by foot soldiers in the 14th century and later **vouges**
VOULGE *n* type of medieval weapon **voulges**
VOULU *adj* deliberate
VOUVRAY *n* dry white French wine
VOW *n, vb* **vowed**
VOWEL *n, vb* **vowelly, vowels**
VOWER ▸ vow
VOWERS ▸ vow

VOWESS *n* nun
VOWING ▶ **vow**
VOWLESS ▶ **vow**
VOWS ▶ **vow**
VOX *n* voice or sound

> Along with **vex**, this Latin word for voice is the highest-scoring three-letter word beginning with V.

VOXEL *n* term used in computing imaging **voxels**
VOYAGE *n*, *vb* **voyaged, voyager, voyages**
VOYEUR *n* **voyeurs**
VOZHD *n* Russian leader **vozhds**

> This unlikely looking word is Russian for a chief or leader, and may provide a great score from an apparently difficult rack.

VRAIC *n* type of seaweed **vraics**
VRIL *n* life force **vrils**
VROOM *interj* exclamation imitative of a car engine revving up ▷ *vb* move noisily and at high speed **vroomed, vrooms**
VROT *adj* South African slang for rotten
VROU *n* Afrikaner woman, esp a married woman **vrous**
VROUW *n* woman **vrouws, vrow**

> The heart of any Scrabble player sinks to see a combination of U, V and W on the rack, as there are relatively few words that use even two of these letters. But **vrouw**, a word of Dutch origin for a woman or goodwife, may get you out of the mess.

VROWS ▶ **vrow**
VUG *n* small cavity in a rock or vein, usually lined with crystals **vugg, vuggier**

> This unusual word of Cornish origin, meaning a cavity in rock, is another that can be useful when you have an uninspiring combination of letters. And it has a variant **vugh** and can be extended to **vuggy** or **vughy**.

VUGGS ▶ **vugg**
VUGGY ▶ **vug**
VUGH = vug
VUGGS ▶ **vugg**
VUGGY ▶ **vug**
VUGHIER ▶ **vugh**
VUGHS ▶ **vugh**
VUGHY ▶ **vug**
VUGS ▶ **vug**
VULCAN *n* blacksmith **vulcans**
VULGAR *adj*, *n* **vulgars**
VULGATE *n* commonly recognized text or version ▷ *adj* generally accepted
VULGO *adv* generally
VULGUS *n* the common people
VULN *vb* wound **vulned, vulning, vulns**
VULPINE *adj* of or like a fox
VULTURE *n*
VULTURN *n* type of turkey
VULVA *n* **vulvae, vulval, vulvar, vulvas, vulvate**
VUM *vb* swear **vummed, vumming, vums**
VUTTIER ▶ **vutty**
VUTTY *adj* dirty
VYING ▶ **vie**
VYINGLY ▶ **vie**
VYINGS ▶ **vie**

Ww

W, like **V**, can be an awkward tile to handle, but at least there are two two-letter words that begin with **W**: **we** and **wo** (5 points each) and two that end with **W**: **aw** and **ow** (5 points each). There are lots of everyday three-letter words that earn good scores: **wiz** (15), **wax** (13) with its two old-fashioned variants **wex** and **wox** (also 13 each) and **way, who, why, wow** and **wry** (9 each). Don't forget **wok** (10) either, which can be as useful on the Scrabble board as in the kitchen!

WAAC *n* (formerly) member of the Women's Auxiliary Army Corp **waacs**
WAB ▸ **web** *n*
WABAIN = **ouabain**
WABAINS ▸ **wabain**
WABBIT *adj* weary
WABBLE = **wobble; wabbled, wabbler, wabbles, wabbly**
WABOOM *another word for* > **wagenboom**
WABOOMS ▸ **waboom**
WABSTER *Scots form of* ▸ **webster**
WACK *n* friend
WACKE *n* any of various soft earthy rocks that resemble or are derived from basaltic rocks
WACKER = **wack**
WACKERS ▸ **wacker**
WACKES ▸ **wacke**
WACKEST ▸ **wack**
WACKIER ▸ **wacky**
WACKILY ▸ **wacky**
WACKO *adj* mad or eccentric ▹ *n* mad or eccentric person **wackos**
WACKS ▸ **wack**
WACKY *adj*
WAD *n, vb*
WADABLE ▸ **wade**
WADD = **wad**
WADDED ▸ **wad**
WADDER ▸ **wad**
WADDERS ▸ **wad**
WADDIE = **waddy**
WADDIED ▸ **waddy**
WADDIES ▸ **waddy**
WADDING ▸ **wad**
WADDLE *vb, n* **waddled, waddler, waddles, waddly**
WADDS ▸ **wadd**
WADDY *n, vb*
WADE *vb, n* **waded**
WADER *n*
WADERS *pl n* long waterproof boots which completely cover the legs
WADES ▸ **wade**
WADI *n*
WADIES ▸ **wady**
WADING ▸ **wade**
WADINGS ▸ **wade**
WADIS ▸ **wadi**
WADMAAL = **wadmal**
WADMAL *n* coarse thick woollen fabric, formerly woven for outer garments **wadmals, wadmel**
WADMELS ▸ **wadmel wadmol, wadmoll**
WADMOL = **wadmal**
WADMOLL = **wadmal**
WADMOLS ▸ **wadmol**
WADS ▸ **wad**
WADSET *vb* pledge or mortgage **wadsets, wadsett**

WADT = **wad**
WADTS ▶ **wadt**
WADY = **wadi**
WAE *old form of* ▶ **woe**
WAEFUL *old form of* ▶ **woeful**
WAENESS *n* sorrow
WAES ▶ **wae**
WAESOME *adj* sorrowful
WAESUCK *interj* alas
WAFER *n, vb* **wafered, wafers, wafery**
WAFF *n* gust or puff of air ▷ *vb* flutter or cause to flutter **waffed**
WAFFIE *n* person regarded as having little worth to society **waffies**
WAFFING ▶ **waff**
WAFFLE *vb, n* **waffled, waffler, waffles, waffly**
WAFFS ▶ **waff**
WAFT *vb, n* **waftage, wafted**
WAFTER *n* device that causes a draught **wafters**
WAFTING ▶ **waft**
WAFTS ▶ **waft**
WAFTURE *n* act of wafting or waving
WAG *vb, n*
WAGE *n, vb* **waged**
WAGER *vb, n* **wagered, wagerer, wagers**
WAGES ▶ **wage**
WAGGA *n* blanket or bed covering made out of sacks stitched together **waggas**
WAGGED ▶ **wag**
WAGGER ▶ **wag**
WAGGERS ▶ **wag**
WAGGERY *n* quality of being humorous
WAGGING ▶ **wag**
WAGGISH *adj* jocular or humorous
WAGGLE *vb, n* **waggled**
WAGGLER *n* float only the bottom of which is attached to the fishing line
WAGGLES ▶ **waggle**
WAGGLY ▶ **waggle**
WAGGON = **wagon**
WAGGONS ▶ **waggon**
WAGING ▶ **wage**
WAGON *n, vb* **wagoned**
WAGONER *n* person who drives a wagon
WAGONS ▶ **wagon**
WAGS ▶ **wag**
WAGSOME *another word for* ▶ **waggish**
WAGTAIL *n*
WAGYU *n* Japanese breed of beef cattle **wagyus**
WAHINE *n* Māori woman, esp a wife **wahines**
WAHOO *n* food and game fish of tropical seas **wahoos**
WAI *n* in New Zealand, water
WAIATA *n* Māori song **waiatas**
WAID ▶ **weigh**
WAIDE ▶ **weigh**
WAIF *n, vb* **waifed, waifing, waifish, waifs**
WAIFT *n* piece of lost property found by someone other than the owner **waifts**
WAIL *vb, n* **wailed, wailer, wailers, wailful, wailing, wails**
WAIN *vb, n*
WAINAGE *n* carriages, etc, for transportation of goods
WAINED ▶ **wain**
WAINING ▶ **wain**
WAINS ▶ **wain**
WAIR *vb* spend **waired, wairing, wairs**
WAIRSH *variant spelling of* ▶ **wersh**
WAIRUA *n* in New Zealand, spirit or soul **wairuas**
WAIS ▶ **wai**
WAIST *n*
WAISTED *adj* having a waist or waistlike part
WAISTER *n* sailor performing menial duties
WAISTS ▶ **waist**
WAIT *vb, n* **waite, waited**
WAITER *n, vb* **waiters**
WAITES ▶ **waite**
WAITING ▶ **wait**
WAITRON *n* waiter or waitress
WAITS ▶ **wait**
WAIVE *vb* **waived**
WAIVER *n* act or instance of voluntarily giving up a claim, right, etc **waivers**

WAIVES ▸ **waive**
WAIVING ▸ **waive**
WAIVODE = **voivode**
WAIWODE = **voivode**
WAKA *n* Māori canoe
WAKAME *n* edible seaweed **wakames**
WAKANDA *n* supernatural quality in Native American belief system
WAKAS ▸ **waka**
WAKE *vb, n* **waked**
WAKEFUL *adj*
WAKEMAN *n* watchman **wakemen**
WAKEN *vb* **wakened, wakener, wakens**
WAKER ▸ **wake**
WAKERS ▸ **wake**
WAKES ▸ **wake**
WAKF = **waqf**
WAKFS ▸ **wakf**
WAKIKI *n* Melanesian shell currency **wakikis**
WAKING ▸ **wake**
WAKINGS ▸ **wake**
WALD *Scots form of* ▸ **weld**
WALDO *n* gadget for manipulating objects by remote control **waldoes, waldos**
WALDS ▸ **wald**
WALE = **weal; waled, waler, walers, wales**
WALI = **vali**
WALIER ▸ **waly**
WALIES ▸ **waly**
WALIEST ▸ **waly**
WALING ▸ **wale**
WALIS ▸ **wali**
WALISE = **valise**
WALISES ▸ **walise**
WALK *vb* move on foot with at least one foot always on the ground ▹ *n* short journey on foot, usu for pleasure **walked**
WALKER *n* **walkers**
WALKIES *pl n as in* **go walkies** a walk
WALKING *adj* (of a person) considered to possess the qualities of something inanimate as specified ▹ *n* act of walking
WALKOUT *n*
WALKS ▸ **walk**
WALKUP *n* building with stairs to upper floors **walkups**
WALKWAY *n*
WALL *n, vb*
WALLA = **wallah**
WALLABA *n* type of S American tree
WALLABY *n*
WALLAH *n* person involved with or in charge of a specified thing **wallahs**
WALLAS ▸ **walla**
WALLED ▸ **wall**
WALLER ▸ **wall**
WALLERS ▸ **wall**
WALLET *n* **wallets**
WALLEYE *n* fish with large staring eyes
WALLIE = **wally**
WALLIER ▸ **wally**
WALLIES ▸ **wally**
WALLING ▸ **wall**
WALLOP *vb, n* **wallops**
WALLOW *vb, n* **wallows**
WALLS ▸ **wall**
WALLY *n* stupid person ▹ *adj* fine, pleasing, or splendid
WALNUT *n, adj* **walnuts**
WALRUS *n*
WALTIER ▸ **walty**
WALTY *adj* (of a ship) likely to roll over
WALTZ *n, vb* **waltzed**
WALTZER *n* person who waltzes
WALTZES ▸ **waltz**
WALY = **wally**
WAMBLE *vb* move unsteadily ▹ *n* unsteady movement **wambled, wambles, wambly**
WAME *n* belly, abdomen, or womb **wamed**
WAMEFOU *Scots variant of* ▸ **wameful**
WAMEFUL *n* bellyful
WAMES ▸ **wame**
WAMMUL *n* dog **wammuls**
WAMMUS = **wamus**
WAMPEE *n* type of Asian fruit tree **wampees**
WAMPISH *vb* wave
WAMPUM *n* shells woven together, formerly used by Native Americans for money **wampums**
WAMPUS = **wamus**
WAMUS *n* type of cardigan or jacket **wamuses**
WAN *adj, vb*
WAND *n*
WANDER *vb, n* **wanders**
WANDLE *adj* supple

WANDOO *n* eucalyptus tree of W Australia, having white bark and durable wood **wandoos**
WANDS ▸ **wand**
WANE *vb* **waned, wanes, waney**
WANG *n* cheekbone
WANGAN = **wanigan**
WANGANS ▸ **wangan**
WANGLE *vb, n* **wangled, wangler, wangles**
WANGS ▸ **wang**
WANGUN = **wanigan**
WANGUNS ▸ **wangun**
WANHOPE *n* delusion
WANIER ▸ **wany**
WANIEST ▸ **wany**
WANIGAN *n* provisions for camp
WANING ▸ **wane**
WANINGS ▸ **wane**
WANION *n* vehemence **wanions**
WANKLE *adj* unstable
WANLE = **wandle**
WANLY ▸ **wan**
WANNA *vb* spelling of **want to** intended to reflect a dialectal or informal pronunciation
WANNABE *adj* wanting to be, or be like, a particular person or thing ▹ *n* person who wants to be, or be like, a particular person or thing
WANNED ▸ **wan**
WANNEL = **wandle**
WANNER, wanness, wannest, wanning ▸ **wan**
WANNION ▸ **wanion**
WANNISH *adj* rather wan
WANS ▸ **wan**
WANT *vb, n*
WANTAGE *n* shortage
WANTED ▸ **want**
WANTER ▸ **want**
WANTERS ▸ **want**
WANTIES ▸ **wanty**
WANTING *adj* lacking ▹ *prep* without
WANTON *adj, n, vb* **wantons**
WANTS ▸ **want**
WANTY *adj* belt
WANY ▸ **wane**
WANZE *vb* wane **wanzed, wanzes, wanzing**
WAP *vb* strike
WAPITI *n* large N American deer **wapitis**
WAPPED ▸ **wap**
WAPPEND *adj* tired
WAPPER *vb* blink **wappers**
WAPPING ▸ **wap**
WAPS ▸ **wap**
WAQF *n* endowment in Muslim law **waqfs**

> An Arabic word meaning the donation of land, property or money for charitable purposes. As one of the Q words without a U, this comes up surprisingly often. It can also be spelt **wakf**.

WAR *n, adj, vb*
WARAGI *n* Ugandan alcoholic drink made from bananas **waragis**
WARATAH *n*
WARB *n* dirty or insignificant person **warbier**
WARBIRD *n* vintage military aeroplane
WARBLE *vb, n* **warbled**
WARBLER *n*
WARBLES ▸ **warble**
WARBS ▸ **warb**
WARBY ▸ **warb**
WARD *n, vb* **warded**
WARDEN *n, vb* **wardens**
WARDER *vb, n* **warders**
WARDIAN *n as in* **wardian case** type of glass container for housing delicate plants
WARDING ▸ **ward**
WARDOG *n* veteran warrior **wardogs**
WARDROP *obsolete form of* > **wardrobe**
WARDS ▸ **ward**
WARE *n, vb* **wared**
WAREHOU *n* any of several edible saltwater New Zealand fish
WARES *pl n* goods for sale
WAREZ *pl n* illegally copied computer software
WARFARE *vb, n*
WARHEAD *n*
WARIER ▸ **wary**
WARIEST ▸ **wary**
WARILY ▸ **wary**
WARING ▸ **ware**

WARISON *n* (esp formerly) a bugle note used as an order to a military force to attack
WARK *Scots form of* ▸ **work**
WARKED ▸ **wark**
WARKING ▸ **wark**
WARKS ▸ **wark**
WARLESS ▸ **war**
WARLIKE *adj* of or relating to war
WARLING *n* one who is not liked
WARLOCK *n*
WARLORD *n* military leader of a nation or part of a nation
WARM *adj, vb, n*
WARMAN *n* one experienced in warfare
WARMED ▸ **warm**
WARMEN ▸ **warman**
WARMER, warmers, warmest, warming, warmish, warmly, warms ▸ **warm**
WARMTH *n* **warmths**
WARMUP *n* preparatory exercise routine **warmups**
WARN *vb* **warned, warner, warners**
WARNING *n, adj*
WARNS ▸ **warn**
WARP *vb, n* **warpage**
WARPATH *n*
WARPED, warper, warpers, warping, warps ▸ **warp**
WARRAN = **warrant**
WARRAND = **warrant**
WARRANS ▸ **warran**
WARRANT *n, vb*
WARRAY *vb* wage war on **warrays**
WARRE = **war**
WARRED ▸ **war**
WARREN *n* **warrens**
WARREY = **warray**
WARREYS ▸ **warrey**
WARRING ▸ **war**
WARRIOR *n*
WARS ▸ **war**
WARSAW *n* type of grouper fish **warsaws**
WARSHIP *n*
WARSLE *dialect word for* ▸ **wrestle**
WARSLED ▸ **warsle**
WARSLER ▸ **warsle**
WARSLES ▸ **warsle**
WARST *obsolete form of* ▸ **worst**
WARSTLE *dialect form of* ▸ **wrestle**
WART *n* **warted**
WARTHOG *n* wild African pig with wartlike lumps on the face
WARTIER ▸ **wart**
WARTIME *n, adj*
WARTS ▸ **wart**
WARTY ▸ **wart**
WARWOLF *n* Roman engine of war
WARWORK *n* work contributing to war effort
WARWORN *adj* worn down by war
WARY *adj*
WARZONE *n* area where a war is taking place or there is some other violent conflict
WAS ▸ **be**
WASABI *n* Japanese cruciferous plant cultivated for its thick green pungent root **wasabis**
WASE *n* pad to relieve pressure of load carried on head **wases**
WASH *vb, n*
WASHDAY *n* day on which clothes and linen are washed, often the same day each week
WASHED ▸ **wash**
WASHEN ▸ **wash**
WASHER *n, vb* **washers**
WASHERY *n* plant at a mine where water or other liquid is used to remove dirt from a mineral, esp coal
WASHES ▸ **wash**
WASHIER ▸ **washy**
WASHILY ▸ **washy**
WASHIN *n* increase in the angle of attack of an aircraft wing towards the wing tip
WASHING *n*
WASHINS ▸ **washin**
WASHOUT *n*
WASHPOT *n* pot for washing things in
WASHRAG = **washcloth**
WASHTUB *n* tub or large container used for washing anything, esp clothes
WASHUP *n* outcome of a process **washups**
WASHY *adj*
WASP *n*

WASPIE *n* tight-waisted corset
WASPIER ▸ **wasp**
WASPIES ▸ **waspie**
WASPILY ▸ **wasp**
WASPISH *adj*
WASPS ▸ **wasp**
WASPY ▸ **wasp**
WASSAIL *n* formerly, festivity when much drinking took place ▹ *vb* drink health of (a person) at a wassail
WASSUP *sentence substitute* what is happening?
WAST *singular form of the past tense of* ▸ **be**
WASTAGE *n*
WASTE *vb, n, adj* **wasted**
WASTEL *n* fine bread or cake **wastels**
WASTER *vb* waste ▹ *n* layabout **wasters**
WASTERY *n* extravagance
WASTES ▸ **waste**
WASTING *adj*
WASTREL *n* lazy or worthless person
WASTRIE = **wastery**
WASTRY *n* wastefulness
WASTS ▸ **wast**
WAT *adj* wet; drunken
WATAP *n* stringy thread made by Native Americans from the roots of conifers **watape**
WATAPES ▸ **watape**
WATAPS ▸ **watap**
WATCH *vb, n* **watched**
WATCHER *n* person who watches
WATCHES ▸ **watch**
WATCHET *n* shade of blue
WATE ▸ **wit**
WATER *n, vb* **watered, waterer, waters**
WATERY *adj*
WATS ▸ **wat**
WATT *n*
WATTAGE *n*
WATTAPE = **watap**
WATTER ▸ **wat**
WATTEST ▸ **wat**
WATTLE *n, adj, vb* **wattled, wattles**
WATTS ▸ **watt**
WAUCHT = **waught**
WAUCHTS ▸ **waucht**
WAUFF = **waff**
WAUFFED ▸ **wauff**
WAUFFS ▸ **wauff**
WAUGH *vb* bark **waughed, waughs**
WAUGHT *vb* drink in large amounts **waughts**
WAUK *vb* full (cloth) **wauked, wauker, waukers, wauking, wauks**
WAUL *vb* cry or wail plaintively like a cat **wauled, wauling**
WAULK = **wauk**
WAULKED ▸ **waulk**
WAULKER ▸ **waulk**
WAULKS ▸ **waulk**
WAULS ▸ **waul**
WAUR *obsolete form of* ▸ **war; waured, wauring, waurs, waurst**
WAVE *vb, n* **waved**
WAVELET *n* small wave
WAVEOFF *n* signal or instruction to an aircraft not to land
WAVER *vb, n* **wavered, waverer, wavers**
WAVERY *adj* lacking firmness
WAVES ▸ **wave**
WAVESON *n* goods floating on waves after shipwreck
WAVEY *n* snow goose or other wild goose **waveys**
WAVICLE *n* origin of wave
WAVIER, wavies, waviest, wavily ▸ **wavy**
WAVING ▸ **wave**
WAVINGS ▸ **wave**
WAVY *adj, n*
WAW *another name for* ▸ **vav**
WAWA *n* speech ▹ *vb* speak **wawaed, wawaing, wawas**
WAWE = **waw**
WAWES ▸ **wawe**
WAWL = **waul**
WAWLED ▸ **wawl**
WAWLING ▸ **wawl**
WAWLS ▸ **wawl**
WAWS ▸ **waw**
WAX *n, vb* **waxable**
WAXBILL *n* any of various chiefly African finchlike weaverbirds
WAXED ▸ **wax**
WAXEN *adj*
WAXER ▸ **wax**
WAXERS ▸ **wax**
WAXES ▸ **wax**

WAXEYE *n* small New Zealand bird **waxeyes**
WAXIER ▶ **waxy**
WAXIEST ▶ **waxy**
WAXILY ▶ **waxy**
WAXING ▶ **wax**
WAXINGS ▶ **wax**
WAXLIKE ▶ **wax**
WAXWEED *n* type of wild flower
WAXWING *n* type of songbird
WAXWORK *n*
WAXWORM *n* waxmoth larva
WAXY *adj*
WAY *n, vb*
WAYBILL *n* document stating the nature, origin, and destination of goods being transported
WAYED ▶ **way**
WAYFARE *vb* travel
WAYGONE *adj* travel-weary
WAYING ▶ **way**
WAYLAID ▶ **waylay**
WAYLAY *vb* **waylays**
WAYLESS ▶ **way**
WAYMARK *n* symbol or signpost marking the route of a footpath ▷ *vb* mark out with waymarks
WAYMENT *vb* express grief
WAYPOST *n* signpost
WAYS ▶ **way**
WAYSIDE *n*
WAYWARD *adj*
WAYWODE *n* Slavonic governor
WAYWORN *adj* worn or tired by travel
WAZIR *another word for* ▶ **vizier**
WAZIRS ▶ **wazir**
WAZZOCK *n* foolish or annoying person
WE *pron*
WEAK *adj*
WEAKEN *vb* **weakens**
WEAKER ▶ **weak**
WEAKEST ▶ **weak**
WEAKISH ▶ **weak**
WEAKLY *adv* feebly ▷ *adj* weak or sickly
WEAKON *n* subatomic particle **weakons**
WEAL *n*
WEALD *n* open or forested country **wealds**
WEALS ▶ **weal**
WEALTH *n* **wealths**
WEALTHY *adj*
WEAMB = **wame**
WEAMBS ▶ **weamb**
WEAN *vb* **weaned**
WEANEL *n* recently-weaned child or animal **weanels**
WEANER *n* person or thing that weans **weaners**
WEANING ▶ **wean**
WEANS ▶ **wean**
WEAPON *vb, n* **weapons**
WEAR *vb, n* **weared, wearer, wearers**
WEARIED, wearier, wearies, wearily ▶ **weary**
WEARING *adj, n*
WEARISH *adj* withered
WEARS ▶ **wear**
WEARY *adj, vb*
WEASAND *former name for the* ▶ **trachea**
WEASEL *n, vb* **weasels, weasely**
WEASON *Scots form of* ▶ **weasand**
WEASONS ▶ **weason**
WEATHER *n, vb*
WEAVE *vb* **weaved**
WEAVER *n* **weavers**
WEAVES ▶ **weave**
WEAVING ▶ **weave**
WEAZAND = **weasand**
WEAZEN = **wizen**
WEAZENS ▶ **weazen**
WEB *n, vb* **webbed**
WEBBIE *n* person who is well versed in the use of the World Wide Web
WEBBIER ▶ **webby**
WEBBIES ▶ **webbie**
WEBBING *n*
WEBBY *adj* of, relating to, resembling, or consisting of a web
WEBCAM *n* camera that transmits images over the internet **webcams**
WEBCAST *n* broadcast of an event over the internet ▷ *vb* make such a broadcast
WEBER *n* SI unit of magnetic flux **webers**
WEBFED *adj* (of printing press) printing from rolls of paper
WEBFEET ▶ **webfoot**
WEBFOOT *n* foot having the toes connected by folds of skin

WEBHEAD *n* person who uses the Internet a lot
WEBIFY *vb* convert (information) for display on the internet
WEBINAR *n* interactive seminar conducted over the World Wide Web
WEBLESS ▸ **web**
WEBLIKE ▸ **web**
WEBLISH *n* shorthand form of English that is used in text messaging, chat rooms, etc
WEBLOG *n* **weblogs**
WEBMAIL *n* system of electronic mail accessed via the internet
WEBPAGE *n* page on website
WEBRING *n* group of websites organized in a circular structure
WEBS ▸ **web**
WEBSITE *n*
WEBSTER *archaic word for* ▸ **weaver**
WEBWORK *n* work done using the World Wide Web
WEBWORM *n* type of caterpillar
WEBZINE *n* magazine published on the Internet
WECHT *n* agricultural tool **wechts**
WED *vb* **wedded**
WEDDER *dialect form of* ▸ **weather**
WEDDERS ▸ **wedder**
WEDDING ▸ **wed**
WEDEL *variant of* ▸ **wedeln**
WEDELED ▸ **wedel**
WEDELN *n* succession of high-speed turns performed in skiing ▹ *vb* perform a wedeln **wedelns**
WEDELS ▸ **wedel**
WEDGE *n, vb* **wedged, wedges**
WEDGIE *n* wedge-heeled shoe
WEDGIER ▸ **wedge**
WEDGIES ▸ **wedgie**
WEDGING ▸ **wedge**
WEDGY ▸ **wedge**
WEDLOCK *n*
WEDS ▸ **wed**
WEE *adj, n, vb*
WEED *n, vb* **weeded, weeder, weeders**
WEEDERY *n* weed-ridden area
WEEDIER ▸ **weedy**
WEEDILY ▸ **weedy**
WEEDING ▸ **weed**
WEEDS *pl n* widow's mourning clothes
WEEDY *adj* (of a person) thin and weak
WEEING ▸ **wee**
WEEK *n, adv*
WEEKDAY *n*
WEEKE = **wick**
WEEKEND *n, vb*
WEEKES ▸ **weeke**
WEEKLY *adv, n, adj*
WEEKS ▸ **week**
WEEL *Scot word for* ▸ **well**
WEELS ▸ **weel**
WEEM *n* underground home **weems**
WEEN *vb* think or imagine (something) **weened**
WEENIE *adj* very small ▹ *n* wiener
WEENIER ▸ **weeny**
WEENIES ▸ **weenie**
WEENING ▸ **ween**
WEENS ▸ **ween**
WEENSY = **weeny**
WEENY *adj* very small
WEEP *vb, n*
WEEPER *n* person who weeps, esp a hired mourner **weepers**
WEEPIE, weepier, weepies, weepily ▸ **weepy**
WEEPING *adj*
WEEPS ▸ **weep**
WEEPY *adj, n*
WEER ▸ **wee**
WEES ▸ **wee**
WEEST ▸ **wee**
WEET *dialect form of* ▸ **wet**
WEETE = **wit**
WEETED ▸ **weete**
WEETEN = **wit**
WEETER, weetest, weeting, weets ▸ **weet**
WEEVER *n* type of small fish **weevers**
WEEVIL *n* **weevils**
WEEVILY *another word for* > **weevilled**
WEEWEE *vb* urinate **weeweed, weewees**
WEFT *n, vb*
WEFTAGE *n* texture

WEFTE *n* forsaken child
WEFTED ▸ **weft**
WEFTES ▸ **wefte**
WEFTING ▸ **weft**
WEFTS ▸ **weft**
WEID *n* sudden illness **weids**
WEIGELA *n* type of shrub
WEIGH *vb* **weighed, weigher, weighs**
WEIGHT *n, vb* **weights**
WEIGHTY *adj*
WEIL *n* whirlpool **weils**
WEINER = **wiener**
WEINERS ▸ **weiner**
WEIR *vb, n*
WEIRD *adj, vb* **weirded, weirder**
WEIRDIE = **weirdo**
WEIRDLY ▸ **weird**
WEIRDO *n* **weirdos**
WEIRDS ▸ **weird**
WEIRDY *n* weird person
WEIRED ▸ **weir**
WEIRING ▸ **weir**
WEIRS ▸ **weir**
WEISE = **wise**
WEISED ▸ **weise**
WEISES ▸ **weise**
WEISING ▸ **weise**
WEIZE = **wise**
WEIZED ▸ **weize**
WEIZES ▸ **weize**
WEIZING ▸ **weize**
WEKA *n* flightless New Zealand rail **wekas**
WELAWAY = **wellaway**
WELCH = **welsh**
WELCHED ▸ **welch**
WELCHER ▸ **welch**
WELCHES ▸ **welch**
WELCOME *vb, n, adj*
WELD *vb, n* **welded, welder, welders, welding, weldor**
WELDORS ▸ **weldor**
WELDS ▸ **weld**
WELFARE *n*
WELK *vb* wither; dry up **welke, welked**
WELKES ▸ **welke**
WELKIN *n* sky, heavens, or upper air
WELKING ▸ **welk**
WELKINS ▸ **welkin**
WELKS ▸ **welk**
WELKT *adj* twisted
WELL *adv, adj, interj, n, vb* **welled**
WELLIE *n* wellington boot
WELLIES ▸ **welly**
WELLING ▸ **well**
WELLS ▸ **well**
WELLY *n*
WELS *n* type of catfish
WELSH *vb* **welshed, welsher, welshes**
WELT = **weal**
WELTED ▸ **welt**
WELTER *n, vb* **welters**
WELTING ▸ **welt**
WELTS ▸ **welt**
WEM = **wame**
WEMB = **wame**
WEMBS ▸ **wemb**
WEMS ▸ **wem**
WEN *n* cyst on the scalp
WENA *pron* South African word for you
WENCH *n, vb* **wenched, wencher, wenches**
WEND *vb* **wended**
WENDIGO *n* evil spirit or cannibal
WENDING ▸ **wend**
WENDS ▸ **wend**
WENGE *n* type of tree found in central and West Africa **wenges**
WENNIER, wennish, wenny, wens ▸ **wen**
WENT *n* path **wents**
WEPT ▸ **weep**
WERE *vb*
WERGELD = **wergild**
WERGELT = **wergeld**
WERGILD *n* price set on a man's life, to be paid as compensation by his slayer
WERO *n* challenge made by an armed Māori warrior to a visitor to a marae **weros**
WERSH *adj* tasteless **wersher**
WERT *singular form of the past tense of* ▸ **be**
WERWOLF = **werewolf**
WESAND = **weasand**
WESANDS ▸ **wesand**
WESKIT *informal word for* > **waistcoat**
WESKITS ▸ **weskit**
WESSAND = **weasand**
WEST *n, adj, adv, vb* **wested**
WESTER *vb* move or appear to move towards the west ▷ *n* strong wind or storm from the west
WESTERN *adj, n*
WESTERS ▸ **wester**
WESTING *n* movement, deviation, or distance covered in a westerly direction

WESTLIN *Scots word for* ▶ **western**
WESTS ▶ **west**
WET *adj, n, vb*
WETA *n* type of wingless insect **wetas**
WETHER *n* male sheep, esp a castrated one **wethers**
WETLAND *n* area of marshy land
WETLY ▶ **wet**
WETNESS ▶ **wet**
WETS ▶ **wet**
WETSUIT *n* body suit for diving
WETTED, wetter, wetters, wettest ▶ **wet**
WETTIE *n* wetsuit **wetties**
WETTING ▶ **wet**
WETTISH ▶ **wet**
WETWARE *n* humorous term for the brain
WEX *obsolete form of* ▶ **wax**

> **Wex** is an old word for **wax**, in the sense of grow. It gives a very good score for a three-letter word, and can be extended to **wexe**.

WEXE *obsolete form of* ▶ **wax**
WEXED ▶ **wex**
WEXES ▶ **wex**
WEXING ▶ **wex**
WEY *n* measurement of weight
WEYARD *obsolete form of* ▶ **weird**
WEYS ▶ **wey**
WEYWARD *obsolete form of* ▶ **weird**
WEZAND *obsolete form of* ▶ **weasand**
WEZANDS ▶ **wezand**
WHA *Scot word for* ▶ **who**
WHACK *vb, n* **whacked, whacker**
WHACKO *n* mad person **whackos**
WHACKS ▶ **whack**
WHACKY *variant spelling of* ▶ **wacky**
WHAE = **wha**
WHAISLE *Scots form of* ▶ **wheeze**
WHAIZLE = **whaisle**
WHALE *n, vb* **whaled**
WHALER *n* ship or person involved in whaling **whalers**
WHALERY *n* whaling
WHALES ▶ **whale**
WHALING *n, adv*
WHALLY *adj* (of eyes) with light-coloured irises
WHAM *interj, n, vb* **whammed**
WHAMMO *n* sound of a sudden collision **whammos**
WHAMMY *n* devastating setback
WHAMO = **whammo**
WHAMPLE *n* strike
WHAMS ▶ **wham**
WHANAU *n* (in Māori societies) a family, esp an extended family **whanaus**
WHANG *vb* strike or be struck so as to cause a resounding noise ▷ *n* resounding noise produced by a heavy blow
WHANGAM *n* imaginary creature
WHANGED ▶ **whang**
WHANGEE *n* tall woody grass grown for its stems, which are used for bamboo canes
WHANGS ▶ **whang**
WHAP = **whop**
WHAPPED ▶ **whap**
WHAPPER = **whopper**
WHAPS ▶ **whap**
WHARE *n* Māori hut or dwelling place **whares**
WHARF *n, vb* **wharfed**
WHARFIE *n* person employed to load and unload ships
WHARFS ▶ **wharf**
WHARVE *n* wooden disc or wheel on a shaft serving as a flywheel or pulley **wharves**
WHAT *pron, interj, adv, n*
WHATA *n* building on stilts or a raised platform for storing provisions **whatas**
WHATEN *adj* what; what kind of **whatna**
WHATNOT *n* similar unspecified thing
WHATS ▶ **what**
WHATSIS *US form of* ▶ **whatsit**
WHATSIT *n* person or thing the name of which is temporarily forgotten

WHATSO *n* of whatever kind
WHATTEN = **whaten**
WHAUP *n* curlew **whaups**
WHAUR *Scot word for* ▸ **where**
WHAURS ▸ **whaur**
WHEAL = **weal**
WHEALS ▸ **wheal**
WHEAR *obsolete variant of* ▸ **where**
WHEARE *obsolete variant of* ▸ **where**
WHEAT *n*
WHEATEN *n* type of dog ▹ *adj* made of the grain or flour of wheat
WHEATS ▸ **wheat**
WHEATY *adj* having a wheat-like taste
WHEE *interj* exclamation of joy, thrill, etc
WHEECH *vb* move quickly **wheechs**
WHEEDLE *vb*
WHEEL *n, vb*
WHEELED *adj* having or equipped with a wheel or wheels
WHEELER *n* horse or other draught animal nearest the wheel
WHEELIE *n* manoeuvre on a bike in which the front wheel is raised off the ground
WHEELS ▸ **wheel**
WHEELY *adj* resembling a wheel
WHEEN *n* few
WHEENGE *Scots form of* ▸ **whinge**
WHEENS ▸ **wheen**
WHEEP *vb* fly quickly and lightly **wheeped**
WHEEPLE *vb* whistle weakly
WHEEPS ▸ **wheep**
WHEESH *vb* silence (a person, noise, etc) or be silenced **wheesht**
WHEEZE *vb, n* **wheezed, wheezer, wheezes**
WHEEZLE *vb* make hoarse breathing sound
WHEEZY ▸ **wheeze**
WHEFT = **waft**
WHEFTS ▸ **wheft**
WHELK *n*
WHELKED *adj* having or covered with whelks
WHELKS ▸ **whelk**
WHELKY ▸ **whelk**
WHELM *vb* engulf entirely with or as if with water **whelmed, whelms**
WHELP *n, vb* **whelped, whelps**
WHEMMLE *vb* overturn
WHEN *adv, pron, n*
WHENAS *conj* while; inasmuch as
WHENCE *n, adv, pron* **whences**
WHENS ▸ **when**
WHENUA *n* land **whenuas**
WHENWE *n* White immigrant to South Africa from Zimbabwe **whenwes**
WHERE *adv, pron, n*
WHEREAS *n*
WHEREAT *adv* at or to which place
WHEREBY *pron, adv*
WHEREIN *adv* in what place or respect? ▹ *pron* in which place or thing
WHEREOF *adv* of what or which person or thing? ▹ *pron* of which person or thing
WHEREON *adv* on what thing or place? ▹ *pron* on which thing, place, etc
WHERES ▸ **where**
WHERESO *adv* in or to unspecified place
WHERETO *adv* towards what (place, end, etc)? ▹ *pron* which
WHERRET *vb* strike (someone) a blow ▹ *n* blow, esp a slap on the face
WHERRIT *vb* worry or cause to worry
WHERRY *n* any of certain kinds of half-decked commercial boats ▹ *vb* travel in a wherry
WHERVE = **wharve**
WHERVES ▸ **wherve**
WHET *vb, n*
WHETHER *conj*
WHETS ▸ **whet**
WHETTED ▸ **whet**
WHETTER ▸ **whet**
WHEUGH = **whew**
WHEUGHS ▸ **wheugh**
WHEW *interj* exclamation expressing relief, delight, etc ▹ *vb*

express relief **whewed, whewing, whews**
WHEY *n* **wheyey, wheyier, wheyish, wheys**
WHICH *pron, adj*
WHICKER *vb* (of a horse) to whinny or neigh
WHID *vb* move quickly
WHIDAH = **whydah**
WHIDAHS ▸ **whidah**
WHIDDED ▸ **whid**
WHIDDER *vb* move with force
WHIDS ▸ **whid**
WHIFF *n, vb* **whiffed, whiffer**
WHIFFET *n* insignificant person
WHIFFLE *vb* think or behave in an erratic or unpredictable way
WHIFFS ▸ **whiff**
WHIFFY *adj* smelly
WHIFT *n* brief emission of air **whifts**
WHIG *vb* go quickly **whigged, whigs**
WHILE *n* **whiled**
WHILERE *adv* a while ago
WHILES *adv* at times
WHILING ▸ **while**
WHILK *archaic and dialect word for* ▸ **which**
WHILLY *vb* influence by flattery
WHILOM *adv* formerly ▹ *adj* one-time
WHILST = **while**
WHIM *n, vb* **whimmed**
WHIMMY *adj* having whims
WHIMPER *vb, n*
WHIMPLE = **wimple**
WHIMS ▸ **whim**
WHIMSEY = **whimsy**
WHIMSY *n, adj*
WHIN *n* gorse
WHINE *n, vb* **whined, whiner, whiners, whines**
WHINEY = **whiny**
WHINGE *vb, n* **whinged, whinger, whinges**
WHINGY *adj* complaining peevishly, whining
WHINIER ▸ **whiny**
WHINING ▸ **whine**
WHINNY *vb, n, adj*
WHINS ▸ **whin**
WHINY *adj* high-pitched and plaintive
WHIO *n* New Zealand mountain duck with blue plumage **whios**
WHIP *n, vb*
WHIPCAT *n* tailor
WHIPPED ▸ **whip**
WHIPPER ▸ **whip**
WHIPPET *n*
WHIPPY *adj* springy
WHIPRAY *n* stingray
WHIPS ▸ **whip**
WHIPSAW *n* any saw with a flexible blade, such as a bandsaw ▹ *vb* saw with a whipsaw
WHIPT *old past tense of* ▸ **whip**
WHIR *n* prolonged soft swish or buzz ▹ *vb* make or cause to make a whir
WHIRL *vb, n* **whirled, whirler, whirls**
WHIRLY *adj* characterized by whirling
WHIRR = **whir**
WHIRRED ▸ **whir**
WHIRRET *vb* strike with sharp blow
WHIRRS ▸ **whirr**
WHIRRY *vb* move quickly
WHIRS ▸ **whir**
WHIRTLE = **wortle**
WHISH *less common word for* ▸ **swish**
WHISHED ▸ **whish**
WHISHES ▸ **whish**
WHISHT *interj* hush! be quiet! ▹ *adj* silent or still ▹ *vb* make or become silent **whishts**
WHISK *vb, n* **whisked**
WHISKER *n*
WHISKET = **wisket**
WHISKEY *n* Irish or American whisky
WHISKS ▸ **whisk**
WHISKY *n*
WHISPER *vb, n*
WHISS *vb* hiss **whissed, whisses**
WHIST = **whisht**
WHISTED ▸ **whist**
WHISTLE *vb, n*
WHISTS ▸ **whist**
WHIT *n*
WHITE *adj, n*
WHITED *adj as in* **whited sepulchre** hypocrite
WHITELY ▸ **white**
WHITEN *vb* **whitens**
WHITER ▸ **white**

WHITES *pl n* white clothes, as worn for playing cricket
WHITEST ▸ **white**
WHITHER = **wuther**
WHITING *n*
WHITISH ▸ **white**
WHITLOW *n* inflamed sore on a finger or toe, esp round a nail
WHITRET *n variant of* > **whittret**
WHITS ▸ **whit**
WHITTAW = **whittawer**
WHITTER *variant spelling of* ▸ **witter**
WHITTLE *vb, n*
WHIZ = **whizz**
WHIZZ *vb, n* **whizzed, whizzer, whizzes**
WHIZZO ▸ **whizzy**
WHIZZY *adj* using sophisticated technology
WHO *pron*
WHOA *interj*
WHOEVER *pron*
WHOLE *adj, n* **wholes**
WHOLISM = **holism**
WHOLIST = **holist**
WHOLLY *adv*
WHOM *pron*
WHOMBLE = **whemmle**
WHOMMLE = **whemmle**
WHOMP *vb* strike; thump **whomped, whomps**
WHOMSO *pron* whom; whomever
WHOOBUB = **hubbub**
WHOOF = **woof**
WHOOFED ▸ **whoof**
WHOOFS ▸ **whoof**
WHOOP *n, vb* **whooped**
WHOOPEE *n*
WHOOPER *n* type of swan
WHOOPIE = **whoopee**
WHOOPLA *n* commotion; fuss
WHOOPS *interj* exclamation of surprise or of apology
WHOOSH *n* hissing or rushing sound ▹ *vb* make or move with a hissing or rushing sound
WHOOSIS *n* thingamajig
WHOOT *obsolete variant of* ▸ **hoot**
WHOOTED ▸ **whoot**
WHOOTS ▸ **whoot**
WHOP *vb* strike, beat, or thrash ▹ *n* heavy blow or the sound made by such a blow **whopped**
WHOPPER *n*
WHOPS ▸ **whop**
WHORE *n, vb* **whored, whores, whoring, whorish**
WHORL *n* **whorled, whorls**
WHORT *n* small shrub bearing blackish edible sweet berries
WHORTLE *n* whortleberry
WHORTS ▸ **whort**
WHOSE *pron, determiner*
WHOSIS *n* thingamajig
WHOSO *archaic word for* ▸ **whoever**
WHOT *obsolete variant of* ▸ **hot**
WHOW *interj* wow
WHUMMLE *vb variant of* ▸ **whemmle**
WHUMP *vb* make a dull thud ▹ *n* dull thud **whumped, whumps**
WHUP *vb* defeat totally **whupped, whups**
WHY *adv, pron, n*
WHYDAH *n* type of black African bird **whydahs**
WHYEVER *adv* for whatever reason
WHYS ▸ **why**
WIBBLE *vb* wobble **wibbled, wibbles**
WICCA *n* cult or practice of witchcraft
WICCAN *n* member of wicca **wiccans**
WICCAS ▸ **wicca**
WICE *Scots form of* ▸ **wise**
WICH *n* variant of wych **wiches**
WICK *n, adj, vb*
WICKAPE = **wicopy**
WICKED *adj, n* **wickeds**
WICKEN = **quicken**
WICKENS ▸ **wicken**
WICKER *adj, n* **wickers**
WICKET *n* **wickets**
WICKIES ▸ **wicky**
WICKING ▸ **wick**
WICKIUP *n* crude shelter made of brushwood, mats, or grass and having an oval frame
WICKS ▸ **wick**
WICKY = **quicken**

WICKYUP = **wickiup**
WICOPY *n* any of various North American trees, shrubs, or herbaceous plants
WIDDER = **widow**
WIDDERS ▸ **widder**
WIDDIE = **widdy**
WIDDIES ▸ **widdy**
WIDDLE *vb* urinate ▹ *n* urine **widdled, widdles**
WIDDY *vb* rope made of twigs
WIDE *adj* large from side to side ▹ *adv* the full extent ▹ *n* (in cricket) a ball outside a batsman's reach **widely**
WIDEN *vb* **widened, widener, widens**
WIDEOUT *n* footballer who catches passes from the quarterback
WIDER ▸ **wide**
WIDES ▸ **wide**
WIDEST ▸ **wide**
WIDGEON = **wigeon**
WIDGET *n* any small device, the name of which is unknown or forgotten **widgets**
WIDGIE *n* female larrikin or bodgie **widgies**
WIDISH ▸ **wide**
WIDOW *n, vb* **widowed**
WIDOWER *n*
WIDOWS ▸ **widow**
WIDTH *n* **widths**
WIEL = **weel**
WIELD *vb* **wielded, wielder, wields**
WIELDY *adj* easily handled, used, or managed
WIELS ▸ **wiel**
WIENER *n* kind of smoked beef or pork sausage, similar to a frankfurter **wieners, wienie**
WIENIES ▸ **wienie**
WIFE *n, vb* **wifed**
WIFEDOM *n* state of being a wife
WIFELY ▸ **wife**
WIFES ▸ **wife**
WIFEY *n* wife **wifeys**
WIFIE *n* woman **wifies**
WIFING ▸ **wife**
WIFTIER ▸ **wifty**
WIFTY *adj* scatterbrained
WIG *n, vb*
WIGAN *n* stiff fabric **wigans**
WIGEON *n* duck found in marshland **wigeons**
WIGGED ▸ **wig**
WIGGERY *n* wigs
WIGGIER ▸ **wiggy**
WIGGING ▸ **wig**
WIGGLE *vb, n* **wiggled, wiggler, wiggles, wiggly**
WIGGY *adj* eccentric
WIGHT *vb* blame ▹ *n* human being ▹ *adj* strong and brave **wighted**
WIGHTLY *adv* swiftly
WIGHTS ▸ **wight**
WIGLESS ▸ **wig**
WIGLET *n* small wig **wiglets**
WIGLIKE ▸ **wig**
WIGS ▸ **wig**
WIGWAG *vb* move (something) back and forth ▹ *n* system of communication by flag semaphore **wigwags**
WIGWAM *n* **wigwams**
WIKI *n* **wikis**
WIKIUP = **wickiup**
WIKIUPS ▸ **wikiup**
WILCO *interj* expression indicating that the message just received will be complied with
WILD = **wield**
WILDCAT *n, adj, vb*
WILDED ▸ **wild**
WILDER *vb* lead or be led astray **wilders**
WILDEST ▸ **wild**
WILDING *n* uncultivated plant
WILDISH ▸ **wild**
WILDLY ▸ **wild**
WILDS ▸ **wild**
WILE *n* trickery, cunning, or craftiness ▹ *vb* lure, beguile, or entice **wiled**
WILEFUL *adj* deceitful
WILES ▸ **wile**
WILFUL *adj*
WILGA *n* small drought-resistant tree of Australia **wilgas**
WILI *n* spirit
WILIER ▸ **wily**
WILIEST ▸ **wily**
WILILY ▸ **wily**
WILING ▸ **wile**
WILIS ▸ **wili**
WILJA ▸ **wiltja**
WILJAS ▸ **wilja**
WILL *vb, n*

WILLED *adj* having a will as specified
WILLER ▸ **will**
WILLERS ▸ **will**
WILLEST ▸ **will**
WILLET *n* large American shore bird **willets**
WILLEY = **willy**
WILLEYS ▸ **willey**
WILLFUL = **wilful**
WILLIAM *n as in* **sweet william** flowering plant
WILLIE *n* informal word for a penis
WILLIED ▸ **willy**
WILLIES ▸ **willy**
WILLING *adj*
WILLOW *n, vb* **willows**
WILLOWY *adj*
WILLS ▸ **will**
WILLY *vb* clean in willowing-machine
WILT *vb, n* **wilted, wilting**
WILTJA *n* Aboriginal shelter **wiltjas**
WILTS ▸ **wilt**
WILY *adj*
WIMBLE *n* any of a number of hand tools used for boring holes ▷ *vb* bore (a hole) with or as if with a wimble **wimbled, wimbles**
WIMBREL = **whimbrel**
WIMMIN *n* common intentional literary misspelling of 'women'
WIMP *n, vb as in* **wimp out; wimped, wimpier, wimping, wimpish**
WIMPLE *n, vb* **wimpled, wimples**
WIMPS ▸ **wimp**
WIMPY ▸ **wimp**
WIN *vb, n*
WINCE *vb, n* **winced, wincer, wincers, winces**
WINCEY *n* plain- or twill-weave cloth **winceys**
WINCH *n, vb* **winched, wincher, winches**
WINCING ▸ **wince**
WIND *n, vb*
WINDAC = **windas**
WINDACS ▸ **windac**
WINDAGE *n* deflection of a projectile as a result of the effect of the wind
WINDAS *n* windlass
WINDBAG *n*
WINDED ▸ **wind**
WINDER *n* person or device that winds, as an engine for hoisting the cages in a mine shaft **winders**
WINDGUN *n* air gun
WINDIER ▸ **windy**
WINDIGO = **wendigo**
WINDILY ▸ **windy**
WINDING ▸ **wind**
WINDLE *vb* wind something round continuously **windled, windles**
WINDOCK = **winnock**
WINDORE *n* window
WINDOW *n, vb* **windows, windowy**
WINDROW *n* long low ridge or line of hay or a similar crop ▷ *vb* put (hay or a similar crop) into windrows
WINDS ▸ **wind**
WINDSES *pl n* ventilation shafts within mines
WINDUP *n* prank or hoax **windups**
WINDWAY *n* part of wind instrument
WINDY *adj*
WINE *n, adj, vb* **wined**
WINERY *n* place where wine is made
WINES ▸ **wine**
WINESAP *n* variety of apple
WINESOP *n* old word for an alcoholic
WINEY *adj* having the taste or qualities of wine
WING *n, vb*
WINGBOW *n* distinctive band of colour marking the wing of a bird
WINGE = **whinge**
WINGED *adj* furnished with wings
WINGER *n* **wingers**
WINGES ▸ **winge**
WINGIER ▸ **wingy**
WINGING ▸ **wing**
WINGLET *n* small wing
WINGMAN *n* player in the wing position in Australian Rules **wingmen**
WINGS ▸ **wing**
WINGTIP *n* outermost edge of a wing
WINGY *adj* having wings

WINIER ▸ **winy**
WINIEST ▸ **winy**
WINING ▸ **wine**
WINISH ▸ **wine**
WINK *vb, n* **winked**
WINKER *n* person or thing that winks **winkers**
WINKING ▸ **wink**
WINKLE *n, vb* **winkled**
WINKLER *n* one who forces person or thing out
WINKLES ▸ **winkle**
WINKS ▸ **wink**
WINLESS *adj* not having won anything
WINN *n* penny
WINNA *vb* will not
WINNARD *n* heron
WINNED ▸ **win**
WINNER *n* **winners**
WINNING *adj*
WINNLE = **windle**
WINNLES ▸ **winnle**
WINNOCK *n* window
WINNOW *vb, n* **winnows**
WINNS ▸ **winn**
WINO *n* **winoes, winos**
WINS ▸ **win**
WINSEY = **wincey**
WINSEYS ▸ **winsey**
WINSOME *adj*
WINTER *n, vb* **winters**
WINTERY = **wintry**
WINTLE *vb* reel; stagger **wintled, wintles**
WINTRY *adj*
WINY = **winey**
WINZE *n* steeply inclined shaft, as for ventilation between levels **winzes**
WIPE *vb, n* **wiped**
WIPEOUT *n* instance of wiping out
WIPER *n* any piece of cloth, such as a handkerchief, towel, etc, used for wiping **wipers**
WIPES ▸ **wipe**
WIPING ▸ **wipe**
WIPINGS ▸ **wipe**
WIPPEN *n* part of hammer action in piano **wippens**
WIRABLE *adj* that can be wired
WIRE *n, vb*
WIRED *adj* excited or nervous
WIREMAN *n* person who installs and maintains electric wiring, cables, etc **wiremen**
WIRER *n* person who sets or uses wires to snare rabbits and similar animals **wirers**
WIRES ▸ **wire**
WIRETAP *vb* obtain information secretly via telegraph or telephone
WIREWAY *n* tube for electric wires
WIRIER ▸ **wiry**
WIRIEST ▸ **wiry**
WIRILDA *n* SE Australian acacia tree with edible seeds
WIRILY ▸ **wiry**
WIRING *n, adj* **wirings**
WIRRA *interj* exclamation of sorrow or deep concern
WIRRAH *n* Australian saltwater fish with bright blue spots **wirrahs**
WIRY *adj*
WIS *vb* know or suppose (something)
WISARD *obsolete spelling of* ▸ **wizard**
WISARDS ▸ **wisard**
WISDOM *n* **wisdoms**
WISE *vb, adj, n*
WISEASS *n* person who thinks he or she is being witty or clever
WISED ▸ **wise**
WISEGUY *n* person who wants to seem clever
WISELY ▸ **wise**
WISENT *n* European bison **wisents**
WISER ▸ **wise**
WISES ▸ **wise**
WISEST ▸ **wise**
WISH *vb, n*
WISHA *interj* expression of surprise
WISHED, wisher, wishers, wishes ▸ **wish**
WISHFUL *adj* too optimistic
WISHING ▸ **wish**
WISHT *variant of* ▸ **whisht**
WISING ▸ **wise**
WISKET *n* basket **wiskets**
WISP *n, vb* **wisped**
WISPIER ▸ **wispy**
WISPILY ▸ **wispy**
WISPING ▸ **wisp**
WISPISH ▸ **wisp**

WISPS ▸ **wisp**
WISPY *adj* thin, fine, or delicate
WISS *vb* urinate
WISSED ▸ **wis**
WISSES ▸ **wis**
WISSING ▸ **wis**
WIST *vb* know **wisted**
WISTFUL *adj*
WISTING ▸ **wist**
WISTITI *n* marmoset
WISTLY *adv* intently
WISTS ▸ **wist**
WIT *vb, n*
WITAN *n* Anglo-Saxon assembly that met to counsel the king **witans**
WITCH *n, vb* **witched**
WITCHEN *n* rowan tree
WITCHES ▸ **witch**
WITCHY *adj* like a witch
WITE *vb* blame **wited, wites**
WITGAT *n* type of S African tree **witgats**
WITH *prep, n*
WITHAL *adv* as well
WITHE *n* strong flexible twig suitable for binding things together ▷ *vb* bind with withes **withed**
WITHER *vb*
WITHERS *pl n* ridge between a horse's shoulder blades
WITHES ▸ **withe**
WITHIER ▸ **withy**
WITHIES ▸ **withy**
WITHIN *adv, prep, n*
WITHING ▸ **withe**
WITHINS ▸ **within**
WITHOUT *prep, adv, n*
WITHS ▸ **with**
WITHY *n* willow tree, esp an osier ▷ *adj* (of people) tough and agile
WITING ▸ **wite**
WITLESS *adj*
WITLING *n* person who thinks himself witty
WITLOOF *n* chicory
WITNESS *n, vb*
WITNEY *n* type of blanket; heavy cloth **witneys**
WITS ▸ **wit**
WITTED *adj* having wit
WITTER *vb, n* **witters**
WITTIER ▸ **witty**
WITTILY ▸ **witty**
WITTING *adj* deliberate
WITTOL *n* man who tolerates his wife's unfaithfulness **wittols**
WITTY *adj*
WITWALL *n* golden oriole
WIVE *vb* marry (a woman) **wived**
WIVER *another word for* ▸ **wivern**
WIVERN = **wyvern**
WIVERNS ▸ **wivern**
WIVERS ▸ **wiver**
WIVES ▸ **wife**
WIVING ▸ **wive**
WIZ *shortened form of* ▸ **wizard**

> **Wiz** is a short form of **wizard**. This is the highest-scoring three-letter word beginning with W, and can be especially useful when there isn't much room to manoeuvre.

WIZARD *n, adj* **wizards**
WIZEN *vb* make or become shrivelled ▷ *n* archaic word for 'weasand' (the gullet)
WIZENED *adj*
WIZENS ▸ **wizen**
WIZES ▸ **wiz**
WIZIER = **vizier**
WIZIERS ▸ **wizier**
WIZZEN = **wizen**
WIZZENS ▸ **wizen**
WIZZES ▸ **wiz**
WO *archaic spelling of* ▸ **woe**
WOAD *n*
WOADED *adj* coloured blue with woad
WOADS ▸ **woad**
WOADWAX *n* small Eurasian leguminous shrub
WOALD = **weld**
WOALDS ▸ **woald**
WOBBLE *vb, n* **wobbled, wobbler, wobbles**
WOBBLY *adj, n*
WOCK = **wok**
WOCKS ▸ **wock**
WODGE *n* **wodges**
WOE *n*
WOEFUL *adj*
WOENESS ▸ **woe**
WOES ▸ **woe**
WOESOME *adj* woeful
WOF *n* fool **wofs**
WOFUL = **woeful**
WOFULLY ▸ **woful**
WOGGLE *n* ring of leather through which a Scout neckerchief is threaded **woggles**
WOIWODE = **voivode**
WOK *n*
WOKE ▸ **wake**

WOKEN ▸ **wake**
WOKKA *modifier as in* **wokka board** a piece of fibreboard used as a musical instrument
WOKS ▸ **wok**
WOLD = **weld**
WOLDS ▸ **wold**
WOLF *n, vb* **wolfed**
WOLFER = **wolver**
WOLFERS ▸ **wolfer**
WOLFING ▸ **wolf**
WOLFISH ▸ **wolf**
WOLFKIN *n* young wolf
WOLFRAM *another name for* > **tungsten**
WOLFS ▸ **wolf**
WOLLIES ▸ **wolly**
WOLLY *n* pickled cucumber or olive
WOLVE *vb* hunt for wolves **wolved**
WOLVER *n* person who hunts wolves **wolvers**
WOLVES ▸ **wolf**
WOLVING ▸ **wolve**
WOLVISH = **wolfish**
WOMAN *n, adj, vb* **womaned**
WOMANLY *adj*
WOMANS ▸ **woman**
WOMB *vb, n*
WOMBAT *n* **wombats**
WOMBED ▸ **womb**
WOMBIER ▸ **womby**
WOMBING ▸ **womb**
WOMBS ▸ **womb**
WOMBY *adj* hollow; spacious
WOMEN ▸ **woman**
WOMERA = **woomera**
WOMERAS ▸ **womera**
WOMMERA = **woomera**
WOMMIT *n* foolish person **wommits**
WOMYN = **woman**
WON *n* standard monetary unit of North Korea ▹ *vb* live or dwell
WONDER *vb, n, adj* **wonders**
WONDRED *adj* splendid
WONGA *n* money **wongas**
WONGI *vb* talk informally **wongied, wongis**
WONING ▸ **won**
WONINGS ▸ **won**
WONK *n* person who is obsessively interested in a specified subject
WONKIER ▸ **wonky**
WONKS ▸ **wonk**
WONKY *adj*
WONNED, wonner, wonners, wonning, wons ▸ **won**
WONT *adj, n, vb*
WONTED *adj* accustomed or habituated (to doing something)
WONTING ▸ **wont**
WONTON *n* dumpling filled with spiced minced pork **wontons**
WONTS ▸ **wont**
WOO *vb*
WOOBUT = **woubit**
WOOBUTS ▸ **woobut**
WOOD *n, adj, vb*
WOODBIN *n* box for firewood
WOODBOX *n* box for firewood
WOODCUT *n*
WOODED *adj*
WOODEN *adj, vb* **woodens**
WOODHEN *another name for* ▸ **weka**
WOODIE *n* gallows rope
WOODIER ▸ **woody**
WOODIES ▸ **woodie**
WOODING ▸ **wood**
WOODLOT *n* area restricted to the growing of trees
WOODMAN = **woodsman**
WOODMEN ▸ **woodman**
WOODRAT *n* pack-rat
WOODS *pl n* closely packed trees forming a forest or wood
WOODSIA *n* type of small fern with tufted rhizomes and wiry fronds
WOODSY *adj* of, reminiscent of, or connected with woods
WOODWAX = **woodwaxen**
WOODY *adj*
WOOED ▸ **woo**
WOOER ▸ **woo**
WOOERS ▸ **woo**
WOOF *vb* **woofed**
WOOFER *n* loudspeaker reproducing low-frequency sounds **woofers**
WOOFIER ▸ **woofy**
WOOFING ▸ **woof**
WOOFS ▸ **woof**
WOOFY *adj* with close, dense texture

WOOHOO *interj*
WOOING ▶ **woo**
WOOINGS ▶ **woo**
WOOL *n*
WOOLD *vb* wind (rope) **woolded**
WOOLDER *n* stick for winding rope
WOOLDS ▶ **woold**
WOOLED = **woolled**
WOOLEN = **woollen**
WOOLENS ▶ **woolen**
WOOLER = **woolder**
WOOLERS ▶ **wooler**
WOOLFAT = **lanolin**
WOOLHAT *n* poor white person in S States
WOOLIE *n* wool garment
WOOLIER ▶ **wooly**
WOOLIES ▶ **wooly**
WOOLLED *adj* (of animals) having wool
WOOLLEN *adj, n*
WOOLLY *adj, n*
WOOLMAN *n* wool trader **woolmen**
WOOLS ▶ **wool**
WOOLSEY *n* cotton and wool blend
WOOLY = **woolly**
WOOMERA *n*
WOON = **won**
WOONED ▶ **woon**
WOONING ▶ **woon**
WOONS ▶ **woon**
WOOPIE *n* well-off older person **woopies**
WOOPS *vb* (esp of small child) vomit **woopsed, woopses**
WOORALI *less common name for* ▶ **curare**
WOORARA = **wourali**
WOORARI = **wourali**
WOOS ▶ **woo**
WOOSE = **wuss**
WOOSEL = **ouzel**
WOOSELL = **ouzel**
WOOSELS ▶ **woosel**
WOOSES ▶ **woose**
WOOSH = **whoosh**
WOOSHED ▶ **woosh**
WOOSHES ▶ **woosh**
WOOT *vb* wilt thou?
WOOTZ *n* Middle-Eastern steel **wootzes**
WOOZIER ▶ **woozy**
WOOZILY ▶ **woozy**
WOOZY *adj*
WORD *n* smallest single meaningful unit of speech or writing ▷ *vb* express in words
WORDAGE *n* words considered collectively, esp a quantity of words
WORDED ▶ **word**
WORDIER ▶ **wordy**
WORDILY ▶ **wordy**
WORDING *n*
WORDISH *adj* talkative
WORDS ▶ **word**
WORDY *adj*
WORE ▶ **wear**
WORK *n, adj, vb*
WORKBAG *n* container for implements, tools, or materials **workbox**
WORKDAY *another word for* > **workaday**
WORKED *adj* made or decorated with evidence of workmanship
WORKER *n* **workers**
WORKFUL *adj* hardworking
WORKING *n, adj*
WORKMAN *n* **workmen**
WORKOUT *n*
WORKS ▶ **work**
WORKSHY *adj*
WORKTOP *n* surface used for food preparation
WORKUP *n* medical examination **workups**
WORLD *n, adj*
WORLDED *adj* incorporating worlds
WORLDLY *adj, adv*
WORLDS ▶ **world**
WORM *n, vb* **wormed, wormer, wormers**
WORMERY *n* piece of apparatus in which worms are kept for study
WORMFLY *n* type of lure dressed on a double hook
WORMIER ▶ **wormy**
WORMIL *n* burrowing larva of type of fly **wormils**
WORMING ▶ **worm**
WORMISH ▶ **worm**
WORMS *n* disease caused by parasitic worms living in the intestines
WORMY *adj* infested with or eaten by worms
WORN ▶ **wear**
WORRAL *n* type of lizard **worrals, worrel**
WORRELS ▶ **worrel**
WORRIED ▶ **worry**

WORRIER ▸ **worry**
WORRIES ▸ **worry**
WORRIT *vb* tease or worry **worrits**
WORRY *vb, n*
WORSE *vb* **worsed**
WORSEN *vb* **worsens**
WORSER *archaic or nonstandard word for* ▸ **worse**
WORSES ▸ **worse**
WORSET *n* worsted fabric **worsets**
WORSHIP *vb, n*
WORSING ▸ **worse**
WORST *n, vb*
WORSTED *n*
WORSTS ▸ **worst**
WORT *n* any of various plants formerly used to cure diseases
WORTH *prep, n, vb* **worthed, worths**
WORTHY *adj, n, vb*
WORTLE *n* plate with holes for drawing wire through **wortles**
WORTS ▸ **wort**
WOS ▸ **wo**
WOSBIRD *n* illegitimate child
WOST *vb* wit, to know
WOT *vb* wit, to know
WOTCHA ▸ **wotcher**
WOTCHER *sentence substitute* slang term of greeting
WOTS, wotted, wottest, wotteth, wotting ▸ **wot**
WOUBIT *n* type of caterpillar **woubits**
WOULD ▸ **will**
WOULDS = **wouldst**
WOULDST *singular form of the past tense of* ▸ **will**
WOUND *vb, n*
WOUNDED *adj* suffering from wounds
WOUNDER ▸ **wound**
WOUNDS ▸ **wound**
WOUNDY *adj* extreme
WOURALI *n* plant from which curare is obtained
WOVE ▸ **weave**
WOVEN *n* article made from woven cloth **wovens**
WOW *interj, n, vb* **wowed, wowee**
WOWF *adj* mad **wowfer, wowfest**

> This is a Scots word meaning crazy: you are not likely to get the chance to play this very often but if your opponent plays **wow** and you have an F you would be wowf to miss the opportunity of the hook!

WOWING ▸ **wow**
WOWS ▸ **wow**
WOWSER *n* puritanical person **wowsers**
WOX ▸ **wax**

> **Wox** is an old past tense of the verb **wax**, to grow, and is another of the key words using X.

WOXEN ▸ **wax**
WRACK *n* seaweed ▹ *vb* strain or shake (something) violently **wracked, wracks**
WRAITH *n* **wraiths**
WRANG *Scot word for* ▸ **wrong**
WRANGED ▸ **wrang**
WRANGLE *vb, n*
WRANGS ▸ **wrang**
WRAP *vb, n* **wrapped**
WRAPPER *vb, n*
WRAPS ▸ **wrap**
WRAPT = **rapt**
WRASSE *n* colourful sea fish **wrasses**
WRASSLE = **wrestle**
WRAST = **wrest**
WRASTED ▸ **wrast**
WRASTLE = **wrestle**
WRASTS ▸ **wrast**
WRATE ▸ **write**
WRATH *n, adj, vb* **wrathed, wraths**
WRATHY = **wrathful**
WRAWL *vb* howl **wrawled, wrawls**
WRAXLE *vb* wrestle **wraxled, wraxles**
WREAK *vb* **wreaked, wreaker, wreaks**
WREATH *n*
WREATHE *vb*
WREATHS ▸ **wreath**
WREATHY *adj* twisted into wreath
WRECK *vb, n*
WRECKED *adj* in a state of intoxication induced by drugs or alcohol
WRECKER *n* formerly, person who lured ships onto the rocks in order to plunder them
WRECKS ▸ **wreck**
WREN *n*

WRENCH *vb, n*
WRENS ▸ **wren**
WREST *vb, n* **wrested, wrester**
WRESTLE *vb, n*
WRESTS ▸ **wrest**
WRETCH *n*
WRETHE = **wreathe**
WRETHED ▸ **wrethe**
WRETHES ▸ **wrethe**
WRICK *variant spelling (chiefly Brit) of* ▸ **rick**
WRICKED ▸ **wrick**
WRICKS ▸ **wrick**
WRIED, wrier, wries, wriest ▸ **wry**
WRIGGLE *vb, n* **wriggly**
WRIGHT *n* maker **wrights**
WRING *vb* **wringed**
WRINGER = **mangle**
WRINGS ▸ **wring**
WRINKLE *n, vb* **wrinkly**
WRIST *n* **wrists**
WRISTY *adj* characterized by considerable movement of the wrist
WRIT *n*
WRITE *vb*
WRITER *n* **writers**
WRITES ▸ **write**
WRITHE *vb, n* **writhed**
WRITHEN *adj* twisted
WRITHER ▸ **writhe**
WRITHES ▸ **writhe**
WRITING ▸ **write**
WRITS ▸ **writ**
WRITTEN ▸ **write**
WRIZLED *adj* wrinkled
WROATH *n* unforeseen trouble **wroaths**
WROKE ▸ **wreak**
WROKEN ▸ **wreak**
WRONG *adj, adv, n, vb* **wronged, wronger, wrongly, wrongs**
WROOT *obsolete form of* ▸ **root**
WROOTED ▸ **wroot**
WROOTS ▸ **wroot**
WROTE ▸ **write**
WROTH *adj* angry
WROUGHT *adj*
WRUNG ▸ **wring**
WRY *adj, vb*
WRYBILL *n* New Zealand plover whose bill is bent to one side
WRYER, wryest, wrying, wryly ▸ **wry**
WRYNECK *n* woodpecker that has a habit of twisting its neck round
WRYNESS ▸ **wry**
WRYTHEN *adj* twisted
WUD *Scots form of* ▸ **wood**

> W and U are a horrible combination to have on your rack, so this Scots word for wood can be a godsend. And remember that it can also be a verb, meaning to load with wood, so you have **wuds, wudding** and **wudded**.

WUDDED ▸ **wud**
WUDDING ▸ **wud**
WUDJULA *n* Australian word for a non-Aboriginal person
WUDS ▸ **wud**
WUDU *n* practice of ritual washing before daily prayer **wudus**
WULL *obsolete form of* ▸ **will**
WULLED ▸ **will**
WULLING ▸ **will**
WULLS ▸ **will**
WUNNER = **oner**
WUNNERS ▸ **wunner**
WURLEY *n* Aboriginal hut **wurleys, wurlie**
WURLIES ▸ **wurlie**
WURST *n* large sausage, esp of a type made in Germany, Austria, etc **wursts**
WURZEL *n* root **wurzels**
WUS *n* casual term of address **wuses**
WUSHU *n* Chinese martial arts **wushus**
WUSS *n* feeble or effeminate person **wusses**
WUSSIER ▸ **wussy**
WUSSIES ▸ **wussy**
WUSSY *adj* feeble or effeminate ▹ *n* feeble person
WUTHER *vb* (of wind) blow and roar **wuthers**
WUXIA *n* Chinese fiction concerning the adventures of sword-wielding heroes **wuxias**

> This Chinese word for a genre of fiction may get you a decent score from a very difficult-looking rack.

WUZZLE *vb* mix up **wuzzled, wuzzles**
WYCH *n* type of tree having flexible branches **wyches**
WYE *n* y-shaped pipe **wyes**

If you have W and Y on your rack, look for an E on the board that will allow you to play this name for the letter Y, especially if you can land on a bonus square as a result.

WYLE *vb* entice **wyled, wyles, wyling**
WYN *n* rune equivalent to English 'w'
WYND *n* narrow lane or alley **wynds**
WYNN = **wyn**
WYNNS ▸ **wynn**
WYNS ▸ **wyn**
WYTE *vb* blame **wyted, wytes, wyting**
WYVERN *n* heraldic beast **wyverns**

Worth 8 points on its own, **X** is one of the best tiles in the game. It doesn't, however, start many two- and three-letter words. There are only two valid two-letter words, **xi** and **xu** (9 points each) beginning with **X**, and only one three-letter word, **xis**. Therefore, if you have an **X** on your rack and need to play short words, you're probably better off thinking of words that end in **X** or have **X** in them rather than those that start with **X**. Particularly good to remember are **zax, zex** (19 points each) and **kex** (14 points).

XANTHAM *n* acacia gum **xanthan**
XANTHIC *adj* of, containing, or derived from xanthic acid
XANTHIN *n* any of a group of yellow or orange carotene derivatives
XEBEC *n* small three-masted Mediterranean vessel with both square and lateen sails, formerly used by Algerian pirates and later used for commerce **xebecs**

> A kind of small boat, and a good high-scoring word that can easily be missed, as we tend to be slow to consider words beginning with X.

XENIA *n* influence of pollen upon the form of the fruit developing after pollination **xenial, xenias**
XENIC *adj* denoting the presence of bacteria
XENIUM *n* diplomatic gift
XENON *n* **xenons**
XENOPUS *n* African frog
XERAFIN *n* Indian coin
XERARCH *adj* (of a sere) having its origin in a dry habitat
XERASIA *n* dryness of the hair
XERIC *adj* of, relating to, or growing in dry conditions
XEROMA *n* excessive dryness of the cornea **xeromas**
XEROSES ▶ **xerosis**
XEROSIS *n* abnormal dryness of bodily tissues, esp the skin, eyes, or mucous membranes **xerotes, xerotic**
XEROX *n* tradename for a machine employing a xerographic copying process ▷ *vb* produce a copy (of a document, etc) using such a machine **xeroxed, xeroxes**
XERUS *n* ground squirrel **xeruses**
XI *n* 14th letter in the Greek alphabet

XIPHOID *adj* shaped like a sword ▷ *n* part of the sternum
XIS ▶ **xi**
XOANA ▶ **xoanon**
XOANON *n* primitive image of a god supposed to have fallen from heaven

> One of the few words starting with X. But be careful: the plural is **xoana** not **xoanons**.

XRAY *n* code word for the letter X **xrays**
XU *n* Vietnamese currency unit
XYLAN *n* yellow polysaccharide consisting of xylose units **xylans**
XYLEM *n* **xylems**
XYLENE *n* type of hydrocarbon **xylenes**
XYLENOL *n* synthetic resin made from xylene
XYLIC ▶ **xylem**
XYLIDIN = **xylidine**
XYLITOL *n* crystalline alcohol used as sweetener
XYLOGEN = **xylem**
XYLOID *adj* of, relating to, or resembling wood
XYLOL *another name (not in technical usage) for* ▶ **xylene**
XYLOLS ▶ **xylol**
XYLOMA *n* hard growth in fungi **xylomas**
XYLONIC *adj* denoting an acid formed from xylose
XYLOSE *n* white crystalline sugar found in wood and straw **xyloses**
XYLYL *n* group of atoms **xylyls**
XYST *n* long portico, esp one used in ancient Greece for athletics

> A kind of court used by ancient Greek athletes for exercises, this is a lovely high-scoring word to play. And if your opponent plays it, remember that you can put an I on it to make **xysti**, as well as an S to make **xysts**.

XYSTER *n* surgical instrument for scraping bone **xysters**
XYSTI ▶ **xystus**
XYSTOI ▶ **xystos**
XYSTOS = **xyst**
XYSTS ▶ **xyst**
XYSTUS = **xyst**

Y can be a useful tile to have on your rack, particularly if you are short of vowels, but it can make it difficult to find bonus words scoring that extra 50 points, and you will normally want to play it off as soon as a good score offers itself. There are only four two-letter words beginning with **Y**, but these are easy to remember as there's one for every vowel except **I**: **ya, ye, yo** and **yu** (5 points each). There are quite a few useful three-letter words: **yew** (9) and **yob** (8) and remember that **yob** was originally **boy** backwards: if you can't fit in **yob**, you may be able to use **boy** instead. And while his half-brother the **zo** (or **dzo** or **dso** or **zho**) gets all the attention, don't forget that the **yak** (10) earns quite a decent score!

YA *pron* you
YAAR *n* in informal Indian English, a friend **yaars**
YABA *n* informal word for 'yet another bloody acronym' **yabas**
YABBA *n* form of methamphetamine **yabbas**
YABBER *vb* talk or jabber ▷ *n* talk or jabber **yabbers**
YABBIE = **yabby**
YABBIED ▶ **yabby**
YABBIES ▶ **yabby**
YABBY *n, vb*
YACCA *n* Australian plant with a woody stem **yaccas**
YACHT *n, vb* **yachted, yachter**
YACHTIE *n* yachtsman
YACHTS ▶ **yacht**
YACK = **yak**
YACKA = **yacca**
YACKAS ▶ **yacka**
YACKED ▶ **yack**
YACKER = **yakka**
YACKERS ▶ **yacker**
YACKING ▶ **yack**
YACKS ▶ **yack**
YAD *n* hand-held pointer used for reading the sefer torah **yads**
YAE = **ae**
YAFF *vb* bark **yaffed, yaffing**
YAFFLE *n* woodpecker with a green back and wings **yaffles**
YAFFS ▶ **yaff**
YAG *n* artificial crystal
YAGER = **jaeger**
YAGERS ▶ **yager**
YAGGER *n* pedlar **yaggers**
YAGI *n* type of highly directional aerial **yagis**
YAGS ▶ **yag**
YAH *interj* exclamation of derision or disgust ▷ *n* affected upper-class person
YAHOO *n* crude coarse person **yahoos**
YAHS ▶ **yah**
YAIRD *Scots form of* ▶ **yard**

YAIRDS ▶ **yaird**
YAK *n, vb*
YAKHDAN *n* box for carrying ice on a pack animal
YAKKA *n* **yakkas**
YAKKED ▶ **yak**
YAKKER = **yakka**
YAKKERS ▶ **yakker**
YAKKING ▶ **yak**
YAKOW *n* animal bred from a male yak and a domestic cow **yakows**
YAKS ▶ **yak**
YAKUZA *n* Japanese criminal organization
YALD *adj* vigorous
YALE *n* mythical beast with the body of an antelope (or similar animal) and swivelling horns **yales**
YAM *n*
YAMALKA = **yarmulke**
YAMEN *n* (in imperial China) the office or residence of a public official **yamens**
YAMMER *vb* whine in a complaining manner ▷ *n* yammering sound **yammers**
YAMPIES ▶ **yampy**
YAMPY *n* foolish person
YAMS ▶ **yam**
YAMULKA = **yarmulke**
YAMUN = **yamen**
YAMUNS ▶ **yamun**
YANG *n* (in Chinese philosophy) one of two complementary principles maintaining harmony in the universe **yangs**
YANK *vb, n* **yanked**
YANKEE *n* code word for the letter Y **yankees**
YANKER ▶ **yank**
YANKERS ▶ **yank**
YANKIE *n* shrewish woman **yankies**
YANKING ▶ **yank**
YANKS ▶ **yank**
YANQUI *n* slang word for American **yanquis**
YANTRA *n* diagram used in meditation **yantras**
YAOURT *n* yoghurt **yaourts**
YAP *vb, n, interj*
YAPOCK = **yapok**
YAPOCKS ▶ **yapock**
YAPOK *n* type of opossum **yapoks**
YAPON = **yaupon**
YAPONS ▶ **yapon**
YAPP *n* type of book binding
YAPPED ▶ **yap**
YAPPER ▶ **yap**
YAPPERS ▶ **yap**
YAPPIE *n* young aspiring professional
YAPPIER ▶ **yap**
YAPPIES ▶ **yappie**
YAPPING ▶ **yap**
YAPPS ▶ **yapp**
YAPPY ▶ **yap**
YAPS ▶ **yap**
YAPSTER ▶ **yap**
YAQONA *n* Polynesian shrub **yaqonas**
YAR *adj* nimble
YARD *n, vb*
YARDAGE *n* length measured in yards
YARDANG *n* ridge formed by wind erosion
YARDARM *n* outer end of a ship's yard
YARDED ▶ **yard**
YARDER ▶ **yard**
YARDERS ▶ **yard**
YARDING *n* group of animals displayed for sale
YARDMAN *n* farm overseer **yardmen**
YARDS ▶ **yard**
YARE *adj* ready, brisk, or eager ▷ *adv* readily or eagerly **yarely, yarer, yarest**
YARFA *n* peat **yarfas**
YARK *vb* make ready **yarked, yarking, yarks**
YARN *n, vb* **yarned, yarner, yarners, yarning, yarns**
YARPHA *n* peat **yarphas**
YARR *n* wild white flower
YARRAN *n* type of small hardy tree of inland Australia **yarrans**
YARROW *n* wild plant with flat clusters of white flowers **yarrows**
YARRS ▶ **yarr**
YARTA *Shetland word for* ▶ **heart**
YARTAS ▶ **yarta**
YARTO = **yarta**
YARTOS ▶ **yarto**
YASHMAC = **yashmak**
YASHMAK *n* **yasmak**
YASMAKS ▶ **yashmak**
YATAGAN = **yataghan**

YATE *n* type of small eucalyptus tree yielding a very hard timber **yates**
YATTER *vb* talk at length ▷ *n* continuous chatter **yatters**
YAUD *Scots word for* ▶ **mare**
YAUDS ▶ **yaud**
YAULD *adj* alert, spritely, or nimble
YAUP *variant spelling of* ▶ **yawp; yauped, yauper, yaupers, yauping**
YAUPON *n* southern US evergreen holly shrub **yaupons**
YAUPS ▶ **yaup**
YAUTIA *n* Caribbean plant cultivated for its edible leaves and underground stems **yautias**
YAW *vb, n* **yawed**
YAWEY ▶ **yaws**
YAWING ▶ **yaw**
YAWL *n* two-masted sailing boat ▷ *vb* howl, weep, or scream harshly **yawled, yawling, yawls**
YAWN *vb, n* **yawned, yawner, yawners, yawnier, yawning, yawns, yawny**
YAWP *vb* gape or yawn, esp audibly ▷ *n* shout, bark, yelp, or cry **yawped, yawper, yawpers, yawping, yawps**
YAWS *n* **yawy**
YAY *interj* exclamation indicating approval or triumph ▷ *n* cry of approval **yays**
YBET *archaic past participle of* ▶ **beat**
YBLENT *archaic past participle of* ▶ **blend**
YBORE *archaic past participle of* ▶ **bear**
YBOUND *archaic past participle of* ▶ **bind**
YBRENT *archaic past participle of* ▶ **burn**
YCLAD *archaic past participle of* ▶ **clothe**
YCLED *archaic past participle of* ▶ **clothe**
YCLEEPE *archaic form of* ▶ **clepe**
YCLEPED = **yclept**
YCLEPT *adj* having the name of
YCOND *archaic past participle of* ▶ **con**
YDRAD *archaic past participle of* ▶ **dread**
YDRED *archaic past participle of* ▶ **dread**
YE *pron, adj*
YEA *interj, adv, sentence substitute, n*
YEAD *vb* proceed **yeading, yeads**
YEAH *n* **yeahs**
YEALDON *n* fuel
YEALING *n* person of the same age as oneself
YEALM *vb* prepare for thatching **yealmed, yealms**
YEAN *vb* (of a sheep or goat) to give birth to (offspring) **yeaned, yeaning, yeans**
YEAR *n*
YEARD *vb* bury **yearded, yeards**
YEAREND *n* end of the year
YEARLY *adv* (happening) every year or once a year ▷ *adj* occurring, done, or appearing once a year or every year ▷ *n* publication, event, etc, that occurs once a year
YEARN *vb* **yearned, yearner, yearns**
YEARS ▶ **year**
YEAS ▶ **yea**
YEAST *n, vb* **yeasted, yeasts**
YEASTY *adj* of, resembling, or containing yeast
YEBO *interj* yes ▷ *sentence substitute* expression of affirmation
YECCH = **yech**
YECCHS ▶ **yecch**
YECH *n* expression of disgust
YECHIER ▶ **yechy**
YECHS ▶ **yech**
YECHY ▶ **yech**
YEDE = **yead**
YEDES ▶ **yede**
YEDING ▶ **yede**
YEED = **yead**
YEEDING ▶ **yeed**
YEEDS ▶ **yeed**
YEELIN *n* person of the same age as oneself **yeelins**

YEGG *n* burglar or safe-breaker **yeggman**
YEGGMEN ▶ **yeggman**
YEGGS ▶ **yegg**
YEH = **yeah**
YELD *adj* (of an animal) barren or too young to bear young
YELK *n* yolk of an egg **yelks**
YELL *vb, n* **yelled, yeller, yellers, yelling**
YELLOCH *vb* yell
YELLOW *n, adj, vb*
YELLOWS *n* any of various fungal or viral diseases of plants
YELLOWY ▶ **yellow**
YELLS ▶ **yell**
YELM = **yealm**
YELMED ▶ **yelm**
YELMING ▶ **yelm**
YELMS ▶ **yelm**
YELP *n, vb* **yelped, yelper, yelpers, yelping, yelps**
YELT *n* young sow **yelts**
YEMMER *southwest English form of* ▶ **ember**
YEMMERS ▶ **yemmer**
YEN *n, vb* **yenned, yenning, yens**
YENTA *n* meddlesome woman **yentas, yente**
YENTES ▶ **yente**
YEOMAN *n* **yeomen**
YEP *n* affirmative statement **yeps**
YERBA *n* stimulating South American drink made from dried leaves **yerbas**
YERD *vb* bury **yerded, yerding, yerds**
YERK *vb* tighten stitches **yerked, yerking, yerks**
YES *interj, n, sentence substitute, vb* **yeses**
YESHIVA *n* traditional Jewish school
YESK *vb* hiccup **yesked, yesking, yesks**
YESSED ▶ **yes**
YESSES ▶ **yes**
YESSING ▶ **yes**
YEST *archaic form of* ▶ **yeast**
YESTER *adj* of or relating to yesterday **yestern**
YESTS ▶ **yest**
YESTY *archaic form of* ▶ **yeasty**
YET *adv*
YETI *n* **yetis**
YETT *n* gate or door
YETTIE *n* young, entrepreneurial, and technology-based (person) **yetties**
YETTS ▶ **yett**
YEUK *vb* itch **yeuked**
YEUKIER ▶ **yeuky**
YEUKING ▶ **yeuk**
YEUKS ▶ **yeuk**
YEUKY ▶ **yeuk**
YEVE *vb* give **yeven, yeves, yeving**
YEW *n*
YEWEN *adj* made of yew
YEWS ▶ **yew**
YEX *vb* hiccup **yexed, yexes, yexing**

> This word meaning to hiccup gives you a good score, and the verb forms offer the chance to expand it if someone else plays it, or if you get the chance later on.

YFERE *adv* together
YGO *archaic past participle of* ▶ **go**
YGOE *archaic past participle of* ▶ **go**
YIBBLES *adv* perhaps
YICKER *vb* squeal or squeak **yickers**
YIDAKI *n* long wooden wind instrument played by the Aboriginal peoples of Arnhem Land **yidakis**
YIELD *vb, n* **yielded, yielder, yields**
YIKE *n* argument, squabble, or fight ▷ *vb* argue, squabble, or fight **yiked**
YIKES *interj* expression of surprise, fear, or alarm
YIKING ▶ **yike**
YIKKER *vb* squeal or squeak **yikkers**
YILL *n* ale **yills**
YIN *Scots word for* ▶ **one**
YINCE *Scots form of* ▶ **once**
YINDIE *n* person who combines a lucrative career with non-mainstream tastes **yindies**
YINS ▶ **yin**
YIP *n* emit a high-pitched bark
YIPE = **yipes**
YIPES *interj* expression of surprise, fear, or alarm

YIPPED ▸ **yip**
YIPPEE *interj*
YIPPER *n* golfer who suffers from a failure of nerve **yippers**
YIPPIE *n* young person sharing hippy ideals **yippies**
YIPPING ▸ **yip**
YIPPY = **yippie**
YIPS ▸ **yip**
YIRD *vb* bury **yirded, yirding, yirds**
YIRK = **yerk**
YIRKED ▸ **yirk**
YIRKING ▸ **yirk**
YIRKS ▸ **yirk**
YIRR *vb* snarl, growl, or yell **yirred, yirring, yirrs**
YIRTH *n* earth **yirths**
YITE *n* European bunting with a yellowish head and body and brown streaked wings and tail **yites, yitie**
YITIES ▸ **yitie**
YITTEN *adj* frightened
YLEM *n* original matter from which the basic elements are said to have been formed **ylems**
YLIKE *Spenserian form of* ▸ **alike**
YLKE *archaic spelling of* ▸ **ilk**
YLKES ▸ **ylke**
YMOLT *Spenserian past participle of* ▸ **melt**
YMOLTEN *Spenserian past participle of* ▸ **melt**
YMPE *Spenserian form of* ▸ **imp**
YMPES ▸ **ympe**
YMPING ▸ **ympe**
YMPT ▸ **ympe**
YNAMBU *n* South American bird **ynambus**
YO *interj* expression used as a greeting ▹ *sentence substitute* expression used as a greeting
YOB *n*
YOBBERY *n* behaviour typical of aggressive surly youths
YOBBISH *adj* typical of aggressive surly youths
YOBBISM ▸ **yob**
YOBBO = **yob**
YOBBOES ▸ **yobbo**
YOBBOS ▸ **yobbo**
YOBS ▸ **yob**
YOCK *vb* chuckle **yocked, yocking, yocks**
YOD *n* tenth letter in the Hebrew alphabet
YODE ▸ **yead**
YODEL *vb, n* **yodeled, yodeler, yodels**
YODH = **yod**
YODHS ▸ **yodh**
YODLE *variant spelling of* ▸ **yodel; yodled, yodler, yodlers, yodles, yodling**
YODS ▸ **yod**
YOGA *n* **yogas**
YOGEE = **yogi**
YOGEES ▸ **yogee**
YOGH *n* character used in Old and Middle English to represent a palatal fricative **yoghs**
YOGHURT = **yogurt**
YOGI *n*
YOGIC ▸ **yoga**
YOGIN = **yogi**
YOGINI ▸ **yogi**
YOGINIS ▸ **yogi**
YOGINS ▸ **yogin**
YOGIS ▸ **yogi**
YOGISM ▸ **yogi**
YOGISMS ▸ **yogi**
YOGURT *n* **yogurts**
YOHIMBE *n* bark used in herbal medicine
YOICK *vb* urge on foxhounds **yoicked**
YOICKS *interj* cry used by huntsmen to urge on the hounds ▹ *vb* urge on foxhounds
YOJAN *n* Indian unit of distance **yojana**
YOJANAS ▸ **yojana**
YOJANS ▸ **yojan**
YOK *vb* chuckle

> A useful short word meaning to laugh, with an alternative spelling **yuk**.

YOKE *n, vb* **yoked**
YOKER *vb* **yokered**
YOKERS, yokes, yoking, yokings ▸ **yoke**
YOKKED ▸ **yok**
YOKKING ▸ **yok**
YOKS ▸ **yok**
YOKUL *Shetland word for* ▸ **yes**
YOLD *archaic past participle of* ▸ **yield**

YOLK *n* **yolked, yolkier, yolks, yolky**
YOM *n* day **yomim**
YOMP *vb* walk or trek laboriously **yomped, yomping, yomps**
YON *adj, adv, pron* **yond**
YONDER *adv, adj, determiner, n* **yonders**
YONI *n* female genitalia, regarded as a divine symbol of sexual pleasure
YONIC *adj* resembling a vulva
YONIS ▸ **yoni**
YONKER = **younker**
YONKERS ▸ **yonker**
YONKS *pl n* very long time
YONNIE *n* stone **yonnies**
YONT = **yon**
YOOF *n* non-standard spelling of youth **yoofs**
YOOP *n* sob **yoops**
YORE *n, adv* **yores**
YORK *vb* bowl or try to bowl (a batsman) by pitching the ball under or just beyond the bat **yorked**
YORKER *n* ball that pitches just under the bat **yorkers**
YORKIE *n* Yorkshire terrier **yorkies**
YORKING ▸ **york**
YORKS ▸ **york**
YORLING *n as in* **yellow yorling** yellowhammer
YORP *vb* shout **yorped, yorping, yorps**
YOU *pron, n*
YOUK *vb* itch **youked, youking, youks**
YOUNG *adj* in an early stage of life or growth ▹ *n* young people in general; offspring **younger**
YOUNGLY *adv* youthfully
YOUNGS ▸ **young**
YOUNGTH *n* youth
YOUNKER *n* young man
YOUPON = **yaupon**
YOUPONS ▸ **youpon**
YOUR *adj*
YOURN *dialect form of* ▸ **yours**
YOURS *pron*
YOURT = **yurt**
YOURTS ▸ **yourt**
YOUS *pron* refers to more than one person including the person or persons addressed but not the speaker **youse**
YOUTH *n*
YOUTHEN *vb* render more youthful-seeming
YOUTHLY *adv* young
YOUTHS ▸ **youth**
YOUTHY *Scots word for* ▸ **young**
YOW *vb* howl
YOWE *Scot word for* ▸ **ewe**
YOWED ▸ **yow**
YOWES ▸ **yowe**
YOWIE *n* legendary Australian apelike creature **yowies**
YOWING ▸ **yow**
YOWL *n, vb* **yowled, yowler, yowlers**
YOWLEY *n* yellowhammer (bird) **yowleys**
YOWLING ▸ **yowl**
YOWLS ▸ **yowl**
YOWS ▸ **yow**
YPERITE *n* mustard gas
YPIGHT *archaic past participle of* ▸ **pitch**
YPLAST *archaic past participle of* ▸ **place**
YPLIGHT *archaic past participle of* ▸ **plight**
YPSILON = **upsilon**
YRAPT *Spenserian form of* ▸ **rapt**
YRENT *archaic past participle of* ▸ **rend**
YRIVD *archaic past participle of* ▸ **rive**
YRNEH *n* unit of reciprocal inductance **yrnehs**
YSAME *Spenserian word for* > **together**
YSHEND *Spenserian form of* ▸ **shend**
YSHENDS ▸ **yshend**
YSHENT ▸ **yshend**
YSLAKED *archaic past participle of* ▸ **slake**
YTOST *archaic past participle of* ▸ **toss**
YTTRIA *n* insoluble solid used mainly in incandescent mantles **yttrias**
YTTRIC ▸ **yttrium**
YTTRIUM *n* silvery metallic element used in various alloys
YU *n* jade
YUAN *n* standard monetary unit of the

People's Republic of China **yuans**
YUCA = **yucca**
YUCAS ▸ **yuca**
YUCCA *n* **yuccas**
YUCCH *interj* expression of disgust
YUCH *interj* expression of disgust
YUCK *interj* exclamation indicating contempt, dislike, or disgust ▹ *vb* chuckle **yucked, yucker, yuckers**
YUCKIER ▸ **yucky**
YUCKING ▸ **yuck**
YUCKO *adj* disgusting ▹ *interj* exclamation of disgust
YUCKS ▸ **yuck**
YUCKY *adj* disgusting, nasty
YUFT *n* Russia leather **yufts**
YUG = **yuga**
YUGA *n* (in Hindu cosmology) one of the four ages of mankind
YUGARIE *variant spelling of* ▸ **eugarie yugas**
YUGS ▸ **yug**
YUK = **yuck**
YUKATA *n* light kimono **yukatas**
YUKE *vb* itch **yuked, yukes**
YUKIER ▸ **yuky**
YUKIEST ▸ **yuky**
YUKING ▸ **yuke**
YUKKED ▸ **yuk**
YUKKIER ▸ **yukky**
YUKKING ▸ **yuk**
YUKKY = **yucky**
YUKO *n* score of five points in judo **yukos**
YUKS ▸ **yuk**
YUKY *adj* itchy
YULAN *n* Chinese magnolia with white flowers **yulans**
YULE *n* Christmas **yules**
YUM *interj* expression of delight
YUMMIER ▸ **yummy**
YUMMIES ▸ **yummy**
YUMMO *adj* tasty ▹ *interj* exclamation of delight or approval
YUMMY *adj, interj, n*
YUMP *vb* leave the ground when driving over a ridge **yumped**
YUMPIE *n* young upwardly mobile person **yumpies**
YUMPING ▸ **yump**
YUMPS ▸ **yump**
YUNX *n* wryneck **yunxes**
YUP *n* informal affirmative statement
YUPON = **yaupon**
YUPONS ▸ **yupon**
YUPPIE *n, adj*
YUPPIES ▸ **yuppy**
YUPPIFY *vb* make yuppie in nature
YUPPY = **yuppie**
YUPS ▸ **yup**
YUPSTER ▸ **yindie**
YURT *n* circular tent consisting of a framework of poles covered with felt or skins **yurta, yurtas, yurts**
YUS ▸ **yu**
YUTZ *n* Yiddish word meaning fool **yutzes**
YUZU *n* type of citrus fruit **yuzus**
YWIS *adv* certainly
YWROKE *archaic past participle of* ▸ **wreak**

Zz

Scoring the same as **Q** but easier to use, **Z** is normally a good tile to have, but it is not the best when it comes to making bonus words scoring that extra 50 points, so you will normally want to play it off as soon as a good score offers itself. There are only two two-letter words beginning with **Z**, **za** and **zo** (11 points), and remembering this will save you wasting time looking for others. There some very good three-letter words starting with **Z**, however. These include another variant of **zo, zho** (15), as well as **zax** and **zex** (19 each), **zap** (14), **zep** (14), **zip** (14) and **zoo** (12).

ZA *n* pizza
ZABETA *n* tariff **zabetas**
ZABRA *n* small sailing vessel **zabras**
ZABTIEH *n* Turkish police officer
ZACATON *n* coarse grass
ZACK *n* Australian five-cent piece **zacks**
ZADDICK *adj* righteous
ZADDIK *n* Hasidic Jewish leader **zaddiks**
ZAFFAR = **zaffer**
ZAFFARS ▸ **zaffar**
ZAFFER *n* impure cobalt oxide, used to impart a blue colour to enamels **zaffers, zaffir**
ZAFFIRS ▸ **zaffir**
ZAFFRE = **zaffer**
ZAFFRES ▸ **zaffre**
ZAFTIG *adj* ripe or curvaceous
ZAG *vb* change direction sharply **zagged, zagging, zags**
ZAIKAI *n* Japanese business community **zaikais**
ZAIRE *n* currency used in the former Zaïre **zaires**
ZAITECH *n* investment in financial markets by a company to supplement its main income
ZAKAT *n* annual tax on Muslims to aid the poor in the Muslim community **zakats**
ZAKUSKA ▸ **zakuski**
ZAKUSKI *pl n* hors d'oeuvres, consisting of tiny open sandwiches
ZAMAN *n* tropical tree **zamang**
ZAMANGS ▸ **zamang**
ZAMANS ▸ **zaman**
ZAMARRA *n* sheepskin coat **zamarro**
ZAMBUCK *n* St John ambulance attendant **zambuk**
ZAMBUKS ▸ **zambuk**
ZAMIA *n* type of plant of tropical and subtropical America **zamias**
ZAMOUSE *n* West African buffalo
ZAMPONE *n* sausage made from pig's trotters **zamponi**
ZANANA = **zenana**

ZANANAS ▸ **zanana**
ZANDER *n* European freshwater pikeperch, valued as a food fish **zanders**
ZANELLA *n* twill fabric
ZANIED, zanier, zanies, zaniest, zanily ▸ **zany**
ZANJA *n* irrigation canal **zanjas**

> An irrigation canal in Spanish America, notable for combining the J and Z.

ZANJERO *n* irrigation supervisor

> Someone who supervises the distribution of water in a **zanja** or irrigation canal. This has a fair chance of coming up in actual play, and would make a great bonus.

ZANTE *n* type of wood **zantes**
ZANY *adj, n, vb* **zanying, zanyish, zanyism**
ZANZA = **zanze**
ZANZAS ▸ **zanza**
ZANZE *n* African musical instrument **zanzes**
ZAP *vb, n, interj*
ZAPATA *adj* (of a moustache) drooping
ZAPATEO *n* Cuban folk dance
ZAPPED ▸ **zap**
ZAPPER *n* remote control for a television etc **zappers**
ZAPPIER ▸ **zappy**
ZAPPING ▸ **zap**
ZAPPY *adj* energetic
ZAPS ▸ **zap**
ZAPTIAH = **zaptieh**
ZAPTIEH *n* Turkish police officer

> Watch out for this Turkish policeman, who can also be spelt **zabtieh** or **zaptiah**.

ZARAPE *n* blanket-like shawl **zarapes**
ZAREBA *n* stockade or enclosure of thorn bushes around a village or campsite **zarebas, zareeba**
ZARF *n* (esp in the Middle East) a holder, usually ornamental, for a hot coffee cup **zarfs**
ZARI *n* thread made from fine gold or silver wire
ZARIBA = **zareba**
ZARIBAS ▸ **zariba**
ZARIS ▸ **zari**
ZARNEC *n* sulphide of arsenic **zarnecs, zarnich**
ZAS ▸ **za**
ZATI *n* type of macaque **zatis**
ZAX *variant of* ▸ **sax**

> A chopper for trimming slate, and a great word combining X and Z. It has a variant **zex**.

ZAXES ▸ **zax**
ZAYIN *n* seventh letter of the Hebrew alphabet **zayins**
ZAZEN *n* deep meditation undertaken whilst sitting upright with legs crossed **zazens**
ZEA *n* corn silk
ZEAL *n*
ZEALANT *archaic variant of* ▸ **zealot**
ZEALFUL ▸ **zeal**
ZEALOT *n* **zealots**
ZEALOUS *adj* extremely eager or enthusiastic
ZEALS ▸ **zeal**
ZEAS ▸ **zeal**
ZEATIN *n* cytokinin derived from corn **zeatins**
ZEBEC *variant spelling of* ▸ **xebec**
ZEBECK = **zebec**
ZEBECKS ▸ **zebeck**
ZEBECS ▸ **zebec**
ZEBRA *n*
ZEBRAIC *adj* like a zebra
ZEBRANO *n* type of striped wood
ZEBRAS ▸ **zebra**
ZEBRASS *n* offspring of a male zebra and a female ass
ZEBRINA *n* trailing herbaceous plant
ZEBRINE ▸ **zebra**
ZEBROID ▸ **zebra**
ZEBRULA *n* offspring of a male zebra and a female horse **zebrule**
ZEBU *n*
ZEBUB *n* large African fly **zebubs**
ZEBUS ▸ **zebu**
ZECCHIN = **zecchino**

ZECHIN = **zecchino**
ZECHINS ▸ zechin
ZED *n* British and New Zealand spoken form of the letter z

> A name for the letter Z, and one of the most commonly played Z words.

ZEDOARY *n* dried rhizome of a tropical Asian plant
ZEDS ▸ zed
ZEE *the US word for* **▸ zed**

> This word can be very useful because E is the most common tile in Scrabble, so keep it in mind if you draw a Z. Zee scores 12 points.

ZEES ▸ zee
ZEIN *n* protein occurring in maize **zeins**
ZEK *n* Soviet prisoner **zeks**
ZEL *n* Turkish cymbal
ZELANT *alternative form of* **▸ zealant**
ZELANTS ▸ zelant
ZELATOR = **zelatrix**
ZELKOVA *n* type of elm tree
ZELOSO *adv* with zeal
ZELS ▸ zel
ZEMSTVA ▸ zemstvo
ZEMSTVO *n* council in Tsarist Russia
ZENAIDA *n* dove
ZENANA *n* part of Muslim or Hindu home reserved for women and girls **zenanas**
ZENDIK *n* unbeliever or heretic **zendiks**
ZENITH *n* **zeniths**
ZEOLITE *n* any of a large group of glassy secondary minerals
ZEP *n* type of long sandwich
ZEPHYR *n* **zephyrs**
ZEPPOLE *n* Italian fritter **zeppoli**
ZEPS ▸ zep
ZERDA *n* fennec **zerdas**
ZEREBA = **zareba**
ZEREBAS ▸ zereba
ZERIBA = **zareba**
ZERIBAS ▸ zeriba
ZERK *n* grease fitting **zerks**
ZERO *n, adj, vb, determiner* **zeroed, zeroes, zeroing, zeros**
ZEROTH *adj* denoting a term in a series that precedes the term otherwise regarded as the first term
ZEST *n, vb* **zested**
ZESTER *n* kitchen utensil used to scrape fine shreds of peel from citrus fruits **zesters**
ZESTFUL, zestier, zestily, zesting, zests, zesty ▸ zest
ZETA *n* sixth letter in the Greek alphabet **zetas**
ZETETIC *adj* proceeding by inquiry ▷ *n* investigation
ZEUGMA *n* figure of speech in which a word is used with two words although appropriate to only one of them **zeugmas**
ZEUXITE *n* ferriferous mineral

> This mineral, a kind of tourmaline, makes an excellent bonus.

ZEX *n* tool for cutting roofing slate **zexes**
ZEZE *n* stringed musical instrument **zezes**
ZHO = **zo**

> A cross between a yak and a cow; the other forms are **dso, dzo** and **zo,** and it's worth remembering all of them.

ZHOMO *n* female zho **zhomos**
ZHOS ▸ zho
ZIBET *n* large civet of S and SE Asia **zibeth**
ZIBETHS ▸ zibeth
ZIBETS ▸ zibet
ZIFF *n* beard
ZIFFIUS *n* sea monster
ZIFFS ▸ ziff
ZIG = **zag**
ZIGAN *n* gypsy
ZIGANKA *n* Russian dance
ZIGANS ▸ zigan
ZIGGED ▸ zig
ZIGGING ▸ zig
ZIGS ▸ zig
ZIGZAG *n, vb, adj, adv* **zigzags**
ZIKURAT = **ziggurat**
ZILA *n* administrative district in India **zilas**
ZILCH *n* nothing **zilches**

ZILL *n* finger cymbal
ZILLA = **zila**
ZILLAH = **zila**
ZILLAHS ▸ **zillah**
ZILLAS ▸ **zilla**
ZILLION *n* extremely large but unspecified number
ZILLS ▸ **zill**
ZIMB = **zebub**
ZIMBI *n* cowrie shell used as money **zimbis**
ZIMBS ▸ **zimb**
ZIMOCCA *n* bath sponge
ZIN *short form of* > **zinfandel**
ZINC *n, vb*
ZINCATE *n* any of a class of salts derived from the amphoteric hydroxide of zinc
ZINCED ▸ **zinc**
ZINCIC ▸ **zinc**
ZINCIER ▸ **zinc**
ZINCIFY *vb* coat with zinc
ZINCING ▸ **zinc**
ZINCITE *n* red or yellow mineral
ZINCKED ▸ **zinc**
ZINCKY ▸ **zinc**
ZINCO *n* printing plate made from zincography
ZINCODE *n* positive electrode
ZINCOID ▸ **zinc**
ZINCOS ▸ **zinco**
ZINCOUS ▸ **zinc**
ZINCS ▸ **zinc**
ZINCY ▸ **zinc**
ZINE *n* magazine or fanzine
ZINEB *n* organic insecticide **zinebs**
ZINES ▸ **zine**
ZING *n, vb*
ZINGANI ▸ **zingano**
ZINGANO *n* gypsy
ZINGARA = **zingaro**
ZINGARE ▸ **zingara**
ZINGARI ▸ **zingaro**
ZINGARO *n* Italian Gypsy
ZINGED ▸ **zing**
ZINGEL *n* small freshwater perch **zingels**
ZINGER ▸ **zing**
ZINGERS ▸ **zing**
ZINGIER ▸ **zingy**
ZINGING ▸ **zing**
ZINGS ▸ **zing**
ZINGY *adj* vibrant
ZINKE *n* cornett
ZINKED ▸ **zinc**
ZINKES ▸ **zinke**
ZINKIER ▸ **zinc**
ZINKIFY *vb* coat with zinc
ZINKING ▸ **zinc**
ZINKY ▸ **zinc**
ZINNIA *n* plant of tropical and subtropical America **zinnias**
ZINS ▸ **zin**
ZIP = **zipper**
ZIPLESS ▸ **zip**
ZIPLOCK *adj* fastened with interlocking plastic strips ▹ *vb* seal (a ziplock storage bag)
ZIPPED ▸ **zip**
ZIPPER *n, vb* **zippers**
ZIPPIER ▸ **zippy**
ZIPPING ▸ **zip**
ZIPPO *n* nothing **zippos**
ZIPPY *adj* full of energy
ZIPS ▸ **zip**
ZIPTOP *adj* (of a bag) closed with a zip
ZIRAM *n* industrial fungicide **zirams**
ZIRCON *n* **zircons**
ZIT *n* spot or pimple

> This little word for a pimple can be very useful for disposing of the Z.

ZITE = **ziti**
ZITHER *n* **zithern, zithers**
ZITI *n* type of pasta **zitis**

> Another very useful word for disposing of the Z, **ziti** is a type of pasta. It has a variant **zite**. Remember that **ziti** takes an S to form **zitis**, but **zite** does not take an S.

ZITS ▸ **zit**
ZIZ = **zizz**
ZIZANIA *n* aquatic grass
ZIZEL *n* chipmunk **zizels**
ZIZIT = **zizith**
ZIZITH *variant spelling of* > **tsitsith**
ZIZZ *n* short sleep ▹ *vb* take a short sleep, snooze **zizzed, zizzes, zizzing**
ZIZZLE *vb* sizzle **zizzled, zizzles**
ZLOTE ▸ **zloty**
ZLOTIES ▸ **zloty**
ZLOTY *n* monetary unit of Poland **zlotych, zlotys**

ZO *n* Tibetan breed of cattle
ZOA ▶ **zoon**
ZOAEA = **zoea**
ZOAEAE ▶ **zoaea**
ZOAEAS ▶ **zoaea**
ZOARIA ▶ **zoarium**
ZOARIAL ▶ **zoarium**
ZOARIUM *n* colony of zooids
ZOBO = **zo**
ZOBOS ▶ **zobo**
ZOBU = **zo**
ZOBUS ▶ **zobu**
ZOCALO *n* plaza in Mexico **zocalos**
ZOCCO *n* plinth **zoccolo, zoccos**
ZODIAC *n* **zodiacs**
ZOEA *n* free-swimming larva of a crab or related crustacean **zoeae, zoeal, zoeas**

> One of the most frequently played words in Scrabble, along with its friends **zoaea** and **zooea** and the various inflections: remember that these words can take an E in the plural as well as S, giving **zoeae, zoaeae** and **zooeae**.

ZOECIA ▶ **zoecium**
ZOECIUM = **zooecium**
ZOEFORM ▶ **zoea**
ZOETIC *adj* pertaining to life
ZOFTIG *adj* ripe or curvaceous
ZOIC *adj* relating to or having animal life
ZOISITE *n* grey, brown, or pink mineral
ZOISM *n* belief in magical animal powers **zoisms, zoist, zoists**
ZOL *n* South African slang for a cannabis cigarette **zols**
ZOMBI = **zombie**
ZOMBIE *n* **zombies**
ZOMBIFY *vb* turn into a zombie
ZOMBIS ▶ **zombi**
ZONA *n* zone or belt **zonae**
ZONAL *adj* of, relating to, or of the nature of a zone **zonally, zonary**
ZONATE *adj* marked with, divided into, or arranged in zones **zonated**
ZONDA *n* South American wind **zondas**
ZONE *n, vb* **zoned**
ZONER *n* something which divides other things into zones **zoners**
ZONES ▶ **zone**
ZONING ▶ **zone**
ZONINGS ▶ **zone**
ZONK *vb* strike resoundingly
ZONKED *adj* highly intoxicated with drugs or alcohol
ZONKING ▶ **zonk**
ZONKS ▶ **zonk**
ZONOID *adj* resembling a zone
ZONULA *n* small zone or belt **zonulae**
ZONULAR ▶ **zonule**
ZONULAS ▶ **zonula**
ZONULE *n* small zone, band, or area **zonules**
ZONULET *n* small belt
ZONURE *n* lizard with ringed tail **zonures**
ZOO *n*
ZOOEA = **zoea**
ZOOEAE ▶ **zooea**
ZOOEAL ▶ **zooea**
ZOOEAS ▶ **zooea**
ZOOECIA > **zooecium**
ZOOEY ▶ **zoo**
ZOOGAMY *n* sexual reproduction in animals
ZOOGENY *n* doctrine of formation of animals
ZOOGLEA = **zoogloea**
ZOOGONY = **zoogeny**
ZOOID *n* any independent animal body, such as an individual of a coral colony **zooidal, zooids**
ZOOIER ▶ **zoo**
ZOOIEST ▶ **zoo**
ZOOKS *short form of* > **gadzooks**
ZOOLITE *n* fossilized animal
ZOOLITH *n* fossilized animal
ZOOLOGY *n*
ZOOM *vb, n* **zoomed, zooming, zooms, zoon**
ZOONAL ▶ **zoon**
ZOONED ▶ **zoon**
ZOONIC *adj* concerning animals

ZOONING ▸ **zoon**
ZOONITE *n* segment of an articulated animal
ZOONOMY *n* science of animal life
ZOONS ▸ **zoon**
ZOOPERY *n* experimentation on animals
ZOOS ▸ **zoo**
ZOOT *n as in* **zoot suit** man's suit consisting of baggy trousers and a long jacket
ZOOTAXY *n* science of the classification of animals

> The science of classifying animals. An unlikely word to appear on your rack, but you never know, and it would make an impressive bonus!

ZOOTIER ▸ **zooty**
ZOOTOMY *n* branch of zoology concerned with the dissection and anatomy of animals
ZOOTY *adj* showy
ZOOTYPE *n* animal figure used as a symbol
ZOOZOO *n* wood pigeon **zoozoos**
ZOPPA *adj* syncopated **zoppo**
ZORBING *n* activity of travelling downhill inside a large air-cushioned hollow ball
ZORGITE *n* copper-lead selenide
ZORI *n* Japanese sandal
ZORIL = **zorilla**
ZORILLA *n* skunk-like African musteline mammal having a long black-and-white coat **zorille**
ZORILLO = **zorille**
ZORILS ▸ **zoril**
ZORINO *n* skunk fur **zorinos**
ZORIS ▸ **zori**
ZORRO *n* hoary fox **zorros**
ZOS ▸ **zo**
ZOSTER *n* shingles; herpes zoster **zosters**
ZOUAVE *n* (formerly) member of a body of French infantry composed of Algerian recruits **zouaves**
ZOUK *n* style of dance music that combines African and Latin American rhythms **zouks**
ZOUNDS *interj* mild oath indicating surprise or indignation
ZOWIE *interj* expression of pleasurable surprise
ZOYSIA *n* type of grass with short stiffly pointed leaves, often used for lawns **zoysias**
ZUFFOLI ▸ **zuffolo**
ZUFFOLO = **zufolo**
ZUFOLI ▸ **zufolo**
ZUFOLO *n* small flute
ZULU *n* (in the NATO phonetic alphabet) used to represent z **zulus**
ZUPA *n* confederation of Serbian villages
ZUPAN *n* head of a zupa **zupans**
ZUPAS ▸ **zupa**
ZURF = **zarf**
ZURFS ▸ **zurf**
ZUZ *n* ancient Hebrew silver coin **zuzim, zuzzim**
ZYDECO *n* type of Black Cajun music **zydecos**
ZYGA ▸ **zygon**
ZYGAL ▸ **zygon**
ZYGOID = **diploid**
ZYGOMA *n* slender arch of bone on each side of the skull of mammals **zygomas**
ZYGON *n* brain fissure
ZYGOSE ▸ **zygosis**
ZYGOSES ▸ **zygosis**
ZYGOSIS *n* direct transfer of DNA between two cells that are temporarily joined
ZYGOTE *n* fertilized egg cell **zygotes, zygotic**
ZYMASE *n* mixture of enzymes that is obtained as an extract from yeast and ferments sugars **zymases**
ZYME *n* ferment **zymes, zymic**
ZYMITE *n* priest who uses leavened bread during communion **zymites**
ZYMOGEN *n* any of various inactive precursors of enzymes activated by a kinase

ZYMOID *adj* relating to a ferment

ZYMOME *n* glutinous substance that is insoluble in alcohol **zymomes**

ZYMOSAN *n* insoluble carbohydrate found in yeast

ZYMOSES ▸ **zymosis**

ZYMOSIS = **zymolysis**

ZYMOTIC *adj* of, relating to, or causing fermentation ▹ *n* disease

ZYMURGY *n* study of fermentation processes

ZYTHUM *n* Ancient Egyptian beer **zythums**

ZYZZYVA *n* American weevil

ZZZ *n* informal word for sleep **zzzs**